BUSINESS Essential

BUSINESS Essential

A & C Black • London

First published in Great Britain 2009

A & C Black Publishers Ltd
36 Soho Square, London W1D 3QY
www.acblack.com

A CIP record for this book is available from the British Library.

ISBN: 9–781–4081–1404–9

This book is produced using paper that is made from wood grown in managed, sustainable forests. It is natural, renewable and recyclable. The logging and manufacturing processes conform to the environmental regulations of the country of origin.

Design by Fiona Pike, Pike Design, Winchester
Typeset by RefineCatch Ltd, Bungay, Suffolk
Printed in China by C & C Offset Printing Co Ltd

Contents

User Guide

Aimed at time-pressed managers and students, the two aims of BUSINESS are straightforward ones: to help you become more effective in your job, and to help you get ahead in your career – even in these challenging financial times.

The book includes the following five key sections:

BEST PRACTICE

Putting the expertise of the world's leading business writers to work for you

The primary objective of the Best Practice Section is to provide you with overviews of key problems and business issues you are likely to face at some point in your working life – from managing change to developing leadership skills to implementing strategy in challenging times.

The articles included present a powerful array of practical business advice, opinion, and original thinking from some of the world's leading business writers and practitioners. They are not designed to be the last word on the subject, but concise and practical introductions from experts in each respective topic.

Our aim in this section is to stimulate, to provoke, and to inspire.

ACTIONLISTS

Finding practical solutions for everyday business problems

The Actionlists provide you with a comprehensive handbook of practical answers to everyday business challenges – from revitalising your CV to decision-making and problem-solving.

They address key management tasks in detail, with an emphasis on e-business, marketing, finance, and personal development. The section on personal development will be invaluable if you are looking for practical advice on furthering your career, looking for a new job, or improving the quality of your working life.

Actionlists include a series of frequently asked questions (and direct answers), as well as helpful suggestions on how to avoid common mistakes.

MANAGEMENT LIBRARY

Summarising the most influential business books of all time

There is a vast literature covering business and the world of work, and thousands more new publications emerge every year. However, only a handful of books become landmarks – forever changing the ways in which management is conceived and practised.

This section distils the main lessons from the best and most important business books ever published. It includes both influential modern titles such as *The Wisdom of Crowds* and *The Tipping Point*, as well as time-honoured classics such as Drucker's *Practice of Management* and F.W. Taylor's *Principles of Scientific Management*.

Each summary includes a quick analysis of the book's contribution to management thinking and practice, as well as a list of the key points emerging from the work.

GURUS

Profiling the top management thinkers

This section provides concise summaries of careers and thinking of the most important and influential writers on management, as well as an assessment of their contributions to business theory and practice. We also provide a list of key works and sources of additional information.

DICTIONARY

Defining business

The **Management Dictionary** provides jargon-free definitions to more than 7,000 international business terms, abbreviations, and acronyms.

---

management the use of professional skills for identifying and achieving organisational objectives through the deployment of appropriate resources.

Management involves identifying what needs to be done, and organising and supporting others to perform the necessary tasks. A manager has complex and ever-changing responsibilities, the focus of which shifts to reflect the issues, trends, and preoccupations of the time. At the beginning of the 20th century, the emphasis was both on supporting the organisation's administration and managing productivity through increased efficiency. Organisations following Henri Fayol's and Max Weber's models built the functional divisions of personnel management, production management, marketing management, operations management, and financial management. At the beginning of the 21st century, those original drivers are still much in evidence. Although management is a profession in its own right, its skill-set often applies to professionals of other disciplines

---

Special features:

- **Abbreviations**, acronyms and their expansions are shown in full and cross-referred for ease of use
- **Extended entries** explain more complex concepts and help you get to grips with ideas quickly
- **Biographical entries** to detail the lives and careers of key business thinkers and leaders

FREE E-BOOK EDITION

As a user of the print version of BUSINESS Essential, you also are entitled to a FREE electronic edition of the book: all the information will be ready when you are, either on your desk or desktop.

To register for the e-book, go to the registration page on our website **www.ultimatebusinessresource.com/register**, type in your e-mail address, and add in your password: **acbBE10**

FEEDBACK

All the information in the book was correct at the time of going to press. However, we welcome any comments you may have about how BUSINESS might be improved. Let us know too if you disagree with any of the points made or have any correction – we want to hear your views. Write to us at **editorial@ultimatebusinessresource.com**.

Contributors

Meredith Belbin is a partner in Belbin Associates, a company known principally as the producer of Interplace – a company-based, team-role advice system, used internationally. He has written several successful business books, including the European bestseller, *Management Teams: Why They Succeed or Fail* (2nd ed, Butterworth-Heinemann, 2003) and, most recently, *Managing without Power* (Butterworth-Heinemann, 2001). He has been a consultant to the European Commission, the US Department of Labor and the OECD, is senior associate professor at Cambridge University, and Honorary Fellow of Henley Management College.

University Professor and Founding Chairman of The Leadership Institute, USC, **Warren Bennis** is also Chairman of the Advisory Board of the Center for Public Leadership at Harvard's Kennedy School. He has written over 25 books and many articles on leadership, change, and creative collaboration. He is a consultant for Fortune 500 companies and has served on four US Presidential Commissions. His book, *Leaders* (reissue, HarperCollins, 2004), was designated by the *Financial Times* as one of the top 50 business books of all time. *An Invented Life* (Addison-Wesley, 1993) was nominated for a Pulitzer. *Forbes Magazine* refers to him as the 'Dean of leadership gurus'. His recent book, *Geeks & Geezers* (Harvard Business School Press, 2002), is about leaders 70 years and older and 32 years and younger. In 2005, HarperCollins published his series of conversations with the late Bob Townsend, *Reinventing Leadership*. He is now completing a book on leadership judgment. In May 2000, the *Financial Times* referred to Bennis as 'the professor who established leadership as a respectable academic field'.

Drayton Bird is founder of Drayton Bird Associates, an agency specialising in direct marketing. For seven years he was a partner of Trenear-Harvey, Bird & Watson, a firm which was sold to Ogilvy and Mather in 1985. As vice-chairman and creative director, he helped O & M Direct become the world's largest direct marketing agency network, and was elected to the worldwide Ogilvy Group board. Drayton is a celebrated speaker and regularly contributes articles to international journals. His three books include the bestseller, *Commonsense Direct and Digital Marketing* (5th ed, Kogan Page, 2007). Visit www.draytonbird.com for more information.

Dr Peter Bunce (peterbunce@bbrt.org) is a chartered engineer who has worked in industry as a manufacturing engineer and in collaborative research programmes on technical and management issues with CAM-I (a US-based research consortium). With Jeremy Hope and Franz Röösli, he is a director of the BBRT, an international research and membership collaborative.

Sir Adrian Cadbury joined the Cadbury business in 1952, became chairman of Cadbury Limited in 1965 and retired as chairman of Cadbury Schweppes in 1989. He was a director of the Bank of England 1970–1994, chairman of the UK Committee on Corporate Governance 1991–1995, and a member of the OECD Business Advisory Group on Corporate Governance. He received the International Corporate Governance Network Award in 2001 and the Laureate Medal for Corporate Governance in 2005. He is the author of *Corporate Governance and Chairmanship; A Personal View* (Oxford University Press, 2002).

Susan Cartwright is Professor of Organizational Psychology and Well Being, Director of Centre for Organizational Health and Well-Being at Lancaster University.

Subir Chowdhury is chairman and CEO of ASI Consulting Group, executive vice-president at the international consultancy firm ASI (American Supplier Institute). As well as being a renowned consultant in the field of quality management and leadership, Chowdhury has written several books on these subjects, including *The Power of Six Sigma* (Financial Times/Prentice Hall/Dearborn Trade, 2001), *The Talent Era* (Financial Times/Prentice Hall, 2001), and *The Ice Cream Maker: An Inspiring Tale about Making Quality the Key Ingredient in Everything You Do* (Currency, 2005).

Besides his professorship, **Cary Cooper** CBE is pro vice-chancellor of Lancaster University. He specialises in stress management, regularly contributing to national newspapers, academic journals, TV, and radio. His many publications include *Organizational Stress* (with Philip Dewe and Michael O'Driscoll; Sage, 2001) and *Work and Health Psychology: The Handbook* (with James Aaron Quick and Marc J. Schabracq, eds; Wiley, 2009).

Robert Cooper is a Professor Emeritus of Marketing and Technology Management at the Michael G. DeGroote School of Business, McMaster University, Ontario, Canada. Creator of the widely employed Stage-Gate® product development process, he is the author of several books, including *Winning at New Products* (3rd ed, Perseus, 2001).

Alan Downs PhD is a management psychologist and consultant who specialises in strategic human resources planning and helping business executives reach their maximum potential. He has written numerous books, including *Corporate Executions* (AMACOM, 1995), the much-acclaimed exposé on downsizing, *The Seven Miracles of Management* (Prentice Hall, 1998), *The Fearless Executive* (AMACOM, 2000), and *Secrets of an Executive Coach: Proven Methods for Helping Leaders Excel Under Pressure* (AMACOM, 2005).

Scott Edgett is CEO and co-founder of the Product Development Institute and co-founder of Stage-Gate Inc, along with Robert Cooper. As well as a noted speaker and consultant worldwide on new product development and portfolio management, Scott is the co-author, with Robert Cooper, of two books on these topics, including *Portfolio Management for New Products* (2nd ed, Basic Books, 2002).

John Elkington is the founder of SustainAbility, one of Europe's leading think tank and consultancy firms focusing on business strategies for sustainable development. He has written or co-authored over 30 books and published reports, including bestseller *The Green Consumer Guide* (Gollancz, 1988) and *Cannibals with Forks* (Capstone, 1997), which introduces the triple bottom line, and *The Power of Unreasonable People* (Harvard Business School Press, 2008). Visit www.johnelkington.com for more information.

Robin Fraser (robinfraser@bbrt.org) is a management consultant and co-author with Jeremy Hope of *Beyond Budgeting*, published by Harvard Business School Press in 2003. He was formerly a partner with Coopers & Lybrand (now PwC) in the UK. He is a former director of BBRT, an international research and membership collaborative.

Mike Freedman is responsible for the worldwide strategy practice of Kepner Tregoe Inc, a global consultancy firm. He is the author of *The Art and Discipline of Strategic Leadership* (McGraw-Hill, 2003).

The late **Sir John Harvey-Jones** joined ICI as a work study officer in 1956, after 19 years in the navy. He rose to be chairman in 1982, and was largely responsible for reshaping the company, doubling the price of ICI shares and turning a loss into a billion-pound profit after only 30 months in the job. After receiving his knighthood in 1985, Sir John wrote several books, including the bestsellers *Making It Happen* (HarperCollins, new edition, 1994) and *Getting It Together* (Ulverscroft, 1992). He also took part a TV series entitled *Troubleshooter*, where he was invited to visit and advise businesses.

Jeremy Hope is a chartered accountant, formerly working with venture capital company 3i and then running his own business. He is the author of several management books, all published by Harvard Business School Press. With Peter Bunce and Franz Röösli, he is a director of the BBRT, an international research and membership collaborative.

Robert Kaplan is Baker Foundation Professor at Harvard Business School. His research, teaching, and consultancy focus on linking cost and performance measurement systems to strategy implementation and operational excellence. With David Norton, Kaplan developed the Balanced Scorecard, an aid to achieving strategy by showing how key measures inter-relate to track progress towards strategy, and both Kaplan and Norton serve as directors with the Balanced Scorecard Collaborative – a global network to support organisations implementing the method. Their books include *The Strategy-focused Organization* (Harvard Business School Press, 2001) and *The Balanced Scorecard* (Harvard Business School Press, 1996).

Former director of e-commerce for Great Universal Stores plc (GUS) and managing director of AKQA, **Michael de Kare-Silver** is a highly experienced marketer. Michael has also written widely, most notably *E-Shock* (AMACOM, 1999) and *Streamlining* (Palgrave Macmillan, 2002).

Allan Kennedy is a Boston-based management consultant and writer. He is co-author with Terrence Deal of *Corporate Cultures* (reissue, Perseus, 2000) and *The New Corporate Cultures* (Perseus, 1999). He has also written *The End of Shareholder Value* (Perseus, 2000) and numerous articles.

Philip Kotler is S.C. Johnson and Son Distinguished Professor of International Marketing at the J.L. Kellogg Graduate School of Management, Northwestern University, Illinois. His extensive canon runs to more than 40 books, and includes the classic marketing textbook *Marketing Management: Analysis, Planning, Implementation, and Control* (now in its 13th edition, Prentice Hall, 2008).

He has also published more than 100 articles in leading journals such as the *Harvard Business Review* and the *Journal of Marketing and Management Science*.

Formerly a partner at McKinsey & Company, **Max Landsberg** is now a business author and partner at Heidrick & Struggles. His guide to coaching, *The Tao of Coaching* (new edition, Profile Business, 2003), first published in 1996, has become a classic.

Costas Markides is Professor of Strategic and International Management and holds the Robert P. Bauman Chair of Strategic Leadership at the London Business School. His books include *Diversification, Refocusing and Economic Performance* (MIT Press, 1995), *All the Right Moves: A Guide to Crafting Breakthrough Strategy* (Harvard Business School Press, 1999), *Strategic Thinking for the Next Economy* (Jossey-Bass, 2001), and *Fast Second: How Smart Companies Bypass Radical Innovation to Enter and Dominate New Markets* (with Paul Geroski; Jossey-Bass Wiley, 2005), which was shortlisted for the *Financial Times* Management Book of the Year Award.

Malcolm McDonald is Professor Emeritus of Marketing at Cranfield University School of Management. He is Chairman of six companies and spends much of his time working with the operating boards of the world's biggest multinational companies, such as IBM, Xerox, BP and the like, in most countries in the world, including Japan, the United States, Europe, South America, ASEAN and Australasia. He has written or co-written many books, including the best-selling title, *Marketing Plans: How to Prepare Them, How to Use Them* (6th ed, Butterworth-Heinemann, 2007), and many of his papers have been published.

Regis McKenna (www.regis.com) founded his own high tech marketing firm, Regis McKenna Inc, in Silicon Valley in 1970. Over the next 30 years, his firm evolved from one focused on high tech start-ups to a broad-based marketing strategy firm servicing international clients in many different industries and countries. McKenna retired from consulting in 2000 and is concentrating his efforts on high-tech entrepreneurial seed-ventures. Regis has written and lectured extensively on the social and market effects of technological change. He pioneered many of the theories and practices of technology marketing that have become integrated into the marketing mainstream.

Ian Mitroff is Professor Emeritus at the Marshall School of Business. He is generally recognised as one of the founders of the field of crisis management. He has published many hundreds of articles and 26 books, including *Why Some Companies Recover Faster and Better from Crises: Seven Essential Lessons for Avoiding Disaster* (AMACOM, 2001).

Geoffrey Moore is a frequent speaker at industry conferences and his books are required reading at leading business schools. These books include *Crossing the Chasm* (revised edition, 1999), *The Gorilla Game* (revised edition, 1999), and *Living on the Fault Line* (2002), published by HarperBusiness, and *Dealing with Darwin: How Great Companies Innovate at Every Stage of Their Evolution* (Capstone, 2006).

Sue Newell is currently the Cammarata Professor of Management at Bentley College in the United States. She is a chartered psychologist and has previously worked at Warwick, Aston, and Nottingham Business Schools. Her research interests are varied, covering innovation, knowledge management, human resource management and business ethics. Sue has published many journal articles on these topics, as well as a book entitled *Creating the Healthy Organisation* (2nd ed, International Thomson Business, 2001).

David Norton is president of Palladium, a consulting firm focused on Strategy Execution, and is the former president of Renaissance Solutions Inc, a management consultancy and systems integration firm. Prior to Renaissance, Norton co-founded and spent 17 years as president of Nolan, Norton & Company, which was acquired by Peat Marwick. Together with Robert Kaplan, Norton developed The Balanced Scorecard, an aid to achieving strategy by showing how key measures interrelate to track progress. Both Norton and Kaplan are directors of the Balanced Scorecard Collaborative, a global network which supports organisations implementing the method. Their books include *The Strategy-focused Organization* (Harvard Business School Press, 2001) and *The Balanced Scorecard* (Harvard Business School Press, 1996).

Joseph O'Connor is an internationally recognised author, trainer and consultant. He is a leading author in the field of Neuro Linguistic Programming (NLP), systemic thinking and coaching, and the author of seventeen books published in 25 languages. He is a Master Trainer of NLP, and co-founder of the International Coaching Community (ICC) with coaches in 31 countries. Visit www.lambentdobrasil.com for more information.

Wally Olins is one of the world's most experienced experts on corporate identity and branding. His main interests are the big ideas behind organisations, mergers, and acquisitions, and he has a particular fascination with the branding of regions and nations. His publications include *On Brand* (Thames & Hudson, 2003).

Jeffrey Pfeffer is the Thomas D. Dee II Professor of Organisational Behaviour in the Graduate School of Business at Stanford University, and author of numerous books, including *The Human Equation: Building Profits by Putting People First* (Harvard Business School Press, 1998).

Kathleen Kelley Reardon, Professor of Management and Organisation at the University of Southern California Marshall School of Business, has served on the faculty of the MBA, Executive MBA, and International MBA Programmes. She is a leading authority on persuasion, politics in the workplace, negotiation, and interpersonal communication. Her five books include *Persuasion in Practice* (2nd ed, Sage, 1991) and *The Skilled Negotiator* (Jossey-Bass, 2004).

Prof. Franz Röösli is head of the Competence Centre for Controlling at the University of Applied Sciences Northwest Switzerland in Basel, Switzerland. He has also held senior positions in Finance in several major companies in Switzerland. With Peter Bunce and Jeremy Hope, he is a director of the BBRT, an international research and membership collaborative.

Philip Sadler is former chief executive of Ashridge Management College, where for many years he led the team which built the college's reputation as one of the world's leading business schools. He now heads Philip Sadler Associates, a UK-based consultancy firm with core competencies in leadership development, organisation design, and strategic human resource management. He has also written several books, including *Designing*

Organizations (Kogan Page, 1994) and *The Seamless Organization: Building Tomorrow's Company* (Kogan Page, 2002).

John Simmons is a consultant and author whose books have been internationally influential. A former director of identity company Newell and Sorrell, then of leading brand consultancy Interbrand, he established the discipline of verbal identity as part of a brand. Working with clients such as Diageo, Unilever, 3 Communications, and Air Products, he has helped brands to create a distinctive tone of voice and to tell their stories better. Now an independent consultant and director of brand language at www.thewriter.co.uk, he writes regularly for the media and runs writing workshops for individuals and businesses. He is a co-founder of 26 (www.26.org.uk), a non-profit collective that champions the cause of better writing in business.

Thomas Stewart is former editor of the *Harvard Business Review* and fellow of the World Economic Forum. He is the author of *Intellectual Capital* (2nd rev ed., Nicholas Brealey, 1998).

Paul Stobart, a qualified chartered accountant, spent seven years with a London-based merchant bank before moving to Interbrand, an international branding and marketing services consultancy firm. During eight years at Interbrand he held a number of positions, latterly chairman of European operations. He is now CEO of Sage UK & Ireland. Paul is the editor of *Brand Power* (New York University Press, 1994), a book examining the branding strategies of leading international brand owners.

Merlin Stone is one of the United Kingdom's most experienced consultants, lecturers and trainers in CRM, database marketing and customer service. He is the author of many articles and books on marketing and customer service, including *Up Close and Personal: CRM @ Work* (with Paul Gamble, Neil Woodcock, and Bryan Foss; Kogan Page, 2006), *Customer Relationship Marketing* (Kogan Page, 2000), and *Successful Customer Relationship Marketing* (Kogan Page, 2001).

Donald N. Sull is professor of management practice at London Business School. He is the author of *Made in China: What Western Managers Can Learn from Trailblazing Chinese Entrepreneurs* (Harvard Business School Press, 2005).

John Surdyk is director of INSITE (Initiative for Study in Technology Entrepreneurship) at the University of Wisconsin-Madison School of Business.

Robert I. Sutton is Professor of Management Science and Engineering at Stanford University and author of *Weird Ideas That Work: 11 and $1/2$ Practices for Promoting, Managing and Sustaining Innovation* (Free Press, 2001). Together with Jeffrey Pfeffer, he is co-author of *The Knowing-Doing Gap* (Harvard Business School Press, 2000).

John Wells is President of IMD in Lausanne, Switzerland and holds the Nestlé Professor Chair. He has taught at Harvard Business School and was a senior partner with Netdecisions, a global strategy and technology company responsible for strategy, knowledge management, innovation, and learning. His career started at Unilever in London, where he trained as a cost and management accountant. During his management career Wells has worked within numerous companies, including the Boston Consulting Group, PepsiCo, and the Thomson Travel Group. He also co-founded The Monitor Company (with Michael Porter and Mark Fuller), a strategy consulting practice, and Datapaq, a leading digital data acquisition company serving the automotive and packaging industries that continues to be a leader in its field.

Best Practice

Managing Stress by Cary Cooper and Susan Cartwright

EXECUTIVE SUMMARY

- Recognising the symptoms of stress is an essential measure in taking immediate action to improve the situation.
- Understanding the causes and common sources of workplace stress is vital in preventing it becoming an issue.
- The changing nature of work makes stress more complex, varied, and quite possibly more common – and dealing with it quickly, early, and effectively is more important now than ever.
- There is a range of techniques and approaches to managing personal stress and these are explored in this section.

INTRODUCTION

The enterprise culture has entailed a substantial personal cost for many individuals. The cost is captured by a single word 'stress'. Indeed, stress has found as firm a place in our modern lexicon as 'fast food', 'mobiles', and 'DVDs'. 'It's a high-stress job', someone says, awarding an odd sort of prestige to his or her occupation. But to those whose ability to cope with day-to-day matters is at crisis point, the concept of stress is no longer a casual one; for them, stress can be translated into a four-letter word – *pain*.

BEHAVIOURAL AND PHYSICAL SYMPTOMS OF STRESS

Pressure is motivating, stimulating and energising, but when pressure exceeds an individual's ability to cope we are in the stress arena. When a number of the following behavioural and physical symptoms are frequently or nearly always experienced by an individual, it can indicate that he/she has crossed the line between mere pressure and harmful stress.

IDENTIFYING THE SOURCES OF WORKPLACE STRESS

Once an individual acknowledges that they are not coping with the everyday pressures of work, the next step is to identify the source(s) of the stress at work. Once this is done, the individual can draw up a plan of action to minimise or eliminate the excess pressure or damaging source of stress. Table 2 identifies some possible daily hassles at work. There are of course more significant problem areas as well, such as coping with redundancy, dealing with a bullying boss, or trying to cope with a dysfunctional corporate culture (for example, excessive working hours, autocratic management style).

Table 1

Behavioural Symptoms	Physical Symptoms
Constant irritability with people	Lack of appetite
Difficulty in making decisions	Craving for food when under pressure
Loss of sense of humour	Frequent indigestion or heartburn
Suppressed anger	
Difficulty concentrating	Constipation or diarrhoea
Inability to finish one task before rushing into another	Insomnia
	Tendency to sweat for no good reason
Feeling targeted by other people's animosity	Nervous twitches, nail biting, etc.
Feeling unable to cope	
Wanting to cry at the smallest problem	Headaches
	Cramps and muscle spasms
Lack of interest in doing things after returning home from work	Nausea
	Breathlessness without exertion
Waking up in the morning and feeling tired after an early night	Fainting spells
	Impotency or frigidity
Constant tiredness	Eczema

Table 2

Daily Hassles at Work	
Trouble with client/customer	Travelling associated with the job
Having to work late	Making mistakes
Constant people interruptions	Conflict with organisational goals
Trouble with boss	
Deadlines and time pressures	Job interfering with home/family life
Decision-making	Can't cope with in-tray
Dealing with the bureaucracy at work	Can't say 'no' to work
Technological breakdowns, e.g. computer	Not enough stimulating things to do
Trouble with colleagues	Too many meetings
Tasks associated with job not stimulating	Don't know where career is going
Too much responsibility	Worried about job security
Too many jobs to do at once	Spouse/partner not supportive about work
Telephone interruptions	Family life adversely affecting work
Travelling to and from work	Having to tell subordinates unpleasant things, e.g. redundancy

PERSONAL STRESS: MANAGING THE DAILY HASSLES

Time management

Of all the daily hassles experienced by managers, one of the most stressful is poor time management. Time wasters fall into several categories, requiring different solutions.

The Mañanas. Individuals in this category cause themselves problems because they procrastinate, preferring to 'think' about work rather than 'do' it. Procrastination often stems from boredom, a lack of confidence, or reluctance to seek clarification. For Mañanas, here are some basic tips to effective time management.

- Break up overwhelming tasks into smaller jobs.
- Draw up a 'to do' list of all the tasks you need to complete in the short term (that is, within the next week) and in the long term.
- When planning your work schedule, attempt to balance routine tasks with the more enjoyable jobs.
- Accept that risks are inevitable and that no decisions are ever made on the basis of complete information.

The Poor Delegators. Individuals in this category waste a considerable amount of their time doing work that could easily and more effectively have been done by somebody else. They should consider some of the following.

- Delegation does not mean abdication.
- Always take time out to explain exactly what is required; poor delegators are often also poor communicators, which is why they are frequently disappointed with the efforts of others.
- Having delegated a job, leave the person to get on with it.
- Avoid taking on unnecessary work that does not fulfil their objectives or that could be done by others by learning to say 'no' politely and assertively.

The Disorganised. Individuals in this category are instantly recognisable by the mounds of paper that form barricades around their desks. Disorganised individuals frequently miss or are late for appointments. They frequently think their problems are due to work overload rather than their own poor organisational skills. They need to:

- plan effectively before taking action
- make a 'to do' list regularly at the start of each day and review it each evening
- stick to one task and finish it!
- think before they telephone and draw up a list of all the information they require from the caller
- identify their prime time for working, when their energy levels are high for the complex task, and save the trivial routine tasks for non-prime time
- when making an appointment in their diaries, enter a finish time as well as a start time

The Mushrooms. Individuals in this category are usually unclear about the purpose and objectives of what they are required to do. They constantly speculate and inwardly question what they should do rather than do it. They basically lack assertion and communication skills. The two most important things for them to do are:

- learn to say 'I don't know', when you don't know something
- learn to say 'I don't understand' when you don't understand a task, a role, or objective

Managing interruptions

Another source of personal stress at work for many managers are 'constant interruptions', from the telephone, e-mail, drop-by colleagues, etc.

New technology

With voice mail, e-mail, mobile phones, instant messaging, and the like, it is important to manage the technology rather than let the technology manage you. There are some general rules that apply to each of the technologies most of us work with and which create unnecessary personal pressure.

For telephone calls: batch phone calls; plan what you are going to say and need to know in advance, and deliberately discipline yourself by placing specific time limits on the length of a call.

For voice mail: use this when you need space to carry out complex tasks requiring your full attention, and don't be tempted to access your voice mail messages every 10 minutes! Also deal with those messages that are most important first; deal with the others later.

For e-mails: prioritise your e-mails in terms of your objectives, then reply to them in this order. All too often, individuals reply to e-mails in order of their arrival and not in terms of their importance.

For mobiles and instant messaging: don't have your mobile on all the time, as it could interrupt some important meeting or activity. Use it on journeys or during other periods of downtime to deal with issues that would otherwise have to be dealt with back at work.

Drop-by colleagues

Although being interrupted can provide a welcome diversion from a boring or tedious task, too many interruptions are a waste of time, distracting, and frequently irritating. There is a range of strategies for controlling these kinds of interruptions.

- Establish quiet hours during which you can work undisturbed. This may mean closing your door and putting a notice outside.
- Establish visiting hours when you are available for drop-in visitors.
- Arrange meetings away from your desk or office; this enables you to take control and leave when you want to.
- Do not hesitate to curb wafflers, in a polite and friendly manner, by asking them to make their main point(s).
- When unexpectedly interrupted, ask the person how much time he or she needs and, if you haven't got the space, then rearrange the meeting.

Interruptions

Interruptions occur for a number of reasons. The person involved may

- want to exchange information
- need reassurance or clarification
- lack confidence about a task
- want a casual chat because they need a break or are bored, etc.

It is important to attempt to differentiate these; so, if it is important to their doing their job properly, you may need to spend some of your time with them, if not, then use some of the above suggestions.

THE CHANGING NATURE OF WORK

Finally, one of the major overriding sources of stress for managers and others today is the fact that jobs are no longer for life – that job security is a vestige of the past. Under the terms of the 'new' psychological contract, organisations expect employees to be more flexible, more accountable, and to be hardworking and committed; at the same time, employers offer increasingly limited (or no) assurances or expectations of employment security and career development opportunities. It is not hard to imagine that for significant numbers of future workers the job is likely to become a freelance activity in the form of a series of temporarily or discretely defined tasks or projects undertaken either successively or concurrently for single or multiple employers. For this, the individual receives financial payment, negotiated in advance, either on a fixed-cost basis or dependent on results achieved.

For individuals currently working in 'delayered' organisational structures, coping with changed career expectations requires considerable personal adjustment: one must accept that the onus for career management and training now rests with oneself rather than with the organisation. This requires a greater degree of self-initiative and personal planning and control. Although the prospect of pursuing a self-determined career outside the structure of an established organisation might seem daunting, research evidence based on experiences of mid-life career changes suggests that increased job and life satisfaction is frequently gained from a move to freelancing and self-employment.

MAKING IT HAPPEN
To minimise and handle your own stress you should:
- **Understand yourself** - understand what causes *you* stress, when you are likely to become stressed, and how you can avoid these situations. To help, it can be useful to think about previous times that were stressful for you and remember how you felt, how you reacted and behaved, what the result was, and whether, with the benefit of hindsight, you handled it in the best way possible.
- **Take responsibility** - too often people either deny their problem, in which case it will almost certainly worsen, or blame someone (or something) else. Even if it is the fault of someone else, *you* are being affected and *you* need to resolve it. People are often too afraid, ashamed, or uncertain to admit that they are suffering from stress, but the longer they delay, the worse the effects of the downward cycle.
- **Consider what is causing stress** - is it resulting from the job, your role, work relationships, change, or something else, perhaps not work-related at all? Knowing the symptoms and acknowledging the existence of stress is really only the start: the next key step is to identify the source of the stress. This is often complicated by the fact that stress is often caused by an accumulation of factors. The solution is to rationally consider how to take down the wall that is encircling you, brick by brick. Stress is rarely removed in one go but often requires action in a range of areas.
- **Anticipate stressful periods (either at work or home) and plan for them** - this may include getting temporary resources or people with specific skills to help during a particular period.

- **Understand and use management techniques to prevent or reduce stress** - time management and assertiveness are two of the most important skills in reducing and handling stress, as many difficulties are caused either by time pressures or relationship issues that could be prevented by more assertive, controlled behaviour. Communication, decision-making and problem-solving also have much to offer once the problem has been acknowledged and the sources of stress identified.
- **Relax** - easier said than done, but the key is to understand that you need to *work* at relaxing! This may mean planning a holiday or finding a hobby or club that suits you and then *absorbing* yourself in it. Time away from the causes of stress can help to put the situation in perspective and lead to a new approach that provides a solution.

If you are responsible for preventing and reducing stress within organisations, you should:
- **Acknowledge stress in others** - as a leader you should not be afraid to comment to someone if you think they are suffering from stress, and then be prepared to help and support them in breaking the downward cycle. Often, just acknowledging the existence of stress and showing understanding can provide enough energy to see the solution, remove the stress, and ultimately overcome the problem.
- **Build a positive team or work environment** - as a leader it is possible to reduce stress for others by developing good communication systems, a supportive team approach, a blame-free environment, and a clear sense of involvement and responsibility. Other factors that can also help include mentoring schemes that prevent, identify, and treat cases of stress; appraisal systems and simply knowing and understanding the people that work with you. For some senior managers in large organisations this may not be possible, in which case these values need to be passed down the chain of command so that they are supported throughout the organisation.

CONCLUSION
In the end, we should begin to truly understand what John Ruskin said in 1851:

'In order that people may be happy in their work, these three things are needed: they must be fit for it; they must not do too much of it; and they must have a sense of success in it'.

THE BEST SOURCES OF HELP
Books:
Campbell Quick, James et al. *Managing Executive Health*. Cambridge: Cambridge University Press, 2008.
Cartwright, Susan, and Cary Cooper. *Oxford Handbook of Personnel Psychology*. Oxford: Oxford University Press, 2008.
Cooper, Cary, and S. Palmer. *How to Deal with Stress*. London: Kogan-Page, 2007.

Taking Charge of Your Career by Andrew Lambert

EXECUTIVE SUMMARY

- In an increasingly uncertain world, build on your employability by accumulating skills and experience. Expect to change career direction at least once.
- Don't expect to plan specific job moves far in advance. Be open to new opportunities that may arise, including events you can't control such as mergers and restructuring.
- Be clear about what you want out of life as well as work. Reassess this from time to time so that your career genuinely matches your needs as they change.
- Do something you enjoy (you won't succeed for long otherwise) and recognise when it's time to move on.
- Endeavour to stay in control of your destiny – you're the person who's most likely to be concerned about your future. Market your talents with conviction.
- If you're a specialist, beware of dead-ends and glass ceilings. Alternatively, try not to be too much of a generalist, that is, a jack-of-all-trades but master of none.
- Be realistic about what an employer can offer you (for example, adding value to your CV) and about whether you want to be your own boss: do you have what that takes?

INTRODUCTION

The quickening pace of market change means that both organisations and individuals need to focus harder than ever on how to adjust, or even reinvent what they do, if they are to continue to prosper. Just as the average lifespan of employing organisations is decreasing rapidly, with new corporations and public-sector bodies emerging to take the place of those that fail, so individuals face the danger of losing not only their job, but also their knowledge and skills, if they don't attune to the needs of the future. The impact of recession in 2008 and 2009 highlights the need to keep skills and attitudes current, as a way of insulating your career from sudden changes in the economy and your organisation.

What is a career in this context? It *is* still valid to envisage a path that follows a broadly consistent direction. However, this is no longer likely to be with one employer, or even in the same industry and specialism. This means being flexible and adaptive, and adjusting any career plan regularly in the light of changing circumstances, both personal and market-related. Additionally, circumstances may require a complete change of direction.

Choosing a career

With or without economic, peer, and family pressures, some people find it easy to make up their minds early and pursue a path accordingly; others don't, and need time to find a path. Either approach is valid: if you're going to be successful it's important to do something you enjoy, something that will inspire your thoughts and energy.

If you're an early chooser, don't let enthusiasm blind you to some of the hard decisions you may have to take. Research your chosen area thoroughly, identifying the stepping stones and obstacles to making progress, and the lifecycle of jobs in the field. Remember also that you may have to shift direction later.

There are advantages in being a late developer in that you can test the waters before committing yourself. Realistically, career planning is often about making opportunistic choices as you progress, not about sticking to a single idea. Many successful people had little idea at the outset that they would end up where they did. They learned from the positive and negative experiences they encountered and made their choices accordingly. However, once they did decide what to head for, they were single-minded.

The importance of academic qualifications varies depending on the country you're in and whether or not you are following a specialist path. Some employers see degrees (even MBAs) primarily as a way of choosing among a large number of applicants. As you progress through your career, your track record assumes greater importance.

Specialists and generalists

If you're expert in something, an employer has a good reason to hire and retain you – at any stage in your career. You will face choices both about how to maintain your specialist edge and how to broaden your managerial skills.

In a corporate context there tend to be two broad types of specialism. Some competences are core to what the organisation does (for example, engineering, science, distribution and logistics, trading). Others are the classic support function competences (finance, marketing, IT, personnel, communications, facilities and property management, etc.). All of these have subsets that are more genuinely specialist.

If you continue to specialise, the availability of jobs on offer in companies will steadily reduce until you hit a glass ceiling. You may then need to move into general management or consultancy. As you climb the managerial ladder, it's increasingly important to acquire and display general management capabilities such as effectiveness in leading and motivating teams, managing change and projects, and understanding the commercial and systems context.

If you want to lead a support function – such as finance or marketing – first become a generalist within the function by experiencing a number of relevant specialisms. If it's your ambition to be a consultant anyway, bear in mind that the real money and status derives from being an owner or partner, and that may not be easy if you enter the arena quite late.

Important planning factors

Whether you're moving within or between organisations, you need to provide evidence of your ability to handle varied challenges, demonstrate responsibility as well as initiative, learn from experience, motivate teams, and above all, achieve results. Whatever your level of ambition, be continuously aware of the qualities, knowledge, and skills that will be valuable in the future – don't let yourself become outdated.

Consider:

- what you're working for – job satisfaction, status, material comfort, real wealth, or the buzz of acquiring power
- whether you intend to have a family at some point (and when)
- whether you feel the need to own a business (large or small), become the leader of an organisation, or just be part of one
- whether you want to stay in a certain geographical area or try pastures new
- personal profiling and psychometric assessment to help you to understand your long-term capabilities and values

Choosing an employer

Building your CV principally means two things: progressing steadily through professional roles, gathering experience and responsibility on the way; and doing so for recognised and well-respected employers. The competition to work for high-profile employers can be fierce, particularly for graduates.

Money is, of course, a key determinant of people's decisions, particularly early on or when family finances are demanding. Benefits such as pensions and career development are important too, though. However, people choose to leave organisations more often because they're unhappy with the opportunities they face or with the attitude of their boss than on purely financial grounds.

So check out what life is really like inside a company, specifically in the area you are joining, before you accept an offer (especially if you're concerned about diversity). Some employers' reality doesn't match their reputation, and getting that 'notch' on your CV can prove punishing, whatever the salary.

Staying in control

It's ever more likely that an organisation you join will undergo takeover, merger, or some other form of restructuring that will affect your progression directly or indirectly. Use any such event as an opportunity to learn – or make sure you move early before the rush. Remember that ultimately you can rely only on yourself to market your talent and achievements – no one else will be as interested as you are!

MAKING IT HAPPEN

- Don't expect that your career will be with one employer, or necessarily in the same industry and specialism. Plan accordingly.
- Be rigorous in identifying ways to progress, and form an idea of the stepping-stones and the lifecycle of jobs in the field.
- Be prepared to make opportunistic choices as you progress, rather than sticking to one single idea.

- It's important to become expert at something, and to maintain and expand your expertise, in order to give employers a good reason to hire and retain you.
- Learn how to lead and motivate teams as a manager of change and projects, and to deploy your specialist knowledge in a broad context.
- Fit your career plan to a realistic assessment of your abilities and potential. Be confident of your ability to achieve and succeed. It should also fit the level of your personal and financial ambition.

CONCLUSION

Taking charge of your career is increasingly important at a time when traditional loyalty from employees is much reduced, and when employers are learning (and having to learn) to show greater flexibility about employment patterns. Cradle-to-grave employment and automatic promotions are now, in virtually every area of life, a thing of the *recent* past. So, if your employer is now less likely to map out a career path for you, who will? The answer, of course, is the individual, and to take charge for the future requires a clear focus on oneself. There are several key points to remember when taking charge of your career:

- **Understand, value, and develop your own skills** – know what you do well, what you enjoy, and why. Letting these guide you will help to find a satisfying career path.
- **Recognise all of the factors that are important to you** – for example, geographical mobility, family time, vocational work.
- **Don't be afraid to discuss this with others** – friends and family can provide a useful sounding board, as they often recognise things about you that you may have missed yourself!
- **Plan your career – but not too much!** See opportunities and cope with change, positive or negative, that may arise and impact on this plan.

Finally, staying in control and making it happen are vitally important. Rarely will anyone else help you out or ensure that your career is looked after exactly as you would wish. The responsibility for acting, or reacting to changing circumstances, is yours.

THE BEST SOURCES OF HELP

Books:

Asher, Donald. *Who Gets Promoted, Who Doesn't and Why: 10 Things You'd Better Do If You Want to Get Ahead.* Berkeley: Ten Speed Press, 2007.

Berman Fortgang, Laura. *Take Yourself to the Top.* Revised ed. New York: Tarcher, 2005.

Lore, Nicholas. *The Pathfinder: How to Choose or Change Your Career for a Lifetime of Satisfaction and Success.* London: Simon & Schuster, 1998.

Websites:

Career Builder: **www.careerbuilder.com**

Monster.co.uk: **www.monster.co.uk**

Working Careers.com: **www.workingcareers.com**

Mentoring by Max Landsberg

EXECUTIVE SUMMARY

As the traditional career ladder crumbles and is replaced by an ever more organic and fluid structure, individuals and firms are increasingly institutionalising the once informal relationship known as mentoring, having a noticeable impact on the way firms implement management and leadership.

- Mentoring is important in developing and retaining employees.
- Corporate mentoring schemes match seasoned employees with younger colleagues new either to the organisation or to a level of responsibility, designed to have a measurable impact upon the organisation.
- Mentors give advice on goal setting and strategising, sharing their wisdom.
- Mentees gain advice, access to established networks, and broader personal and professional perspective.

INTRODUCTION

When Odysseus departed to fight the Trojans, he entrusted his son to Mentor, his wisest friend. Mentor counselled Odysseus's son for 13 years, lending his name to the guidance and support one might expect from a wise uncle. Mentoring is defined as the process whereby the leader offers guidance and support to facilitate the understanding of another. Mentoring is vital to delegating and to a range of other management situations – for example, team building, development of people, and managing change.

Most of us probably acquired our mentors more by luck than through planning. But with the erosion of traditional career ladders and the increasingly organic and unstructured composition of the modern firm, individuals and companies alike are seeing ever-greater merits in institutionalising this once-informal relationship called mentoring. In fact, in times of recession, mentoring is a simple and very cost-effective way to develop and retain talented employees.

THE SCOPE OF THE MENTORING RELATIONSHIP

Mentoring is the provision of counsel regarding major career or life issues by a wise and experienced adviser to someone who is typically outside the adviser's direct line of responsibility. In a corporate setting a mentoring relationship focuses on skills and career and personal development.

At the start of their relationship neither mentor nor mentee can anticipate all the issues they'll end up discussing. Nevertheless, both parties should be aware of the topics that they might fruitfully discuss or that may emerge.

These topics fall into two broad categories: helping the mentee to achieve learning and career goals, and building the mentee's confidence and self-awareness.

Career issues most typically include:

- whether the mentee's career vision and goals seem relevant and viable
- how to decode the organisation's feedback to the mentee, for example, from an annual appraisal or from a promotion received or missed
- what experience and expertise to acquire in the short and long terms
- where to find role models the mentee can identify with
- whether to accept an internal (or external) job offer
- how best to promote a corporate initiative that the mentee has conceived
- how the mentee can best interact with his or her line manager
- how to react to unacceptable behaviour experienced by the mentee, for example, apparent bias, favouritism, or harassment
- how to deal with the effects of a family problem or disaster, for example, how best to ask for paid or unpaid leave

Confidence and self-awareness issues may include:

- how the mentee can frankly review personal strengths and weaknesses
- whether feedback about the mentee's personal style is accurate or not
- how to overcome apparent career setbacks or feelings of isolation or depression
- how to project greater charisma

Despite this great breadth, mentoring relationships do have their limits. Organisations do not condone nepotistic relationships in which the mentor exerts undue influence in favour of the mentee. The mentor should focus on advice rather than rescue, directing the mentee to a professional counsellor if needed.

THE FOUR OPTIONS FOR MENTORING

There are four main types of mentoring an individual may seek or an organisation may wish to promote. It's important to recognise that these four models are not mutually exclusive. Furthermore, most people have more than one mentor, and those mentors may play complementary roles.

1. **Informal mentoring** takes place when an experienced person decides to take someone less experienced under his or her wing, often to give career advice. Such relationships sometimes form spontaneously, usually based on similar interests, expertise, or personal history. They tend to grow and flourish, often enduring after one person has left the organisation.

2. **Positional mentoring** occurs when the mentor is the mentee's line manager. All good managers mentor their team members to some extent, but there are natural constraints to the effectiveness of this approach. First, the mentee may find it difficult to raise issues of switching jobs or roles. Second, the mentor can't provide an impartial view of their professional relationship. Third, the

manager may be accused of favouritism if one mentee advances more rapidly than another.

3. **Formal mentoring** programmes emerged during the 1990s in an attempt to gain the advantages of natural mentoring while recognising the limitations of positional mentoring. Formal mentoring is discussed in more detail below.

4. **Situational mentoring** provides advice for a specific circumstance, for example, when the mentee has to implement a new computer system or take up a foreign posting. Although such a relationship is often by definition short term, it sometimes develops into a longer-term connection.

THE BENEFITS OF MENTORING

The benefits of mentoring accrue most obviously to mentees: advice, guidance, access to contacts and networks, reassurance, and a broader perspective.

But corporations also benefit through better recruitment, induction, and retention of staff, better communication across vertical and horizontal boundaries, faster organisational learning, and a stronger corporate culture.

Finally, mentors often benefit by enhancing their interpersonal skills, gaining insight into the workings of their organisation and teams, and enjoying the satisfaction of seeing others grow.

TECHNIQUES FOR ENSURING SUCCESS

At different times the mentor's role is to be a coach, motivator, guide, counsellor, role model, and – possibly – provider of contacts.

In playing these roles the excellent mentor:
- helps the mentee to focus efforts and clarify goals
- prompts the mentee to develop effective strategies, and acts as devil's advocate to challenge them
- helps the mentee to identify appropriate resources, contacts, and role models
- shares knowledge and wisdom based on his or her own experiences
- acts as a source of inspiration and motivation while maintaining confidentiality

Mentors do this in the following ways: by asking penetrating questions that help mentees to distinguish real issues from apparent ones; by accepting the mentees unconditionally, asking *how* or *what* rather than *why*; by listening actively to mentees' feelings as well as their words; and by volunteering observations when appropriate.

Mentors are unlikely to be effective in the long term if they try to become personal fixers of their mentees' problems.

In obtaining maximum value from the relationship, the three most important attributes of the excellent mentee are openness, initiative, and consideration for the mentor's time.

Mentees clearly need to be open about their objectives and aspirations. But they also need to be open to feedback or other observations by their mentor. If a mentor finds that frank comments are met with defensiveness, the relationship soon withers.

In taking the initiative, the excellent mentee is proactive in meeting with and relating to the mentor, arriving at meetings fully prepared with clear objectives, and taking the lead in suggesting new ways of viewing personal issues. Part of a mentee's task is to follow up on any ideas generated in the meetings and keep the mentor informed about progress.

Finally, the excellent mentee shows consideration for the mentor's investment of time. This involves identifying what the mentor wants to derive from the relationship, accommodating the mentor's schedule when arranging meetings, and providing feedback, praise, and thanks in an appropriate way.

ESTABLISHING MENTORING PROGRAMMES

Organisations increasingly aim to reap the benefits of mentoring by setting up formal programmes. Contrary to natural mentoring, formal mentoring tends to focus on specific objectives and aim at a measurable impact, for example, employee retention. It usually runs for a limited period, involves professional discussions, and is based on pairing, balanced in favour of the mentee.

Such programmes typically aim to support employees who are new to the organisation or a particular role, or who are part of a group that is in some way specialised or disadvantaged. Formal efforts to provide mentoring for all employees in an organisation rarely succeed because of the lack of sufficient mentoring time.

When designing a corporate mentoring programme:
- decide whether to adopt a formal programme or one that includes an element of natural mentoring
- develop simple criteria for eligibility to participate and for the maximum number of mentees per mentor
- agree whether mentees are to choose mentors (recommended) or vice versa, and establish a matching process that is patently fair
- explain the ground rules clearly, such as commitment to a duration of one year, ability to terminate the relationship at any time without blame, or complete confidentiality
- provide training for mentors and mentees and specify the expected benefits of the programme.

MAKING IT HAPPEN
- As a mentor, concentrate on helping the employee to achieve learning and career goals, and to build confidence and self-awareness.
- Some mentoring of team members is desirable, but recognise that the line manager, as a superior, can't provide an impartial view of the relationship.
- Use mentoring to enhance the mentor's own interpersonal skills and insights into the workings of the organisation and its teams.
- Consciously move between six roles as needed: coach, motivator, guide, counsellor, role model, and (possibly) provider of contacts.
- Ensure that the mentee arranges meetings with the mentor, comes fully prepared, and follows up on any ideas that emerge.

Use formal mentoring programmes only for selected employees – there won't be enough mentoring time for everybody. The following factors are critical to the success of corporate mentoring schemes:

- a supportive culture and work environment
- visible top management commitment, support and leadership
- participants are volunteers
- the mentoring scheme is designed to meet clearly envisioned, critical objectives within an effective time frame
- agreed terms of reference and ongoing support is provided for mentors
- the scheme is regularly monitored and evaluated for successes and drawbacks and inadequacies, and change is implemented on a regular basis

Key questions to consider when implementing a mentoring scheme are:

- what are the specific goals of the scheme?
- have all the people who need to be involved been identified?
- what are the metrics for the scheme's success and, accordingly, how will the scheme be evaluated?
- is there commitment from the top management?
- what are the necessary resources, and are they present?
- how will prospective mentors be trained?
- how will mentors and mentees be paired?
- have the guidelines for the scheme's operation been properly communicated to all parties involved?

Corporate mentoring schemes should be goal-focused and, providing the above points are recognised and effectively incorporated into the process, increase productivity and facilitate efficiency.

CONCLUSION

It is important to remember that corporate mentoring schemes should be clearly envisioned and constructed to meet the actual requirements of an organisation. They are currently being implemented in an increasing number of organisations where they are an invaluable asset – a trend that is sure to continue in the future as old-fashioned management structures are eroded and replaced by organic and dynamic modern constructs. Corporate mentoring schemes are a crucial part of such constructs and their benefits are certain to be reaped both in the short term and in the future.

THE BEST SOURCES OF HELP

Books:

Clutterbuck, David. *Everyone Needs a Mentor*. 4th ed. London: Chartered Institute of Personnel and Development, 2004.

Maxwell, John C. *Mentoring 101*. London: Thomas Nelson, 2008.

Website:

Chartered Institute of Personnel Development: **www.cipd.co.uk**

Coaching by Max Landsberg

EXECUTIVE SUMMARY

Coaching is an integrated set of actions, aimed at boosting the performance of an individual or team. Coaching includes:

- a context of trust and understanding
- use of 'ask', not only 'tell'
- agreement on the goals
- optimising opportunities to perform
- ongoing, ad hoc, feedback
- periodically, coaching sessions of greater depth
- a recognition by the line manager of the obligation to coach, and the incentives to do so

INTRODUCTION

Coaching is an integrated set of actions aimed at boosting a colleague's performance – so that the person being coached (the 'learner') reaches his or her full potential, or even redefines that view of said potential. In the business world, coaching is a systematic form of on-the-job training, provided by professional outsiders, by peers, or (preferably) by the learner's line manager. Coaching typically aims to build skills in communications (written and oral), problem-solving, teamwork, and selling, or even to enhance personal characteristics such as 'impact'. Here we will examine the very elements of successful coaching.

A CONTEXT OF TRUST AND UNDERSTANDING

For coaching to be effective, the coach and learner must first agree explicitly on how the coaching will be delivered. A brief discussion will normally suffice if the coach is the coachee's line manager. However, if the coach is an external professional, a written contract is advisable.

In addition, however, the coach and learner need to trust and understand each other.

Firstly, and most importantly, the learner needs to trust that the coach is not continually trying to evaluate him or her. In companies or teams in which the culture is highly evaluative, junior people typically do not ask their line managers for coaching support – they avoid showing weakness or ignorance.

Secondly, the coach needs to understand what motivates the learner to perform strongly in the relevant areas – and whether any under-performance derives from a lack of skill, or from a lack of will (since the approach to coaching might differ in these two cases).

Finally, the learner needs to understand how the coach most likes to deliver coaching. This topic is often overlooked – but the truly great coach-cum-manager typically helps the learner to understand his or her preferences.

ASK – DO NOT JUST *TELL*

In all aspects of coaching, the effective coach will more often ask questions than provide, or 'tell', answers. This applies both when providing feedback about the learner's prior under-performance, as well as when generating ideas about how to improve that performance.

AGREE SPECIFIC GOALS

Crucial to the coaching process are explicit goals for the learner. This may spring from a recent annual appraisal, from the requirements of a new role, or from some new aspiration by the learner.

It is worth remembering that the best goals are Specific, Measurable, Achievable, Results-driven, and Time constituted – the memorable 'SMART' acronym.

OPTIMISE OPPORTUNITIES

Practice makes perfect – but feedback alone will not. Central to any increased performance by the learner is the opportunity to confront new challenges in the skill area on which he or she is working. This is why line managers are potentially the best coaches of their team members – they can directly assign tasks which will allow the learner to hone the relevant skills.

PROVIDE AD HOC FEEDBACK

Feedback is one of the coach's most important techniques. Ad hoc feedback means regular constructive and considered comments. Ineffective managers tend to provide feedback using generalities ('Your presentations lack impact.'). Such negative forms of feedback leave the learner feeling blamed, defensive, uncertain, and lacking in confidence and self-esteem.

By contrast, constructive feedback focuses on specific skills and improvements needed. It clarifies 'where the learner stands' and what to do next, and leaves the person feeling helped rather than merely judged. With this in mind, effective coaches can deliver constructive feedback in three discrete parts.

1. Firstly, the coach is specific in replaying actions that the learner took. ('During your last presentation you avoided answering a direct question and instead presented another chart.')
2. Secondly, the coach highlights the implications. ('This made the audience feel that you were uncertain about your material and uninterested in their concerns.')
3. Finally, the coach suggests a desired outcome. ('Next time try to allow time for questions and respond to them clearly.')

This three-part approach (*Action, Impact, Desirable outcome* – or *AID* for short), is the key to providing useful feedback. It is particularly effective if the three points can be elicited using 'ask' mode, ('Which parts of your presentation worked best? Which parts of it worked least well? What was the impact of this? What could you do differently next time?')

Even when delivering positive feedback (that is, praise), effective coaches use the first two steps of this approach. By specifically highlighting the Action and the Impact, the coachee can more fully understand why he or she has 'done a good job'.

DELIVER IN-DEPTH SESSIONS

Periodically the coach and coachee will decide to complement ad hoc feedback with a 30–60-minute coaching 'session'.

To ensure a relevant focus and clear outcomes, effective coaches typically use a four-step agenda that covers **G**oals, **R**eality, **O**ptions, and **W**rap-up: the GROW model.

In the first step (**Goals**), coach and learner agree on the topic for discussion and the objective for the session ('Let's find ways to further develop your presentation skills. Let's find at least three ideas in the next half-hour.'). They might also review or amend the longer-term goal ('Let's establish as a goal that you feel able to present the division's results to the board meeting next month.').

In the second step (**Reality**), the coach and learner take stock of the coachee's current strengths and weaknesses. The effective coach invites the learner to do most of the talking, starting with a self-assessment. If the coach does provide feedback, it takes the form of specific examples, either in ask mode ('What did you feel about the question-and-answer session at the end of your last presentation?') or in tell mode ('You could have allowed more time for questions.').

In step three (**Options**), coach and learner both brainstorm ways forward. What can the coachee do to change the situation? What alternatives are there to that approach? Who could help? The coach's role is not primarily to provide answers. It is rather to stimulate creative ideas from the learner – possible actions that the learner will more naturally buy into.

Finally (**Wrap-up**), the coach helps the learner to choose an option and commit to action. This involves identifying possible obstacles, making the next steps specific, agreeing timing, and identifying any support needed. In subsequent sessions the coach will naturally vary the length of each step as needed.

UNDERSTAND OBLIGATIONS AND INCENTIVES

The autocratic manager is fast becoming a dinosaur; all managers are now obliged to coach their teams. This stems from two changes in the business climate. Firstly, employees are now even more avid to acquire skills, and even more likely to change employer if they are disappointed. Thus, coaching is crucial to the retention of talented people. Secondly, the rapid pace of business and the greater prevalence of job rotation and cross-functional teamwork mean that traditional off-the-job training can rarely be scheduled in a timely way.

Strong managers recognise their obligation to coach. They also realise the benefits to themselves: more time because of having a stronger team to which to delegate; less time spent on recruiting replacements; a more positive and enjoyable work environment; and stronger interpersonal skills honed through coaching.

MAKING IT HAPPEN

There are many questions that coaches can ask to focus the coaching process. The same questions can also be used for self-coaching – all you need to do is consider a major issue or ongoing behaviour that you would like to resolve.

- What are you trying to achieve?
- How will you know when you have achieved it?
- Would you define it as an end goal or a performance goal?
- If it is an end goal, what performance goal could be related to it?
- Is the goal specific?
- In what way is it measurable?
- To what extent can you control the result, What sort of things won't you have control over?
- Do you feel that achieving the goal will stretch or break you?
- When do you want to achieve the goal by?
- What are the milestones or key points on the way to achieving your goal?
- Who is involved and what effect could they have on the situation?
- What have you done about this situation so far, and what have been the results?
- What are the major constraints in finding a way forward?
- Are these constraints major or minor? How could their effect be reduced?
- What other issues are occurring at work that might have a bearing on your goal?
- What options do you have?
- If you had unlimited resources, what options would you have?
- Could you link your goal to some other organisational issue?
- What would be the perfect solution?

Once the position has been assessed, the time comes to select the best option and take action. The following questions may then be useful:

- What are you going to do?
- When are you going to do it?
- Who needs to know?
- What support and resources do you need, and how will you get them?
- How will the above help you to achieve your goals?
- What obstacles might hinder you and what strategies do you have for countering these?

CONCLUSION

Coaching has much to do with mentoring and it has a great deal to do with counselling. All three are about supporting individuals to overcome problems, achieve success, and realise their full potential. Common skills for coaches, mentors, and counsellors are strong interpersonal skills, and include:

- good listening skills
- good questioning – getting the learner to open up by asking open questions and avoiding 'yes' or 'no' answers
- suspending judgment
- giving constructive feedback
- checking understanding
- providing focus

The value of all these attributes is that they clarify issues, solve problems by creating options, change patterns of behaviour, and help the individual to learn, and develop action plans to ensure that progress is made.

Coaching relies on the agenda being set by the learners. They should discover their own way forward, and should feel commitment to their course of action because they have been the one responsible for establishing it. Coaching can be seen as having four main phases:

1. Set **goals** both for the overall coaching relationship and for each session.
2. Explore the current position of the learner: the **reality** of their circumstances and their concerns.
3. Generate strategies, action plans, and **options** for achieving the desired goals.
4. Decide **what** is to be done, by whom, how, and when.

THE BEST SOURCES OF HELP
Books:
Bossons, Patricia, Jeremy Kourdi and Denis Sartain. *Coaching Essentials*. London: A & C Black, 2009.
Landsberg, Max. *The Tao of Coaching*. London: Economist Books, 2005.
O'Connor, Joseph, and Andrea Lages. *How Coaching Works: The Essential Guide to the History and Practice of Effective Coaching*. London: A & C Black, 2007
Whitmore, Sir John. *Coaching for Performance*. 4th ed. London: Nicholas Brealey, 2009.

Website:
International Coach Federation:
www.coachfederation.org

Downsizing with Dignity by Alan Downs

EXECUTIVE SUMMARY

- Downsizing (or redundancy) is a toxic solution. Used sparingly and with planning it can be an organisational lifesaver, but when used repeatedly without a thoughtful strategy it can destroy an organisation's effectiveness.
- One outcome of downsizing must be to preserve the organisation's intellectual capital.
- How downsized employees are treated directly affects the morale and retention of valued, high-performing employees who are not downsized.
- Downsizing should never be used as a communication to financial centres or investors of the new management's tough-minded, no-nonsense style of management – the cost of downsizing far outweighs any benefits thus gained.

INTRODUCTION

Make no mistake: downsizing is extremely difficult, even in challenging financial times. It taxes all of a management team's resources, including both business acumen and humanity. No one looks forward to downsizing. Perhaps this is why so many otherwise first-rate executives downsize so poorly. They ignore all the signs pointing to a layoff until it's too late to plan adequately, then act hastily to reduce the financial drain of excess staff. The extremely difficult decisions of who must be laid off, how much notice they will be given, the amount of severance pay, and how far the company will go to help the laid-off employee find another job are given less than adequate attention. These critical decisions have as much to do with the future of the organisation as they do with the future of the laid-off employees, so they must be considered carefully.

So what happens? These decisions often are handed to the legal department, whose primary objective is to reduce the risk of legal proceedings, not to protect the morale and intellectual capital of the organisation. Consequently downsizing is often executed with a brisk, compassionless efficiency that leaves laid-off employees angry and surviving employees feeling helpless, demotivated, and poorly prepared to start rebuilding the business.

Helplessness is the enemy of high achievement. It produces a work environment of withdrawal, risk-averse decisions, severely impaired morale, and excessive blaming. All of these put a stranglehold upon an organisation that now desperately needs to excel. Thus downsizing becomes a contributor to an organisation's downfall rather than a catalyst for growth and profitability.

AVOIDING THE PITFALLS

Ineffective methods of downsizing abound. Downsizing malpractices such as those that follow are common; they are also inefficient and very dangerous.

Allowing legal concerns to design the redundancies

Most corporate lawyers advise laying off employees on a last-hired, first-fired basis across all departments. The method for downsizing that is most clearly defensible in a court of law, for example, is to lay off 10 per cent of employees across all departments on a seniority-only basis. This way no employee can claim to have been made redundant for discriminatory reasons. Furthermore, lawyers advise against saying anything more than what's absolutely necessary to either departing employees or survivors. This caution protects the company from making any implied or explicit promises that aren't then kept. By strictly scripting what is said, the company protects itself from verbal slips by managers who are themselves stressed at having to release valued employees.

This approach may succeed from a legal perspective, but not necessarily from the more important one of organisational health. First, laying off employees by a flat percentage across different departments is irrational. How can it be that accounting can do with the same proportion of fewer employees as human resources? Could one department be externalised and the other left intact? The decision of how many employees to lay off from each department should be based on an analysis of business needs, not an arbitrary statistic.

The concept of laying off employees strictly on the basis of seniority is also irrational. The choice of employees for redundancy should be based on a redistribution of the work, not the date the employee was hired. Sometimes an employee of 18 months has a skill far more valuable than one with 18 years' seniority.

Giving as little notice as possible

Out of fear and guilt many executives choose to give employees as little forewarning as possible about upcoming redundancies. Managers fear that if employees know their fate ahead of time, they may become demoralised and unproductive – they may even sabotage the business. However, there is no documented evidence that advance notice of redundancies increases the incidence of employee sabotage.

The lack of advance notice, however, does dramatically increase mistrust of management among surviving workers. Trust is based on mutual respect. When employees discover what has been brewing without their knowledge or input (and they will when the first person is let go), they see a blatant disrespect for their integrity, destroying trust. By not giving employees information that could be enormously helpful to them in planning their own lives, management initiates a cycle of mistrust and helplessness that can be very destructive and require years to correct.

Acting as if nothing happened

Many managers believe that after redundancies, the less said about them the better. With luck, everyone will just forget and move on. The reality is that surviving employees will talk about what's happened whether the management team does or doesn't. The more the company tries to suppress these discussions and act as if nothing has happened, the more subversive the discussion becomes. Remaining employees will react to what has happened regardless of whether the management does.

Recovery from redundancies is greatly hastened if managers and employees are allowed to speak their minds freely about what's happened. In fact, it can be a great opportunity for the survivors to pull together and renew ties. When management refuses to acknowledge what has really taken place, it appears emphatically heartless, feeding the employees' sense of helplessness. If management won't talk about it even after the fact, what else is it hiding?

DOWNSIZING EFFECTIVELY
An organisation that isn't functioning at optimal efficiency and is thinking that redundancies are needed must keep in mind a few key principles.

Is the problem too many people or too little profit?
This is the critical first question to ask before any redundancies. Using redundancies as a cost-cutting measure is utterly foolish: throwing away valuable talent and organisational learning only makes a bad situation worse. When your business lacks revenue, annihilating intellectual capital and thus reducing the efficiency of remaining resources as well as the potential for future growth is not the solution.

If the answer is too many employees, then you've begun the process of a well-thought-out strategy for change. To legitimately determine if you have too many employees, look at the organisation's business plan, not its headcount. What product and services will you offer? Which of these products and services is likely to be profitable? What talent will you need to run the new organisation? These questions will help you plan for the future after redundancies. These issues will enable a quick turnaround from the inevitably negative effects of downsizing to positive growth in value.

What will the post-redundancies company look like?
Having a clear, well-defined vision of the new company is imperative *before the redundancies take place*. Management should know what it wants to accomplish, where the emphasis will be in the new organisation, and what staff will be needed.

If not directed according to a clear vision of the future, the new organisation is likely to carry forward some of the same problems that initially created the need for the redundancies. Unfortunately, many managers underestimate the momentum of the old organisation to recreate the same problems. Without a clearly defined, shared vision of the new company among the entire management team, the past will be likely to sabotage the future and create a cycle of repeated redundancies with little improvement in organisational efficiency.

Always respect people's dignity
The methods employed in many poorly executed redundancies treat employees like children. Information is withheld and doled out. Managers' control over their employees is violated. Human-resource representatives scurry from one hush-hush meeting to another. How management treats laid-off employees is how it vicariously treats remaining employees – in a successful layoff, everything is done in the arena, with everyone observing.

Why does this matter? Because careful planning will keep the organisation going and improve its results. You must keep exceptional talent, who are also the employees most marketable to other organisations. When they see the company treating laid-off employees poorly, they'll start looking for a better place to work.

Respect the law
While it's important not to allow the legal department to design a redundancy package, it's nevertheless important to respect the employment laws. In different countries such laws include entitlements tied to civil rights, age discrimination, disabilities, worked adjustment, and retraining. These laws should be respected for what they intend as well as what they prescribe – or proscribe. If you plan your layoff according to business needs, and not on headcount or seniority, you should have no problem upholding the law. You will almost always find yourself in legal trouble when you base redundancies on factors other than business needs.

MINI-CASES
Good examples
During the merger of *BB&T Financial Corporation* and *Southern National Corporation*, redundant positions were eliminated through the strategic use of a hiring freeze.

Hewlett-Packard implemented a so-called fortnight programme in which all employees were asked to take one day off without pay every two weeks until business revenue increased. Similarly, during 2009 when auto manufacturers worldwide were struggling with falling demand for their vehicles, several major corporations (such as Honda) asked workers to take time off on reduced pay, in the hope of weathering the recessionary storm and retaining the skills they would need when the business cycle improved.

Bad examples
Eastman Kodak has laid off thousands of employees in the past 20 years without seeing any significant rise in productivity or profitability as a result. Virtually all the redundancies were administered by company-wide mandated percentage of employees to be laid off.

Perhaps the classic bad-case example remains *Scott Paper*. It conducted a layoff of 10,500 employees in the mid-1990s. In the years that followed Scott was unable to introduce any new products and saw a dramatic decrease in profitability, until it was eventually bought out by competitor Kimberly-Clark.

MAKING IT HAPPEN

- Plan for the future, including a shared vision of the company post-layoff. Consider how best to motivate and reward employees after downsizing and how to retain the most talented and valuable employees.
- Treat all employees with dignity and respect. Communicate too much rather than withholding information.
- Research applicable laws and follow the spirit of the legislation.
- Afterwards, give employees the psychological space to accept and discuss what has happened.
- Understand what the downsizing process must achieve – and what it must avoid.

CONCLUSION

There are two important factors to keep in mind when planning redundancies: respecting employee dignity,

and business planning. No one, from the mailroom to the boardroom, enjoys downsizing; but when it is unavoidable, redundancies can be accomplished in such a way that the problem is fixed and the organisation excels.

THE BEST SOURCES OF HELP

Books:

Essentials of Employment Law. London: Chartered Institute of Personnel Development, 2008.

Marchington, Mick, and Adrian Wilkinson. *Human Resources Management at Work*. 4th ed. London: Chartered Institute of Personnel Development, 2008.

Palca, Julia and Catherine Taylor. *Employment Law Checklists 2009*. 4th ed. Oxford: OUP, 2009.

Saleni, Rey. *Leading After a Layoff*. Avon, Massachusetts: Adams Media, 2005.

Website:

Chartered Institute of Personnel Development: **www.cipd.co.uk**

Viewpoint: Philip Kotler Making Marketing Manageable

Philip Kotler is the world's pre-eminent marketing thinker. A professor at the J.L. Kellogg Graduate School of Management, Northwestern University, Kotler's reputation as one of the world's foremost marketing experts is substantially based on the definitive textbook *Marketing Management: Analysis, Planning, Implementation, and Control*. Now in its 13th edition, it remains the definitive work on the subject. He has published over 40 other books, covering such topics as the marketing of places, persons, social causes, and cultural institutions.

Kotler has done more than virtually anyone to cement marketing's reputation as a serious business discipline. 'When I am asked to define marketing in the briefest possible way, I say marketing is "meeting needs profitably". A lot of us meet needs – but businesses are set up to do it profitably. . .marketing is the homework that you do to hit the mark that satisfies the needs of the target market exactly.'

What is the most important thing and who is the most important person to have influenced your thinking on business and management?

Businesses are finally grasping that winning companies choose target segments and customers and make them central to developing their strategy and operations. Customer focus is critical in a world no longer marked by a shortage of goods but by a shortage of customers.

I am deeply influenced by the late Peter Drucker, who observed some decades ago that 'marketing. . .is the

whole business seen from the point of view of its final result, that is, from the customer's point of view'. Drucker insisted that a company has only two functions: innovation and marketing. I have been called the Father of Modern Marketing. But if that's the case, Peter Drucker is The Grandfather of Modern Marketing.

Compared to the last 50 years, how will business be different in the 21st century?

Technology will have the deepest impact on business. We have already witnessed the impact of lean and flexible manufacturing, computers, mobiles phones, the Internet, and wireless. Business success in the future will require knowledge workers who are skilled in specific technologies that might confer a competitive advantage to the firm.

The other force having a deep impact on business is globalisation. Today a producer of a product or service needs to think of the world market, not just the domestic market. The producer may be able to sell additional units in select other countries. Also, the producer needs to worry about foreign producers coming into his market.

What effect has the advent of the new economy and the Internet had on your thinking and on marketing?

I became fascinated with the potentials of e-business to create new competitive advantages. Companies are making increasing use of such digital media as websites, podcasts, blogs, webcasts, social media, and mobile marketing. They continue to use traditional media but are now adding a whole layer of digital media to target specific buyers with timely and relevant information and promotion. The company's website is its face to the world.

In my 13th edition of *Marketing Management*, I show how customers, companies, competitors, and marketplaces all gain from the digital revolution. Consumers can compare suppliers and their prices from around the world. Companies can quickly gain information on consumers, competitors, suppliers and distributors. The digital revolution is without a doubt increasing marketing productivity.

Are these changes reflected in your current research?

I am doing research on the ability of companies to manage their future through information. I have formulated a concept called 'holistic marketing', where companies are able to find, create, and deliver value by linking demand management, resource planning, and partner alliances. Central to holistic marketing is the use of the Internet, the company Intranet, and various Extranets to drive the company to profitable growth.

My research is taking two directions. One is to develop real-time marketing information 'dashboards' where managers can continuously monitor sales, prices, and costs in different geographical and segment markets. This will help managers spot growth opportunities as well as problems emerging in the field.

The other research direction is to create 'planning dashboards', to be used by brand and product managers to develop stronger marketing plans. They can click to find out how to do any procedure, such as test a marketing concept, develop a sales promotion, test the effectiveness of an ad, or run a test market. The planning dashboard would open a marketing encyclopaedia of best marketing practices on the computer screen.

I have also been developing a Chaotics Management and Marketing System designed to help companies adjust their marketing in The Age of Turbulence. I warn against across-the-board cost cuts and emphasise that turbulent conditions present new opportunities as well as new threats.

What new skills will be needed to cope with these changes? How can managers best develop these required skills?

Marketers will need skills beyond the four traditional ones of marketing research, sales management, advertising, and sales promotion. Needed are skills in:
- database marketing and data mining
- customer relationship management (CRM)
- partner relationship management (PRM)
- telemarketing and call centre management
- integrated marketing communications (IMC)
- public relations marketing (including event and sponsorship marketing)

- profitability analysis applied to customers, market segments, channels, geographical area, and order sizes
- customisation of offerings, services, and messages
- experiential marketing (creating a total experience)

Are there new management questions we should be asking? If so, what are they?

Here are a few questions, not necessarily new ones, that management should think through better:
- How much should companies invest in social responsibility programmes? How can the payoff be measured?
- Would companies be more profitable if they spent less on traditional advertising and promotion and more on innovation and improving their products and services so that customer word-of-mouth can serve as the engine for growth?
- How can companies move more of their customers to using less costly channels?
- How can companies speed up the digitalisation of their production, marketing, and distribution and service systems?

What will happen to the concept of the career in the future? What career advice would you offer tomorrow's managers?

Fewer managers will spend their whole career within one company. Managers will be more attached to their knowledge speciality than to their current company. There will be active markets for each knowledge speciality, and managers will be on the lookout for advancement opportunities. The key then is for tomorrow's managers to study the various knowledge specialities and choose the one or two that will yield the most long-run market value and personal satisfaction. Companies will need to develop better inducement packages and conditions for retaining their most valued knowledge workers.

How can companies best promote enterprises that are a) profitable and b) good places for people to work?

Profitability and a good place to work are more compatible than profitability and a bad place to work. In the old days zero sum thinking prevailed, in that manufacturers thought that they would make the most money by paying the least to their suppliers, employees, and distributors. But this led to poorer inputs and outputs and lots of resource turnover. Smart companies today practise positive sum thinking and treat their suppliers, employees, and distributors as partners who are motivated to deliver superior value to target customers. 'Win-win-win' thinking will prevail over 'I win, you lose' thinking.

THE BEST SOURCES OF HELP

Kotler, Philip, and Kevin Keller. *Marketing Management: Analysis, Planning, Implementation, and Control*. 13th ed. Harlow: Prentice Hall, 2009.

Managing 1 : 1 Marketing by Drayton Bird

EXECUTIVE SUMMARY

- Direct marketing is a special marketing discipline, not just a medium.
- The aim is to increase customer value.
- It focuses on individuals, not masses.
- Direct marketing builds brands; it must be integrated with other disciplines.
- Its principles apply to e-commerce.
- Building and enhancing the database is key.
- Testing and accurate measurement reduce risk and increase return on investment.

INTRODUCTION

Virtually all organisations in advanced economies – and many in less-developed ones – use direct marketing. In the United Kingdom alone, the industry employs an estimated 800,000 people and generates a total annual spend of over £100 billion (Young Direct Marketing Awards, 2009).

Today's direct marketing is really a fusion of traditional mail-order selling and direct mail. Yet it's more than a sales process or medium: it's a marketing discipline with special characteristics. It uses all media. It's personal, focusing on individuals, not masses. Every message is coded, so you can gauge return on investment exactly. And it looks to long-term customer value rather than the value of individual sales. It is growing in importance because e-commerce, also conducted directly with individuals, is accelerated direct marketing. Brands like Amazon, Dell, and eBay are all direct marketers.

Increasingly, as businesses face greater competition and products and services can be copied quickly direct marketing makes great sense, as it focuses more on the customer than on what is actually being sold. It is not always a cheaper way of marketing. But when properly managed, it directs your efforts more accurately, giving you more for your marketing money. It does this in three stages.

Three steps to success

1. First, you identify those customers, including organisations and the individuals within them, that your offering is most likely to appeal to. You store relevant data about them on a database, which you continually enrich with added information. So, for example, you can offer what they are most likely to want when they are most likely to want it with growing confidence, eliminating junk messages.
2. Second, by communicating with customers in an increasingly relevant way as you learn more, you strengthen and lengthen your relationship with them. This is important, as retaining customers is far more profitable than attracting them. This fact has helped fuel today's greater focus on the customer.
3. Third, you reduce risk by rigorous measurement, testing on small numbers before spending big money, and comparing different approaches. Seemingly trivial changes can make big differences. Adding – or removing – an element in a mailing may increase return on investment by as much as 90 per cent. Running one TV commercial rather than another, or changing the time it runs, may transform loss into profit. Changing just one word in a headline can have the same effect. Altering the timing and heading to an e-mail can increase response as much as 260 per cent.

WHERE AND HOW IT WORKS

Direct marketing is ideal for anything complex calling for detailed explanation to be studied at leisure. It also works where potential customers feel pressurised by salespeople. Insurance and investment are good examples – financial services are the biggest direct marketers.

It's a good technique to use when distance is involved. It's also good for products people are shy about buying in person – slimming remedies and other health-related products, or exotic lingerie.

Since the database means you can vary messages to suit individuals, direct marketing works well if you sell to businesses where decision-makers have varying motives – value for money matters to finance directors, while managing directors may care more about efficiency.

Direct marketing complements personal selling. You can use various means – direct-response advertising, faxes, banner ads on a website, the phone, e-mail, or direct mail – to acquire leads, keep in touch with customers between calls, or deal with lower-value customers who don't merit expensive personal visits.

Direct messages are advertising and can build brands fast – Dell and Direct Line insurance are good examples of this. Direct marketing must be integrated with other disciplines. The creative work need not slavishly follow your advertising, but should have the same tone and positioning.

Long copy generally works best, as you seek an immediate response, by using and repeating every relevant argument. That's why effective mailings often incorporate many pieces. The letter, being personal, is normally the critical element in a mailing. Response rates vary greatly depending on the proposition: getting someone to buy something costly is far harder than offering them a free chance to win a lottery.

THE DATABASE IS CENTRAL

At the heart of direct marketing lies the database, holding details of each individual or business. You use it to communicate with people by mail, e-mail, fax, or phone. Recording all relevant information is vital. Success turns on how persuasive, relevant, and timely your messages are, and this is determined largely by how well you capture, store, and use the right details.

You develop your database in the same way you develop your knowledge of other people. It starts as just names and addresses; each added scrap of information makes it more valuable. You overlay it with data already in the public domain or gathered by private enterprise.

The electoral roll gives you simple but essential information such as whether names and address are accurate and how many people live in a particular household. Other valuable data derive from the likely characteristics of different addresses. Some areas are more prosperous than others; in the United Kingdom, generally someone in a house with a name is wealthier than someone in one with a number; they in turn are richer than a flat-dweller; and a property-owner is more prosperous than a tenant.

You enrich your database with relevant facts, such as who buys what, how often, and when; how long they remain loyal customers; what else they have bought – thus building a complete picture of their nature and value. This information also helps you to predict behaviour; similar individuals behave similarly.

CUSTOMER LIFE-TIME VALUE

Strategically, the most interesting aspect of direct marketing may be its emphasis on customer value. Whereas firms have traditionally measured performance by current sales or profits, direct marketers have always thought in terms of how profitable a customer is over time.

One reason is because the best early direct marketers were book clubs and catalogue companies. They lured customers with incentives, which obviously made the first transaction unprofitable – their strategy was to lose money initially in order to make money eventually. Incentives to buy, or enquire, or simply give information, are important in direct marketing. Thus, a car firm may want to know what car a prospect has, what car he or she is thinking of buying next and when, and how much money the next car is likely to cost.

The early direct marketers measured loyalty (how long a customer stayed with them – usually between five and seven years) and what they could afford to pay to acquire a customer. In the same way banks, credit-card companies, and insurance companies look to long-term relationships, and car firms look to keep customers buying their marque.

Customer value varies enormously. A small percentage of customers generally buys most of any product or service, and by identifying those individuals you can concentrate your efforts and reap disproportionate rewards. You can lower or eliminate expenditure on less valuable customers and increase it on more valuable ones.

A MORE PRECISE TOOL

Direct marketing is more precise than mass advertising. Mass advertisers concentrate on the most effective media (those more likely to be read or viewed by customers), but this is inevitably imprecise, as they're always looking at masses or groups.

Direct marketing aims to isolate individuals and place them in groups. The categories will vary according to your purpose. Thus, on a database you could isolate all the individuals over 50 with an income above £40,000 per annum within 15 miles of Manchester and offer them the opportunity to buy a car direct from their nearest showroom. Thus you eliminate waste.

Marketers often spend millions on huge campaigns without knowing in advance what will happen. Intelligent speculation or a hunch can be backed by research predicting likely customer behaviour. Very often, though, research fails. Customers can tell you what they think or believe, but not what they will do when asked to part with money, especially with a new product.

The direct marketer tests on a small scale first. Test results tell you pretty exactly what will happen – before you spend. You can discover which treatments and media work best and when. Nobody knows in advance which message will work best – and there's often great discrepancy between the media that research ranks as best and those that generate most response. Equally, customers recruited in different media or with different messages usually tend to have differing lifetime value.

There's ample room for confusion because different organisations use different names for very similar activities. Some names describe the process, for example, as database marketing, dialogue marketing, and one-to-one marketing. Others, such as loyalty marketing and relationship marketing (often labelled customer relationship management), relate to the objective. All rely on direct-marketing methods, but some neglect testing and measurement.

MAKING IT HAPPEN

- Identify the customers and organisations (and individuals within) most likely to want your offering, and store the data on a continually enriched database.
- Use direct marketing to strengthen and lengthen your relationship with profitably retained customers.
- Reduce marketing risk by rigorous testing before spending big money.
- Use direct response advertising, phone, fax, e-mail, or direct mail to complement personal selling by getting leads, keeping in touch, and serving lower-value customers.
- Generally, treat the personal letter as the critical element in a mailing.
- Put your emphasis on customer value – how profitable a customer is over time – not on current sales or profits. Customer value is the cornerstone of long-term success.

CONCLUSION

Direct (or one-to-one) marketing involves market segmentation down to the smallest element: the individual. Individuals with similar characteristics are placed in groups, which are analysed carefully, leading to a more detailed understanding of their needs and wants. They are then communicated with, based on the knowledge gained. This makes messages more relevant, leading to greater profitability and long-term competitive advantage. Good direct marketers test and measure constantly to optimise ROI. Without direct marketing, many organisations will not maximise their potential. Even packaged good marketers wedded to mass advertising like Procter and Gamble, Nestle, and Mars realise that direct marketing has a role to play. No intelligent marketing strategy should ignore it; some depend utterly on it. As markets become increasingly global, diverse, and complex, direct marketing has become increasingly valuable in creating effective marketing strategies.

THE BEST SOURCES OF HELP
Books:
Bird, Drayton. *Commonsense Direct and Digital Marketing.* 5th ed. London: Kogan Page, 2005.
Meisner, Chet. *The Complete Guide to Direct Marketing: Creating Breakthrough Programs That Really Work.* New York: Kaplan Business, 2006.
Stone, Bob, and Ron Jacob. *Successful Direct Marketing Methods: Interactive, Database, and Customer Marketing for the Multichannel Communications Age.* 8th ed. New York: McGraw-Hill Professional, 2008.

On Writing as an Essential Business Skill
by John Simmons

EXECUTIVE SUMMARY

- Brands need to manage both visual and verbal identity (images and words) to achieve recognition and differentiation.
- Creative management of a brand's written language – tone of voice – can build loyalty with audiences.
- Tone of voice needs to develop from the brand's personality and values, and to be consistent across all media, internal and external.
- Inconsistent application through everyday contacts can undermine a brand's credibility.
- All individuals represent a brand through the words they use – it is important at least to recognise when the right tone of voice is not being achieved.
- Champions – individuals able to write in the brand's tone of voice and to tell the brand's story – need to be established through development and training.
- Creativity, particularly the creativity of its own people, is the main means by which a modern business can make itself distinctive.
- Nurturing of creative writing skills at work achieves business objectives and provides opportunities for personal development.

INTRODUCTION
Why words matter
Words are the essential tools of communication. But they are so much more. They convey information, they express emotion; they influence, persuade, motivate. They do all the things that a successful business wants to do – if they are used well. Or, if they are used badly, they undermine a business.

After decades of obeisance to the notion that we 'live in a visual world', the word has struck back. From 'a picture is worth a thousand words', business is returning to a position closer to that articulated by Bill Bernbach in the 1950s: 'But not necessarily worth one word. The right word'.

VERBAL IDENTITY
Many businesses, particularly those that adhere to principles of branding, now attach equal importance to words and images. Visual identity – the consistent use of logos, colours, typefaces, photography – is an established management discipline. Verbal identity – managing a brand's tone of voice through style, vocabulary, names, and the use of stories – is in its relative infancy.

Combining the visual and the verbal provides the means to make brands that really work. A prime objective of any modern brand is to create better relationships with its consumers. Companies use their brands to create and maintain better relationships through conversations, just as individuals do. Many of those conversations are conducted in written form, whether in print, in e-mails or on the Internet. But, as 'conversations' implies, they need to be written as if they were spoken – a more informal approach to language than business practices of the previous century.

The words used in those conversations – through all experiences, including the Internet – are reflections of a brand's personality. When products and services are basically similar, words can be the principal means of differentiating one company from another.

A case study
In 1998 three college friends formed a company that makes fruit smoothies. A very simple business and, at

that time, a tiny market for the product. They called the company Innocent Drinks. They had little money to spend on visual identity, but the founders had a playful approach to words. They channelled their creative effort into writing words – humorous little stories – that appeared on the labels of their products.

Innocent's verbal identity begins with its name. They are innocent in the sense of being the little guys up against big corporations – but also in believing in the natural goodness of pure fruit, with no nasty additives. All their words reinforce this proposition through the disarming use of humour. A very clear sense of the Innocent personality emerges through every word they use, even down to a distinctive, honest but funny way of listing the ingredients of their products.

The news about Innocent spread, appropriately enough, by word of mouth. People talked about them, shared the humour of the labels (which changed constantly) and became loyal fans. Innocent got other things right too, particularly distribution. In a matter of a few years they were ubiquitous, the United Kingdom's fastest-growing food and drink company.

WORDS ARE SLIPPERY

Many businesses have since tried to copy Innocent, but Innocent's success is built on the consistency of its tone of voice and its absolute rightness for what it does. Different brands need different personalities and different words. Those words also need to be consistent across the brand's disciplines and range of activities. Otherwise the wrong words can undermine a brand.

It is relatively easy to manufacture a tone of voice that works in external communication such as advertising. People regard advertising – particularly on TV – almost as a form of entertainment. Naturally good advertising uses words creatively. But there is a danger if a brand's advertising sends a message of, say, off-beat friendliness and if a consumer's subsequent encounter with a brand representative or communication is disappointingly dull or unfriendly.

THE INDIVIDUALITY OF WORDS

A brand's tone of voice needs to work from the inside outwards, if it is to have real credibility. It should start with a brand personality that is distinctive and owned by the individuals responsible for shaping the company. But every individual has a role to play, because everyone represents the brand through the words that they choose to use. If a brand such as Apple promises to 'Think different', for example, this places responsibility on the behaviour of everyone representing the brand. The consumer has a right to expect a degree of creativity from all the brand's representatives. And words are the most *available* creative resource for any company to use.

Content matters as well as style. Even if, for example, Apple and Innocent had created an identical brand personality for themselves, their words would be made different by the fact that Apple would describe music or computer technology, whereas Innocent would write about fruit and the making of juice. Content influences vocabulary, the choice of individual words. These words are further ordered by structure and they are connected by style.

For a brand to achieve true differentiation in its tone of voice, all these elements need to be combined with craft. The outcome should be a playful richness of language rather than approaches that masquerade as verbal identity by restricting vocabulary to an approved list of words. Brands, and their representatives, need to see what they do as storytelling.

TELLING THE STORY

Stories are one of the most fundamental forms of communication. Through stories, individuals and businesses can understand the world better and engage more effectively with audiences. Stories can be used to achieve a number of important business objectives:

- provide starting points for brands and continuing touchpoints of inspiration as companies grow
- become a means of encouraging personal creative expression by employees, and therefore increased motivation
- clarify the purpose of a business and inspire greater internal and external loyalty
- illuminate the meaning of business strategies and principles so that they are more easily understood

DEVELOPING SKILLS

It is clear that the need to establish a distinctive verbal identity (including the use of storytelling) makes demands of a company and its individuals. Not everyone can be a fluent, skilful writer. But we all use words as part of our work – it is an inescapable fact of modern working life.

Companies need to look at the way they manage the words that individuals produce on their behalf. Champions – discipline by discipline, department by department – have to be given responsibility for setting and maintaining a high standard of written communication, internal and external. They need to create and adhere to an agreed tone of voice that projects a consistent brand personality. Skills need to be nurtured through guidelines, training, books, and online learning.

CONCLUSION
Creativity is fundamental

Fifty years ago, 'creativity' was required only in an advertising agency. Today every business needs to be creative and it needs to inspire and harness the creativity of all its people. This is not an optional extra, but an essential requirement for survival, growth and reinvention. Businesses that lack creativity will increasingly struggle to survive.

Creative skills therefore need to be nurtured and developed in businesses of all kinds. Writing is the creative skill that is, literally, closest at hand for any business. By developing people to express themselves more creatively through words, businesses can unlock the potential of innovation, increase the impact of communication and become more effective in winning business.

The business benefits are reinforced by the additional advantage of personal development. Businesses are increasingly reliant on the quality of people, and they need to make sure that people feel that they are fulfilling their potential. Writing is an effective way to help people in a business to achieve personal development.

THE BEST SOURCES OF HELP
Books:
Ogilvy, David. *The Unpublished David Ogilvy*. London: Sidgwick & Jackson, 1980.
Simmons, John. *Dark Angels*. London: Cyan Books, 2005.
Vincent, Laurence. *Legendary Brands: Unleashing the Power of Storytelling*. New York: Dearborn, 2002.
Whyte, David. *Crossing the Unknown Sea: Work and the Shaping of Identity*. London: Penguin, 2002.

How to Plan Marketing by Malcolm McDonald

EXECUTIVE SUMMARY
- Organisations operate in a complex and fast-changing environment and managers need some way of interacting with their environments.
- Marketing planning is merely a managerial process for coping with environmental uncertainty.
- Strategic marketing planning needs to precede tactical marketing planning.
- The output of the process (the plan) spells out how an organisation expects to achieve its objectives.
- Academic researchers agree that there is a link between marketing planning and long-term organisational success.
- The planning process is universal, although the formality of its implementation may vary between organisations.
- Organisational culture is the biggest barrier to implementing effective marketing planning.

INTRODUCTION
All organisations operate in a complex environment in which hundreds of external and internal factors interact to affect their ability to achieve their objectives. Managers need some understanding or view about how all these variables interact. They must try to be rational in making decisions, no matter how important intuition, feel, and experience are as contributory factors. Most managers accept that some kind of procedure for planning the organisation's marketing helps to sharpen this rationality, making the complexity of business operations manageable and adding a dimension of realism to the organisation's future plans.

This procedure is known as marketing planning.

THE ESSENCE OF MARKETING PLANNING
The contribution of marketing planning to the success of an organisation, whatever its area of activity, lies in its commitment to detailed analysis of future opportunities to meet customer needs. It offers a wholly professional approach to selling to well-defined market segments those products or services that deliver the desired benefits. Such commitment and activities shouldn't be mistaken for budgets and forecasts, which have always been a commercial necessity. Marketing planning is a more sophisticated approach concerned with identifying what sales are going to be made in the longer term and to whom, in order to give revenue budgets and sales forecasts a real chance of being achieved.

MARKETING PLANNING IS A MANAGERIAL PROCESS
In essence marketing planning is a managerial process, the output of which is a marketing plan. As such it is a logical sequence, a series of activities leading to the setting of marketing objectives and the formulation of plans for achieving them. Conceptually, the process is very simple and is achieved by means of a planning system. The system is little more than a structured way of identifying a range of options for the organisation, of making them explicit in writing, of formulating marketing objectives consistent with the company's overall objectives, and of scheduling and costing the specific activities most likely to bring about the achievement of the objectives. The systemisation of this process lies at the heart of the theory of marketing planning.

TYPES OF MARKETING PLAN
There are two principal kinds of marketing plan:
1. **The strategic marketing plan**
A strategic marketing plan is a plan for three or more years. It is a written document outlining how managers perceive their own position in the market relative to their competitors (with competitive advantage accurately defined), what objectives they want to achieve, how they intend to achieve them (strategies), what resources

are required (budget), and what results are expected. Three years is the most common strategic planning period. Five years is the longest, but is becoming less common because of the speed of technological and environmental change. Strategic marketing-driven plans are not to be confused with scenario planning or the kind of very long-range plans formulated by a number of Japanese companies (which often have planning horizons of between 50 and 200 years!).

2. **The tactical marketing plan**

A tactical marketing plan is the detailed scheduling and costing of the actions necessary for achieving the first year of the strategic marketing plan. The tactical plan is thus for one year.

THE CORRECT SEQUENCE OF MARKETING PLANS

Research into the marketing planning practices of organisations shows that successful companies complete the strategic plan before the tactical plan. Unsuccessful organisations often don't bother with a strategic marketing plan at all, relying largely on sales forecasts and the associated budgets. The problem with this approach is that many managers sell the products and services they find easiest to sell, concentrating on those customers who offer the least resistance. By developing short-term tactical marketing plans first and then extrapolating them, managers merely succeed in extrapolating their own shortcomings. This is just about acceptable when markets are growing rapidly or are regulated in such a way that little effort is required to grow sales. Today, however, few such markets exist. Preoccupation with preparing a detailed short-term marketing plan first is typical of companies that confuse sales forecasting and budgeting with strategic marketing planning.

THE CONTENTS OF A STRATEGIC MARKETING PLAN

The contents of a strategic marketing plan are as follows:

- **mission statement,** setting out the raison d'être of the organisation and covering its role, business definition, distinctive competence, and future indications
- **financial summary,** summarising the financial implications over the full planning period
- **market overview,** providing a brief picture of the market, including market structure, market trends, key market segments, and (sometimes) gap analysis
- **SWOT analysis,** analysing the strengths and weaknesses of the organisation compared with competitors against key customer success factors, and considering opportunities and threats, usually for each key product or segment
- **issues to be addressed,** derived from the SWOT analysis and usually specific to each product or segment
- **portfolio summary,** offering a pictorial summary of the SWOT analysis that makes it easy to see at a glance the relative importance of each of the four elements; it is often a two-dimensional matrix in which the horizontal axis measures the organisation's comparative strengths and the vertical axis measures its relative attractiveness

- **assumptions,** listing the underlying assumptions critical to the planned marketing objectives and strategies
- **marketing objectives,** usually consisting of quantitative statements (in terms of profit, volume, value, and market share) of what the organisation wishes to achieve; they are usually given by product, by segment, and overall
- **marketing strategies,** stating how the objectives are to be achieved; they often involve the four Ps of marketing: product, price, place, and promotion
- **resource requirements and budget,** showing the full planning-period budget, giving in detail the revenues and associated costs for each year

THE CONTENTS OF A TACTICAL MARKETING PLAN

The contents of a tactical marketing plan are very similar, except that they often omit the mission statement, the market overview, and SWOT analysis, and the plan goes into much more detailed quantification by product and segment of marketing objectives and associated strategies. An additional feature is more detailed scheduling and costing of the tactics necessary to achieve the first year's planned goals.

STRATEGIC MARKETING PLANNING: A REVIEW OF CURRENT THINKING

From an extensive review of the current research into strategic marketing planning, five principal conclusions emerge:

- There is a clear consensus about the desirable outputs of the strategic marketing planning process.
- Strategic marketing planning and the marketing orientation that accompanies it are clearly associated with improved organisational performance across most market situations.
- In unsuccessful companies the prescriptive process of strategic marketing planning is poorly adhered to in practice and is frequently used as a pretext for inadequate budgeting and tactical programmes.
- The primary barrier to strategic marketing planning lies in the organisational culture of the company and the values that stem from that culture.
- Although the degree of formality of the process can range from a highly creative, entrepreneurial approach to the more structured, rational process described here, there is universal consensus among strategic thinkers and planners that some kind of managerial planning process has to be used to manage the link between an organisation and its environment.

Hence, in large, multi-national, multi-product, multi-cultural organisations it is usual to find a structured process for marketing planning; in smaller organisations with less complex products or markets the management of the process tends to be much less formalised and structured. The process and the steps, however, are the same in all consistently successful organisations.

MINI-CASE

Everyone has an opinion about why the once-mighty IBM lost billions of dollars in the 1990s. Indeed, the two books about IBM published at the time both predicted the end of the company. The arrival of Lou Gerstner as chairman and CEO, however, heralded a reversal in its fortunes. Like all good managers, he stopped the financial bleeding by introducing operational efficiencies. He came from a consumer-goods background, and it wasn't long before he insisted that his business unit managers introduce the kind of classical market-based planning procedures described here, including the major basis for successful marketing planning – market segmentation. IBM is, due to Lou Gerstner, once again a major global player in the communications market.

Other firms – from Apple to Toyota and Google – have also succeeded and become market leaders by applying a combination of a strong strategy, innovative products, and operational efficiencies, combined with successful marketing planning.

MAKING IT HAPPEN

- Identify what sales will be made in the longer term and to whom, in order to turn revenue budgets and sales forecasts into reality.
- Analyse your strengths and weaknesses compared with competitors' against key customer success factors, and similarly review the organisation's opportunities and threats.
- Complete the strategic marketing plan before the tactical plan. Write your strategic marketing plan to cover three or more years, defining competitive advantage, objectives, strategies, and budgets.

- Build marketing strategies round the four Ps of marketing: product, price, place, promotion.
- Write a tactical marketing plan, detailing schedules and costing for the specific actions necessary to achieve the first year of the strategic plan.

CONCLUSION

Successful marketing planning is the cornerstone of developing strong, durable, and robust organisations. Overcoming an organisational culture that acts as a barrier to effective marketing planning is essential if performance is to be optimised and long-term goals are to be achieved. Given the complexity of the rapidly changing business environment and the high number of variables that influence business performance, it is necessary for managers to have an effective means of making the situation manageable. Thorough and detailed analysis of how to meet future customer needs provides a sophisticated and reliable method for building long-term success. Marketing planning enables the organisation's vision to become a reality.

THE BEST SOURCES OF HELP

Books:
McDonald, Malcolm. *Marketing Plans: How to Prepare Them, How to Use Them.* 6th ed. Oxford: Butterworth-Heinemann, 2007.
Piercy, Nigel. *Market-Led Strategic Change.* 4th ed. Oxford: Butterworth-Heinemann, 2008.

Creating Powerful Brands by Paul Stobart

EXECUTIVE SUMMARY

- A brand is defined as the sum of the functional and emotional characteristics that a consumer attributes to a product or service.
- Brands are important both to companies, as a source of competitive advantage, and to consumers, as an aid in making purchase decisions.
- A critical factor in creating powerful brands is a company's ability to differentiate the product and/or service elements of its offerings from those of its competitors.

- Key building blocks in the creation of a brand are brand proposition, brand positioning, and brand identity.
- Brand managers have a number of tools at their disposal, including product design, packaging, and advertising.
- It is important for companies to track their brand equity over time, particularly brand awareness and brand image measures.
- The Internet represents a powerful new medium for creating brands, but it's also encouraging consumers to demand a two-way dialogue with brand owners.

WHAT IS A BRAND?

Put simply, a brand is the difference between a bottle of sugared, flavoured, fizzy water and a bottle of Coca-Cola. It is the sum of the functional and emotional characteristics, both tangible and intangible, that a consumer attributes to a product or service. These characteristics are embodied in a name, trademark, symbol, or design, or any combination of these.

However, this definition is being increasingly stretched. As the Internet grows ever more pervasive, many online brands have virtually no tangible attributes. It could be argued that brands such as Amazon and Google exist purely in virtual reality. Moreover, the concept of branding can no longer be restricted to products and services. Film stars, politicians, and company executives are all realising that success is dependent on their ability to market themselves as brands.

MINI-CASE

The organisation as brand

Many companies, and particularly those that have system brands, are realising that creating a successful brand franchise involves mobilising the entire organisation. Every aspect of the organisation, from the premises through the behaviour of the employees (particularly those who work in customer-facing roles) to company letterheads and formal marketing communications, should reflect and reinforce the values of the brand.

A good example of the organisation as brand is Sage, a leading supplier of accounting and payroll software. Unusually for the software industry, where marketing tends to focus on product features, Sage's brand identity communicates a feeling of confident control, leading to peace of mind. Most customers who buy Sage software also purchase an annual telephone support contract. When they phone the hotline the support technician's ability to resolve their problem serves to reinforce the brand promise.

Another example is provided by Dyson, the British industrial design firm. A highly innovative approach to redesigning ordinary products (such as wheelbarrows and vacuum cleaners) permeates the whole business and is combined with careful marketing planning. (For example, Dyson's innovative 'cyclonic' vacuum cleaner was first launched in Japan, where it gained prominence and awards, before being launched worldwide.) The business has developed a strong brand widely known for its practical, innovative approach.

WHY ARE BRANDS IMPORTANT?

For most companies brands are their primary source of competitive advantage and their most valuable strategic asset. Without brands we'd live in a world of commodities – undifferentiated products that are traded solely on price, according to the laws of supply and demand. Branding enables companies to actively influence the demand side of the equation by encouraging consumers to base their purchase decisions on factors other than price.

Brands are also important for consumers. They enable consumers to make informed purchase decisions and help them to navigate their way through the bewildering number of alternatives that exist in any product category. It can also be argued that brands enrich our lives. In a world in which our basic needs have been satisfied, brands give us something to which we can aspire and help in defining our own identities. This, however, is a question of ideology, and many would disagree.

SOURCES OF DIFFERENTIATION

Differentiation is the most important concept in the creation of powerful brands. Essentially brands can be differentiated in terms of product and/or service, leading to four generic types.

1. One in which an offering is differentiated neither in terms of product nor service: it is a **commodity**. Precious metals and staple food products are still largely traded as commodities (though the increasing demand for organic produce is changing this).

2. One in which an offering is differentiated in product, but not in service terms: it is a **product brand**. Product brands can be further differentiated in terms of intrinsic (or functional) benefits and extrinsic (or emotional) benefits. In practice most consumer goods are product brands, and most contain elements of both intrinsic and extrinsic differentiation. Hi-fi manufacturers focus primarily on the functionality of their products, whilst most mainstream soft-drink brands are differentiated largely in terms of image. The marketing of cars, one of the most potent symbols of status and way of life, plays on both function and emotion.

3. An offering based on providing an intangible service is a **service brand**. Financial services are classic examples. Creating service brands can prove difficult because, unlike packaged goods, delivering a service to the consumer relies heavily on humans and humans are a lot less standard than products. Service brands are most often measured in terms of their perceived value and/or perceived quality of the experience.

4. An offering differentiated in both product and service terms is a **system brand**. The McDonald's experience is based on a combination of the quality of the food, the speed of the service, and the cleanliness of the restaurant.

THE BUILDING BLOCKS OF BRAND CREATION

The **brand proposition** is the statement of the functional and emotional benefits that a company believes its product or service offers to the consumer. Coca-Cola's brand proposition is a mixture of functional benefits (taste, refreshment) and emotional benefits (good wholesome fun).

Brand positioning is a description of those at whom the brand is aimed (the target audience) and where it stands relative to the competition.

Brand identity (or **brand image**) is the aggregation of the words, images, and ideas that the consumer associates with a brand. There is an increasing tendency to personify brands, and companies talk about brand personality and brand attitude. This is particularly important in youth markets, in which consumers regard brands as statements of their beliefs and preferences.

THE BRAND-BUILDER'S TOOLBOX

Successful brand creation starts with product design. But it's not just about how the product performs, it's also about how it looks. When Dyson turned the vacuum cleaner market upside down, it was due not only to the revolutionary technology, but also to the fact that its products looked like nothing else on earth!

In the fast-moving consumer-goods sector, packaging is also a key source of differentiation, both as a powerful tool for creating brand identity and as a means whereby brands can stand out from the crowd on increasingly cluttered supermarket shelves.

Advertising is perhaps the brand manager's most potent tool. Print and broadcast media not only represent a cost-effective mechanism for reaching mass audiences, they also have the power to influence consumer behaviour. The press is a particularly effective medium for communicating complex messages, while TV advertising, with its beguiling interplay of sounds and pictures, is ideal for building brand image.

In recent years, however, the brand manager's task has become increasingly complex. Brands have proliferated, media have fragmented, and consumers have become more cynical. Brand owners have had to become more innovative, constantly reinventing their brands to keep one step ahead of their competitors and their consumers.

Advances such as the arrival of the Internet into more than 50 per cent of our homes and the growing power and penetration of mobile phone technology has facilitated increasingly sophisticated segmentation as well as 24-hour messaging and communication. With the power of database profiling technologies, many brand owners are being able to jump the chasm from a one-to-many to a one-to-one marketing model.

MEASURING BRAND EQUITY

If brands are a company's most valuable strategic asset, then it makes sense to take good care of them. While it is difficult to prove a statistical relationship between advertising and sales because of the sheer number of variables involved, it is possible to prove a relationship between advertising and awareness and between awareness and sales. For this reason most companies track brand awareness levels, together with other measures such as brand loyalty and purchase intention.

It is also important to track brand image, to ensure that the differentiating elements of brand identity a company is attempting to communicate are being received accurately by the consumer. One reason for doing this is to gauge to what extent brand equity can be leveraged into line extensions or new products. Virgin is the classic example of this, with the brand now spanning airlines, trains, and soft drinks.

In recent years, many brand owners have attempted to assign an economic value to their brands on the balance sheet. The brand consultancy Interbrand have been at the forefront of this process, though the accounting profession has yet to fully embrace the concept.

MAKING IT HAPPEN

- Seek above all to differentiate the product and/or service elements of your offerings from those of your competitors.
- Build the brand proposition from the functional and emotional benefits you believe your product or service offers to customers.
- Use sophisticated consumer segmentation techniques to move from a one-to-many to a one-to-one marketing model.
- Track brand image to ensure that the differentiating elements of brand identity are being received accurately by the consumer.
- Harness the Internet to extend the customer franchise of your most successful offline brands.
- Work on every aspect of the organisation, from employee behaviour to premises, so as to reflect and reinforce brand values.

THE FUTURE OF BRANDS

While brands are undoubtedly here to stay, there is growing evidence of a consumer backlash. Ironically it's the Internet that's encouraging consumers, sick of being marketed to by faceless corporations, to demand a dialogue with brand owners.

Moreover, disgruntled consumers are using the Internet to undermine the brand equity that has been expensively created by these same faceless corporations. Customer feedback boards, message boards, and blogs have all been used to great effect by unhappy customers to get their point across and, in the case of Dell (following the fabled Jeff Jarvis 'Dell Hell' posting in 2005) bring about change in corporations.

THE BEST SOURCES OF HELP

Books:

Aaker, David. *Building Strong Brands*. London: Simon & Schuster, 2002.

Adamson, Allen P. *BrandSimple: How the Best Brands Keep it Simple and Succeed*. London: Palgrave Macmillan, 2007.

de Chernatony, Leslie. *From Brand Vision to Brand Evaluation*. 2nd ed. Oxford: Butterworth-Heinemann, 2006.

Managing the Customer by Merlin Stone

EXECUTIVE SUMMARY

- As competition in all its forms intensifies, customer management holds the key to increasing revenues *in a way that also drives profitability.*
- Whether cross-selling or upselling additional products to customers, retaining existing customers, attracting new ones, using customers to help develop new products, or simply providing the same products more efficiently and at less cost – the importance of customer focus and management is without parallel.
- At a time when the number of sales channels is increasing significantly and many other factors are impacting on traditional sales and marketing issues, the need for customer service that is 24/7 and manages the customer is as challenging as ever.

INTRODUCTION

There's no ideal way of managing customers. Marketers have been brought up on consumer-goods branding, retail marketing, and sales-force management. Along comes customer-relationship marketing with the claim to replace or substantially supplement these tried and tested ways of doing business. However, there are many ways of managing customers. The main ways are listed below. In practice many companies combine several.

MODELS FOR MANAGING THE CUSTOMER

One-to-one

Here most aspects of the marketing mix are actively attuned to the individual, based on information given by the individual before or during contacts, perhaps supplemented by other data (for example, inferred data). Some – but not all – customers are considered receptive to this, that is, customers have different propensities to respond in terms of returning more value. The principles work when applied to large customers whose value justifies the degree of customisation implied by this approach.

Transparent marketing

Many customers would like to manage their relationship with companies rather than the other way round. They try to do this by soliciting information from them and customising the offer made to them (content, timing, etc.), but they're not usually allowed to do so. Where it is possible (for example, via advanced call centres or the Web) some customers are very responsive. However, most companies do not offer this to their customers, and even waste large amounts of money trying to guess what customers want based on inadequate information.

Customer-relationship marketing (CRM) through a few segmented offers

This is still the aspiration of most companies. Although most companies make slower progress than they would like, many get solid gains by prioritising those areas of the relationship in which the offer for target customers (for example, positive- and/or high-value) is most at variance with the need. This model recognises that the relationship is only one part of the marketing mix, and that there are often situations in which classic elements of the marketing mix are more critical for marketing success.

Personalised communication and targeting

Campaign selection and tailored packaging of standard offers are examples of personalised communication and marketing. The practice grew from good practice in direct mail and telemarketing. It involves good use and management of customer data. It can raise response and conversion rates and save communication costs. In its most advanced form, data given by the customer at the point of contact is used to create or modify the profile and hence the offer made.

Top vanilla

In this method, leadership is gained by offering excellent customer management (before, during, and after the sale), but to standards available to everyone in the target market rather than just a few selected customers. In some cases this is combined with one of the other approaches for one or more small segments of highly valuable customers. This approach is characteristic of companies that manage their customers entirely by direct-marketing techniques such as telemarketing, direct mail, and the Internet.

Spot-sell within managed roster

For some or all of the products they buy, some customers prefer to get the best deal (value for money, not necessarily lowest price) at the time of purchase, but only from a selected roster of suppliers. This is characteristic of heavy users of fast-moving consumer goods (FMCG) or shopping goods, but also of many industrial purchases in which a roster of suppliers is used to ensure optimal variety, product quality, and service. In such situations attempts to develop behavioural loyalty (so that a customer buys more than the usual proportion from one supplier) usually require some promotional incentive.

Branding is usually a critical determinant of inclusion in the roster. For products bought through intermediaries, the supplier's aim is to ensure availability through intermediaries in the customer's roster. Note that the final customer may have a roster of products/brands and a roster of intermediaries. In this model, marketing focuses on getting on the customer's roster and providing best value compared to other companies on the roster. Top vanilla service can add competitive edge. CRM can be used to reinforce the supplier's or intermediary's position in the roster, though it may not help in gaining profit. However, if the supplier's product or the intermediary's offer is good value for money, a fair share of the business can be obtained, so the returns to CRM can be good.

Spot-sell managed by agent

In some cases drawing up the roster can be a complex task, with which customers feel they need the help of an agent, whether for expert advice, bargaining expertise, or just to delegate some of the transaction management. Some modes of purchase may require the customer to sign on as a registered customer (for example, buying via telephone or the Web), but the customer prefers to register with an independent agent rather than the original product or service supplier. So the customer appoints one intermediary to act as an agent, and the agent then draws up the roster. However, CRM techniques can be used very successfully with the intermediaries. This approach can often be combined with top vanilla service for final customers and agents. In an increasing number of cases, the agent may be Web-based.

Pure spot-sell

Here the customer rejects all relationships and buys (whether from original supplier or intermediary) purely on the basis of current perceived value. This in turn is strongly influenced by classic marketing-mix variables – brand, perceived product quality, price (including promotional discounts), availability, etc. To avoid being drawn into this situation, suppliers must seek to differentiate their offer such that the customer sees pure spot-buying as being risky.

The partnership model

This is a model that seems to have a very good pedigree, but it is quite difficult to implement. It is suggested as a model where both supplier and intermediary have strong visibility of and to the final customer, as in the automotive industry or in financial services.

CLASSIC MARKETING MODELS

There are several classic marketing models in which the nature of customer management is not specified explicitly but there is a very strong implicit model of customer management. These include:

- retailing
- sales-force management
- mail order
- consumer-product and company-brand management
- business-product management (closely related to technical innovation models)

ADOPTING THE RIGHT APPROACH

Obviously, these approaches to managing customers overlap, and suppliers may find they need to combine

them in different ways for managing different customers and for different products. However, each has characteristic and very different patterns of marketing investment and return.

The choice is affected by factors such as the following:

- **state and rate of change of product technology,** which can lead customers to require uncertainty reduction – available through relationship or agents – but it can also create big differences in spot value
- **underlying production and distribution techniques and costs,** for example, costs of variety, economies of scale
- **rate of entry of new-to-category customers,** which affects the role of experience
- **market structure fundamentals,** for example, patterns of competition or regulation
- **transfer of learning and expectations of customers** between different paradigms of management that customers expect
- **customer behaviour and psychographics** or, more simply, what they think and feel, how they buy, their need to give or take control, and associated way-of-life and life-cycle issues
- **timing issues** – how quickly customers' needs can be identified, and how quickly they can be responded to
- **customer expertise** – whether customers are good at identifying their own needs (and if so, how long it takes) and associated learning issues
- **sector** – the strong tendency in some complex business-to-business relationships for customers to prefer a CRM-managed repertoire with spot-buying
- **state of intermediation** – type of intermediation (for example, by agents, Web-based) and amount and type of value added by intermediaries
- **relationship between risk and value,** for example, whether customers have high risks (credit, insurance, etc.) attached to them as individuals; what the balance is between good and bad customers and between good and bad customer characteristics
- **data issues** – quality, legal issues
- **staffing** – current skill levels, possibilities of recruiting new skill sets, training options, etc.
- **systems culture of the supplier,** for example, whether managers are able to cope with the latest call-centre and Web-based technology.

MAKING IT HAPPEN

- Build customer management by combining different approaches in different ways for managing different customers and products.
- Treat one-to-one marketing as an ideal target rather than a practical means of returning more value.
- Don't guess what customers want, but build an accurate picture from well-researched data.
- Recognise that the customer relationship is only one part of the marketing mix, and that other elements may be more critical.
- If possible, offer excellent customer management (before, during, and after the sale) to everyone in the target market, not just a few.
- Review the success of different approaches in your own and parallel markets as part of general corporate strategy reviews.

CONCLUSION

No one paradigm dominates another – horses for courses is the key. Our research indicates that companies should consider the variety of models of customer management that might work in their market, identifying which might be best for their market as a whole and for particular segments. They should review the extent to which these approaches have really been successful in their own and parallel markets. This review should take place as part of a general corporate strategy review, for each paradigm requires its own operational structure, processes, systems, and policies. There's no point choosing a marketing model that sits badly with other functional strategies. Perhaps most important of all, companies should keep a close watch on the preferred paradigms of their most valued customers – but with a sceptical eye. Often a paradigm works only because customers have been offered nothing better.

THE BEST SOURCES OF HELP
Books:
Bird, Drayton. *Commonsense Direct and Digital Marketing*. 5th ed. London: Kogan Page, 2007.
Meisner, Chet. *The Complete Guide to Direct Marketing: Creating Breakthrough Programs That Really Work*. New York: Kaplan Business, 2006.

Marketing in the Internet Age by Regis McKenna

EXECUTIVE SUMMARY
- Traditional marketing is event- rather than process-oriented. A new form of information logistics is replacing the old marketing. Marketing people haven't as yet caught on.
- The Internet offers a major new vehicle for marketing to reassert its central role in enhancing firm value around core assets such as customers, value propositions, partnerships, and brands.
- Successful marketing companies use technology to build, leverage, and promote a powerful, customer-oriented business infrastructure.

INTRODUCTION

Almost everyone recognises the Internet as a powerful communications tool, but when it comes to marketing, two questions need to be asked:
1. How does the Internet affect or change the marketing process?
2. How is marketing practised on the Internet and what room is there for improvement?

Perhaps the most important thing to say at the start is that *true* marketing is not about hype. Hype, of course, dominates the way many people think of marketing and, in particular, Internet marketing. Buzzword solutions, promoted as brands themselves and dispensed by branding consultants, proliferate. Too often, they end up cluttering the customer's inbox with junk mail. Don't go there. Marketing via the Internet offers the potential of a real-time connection to the customer and the enterprise value chain; the Internet increases the urgency and criticality of that role. Marketing should embrace activities ranging from managing the product/service analysis and user feedback, real-time interchange with solution partners, and alliances scaling demands, supply logistics, relationships management, and other key business processes that get little mention in the Internet marketing debate. If anything, Internet marketing magnifies the need for focused attention on the core essentials.

THE INTERNET: A UNIQUE VEHICLE

The Internet affects every facet of a firm's value-delivery system, providing critical feedback and insight about the company and its partners/channels: the efficiency and effectiveness of its product/service design and delivery; who the customers are, what they think, and what they value; and how the competition is performing. Companies become great because they build sustainable business and service infrastructures that are superior to their competitors and leverage those infrastructures to deliver more value to each customer. The infrastructures that matter most are processes such as logistics, distribution, and services. The quality and customer's experience resulting experience of those business processes is what customers perceive as a company's 'position'. Marketing should be critically linked to, if not driving, these processes, because it is visible to the customer and shapes the customer's perspective of the brand.

The Internet is, above all else, a unique vehicle for facilitating and enhancing the customer's role as an integral part of the processes and market infrastructure. I like to think about the network as a 'learning channel' whereby the customer learns about the benefits of your products and service and you, the producer, gain knowledge about your customers in order to be responsive. It helps companies with strong and targeted value propositions develop much richer dialogue with their customers and, as a result, improve innovations in products and services to make the consumer experience richer and more relevant. Companies like Wal-Mart, Apple,

Amazon, and Google, with thousands of customer inter-actions each day, have become places where those in charge of their Internet site must be total access archi-tects stitching the entire corporate infrastructure to the advantage of the online customer. For example, Wal-Mart updates its customer database every 90 minutes and uses that to keep its stock at the optimum level. Old-style mar-keting could never keep track of a customer that rapidly, and neither could companies that simply market by buzzwords.

CURRENT INTERNET MARKETING: MUCH ROOM FOR IMPROVEMENT

Much of today's marketing activities such as branding and media advertising are, in my view, disconnected from reality. As consumers, we are well aware that rarely do products and services meet, much less exceed our expectations. Promotion, however, must have a certain 'unreality' about it in order to attract attention. However, attention does not necessarily lead to brand loyalty. Advertising, for example, is often considered 'the sizzle' and not the 'steak'. Too many marketing people are not prepared for the information age. Too many know very little about the real benefits of the product/service they are promoting, or about the competition's strengths and weakness, or about the support infrastructure required to achieve consistent customer satisfaction. As a result, much of promotion we see today is pure cos-metic fantasy – that's essentially what many marketers call branding.

Because it is a radically new landscape, the networked marketplace or Internet has yet to see a consistent set of marketing principles applied to it. As a result, a series of myths have grown up around the Internet as a market-ing medium, myths that have proven expensive and often disastrous to many marketers who have not taken the time to understand this new medium.

Myth 1: The Internet is a great customer acquisition vehicle

True, it is easier and cheaper to use the Internet than, say, television advertising. However, I would contend that long-term customer relationship building is an invest-ment and must be continually adapted, constantly renewed and reviewed, as well as addressed in multiple ways and modes. The Internet is a great communicating vehicle once the customer has established a need or want. But even that does not build long-term loyalty. Loyalty or brand building is not easy. 'Brand', by its very nature, implies loyalty over time. That means that the producer and consumer must establish a history of reliable and responsive experiences. On the other hand, the Internet encourages competitive shopping and has an anonymity that screens the customer's decision-making process from direct influence. In effect, the Internet often encourages disloyalty because of the almost limitless choices it presents. The consumer abandons a very high percent-age of online 'shopping carts'. This new media is

presently an entirely new experience for both producers and consumers.

Myth 2: The Internet is a great messaging and advertising medium

The Internet is more complex than any broadcast media. First of all, the Internet is real-time interactive. Second, whereas a few hundred channels limit broadcast media at most with fixed content, there are millions of channels (sources of information) available to access on the Internet and those channels are not limited by geographic bound-aries. Second, the content on the Internet is a virtual tsunami of information that is – by and large – generated by the consumers themselves. Third, the Internet is not limited by 'viewing times'. Most studies show today that consumers are multiplexing their time. That is surfing the Internet while listening to music or watching television or talking on their mobile phones. This is particularly true of younger consumers. Search engines have become the new 'link' to engaging the consumer. As the consumer surfs the Internet, his or her *interests* are responded to by the intelligent listening nature of the search engine that links those interests to specific products or solutions. The consumer – or what I call 'market driven', not 'marketing driven' – drives the process. Thus, access replaces broad-cast. We are still learning how to use this new medium effectively and wisely so as to engender trust from the consumer.

Myth 3: The Internet makes 1 : 1 marketing a reality

The programmability aspect of computers and software applications makes 1:1 marketing possible. CRM (Customer Relationship Management), after all, is a soft-ware approach to managing a large customer base as well as enabling those services represented in software to adapt to each customer's need. 'Web services' is the infra-structure management system that co-ordinates all the underlying functions for compliance, security, referencing customer history, and so forth. Listening and responding technologies are now pervasive, from the ATM to the checkout counter to the remote network-management con-sole. Marketing as a promotional game has yet to recognise these systems as the new tools for building brand.

MARKETING IN THE INTERNET AGE

Such myths make most current Internet marketing prac-tices only marginally valuable and successful. We need to think not about Internet marketing but about *marketing in the Internet age* – the totality of the marketing chal-lenge in an age where business processes are increas-ingly mediated by the Internet and its underlying intelligent infrastructure.

The challenge for marketers in the Internet age is *marketing at the core*. It requires an understanding of customer pain points (an ability to listen rather than talk), a more-than-passing familiarity with the econom-ics of cost-to-serve and, above all, an approach to customers that is based upon a life-cycle relationship management process.

The US-based online retailer, Amazon.com, has redefined bookselling. Its culture appreciates the potential of technology, with the company using information in four key ways:

1. to minimise risks by analysing information from millions of customers to see how and when they purchase, enabling Amazon.com to reduce the level of risk;
2. to reduce costs by using technology to control the way it manages its inventory and suppliers;
3. to add value and help customers by offering reviews of books and free downloadable information and by treating each customer's website as an individual shop front – for example, by tailoring lists of suggested titles that the customer may enjoy based on previous purchases;
4. to innovate. Amazon believes that to rival its competitors, an innovative approach is essential in order to improve the value and service offered to consumers.

What matters is not simply what information exists but how that information is used to build competitive advantage. Many other retailing companies have now followed Amazon's lead. For example, Apple's iTunes and iStore has done for music retailing what Amazon did for bookselling using many of the same principles.

MAKING IT HAPPEN

To separate hype from true Internet marketing, you must answer at least seven questions:

- How does the Web deliver value to customers, business partners, and my own company?
- Who am I serving with my Web presence, and do the economics deliver enough return to the value network to justify the use of the Web?
- What is the whole product that I need to bring to my Web business, including, where necessary, non-Web and partnership components?
- How do I ensure extraordinary value delivery on the Web, manage that value delivery over time for my customers, and build brand value from that total customer experience?
- How does the Web fit into that total relationship with the customer and why? What roles should it play at different stages of the relationship?
- Where should the Web fit organisationally so that it leverages and enhances my total marketing strategy and implementation plan?

- How do I measure success in terms of new customers, repeat customers, loyal customers, total revenue and margin growth, new product success rates, partner business and profitability growth?

The Web is indeed a revolutionary technology: millions of people are now online worldwide. The next millions will surely be from emerging economies in India, China, Latin America, and elsewhere. This expansion will present yet another challenge for marketers. All the new technologies such as search engines, CRM, and web services have emerged from software developers and not from the traditional sources of marketing expertise. Future marketers will have to learn how to apply creative skills within the context of real-time information networks where the consumer controls the dialogue.

CONCLUSION

Marketing, like TQM, has become 'everybody's job'. From the CEO and CIO to the salesperson and retail partner, the strategy and implementation must be well understood and renewed everyday. Competition is going to get more global and more intense, and only those who excel as a total business entity will be successful.

Finally, the new, interactive and digital technologies have enabled the convergence of marketing and IT. With that in mind, I suggest marketers redefine marketing as a continuous process of organisational learning and the subsequent adaptation of the business to technological, market and customer ever-changing dynamics.

Marketing is a business process rather than an event, enabling product and service providers to acquire and apply knowledge efficiently by interacting with customers and the marketplace. They are then able to innovate and respond competitively, reliably, consistently, and profitably.

THE BEST SOURCES OF HELP

Books:

Hanson, Ward and Kirthi Kalyanam. *Internet Marketing and e-Commerce*. South-Western College Publishing, 2006.

Meerman Scott, David. *The New Rules of Marketing and PR: How to Use News Releases, Blogs, Podcasting, Viral Marketing and Online Media to Reach Buyers Directly*. Hoboken: Wiley, 2008.

Website:

Regis.com: **www.regis.com**

Intellectual Capital by Thomas Stewart

EXECUTIVE SUMMARY
- Intellectual capital is knowledge that transforms raw materials and makes them more valuable.
- To be considered intellectual capital, knowledge must be an asset.
- Intellectual capital's raw materials might be physical or intangible, like information.

INTRODUCTION

Intellectual capital is just that: a capital asset consisting of intellectual material. To be considered intellectual capital, knowledge must be an asset – able to be used to create wealth. Thus intellectual capital includes the talents and skills of individuals and groups; technological and social networks and the software and culture that connect them; and intellectual property such as patents, copyrights, methods, procedures, archives, etc. It excludes knowledge or information not involved in production or wealth creation. Just as raw material such as iron ore should not be confused with an asset such as a steel mill, so knowledge materials such as data or miscellaneous facts ought not to be confused with knowledge assets.

INTELLECTUAL CAPITAL AS AN ASSET

From the standpoint of traditional accounting, intellectual capital frequently does not fit the definition of an asset. Generally, under accounting rules, an asset must be tangible; it must have been acquired in one or more transactions, so that it has a known cost or a market value, and it must be under the control of the party whose asset it is said to be. Thus scientific skill is not an accounting asset, but laboratory equipment is.

Intellectual capital theory argues that this definition is too narrow and hinders businesses from seeing, managing, or building knowledge assets. This in turn inhibits companies' ability to compete and prosper in an economy in which knowledge has become an important source of profits. The intellectual capitalists use a looser definition: an asset is something that transforms raw material into something more valuable. It is a magician's black box. Inputs get put in – a few handkerchiefs, say; the asset does something to transform them; and out come outputs worth more than the inputs – rabbits, maybe. The question of ownership and control matters less than the question of access. A corporation might not own scientific expertise (in the form of a cadre of employees, for example), but it has the use of it and can exert a quasi-proprietary influence over how it is used.

Intellectual capital, then, is knowledge that transforms raw materials and makes them more valuable. The raw materials might be physical – knowledge of the formula for Coca-Cola is an intellectual asset that transforms a few cents' worth of sugar, water, carbon dioxide, and flavourings into a dollar's worth of refreshment. The raw material might be intangible, like information. Knowledge of the law is an intellectual asset; a lawyer takes the facts of a dispute (raw material), transforms them through his knowledge of the law (an intellectual asset), to produce an opinion or a legal brief (an output of higher value than the facts by themselves).

Though financial accounting does not measure intellectual capital, markets clearly do. Shares of companies in the pharmaceutical industry, for example, generally trade at a high premium over the book value of their assets, and the companies' return on net assets is abnormally high; but if their spending on research and development is added to their capital, both their market-to-book ratios and their returns on assets come to resemble those of less knowledge-intensive companies.

Indeed, it was the unusual behaviour of the equities of knowledge-intensive companies that first drew the attention of analysts to intellectual capital. The term seems to have been employed first in 1958, when two financial analysts, describing the stock-market valuations of several small, science-based companies, concluded that 'The intellectual capital of such companies is perhaps their single most important element', and noted that their high stock valuations might be termed an 'intellectual premium'. (Morris Kronfeld and Arthur Rock, 'Some considerations of the infinite', *The Analyst's Journal*, November 1958, p. 6.) The idea lay dormant for a quarter of a century. In the 1980s, Walter Wriston, the former chairman of Citicorp, noted that his bank and other corporations possessed valuable intellectual capital that accountants (and bank regulators) did not measure.

INTELLECTUAL CAPITAL ANALYSED

Karl-Erik Sveiby, a Swede, intrigued by the anomalous stock-market behaviour of knowledge-intensive companies, began an investigation that produced the first analysis of the nature of intellectual capital. Sveiby, his colleagues, and *Affärsvärlden*, Sweden's oldest business magazine, noticed that the magazine's proprietary model for valuing initial public offerings broke down for high-tech companies. Sveiby concluded that these companies possessed assets not described in financial documents or included in the magazine's model. With a like-minded group of associates, he sat down to puzzle out what these might be. In 'Den Osynliga Balansräkningen Ledarskap' ('The invisible balance sheet'), 1989, they laid the foundation stone for much of what has come after by coming up with a taxonomy for intellectual capital. Knowledge assets, they proposed, could be found in three places: the competencies of a company's people, its internal structure (patents, models, computer and administrative systems), and its external structure (brands, reputation, relationships with customers and suppliers).

After some tinkering by others – the pieces are now usually called human capital, structural (or organisational) capital, and customer (or relationship) capital – Sveiby's model still stands. It has made managing intellectual capital possible by naming its component parts. Shortly thereafter, Leif Edvinsson, an executive at the Swedish financial services company Skandia, persuaded his management to appoint him 'Director, Intellectual Capital'; Skandia became the business world's most conspicuous laboratory for intellectual capital studies.

Ideas whose time has come flower everywhere at once. Ikujiro Nonaka and Hirotaka Takeuchi in Japan began investigations of how knowledge is produced that resulted in 'The knowledge-creating company' (*Harvard Business Review*, November–December 1991) and Thomas A. Stewart synthesised US research in intellectual capital in 'Brainpower: How intellectual capital is becoming America's most important asset' (*Fortune*, 3 June, 1991).

Every company or organisation possesses all three forms of intellectual capital. Human capital consists of the skills, competencies, and abilities of individuals and groups. These range from specific technical skills to 'softer' skills, like salesmanship or the ability to work effectively in a team. An individual's human capital cannot, in a legal sense, be owned by a corporation; the term thus refers not only to individual talent but also to the collective skills and aptitudes of a workforce. Indeed, one challenge faced by executives is how to manage the talent of truly outstanding members of their staff: how to use it to the utmost without becoming overdependent on a few star performers, or how to encourage stars to share their skills with others. Skills that are irrelevant to a company's business – the fine tenor voice of an actuary, for example – may be part of the individual's human capital, but not of his employer's.

Structural capital comprises knowledge assets that are indeed company property: intellectual property such as patents, copyrights, and trademarks; processes, methodologies, models; documents and other knowledge artefacts; computer networks and software; administrative systems; and so forth. A data warehouse is structural capital; so is the decision-support software that helps people to use the data. One knowledge-management process is converting human capital – which is usually available to just a few people – into structural capital, so it becomes shareable. This happens, for example, when a team writes up the 'lessons learned' from a project so that others can apply them. Some structural capital can be said to be owned in common; open-source software is an example. In general, however, proprietary assets, whether intellectual or otherwise, are of more strategic value than assets equally available to rivals.

Customer capital is the value of relationships with suppliers, allies, and customers. Two common forms are brand equity and customer loyalty. The former is a promise of quality (or some other attribute) for which a customer agrees to pay a premium price; the value of brands is measurable in financial terms. The loyalty of a base of customers is also measurable, using discounted cash-flow analysis. Both are frequently calculated when companies are bought and sold. In a sense, all customer capital should eventually reflect itself either in a premium price or an enduring buyer–seller relationship.

Every organisation possesses intellectual capital in all three manifestations, but with varying emphasis, depending on its history and strategy. For example, a chemical company might have as a knowledge asset the ability to concoct custom chemical compounds that precisely match its customers' needs. That asset might be people-based, residing in the tacit knowledge of dozens of skilled chemists; it might be structural, found in an extensive library of patents and manuals, or databases and expert systems; it might be relationship-based, found in the company's intimate ties to customers, suppliers, universities, etc. Most likely, of course, the asset – skill at making custom chemicals – is a combination of the three. A company that takes a strategic approach to intellectual capital will examine its business model and the economics of its industry to manage the combination of human, structural, and customer capital in such a way as to create value that competitors cannot match.

At least three characteristics of intellectual capital give it extraordinary power to add value. First, companies that use knowledge assets deftly can reduce the expense and burden of carrying physical assets, or can maximise their return on them. For example, transportation companies can use information networks and skill in logistics and load management to maximise their utilisation of assets like railway carriages and containers. Second, it can be possible to get enormous leverage or gearage from knowledge assets. The value of an aircraft can be realised over just one route at a time, whereas that of an airline's reservation system is limited only by the number of people in the world. In a study of the chemical industry that examined 83 companies over 25 years, Baruch Lev, professor of accounting at New York University, found that R&D spending (one form of investment in intellectual capital) returned 25.9 per cent pretax, whereas capital spending earned just 15 per cent (about 10 per cent after tax, approximately the cost of capital).

Third, human and customer capital are the primary sources of innovation and customisation. The increasing sophistication of machinery and information technology has led to the automation of more and more repetitive tasks. These manufacturing economies of scale are sources of competitive advantage in industrial processes. At a certain point, however, their value diminishes: the more it is possible to do a task the same way twice, the harder it is for one company to differentiate its offerings from that of its competitors. When this happens the value of innovation, customisation, and service increases; all are highly dependent on intellectual capital.

MAKING IT HAPPEN
• Treat knowledge as an asset only if it is capable of yielding an economic return.

- Build human capital by developing skills, competencies, abilities of individuals and groups who deliver value to customers.
- Convert human capital into structural capital, by organising the exchange and sharing of knowledge.
- Optimise customer capital – the value of relationships with suppliers, allies, and customers – by building brand equity and customer loyalty.
- Use knowledge assets to reduce the expense and burden of carrying physical assets, or to maximise return on those assets
- Look for competitive advantage from innovation, customisation, and service rather than from economies of scale.

THE BEST SOURCES OF HELP
Books:
Moore, Lindsay and Lesley Craig. *Intellectual Capital in Enterprise Success: Strategy Revisited*. Chichester: Wiley, 2008.
Roos, Göran Roos, Stephen Pike, and Lisa Fernstrom. *Managing Intellectual Capital in Practice*. Oxford: Butterworth-Heinemann, 2006.

Website:
www.intellectualcapital.nl

How to Get Lucky by Donald N. Sull

EXECUTIVE SUMMARY
- Luck is too important to leave to chance.
- The most successful terms use the strategy of active waiting instead.
- Whatever your chosen strategy, remember that timing is everything: too early can be as bad as too late.

INTRODUCTION

In highly volatile markets, a company's success or failure is often attributed to luck. As no one can foresee the twists and turns the future holds, it is all a bit of a crap shoot. Turbulent markets throw out opportunities and threats, whose timing, nature, and magnitude managers can neither predict nor control. In such a competitive casino, you place your bets and hope for the best.

The importance of luck in volatile situations is not new. Napoleon explained that he consistently won battles despite the disorder, uncertainty, and friction of war because he picked lucky generals. At first glance, this seems an odd explanation. How was Napoleon able to pick lucky generals any more than directors are able to pick lucky CEOs?

Yet Napoleon was on to something important. Some firms consistently seize major opportunities and skirt crises that undo less-fortunate rivals. Over recent years I have studied more than 20 pairs of comparable companies in unpredictable industries (for example, telecommunications, airlines, enterprise software) and countries (for example, China and Brazil). By pairing similar firms, I could study how they responded differently to unforeseen threats and opportunities that both faced. Indeed, the more successful firms were luckier, in the sense that they consistently responded more effectively to volatile factors that influenced performance, such as unexpected

shifts in regulation, technology, competition, and macroeconomics. They did not win through greater insight into the future – the executives at the more successful companies strenuously denied their ability to pierce the fog of an unpredictable future.

Luck is too important to leave to chance. The most successful firms exemplified *active waiting,* a strategy in highly unpredictable markets that consists of anticipating and preparing for opportunities and threats that executives can neither fully predict nor control. Rather than deluding themselves that they could make long-term predictions, executives in the more successful firms proceeded like generals leading armies forward into war. They conducted reconnaissance into the future to anticipate threats and opportunities that might emerge; they built a reserve of capital and managers to deploy when a golden opportunity or life-threatening crisis arose; they kept the troops battle-ready during lulls in the action; and periodically they committed their reserves to seizing a golden opportunity.

TIMING IS EVERYTHING

An executive is sometimes compared to the captain of a ship, standing at the helm in clear weather, peering through a telescope to the distant horizon and setting a clear course for the future. In many markets, however, the future is obscured by dense fog, and managing resembles driving a racing car along a treacherous route in an impenetrable mist. The fog descends when multiple variables interact in ways that produce unpredictable opportunities and threats. Consider the telecommunications industry. Shifting regulations, continuous technological change, entry by non-traditional rivals like Google, competitive thrust and parry among established players, and shifts in consumer preferences combine and recombine in countless permutations to throw out a steady stream of unforeseen opportunities and threats.

The good news is that unpredictable markets generate opportunities. Demand for automobiles in China, for example, arose from the confluence of increased disposable income, government investment in infrastructure, rising middle-class aspirations, easy credit, and the demise of employer-provided housing. Turbulent markets often generate new resources, such as innovative technology like the Internet or privatised assets. Shifting contextual factors open new gaps in the market and new resources enable firms to fill these gaps.

But these opportunities are not created equal. Scientists studying a range of complex systems have found that the frequency of an event tends to be inversely related to its magnitude – tectonic fault lines, for example, experience many small tremors, regular mid-sized earthquakes, and the rare major one. The same holds for volatile markets. Firms face countless small opportunities, regular mid-sized ones, and the periodic golden opportunity – a chance to create value disproportionate to the resources invested in a short period of time. Typical golden opportunities include acquisition of a major competitor to gain global scale; seizing explosive demand in an emerging market like China; pioneering a new product or service such as the iPod™; or consolidating an industry as Oracle has done in enterprise software.

Golden opportunities are rare; they occur only when external circumstances open several windows at once. Consider the golden opportunity for middleware – software linking an enterprise's disparate applications – an opportunity that IBM and BEA converted into billion-dollar businesses. The middleware opportunity arose when, simultaneously, the Internet created demand for software that could link applications; available technology was up to the task; early leaders like NCR and Novell were distracted by other markets; and the paucity of venture capital at that juncture prevented a few start-ups from chasing the same market. Golden opportunities are the mirror image of major crises – when multiple variables go south simultaneously. The crisis in the global airline industry, for example, resulted from the unfortunate combination of 9/11, SARS, and rapidly rising fuel prices.

Golden opportunities are not only rare, they are also fleeting. Timing is everything when going for the gold. Too early can be as bad as too late. Had IBM or BEA entered the middleware market a year or two earlier, customers' pain would have been less acute and the technology fix less developed. A few years later, and new entrants flush with venture capital cash might have established a lead, or early leaders might have focused their effort on the segment.

THE STRATEGY OF ACTIVE WAITING

Seizing a golden opportunity can provide a firm with a decisive advantage. But there is a catch. Executives can neither predict nor control the precise form, magnitude, or timing of these golden opportunities. Executives can rarely open the contextual windows that give rise to golden opportunities. Even mighty IBM could not have

affected the speed of Internet adoption, stopped venture capitalists from funding start-ups, or deterred NCR or Novell from building on their early lead. Executives should, of course, take whatever steps they can to nudge a golden opportunity along, by, for example, lobbying governments, guiding industry standards, or pre-empting competitors. But it is rank hubris for an executive to think he or she can conjure up a golden opportunity when the core business is declining or investors are clamouring for a big hit. Attempting to force an opportunity when the contextual stars are not aligned generally ends in tears.

That said, there is much executives *can* do to prepare their firms to capitalise on a golden opportunity (or weather a major crisis) when one arises. The secret to success lies not in heroic efforts in the midst of storms, but rather the quiet actions taken during periods of relative calm between them.

MAKING IT HAPPEN
Keep the vision fuzzy

Managers must first acknowledge that they cannot predict or control how the future will unfold by articulating a fuzzy vision – a company's domain, geographic scope, and aspiration – in broad terms: 'We aspire to global leadership (or excellence or quality) in our industry'. A fuzzy vision provides general direction and sets aspirations without prematurely locking the company into a specific course. In contrast, overly detailed long-term visions cause more problems than they solve. They induce executives to bet too big too early, distract employees from emerging changes inconsistent with the vision, and provide a false sense of security that the world is more certain than it is. A crystal clear long-term vision often ensures that companies get to the wrong place faster than their competitors.

Keep the priorities clear

In unpredictable markets, managers often try to hedge against every possible contingency by running multiple experiments and unleashing a flurry of new initiatives. Taken in isolation each initiative makes sense, but collectively they lead to priority proliferation. Employees and managers find themselves overwhelmed by multiple, often conflicting priorities. In attempting to pursue too many priorities simultaneously, organisations spread their chips too thin and hinder co-ordination across units. The point of prioritisation is not to choose what to do and what not to do, but what to do *when*. Managers must exercise discipline and choose a small number of objectives to pursue first, and let others wait for now (recognising that changing circumstances could force a reordering of priorities). Equally important, managers must decide what to stop doing to free up time, attention, and resources so that the critical objectives are met.

Conduct reconnaissance into the future

Reconnaissance, in military parlance, is the activity of sending troops ahead of an advancing army to investigate the terrain, enemy disposition, and other factors that lie ahead. Reconnaissance into the future is the process of probing the fog to discover an emerging situation. Four principles capture the essence of conducting reconnaissance into the future:

1. **Jump into the action:** Rather than spending years conducting market research, companies should make exploratory forays by investing or partnering with start-ups, or conducting small-scale experiments to test the market.

2. **Send out multiple probes:** A prudent general sends out probes in different directions to broaden the search for opportunities. Executives should likewise avoid betting the company in pursuing a single path.

3. **Interrogate anomalies:** When conducting reconnaissance, managers must above all remain alert to anomalies: new information that surprises them or doesn't jibe with expectations; things that should work but don't or that shouldn't work but do. In turbulent markets, a manager's mental map can quickly become outdated. Anomalies provide clues as to where a mental map is wrong, and managers who discover and act on these clues can seize the initiative from rivals slower to abandon their assumptions. When managers observe an anomaly, they must investigate it first hand until they are satisfied they understand the source of the discrepancy.

4. **Pass surfaces but swarm gaps:** Reconnaissance into the future resembles a process of probing a wall of resistance for gaps. Most of the time, a company encounters hard surfaces, such as competitors who won't get out of the way, customers who don't want to buy, technologies that won't work. Rather than exhaust resources trying to smash through the wall, executives should probe for gaps. When they do find a gap, managers should swarm through it, pulling other resources in their wake.

KEEP A RESERVE

During periods of relative calm, executives should build a war chest of cash to deploy quickly when faced with a golden opportunity or sudden-death threat. Building and preserving a war chest requires restraint. To avoid spreading a company's chips across too many probes, thereby leaving little cash in reserve, senior executives should scrutinise the firm's resource allocation process, monitor the number of probes, cap the investment allocated to probes, and increase investment only after explicit evaluation. Managers must also build sufficient credibility with investors to allow them to hold on to the cash.

Keep the troops battle-ready

During periods of active waiting, executives must relentlessly drive operating improvements – cutting costs, strengthening distribution, improving products. The cumulative effect of incremental operating improvements can prove decisive in the long run. Efficient companies can survive long enough to have a shot at the next golden opportunity. Operating improvements during lulls contribute to the war chest, of course, but also build the credibility required to seize the golden opportunity. The Royal Bank of Scotland, for example, did not make the highest bid to acquire NatWest, but the Scottish bank's track record of execution convinced the capital markets that they were the buyer most likely to make the deal work.

Declare the main effort

One of the greatest challenges in active waiting is deciding when to commit reserves and go for broke. Executives conducting reconnaissance into the future will detect countless opportunities and threats that never rise above the routine. Periodically, however, they will encounter an opportunity or threat so important that it demands the company's full focus. Executives provide this focus by declaring the opportunity or threat the main effort for a period of time. This creates a sense of urgency, focuses the organisation, prioritises resource allocation, lays the groundwork for co-ordinated effort, and increases the odds of winning big. Declaring the main effort requires judgment. If managers wait for complete certainty before they commit, nimbler rivals will seize the initiative. Many leaders say that declaring a golden opportunity the main effort was the most difficult decision they ever made. Playing it safe in the short term, however, can prove hazardous in the long term. Companies that pass on every golden opportunity will eventually find themselves eclipsed by players that can both wait actively and strike decisively.

CONCLUSION

Leading a company into the fog of the future remains risky. By waiting actively during periods of relative calm, however, executives can increase their chances of success.

THE BEST SOURCES OF HELP
Book:
Sull, Donald N. *Made In China: What Western Managers Can Learn from Trailblazing Chinese Entrepreneurs*. Cambridge, Massachusetts: Harvard Business School Press, 2005.

Strategy in Turbulent Times by Costas Markides

EXECUTIVE SUMMARY

- Strategy is important even during times of uncertainty.
- Strategy is about making difficult choices in the face of uncertainty, then learning as you go along and adjusting your original choices.
- Successful companies are those which process the information they receive differently and, by doing so, create differentiated strategies.
- Creativity and innovation are different. Innovation is deciding which ideas to pick on and implement to create value.
- Innovation is not just coming up with ideas, but also scaling them up to create big markets.

INTRODUCTION

In our turbulent and uncertain times it is tempting for companies to wonder whether they do actually require a strategy. They do.

By way of proof, imagine that you find yourself in the middle of a dark and hostile jungle. If you want to get out of the jungle, do you need a strategy?

Think about it. In the dense foliage you cannot see further than a few feet. You want to get out of this jungle, but you don't know how and you don't know which way to turn. There is total uncertainty. How then can you get out alive? Well, the last thing you want to do is to stay still, paralysed by uncertainty. You need to analyse your position based on the available information and then decide on a direction. That's the first principle of strategy – the need to make difficult choices based on what information you have at the time. You take stock, gather information based on that, and then start walking. The worst thing is to stay still. That's the second principle of strategy – the need to stop analysing and start doing, even if you are not entirely sure that what you are doing is going to turn out to be the right thing.

After you start walking, new information comes your way. The new information may allow you to revise your original direction. That's the third principle of strategy – the need to learn as you go along and modify your strategy through trial and error. If you meet a wild animal or run into a canyon, your strategy (or direction) has to change. Therefore, strategy is all about making difficult choices in the face of uncertainty and then learning as you go along and adjusting your original choices. When you think of it like this, it's obvious that you need a strategy – even (or especially) in times of uncertainty.

THE SEARCH FOR DIFFERENCE

If strategy is necessary, the next question is how to come up with a *differentiated* strategy.

In many industries, competing companies have the same suppliers, are structured in much the same way, receive their information from the same sources, use the same consultants, and so on. They receive much the same information. And yet some pursue genuinely different strategies.

The difference lies in mental processing. How companies process the information around them will determine what they do.

Indeed, this is what differentiates innovators from other companies. Most companies try to become better than their competitors. But for almost all companies other than the established leader, being better is not the right way. They need to play a different game. Look at EasyJet, e*trade, or Schwab. These are companies intent, not on being better, but on playing a different game. They thought of new ways of playing the game. The managers of these companies face the same information as everyone else in their industries, yet they process this information differently and come up with differentiated strategies. Companies get the same inputs, but it's what they do with the inputs to change the rules of the game that matters.

ESTABLISHED BUT DIFFERENT

Many established companies develop a winning strategy and then spend all their time trying to improve it and make it better. They rarely consider 'cannibalising' their current strategy in favour of a different one. They judge the risks of doing so to be too high. Yet all around us established companies are being toppled by newcomers that adopt different strategies.

The solution? Companies must continue to improve their existing strategies, but they must also continuously strive to discover new or different strategies. They should try to be better and different at the same time.

PLAYING TWO GAMES

How can a company play two games simultaneously? Harvard Business School's Michael Porter suggests that doing this is so difficult that most companies attempting it will fail. His advice is for companies to focus on only one game. His Harvard colleague Clay Christensen suggests that a company can play two games at the same time, but that the new game needs to be separate from the main business.

My own research suggests that although it's difficult, companies can still play two games without necessarily separating them. More importantly, it implies that when established companies are attacked by a new way of playing the game, they do not necessarily have to respond by adopting the new game.

What established companies need to appreciate is that the new, disruptive ways of playing the game are not God-sent. The new ways are not pre-ordained to win. Established companies could respond by killing off the new ways. For example, why is Internet banking the game of the future? Is it more convenient or more efficient than traditional banking? Why don't banks respond to Internet banking, *not* by adopting it, but by making their traditional operations so good that consumers simply wouldn't find banking over the Internet an attractive proposition?

CONFUSING CREATIVITY AND INNOVATION

One of the problems is that the difference between innovation and creativity (or invention) is often misunderstood. Creativity is about coming up with new ideas. Innovation is deciding which ideas to select and implement to create value. A lot of research tends to emphasise creativity rather than innovation.

Innovation is about selecting new ideas and then finding ways to scale them up to create mass markets out of them. For example, consider the market for PCs. Who is the innovator in this market? Most people think that the answer is Apple, or perhaps Osborne. But who really created the mass market for PCs? Who should be credited with the fact that the personal computer is not some high-tech gimmick that only nerds use, but is instead a fixture in every home? The answer is simple – IBM. IBM scaled it up. IBM created the mass market. Yet, nobody considers IBM an innovator.

Therefore, innovation is not just about the selection of new ideas: it's also about scaling them up to create big markets. Most of the dot-coms failed because they didn't know how to sell to customers, to bring ideas to a mass market.

The trouble is that the act of scaling ideas up into big markets is not celebrated as innovative. Even worse, scaling up – rather than coming up with new ideas – is what big companies are good at, but they often forget this and try instead to become brilliantly creative like the small start-up companies. Instead of taking the ideas of others and converting them into big markets, they focus on coming up with ideas themselves. Unfortunately, this is what small firms excel at.

CONVERTING BIG FIRMS INTO SMALL FIRMS

Over the last 10 years we have tried to convert big firms into small firms. There's a lot of talk about injecting big corporations with the entrepreneurial culture of the small firm, or breaking up the big ones to make them as agile and flexible as the small ones. This won't happen. The big firm will never become as creative as the small firm. What the big corporation is good at is scaling up, not creativity. Our attention should shift towards making the big corporation better at what it is good at – not making it like the small ones.

We have a cultural bias in favour of coming up with ideas, and a real lack of appreciation for the challenging task of taking the idea and converting it into a mass market. Similarly, there is a bias in defining innovation as something new. But the real trick is how to convert something new from being a plaything of the few into the mass market.

MAKING IT HAPPEN

CEOs know how to encourage innovation in their organisations – allow experiments, reward new ideas, do not punish mistakes, and so on. The problem is, it doesn't happen. This is because innovation carries huge personal risk – and people also tend to be evaluated on delivering results, rather than coming up with innovative ideas. As a result, few have the courage to focus solely on innovation. To make it happen, we need to rethink totally how we manage corporations.

- We require corporations which have different structures, processes, mindsets, and behaviours than has been the norm for the last 50 years.
- We need to train people *how* to think, not what to think.
- We need to give people a sense that organisations are not there simply to make money, but that they have a social purpose too. The important thing is for young people to get into business not only because it's a good way to make money, but also because through their companies, they can help create something that improves the state of the world. For example, the young people that developed the Apple Mac were not just making a computer. They were on a mission to change the way people thought about computers.
- The modern corporation must be able to make an accurate assessment of the external environment so that it takes the right strategic position. In addition, it must remain true to the unwritten moral contract with employees, which promises to provide an environment which sustains them and allows them to grow as individuals.
- To be flexible and fluid, companies need to become amoeba-like – able to move one way while always responding to local stimuli and changing direction in response to new information from the environment.

This can only be achieved by giving people autonomy, and the freedom to monitor what's going on around them and respond as they see fit.

THE BEST SOURCES OF HELP

Books:
Hamel, Gary, and C.K. Prahalad. *Competing for the Future*. Revised ed. Cambridge, Massachusetts: Harvard Business School Press, 1996.
Markides, Costas, et al. *Strategy, Innovation, and Change: Challenges for Management*. Oxford: OUP, 2008.

Organic Growth Versus Acquisition by Peter Bebb

EXECUTIVE SUMMARY

- If they are to survive and succeed, businesses need to find ways to rapidly, radically, and measurably change their strategy, processes, and roles. Individuals need to know precisely what to produce and what reward they'll get for doing so.
- Companies acquiring, merging, and de-merging need long-term ways of enhancing shareholder value once the initial and obvious savings have been made.
- Organic growth and growth by acquisition should be complementary strategies. The successful execution of both depends on aligning everyone and everything around a single set of corporate goals, and so achieving these goals faster, better, and cheaper.
- Many organisations suffer from acquisition indigestion, having failed to absorb and make the best of their acquisitions or mergers. All organisations have more scope for organic growth than they realise.

INTRODUCTION

Organisations exist in a rapidly changing environment, necessitating responsive and often radical strategic capabilities. To realise potential, organisations can be beset with common difficulties, such as strategic confusion and preoccupation with day-to-day activities. Despite many attempts to push organisations forwards, shareholder value often stagnates or even declines. The solution lies not in focusing on improving the current situation but rather in taking the step-changes necessary to realise the future requirements of the organisation.

UNDERSTANDING THE PROBLEMS

Dysfunctional organisations

Most people have difficulty stating their organisation's strategy: what the organisation wants to become, how it would like its people to behave, and what it will provide to which customers in the future. The reality is that the organisation's business and operating units march to priorities different from, if not contradictory to, those implied by its strategy. The majority of the people in an organisation focus on day-to-day operational matters and their individual aspirations. Consequently the strategy is never realised.

Frustrated by the lack of forward progress, executives launch new communication, reorganisation, process redesign, or technology initiatives. Everyone is doing more, and yet performance stagnates or even declines.

Losing the value of mergers and acquisitions

Research by the consultancy KPMG found that, though 82 per cent of respondents believed the deal they had transacted was a success, 83 per cent of the same mergers failed to increase shareholder value. Of these transactions, 30 per cent produced no discernible difference in shareholder value and 53 per cent actually reduced value.

Acquiring, merging, and demerging companies need long-term ways of enhancing shareholder value once the initial and obvious savings have been taken. But they usually focus on tactical integration (for example, of organisational structure, support services, policies), rather than on strategic integration (customers, products, people, systems). However, to succeed, both are needed.

The performance management gap

There is a gap between *business* performance *management* and *individual* performance *management* in all businesses, leading to a gap between business performance and individual performance. Business performance management is usually driven through an annual business planning process, which sets financial targets without specifying how they are to be achieved. Individual performance management is carried out through a performance appraisal process that sets mainly non-financial personal targets without explaining how they link to financial targets. Both focus on improving the present situation rather than initiating the step-change today's organisations must make if they want to succeed in the future.

THE SOLUTION: TRANSLATING STRATEGY INTO ACTION

Business alignment

Business alignment is a unique new approach that:

- defines the issues and resources that are of value, allocating crystal-clear responsibility for them and measuring progress towards their delivery
- empowers people to set their own objectives in the context of corporate goals
- creates a results-oriented performance culture, rewarding the delivery of outcomes rather than the management of resources
- organises around results rather than skills
- challenges and justifies partners' and support units' outcomes, replacing adversarial service-level agreements
- integrates and automates planning, budgeting, resourcing, measuring, reporting, and rewarding, thus releasing managers and support staff to deliver growth outcomes
- combines business and individual performance management
- identifies core processes and prioritises initiatives
- continuously reveals duplication, streamlines processes, and optimises the allocation of resources
- aligns information technology with the business through the IT alignment matrix
- integrates people and other resources around common goals after a merger or acquisition

Business alignment gets everyone to specify what their organisation needs to do to produce what it needs to deliver to stakeholders in the future. It defines precisely what should be done to extract value from a merger or acquisition once the initial cost savings have been taken, and so enables long-term growth in shareholder value.

By applying business alignment before a merger, the organisation goes into the merger negotiation knowing more precisely what it wants out of the merger, and thus is better prepared to extract value from the merger after the event.

APPLYING THE BALANCED SCORECARD

Translating strategy into business results with the balanced scorecard is a four-part process.
1. Leaders build and align around an architecture for change.
2. Required outcomes are linked to the activities that will deliver them, and resources are allocated to carry them out.
3. The organisation is mobilised for action.
4. A feedback and learning system is built to make strategy development and implementation a continuous process.

BUILDING AND ALIGNING LEADERSHIP – AN ARCHITECTURE FOR CHANGE

Building an architecture for change involves defining strategy as an integrated set of hypotheses that describe an organisation's evolution from the present to the future. The hypotheses are captured in a balanced scorecard, which defines the causal relationships between the things of value to the business, thus enabling value-based and activity-based management. It also defines how these things of value should be measured, thus providing key performance indicators.

Linking to business planning – making strategy operational

Business process re-engineering, activity-based costing, and workflow
The organisation's leaders decide on the corporate processes and initiatives required to deliver the outcomes. They use these to assess the relevance of current corporate processes, to prioritise existing initiatives, and to define new initiatives needed for achieving the strategy. Some initiatives and processes are found to be irrelevant to the future of the organisation and can be removed, following Hammer's principle, 'Don't automate, obliterate'. Activity-based costing is used to determine which resources are released by the removal of the activity, and workflow software is applied to the new and remaining processes after their definition or improvement.

Focusing on organisational development
Processes are associated with the outcomes they deliver, and in so doing they suggest an organisation that allocates resources to the delivery of strategic outcomes. This is usually radically different from, and more productive than, the functional organisation.

IT alignment matrix
The IT alignment matrix (ITAM) defines the knowledge communities of the future and the structure and content of the data warehouses required to inform them. The ITAM reveals the gap between the current databases and those required to deliver outcomes defined in the balanced scorecard.

Enterprise resource planning
The types of resource – people and things – needed to deliver the future outcomes are then identified and valued in monetary terms to define a budget. Note that this turns the business planning process on its head, since the traditional process starts with money (and involves too much guesswork). Starting with outcomes enables a rational debate about what should be produced and in what quantity. Information from enterprise resource-planning is used to calculate the budget.

Investing in people
Discretionary pay and bonuses are dependent on the delivery of balanced-scorecard outcomes and targets. At the executive level the change is the addition of non-financial targets. At lower levels the change is more significant, involving specific rewards for deliverables that individuals can influence.

Business alignment integrates individuals with performance management by empowering them to say what they can contribute to outcomes. Instead of being told what to do, people are invited to say what they can produce. Consequently they have a real opportunity to create their own careers.

Cascading and mobilisation – linking the boardroom to the front line

Now the organisation is aligned around the strategic outcomes. There is no formal reorganisation in the traditional sense, since this rarely produces positive changes in behaviour. Instead, individuals are appointed to lead the delivery of the strategic themes, and the rest of the organisation are invited to say what they can produce that will assist the delivery of the themes.

Over time, status and rewards are aligned with the delivery of outcomes that help to deliver the themes, and people and other resources gravitate towards the themes. Level by level, organisations achieve strategic focus and alignment. Non-strategic outcomes and activities are eliminated, freeing up resources that are then redirected to strategic outcomes.

Feedback and learning – linking the front line to the boardroom

People at all levels are now aligned to the strategy. What remains is to link them through feedback and learning, using a dynamic enterprise performance-management system. Information about outcomes, activities, and resources is stored electronically, enabling the organisation to outpace its peers. Measures, progress assessments, recommendations, and insights flow from the grass roots to the executive team. Meetings solely for reporting results are replaced by working sessions to solve problems of which everyone is already aware.

MAKING IT HAPPEN
- Work out what customers will buy from the company, and what internal processes are critical to delivering those purchases.
- Decide what the organisation must learn in order to carry out the core processes effectively.
- Draw a strategy map to show what outcomes the organisation must achieve to deliver its strategy, and which outcome leads to another.
- Measure performance against the parameters in the last full reporting period before the development of the balanced scorecard.

- Cascade the corporate outcomes, activities, and resources to the front line so that the people responsible for delivery to customers change their behaviour.
- Appoint the CEO as champion of the balanced scorecard and leader of the workshop activity.

THE BEST SOURCES OF HELP
Books:
Bakker, Hans, Martijn Babeliowsky, and Frank Stevenaar. *The Next Leap: Achieving Growth Through Global Networks, Partnerships and Co-operation.* London: Cyan Books, 2004.
Bruner, Robert F. *Deals from Hell: M & A Lessons That Rise Above the Ashes.* Chichester: Wiley, 2009.
Kaplan, Robert S., and David P. Norton. *The Balanced Scorecard: Translating Strategy into Action.* Cambridge, Massachusetts: Harvard Business School Press, 1996.

Why Mergers Fail and How to Prevent It
by Susan Cartwright

EXECUTIVE SUMMARY
- Mergers and acquisitions (M&A) are increasing in frequency, yet at least half fail to meet financial expectations.
- The United States and the United Kingdom continue to dominate M&A activity. As the number of cross-border deals increases, however, many other national players are entering the field, further highlighting the issue of cultural compatibility.
- Financial and strategic factors alone are insufficient to explain the high rate of failure; more account needs to be taken of human factors.
- The successful management of integrating people and their organisational cultures is the key to achieving desired M&A outcomes.

INTRODUCTION
Many businesses and even whole industries have endured a rollercoaster ride over the last decade. Firms have been profoundly affected by the emergence of new markets and competitors in fast-developing economies, massive increases in productivity resulting from technological developments, the rise of shareholder value and influence and, most notably, the first global recession of the 21st century. Against this background of tumultuous change the popularity of mergers has endured – and they have even come to be seen as a way to stave off business failure. For example, governments have actively promoted mergers in the financial services sector as a way of ensuring economic stability and confidence. While the motives for merger can variously be described as practical, psychological, or opportunist, the objective of all related M&A is to achieve synergy, or what is commonly referred to as the 2 + 2 = 5 effect. However, as many organisations learn to their cost, the mere recognition of potential synergy is no guarantee that the combination will actually realise that potential.

MERGER FAILURE RATES
The burning question remains – why do so many mergers fail to live up to shareholder expectations? In the short term, many seemingly successful acquisitions look good, but disappointing productivity levels are often masked by one-off cost savings, asset disposals, pension-fund holidays, or astute tax manoeuvres that inflate balance-sheet figures during the first few years.

Merger gains are notoriously difficult to assess. There are problems in selecting appropriate indices to make any assessment, as well as difficulties in deciding on a suitable measurement period. Typically the criteria selected by analysts are:
- profit-earning ratios
- share-price fluctuations
- managerial assessments

Irrespective of the evaluation method selected, the evidence on M&A performance is consistent in suggesting that a high proportion of M&As are financially unsuccessful. US sources place merger failure rates as high as 80 per cent, with UK evidence indicating that around half of mergers fail to meet financial expectations. A much-cited McKinsey study presents evidence arguing that most organisations would have received a better return on their investment if they had merely banked their money instead of buying another company. Consequently, many commentators have concluded that the true beneficiaries from M&A activity are those who sell their shares when deals are announced and the marriage brokers – the bankers, lawyers, and accountants – who arrange, advise, and execute the deals.

TRADITIONAL REASONS FOR MERGER FAILURE

M&A is still regarded by many decision-makers as an exclusively rational, financial, and strategic activity, and not as a human collaboration. Financial and strategic considerations, along with price and availability, therefore dominate target selection, overriding the soft issues such as people and cultural fit. Explanations of merger failure or underperformance often tend to focus on re-examining the factors that prompted the initial selection decision, for example:
- payment of an over-inflated price for the acquired company
- poor strategic fit
- failure to achieve potential economies of scale because of financial mismanagement or incompetence
- sudden and unpredicted changes in market conditions

This ground has been well trodden, yet the rate of merger, acquisition, and joint-venture success has improved little. Clearly these factors may contribute to disappointing M&A outcomes, but this conventional wisdom only part explains what goes wrong in M&A management.

THE FORGOTTEN FACTOR IN M&A

The false distinction that has developed between hard and soft merger issues has been extremely unhelpful in extending our understanding of merger failure, as it separates the impact of the merger on the individual from its financial impact on the organisation. Successful M&A outcomes are linked closely to the extent to which management is able to integrate organisational members and their cultures and sensitively address and minimise individuals' concerns.

By representing sudden and major change, mergers generate considerable uncertainty and feelings of powerlessness. This can lead to reduced morale, job and career dissatisfaction, employee stress, and uncertainty. Rather than increased profitability, mergers have become associated with a range of negative behavioural outcomes such as:
- acts of sabotage and petty theft
- increased staff turnover, with rates reported as high as 60 per cent
- increased sickness and absenteeism

Ironically, this occurs at the very time when organisations need and expect greater employee loyalty, flexibility, co-operation, and productivity.

PEOPLE FACTORS ASSOCIATED WITH M&A FAILURE

A wide range of people factors have been identified with unsuccessful M&A. These include:
- underestimating the difficulties of merging two cultures
- underestimating the problem of skills transfer
- demotivation of employees
- departure of key people
- expenditure of too much energy on doing the deal at the expense of post-merger planning
- lack of clear responsibilities, leading to post-merger conflicts
- too narrow a focus on internal issues to the neglect of the customers and the external environment
- insufficient research about the merger partner or acquired organisation

DIFFERENCES BETWEEN MERGERS AND ACQUISITIONS

In terms of employee response, whether the transaction is described as a merger or an acquisition, the event will trigger uncertainty and fears of job losses. However, there are important differences. In an acquisition, power is substantially assumed by the new parent. Change is usually swift and often brutal as the acquirer imposes its own control systems and financial restraints. Parties to a merger are likely to be more evenly matched in terms of size, and the power and cultural dynamics of the combination are more ambiguous. Integration is a more drawn-out process.

This has implications for the individual. During an acquisition there is often more overt conflict and resistance and a sense of powerlessness. In mergers, however, because of the prolonged period between the initial announcement and actual integration, uncertainty and anxiety continue for a much longer time as the organisation remains in a state of limbo.

CULTURAL COMPATIBILITY

The process of the merger is often likened to marriage. In the same way that clashes of personality and misunderstanding lead to difficulties in personal relationships, differences in organisational cultures, communication problems, and mistaken assumptions lead to conflicts in organisational partnerships.

Mergers are rarely a marriage of equals, and it's still the case that most acquirers or dominant merger partners pursue a strategy of cultural absorption; the acquired company or smaller merger partner is expected to assimilate and adopt the culture of the other. Whether the outcome is successful depends upon the willingness of organisational members to surrender their own culture and at the same time perceive that the other culture is attractive and therefore worth adopting.

Cultural similarity may make absorption easier than when the two cultures are very different, yet the process of due diligence rarely extends to evaluating the degree of cultural fit. Furthermore, few organisations bother to try to understand the cultural values and strengths of the acquiring workforce or their merger partners in order to inform and guide the way in which they should go about introducing change.

MAKING IT HAPPEN

Making a good organisational marriage currently seems to be a matter of chance and luck. This needs to change so that there is a greater awareness of the people issues involved and consequently a more-informed integration strategy. Some basic guidelines for more effective management include:

- extension of the due diligence process to incorporate issues of cultural fit
- greater involvement of human resource professionals
- the conducting of culture audits before the introduction of change management initiatives
- increased communication and involvement of employees at all levels in the integration process
- the introduction of mechanisms to monitor employee stress levels
- fair and objective reselection processes and role allocation
- providing management with the skills and training to sensitively handle M&A issues such as insecurity and redundancy
- creating a superordinate goal which will unify work efforts

MINI-CASE

Paul Hodder was involved as director of human resource management in the formation of Aon Risk Services, a merger of four rather different retail-insurance-broking and risk-management companies. A major theme of their integration process was the formation of a series of task groups to review and identify best practice. Another part involved an organisation-wide training programme to provide individuals with life skills to help them initiate and cope with change, to improve teamwork,

and to develop support networks. Enthusiasm for the programme provided several hundred change champions to lead change projects and assume support and mentoring roles. Good communication of early wins and successes has reassured organisational members that the changes are working and are beneficial.

CONCLUSION

Despite thorough pre-merger procedures, mergers continue to fall far short of financial expectations. The single biggest cause of this failure rate is poor integration following the acquisition. The identification of the target company, the subsequent and often drawn-out negotiations, and attending to the myriad financial, technical, and legal details are all exhausting activities. Once the target company has been acquired, little energy or motivation is left to plan and implement the integration of the people and cultures following the merger. It seems nonsensical to waste all the resources and energy that has gone into the merger, through inadequate planning of the integration stage of the process, yet all too often organisations do just that. Without a properly planned integration process or its effective implementation, mergers will not be able to achieve the full potential of the acquisition.

THE BEST SOURCES OF HELP
Books:
Brady, Chris, and Scott Mueller. *Intelligent M&A: Navigating the Mergers and Acquisitions Minefield*. Chichester: Wiley, 2007.
Rankine, Denzil, and Peter Howkin. *Acquisition Essentials: A Step-by-Step Guide to Smarter M&A Deals*. Harlow: FT Prentice Hall, 2005.

The Power of Identity by Wally Olins

EXECUTIVE SUMMARY
- Corporate identity is the unique identity of a firm that differentiates it from its competitors; it is a valuable asset and influences the organisation's strategy, structure, and vision. Today, it is often replaced by the word 'brand'.
- A corporate identity or branding programme enables a corporation's individual identity to be managed and projected.
- In order to develop an effective identity or branding programme, organisational builders must have a clear idea about what drives the organisation – they must have a vision and a sense of strategic direction.
- Organisational builders can consciously construct a structure that enables the organisation to project its identity both internally and externally.

INTRODUCTION

Organisations have a unique identity that can be employed as a valuable asset. Companies currently face challenges to their identity from all sides. These challenges are increasingly prompting company boards to regard identity or brand as an important topic. These are the most common problems regarding identity management.

- Products and services are increasingly becoming more similar, persuading customers to purchase products on an emotional basis – a projected sense of corporate personality and rapport with customers boosts business.
- Corporate mergers are on the rise, charging leaders with the problem of how to create a new identity from two old ones.
- Organisations are forced through changing technologies, deregulation, and globalisation to alter the nature of their

business and to manage corporate identity through change and uncertainty.

Corporate identity or branding provides a bedrock of valuable resources, such as goodwill, loyalty, and respect among customers, while internally providing a strategic direction.

WHAT IS IDENTITY?

Every organisation carries out thousands of transactions every day: it buys, it sells, it hires and fires, it makes, it promotes, it informs through advertising and the Web. In each transaction the organisation is in some way presenting itself – or part of itself – to the various groups of people it deals with. The totality of the way the organisation presents itself can be called its identity. What different audiences perceive is often called its image.

Because the range of its activities is so vast, and the manifestations of identity are so diverse, the corporation needs to actively and explicitly manage its identity or brand.

Identity can project four ideas:
• who you are
• what you do
• how you do it
• where you want to go

THE FOUR VECTORS

Identity or brand manifests itself primarily through four main vectors:
• products and services
• environments – where you make or sell your products or services
• communications – how you talk about your product
• behaviour – how you behave to your employees and the world

The balance between these four is rarely equal, and a priority early on in creating any identity programme is to determine which predominates.

The central idea/vision

The idea behind an identity programme is that in everything the organisation does or produces, it should project a clear idea of what it is and what its aims are.

Name/logo

At the heart of the visual identity is the hierarchy and identification system and the way it is reflected in symbols, logotypes, and marks. The symbol is highly visible. Its prime purpose is to present the idea of the corporation with impact, brevity, and immediacy.

It is sometimes necessary to change the symbol in order to signify a change in direction, as, for example, BP did. In other cases (for example, Renault or Shell) modification may be more appropriate.

Sometimes it's appropriate to change the name of a corporation for legal reasons (for example, Andersen Consulting becoming Accenture). Name changes are, however, frequently misunderstood and always excite high levels of emotion, particularly in the media.

Audiences

The audiences of an organisation are those people who come into contact with it in any way. It is often assumed that the most important audience for any company is its customers. In a service business, however, employees are by far the most significant audience. They transmit the identity of the organisation to customers, so they have to live it.

There are both internal and external audiences. The internal audience comprises staff and their families. External audiences include shareholders, competitors, suppliers, and partners, the financial world, and opinion-formers of all kinds. These audiences are not always separate and independent; to some extent they overlap.

Types of corporate identity (or 'Brand Architecture')

The identity of most companies can be assigned to one of three general categories: monolithic, endorsed, or branded.

Monolithic identity. Here the organisation uses one name and one visual system throughout all of its interactions. Because everything that the organisation does has the same name, style, and character, each part supports the other. Virgin is the most high-profile example of this type of identity. The name and identity of Virgin is not associated so much with what it does, but with what it is, how it behaves, and what it seems to stand for.

Endorsed identity. Most companies grow at least partly by acquisition. The acquiring company is often eager to preserve the goodwill (equity) associated with its acquisitions. Under an endorsed identity strategy, the parent endorses its subsidiaries with the corporate name and sometimes its visual style. Accor is an example of an organisation that uses the endorsed system.

Branded identity. Some companies, especially those in the consumer products field, separate their corporate identity from the identities of the brands they own, for example, Unilever, Diageo, and LVMH. The final customer identifies with the brand, other audiences with the corporation. Brands have names, reputations, life cycles, and personalities of their own, and they may even compete with other brands from the same company.

STARTING AND MANAGING A PROGRAMME

The following points should be considered when implementing a corporate identity programme:
• Is it part of a corporate turnaround?
• Does it inspire, invigorate, and create more cohesion internally?
• Is it intended to increase the share price?
• Is it focused on helping to integrate newly acquired companies?
• Is it a response to competitive pressures?

When a corporate identity programme is initiated, a senior individual in the organisation must be appointed to manage it, and change should be implemented in a clear and goal-focused manner. Organisations are rarely sufficiently objective, self-aware, or experienced to carry out all this work by themselves. They usually need outside assistance from branding, identity, or design consultants. As with every corporate activity, the identity programme needs a power base, financial controls, and clear lines of authority. A working party should be formed, which should report to a steering group.

THE STAGES OF WORK

Stage One: Investigation, analysis, and strategic recommendations

The organisation has to take an objective look at how it is perceived by its various audiences and how these perceptions compare with its aspirations. If the existing identity is seen as unclear, old fashioned, or ineffective, senior managers need to agree on the action required to change perceptions. Stage One ends with recommendations for action.

Stage Two: Development

Depending on the results of Stage One, it may be necessary to change the identity of the company completely, including name and visual style (Accenture), to keep the same name but change the identity visually (BP Amoco), or simply to make some changes.

Changes of name and visual style are expensive and time consuming, and they clearly signal to the marketplace that the organisation is making a new promise or moving in a new direction. This kind of change makes a promise of changed performance that has to be fulfilled. Never promise more than you can deliver.

On the basis of the recommendations made in Stage One, consultants develop an identity system based on the endorsed or branded model. The identity system usually consists of a name (or names), mark or logo, main and subsidiary typefaces, and colours. These will be applied to materials such as letterheads, websites, and products.

Stage Three: Implementation

The new identity has to be codified so that it can be used in the organisation and by relevant outside suppliers. Manuals are prepared containing all the identity elements and their precise specifications for a variety of applications. The manual should also demonstrate the spirit that lies behind the organisation.

Stage Four: Launch

If the new corporate identity programme is to work, it has to be launched with enthusiasm and commitment. The launch is the first major opportunity for the company's leaders to present the identity as a significant corporate resource and to integrate it into the organisational structure.

Never trivialise your corporate identity. Explain that the new identity is the outward sign of change and explain what that change means. Internal audiences want to know what, why, and particularly how it will affect them as individuals. External audiences only want to know why and how much.

MAKING IT HAPPEN

- Develop your corporate identity to project the company's approach, values, distinctiveness, and direction.
- Concentrate primarily on three 'tangibles': your products and services, the environments where you make or sell them, and communications.
- Treat the intangibles of behaviour – how you behave to your employees and the world outside – as vital.
- As a priority, determine early which of the above four tangible and intangible factors predominates.
- Before starting a corporate identity programme, decide what you want it to achieve in the longer term.
- Construct the programme in the four stages recommended above.

CONCLUSION

All companies have an identity, whether or not they control it. By developing a desirable corporate identity, projecting it to customers, and employing it as a tool to provide internal direction, organisational efficiency can be raised. A corporate identity programme harnesses and manages a valuable corporate asset.

THE BEST SOURCES OF HELP

Books:

Olins, Wally. *On Brand*. London: Thames & Hudson, 2003.

Wheeler, Alina. *Designing Brand Identity: A Complete Guide to Creating, Building, and Maintaining Strong Brands*. Hoboken: Wiley, 2006.

Strategic Agility by John Wells

EXECUTIVE SUMMARY

- Whenever there's an economic slump, management focus shifts to cutting costs.
- This is only of benefit if at the same time the opportunity is taken to build a more agile business platform.
- There are several different levels of approach to cost management, from talking about it to taking the long-term strategic view.
- Most of these approaches have an impact on systems architecture – or should do.

INTRODUCTION

With the crash of the global financial services sector turning into a general economic slump, top management focus shifted from investing in new technology and business ideas to cutting costs. When the pressure is on to cut costs, a CEO has a tough choice to make: simply make bold cuts without consideration of future needs, or invest in taking the first steps to building a much more agile business platform that will allow the firm to exploit future opportunities and respond more quickly to change.

MAKING IT HAPPEN

Level Zero cost management: talking about it

The simplest and least-disruptive approach to cost-cutting is to talk about it but not actually do much. This is common behaviour in companies who acquire other businesses with the promise of major cost-reduction synergies that then fail to materialise. For instance, Bank of America, which grew from Nations Bank into the number one US consumer bank in a 30-year binge of more than 100 acquisitions, never realised major cost synergies until a new management came in.

Level One cost management: arbitrary cuts

A more dramatic approach to cost management is to cut all discretionary expenses (consultants, bowls of fresh fruit) and demand headcount reductions across the board. But cutting costs without tackling the underlying causes is often a short-lived solution. Costs have a nasty habit of growing back. Savings promised by the majority of cost-reduction programmes disappear within two years, never delivering the returns required to justify the high price paid for them.

Level One cost management is fast, decisive, and sometimes very necessary in a crisis, but it's seldom optimal. While it may be a short-term palliative for investors, it is seldom in the best long-term interests of the firm.

Level Two cost management: redesign business processes to meet today's needs

Rather than simply cutting costs, the challenge is to deal with the underlying causes of cost. This takes re-engineering business processes to design costs out. Rather than simply reducing the amount of resource allocated to an old process in the hope that it will work harder, the objective is to redesign the process so that it requires less resource in the first place. This is more thoughtful – and more effective – cost-cutting.

Level Three cost management: redesign business processes to meet tomorrow's needs

There is a danger of changing processes to meet today's immediate needs without paying attention to the future, so that when business improves another expensive process redesign is required. Every CEO knows there are a host of actions that must be taken if the firm is to prosper, but some must be deferred until financial conditions improve and shareholders have more of an appetite for investment.

The process redesign should take these into account, ensuring that the firm is ready to expand its activities when the time is ripe.

Level Four cost management: meeting unforeseen needs

But how can an organisation *really* be future-proof? What about those unforeseen events that demand sudden changes? It's not possible to design a set of business processes to meet every eventuality. And yet an organisation can't afford to redesign all of its processes every time it encounters change. The challenge is to shape a process architecture that can be more easily adapted to change.

The way to achieve this is to shape processes in a way that decouples them from each other as much as possible, allowing local changes to be made in a single process without major redesign of the total system. This is component-based process architecture.

Level Five cost management: self-adaptive systems

Decoupling various processes also allows the team of people responsible for operating each process to look for improvements continuously. If they are incentivised to behave in this way, then when changes occur the process is quickly modified to meet the new needs. The process and the people who operate it form a component of the organisation.

To be really adaptive, the component team must have the ability to modify and improve the process themselves. This makes for really rapid response. The component, and the organisation as a whole, then become much more agile and adaptive.

MINI-CASE

Wells Fargo saw the opportunity to offer loans to small businesses on the Web, collecting credit-worthiness information on each applicant in real time to decide on whether to approve a loan. The company envisaged an automated loan manager and backroom support service that were much more cost effective than the human variety.

The initial service was very well received. Not only did it cut costs, but it provided much quicker response to the customer, and it began driving up market share.

The next challenge came when Wells Fargo wanted to change its criteria for making loans. This process had traditionally taken up to six months, limiting flexibility and responsiveness to changing market demands. One solution would have been simply to wire in the new loan criteria. However, sufficiently dissatisfied by its past experience, in this phase Wells Fargo sought to componentise the system, isolating the criteria from the rest of the system so that they could be changed more easily. Moreover, rather than simply inserting a new set of criteria into the criteria module, the company built a criteria generator. Instead of requiring expensive IT resource to change the criteria, the department managers could do it themselves, taking days instead of months.

Far from limiting the number of criteria, Wells Fargo made its solution even smarter by making sure that the criteria component allowed the addition of more, as yet unidentified, criteria, providing the system with the agility to react to the unknown. The bank avoided the temptation to implement a Level Two solution and moved directly to a Level Five solution, dealing with known changes and changes as yet unknown, while empowering the management team to look continuously for improvements.

The implications for information systems: componentised systems architecture

Redesigning processes almost always means changing the information systems that support the processes. And the trouble is that old legacy systems get in the way. Hence the frustration with IT departments. Rather than being seen as the driver of change, IT is often seen as the greatest impediment to change in large organisations.

Old legacy platforms are typically hugely complex systems tied together to help run the company. A minor change in one part of the system can have major and unpredictable impact on other parts, rather like the proverbial butterfly that starts a hurricane in the Caribbean by fluttering in South America.

The challenge for legacy IT systems is the same as for organisational processes: to be able to break them down into loosely coupled components, so that each component can be changed without affecting the organisation as a whole.

The IT components must map 100 per cent on to organisational process components, so that when a department component sees opportunities for improvement it can change without disrupting the whole organisation. The IT system can be adapted in parallel to support the change without changing the whole IT system. The capacity for change when this alignment is achieved is obviously very large.

CONCLUSION
Deal with today's challenge with tomorrow in mind

When a company is facing major economic challenges, how can it find time to worry about turning its IT platform into components? The reality is that a company must be guided by its component architecture whenever it makes change. Take the current plethora of legacy systems and identify the role each will play in a more flexible componentised architecture. In the context of a clear long-term view, legacy systems can be changed in ways that contribute to the long-term agenda.

THE BEST SOURCES OF HELP
Books:
Chaffey, Dave. *E-Business and E-Commerce Management: Strategy, Implementation and Practice.* 4th ed. Harlow: FT/Prentice Hall, 2009.
Doz, Yves and Mikko Kosonen. *Fast Strategy: How Strategic Agility Will Help You Stay Ahead of the Game.* Philadelphia: Wharton School Publishing, 2008.
Laudon, Kenneth, and Carol Guercio Traver. *E-Commerce: Business, Technology, Society.* 5th ed. Reading, Massachusetts: Wesley Publishing Company, 2008.
Morgan, Mark, Raymond E. Levitt, and William Malek. *Executing Your Strategy: How to Break It Down and Get It Done.* Boston: Harvard Business School Press, 2008.
Turban, Efraim, et al. *Electronic Commerce 2010: A Managerial Perspective.* 6th ed. Harlow: Prentice Hall, 2009.

Return on Talent by Subir Chowdhury

EXECUTIVE SUMMARY
- The performance of an organisation is determined by the performance of its employees.
- Organisations must therefore measure return on talent (ROT) as well as return on investment (ROI).
- Knowledge is one of the most important factors for business success. If knowledge assets are increased, related factors such as sales will also increase.
- Talent – or intellectual capital – has fast become one of the most significant areas of business activity and competition.

INTRODUCTION

The performance of an organisation is entirely determined by the performance of its employees. This bold statement deserves further study. If the determinant of corporate performance is not its employees, what is? Is it strategic intent? Core competencies? Manufacturing? Is it proprietary technologies? The best equipment and laboratories? A visionary CEO? Yes, it's all of these things. And all of these things are created and constantly improved by employees. Talented employees are the change agents. Good employees join in to help implement new initiatives. Others follow at various times, depending on when they can break the bonds of their comfort zone to enter the area of change, uncertainty, and opportunity. They fall by the wayside because they were in the wrong job.

It is broadly recognised that past performance is not a reliable indicator of potential or future success. Yet many organisations continue to use past performance to identify high-potential employees. How much true talent is overlooked by this practice? Overlooked and misplaced high-potential employees stagnate. The problem of identifying, positioning, and compensating high-potential employees spans all disciplines and levels, from the mail room to the boardroom. Lost and underused employees represent enormous, largely unattended financial loss. A second problem is the difficulty in measuring the financial contribution of employees beyond global measures such as revenues per employee.

To focus a successful organisation, managers must use a new tool called return on talent (ROT). Most organisations focus on return on investment (ROI) and fail to understand the key strategy of how to increase ROI by increasing ROT. By harnessing talent and realising the value of knowledge, everyone can benefit.

HARNESSING TALENT

ROT has the power to revolutionise business. ROT is calculated by dividing the knowledge generated and applied by the investment in talent. You need to address the dilemma of how to measure an intangible asset and how to generate high ROT value. For decades, organisations have used key metrics like ROI and ROA (return on assets) to determine value. But increasingly an effective new-economy organisation will use ROT. Current business measurements merely measure the use of capital, but ROT is expressed as follows:

ROT = knowledge generated & applied/investment in talent

If you have talented people, knowledge is just one component. The generation of knowledge is the most important thing talent can provide. Now you may realise that knowledge generated by the talent doesn't equal knowledge applied, right? And if knowledge isn't applied, then the company loses most of the market value of that knowledge. Whatever knowledge a person generates in a year divided by how much is invested in that particular person is the value.

If an employee generates many innovative ideas but never implements any of them, that person fails to generate any value, because the return to the company is zero. Knowledge generated does not necessarily mean knowledge applied. So value is knowledge generated *and* applied. Knowledge becomes an asset only when it's captured and used effectively; if it isn't effectively applied, it can't generate any yield or ROI. Generating a lot of knowledge within organisations doesn't add any value unless that knowledge is used in effective strategy for-

mulation. Knowledge assets, like money or equipment, are worth cultivating only in the context of strategy. You can't define and manage intellectual assets unless you know what you are trying to do with them. This is the backbone of the knowledge economy; success in this field depends on mastery of talent, just as success in manufacturing relies on the skilful employment of plant and supply chains.

THE VALUE OF KNOWLEDGE
Return on talent

The value of knowledge generated increases with its effective deployment. Effective knowledge generated means high ROT. It leads to a creative workforce, innovations, smooth processes, continuous product improvements, and improved communications. It helps management to be flexible, to capitalise on opportunities, and to keep pace with the changing business climate. Talented people influence those around them, and their knowledge is shared over time. Top knowledge generators should be rewarded. If managers expect top talents to achieve their maximum performance and produce maximum return, they must not place them in routine jobs.

ROT measures the payback from investment in people; it shows whether managers are hiring the right people and how effectively they use them to achieve business success. It can be a quantitative or qualitative measurement, based on management's viewpoint. Are managers getting the maximum payback on their investment? If managers want to see quantitative results, they must put a price on knowledge generated, based on the results achieved. Talent generates knowledge, which is one of the greatest assets in the global economy. True knowledge brings creativity and innovation and adds value to the company. Knowledge has become a key production factor, along with traditional resources such as raw materials, buildings, and machinery. Companies that measure the knowledge generated and applied by their talent can make their investments in talent more profitable. Further, companies cannot improve what they do not measure.

Effective managers use ROT measurements to make their investments in talent more profitable. ROT measurements help to monitor performance, forecast opportunity, and determine the profitability of their investment in talent. To make their investment more profitable, management must constantly measure ROT, continuously improve ROT, and nurture, develop, and refresh talent.

Return on knowledge

Return on knowledge generated and applied is more difficult to calculate and track. Knowledge creates real wealth through multiple applications, for example, repeating the same application pervasively through a corporation, or finding new applications to new situations. Knowledge applications have breadth (across organisations) and length (in time). Years may pass between the generation of knowledge and its first application, let alone subsequent applications.

In order to properly account for the value of knowledge generated, initial estimates need to be made and refined yearly as applications appear on the horizon and then are realised. Leading indicators of return are based on projections of the probability of each anticipated application and the monetary value of each application summed over all anticipated applications.

Forward-looking projections and backward-looking allocations are both judgments, and there's no reason to believe that one is any better than the other. Indeed, projections made while focusing on the knowledge generated may be the more reliable of the two. It is certain that the combination of early projections, after-the-fact allocations, and annual updating and tracking between knowledge generated and the first of a series of applications, greatly improves the capability to measure and link return on knowledge generated and applied, and investment in talent.

MAKING IT HAPPEN

1. **Build a team focused on developing talent.** To reach high ROT scores, you need a talent team. Often you find one or two good people who can generate knowledge and perhaps even apply that knowledge, but you don't have a talent team that can leverage their ideas. Most of the individual talent in a company can be innovative if the team dynamics are right. If you have a low ROT score, you may have a dysfunctional team. ROT scores are not fixed; they change over time.

2. **Measure and monitor ROT.** If you are a manager who hires and invests in talent, you need to monitor ROT closely. In a company the size of General Motors or General Electric, you probably view salaries as a regular fixed cost that is standard. The portion that may vary is how much you invest in certain ideas. If you see that certain employees are not generating enough knowledge and success relative to your investment in them, that should be a big red flag, because your ROT value might become negative, or much lower than your competitor's ROT value.

3. **Decide how to increase ROT throughout the organisation.** If you were hired to manage talent with a low ROT score (perhaps even a negative value), you need to do some things to boost the ROT fast. How do you turn around an organisation and achieve higher ROT scores? You do it person by person, function by function. You have to assess the talent on your team and find out who and what is bringing the most profit to the company, who and what is winning and keeping the best customers. Your first task is to perform talent diagnostics. You might easily spend six months identifying all your talent and determining which ones you can work with to turn the company around. But usually you don't have six months to do talent diagnostics. So you need to do it faster, even in a large company. There is much to be said for focusing on quick, high-profile actions that build support and momentum behind the need to increase ROT.

Many managers assess employees' talent intuitively – they don't necessarily need a measurement tool. Every manager, however, benefits from having a tool to measure and monitor ROT. Apple soared when Steve Jobs was CEO, and faded when he left. It soared again when he returned as Apple's CEO. It doesn't mean that Jobs was a good or bad person. He was a very effective person in that environment. Many good CEOs fail in environments in which there is no structure. They go by intuition. After you identify the key talent, give them the authority and resources to boost the ROT team score. The talent diagnostic may show that in one division you have a lot of talented people, while in a different division you have very few. You have to cross functions, making sure you balance the talent according to the needs of the organisation, and then challenge each talent and team to reach a financial goal.

CONCLUSION

Organisations that constantly improve ROT grow at a rapid rate. Management can monitor the performances of individuals as well as teams. Knowledge is one of the most important factors for business success. If knowledge assets are increased, then all other related factors like production and sales will be automatically increased. Consequently, organisations should try to improve ROT continuously to sustain sales growth. ROT is a superb key performance indicator, and one that is set to be measured and managed in much the same way as financial issues.

THE BEST SOURCES OF HELP
Book:
Brockbank, Wayne, and David Ulrich. *The HR Value Proposition*. Cambridge, Massachusetts: Harvard Business School Press, 2005.

Budgeting by Jeremy Hope, Robin Fraser, Peter Bunce, and Franz Röösli, Beyond Budgeting Round Table (BBRT)

EXECUTIVE SUMMARY

- **The 'Command and Control' model.** This management model emerged in the early 1900s to help companies meet rising demand and maximise profitability. With its main focus on efficiency, it introduced division of labour, incentives linking pay to performance, functional organisation, and centralised decision-making. It led to dramatic increases in productivity, but it also dehumanised work. The annual planning and budgeting process that ties it all together is its defining characteristic and the source of many of its problems today.
- **The changing environment.** In conditions of discontinuous change, unpredictable competition, and fickle customers, few companies can plan ahead with any confidence. Yet most organisations today remain locked into a traditional 'plan-make-and-sell' management model that involves a protracted annual planning and budgeting process based on negotiated targets and resources, which act as a constraint on responsiveness.
- **The barriers to change.** Organisations need to find a new model that effectively empowers front-line managers to make quick decisions based on fast, relevant information. But the annual planning and budgeting process and the resulting 'fixed performance contract' act as barriers to change, both mental and systemic.
- **The 'Devolved Leadership' model.** A number of companies have broken free from the traditional model and created a model that is much better aligned with today's competitive success factors. They have done this by devolving accountability to front-line managers and replacing annual planning and budgeting with alternative steering mechanisms. The BBRT has studied these cases, seen what huge competitive advantage they have gained from this model, and identified the principles on which it operates.
- **Making it happen.** The BBRT has identified some of the best cases worldwide and developed a pragmatic, scientifically based approach to implementing the model and gaining real competitive advantage from it.

THE COMMAND AND CONTROL MODEL

The traditional Command and Control model was designed to execute a *producer-led* approach to business. It was influenced to a large extent by Frederick W. Taylor and the Scientific Management movement. The multi-divisional organisation (or M-form) coped with increasing complexity by placing the activities of each distinct product line, region, or technology into a separately managed compartment and subjecting all these compartments to the financial discipline of a strong corporate staff. The underlying thread was control. The mission statement agreed by senior executives was translated into the strategic plan by the planners and handed down the hierarchy to operational managers, who then prepared their plans and budgets. Once these were agreed, all that was demanded was adherence to the plan. Head office did not like surprises. Control reports were constantly fed back up the line, and if they showed that performance was veering off track, new directives would be issued.

The model led to dramatic increases in productivity, but division of labour led to the 'dehumanisation' of work. Ways have been found to ameliorate this problem to some degree, but the design of the model is fundamentally one that works *against*, not *with*, the best in human nature. Douglas McGregor maintained in the 1960s that most managers tend towards Theory X (assuming the worst in human nature) and generally get poor results, while enlightened managers use Theory Y (assuming the best), which produces better performance and results, and allows people to grow and develop. Much of his message was misinterpreted or ignored, but he hoped that a time would come when significant changes in leadership philosophy would become a requirement for survival, because they would benefit organisations and workers alike. Today, these conditions exist. Workers are no longer the un-automated parts of production processes, as they were in the industrial age. Most are now 'knowledge workers' (i.e. professionals). As Peter Drucker forecast decades ago, they must lead in the information age, and this leadership has to be visionary and completely different from the traditional ways of leadership and management applied in the Command and Control model.

THE CHANGING ENVIRONMENT

The traditional model worked well when market conditions were stable, competitors were known and their actions predictable, relatively few people took decisions, prices reflected internal costs, strategy and product life cycles were lengthy, customers had limited choice, and the priority of shareholders was good stewardship. But these conditions no longer apply. Many people are required to take decisions, the pace of innovation is increasing, costs reflect market pressures, customers are fickle, and shareholders are more demanding. To compete more effectively in the information economy, firms must transform their centralised, functional hierarchies into networks of relatively autonomous units accountable for customer outcomes. They must also break free from the incremental planning and budgeting mentality, and involve all their people in building a new platform for sustainable improvement.

THE BARRIERS TO CHANGE

While most senior executives want their organisations to be more adaptive (and thus more devolved), few know how to turn management rhetoric into operating reality. While they talk about fast response, empowerment, innovation, operational excellence, customer focus, and shareholder value, their management processes (for example, targets, plans, measures, and rewards) all too often remain stuck in the past. Fixed strategies prevent fast responses; rigid organisational structures turn off managers who seek challenge and development; bureaucracies stifle innovation; entrenched functions undermine cross-functional processes; an emphasis on product targets works against customer loyalty programmes; and short-term performance contracts fail to support long-term value creation. Nor do the millions spent every year on re-engineering, team-building, enterprise-wide systems, customer relationship management, value-based management, and balanced scorecards seem to overcome these problems. In fact, the vast majority of these initiatives fail for exactly the same reason – they support the rhetoric but founder as they collide with the immovable forces of centralised decision-making and 'fixed performance contracts'.

THE DEVOLVED LEADERSHIP MODEL

The Devolved Leadership (or Beyond Budgeting) model is designed to overcome these barriers and create a flexible and adaptive organisation. Unlike the Command and Control model, Devolved Leadership works with, not against the best side of human nature (McGregor's Theory Y); it is suitable for post-industrial knowledge-based organisations; it supports the success factors that must be met in highly competitive business conditions; and it is also consistent with cybernetics and systems theory – the most relevant management science. Twelve principles provide managers with a robust, albeit empirical framework for evaluating where their organisations stand today, and guiding them towards an alternative management model.

Principles of the devolved leadership model

Leadership principles

1. **Customers.** Focus everyone on improving customer outcomes, *not on hierarchical relationships*.
2. **Organisation.** Organise as a network of lean, accountable teams, *not around centralised functions*.
3. **Responsibility.** Enable everyone to think and act like a leader, *not merely follow 'the plan'*.
4. **Autonomy.** Give teams the freedom and capability to act; *don't micro-manage them*.
5. **Values.** Govern through a few clear values, goals and boundaries, *not detailed rules and budgets*.
6. **Transparency.** Promote open information for self-management; *don't restrict it hierarchically*.

Process principles

1. **Goals.** Set relative goals for continuous improvement; *don't negotiate fixed performance contracts*.

2. **Rewards.** Reward shared success based on relative performance, *not on meeting fixed targets*.
3. **Planning.** Make planning a continuous and inclusive process, *not a top-down annual event*.
4. **Controls.** Base controls on relative indicators and trends, *not variances against plan*.
5. **Resources.** Make resources available as needed, *not through annual budget allocations*.
6. **Co-ordination.** Co-ordinate interactions dynamically, *not through annual planning cycles*.

MINI-CASES

Since its formation in 1998, the Beyond Budgeting Round Table (BBRT) has made numerous case studies of organisations that have moved or started to move towards a Devolved Leadership model. These include Svenska Handelsbanken and ALDI. *Svenska Handelsbanken*, the most successful Nordic bank, introduced its 'Devolved Leadership' model in 1970. Although a regional rather than a global player, Handelsbanken's performance is nevertheless quite exceptional. They have achieved their corporate goal of making a higher return on equity than the average of their competitors every year for three consecutive years. Their cost-to-income ratio is one of the lowest among European banks. In Sweden, they have had more satisfied customers, both business and private, than the average of their competitors in every single year since 1989. They have had lower loan losses than their competitors since the early 1980s. But the key point is that their sustained, high performance, through good times and bad, results directly from their 'Devolved Leadership' model. At Handelsbanken their model is their strategy and the main source of their competitive advantage. Theirs is a coherent model, and under consistent leadership for over three decades, they have evolved and deepened it.

ALDI, with Wal-Mart, is the most successful retailer in the world. Its founders, Karl and Theo Albrecht, are among the wealthiest men in the world, according to *Forbes*. Their model has been derived from the thrift and entrepreneurship that was necessary at the time the business was founded. It has evolved into what has been described as the retail idea of the century. The fundamental principle is always to keep it as simple as possible. Continual improvements ensure that the 'simple' is not only well executed but perfected. The customer is always the prime consideration in all decisions. They reduce the amount of communication and co-ordination and the risk of bad decisions being taken remotely by establishing small autonomous units. It allows closer contact to the market and customer as well as being faster than their competitors. It is also one of the best ways to reduce unnecessary complexity, and it enables many more people to feel they are 'running their own business'. They achieve this through 'cell division' from ALDI headquarters, as soon as a certain size is reached in a region (50 or 60 branches, for example). Chiefs of staff and controllers for supporting responsible line managers do not exist. Their leadership is recruited from inside the company. Accordingly, they have an outstanding knowledge of the business, a common doctrine and an unconditional interest in the company. The strong company culture gives ALDI a strategic and competitive advantage which is not easily imitated. They manage by means of their culture and values; there are no budgets and formally agreed plan and there never have been.

MAKING IT HAPPEN

A well-functioning management model is a delicate and intricate system. Every part of it must steer in the same direction. Only then can the organisation minimise its internal conflicts and maximise its potential. You cannot, therefore, 'pick and mix' among the principles. All 12 are necessary to bring about and sustain a complete change from the Command and Control model to Devolved Leadership. Unless the model is coherent, it will not be fully effective and it may regress. So, 'making it happen' requires:

- **initiation.** Build awareness of the gravity of the problems with the organisation's management model; raise a real sense of urgency to improve it; and make a compelling case for change.
- **change process.** Create a coalition of people in the organisation that is strong enough to guide the changes needed; work with them to create a clear vision of the new model; communicate it credibly and widely; and importantly 'do it together', rather than impose it from the top.
- **design.** Tackle the design *holistically*; address the leadership issues before the management processes and the management processes before the systems and tools. Each element must cohere to support the new, not the existing model.
- **implementation.** Don't implement anything until an overall vision and outline design have been agreed by the leadership, including the guiding team. Use 'trial and error' rather than 'delayed perfection', to find the most workable solutions.
- **evolution.** Don't let go until the model is implemented and embedded into the organisation. Even then the model must be continually improved and deepened if the organisation is to sustain competitive advantage from it.

CONCLUSION

Devolving accountability for results and replacing 'fixed performance contracts' with more adaptive steering mechanisms will create a management model that will enable an organisation to:

- respond more quickly to change and be better able to deal with increasing levels of uncertainty and complexity
- attract more talented managers and potential strategic partners
- generate a far better climate for breakthrough strategies aimed at improvement and growth
- operate at lower cost
- find and keep the right customers
- minimise dysfunctional behaviour, and encourage ethical behaviour
- create sustained growth in shareholder wealth

It is always a risk to make changes as profound as those required in introducing a Devolved Leadership model, but the greater risk in the long run is to continue to use a management model that is not aligned with today's critical success factors (CSFs), and works against human nature.

As increasing numbers of organisations adopt a management model that supports today's competitive success factors, those who do not must fall behind and eventually be forced to change, or fail to survive. Those who adopt it early will gain the greatest relative advantage, because its potential benefits are so great and it is very hard to copy. So it is not really a matter of whether or even when: it's now! Its time has come.

THE BEST SOURCES OF HELP
Website:
BBRT: **www.bbrt.org**.

Finding and Keeping Top Talent by Philip Sadler

EXECUTIVE SUMMARY

Just as organisations have changed dramatically in nature over the last 25 years, so have people's attitudes to their employers – and the attitudes of the most talented people are no exception.

- Talented employees are increasingly aware of their value and are prepared to move to other organisations if they feel they will receive greater respect and reward. Cradle to grave loyalty, if it ever existed at all, is certainly very scarce.
- Knowledge is more important than ever before and a major source of competitive advantage. Attracting, finding, and retaining talented people is therefore vital for success. Not only are people the most decisive and expensive resource, they also determine the success of every activity within the organisation.
- Although money remains important, talented people value much more; an increasingly complex range of factors affects their loyalty, motivation, and effectiveness.
- A disappointingly large number of talented people are already within organisations, their potential largely unfulfilled.

INTRODUCTION

In the past, the typical wealth-creating enterprises of the advanced industrial societies were either labour-intensive – such as coal mining or textiles – or capital-intensive – such as chemicals and steel. Today, many of the world's major corporations are best described as knowledge-intensive or talent-intensive. The obvious examples are companies in fields such as software, pharmaceuticals, business and professional services, music publishing, entertainment, and professional sports. The management of knowledge has become a lucrative field for management consultants and academic gurus in recent years and it is obviously important that a company should exploit its knowledge capital to the greatest extent possible. Sooner or later, however, all today's knowledge is obsolete. The competitive edge lies with companies that are focused on creating new knowledge. The value of a research laboratory to a potential investor is the ability of its scientists to make new discoveries and develop new products in the future.

In a world in which there is no shortage of capital for investment, talent is the only remaining scarce resource. However, the kind of talent needed by many of today's businesses is not necessarily of the kind that was in demand in the past. Fashion designers, international footballers, creative writers, inventors such as James Dyson, entrepreneurs such as Richard Branson, boy bands, website designers, and others possess marketable skills that have little to do with their ability to absorb knowledge. This explains why outstanding performers in many fields did not enjoy academic success in their schooldays.

CHARACTERISTICS OF TALENT-INTENSIVE ORGANISATIONS

Talent-intensive organisations share several characteristics.

- Their principal assets (that is, their talented people) do not appear on the balance sheet (although they are, or should be, the main determinants of the company's market valuation).
- These key assets are mobile. They can, despite contracts of service, simply walk away.
- Talent-intensive organisations rely particularly on creativity and imagination.
- The success criteria for talent-intensive organisations stretch far beyond the accountants' bottom line. Winning a Nobel Prize, an Oscar, a fashion design award, or the World Cup may weigh far more than profit or cash flow do.

THE INTERNATIONAL DIMENSION

Like so many other activities, recruiting is now affected by globalisation. Companies increasingly understand that they must adapt their human resources policies to a highly competitive global market for talent. There is a constant flow of talented people from countries with lower living standards or higher levels of personal taxation to countries where talent can enjoy a higher reward – the so-called 'brain drain'. Recruiting managers should try to include at least one global candidate in every key search. They should also consult with senior management on the question of where in the world the work (and the workforce) should be positioned in order to maximise its cost-effectiveness.

RECRUITING AND FINDING TALENT

The distinction between recruiting talent and finding it is important. Sometimes an organisation looks outside for new talent when the potential for outstanding performance already exists unrecognised among existing employees.

Recruitment itself can be separated into two quite distinct processes. The first is that of attracting people whose exceptional talent has already been established and recognised elsewhere. This can be called the transplanting type of recruiting – equivalent to digging up a mature tree in the quest for an instant garden. In such instances, companies often make the mistake of assuming that the cash nexus is the most important factor. While it is obviously true that an outstanding performer in any field is unlikely to move from one organisation to another if it involves a drop in remuneration, it remains the case that other factors are seldom given enough weight or consideration. For example, in the case of highly talented people, a key influence on the decision whether or not to move jobs is the reputation of the recruiting organisation in its particular field. Is it at the leading edge, does it set the pace for its industry, does the individual feel honoured to have been approached? Reputation building, therefore, is a key element in recruiting strategy. Top firms like Starbucks, Intel, Cisco, Marriott, Dell, Wal-Mart, and Microsoft have been focusing on employment branding for years. Nothing has a greater impact than being talked about in the media as a well-managed firm that is also a good place to work. Research shows that the best source of quality applicants comes from an organisation's existing employees. If employees are proud of their employer and enjoy a high level of job satisfaction, the result will be one or two quality employee referrals for every vacancy.

The 'nursery' approach

The second process can be termed the 'seed bed' or 'nursery' approach: recruiting young people straight from school or university, nurturing or developing their emerging talent and bringing it to fruition. This is clearly a longer-term approach and one fraught with obvious risks, one of which is the difficulty of predicting ultimate success. The obstacles in the way of successful prediction are many, including:

- different rates of maturing of individuals' abilities – late developers are often missed
- the relative weakness of psychometric tests when it comes to predicting things like creativity and entrepreneurial ability

- the tendency to give too much weight to academic qualifications
- failure to value diversity with regard to the workforce – a great deal of fine talent is overlooked among ethnic minorities, particularly when the selection process involves using psychometric instruments that have been validated within the Anglo-American culture
- the fact that motivation and drive may well be more powerful determinants of performance than sheer ability

Talent spotting
Somewhat less risky is the process of finding talent among existing employees. Assuming they have been in employment for some time, a well-designed appraisal and development procedure can be effective in selecting promising candidates for accelerated development.

Michael Howe, Reader in Human Cognition at Exeter University, is one of the world's leading experts on the subject of talent. He points to the danger of seeing talent in any field as a gift which you either have or not, as the case may be. 'We are easily convinced that the most striking feats must depend on circumstances which, except for certain rare individuals, are entirely unattainable. Some of the most widespread beliefs about exceptional people revolve around the view that certain individuals are not only remarkable but inherently so, while the remainder of us are doomed to ordinariness.' Howe challenges such beliefs and produces compelling evidence that appropriate training and development can bring about exceptional performance. His views are borne out by the achievements of participants in the TV series *Faking It* in which, for example, a go-go dancer with no previous experience of horse riding became a successful show jumper within a few weeks.

KEEPING TALENT
When it comes to retaining talent, it goes without saying that there has to be an adequate rewards package. What makes the real difference in keeping talented employees loyal is the extent to which the company provides them with a working environment favourable to creativity, self-expression, and the exercise of initiative. The paradox facing organisations, particularly very large ones, is that they are hierarchical, bureaucratic, and conformist in order to achieve efficiency and uniformity, yet it is just these characteristics that turn off highly creative people.

The term 'skunk works' has entered the language of organisations to describe small, informal, tightly knit teams that are shielded from standard company practices and rules in order to foster their creative energies. Warren Bennis gives a graphic description of the very

first skunk works, set up by Lockheed to develop the first US jet fighter during the Second World War. Lockheed's chief designer selected a team of 23 engineers and 30 support staff. They built makeshift quarters from discarded engine boxes roofed with a circus tent. They worked in secrecy, doing their own cleaning and secretarial work. Bennis describes the designer Johnson as 'a visionary on at least two fronts: designing aeroplanes and organising genius. Johnson seemed to know intuitively what talented people needed to do their best work, how to motivate them, and how to make sure the desired product was created as quickly and cheaply as possible.' His unit was characterised by the egalitarian treatment of people, an absence of paperwork, informality of dress, and open debate. The culture of an organisation is an important factor in its ability to retain talent. The chief characteristics of a culture that nurtures talent are:
- highly cohesive work teams
- authority residing in expertise and competence rather than rank or status
- elites recognised without elitism in that talented people respect and recognise the contribution of those less gifted colleagues who support them
- respected leadership: talented people are critical people who do not follow blindly, and know when the emperor has no clothes
- freedom, autonomy, space, and flexibility
- openness and trust
- encouragement of risk-taking

In other words, the right approach for organisations anxious to retain their most talented people is not so much to create a skunk works inside the company, but to make the company as a whole as much like a skunk works as possible.

THE BEST SOURCES OF HELP
Books:
Bennis, Warren, and Patricia Ward Biederman. *Organizing Genius: The Secrets of Creative Collaboration.* Cambridge, Massachusetts: Perseus, 1998.
Capelli, Peter. *Talent on Demand: Managing Talent in an Age of Uncertainty.* Boston: Harvard Business School Press, 2008.
Howe, Michael J.A. *The Origins of Exceptional Abilities.* Oxford: Blackwell, 1990.
Lawler, Edward E. III. *Talent: Making People Your Competitive Advantage.* San Francisco: Jossey-Bass, 2008.

The Critical Factors That Build or Break Teams
by Meredith Belbin

EXECUTIVE SUMMARY
- 'Team' and 'teamwork' too easily become glib terms. Check their meaning.
- Find out what work really requires a team.
- Some people flourish in teams, others don't.
- Teams need to be empowered and enabled to work within boundaries.
- Balanced teams need to be developed into mature teams.
- Effective teams need to understand both team roles and work roles.

INTRODUCTION

The problem with the word 'teamwork' is that it has become too popular and has therefore lost its meaning. A person deemed good at teamwork is all too often someone who fits into a group and keeps out of trouble. Ideal behaviour is often judged as complying with majority decisions and being willing to do anything that's required. Yet if everyone behaved like that, you'd have good reason to doubt that the team would function effectively. A flock of sheep may hang together well, but their only accomplishment is to eat grass.

For anyone interested in productive teamwork, it's often better to start with the work rather than the team. First of all, does the work call for a team? There are many types of repetitive operation, unskilled work, and specialist activities that are best performed by loners. Rounding up such people and making them members of a team risks producing a double disadvantage: their personal productivity falls and their privacy is invaded. Such social engineering may accord with the prevailing culture, but it's difficult to see any other benefit. Of course, it may be argued that isolated workers need a social dimension to their work. If this is true, it implies that individuals engaged on such jobs have been wrongly placed. Introverts need work suitable for introverts, while extroverts need work appropriate to extroverts.

DESIGNING WORK TO FIT THE PERSON

It is important to ensure that people have the right fit in the organisation, if not, difficulties may arise. The example below provides an illustration of this.

Introverts and extroverts look for different things in a job. Lighthouse-keeping and leading tour groups are contrasting jobs calling for different personalities. In the case of most jobs, of course, the relationship between work demands and personal characteristics is less pronounced. The reality is that most jobs entail some degree of individual work and responsibility along with a degree of liaison activity and some shared responsibilities. Such

a mixture of demands not only makes it difficult to find candidates with the ideal profile, but there are intrinsic problems in setting up jobs encompassing such different constituents. Most employers make few attempts to define the boundaries, and, even if they are laid down in advance, people who work in close association are inclined to move them at will. That's why colleagues are often cited as the biggest aggravation at work. When conflicts result, one party or another will be blamed as a poor teamworker.

The best starting point for establishing good teamwork is to begin with the principal demands of a broad work area. What are its structural characteristics? Do some responsibilities need to be shared? If so, which responsibilities, and with whom? Which responsibilities can be assigned to individuals and made subject to personal accountability? Which tasks are critical in their timing and mode of treatment and require a prescriptive approach based on best practice? These are all basic questions. They can either be asked and answered with the manager as the sole decision-maker, or such decision-making can be carried out in consultation with others. Either way, there's a risk that a busy manager will cut corners and make hasty decisions that are out of touch with operational realities. That's why it is often better to assign a group of workers to address these basic questions and seek to find answers. Those at the sharp end will be most familiar with the demands and pressures of the work. They are often better placed to decide how work should be shared out.

MINI-CASE

I was engaged on a project to facilitate the introduction of a cargo-handling computer system at a large airport. The perceived problem was that the labourers whose jobs were to be converted were both computer-illiterate and highly unionised. Devising a suitable form of training proved a challenge, but once this had been accomplished the introduction went without a hitch. The main problem arose in the way in which the design engineers had devised the work itself. The physical arrangement required these social labourers to sit in isolation at consoles. They soon tired of it and chose instead to bypass the information system by riding on the mechanical handling equipment in order to conduct personal inspections of the cargo bays. Such bravado may have been exhilarating, but it was also dangerous practice.

Clearly, it is not only vitally important to understand the nature of the work being undertaken, but also the skills, experience, and approach of those doing the work. Taking account of people's strengths and motivations can certainly help to build or break teams.

TEAMS NEED TO BE GIVEN SCOPE

The team approach for organising work depends on empowerment; it relies on trust, the confidence that a manager places on the qualities and calibre of the workforce. It also depends on how well members of a group have developed an understanding of each other's strengths and weaknesses. That's why training in teamwork is so important and why it helps to understand the language of team roles. People make different contributions to teams, and it's important that every team plays to the best strengths of its individual players. Diversity in the range of available team roles lays the foundation for a balanced team. But diversity does not automatically produce harmony or balance. It can just as well produce conflict as different individuals strive to do their own thing. This is where the manager becomes so important, in creating the vision and the ethos. The role of the manager is to turn a potentially balanced team into a mature team.

Mature teams have the capacity to make local decisions in distributing the overall workload and its various elements appropriately. This is impossible unless the manager has set the stage, believes in empowerment, and knows how to put it into effect. The key to success lies in managing the interface between team roles and work roles. The manager has to understand this before the team can be expected to respond with appropriate action. Managers sometimes fear that workers will lack the will to take tough decisions, for example, when one person is not up to a particular aspect of the job. The surprise is often that workers prove more intolerant of a slacker or a poor performer than the manager. The group builds up a body of opinion that's a powerful force in its own right. Such a force can operate against the interests of management, but it can equally well reinforce the policies and strategies that management favours. The more autocratic the management, the greater the likelihood that the group will combine to become a counterforce. The greater the level of empowerment, the more likely will be the team's sense of ownership and pride, and the greater its commitment to the responsibilities undertaken. Without empowerment, balanced groups cannot be developed into mature teams.

REWARDING TEAMS APPROPRIATELY

All teams need to be assessed. The question is, how should it be done so that it is positive and constructive? One way is to set objectives for teams and judge how well these have been met. Such a view prevails in the top-down school of management and is given added impetus by performance-related bonuses. The argument put forward is that teams need fixed incentives to perform well, an assumption linked with the converse view that without such an incentive the team will not perform satisfactorily. This mechanistic view of human motivation is mistaken and is likely to backfire. Success in meeting given criteria depends

partly on circumstances and contingencies. Success may not be commensurate with effort or skill. Objectives may be too easy to reach or too difficult. In the end, people may focus more on the shortcomings of the incentive than on the sense and purpose of their work. Retrospective awards for teams performing well are better received than prospective rewards for teams given set targets.

MAKING IT HAPPEN

- Start with the work, not the team. Ask first whether the work calls for a team at all.
- If a team is required, determine which responsibilities need to be shared and by whom.
- Decide which remaining responsibilities can be assigned to individuals, and make them subject to personal accountability.
- Use training in teamwork and team roles to ensure that every team plays to the best strengths of its individual players.
- Understand the team's strengths, weaknesses, and sense of 'self-awareness' to improve.
- Maximise empowerment to develop ownership, pride, and maximum commitment to the team's responsibilities.
- Delegate work efficiently, and enable people to succeed.
- Understand what motivates the team, providing them with impetus and momentum.
- Give retrospective rewards for teams performing well rather than incentive rewards linked to set targets.

CONCLUSION

In recent years we have developed an approach to work that hinges on understanding and mastering two languages: the language of contributors to team effort – team roles – and the language of the work demands themselves – work roles. Essentially this approach offers a framework for deciding who does what. Unless people decide for themselves, or at least share in that decision-making, there will be no commitment to the work itself.

THE BEST SOURCES OF HELP

Books:

Belbin, R. Meredith. *Management Teams: Why They Succeed or Fail.* 2nd ed. Oxford: Butterworth-Heinemann, 2004.

Belbin, R. Meredith. *The Coming Shape of Organisation.* Oxford: Butterworth-Heinemann, 1998.

Katzenbach, Jon R., and Douglas K. Smith. *The Wisdom of Teams: Creating the High-performance Organization.* Maidenhead: McGraw-Hill Education, 2005.

Film:

To facilitate an understanding of these issues, Belbin Associates have made two films in association with Video Arts: *Building the Perfect Team* (1991) and *Selecting the Perfect Team* (1993). A new DVD, *Fire, Toast and Teamwork*, is also available.

Viewpoint: Warren Bennis

LEADING MANAGERS TO ADAPT AND GROW

Warren Bennis is practically synonymous with leadership. A student and protégé of Douglas McGregor, he was invited by McGregor in 1959 to establish a department of organisation studies at MIT's Sloan School of Management. After serving in administrative positions in the 1960s and 1970s, he returned to research and teaching in 1979, joining the University of Southern California, where he continues to pursue his groundbreaking work on leadership, organisational life, and personal development. He is author of dozens of articles and over 30 books on leadership, including *Leaders, On Becoming a Leader, Geeks and Geezers, Managing the Dream*, and *Organizing Genius*. Here he reflects on the factors that have most profoundly influenced this thinking, as well as on the qualities that people and organisations must nurture in order to create meaningful work.

Like everyone else, I'd have to say that there's no one thing that has influenced my thinking. And that's probably true of life. In my own case, I think there were several factors that came out along the way and that, in looking back, seem like a set of eccentric precursors instead of a kind of single-willed, purposeful, I-know-what-I-want-to-do path. I'll start off from how I grew up. There were giants in the air. It was during the Second World War and these iconic figures dominated the world – some for great evil and some for great good. We happened to be on the side of great good, when you think about Churchill and Roosevelt. I'm reminded of how grateful we should be for their examples of leadership and how wary we should be of dictators and demagogues like the Hitlers and Mussolinis. In those days, very like as recently as 11 September 2001, we turned our eyes to public figures.

This was true when I was a young man. As I was born in 1925, it was very clear that the Depression and the Second World War were influential in my development. Those of us growing up in those formative years saw horrors with Mussolini, Hitler and, later on, with Stalin. Listening to Hitler giving his speeches during the 1930s before the Second World War was very, very scary.

So, I grew up at a time when you saw how influential leaders could be and how influential their activities, their political entities, their organisations could be – potentially virulent and toxic; how much pathogen could be spread by one person and how many healthy white cells by the other. That was just part of it, part of the zeitgeist, part of the era. It was very important, though largely unconscious to us.

There were other things – of a more 'micro', interpersonal nature. I happened to go to a college where the president was one of the men who laid the foundation for our field of organisational behaviour and leadership. That was Douglas McGregor, who was the president of the college that I went to and had come from MIT. Well,

it was no accident that I also became a college president and also did my PhD at MIT. He was very interested in group dynamics and leadership – wrote a lot about it – and certainly the 'McGregorian chants', as I called them, were very influential. Being at MIT, being in Cambridge, Massachusetts, during the 1950s and 1960s certainly influenced my thinking. I was fascinated by how, under certain conditions, groups can do the most creative, the most spectacular things and reach the most extraordinary heights of achievement – if they can create the right conditions for it. *Organizing Genius*, for example, was really the fruit, the result of those early years of thinking about groups. I became very interested to see how organisations, where we spend at least a third of our life, if not more, can be less toxic, more healthy, and provide more opportunities for people's growth, so that they can reach the frontiers of human possibility.

Three words leaders have trouble dealing with: 'I don't know'. I think good leadership will often start with questions whose answer is: 'I don't know, but we're going to find out'. Even before September 11, we were living in a world characterised by mystery, doubt, complexity, uncertainty, and chaos. Think about the transformation from an analogue to a digital society. In 1989, for example, there were only 400 users of the Web; now, as Shakespeare wrote in the 16th century, 'we are a girdled globe'. Before September 11 there were something like 40 ongoing border disputes around the world. Globalisation. Disruptive technologies. People are going to have to deal with doubt and uncertainty.

Organisations, organisational leadership, and organisational culture will have to be people factories – generating, nourishing, and nurturing terrific talent. They have to be education factories where that talent will be continually going to school. They will have to be led by leaders with enough emotional intelligence and cognitive capacity to be able to hold two divergent ideas in their heads at one time. I think those are going to be the critical aspects.

I'm going to add from my own work what I consider to be four critical aspects of leadership, which came out of a study about leadership and learning. I think they're important. And I want to argue that these four factors, which I think are critical for leading in this new world, are context- and culture-free. One is the adaptive capacity, which I think is probably the *sine qua non*, absolutely the most essential and central aspect of leadership in this environment of complexity and turbo-change. The adaptive capacity has a lot of things under it. It means a sense of resilience, hardiness, and creativity. It means seizing opportunities. It means learning learning.

The second critical ingredient is the capacity to engage followers in shared meaning – to align the stars around a common, meaningful goal. Not just any old goal. Think of Henry V at Agincourt: 'a mission from God'. Third, leaders are really going to have to spend a long time – and it's a continual process – finding out who they themselves are: learning their own voice, learning how they affect other people, learning a great deal about emotional intelligence. And finally, leaders will have to rely on a moral compass, a set of principles, a belief system, a set of convictions. Every good leader is going to have to – one way or another – learn these capacities. Now, I do think there are contextual and cultural factors, but I'm saying that, regardless of culture and context, these four factors are essential. They are necessary, but not sufficient. For example, if you're interested in leading a ballet company, you must know something about choreography and about the art world. There's a whole ecology around ballet, around science, around being a baseball manager. Nevertheless, these four factors are, across the board, essential, whether talking about George Washington or Margaret Thatcher.

Managers need to ask themselves: Do you really want to lead? Are you aware of the sacrifices, the time demands, the complexity? Do you have a true commitment to abandon your ego to the talents of others? Do you love what you're doing? Do you

enjoy trying to understand the social etiquette of bureaucracy? Do you really enjoy engaging others? Any great place to work can be profitable. In fact, the most profitable *are* great places to work. I remember a former president of MIT once said to me, without a trace of grandiosity, that MIT 'has had the habits of success'. There's something about being successful that tends to perpetuate itself. I think that what will make a workplace great is when people really feel down deep that the company is on their side, that they will be treated equitably and fairly, that they are being given many opportunities for self-development and organisational development, where people are encouraged to 'talk truth to power'. If they're going to be putting in a lot of work at a place, not only do people need to have a licence to tell the truth, they want to be in a place where they really feel they're going to be learning. People want to feel nurtured, that they're growing, and that there are enormous developmental opportunities available to them. To use my friend, Charles Handy's, book title, I think we're all 'hungry spirits'. Deep down, we all want to make a difference; if there's no meaning at work, people will leave their hearts at the door.

Leading in Interesting Times by Chris Turner

EXECUTIVE SUMMARY
- Companies continue to talk about teams, thinking out of the box, and empowerment, while modelling management and leadership styles which are controlling, structured, and hierarchical.
- Neither model is right or wrong, but we must think and act in ways that recognise the paradoxical nature of converging approaches.

INTRODUCTION

There is an old Chinese saying that is considered both a blessing and a curse:

'May you live in interesting times.'

And that is where we find ourselves – in a world that is messy, unpredictable, often incomprehensible, and incredibly interesting; a world where old ideas of leadership and management no longer serve us; a world that calls for a rethinking of all our assumptions about the nature of organisations and our roles within them.

Just as the era of the technology boom was challenged by the dotcom collapse in the early 2000s, so it is that the era of economic growth, globalisation and increases in productivity was challenged by the credit crunch and recession. The rise of the Internet is a good example of the significant changes that have reshaped businesses

over the last 20 years, and are now challenging the way organisations are managed and led.

The Internet originally sprang from people's need to communicate and share information. It is a network of relationships and conversations: dynamic, emergent, adaptive, complex, collaborative, and self-organising. Nobody is in charge. Most business enterprises, by contrast, have roots in the industrial age. The mindset leans towards the mechanistic: control, predictability, and internal competition are valued. Even in flattened organisations, reporting lines and hierarchy are carefully defined. These companies are laced with masculine norms and values.

Yet ask any CEO what's required to succeed in the future and he or she will inevitably say that the ability to innovate, to change direction on a dime, and to manage across cultures are imperative. They will talk of tapping the power of the Internet; but many fail to recognise the dissonance created when systems with very different operating assumptions converge: masculine versus feminine; controlled versus messy; engineered versus self-organising; convergent versus divergent. Michael Lewis's book, *Next*, illustrates how the very existence of the Internet challenges institutions as we have known them.

Neither the industrial age model nor the Web model is right or wrong. This is not an either/or proposition. To be successful in the future, we must think and act in ways that recognise the paradoxical nature of converging approaches.

MAKING IT HAPPEN

Because I work in many companies, I have the opportunity to observe individuals who navigate this paradoxical world quite well, who are leading effectively in these interesting times. Some lead from powerful positions; others lead informally and have huge influence on their organisations:

• Leaders don't take themselves too seriously

Sometimes I ask people 'Did you ever feel like a big sham?' Leaders inevitably have hilarious stories about such moments.

One friend tells about being invited to a very prestigious conference. When he mentioned the meeting to friends and family, their responses were maddeningly similar, 'How did *you* get invited?'

He recalled that during the big gathering he kept waiting for everyone to turn to him and say, 'You don't belong here. You're nothing but a big sham. Please leave.'

• Leaders sometimes manage grudgingly

These leaders are imaginative, visionary, and have active intellectual lives. They will often say that managing is both the most rewarding and the toughest part of the job, and they tend, over a career, to move between management and non-management positions.

One of the finest leaders I know recently sold his enterprise for big money but has agreed to stay around for four to five years to ensure success. I asked him what he wants to do next. He put his head in his hands and said, 'Anything where I don't have a bunch of people reporting to me.' It was one of those days.

• Leaders are good at conversations and relationships

These leaders have mastered the art of hanging out. They make opportunities for casual conversation. They do lunch. They nurture relationships. They aren't all extroverts, nor do they walk around slapping people on the back. On the contrary, many seem quiet when you first meet them. Their approach is often gentle, sometimes even deferential. But because they are great listeners, people gravitate to them.

An organisation is really nothing more than a network of conversations and relationships, so it is unsurprising that these 'hanger-outers' become the go-to people in enterprises. They know what's up, they know how to make things happen, they can get things done. They move comfortably through chaos.

• Leaders don't hang on to their own assumptions and beliefs

Despite the fact that these leaders are powerful, either formally or informally, they don't get overly attached to their own assumptions about 'the way things are'.

Recently in a meeting with a CEO and his senior staff, the CEO was under incredible pressure. When his colleagues suggested that a planning process would take several weeks, he snapped, 'We can finish that in 15 minutes.' A softly spoken staffer commented, 'Well, it's just not that easy.' The CEO retreated and within moments was laughing at the absurdity of his statement. He is a person of strong opinions with a powerful job; yet people are not afraid to challenge him because he is down-to-earth,

self-aware, and really smart. He listens – even when he doesn't like the message.

• Leaders are politely tenacious

These new leaders are quietly upbeat. That's not to say they don't get discouraged, even depressed at times. If they think an organisational approach is misguided, they either figure out how to work around the craziness or they focus on how to present their viewpoints more convincingly. They ask questions like, 'Help me to understand why you think this strategy will be successful.' They probe the assumptions that have led the organisation to a certain place and remain open to seeing things differently. At the same time, they are not afraid to challenge the status quo or to accept responsibility for their own mistakes.

• Leaders thrive on ambiguity

Although many of these leaders have grown up in organisations that are obsessed with control and prediction, they themselves tolerate ambiguity quite well. They analyse; they look at data; they study the situation; they pick people's brains; they solicit feedback. If they need approval, they are masterful at selling their ideas – even within risk-averse organisations. They understand that most decisions are about playing the odds – that nothing is a sure thing.

• Leaders are curious, always learning

The next time you take a trip, notice the person across the aisle madly tearing articles out of newspapers and quizzing the flight attendants on the airline survey. The odds are that this person is one of these new leaders I'm talking about. These people are hugely curious and ever in search of new information, new points of view. Walk into their offices and you'll see stacks of books and publications; prepare yourself to hear stories about their latest discoveries. They are ever learning.

Many of these leaders seem to have minds that are more divergent than convergent. Engineers are often convergent. They work to connect all the dots. Artists are more commonly divergent. If they even see the dots, they figure that trying to connect them perfectly is a waste of time. In one of Gore Vidal's essays, republished in his most recent book, *Empire*, he contrasts the convergent mind of Jimmy Carter with the divergent minds of Kennedy and Clinton. He suggests that Carter's obsession with connecting all the dots contributed to his ineffectiveness in a dynamic role. Whatever a leader's style, he or she is careful to listen and to surround himself or herself with colleagues with diverse points of view. He or she understands the value of balance.

• Leaders understand that fear is corrosive

Leaders are never punitive. The Chilean biologist, Humberto Maturana, says that 'love is the only emotion that expands human intelligence'. Leaders understand this at a gut level – although some might hesitate to use the word 'love'.

As managers, these folks are careful about the way compensation policies are designed. They understand that sharing wealth creates more wealth, not less. If someone is in the wrong job or underperforming, these leaders help the person to find another position or work out a way for them to depart gracefully with a generous package. They recognise that punitive behaviour creates fear that, in turn, stifles the creativity they so value.

• **Leaders talk like real people**

Companies are like families; they each have their own language, their own acronyms, their own shorthand. Sometimes people in organisations become so steeped in buzzwords and jargon that, to the uninitiated, they sound like soulless droids from outer space.

These new leaders have a knack for avoiding institutional language. They talk in plain speak. This is part of their appeal, part of the reason that people gravitate to them. They are accessible. They have no need to impress others with insider words. They understand this quote from *The Cluetrain Manifesto* (FT.com, 2000): 'In just a few years, the current homogenised "voice" of business – the sounds of mission statements and brochures – will seem as contrived and artificial as the language of the 18th-century French court.'

• **Leaders understand the power of context**

Workplaces are embedded with messages. I'm always amazed to hear people say they want their organisation to be more innovative while working in offices that are absolutely dismal. To inspire innovation, these companies typically schedule creativity workshops.

If we think of an organisation as a fish tank, many efforts to improve enterprises focus on the fish and ignore the water. The true power for change resides in the water, the environment in which the fish live. The water is the context.

I was recently with a group who were ruminating about leadership, wishing for discipline in their organisation. When their lunchtime meeting was over, they all departed leaving their lunch mess behind. With this particular group, their leadership efforts need to start with cleaning up after themselves. Their lack of discipline in caring for the physical environment sends signals that affect the organisation exponentially.

As Malcolm Gladwell points out in his great book *The Tipping Point*, 'We are all more than just sensitive to changes in context. We're exquisitely sensitive to them'. Alan Kay, one of the original innovators in Silicon Valley, says, 'Context is worth 50 IQ points.' Leaders pay attention to environmental details. They invest in making the workplace more inviting, whether by painting it in bright colours, putting good art on the walls, or taking interior desks so the windows can be shared by everyone. They are attentive to how meetings are conducted, the forms their communications take, the culture's graphic identity. They tell stories and encourage storytelling because stories contribute to context. They tinker with the environment constantly. Recently a CEO showing me around her facility paused to pick up a scrap of paper on the stairs. She didn't see the paper as paper; she understood it to be a message about the organisation.

CONCLUSION

I don't have a neat seven-step approach to cultivating the attributes and behaviour detailed here; but what I notice about these leaders is that they are acutely self-aware and very present. They think. They recognise their own strengths and weaknesses. They constantly look for ways to improve themselves because they subscribe to the discipline of personal mastery. Their leadership comes from who they are as much as what they know.

THE BEST SOURCES OF HELP
Books:

Ehrenreich, Barbara. *Nickel and Dimed*. London: Granta Books, 2002.
Gladwell, Malcolm. *The Tipping Point*. London: Little, Brown, 2000.
Lewis, Michael. *Next: The Future Just Happened*. New York: W.W. Norton, 2002.

Managing Internal Politics by Kathleen Kelley Reardon

EXECUTIVE SUMMARY
- Advancing business and career goals often necessitate acting politically.
- Those managers who reject – or fail to understand – internal politics do so at their own peril.
- The nature of the political arena affects the productivity, morale, and success or failure of individual employees.
- Career success depends on matching the individual's political style to the firm's environment.
- Smart managers familiarise themselves with the warning signs of political pathology before it's too late.

INTRODUCTION

Many of the hurdles managers must face and overcome have little to do with technical competence. Rather, they have to do with politics. Internal politics is a fact of life in organisations, yet many managers and CEOs will tell you their success is largely due to allowing 'no politics' in their firms. They'll regale you with stories of how they use and encourage 'people skills' to create a desired environment and accomplish organisational goals. What they're really talking about is how they use politics.

In common vernacular, 'politics' is used to describe what people do to influence decision-makers, accomplish hidden agendas, and surreptitiously advance their careers, often to the detriment of others. But politics is not always so sinister. By its very nature, politics involves going outside usual, formally sanctioned channels to accomplish objectives, but not necessarily in a secretive manner and often to the benefit of all involved. When used to influence people in the service of valid company goals, politics becomes a positive tool indeed. The team leader who makes valuable connections with people who can advance the team's efforts is acting politically.

While a high level of field-based competence is required, given two competent persons, the one who has political savvy, agility in the use of power, and the ability to influence others is more likely to succeed as a senior manager. Indeed, to the successful senior manager in a competitive organisation, day-to-day life *is* politics. That's why smart business people think like Caroline Nahas, managing director of Korn/Ferry International, southern California. To be politically astute, you need to 'read where the trend lines are' and 'be ahead of the game'.

Of course, politics is not always positive. Sometimes, people must defend themselves from political manoeuvring. When surrounded or targeted by colleagues playing underhand political games, job survival may require one to respond in politically astute, sometimes unpreferred ways. In organisations where biases or favouritism dictate who gets key assignments and promotions, political-style flexibility is required to get into the loop. The organisational political arena merely requires the use of relational strategies, sometimes uncomfortable ones, to advance oneself. In short, the astute manager must understand how politics functions in organisations and how to advance his or her and the firm's own goals.

SIZING UP THE POLITICAL ARENA

The first step in acquiring political acumen is learning to identify the kind of political arena in which you operate. Without this knowledge, managers operate in the dark, wondering why opportunities were lost. All four primary political arenas – minimally, moderately, highly, and pathologically political – often coexist inside a large organisation.

In a **minimally politicised** arena, the atmosphere is amicable. Conflicts rarely occur and don't usually last long. There's an absence of in- and out-groups, and one person's gain isn't seen as another's loss. Rules may be bent and favours granted, but people treat each other with regard and rarely resort to underhand political means. These are excellent environments for people uncomfortable with aggressive politics. Unfortunately, such organisations are more the exception than the rule.

Moderately politicised organisations operate on commonly understood and formally sanctioned rules. They often include smaller, fast-moving firms and large ones focused on organisational agility. Where customer focus,

results, teamwork, and interpersonal trust are priorities, politics are rarely destructive, and often focus on surfacing worthwhile ideas. Achieving objectives via unsanctioned methods isn't unusual, but tends to be subtle and deniable. When conflicts get out of hand, managers will invoke sanctioned rules or shared mores for resolution.

As a manager, however, when such an arena becomes dysfunctional, you will see considerable denial before unspoken political rules surface to where you can identify and address them constructively.

In a **highly politicised** culture, conflict is pervasive. Instead of applying formal rules consistently, political players only invoke them when convenient. In-groups and out-groups are clearly defined. Few people dare to communicate directly with senior managers. 'Who' is more important than 'what' you know, and work is often highly stressful, especially for those in out-groups. When there's conflict, people rely on aggressive political methods and involve others in the dispute. Highly political organisations usually have difficulty resolving conflicts constructively. They place blame and terminate losers. Such quick fixes rarely alter the dysfunctional pattern.

Pathologically politicised organisations are often on the verge of self-destruction. Productivity is suboptimal and information massaging is prevalent. People distrust each other, interactions are often fractious, and conflict is long-lasting and pervasive. People must circumvent formal procedures and structures to achieve objectives. They spend much time covering their backs. Management uses a carrot-and-stick approach to control people. Subordinates are seen as stubborn, wilful – even stupid. In the classic *Harvard Business Review* article, 'Asinine Attitudes Toward Motivation', Harry Levinson described this as the 'jackass fallacy'.

IDENTIFYING POLITICAL PATHOLOGY

To avoid political pathology, managers must recognise its encroachment. Here are five indicators that it's time to alter the political environment in order to save it from self-destruction.

1. **Frequent flattery** of persons in power, coupled with abuse of people in weaker positions.
2. **Information massages**. Anything that might rock the boat is actively discouraged and the common means of communication is hint and innuendo.
3. **Malicious gossip** and backstabbing are common, even where little overt conflict appears.
4. **Cold indifference**, where no one is valued and everyone is dispensable, indicates the area has been systemically polluted by people in charge. Survival is based on obsequiousness, and getting others before they get you.
5. **Fake left, go right**. People, even entire departments, purposely mislead others in order to look good when they fail. Teamwork is absent. Managers sacrifice subordinates' careers to avoid looking bad.

MATCHING POLITICAL STYLE TO POLITICAL CULTURE

The second crucial step in learning to manage politics is identifying individual political styles. The mix of styles and their 'fit' with the predominant political arena exert considerable influence on goal achievement.

The purist

The least political are 'purists', who believe in getting ahead through hard work. They shun politics, and rely on following sanctioned rules to get things done. Purists are usually honest and in highly political or pathological organisations are perceived as naively so. They believe in getting ahead by doing their job well. Purists tend to trust other people and prefer to work with those who do the same. Behind the scenes grappling for power and prestige is not of interest, hence purists are best suited to minimally political climates.

The team player

'Team players' believe you get ahead by working with others and using politics that advance the goals of the group. They rarely put career needs ahead of group needs. Team players prefer to operate by sanctioned rules, but will trade favours or engage in other relatively benign politics to achieve team goals. Focused on doing the job right and creating conditions for team member advancement, team players are best suited to moderately political environments.

The street fighter

An individualist, the 'street fighter' believes the best way to get ahead is via rough tactics. The street fighter relies more on subliminal politics than the purist and the team player, but is just as likely to invoke sanctioned rules when they serve personal goals. Street fighters watch their backs, push hard to achieve personal goals, and are slow to trust others. They thrive on the 'cut and thrust' of business, enjoy intrigue, and derive gratification from working the system. The street fighter is comfortable in highly political arenas and can survive in pathological ones as well.

The manoeuvrer

The 'manoeuvrer' is also an individualist, one who believes in getting ahead by playing political games in a skilful, unobtrusive manner. Subtler than the street fighter, but uninhibited about using politics to advance personal objectives and favoured team objectives, manoeuvrers prefer to do so in deniable ways. They look for ulterior motives in others, have little regard for sanctioned rules, and rely largely on subliminal politics. These smooth operators are less committed to hard work than purists, and only operate as team players when it suits their agendas. People get in the way of a manoeuvrer at their own peril unless they too are capable of manoeuvrering. The manoeuvrer is best suited to highly political and pathological arenas.

The task of all managers with regard to politics is to assess the arena prevalent in their division, and that of the larger organisation. Is it becoming highly political or pathological? If so, is this because opinion leaders are of the street fighter or manoeuvrer styles? There's nothing inherently wrong with street fighters and the occasional manoeuvrer may be an asset if he or she is not a threat to the group. A predominance of these styles, however, can tip a division or organisation closer to pathology, a condition that is difficult if not impossible to reverse. Savvy managers familiarise themselves with political warning signs and they take steps to stem the tide of political self-destruction.

MAKING IT HAPPEN

- Assess the degree to which your organisation is politicised. Is the atmosphere amicable or distrustful? Is the workforce productive, or does conflict prevent work getting done?
- Recognise the signs of impending political pathology: flattery of superiors, malicious gossip, information massaging, indifference, and purposeful misleading.
- Take steps to detoxify the workplace: communicate more openly and directly, invoke sanctioned rules or shared mores to resolve conflict, and emphasise solving problems over placing blame.

CONCLUSION

Politics are a reality in the workplace and, consequently, one must manage the conflicts that arise from political behaviour. Politics, in and of itself, is not bad if it works to serve company goals by making sure that the workplace is productive and that morale remains high. Politics must never be allowed to degenerate into a self-destructive process.

THE BEST SOURCES OF HELP
Books:

Jay, Antony. *Management and Machiavelli*. London: Penguin, 1973.

Reardon, Kathleen Kelley. *The Secret Handshake: Mastering the Politics of the Business Inner Circle*. New York: Random House, 2001.

Reardon, Kathleen Kelley. *It's All Politics: Winning in a World Where Hard Work and Talent Aren't Enough*. New York: Doubleday, 2005.

Response Ability – How Managers Stay Up When Times Are Down by Paul Stoltz

EXECUTIVE SUMMARY

- Adversity in business is increasing. Managers in dozens of industries worldwide are facing a more difficult, chaotic, uncertain, and demanding future.
- Today, managers must have *Response Ability* – the ability to respond optimally to whatever happens the moment it strikes.
- The most important variable in unleashing and building human capital is how people respond to growing levels of adversity.
- Adversity Quotient (AQ) is a measure of a person's hardwired pattern of response to adversity and a measure of Response Ability.
- AQ can be measured, permanently rewired, and strengthened, affecting individual and collective performance, agility, and resilience.

INTRODUCTION

Adversity, ranging from annoyance to tragedy, has become the rule in corporate life. Adversity is everything that gets in the way of, or blocks, an organisation's quest to fulfil its vision, achieve its goals, and accomplish its strategic plan. To keep these imperatives alive requires greater resilience than most managers possess. Given that managing adversity lies at the heart of management's ability to unleash human capital, how can managers learn to harness adversity to launch new levels of opportunity and momentum? As adversity rises, every manager's and organisation's resilience and effectiveness hinges on *Response Ability,* the ability to respond optimally to whatever happens the moment it strikes. Response-Able managers thrive amid the same difficulties that paralyse their less Response-Able counterparts.

MANAGING IN ADVERSITY
The silent toll

While today's workplace is arguably more dynamic and exciting, it is also exacting a growing toll. A Gallup Poll revealed that 19 per cent of workers are 'actively disengaged' – they are delivering a small fraction of their talents at work. Furthermore, 61 per cent (or more) are at least partially disengaged. The estimated cost to corporations in the United States alone is $350 billion; multiply that several times over for a worldwide estimate.

As adversity rises, workers feel increasingly stretched. Their work and their lives become more complex, chaotic, uncertain, and demanding. Their entire world demands that they do more, faster, and better. The physical toll that adversity takes upon the majority of the workforce includes a multitude of dismal symptoms, including diminished immune functions (with increased sick days), sapped energy, insomnia, and stress. Inside most people, today's levels of adversity create a chronic and toxic biochemical reaction that holistically degrades their performance deeply.

The psychological toll of the adversity trend manifests itself as depression, restlessness, anxiety, and pessimism – all psychosocial phenomena which are occurring at epidemic levels and growing. These conditions are also symbiotic, feeding off and flourishing in each other's presence. Overall the grand-scale toll of adversity in organisations, their capacity, and human capital is inestimable. Fortunately, it is also largely unnecessary.

The truth about motivation

Nearly every manager perceives motivating others as an important and essential duty. Yet, intuitively, we know that we cannot motivate others: authentic motivation originates and is sustained from deep within the self. Attempting to motivate others can be like painting your car red to make it go faster. It may *feel* faster, but very little has happened to strengthen performance.

To fully understand the myth and challenge of motivation, we must consider three forms of capacity. A person's *Required Capacity* is what the world demands of them, or what is required of them to perform their job effectively. As adversity mounts, most people's required capacity is growing at an accelerated rate, making it harder to remain fully engaged and motivated.

When we motivate others, we are striving to help them tap and deliver their *Existing Capacity* – their talents, aptitudes, competencies, experience, knowledge, wisdom, and energy – to the challenge at hand. People are hired for their Existing Capacity under two assumptions: that they will tap most, if not all, of it on a regular basis and that they will build on it to meet or exceed the Required Capacity.

The portion of their capacity that a person actually taps and delivers is called their *Accessed Capacity.* Anyone who has hired someone knows that many people fail to access their best abilities at work. This is a chronic source of frustration among managers and the major source of lost or under-utilised human capital. The quest of every manager must be to hire and grow Response-Able people who can consistently tap and build on their Existing Capacities. Clearly traditional methods of motivation, screening applicants, and training employees fall critically short of what is required.

ACHIEVING SUCCESS AND RESPONSE ABILITY

Fortunately, there is a way to assess and strengthen how people respond to adversity, or their Response Ability. Beyond your IQ, experience, or skill-set, it is your Adversity Quotient, or AQ, that most directly predicts and determines your ability to weather and harness the current storm for future gains.

AQ is scientifically valid, a reliable measure of your hardwired pattern of response to adversity. More than 100,000 employees in dozens of companies representing a broad range of industries have measured their AQs and learned about how their CORE affects their Response Ability, capacity, and resilience.

A Response-Able culture is one in which. . .

1. *People thrive on adversity.* The greater the challenges, the more energised and engaged people become. In fact, people get bored if things are too calm for too long.
2. *Challenges unleash greatness.* People are at their best in trying situations and times. They consistently dig deep and bring out their greatest talents and capacity when faced with the impossible.
3. *There's calm in the storm.* There is a norm of cool-headed decision-making. People are not easily fazed or thrown off by unexpected turns of events.
4. *There are stories of overcoming.* There is likely to be a history of resilience, with sagas of heroes who overcame adversity to create pivotal advancements.
5. *Managers hire and keep the best.* Self-motivated, fully engaged people are attracted to and are likely to stay with the organisation.

A LOW AQ CULTURE IS ONE IN WHICH. . .

1. *People crumble under pressure.* When adversity strikes, people are stunned, angry, resigned, and uninspired.
2. *Situations bring out the worst.* As adversity mounts, people act in selfish, distant, panicked, mean, and disengaged ways. Conflicts arise, panic spreads, helplessness grows, and problems fester.
3. *It seems like a blame game.* Adversity makes people point fingers and sidestep blame. The greater the adversity, the more accountability, trust, and agility suffer.
4. *The bleeding edge moves in.* Despite efforts to reward self-motivated top performers, there is a history of losing these people. Turnover remains a chronic, incalculable loss of human capital and potential.
5. *Excitement reduces to passionless pursuit.* People go through the motions, but the culture lacks passion, excitement, risk-taking, and a compelling sense of purpose. A mere 5–20 per cent of the workforce drives the success of the entire organisation.

ADVERSITY QUOTIENT: THE CORE OF RESPONSE ABILITY

AQ is comprised of four CORE dimensions, which together determine and drive Response Ability. Each dimension plays a unique role in a person's resilience, performance, innovation, and strength.

C = Control: *To what extent do I perceive I can influence the situation at hand?*

This dimension of AQ assesses perceived control, not actual control. It pinpoints your propensity for self-determination on the one hand and helplessness on the other.

O = Ownership: *To what extent can/should I play a role in improving this situation?*

This dimension assesses propensity for inner accountability. In contrast to blame, which is about pinpointing the source of the problem, ownership is about playing even the smallest role in improving the situation, regardless of its cause.

R = Reach: *How far does this adversity reach and affect other areas of work or life?*

This dimension pinpoints the perceived size or magnitude of the adversity, which has a dramatic impact on the likelihood of taking meaningful action.

E = Endurance: *How long can you continue to confront adversity in a positive way?*

This dimension provides a reading on how you will deal with the next challenge, obstacle, or difficult personality.

When we measure these four characteristics, individually and collectively, basic patterns emerge. A company can be seen as either having a Response-Able culture, or not.

MINI-CASES
Organisations building Response Ability

ADC Telecommunications successfully positioned itself to provide vital hardware and services to technology businesses such as Sprint and AT&T. Yet, when the entire sector lost 70 per cent of its market value in a matter of a few months, ADC's stock plummeted, despite record earnings. ADC decided that creating a Response-Able, resilient sales force would position them for a superior and quicker comeback against competitors. In classes in Singapore, Spain, China, Canada, and the United States, ADC's global sales force from 16 countries learned new ways to get, keep, and develop people who can thrive in a demanding, dynamic industry.

Marriott International recognised that the defining factor in sustaining their aggressive growth curve while maintaining their high standard of service during an economic downturn would be their associates' and leaders' Response Ability.

Many other organisations – including FedEx and Deloitte & Touche – have focused on how well their employees and managers handle adversity, resulting in improved performance, retention, agility, innovation, problem-solving, resilience, and accelerated change.

MAKING IT HAPPEN

Growing a Response-Able workforce that can not only cope with but thrive in adversity-rich times requires a commitment to forego the comforts of mediocrity and the courage to reinvent existing norms regarding Control, Ownership, Reach, and Endurance – the pattern of response to adversity. To start to build Response Ability, managers must:

- assess the Adversity Quotient of their current workforce
- hire high AQ people
- nurture high AQ, Response-Able leaders
- pay attention to how people respond to adversity the moment it strikes, assessing Control, Ownership, Reach, and Endurance
- focus on what facets of a situation can be influenced, no matter how impossible it may seem
- establish norms for people stepping up to improve and address difficulties the moment they arise
- contain each adversity in scope immediately
- be the first to recognise and seize the opportunity embedded in each adversity
- strategise around worst-case scenarios in a matter-of-fact way

CONCLUSION

Adversity is on the rise, and that's the *good* news! Great companies and managers are – and increasingly will be – those who can harness the force of adversity to create even greater opportunity. They assess and strengthen their Adversity Quotients to become more Response Able. And they use their growing Response Ability to optimise their human capital and to stay up when times are down.

THE BEST SOURCES OF HELP
Books:
Bibb, Sally, and Jeremy Kourdi. *A Question of Trust*. London: Cyan, 2006.
Maddi, Salvatore. *Resilience At Work: How to Succeed No Matter What Life Throws At You*. New York: AMACOM, 2005.
Seligman, M.P. *Learned Optimism: How to Change Your Mind & Your Life*. New York: Pocket Books, 1998.

How NLP Can Contribute to Best Management Practice by Joseph O'Connor

EXECUTIVE SUMMARY

Neuro-linguistic programming (NLP) is the systemic study of human communication. It studies the interrelationship between thinking, language, and achievement and models best practice to make it available to others.

This article will summarise the main contributions of NLP to best management practice.

- NLP helps managers to understand people and how to motivate them.
- It models best practice so that important skills can be passed on to others.
- It models the business system to see how it can be improved.
- NLP helps managers to generate business and personal goals, and to integrate individual and organisational goals and values.
- It gives skills to make meetings shorter and more productive.
- It gives managers the skills to coach their people.

INTRODUCTION

NLP was created in the mid-1970s in California by John Grinder, a professor of linguistics at the University of California and Richard Bandler, a student at that university. They wanted to know: how is it that some people are extremely good at a skill and others are not? The power of this question was in the 'how' rather than 'why'. They modelled some of the best communicators of the time, to describe how they were so good, so that the skills could be taught to others.

NLP is now used internationally and NLP practitioners have modelled excellence in many different fields – sports, education, leadership, sales, and, naturally, management. What makes a good manager? What is best management practice? NLP is in a unique position to answer these questions. It does not only study their behaviour; it explores the goals, values, and motivations. Nor is NLP satisfied with the rationalisations that people give. Typically the very best in every profession do not know how they do it so well. They show you, they do not tell you.

WHAT IS NLP?

NLP is the systemic study of human communication. There are four main aspects.

1. *An attitude of curiosity.* How do people do what they do? How is it that some days you are very good, and other days you are not? Human thinking is not random; there must be a structure. NLP discovers this. Then you can have many more of your best days.

2. *A methodology of modelling.* NLP explores the ideas and actions of the person to find out how he or she operates.

3. *A vision.* Everybody has access to the best possible methods. No one has to reinvent the wheel every time he or she assumes a management position. Everybody learns how to learn and be the best he or she can be.

4. *A set of tools.* NLP has a tool set and modelling excellence itself produces more tools.

NLP stands for neuro-linguistic programming.

• 'Neuro' is the mind.

• 'Linguistic' is language.

• 'Programming' is how we put together sequences of actions to achieve goals.

How does this help managers? Management is getting things done through others. Managers stand or fall by the business results they get, but those results are produced by the people they manage, not by themselves. Managers are paid to communicate. The best managers are the best at communicating. This is NLP territory.

MOTIVATION AND COMMUNICATION

'Management practice' is what NLP would call a double nominalisation. Both words are abstractions; they cannot be seen, heard, nor touched. Try this small NLP thought experiment. Think of 'management'. What does it mean to you? Let the pictures, sounds, and feelings that go with this word come into your mind. Now think about 'managing'. The odds are when you think of the verb, your mental pictures spring to life. Things start moving. Managing is about execution.

The best managers are often not noticed or appreciated. Why? Because there are no dramatics, no last-minute saves, no fire fighting, no disasters. They seem lucky. Most projects go smoothly. The managers who get noticed are the ones who skirt on the edge of disaster, who rescue the project at the eleventh hour. While this may be necessary, the best managers stay away from the edge and are on top of the job well before the eleventh hour.

Good managers motivate and communicate. To succeed, every manager has to balance two elements.

First is task. They need to get the job done, and give clear instructions. Misunderstanding can be very costly. NLP has *the Meta Model,* a series of precision questions to ensure a clear understanding. Most misunderstandings happen because we assume the other person means what we think he or she means, instead of asking questions to clarify.

Second is relationship. All communication is embedded in relationship and NLP has studied how relationships of *trust, rapport,* and respect are developed.

The best managers network well and are respected. They have good relationships. A good relationship makes the task more pleasant and easier. In Western European and US culture, the relationship is supposed to flow from the shared task. In Latin and many other cultures, the best work comes from good relationships that are established beforehand.

MODELLING BEST PRACTICE

NLP came about as a result of modelling. The practitioners of NLP search for people who are exceptional in their field and discover how they are able to get the results they do. NLP is pragmatic. An NLP model is eval-

uated by whether it works or not – you must get the same class of results as the person modelled. If you want your managers to be the best, don't use a theoretical model, use one that works, one that comes from real managers.

NLP modelling is used in two ways.

1. *Modelling the best people.* For example, model the best managers or salespeople, then using the model to train the average performers to be better. This model can also be used to recruit the people that will be best in the organisation.

2. *Systemic audit for the business.* This is an NLP model of the business system that can act as a sophisticated needs analysis. It identifies where the business is working well, and where it is not, by analysing the communication systems. It analyses what people do and think, not what they should be doing and thinking. It gives a real-time photograph of the business.

GOAL AND VALUES

Goals are one of the keystones of NLP. Everyone acts to achieve something. They may not be doing it very well and they may not get the results they intend. NLP has a set of principles and tools to ensure that business goals are clear, measured, challenging, and achievable. These goal-setting tools are essential in appraisals, teamwork, and strategic planning.

NLP also gives insight into individual and organisational values. Many businesses have excellent mission and vision statements, but somehow these are never able to connect with the minds and the hearts of the people who are responsible for realising them. Values are the keys to motivation and creative work. They are the reason companies change hands for millions of dollars when the products and bricks and mortar that comprise the business are worth only a fraction of the price.

Imagine a Monday morning when only 50 per cent of your work force came to work. Disaster. Then imagine on Tuesday, everyone came to work but with only 50 per cent of their energy and creativity. This is still a disaster, but it is invisible. It never gets noticed. NLP helps to explore and integrate the goals and values of the organisation so that everyone is aligned.

MEETINGS

Many business meetings are unnecessary, and many take longer than necessary. NLP has modelled negotiation skills, so people know how to get the most from their meetings. These skills can also be used to deal with difficult people and situations in the workplace, and in negotiations with competitors.

COACHING

Coaching is growing increasingly popular in business and rightly so. It is a cost-effective way of getting the best from people. External coaches work with executives and managers to help them to give their best. Managers need coaching skills to get the best from their people.

NLP has contributed a great deal to best practices of coaching, particularly in its study of effective language and the use of powerful questions. NLP helps people to explore how their habitual ideas are holding them back, so that they can become more productive, happier, and effective at work. It also helps them achieve a work–life balance. An unhappy manager will not be so effective, regardless of his or her skill level.

The new management paradigm
The old paradigm of management was to get your people to explain the problem to you. You asked questions to help you understand it, and then you told them what to do. The new paradigm, in which the manager is a coach, is to ask open questions to help the person understand the problem so *he* or *she* can find the solution. This not only solves the problem, but also solves the limited thinking that gave rise to the problem in the first place. It makes people more creative, productive, and self-sufficient.

CONCLUSION
Here are some of the patterns shared by successful managers:
- *They take multiple perspectives.* They look to the short (next month), medium, (next year) and long term (next five years) when making goals and assessing plans. They also look at problems from many different viewpoints as well as their own (for example, customer, shareholder, CEO, manufacturer etc.).
- *They motivate through values.* They do not rely simply on the carrot and the stick. The strongest motivation comes from the inside and people work best when they feel engaged.
- *They are purpose driven rather than problem driven.* They think in terms of achievements and goals rather than what is wrong. They do not blame.
- *They believe in themselves and their business.* They believe in their own skills and they believe in their organisation. They are congruent about what they do.
- *They learn on two levels.* They learn how to solve problems and how to stop the kind of thinking that gave rise to the problem in the first place.
- *They balance task and relationship.* They know that both are necessary for the best results.
- *They can tolerate uncertainty and ambiguity.* They know they do not have to know everything. And they do the best they can in the present moment, using all the resources they have.

THE BEST SOURCES OF HELP
Book:
O'Connor, Joseph, and Andrea Lages. *How Coaching Works.* London: A & C Black, 2007.

Website:
Lambent.com: **www.lambent.com**

CSR: More than PR, Pursuing Competitive Advantage in the Long Run by John Surdyk

EXECUTIVE SUMMARY
- Consumers increasingly expect companies to act in 'responsible' ways.
- Because of their scale and reach, companies have unusual opportunities to address social concerns in innovative and productive ways.
- Evidence suggests corporate social responsibility (CSR) practices produce long-term benefits with financial performance gains.
- Advancing CSR is made easier with modern risk management tools, reporting guidelines, and committed leadership and employees.

THE EMERGENCE OF CORPORATE SOCIAL RESPONSIBILITY
Global greenhouse gas emissions continue to rise. Diseases wreak havoc across entire continents. An entire host of seemingly intractable issues confront governments throughout the world, who are sometimes unable to effect positive changes. With the emergence of companies as some of the most powerful institutions for innovation and social change, more shareholders, regulators, customers and corporate partners are increasingly interested in understanding the impact of these organisations' regular activities upon the community and its natural resources. With the world's largest 800 non-financial companies accounting for as much economic output as the world's poorest 144 countries, the importance of these organisations in addressing trade imbalances, income inequality, resource degradation and other issues is clear. While companies are not tasked with the responsibilities of governments, their scale and their ability to influence these issues necessitate their involvement and create opportunities for forward-looking organisations to exercise great leadership.

In public opinion surveys, consumers admit that they

prefer to buy products and services from companies they feel are socially responsible (72 per cent) and that they sell shares of those companies they feel don't pass muster (27 per cent). Challenging Nobel Laureate Milton Friedman's notion that companies' only responsibility is to make profit, executives are increasingly seeking ways to combine economic gain with social well-being in ways that will produce more customer loyalty, better relationships with regulators, and a host of other advantages. CSR practices may, in fact, prove pivotal to the success of a company.

Sometimes described simply as 'doing well by doing good', corporate social responsibility initiatives gained traction in the 1990s as consumer interest in management practices erupted in the wake of several substantial incidences of executive malfeasance and of escalating environmental challenges. While originally focused on environmental factors, CSR reports increasingly include social measures. Likewise, company leaders today express interest in business models that weave together explicit goals for profit, environmental performance, and social factors, at the same time recognising that these efforts are unlikely to yield any short-term financial benefits but rather long-term performance improvements.

A CLOUDY CONCEPT BEGINS TO CRYSTALLISE

The phrase 'corporate social responsibility' describes both:
- a social movement
- a collection of specific management practices and initiatives

Business leaders, government professionals and others use these principles and tools to assess and report upon organisations' impact on society.

Globally, CSR is an evolving concept without a clear definition, yet it describes a set of corporate obligations and practices somewhere on the spectrum between traditional charitable giving on one hand and merely strict compliance with laws on the other.

While operating definitions remain elusive, the term 'CSR' generally refers to a company's efforts to explicitly include social and environmental concerns in its decision-making along with a commitment to increasing the organisation's positive impact on society. Beneath these efforts is a realisation that improved CSR reporting and better risk-management systems generally promote the transparency and accountability essential to good company governance and improved financial performance. These systems, in effect, enable a company to anticipate and respond to opportunities when it senses that society's expectations aren't being met by its performance.

BENEFITS FROM CSR

Benefits of corporate social performance reporting can spread over an entire organisation.

Areas of greatest gain for a company's market value, operational efficiency, access to capital, and brand value typically come from:

- establishing ethics, values and principles for the organisation
- improving environmental processes or reducing environmental impact
- improving workplace conditions

Other efforts, such as better governance measures, also tend to yield positive benefits for companies.

MAKING CSR REAL

Traditional rhetoric about 'private versus public' responsibilities is diminishing while companies operate more and more with an understanding of an acknowledged (if tacit) role to play in society. In the United States, many people feel companies should be doing more to improve society through changing their business practices.

While implementing CSR initiatives in modern companies is a daunting prospect because of their increasingly complex and global operations, many CSR management frameworks have moved on to the international stage. Approximately 400 companies – including many of the world's largest – use all or some of the Global Reporting Initiative (GRI), and combined environmental and social reports are increasingly common alongside companies' regular sustainability reports. Launched in 1997 by the Coalition of Environmentally Responsible Economies, the GRI report contains 50 core environmental, social, and economic indicators for a broad range of companies. It also offers additional modules with distinct metrics for companies, depending upon their industry sector and operations. The price range for producing a report spans from $100,000 for a basic GRI to more than $3 million for complex organisations like Shell.

Other major initiatives and reporting standards provide helpful guidance and principles, among them are:
- the United National Global Compact
- Global Environmental Management Initiative
- International Standards Organization guidelines (for example, ISO14000)

The continued growth of the socially responsible investment movement, especially in the United States and Europe, is stimulating companies' adoption of GRI and other instruments. In the United States alone, capital available to socially responsible companies reached $2.29 trillion in 2005.

MINI-CASE

Beginning with $1,000 in a garage in 1990, Greg Erickson founded a new energy bar company, Clif Bars Inc., in Berkeley, California. Committed to exercising environmental stewardship, Greg made expensive investments in organic ingredients and renewable energy while pursuing progressive employment practices such as six-month sabbaticals for employees. Refusing acquisition overtures from other companies, Clif Bars' commitments to corporate responsibility laid a strong, long-term foundation for the growing $100 + million company and its meteoric rise against titans like Kellogg and Quaker Oats.

BENEFITS OF CSR Business Area	Reduce Costs	Create Value
Licence to Operate	More favourable government relations; reduced shareholder activism; reduced risk of lawsuits	Increased community support for the company's operations ('a bank account of goodwill')
Reputational Capital	Reduced negative consumer activism/boycotts; positive media coverage/'free advertising'; positive 'word-of-mouth' advertising	Increased customer attraction; increased customer retention
Human Resources	Increased employee retention and morale	Enhanced recruitment; increased productivity
Finance	Social screens and investment funds are attracted to companies perceived as good social performers	

CHALLENGES TO CSR

The majority of corporations in the world do not produce any reports on their CSR practices. Executives often cite several concerns, including those below.

- Fear they may undertake a CSR scheme while competitors do not, meaning they incur expenses and refocus management talent that may place them at a competitive disadvantage.
- No feeling of urgency to act on many societal issues.
- No accepted standard of what type of information should be reported or at what depth.
- Concern that if they only achieve goals they largely establish for themselves, they may appear only half-heartedly committed – or they may even open themselves to lawsuits.
- Trouble identifying stakeholders, meaning the audience for their reports may be ambiguous which may, in turn, undermine the quality of the reporting generally.
- Belief that traditional philanthropy fulfils an organisation's commitment to society.
- Reporting upon the entire scope of a company's impact upon society and the environment is increasingly complex.

Recognising 'that one size does not fit all', more companies are exercising greater discretion in reporting initiatives to highlight key information for their sector or the parts of the world in which they operate.

HOW TO GET STARTED

These principles must be grounded in an organisation for CSR management frameworks to yield their maximum benefit.

- Ensure long-term organisational commitment by involving the top leadership *and* the employees.
- Don't adopt every reporting system: select one that makes the most sense for your industry and scale.
- Carefully identify stakeholders to help develop feedback loops so you can adjust your course.
- Consider benchmarking against peer companies.
- Communicate your results widely.
- Don't be afraid to revise standards or develop new metrics of your own.

MAKING IT HAPPEN

There is no consensus among government bodies, companies, or consumers about what precisely constitutes a definition – or even a consistent set of management topics – under the umbrella of corporate social responsibility.

Several inter-governmental bodies, company federations, and non-profits have advanced competing definitions. Among the most influential are:

World Bank. 'Corporate Social Responsibility, or CSR, is the commitment of business to contribute to sustainable economic development, working with employees, their families, the local community, and society at large to improve their quality of life, in ways that are both good for business and good for development.'

World Economic Forum. 'Corporate Citizenship can be defined as the contribution a company makes to society through its core business activities, its social investment and philanthropy programmes, and its engagement in public policy. The manner in which a company manages its economic, social, and environmental relationships, as well as those with different stakeholders, in particular shareholders, employees, customers, business partners, governments, and communities, determines its impact.'

Business for Social Responsibility. 'CSR is operating a business in a manner that meets or exceeds the ethical, legal, commercial, and public expectations that society has of business. CSR is seen by leadership companies as more than a collection of discrete practices and occasional gestures, or initiatives motivated by marketing, public relations, or other business benefits. Rather, it is viewed as a comprehensive set of policies, practices, and programmes that are integrated throughout business operations, and decision-making processes that are supported and rewarded by top management.'

Center for Corporate Citizenship at Boston College. 'Corporate Citizenship refers to the way a company integrates basic social values with everyday business practices, operations, and policies. A corporate citizenship company understands that its own success is intertwined with societal health and well-being. Therefore, it takes into account its impact on all stakeholders, including employees, customers, communities, suppliers, and the natural environment.'

International Business Leaders Forum. 'Corporate Social Responsibility means open and transparent business practices that are based on ethical values and respect for employees, communities, and the environment. It is designed to deliver sustainable value to society at large as well as to shareholders.'

United Nations. While not advocating a particular definition of corporate social responsibility, the United Nations uses the term 'global corporate citizenship' to describe international companies' obligations to respect human rights, improve labour conditions and protect the environment. The UN Research Institute for Sustainable Development, which follows academic work in this area, typically concentrates upon ethical issues and principles guiding how a company's management engages stakeholders.

CONCLUSION

Evidence is mounting that CSR provides tangible benefits and lasting competitive advantage to organisations. While difficult to implement, corporate social responsibility practices and frameworks provide companies with a chance to influence the rules of competition positively while playing a crucial – and increasingly expected – role in the world.

THE BEST SOURCES OF HELP
Book:
United Nations Conference on Trade and Development. *Disclosure of the Impact of Corporations on Society: Current Trends and Issues.* Geneva: New York, 2004

Websites:
Business for Social Responsibility: **www.bsr.org**
Business in the Community:
  www.bitc.org.uk/index.html
CSR Network: **www.csrnetwork.com/default.asp**
Ethical Corp: **www.ethicalcorp.com**
Social Investment Forum: **www.socialinvest.com**
SustainAbility: **www.sustainability.com**
World Business Council for Sustainable Development:
  www.wbcsd.org

Business Ethics by Sue Newell

EXECUTIVE SUMMARY
- Business ethics focuses on identifying the moral principles by which we can evaluate business organisations.
- Companies often behave unethically, having a harmful effect on people or the environment.
- Unethical behaviour is typically not caused by a single 'bad apple', but is rather the outcome of complex interactions between individuals, groups, and organisations.
- Ethical behaviour can be defined either as behaviour that maximises happiness and minimises harm or as behaviour that is motivated by principles of duty.
- While behaving unethically may have some short-term benefit for a company, in the long term it will harm stakeholder support.
- Long-term sustainability comes from concentrating on the *triple bottom line*: being concerned with the social and environmental as well as the economic impact of a business.

INTRODUCTION

Look in the newspaper on virtually any day of the week and you will find at least one business scandal in which a company appears to have challenged the regulators or violated the standards of behaviour generally accepted by society. For example, financiers such as Bernard Madoff have continued the criminality shown some time ago by firms such as Enron, Worldcom, and others. It seems that in good times and bad, company finances have been manipulated in order to show a better balance sheet than actually exists, toxic waste has been allowed to flow into a river, bribes have been paid in order to secure a business deal, employees have misused the

company intranet to send pornographic pictures, child labour has been used to assemble a product, discriminatory practices have prevented the employment or promotion of members of a particular group, goods or services have been sold that do not match the specifications, and so on. In other words, businesses regularly behave unethically, that is, they behave in ways that have a harmful effect upon others and that are morally unacceptable to the larger community. Moreover, the impact of companies is increasing as they become larger (indeed, global) and as profit-making concerns take over functions that were once publicly controlled such as the railways, water provision, and health care. Increasingly it is business (for-profit companies) that determines the quality of the air we breathe, the water we drink, our standard of living, and even where we live and how easily we can move around.

COMMON ETHICAL PROBLEMS WITHIN COMPANIES

Given the increasing social impact of business, business ethics has emerged as a discrete subject over the last 20 years. Business ethics is concerned with exploring the moral principles by which we can evaluate business organisations in relation to their impact on people and the environment. Trevino and Nelson categorise four types of ethical problems common in business organisations (*Managing Business Ethics*, 4th ed. Wiley, 2006).

First are human resourcing ethical problems, which relate to the equitable and just treatment of current and potential employees. Unethical behaviour here involves treating people unfairly because of their gender, sexuality, skin colour, religion, ethnic background, and so on.

Second are ethical problems arising because of conflicts of interest. Here, particular individuals or organisations are given special treatment because of some personal relationship with the person or group making a decision. A company might get a lucrative contract, for example, because a bribe was paid to the management team of the contracting organisation, not because of the quality of its proposal, or a person is hired because he is the son of the finance director, not because he is the best candidate.

Third are ethical problems that involve customer confidence, with companies behaving in ways that show a lack of respect for customers or a lack of concern with public safety. Examples here include advertisements that lie (or at least conceal the truth) about particular goods or services, and the sale of products, such as drugs, that a company knows to be unsafe (or at least not completely safe).

The financial scandals that have rocked the corporate world (Madoff, Enron, and WorldCom for example) involve a number of these different ethical issues. In these cases senior managers have engaged in improper book-keeping, making companies look more financially profitable than they actually are. This increases the shareholder value of the company so that anyone with shares profits directly. Those profiting will include those making the decisions to manipulate the accounts and so there is a conflict of interest. However, the fall-out from the downfall of these companies affects shareholders, employees and society at large negatively, with innocent people losing their pension funds and/or savings, and employees losing their jobs.

Finally, there are ethical problems surrounding the use of corporate resources by employees who make private phone calls at work, submit false expense claims, take company stationery home, etc.

ACCOUNTING FOR ETHICAL AND UNETHICAL BEHAVIOUR

While it may be very easy to identify and blame an individual or small group of individuals and to see these individuals as the perpetrators of an unethical act – the 'bad apple' – and hold them responsible for the harm caused, this response is an over-simplification. Most accounts of unethical behaviour that are restricted to the level of the individual are inadequate. Despite popular belief, decisions harmful to others or the environment that are made within organisations are not typically the result of an immoral individual seeking to gain personal benefit. While individual influences such as the employee's level of moral maturity or the locus of control may be factors, we also need to explore the decision-making context in order to understand why an unethical decision was made. Group dynamics, for example, very often influence the decision-making process.

A particularly important group-level influence is *groupthink*, a phenomenon identified by Irving Janis in his research on US foreign policy groups (*Groupthink: Psychological Studies of Policy Decisions and Fiascoes*,

Houghton Mifflin College, 1982). The research demonstrates the presence of strong pressures towards conformity in these groups; individual members suspend their own critical judgment and right to question, with the result that they make bad and/or immoral decisions. Janis defines groupthink as 'the psychological drive for consensus at any cost that suppresses dissent and appraisal of alternatives in cohesive decision-making groups' (Janis, 1982).

Aside from these immediate group pressures, the degree to which decisions are ethical is also influenced by organisational factors, in particular organisational culture. Smith and Johnson differentiate three general approaches that organisations take to corporate responsibility (*Business Ethics and Business Behaviour*, International Thomson Business Press, 1996):

1. **social obligation**: the company does only what is legally required
2. **social responsiveness**: the company responds to pressure from different stakeholder groups
3. **social responsibility**: the company has an agenda of pro-actively trying to improve society

In a company in which the dominant approach to business ethics is social obligation, it is likely to be difficult to justify a decision based on ethical criteria; morally irresponsible behaviour may be condoned as long as it does not break the law. Legal loopholes, for example, may be exploited in such a company if these can benefit the company in the short term, even if they might negatively influence others in society.

ETHICAL DILEMMAS

In some instances it is clear that a business has behaved unethically, for example where a drug is sold illegally, the company accounts have been falsely presented, or where client funds have been embezzled. Of more interest, however, and much more common, are situations that pose an ethical dilemma: situations presenting a conflict between right and wrong or between values and obligations, so that a choice is necessary. For example, a company may want to build a new factory on a previously undeveloped and popular tourist site in a location where there is large-scale unemployment among the local population. Here we have a conflict between the benefits of wealth and job creation in a location in which these are crucial and the cost of spoiling some naturally beautiful countryside. Philosophers through the ages have been concerned with evaluating such dilemmas and prescribing how we can ethically resolve them. They have attempted to develop prescriptive theories providing universal laws that enable us to differentiate between right and wrong, and good and bad in these situations.

PRESCRIPTIVE ETHICAL THEORIES

Essentially there are two schools of thought. The consequentialists argue that behaviour is ethical if it maximises the common good (happiness) and minimises harm. Opposing non-consequentialists argue that behaviour is ethical if it is motivated by a sense of duty or a set of moral principles about human conduct – regardless of the consequences of the action.

Consequentialist accounts of ethical behaviour

Philosophers who adopt the consequentialist approach (sometimes also referred to as utilitarianism) consider that behaviour can be judged ethical if it has been enacted in order to maximise human happiness and minimise harm. Jeremy Bentham (1748–1832) and John Stuart Mill (1806–73) are two of the best-known early proponents of this view. Importantly it is the common good, not personal happiness, that is the arbiter of right and wrong. Indeed, we are required to sacrifice our personal happiness if doing so enhances the total sum of happiness. For a person forced with a decision choice, the ethical action is thus to weigh up the impact on others of all the possible options and choose the one that maximises happiness and minimises harm. Common criticisms of this approach are that it is impossible to measure happiness adequately and so assess the relative impact of different action choices, and that it essentially condones injustice – harm to a minority – if this is to the benefit of the majority.

Non-consequentialist accounts of ethical behaviour

Philosophers who adopt a non-consequentialist approach (also referred to as deontological theory) argue that behaviour can be judged as ethical if it is based on a sense of duty and carried out in accordance with defined principles. Immanuel Kant (1724–1804), for example, articulated the principle of *respect for persons*, which states that people should never be treated as a means to an end, but always as an end in themselves. The idea here is that we can establish moral judgments that are true because they can be based on the unique human ability to reason. One common criticism of this approach is that it is impossible to agree on the basic ethical principles of duty or their relative weighting in order to direct choices when multiple ethical principles are called into question at the same time.

MAKING IT HAPPEN

While these two approaches to evaluating behaviour are clearly different, they can be integrated to create a checklist that will help an individual or group to make sound ethical decisions. Thus, in any choice situation you or your team should take the following steps.

- Gather the facts: what is the problem, and what are the potential solutions?
- Define the ethical issues. (This is a step that is often neglected, so that the ethical dilemmas raised by a particular decision are never even considered.)
- Identify the various stakeholders involved.
- Think through the consequences of each solution: what happiness or harm will be caused?
- Identify the obligations and rights of those potentially affected: what is your duty here?
- Check your gut feeling.

The last step is crucial. Those involved need to ask themselves what they would feel like if friends or family found out they had been involved in making a particular corporate decision, whether personally or collectively.

WHY BEHAVING ETHICALLY IS IMPORTANT FOR BUSINESS

Choosing to be ethical can involve short-term disadvantages for a company. Yet in the long term it is clear that behaving ethically is the key to sustainable development. When you're faced with an ethical dilemma in which the immoral choice looks appealing, ask yourself three questions:

1. **What will happen when (not if) the action is discovered?** Increasingly the behaviour of companies is coming under scrutiny from their various stakeholders – customers, suppliers, shareholders, employees, competitors, regulators, environmental pressure groups, and the general public. People are less willing to keep quiet when they feel an injustice has been done, and the Internet and other media give them the means to make their concerns very public, reaching a global audience. Companies that behave unethically are unlikely to get away with it, and the impact when they are discovered can be catastrophic. This leads to the second question.

2. **Is the decision really in the long-term interests of the company?** Many financial services firms in the United Kingdom generated short-term profits in the 1990s by mis-selling personal pensions to people who would have been better off staying in their company's pension scheme. However, in the long term these firms have suffered by having to repay this money and pay penalties. Most significantly, the practice has eroded public confidence.

3. **Will organisations that behave unethically attract the necessary employees?** Companies that harm society or the environment are actually harming their own employees, including those who are making the decisions. Companies that pour toxins into the air are polluting the air their employees' families breathe, companies that discriminate unfairly on the basis of sexual orientation are potentially discriminating against members of employees' own families and so on. Ultimately a company relies on its human resources. If a company cannot attract high-quality people because it has a poor public image based on previous unethical behaviour, then it will certainly flounder.

Behaving ethically is clearly key to the long-term sustainability of any business. Focusing on the triple bottom line – the social and environmental as well as the economic impact of a company – provides the basis for sound stakeholder relationships that can sustain a business into the future.

THE BEST SOURCES OF HELP
Books:
Elkington, John. *Cannibals with Forks: The Triple Bottom Line of 21st Century Business*. Oxford: Capstone, 1998.

Ferrell, O.C. and John Fraedrich. *Business Ethics: Ethical Decision Making and Cases*. South-Western College Publishing, 2007.
Trevino, Linda K. and Katherine A. Nelson. *Managing Business Ethics: Straight Talk About How to Do It Right*. 4th ed. Chichester: Wiley, 2006.

Boardroom Roles by Adrian Cadbury

EXECUTIVE SUMMARY
- The role of the board is to direct, not to manage.
- Balance of board smembership and choice of individuals are key.
- The chairman is responsible for the effectiveness of the board.
- Non-executive directors have a particular contribution to make to the work of a board.
- Board committees are important structurally and for the tasks they undertake.
- Executive directors should be appointed solely for the value they can add to the board.
- Board members have different roles; what matters is how they combine to form the board team.

ROLE OF THE BOARD
The crispest definition of a board's role is that of the late Sir John Harvey Jones: 'to create tomorrow's company out of today's'. A fuller description can be found in Boards at Work: 'Boards, by general agreement, have three key roles: strategy – responsibility for monitoring and influencing strategy; control – maintaining control over the management of the company; and service – providing advice and counsel to executives, and providing an institutional face for the organisation.' To this I would add that boards set the tone for their organisations and are guardians of their values.

Boards are in place to direct and not to manage. Boards have the task of defining the purpose of their enterprises and of agreeing the strategy for achieving that purpose. They are responsible for appointing executives to turn strategic plans into action, for supporting and counselling them in so doing and if necessary for replacing them. Above all, boards are there to provide leadership and it is in that context that the roles of board members need to be considered.

BOARD COMPOSITION
A single board at the head of a company is the commonest structure. Unitary boards of this nature are made up of executive and non-executive, or outside, directors. Two-tier boards separate these two kinds of director and their structure is covered briefly in the Mini-case. Given that both executive and outside directors sit on unitary boards, the first issue is the balance between them. The ratio on UK boards before the present interest in corporate governance was around two-thirds executive directors and one-third outside directors. This balance has now moved through parity to a position where outside directors are in the majority. This is in response to the provision of the UK Combined Code On Corporate Governance that, except for smaller companies, 'At least half the board, excluding the chairman, should comprise non-executive directors determined by the board to be independent'. In the United States, the chief executive and the chief financial officer are often the only executives on the board, and the chief executive is usually its chairman as well.

In addition to the question of balance, there is the question of size. There is a clear move to smaller boards in both the United Kingdom and the United States. Martin Lipton and Jay W. Lorsch in their 'Modest proposal for improving corporate governance' (*The Business Lawyer*, volume 48, pages 59–77) recommend a maximum board size of 10 and favour eight or nine. The argument for smaller boards is that they enable all the directors to get to know each other and to contribute effectively in board discussions, thus arriving at a true consensus. The crucial point is that boards are teams and provide collective leadership. So the balance of membership and choice of individuals are key to forming the team.

MINI-CASE
Two-tier boards
Two-tier boards consist of a supervisory board whose members are all non-executive and a management board made up of executive directors. The management board is responsible for strategy and for running the business. The supervisory board appoints and can dismiss the members of the management board and no one can be on both boards. The legal responsibilities of the two boards and of their directors are different, whereas with a unitary board all directors have the same legal duties

however the board is structured. Since supervisory boards can have employees as members, this raises the question of their role on boards. In Germany, for example, where companies have more than 500 employees, employees are by law represented on the board. There is a variety of means of involving employees at board level in some other European countries. The anomaly of such arrangements for international companies is that it is only practicable for their home country employees to be represented. I believe that employee participation is genuinely of value, but question whether it is not more effective at levels below the board, where the decisions are taken that affect employees most directly and to which they can contribute most knowledgeably.

THE CHAIRMAN'S ROLE

The chairman is responsible for the effectiveness of the board. This responsibility rests with the chairman, whatever his or her other duties may be. It leads on to the point that all companies are different and the issues they face are constantly changing. Individual boards have to follow accepted board principles, but in ways which meet their particular circumstances. It is the chairman who has the responsibility of ensuring that the make-up of the board is appropriate for the challenges ahead. Similarly, it is the chairman who has the task of welding the directors into an effective team. Effective boards are not brought into being simply by seating competent individuals around a board table. Creating effective boards requires effort by board members, but above all coaching and leadership by their chairmen. It is difficult for busy chief executives who are also chairmen to devote sufficient time to these aspects of their role.

The chairman is responsible for the running of the board. Responsibilities include the agenda, the provision of adequate and timely information to all directors and the actual conduct of board meetings. The chairman is also, provided he or she is not chief executive, responsible for putting in place a means by which boards can evaluate their own collective performance and that of individual directors. Where the chairman is also chief executive, his or her duties in relation to their board remain the same, but a deputy or a senior outside director would be responsible for the appraisal of the chief executive and for the review of the board's performance.

ROLE OF OUTSIDE DIRECTORS

All directors are equal in that they all carry the same legal responsibilities. Outside or non-executive directors are in that sense no different from their executive colleagues. They do however have particular contributions to make to their boards by virtue of standing further back from the business. One of these is reviewing the performance of the chief executive and the executive team; clearly the outside directors are the only board members in a position to do this objectively.

Another contribution is in relation to potential conflicts of interest, such as those between the interests of the executives and those of the shareholders. Examples are directors' pay, dividends versus re-investment, and whether top appointments should be made from within or outside the company. Decisions on these matters are ultimately decisions of the whole board, but the outside directors are well placed to give a lead on where the best interests of the company – to which all directors owe their duty – lie.

Outside directors bring with them their experience in fields which are different from those of the executive directors, and this external experience is of particular value in strategy formulation. The potential advantage which the unitary board has over the two-tier board is that it provides the opportunity to combine, in the same body, the depth of knowledge of the business of the executives with the breadth of experience of the outside directors. Once again, it is up to chairmen to make the most of these different viewpoints by the way they structure board debates.

The role of outside directors in helping to resolve conflicts of interest does not imply that their standards are in some way higher than those of their executive colleagues. The difference is simply that they can judge such matters more objectively because their interests are involved less directly. There are however differences between outside directors themselves. The UK Combined Code provides that: 'The board should identify in the annual report each non-executive director it considers to be independent. The board should determine whether the director is independent in character and judgment and whether there are relationships or circumstances which are likely to affect, or could appear to affect, the director's judgment.' Non-executive directors who do not meet these tests may well be valued board members in their own right but they cannot be classed as independent, when it comes to meeting Code provisions over the proportion of independent directors on boards and their committees.

The Combined Code further provides that the board should appoint a senior independent director. to whom shareholders can convey concerns which they cannot resolve through the normal channels. This new role is particularly important, when the posts of chairman and chief executive are combined, as it makes clear to whom directors or investors should go if there are perceived to be problems at the head of a company.

ROLE OF BOARD COMMITTEES

As the responsibilities of directors have become more demanding, boards have increasingly formed committees to deal with some of their more detailed work. The Combined Code requires all quoted companies to establish audit and remuneration committees and, unless they have a small board, nomination committees. These committees strengthen the position of the outside directors, of whom they are made up, and are important for the work they do. The essential point is that they are committees *of* the board. It is the board which appoints them, sets their terms of reference and turns their recommendations into decisions.

ROLE OF EXECUTIVE DIRECTORS

The duties of executive directors are the same as those of the outside directors. They are as responsible for the monitoring task of the board as the outside directors, who in turn are as responsible for the strategy and leadership of the company as the executives. This means that executive directors have to take their executive hats off on entering the boardroom and put on their directorial ones. They should only be appointed for the contribution they can make to the board and they are there to further the company's interests – not those of their function or department. It is not an easy transition to make and executive directors can be helped in the adoption of their new non-managerial role through appropriate training or through a non-executive directorship elsewhere.

ROLE OF THE COMPANY SECRETARY

Chairmen and board members should be able to look to the company secretary for impartial and professional guidance on their responsibilities and all directors should have access to the advice and services of a company secretary, who is responsible for ensuring that board procedures are kept up to date and followed.

MAKING IT HAPPEN

- Ensure the board concentrates on those issues for which it alone is responsible, such as corporate purpose and values, strategy, executive selection, and succession.
- Elect a chairman who is not chief executive, and who will put in place effective measures of board performance.
- Keep the board preferably to a maximum of 10 members, with a majority of external, non-executive directors.
- Ensure that non-executive directors are independent of management and free from connections that may affect their judgment.
- Use the whole board to select new appointees, who should add value by filling gaps in the experience and backgrounds of existing directors.
- Offer executive directors training on joining the board and encourage them to accept a non-executive post in another company.

CONCLUSION

Although board members have different roles, what counts is the way those roles are combined in the board team. This is why board selection is so fundamental. Directors should only be appointed for the value they can add to their boards. All directors should have terms of office to enable renewal to take place, although I am personally against rigid rules tying retirement to age or length of board service, preferring to leave this to board judgment.

The search for outside directors should be purposeful, with the aim of filling gaps in the experience and backgrounds of the existing directors, and their selection should involve the board as a whole. Chairmen, however, have a particular responsibility for the choice of board members since it is they who have to turn them into an effective team.

THE BEST SOURCES OF HELP

Books:

Carver, John. *On Board Leadership*. Chichester: Jossey-Bass, 2002.

Charan, Ram. *Boards That Deliver: Advancing Corporate Governance From Compliance to Competitive Advantage*. San Francisco: Jossey-Bass, 2005.

Harvey-Jones, John. *Making It Happen: Reflections on Leadership*. London: Profile, 2005.

Mina, Eli. *101 Boardroom Problems and How to Solve Them*. New York: AMACOM, 2008.

Stiles, Philip, and Bernard Taylor. *Boards At Work: How Directors View Their Roles and Responsibilities*. Oxford: Oxford University Press. 2001.

Websites:

www.boardmember.com: this is the site of *Corporate Board Member* magazine – a useful resource for board members of US public companies.

www.iod.com: the UK Institute of Directors offer practical advice on how to run boards.

www.ecgi.org: the European Corporate Governance Institute website gives details of codes country by country including the UK Combined Code.

Environmental Management by John Elkington

EXECUTIVE SUMMARY

Some management trends start at the top and cascade down; others evolve from the bottom up. Sustainable development (SD) has come from both directions. In the process it has caught a growing number of well-known companies off balance – among them Shell, Monsanto, and Nike. More positive has been the foundation of the World Business Council for Sustainable Development (WBCSD); and the World Economic Forum in Davos routinely covers sustainable-development issues. But, in many respects, this business story has only just begun. Consider some of the conclusions from the 2002 Earth summit in Johannesburg; the issues raised then remain squarely on the mind of anyone concerned with the weight of SD issues:

- Demographic pressures will create enormous new risks and opportunities. During the 20th century the planet's human population rose from 1.6 billion to 6 billion. There is likely to be a further 50 per cent increase by 2030.
- A growing range of environmental problems – including ozone depletion, climate change, the collapse of fisheries, and loss of forests – signal that today's economic and business models are unsustainable.
- The end of communism in many countries means that the one-third of humanity who used to live in the old communist world is now playing a growing role in the global economy. In total there are some 4 billion people living in the poorer parts of the world; it will be necessary to meet their needs.
- Business is increasingly in the spotlight – and is expected to play a key role in defining and delivering sustainable development. Paradoxically, the governance vacuum created by accelerating globalisation will increase the pressures on brand-name companies and on financial markets to act responsibly and effectively.
- At the same time, however, growing resistance to current forms of economic globalisation represents a profound challenge to free market capitalism.
- As a result, growing numbers of companies are adopting *triple-bottom-line* strategies, focusing simultaneously on economic prosperity, social equity, and environmental protection.

THE SUSTAINABILITY AGENDA

Boardrooms have been buzzing with questions since the SD agenda first began to appear on corporate radar screens. Some business leaders see SD as simply the environmental agenda in new colours, but others speak of a profound shift, with new forms of corporate responsibility and accountability emerging. Here are some key questions and answers.

What is sustainability?

The answer, first laid out in the 1987 report of the World Commission on Environment and Development, is that sustainability is the principle of ensuring that our actions today do not limit the range of economic, social, and environmental options open to future generations.

Why is it important?

Simply stated, SD is the emerging 21st-century business paradigm. It is increasingly proposed by governments and business leaders as a solution for problems now racing up the international agenda. These range from climate change to human-rights issues.

Surely this is a job for politicians and legislators?

In part, of course, it is, but industry's lobbying over the years for less regulation and in some cases active deregulation may now be coming back to haunt it.

What has SD got to do with capitalism?

Simply put, traditional capitalism dealt with financial and physical forms of capital. Increasingly, however, companies are expected to manage, account for, and grow multiple forms of capital, for example, financial, physical, human, intellectual, natural, and social capital.

How can we sell this to the financial markets?

It's tough, but in the coming decades the world's financial markets will adopt triple-bottom-line models to assess value creation. Insurers and reinsurers have been badly affected by issues like asbestos, contaminated land, and toxic and nuclear wastes. Leading banks are increasingly sensitive both to new forms of risk and to emerging opportunities created by new environmental and social standards. And while some financial analysts have been slow on the uptake, the entry of players like the Dow Jones Sustainability Group is providing a wake-up call.

WHAT THE GURUS SAY

The ways in which the environmental and wider sustainability agendas have been engaged by business have reflected the priorities of those held responsible at the time in the corporate world. To help to simplify the evolutionary history, let's focus on three main phases.

Phase 1 – Denial

From the early 1970s, environmental and social issues were handled on the corporate periphery by lawyers or PR people. Most companies were in denial: pollution problems either were not their fault or, if they were, were seen as the price of wealth creation. Key issues include compliance, a company's licence to operate, and risk to reputation.

Phase 2 – Cleaning up

From the late 1970s, the spotlight shifted to plant siting, production processes, and products. As a result, companies tended look to field planners, engineers, and new product development (NPD) specialists, who used a growing range of tools such as impact assessments, audits, life-cycle assessments, and so-called clean technology. Eco-efficiency concepts introduced by the WBCSD were adopted by a growing number of companies. Phase 2 activity continues to build, with the European Commission introducing new strategic impact assessment requirements for major industrial projects.

Phase 3 – Governance

During the 1990s, concepts like that of the triple bottom line began to draw in more senior business people. CEOs and their boards began to pay attention, often because of the difficult trade-offs involved. A water pollution control investment, for example, might result in higher carbon dioxide emissions, raising climate change issues. Accountants have also been increasingly involved. In the process, the SD agenda has begun to cross-connect with corporate and global governance agendas.

Most mainstream management writers have overlooked these trends. In their classic text *In Search of Excellence*, first published in 1982, Tom Peters and Robert Waterman made not a single reference to environmental issues. By 1991, however, Peters had published *Lean, Clean, and Green*. Other mainstream management gurus were soon nibbling at corners of the agenda, including Charles Handy (what is a company for?), James Collins and Jerry Porras (guidelines for long-lived companies), James Moore (business ecosystems), Francis Fukuyama (the role of trust and other forms of social capital), Peter Schwartz (the art of t he long view, scenarios), Michael Porter (value chains, green competition), and Peter Senge (organisational learning).

However, the greatest impact has come from a number of SD experts whose books are beginning to be accepted as mainstream management texts. They include Claude Fussler (eco-efficiency, eco-innovation), Ernst Ulrich von Weizacker (Factor 4–10), and Paul Hawken and Amory and Hunter Lovins (natural capitalism).

Organisations like the WBCSD now produce a huge amount of material on the SD agenda for business (**www.wbcsd.ch**). For those who want to see SD in action, take a look at the work of eco-architect Bill McDonough and his colleague Michael Braungart (**www.mbdc.com**). Having designed buildings for companies such as Gap, Nike and Ford, McDonough and his associates represent a truly new kind of architectural firm.

MAKING IT HAPPEN

- Adopt a triple-bottom-line strategy, focusing simultaneously on economic prosperity, social equity, and environmental protection.
- Make environmental and social issues a central boardroom concern, with compliance, the licence to operate, and reputational risk as key issues.
- Take the initiative by adopting policies that will meet the criteria of sustainable development.
- Use tools like impact assessments, audits, life-cycle assessments, and clean technology to obtain eco-efficient plant siting, production processes, and products.
- Consider what sustainable development may mean for your business, the areas to take action, the people to involve, and the benefits that may result.
- Closely monitor the new requirements for major industrial projects stemming from governmental bodies, including the European Commission.
- Accept that difficult trade-offs may be required, and face up to the consequences sooner rather than later.

CONCLUSION

The floodgates are opening. The first major article in the *Harvard Business Review* on the SD agenda was by Professor Stuart Hart in 1997; the number has been growing ever since. Some key issues for the coming years include: developing the business case for SD; exploring the overlap between organisational learning and SD agendas (**www.solonline.org**); and engaging corporate boards in the governance dimensions of SD. Sustainable development is set to become an increasingly significant strategic priority facing organisations. It offers a more efficient system for growth that is acceptable to stakeholders and is proven to be both viable and commercially advantageous.

THE BEST SOURCES OF HELP

Books:

Brown, Lester R. *Plan B 2.0: Rescuing a Planet Under Stress and a Civilization in Trouble*. London: W.W. Norton, 2006.

Hawken, Paul, et al. *Natural Capitalism: Creating the Next Industrial Revolution*. 2nd ed. London: Earthscan, 2008.

Porritt, Jonathon. *Capitalism As If the World Matters*. 2nd ed. London: Earthscan, 2007.

Rainey, David L. *Sustainable Business Development: Inventing the Future Through Strategy, Innovation, and Leadership*. Cambridge: Cambridge University Press, 2006.

Worldwatch Institute. *Vital Signs 2009*. Washington, DC: Worldwatch Institute, 2009.

Websites:

International Institute for Sustainable Development: **www.iisd.org**

Rocky Mountain Institute: **www.rmi.org**

Worldwatch Institute: **www.worldwatch.org**

World Resources Institute: **www.wri.org**

Creating Strategic Excellence by Mike Freedman

EXECUTIVE SUMMARY
- Organisations need strategy in order to prosper, rather than survive.
- The right environment is essential.
- Strategy, planning, and operational activities must be integrated.
- Develop a strategic culture to ensure success.

THE NEED FOR STRATEGIC EXCELLENCE

Survival or prosperity?

Organisations can survive without a strategy, but that's about all they will do. They will never prosper over the long term and will always perform sub-optimally – indeed, some may head in the wrong direction fast and finish up nowhere. With a clear strategy, effectively communicated, well planned, and carefully implemented, the chances of superior performance are enhanced immensely. Setting and implementing strategy, however, is not easy, requires considerable time and effort by an organisation's leadership, and demands outstanding thinking skills by all involved.

The right environment

An appropriate performance environment is required to achieve strategic clarity, coherence, and co-ordination throughout the organisation. The environment needs to encourage and stimulate those involved and balance strategic and operational imperatives, which are often in conflict for time, attention, resources, and thinking efforts. CEOs must lead by example, for there is nothing more important in their role than to ensure strategy is set and a leadership team is in place to help in that process and subsequently to direct its implementation.

STRATEGY DEFINED

Working on a global basis with many of the world's leading companies and government bodies, we have found that the following definitions have stood the test of time over the past 30 years.

Mission

The mission establishes the overall purpose of an organisation in a simple, clear statement of intent. It guides strategy formulation but is not a substitute for it. It must be meaningful. One client had as its mission 'to redefine, build, and own the greetings category globally'. This provided direction and motivation and gave a sense of what needed to be covered in its strategic vision.

This compares favourably with the mission of a Japanese car manufacturer: to 'kill Porsche'. A dramatic statement, but somewhat simplistic.

Strategy

Strategy is defined as 'a framework within which the choices about the nature and direction of an organisation are made'. *Framework* here means boundaries or parameters that help determine what lies inside or outside the scope of the organisation's strategy. Clear criteria are developed to apply in this initial decision-making filter. The choices to be made are what products and/or services will and will not be offered, what markets (customers, consumers, and geographies) will and will not be served, and what key capabilities are needed to take products to markets. The *nature* of an organisation is its very essence. McDonald's is defined by its fast-food essence, Dunhill by luxury goods, and Goldman Sachs by financial services. *Direction* refers to where an organisation is headed and how it might retain or change its nature and/or the scope of its activities.

A MODEL FOR STRATEGY FORMULATION AND IMPLEMENTATION

The role of a model

Having a proven model and the processes to support it eases the burden of a CEO and the top management team and produces a superior result. It also ensures that the necessary links are made and that the organisation's mission, strategic vision, planning processes, day-to-day decision-making, and human performance system are all aligned. Such an approach also facilitates continuous monitoring, review, and updating of the strategy, vital in today's climate of constant and rapid change.

A five-phase model

The model described below has been used effectively by many of the world's great corporations, including Corning, Hallmark, Hong Kong-based Towngas, the Venezuelan state oil company Lagoven, the Irish Development Agency, Kennametal, and Dunhill.

It has considerable advantages over many other well-known models such as those proposed by Michael Porter, Hamel and Prahalad, the Boston Consulting Group, General Electric, and McKinsey. Each of those focuses on only one or two elements of the Kepner–Tregoe model, typically omitting either planning the execution of the strategy or its actual implementation. They are thus incomplete. Our experience indicates that all five phases must be in place if there is to be a realistic chance of achieving strategic excellence. The model is as follows:

- Phase 1: Strategic intelligence gathering and analysis
- Phase 2: Strategy formulation
- Phase 3: Strategic master project planning
- Phase 4: Strategy implementation
- Phase 5: Strategy monitoring, review, and updating

The model is not linear, but iterative. A continuous feedback loop links each phase to the next.

Strategic intelligence gathering and analysis

This phase ensures that the depth and breadth of information on which strategic decisions are based is up to date, accurate, and relevant; the quality of strategic decisions depends very largely on the quality of this information. The intelligence covered includes competition, technology, markets, macro-economic, political, and social information and trends, and regulation, among other subjects specific to each organisation. Key to this phase is determining the implications of this intelligence to the organisation within its strategic time frame.

Strategy formulation

Using our definition of strategy, this phase results in the creation of a strategic vision or profile that builds on the strategic mission developed as its starting point. Such a vision answers nine key questions:

1. What are our fundamental beliefs and values?
2. What are the assumptions upon which we will make our future strategic decisions? (These are drawn from Phase 1.)
3. What products and/or services will we and will we not offer and what are their characteristics?
4. What customers and end-user groups (if they are different) will we serve and not serve and what are their characteristics?
5. What is our geographic scope?
6. What products/services and markets represent the greatest potential for growth and require the most investment and resource allocation?
7. What competitive advantage(s) will enable us to succeed?
8. What key capabilities do we need to ensure we take our products/services to market and to support our competitive advantage(s)?
9. What financial and non-financial goals (for example, market share, technology leadership) do we aim to achieve?

STRATEGIC MASTER PROJECT PLANNING

This phase encompasses the development of the plan for strategy implementation.

A significant number of projects emerge (often several hundred), the execution of which leads to successful implementation. Creating a strategic master project plan and developing an optimal project portfolio help to guide the organisation in prioritising, defining in detail, sequencing, scheduling, researching, executing, and monitoring these projects.

A strategic master project plan can contain projects covering a wide variety of activities, including:

- launching new products and markets
- filling capability gaps
- aligning organisational structure with strategy
- reducing complexity
- managing costs
- synchronising planning and budgeting with the strategy process

- developing functional strategy
- redefining and realigning IT hardware, software, and information requirements
- repositioning the company externally
- branding
- managing merger, acquisition, and disposal activities
- creating strategic alliances
- training and developing mid-level executives in strategy
- phasing out products and markets
- establishing an appropriate performance system

Strategy implementation

This phase involves taking planned actions, monitoring implementation, and modifying the strategic master project plan as circumstances change and projects are amended, completed, or abandoned and new ones added. Involving significant numbers of employees in the implementation phase is a vital ingredient in successful execution. The more strongly employees feel ownership of the strategy, the more they will be committed to play their part. Ownership, commitment, and involvement begin with a major communications exercise to ensure all employees fully understand the strategy and each can answer the question, 'What does this mean for me?' This phase often involves considerable training to empower employees to play their role.

Strategy monitoring, review, and updating

Given the rate and pace of change in the 21st century, this phase is a vital requirement. Continuous monitoring of strategic progress, goals, and indicators of success is a full-time task and a key input to regular, generally quarterly, reviews. Such reviews not only assess ongoing implementation, but examine whether the assumptions used to underpin the strategy are still valid and whether the organisation's strategic direction is still robust and viable. Strategic updates are an output of the monitoring and review process.

INTEGRATING STRATEGY, PLANNING, AND OPERATIONAL ACTIVITIES

Clearly the strategic dimension of an organisation is not an isolated set of activities. Strategic alignment requires the integration of every organisational component.

Constant internal and external communication is a key feature of successful strategic leadership and must accompany each phase of the process.

STRATEGY COMMUNICATION

What to communicate, to whom, by whom, when, how, and where are key questions in achieving strategic excellence. Many internal and external constituencies can and must play a role in effective strategy implementation. A pre-condition is that they all understand the message and know their role and what's in it for them. At Kepner Tregoe we use a communications matrix to guide this exercise. Each cell in the matrix requires a detailed project plan; this ensures that all key questions are answered. For more information about this, see **www.kepner-tregoe.com**.

MAKING IT HAPPEN

As the glue to the whole strategic environment, creating a strategic culture helps an organisation to achieve its goals. Strategic culture is defined as 'the combined effect of behaviours, norms, beliefs, values, heritage, thinking, and relationships and the way they manifest themselves in an organisation and its strategic performance'.

Its facets are:

- basic beliefs and values
- thinking patterns
- organisational structure
- management style
- management processes and systems
- education, training, and development
- goal setting and appraisals
- reward systems
- myths, stories, legends, and symbols
- information and knowledge
- agendas and meetings

- behaviours
- external manifestations to outside constituencies

When these align with, and support, an organisation's strategy efforts, then strategic success is assured.

THE BEST SOURCES OF HELP

Books:

Johnson, Spencer. *Who Moved My Cheese?: An Amazing Way to Deal with Change in Your Work and in Your Life*. London: Vermilion, 2002.

Kourdi, Jeremy. *Business Strategy*. 2nd ed. London: Profile Books, 2009.

Mintzberg, Henry, Bruce Ahlstrand, and Joseph Lampel. *Strategy Safari: A Guided Tour through the Wilds of Strategic Management*. London: Financial Times Prentice Hall, 2001.

Website:

www.kepner-tregoe.com has many supplementary articles on strategic approach.

Turnaround Strategies by Sir John Harvey-Jones

EXECUTIVE SUMMARY

- In a crisis situation, the leader of a business tends to be the first casualty and outsiders are brought in to sort out the situation.
- However, remedies are usually best applied by those already within the organisation.
- A turnaround situation is one of pointing out a new direction.
- The reason many companies find themselves in trouble is almost always due to problems right at the top.
- Any solution must be one to which all parties (particularly within the company) can offer their support.
- You only get one shot at trying to turn around a business.
- Everything has to be up for grabs, and fear and tradition must not be allowed to inhibit action.

INTRODUCTION

The area of business which, mercifully, few of us have any experience of is turning a business around before it goes under – but when the rocks ahead are clearly visible. In these situations, the first casualty tends to be the current leader. He or she is usually replaced by a hired 'hard man' to do the dirty work. The result is all too often far below what could be achieved by someone already within the organisation, who would have been aware of the culture which has led to the decline in the first place.

The in-house candidate (a role I have personally filled) is desirable because he or she has the best chance of sav-

ing the largest proportion of what may be salvageable. After all, insolvency practitioners, or at least the good ones, could be described as managing turnarounds, but at a cost which most of us would attempt to avoid. The greatest difficulty the in-house employee faces is the problem of analysing the causes of the downfall with sufficient clarity and over a long enough time. The elapsed time from the first business mistake to eventual collapse varies enormously. Very large organisations can carry on for a surprising time before events overwhelm them, while in the case of the small business retribution tends to strike much more quickly. What is certain is that both the stock market and the banks have less and less tolerance of business mistakes, and the time available to demonstrate an effective recovery plan is becoming ever shorter. Moreover the judgment of the chances of success is made by business analysts and the press, who probably have very little knowledge of the real situation which has led to the visible signs of failure. In reality, these are all too often symptoms rather than causes.

It is the people within the organisation itself who know the myriad problems which must be overcome and the actions to be taken. Therefore the turnaround problem becomes one of pointing out the new direction. This is where being able to call on the knowledge, drive, and enthusiasm of existing employees can be so valuable. This is obviously far more difficult when all of your employees are worrying about the future, and the best and most self-confident are voting with their feet for a safer environment. The reason many companies find themselves in trouble is almost always due to problems right at the top. I have yet to meet such a situation which was caused by the employees. Employee dissatisfaction is largely caused by mismanagement or frustration. No employee actually wants to do a bad job, or to be seen to be doing one. Obviously no employee actually wants the company to fail or to find themselves faced with enforced redundancy on minimal terms.

Diagnosis and solution

If you find yourself managing a turnaround, the first two points on which you have to concentrate are your diagnosis of the problem and endeavouring to ensure that you have a reasonable time gap in which to carry out your chosen solution. For the diagnosis, you need every scrap of information, opinion, and statistical analysis you can lay your hands on. The views and openness of those on the shop floor are as important – or in some cases, more important – than those at the top. Individuals in these situations are astonishingly honest with themselves, and it is from this apparently inchoate mass of opinion and fact that a first 'rough cut' analysis will appear. The strategy has to be concise and simple, for it is essential that everyone inside or outside the company should understand the aims. The detail is best left to those who will have to deliver it.

Self-evidently you cannot turn around a company by doing more of what has already landed you in trouble, although it is extraordinary how often the existing management blame their own ineffectiveness and not the strategy which has so obviously failed.

Few individuals are so closed-minded that they won't give you a chance if you explain your thinking, and in any case, no recovery plan is a single unique solution. The eventual solution you decide upon can, and must, be one to which all parties (particularly within the company) can offer their support.

Remember that your advent has kindled hope in those who work for you, coupled with probably unrealistic assumptions of a miraculous and speedy change in the situation.

Where does everybody stand?

A positive strategy with clear delegation for action and a lot of trust in your employees can change things surprisingly quickly. The next, and very difficult, action is entirely within your own outfit. It is absolutely vital that everyone knows where they stand. Start with the key 10–20 per cent, who you are sure need to be on board. Make clear that as long as you have a business, you need them and they are as secure as anyone in these times can be. Then address the 10–15 per cent most at risk. It is almost certain you will have to reduce cash, but generally a pay-out of under 20 per cent will do the trick. Remember that starting at the top involves fewer people and releases more money. Those most at risk deserve the earliest warning and the most help. Sharing the task of helping them to find alternatives eases the pain, as does the maximum affordable financial aid.

The remainder should be told that they are not at immediate risk, and that the risk to them depends almost entirely on the success of the turnaround.

The financial state of the company should be known to everyone, as should the direction and amount of change which will be required. Don't be trapped by the fear of lack of security on data. Bad news travels like lightning and all too often is far exceeded by the rumours and ill-concealed *Schadenfreude* of those in the outside world. You only get one go at trying to turn around a business, and concealment of the reality is not a help.

Delegation and trust

Once you have decided the strategy, the aim, and the team, delegate furiously. People have to know they are trusted and that all depends upon them.

Do not allow the inevitable attempts to 'delegate upwards'. You must keep on pushing the problem back to employees, while reiterating your commitment and support for their actions. The world is littered with examples of individuals who have achieved what you and others felt was impossible. Problems are only, and can only be, solved by those who 'own' them, and your leadership role is to reinforce that ownership.

Leading by example

You now enter what is probably the most personally difficult phase of all. Both inside and outside the company, you have to radiate confidence and realism while encouraging people to increase their speed of activity. This is helped by removing the brakes, simplifying the structure, reducing the senior management numbers and levels, and increasing the tempo.

Example is all. You cannot expect everyone else to throw themselves at the problem if you turn up late and go off early to enjoy a liquid lunch. The drum beat is taken from the top. In my own case, I have reduced my pay level and given back money I had been awarded until the business results had turned. You need a few dramatic examples from the top. Don't expect that stopping tea and biscuits will be greeted with anything other than cynicism. Selling the headquarters or the board cars is more likely to hit a responsive chord.

It is the board that has led the business into the mess, and it is the board who must be seen to take the medicine and be totally committed to the change. In my own case, a 50 per cent reduction in the number of executive board members and a refusal to allow deputies both increased our speed of response and demonstrated that there were no sacred cows.

Everything has to be up for grabs, and fear and tradition must not be allowed to inhibit action.

The whole problem is to achieve ownership of a new plan and a new pace of action – and all must be results oriented. Turnarounds are difficult, and test both the imagination and courage, but once it is evident you have started on the way up again there is no limit to how far and how fast you can go.

MAKING IT HAPPEN

- Act in the certainty that people within the organisation itself know the myriad problems which must be overcome and the actions to be taken.
- Concentrate first on your diagnosis of the problem and ensure a reasonable time to execute your chosen solution.
- Ensure that the solution is one which all parties, particularly within the company, can support.
- Start your programme by telling the key 10–20 per cent that you need them on board. Then address the 10–15 per cent whose jobs are most at risk.
- Once you have decided the strategy, the aim, and the team, delegate intensively to people who know they are trusted and that all depends upon them.
- Remove the brakes, simplify the structure, reduce senior management numbers and levels, increase the tempo – and be ready to implement a few dramatic examples from the top.

THE BEST SOURCES OF HELP

Books:

Deming, W. Edwards. *Out of the Crisis*. Cambridge, Massachusetts: MIT Press, 2000.

Kim, W. Chan and Renée Mauborgne. *Blue Ocean Strategy: How to Create Uncontested Market Space and Make Competition Irrelevant*. Boston: Harvard Business School Press, 2005.

Website:

www.turnaround.org: this is the site of the Turnaround Management Association, an international non-profit association that advocates the use of professional turnaround specialists in a crisis. The site includes a Journal of Corporate Renewal page and links to other sites.

Core Versus Context: Managing Resources in a Downturn by Geoffrey A. Moore

EXECUTIVE SUMMARY

- *Core* processes create competitive advantage through differentiation.
- *Context* processes are necessary to meet competitive market standards, but do not differentiate.
- Investors wish the bulk of their capital to go to core processes, as only those can raise stock prices.

INTRODUCTION

Executives well understand the value of focusing on core business issues and activities, although they sometimes fail to distinguish between core as competitive advantage versus core competence. The former is what the market rewards, the latter what the company is good at. One of the toughest challenges in business occurs when core competence is no longer core. Competition has caught up with you to such an extent that what was once core has now become context. The market still demands the process, but it's no longer willing to pay a premium for it.

Companies thus find themselves with an increasing portion of their asset base – sometimes in equipment, always in personnel – that no longer generates attractive returns. What was once differentiated and at a premium has now been commoditised. This in turn causes investors to bid down the value of their stock, since they see an increasingly large portion of their capital going to fund processes that are at best financially inert and are potentially a financial sinkhole.

Lest anyone feel superior to executives struggling with this challenge, we should note that every company is subject to erosion of core into context; the very nature of competitive markets works to neutralise differentiation over time as competitors find ways to mimic or substitute for the value created and thereby re-level the playing field. The knee-jerk response of most management teams is to make or find new core, which is necessary but insufficient. What they must also do is systematically work to shed themselves of context or face a perpetually deteriorating core/context ratio, with loss of attractiveness to investors and, ultimately, an uncompetitive cost of capital. In this article we will outline the impact of core versus context, and the actions that companies must take.

THE IMPACT ON COMPANIES

Companies get trapped by context from various causes, many attributable to organisational inertia. Such processes were once their bread and butter, making it hard to abandon them. Moreover, if the alternative is to outsource the work (the fundamental domain in which context shedding is accomplished), there are inevitable concerns about cost. Rarely do in-house teams *not* assert that they can perform a given function cheaper, faster, and better than outsourcers.

Long term, however, this is not the case. Where one company's context is another company's core, market dynamics ultimately favour the latter's position. That company can invest in productivity-improving systems and processes with full support of its investors, whereas the other company cannot. Moreover, it can attract the best people because it can provide them with an upwardly mobile career path, whereas the latter company cannot. Finally, it can amortise investments across a broad base of customers, whereas the other company cannot.

Thus, in the long term, failing to outsource is a losing game. Only in the short term – specifically, in the current quarter – is it often more expensive, in part for reasons of transition costs, in part because prices and offerings are not as competitive as one would want until market forces have a chance to work. The end result: unless the outsourcer makes a short-term sacrifice, it's unlikely the deal goes forward.

Most executives are wise to this game, but few appreciate how pernicious it is to accede to it. They don't see how every context process not outsourced creates a tax on the asset base of the company. Worse, they don't see how failure to manage context aggressively leads necessarily to a loss of agility in their corporate culture and a corresponding rise in stifling bureaucracy and administration. Why?

Context processes have no upside, but they do have downside. Just because the safety valve on a machine doesn't differentiate it (and therefore can't be leveraged for premium value) doesn't mean it can be neglected. Context carries liability just as core does. The difference is that core also transfers competitive advantage, which context does not. Thus, if you're managing core, you're always in search of the efficient frontier of risk versus reward. But what is the best strategy for managing context?

Darwinian natural selection will drive context managers to increasingly risk-averse strategies, those being the most suitable for managing processes that have a downside but no upside. As a company's core/context ratio deteriorates, its population of managers will thus become increasingly risk-averse. They are happy for other people to take risks, but not themselves (and not others if that's going to put their area in the line of fire). The result? Large corporations become stultified and unresponsive.

SUCCESSFULLY MANAGING THE CORE/CONTEXT RATIO

The proving ground for outsourcing context today is contract manufacturing in the electronics industry, with companies like Cisco and Dell, and outsourcers like Solectron and Flextronics, leading the way. What these companies are exploiting is the premise that whatever is one company's context can be another company's core. In this relationship, whenever a business process is transferred from one to the other, the investors of both companies applaud, one because it went off their balance sheet, and the other because it went on to theirs.

Drill down into the systems investments that have enabled these early adopters to steal a march on their competitors and we see that they focus on two critical issues: *control* and *visibility*. The following cases provide examples.

Beyond manufacturing, more companies are looking to outsource IT and financial and human resources services. Payroll has long been a function considered outsourceable, as companies like ADP, Paychex, and Ceridian can testify. For example, a visible departmental outsourcing deal is that between British Petroleum with PricewaterhouseCoopers for human resources. Here, the best strategy is to determine for each function what is still core and what is legitimately context, so that you don't outsource the baby with the bath water (particularly critical in the case of IT).

Early outsourcing relationships between EDS and General Motors and between IBM and Kodak have been strongly criticised and provide some important lessons. In both cases the corporations were fed up with their in-house organisation and wanted a better substitute at a fixed price. They made no attempt to segregate core from context. Instead they focused on price, which was negotiated as low as possible. This in turn motivated the outsourcers to cut corners or penny-pinch the end users on change requests, leading to bad relationships and bad outcomes. The end result was annoying when it came to context processes, but it was devastating when it ended up holding core projects hostage.

Conversely, outsourcing IT infrastructure looks to be a major growth market. Moreover, specialised services like 24/7 performance monitoring and security management both lend themselves to third-party provisioning. The key is that these functions, although frequently mission-critical, are almost never core. This is where outsourcing shines.

KEY POINTS WHEN MANAGING THE CORE/COMPETENCE RATIO

1. **Be prepared to delegate core activities.** Top management can delegate core to middle management. Of course, it rarely wants to, because this is the fun stuff. The truth is that the middle of the organisation has a better view of emerging market trends than the top; if you empower it, it will do a better job than you.

2. **Outsource and manage context.** Top management's most powerful lever is the outsourcing of context. This is not the fun stuff. But middle management is never positioned to act on this directive, as it can't afford to put its political capital at risk. Only top management can drive these initiatives correctly, working with support from the board, always with an eye towards repurposing reclaimed resources into the next generation of core work.

3. **Distinguish between mission-critical and supporting activities.** To the distinction between core and context needs, we need to add the distinction between *mission-critical* and *supporting*. The former applies to processes that can directly damage customer outcomes or corporate capabilities. These must be kept under managerial control. The latter, by contrast, can be readily outsourced with only modest controls. The big

challenge in core/context ratio management comes with the need to outsource mission-critical context. Indeed, executives often confuse mission-critical with core because they're sure they *can't* outsource such processes. But to manage their core/context ratio, they must. This demands new best practices in outsourcing, enabling customers to retain control and visibility, while transferring the bulk of work to another organisation.

4. **Harness the benefit of technology.** The technology key to the new best practices is for the company and its outsourcer to create information systems that give the company short-term adaptive controls and long-term visibility into its risk positions. The Internet provides a backbone for enabling such systems. The business logic that must ride on that backbone is just now coming to market. Early adopters may well have to write their own systems in order to get ahead of their competition.

MINI-CASES

In Cisco, early work with outsourcing was based on the company transferring in-house control systems (not manufacturing systems) to the outsourcer. These systems simply do not print shipping documents until and unless automated testing proves the equipment matches the customer order. Thus build-to-order manufacturing gets protected against a raft of customer returns.

Dell has used IT to develop end-to-end visibility into their inventory positions and used their market power to force suppliers to hold that inventory until the last second. This would be intolerable for the supplier were it not for Dell giving them near-real-time visibility into the emerging order mix, which is made possible by configuration software, now web-enabled, that funnels customer demand from an infinite array of selections into a finite and manageable set of options.

MAKING IT HAPPEN

1. **Start with a questioning analysis of core and context activities, at three levels:**
   - **Top level:** which of our businesses are still core? Which have become context?
   - **Business unit level:** which of our line functions are the real basis for our competitive differentiation? Which are not?
   - **Function level:** which of our processes are the source of differentiation? Which are driven by more compliance?

   - **Departmental and, if useful, individual levels:** how much time is spent on context activities?
2. **Consider two key ideas to help guide this process, asking the questions:**
   - If we were entirely free of current obligations, what could we do to increase the competitive advantage of our company? This helps people to see the possible sources and types of core activity, and may help start the journey to get there. It also identifies the task work that should be passed on or left alone, leading to the second question:
   - What work would we be willing to surrender if we were assured that someone else would handle it appropriately? This becomes a lightning rod to attract context processes that, once aggregated, can be analysed for disposal.
3. **Implement and monitor the results.** It helps to understand from the outset that the process of detailed implementation will invariably result in a course correction later. Also, not only does the process of implementation need to be monitored to ensure that it remains on track, but the core/context ratio needs to be regularly assessed, as competitive markets are far from static. One of the keys to successful implementation is to assemble a sufficient amount of work to motivate an outsourcer to put their best efforts into the work. At the same time it is important not to create such organisational shocks that will risk losing momentum or upset customers.

CONCLUSION

Executives must learn to manage the core/context ratio. Regardless of how superior their core is, eventually its impact will be dwarfed by an ever-expanding context. It's like cholesterol: if you do not manage context, it will finish you.

THE BEST SOURCES OF HELP

Books:

Christensen, Clayton M. *The Innovator's Dilemma*. Rev. ed. London: HarperBusiness, 2003.

Christensen, Clayton M. and Michael E. Raynor. *The Innovator's Solution: Creating and Sustaining Successful Growth*. Boston: Harvard Business School Press, 2003.

Moore, Geoffrey A. *Crossing the Chasm*. London: Collins Business, 2002.

Snapping Managerial Inertia
by Jeffrey Pfeffer and Robert I. Sutton

EXECUTIVE SUMMARY

- Despite the billions of dollars that industry spends on executive education, leadership development, and knowledge-management efforts each year, very little change takes place.
- Executives must use plans, analysis, meetings, and presentations to inspire achievement, not to substitute for action.
- To accomplish this, companies must eliminate fear, abolish destructive internal competition, measure what matters, and promote leaders who understand the work employees do.

INTRODUCTION

Why do so many managers understand so much about employee and organisational performance and work so hard, yet do so much to undermine performance? Why do so many companies sponsor training programmes and knowledge-management initiatives, yet see no impact from those efforts? Knowing what to do isn't enough. Companies must inspire action to turn all of that individual and collective knowledge into achievements that affect the company's business results.

What happens in many companies is that managers spend so much time fighting internal battles that they have little time left to fight the company's competitors. In too many companies, points are scored on the elaborateness of internal presentations (meaning that people spend inordinate amounts of time preparing those presentations to impress their bosses and peers) instead of tangible business results. In many other companies, the penalty for failure is so great that managers spend their time preserving the status quo rather than trying to find new and better ways of affecting business results. Further, the 'not invented here' (NIH) syndrome prevents people from learning from each other for fear that they'll give credit to some other person in the company who has developed a better method – for fear they'll admit the other person deserves more recognition and, perhaps, a greater share of the available rewards.

It doesn't have to be this way. Many companies are finding ways of overcoming the knowing–doing gap. Knowing how to bridge this gap will make a positive difference to your company's business results and your effectiveness as a manager.

GUIDELINES FOR ACTION
Recognise the importance of philosophy

Many companies have undertaken experiments in one division or location to implement high-performance work teams. While many such efforts have shown outstanding results, few of these companies have been successful in transferring these new work methods to other plants, divisions, or locations. A prime example of this is that few of the innovations from Saturn and NUMMI have ever been adopted by other parts of the General Motors organisation. What's missing is a company-wide understanding of the basic philosophy of the new methods and a frank and open discussion of why the new methods are important and must be replicated throughout the company.

Companies that don't accept talk as a substitute for action often do one or more of the following:

- promote people who have developed a real-world understanding of the organisation's work processes because they have performed them themselves
- build a culture that values simplicity (and doesn't reward complexity), uses simple, clear, and direct language, and values common sense
- use action-oriented language and follow up to ensure that decisions are implemented
- refuse to accept excuses for why things won't work, instead encouraging employees to reframe objections into challenges to be overcome

Act and teach others how to act

Too many companies place great value on conceptual frameworks, fancy graphic presentations, and lots of words, but little value on action. Why are so many change efforts approved in the boardroom and never implemented? Honda puts employees into suppliers' organisations so they can see how the suppliers make parts and what work methods they use. Being closely involved with the supplier is imperative for real understanding and learning.

Plans and concepts count less than action

Too many companies are stymied by analysis paralysis, the feeling that plans must be complete and bullet-proof before any action is taken. The more successful companies encourage action to foster learning by doing. In many of these companies it is believed that an 80 per-cent solution today is better than a 100 per-cent solution months or years from now. Former Continental Airlines COO Greg Brenneman spoke of the airline's turnaround in this way: 'If you sit around devising elegant and complex strategies and then try to execute them through a series of flawless decisions, you're doomed. We saved Continental because we acted and we never looked back.'

Tolerate errors as a sign that learning is taking place

Does your company treat mistakes so harshly that people continuously analyse and discuss plans instead of taking action? Thomas Edison tried thousands of materials for light-bulb filaments before discovering tungsten. When someone asked him how he overcame so many failures, he said that he never failed – he just learned. Roger Sant, co-founder of AES, fosters a culture of forgiveness, noting, 'You would be amazed at how quickly people support and forgive one another here.'

Drive fear out of your organisation

If employees fear that any new idea that doesn't work perfectly at the first attempt will result in punishment or dismissal, they'll never try anything new. Rapid prototyping is a manufacturing design method in which new ideas can be tried out quickly and relatively inexpensively and plans modified based on results. Failure of a new idea is viewed as part of the learning process, not as something to be feared. Successful companies encourage risk-taking and encourage employees to try new ideas without an overwhelming fear of retribution should they fail.

Companies that work to drive fear out of their organisation often try some of these approaches:

- rather than shooting the messenger, reward employees who deliver bad news – if the company doesn't know about a problem, it can't solve it
- punish inaction, not unsuccessful actions – an unsuccessful action should be viewed as a learning experience
- share failures – when leaders share their failures, they give permission to others to fail and encourage them to try
- banish anyone, at any level, who humiliates others
- learn from, and even celebrate, mistakes – especially when trying something new

Fight the competition, not each other

Because competitive free enterprise has triumphed as an economic system, many companies have adopted internal competition as a way of life. This is typified by such practices as normal-curve performance rating systems, recognition for relatively few employees, and individual measurements and rewards that set people against each other. These practices take the focus away from the real opposition: external competitors. There are exceptions, however.

Measure action and what turns knowledge into action

Many companies are awash with data measuring every conceivable action. Amid so many measures employees spend far too much time focused on the numbers and how they'll look rather than on actions that can help to improve the business and meet overall goals. More successful companies focus on a few key measures of company performance, believing that if those key measures are met, everything else will fall into line.

Leadership is the key

Successful leaders create a positive learning environment that not only helps employees learn but also helps them apply that learning to their work to make a positive difference in business results. They lead by their own example and teach others how to act.

MINI-CASES

At Men's Wearhouse the emphasis is on team selling; employees succeed only as their colleagues succeed. Customers don't care who gets the commission, they want great service from every employee.

The SAS Institute has a very low turnover rate, based partly on employees' preference not to have to constantly look over their shoulder to see which colleague is getting ready to subvert their work in order to look better themselves.

Southwest Airlines focuses on key measures such as lost bags, customer complaints, and on-time performance.

AES focuses on uptime of their power plants, new business development, and environmental and safety factors.

Measurements that can help to turn knowledge into action include those that are:

- focused on organisational success rather than individual success. This encourages teamwork and interdependence.
- focused more on processes and means to ends, not on end products and final outcomes. This helps to facilitate learning and provides data that can better guide action and decision-making.
- focused on the business model, culture, and philosophy of the firm. This means that measurements will vary from firm to firm and will generally depart from traditional accounting-based indicators.
- focused on a mindful, ongoing process of learning from experience and experimentation. No process is ever viewed as complete or final.

When David Kearns was CEO at Xerox, he applied quality principles to the top management team as he encouraged their implementation throughout the company.

The CEO of General Motors teaches in GM University, demonstrating his personal commitment to knowledge building and sharing.

CONCLUSION

Many readers will finish this article and start nodding: How did they know what's happening in my company? But recognising that the problems exist isn't enough. Going back over 20 years, Peters and Waterman, in their book *In Search of Excellence*, recognised that the most successful companies have a 'bias for action'. And that's what you need to snap your company's managerial inertia. Start right now!

THE BEST SOURCES OF HELP
Books:
Bossidy, Larry, Ram Charan, and Charles Burck. *Execution: The Discipline of Getting Things Done.* London: Crown Business, 2002.
Collins, Jim and Jerry I. Porras. *Built to Last: Successful Habits of Visionary Companies.* London: Collins Business, 2004.

The End of Growth: Why Does It Always End? What Can You Do About It? by Robert M. Tomasko

EXECUTIVE SUMMARY
- All growth trajectories follow a life-cycle.
- Business growth invariably slows.
- If you anticipate the inevitable decline, you can push it further into the future.
- Sustained growth ultimately requires the courage to abandon one growth path for another.

INTRODUCTION

Why do bubbles burst? Because as they grow their surface area becomes so large that increasing amounts of energy are diverted away from keeping the structure intact and into expanding its size. Some bubbles find an equilibrium point and persist, but those that keep trying to grow collapse. This collapse has little to do with outside intervention. It's caused by trying too hard. Many businesses similarly try too hard, fighting the nature of their markets and organisation, and find their growth trajectory coming to a crashing halt.

All growth efforts eventually slow. But neither your business nor your career has to decline in tandem with them as long as you stay alert to the dynamics that are in play and cultivate the ability to adapt.

MINI-CASES

Sainsbury, once the United Kingdom's largest supermarket chain, discovered that an attempt to maintain family control of its top management, while expanding abroad and diversifying at home, was more than its growth path could endure. The result: a fall from the top as the UK market-share leader and a change to an outside CEO.

Many banks and financial service businesses, once one of the fastest-growing and most profitable sectors in the global economy, went hurtling to disaster through a combination of hubris and an over-expansion into new products and markets that were only lightly regulated. The result: a credit crunch and a catalyst for global recession.

Swissair, the long-time standard-setter for classy air travel, attempted to fuel its growth with an ill-thought-out plan to buy parts of a dozen small, struggling airlines. Financial chaos from cascading losses ensued, along with a CEO-firing and resignation of the directors who endorsed such a blind-alley strategy.

THE LAWS OF GRAVITY ALSO APPLY TO BUSINESS

Hitting the growth wall is a problem that eventually plagues every business.
- City analysts hate hearing from executives with no visibility about their next quarter's prospects.
- Underwater stock options demoralise.
- Unreachable sales quotas squash motivation.

- Just as rapid growth creates its own forward momentum, generating new fast-track career paths, ambitious top performers are often the first to jump ship at the prospect of a business slowdown. Net result: fewer seasoned business growers available to rebound the business.

The cumulative impact of poor publicity, talent loss, and demoralisation serves only to reinforce this negative spiral. The dynamics behind the global recession aren't all that different from the forces that resulted in the turn-of-the-millennium e-business slowdown, the limited expansion of the mainframe computer industry in the 1990s, energy companies in the 1980s, consumer-goods makers in the 1970s, and, over a century ago, the steam railways.

Sudden, out-of-the-blue shocks are blamed for many business slowdowns. However, in reality these are few and far between. The Internet, a favourite scapegoat, has caused far more businesses to grow than it has destroyed. Every market runs on a life-cycle. So does every business, in a cycle of:
- ramp-up
- rapid growth
- mature stability
- gradual decline

When the two cycles – the company's and its industry's – are out of sync, growth inevitably slows and economic performance suffers. This is the story of Apple Computer before its iPod days, and the Internet-based grocer Webvan. It's a lesson that retailer Target has learned and K-Mart has not. Cataclysmic events and life-cycle misfits are outside-the-company growth retarders. They can sting, but the enemy to be most wary of is lurking within. Most businesses don't need competitors to steal their growth opportunities. They do it to themselves, making errors of both omission and commission.

UNDERSTANDING THE POTENTIAL FOR SELF-INFLICTED WOUNDS

What's most commonly missing among managers and executives of slow-growth companies is the ability to engage in systems thinking.

These people tend to
- treat each happening in the business as an isolated event (or problem to be solved) rather than seeing it as part of a chain extending over a long time period;
- focus on the needs of their own company, department, or job rather than seeing themselves and their business as part of a network of interconnected players.

This mentality puts a brake on growth. It forgets that every driver of growth is accompanied by some kind of limiting process, such as:
- an awakened competitor
- an overtaxed supplier

- an extra-vigilant regulator
- an internal capacity constraint (usually cash or talent)

It's also important to be wary of growth substitutes. Among the most common are:

- **Accounting trickery.** Managing earnings instead of growth creates the appearance of profit increases through restructuring charges, hidden reserves, and changes in pension-funding policies.
- **Stock buy-backs.** Earnings per share do rise when the number of shares shrinks, but this is not the same as increases due to profitable revenue growth.
- **Merger mania.** Acquisitions and mergers, as CitiGroup, RBS and many other firms have learned, are often more of a long detour than a direct path to real growth.
- **Cost-cutting.** This source of short-term gain destroys more seeds of future growth than any aggressive competitor might.

AVOIDING A TOXIC TREATMENT

Why does cost-cutting bite back? There are times when it's the right remedy, but like some popular medicines it's over-prescribed as a cure for stalled growth. Profits can grow in the short term through cost-cutting, of course, at least until the business runs out of expendables. No amount of down-sizing can make up for General Motors' inability to build cars that people really want to buy. Profits resulting from creating hard-to-duplicate benefits that are conveyed to customers are a sustainable, renewable resource. But they are renewable only as long as the business growers who create them are kept in place and motivated. But when the cost-cutting fixer mentality dominates with its often mindless, across-the-board slashes, good growers run for cover. The growth mindset cultivates carefully nurtured, experience-based, invest-now-for-future-return behaviour.

Responding to the end of growth

If you're facing market collapse

- Remember that it's better to yield to some trends, rather than engaging in an unwinnable war.
- Even if you're facing total economic collapse, don't throw in the towel until you study the lessons of Brazilian and Lebanese businesses. Both are world-class improvisers – the best strategy when everything seems up in the air.
- If regulatory straitjackets seem insurmountable obstacles, look hard at the ways of northern Italy's virtual keiretsu and France's highly automated manufacturers.

If your market's life-cycle is at war with your plans

- Sustain your growth by getting out ahead of the curve.
- Consider the first hints of growth deceleration as nature's way of telling you to shift gears. Nokia did this, growing in the same mobile phone manufacturing marketplace that was a quagmire for Ericsson and Motorola.
- When the market seems to have had enough of innovative products, consider reorienting around customer-defined requirements rather than inner vision.
- When growth slows because everyone in the industry seems to be following the same formula, follow the lead of upstarts like Southwest Airlines and Ryanair, and rethink your offerings from the ground up.
- When industry domination becomes too costly to sustain, pick off the most profitable segments, focus exclusively on customers' needs, and reap the high-margin rewards that come to specialist companies like Rolex and Germany's famous Mittelstand.

If your company seems to be its own worst enemy

- Don't throw away that next invitation to a seminar on systems thinking. Go, and you'll never think about your business in the same way again.
- Keep multiple sets of books if you have to (as your country's laws allow, of course), but don't confuse the kinds of growth accountants create with the real thing.
- Resist the urge to merge until it's crystal clear how the acquisition will enable growth. Don't let size become an end in itself.
- Never cut costs as an end in itself, only as a subordinate component of an overall growth plan.
- Never confuse stock-price growth with business growth.
- Don't waste energy whining when the market tanks your shares.
- 'Take no prisoners' is an order that belongs to the cinema, not the boardroom. Microsoft's growth was much more sustainable when its standard-setting opened up profitable market segments for business allies clustering under its umbrella. Taking a live-and-let-live perspective on the competition is a great way to expand the size of everyone's market. Coke and Pepsi need each other, and they both know it. Virgin and British Airways do, too, but they may not be quite as aware of the need. Wal-Mart needs vibrant speciality retailers on the high street, but has ignored that reality, generating opposition to its growth because of it.

MAKING IT HAPPEN

The following steps can help successful growth to continue, or to be rekindled:

1. **Review current business activities:** this may involve analysing strengths, weaknesses, opportunities, and threats, as well as assessing the business's relative market share. It can also mean answering the following questions:
   - Where are the most profitable parts of the business?
   - What are the prospects in the short, medium, and long term for those products and markets?
   - How precarious is the business – for example, does it rely on too few products, customers, or distribution channels?
   - How clearly focused is the business – is it over-burdened with too many products, markets, and initiatives, or is it running on empty with too few opportunities?
   - What is likely to be the best method of expansion – is it affordable (not just in terms of money)?
   - What are the advantages and disadvantages of expanding?

2. **Decide the best method of achieving growth:** discuss the options with senior managers and shareholders, refining potential opportunities and deciding how to approach problems.

3. **Plan for growth:** decide what action is needed to achieve growth. This will certainly involve leadership qualities to communicate and mobilise resources.

4. **Act decisively and consistently:** once the course has been set it needs to be rigorously followed. One of the greatest obstacles to growth is inertia, often in the form of attachment to heritage and past activities. However, Sir John Harvey-Jones, former CEO of ICI and one of the United Kingdom's most successful businessmen, emphasised that any business is only as good as its next three months' order book.

It is also necessary to pay attention to the details of any strategy for growth. Understand how the changes affect people. Decisive action is vital, but this needs to include an understanding of how to maintain people's commitment and motivation. If people feel threatened, or insecure, then however sensible the strategy for growth and the plan for implementation it simply will not be achieved. It is vital to treat people with respect. It is also worth communicating what is happening to people so that they understand their role and how they can contribute. Also, monitor the situation: time lags need to be understood and planned for, and the strategy must be supported in the long term.

CONCLUSION

Growth always ends. For some businesses it comes with a bang, for others, with a whimper. The ideas here will assist in prolonging the end game. Apply them, but do so with your eyes open. Ramping down is just as much a part of the business landscape as ramping up. Knowing when to let go, and recycling your efforts in a more promising direction, is the secret of long-term happiness in a business career. There are many market, industry, and organisational indicators you can watch for, clues that bail-out time is near. Look hard at them, but in the end the best litmus test is to ask yourself a simple question: Am I still having fun? If the honest answer is no, then you know what you need to do.

THE BEST SOURCES OF HELP

Books:
Christensen, Clayton M. *The Innovator's Dilemma*. Rev. ed. London: HarperBusiness, 2003.
Greenwald, Bruce, and Judd Kahn. *Competition Demystified*. New York: Portfolio, 2005.
Kourdi, Jeremy. *Surviving a Downturn*. London: A&C Black, 2007.
Tomasko, Robert. *Bigger Isn't Always Better*. New York: AMACOM Books, 2006.

Websites:
The McKinsey Quarterly:
   www.mckinseyquarterly.com
Robert Tomasko.com: **www.roberttomasko.com**

Managing New-product Portfolios
by Robert G. Cooper and Scott J. Edgett

EXECUTIVE SUMMARY

- New-product portfolio management is about how you invest your business's product development resources through project prioritisation and allocating resources across development projects.
- There are four goals in portfolio management: maximising the value of the portfolio; seeking the right balance of projects; ensuring that your portfolio is strategically aligned, and making sure you have the appropriate number of projects for your limited resources.
- There are many tools – some quantitative, others graphical, some strategic – designed to help you choose the right portfolio of projects.
- Your new-product process or 'stage-gate' system must be working in order to achieve effective portfolio management. It must deliver data integrity and also weed out the bad projects early.

INTRODUCTION

How should you most effectively invest your product development resources? And how should you prioritise your development projects and allocate resources among them? These are crucial issues in new-product portfolio management. Much as for a stock market portfolio manager, those senior executives who manage to optimise their R&D investments, selecting winning new-product projects and achieving the ideal balance and numbers of projects, will win in the long run.

Portfolio management is a critical senior management challenge. This is why:
- a successful new-product effort is *fundamental to business success*. This logically translates into portfolio management – the ability to select today's projects that will become tomorrow's new-product winners.

- new-product development is the *manifestation of your business's strategy*. If your new product initiatives are wrong – either the wrong projects or the wrong balance – then you fail at implementing your business strategy.
- portfolio management is about *resource allocation*. In a business world preoccupied with value to the shareholder and doing more with less, technology and marketing resources are simply too scarce to waste. The consequences of poor portfolio management are evident: you squander scarce resources and, as a result, starve the truly deserving projects.

MAKING IT HAPPEN

There are four goals of portfolio management to aim for.

Goal 1: maximise the value of your portfolio. Here the goal is to select new product projects to maximise the sum of the values or *commercial worth* of all active projects in your development pipeline in terms of some business objective. Tools used to assess 'project value' include:

- *Net present value (NPV).* Determine the project's NPV and then rank projects by NPV divided by the key or constraining resource (for example, the R&D costs still left to be spent on the project; that is, by NPV/R&D). Projects are rank-ordered according to this index until resources run out, thus maximising the value of the portfolio (the sum of the NPVs across all projects) for a given or limited resource expenditure.
- *Expected Commercial Value (ECV).* This method uses decision-tree analysis, breaking the project into decision stages – for example, development and commercialisation. Define the possible outcomes of the project along with probabilities of each occurring – for example, probabilities of technical and commercial success. The resulting ECV is then divided by the constraining resource (as in the NPV method), and projects are rank-ordered according to this index in order to maximise the 'punch per pound'. This method also approximates *real options theory*, and thus is appropriate for handling higher-risk projects.
- *Scoring Model.* Decision-makers rate projects on a number of factors that distinguish superior projects, typically on 1–5 or 0–10 scales. Add the ratings for each factor to yield a quantified 'project attractiveness score', which must clear a minimum hurdle. This score is a proxy for the 'value of the project' but incorporates factors beyond just financial measures. Projects are then rank-ordered according to this score until resources run out. Typical factors are: strategic alignment; product/competitive advantage; market attractiveness; leverage or synergies; technical feasibility, and risk versus return.

Goal 2: seek balance in your portfolio. Here the goal is to achieve a desired balance of projects in terms of a number of parameters. For example, long-term projects versus short ones, or high-risk versus lower-risk projects. Balance can also be sought across various markets, technologies, product categories and project types. Pictures portray balance much better than numbers and lists, so the techniques used here are largely graphical in nature.

- **Bubble diagrams:** Display your projects on a two-dimensional grid as different-size bubbles (the size of the bubbles denotes the spending on each project). The axes vary but the most popular chart is the risk-reward bubble diagram, where NPV is plotted versus probability of technical success. Then seek an appropriate balance in numbers of projects (and spending) across the four quadrants.
- **Pie charts:** Show your spending breakdowns as slices of pies in a pie chart. Popular pie charts include a breakdown by project types, by market or segment, and by product line or product category.

Unlike the maximisation tools described under Goal 1, bubble diagrams and pie charts are not decision models, but rather information display. They depict the current portfolio and where the resources are going – the 'what is'. These charts provide a useful beginning for the discussion of 'what should be' – how your resources should be allocated.

Goal 3: your portfolio must be strategically aligned. Being strategically aligned means that all your projects are 'on strategy', and that your breakdown of spending across projects, areas, markets, and so on must mirror your strategic priorities. Several portfolio methods are designed to achieve strategic alignment.

- **Top-down, strategic buckets:** Begin at the top with your business's strategy and from that, your product innovation strategy – that is, its goals, and where and how to focus your new product efforts. Next, make splits in resources: given your strategy, where should you spend your money? These splits can be by project types, product lines, markets or industry sectors, and so on. Thus, you establish strategic buckets of resources. Within each bucket, list all projects – active, on-hold and new – and rank these until you run out of resources in that bucket. The result is multiple portfolios, one portfolio per bucket. Another result is that your spending at year-end will truly reflect the strategic priorities of your business.
- **Top-down, product roadmap:** Once again, begin at the top, with your business and product innovation strategy. But now the question is, given that you have selected several areas of strategic focus (markets, technologies, or product types), what major initiatives must you undertake in order to be successful here? The end result is a mapping of these major initiatives along a timeline of several years – the product roadmap. The selected projects are 100 per cent strategically driven.
- **Bottom-up:** 'Make good decisions on individual projects, and the portfolio will take care of itself' is a commonly accepted philosophy. That is, make sure that your project gating system is working well – that gates are accepting good projects and killing the poor ones – and the resulting portfolio will be a solid one. To ensure strategic alignment, use a scoring model at your project reviews and gates (as in Goal 2), and include strategic questions in this model. Strategic alignment is all but assured: your portfolio will indeed consist of all 'on strategy' projects (although spending splits may not coincide with strategic priorities).

Note that regardless of the strategic approach, all of these methods presuppose that your business has a product innovation strategy, something that many businesses lack.

Goal 4: pick the right number of projects. Most companies have too many projects under way for their limited available resources. The result is pipeline gridlock: projects take too long to reach the market, and key activities are omitted because of a lack of people and time. Thus an overriding goal is to ensure a balance between resources required for the active projects and resources available. The following are two ways of achieving this goal.

- **Resource limits:** The value maximisation methods (Goal 1) build in a resource limitation. Using them means ranking your projects until you run out of resources. The same is true of bubble diagrams (Goal 2). The sum of the areas of the bubbles – the resources devoted to each project – should be a constant, and adding one more project to the diagram requires that another be deleted.
- **Resource capacity analysis:** Determine your resource demand by prioritising projects and adding up the resources required by each department for all active projects (usually expressed in person-days per month). Portfolio management software enables this round-up of resource requirements. Then determine the available resources per department – how much time people have to work on these projects. A department-by-department and month-by-month assessment usually reveals that there are too many projects. It suggests a project limit (the point beyond which projects in the prioritised list should be put on hold), and it identifies which departments are the bottlenecks.

YOUR NEW-PRODUCT PROCESS MUST WORK

Before you charge ahead with portfolio management, put first things first: make sure that your new-product process or 'gating system' is working well. An effective new-product process is central to portfolio management for the following reasons:

- regardless of the sophistication of the portfolio models used, your input data must be sound. Look to your new-product process to deliver *data integrity.*
- your gating process should at minimum kill or cull out the bad projects and, in so doing, yield a better portfolio.

Data integrity means that the up-front homework in projects must be done. Many companies have improved the quality of execution and at the same time provided far better data for project selection by implementing a systematic Stage-Gate® new-product process. Build two stages of homework into your process prior to the beginning of development:

- the scoping stage, which entails a preliminary market, technical, and business assessment;
- building the business case, which involves much more detailed market research (a user-needs-and-wants study, competitive analysis, concept tests) along with technical and manufacturing assessments.

An effective new-product process also means effective gates. In best-practice businesses, this translates into a menu of specified deliverables for each gate; visible 'go/kill' and prioritisation criteria at the gates (many companies use scorecards to rate projects at gate meetings); defined gatekeepers per gate; clear gate outputs, and even 'rules of engagement' for the gatekeeping or leadership team of the business.

CONCLUSION

Portfolio management is fundamental to new-product success. But it's not as easy as it first seems. Not only must you seek to maximise the value of your portfolio, but the development projects in your portfolio must be appropriately balanced; there must be the right number of projects and, finally, the portfolio must be strategically aligned. No one model can deliver on all four goals, and so best-practice businesses tend to use multiple methods to select their projects.

THE BEST SOURCES OF HELP
Books:
Aaker, David A. *Brand Portfolio Strategy: Creating Relevance, Differentiation, Energy, Leverage and Clarity.* New York: Simon & Schuster, 2004.
Cooper, R.G., S.J. Edgett, and E.J. Kleinschmidt. *Portfolio Management for New Products.* 2nd ed. Cambridge, Massachusetts: Perseus, 2002.
Cooper, R.G. *Winning at New Products: Accelerating the Process from Idea to Launch.* 3rd ed. Cambridge, Massachusetts: Perseus, 2001.
Cooper, R.G., and S.J. Edgett. *Lean, Rapid and Profitable New Product Development.* Hamilton, Ontario: Product Development Institute, 2005.

Website:
www.prod-dev.com: this is the official website of the widely used *Stage-Gate* Process Model developed by Robert G. Cooper.

From Crisis Management to Crisis Leadership
by Ian Mitroff

EXECUTIVE SUMMARY
- Over 20 years ago, the Tylenol poisonings prompted the field of crisis management. Although much has been learned since, many organisations still have not adopted pro-active crisis-leadership programmes.
- Until organisations do so, they will be crisis prone, susceptible to an ever-growing number of crises.

INTRODUCTION

Crisis management is no longer sufficient to respond to the crises today's organisations face. The difference between crisis management and crisis leadership is directional: crisis management is largely reactive, responding to crises after they have occurred. In contrast, crisis leadership is pro-active, seeking to plan as carefully as possible before crises occur. Crisis management tends to consider individual crises in isolation, while crisis leadership considers the big picture – how individual crises interact.

Unless your organisation takes a position of crisis leadership, you cannot respond properly when a crisis hits. Among the more important steps you can take now is anticipating the broadest possible range of potential crises. If your focus becomes too narrow you won't be able to respond appropriately when crises hit – and they will. If you aren't prepared to handle a crisis before it occurs, you won't be able to respond effectively when it arrives.

WHY EVERY ORGANISATION NEEDS TO HAVE A CRISIS PORTFOLIO

Research demonstrates that crises fall into general categories or families (see table opposite). Within each general family, the specific crises share strong similarities. On the other hand, there are sharp differences between the general categories, families, or types of major crises.

The table leads us to a number of key lessons that crisis-prepared organisations have learned.

Lesson 1: Prepare for at least one crisis in each of the families

Research has demonstrated unequivocally how the best organisations plan and prepare for major crises. Most organisations consider only one or two crisis families, for example, natural disasters such as fires or earthquakes. This is undoubtedly a major focus because natural disasters not only occur with great regularity, but they're equally likely to strike all organisations. There's no blame associated with them as there is with other types of disaster, for example, workplace violence. Nonetheless, even earthquakes can attract some degree of human blame: humans are still charged with the responsibility of designing appropriate buildings that will withstand their worst effects and with designing appropriate recovery efforts for the survivors.

Lesson 2: It isn't sufficient to prepare only for industry-specific crises

When organisations do broaden their preparations to cover crises other than natural disasters, more often than not it's to cover core or normal disasters specific to their industry. For instance, you rarely have to prod chemical companies to prepare for explosions and fires, which can easily arise from their day-to-day operating experience. No one has to prod fast-food companies to prepare for food contamination and poisoning, since such incidents are an ever-present threat in businesses that handle food. This kind of anticipation, while necessary, is too specific to count as complete preparation.

Lesson 3: Prepare for the simultaneous occurrence of multiple crises

Major crises occur not only because of what an organisation knows, anticipates, and plans for, but because of what it does not know and does not anticipate. Even if you've prepared for a particular type or form of crisis, major crises will still occur, because new environmental factors are constantly emerging to give a new wrinkle to old forms. It's not only the crises that you've planned and prepared for that constitute a threat – crises you've never even thought about may be even more serious.

Lesson 4: The purpose of definitions is to guide, not predict

It isn't possible to give a precise definition of a crisis, because it isn't possible to predict with exact certainty how a crisis will occur, when, and why. Nonetheless, as a guiding definition, a crisis is any adverse event that affects or has the potential to affect the *whole* of an organisation. If something affects only a small, isolated part of an organisation, it may not be a major crisis. In order for a problem to be judged a crisis, it must exact a major toll on human lives, property, financial earnings, the reputation, and the general health and well-being of an organisation. Most often, all of these suffer damage simultaneously. A major crisis is something that *cannot be completely contained within the walls of an organisation*. For example, a single rogue trader has the potential to destroy an entire organisation.

Lesson 5: Every type of crisis can happen to every organisation

Every organisation needs to plan for the occurrence of at least one crisis in each family, because each type

MAJOR CRISIS TYPES/RISKS						
Economic	Informational	Physical (loss of key plant and facilities)	Human resources	Reputation	Psychopathic acts	Natural disasters
Labour strikes	Loss of proprietary and confidential information	Loss of key equipment, plant, and material supplies	Loss of key executives	Slander, gossip	Product tampering	Earthquakes
Labour unrest	False information	Breakdown of key equipment, plant, etc.	Loss of key personnel	Sick jokes	Kidnapping	Fires
Labour shortage	Tampering with computer records	Loss of key facilities	Rise in absenteeism	Rumours	Hostage-taking	Floods
Major decline in stock price and price fluctuations	Loss of key computer information with regard to customers, suppliers, etc.	Major plant disruptions	Rise in vandalism and accidents	Damage to corporate reputation	Terrorism	Explosions
Market crash	Y2K	Workplace violence	Tampering with corporate logos	Workplace violence		Typhoons
Decline in major earnings						Hurricanes

Source: Pauchant and Mitroff (1992)

could actually happen. Furthermore, you must consider all the types broadly and not literally. Consider, for instance, product tampering, which can impact a company in multiple ways.

Lesson 6: No type of crisis should be taken literally

Product tampering doesn't apply only to food or to pharmaceutical companies. Any organisation can be the victim of some form of product tampering. Computers, for example, are integral to every organisation, yet the true value of computers is not the cost of the hardware or software: it's the information they contain regarding customers and other key stakeholders. If someone were to gain access and tamper with these records, the company's products and services could be seriously affected. Consider the French publisher Larousse. The French are avid eaters of mushrooms; at times they search the forests with Larousse encyclopedias. One article in the encyclopedia has two facing pages of illustrations, one showing mushrooms that are safe to eat, the other those that are unsafe. Once, the labels on the two pages were reversed. The moral is clear: you ignore any or all of the types of major crisis at your peril.

Lesson 7: Tampering is the most generic form or type of all crises

Tampering – significantly altering the properties of information or of an object, person, product, etc. – is the most

important crisis type. Tampering essentially converts properties that are acceptable and safe into properties that are unacceptable or dangerous; in this broad sense every crisis listed in Table 1 can be viewed as a form of tampering. Tampering thus threatens everything connected with an organisation.

Lesson 8: No crisis ever happens in the precise way you plan for it, so it's not simply crisis planning that's important, it's thinking about the unthinkable

Fortunately you don't have to prepare for every specific type of crisis within each of the families. If this were required, then crisis leadership would be overwhelming. It's acceptable to limit your preparations to one or more types of crisis within each of the families. Why? If a crisis seldom happens exactly according to plan, then the critical thing is doing your best to think about the unthinkable. This exercise makes you better able to think on your feet when a crisis does hit, and hence to recover faster without being paralysed. If the specific types of crises within a particular family share strong similarities, then giving serious consideration to each of the families is the most helpful kind of preparation. It's still important to prepare for a broader and wider range of crises, although to start on the difficult road of crisis leadership it's not necessary to prepare for everything simultaneously. In fact, trying to prepare at once for every eventuality might well lead you to conclude that the task is overwhelming and hopeless – it's not.

Lesson 9: Every crisis is capable of being both the cause and the effect of any other crisis

The best organisations don't prepare for a single crisis, they attempt to prepare for the simultaneous occurrence of multiple crises. Organisations that are well prepared study past crises, looking for patterns and interconnections. They generate visual maps to understand better how crises unfold over time and how they are interrelated. In today's world, no individual crisis ever happens in isolation and independently of any other crisis. You need to consider the potential impact of every crisis in your organisation's crisis portfolio on every other crisis.

Lesson 10: Crisis leadership is systemic

Like total quality management or environmentalism, if crisis leadership is not undertaken systemically, then it is basically not being done, let alone being done well.

MAKING IT HAPPEN

- Assemble and train a cross-functional, cross-divisional crisis team.
- Poll individual members of the team with regard to the crises they can envision because of their distinct vantage points.

- Produce at least three or four general maps or big pictures showing how each of the individual crises that the various team members envision might interact so as to set off a chain reaction.
- Referring to the overall maps, determine what pieces of data can be used as early warning signals to announce the beginning stages of each individual crisis and indicate the likelihood that it will set off a chain reaction of other crises.

THE BEST SOURCES OF HELP

Book:

Mitroff, Ian I., et al. *Why Some Companies Recover Faster and Better from Crises: Seven Essential Lessons for Avoiding Disaster*. New York: AMACOM, 2005.

Websites:

Center for Global Education: **www.globaled.us**
Comprehensive Crisis Management site: **www.compcrisis.com**

The Balanced Scorecard
by Robert S. Kaplan and David P. Norton

EXECUTIVE SUMMARY

- The balanced scorecard is a powerful framework for aligning strategic objectives, management systems, and corporate performance, resulting in robust long-term growth and value creation.
- Implementing the balanced scorecard successfully is a function of five core principles: mobilising change through executive leadership; translating strategy into operational terms; aligning the organisation to the strategy; making strategy everyone's everyday job; and making strategy a continual process.
- The balanced scorecard enables organisations to become more adaptive and responsive to the needs of both internal and external constituencies, resulting in greater opportunities for problem solving and innovation.

INTRODUCTION

The balanced scorecard is a performance measurement and management system using objectives and measures in four interrelated perspectives – financial, customer, internal process, and learning and growth. We introduced the balanced scorecard in the early 1990s because we believed that an exclusive reliance on financial measures in a management system would be insufficient for the 21st century. Strategies for creating value had shifted from managing tangible assets to knowledge-based strategies that created and deployed an organisation's intangible assets, including customer relationships, innovative products and services, high-quality operating processes, and the skills, knowledge, and motivation of its workforce.

Organisations such as Mobil North American Marketing and Refining, Cigna Property and Casualty Insurance, Brown and Root Engineering Services, and Chemical (Chase) Bank implemented the balanced scorecard, embedded it into their management systems, and achieved breakthrough performance within two years. Our research has revealed a set of five principles, built around the balanced scorecard system, that enabled these and other organisations to execute their strategies rapidly and effectively.

Principle 1: mobilise change through executive leadership

The single most important condition for success is the ownership and active involvement of the executive team. A balanced scorecard programme starts with the recognition that it is not a 'metrics' project; it's a change project. Initially, executive leaders must *mobilise* the organisation, creating momentum to get the process launched. Once mobilised, leadership focus shifts to *governance* to install the new performance model. Gradually a new management system evolves – a *strategic management system* that institutionalises the new cultural values and processes into a new system for managing. Convergence to the new management system can take two to three years.

Principle 2: translate the strategy into operational terms

The objectives and measures on a balanced scorecard help executive teams to better understand and articulate their strategies. The scorecard provides a framework for organising strategic objectives into four perspectives:

1. *Financial* – the strategy for growth, profitability, and risk, viewed from the perspective of the shareholder.
2. *Customer* – the strategy for creating value and differentiation from the perspective of the customer.
3. *Internal business processes* – the strategic priorities for various business processes that create customer and shareholder satisfaction.
4. *Learning and growth* – the priorities to create a climate that supports organisational change, innovation, and growth.

From work done with an initial set of implementers, we developed a strategy map to provide a graphical representation of a well-constructed balanced scorecard. A strategy map, a logical and comprehensive architecture for describing strategy, specifies the critical elements and their linkages for an organisation's strategy. It creates a common and understandable point of reference for all organisation units and their employees.

Organisations build strategy maps from the top down, starting with the destination and then charting the routes that lead there. Corporate executives first review their mission statement (why their company exists) and core values (what their company believes in). From that information, they develop their strategic vision (what their company wants to become). This vision creates a clear picture of the company's overall goal.

Once the strategy map has been defined and agreed to by the executive team, the design of a scorecard with measures and targets is a straightforward process. The strategy map approach illustrates the idea that balanced scorecards should not just be collections of financial and non-financial measures organised into four perspectives. Balanced scorecards should reflect the strategy of the organisation. A good test is whether you can understand the strategy by looking only at the scorecard and its strategy map.

Principle 3: align the organisation to the strategy

The balanced scorecard is a powerful tool to describe a business unit's strategy. But organisations consist of numerous sectors, business units, and specialised departments, each with its own operations and often its own strategy. For synergy to occur across these diverse units, the strategies across these units need to be co-ordinated. The balanced scorecard helps to define the strategic linkages that integrate the performance of multiple organisations. Each unit formulates a strategy appropriate for its target market in light of the specific circumstances it faces – competitors, market opportunities, and critical processes – but that is consistent with the themes and priorities of the corporation or division. The measures at the individual business unit levels do not have to add to a corporate or divisional measure, unlike financial measures that aggregate easily from sub-units to departments to higher organisational levels. The business unit managers choose local measures that *influence,* but are not necessarily identical to, the corporate scorecard measures.

Beyond aligning the business units, strategy-focused organisations must also align their staff functions and shared-service units, such as human resources, information technology, purchasing, environmental, and finance. Often this alignment is accomplished with a service agreement between each functional department and the business units. The service agreement defines the menu of services to be provided, including their functionality, quality level and cost.

When this process is complete, all the organisational units – line business units and staff functions – have well-defined strategies that are articulated and measured by balanced scorecards and strategy maps. This alignment allows corporate-level synergies to emerge, in which the whole exceeds the sum of the individual parts.

Linkages can also be established across corporate boundaries to define relationships with key suppliers, customers, outsourcing vendors and joint ventures. Companies use such scorecards with external parties to be explicit about (1) the objectives of the relationship and (2) how to measure the contribution and performance of each party to the relationship in ways other than just price or cost.

Principle 4: make strategy everyone's everyday job

The CEOs and senior leadership teams of organisations that adopted the balanced scorecard understood that they could not implement the new strategy by themselves. They wanted contributions – actions and ideas – from everyone in the organisation. This is not top-down *direction*. This is top-down *communication* and bottom-up *implementation*. Three processes are required.

- **Use communication and education to create awareness.** A prerequisite for implementing strategy is that all employees understand the strategy. A consistent and continuing communication programme is the foundation for organisational alignment.
- **Align personal objectives with the strategy.** Companies challenge individuals and departments at lower levels to develop their own objectives in light of the broader priorities; in

some cases, personal scorecards are used to set *personal objectives*.

• **Link compensation to the scorecard.** To modify behaviour as required by the strategy and as defined in the scorecard, change *must* be reinforced through incentive compensation. When the incentive compensation programme becomes linked to the balanced scorecard, interest in the details of the strategy increases.

Principle 5: make strategy a continual process

Companies adopt a new 'double-loop process' to manage strategy. The first step *links strategy to the budgeting process*. Managers use the balanced scorecard as a screen to evaluate potential investments and initiatives that will develop entirely new capabilities, reach new customers and markets, and make radical improvements in existing processes and capabilities. This distinction is essential. Just as the balanced scorecard attempts to protect long-term objectives from being diluted to suit short-term needs, the budgeting process must protect the long-term initiatives from the pressures to deliver short-term financial performance.

The second step introduces a *simple management meeting* to review strategy. As obvious as this step sounds, such meetings didn't exist in the past. Now management meetings are planned on a monthly or quarterly basis to discuss the balanced scorecard, so that a broad spectrum of managers comes together to monitor organisational performance against the short-term targets for the scorecard's financial and non-financial measures. This process creates a focus on the strategy that did not exist before.

Information feedback systems change to support the new management meetings. Many organisations create an *open reporting* environment, in which performance results are made available to everyone in the organisation. Building upon the principle that 'strategy is everyone's job', they empower 'everyone' by giving them the knowledge needed to do their jobs.

Finally, a *process for learning and adapting the strategy* evolves. As the scorecard is put into action and feedback systems begin their reporting on actual results, the organisation tests the hypotheses underlying its strategy, to see whether the strategy is delivering the expected results.

A new kind of energy is created. People use terms like 'fun' and 'exciting' to describe the management meetings. One senior executive reported that the meetings became so popular, there was standing room only . . . he could have sold tickets to them.

Companies also use the meetings to search for new strategic opportunities that aren't currently on their scorecard. New challenges arise externally, and ideas and learning emerge internally from within the organisation. Rather than waiting for next year's budget cycle, the priorities and the scorecards are updated immediately. Much like a navigator guiding a vessel on a long-term journey, constantly sensing the shifting winds and currents and constantly adapting the course, the executives of successful companies use the ideas and learning generated by their organisation to fine-tune their strategies. Instead of being an annual event, strategy formulation, testing, and revision became a continual process.

CONCLUSION

The balanced scorecard enables organisations to introduce a new governance and review process – one focused on strategy, not tactics. The new governance process emphasises learning, team problem-solving, and coaching. Review meetings look into the future – exploring how to implement strategy more effectively, and identifying the changes to be made to the strategy – based on what has been learned from the past.

This is a management process attuned to the needs of contemporary businesses. The essential ingredient is a simple framework – the balanced scorecard and its representation on a strategy map – that allows strategy to be clearly articulated. The balanced scorecard becomes the heart of the management system that strategy-focused organisations will use to build their future.

THE BEST SOURCES OF HELP

Books:
Kaplan, Robert, and David Norton. *The Balanced Scorecard: Translating Strategy into Action*. Cambridge, Massachusetts: Harvard Business School Press, 1996.

Kaplan, Robert, and David Norton. *The Strategy-focused Organisation: How Balanced Scorecard Companies Thrive in the New Business Environment*. Cambridge, Massachusetts: Harvard Business School Press, 2000.

Journal article:
Kaplan, Robert, and David Norton. 'Having trouble with your strategy? Then map it'. *Harvard Business Review* (September–October 2000).

Website:
The Palladium Group:
www.thepalladiumgroup.com

Setting Objectives for a Business by Allan A. Kennedy

EXECUTIVE SUMMARY

- Managing inherently involves setting a goal or objective and then executing a series of actions to meet it. Establishing the right objective is critical to successful management of any business.
- Successful long-term businesses almost always started with a set of non-financial objectives (sometimes referred to as a vision or mission) and derived financial objectives consistent with pursuit of their broader goals.
- Setting only financial objectives is risky for a business because single-minded pursuit of financial objectives can lead to actions that undermine long-term viability.

INTRODUCTION

Managing is the task of moving an enterprise towards a defined objective. Most of the disciplines of management – budgeting, strategic planning, performance monitoring – take as a given that an appropriate objective has been set. Given the central role that objectives or targets play in most management actions, it is critical that they be set correctly. It may seem trite to point out, but it is none the less valid: if inappropriate objectives are set for a business, inappropriate outcomes will occur.

What constitutes appropriate objectives for a business? As business and management have evolved, thinking about what constitutes an appropriate objective has evolved as well. Throughout this evolution, there has been an ongoing tension between financial goals and objectives and non-financial objectives. If business exists primarily or solely to make a profit (a highly quantifiable outcome) then relatively simple financial objectives suffice, argue some. Others say that business exists to serve simultaneously the needs of various constituencies – shareholders, customers, suppliers, employees, communities. The interests of these various legitimate constituencies are not always quantifiable, leading to a school of thought that puts greater emphasis on non-financial objectives. The history of business would suggest that both types of objectives are important.

A BRIEF HISTORY OF BUSINESS OBJECTIVES

Most businesses that were launched in the 19th century began their life as some form of family enterprise. As family businesses, their objectives were quite clear: to provide an ongoing source of income and, where necessary, employment for current and future members of the family.

As the technology of management has evolved, ideas about what constitutes the right objective for a business have changed. In his book *Concept of the Corporation*, first published in 1946, Peter Drucker described the purpose of a corporation as generating the maximum profit achievable from its operations. He went on to comment on the potential conflict between this purpose and society's expectation that the job of business was to maximise the production of cheap goods and services for consumption. To a modern observer, Drucker's thinking seems simplistic.

Drucker based his comments on work he had done with General Motors (GM), then the largest industrial enterprise in the world. The people he worked with in GM were convinced he got it wrong. To set the record straight, the legendary leader of General Motors from 1923 until 1946, Alfred Sloan Jr, wrote his own account of the GM system of management, which he called *My Years with General Motors*. In that book, Sloan described a high-level task force effort he led in 1920 to define the concept of GM's business. He articulated a purpose for GM's business quite different from Drucker's version. 'We made the assumption . . . that the first purpose in . . . establishment of a business [is that it] will pay *satisfactory* dividends and *preserve* and *increase* its capital value' [emphasis added].

As a reflection of Sloan's influence in the business world, in the 1950s and 1960s most businesses sought to operate with a conservative balance sheet while showing steady signs of growth in sales, assets, profits, dividends, and shareholder equity.

During the 1950s and 1960s, new types of companies emerged on the business landscape. These companies were young, entrepreneurial, and managed by hands-on practitioners, each in his own fashion on a mission. This new breed included the likes of Hewlett-Packard, a company set up to make useful technical contributions in a variety of engineering markets. It also included companies like Wal-Mart, whose driving rationale was providing superior value to its customers.

All of these new companies were in business to make a profit, both as a return to their investors and as a measure of the value of what they were doing as a company. These financial objectives were, however, secondary to their broader institutional objectives. Because many of these new companies grew very rapidly and became, relatively speaking, darlings of the stock market, many established companies modified their traditional objectives to focus on achieving specified levels of growth in revenues and profits in an attempt to keep pace.

In the late 1970s, a new theory about appropriate objectives for business was developed by academics specialising in the complex area of accounting. Their theory held that since shareholders owned companies, the real objective of business should be maximising shareholder value. They went on to point out that conventional accounting measures of profitability, such as earnings per share of public companies, were very poor proxies indeed for the true value of a company. Instead they urged business people to focus on the present value of future cash-flow streams as a truer measure of value. Most managers ignored this advice for all practical purposes, but some specialised investment bankers, who came to be known as 'corporate raiders' or 'leveraged buyout bankers', took the insights of the academics very seriously.

The immediate result was an unprecedented wave of corporate takeovers during the 1980s. The longer-term result was a fundamental rethinking of what business was all about by most managers, as they adopted share-holder-value thinking as a means of defending them-selves from the corporate raiders.

Throughout the 1990s and into the 2000s, maximising shareholder value was the driving purpose of most busi-nesses, and managers did virtually anything they could to ensure that their stock price – the most direct proxy for shareholder value – rose steadily. This continued during the 2000s, when the emphasis on maximising shareholder returns – notably in the financial services sector but also other businesses such as retail, technol-ogy and manufacturing – continued unabated.

LIMITATIONS OF RELYING SOLELY ON FINANCIAL OBJECTIVES

The stock market boom of the early 2000s seemed to prove that focusing on shareholder value was the right way to run a business. But the boom of the 2000s gave way to the economic slow-down and stock market cor-rections that began in 2008. With the change in the busi-ness climate, the problems associated with over-reliance on maximising shareholder value became apparent. With an exclusive focus on rewarding shareholders, many companies simply failed to take care of the legitimate needs of the other constituencies they depended on to provide them with a profitable future.

THE STAYING POWER OF NON-FINANCIAL OBJECTIVES

Why do some companies seem to thrive over a very long period of time, while others have a brief moment in the sun and then recede into obscurity? There are a number of factors that account for this long-term pattern of suc-cess, including leadership, the quality of management, and the dynamics of the markets they serve. James Collins and Jerry Porras in their landmark book, *Built to Last*, suggest there is one common element. Companies that thrive for a long time all have a non-financial vision of what they are in business to accomplish. The 3M com-pany exists to create useful products through innovation. Boeing exists to be at the leading edge of the aeronautics field. Marriott has a mission to make its customers feel as if they have a home away from home. Johnson & Johnson exists to help alleviate pain and suffering. All of these companies, and the others cited by Collins and Porras, also work hard to make a profit and return value to their shareholders. However, producing profits and generating value for their shareholders was a by-product of the broader objectives each of these companies sought to pursue.

Why this should be so is actually quite simple. Most people who work for companies need a broader goal than purely a financial one to motivate them to perform at their best. The companies profiled by Collins and Porras provided their people with just such a broader mission, treated them as full partners in the pursuit of this broader goal, and as a result realised higher levels of commitment and motivation from them. The companies reward this higher level of commitment and loyalty with policies appropriate to maintaining an ongoing partnership. To be viable and successful, every business must set and work hard to achieve a series of financial goals and objectives. But having financial objectives alone will not produce superior performance over the long term.

MAKING IT HAPPEN

How can a manager at any level of business decide whether or not the objectives set for the business are sound? There are no firm rules to rely on, but there are some commonsense tests any manager can apply to determine whether the objectives set are:

- Compelling – capable of getting someone's attention
- Motivating – likely to inspire someone to put in extra effort
- Consistent – able to be met without compromise
- Achievable – reachable with reasonable levels of effort and commitment
- Distinguishing – something that when achieved will set the company or business apart from others
- Competitively superior – difficult enough to attain so that the achievement will produce superior rewards from the markets served and the investing public
- Satisfying – of such a nature that the achievement of the objective will produce a personal sense of satisfaction among those who contributed
- Lasting – likely to pass the test of time

Tests like these are applicable to financial as well as non-financial objectives.

CONCLUSION

Making a profit and delivering value to shareholders is motivating indeed for anyone engaged in business. However, it is simply not a sufficient motivator to pro-duce the kind of extra effort over a long period of time that produces superior long-term performance.

THE BEST SOURCES OF HELP

Books:

Collins, James C., and Jerry I. Porras. *Built to Last: Successful Habits of Visionary Companies*. London: Random House Business Books, 2005.

Davidson, Bill. *Breakthrough: How Great Companies Set. Outrageous Objectives – and Achieve Them*. Chichester: Wiley, 2003.

Drucker, Peter. *Concept of the Corporation*. Reprint. Somerset, New Jersey: Transaction Publishers, 2001.

Roberts, John. *The Modern Firm: Organisational Design for Performance and Growth*. Rev. ed. Oxford: Oxford University Press, 2007.

Profiting from Prices by Michael de Kare-Silver

EXECUTIVE SUMMARY

- In an attempt to boost profits, many companies have tried to reduce costs through re-engineering, outsourcing, downsizing, etc.
- Companies are becoming aware of the opportunity and potential of the top line (as opposed to the bottom line).
- Pricing is an undiscovered weapon in the search for higher revenues.

INTRODUCTION

In recent years many companies have not found it easy to increase revenues. Economic conditions, government policies against inflation, increased competition on pricing (including producers from less-developed countries), and globally more sophisticated customers have all put pressure on volume and price in many industries. Not surprisingly, companies have turned to levers more directly in their control – such as reducing costs and better process management – as sources of profit growth. Hence the fads and focuses on re-engineering, downsizing, outsourcing, etc.

But those cost/process levers can only go so far in boosting profits. As their markets strive for growth, companies are increasingly challenging revenue performance and realising that the top line has not received the same close examination and insight as the bottom line in recent times. There is a growing awakening to the fact that more opportunity and potential may lie on the top line.

What can be realistically achieved? Is the search for higher revenues a futile battle against macro-economic forces and competitive pressures? Analysis shows the contrary. Pricing, especially, is an undiscovered weapon. There is significant profit potential for companies in challenging this area, and in 're-engineering' their price position.

OPPORTUNITIES IN PRICING

Choosing the best pricing strategy is always challenging and vitally important – and never more than during an economic slowdown. Looking at pricing is, in principle, much more attractive than downsizing. There are no severance costs, no people/organisation issues, no impact next Monday morning: a quick win flows straight through to the bottom line.

In any event, opportunities to improve profitability principally through cost and process management may have peaked for the time being. Many re-engineering projects have disappointed. Research among UK and US companies shows that:

- no more than two in 10 companies achieve breakthrough improvements in performance
- less than 30 per cent claim to be satisfied with either the change process itself or the results

ROUTES TO EFFECTIVE PRICING

The more you know about which products make money and which lose, the more you can adopt a better strategic and selective pricing policy. Three main routes can be identified that lead to more effective pricing:

- exploiting market advantages
- changing the decision-making process on pricing
- testing whether all the different pricing options are being proactively pursued

Of course, some companies enjoy market or structural circumstances that make pricing management easier. Have they just fallen by luck into those situations, or have their advantages been 'engineered' more deliberately? Some companies have used strategic alliances to create market and structural barriers deliberately – by locking up a vital supply of raw materials, say, and making it hard for others to function. Procter & Gamble thus used an alliance to tie up the Japanese supplier of scarce polyacrylate material. As a result, it was able to block competitors and recover market leadership.

Even without market or structural advantage, significant untapped pricing potential exists. How can this be exploited? Many factors are *prima facie* within executive control, and can be changed to enable more effective pricing management. For example, internal structures could be adjusted to facilitate more effective pricing. Several roadblocks operate within the organisation – such as:

- responsibility for pricing is left to the sales department. (Who has ever met a salesman who wanted to increase prices?)
- there is little or no finance department involvement to balance decision-making
- senior management's remoteness from the detailed market circumstances makes it difficult to challenge sales views
- no systems/mechanisms are available to easily assess more aggressive pricing opportunities
- data on the true net profitability of individual services/products to either company or customer is limited

Indeed, not only could companies make structural moves that are more easily within their control; research shows that as many as 12 different pricing strategies are available. They often appear to be underexploited. The challenge is frequently not lack of familiarity with the particular pricing option. It is more about:

- having enough management time to check whether the particular pricing options have been fully considered
- understanding the pricing relationship to competitors and what drives it
- examining price opportunities and developing insights on an *individual* product line basis, rather than across a range
- management's ability to challenge sales-led pricing decisions
- the effectiveness and rigour with which the pricing strategies are implemented
- the information base and systems needed to do all this

PRICING STRATEGIES

Many of the 12 different pricing strategy options are geared to medium/long-term profit-building; few can have immediate effect. The pricing options that follow are relatively simple illustrations to highlight sources of pricing opportunity.

Pricing strategies fall into three main groups:

- customer information management
- exploiting structural advantages
- innovation and leadership

CUSTOMER INFORMATION MANAGEMENT

There are four approaches to consider:

1. **category segmentation**: use detailed product-line profitability and pricing to achieve analysis and insight, developed separately for *each* product line.
2. **customer segmentation**: use detailed customer segmentation to identify pricing opportunities.
3. **bundling**: in medical products, as core product/service prices have come under pressure, companies have added related products and services where pricing is more robust (and which equally reinforce the core product/service value proposition). Similarly, some leading Internet software suppliers provide free access software but charge for use of related products and services.
4. **trade terms management**: manage the level of discounts given to customers to get a better return.

EXPLOITING STRUCTURAL ADVANTAGES

Four options are highlighted here:

1. **lowest cost/lowest price**: cost advantages enable invaders to price lower and grow share rapidly.
2. **supply and demand management**: as an illustration, better hotel occupancy/yield management systems have enabled leaders to quote more aggressive room tariffs.
3. **supplier–customer 'balance of power'**: this can be exploited to ensure that suppliers 'contribute' to gross margin success. Tough management of the supply price provides greater flexibility in end-consumer pricing.
4. **'open-book' and partnership-pricing**: the open-book approach was pioneered in the automotive industry. Sharing information about costs has enabled better suppliers to justify and push through selective price increases.

INNOVATION AND LEADERSHIP

This area offers two zones of higher comfort:

1. **branding**: consistent high levels of branding and advertising enable a company to maintain a price premium.
2. **total value proposition**: where five strategies can be singled out:
   - *technology-driven*: continuous development of niche, technically advanced products can give strong gross margin advantages.
   - *first in*: continual focus on being first to market gives initial pricing advantages, as well as other benefits.
   - *best at*: leadership on all features valued by the customer can give price leadership in both 'value pricing' of certain products and 'premium pricing' for certain others.
   - *share leadership*: restructuring the product portfolio to focus only on market-share leaders where you have more control over pricing and other levers.
   - *innovative consumer value*: provide a clear mixing of quality, value, and service to lead in the eyes of the customer.

There are at least a couple of shorter-term options, too:

1. **price squeeze**: in one turnaround, the new CEO insisted that each product-line price be 'squeezed' up 1 per cent. Despite initial internal resistance, this was successfully implemented, immediately impacting the bottom line.
2. **price elasticity**: is the price/volume equation effectively analysed and balanced? For example, low-margin products can be priced up relatively aggressively with less impact on contribution from any volume lost.

Research shows that many of these pricing strategies are in fact applicable in most industries and most company situations, but that surprisingly few are being proactively investigated and implemented.

USING PRICING OPPORTUNITIES

How can a company check whether it is fully utilising its pricing opportunities? This initial checklist looks first internally – for example, at the priority that pricing decision-making has in the organisation:

1. What percentage of senior management time is spent on pricing?
2. How much senior management time is spent with customers?
3. Is there an information base in place which tracks pricing for each product line and its relationship with volume?
4. Is competitor pricing tracked in similar detail?
5. How frequently is pricing specifically and rigorously reviewed?
6. Is the company organised in a way that ensures that a 'balanced' pricing decision is made?

The other questions are directed at the external market potential:

1. Are competitors' future pricing strategies and plans understood?
2. Is there a clear understanding and alignment between what the company sees as added value, compared to what the customer sees?
3. Does the company have a clear pricing strategy differentiated for the circumstances and market position of each product group and each customer?

As global competition intensifies to the end of this decade and beyond, close attention to the detail, the 'micro-management', will become increasingly important. 'Discovering' pricing and systematising and institutionalising its proactive exploitation in the business will become a key distinguishing factor among the more successful corporations.

MAKING IT HAPPEN

- When seeking to boost financial performance, look at pricing possibilities before cutbacks in costs.
- Investigate three main routes: (1) exploiting market advantages; (2) improved decision-making process; (3) pursuing all pricing options proactively.
- Share responsibility for pricing between sales, finance, and a fully informed senior management.
- Develop high-quality data on true net profitability of individual services/products to both the company and the customer.
- Look for price opportunities on an individual product-line basis, rather than across a range.
- Seek superior strategies by: (1) managing customer information; (2) exploiting structural advantages; (3) innovation and leadership.

CONCLUSION

Price decisions are too often made by too few people. Only by sharing the responsibility for pricing can man-agers begin to understand the importance that pricing can have on the success of any business. Ultimately, decisions on pricing must be measured against other critical factors, such as data on customers. In the final analysis, pricing can be an exercise in both innovation and leadership.

THE BEST SOURCES OF HELP

Books:

Baker, Ronald J. *Pricing on Purpose: Creating and Capturing Value*. Chichester: Wiley, 2006.

Cram, Tony. *Smarter Pricing: How to Capture More Value in Your Market*. Harlow: Financial Times/Prentice Hall, 2005.

Dolan, Robert J., and Hermann Simon. *Power Pricing: How Managing Price Transforms the Bottom Line*. New York: Free Press, 1996.

Nagle, Thomas T., and Reed K. Holden. *The Strategy and Tactics of Pricing: A Guide to Profitable Decision Making*. 4th ed. London: Pearson, 2005.

Actionlists

Finding Your Dream Job

GETTING STARTED

Do you wake up in the morning full of excitement and enthusiasm about your day? Or do you dread going to work? If your job is sapping the life out of you, then it is time to reassess your life and your work. If you feel like an old dream is stirring and just won't go away, you need to discover and pursue your calling. The following questions provide thoughts for reflection as you start to mull this over:

- What keeps you in your current job, even though you are unhappy?
- What skills and talents are unused?
- What dreams have you buried because they weren't 'practical'?
- What would a 'dream job' look like to you?
- What are you willing to sacrifice in order to have a dream job?

FAQS

Isn't work supposed to be painful? Isn't that why they call it work?

No, work is not supposed to be painful, even in these challenging times. If you believe that, then you will settle for less and never be completely satisfied. Work is as natural to human beings as breathing. We feel bored, dissatisfied, and empty if we cannot contribute to the world in some meaningful way.

I'm just getting started in my career. Don't I have to serve my time first before I can find work I really enjoy?

Certainly you shouldn't expect to jump into the job of your dreams straight out of university. Unless, of course, you started the company! You do need to spend time in a new job learning the ropes and making connections. But don't ever think of it as 'serving my time'. This kind of thinking encourages staying in a job that may not really suit you. You should expect to be excited about going to work each day.

I'm getting near retirement. Isn't it a little late to be thinking about finding my calling?

Many people who are nearing retirement grew up in a culture where work was expected to be a drudge. You may have sacrificed your dreams for most of your life, but now is your chance to take the time to do something you really love. You might consider volunteer work, being a mentor to someone getting started, or finding a company that really appreciates the wisdom of older people.

MAKING IT HAPPEN

Assessment

Begin by assessing your skills and talents. Make a list of all the things you have been good at in your life. On this same piece of paper, make three columns. The first one is labelled 'Current Job'. In this column put a tick next to all the skills and talents you are currently using. The second column is labelled 'Joy and Meaning'. Here put a tick next to any skill that brings you joy and a sense of meaning when you are using it. This includes skills that you may not currently be using in your job. The third column is labelled 'Dream Job'. In this column put a tick next to any skills that you would like to use in a 'dream job'. As you are doing this exercise, you may think of other skills and you can add them to the list. After completing the ticks, make some notes for yourself about any thoughts and ideas that came up about what a dream job might be.

Be of service

Focus on the principle of service. All vocational callings have a strong element of service in them. Whom do you serve? How can you use your gifts and talents to serve them? What issues in the community, in business, or in society do you care about? Have you ever wished you could make a difference? These are clues to your calling.

Do what you love

In order to be of service to others, we first have to do what we love. So do what pleases you, and you will probably find that you are acquiring knowledge and skills that will help you to be of service to others in the future. And sometimes it is enough just to know that if you do what brings you satisfaction, even if it is not of service to anyone else, the world is a better place.

Make it real

Make your dream real in some concrete way. Write down a description of your dream job. Write in your diary about what 'calls' to you. Tell other people about your dream job. You will find that as you get more and more detailed about what you are looking for, opportunities will 'coincidentally' appear. Make sure you are paying attention to these opportunities.

Talk to others

Don't be afraid to tell others about your calling. The more you tell others about your dreams, the more real they become, and the more likely you are to notice opportunities that will help you fulfil your dreams. Also, by telling others about the job you would love to have, you are increasing the chances of finding someone who has the right piece of information, or the right connection for you.

Learn to fly

Remember the rule of the bumblebee. According to the laws of mathematics and aerodynamics, it is physically impossible for bumblebees to fly. Fortunately, no one ever explained that to a bumblebee. Keep in mind that the most successful business people were frequently told that what they wanted to do was 'impossible'.

Let go

In order to follow your calling, there are always necessary sacrifices that must be made. Before you make the move to another job or to starting your own business, spend some time thinking about what are absolute necessities in your life and work. Is it essential that you have high earnings, or are you willing to earn less money to do work that is more meaningful? Is it essential that you have a steady income, or could you cope with the risk and potential that comes with working for a small start-up organisation? Is it essential that you work with people, or are you content to work alone? What things are absolutely necessary to you in your work, and what can you let go of? Make a list of five things that are necessary and five things that you are willing to let go of.

Look in your own backyard

There's an old song that goes, 'If you can't be with the one you love, love the one you're with'. This can apply to your job too. Many people cannot easily leave their current working situation. The challenge, then, is how to see your current work as your calling. Once again, the principle of 'service' can be very helpful. If you need to stay with your current job, write yourself a brief reminder about how the work you do is of service to others, and keep it somewhere nearby.

COMMON MISTAKES

Many people think that their dream job already exists, and that they just have to look around hard enough until they find it. The truth is that most people who have found their calling have actually created the work that they do. Do not go looking in the classified advertisements for the dream job. You must network, make connections, and tell other people about your dreams.

When you begin to follow your calling, there will always be people who will tell you that you are impractical, unrealistic, idealistic, or selfish. It would be a mistake to listen to them. They are the people who want to tell the bumblebee that it can't fly. Remember that, just because it's never been done before, it doesn't mean that you can't do it.

Beware of a job that is too good to be true, especially if you are being asked to put in your own money or to work for very low amounts at first. Con men understand the hunger that people have for a dream job, and they can play on that. If you are being offered a job that really seems to fit what you are looking for, make sure that you are going to be paid what you are worth.

Sometimes people get too attached to their idea of what a 'perfect job' would look like. Beware of being too picky and of passing up opportunities that could turn out to be even better than the job you are looking for. Keep an open mind, but at the same time don't settle for something that doesn't fit your values, or that doesn't really use your most important skills and talents.

THE BEST SOURCES OF HELP
Book:
Green, Graham. *The Career Change Handbook: How to Find Out What You're Good at and Enjoy – Then Get Someone to Pay You for It*. 4th ed. Oxford: How To Books, 2008.

Creating a Career Plan

GETTING STARTED

When jobs were for life, you decided what line of work you wanted, worked hard, and the career path was pretty much mapped out for you. The working world has changed, and the recent global financial crises are changing it ever more rapidly. Now individuals wanting to maximise their potential will take a much more active part in mapping out their career. Career planning today needs to be a frequent, dynamic process of self-awareness, market and trend analysis, planning, development, and self-marketing.

The good news is that career paths are more flexible. Individuals can choose a spiral one, stepping through different fields or functions. Many employers encourage cross-fertilisation of ideas through diversity in their workforce. They also value the different perspectives offered by those from outside their industry.

As career breaks are more common today, even transitory career paths are possible. These are popular with people who like variety, novelty, or have other worthwhile priorities. If you require periods of employment, interspersed by breaks, be it for study, travel, raising a family, starting a business, or caring for elderly or unwell family members, this option could be for you.

There are, however, still expert career paths for those who want to specialise in a particular field and linear careers for those who enjoy the challenge, responsibility, and status of climbing the hierarchical ladder. Whatever your set of circumstances, think about this: what does your career need to do for *you*?

FAQS

What's the difference between a career plan and a development plan?

Your career plan maps out long-term objectives, your more immediate objectives, and how you want your life and work to fit together. Your development plan maps out the skills and experience gaps for the different steps along the way and how you will address those. In effect, the development plan enables the career plan to work.

How do I find out what jobs I might be suitable for?

If you are naturally outgoing, start your research by talking to people. Make use of your contacts and ask for names and contact details of people who might be able to help with each of the options you're considering. This approach not only increases your network but it also gets you the targeted information you need. It may also put you in touch with contacts who can often open doors for you.

On the other hand, you may prefer to get started with some Internet or library research and save the networking until you feel a little better informed about your possibilities. Neither approach is right nor wrong, but people who use *both* approaches are likely to be the best prepared, most knowledgeable, and 'luckiest' when it comes to opportunities.

Will frequent job moves look bad on my CV?

It depends on what is 'normal' for your market. In IT, for example, regular moves are common. A CV that shows frequent moves is less likely to be frowned on if the skills offered and achievements shown are relevant to the job you're applying for now. If it is clear that in each role you've occupied you've been promoted or selected for specific strengths or skills, then employers will see you as a sought-after individual rather than a job hopper.

MAKING IT HAPPEN

Be self-aware

Review your career so far, asking yourself some key questions. For example, what expertise do you have? What achievements are you proud of? What work have you received praise and recognition for? What were the outcomes of these achievements for your clients, team, or organisation? What flair or talents have you not yet fully used? Do you have areas of untapped potential?

Also think about the skills you've used throughout your career so far and any differences in the way you've worked from job to job. Go through a typical working week writing down on a separate piece of paper or Post-it™ note each skill, strength, or knowledge area that you have used. Do this for each job you've held. You can then cluster your notes, grouping those that fit together and giving each group a title, such as 'Organising', 'Communicating', or 'People skills'. Doing this will identify and organise your transferable skills and help you to be clearer about what you're offering other employers.

Finally, draw other elements into the mix. What does your career need to do for you (and your family)? What do you value in work? What makes a job satisfying? What would you or do you hate in a job? Thinking about these questions will help you to identify your needs and constraints, such as financial obligations or geographical preferences.

Do a market and trend analysis

Next you need to think about the market you're working in and which way that seems to be moving. What do you like about the market you're currently in? What are the trends within the industry? How might these affect your prospects going forward? Think in broad terms about who might have a need for your skills. What goals or problems could you help them with and what else can you offer them?

These are big and wide-ranging questions; so, to help you focus on them, do some research. Use the Internet and your network of friends and colleagues to expand your knowledge of companies and organisations, and of their internal trends and needs. Read all you can in journals and newspapers about the markets you are most interested in and identify relevant professional bodies for information on trends and the market for relevant skills. Libraries and Chambers of Commerce can be good sources of local information. The more questions you ask, the more you will know what other information you need, and research often gets easier as you go along.

Plan ahead

Be clear about how you want your research and planning to fit together. Ask yourself what you'd like your life to be like in three years' time and write down what comes to mind in as much detail as you can. Write in the present tense, as if it has already happened. Then repeat this for one year's time, six months' time, and one month's time. This '3161' plan gives clarity and motivation for the long-term future. It breaks down the bigger picture of your life into an actionable plan that you can start on right now.

A 'reality check' will help you recognise the right opportunity when it arises. Spend time on this when you are job hunting. Divide a page into four quadrants, headed 'Role', 'Organisation', 'Benefits package', and 'Boss'. Now ask yourself what you want from your next career move. Think about the 'ingredients' that make up your ideal role, putting these into the quadrants on your page. Once your criteria are mapped out in this way, you'll have visual aid that will help you to weigh up the opportunities that come your way. When you're invited to interview for a new job, you can use the sheet to come up with strong, targeted questions about the potential role and the organisation.

Develop yourself

You have identified your own skills and your immediate and longer-term goals. Is there a direct match already or will employers see gaps? If they might, specify what those gaps are and prioritise them, working out what you need to learn. Divide each missing skill into bite-sized chunks of learning or experience required.

Next, think about how you learn best. Do you prefer to read books, listen to an expert, try things out yourself, or practise with supervision? Knowing your preferred learning style is important to your planning.

Finally, you have to be sure that you're motivated to do this learning. If you are, go back to your '3161' plan and write in what it will be like to have filled these gaps at the relevant stages. If, on the other hand, you have more to do than you think you'll realistically be motivated to do, your plan is unrealistic and needs to be changed. Don't think, though, that all changes need to be drastic – sometimes a realistic timescale is the only tweak needed to your plan to allow your dream to happen.

Market yourself
Identify the stage you are at and your objectives. Let's look at three examples.

- During the honeymoon period in a new job, your objective is to establish good communication channels with your new colleagues and contacts and build a practical network. Here, then, marketing yourself will focus on attracting the interest of people who will make your work easier.
- Once you feel established in your new role, your objective is to make sure that interesting work is offered to you, so self-marketing in *this* context will focus more on bringing your successes and achievements to light.
- When looking for new roles, your objective is to attract offers that meet your criteria. Your self-marketing now will focus on getting noticed by the right employers.

As we can see, self-marketing is continuous, but it will change in nature depending on where you are in your career and what your ideal next step is. Whatever you're doing, though, think about your 'audience' and what is important to them. You may be offering to solve problems, deliver a product or service, improve quality or develop something new. To grab and maintain their attention, you need to focus on the relevant outcomes of your activities: increased profits, customer satisfaction and retention, or improvements in efficiency.

COMMON MISTAKES
You forget to market yourself
Don't assume that your work alone will get you noticed. Self-marketing is what makes the difference between a good job well done and a good job resulting in a promotion (if that's what you want). If you are looking for a move up the ladder, keep up the momentum and don't wait to market yourself until you need your next role urgently – try to get into the habit of doing it and of raising your profile gradually but consistently.

You have unrealistic ambitions
If you can't be bothered to identify trends and their impact on your market, you'll end up with a career plan that's completely unrealistic. The wealth of information on the Internet in particular means that there's little excuse for remaining ignorant about issues that may affect your future success. Even if you're not online at home, you can use an Internet café or just visit your local library to find out what you need to know. Make it your business to be informed and don't be afraid to ask 'difficult' questions of people in the know.

You don't do anything
A plan works by provoking specific and related actions which together create the desired effect. There's absolutely no point in writing a plan, carrying out the first action, then leaving it to gather dust.

THE BEST SOURCES OF HELP
Website:
TotalJobs.com: **www.totaljobs.com**

Enter an Entirely New Field

GETTING STARTED
It wasn't so long ago that employment stability was the hallmark of emotional maturity and reliability. Changing jobs frequently, even within the scope of a single career path, was generally frowned on, unless the transition was on a clearly upward path. Changing careers entirely was almost unthinkable. The prevailing wisdom was: 'Pick one thing, do it well, and put away your childish notions of further adventures into discovery.'

Now, however, most people are expected to change jobs several times during their working lives, and maybe their career. There are many reasons for this shift. We're healthier and more productive for longer, so we have time to build a body of several types of work, not just one. The marketplace changes so rapidly that many careers are unrecognisable from their forms even five years ago, and some have disappeared altogether. Some people are being forced into career transitions. But most can't resist the siren call of new discoveries and new opportunities to expand the frontiers of their potential.

The following points are key questions to ask yourself while considering whether you should make a career transition:
- What aspects of your current career do you especially enjoy?

- What attracts you to a different career prospect? Can you isolate those elements and find ways to experience them in your current work?
- Where are you in your career life? Do you expect to have enough working years ahead of you to become fully functional in your new career choice?
- Does the time required for education and training reduce your potential for seeing a return on your investment? If so, is there an alternative choice that can give you the same satisfaction without the necessary investment of years of training before you can start?
- Will the career transition be the change that will give you the happiness you seek? Or are there other issues that you must address as well?

FAQS

Is it too late to change career?

This depends on what else you want to do with your life, and what you're willing to sacrifice. It's possible, for instance, to become a lawyer in your late 50s and early 60s, but that would require giving up or postponing the rewards of a leisurely retirement or the benefits of a senior position that you've earned in the years you've already invested in your current career.

What happens if I make the change and discover that I don't like it?

It's possible that you can find a way to return to your previous career. Or perhaps you can take your additional self-awareness and launch yourself into yet a third career. Continue thinking of this process as an ongoing journey.

MAKING IT HAPPEN

Focus on what goes right in the career you have now

Make a list of the elements of your current work that give you satisfaction. Is it the people you work with? The tasks you perform? The way you feel about yourself when you've achieved a goal? The geographical location of your job? The nature of the industry? How your work benefits your customers?

Isolate those things you dislike about your career

Consider the elements about your current work that you don't enjoy. Can you simply remove them or reduce them so that the positive elements are more prominent and you can renew your sense of satisfaction in your work?

Remember your earlier dreams

Think back to those careers you dreamed about when you were young. You probably had some big, idealistic ideas for your future as a child, and you might have abandoned them prematurely in favour of more seemingly practical choices. But perhaps the time to realise your dreams has arrived. Refresh your memory of what those early dreams were and how they made you feel about

yourself when you imagined doing your dream work. Now that you're equipped with more world-knowledge and a more adult intellect, how many different real careers can you list that would realise those dreams?

Research your dreams

Use the vast resources available online. The Web continues to expand its content every day, so you should be able to discover the necessary information about any type of career you're interested in. Additionally, you can research the thousands of associations and professional groups that support and promote practitioners in careers that interest you. A good place to start is the European Society of Association Executives (**www.esae.org**).

Ask around

Talk to the people who are already engaged in the work that interests you. Go to association receptions. Set up interviews with practitioners in the field of your dreams. Don't be shy. Most people who love their work consider it a pleasure and a welcome duty to promote their field to others. Encourage them to discuss their work on two levels: not only the practical how-tos and to-dos, but also the intangible rewards.

Seek out the necessary financial support to help you get the education you need

It's possible that you'll need to get additional education to prepare for your career transition. That could be an expensive proposition, but there are alternatives to paying for it entirely by yourself. There are sources of financial support available to you, and the Web is a good place to research sources of scholarships, grants, and other forms of financial aid.

Don't give up

Once you've identified the next career transition that fires your imagination and your enthusiasm, keep the feeling of excitement about your future alive and well. You may go through moments of uncertainty or doubt, but try to consider those feelings as temporary dips in the transition process. Transition is a journey into the unknown, but the rewards will be well worth it.

COMMON MISTAKES

You're in such a hurry to make a change that you neglect to make an improvement

Moving from one career to an entirely different one is more than simply changing jobs. It involves changing one of the most fundamental aspects of how you define yourself. You'll be changing the environment you work in, many of your social and business contacts, much of your everyday vocabulary, your process of prioritising conflicting demands. If you're like most people, you entered your first career in a hurry, without full knowledge about all the options available to you. Take this opportunity to make this a positive adventure in discovery, as well as a way of finding a new livelihood.

You rely on the wrong help or advice

Placement agencies and search firms, for instance, are in the business of filling positions, not helping you discover yourself and your new role. Many career counsellors are underqualified and merely process you through questionable pencil-and-paper aptitude tests.

You rely on no outside help or advice

Don't try to do it all on your own. If you have a high-quality outplacement firm available to you through your employer, be sure to make full use of its services. Additionally, many colleges support alumni networking groups where you can investigate the pros and cons of possible new career paths with people already in those fields. Confer with those closest to you – people who have observed those things that have brought you satisfaction and enjoyment throughout your recent years.

You pursue careers mentioned in 'hot career' lists, thinking that they'll promise financial security

Recent history has shown that those 'hot career' lists reflect the best of limited thinking for a limited time. As those lists are published, the market experiences a flood of candidates seeking those career options, and suddenly there isn't quite the demand for qualified candidates that was originally expected. If you're fortunate enough actually to land one of those hot jobs, you may discover that, financially lucrative as it might be, you're still left with that familiar discomfort that comes with the wrong fit.

You lose heart

Try to keep in mind that you're in a far better position to seek out satisfying work the second or third time around than you were the first time you took on a new career. You're more mature, and you're equipped with deeper self-knowledge as well as with additional marketable skills and experience.

Discovering and exploring career options that you might love should never be a once-only exercise. It should be an ongoing part of your life's journey, leading you to even more exciting revelations about your potential to contribute to the world and make a difference, while making a living.

THE BEST SOURCES OF HELP

Websites:

iVillage.co.uk: **www.ivillage.co.uk/workcareer/ survive/persondev/articles/ 0,,182_163242,00.html**

Monster.co.uk: **www.content.monster.co.uk/ career_change**

workthing.com: **www.workthing.com/career-advice/career-change**

Researching the Job Market

GETTING STARTED

Finding out about the job market today has been made immeasurably easier by the amount of information available online and the ease with which most people can access it. That said, for the best results, you'll need to be focused and narrow down your information gathering. Ask yourself:

- What do I need to know about the industry I want to work in that will help me to ask and answer intelligent questions?
- Where can I find out more information about the companies I have selected?
- What kind of information do I want to know about each of these companies?
- What would I like to know about the personnel officer that will help me to write a more effective covering letter and to perform most effectively at interview?

FAQS

Do I really have to research the job market? Isn't it enough just to scan through job ads online or have them e-mailed to me?

Only a small percentage of people find jobs that they love through ads. If you research the job market thoroughly, you will have a clearer idea of what is really out there and what you are attracted to. You'll also be able to design your CV and covering letter more effectively and intelligently because of the information you have gathered.

Why do I need to research industry trends?

First of all, it will help you to decide whether or not you want to stay in the industry you have chosen, or if you want to move to something entirely new. If the trends show that you are in a declining industry, it may be time for a change. Secondly, when you have an interview, it will help you to ask informed questions (which always impresses recruiters), and will help you to answer questions from a more rounded perspective.

How much time should I spend on this research?

It depends, of course, on the level of the job you are seeking. If you are seeking a very high level executive position in the same industry, you may already know most of the required information. If you are seeking a high level position in a new industry, you may need to spend several weeks on your job market research. If you are seeking a specialised position, you may not need to know as much about industry trends, but you will want to do several days' research on your chosen organisations.

MAKING IT HAPPEN
Start broadly and then narrow down your research
In the early stages of your research, you will begin by researching industry trends. The main things you will be looking for are:
• the major growth areas
• the major players
• the major challenges and problems for this industry.

If you are not sure which industry you want to work in, there are several good references and reports on attractive jobs and desirable companies. The *Financial Times* website (www.ft.com/companies) provides valuable information on this topic, as does the UK Trade & Investment website (www.uktradeinvest.gov.uk), which has well-organised information about trends in various business sectors. *The Economist* website is another useful resource, providing business briefings by country (www.economist.com/countries). In addition to these resources, some of the top business schools have websites that give good guidance on where to go and which directories to look at. Other useful sites include Hoovers, Bloomberg, Reuters, Forrester, and Keynote.

Research your chosen companies
The next step is to narrow your research by gathering information about the specific companies that you are aiming for in your job search. The key facts you will probably want to know about each of these organisations are:
• size of the organisation (sales, profits, market share, numbers of employees)
• strong and weak points
• key competitors
• organisational culture
• how the company is organised
• key strategic challenges

Much of this information is now easily available online. Once you've found an organisation that you are interested in, get hold of a copy of their annual report. If they don't have it on their website, simply phone the company and ask them to send you a copy.

If you have chosen a local company, you may know some employees (or know someone else who knows one!) who can tell you what it's like to work there and what its strengths and weaknesses are. You can also ask them about competitors, and about the key strategic challenges that the company is facing. If you don't know anyone who works there, it may be worth attending a few local business meetings such as the Chamber of Commerce meetings, or other professional gatherings.

The 'best company' websites listed at the end of this Actionlist will provide information about good companies to select, if you are not sure where to start.

Research information about a specific job
If you are looking for a specific job in a specific company, you'll want to know:
• What would my tasks and responsibilities be?
• What qualifications are needed? What is the typical salary for a job like this?
• What can I find out about the human resources manager?

Most of these questions will be answered when you are at the interview, but if you can gather information about them ahead of time, you're already one step ahead when you're preparing your covering letter, your CV, and your interview. If you saw the job advertisement, then the tasks and responsibilities were probably spelled out. If you know for sure that there is a job opening, you can phone and ask the company to send you a copy of the job description.

You will want to find out as much as you can about the human resources manager, and you may be able to do this through some of the business reference books mentioned above, if he or she is at a high-enough level. You can also do an Internet search to see if he or she has been mentioned in any publications, or has written any publications in your field. Professional associations may have information on this person if he or she is active in your professional field. And if you know other people in the company, you can contact the company and ask someone to send you a copy of the job description.

COMMON MISTAKES
Your research is not thorough enough
If you do not do enough research about the industry, the company, and the job, you may say or do something that shows your ignorance and jeopardises your chances. If you can demonstrate that you have done your homework, you will really stand out from the crowd and will have a better chance of being taken on.

You do so much research that you can't keep track of it all
It is helpful to create files for each of the industries and companies that you are researching. Systematise your information so that you can find what you need quickly. This is especially important when you are preparing for an interview. You might want to prepare a set of index cards listing key points that you want to remember. Carry these cards with you wherever you go to help you to learn and remember important information.

THE BEST SOURCES OF HELP
Book:
Bolles, Richard. *What Color is Your Parachute? A Practical Manual for Job-Hunters and Career-Changers.* Revised ed. Berkeley, California: Ten Speed Press, 2008.

Websites:
International jobsearch information:
  DirectGov: **www.direct.gov.uk**
  Job Search: **www.jobsearch.co.uk**
  Jobs-by-email: **www.jobs-by-email.co.uk/**

Sunday Times Best 100 Companies to Work For:
  http:// business.timesonline.co.uk/tol/
  business/career_and_jobs/best_100_companies

Building a Fantastic Contact List

GETTING STARTED

Throughout your career, you will always need to have a contact list. It is useful for job searching, for marketing and selling products and/or services, and for networking of all kinds. People who have good contacts in their profession are admired and considered powerful. It really is important who you know.

In preparing your contact list and setting up your system, here are some questions to keep in mind:

- What are your major career issues right now?
- What are your major career goals at this point in your life?
- What networks do you have that can be helpful to you?
- What networking activities can you participate in that will build up your contact list?
- What system do you have in place to record and maintain your contact list?
- What do you have to offer to people on your contact list?

FAQS

How can my contact list help me with my job search?

Contacts can help in many ways. They can provide information on industry trends, the rewards and drawbacks of a particular kind of job, the likelihood that a particular organisation might be recruiting, and on specific job openings.

I'm happy with my current job and am not involved in a job search at the moment. Why do I need a contact list?

First of all, these days you never know when you might suddenly find yourself looking for a job. If you have kept in contact with people while you are gainfully employed, they are more likely to help you when you are job hunting. And contact lists are useful for many reasons besides job hunting.

Your contacts can help you throughout your career. People in your field who are not in your organisation can give you a broader perspective on your profession. People who are in your organisation can provide important strategic information that will help you make effective career decisions. People who are in professional associations can encourage you to get more involved and can increase your visibility and help you to gain more knowledge.

What is the best way to develop contacts outside my organisation?

Generally, the best way to develop contacts is to join a professional association, get involved with social networking (see p.111), and to get involved by volunteering for committees or running for office.

People tell me that human resources professionals are the best point of contact in an organisation. Is that true?

It is true if you are looking for a position in human resources. Otherwise, if you are job hunting, you should be developing contacts with people who make the recruiting decisions.

MAKING IT HAPPEN

Identify your major career issues

It is important to understand your reasons for building a contact list. The two key reasons people use contact lists are (1) job hunting and (2) professional development. If you are job hunting, your contact list will be focused on people who can provide you with information about the job market and who may be able to help you locate specific job openings. If you are not job hunting, you will most likely be using your contact list to help you to learn more about your field, to solve particular professional problems, or to get mentoring from people in your profession.

Develop relationships before you need help

Ideally, you want to begin building your contact list before you need to call on people for help or advice. In today's fast-paced climate, people have limited time to help others and are more likely to respond to someone they know and trust than to a stranger who is asking for help. As you begin to build contacts, keep in touch regularly with people just for the sake of keeping in touch.

Then, when you really need their help, they will be glad to give you their time and energy.

Identify your different networks and create a list of everyone you know for each

We each belong to three basic types of network: a personal network, a professional network, and a work–life network. Create a separate sheet of paper or computer document for each of these networks, and identify everyone you know within each one.

First, make a list of people in your personal network, which includes your family, friends, neighbours, and others with whom you interact in your personal life. This might include people who are involved in community organisations in which you volunteer, people from your place of worship, and people connected to your children's school.

Next, make a list of people from your professional network. This can include former and current colleagues and supervisors, teachers or professors, and colleagues who are members of professional organisations. You also might add suppliers or customers of your organisation, consultants, speakers, and authors in your field.

Finally, make a list of people who are in your work–life network. These are people who are professionals in the career and outplacement field, such as executive recruiters, and career counsellors.

Create a system for keeping track of your contacts

Some people cling to the good old index card system, but these days the most common systems are:
- computer software systems, such as Microsoft Access™ or Microsoft Outlook™
- personal digital assistant (PDA), such as a smartphone or BlackBerry®, or electronic organiser systems

Online, you can use social networking sites, such as LinkedIn or Facebook.

You must decide whether you will do most of your contact work from your desk in the office or at home, or even when you're out on the road. If you need to be more portable, the PDA is probably the best system to use. Otherwise, it is just personal preference.

Your system should allow you to record the person's name, address, phone numbers, e-mail, website address, pager number, and any other contact information that you might need. It also should allow you to include personal information such as birthday, names of family members, hobbies, or other details that will jog your memory about personal connections with this contact. Finally, you need room to include information about when you contacted the person, what transpired, and when you should get back to them.

Consider creating a 'tickler file'

If you need to connect with people in your contact list on a regular basis, for example, once a month, you might want to create a 'tickler' file. Let's say you are using a traditional index card system. Instead of filing names

alphabetically, you divide up your contacts into four groups, one for each week of the month. During week one, you call all the people in the first group. During week two, you call all the people in the second group, and so on. This system is particularly good for people who are in sales or public relations, but it also might be useful occasionally for people who are job hunting.

Have something to offer the people on your contact list

Remember that working with your contact list means working with relationships, and relationships are two-way streets. If you call only because there is something you want, people will eventually think of you as an energy drain and will avoid you. Always think about what you can give. When you ask a contact for help, also ask if there is anything that you can do in return. Each time you call, make sure you take the time truly to listen to the person you have called.

Don't forget to say 'thank you'

Every time you interact with someone on your contact list, make sure you find a way to say 'thank you'. People have so little time these days, and they are much more likely to be responsive to your calls in the future if they feel as if their time is respected and appreciated.

COMMON MISTAKES

You use the 'shoebox' method of creating a contact list

This is the method of writing people's contact information down on a slip of paper and then throwing it in a box or a drawer to look at later. Usually business cards get tossed into this pile as well. The difficulty is finding a particular piece of information when you want it. It's best to set a specific time aside to transfer the information from paper scraps and business cards to your master file on a regular basis.

You have a brilliant system, but you don't use it

Some people love setting up wonderful systems with colour-coding and dividers and cross-referencing and so on, but they find they freeze up when it comes actually to making the call or connection. Commit to a certain time of the day when you will make your calls, and give yourself motivational incentives for doing the work.

You don't follow up

The worst thing in the world is making the initial contact with someone, getting their promise of help, and then not following up. All the hard work is in making the first call. If you don't follow up and keep your commitments to stay in contact, you lose credibility with the people in your networks. This is where the tickler file or a similar system can come in handy. Make sure that follow-up calls are on your calendar or on your daily to-do list.

THE BEST SOURCES OF HELP
Book:
D'Souza, Steve. *Brilliant Networking*. Harlow: Prentice Hall, 2007.

Website:
Monster Career Centre:
www.content.monster.co.uk/career/networking/newcontact

Social Networking

GETTING STARTED

Social networks have existed for as long as human beings have inhabited the planet. There is undeniably 'safety in numbers'. Throughout history, social networks have enabled us to form stronger tribal and national identities, harvest and kill food more efficiently, defend our territory, and engage in group activities for fitness, pleasure, and relaxation. These networks also pass memories, learning, and wisdom down the line so that patterns of survival can be repeated without societies having to learn them from scratch each time a new generation is born.

Generation 'X', typically defined as those born between the early Sixties and late Seventies, is probably the last generation to have experienced the traditional style of social networking. Roughly speaking, this was characterised by relatively stable family units, low mobility, and a kind of constancy that is absent from most of our social networks today.

Generation 'Y' on the other hand, the current 20- and 30-somethings, has been raised in a totally different social atmosphere driven by a high level of technological and material sophistication, instant communication, and networks that stretch right across the globe. This generation has quickly become used to both face-to-face social networking and interacting via 'virtual' networks on the Internet.

FAQS

Isn't social networking just an opportunity to get what you want by using other people's knowledge, skills, and talents?

Not at all. It's an important way of making new friends, keeping in touch with old ones, finding contacts, and becoming more involved with both local and wider-scale communities.

Of course, if you constantly use someone for personal gain, they will soon become tired of serving your purposes and become less willing to help. You may get something from them in the short term but you are also likely to receive some long-term resentment! There may come a time when you really need this person to help you, so make sure that the give and take of your relationship is evenly balanced.

I'm not gregarious and don't like networking at all. How can I overcome this?

Many people find social networking a strain because they are not naturally confident or extrovert. However, if you think of it as a task rather than expecting it to be a pleasure, you may find it less daunting, particularly if you know why you're doing it. Network with a clear objective and a strategy – along with a contingency plan in case things don't work out the way you wanted them to.

I am relocating due to a new job and won't know anyone in the area. How can I create a network out of nowhere?

If you are moving with your work, you already have the makings of a social network. However, if you'd rather keep work and personal life separate, seek out clubs and societies and attend a few events to get yourself going. You may decide not to continue with these in the long term, but the chances are that you'll meet a few new people, who will then introduce you to *their* social network.

My network doesn't seem to be delivering what I want. How can I breathe life back into the relationships that I have?

If your network is not giving you what you want, firstly ask yourself if *you* are giving it what *it* wants. Is the effort you are putting in as great as the benefit the network brings you? You may find that you have outgrown your network and that it's time to move on. Sometimes people may be holding you back for one reason or another, or relationships might have started to go sour. Be clear about what you want from your network and don't be afraid to move on when it's time to do so.

MAKING IT HAPPEN
Understand virtual networking

In the last few years, social networks have metamorphosed from the relatively small confines of family units and close circles of friends to worldwide virtual communities. There remains a crucial similarity between the two types of network: both enable us to connect with each other in a way that brings more support and opportunities into our lives. Examples include:

- *Friends Reunited* (www.friendsreunited.com) was the first important virtual social network on the Internet. Launched in 2000, it grew rapidly and has put many people back in touch with each other by repairing broken social networks in a completely new way. This success inspired many more virtual networks where people could find each other and communicate across the globe as well as across cultures, age groups, and different levels of social, educational, and physical advantage.
- *Facebook* (www.facebook.com) Launched in 2004 Facebook now has an astounding membership of over 30 million people. It is an ever-growing social networking tool allowing those registered to keep in contact with and find out more about acquaintances who work, live, and study both in the same area and further afield. Made up of a number of networks, each based around a company, area, or place of education, it allows users to create a personal profile, contact each other, upload an unlimited number of photos, and share links and videos.
- *MySpace* (www.myspace.com) was launched in 2004 and was so successful that it was sold two years later for a staggering $580 million. It uses personal profiles, chat rooms, e-mails, and blogs to enable friends and families to talk online, orchestrate meetings with new people, or look for those with whom they have lost contact. Allowing users to upload music files, MySpace is a site that is highly regarded by the music industry for finding new artists and keeping fans updated on popular bands' activities. Many artists have their own pages where fans can contact them and find out about them and their upcoming projects.
- *LinkedIn* (www.linkedin.com) is a business orientated networking site aimed at helping people to get the most out of their everyday work, and use existing contacts to further themselves professionally. Encompassing more than 150 industries, LinkedIn has over 12 million professional members from all over the globe, linking the member to their own contacts, and those of their connections. This site allows people to make a personalised profile summarising their career achievements, through which they can keep in touch with old colleagues, search for clients, jobs, inside connections, and passive candidates whilst being available to be found for a different work position.
- *Twitter* (http://twitter.com) is a social networking and microblogging site that has a growing number of business users. Members communicate by sending 'tweets'.

Remember the seven principles of social networking

Even though we have taken social networking into the stratosphere, the principles that underpin both real and virtual social networking remain the same. Think of them as the seven 'R's:

1. **Reciprocity.** This is the 'do as you would be done by' principle. People are much more likely to be willing to befriend and assist you if they feel that their efforts will be rewarded in equal measure. If you want to show your willingness to enter a reciprocal relationship, look for opportunities to respond to someone's interest or need. Try not to pin your hopes on having the favour returned straightaway, and give unconditionally. If you approach this as a calculated business transaction, you might find yourself being disappointed, but if you give freely you may be surprised and delighted by what comes back to you. Don't forget, either, that if you want something, you can ask for it. You don't have to rely on manoeuvring someone into a position where they are compelled to meet your needs. Most people like to be given the opportunity to assist others and are pleased to help out!

2. **Respect.** Social networking should not be undertaken selfishly or cynically. You may sometimes have to acknowledge that people have a different perspective on life and that your way is not their way. This doesn't mean to say that you can't enjoy a mutually beneficial relationship. Try not to be judgmental or dismissive of someone else's values and beliefs, and see things from their point of view. This means not making assumptions, jumping to conclusions or making hasty judgments. Listen attentively to what others have to say and be open to the possibility of changing your mindset.

3. **Reliability.** When you say you're going to do something for someone, make sure that you honour your promise and deliver. Social networks are voluntary, not compulsory, so it's all too easy to waive a commitment when there are unlikely to be any professional repercussions. However, if you get a reputation for over-promising and not coming up with the goods, you'll soon find that you won't be taken seriously and others' willingness to help you will diminish.

4. **Relationships.** Networks are sustained through effective relationships. These can only flourish with good communication, which in practice means staying in regular touch with people and treating them thoughtfully. Show that you have someone's interests at heart by sending them an article they might like, a congratulatory note, or an invitation to an event or dinner. It is very easy to stay in touch more informally nowadays using e-mails and text messages – and don't forget those social networking sites! These are great ways of reminding someone that you are still around, whilst also allowing the person to get back to you in his or her own time.

5. **Records.** If you have a poor memory, you might find it useful to devise a system that will prompt you when important occasions are coming up for people in your social network. There are many paper and electronic tools available to make sure you keep on top of what is happening when. By being thoughtful and proactive about your communication, you will be able to demonstrate that you care and that you are willing to put yourself out for the relationship. For example, you might send somebody a message to ask how a

particular important event went. Listen out for and take a note of important dates or events when they come up in conversation. Try to be disciplined and record these dates as soon as you hear about them.

6. **Results and rewards.** The results of social networking vary from tangible and exciting rewards and opportunities to a feeling of inclusion. Be clear about what you want from your networking activities so that you can judge whether or not your efforts are being well spent.

7. **Review.** Social networks are dynamic structures and they require our attention if we are to get the best from them. Be prepared to *raze*, *renovate*, and *repair*. If you find that you have a contact who is absorbing too much of your time and is not giving you what you want, don't continue to pour your energy into the relationship. Sometimes we have to prune our networks in order to keep them manageable. Equally, there will be times when you need to build your social network. You can do this by attending events, hosting functions, or volunteering your services. Your networks are bound to ebb and flow according to your life stage or circumstances. You may lose some people from your social network and gain others. Sometimes, people reconnect with past relationships years down the line.

First impressions are also very important. Remember, it takes only a few seconds for people to make up their minds about you and once they've done so, it is very difficult to shift their perceptions. You may want to think about how you create first impressions and whether these are helping or hindering you. Perhaps you could ask a trusted friend to give you some feedback.

The most important thing is to leave people feeling valued. This means being honest about your motivations, and entering relationships sincerely.

COMMON MISTAKES
Your network gets too big
It may become impossible to maintain all your relationships at once. Rather than run the risk of people feeling ignored or let down, think about how you can manage their expectations. You might disclose that you are going through a particularly intense or busy time and that you won't be around as much as usual for a while. Let people know what's going on for you, and then go back to them when time or circumstance allows.

You are unable to say 'no'
If you take on too much for other people, this can leave you feeling overburdened and stressed. You don't *have* to agree to everything people ask of you. Practice assertive communication and manage your boundaries so that you don't become overwhelmed.

You give up too easily
People sometimes get disheartened if someone in their network declines a request or is unable to help them achieve something they had hoped for. Although this may feel a bit like a dead end, ask your contact who they'd recommend you approach next. They may put you in touch with somebody new, giving you the opportunity to build new relationships.

You demand too much
Being over-demanding when you need a favour can exhaust the goodwill in your social network. Be vigilant about giving back to somebody who has helped you. If you have developed a relationship well, you will know just what to do in return, leaving your friend or contact feeling valued and the relationship strengthened.

THE BEST SOURCES OF HELP
Websites:
Directory of social networking websites:
  http://en.wikipedia.org/wiki/List_of_social_net working_websites
Facebook: **www.facebook.com**
Friends Reunited: **www.friendsreunited.com**
LinkedIn: **www.linkedin.com**
My Space: **www.myspace.com**
Networking knowledge: **www.networking-knowledge.com/basics.html**
Positive networking skills:
  www.saleslobby.com/Mag/0502/FEAN.asp
Social networking weblog: **www.socialnetworking-weblog.com**
Twitter: **http://twitter.com**

Learning How to Network

GETTING STARTED

No matter what your organisational position, and no matter what your career goals are, you can always benefit from networking and marketing yourself. In today's world, business is driven by relationships. Networking and marketing yourself require you to build strong and meaningful relationships – many that will be long term. The following points are questions to consider as you prepare to network and market yourself:

- Why am I networking? What's my personal or professional goal?
- What are the strengths that will help me to market myself?
- What organisations or events will be valuable places for networking?
- How much time do I want to spend on networking, and when will I do it?
- How will I know when I've been successful?

FAQS

Why should I bother to network and to market myself?

Research has shown that people who have a vast network of contacts, who are involved in professional and community activities outside their organisation, and who look for opportunities to be visible are more successful in their careers and contribute more effectively to their organisation.

Isn't networking blatant self-promotion, and won't it look bad?

No. Networking is done for the good of the organisation or your professional field, rather than for personal gain. If you're a successful networker, people are drawn to you because they know you're well connected and that you have good resources.

When is the best time to network?

Networking should become a way of life, a way of being. You should be networking all the time. As you build professional relationships, be constantly thinking: 'What can I offer this person?', 'How can I be of help?' The more you try to be of service to others, the more people will want to do things for you.

MAKING IT HAPPEN

Clarify the purpose of your networking and why you're marketing yourself

There are many reasons for networking and for marketing yourself. They can include finding a new job, seeking a promotion, or gaining support for a major project. Although it's important to build relationships continually, it's much more effective to know why you're building these relationships and what you hope to

accomplish. Everyone has limited time, and this will help you to decide how to prioritise your networking activities.

Make a list of your strong points

It's important to have a sense of who you are and what your strengths are when you're networking and marketing yourself. What are your special skills and abilities? What unique knowledge do you have? What experiences will other people find valuable? What characteristics and beliefs define who you are? Once you've made this list, make copies for your bathroom mirror, for your car dashboard, and for your wallet. Knowing your strengths helps you to remember that other people will value what you have to offer.

Never network from a position of weakness; always network from a position of strength. Have something of value to offer; otherwise people will see you as an annoyance. And remember to begin networking before you need anything from other people. Join or create a network to build relationships, and do what you can to help others or the organisation.

Network online

The Internet is a great place to make connections and is particularly valuable if you are nervous about networking in person. There may be sites particularly relevant to the industry you work in, but LinkedIn and even Facebook are a good place to start (see p.112). And why not start your own blog?

Make a list of organisations and events for networking

Identify professional organisations and events that may be helpful to you in your career or with your project. Look for special interest groups, like those for 'entrepreneurial women' for example. Get involved. When you're at professional events, make sure that you attend social functions, that you join people for dinner, and that you seek out volunteer opportunities. If you're networking within your own organisation, find special interest groups or social groups to join. Look for committees to be involved in, and don't be shy about asking questions and making suggestions.

If you aren't sure where to begin on this step, ask for advice from a mentor, from your boss, and from trusted colleagues.

Create a contact list

Keeping in mind your reasons for networking, brainstorm all the people you know who might be of help to you. Prioritise the list according to who is most likely to be helpful. Think about people you've done favours for in the past who might not be of direct help, but who may know someone who can be. After you've spoken to each person, ask him or her, 'Who else do you know that can be of help to me?'

Create an action plan with a schedule

Take your list of organisations and events and your contact list, and put together an action plan for making connections. Schedule networking events in your diary, along with organisational meetings, conferences, and so on. Using your contact list, set up a timetable for making a certain number of calls per day or per week.

Meet up with people and attend events

Before you meet up with someone or attend an event, review your list of strengths, and focus on your purpose for networking and marketing yourself. It helps to visualise or picture a successful outcome. Be friendly and professional, but most of all, be yourself. Spend time connecting with people on a personal level before asking for help or sharing your reason for networking. If you're meeting in person with someone on your contact list, always bring a gift – something they can remember you by.

Market yourself

The actions you take depend on why you're marketing yourself, but think of yourself as a brand: 'Brand You'. When marketers are marketing a product, they look for the 'Unique Selling Proposition' (USP). A USP is something relevant and original that can be claimed for a particular product or service. The USP should be able to communicate: 'Buy our brand and get this unique benefit'. When marketing yourself, you need to define who your 'customers' are and what your Unique Selling Proposition is. Your list of strengths should give you some clues, but the USP needs to be stated in a short phrase. People who are closest to you can often give you suggestions. It might be something like: 'My leadership brings out the best in others', or 'I solve problems quickly and simply'.

Once you know your USP, brainstorm ways that you can market yourself and your unique qualities. The key is to let people know what you have to offer. Write an article for the company newsletter or a professional newsletter related to your USP. Volunteer to give a talk. Design a project that uses your talents and propose it to the right people. Be visible.

Assess your progress towards networking goals

You may wish to keep a notebook of your action plans and your progress. It also helps to have someone as a sounding board. That person can be a friend, your boss, a mentor, or a professional adviser. When we feel accountable for our actions to someone we trust, we're much more likely to follow through. It also helps to have someone who is willing to celebrate your successes and accomplishments with you.

Always say 'thank you'

As you network, many people will offer you information, opportunities, and valuable contacts. In your notebook, keep track of the favours that people have done for you and make sure that you write each one a short and simple thank-you letter or e-mail. People are always more willing to help someone who has been appreciative in the past.

Be patient

Networking is a long-term activity. Steven Ginsburg of the *Washington Post* describes networking as 'building social capital'. You may not see results overnight, and at first should expect to give more than you get. But over time, your network will become one of your most valued assets.

COMMON MISTAKES

You don't want to bother anyone

Remember that people love to help others. Don't take up too much of their time, and come well prepared. When you ask for someone's time, be specific. Say, 'I'd like 30 minutes of your time', and then stick to it. Don't outstay your welcome. Whenever you meet up with someone, always be thinking, 'Is there something I can do to help this person?' Create a win–win situation.

You come on too strong

Networking isn't about selling someone something they don't want. You're looking for opportunities to create a mutual relationship, where there is give and take. In order for networking to be successful, you have to be interested in developing a long-term connection. Remind yourself that your focus is on relationship building, not on immediate results.

You don't come on strongly enough

You put yourself in networking situations, but never talk about your needs or interests. This may be because you aren't clear enough about why you're networking, or you're networking for reasons that aren't particularly important to you. Go back to the first stage and clarify your purpose.

THE BEST SOURCES OF HELP

Websites:
Business Link: **www.businesslink.gov.uk/bdotg/ action/home**
City Women's Network: **www.citywomen.org**
LinkedIn: **www.linkedin.com**
Networking People UK: **www.npuk.com**

Finding and Working with Search Organisations

GETTING STARTED

When you begin the job-search process, it is common to feel haunted by the so-called 'hidden job market', that exclusive network that links the favoured few with the very best job opportunities. There are legitimate reasons for feeling that way. Only a small percentage of open jobs are publicly announced. The very best jobs usually require a special set of skills or background, and companies use refined recruitment techniques to attract candidates for such unique positions.

One of those techniques is the retention of search organisations that specialise in ferreting out the best candidates for the open position. The trouble is that it is not easy to know about, much less apply for, these particular opportunities. And, among the very best search organisations, the general message to the public is: 'Don't find us. We'll find you'.

Indeed, the mere fact that you reach out to a search organisation renders you undesirable in the eyes of many of these companies. Just as banks only like to lend money to people who do not really need it, search organisations like to recruit candidates who are not really looking for jobs.

With that closed-club impression, it is natural to feel as though actively setting out to attract the attention of search organisations is probably counterproductive. However, there are ways to use the connections and power of search organisations to promote your own career.

The following points are questions to consider as you prepare to look for your next job with the help of one or more search organisations:
- Do I need a search organisation to help me find my next job?
- How quickly do I need a new job?
- Should I work with a contingency organisation or a retained search organisation?

FAQS

How much should I expect to have to pay a search organisation for helping me?
Nothing. The client is the recruiting company. Never pay a search organisation. Search organisations receive their fees from the company, valued at roughly 30 per cent of the new employee's first year's salary.

What's the difference between a contingency search organisation and a retained search organisation?
A contingency search organisation only makes its money when it successfully places a candidate. Contingency organisations usually fill junior to middle-level executive positions, with salaries ranging from £35,000 to £100,000. A retained search organisation works with more senior positions, receiving its fee regardless of whether certain positions are successfully filled. Both are legitimate forms of business; however, it is generally agreed that retained search organisations have a higher-quality relationship with their client company – a long-term interest in which the mutual goal is the company's prosperity. With a contingency search organisation, the emphasis is more likely to be on the individual placement. So both you and the recruiting company could find yourselves in a wrong match.

Can I work with more than one search organisation at a time?
In most cases, yes. You are the one still in charge of your own future. Seriously reconsider signing with a search organisation that insists on an exclusive contract with you. Because you are not the paying client, your own personal interests are not part of the organisation's business concerns. Therefore, you should be able to market and represent yourself freely elsewhere.

MAKING IT HAPPEN

Identify the best search organisations for the type of position you are seeking
Use word of mouth and other indirect marketing techniques for identifying the best search organisations and helping them find you. Ask your friends, colleagues, and college career centres to introduce you to the services they found to be satisfactory. Go where search organisation consultants go. Attend high-profile business receptions, go to human resource seminars in your community or industry. Participate as a speaker (or even a volunteer) at business symposia. Write articles for your industry journal.

Contact the search organisation
The best way to initiate contact with a search organisation is to phone a search organisation consultant specifically recommended to you by a friend or colleague. Have an expertly prepared CV ready to send immediately. If you do not have a personal introduction, send the CV with a covering letter describing your overall credentials and abilities.

Be prepared
You may be invited to come in for an interview immediately. Or you may be notified that your CV has been keyed into the organisation's database. Assuming that your CV contains the important keywords associated with your career path, your information will then come up the next time a suitable position is researched. Working with search companies is likely to be a long-term proposition, where both you and the consultant will find success if and when a compatible opening is available at a client company.

Know how to evaluate a search organisation
When you are contacted by a search organisation that you are unfamiliar with, be sure to assess the organisation's

ability to serve your interests well. An excellent question to ask is who their client companies have been. The organisations you want to work with will freely offer a shortlist of prestigious client companies.

Select only a few search organisations to work with
While you should never succumb to the pressure of signing an exclusive deal with only one organisation, you also should sign with only a small number of organisations, so that you can stay focused and in control of your schedule of interviews.

Follow up
After the initial interview with the recruiting company, follow up with that company in the standard ways, such as a thank-you letter. Search organisations should not try to stand in the way of the relationship you cultivate with the recruiting company. The successful recruitment will benefit all three parties, and it continues to be up to you to do your part to improve the chances of receiving an offer.

Listen to consultant feedback and accept recommended training
The consultant may see you as the best possible candidate for an ideal position; however, there may be a small element in your personal demeanour, grooming, or body language that could spoil your chances. If the consultant's recommendations do not require a fundamental shift in your basic nature or values, seriously consider following the advice.

COMMON MISTAKES
You waste your time with low-quality consultants and search organisations
Insist on a personal meeting at their offices. If they insist, in return, on a telephone relationship, or if you find that their offices are shabby, these are excellent indicators that their clients will probably not be top-market employment opportunities for you.

You wait until you need to find a new job before cultivating a relationship with a search-organisation consultant
Some of the most successful search organisations receive up to 300 CVs a day, so you have to compete for their attention. Additionally, there may not be any openings for positions that you are best qualified for. The coincidence of availabilities is rare enough that you should be in the search organisation's system long before you are desperate for a new job.

You try to camouflage an irregular career path with clever answers
Most consultants and recruiting managers have heard the language typically used to camouflage a firing or a dismissal for a company's downsizing. If you are available now because you were dismissed or fired, be as candid as possible.

You drop your search organisation consultant after you have accepted your new position
If you have achieved a mutually satisfactory relationship with your search organisation consultant, stay in touch with that person. Send them excellent candidates for other positions that may become available. Meet for lunch now and then. You don't have to make that person your best friend. But the days of working for one company for the rest of your life are over. The chances are that you will be searching for a new position within a few years. Use that earlier relationship to keep moving forward along your career path towards your future.

THE BEST SOURCES OF HELP
Websites:
Executive Grapevine: **www.askgrapevine.com**
Global Executive: **www.economist.com/ globalexecutive**

Getting the Most from a Professional Career Adviser

GETTING STARTED
Sometimes the best way to reach a goal is to call in professional help. Professional career advisers can help you work out what kind of career you should be in, set career goals, and prepare for a new job or promotion if that is what you want. Career advisers can have different approaches and views, so make sure that you choose someone who is really right for your situation and with whom you feel a sense of compatibility and trust. They're also not cheap, so you want to make sure that you get the most for your money. Think about

the following questions as you set out to work with a career adviser:
• What is your goal in working with a professional career adviser?
• What are some of the services typically offered by career advisers?
• How do you find the right person?
• How do you manage the relationship effectively?
• How do you know when your goal has been achieved?

FAQS

When do people typically use a professional career adviser?

Career advisers are most frequently used when someone is considering changing careers or when they are between jobs and looking for a new position, as many people are currently. However, career advisers can also be used as a sounding board for your current career. And some people use career advisers once or twice a year for career 'MOTs'.

How much does a professional career adviser cost?

Career advisers usually charge by the hour (often up to £200 per hour or offer a flat fee for courses of advice lasting for several months. An initial consultation is, typically, free. Sometimes an adviser might, however, ask you to pay a large fee before a consultation. Before you agree to do that, you may wish to interview several career advisers and find out what their fees are. The only exception to this is if the career adviser is going to offer you a battery of tests to help you understand your skills and your personality style, and to conduct a self-assessment that can guide you in deciding what kind of career you will be successful in. The battery of tests will cost several hundred pounds, but these are not always necessary.

How do I find a professional career adviser?

The best way to find a career adviser is through personal referral. If you know someone who has successfully used a career adviser, you can ask them to give you the person's name and number. Some people call themselves career coaches or career counsellors rather than career advisers, so you can look these terms up in your Yellow Pages and on the Internet.

MAKING IT HAPPEN

Set a concrete goal for working with your professional career adviser

Define your goal in results-oriented language. Be as clear and specific as possible so that you will know when you have met your goal. Some examples are:

- to find a new job
- to obtain a promotion and a pay rise
- to change careers to something more fulfilling

Become knowledgeable about the different kinds of services that professional career advisers offer

First of all, be sceptical about any career advisers who promise a quick fix, easy money, CVs that get speedy results, or other come-ons. Career issues are complex and often take time to work through. And professional career advisers require extensive training and education.

Make a list of potential career advisers and research their qualifications

After identifying sources for finding career advisers as described in the FAQs, narrow your list down by checking on the qualifications of each of the potential advisers. You also may call potential advisers and enquire about their training and experience.

Select a professional career adviser from your list

After screening candidates based on their background, conduct a telephone interview with the remaining people on your list and explain your goal to them. Ask them about their methodology, what their costs are, and how their background will help them to help you. Ask yourself how comfortable you feel with each person, and pay attention to what your instincts or intuition tell you. You want to choose someone that you can trust and who will challenge you to reach your full potential. If you are having difficulty deciding between two or three potential career advisers, then make a face-to-face appointment with each in order to make your final decision. Most professional career advisers will not charge you for an exploratory meeting.

Set clear goals and expectations with your professional career adviser

Explain your goals to your career adviser. They will describe clear expectations about how they want to work with you and what they expect you to do between sessions. If you have any expectations about how you want to work together, make sure that you make them clear from the start. Also find out how much you'll have to pay and when. Will you pay session by session, or will they send you an invoice at the end of each month, for example? Usually, most career advisers expect you to pay something before the sessions as a sign of your commitment, and many will ask you to sign a contract. Only sign the contract if you are comfortable with all elements of it, and feel free to question any items that you don't understand or don't like.

Plan for the ending of your engagement with the professional career adviser

Since you have set a clear goal in the beginning, it will be obvious when your work together is done. However, sometimes new goals arise as a result of your work together, and you may decide to create a new contract. Or you may decide that you want to meet every six months, or on an 'as needed' basis. Because the relationship with a professional career adviser can be very personal and very rewarding, it's always nice to end with a little celebration or with a gift as a way of showing your appreciation.

COMMON MISTAKES

Your goals are unclear

Some people go into this relationship because they have been made redundant from their job and the company pays for them to have a career adviser as part of the severance package. The danger here is that you meet with your adviser regularly just because he or she is there, and nothing gets accomplished. A really good career adviser will guide you into setting goals right at the beginning, if you haven't done that already. If you find yourself meeting for over a month and not sensing any progress, then it's time to choose a new career adviser.

You are not really committed to your own career development

You meet weekly with your adviser and you agree to take certain actions such as working on your CV or making five phone calls. But the following week when you meet again you have not done anything that you promised you would do. If this becomes a regular pattern, you need to take a serious look at your goal. You may have set a goal that is not really what, in your heart, you want. In your next meeting with your career adviser, ask for help evaluating the appropriateness of your goal.

You don't know how to let go

If the relationship has been really successful, you will have developed a powerful bond with your career adviser, and it will be difficult to end the relationship when your goal is met. But it is healthy for you to move on and to begin to apply on your own the things you have learned in this relationship. Having a celebration dinner is a nice way to symbolise the ending of your working together, and you can always book career 'tune-ups' if you need them.

Revitalising Your CV

GETTING STARTED

If you're embarking on a job hunt, there are lots of options open to you as you look for the right way to display your fantastic skills and experience. There are many different styles of CV, but why do you need to know how to prepare them? Because every person's career history is different, and you want a CV that puts your career history in the most marketable and attractive light. It's important to think carefully about which style to use when you apply for a job. A carefully written and targeted CV will impress a personnel officer much more effectively than a random story of your life.

Your particular job search and career goals are also unique. The stage you're at in your career is also a factor to bear in mind. As you decide which type of CV to prepare, think about whether you plan on staying in the same field or whether you're changing careers. Have you had a fairly standard career development, or has your career been less traditional? Is this your first job? Are you aiming for a specific job in a specific company or are you on the look-out for something new and challenging? Is it a while since you've updated your CV and do you feel a bit behind the times?

All these factors will help you decide which type of CV is most likely to get you the interview that will lead to your perfect job.

FAQS

How many types of CV are there?

There are many different types of CV, but we'll be focusing on the following:
- chronological
- functional
- targeted
- capabilities

A chronological CV is still the most popular type of CV by far, but knowing how to put together the other types will stand you in good stead as you progress through your career and come across different job opportunities. These days people may have several different careers (not just jobs) in the course of their working lives, so if you're thinking about dramatically changing what you do, a non-traditional CV may suit your needs best. Keep your CV to two pages, ideally.

How do the CV types differ?

You should use a **chronological CV** when you're staying in the same field rather than making a major career change. This type of CV also works well when you've progressed steadily up a standard career ladder. For example, if you began your career as a junior designer, you moved on to become senior designer, and you're hoping to become design manager, this is the CV type for you. You would also use this kind of CV when you've worked for the same company for most of your career, even though you may have had several different kinds of job within that company. If you're starting off on your career path, looking for your first or second job, this CV is probably most appropriate to your experience.

A **functional CV** is the better choice when you're looking for your *first* professional job, as it stresses your skills rather than your experience. It's also a good choice when you're making a fairly major career change, for the same reasons. If you've changed employers frequently, followed a less traditional career path, or are concerned that your career history has been a bit patchy, you may be better off with this type of CV.

You should use a **targeted CV** when you're very clear about your job direction and when you need to make an impressive case for a specific job. It's hard work writing this kind of customised CV, especially if you're applying for several jobs, but it can make you and your abilities stand out from all the others in the pile.

Actionlists

If you're aiming for a specific job or assignment within your current organisation, the best CV to use is the **capabilities CV**. Remember, though, that you need to make time to customise your CV for the situation.

Do I need to create a CV for each of these types?

Not normally, no. The only exception to this is when you've created one of the standard formats (either a chronological or a functional CV) and a unique opportunity comes up for which one of the customised CVs (either a targeted or a capabilities CV) is better.

What's a job search 'objective'?

These were a CV must-have a few years ago. A job search objective is a short paragraph at the top of your CV that explains exactly what type of job you're looking for. It's particularly useful if you're writing to someone speculatively, but isn't always appropriate, so think carefully about whether you need to include one or not. If you want to add one to your CV, make sure it's concise, specific, and above all, honest. For example, the following objective is too general:

Seeking position in broadcasting industry.

That's not going to do you many favours. An improved version could be:

An experienced broadcasting professional is seeking a position to make full use of an in-depth background as a television producer, production manager, scriptwriter, and networker. I am looking for a challenging production manager position that will enable me to use and expand my creative skills and international experience in the broadcasting industry.

MAKING IT HAPPEN

Create a chronological CV

- Write your name and contact details at the top. Don't use your work e-mail address as part of these; it will look as if you're taking advantage of your current employer. Use your home e-mail address instead or an Internet-based one such as Googlemail or Hotmail.
- If you're applying speculatively, you may want to include a job search 'objective'.
- Write your employment history. Start with your present or most recent position, and work backwards.
- For each position listed, describe your major duties and accomplishments, beginning with an action verb. Keep to the point and stress what you've achieved.
- Keep your career goals in mind as you write and, as you describe your duties and accomplishments, emphasise those which are most related to your desired job.
- Include your education in a separate section at the bottom of the CV. If you have more than one degree, they should be listed in reverse chronological order. List any professional qualifications or training you've undertaken separately.

If you've been working for some time, you only need to write in detail about your last four or five positions, covering the last 10 years or so. It's fine just to summarise the rest of your career history that goes back beyond that.

Create a functional CV

- Write your name and contact details at the top.
- As this type of CV is well suited to people starting out in their careers, you may want to state your job search 'objective' clearly.
- Write between three to five separate paragraphs, each one focusing on a particular skill or accomplishment.
- List these 'functional' paragraphs in order of importance, with the one most related to your career goal at the top.
- Provide a heading for each paragraph.
- Within each functional area, emphasise the most relevant accomplishments or results produced.
- Add in a brief breakdown of your actual work experience after the last functional area, giving dates (years), employer, and job titles only.
- Include your education in a separate section at the bottom of the CV. Again, if you have more than one degree, they should be listed in reverse chronological order.

Using this CV style means that you can include information about your skills and accomplishments without identifying which employer or situation it was connected to. This is especially helpful if you've signed a non-disclosure agreement with your current or previous employer, in which you undertake not to reveal specific information about a job or project to potential competitors. Non-disclosure agreements are particularly common in high-tech or research companies.

Create a targeted CV

- Begin by brainstorming a list of key points. For example, what have you done that is relevant to your job target? Are you proud of what you've achieved? Have you achieved anything in another field that is relevant to your job target? Think about what you do that demonstrates your ability to work with people.
- Write your name and contact details at the top.
- Think carefully about whether you need to include a job search 'objective' here; as this type of CV is best geared to an application for a specific job, you may not need to include one and could use the space more usefully.
- From your brainstormed list, select between five and eight skills/accomplishments that are the most relevant to your job target. Make sure that the statements focus on action and results.
- Briefly describe your actual work experience beneath each skills/accomplishment item, giving dates (years), employer, and job titles only.
- Include your education in a separate section at the bottom of the CV, listed in reverse chronological order.

Create a capabilities CV

- To develop a capabilities CV, you first need to learn all you can about the internal job that you're applying for.
- List your name and contact details at the top.
- Think carefully about whether you need to include a job search 'objective' here; as this type of CV is best geared to an application for a specific job, you may not need to include one.
- Next, list your five top accomplishments, focusing on actions taken and results achieved that are relevant to the position you're interested in.

- Write a brief paragraph about any relevant work experience you've had in your current position. If you haven't been at the company for long, you should provide a complete synopsis of your work experience as described for the targeted CV.
- Include your education in a separate section at the bottom of the CV in reverse chronological order.

Think about the look and feel

Once you've decided on the best CV type for you and the job you want, spend a little time making sure that you think about the details and present all the information to its best advantage.

- Most CVs are submitted via e-mail these days, but if you're asked to send your CV by post, print the document on high-quality white or cream paper. This will make sure that your CV can easily be read, photocopied, or scanned by the recruiter.
- Buy your own stationery. Don't use headed notepaper or address labels from your current place of work when you're printing out or posting your CV to another company or agency. Just like using your work e-mail as part of your contact details, this will give a strong impression that you're taking advantage of your present employer and his or her facilities.
- Take care with the formatting of your CV. Use a 'clean' looking font that is easy to read (some people prefer a sans serif, such as Arial), and make sure that the type size you use isn't too small. Draw attention to your achievements by using a bold face to highlight positions you've held or qualifications you've gained. Emphasise key points in lists by using bullets.
- Make sure you read over your CV once you've finished working on it to check for spelling or grammatical errors – these, above all, will mean your CV ends up in the bin rather than on the right person's desk. It's always a good idea to ask someone else to read over your finished CV too; he or she may spot something you've overlooked as you've become so familiar with what you've written.
- Try not to rely on computer spellcheckers. While they'll pick up on a good many mistakes in spelling and usage, remember that they won't pick up on words that are spelt correctly but used in the wrong way or the wrong place. For example, if you write 'there' when you actually mean 'their', the spellchecker won't realise that you've made a mistake.
- Unless you're *specifically* asked by a recruiter to submit a hand-written CV or covering letter, use a computer to give a more professional finish.
- Follow your own instincts. By all means ask friends or family members to read through your CV but remember that, if you ask 20 people what they think, you'll get 20 (probably different) opinions. In the end *you* are the one who needs to feel comfortable with it.

COMMON MISTAKES

You try to include *everything*

Like many people, you may want to tell a potential employer everything you have ever done to try to impress them. A recruiter or employer will be looking for someone who can get to the point and express him or herself clearly and effectively, though, so remember to keep it simple and focus on those things that are most likely to get you an interview.

You don't use any particular format

If you haven't had much experience in writing CVs, you may create one that is a mixture of job listings, skills, and accomplishments. This will only confuse your reader. Rather than leap straight in, work out which type of CV suits your job search or your target vacancy best.

If you're still concerned about which CV you think will suit you best, it might be worth visiting a career adviser. If you're still a student, your local further education college may well have a career adviser who can help you for free. Otherwise, the reference library may be able to suggest where to find help. If you're working already, bear in mind that you'll have to pay for this type of service, and rates can vary quite dramatically.

You don't follow up

This is the commonest and most serious mistake. If you said you would phone to arrange an interview in your covering letter, make a note of the date and follow up. Although it can be difficult to make the call because of fear of rejection, you'll never get the job if you don't!

You become disheartened

Sales people have learned that you have to take a certain number of rejections before you get a 'yes'. Finding a job is the same thing. If you receive a 'no' after making a phone call for an appointment, tell yourself, 'Well, that's a shame, but it's one less "no" that I have to hear before I get a "yes"'.

THE BEST SOURCES OF HELP

Book:

Bolles, Richard. *What Color is Your Parachute? A Practical Manual for Job-Hunters and Career-Changers*. Revised ed. Berkeley, California: Ten Speed Press, 2008.

Websites:

Monster.co.uk: **http://content.monster.co.uk/ section328.asp**

Total Jobs: **http://careers.msn.com**

Creating Covering Letters That Sell

GETTING STARTED

When you apply for a new job, you're usually asked to submit a CV and covering letter. The two work together well: the CV gives an outline of your experience and qualifications, while in the covering letter you're able to explain what attracts you to the job in question and give more of a sense of yourself. Today, 'letter' is a misnomer as the vast majority of CVs are submitted by e-mail, but the principles are the same and we'll use this phrase to cover both print and electronic versions in this actionlist. To make the best of a covering letter, ask yourself the following:

- What tone do I want to convey in my letter?
- Have I done my research about this company and this position?
- What is unique about me that would interest this employer?

FAQS

Why is a covering letter important?

The covering letter is the very first thing a personnel officer or a recruiter reads. It must capture his or her attention and make him or her want to read your CV. It is your first chance to stand out from the crowd.

Is the appearance of the covering letter important?

Yes, it is extremely important. Just as you put on your best professional clothes to go to an interview, if you're asked to submit a hard copy covering letter, use the best paper you can find, the most professional-looking fonts and make sure the document is error free. This is your chance to send an unspoken message that you are a top-quality candidate.

Do I use a covering letter in every job application situation?

No. In some cases you may send a letter to an organisation enquiring about whether or not they have any job openings. You would also ask who to send your CV to. You would not use a covering letter if you visit an organisation in person and are asked to fill in a job application, and it's highly unlikely you'd ever need one in an online job search.

MAKING IT HAPPEN

The guidelines for writing a covering letter that really sells are fairly straightforward, but they do require you to do your homework.

Each covering letter that you write should be uniquely tailored to the specific position that you are applying for. When you combine well-written letters or e-mails with effective face-to-face and telephone networking, your job campaign will stand a much better chance of success.

Identify a specific person to receive your covering letter and CV

Covering letters addressed to 'Dear Sir', or 'To Whom It May Concern', get quickly thrown into the bin. If you do not know a specific person within the company (which may be the case if you're sending in a speculative application), look online or ring the company and ask.

Get to the point

An effective covering letter is typically two or three paragraphs long. In the very first line of your covering letter you will explain its purpose. It may read something like, 'I am very interested in the position of Production Manager as advertised on your website'. Or, 'I was given your name by Mary Bettencourt regarding the position in Human Resource Information Systems'.

Show your understanding of the company's business issues

In order to stand out from the stack of letters and CVs that the personnel officer has on his or her desk, you must show that you have done your homework about the company and their current business issues and challenges. The Internet is a marvellous tool for learning more about a particular company. The first step is to go to the company's website. Most companies have a section for recent news articles about them, particularly their press releases. You should also be reading the best business newspaper and magazines available. They will give you a sense of the major industry issues, and they may also have particular information about companies that you are targeting.

It is a good idea to save these articles in a file for each company. They are valuable to review if you actually get an interview. You can also use your friendly reference librarian to help you research some basic information about the company in business reference books.

Describe your qualifications

Very early in the covering letter you must interest the personnel officer in your qualifications. Explain how your qualifications will help this organisation achieve its goals. For example, 'I understand that your company is planning on creating a web presence to support your sales. In my current position as Director of Internet Sales for Speedy Sales Company, I have helped to increase our market share by 13 per cent in the past year'. Show how you specifically can help this organisation with the issues or challenges it is facing.

Ask for an interview

There are several ways to do this. You might say that you are going to be in their area during a specific time period and that you would be available for an interview. Or you can simply say, 'I look forward to discussing how my qualifications can help your organisation to be more successful. I will telephone you within a week to set up an appointment'.

Be yourself
CVs are cut and dried, and only convey your experiences and your accomplishments. Your covering letter is your one opportunity to convey something about your personality and your uniqueness before you actually go to the interview. Keep it professional, but don't be afraid to show your enthusiasm, your willingness to work hard, and your interest in the position. Potential employers are really attracted to job applicants who show an interest in them and who seem very eager to be a part of the company.

Present a professional appearance in your covering letter
First of all, make absolutely certain that there are no grammatical or spelling errors. Fortunately, most word processing programs catch and correct these problems, but make sure that you proofread the letter before you send it out. If you need to send hard copies, use the highest quality paper that you can find. Unless you are applying for a specialised job in the arts or advertising field, you will probably want to use a quiet, neutral-toned paper such as white or cream. Use a standard and easily readable font such as Times New Roman or Helvetica.

If you are posting the covering letter and CV, send them in a large flat envelope. And send two copies. Many personnel officers will need to circulate your letter and CV. Photocopies are better if the originals have not been folded.

COMMON MISTAKES
You use a covering letter template from a book
Reading through books of sample letters will certainly help you get a feel for the kinds of information people include as well as layout and tone, but it's worth starting your own letters from scratch. Experienced managers have seen hundreds of covering letters, and they are tired of hearing the same old textbook phrases. Personalise each of your covering letters so that they are targeted to a particular person, and so that they represent you and your unique skills.

You use the same covering letter for all your job applications
Recruiters will easily be able to tell if you are 'recycling' a letter you've used for other job applications. Take time to understand each company you contact and to tailor your letter appropriately.

THE BEST SOURCES OF HELP
Website:
CareerWeb.com, 20 Deadly Letter Mistakes Job
  Seekers Make: **www.careerweb.com/rescen/
  car_advice/ jobsearch/20dead.html**

Making an Impact in Interviews

GETTING STARTED
Well done! You've cleared the first hurdle in your job search with a great CV and a covering letter, and have been invited for an interview - you've already found some way to stand out from the crowd. Now you need to build on this success. This actionlist will help you prepare mentally and emotionally for your interview. Read on to find out how to make a real impact with prospective employers.

FAQS
Are there any interview questions that I should prepare for whatever type of job I'm going for?
Obviously there are no hard and fast rules about what an interviewer will ask you, but there are a few things that you should get straight in your head as you start your interview preparation. Keep these questions in mind:
• Why do you think you're the best person for the job?
• What is it about this job that attracts you?
• What is it about this organisation that has made you apply for the position?
• Who will interview you and what do you know about them?
• What is the appropriate dress and/or image for this organisation?

MAKING IT HAPPEN
Refresh your memory about your CV or application form
As a first step, remind yourself thoroughly of all the information on your CV or application form (it's a good idea to keep a photocopy of anything you send to a prospective employer for this very reason). It may have been some time since you applied for the job, so it's no bad idea to look back over what you said way back when. Think about what questions you might be asked based on your education or work history. Some questions that might be difficult to answer include, 'Why did you choose to study this subject?', 'Why did you leave your last job?', or 'Why did you have a period of unemployment?'. Write notes about what you're going to say and practise your answers with a friend or family member.

Research the organisation

Finding out as much as you can about the company you're visiting will not only help you decide if it's the sort of organisation you'd like to work for, but may give you some ideas for questions to ask the interviewer. If you find an opportunity to show that you've done your research, this will signal to the interviewer that you're enthusiastic about the job, as well as knowledgeable about the market.

The best place to start looking is the company website. Focus on the annual report, news, press releases, and biographies of key members of staff. This will give you a feel for the organisation – its values, its success factor, and its people. If the company doesn't have a website, ring them and ask to be sent this information along with their most up-to-date catalogue.

If you have time, it's also a good idea to cast your net a bit wider and to research current factors that might affect the organisation. These can include industry trends, competitive issues, strategic direction, and particular challenges or opportunities.

Set yourself the challenge of finding out about these five essential questions before the interview:

- How large is the organisation?
- How is the organisation structured?
- What is its main business?
- Who are its major competitors?
- What is the organisation's work culture like?

Decide what *you* want to get from the interview

In their nerves before an interview, candidates often forget that there are two sides to the process: clearly, the prospective employer wants to suss you out, but you too need to work out if you want to work with them. It's a good idea to prepare a list of questions that will help you decide whether or not this job is a good fit for your personality and your career goals. For example, you might want to ask your interviewers what progression prospects they see for the eventual post-holder, what the company's values are, or what the professional development policy is. In general, it's a good idea not to ask about benefits and salary at a first interview, unless the interviewer brings them up. Get the offer first, then talk about money!

You also need to work out the key points you want to make about your strengths and skills. When you prepared your CV, you listed the principal strengths and skills that you thought an employer would be looking for. Look at that list again, choose a skill, and think of a recent situation you've been in that will demonstrate that strength or skill to an interviewer. If possible, include any concrete results you achieved through using it.

Even though you may feel under pressure at points, always focus on the positive in your answers, even when you've been asked to talk about a difficult situation or your weaknesses. That way, you'll come across as someone who rises to a challenge and looks for opportunities to improve and develop.

Prepare yourself mentally

Many people, including athletes and salespeople, prepare themselves for challenging situations by mentally picturing a successful result. This is a great method that can also be used to help you to perform well in an interview.

Before the interview, imagine yourself being professional, interesting, and enthusiastic in your interview. Also imagine yourself leaving the interview with a good feeling about how you did. This will put you in a positive frame of mind and help you to be at your very best in the interview.

Practise!

If possible, ask a friend or family member to role-play the interview with you. If you have a career counsellor or coach, they'll also be able to help you out here. Give the other person a list of questions that you think you might be asked (and ask them to throw in a few of their own so that you have to get used to thinking on your feet!), and then role-play the interview, asking your friend afterwards for honest feedback. Film the role-play if you can so that you can watch your body language; this is often more telling than you realise.

Start the ball rolling with some standard questions that interviewers often ask:

- Tell me a little bit about yourself.
- Where do you see yourself in your career five years from now?
- What are you most proud of in your career?
- What is your greatest strength?
- What is your biggest weakness?
- Describe a difficult situation and how you handled it.
- Can you tell me about a time when you had to motivate a team?

You don't need to go right back to your junior years if someone asks you to tell them a bit about yourself: use it to give a very brief overview of yourself including a short history of recent employment.

Create a positive impression on the day itself

When the day of the interview dawns, be punctual. Better still, be early to give yourself some preparation and relaxation time. If you're not sure of the location of the company, you might want to do a practice run of the journey so you can be sure to leave yourself enough time. Have a glass of water, flick through company magazines if they're available, and try to get a feel for the atmosphere, as this will help you to decide if it's the sort of place you can see yourself being happy working in. It will also give you an idea of what to expect in the interview, and the sort of candidate the interviewers will be looking for. If he or she isn't too busy, take some time to talk to the receptionist, who is often asked by recruiters to act as an extra 'screen' during the recruitment process; if candidates are rude to the receptionist, they often don't get much further.

Be enthusiastic

You know why you're interested in this job, and you need to convey that interest to the recruiters – interviewees who are excited about the organisation get job offers! Even if it's true, don't say that you're keen on the job because it pays well. Instead, be ready to talk about what you can offer the company, how the position will expand your skills, and why this kind of work would be satisfying and meaningful to you. Don't overdo it, though, as this may come across as insincere or overconfident.

Be honest

The overall impression you're trying to create is of an enthusiastic, professional, positive, and sincere person. These things will come across from the word go if you follow the basic rules of giving a firm handshake, a friendly smile, and maintaining good eye contact throughout the interview. Never lie in the interview or attempt to bluff your way through difficult questions – it's just not worth it. Good preparation should ensure that you don't have to resort to this. Speak clearly and respectfully to the interviewers and remember that swearing and flirting are definite no-nos.

Wherever possible, back up your responses to questions with evidence-based replies. For example, if an interviewer asks you how you manage conflict within a team, it's best to give a brief general response and then focus on a specific example of how you've done this in the past. Illustrating your answers with real examples gives you the opportunity to focus on your personal contribution, and will be more impressive than giving a vague, hypothetical reply.

Look *and* sound the part

Even though what you're saying in an interview is the main thing, it's important to look professional as well. You should feel comfortable in what you wear, but it's better to turn up 'too smart' than 'too casual' – people will take you seriously if you dress respectably. If you're applying for jobs in media or the arts a suit may not be necessary, but dressing smartly will always give the impression that you care about getting this job.

It's always a good idea to take some anti-perspirant with you to an interview, as when people are nervous they tend to sweat. You may also find yourself a bit hot and dishevelled if you had to rush to get to the interview in good time (although if you've prepared your journey well, this shouldn't happen!). Make sure you have time to freshen up before the interview. This will help your confidence, and spare the interviewers from a sweaty handshake or, worse still, a bad odour when you enter the room. And remember, don't go overboard on the perfume or aftershave – that would count as a bad odour, too.

COMMON MISTAKES

You 'misread' the interviewer

People tend to underestimate the level of formality and professionalism required in an interview, and some interviewers even create a more social than professional situation to catch you off guard. If you find yourself in an interview with a more casual approach than is appropriate, change your behaviour as soon as you notice. The interviewers are more likely to remember your behaviour at the end of the interview than at the beginning. On the other hand, if the environment or the interviewer is more casual than you realised, don't worry. You're *expected* to look and act in a highly professional and formal way in an interview. Use your instincts to judge how much you need to change your behaviour to show that you'd fit into the company culture.

You use humour inappropriately

To make a situation less tense, people sometimes use humour to lighten the mood. If you've said something you think is funny and received a negative reaction, though, it's best not to call attention to the situation by apologising. Try to act as if nothing happened and go back to behaving professionally. Whatever you do, don't follow inappropriate humour with more humour.

You didn't do your homework

You get to the interview and realise that you really know nothing about this organisation. Hopefully, you arrived early and have some time in reception. Often, booklets and leaflets found in receptions provide quite a bit of information about the company, its industry, its products and services. Look at them, look around, and learn everything you can. Talk to the receptionist and ask him or her questions that may be helpful to you in the interview. It's possible to learn quite a bit about the organisation on the fly, but nothing works better than doing your homework.

You criticise your former employer

Avoid this at all costs. It gives the interview a very negative feeling, and will leave the interviewer wondering if you would criticise his or her organisation when you left. This kind of criticism usually happens when someone is asked why they're leaving (or have left) their last position. The best way to answer this is to talk about the future rather than the past, and to show your eagerness to take on challenging career opportunities.

THE BEST SOURCES OF HELP

Book:
Bolles, Richard. *What Color is Your Parachute? A Practical Manual for Job-Hunters and Career-Changers*. Revised ed. Berkeley, California: Ten Speed Press, 2008.

Website:
Monster.co.uk: **http://content.monster.co.uk/ Job_hunting/articles2/coping_with_interviews**

Preparing for Different Types of Interview

GETTING STARTED

Looking for a new job can be a long and tiring process, but when you get to the interview stage, you know that the end is in sight, whatever happens. Quite understandably, some people find interviews nerve-wracking; it's not easy to see your professional life laid out before you on your CV and then have a series of questions fired at you. Preparation can help, though, and part of that process is being aware of the different types of interviews that you may be asked to attend. Some of them are industry-specific, some are more suitable for experienced employees, some are designed to root out the best first-jobbers. This actionlist gives you an overview of the different types of interview out there and what you need to do to let your natural talent shine.

FAQS

I feel much more comfortable talking to one person than a group of people, but I've been asked to attend a panel interview. I'm really nervous. What can I do to help myself?

First of all, don't panic. You'll just tire yourself out. Keep calm and remember how well you've done to get to this stage – lots of other candidates won't have got this far! Next, find out as much as you can about who you'll be meeting and then plan what you need to say to impress them. This doesn't mean pretending to be someone you're not; rather that you're good at what you do, on top of your game, and you'd like to work with them. If you feel nervous, take plenty of deep breaths before you go in and before you speak. If you don't hear a question clearly or aren't sure if you understand it, don't be afraid to check. Read on for more help!

MAKING IT HAPPEN

Deal with telephone interviews

Initial interviews by telephone are becoming more common, but they're quite challenging for both parties. You probably normally use the phone either to talk with friends whom you know, and can visualise, or for business calls with people you don't need to know. Getting to know someone on the phone can be awkward: the absence of visual feedback is disconcerting. As always, preparation and practice will provide some help.

Be well equipped

• Have everything ready before you start: papers, pen, information you'll need to put across accurately, dates, and so on.
• Think carefully about the likely shape of the interview. What information do you need to give? What questions do you need to ask?
• Make sure you find a quiet room to take the call in, where you won't be interrupted or have any distractions. You may need to refer to some notes, but try not to rustle your papers too

much. It may be best to arrange to take the call at lunchtime or at home after work. Most HR professionals are used to having to interview clients later in the day, so this may be a good option for you.

Be aware of your own voice

• It may sound strange, but don't talk too much! Pauses – even very short ones – are awkward on the phone and with no visual cues to guide you it's tempting to fill spaces with words. You may end up saying more than you mean to.
• Take care not to become monotonous – your voice is important because you cannot make an impression visually. As you would in any face-to-face interview, sound positive, friendly, and business-like.

Listen to the interviewer

• Since you get no visual information on the phone, you should pay careful attention to the non-verbal aspects of speech – tone, pitch, inflection, for example – to pick up clues about what the interviewer is interested in.
• Make notes of important facts and agreements – it's easy to forget things when there is no 'picture' to reinforce them.

Cope with competence-based interviews

The idea behind competence-based interviews (often called behavioural interviews) is to determine how well suited you are to a job based upon what you've learned from situations in the past. Most interviews incorporate some competence-based questions, because research shows that they seem to be the most effective form of assessment – your knowledge and experience are being judged against the specific criteria of the job. Competence-based questions usually start 'Give me an example of when. . .' or 'Describe a situation where. . .'

As a rule of thumb, there are certain competences that almost all employers will be interested in. A shortlist of favourites is planning and organising; decision-making; communicating; influencing others; teamwork; achieving results; leadership.

Prepare examples

Given that the interview will focus on past experience, it's useful to think about examples you could use to show how you've developed the core competences outlined in the list above. When you look back at these experiences, ask yourself the following questions:

• What did you do personally?
• How did you overcome barriers or pitfalls?
• What did you achieve?
• Is there anything you would have done differently?
• What did you learn from the experience?

Whilst you may not be asked precisely these questions, they'll prepare you for areas of questioning that you're very likely to encounter in the interview.

Know the job

Before an interview of this type, read the job description very carefully and focus on the specific requirements of the post. Think about the issues and responsibilities related to the job. You can try to anticipate the sorts of questions you may be asked based on those requirements and responsibilities. Also think about your present job and in particular how your role fits within the team.

Cope with internal interviews

Some companies like to use an interview process for filling internal vacancies or making career plans. Within an organisation there can be all sorts of assumptions that may complicate this process. For example, some people feel that the company should know them well enough from experience and appraisals to make an interview unnecessary. Others worry about the politics of the situation, and the consequences of failure. Some may be inclined to treat it too informally or lightly.

The general rule is to treat these interviews as you would an external application until you have definitive information that things are different. It's much better to err on the side of formality until you're sure what is required.

As ever, remember to do your homework beforehand and find out as much as you can about the job. If you have a human resources department, they'll probably be the best source of information. It's also a good idea to

- talk to your boss about your intended move if your interview is for a job in a different department. It could create a very nasty atmosphere if he or she finds out from someone else.
- find out what's required from you and how the decision-making process works.
- anticipate what the interviewer knows already and what he or she will want to know about your experience and competence. Don't take too much for granted in this area.

Don't panic in stress interviews

Stress interviews involve putting the candidates under pressure to see how they respond to difficult people or unexpected events. Organisations should only use this technique when they can clearly show the need for it, and even then they should be careful how it is handled, taking account of the sensitivities of the interviewee. It can be an unnerving experience, but being aware that this is a recognised interviewing technique for some firms will help you to cope should you come across it. The sorts of industries that may employ this technique include banking and some security firms.

Stress questions often come in the form of a role-play, when the interviewer, *in his or her role*, may say something like: 'I think your answer is totally inadequate: it doesn't deal with my concerns at all, can't you do better than that?' The interviewer is testing your ability to manage surprises and ambiguity. He or she will want to see you keep the initiative and take responsibility for dealing with the situation appropriately.

The trick is not to take the remarks personally but to recognise that you're required to play a role. Take a deep breath, pause, keep your temper, and respond as naturally and accurately as you can.

Keep your wits about you because the technique is designed to catch you off guard. Create time for yourself to balance logic and emotion calmly in framing your response. If you can, try to anticipate what the next problem will be and keep ahead of the game.

Make your mark at assessment centres

This method of selection usually involves a group of candidates performing a number of different tasks and exercises over the course of one to three days. Assessment centres were traditionally used at the second stage of recruitment, but nowadays candidates are often asked to one at the first stage.

Assessment centres usually include:

1. Group exercises: role-playing, discussion, leadership exercises
2. Individual exercises. For example:
   - written tests (such as report writing based on case studies)
   - in-tray exercises (a business simulation where you're expected to sort through an in-tray, making decisions about how to deal with each item)
   - presentation of an argument or data analysis
   - psychometric tests
   - interviews
3. Social events
4. Company presentations

You'll be assessed most of the time – the administrator should clarify this for you – so there's rarely an opportunity to let down your guard.

You can make these events a little less stressful with a few simple rules:

- The organisation will probably tell you what they're looking for in their career literature or their invitation. Make sure you've read this, thought about it, and worked out how you show the behaviour they're interested in.
- Behave naturally but thoughtfully. Do not attempt to play an exaggerated role – it's never what the assessors want to see!
- Make sure that you take part fully in all activities; assessors can only appraise what you show them.
- Don't be over-competitive. The assessors are likely to be working to professional standards, not looking for the 'winner'. Unnatural behaviour quickly becomes inappropriate and boorish.
- Take an overview. Most of the exercises have a purpose wider than the obvious. Try to stand back and look at things in context rather than rush straight in. With the in-tray exercise, for example, you'll probably find that some items are related and need to be tackled together.

Tick all the boxes at technical interviews

In this type of an interview you'll be asked specific questions relating to technical knowledge and skills. As you'd imagine, this approach is common and extremely useful in research and technology companies' selection processes.

The organisation will normally tell you in advance that they have a technical interview or if they want you to give a presentation on your thesis or experience. You need to be prepared for 'applied' questions that ask for knowledge in a different form from the way you learned it at college. For example, 'How would you design a commercially viable wind turbine?' or 'How would you implement the requirements of data protection legislation in a small international organisation?' Consider the 'audience' and how your knowledge fits with their likely interests and priorities. What questions are they likely to ask?

Sometimes these presentations go wrong when interviewers ask very 'obvious' questions; or one of them has a favourite or 'trick' question. It's easy to be irritated by these, but you should remain calm and courteous. Try to see the interviewers as your 'customer' and respond with patience.

As always, preparation and anticipation are the keys to success. Work out what your interviewers will want to know and make sure your knowledge is up to scratch in the correct areas.

Think on your feet in panel interviews

When you're looking for a job, sooner or later you may be asked to attend a panel interview. These are becoming more popular, as they

- save time and are efficient. Several interviewers meet in one place at one time, so the applicant does not need to be shuffled around from office to office and there is no schedule to follow or overrun.
- provide consistent information. You, as the job applicant, only need to tell your story once instead of repeating it over and over again in private meetings with each interviewer.

Although it can be quite daunting to walk into an interview where several people are present, a panel interview is also an excellent opportunity to show your strengths to a number of interviewers at once. A successful panel interview is one in which you come across as cool and confident and able to handle whatever is thrown your way.

To take the sting out of panel interviews, find out about the organisation as well as the position you're applying for. Start with the company's website, if it has one, and try to get a copy of its annual report. Talk to people who may be familiar with the organisation. Go to the library and see if any recent articles have been written about it.

Next, begin to prepare mentally for the possibility of a panel interview. Ask yourself what your major selling points are. How can you get these across to each member of the panel? This is particularly useful if you know beforehand who you're going to meet and what their responsibilities are. If, for example, you'll be meeting a sales director and a finance director, you might want to explain how you can do things in such a way that you achieve maximum sales of a product or service cost-effectively. If you like, see the panel interview as a type of presentation, and keep your audience in mind at all times.

If the prospect of this type of interview makes you nervous, try to combat your nerves with 'visualisation'. This is a very good way of helping you feel and appear relaxed and confident. Before your interview, imagine what a panel interview might be like. Visualise yourself in a conference room with several people sitting around a large table. Imagine answering each question easily, bonding with each interviewer and having a successful interview.

Some people are uncomfortable using the visualisation technique, but it's a really effective method. Remember, Jack Nicklaus claims that much of his golf success comes from mentally rehearsing each shot before he actually picks up a club. What has worked so well for him can work for you, too.

Answer the questions

Sometimes in a panel interview it can feel as though questions are coming at you from all directions. Try to take the first question, answer it, then build on that answer to respond to the second interviewer. Make sure you answer every question so that none of the interviewers thinks you ignored his or her question.

Clarify questions if necessary. If you find a question confusing, don't be afraid to ask for further explanation; it shows that you're coping under pressure and also it will save time all round. Phrases such as, 'Just to clarify. . .' or, 'If I understand correctly, you want to know. . .' can help you to understand exactly what information the interviewers are looking for. If you're still unsure, you might want to check that your answers were understood and that you've answered the question fully. Simply ask the appropriate person, 'Did I answer your question?'

As you're talking, make eye contact with each member of the panel in turn. This means catching the gaze of a particular member of the panel, holding it for about three seconds, and then moving to the next panel member. In reality, it's actually very difficult to look someone in the eye, count to three, and then move on, all while answering a challenging question, but with some practice it will become second nature. It's a really useful skill to develop for meetings of all types and for public speaking.

Resist the temptation to take the less-pressurised route by letting members of the panel do all the talking. Remember, you're there to sell yourself and to do that you need to get your point across. If the people on the panel do all the talking, all they will remember about you is that you may be a good listener. Of course, you should certainly not interrupt members of the panel, but do make sure you discuss your strengths and the reasons they should employ you. Sell yourself as you would in an individual interview.

Keep calm in 'scenario-based' interviews

Most interviewers have been carefully trained to look only for evidence and facts from the candidates' past and therefore *never* to ask hypothetical questions. But sometimes – and especially with younger candidates who don't have much past work experience – an organisation will be more interested in what the person can become in the future rather than what he or she is now.

There are techniques for doing this. They normally focus on exploring how you think and act when confronted with problems you haven't experienced before – *how* rather than *what* you think and do. The logic is that in order to learn from a new experience you must be able to understand the experience thoroughly. These interviews assess the level of complexity at which you can think – and therefore understand the issues and learn how to deal with them.

Typically you'll be asked in these interviews to take part in a conversation that gets more complex and wide-ranging as it progresses. You build a scenario further and further into the future. There are no right answers of course: the interviewer is looking for an ability to spot the right questions.

Knowing that the interview will take this form is some help, but there is really little that you can do to prepare

for it. Being well rested and alert, relaxing and enjoying the challenge are the best tips.

COMMON MISTAKES
You think you can wing it
You can't. You have to prepare for interviews if you want to do well. The amount of preparation you do will depend on the type of interview you're having or the type of job you want, but you have to show that you not only understand what the prospective job is about, but what you can bring to it, what challenges the business faces, what the state of the relevant industry is, and so on. You must be professional and show that you're the complete package.

THE BEST SOURCES OF HELP
Websites:
Monster.co.uk: **http://content.monster.co.uk/ section323.asp**
University of Bradford: **www.careers.brad.ac.uk/ student_hunt_interview**

Answering Tricky Interview Questions

GETTING STARTED
Job interviews are the single most important part of the selection process - for both you and your future employer. Once your CV (or personal referral by someone whose opinion the recruitment manager trusts) has established that you meet the basic skills and background requirements, it is the interview that establishes you as a candidate who will fit well into an organisation's culture and future plans.

While most interview questions are generally straightforward, unambiguous inquiries, some interviewers will throw in surprises specifically intended to explore your thinking and expectations at a deeper level. Or they may be meant to throw you off guard to see how you react in high-stress or confusing circumstances. Or they may not be intentionally tricky at all. They may merely be invented by the interviewer, or borrowed from lists of questions available on the Internet, with no idea what their value is, or how to

assess your response as it relates to the requirements of the job.

How you answer tricky questions could determine whether you will receive an offer from the organisation. But it's also important to remember that what those questions are, and how your answers are received, can tell you volumes about whether this is a company you want to work for.

Here are some of the questions you might want to consider as you're preparing yourself for a job interview:
- What aspects of your career do you feel especially good about, and how can you make sure those are discussed in the interview?
- What aspects of your career so far do you feel especially worried about discussing?
- Can you formulate answers to questions about those aspects in advance?
- How can you use the interview to learn about the potential employer?

FAQS
What if I don't understand how the question relates to the job I'm applying for?
Some questions – especially questions in which you are given a scenario and asked to think your way through to a solution – are designed to help the interviewer

understand your ability to make tough decisions, or be a leader in high-pressure situations.

True, it's reasonable to expect that you won't ever find yourself stranded in a lifeboat, charged with deciding which fellow survivor to throw overboard to conserve rations. But the way you reason out your decision may tell the interviewer much about you, for example, how you would choose which product to take out of stock to conserve valuable warehouse space. Try to answer these kinds of questions based on business strategy.

Some questions ask me to divulge my greatest weakness. How can I answer these questions without disqualifying myself for the job?

Such questions are usually designed to discover the extent of your self-knowledge. We all have weaknesses, and it's unreasonable to expect you to be perfect in every way. Keep your answer short and dignified. Identify only one area of weakness that you're aware of, but also describe what you are doing to strengthen that area. Don't try to be too clever by turning a negative into a positive, saying things like, 'My biggest weakness is that I'm a determined worker and won't give up until the job is done well and completely.' You aren't fooling anyone.

Sometimes I get the impression that the interviewer doesn't know why I'm being asked a certain question, and that my answer would be beyond his or her understanding. How do I salvage that situation?

A company that uses unqualified interviewers to select qualified candidates may not be one you would like to work for, so you may not want to salvage such a situation. But if you're determined to give yourself the best chance to work at this organisation, help the interviewer out by exploring the reasons behind the question and what exactly is being looked for in the way of response.

Even though you may not answer the question itself, you will still benefit from the conversation. You will position yourself in the interviewer's mind as someone who is not rattled by ambiguity, but instead works calmly and co-operatively with team members to arrive at the best possible outcome.

MAKING IT HAPPEN
Understand the purpose of the interview

The best job interviews are respectful encounters that allow mutual discovery. It may feel as though the employer has all the power – after all, it's the employer who will decide whether to offer you the job. Ultimately, however, it is you who holds the power, because it will be you who decides whether to accept the job. So interviews are just as important for you in the selection process as they are for the interviewer.

Keep that power balance in mind, and it will help you to stay calm, dignified, and clear-headed when tricky questions are asked.

Assume that the interviewer is probably as uncomfortable with the process as you are

Put yourself in the interviewer's shoes, and assume that he or she is slightly uncomfortable with the process as well. Few people relish meeting someone new and peppering them with probing questions. You may be

the 25th candidate for a job, so the interviewer may feel tired of the same old questions and the same pat, rehearsed answers. Remember also that the interviewer was once sitting in your seat, applying for his or her job in the company and worrying about the same surprise questions that you are. The resulting empathy will help break down the barriers of tension and perceived judgmentalism.

Prepare yourself in advance by identifying the topic areas that might be the trickiest for you. Then think carefully about how you might answer them. Broadly speaking, there are eight areas of questioning that could pose a challenge for you:

- your experience and management skills
- your opinion about industry or professional trends
- the reasons why you are leaving your current job
- financial or other value of your past achievements
- your work habits
- your salary expectations
- your expectations for the future
- your personality and relationship skills or problems

Imagine which of these areas might be discussed and formulate in advance the general thoughts and responses you want to express. But don't rehearse answers to anticipated questions word for word.

Never lie

Many interviewers do this work for a living, so they are more experienced at hearing the answers that candidates think they want to hear than you are at delivering them. Be candid and clear, and use lengthy answers only when you see that demonstrating your strategic thought process in detail will add valuable information.

When in doubt, try to understand the business reason behind the question. Ask questions of your own

'What do you mean?' or 'Could you rephrase that question?' are perfectly acceptable queries in any civilised conversation. Job interviews are no different.

Be prepared to answer questions about salary

During the interview process you want to keep the focus on your worth, not your cost. Early in the process, politely decline to go into details about past salary and future expectations. Many companies have a policy of offering salaries only at a certain percentage above a candidate's previous salary. If your previous salary, for whatever reason, was below market average or below your worth, you shouldn't have to be forced to accept a lower salary in the future.

If a question comes up about your salary expectations, make sure you have done your homework. You should have decided ahead of time on a salary range that is acceptable to you. Make sure the top of the range is well above the figure you would be thrilled to accept, and the bottom of the range slightly above your predetermined 'walk-away' figure.

Study question lists

Many lists of questions are available online. Interviewers use them, and you can, too. Although you may not be asked those specific questions during the interview, the knowledge that you have done everything you can by preparing in advance will help you feel relaxed, confident, and capable – which is basically what the employer is looking for in the first place!

COMMON MISTAKES

You criticise your former employer or colleagues

If you are asked why you are looking for a new job, focus on your positive ambitions, not any resentments or grudges you may harbour. Talk in terms of what has worked in your career, not what has failed.

You get angry or defensive

A job interview is part gamesmanship, part blind date, part tea party. Use your social skills to smooth over edgy moments or bristly reactions to possibly offensive questions. And don't take anything personally.

You give away your power

You are at the interview to assess the desirability of the job, just as much as to sell your own desirability to the company. Remembering that will help you to keep your dignity and protect you from feeling compelled to answer inappropriate, irrelevant, or intrusive questions.

You use scripted answers to anticipated questions

These are artificial, and the interviewer has heard them all before. Original responses, even if they are slightly clumsy, will be more valuable to both you and the interviewer. They are a more accurate guide as to whether there is indeed a match between you and your potential new employer.

THE BEST SOURCES OF HELP

Books:

Fry, Ronald. *101 Great Answers to the Toughest Interview Questions*. 5th ed. Franklin Lakes, New Jersey: Career Press, 2006.

Yate, Martin John. *Great Answers to Tough Interview Questions*. 7th ed. London: Kogan Page, 2008.

Website:

Monster Career Centre – answering interview questions: **www.content.monster.co.uk**

Negotiating the Best Deal in Your New Job

GETTING STARTED

When you start a new job, you have a unique opportunity to position yourself as a valuable asset in the organisation and to set your level of pay accordingly. To achieve this you need to establish an appropriate asking price. On the one hand, you don't want to oversell yourself and price yourself out of the market. On the other, you need to avoid selling yourself short, for it's extremely difficult to change your position significantly once you're placed in a complex pay structure.

There are no hard and fast rules about how or when to conduct your negotiation. Every situation is different and each employer will have their own set of thresholds. Understanding the context in which your negotiation is going to take place and being sensitive to the culture of the organisation is therefore essential.

Having said that, there are some practical steps you can take to position yourself sensibly.

FAQS

I am in the process of applying for a new job. How should I prepare for the negotiation on the package?

You need to do your research before entering the negotiation so that you're supported by accurate, current information. This means familiarising yourself with the company itself, as well as the range of salary and benefit options that are being offered. You may be able to tinker with the combination of benefits, if not the salary itself. Don't assume you'll be offered more than your former salary, especially if you're competing with someone who is equally qualified but willing to work for less. If the salary offered is less than you had hoped for, you can discuss the benefits package and make provision for an early salary review.

I feel extremely uncomfortable talking about how much I'm worth. What can I do to make this easier?

Many people dislike the negotiation phase of finding a new job. However, here are some simple steps you can take to make this easier.

- Try to avoid discussing your package until you've been offered the position.
- When you start negotiating, make sure you have in mind the minimum acceptable salary to you. (Don't reveal this figure, though!)
- Try to elicit the salary information first. If you're offered a range, go high or even slightly above the top end. If you're offered a specific figure, assume this is mid-range and try to push it up.

- If you're asked to name a figure, don't lie, but offer a range within which you'd be prepared to negotiate.
- If you're successful in your negotiations, ask for the agreed terms and conditions confirmed in writing – before you resign from your current position.

I am applying for a position that is a dream come true, and I don't want to put off my prospective employer by asking for too much. How can I safely position my worth?

You can put off a prospective employer by pitching too high *or* too low, so it's important to get your level right. Look at the job pages to get a feel for the market rate, and draw information from your professional network. You'll also find some listings on the Web that will help you. Some of these are indicated below.

MAKING IT HAPPEN
Position yourself

When you're going for a job, you are effectively a salesperson promoting a product, and it's up to you to demonstrate that the 'product' is valuable, high quality, and superior to anything a competitor could offer. Potential employers, or 'buyers', are looking for the best value for their money, so will be driving the deal in the opposite direction. However, if you've positioned yourself well, they won't risk losing you and will be prepared to settle at the top of the market rather than at the bottom.

Leave the salary discussions as late as possible

It's preferable to leave salary discussions until the point at which you're offered the job. However, it isn't always the case that this will be left until the final stages of the process. Many recruiters ask for salary expectations and details of current salary early in the process. Some even screen people out on this basis. If this is the case, you may need to spend some time researching the question of salary at the application stage or before the first meeting. This will require you to think about your aspirations and be absolutely sure of the territory you'd like to cover, the experience you'd like to gain, and the context in which you'd like to work.

If you're forced to answer a question about your salary hopes at the beginning of your interaction, have a figure ready that is at the higher end of the scale. You can always supplement this with a request for a particular benefits package.

Consult the right sources

When seeking an entry point for your salary, there are several sources that will help you find an appropriate figure.

- Look at the range of packages offered for similar positions in the adverts on the jobs page.
- Ask for advice from people in your professional and personal network.
- Ask your mentor, if you have one, to advise you – or use his or her own network to access the information.

- Approach your local Training and Enterprise Council.
- If you're a member of a union, it will have information on acceptable salary ranges for your profession.
- Go to some of the Web-based salary information services, like the one listed at the end of this actionlist.

Consider the package, not just the salary

Some employers have fixed-scale salaries, in which case there is little room for negotiation. However, you may find that the total package of pay and benefits raises the worth of the salary to an acceptable level. For instance, you may be offered private health cover, a non-contributory pension, a fully financed car, and significant bonus potential. You may be able to negotiate a cash equivalent in place of a benefit, particularly in a smaller organisation that doesn't have inflexible systems in place. When bonuses are mentioned, you may want to discuss the basis on which the bonus is paid so that you're absolutely clear of the terms and conditions attached to it. Some bonus schemes spread the payments over several years as an incentive to stay with the business. Such complexities can be very off-putting.

Remember the tax implications

It's worth remembering that all the benefits included in a package are taxed as 'benefits in kind'. Company cars are taxed on the basis of the price of the model when first registered. You may want to consider whether you need a car with a large capacity, or whether running a car with a smaller engine could improve your income tax situation. As a result of the rapid depreciation of new cars, many people are now opting for a salary increase instead of a car allowance. Private health insurance is taxed at its cash value. This would make another impact on your tax bill.

Explore the boundaries

Adverts usually carry salary ranges to give applicants an idea of the boundaries of the negotiation. You can be sure, however, that the negotiation will start at base level. If you find that potential employers aren't responding to your sales pitch, you could negotiate an early pay review instead: for instance, if you demonstrate your worth against certain criteria in the first six months of employment, they'll agree to a particular salary increase. Ensure that the criteria are clearly set, though, and make sure this is included in your contract of employment.

Some adverts state that the salary is 'negotiable'. The onus is then on you to move in with an offer. Again, try to leave it to the end of the recruitment process, and be sure that you've studied the equivalent packages for the type of role and industry sector you're applying for.

Stay calm

When negotiating for a package, try to do it calmly and assertively. Appearing too eager can defeat your negotiation. Being too laid back or diffident can portray a lack of professionalism or self-confidence. Either behaviour can damage your case.

COMMON MISTAKES

You don't do your research

Thinking that requesting a high salary will convey your worth is often misguided. Your prospective employer will naturally look for reasons to back up your assertion that you're worth so much. If you don't have a rational argument, you will look ill prepared and unprofessional. Time spent in research is always well spent. In this way, you can argue your case logically and professionally.

You try to bluff

Don't bluff in your negotiation and try to play off fictitious job offers against the real one you're hoping to get. Employers generally don't respond to this kind of pressure, and instead of receiving a speedy offer you're likely to be left with nothing.

You show too much interest in the package

Behaving as if you're more interested in your benefits package than in the role you're being recruited for is a mistake. Every employer knows that you will want a fair package, but you need to demonstrate that your financial concerns are balanced with a genuine desire for the job.

THE BEST SOURCES OF HELP

Websites:
Monster.co.uk:
 **http://content.monster.co.uk/
 section325.asp**
Salary.co.uk:
 www.salarysearch.co.uk

Moving Sideways: Benefiting from a Lateral Move

GETTING STARTED

Today's career environment requires more creativity, flexibility, and originality than ever before. The notion of a 'job for life' has vanished. So, fortunately, has the rigid assumption that there is only one way to succeed in a company, that is, by promotion. Previously, if you were not moving up, you were almost certainly fast-tracked in another direction: out of the door.

But today both employers and employees are discovering that lateral career moves are a creative way to build exciting companies and rewarding futures. For their part, individuals recognise that the more varied their skill-sets and experiences, the more value they can bring to their employers. This translates into increased marketability, as well as additional job security in changing times. Your willingness to move laterally may protect you from being made redundant as your company downsizes in one department while expanding operations in other, more profitable divisions.

Employers, by contrast, are coming to recognise lateral moves as a way of retaining valuable employees (as well as protecting themselves from losing valued talent to their competitors). Top talent is difficult and expensive to identify, recruit, and retain. Top talent is also hungriest for new challenges and growth opportunities and will be quick to leave if not fed with them. Employers are beginning to understand that moving eager and interested employees within the organisation is an extremely valuable approach to employee development, and one which will serve them well in the future.

The following points are key questions to ask yourself when considering the option to move sideways within the organisation – perhaps, in certain circumstances, even down the ladder:

- If your company is downsizing, or if there are other elements in your life requiring more of your attention and energy, will a lateral move help you stay happily employed?
- Will a lateral move give you valuable on-the-job exposure to business functions that will help you to accelerate your upward mobility?
- How receptive is your employer to the principle of recruiting from within and providing lateral experience in order to develop employees?
- Is there a monitoring system in place within the management so that your career path will be tracked and your new skills set will be expanded further later on?

FAQS

Wouldn't a lateral move reflect negatively on me?

Not necessarily. As with almost every business decision, you get the best value if you make your choice for strategic reasons and then learn from the experience. A lateral move can be made for any number of reasons, and you may experience some surprising benefits in the process (understanding the ways other parts of the business are run, for example). Capture those benefits as added strategic value and you may actually boost your career prospects in the long run.

How can I be sure that my company won't just assume I belong permanently on the slow track?

Employers that support skills development and communication across the whole business are the most likely to understand the value of placing their high-potential employees in a wide variety of their business operations. After all, the best CEOs are the ones with the broadest exposure to the spectrum of corporate functions. However, if you observe that your company's most senior leaders have achieved their success via single channels of departmental experience, you might consider either staying on your departmental ladder or changing employers if your career plan involves wide variety.

MAKING IT HAPPEN

Identify the reasons why you'd like to explore the option of a lateral move

Does the next logical upward step in your career path require certain experience that you don't yet have? Have you just finished a protracted period of high-pressure productivity and need a lighter load for a short time? Are you studying hard to increase your market value in the long run and need a less strenuous set of responsibilities during your workday? Are family needs preventing you from keeping up a demanding travel schedule? Are you committed to the company in the long run and want to understand as much of it as you can? Or do you simply want some variety?

Investigate internal employment policies

Find out if there is a policy in place that supports lateral moves. Talk to employees who have made that choice to discover whether their long-term career ambitions are still being protected.

Discover which functions and divisions of your company are growing

You want to seek out opportunities in areas in which your company is thriving or continuing to expand. Talk to other employees in those divisions to discover what the environment is like and whether senior management is supportive of individual ambition and career development.

Consider the desirability of the openings that are available

Would you have to take a pay cut? How long do you think you'd remain interested in that particular work? Does the new department show promise for continued growth and opportunity? Is the management team of your chosen department well received and respected among their own superiors?

Identify what you enjoy about your current work

Think about what you like best about your job as it stands and try to work out if you'll find the same elements in your prospective new assignment. How will you stay in touch with your current team members? Would you be able to return to your present assignment when and if you desire? If not, would that make an important difference to you?

Identify your potential for success and failure in your possible new assignment

Work out roughly how long it will take to achieve your current level of proficiency in your new assignment. Are the measures of success acceptable to you? Are the requirements for upward mobility on this new ladder attractive to you?

Identify your prospects for development outside the company

Does this new ladder present opportunities for expanding your marketability in the external job market? Will it provide you with technical training and experiences to boost your competence, therefore rewarding you sufficiently for the risk you'd be taking now?

Plan for transitions

Be sure you and your new manager have worked out a plan to integrate you into the new team as smoothly as possible. You may have put a great deal of advance thought and work into making the transition, but your new colleagues may not be so ready for you as a new player.

Don't assume that just because you're a long-standing employee in the company, you're at home in this new division. If you're replacing a popular former colleague, you may run up against additional resistance to your presence. Do as much as you can to make yourself welcome in the group.

COMMON MISTAKES

You leave a secure position only to discover that your new job will be a casualty of a downsizing exercise

Thoroughly investigate the prospects of this new assignment, just as you would if you were applying for the job from the outside. Understand the roles that this particular position and the department play in the company's long-term plans. If you cannot see how this work serves your employer's strategic objectives, hold out for another opportunity.

You become unintentionally slow-tracked

If you make a lateral move, especially if it is to reduce your stress load temporarily for a personal reason, you may find yourself accidentally on the list of expendable employees. Be sure to invest time regularly to market yourself to colleagues throughout the business. For example, go to key meetings on a regular basis or have lunch with your former manager to stay in touch with developments in your original department. Stay up to date with your company's developments and objectives and position yourself to make another jump into a more senior job as soon as you can.

You make too many lateral moves with no apparent growth or progression

Remember that, desirable as lateral moves may be, your career path must still show regular upward mobility.

When you make lateral moves, try to take a job that pays in some way, even though it's on the same level in the organisational chart. Or take a lateral move to learn more management skills elsewhere, and then return to your original department at a higher rank. Lateral career moves shouldn't be used routinely as a preventive measure against losing your job, or as a way to tread water for longer than during a very short downturn in the economy or your industry. Lateral career moves should be used as a valuable strategic career-management tool and, when you're able to discuss your recent career path in those terms, you'll find that a lateral move can be an excellent springboard to an even better future.

THE BEST SOURCES OF HELP
Book:
Bolles, Richard. *What Color is Your Parachute? A Practical Manual for Job-Hunters and Career-Changers*. Revised ed. Berkeley, California: Ten Speed Press, 2008.

Website:
PersonnelToday.com: **www.personneltoday.com**

Making Yourself Promotable

GETTING STARTED

Being good at your job is not enough to guarantee a promotion these days. Being *promotable*, on the other hand, increases your chances of success and assists you in taking the career steps that you desire.

Being promotable draws together your professional skills and competences with your business sense and ability to build good relationships to create the impression of someone who will be valuable to your organisation at increasingly senior levels. When you're recognised for your specialist expertise and have a track record of success, you're no doubt likely to be seen as a candidate for the succession line. However, other personal attributes that go well beyond your current role will be taken into consideration. To get ahead, you'll need to demonstrate business acumen, political sensitivity, the ability to manage change, and loyalty to your employing organisation. These attributes go hand-in-hand with the need to communicate and network effectively and the ability to cement critical relationships with those who will sponsor and support you as you move along your career path.

FAQS

I am very keen to be promoted and think I have done everything I can to get noticed. Competition is fierce, though, so how can I make sure I'm considered a suitable candidate for a new appointment?

Blowing your own trumpet too loudly isn't always the most effective way of influencing events. Being clear about what you want and why you deserve to be promoted is, of course, very important, but a subtle approach can also reap rewards. You could, for example:

- find a mentor or sponsor in the organisation with whom you can work
- approach your line manager and discuss your development plan in the light of your conviction that you have more to offer the business
- observe those that have been promoted and ask yourself if you're displaying the same personal attributes

Try to become more visible by ensuring that you take the opportunity to mix with decision-makers and by sharing stories of your success at appropriate times. Don't make too much of your achievements or you may turn off the very people you need to court.

I am working on becoming promotable but am having difficulty becoming more visible. Do you have any ideas?

While increasing your 'visibility' within the boundaries of your organisation is important, you don't need to confine yourself to just that. Why not publish articles in your trade or professional magazine, or accept invitations (or volunteer) to speak at conferences? If you want to raise your visibility closer to home to demonstrate your commitment to the community, you could get involved in local politics.

I work in an organisation where promotion is a thing of the past for all but a very few. How can I work my way into the senior management tier?

It sounds as if you're working in a flat organisation (where there are fewer levels in the hierarchy) or in a matrix organisation (where the business is structured according to common activities rather than discrete business units. Project teams are made up from specialists across a business). In these cases, promotability takes on a new meaning as there is often no longer a clear succession route. There may be prestigious and exciting areas to be associated with, however, or some career-enhancing assignments that you could target. Take a step back and examine the patterns and trends of progressive career paths in your organisation. Once you've identified the 'hot spots', you can work out which suit you best and plan your approach to reach them.

MAKING IT HAPPEN

Making yourself promotable is not an easy task because it implies a very wide development agenda. Aspects of this include familiarising yourself with the broader business arena and general management issues, developing social and political skills that enable you to build effective relationships, and finding a personal leadership style that you're comfortable with and can develop into a distinctive personal 'brand' in the long run.

It's a sad fact that the personal skills and attributes that have carried you to the point in your career where you're looking at a more senior appointment are the very skills and attributes that can sabotage your success at this level. These include having too high a dependence on your specialist expertise, an individualistic approach that differentiates you from your peers, and an inclination to challenge the organisational status quo. Shedding some of these traits, therefore, may be the key to becoming promotable.

In addition to these features, past research has highlighted several derailment factors that can prevent an otherwise capable person from further advancement. These include: 'problems with interpersonal relationships, failure to meet business objectives, failure to build and lead a team and an inability to change or adapt during a transition'. ('Why Executives Derail: Perspectives Across Time and Cultures', *Academy of Management Executive*. 1995. Volume 9, Number 4, pp. 62–72.) Two further derailment factors that were considered to reflect the changing business environment were later identified. These were the failure to *learn* to deal with change and complexity and overdependence upon a single boss or mentor. If you tackle each of these five factors in turn, you can be sure that you'll be building the personal capabilities that will enhance your promotability and distinguish you as a future leader.

Develop good interpersonal skills

As you progress through your career, a shift occurs in the balance between the expert contribution you make and your ability to build relationships. More senior positions demand a higher level of political sensitivity because, at this level, relationships go beyond the organisational setting and are more likely to have an impact on the long-term viability of the business. Faced with this realisation, many potential leaders try to fake it with an over-confident communication style that conveys nothing but arrogance and authoritarianism. Good interpersonal relationships are built by people who have no axe to grind and who aren't trying to create an illusion of confidence and capability. There's no substitute for genuine self-confidence; people can generally see through bluff and bluster, so it's as well to put the personal development time in to really know yourself well, understand your values, and create a clear picture of what you want. With this knowledge in place, good communication and an easy manner will follow naturally and authoritatively because it will genuinely reflect who you are.

Meet business objectives

In order to make yourself promotable, not only do you have to meet the objectives of your role, but you have to contribute to the wider business, too. This means showing initiative and taking an interest in areas outside your role boundaries. You could do this by volunteering for an important project, chairing a committee, or facilitating a special interest group. If you're seen to be supportive of, and passionate for, the business, you're much more likely to be noticed as someone who could add value at a more senior level. Although it may be unpalatable to some, you may have to consider (subtle) ways in which you can broadcast your willingness to play a more committed part in the fortunes of your business, such as suggesting or volunteering for a special project. This doesn't mean that you have to be sycophantic, but if you act like someone who occupies the type of role you're aiming for, it'll be easier for others to see you in that role.

Build and lead teams

One of the essential skills of a senior executive is the ability to build and lead teams. Without this, the co-operative networks that are vital if an organisation is to achieve its objectives are damaged. Much of a person's success in this area depends on his or her ability to communicate clear objectives as well as understanding the skills, motivations, and personal values of those in their team. Relationships must be open, with a healthy ebb and flow of feedback to ensure that everyone is aligned with the purpose of the team. Milestones and markers need to be part of the plan so that progress can be monitored and successes celebrated.

Learn to manage transition and change

Business and organisational models change in response to developments in the market and economy. The ripple effects of these changes are felt throughout the organisation and have an impact on everyone. Being able to field such changes and use your knowledge and insight to direct people's creative energy towards making them a success are valuable attributes of a leader. Entrenchment and other blocking types of behaviour are not perceived to be helpful, even if you feel that the change is unwise or counter-productive. If you find yourself in a situation like this, you may want to make alternative suggestions and explain the thinking behind them. If your concerns are rejected, though, demonstrate your loyalty by remaining flexible and actively seeking ways of making the changes work. Show that you're prepared to keep people motivated and learn from the new experience rather than demonstrate resentfulness or obstinacy. In short, remaining flexible and actively seeking ways of making (sometimes difficult) things happen, keeping people motivated, and learning from the new experience are all important characteristics of those in the top team.

Loyalty and solidarity are values that are prized in cultures that are subject to transition and change.

Build an effective network of champions or sponsors

We've all seen people who have been promoted on the basis of who they know, not what they know, yet this is no guarantee of future success. Indeed, investing in a nepotistic relationship is all very well when your champion is in favour, but if his or her reputation is damaged for any reason, yours will also be tarnished because of your close association. It's important, therefore, to build a robust network of relationships that will support you purely because of your potential and personal integrity. In this way, you can be sure that you aren't reliant on the perception people have of someone else (over whom you have no control), but that you're judged on your own talent and attributes. Think about your network and identify role models, potential coaches, and mentors for different aspects of your development plan. As you approach them, be open with your request for assistance but beware of projecting self-interest above the interests of the organisation. Frame your request in development terms stating that you feel you have more to offer the business and would appreciate their guidance.

In summary, being promotable does not rely on past success but on your ambassadorial qualities as you represent those in the upper echelons of the organisation. Neither does it rely on over-confidence or bullishness. Being promotable demands that you demonstrate an active interest in the business and an understanding of the strategic issues, an ability to reach stretch targets and build value, a genuinely confident communication style and an ability to build effective personal relationships within your team and among your colleagues.

COMMON MISTAKES

You irritate the people who could help you

Sometimes, people looking for a move up the career ladder make such a fuss about their ambitions that they make a lot of noise around the people who they think can promote them. This won't help their case, and in fact it's very irritating and counter-productive. There are unwritten 'rules' to being promotable, and you need to work these out through observing and adopting some of the tactics of successful people who've gone before you. Find out about the interests of those in authority and reflect these back to them or make yourself known in their philanthropic circles outside the business. For example, if you know that your boss supports a local charity, society, or sports team, why not go along to one of their events?

You're not willing to change

Although a track record of being a maverick may get you noticed, this is usually not a trait that will get you promoted. You need to play down your notoriety and redirect your energies into activities that are seen to support the organisation's best interests. If you're hoping to enter a different cultural zone in the organisation, you have to make sure you're familiar with the values that operate there and demonstrate that they're part of your value set too.

You ignore your team

It's tempting to focus on yourself as you look towards your career horizon and plan for your own success. You'll be judged on your ability to develop the talent in your team, though, so it's foolish to ignore them. You won't succeed by squashing those with potential, so you must trust in your own abilities and let your team flourish too. Doing this will create a loyal group who will support you in the long run. Take care to maintain these relationships as you move through the organisation, as you never know who you'll be working with (or for!) one day.

THE BEST SOURCES OF HELP
Websites:
Dauten.com: **www.dauten.com/pi**
OCJobSite.com: **www.ocjobsite.com/job-articles/ promote-yourself.asp**

Getting the Pay Rise You Deserve

GETTING STARTED

You feel certain that you deserve a pay rise, but you're unsure about how to ask your boss. It's very important to think through a number of issues and to have lots of information available when you make your request. It's also important to know how to respond if you end up receiving a negative answer. Here are some questions that will help you prepare for your negotiations for a higher salary:

- How is your company faring in the current economic downturn?
- When is the right time to ask for a pay rise?
- How has your performance been, and what's the evidence of your accomplishments?
- What's the typical salary range for a job such as yours?
- What's the best way to make the request?

FAQS

Why should I even bother to ask for a pay rise? Won't they give me a pay rise at my annual performance review if I have performed well?

Organisations have to make a trade-off between the need to pay enough money to keep people motivated to stay with the company and the need to keep down labour costs. You have to be your own agent and to promote your own case for why you should receive more money than you're currently making. It's helpful to learn about the salary philosophy of your organisation. For example, does it pay the minimum it can to keep costs down, or does it pay higher than market rate in order to attract the best employees? Does it tend to give pay rises that are close to the cost of living increase for the year (which is really not a pay rise)? Does it require managers to create a hierarchy among their staff and only give pay rises to the highest performers? If you have an understanding of the company philosophy, you can come to your performance appraisal well prepared to negotiate for a meaningful increase in salary. If you don't look out for yourself, the chances are pretty good that no one else will.

The company has not given many pay rises for quite a while. What should I do?

All companies go through boom times and difficult times, and they tend to retrench and cut costs when things are difficult financially: this is particularly the case at the time of writing. But that doesn't mean that you can't *ask for* a pay rise. If you've done a really outstanding job this past year and can point to concrete contributions, it's possible that the company might be able to find some money to reward your hard work. If no money is available, some other improvements in your job terms or benefits may be possible.

I'm not good at asking for things for myself. How do I go about boosting my confidence?

If you go into the salary negotiation meeting with well-prepared documentation of your achievements (see 'Document your contributions to the company' below), you'll have a stronger sense of your worth to the company and will feel more self-assured about asking for a pay rise. If you're really nervous about this, you might consider asking someone to role-play the situation with you so that you can practise beforehand. It's also helpful to visualise the meeting ahead of time and to picture what success would look like. Eliminate any negative talk in your head, such as 'No one ever appreciates what I do' or 'I never get what I want', and replace these ideas with something positive, such as 'I have worked hard for this company this past year, and I can present a strong case for why I should receive a pay rise.'

I was offered a promotion without a pay rise. Should I accept?

There are a lot of factors to take into account in this situation. If the promotion increases your skills, your responsibilities, and your visibility, and if the company is a start-up or is otherwise strapped for cash, you might agree to take the promotion. But you should also get written agreement from your supervisor that you'll have a salary discussion at a predetermined time in the future, for example, in three months.

MAKING IT HAPPEN

Decide on the best timing to ask for a pay rise

The most obvious time to ask for a pay rise is during your performance review discussion with your boss. However, it isn't uncommon for supervisors to put off these discussions for quite a while. It's one of their least favourite things to do. If it has been more than a year since your last performance review and since your last salary increase, you should approach your supervisor about your performance and your salary.

Ask your boss for a meeting

Give your boss time to prepare his or her thoughts for this discussion. Don't ask your boss for this meeting in front of other employees, because it puts him or her on the spot. Tell your boss that you'd like to have a meeting to discuss your performance, your career plans, and your salary, and plan for it to last at least 30 minutes. Don't just drop into his or her office and say, 'I'd like to talk to you about giving me a pay rise'.

Document your contributions to the company

The best way to do this is to keep a job diary or a file of your achievements regularly throughout the year. It's so easy to forget all that you've done, but if you keep track along the way, you'll have an excellent record of what you've contributed. When you ask for a pay rise, you need to build a business case for why the company should pay you more. You need to show what you've done for the business and document why you should be rewarded. Be sure to keep track of measurable results from your actions, such as pounds saved, sales increased, level of quality improved, or percentage of employee retention. Prepare a one-page executive briefing on your accomplishments to take into your meeting.

Know your worth in the marketplace

When companies calculate how much they typically pay for a job, they conduct wage surveys to compare salaries within the industry and geographical area. They also conduct internal pay analyses to make sure that comparable jobs within the company receive comparable pay. Such wage and salary information is now available on the Internet (see the websites below). It's a little bit harder to find out information about the internal pay structure, but you can ask the human resources department for information on what jobs like yours typically pay.

Approach your meeting with your supervisor with a win–win attitude

All successful negotiations end in both parties feeling that they received something of value. Your goal is to get a pay rise. Your supervisor's goal is to have a highly motivated and productive employee. Remember that pay rises are never given for potential or for what you're 'going to do'. Pay rises are given for meeting and exceeding performance goals. When you meet with your boss, you should be thinking about how your actions and accomplishments have helped to fulfil his or her own goals.

Discuss both performance and salary

Begin your discussion with a description of your accomplishments and contributions. Next, discuss how you intend to build on those in the coming year, and what some of your key goals are. Describe your goals in terms of how they'll support your boss and make a difference to the company. Then ask for the amount and percentage of salary increase that you think you deserve and explain why.

Listen

As your boss responds, listen to any objections that are made to your requests. Consider this discussion as a mentoring session and keep an open mind about what you can learn that will help your progress in the company. Before trying to overcome any objections, make sure that you communicate your understanding of those objections through paraphrasing what you've heard. This is the first step in negotiation and objections are a normal response. Be prepared for objections and be prepared to explain why you still deserve a pay rise.

Know what to do if you get a 'no'?

If you're told that you won't be getting a pay rise at this time, then ask what it is you need to do in order to earn one. Write down everything you're told. After the meeting, write a memo thanking your boss for his or her time, and listing the actions you need to take in order to earn a pay rise.

COMMON MISTAKES

You threaten to leave if you don't get the pay rise you deserve

Unless you're really unhappy and were thinking of leaving anyway, this strategy can do you much more harm than good. If you threaten to leave, you're sending the message that you aren't that committed to the organisation and are basically out for yourself. This approach isn't career-enhancing.

You complain to colleagues about your salary

Most organisations are insistent that all salary discussions take place only with your immediate supervisor. If you complain about your salary to your colleagues, you're very often seen as someone who isn't a team player, and who isn't politically astute. It's very unlikely that you'd get promoted or get a pay rise under these circumstances.

You ask fellow employees how much they make

Unless you're in an 'open-book' company, most organisations prefer that salary information be kept private. They're concerned that if employees begin to compare salaries with one another, it may lead some to think that they're being treated unfairly and will therefore lead to lower morale. You can get a better idea of your internal worth by benchmarking similar jobs in your organisation and then doing a search on the Internet for salary ranges for those jobs.

THE BEST SOURCES OF HELP
Websites:
Jobsite: **www.jobsite.co.uk/career/advice/ negotiate.html**
SalarySearch: **www.salarysearch.co.uk**

Leaving with Style: Exiting with Dignity

GETTING STARTED

Probably several times during your career, you will leave one employer for another. Frequently, leaving the organisation will be your choice; sometimes it will be the organisation's. Either way, it is important for you to exit with style and dignity. Whenever you depart from a job, under whatever circumstances, you want to leave a lasting impression of professionalism. The following are questions you should contemplate as you get ready to leave your current employer:

- How do I want my boss and colleagues to remember me after I have moved on to the next job?
- What do I want my boss and colleagues to say about me after I leave the organisation?
- What specific things can I do to demonstrate my professionalism, even when I know that I am leaving?

FAQS

Why should I worry about 'exiting with dignity'? I won't be working there any more anyway

The phrase 'never burn your bridges' became a cliché with good reason. You should always leave a job on the best possible terms. People from the organisation you are leaving may be called to give you references for future jobs. You want to be able to use past employers for references, and to feel assured that they will speak highly of you.

Remember that, even in large industries, it is still a small world. People (especially at higher levels) know each other, and may casually enquire about a former employee. Staff from your former organisation may go to conventions or conferences and meet people from your current organisation. If you leave a negative impression at one company, your new employer may very well hear about it.

Also, suppose your new organisation were to be bought by or merged with your old one? Mergers and acquisitions are becoming more common. You could end up working for and with some of the same people you left when you resigned from the company. Make sure you can face former employers with your head held high.

My boss has been impossible to work with. Should I discuss his or her management errors in the exit interview?

The simple answer is 'no'. What will you gain by bad-mouthing your (soon-to-be) former boss? When asked about working conditions or supervision, always begin and end with positive comments. For example, 'I think we have a great team in the department, even though we've been under some real pressure lately. If there was a bit less pressure, I think the department could really capitalise on the creativity that's already there'. Say as many positive, accurate things as possible.

Should I help my employer to find my replacement?

If your boss asks you to interview candidates for your job, doing it well can go a long way to leaving a positive lasting impression. When talking to candidates for your job, do not discuss negative aspects of the job, colleagues, supervisors, or the organisation. This is the time to be as upbeat as possible. Talk about the positive facets of the work and the organisation. Remember, the person you are interviewing may get the job, and you want his or her impression of you to be that of the consummate professional.

If the interviewee asks you why you are leaving the organisation, never talk about how much more money you will be making, or how much better the working conditions are at your new job. Tell your potential replacement that you were offered an opportunity with some interesting challenges that will build on the skills that you have attained in your current position.

MAKING IT HAPPEN

Prepare your letter of resignation

Always give notice to your employer in writing. Your letter should be brief and professional, and contain the date of your last day of work. End your resignation letter on a positive note by commenting briefly on the valuable learning, or challenging, or growth opportunities the position you are resigning from has afforded you. That's it. Do not go on about how much better the new job is.

Meet with your immediate supervisor

Arrange a time to meet with the person to whom you report directly. Your immediate supervisor always deserves the courtesy of a face-to-face meeting. During this meeting, you should tell your supervisor that you have decided to take another position, and when you will be leaving. This is not the time to tell your boss all the things that are wrong with him or her, how low your salary has been, or how awful the working conditions are in your present organisation. When asked why you are leaving, simply state that an exciting new opportunity has presented itself, one that you just could not refuse.

Always be professional in this meeting. If you have had any problems with your supervisor, forget about them now. The best advice ever given about this meeting is 'let your supervisor save face'. You want your boss to feel as comfortable as possible during this meeting. You also want to assure him or her that you will be finishing certain projects, or continuing to deal with customers, and so on. Perhaps one of the most difficult aspects of exiting with dignity is to keep this meeting positive and upbeat.

Continue to work as if you were staying with the organisation

This is the real key to exiting with dignity and leaving an excellent lasting impression. Continue to work as if you were trying for the next promotion. Finish as many projects as possible; attend all meetings; be an active participant in your work. This is not the time to let things slide.

One outstanding example of an impressive and dignified exit was set by a tutor who did not receive tenure at his university (the academic equivalent of being fired). He attended and actively participated in every meeting, put effort into his teaching, and continued to work enthusiastically with students. In short, he continued to work as if he would be in that job next week, next month, and next year. You should too.

Leave instructions for the next person who will be doing your job

If there are certain projects that are ongoing or you do not complete, leave detailed written instructions. Make the transition for the next person as easy as possible. In doing so, you are leaving the impression that you did not simply abandon the work you could not complete; you recognised it, and took the steps necessary to get the job done.

COMMON MISTAKES

Not giving enough notice when you resign

In a number of professions, the two-week notice is a thing of the past. Many organisations expect a much longer notice. Check your contract discreetly when you start looking for another job. Companies look very unfavourably on employees who give little or no notice before leaving. You should give your employer adequate notice to recruit someone to take over your position.

Talking excessively about your great new job and salary to colleagues

Colleagues will ask you about your new position, and talking about it is natural, but bragging about how much better your new position is than your old one only leaves colleagues feeling resentful and with an overall unfavourable impression of you. Tempting as it is to brag, and excited as you are about your new position, limit your discussions to comments such as 'Well, this is a good opportunity for me'.

Giving your notice or resignation via e-mail

Although e-mail is probably the most popular type of office communication these days, always give your supervisor a formal letter of resignation (see 'Prepare your letter of resignation' above). Also be sure to arrange a meeting to give your notice in person to your direct supervisor (see 'Meet with your immediate supervisor' above).

THE BEST SOURCES OF HELP
Websites:
iResign.com: **www.i-resign.com/uk/letters/**
Job Hunters' Bible: **www.jobhuntersbible.com**

Surviving Redundancy

GETTING STARTED

Redundancy has, unfortunately, become a reality for many people since the global economic crisis really took hold in 2008. No matter whether you're made redundant with no notice, or you know months in advance that your position is going to be eliminated, the actual event of losing your job can be a shock to your physical system, your emotional health, and, of course, your bank account. The steps you take as soon as you get a hint that your job is coming to an end will help to cushion the impact of one of the most stressful times in your life.

The concept of 'strategy' is extremely valuable at this point in your career. It invites you somehow to rise above your sensation of panic and, perhaps, the tendency to feel worthless in the marketplace. It'll also help you take a new, bird's-eye view of your life and career, and see the potential for ultimately better work and greater success. You should consider the following questions as you take important steps to turn this upsetting news into a success story:

- How can you benefit in the long run?
- What can you do to prepare yourself in advance, so you're not taken by surprise?
- What power do you have to decide the terms of your departure?
- Can you be consistent with your own dreams, in the face of a marketplace that is urging you to build a career that doesn't interest you?
- How do your skills, talents, and drive fit into the larger business community?

FAQS

Why is it important to have a strategy in place before I lose my job?

If you're able to design your strategy in a calm environment, you can coolly select the steps and actions to take later when you're most likely to feel panicked and diminished by the event of discovering your employer no longer wants you.

If I'm made redundant by my organisation, does that mean my relationship with my employer is over for good?

No. Many employers who are making people redundant recognise that it's very likely that they'll want to re-employ them when economic conditions improve. Even if that were not to happen, the business world is very small and you are likely to run into your employer in the future at a convention, or even at a different organisation. In fact, it's not unheard of for the redundant employee to be the one to recruit their former superior at a different organisation months or years later. For this reason, it's important never to burn a bridge!

What should I tell my family?

Hundreds of thousands of excellent employees all over the world face unemployment through no fault of their own. If you aren't completely honest with your family, they won't understand the strain and tension that is suddenly in your home and you'll rob them of the opportunity to support you in your time of crisis. Everyone – down to the smallest child – can contribute to the cause of thriving in temporarily reduced circumstances. This could be a golden opportunity to become closer through the teamwork needed to pull through.

MAKING IT HAPPEN
Try to be aware of potential redundancy long before it actually happens
Employers are often reluctant to announce to the workforce that there is going to be a cutback for fear that everyone will disappear en masse, leaving the organisation in chaos. But it's still possible to be aware of trends that might result in unemployment. Is your local newspaper reporting lower profits for your organisation? Is there a merger or acquisition rumoured? Is there a sudden spate of 'closed-door' meetings? Has your boss, or boss's boss, suddenly lost organisational power, no longer being invited to those closed-door meetings? Is your own job a vital link to the organisation's profitability or is it a 'cost centre'? Is your overall industry, or local economy, suffering a downturn? The answers to these questions might help you assess how secure your position really is.

Network
Have a large and intricate network of contacts that you can always draw from, no matter what your employment circumstances. That network could be your advance warning system, or the conduit for information about other jobs and opportunities in good times and bad. Knowing you have that resource at your disposal will reduce the anxiety and panic, should the worst-case scenario of losing your job actually come true. Traditionally, networking was done in person, often as part of being a member of a professional organisation or association, but you can network with people all over the world without leaving your laptop, thanks to sites such as LinkedIn (www.linkedin.com) and Facebook (www.facebook.com) and services such as Twitter (www.twitter.com).

Don't sign the redundancy agreement while in a state of shock
Most employers will tell you the terrible news and then slide a contract under your nose for you to sign before you go away. Remember, they've had plenty of advance warning to devise a separation agreement that benefits the organisation. You deserve at least 24 hours to enable you to consider it carefully, perhaps even with a lawyer.

Remember that many redundancy agreements are negotiable
Perhaps you can convert your job to a contract position. In most cases, after all, the work still has to be done. By offering to do it on an outsourcing basis, you've found a way to generate cash flow for yourself while staying in touch and on good terms with your former employer. Other negotiable details can include the right to continue to use your office space while searching for

new employment (the space may still be available whether you're there or not, and the illusion of being employed adds to your attractiveness to other possible employers); use of company equipment and services, such as the photocopier and voicemail; letters of recommendation or introduction from the organisation's senior executives; or a larger redundancy settlement.

Take advantage of company-sponsored outplacement services
The best outplacement services are highly valuable benefits, largely unavailable to the average individual. This is a once-in-a-lifetime opportunity to have free professional help in designing your job-search plan of action and to receive state-of-the-art aptitude and skills testing – as well as giving you a place to go to every day, where you'll be in a professional office environment with your peers. Outplacement counsellors also know the best and most powerful employers in the area, so you're plugged into a pipeline that's not available to individuals who aren't affiliated with organisations or outplacement services.

Keep your skills up to date
If your employer is offering free or subsidised skills training, take advantage of the offer. If you've been out of the job market for even as little as a year, it's likely that your technical and professional skills would benefit from a refresher course. Seize every learning opportunity that's placed before you. It will give you both a technical edge and the confidence to start your job-search project.

Keep your spirits up
Throw a party for your fellow sufferers, and invite local recruiters to enjoy the gathering as well. It's good to know you're not alone and, even if recruiters don't have any opportunities at the moment, they'll be glad to take a copy of your CV and contact information. The economy goes through cycles, and recruiters will always be glad to have a full file of excellent potential candidates.

Forget those lists of promising, 'hot' careers
They only ever promise a glut on the market of such careers in two to four years' time. Do what you love and build a career around your interests. There will always be a demand for employees who love what they do – they're the most innovative, self-starting, and constantly developing individuals.

COMMON MISTAKES
You fall into despair
Don't tie your sense of self-worth to your career or job. You are who you are, regardless of where your salary is coming from. If you go through a spell of low self-esteem, volunteer your professional expertise to a charity. The time spent with others will get you out of your

gloom. Most important, you'll experience the real bene-fits of your gifts and knowledge, as they'll be received with no other payment than gratitude.

You don't take care of yourself physically
Without routine and regular exercise, the sofa and the remote control become increasingly enticing. But if you maintain a regular routine and exercise programme, your sense of purpose and minute-by-minute priorities will remain clear. The endorphins resulting from your phys-ical exertion will also keep the blues and fear at bay. Eating sensibly will keep your body strong and resistant to the stress that comes with uncertainty.

You let isolation overwhelm your life
Make a point of filling your calendar with business meet-ings every week. Put on presentable clothes every day and go to a local coffee shop, if that's all that is available,

just to be out among people. Meet at least one new person a week: start off online if you need to with some of the sites mentioned above. Find a way to help people you do meet by introducing them to someone in your own network: you'll soon see positive results.

THE BEST SOURCES OF HELP
Book:
Taylor, Andrew. *Burning the Suit: Fighting Back Against Redundancy.* Chichester: Capstone, 2008.

Websites:
Citizens Advice Bureau: **www.citizensadvice.org.uk**
Department for Business, Enterprise and Regulatory Reform: **www.berr.gov.uk**
Laid Off Central: **www.laidoffcentral.com**

Freelancing: Setting Up As a Free Agent

GETTING STARTED
Who wouldn't be seduced by the idea of commuting in a dressing gown and slippers to an office only a few yards away from the breakfast table? On top of this idyllic scene comes the next logical step for many people: leaving their current job to start their own business.

Hundreds of thousands of people choose to work from home these days, and most new businesses start off in the home of their owner–managers. If you're thinking about basing your company in your house to begin with, you'll need to get used to not only a different way of working, but to being the person with whom the buck stops in all work matters. Could you cut the mustard? To start, ask yourself the following questions:
• How much of my freelance fantasy is based on being unhappy with my current situation?
• What is my 'core competency', around which I will begin a freelance business?
• Who employs freelancers in my field of work and do I have enough experience and contacts?
• Who is my competition and what edge do I have over them?
• What are the costs of going into my own business, as well as the benefits?

FAQS
What exactly is a freelancer?
The word 'freelance' comes from the old days of knights-for-hire, but these days it refers to someone in the serv-ice of more than one employer. Nowadays, a freelancer can be a self-employed person in any number of indus-tries, including accounting, writing, film and video,

management consulting, software development, and Internet services.

What sort of personality traits and skills must a person have as a freelancer?
You must be – or quickly become – confident, resource-ful, enterprising, adventurous, flexible, and organised. As a business owner, you also must be a manager, a book-keeper, and a promoter. You'll have to be able to 'multi-task' – juggle a number of diverse projects, each with different deadlines, for your clients.

How do I decide what to charge for my services?
There are books and websites that give guidelines about the value of your profession, in terms of an hourly rate. Another way to determine your starting hourly rate is to work out what people in that field earn per hour as employees, then add 25–50 per cent to account for the overheads you'll have (such as taxes, insurance, retire-ment savings, equipment, and supplies).

Remember, too, that as a business owner, at least a quarter of your workload will involve activities you may not invoice for, such as research, marketing, promotion, and book-keeping. If possible, find out what established freelancers in your field are charging. You may want to start at a reduced rate for the first year, especially if you're going to be competing against more established freelancers.

MAKING IT HAPPEN
Do your research
Making a jump to freelancing requires a kind of 'inside-out' approach:

- Be honest with yourself about your motives for the move. If you feel more excitement about the future than dread of where you are now, you're on the right track.
- Look at your personality assets: you'll need people skills, energy, promotional creativity, a love of your chosen profession, and a devotion to detail.
- Your outside research should include canvassing the industry in which you'll offer your services.
- Determine how big a 'territory' you'll initially serve, and what sort of companies. If possible, ask the advice of anyone already in that field. In the best of all worlds, knowing someone at those companies who knows you from a prior work relationship (and who can therefore recommend you for future work) is a big asset.

Develop your business plan

Once you decide to commit to a life as a freelancer – but before you leave your day job – develop a business plan. Even if you've lined up a client or two, a business plan will plot the first year's goals and activity.

Some people have found it a good idea to start a free-lance business on a part-time basis, so that they can still rely on the income from their other job during the tricky start-up phases. This part-time approach may take on the dimensions of a second full-time job and as a result cut into other areas of your life, but trying it out this way will show you quickly if you have the determination and work ethic to persevere.

Not only will your business plan help you clarify your business's purpose and prepare well for the future, it's also essential if you want to borrow money from the bank or another financial institution. You need to convince other people to be as committed to the business as you are, so remember to:

- be as specific as possible about the kind of business you're starting
- describe your business in terms of a mission statement or 'executive summary' that clearly summarises your business's purpose
- make sure your purpose can be easily understood by you, your customers, and potential investors. If you can't describe your business in this way, you really need to rethink your business idea and focus on the core activities and direction

Use as your starting point your vision of where you might want your business to be in five years' time, so that you can show in your plan how you'd start to move towards that point. For example, you might work towards becoming a market leader, an innovator, a specialist, a large concern, or a top-notch supplier.

Market and promote your business

Whether or not your freelance business is in the same industry you're currently employed in, you'll need to develop a target list of companies that you'd like to work for. Once you've done that, learn all you can about each company, its products and services, its financial health, its challenges, and its history with contract employment. Find out who in those companies makes contract decisions. Aim your marketing and proposals at them; invite them to lunch if they happen to live nearby.

Marketing can also include letters, brochures, or e-mails sent to potential customers, as well as personal networking, advertising, and promotional activities, even a website. Ideally, you'll have built enough of a network before you start your business to reduce the amount of 'cold calling' you must do.

Focus on customer service

Making the move to being a profitable freelancer is largely a matter of time: the longer you're in business, the greater the probability that you'll be successful. Remember that it's far better to keep a client happy than to spend the same amount of time finding another one, so being prompt and delivering a professional product or service for the proposed budget are the cornerstones of a successful freelance business.

Keep up good business practices

As a freelancer, it would be rare to have a consistent client, or set of clients, for a long period of time. Business climates change, and freelancers are vulnerable to shifts in policy and personnel: if your in-house contact moves on, for example, the new person may have his or her preferred freelancers, so you may lose out. Ensure that you always keep on good terms with your contacts, so that they'll want you to 'move' with them if the time comes.

Get used to the idea of losing clients and gaining new ones; it's part of the nature of the business, like an animal shedding a winter coat and growing a new one. To protect themselves against this inevitability, freelancers usually have several irons in the fire. As it often takes six months to a year to secure work with a new prospective client, you should discipline yourself to plan at least six months ahead. Learn to anticipate when clients need more service, but also learn to predict when your tenure may be drawing to a close. Have the foresight to build enough diversity in your client base that the loss of one won't spell disaster for your business.

COMMON MISTAKES

You're cavalier about your home office

Many freelancers begin at home and there's nothing wrong with that. But it's essential that (for HM Revenue & Customs purposes) you create a separate office that has no other purpose. Keep very good records of things you'll want to list as itemised deductions on your business tax return. HM Revenue & Customs doesn't mind you having such a short journey to work (actually, it does mind a little), but it has some specific guidelines under which you may deduct home office expenses.

You rely too much on one client

In the best sense, freelancers bring added value to a company, and companies are willing to pay handsomely for those who can deliver. But don't become complacent.

Valued as you may feel, freelancers are easier to lay off than employees, so be vigilant and prepared for budget tightening or changes in administrative personnel.

You don't save for the lean times

Inevitably, there will be lean times in your freelance business. Putting aside enough money to get you through, say, two or three months of basic expenses is advisable. Besides that, however, remember that as a freelancer, you're also responsible for paying taxes to HM Revenue & Customs. Make sure you're aware of what these are likely to be and create a reserve in readiness for this eventuality. However, don't forget to pay yourself, including your subscription to a private health insurer and appropriate provision for your retirement. Try to save for holidays too; we all benefit from a break.

You let things slide

Just as you must be adept and professional about what you bill your client for, you also must become skilled at running your own business affairs. Plan to devote up to 25 per cent of your time on various administrative and marketing-related activities. When business is booming, it's especially easy to get complacent about record keeping, credit card debt, payment of taxes, developing new business leads, and even collecting from your clients on time. If you don't stay on top of your own business details, you could be ruined very quickly when times are harder.

For tax purposes and others, it's well worth the £150–£300 a year to have a respected accountant look at your business. An accountant can tell you how to avoid tax troubles and will often save you more in deductions than you'll pay him or her in fees. Accountants have a lot of experience advising business people about a variety of issues, so feel free to pump yours for information. If they're reluctant to share, find another one.

THE BEST SOURCES OF HELP
Websites:
BusinessLink: **www.businesslink.gov.uk**
HM Revenue & Customs: **www.hmrc.gov.uk**

Setting Up and Maintaining Your Home Office

GETTING STARTED
Many people choose to work from home these days, and most new businesses start off in the home of their owner-managers. If you're thinking about basing your company in your house to begin with, you may need to get used to a new way of working, especially if you've previously been working in a more formal, structured setting. To start, ask yourself the following questions:
- Can I handle the social isolation of a home office on a full-time basis?
- Am I a self-starter?
- How do I rate as a decision-maker, organiser, book-keeper, and secretary?
- Could I separate business and personal life if both were under the same roof?
- Am I a workaholic and would an office at home worsen that problem?

FAQS
Is working from home as wonderful as it sounds?
Yes and no. For convenience, cost, and comfort, there's nothing quite like a home office. Low overheads, no commuting hassles, no office politics, and setting your own hours are a few of the pluses. On the minus side, there's only you – and if you're not disciplined, you'll be spending more time with the children, the pets, or in front of the fridge than working where you belong. It can be a simple formula for failure.

How can I make a home-based business seem professional to customers?
It depends on the type of business, but start with a professional attitude and then buy some good-looking business cards and stationery. Think about adding an attractive logo and using a two-colour design on business cards, letterheads, and envelopes. Having a well-produced flyer or brochure that describes your business is also a plus: good-quality customer service will do the rest.

E-commerce is relatively easy to conduct from a home office, especially with a website that attracts customers. Clients don't really need to know whether you work at home or in a sophisticated office building, so long as you get the job done for them. As with your other materials, the website should reflect the personality and professionalism of your business.

What sort of investment is necessary to equip a home office?
This, too, depends on the type of activity you'll be doing – whether it be business or teleworking, or a personal or family office. But generally, spending between £1,500 and £3,000 should make you well equipped and comfortable. Make a list and plan a sensible budget beforehand. You don't want to blow your entire savings on setting

up the office, then have nothing to spend on attracting business.

MAKING IT HAPPEN
Plan the layout of your office
Planning a home office involves deciding where to locate the office, how to decorate it, and how to furnish it. You should give lots of thought to this, as it will be the hub of a small business and you'll be spending a lot of time there. Some people even make a scale drawing of the room they intend to use, then place to-scale furniture in there to decide on the best layout.

Take account of tax considerations
As you're planning to use the office for a small business, HM Revenue & Customs will allow you to deduct certain expenses connected to the business. For that reason, the office must be completely dedicated to the business and not merely a spare bedroom with a fold-up desk and your cordless phone. Good record-keeping is very important if you plan to deduct expenses and part of the mortgage interest, utilities, and phone bills for business activity.

Make sure you're comfortable and have the right equipment
Office décor is important. Besides getting the right atmosphere (lighting, paint/wallpaper, floor covering), think about practical items too: do you have enough phone lines and electrical sockets in the room to support the office equipment? Beyond that, having comfortable, functional furniture will allow you to work productively.

Your package of office equipment will depend on the type of business you're in, but will probably include computer(s) and peripherals, software, phones and phone service for voice, fax and computer, and perhaps even a separate copier and/or scanner. Add a digital camera if you plan to put photos of yourself or your products on your website. A broadband connection will make your life easier if you don't have one already: it is available in most places now, although the service can be limited in some rural areas. If you visit **www.broadbandchecker.co.uk**, you can type in your postcode and phone number and you'll be told whether broadband is available in your area, along with a list of service providers. Finally, don't forget that you'll need storage space for files, records, and other general office supplies.

Be disciplined
One of the most difficult aspects of the home office is the home itself – it's all too easy to be distracted by jobs round the house, watch TV, weed the garden, get involved with family things, have a snack in the kitchen, and otherwise avoid the work that awaits you in your office. Two factors will help avoid the home trap: being excited about your office space and the work – and discipline. Set regular office hours, have a separate business phone, organise your time, and stick to your deadlines.

Don't let yourself get isolated
Being isolated in your home office, you may develop a tendency to cocoon yourself in there or to avoid keeping in touch with the outside world, both of which can be unhealthy.

Having a business gives you plenty of opportunity to break away from the office to meet other people socially and professionally. Even if much of your business is conducted over the phone and by computer, it's still important to network. Invite customers and prospective customers to lunch, if they happen to do business nearby. Join a local community group or professional organisation to stay connected and also to generate local interest in your business. Get physical exercise away from the home. Join an evening class. All these things will help keep you connected, bring in new ideas, and generate lots of personal energy – things you'll value when working alone.

COMMON MISTAKES
You go halfway with the office arrangement
Starting a home office on the dining-room table is not a good idea, nor is committing only half-heartedly to making a guestroom into a real office. If you don't treat the office seriously, there's a better than even chance you won't take your work seriously either.

Carve out a separate space and dedicate it as the office. You'll feel better and your work will benefit from that decision.

You succumb to workaholic syndrome
If, while working in an office setting, you've had a tendency to stay there until the work is done, operating from home is a workaholic's dream come true. With the office only a few rooms away, there's a temptation to 'get one last thing done' after dinner or at weekends.

It's important to be professional about your business, but it's also important that you don't let the office become your new home. Set hours, try to manage your workflow into those hours, then shut the door and leave it all behind.

You get swamped by family issues
Lots of women see working at home as the answer to two issues – making a living and raising a family. If it were easy to mix children and work, parents would have been doing it at their offices long ago.

That said, it isn't entirely impossible either. The trick is balance. You can't afford to be at the beck and call of your children, but you certainly don't want them to feel totally ignored. Racing from the office to untangle toys and do the washing every hour will soon turn your work world upside-down. Closing the door and ignoring the family will have an equally unfortunate effect.

Obviously, day care is an option. Consider it for the days that you might need to concentrate on your most important work. On days you set aside for more mundane tasks, such as paying bills, book-keeping, research on the Internet, and so forth, you might find it easier to have the family there.

You lack certain office job skills

When working for other companies, you probably relied on others with jobs that complemented your own. When you are your own boss, working from your home office, you have a lot more duties besides the specific ones that 'bring home the bacon'. You'll be responsible for executive and marketing decisions, financial and administrative details and deadlines, as well as clerical and reception work. Until your business becomes profitable enough to employ other people, it's all down to you.

This is where a business plan makes sense. You need to work out the details of how you'll charge for your products or services. Be careful to account for the 'cost of doing business', which includes the clerical and administrative things, too. Add in a 'fudge factor' and some profit. Assuming that you'll work a 40-hour week, set your sights on making a living in 30 hours, then use the other 10 hours to take care of the other parts of the business –

marketing, promotion, invoicing, book-keeping, and business errands.

If you feel you lack the skills to juggle all of these things, or don't have the interest in becoming your own secretary, perhaps you're not cut out for a home business. But if you want to give it a try, you can certainly learn what you need to know about the care and feeding of a small business from books, the Internet, or your local small-business advisory service.

THE BEST SOURCES OF HELP
Book:
Holmes, Andrew. *Finance for Freelancers: How to Get Started and Make Sure You Get Paid.* London: A&C Black, 2008.

Websites:
Entrepreneur: **www.entrepreneur.com**
HM Revenue & Customs: **www.hmrc.gov.uk/ menus/b_taxpayers.htm**
Money *Guardian*: **www.guardian.co.uk/money**

Looking for Work When You Go Freelance

GETTING STARTED
Going freelance can be an incredibly exhilarating experience, and many people enjoy the freedom and choice that it affords them. On the flipside, it does mean that they're solely responsible for finding work, for balancing their existing workload with the need to find future projects, for keeping an eye on their finances, and for ensuring that they still have a private life!

It can all work out well, however, as long as you work at building relationships and growing your network of contacts. If you have gone freelance and you're not a natural networker, going out of your way to meet others for non-social reasons may not be an attractive option. If you don't put yourself out, however, you run the risk of the work drying up one day, so you need to find ways of building contacts that's as efficient and pain-free as possible. The good news is that there are plenty of ways you can do this, including harnessing the power of the Internet.

FAQS
A huge project has come my way and I'm very keen to do it, but it will dominate my life for several months. What's the best way to manage my work–life balance?
Guaranteed work is manna from heaven for the freelancer, but if the job is genuinely massive, it's

unlikely you'll be able to do it all yourself and still be able to meet your personal commitments at home with family or friends. Tap into your network of contacts to see whether a trusted freelance colleague may be able to help you out with some aspects of the project. You can, of course, check over their work before it goes back to your client to make sure that it meets your own quality standards, but that will still be quicker than taking it on yourself. If you've got an established relationship with the client who has offered you the work, talk to them honestly about the schedule and other deliverables to find a way through that works for you both.

How can I keep an eye on the future while I'm working on a project?
You're right to recognise that it's essential to still put out feelers for work *after* the big project is done. Much of freelance life is characterised by peaks and troughs of intense activity and then fallow periods, so advance planning to keep your schedule more stable is an excellent idea. Why not put aside a morning each week to e-mail or telephone contacts, or to attend networking events?

I've just been made redundant and have decided to go freelance. My first job is with the company that just let me go. Even though we know each

other well, should I still ask them to sign a contract with me for the new work I'm doing?

Yes. It's important that you start your new career on a professional footing and also that you protect your own interests. If things are in a state of flux, there's a chance that your contact at your former employer may move on too. It's therefore essential that you have all the details of your project laid out and confirmed in a signed contract. List out all relevant aspects that have been agreed (time-lines, fees or hourly rates, a description of the work you'll be doing) and also included payment terms and any cancellation conditions. Use the final draft of this contract as a template for future ones.

MAKING IT HAPPEN

Plan ahead

In many industries, the traditional hierarchical workplace just doesn't exist any more, which means that the opportunities for freelancers are growing. Yes, it can be a big leap if you've spent the bulk of your career employed by an organisation, but many people find that they thrive in a freelancing environment and eventually have no wish to return to conventional employment in any case!

To avoid headaches and financial crises, however, you need to make sure you have regular work coming in. The steps below highlight ways you can do that.

Let people know what you can do

Your clients engage you for the range of skills that you have and which they need at that time. However, make sure that people know what else you have to offer, so that you don't get 'typecast'. You don't have to be pushy; just a simple statement will do: 'If you're looking for help with marketing, just let me know. I used to run the marketing and publicity department in my previous job, and I'd be happy to talk to you about extending my contract for a few weeks to take this on'.

Another way of showing how you can contribute further to a client's business is to write a business case that supports your skills and shows how they could be used in a project. If you add some (realistic!) figures to your proposal, you're doing some of the work your client would have to do anyway, so they'll be grateful for your proactive approach. Don't be downhearted if this doesn't work first time: no one gets a win every single time, but you can learn from each pitch and improve them as you go forward.

While it is always good to be invited to work for others, don't be afraid for asking for projects to take on. Many freelancers slip into the habit of simply responding to others' need for work to be done, and are reluctant to go 'cap in hand' to a potential client and ask for work. However, sometimes clients don't realise what value you could add to their business. It may be that you get in touch at just the right moment and land yourself a lucrative job, as well as extending your network of contacts.

Tap into your network

A good deal of freelance work is placed as a result of people's contacts, both within their immediate and extended networks. Take some time to think through the various strands that make up your network: you'd be amazed how many people may be interested in your services, even if only tangentially. Be brave and remind people regularly of who you are, what you do, what news you have, and so on: e-mails, phone calls, and face-to-face meetings are all great ways to do this. As with all networking activity, however, remember that the traffic needs to go both ways. Ask other people how you can help them and they're much more likely to want to help you. Always say thank you for any leads you get – and create leads in return.

Be visible

Taking the initiative is a key part of freelance success. As part of your campaign, attend events tailored to your industry that will allow you to meet like-minded free-lance colleagues and potential clients. If you go to a conference, attend debates so you can keep in touch with new thinking, hot topics, and trends. Talk to other delegates and follow up after the event so that you're actively working towards establishing relationships, rather than expecting people to come to you.

Advertise yourself

On a similar note, why not offer to contribute to these events by giving a presentation or writing an article for the accompanying brochure? Make sure your contact details are listed so that people can get in touch. Also be ready to comment on topical issues relating to your work. While *you* may not feel that you are the 'go to' expert in your field, people will start to perceive you as such.

Benefit from the Internet

Used carefully, the Internet is an absolute boon for free-lancers. It allows you to find out more about existing and potential clients by visiting their sites, and you can network online too, which is a great option if you're new to freelancing or lack confidence in your social skills. Practise online before you try out other networking options. You can also use the Internet to boost your brand, as mentioned above, via your own website, a blog, or networking sites such as Facebook or LinkedIn.

COMMON MISTAKES

You never say 'no'

When the buck stops with you in terms of finding work, it can be hard to turn down opportunities. If you agree to absolutely everything, though, you just won't be able to manage. Your standards may slip, you'll miss deadlines, clients may be reluctant to give you future projects, and you'll end up losing a lot of money in the long term. Saying no to an offer of work won't prevent a client from coming back to you. In fact they'll see that you're busy, and that you're sensible about managing your workload – both of which are points firmly in your favour.

You allow work to take over other areas of your life
If you're rushing to meet a tight deadline, it's almost inevitable that you'll end up working in the evenings or at the weekends. You'll also need to squeeze some time in to look after billing, meet your accountant, and make new contacts. That's a big to-do list. If it sounds familiar to you, schedule some time in your diary every week *during working hours* in which you look after these crucial details. Making sure you take regular holidays will also help you to rest and to keep up with friends and family, so don't put them off.

You put all your eggs in one basket
Take time to regularly look for new opportunities and customers. Even if you have a fantastic relationship with a large client, there are bound to be quieter times in their work schedule, so if you rely on them for all your work you'll soon come unstuck. Don't put off networking or feel that it's a waste of time: being visible and making connections may not reap rewards instantly, but will come in handy in the longer term.

You don't keep on top of the paperwork
Few people enjoy dealing with invoices, contracts, tax returns, and the other admin issues that take up so much time for the self-employed. However, letting this slide can result in payments being delayed or missed, leaving you to pay for all your outgoings while struggling with no income. If your client has agreed that you can bill them for costs and expenses incurred over and above your hourly or daily rate (international phone calls, say, or travel costs), make sure you keep all receipts and that they are submitted with your invoice. Also remember that the sooner you invoice, the sooner you'll be paid. Cash-flow traumas are the number one reason for small business failure, so make sure your business doesn't become another casualty.

THE BEST SOURCES OF HELP
Books:
Ferriss, Timothy. *The 4-Hour Workweek: Escape 9–5, Live Anywhere, and Join the New Rich*. New York: Crown Business, 2007.
Holmes, Andrew. *Finance for Freelancers: How to Get Started and Make Sure You Get Paid*. London: A&C Black, 2008.

Websites:
Facebook: **www.facebook.com**
LinkedIn: **www.linkedin.com**

Working As Part of a Virtual Team

GETTING STARTED
Working as part of a virtual team is obviously something you need to think about if you decide to work from home. In very broad strokes, a virtual team is a group of people who use a range of technologies to collaborate from different work bases. Members of a virtual team may all work for the same company, be a mix of employees and freelances, or be entirely freelance. Team members may be scattered across one country or all around the world.

Virtual teams are becoming more common as businesses open up offices around the world to expand their reach but, in attempts to keep time and cost investments to a minimum, colleagues and team members remain physically isolated from each other.

Although tele- and videoconferencing technology and other forms of electronic communication have improved greatly over the last 10 years, they're poor substitutes for the chemistry that teams create as they work together, getting the best from each person's strengths and characteristics. Building and working in a successful virtual team is a great new skill to add to your bow, and one that can add even more positive aspects to your decision to work from home.

FAQS
I'm worried about feeling isolated – what can I do to avoid this?
If you're working from home for most of the week and you're feeling isolated, try using some of the virtual group technologies that are available to boost your feelings of 'belonging'. Each of these packages has different attributes, so you may want to try a few before finding one that suits you. The technologies create a way of collecting information, advice, guidance, and war stories that bring a human element to your interaction. They also create a sense of team identification, because you have to be a member to have access to them. If you go to the search engine of your choice and put in the keywords: 'virtual teams', 'virtual groups', or 'egroups', you'll find lots of information about available technologies.

MAKING IT HAPPEN
Think about the qualities needed for an effective virtual team
An effective virtual team has the same qualities as a team working in close proximity. Good virtual team members are:

- collaborative in their work. They share information, knowledge, ideas, views, and experiences in order for the team to pull together as a unit.
- trusting of each other. Each member needs to know that the others will meet their promises promptly without personal agendas getting in the way.
- attentive to communication. Each member has to agree priorities and communicate progress regularly. There should be no withholding of information. Good communication only happens when every member takes responsibility for being part of the team and is committed to the team's purpose.
- skilled at building relationships. In the absence of actual face-to-face meetings, the development of strong, trusting relationships will depend even more than usual upon excellent communication.
- agreed on how they'll work together. All team members should agree on ground rules, written down or not, governing how they operate.

'Meet' all members of the team and get to know something about them

Before you start to work as part of a virtual team, it's a good idea to get in touch with your colleagues and get to know them a bit better. Phone them if you can, and if time zones allow. We're all aware of the hazards of communicating by e-mail (such as your tone being misinterpreted, irony not always travelling very well, and so on), so it will help to get a feel of what your colleagues are like in 'real life'.

Look for similarities of values, interests, expertise, or experience so that you have a bridge into the relationship. Building rapport is the first step to being part of an effective team; without this, there's nothing to cement the team together.

If you're about to take responsibility for managing a virtual team, you won't be able to move through traditional team-building phases and will need to think of a back-up plan.

Try setting up an extensive briefing session facilitated via video conference or a training programme that encourages information sharing and collaboration. In this way, you'll put team members in a position where they have to build good communication channels and trust among themselves.

Obviously it's much easier to build trust and rapport when you can actually see someone and communicate spontaneously. You only need do this once or twice to kick-start your relationship and get a handle on how everyone operates. For this reason, it's worth having one videoconference with those members of your team who live in compatible time zones and a second with those who couldn't join you at the first conference. Encourage the others to do the same, passing real-time communication around the team like the baton in a relay race. In this way even though you can't meet everyone at the same time, you can still meet each member face to face.

Agree and assign the different roles in the team

As a group, decide who plays which part in assisting the team to meet its objectives. Work out the resources and support that you'll need in order to play your part effectively. This exercise demands that everyone is honest: it's great to share talents and strengths, but you also need to be aware of knowledge gaps so that you can plug them.

Set boundaries around tasks and agree timescales. Decide collectively how the team will deal with failures to meet its objectives. You may need to call emergency meetings to create contingency plans, set new timescales, or realign the team's objectives.

Agree how regularly you'll check in with each other. These reviews are designed primarily to make sure that all projects are on track, but they'll also act as early-warning systems if something is beginning to go wrong. These sessions are really important, so everyone needs to be committed to taking part in them.

Discuss the possibility of conflict and decide how you'll deal with this. Many people hate even the thought of conflict and tend to ignore the possibility until it actually emerges and needs to be dealt with. Conflict isn't always a negative experience; if it's handled well and sensitively, it can clear the air and be positive in the long run.

Make electronic systems work for you

New electronic communication systems are being developed all the time, many of which can help virtual teams work well. Most people are familiar with tele- and video-conferencing as a way of bringing people together, and of course there are also the mobile phone, fax, and e-mail. There are some other useful technologies that can help people who are based far apart to communicate, though, including:

- **Web conferencing.** This technology enables members of the team to sit at their respective computers and watch the meeting host illustrate his or her message on the screen. This technological aid requires access to two telephone lines, one for the telephone and one for the web connection (unless you have broadband), but is otherwise easy to set up and use.
- **document storage/sharing.** There are a number of online document storage providers that enable team members to store, edit, and access common documents. This prevents the need to create multiple versions of the same document; team members can simply work on the sections they need.
- **group e-mail.** The ability to send e-mail to one or every member of the team greatly enhances the team's ability to communicate.
- **message boards.** Message or bulletin boards enable group members to go to a central place where communication can take place and information is stored.

Celebrate success

It's all too easy for dispersed teams to forget to celebrate their achievements, but it's important to mark the attainment of goals. Celebration allows you to release tension, enjoy your success, and move on to the next challenge.

Organise a video conference and agree to hold a virtual party. Although this may feel a little contrived, it nonetheless allows a form of togetherness and mutual appreciation. It also invites humour as you review what went well and what didn't, so it's a great way of letting things go and getting them into perspective.

Learn from the experience
T.S. Eliot wrote: 'It is possible to have the experience yet miss the meaning'. If you don't learn, you don't develop and grow. Take time to reflect on how you took your part in the team and what you've learned about yourself from doing so. What would you do differently or better next time?

COMMON MISTAKES
You don't build up rapport and trust
Not spending enough time on building rapport and trust will sabotage any team, but it's a definite no-no for a virtual team. It's easy to assume that everyone has the same high level of commitment to the team's formation and purpose as the co-ordinator or team leader, but if you're a leader you need to check that everyone does feel like that, and if you're a team member, you need the chance to tell someone if you're worried about or disheartened by something. Give team members an opportunity to get to know each other so that they can work out how their talents and skills will work together to reach your objectives. This means either a physical team-building meeting or a series of virtual gatherings.

You communicate badly
Forgetting to communicate with virtual colleagues is one of the main reasons that virtual teams fail. In the absence of physical proximity and the ability to pass quick messages or information over a cup of coffee in the office, out of sight can quickly become out of mind. Be sure to schedule regular meetings – and hold them without fail.

You don't establish clear understanding of roles and expectations
It's important that all members understand both their role in the team and the expectations that the team leader and the members have of each other. It's too easy to assume that this is obvious. If you're the team leader, you need to be crystal-clear about this from the outset or the team will disintegrate into conflict.

THE BEST SOURCES OF HELP
Websites:
globalchange.com: **www.globalchange.com/ vteams.htm**
Wally Bock: **www.bockinfo.com/docs/virteam.htm**

Creating and Balancing the Portfolio Career

GETTING STARTED
Job satisfaction takes many forms. For some people, job satisfaction means a relatively secure income; for others, it means the opportunity to concentrate on a single, fascinating career. Then there are those for whom job satisfaction comes from having a variety of different careers (either all at once or consecutively) that allow them to earn a livelihood exploring a wide world of interests.

To critical observers, this approach to career development may appear unfocused and directionless. However, it is an excellent approach to enjoying the many adventures, opportunities, and textures (sights, experiences, friends, diversities, and so on) of modern life. And because the so-called 'job for life' is virtually extinct, the single most compelling argument for suppressing one's curiosity in favour of the illusion of job security has been negated.

In fact, portfolio career practitioners discover that their multiple sources of income provide them with a more secure feeling than depending on the continuing goodwill and loyalty of a single income source. And, even though you're self-employed and indulging your passions and spirit of adventure, that does not necessarily mean that you must trade away financial reward. With multiple sources of income, you may find that you make more money than you would in a traditional career.

The following points are key questions to ask yourself when considering ways to build a portfolio career:
• How high is your tolerance for uncertainty and insecurity?
• Are you self-motivated?
• Do you relish change and meeting new people?
• Do you depend on the social life and intimacy that being a regular member of a single workplace gives you?

FAQS
What protects me from being seen as a dilettante or someone who just can't keep a job?
An overall sense of purpose and big-picture direction is what separates you from idle dabblers. You can dabble and experiment to your heart's content, but when you talk about your work, or even think about it in the privacy of your own mind, always regard your

portfolio career as a unified whole, rather than as a simple collection of 'odd jobs'.

Actually, I am between jobs. And my industry is in a recession at the moment, so it's not a good time to find a full-time job. How can I use the portfolio career concept to improve my marketability later when I'm back on the job market?

Take a strategic approach to designing your portfolio career. Make sure that each assignment you accept gives you additional information, experience, or exposure to key players in your industry. The more varied your experience within a single industry, the better your understanding is of important trends in that industry. Therefore, you will be better qualified for strategic positions later. Industry experts who have a bird's-eye view are often in a better position to command higher salaries.

Can I have a portfolio career even though I have a full-time job?

Yes. Your full-time job could be the keystone to your portfolio career as you build a lifelong CV of ever-increasing experience, responsibility, and variety. Or you can build a portfolio career as a sideline, using your spare time and energy to develop passions that are either related or entirely unrelated to your full-time work.

MAKING IT HAPPEN
You don't have to leave your job at first

Creating a portfolio career is more a matter of perspective and approach than needing to have the courage to 'go public' with an all-or-nothing announcement that you're now a fully committed self-employed individual. While portfolio careers often entail at least one independent source of income, they don't require that you abandon a full-time source of financial security.

Explore the big-picture view of your career

Your big-picture approach to your portfolio career will probably evolve over time, but it's necessary to at least start out with a general idea of what the big picture will look like once you have put all your job puzzle pieces together. Just as a collector gathers items according to some kind of theme, so a portfolio career also requires that, ultimately, your varied experience will contribute to some sort of unified result. Ask yourself, 'What do I want myself to be all about?' and keep that question at the centre of your mind as your career progresses and jobs accumulate.

Give yourself the best chance of success at each of your portfolio jobs

Always be businesslike to the extent that is appropriate to your job. Read industry publications and books. Keep up with trends and speak knowledgeably of the strategic issues facing your industry.

Market yourself as a management consultant would

Socialise, and volunteer to assist in situations that are likely to put you in front of leaders of industry and key decision-makers. Participate in local industry groups. Contribute as much as you can.

Don't waste time

Eliminate drains on your time whenever possible. Unnecessary hours spent in front of the television or reading may prove to be time-expensive luxuries that you can no longer afford.

Learn to say 'no'. And learn to say 'yes'

As you become increasingly successful and popular in your variety of occupations, you'll have to learn to balance the temptations of pursuing exciting opportunities with staying focused on your overall career theme. Choose carefully, but do explore the most tempting offers. The reason why you say 'Yes' may become apparent later; you may meet an important person or learn a new skill that will make the doors to other opportunities swing wide open.

Keep a journal

Some career paths seem to be more like career trenches. You may not see exactly where they are leading you. By keeping a journal, you will be creating a map for retrospective analysis, and it will be in the looking back that you will understand the larger purpose of your journey.

Have fun!

You may be the only person you know who is following an unusual, zigzag pattern of career progression. You may be alone in your values and the choices you make. There could be high costs in choosing this kind of work style. But there is one reward that you have total control over: the ability to enjoy the process. There will be benefits that are available to you only if you have a sense of independence, which often comes with knowing you have an independent source of income: the ability to pick and choose your assignments; the chance to live in beautiful parts of the world; the opportunity to travel, if you wish; and the chance to move freely through corporate hierarchies and meet exciting and powerful people at all levels of organisations.

COMMON MISTAKES
You become strapped for cash

Start this adventure with a cushion of six months' living expenses, if you can. Additionally, follow the practices of management consultants whenever possible: they sell their services by the value of results (not by tasks or time) and they insist on at least 50 per cent in advance of the work.

You become bogged down

It is possible to become overloaded. It's hard to turn down work, especially when you are unsure where and when the next opportunity will come, but overloading yourself robs you of the benefits of this kind of lifestyle and work style. It is important for the sake of your own mental and physical health to take time off and get plenty of exercise and rest.

You become isolated

Employees who work full-time in a congenial work environment have the advantage of everyday camaraderie, companionship, and creative synergy. As a portfolio careerist, it is very important to make sure your business and social networks are current and thriving. You must have friends you can turn to to share ideas with or simply to relax with.

Your skills become out of date

If you were working full-time for a company, you may have enjoyed training and development benefits. As a portfolio careerist, you may be fully self-employed. It is up to you to make sure your skills are current and marketable, and you may be the one who must pay for the necessary training courses or schemes.

THE BEST SOURCES OF HELP
Book:
Handy, Charles. *The Age of Unreason*. New ed. London: Random House Business Books, 2002.
Hopson, Barrie, and Katie Ledger. *And What Do You Do? Ten Steps to a Portfolio Career*. London: A&C Black, 2009.

Website:
A Portfolio Career: **www.creativekeys.net/ portfoliocareer3.htm**

Downshifting: Working Less and Enjoying It More

GETTING STARTED

The traditional definition of success is to work hard, get promoted, make more money, and give more and more of your life and your identity to your organisation. Some call it 'climbing the corporate ladder', or 'making good'. But in the last few years, there has been a growing number of people who are questioning common wisdom. Instead, they are looking for ways to get out of the rat race and to have a more balanced and fulfilling life.

There are many reasons why you might consider downshifting in your career. Quite often, the reason is family demands. Your children require more attention, or your marriage may be shaky because of the time you spend away from the family. Or perhaps an elderly parent requires more care. Conflicts of values can be another major reason for a desire to downshift. You may have been asked to do something by your organisation that goes strongly against deeply held values, and it leads you to question why you are working so hard for this organisation. And, finally, you may be near retirement and it feels as if it is time to begin disengaging from your career and building a new life outside work.

Regardless of the reason for downshifting, it takes a lot of foresight, planning, and courage to make a move towards a simpler life. Consider the following questions as you think through the possibility of downshifting:

- Why do you want to downshift?
- Do you feel called towards something new, or are you wanting to get away from something that no longer works for you?
- What is your current, and long-term, financial situation?
- What are the core values that you want to live by in your new life?
- Do you have a support network of like-minded people?
- What do you want to keep, what do you want to let go of, and what do you want more of?

FAQS

If I downshift, won't I be ruining my career?

If you have to ask this question, then you shouldn't even be considering downshifting. People who downshift generally are no longer interested in climbing the career ladder. It's just not relevant to them. They have emotionally detached themselves from the 'corporate game' and are moving towards a slower, less-demanding way of life. They are not motivated by the traditional definitions and trappings of success.

I am ready to get off the fast track, but won't everyone say I'm mad?

Chances are very good that a number of people will say you are mad. It's as if they are playing Monopoly and you have moved over to another table to play chess. You are each playing by a different set of rules, and, if they think you are still playing Monopoly, then your behaviour looks very strange to them. You must constantly check with your own inner voice and your own values to see if this is right for you. Don't worry about what other people think. It is your life to live. Paul Ray and Sherry Anderson have done research on people's values in the United States and Europe. They found that about 26 per cent of the adult population in these areas have a strong interest in living a slower, simpler life that is more in harmony with nature, family, and community life. So you are not alone.

If I decide that downshifting is not for me, will I be able to get back into my old career path?

You take a risk when you downshift. You are stepping into unknown territory and creating a new lifestyle for yourself. You may not be able to go back the way you came. However, chances are pretty good that this new adventure may lead you to other career paths you never even considered. If you decide that a simpler way of life just doesn't suit you, you can use the same risk-taking and imaginative skills you used in downshifting to create the next inventive step on your path.

MAKING IT HAPPEN

Be clear about why you are thinking about downshifting and involve your family

The decision to downshift is a major lifestyle decision. Take the time to do soul-searching about why you want to slow down and simplify your life. Then discuss it with your family and anyone else who would be directly affected by such a choice. Explain what you find attractive about this new way of life, and then be willing to listen to their concerns and fears.

Downshifting often occurs as a backlash to a corporate lifestyle that doesn't work for you any more. But be sure that you are not just running away from a difficult situation that perhaps you should face. Successful downshifting occurs when there is also a clear vision of a better and more meaningful life. It is important to be as concrete about the new vision as you can.

Make a thorough assessment of your short-term and long-term financial situation

Downshifting requires some risk, but you should not be putting your health and your old age in jeopardy. Give careful consideration to what you might need in an emergency or in case of a long-term illness. But also don't turn so conservative that you become afraid to build a life that you've always dreamed of. Make sure that you have something in savings. And wherever possible, think of ways to develop passive income.

When you first make the move towards downshifting, it may mean leaving your organisation and being on your own for a while. You should have sufficient savings in place to pay your monthly expenses for six months to a year. As a part of downshifting, you will be dramatically reducing your expenses, so your savings should go quite a bit further

Conduct a work–life values assessment

Downshifting requires some major decision-making about your life and your work. If you are going to be

happy with your decision, you will need to be very clear about your core values and how your new life will be in alignment with those values.

Make a decision about whether or not you want to leave your organisation

Downshifting often means leaving your job and becoming a free agent and working out of your home. But it can also mean moving to a lower-pressure less- demanding job in the organisation. Or you might consider moving to an organisation that has a slower paced culture.

Decide what to keep and what to let go of

You can simplify your life by getting rid of possessions you no longer need. There is less to keep track of and care for, and often you can do good by giving these things away. Clean out your cupboards. Give clothes to charity. Cancel magazine subscriptions. At the same time, be sure to keep things that have significant meaning and value for you. Even if it is not practical, you will want to keep those heirlooms that were passed down from your grandmother.

Create an action plan with a schedule

Once you decide what living and working changes you are going to make, you can prepare a timetable of key actions. These might include putting your house on the market, selling furniture, giving notice at your company, and starting up your own business. As you begin to implement your plan, your life will actually get more hectic before it gets simpler. You will be still living your old life while planning for your new life. Be gentle with yourself and do not try to rush things too much. That would be defeating the overall purpose of having a slower, less-stressful life.

Take an annual retreat and continue your life–work assessment

At least once a year, take time off with your family to talk about how this new lifestyle is going. Analyse what is working and what you would like to change. Celebrate your courage for taking the risk to move towards a more balanced life.

COMMON MISTAKES

You get excited about the idea of downshifting and immediately leave your job

Downshifting is a major life change, and requires a lot of thought and planning. Take your time to really think through the kind of life you want to build before doing anything drastic.

You try to do too much at once

Changing jobs and moving are two of life's most stressful activities. If your downshifting plan calls for both of these actions, try not to do them both at once. Plan for gentle transitions where possible.

You make only cosmetic changes and then find yourself right back in the rat race

Old habits are hard to break and many of us are addicted to hard work and stress. You might try to simplify your life by eliminating some of the things you normally do, only to find that you have filled up the spare time with new things to do.

Revisit your core values assessment and spend time envisioning the simpler lifestyle you pictured. You may need to make a more dramatic change in order to have a truly slower lifestyle.

THE BEST SOURCES OF HELP
Books:
Bolles, Richard. *What Color is Your Parachute? A Practical Manual for Job-Hunters and Career-Changers*. Revised ed. Berkeley, California: Ten Speed Press, 2008.

Drake, John. *Downshifting: How to Work Less and Enjoy Life More*. San Francisco, California: Berrett-Koehler, 2001.

Preparing for Retirement Gracefully

GETTING STARTED
Given the recent turbulent economic times, many people have been putting off the idea of retirement for a variety of reasons: they may, bluntly, need the money that their work provides, especially if the value of their pension may be plummeting. If, however, you are still hoping to make the transition to a less work-oriented life in the medium term, ask yourself these few important questions:
- When do I want to retire, and what sort of lifestyle do I want?
- How much money will it take to maintain that lifestyle?
- How much short-term sacrifice can I make for a long-term payoff?
- What sorts of budgeting and investing am I already doing?

FAQS
How can I work out what amount of money I'll need to retire?

Financial planners and retirement-oriented websites have 'calculators' that will give you a ballpark figure of what you'll need. They'll ask you: how much income will you want per year in retirement; how long after retirement will you need that income; what sources of income will you have to draw from? From this and other data, they can tell you the gap that exists between what you will need and what you predict you'll have. It's advisable to consult a financial planner to help you close that gap with investments. Your bank may provide you with some free consultation.

Should I pay off my debts first or start saving?

Generally, it's better to pay off debt first, especially credit cards. Why? Credit card interest (18 per cent–22 per cent) is higher than the interest paid by most savings and investment accounts. Paying off debt saves you the future interest costs you'd be charged. And, when the debt is gone, you'll have made a habit of setting aside a certain amount. That same amount, or more, can then be earmarked for retirement.

There is one exception to that rule: if your employer

has a company retirement plan and matches contributions made by employees, it's wise to put in as much as you can, because the employer's contribution is a bonus.

Besides the financial part, should I be planning for other things in retirement, too?

Retirement can be the life you never had as a working person and as a parent. Those who make the best of their 'golden years' say that having interests beyond work is a key ingredient. Certainly, it may be desirable, or even important, to continue to work part-time. But retirement also gives you the opportunity to do things you've never had the time for before – travel, volunteering, education, reading, physical conditioning, cooking, catching up with friends and family, or starting a hobby. It's probably best if you research a bit now into what may keep you happy and busy in later life, rather than maintaining a 'wait and see' attitude.

MAKING IT HAPPEN
Learn about how much you can earn

Do a little research on your skill level and job title. Look at both the private and public sectors, including the benefit packages available – insurance coverage, pension contributions, bonuses, and incentives. If you're not making what others in your category are, you can lobby for a pay rise or look for greener pastures.

Also consider additional education, if having college qualifications or other training will increase your worth with your employer. Just think, if you aim for a 3 per cent salary increase each year, the difference in your earnings over a 40-year period is thousands of pounds more than if you get no increases whatsoever!

Give some thought to where you want to be in five years, 10 years, and longer

Goal setting has a lot of value when it comes to career and retirement. It's important to separate wishful thinking from practical realities. Once you've decided on the priorities, for example, travel, children and money for their education, losing weight, buying a home or

Actionlists

recreational vehicle, begin to put pound signs to each of them. It may surprise you or shock you. Regardless, having those numbers is an important place to begin building a good life and a good retirement.

Budget properly

To some, the very thought of budgeting is like taking a cold shower. For those who do it religiously, however, budgeting can make the difference between comfort and catastrophe and as the world reels from one economic 'shock' to another, it has never been more crucial. In short, budgeting is more apt to get you those things in life you most desire, and allow you to get there faster and more pragmatically, than buying on 'impulse' as the desire arises. The primary rule of budgeting is to spend less than you earn and avoid debt.

Another rule is to 'pay' yourself first (that is, set aside your savings), rather than paying all the bills and saving what's left. You probably know already that, often, there is nothing left if you pay yourself last. Start with 10 per cent if you can, but start anyway and be consistent with your saving.

Take professional advice about investments

Only the brave are ready to invest heavily in anything at the time of writing: even property, for so long a virtually cast-iron guarantee of a good return of investment, is in a parlous state. So that you're best placed to take advantage of the recovery, when it kicks in, seek expert professional help rather than strike out on your own.

Protecting yourself and your family

Insurance, a will, and even a basic estate plan are also valuable assets to have when developing a life-long strategy. 'Whole life' insurance takes care of dependants in the event of your injury or death by replacing your lost income with insurance payments. 'Term' insurance may be preferable for those without children or other dependants. 'Disability' insurance replaces your income in the event of illness or injury. A will and estate plan make sure that your assets are not gobbled up in probate court and taxes but go instead to the people you want to leave them to.

As in the case of investments, shopping for and finding professional advice you can trust is important: get referrals and don't assume that one planner or agent is as good as the next. Don't buy more insurance than you need for your own particular situation.

Establish a life outside work

Statistically speaking, people whose lives revolve entirely around their careers don't fare as well in retirement as those who have a well-rounded life. Never before have there been so many excellent choices and opportunities for retired people to stay active and engaged in life. How you view the element of time in retirement is largely an issue of attitude, but planning also plays a role.

Community non-profit organisations, churches, schools, and even local government bodies, thrive on volunteers. Volunteering is a way to make a difference in the community, as well as being a way to socialise and continue to learn. Community colleges are designed to open new vistas to learners of all ages. But 'getting a life' after your career takes practice, and if you're not doing so already, start practising now.

COMMON MISTAKES

Waiting too long to begin planning for retirement

The 'play as you go' attitude often leaves too little saved as retirement draws near. Get in the habit of budgeting and saving for retirement, even if you're in your 20s. If you're not investing in your employer's pension plan, you're giving away free money.

If you've already waited longer than is advisable, don't despair – just get started right away. And get creative (legally!) about how to make up some lost time. Given the 2008 stock market crash, find some professional financial help – quickly.

Getting too deep into consumer debt

We all intend to pay off credit card balances each month, but it seldom works out that way. By accumulating more high-interest debt, you end up paying far more for a product or service than if you'd paid cash for it.

Keeping poor records

Failure to keep good records can translate into spending more on taxes than you should. Claiming itemised deductions for legitimate expenses is not a privilege solely for the rich! But you must have records to back up the deduction claim, or HM Revenue & Customs will disallow those deductions should you be audited.

Investing with your heart, not your head

It's sad how much hard-earned money is thrown away each year on bad investments. 'Get-rich-quick' schemes have cheated thousands of investors of many hundreds of millions of pounds.

Be very wary of high-pressure sales from people you don't know, telling you about investments you know even less about. It is better to seek the advice of a professional planner, who can help you make reasoned decisions about investing in a diverse portfolio.

THE BEST SOURCES OF HELP

Books:

Brown, Rosemary. *The Good Non-Retirement Guide.* Rev. ed. London: Kogan Page, 2009.

Cantor, Dorothy, and Andrea Thompson. *What Do You Want to Do When You Grow Up: Starting the Next Chapter of Your Life.* New York: Little, Brown, 2002.

Cullinane, Jay, and Cathy Fitzgerald. *The New Retirement: The Ultimate Guide to the Rest of Your Life.* New York: Rodale, 2004.

Website:

The Motley Fool: **www.fool.co.uk/news/investing/ company-comment/2009/03/16/3-ways-to- destroy-your-retirement.aspx**

Communicating Assertively in the Workplace

GETTING STARTED

Do you find that people get the better of you at work, that you're always the one who draws the short straw and ends up doing things that you'd rather not do? Does this make you resentful or unhappy because you feel helpless and unable to represent yourself strongly enough in the way you communicate?

Assertiveness is an attitude that honours your choices as well as those of the person you're communicating with. It's not about being aggressive and steamrollering your colleague into submission. Rather, it's about seeking and exchanging opinions, developing a full understanding of the situation, and negotiating a win–win situation. Ask yourself these questions to determine your level of assertiveness:

- Do you feel 'put upon' or ignored in your exchanges with colleagues?
- Are you unable to speak your mind and ask for what you want?
- Do you find it difficult to stand up for yourself in a discussion?
- Are you inordinately grateful when someone seeks your opinion and takes it into account?

If you answer 'yes' to most of these questions, you may need to consider becoming more assertive.

FAQS

Won't people think me aggressive if I change my communication style?

There are four types of communication style:

- aggressive – where you win and everyone else loses
- passive – where you lose and everyone else wins
- passive/aggressive – where you lose and do everything you can (without being too obvious) to make others lose too
- assertive – where everyone wins

If you become more assertive, people won't necessarily think that you've become more aggressive because their needs will be met too. All that will happen is that your communication style becomes more effective.

I have had a lifetime of being 'me'. How can I change that now?

If you don't change what you do, you'll never change what you get. All it takes to change is a decision. Once you've made that decision, you'll naturally observe yourself in situations, notice what you do and don't do well, and then you can try out new ways of behaving to see what works for you.

I just don't have the confidence to confront people. Will becoming assertive help me?

This is a bit like the 'chicken and egg'. Once you become assertive, your confidence level will be boosted, yet you need to have sufficient levels of confidence to try it in

the first place. Just try the technique out in a safe environment first so that you get used to how it feels, then you can use it more widely.

It's all right for people who have presence, but I'm small so I'm often overlooked. How can I become assertive?

Many of the most successful people, in business and in entertainment, are physically quite small. Adopting an assertive communication style and body language has the effect of making you look more imposing. Assume you have impact, visualise it, feel it, breathe it, be it.

I find it hard to say 'no' to people. How can I change this?

Until you get used to being assertive, you may find this difficult. However, one useful technique is to say, 'I'd like to think about this first. I'll get back to you shortly.' Giving yourself time and space to rehearse your response can be really helpful.

MAKING IT HAPPEN
Choose the right approach

Becoming assertive is all about making choices that meet your needs and the needs of the situation. Sometimes it's appropriate to be passive. If you were facing a snarling dog, you might not want to provoke an attack by looking for a win–win situation! There may be other occasions when aggression is the answer. However, this is still assertive behaviour as *you*, rather than other people or situations, are in control of how you react.

You may find it helpful to investigate some specially tailored training courses so that you can try out some approaches before taking on a colleague or manager in a 'live' situation. This sort of thing takes practice.

Practise projecting a positive image

Use 'winning' language. Rather than saying 'I always come off worst!' say 'I've learned a great deal from doing lots of different things in my career. I'm now ready to move on'. This is the beginning of taking control in your life. Visualise what you wish to become, make the image as real as possible, and feel the sensation of being in control. Perhaps there have been moments in your life when you naturally felt like this, a time when you've excelled. Recapture that moment and 'live' it again. Imagine how it would be if you felt like that in other areas of your life. Determine to make this your goal and recall this powerful image or feeling when you're getting disheartened. It will re-energise you and keep you on track.

Condition others to take you seriously by creating a positive impression

This can be done through non-verbal as well as verbal communication. If someone is talking over you and you're finding it difficult to get a word in edgeways, you can hold up your hand signalling 'stop' as you begin to speak. 'I hear what you're saying but I would like to put forward an alternative viewpoint. . .' Always take responsibility for your communication. Use the 'I' word. 'I would like. . .', 'I don't agree. . .', 'I am uncomfortable with this. . .' Being aware of non-verbal communication signals can also help you build rapport. If you mirror what others are doing when they're communicating with you, it will help you get a sense of where they're coming from and how to respond in the most helpful way.

Use positive body language

Stand tall, breathe deeply, and look people in the eye when you speak to them. Instead of anticipating a negative outcome, expect something positive. Listen actively to the other party and try putting yourself in their shoes so that you have a better chance of seeking the solution that works for you both. Inquire about their thoughts and feelings by using 'open' questions, that allow them to give you a full response rather than just 'yes' or 'no'. Examples include: 'Tell me more about why. . .', 'How do you see this working out?', and so forth.

Assertiveness also helps you learn to deal with people who have different communication styles. If you're dealing with someone behaving in a passive/aggressive manner, you can handle it by exposing what he or she is doing. 'I get the feeling you're not happy about this decision' or 'It appears you have something to say on this; would you like to share your views now?' In this way, they either have to deny their passive/aggressive stance or they have to disclose their motivations. Either way, you're left in the driving seat.

If you're dealing with a passive person, rather than let them be silent, encourage them to contribute so that they can't put the blame for their disquiet on someone else.

The aggressive communicator may need confronting but do it carefully; you don't want things to escalate out of control. One option is to start by saying 'I'd like to think about it first': this gives you time to gather your thoughts and the other person time to calm down. When you're feeling put upon, it's important to remember that you have as much right as anyone to speak up and be heard.

Conflict is notorious for bringing out aggression in people, but it's still possible to be assertive in this context. You may need to show that you're taking them seriously by reflecting their energy. To do this, you could raise your voice to match the volume of theirs, then bring the volume down as you start to explore what would lead to a win–win solution. 'I CAN SEE THAT YOU ARE UPSET and I would feel exactly the same if I were you. . . however. . .' Then you can establish the desired outcome for both of you.

COMMON MISTAKES

You go too far at first

Many people, when trying out assertive behaviour for the first time, find that they 'go too far' and become aggressive. Remember that you're looking for a win–win, not a you win and they lose situation. Take your time. Observe yourself in action. Practise and ask for feedback from trusted friends or colleagues.

You allow others to react negatively to your assertiveness

Your familiar circle of friends will be used to you the way you were, not the way you want to become. They may try and make things difficult for you. With your new assertive behaviour, this won't be possible unless you let them get away with it. If you find you're in this situation, try explaining what you're trying to do and ask for their support. If they aren't prepared to help you, you may choose to let them go from your circle of friends.

You bite off more than you can chew and get yourself into situations that are difficult to manage

If this happens to you, find a good way of backing down, go away and reflect on what went wrong, rehearse an assertive response, and forgive yourself for not getting it right every time. The more you rehearse, the more assertive responses you'll have in your tool kit when you need them.

THE BEST SOURCES OF HELP

Book:
Back, Ken, and Kate Back. *Assertiveness At Work: A Practical Guide to Handling Awkward Situations.* 3rd ed. Maidenhead: McGraw-Hill, 2005.

Website:
Assertiveness.com:
www.assertiveness.com

Preparing Presentations

GETTING STARTED

Whether you're pitching for business, making a case for funding, or addressing staff meetings, you're giving a presentation. Few people like speaking formally to an audience, but there are many real benefits, and, as you gain experience in giving presentations, you'll probably find that they become less of a worry, and even enjoyable. This actionlist will give you some suggestions for preparing the content of your presentation, looking at the objectives that you hope to achieve, pitching it right for your particular audience, and getting your points across in the best way.

FAQS

What's the best way to start my preparation?

Set some clear objectives. Ask yourself why you're giving the talk, and what you want your audience to get out of it. Also consider whether using speech alone is the best way of communicating your message, and whether your presentation would benefit from using visual aids and slides to further illustrate its main points. When you're planning and giving the presentation, keep your objectives in mind at all times – they'll focus your thoughts. Having clear reasons for giving the presentation will make sure that you're not wasting anyone's time, either your audience's or your own.

What do I need to know about the audience?

Before you plan your presentation try as best as you can to find out who is going to be in your audience, and their expectations. For example, the tone and content of a presentation to the managing director of another company will be very different from one addressed to potential users of a product. It's important that you know the extent of the audience's knowledge about the topic you'll be discussing. Their familiarity with the subject will determine the level at which you pitch the talk. Try to appeal to what will motivate and interest these people.

MAKING IT HAPPEN

Start 'building' your speech

When it comes to presentations, there is no substitute for detailed preparation and planning. While everyone prepares in different ways, all of which develop with experience, here are a few key points to bear in mind while you're preparing.

Start by breaking up the task of preparing your speech into manageable units. Once you know the length of the presentation – say 15 minutes, for example – break the time up into smaller units and allocate sections of your speech to each unit. Then note down all the points you want to make, and order them logically. This will help you to develop the framework and emphasis of the presentation.

Keep your presentation short and simple, if you can, as it'll be easier for you to manage and remember. If you need to provide more detail, you can supply a written handout to be given out at the end. A shorter presentation is usually more effective from the audience's point of view, too, as most people dislike long speeches, and will not necessarily remember any more from them.

Avoid packing your talk with facts and figures – your audience may become confused and you could lose the thread as well. If you do need to back up what you're saying, you could use graphs or charts to get across the message in a clear, pictorial form. Aim to identify two or three key points, and concentrate on getting these across in a creative fashion.

Use visual aids and equipment

With any presentation, you'll need to consider whether to use visual aids, which can range from the simple – such as acetates for an overhead projector (OHP) – to the more sophisticated – such as a computer package like PowerPoint. Remember that visual aids should only be used as signposts during the presentation, to help the audience focus on the main point. It's important not to cram too much information on to one visual aid, as you'll probably lose the attention of your audience while they try to read everything on it. Make sure the audience can see the information by using big, bold lettering, and bear in mind that images are often far more effective than words.

At its most basic, a personal computer can be used to develop and produce a series of slides which can be printed onto acetates for use on an overhead projector. A more common usage is to link up the PC with a projector in order to show the information on a large screen.

If you're going to use slides, you should try to standardise them to make them look more professional. Use templates where possible to make sure that they don't blend together, and again, try not to put too much information on to a single slide, or it will become difficult to read. A sensible guideline is to include no more than six points per slide, and to keep the number of words you use for each point to the absolute minimum. Think of what you're writing as the prompts for what you want to say.

The most common presentation packages are Microsoft PowerPoint and Corel Presentations. Both of these will allow you to develop a presentation using slide templates and give you the option of using charts, graphics, or even photographs to bring your information alive. Packages such as PhotoShop or Paint Shop Pro will also allow you to scan in or manipulate photographs, or you could also use some of the available animations for transitions between slides.

You should pay particular attention to the layout and text on the slides and remain consistent throughout. Select a background that contrasts well with the text, and colours that are strong and stand out. It may also be a good idea to include the business's logo on all of the slides. It's important, always, to proofread your slides and acetates. There is nothing more noticeable, or more unprofessional, than a typo or grammatical error projected to 10 times its original size on a screen!

Practise!
Very few people can wing it, so do make sure you practise at least three times before you give your speech. If possible, ask a friend or colleague to listen to a run-through so that you can adapt your delivery if you need to. Once you're confident that your presentation is right, don't tinker with. Remember, *you* may have heard the speech many times, but the audience will be hearing it for the first time. It's also a good idea to practise your speech using the equipment you intend to use; computers, projectors, and DVD players should be tested in advance to make sure you know how to operate them.

Make sure you have a contingency plan to cope with any unforeseen mishaps. For example, you could take acetates of your slides along with you so that if your computer breaks down and there's an OHP to hand, you can show them that way. Finally, during your rehearsals, time your speech so that you can check that it's neither too long nor too short. If you're a nervous presenter, it can be tempting to bring a print-out of the whole presentation with you, but it's likely that you'll end up just reading this out rather than engaging with your audience. It's better to instead write the main points on some discreet cards that you can flip through if you need a reminder (number the cards clearly in case you drop or fumble with them).

Prepare the venue
If the presentation is happening at your premises or at another venue that you've booked, make sure that an appropriately sized room has been set aside. It should seat the number of attendees comfortably, be bright and tidy, and have either the heating or ventilation you need to deal with the weather expected. Offering some refreshments for participants, such as tea, coffee, and water, is always welcome.

You also need to make sure there will be no interruptions, for example by phone calls, fire drills, or people accidentally entering the room. Whether you're presenting at your own office or elsewhere, you must make sure that any equipment or props you need are available and set up properly before the presentation starts. If you're presenting away from your office, at a conference or a client's premises, for example, it's a good idea to visit the site beforehand to make sure it provides the necessary facilities.

COMMON MISTAKES
You don't research your audience
A good knowledge of the audience is absolutely crucial in finding the correct pitch. It's no good blinding your audience with technical jargon if they only have a basic grasp of the subject. Similarly, a very knowledgeable audience will soon switch off if you spend the first few minutes going over the basics.

You go on for too long
If your presentation absolutely has to be longer than 20 minutes, it may be a good idea to insert some breaks so that your audience remains fresh and interested.

You forget to check the room and equipment
This can be disastrous! Imagine, for example, arriving and finding that there is no facility for delivering PowerPoint presentations, and you have no other method of showing slides. Make sure you're familiar with the environment in which you'll be presenting.

THE BEST SOURCES OF HELP
Books:
Give Great Presentations: How to Speak Confidently and Make Your Mark (Steps to Success series). London: A&C Black, 2005.
Wilder, Claudine, and Jennifer Rotondo. *Point, Click and Wow! A Quick Guide to Brilliant Laptop Presentations*. 3rd ed. Chichester: Wiley, 2008.

Websites:
Mind Tools: **http://www.mindtools.com/CommSkll/PresentationPlanningChecklist.htm**
SpeechTips.com: **www.speechtips.com/preparation.html**

Delivering Presentations

GETTING STARTED

A presentation is an ideal environment for you to promote your ideas, your products, or your services. You have a captive audience, are able to provide them with relevant information, and can answer any questions they may have on the spot. For a presentation to be a success, you need to speak clearly and fluently in order to hold the attention of the audience and to leave them wanting to know more.

Some people are natural presenters, while others find it more difficult, but practice and feedback from previous audiences will help you develop your presentation skills. This actionlist will give you some ideas for structuring, preparing, and delivering your presentation.

FAQS

How should I structure my presentation?

Structure is essential for any presentation: there should be an introduction, a main body, and a conclusion. You can be witty, controversial, or even outrageous if the mood of the presentation allows, but, whatever approach you try, your chief aims are to pique the audience's curiosity and to get your message across.

What's the best way to introduce my presentation?

The introduction to your presentation needs to attract your audience's interest and attention. A good opening is also important for your own confidence, because if you start well, the rest should follow easily. Plan your opening words carefully for maximum impact: they should be short, sharp, and to the point. Let your audience know how long your presentation will take, as this will prepare people to focus for the period of time you expect to speak. Summarise what you'll be discussing, so that they can work out how much information they'll need to absorb. Explaining the key points in the first few sentences will also help your mind to focus on the task in hand, and refresh your memory on the major points of your presentation. It sometimes helps to get started if you can learn your first few sentences by heart. Let your audience know if you're happy to interact with them throughout the presentation. Alternatively, inform them that you'll be holding a question-and-answer session at the end.

What should I do in the main body of the presentation?

The main body of the presentation will be dictated by the points that you want to make. Use short, sharp, and simple language to keep your audience's attention and to ensure that your message is being understood. Include only one idea per sentence and pause after each one so as to make a mental full stop. Use precise language to convey your message, but make sure that your presentation sounds spontaneous – it shouldn't sound like a chapter from a textbook. You need to convey your message clearly, without masking the salient points with waffle. Stick to your original plan for your presentation and don't go off at a tangent on a particular point, and miss the thread of your presentation. Why not try using metaphors and images to illustrate points? This will give impact to what you say, and help your audience to remember it.

How should I conclude my presentation?

You should close by summing up the key points of what you've covered. The closing seconds of your presentation are as crucial as the opening sentence, as they give you a chance to really hammer home your point. To make the most of this, think about what action you'd like your audience to take after the presentation is over and then inspire them to do it.

MAKING IT HAPPEN

Make sure you've practised

Nothing will make you more confident about your presentation than practising. Run through it by yourself a few times or, even better, ask a friend, colleague, or family member to listen to you.

Think about posture and delivery

Once you've practised the core part of your presentation, you can move on to think about some techniques to do with your posture and delivery that can be used to increase its impact. First, keep up good eye contact and address your audience directly throughout your presentation. Try to be aware of your stance, posture, and gestures without being too self-conscious. Don't slouch – you'll look unprofessional – stand up straight: this will make you look more confident and also help you project your voice better. Even if you're nervous, don't fiddle with pens, pencils, your hair, or clothes: all these things are distracting for an audience, and will mean that they're missing important points in your presentation.

Remember that your audience has come to learn something, so be authoritative, sincere, and enthusiastic; if *you* don't sound as if you believe in yourself, your audience won't be interested. Also think about the way in which you're speaking. Most people need to articulate their words more clearly when addressing an audience. There's usually no opportunity for the audience to ask you to repeat a word you've missed, so aim to pronounce the vowels and consonants of words clearly. Also be aware of your vocal expression and try to vary volume, pitch, and speed of delivery to underline your meaning, and so that you maintain your audience's interest. Try not to use too many acronyms that are specific to your business or industry, as you can't be completely sure that everyone in the audience will know what they mean. If you do need to use them, introduce them and explain them early in your presentation so that everyone can keep up.

Close your presentation

It's tempting (and, if you're a nervous presenter, comforting) to have the full version of your speech in front of you, but it's best to avoid this and use cue cards instead. These will have a few headings referring to the main subject areas of your speech, and a few key points. In this way you can remember the key points you want to convey, but you have the freedom to talk naturally about them, rather than speaking from an over-rehearsed script, and this will make you seem more spontaneous. You may, though, want to write out the introduction in full on your first card to get you off to a good start.

Be careful when using visual aids and equipment in the presentation, as these can also be distracting for an audience. Use a pen to point out details on the overhead projector itself, rather than the screen, as this is much clearer. Flipcharts should be written on quickly in long hand, but try not to turn your back on the audience as you write. Commonly available presentation packages often have a facility to enable you to link to specific slides. If a specific topic needs further explanation, you could also have a built-in series of links so that you can move to some extra slides to explain a particular point. If you intend to use sophisticated technology, then have a technician on hand to help out. Make sure you have a contingency plan in case your technology crashes: a back-up disk or extra copies of a handout would be a good plan.

Finish on a high note

As you draw your presentation to a close, remember to summarise briefly your key points and whatever you want your audience to 'take away' from the time you've spent talking to them. You might also want to take a few questions from the audience: in fact, taking all the questions at the end is a good idea for nervous presenters, as it means that they won't have their train of thought interrupted while they're speaking.

We all deal with questions in a different way, but some good general pointers are as follows:

- give your audience an idea of how much time you have to spend on the questions. This may be an issue if you're just one of several people speaking, as, if you run over, everyone will start running late.
- if someone asks you a question and you don't know the answer, be honest and tell them that you'll find out what they need to know and get back to them separately. This will save time, and also prevent you from giving an incorrect answer. Try to get back to them within two working days.
- if the question is a general discussion point, you could always try throwing the question open to the floor; you may be able to get an interesting discussion going between the members of your audience.

COMMON MISTAKES
You lack enthusiasm

If *you* don't have any interest or excitement in your own speech, then don't expect your audience to be interested or excited. Listening to a single voice for 20 minutes or more can be difficult for an audience, so you must try to inject enthusiasm into what you're saying. You could consider planning some kind of interaction with your audience, too, in the form of activities or discussion.

You speak too quickly

Don't rush your presentation; it's important to take your time. It's hard not to rush, especially if you're nervous and want the whole thing to be over as soon as possible, but the audience will find it hard to understand or keep up with you if you talk too fast. Make sure you summarise your main points every five minutes or so, or as you reach the end of a section. This will help to clarify the most important issues for your audience, and it's then more likely that they'll remember the central issues long after you've finished your presentation.

You don't check equipment

There is nothing more irritating for people who have all made an effort to turn up on time, than to have to sit around and wait while you struggle to get your laptop to work or sort your slides out. Make sure everything is exactly in place well before your audience begins to arrive. If you're planning to use sophisticated technology, it might be a good idea to have an expert colleague on hand just in case.

You don't interact with the audience

Be careful not to look at the floor during your presentation, or to direct your speech at one person. Try to draw your whole audience into the presentation by glancing at everyone's faces, in a relaxed and unhurried way, as you make your points. Keeping in tune with your audience in this way will also help you judge if people are becoming bored. If you do detect this, you could try to change the tempo of your presentation to refocus their attention.

THE BEST SOURCES OF HELP
Books:
Give Great Presentations: How to Speak Confidently and Make Your Mark (Steps to Success series). London: A&C Black, 2005.
Wilder, Claudine, and Jennifer Rotondo. *Point, Click and Wow! A Quick Guide to Brilliant Laptop Presentations.* 3rd ed. Chichester: Wiley, 2008.

Websites:
BusinessTown.com: **www.businesstown.com/presentations/index.asp**
iVillage: **www.ivillage.co.uk/workcareer/survive/prodskills/articles/0,,156471_156690,00.html**
SpeechTips.com: **www.speechtips.com/delivering.html**

Negotiating with Confidence

GETTING STARTED

We all negotiate a lot more than we think we do, in all areas of our lives, and developing negotiation skills is an essential part of moving up the career ladder.

Negotiating is the process of trying to find an agreement between two or more parties with differing views on, and expectations of, a certain issue. Good negotiations find a balance between each party's objectives to create a 'win–win' outcome.

Negotiation can be 'competitive' or 'collaborative'. In competitive negotiations, the negotiator wants to 'win' even if this results in the other party 'losing'; this can ultimately end in confrontation. In collaborative negotiations, the aim is to reach an agreement that satisfies both parties, maximising mutual advantage.

There is no one right way to negotiate, and you'll develop a style that suits you. Most negotiations will be a mixture of the collaborative and competitive approaches. In situations where you're negotiating the terms of an ongoing relationship (rather than a one-off deal), it's generally more productive to lean towards collaboration rather than competition.

FAQS

What is competitive negotiation?

This type of negotiation may have an unfriendly atmosphere and each party is clearly out to get the very best deal for him- or herself – the other party's objectives tend not to come into the equation. If you find yourself involved in a competitive negotiation, bear in mind the following:

- **opening.** If you can, avoid making the opening bid as it gives a great deal of information to the other party. Try not to tell the other party too much and aim to keep control of the meeting's agenda.
- **concessions.** Conceding in a competitive situation is seen as a sign of weakness, so do this as little as possible. The size of the first concession gives the opposing parties an idea of the next best alternative, and tells them exactly how far they can push you.
- **conflict.** If conflict flares up, negotiators need to use assertiveness skills to maintain a prime position, and to defuse the situation.

What is collaborative negotiation?

Many people see negotiation as a battle where the stronger party defeats the weaker party, that is, there is a winner and a loser. In some cases, negotiations can break down altogether, such as in industrial disputes which result in strike action. In this scenario, nobody wins, so there are only losers. It needn't be like this, however. In collaborative negotiation, conflict is minimised and the whole idea is to reach a solution where everyone benefits. This approach tends to produce the best results, mainly because there is much better communication between the parties. In addition, it makes for better long-term relations if it's necessary to work together over a long period.

The opening will involve gathering as much information as possible but also disclosing information so solutions can be developed that are acceptable to both parties. This involves:

- considering a number of alternatives for each issue
- using open questions (which do not have yes/no answers)
- being flexible
- helping the other party to expand his or her ideas about possible solutions

Both parties will make concessions if necessary, normally aiming to trade things which are cheap for them to give but valuable to the opposing party, in return for things which are valuable to them (but may not be so cheap for the other party).

By listening, summarising, paraphrasing, and disclosing in collaborative negotiations (for example, 'I would like to ask you a question. . .' or 'I feel that I need to tell you that. . .'), conflict will be kept to a minimum, enabling a mutual advantage to be reached.

MAKING IT HAPPEN

Prepare yourself

As with many business situations, good preparation will help to reduce your stress levels. Don't think that preparation time is wasted time; it's anything but. Begin by working out your objectives, and making sure they are specific, achievable, and measurable. It's also important to have a clear idea of what you're expecting from the other party. Be sure that your expectations are realistic and that their results are easy to assess. It's a good idea to write down objectives and to put them into an order of priority. One way to do this is to classify them as 'must achieve', 'intend to achieve', and 'like to achieve'. For example, a new photocopier has been bought for the office. It breaks down after a week and you need to contact the supplier to sort out the problem. The objectives can be defined as:

- **Must achieve:** The use of a photocopier that works.
- **Intend to achieve:** Get the photocopier repaired.
- **Like to achieve:** Get a replacement photocopier.

Ahead of any negotiation, gather as much information as possible about the subject under discussion. The person with the most information usually does better in negotiations. For example, imagine that two people have each prepared a very important document. Let's see how this situation can progress.

They both need to have them processed by the one desktop publishing operator in the company and couriered to the destination for the following morning. However, there is only time to have one job finished before the daily courier collection at 4pm, so the two argue over whose document is the more vital. If they argue too long, neither job will be finished on time and both would 'lose'. The senior member of staff could pull rank, resulting in the junior being the 'loser', with the possible loss of his or her future co-operation.

If they obtained more information, they would find out that the courier company runs an optional 6pm collection, which also guarantees delivery before 11am the next day. A 'win–win' situation could then be achieved.

Discuss and explore

At the beginning of a meeting, each party needs to explore the other's needs and make tentative opening offers. Remember that these need to be realistic or it's unlikely that the discussion will progress to a successful conclusion for everyone. If both parties co-operate, progress can be made; however, if one side adopts a competitive approach and the other does not, problems may arise. You need, then, to analyse the other party's reaction to what's said.

An opening statement is a good way of covering the main issues at stake for each party, and allows the discussion to develop naturally. At this stage, the issues are just being discussed and not yet negotiated. What you're trying to do is develop a relationship with the other person. Ask questions to help you identify their needs and keep things moving. As a way of doing this, ask open-ended questions that the person can reply to fully, rather than closed questions to which he or she can only answer 'yes' or 'no'. For example, you could begin by saying 'Tell me your thoughts about [the issue under discussion]'.

Make a proposal

Once both parties have had chance to assess the other's position, proposals and suggestions can be made and received. Remember that you need to trade things and not just concede them. The following phrase is valuable: 'If you (give to, or do something for, us), then we'll (give to, or do something for, you)'.

Look for an opportunity to trade things that are cheap for you to give but of value to the other party, in return for things which are valuable to your business. For example, if you are a painter and decorator who needs to rent a reasonably priced flat, you could negotiate with the landlord to paint certain rooms in return for a lower rent. Or say you need to publicise a product and would like to engage someone to do some work for you, but you can't quite afford to pay the job rate they had in mind. If you or your business have a website, you could offer to put a click-through link from your website to theirs so that anyone who reads their article can find out more about them and perhaps offer them more work.

Start the bargaining

After discussing each other's requirements and exchanging information, the bargaining can start (as in the first example above). Generally speaking, the more you ask for, the more you get, while you'll concede less if you don't offer as much at the beginning. For example, let's say you've something to sell to another party. You know you have a premium product, but you're not sure quite how blank the other party's cheque is. If you know you'd be happy to sell for £200, you might want to start off by asking for £300, knowing that:

- you'll be able to look as if you're giving ground to the other party
- they think they're getting a bargain
- you may even get a better deal than you'd thought!

If conflict arises when the bargaining starts, explain that the opening position is just that, an opening position and therefore not necessarily the one that will be adopted at the end of the negotiation. Ultimately, an agreement can be reached only when both parties find an acceptable point somewhere between their individual starting positions.

When you make an offer, be very clear about what's on the table. Avoid using words such as 'approximately' or 'about', as an experienced negotiator will spot an opportunity to raise the stakes quite dramatically. Don't make the whole process harder for yourself. For example, if you can only offer £600 for something, say so, or before you know it you'll be being pressed into agreeing to go up to £700.

Similarly, when the other party makes an offer, make sure you find out exactly what it includes. For example, if you're negotiating with a supplier, check whether or not the cost the supplier is quoting you contains delivery, VAT, and so on. Ask for clarification if there's anything you're not sure about and check that the offer matches all the criteria that you noted down during the preparation stages as being on your list of requirements.

Communicate clearly but openly

When you're negotiating with someone face to face, use open body language and maintain eye contact. Try to avoid sitting with your arms folded and your legs crossed, for example. Also, try to think through what you're about to say before you say it. Don't use language that will annoy the other person. For example, avoid using words like 'quibbling' and 'petty'. Even if you think someone is doing or being either of these things, using these words to them will only make the situation worse. Don't be sarcastic or demean them, their position, or their offer.

Similarly, if you feel that the main discussion is losing its focus and that people are starting to make asides to colleagues, address this by saying 'I sense there's something you're unhappy about. Would you like to discuss it now?'

Listen!

Sometimes when you're nervous about something, you become so focused on what you want to say that you don't pay enough attention to what's being said to you. This can cause all manner of problems, including knee-jerk reactions to problems that aren't really there but which you think you've heard. Active listening is a technique which will improve your general communication skills and will be particularly useful to practise if you have to negotiate a lot. To become an active listener, practice the following.

- Concentrate on what's being said, rather than using the time to think of a retort of your own.
- Acknowledge what's being said by your body language. This can include keeping good eye contact and nodding.
- Emphasise that you're listening by summarising your understanding of what has been said and checking that this is what the communicator intended to convey.
- Empathise with the communicator's situation. Empathy is about being able to put yourself in the other person's shoes and imagine what things are like from their perspective.
- Question and probe to bring forth more information and clear up any misunderstandings about what's being said. If you want to explore someone's thoughts more thoroughly, open questions are helpful. 'Tell me more about…?', 'What were your feelings when…?', 'What are your thoughts…?' These questions encourage the speaker to impart more information than closed questions, that merely elicit a 'yes' or 'no'.
- Don't be afraid of silence. We often feel compelled to fill silences, even when we don't really have anything to say – yet silence can be helpful in creating the space to gather thoughts and prepare for our next intervention.

Call a break if you need to

Sometimes a short break of 10 or 15 minutes may be a good thing if a negotiation is proving to be more complex or contentious than you'd previously thought. A break will give everyone a chance to cool down or recharge his or her batteries as necessary. It'll also give everyone an opportunity to take a step back from the issue under discussion and return to the table with some ideas if there has previously been an impasse.

Reach agreement

As the discussion continues, listen for verbal indications from the other party such as 'maybe' or 'perhaps' – these could be signs of an agreement being in sight. Also look out for non-verbal signs, like papers being tidied away. Now is the time to summarise what has been discussed and agreed and not to start bargaining again.

Summaries are an essential part of the negotiation process. They offer a way of making sure that everyone is clear on the decisions reached and also give all participants a final chance to raise any questions they may have. As soon as possible after the negotiation, send a letter that sets out the final, agreed decision. A handshake on a deal is fine, but no substitute for a written record. Make sure your letter mentions:

- the terms of the agreement
- the names of those involved
- relevant specifications or quantities
- any prices mentioned plus discounts, and so on

- individual responsibilities
- time schedules and any deadlines agreed

COMMON MISTAKES

You open negotiations with an unreasonable offer

Both parties need to see a reasonable chance of getting what they want from the negotiation process. By starting off with an unreasonable offer, you risk killing the process before it starts.

You begin negotiations without enough information about what the other party wants

The early discussion and information gathering phases need to be used properly to ensure that both parties aren't 'talking past each other'. Before negotiation begins, you need to have a broad view of the points you might need to concede on, and what you want the other party to concede to you. These can then be 'traded' in accordance with your bottom line.

You lose your temper

Some people are much easier to negotiate with than others and there's a difference between a serious, probing discussion and a bad-tempered slanging match laced with sarcasm. If someone is rude to you while you're negotiating with him or her, don't rise to the bait (even though it can be tempting). Instead, address them politely but assertively, and challenge their behaviour. You could say something like 'I think that comment was inappropriate and unhelpful. Shall we return to the issue?'

You try to rush negotiations in pursuit of a quick agreement

Both parties need to feel comfortable with the pace and direction of negotiations as they develop. This could mean that one or other party might need time to consider certain points or options before moving on to others. You should respect this need, while at the same time making sure that both parties observe a flexible timeframe for resolution. Endless negotiations will only waste time and money.

THE BEST SOURCES OF HELP

Book:
Fisher, Roger, William Ury, and Bruce Patton. *Getting to Yes*. London: Random House Business Books, 2003.

Websites:
ACAS: **www.acas.org.uk**
learndirect: **www.learndirect.co.uk**
Learning and Skills Council: **www.lsc.gov.uk**

Coping in Difficult Negotiations

GETTING STARTED

However experienced you are at handling negotiations, you'll occasionally run into difficulties. The number of potential problem areas is legion, but the most common ones fall into two categories: difficult people and difficult situations.

Again, the range of possibilities is wide, but some general principles will emerge in each case.

FAQS

I dread negotiating with one particular supplier as she is so abrasive. What can I do to change this?

People are difficult for several reasons. They may have unresolved issues in their personal life that affect their attitudes and commitment to the negotiation. They may lack empathy and make insensitive or inappropriate remarks, or they may simply be unskilled in negotiating and make mistakes. Whatever the cause, try not to over-react, remain professional and remember that you can take your custom elsewhere, ultimately.

MAKING IT HAPPEN

Decide whether you want to save the situation

You've had a long day and things aren't going well. Do you want to rescue what's left of the negotiation? If not, suggest postponing the negotiation to another day. If you do want to persevere, try the following approach.

There are two possible ways of behaving when working with others. When someone asks us for help, or appears to need it, the natural tendency of most people is to try to offer a solution. We generally produce one of the three kinds of behaviour:

• we advise people what to do
• we tell them
• we offer to do something for them under certain conditions

This is called 'solution-centred behaviour' because it focuses principally on finding an answer. Sometimes this works, but it is rather easy to produce a brilliant solution to what later turns out to be the wrong problem. And when this happens, it is, of course, your fault!

An alternative approach is to use 'problem-centred behaviour', which means questioning the other person about how he or she understands the problem.

You can do this either by consulting ('What exactly is the problem?', 'When did it occur?', 'What might have caused it?' and so on) or reflecting ('I can see that you're very angry about this, what's causing it?', 'What aspect of the problem is troubling you most?'). The key message here is to consult about facts, reflect on feelings. The purpose is to make sure that you both share a clear understanding of what the problem is. In fact, helping the other person to clarify his or her thinking about the problem often allows the answer to emerge as if by magic. The other party then feels as if they 'own' the solution, so they feel committed to it and you may not need to use the solution-centred behaviour at all.

Tap into the power of questions

Asking questions is always a good idea if you have to deal with difficult people, as it enables you to control the conversation – if you ask a question, people will usually answer it. This approach avoids confrontation, and it may get you valuable information about the person or the negotiation.

Remember the guidelines

• When in doubt, consult and reflect.
• Ask good, useful, open questions: plan them carefully.
• Ask for the other party's proposals or ideas – don't give yours first.
• Ask for clarification of the other party's proposals rather than saying what is wrong with them.
• Ask about their goals and objectives rather than telling them about yours.
• Ask how you can help them.

Have a back-up plan if all else fails

If the other person is still being 'difficult' and hindering the negotiation, more drastic action is needed. Either he or she doesn't want the negotiation to succeed, or is unable to conduct the discussion properly at this time. In any case, you need to do something to move things along.

Acknowledge that there seems to be a problem and ask three key questions:

• Does he or she want to continue the discussions?
• Would it be better if you spoke with someone else? A more senior member of staff, for example?
• Is there anything you can do that will help him or her feel more comfortable with the negotiation?

Deal with difficult situations

Not all negotiations take place face to face these days; in fact, most negotiations happen over the phone or by e-mail. Here we'll look at negotiating by phone. People sometimes opt for this to save time, but it's very much a second-best situation: avoid it as much as possible, except for simple negotiations.

For these straightforward discussions, telephone contact can have certain advantages:

• it is relatively cheap and usually quite quick
• you can spread your papers out in front of you for easy reference – this is especially useful if you need to refer to price lists, discounts, and so on
• you can use checklists to act as prompts
• you can take notes or make calculations as you wish

- the telephone forces you both to listen well
- decisions can be made promptly

However, there are a number of general disadvantages for both parties, but particularly for the party that has not initiated the discussion. You need to take account of these if put in this situation. The main problems are:

- you have little time to think
- you get no 'feel' for the other person, because you can't see them, and you can't pick up on any non-verbal clues in their behaviour
- the telephone is impersonal; it is difficult to use the 'personal domain'
- many standard negotiation tactics are less effective over the phone
- it is difficult to set and keep to an agenda
- people are more inclined to say 'no' on the phone because they don't get that little extra reassurance that comes from face-to-face contact
- 'what if...?' questions and searches for a 'better deal' can be more difficult on the phone – there is a tendency to stick to the specified business
- it can be difficult to co-ordinate within your own organisation
- there is a danger of distractions: visitors, noise, pending appointments, and so on
- many people feel pressured by time during a phone call
- silences are more threatening in a phone call (and in some countries, may lead to the connection being lost)
- you feel as if you have to make decisions too quickly
- the line may be bad, disrupting the flow of the negotiation, and you don't know who else is listening
- if you forget something, it may be difficult to come back to the point or introduce it later: telephone calls tend to be 'linear' (that is, you may have only one opportunity to say or raise something), whereas face-to-face conversations can go round in loops

If you *have to* negotiate over the phone, arrange a time that will allow you to do some preparation beforehand. If someone 'ambushes' you and you're caught off guard, ask if you can ring them back in half an hour or so.

Have all the necessary paperwork close at hand. For example, if you're discussing the renewal of a contract, make sure you have a copy close by that you can refer to.

Also have plenty of paper nearby that you can make notes on.

Make sure that you won't be disturbed. If you have an office, close the door. If you work in an open-plan office, see if you can book a meeting room elsewhere in the building so that you won't be distracted by other people's conversations around you.

Even though the other party can't see you, use the body language you would use if they were there in person, for example nod if you agree, move your hands as you speak. All of this will filter back in the tone of your voice.

Take a break and arrange to call the other person back if things are getting heated or you've reached a stalemate. Once agreement has been reached, follow up in writing as you would do if you'd conducted a face-to-face negotiation.

COMMON MISTAKES

You battle on when it's just not worth it

While everyone aims to tie up negotiations with the least amount of fuss and wasted time possible, some days it just won't work. On those days, it's important to recognise this, cut your losses, and rearrange for another time.

You don't get to the bottom of why someone is being 'difficult'

Even though your patience may be stretched to its absolute limit, try to put yourself in the other party's shoes to find out why they are acting in the way that they are. Also ask questions that allow the other party to disclose their concerns and motivations – you may actually be able to help them, thus achieving that ideal win–win goal.

THE BEST SOURCES OF HELP
Websites:
The Negotiation Skills Company: **www.negotiation-skills.com/articles.html**
Work911.com: **www.work911.com/cgi-bin/links/jump.cgi?ID = 3323**

Managing Your Time

GETTING STARTED

Time is a man-made concept. Animals don't understand the idea. They live *in* time; they are in the moment; the present is all that counts. Remembering this can be useful in the business world: being able to focus on the present is often an effective way of getting through laborious tasks and not worrying about the past or future.

In business, time is money. Paradoxically, as technology proliferates (with the promise that it will increase productivity), it simultaneously adds complexity to managers' workloads, frequently with fewer support staff to complete the work. The only realistic way out of such a paradox is to make better use of time.

Actionlists

FAQS

How can I be a better time manager?

The *desire* to be good at time management is half the battle, but you need to be aware of the choices you have to make. These relate to your overall life balance and the values you hold.

Look at what you're being asked to do and why. If some requests are outside your area of responsibility or expertise, you may need to speak to your boss to clarify the boundaries. If you're told these new things are now a permanent part of your workload, then something else will have to give way – unless, of course, you can improve your time-management capabilities, or delegate some of the tasks.

Perhaps you'll have to be more realistic about your strengths and capabilities. Rather than deadlines being imposed, try to have input into setting realistic ones. Build some slack in the schedule to give yourself the best possible chance of meeting deadlines.

One of my team members seems incredibly disorganised. What can I do to help?

A good team leader often needs to work with individual team members to help them to understand what's expected. Set realistic goals and give them adequate time and resources to complete the work. Additionally, if possible, ask them to examine their performance objectively and identify patterns of behaviour that contribute to being disorganised. Often time management requires a change in habitual behaviour. This can only be achieved by building awareness, charting a clear route, and rewarding success.

I've recently invested in a BlackBerry® but find I am still using a diary as well. How can I get away from using redundant systems?

Plan the time it will take to learn the new technology and transfer your information. Ask for a tutorial from someone who has made the leap already. Then, over a period of a month, wean yourself off the dual system by omitting the diary. You'll soon find the computerised method more versatile and convenient than anything you've used in the past.

MAKING IT HAPPEN

Conduct a 'time audit'

You may find it useful to conduct a 'time audit' on your life. What's the balance between the demands placed upon you at work and those that define your private life? Does this balance satisfy you, or do you find yourself sacrificing one element for another? One key to good time management is being aware of the wider world in which you live and how the component parts relate to one another. Another key is prioritising – if in fact there isn't enough time to satisfy all competing demands – and then choosing how you apportion your time.

Take a large sheet of paper and write your name in the centre. Write all the demands of your life around it. Include work hours, commuting, socialising, eating, sleeping, household duties, and family commitments. Remember that taking time for family and friends, exercise, hobbies, holidays, and just plain fun is important. Mark the number of hours that you dedicate to each of these areas throughout the day, month, or year. This chart graphically represents your life, in terms of the choices and trade-offs you have made in areas that are important to you.

Ask yourself, is this how I want to live my life? You may decide to sacrifice some important areas in the short term, but be aware of what might happen when a particular phase of your life comes to an end. For example, how will you manage if you get married or divorced; when children grow up and leave home; when you get transferred to another position or take another job in another company or city; when you have an accident or long-term illness; when you retire?

Evaluate what action needs to be taken

Take a highlighter and mark those areas on your chart that need attention. If, for instance, you are spending too much time at work, you need to review your professional objectives and decide how to achieve a better balance.

Life is all about choices. You may find that you can win more time by working from home, if your employer will permit it and your family will respect the necessary home–work boundaries.

You'll probably find that there are other ways to prune hours from the day that are otherwise wasted. For instance, if you like to play sport or keep fit, consider finding a club near work where you can go early in the morning, instead of having to fit this in during the evening.

Look for patterns in the way you use your time. You may find that you're constantly in meetings that run late or that you pick up a lot of extra work because you aren't assertive enough in saying 'no'. If you don't have enough time and your own behaviour is contributing to the shortage, change your patterns of behaviour.

Learn to use the right tools

Time-management tools and techniques are only as useful as the time you invest in using them. Some commercially available tools and techniques include:

- handheld organisers, also known as personal digital assistants (PDAs)
- organisers, both computer-based programs and paper diaries or schedulers
- 'to do' lists
- prioritising work according to its importance, and focusing only on the essential
- shared diaries – team, secretarial, professional groups

If you're a person more accustomed to focusing on 'the moment' rather than the 'big picture', it may be a good idea to learn to stand back and look at time as a continuum, in terms of past, present, and future. Doing so gives you a sense or order, structure, and perspective.

Some dos and don'ts of time management

Do	Don't
Undertake a 'time audit'	Spend time on unnecessary activities or those that don't serve your purpose
Be honest about how long things take	
Build in time for reflecting and learning	Try to undertake the impossible
Build in time for yourself	Blame others for your disorganisation
Delegate wherever you can	
Anticipate the pressure of commitments that you make	Get hung up on process
	Make commitments that you can't meet
Communicate with others where you have time conflicts	Expect others to make up for what you can't do
Plan ahead	Give up

If too much work is the issue, look at your workload, prioritise, and refer back to how it fits your job description. Decide, perhaps together with your manager, which things you're doing that add value to your job and career potential and which would be better delegated to others.

The central point is that planning is essential. Bringing time into consciousness will build awareness, and awareness always precedes action.

COMMON MISTAKES

You buy a new gadget but still rely on old time-management tools

If you're going to buy a new device to help you plan your time better, you need to be disciplined in mastering it and using it daily. Don't buy something just for the sake of it and leave it to gather dust.

You expect too much of yourself and become disenchanted

Change is difficult and often requires a new set of skills. The principles of time management sound completely logical and straightforward, but in fact we lead extremely complex lives, and these simple principles are hard to put in to practice. Don't overwhelm yourself by trying to change everything at once. Instead, establish a series of small, clear goals, and achieve them one by one.

You're not prepared to break bad habits, and don't ask for help

Old habits do die hard, and one of the hardest to break is the way we structure and use our time. Everyone knows people who are always late or always early; those who jump right on to tasks or are terrible procrastinators; those who are stressed-out workaholics or who always seem miraculously refreshed and relaxed. The choices we make in managing our time are connected to the way we view ourselves and the world: making different choices affects our sense of identity and our relationships. Take it slowly, look to family, friends, and work colleagues for support in making these changes, and don't rule out taking workshops or looking for a consultant to help you.

THE BEST SOURCES OF HELP
Books:
Allen, David. *Getting Things Done*. London: Piatkus, 2002.
Tracy, Brian. *Eat That Frog! 21 Great Ways to Stop Procrastinating and Get More Done in Less Time*. San Francisco, California: Berrett-Koehler, 2002.

Websites:
Mind Tools: **www.mindtools.com/pages/main/ newMN_HTE.htm**
Time Management Guide: **www.time-management-guide.com**

Delegating without Guilt

GETTING STARTED

If you have a team working for you, you need to get to grips with delegation. It's a key skill to develop. Delegation isn't about giving tasks to others because you can't be bothered to do them yourself. It *is* about getting a particular job done, clearly, but it's also about encouraging people to learn new skills and reach their potential, all of which helps a business to grow.

Many of us like being in control of everything and find it hard to let go of things we know we can do well ourselves. However, if we want to be successful managers – and preserve our own sanity – that's exactly what we must do.

FAQS

Why do people find it difficult to delegate?

There are many reasons why you may find it difficult to delegate. Often, it seems quicker to do the task yourself than bother to explain it to somebody else and then correct his or her mistakes. You might worry that the person will make a bit of a hash of it, and it'll take a long time to put right the mistakes they make. On the other hand, you may feel threatened by the competence of a person who is quick on the uptake and does well. You may fear that the employee may take over the role of being the person the rest of the staff go to with their problems. They may even find something wrong with the way *you* do things.

If you lack confidence, you may find it hard to give instructions and you'll put off delegating. If you do delegate, and problems arise because the employee fails to do what you've asked him or her to do, you may doubt your own ability to confront the person about his or her actions. If staff have been given increased responsibilities and have done well, you may not be confident of being able to reward them sufficiently. Conversely, you might be reluctant to delegate tasks that you think are too tedious.

Finally, you may realise that delegation is necessary, but you don't know where to start, or how to go about it. You need some kind of method to follow. The following paragraphs will help to put you on the right track.

How can delegation help me?

Delegation offers many benefits. Done well, it will allow you to concentrate on the things you do best and also give you the time and space to tackle more interesting and challenging tasks in the future. You'll be less likely to put off making key decisions and you'll be much more effective. Your staff will benefit too; everyone needs new challenges, and by delegating to them, you'll be able to test their ability in a range of areas and increase their contribution to the business. Staff can make quick decisions themselves, and they'll develop a better understanding of the details concerned. Done well, delegation should improve the overall productivity of employees.

It's all too tempting to withdraw into 'essential' tasks and not develop relations with your team. The bottom line is that it's wasteful for senior staff to be given big salaries for doing low-value work, and passing tasks down the line is essential if other people are to develop. Not knowing how to do this is recognised as one of the biggest obstacles to small business growth. By delegating, you'll have much more time to do your own job properly.

Delegation doesn't make things easier (there will always be other challenges), but it does make things more efficient and effective. Essentially, it represents a more interactive way of working with a team of people, and it involves instruction, training, and development. The results will be well worth the time and effort you invest in doing it properly.

When should I delegate?

Delegation is fundamental to successful management – look for opportunities to do it. If you have too much work to do, or if you don't have enough time to devote to important tasks, delegate. When it's clear that certain staff, particularly new employees, need to develop, or

when an employee clearly has the skills needed to perform a specific task, delegate.

What tasks should I delegate?

Begin with any routine administrative tasks that take up too much of your time. There are likely to be many small everyday jobs which you've always done – you may even enjoy doing them (for example, sending faxes) – but they're not a good use of your time. Review these small jobs and delegate as many of them as you can. Being your company's point of contact for a particular person or organisation, which is important but can be time-consuming, is also an excellent task to delegate.

On a larger scale, delegate projects that it makes sense for one person to handle; these make good tests of people's ability to manage and co-ordinate tasks. Give the person you delegate to something he or she has every chance of completing successfully and, if possible, something for which he or she has a special aptitude. Do not delegate an impossible task at which others have failed and which may well prove a negative experience for the delegatee.

Who should I delegate to?

Make sure you understand the person you're delegating to. He or she must have the skills and ability – or at least the potential – to develop into the role and must be someone you can trust. It's a good idea to test out the employee with small tasks that will help show what he or she can do. Also make sure that the employee is available for the assignment – don't put too much pressure on your most effective workers. Spread out the tasks you delegate among as many people as possible: two or more people could even share a task if it's particularly complicated.

MAKING IT HAPPEN
Be positive

Think positively: you have the right to delegate and, frankly, you must delegate. You won't get it 100 per cent right the first time, but you'll improve with experience. Be as decisive as you can, and, if you need to improve your assertiveness skills, consider attending a course or reading one of the many books on the subject. A positive approach will also give your employees confidence in themselves, and they need to feel that you believe in them.

If you expect efficiency from the person you delegate to, organise yourself first. If there's no overall plan of what's going on, it'll be hard to identify, schedule, and evaluate the work being delegated. Prepare the ground before seeing the person (but don't use this as a ploy to delay!). Assess the task and decide how much responsibility the person will have. Assess the person's progress regularly and make notes.

Discuss the task to be delegated

When you meet the person or people you're delegating to, discuss the tasks and the problems in depth, and explain fully what's expected of them. It's crucial to give people precise objectives, but encourage them to seek these out themselves by letting them ask you questions and participate in setting the parameters. They need to understand why they're doing the task, and where it fits into the scheme of things. Ask them how they'll go about the task; discuss their plan and the support they might need.

Set targets and offer support if necessary

Targets should be set and deadlines scheduled into diaries. Summarise what has been agreed, and take notes about what the person is required to do so everyone is clear. If he or she is given a lot of creative scope and is being tested out, you may decide to be deliberately vague, but if the task is urgent and critical, you must be specific.

How much support you offer and give will very much depend on the person and your relationship with him or her. In the early stages you might want to work with the person and to share certain tasks, but you'll be able to back off more as your understanding of the person's abilities increases. Encourage people to come back to you if they have any problems – while it's important to have time alone, you should be accessible if anyone has a problem or the situation changes. If someone needs to check something with you, try to get back to him or her quickly. Don't interfere or criticise if things are going according to plan.

Monitoring progress is vital – it's very easy to forget all about the task until the completion date, but, in the meantime, all sorts of things could have gone wrong. When planning, time should be built in to review progress. If more problems were expected to arise and nothing has been heard, check with the employee that all is well. Schedule routine meetings with the person and be flexible enough to adjust deadlines and objectives as the situation changes.

How did it go?

When a task is complete, give praise and review how things went. If an employee's responsibilities are increased, make sure he or she receives fair rewards for it. On the other hand, there may be limits on what can be offered, so don't offer rewards you can't deliver. Also bear in mind that development can carry its own rewards. Such career development issues can be discussed with the employee in appraisals, and the results of delegated tasks noted for this purpose. If the person has failed to deliver, discuss it with him or her, find out what went wrong, and aim to resolve problems in the future.

COMMON MISTAKES

You expect employees to do things the way that you do

Managers often criticise the way things are done because it isn't the way they would have done it themselves. Remember that people prefer working in different ways; concentrate on the results rather than the methods used to obtain them.

You don't give people a chance

If you're giving someone something new to do, you must be patient. It'll take time for employees to develop new skills, but it's time that will pay off in the end. Have faith in the people around you.

You delegate responsibility without authority

It's unfair to expect results from someone with one hand tied behind his or her back. If you're going to delegate responsibilities, make sure that those involved know this, and confer the necessary authority upon the person you're delegating to.

THE BEST SOURCES OF HELP
Websites:
businessballs.com: **www.businessballs.com/ delegation.htm**
iVillage: **www.ivillage.co.uk/workcareer/survive/ opolitics/articles/0,,156475_157030,00.html**
Mind Tools: **www.mindtools.com/tmdelegt.html**

Solving Problems

GETTING STARTED

Problem-solving is a key activity of management, as well as of many other jobs. Without problem-solving capabilities, no organisation could exist for very long. Intelligence, common sense, and education help us solve problems in our individual lives, and those same elements can also help us with organisational problems. However, if you're attempting to do something complex, such as reorganise the business or implement a total quality management programme, you need a systematic approach to problem-solving, a process that allows people at all levels to contribute to finding solutions. This actionlist looks at a variety of issues, techniques, and resources to help you to find your own best approach.

FAQS

Why shouldn't I just allow people to solve problems in their own way?

In most situations, it's good to allow people to understand and then solve problems in their own way. However, using tried and tested techniques of problem-solving – ones that are plainly mapped out and used uniformly – makes it easier for others to understand the way in which the problem area is being explored. The process ensures that, whether talking about customer service or production quotas, others can get actively involved in solving the problem at any stage.

Each problem is different; is it really possible to use the same problem-solving technique in each case?

While problems *are* always different, there are some common approaches and processes for solving them. Problems can be diagnosed and the various elements can be mapped – whether you're talking about a manufacturing roadblock or an IT systems failure. Obviously, as an organisation grows in size, so too does the need for more sophisticated techniques.

Isn't problem-solving just for those people who like to spend lots of time thinking? Surely finding a quick and ready solution is more important?

It's true that we often notice the solution more than the problem. That's because problems cause us headaches and can hold us up; solutions allow us to move forward. However, in order to be sure of having the *right* solution, spending time on using problem-solving techniques means you can be certain that you know the full extent of the problem, the possible knock-on effects, and the priorities for managing the situation.

Doesn't a structured approach stifle creativity?

Problem-solving isn't just about logical deductions; it's about finding new and alternative ways of resolving a situation. In fact, creativity can flourish through a structured process. Structure can also be limiting, though, so you must be careful not to preclude a full exploration of the possibilities. If, for example, you're working in a group, don't allow members to become judgmental about ideas and dismiss them too early in the process. Practise letting go of your assumptions, and allow everyone to contribute in a way that suits them best.

MAKING IT HAPPEN

Problem-solving is best done in groups, to ensure that a true win–win situation is achieved. Any problem-solving process requires the following steps.

Identify the problem

Understanding a problem requires an ability to see it in its entirety – in breadth, depth, and context. Here are a number of ways to evaluate the scope of a problem:
• recognition – can you see or feel the problem? Is it isolated, or part of a bigger problem?

• symptoms – how is it showing itself?
• causes – why has it happened?
• effects – what else is being affected by it?

The task then is to break the main problem down into smaller problems, in order to determine whether you're the right person or team to handle it. If not, you need to transfer the problem-solving process to those better equipped to deal with it. If the answer is yes, you need to ask additional questions, including: do you have the right resources? how long might the process take? what are some of the obstacles? what's the anticipated benefit? Once you get answers, move on to the next step.

Find the best way of gathering data

There are two important questions here: what do you need to know, and how are you going to get it? Most information can be accessed, but there are often time and resource issues involved with collecting and analysing it. Remember that data collection may involve investigating the symptoms of the problem, its underlying causes, and/or its overall effects. Each of these may have different implications for how the problem is viewed. Data-gathering techniques include:
• workflow analysis
• surveys and questionnaires
• flow charts
• group and/or one-to-one interviews

Brainstorm the problem

In any problem-solving exercise, there will be a need for brainstorming. There are five golden rules for the brainstorming process:
• anything goes – no evaluation or judgment by others
• hitchhike – build on the ideas of others
• quality – strive for quality
• be off the wall – encourage wild and wacky ideas
• inclusiveness – include other people and encourage participation

Explore options and solutions

Lateral thinking can play an important role in understanding the perspectives of a problem and their implications. Look at what others have done in the past, and don't ignore what may seem a crazy idea. It's best to cast the net wide when exploring solutions, so that there is a richness of ideas and possible options.

Evaluate priorities and decisions

Taking time to identify the most appropriate solution from your range of options is very important. Suggestions need to be winnowed down to a shortlist, containing only the most realistic possibilities.

To do this, set some hard measures. Try to determine the costs and benefits of the suggested solutions. If, for example, you feel that outside investment is needed to solve a particular problem, work out the payback period. You can then assess whether your senior management team will accept it.

Always understand that each possible solution has consequences, some of which may cause additional problems themselves.

Select the best solutions for the situation and context

The chosen solution needs to meet some key criteria. Do you have the necessary people, money, and time to achieve it? Will you get a sufficient return on investment? Is the solution acceptable to others involved in the situation? You should draw up:

- a rationale of why you've reached your particular conclusion
- a set of criteria to judge the solution's success
- a plan of action and contingencies
- a schedule for implementation
- a team to carry out, be responsible for, and approve the solution

Implement the solution and make it happen

Implementation means having action plans with relevant deadlines and contingencies built in. Any implementation needs constant review, and the implementation team needs to be sure it has the support of relevant management. Keep asking the following questions:

- Are deadlines being met?
- Are team members happy, and is communication strong within and from the team?
- Has the team been recognised for its achievements?
- Are the improvements measurable?
- Is the situation reviewed regularly?

Evaluate the solution

This is where the two most important questions are asked:

- How well did it work?
- What did we learn from the process?

All experience can be valuable in terms of adding to an organisation's learning and knowledge banks.

Canvass people's opinions regarding the effectiveness of the process and its outcome. Ask for areas of improvement that could be incorporated into a second phase. Don't be afraid of involving your clients in any evaluation; this can convey a positive message if handled properly, and builds trust in your ability to troubleshoot problems and implement solutions.

Be aware of the pitfalls of problem-solving

There are, of course, pitfalls that can make for ineffective problem-solving. These are:

- failing to involve the right people at the right time, particularly those outside the immediate group
- tackling problems that lie beyond the control of the team
- jumping to conclusions before truly understanding the depth or scope of the problem
- failing to gather sufficient data, either about the problem itself or some of the proposed solutions
- failing to 'right size' the problem; people often work on problems that are too general or too large
- failing fully to support the conclusions reached or the solution identified

COMMON MISTAKES
You use too many techniques

Don't try to use too many techniques. Find one that you feel will work well in the business. Often, when running workshops, the process becomes more important than the ideas and intellectual discussion. Getting the balance right is important.

Your team is too narrow in scope

Don't limit your team to the people you like. Try to get representatives from different parts of the business to give a different angle on the problem. Remember that:

- often the exciting part of problem-solving is identifying innovative solutions. But it's important to focus on the full picture, from problem identification through to final implementation and evaluation. Your ideas are only as good as the results you get.
- creativity can often derail a problem-solving process. Getting the balance right between understanding the problem and finding imaginative solutions requires strong facilitation.
- your solution will have an impact on other parts of the business, or the client. Make sure you think through the implications of the proposed solution and the implementation plan.

THE BEST SOURCES OF HELP
Book:
de Bono, Edward. *Six Thinking Hats*. Revised ed. London: Penguin, 2000.

Making Good Decisions Under Pressure

GETTING STARTED

When we are called on to make decisions under pressure, we often worry that we will make the wrong decision, and that it will come back to haunt us. Most of us prefer to have enough time to analyse the situation and consider the alternatives. When under pressure, however, this luxury is not afforded us and we are expected to make good decisions in a very short space of time.

Yet, some of the best decisions we make are the ones we make under pressure. Pressure can result in focused attention and the use of unconscious reasoning. It forces us to sort the relevant factors from the irrelevant and can result in clear thinking and clear priorities. This actionlist helps you to develop good decision-making practices which will stand you in good stead when you are put under pressure.

FAQS

When I am called to make a decision under pressure I panic and feel overwhelmed by the probability that I will get it wrong. What can I do to overcome these feelings?

What you are probably doing is running through all the disaster scenarios if you make the wrong decision. This clouds your thinking and adds yet more pressure to your decision-making. Try to overcome this by focusing on what the relevant information is, and put the rest to the back of your mind. Should you wish, you can mull it over later – but for now you need to prioritise and focus on the key factors.

How do I avoid having to make hasty decisions under pressure?

'Good' decisions are usually made as a result of un-pressured analysis. If you are in a job where you might be called upon to make decisions under pressure, it would be worth your while to look ahead and consider various potential eventualities, what decisions you might make, and their likely outcomes. Doing this means that, even if you don't encounter the exact situation, you will already have thought through a number of different scenarios so your thinking will be faster, clearer, and more readily accessible.

I think I have good instincts but I tend to override these by spending time gathering information to justify the action I take. Is it safe to use gut instinct to make decisions under pressure?

There are times when your instincts serve you well, especially if you have a long track record of dealing with similar situations – but you need to balance these by considering any extenuating circumstances. Try to remain open to any new information before deciding to follow your instincts.

I am often put under pressure to make fast decisions that meet other people's agendas. I find it hard to think through their motivations fast enough to come to the right conclusions. How can I manage this?

If you don't see the urgency to make a decision yourself, play for time and explore it more fully. In these instances, it is important that there is open communication – especially if your decision has an impact on others. It would be a shame to be called to account for a decision

you made and to have to admit you were pressured to do so by someone else!

MAKING IT HAPPEN

Decision-making is not something that we are all equally equipped to do, but it *is* something we can learn. There are many tools that can help in the decision-making process. They range from *decision trees*, which help you see the ups and downs of different solutions, to a *force field analysis* where the pressures for and against change are highlighted and weighted. However, if these techniques are not put in the light of experience or moderated by a feeling of what will work and what won't, they can be clumsy.

If you are under pressure to make a decision, though, you won't have the time to use any of these approaches. Instead, you will be forced into being reactive and to draw upon your intuition. Some people appear to be fortunate enough to have a good feel for what needs to be done – but if you scratch the surface of their decisions, you'll probably find that they have drawn from their extensive experience and memories of what has worked in the past and what hasn't. If you don't have this background, you will be better served by going through likely decisions 'virtually' before they need to be made. In this way, you can rehearse your responses to different situations in a more leisurely way and determine the best way forward should they arise.

Here are some suggestions that may help you when you are under pressure.

Undertake a risk analysis before any need for a reactive decision arises

To protect ourselves from serious errors when making decisions under pressure, it's a good idea to think ahead and anticipate and rehearse scenarios. This is what the emergency services do when they role-play serious situations or crises. Everything is enacted as if it is really happening so that the parties involved can practice making good decisions under pressure. Then, when the situation occurs in reality, they are able to make decisions rapidly and effectively.

Think through a series of 'disaster scenarios' and come to some conclusions about what you would do if any of them actually happened. This is not a negative activity and, with a bit of luck, none of the situations you have thought about will emerge. However, if they do, you will already have been through the thought processes in your mind and you will be able to access them quickly. Here is a checklist for conducting a risk analysis:

1. Speculate on the threats that you are facing in your situation. These include financial, technical, operational, and human. Ask yourself 'What if. . .' until you have exhausted all possible scenarios.
2. Measure the likelihood of the risk occurring. Think about the combination of the cost and the probability of it happening. By doing this, you will be able to highlight the worst-case scenario and consider this first.

3. Start with the most critical risk and think through the different ways in which you could address it. By going through this exercise before the risk occurs, you may be able to eliminate the risk altogether or devise a contingency plan that will ameliorate the risk.

4. Make contact with anyone who is likely to be involved and inform them of any procedures they need to apply or approaches that they need to take in order to manage the situation effectively. If everyone is pre-warned, informed of their role, and kept briefed about the probability of something occurring, they will be able to help you move swiftly when you have to.

UNDERSTAND THE SITUATION

When something happens that requires your urgent attention, try not to jump to conclusions or go down a path that reflects your fears rather than what is actually going on. Breathe deeply a couple of times, give yourself time to appraise the situation, then decide which of the scenarios you have already thought through most closely matches what has happened. It is difficult to predict a situation precisely, so be prepared to 'mix and match' your prepared responses so that they meet the demands of the situation.

Sort out the relevant from the irrelevant facts

We often get overwhelmed by information in crisis situations; there are usually only one or two important facts on which the decision rests. Don't get waylaid by factors that are irrelevant to the current decision. Discard any information that is clouding your judgment and address it later. By asking yourself 'Is this critical now?' you will be able to reject elements of the situation that do not warrant urgent attention and get to the core of the problem rapidly.

Apply weightings or some other criteria to the issues under consideration

It sometimes helps if you put scores or weightings on the options that are available to you so that you can see clearly which are the most suitable decisions. If the situation is highly pressured you may have to do this in your head – but this activity will focus your mind and help you to make good decisions.

Talk your decision through with a trusted or experienced colleague

To make sure you haven't missed anything in your rush, find someone to check your logic. Just hearing yourself talk about it could further clarify your rationale for making a decision.

Remember that a 'good' decision doesn't necessarily guarantee a satisfactory outcome. Sometimes, even when we have gone through a careful decision-making process to make what we believe to be a good decision, it turns sour. The activity of making a good decision does not protect us from failure; all we can do is stack up the odds in our favour as much as possible and hope that chance or circumstance don't sabotage us.

COMMON MISTAKES

You allow yourself to feel overwhelmed by the need to make a good decision under pressure

If you allow yourself to become overwhelmed, your logic will become clouded and your decision-making ability will be compromised. No matter what the time pressures are, make sure that you listen attentively and collect all the information available before moving into decision-making mode. This will enable you to remain clear headed as you sift through the facts and find out what is really going on. Many mistakes are made by people who assume they know what is happening and stop seeing and hearing what's going on around them. It is well known that we often see and hear what we expect to see and hear!

You don't brief people properly about what is expected of them

This can slow things down and will increase the pressure on anyone involved in the situation – including yourself. If you are making rapid decisions under pressure, the last thing you want is people asking what they should be doing or how they should be doing it.

You get stuck in irrelevant detail

This is one of the common barriers to making good decisions. Although it is true that 'the devil is in the detail', if the detail isn't immediately relevant it should be set aside for the time being. Try to eliminate as much irrelevant detail as possible so that you can see the core of the issue. This will help you focus on what needs to be done and what decisions need to be taken.

THE BEST SOURCES OF HELP
Book:
Adair, John. *Decision Making and Problem Solving Strategies*. 2nd ed. London: Kogan Page, 2007.

Handling Office Politics

GETTING STARTED

The old adage 'if you want to get ahead, you have to work hard' doesn't necessarily apply in modern organisations, especially those that are predisposed towards having a 'political' culture. In these organisations, *who* you know tends to matter more than *what* you know. The *context* in which relationships have been built is also an important factor as these will carry certain kinds of loyalties (or perceived obligations). Family, school, or social networks that intrude into professional territory can embroil people in all sorts of political manoeuvrings that eventually lead to a politically charged work environment.

FAQS

I have unwittingly become involved in a political situation which I fear will compromise my reputation in the business. What should I do?

If you are unable to confront the situation directly, it's important to go through the correct channels to avoid compromising yourself further. Communicate with your supervisor or manager and explain what has happened. If the political situation involves your boss, you may want to approach your human resources department to ask their advice. If you have one, a mentor is often a good sounding board for helping you resolve your dilemma.

I am a woman with a management position in a large organisation, and I am always coming up against 'male' politics. How can I continue to succeed without getting drawn in to ugly gender battles?

Male networks have controlled the power in businesses for hundreds of years and they are almost impenetrable. You may find it helpful to find a mentor, male or female, inside or outside the business, who will champion you and look out for information and opportunities for you. Build your relationships carefully and find ways in which you can make connections that bring value to your male colleagues. Don't let them get away with abusing your gifts; follow up and ask for feedback. In this way, you will build their respect and find a tenable position amongst them.

I am weary of the politics of large organisations, yet I love what I do and want to carry on doing it. How can I find an environment where I can just get on with my work?

You may find that a change of context meets your needs. This doesn't necessarily mean a move out of the organisation entirely, but perhaps you could consider a move to a small-business unit or specialised department where the likelihood of a different political culture exists.

Smaller work units are very often structurally simpler and less political than large ones.

MAKING IT HAPPEN

Watch for signs of office politics

Politics plays a part in all organisations; it is an inevitable effect of putting human beings together in some sort of hierarchical arrangement. Indicators of office politics are often fairly easy to pick up. Comments from people who have been passed over for promotion by the son of the chairman, or by the recruiting manager's former golfing partner, give clues about the undercover workings of the business. Those who succeed by publicly supporting their boss and ensuring that they are always in the right place at the right time again, indicate that hidden agendas are at play.

Find ways to discourage political behaviours

In any context, decision-making based on politics encourages hypocrisy, double dealing, cliques, self interest, and deception. These are the behaviours that need to be reined in if the business is going to survive in the long term. Here are a few ideas for creating change.

- **Promotions** should be given to the candidates who have demonstrated a relevant track record of success. Conduct structured, formal interviews and consult with others affected by the decision. Match the successful candidate to the job description. Remember that although a good working relationship is necessary, the talents and values of the individual do not have to match those of their new line manager.

- **Reward and recognition** must be given for good performance, not in return for favours. All promotions or pay rises must be based on the individual's ability to reach or exceed the key performance indicators set during the performance review. Performance data should be available to those it concerns, with no hidden judgments or decisions.

- **Communication** should be open and transparent. Only unhealthy organisations hide information and spring unpleasant surprises on their employees. Communicate anything that affects your employees and their performance, including bad news, challenges, and initiatives for change.

- **New initiatives**, projects, and ideas should be actioned on the basis of their value to the business, not on the basis of favouritism or possible personal benefit. A formal process for proposing new initiatives and tracing their evaluation and implementation creates confidence in an unbiased outcome.

- **Politicking** can be tempting, especially when you can see an opportunity to benefit either yourself or the organisation as a whole. You might want to 'offload' a member of your team in order to attract someone you feel may perform more effectively. However, this is where the rot sets in. If you manage people on this basis, you will destroy any trust your team has in you and their collective performance will deteriorate.

Ensure your own survival

If your organisation is rife with politics, you can survive by following some simple rules.

- **Observe** the organisation's political style without getting involved until you are sure that you know what is going on. You may have started to notice coincidences or inconsistencies. Bide your time and watch the process so that you can begin to understand what the patterns and motivations are.
- **Keep your own counsel** during this period and work according to your own values; do not try to reconfigure your values to match those of the organisation, as you will only get stressed. Also, under pressure, your own values will reassert themselves forcefully. You can't please everyone all the time, so use your own integrity to make decisions.
- **Build a network** of trusted allies. During your observation phase you will have identified who these people could be. Build a network outside the organisation to create options and opportunities for yourself. This also takes the focus off work for a while and gives you time to reconfirm or realign your values.
- **Expose** other people's politically motivated behaviour. When colleagues say one thing and do another, or seem to be sabotaging your decisions or work relationships, use your assertiveness skills to challenge their motivation: 'You seem to be unhappy with the decisions I've made, would you like to discuss them?' They will either have to deny your assertion or confront it, but at least the issue will be out in the open.
- **Find a mentor** with whom you can discuss your observations and concerns. You may gain a deeper understanding of the political processes at work and some insight into how you can manage these more effectively.

COMMON MISTAKES

You misread a situation and wade in with an accusation of politicking

At best this reveals your naiveté, at worst your own politicking or neuroses. If you think a colleague is politically motivated, observe the person's behaviour until you are sure that you understand it. You may wish to share your thoughts with someone you trust or if it serves a purpose, confront the situation. Sometimes it is best to leave things alone. You will be the best judge of this.

You build a network purely for your own ends

Some people try to short-circuit the path to promotion by building what they believe to be critical relationships. However, there is a big difference between building professional networks and using your contacts shamelessly in headlong pursuit of your own selfish ends. Remember that if you launch yourself into an early promotion without having developed the skills to be successful, you may be setting yourself up for a very public and career-damaging failure. Build your networks prudently and use them to help develop your skills and expose you to new opportunities. It may take a little longer, but it will pay off in the end.

You get involved in the politics too early

When you join a new organisation, try not to get embroiled in the politics at an early stage. Your newness in the business will allow you to ask naive questions that will help you create a picture of the political environment. Keep your relationships open and friendly and build your network with a diverse range of people. Observe the patterns of relationships closely to see where the information lies and where the power sits. After a few months you will probably have a fairly accurate idea of what is going on and you can then make your own decisions about the extent to which you should get involved in organisational politics.

Communication channels are unclear

Poor communication is probably the most common cause of a destructive political culture. In the absence of information or explanation, people will fill the gaps with speculation and rumour which circulate around the grapevine very fast. Maintaining clear channels of communication, that leave people in no doubt about plans or decisions, helps protect an organisation from becoming a breeding ground for politics. Newsletters, bulletin boards on an intranet, and company-wide meetings are all useful vehicles for disseminating information, along with more local activities such as team meetings and personal briefings.

THE BEST SOURCES OF HELP

Websites:
iVillage.co.uk: **www.ivillage.co.uk/workcareer/ survive/archive/0,10391,156475,00.htm**
'Surfing Office Politics', CareerLink.com:
http://careerlink.devx.com/articles/hc1199/hc1 199.asp

Coping with a Nightmare Boss

GETTING STARTED

Many people have a difficult or challenging relationship with their boss. Of all the difficult relationships you may have at work, this will probably be the trickiest and most stressful because of the inherent political dynamic of your relationship. It can be tempting to lay the blame for this unhappy type of situation at the boss's feet because of his or her unreasonable, negative, awkward, or unhelpful behaviour. Whether this view is justified or not, the good news is that, as a significant party in the relationship, there is much you can do to end the bad boss nightmare.

FAQS

My boss is always making negative and derisive comments about the way I do my work. What should I do?

Find a private moment when you can explain clearly how this makes you feel and ask your boss to stop doing it. You could suggest that he or she gives you clear guidelines and constructive feedback that will help you to meet his or her expectations and develop your talents. Point out that constant nagging affects the way you work and that you would be much more effective if he or she took a positive interest in what you do. If the negativity continues, you may decide to lodge a complaint of discrimination against your boss. If you take this route, make sure you have a record of the incidents and a note of the witnesses present. You might also decide to seek further advice from your human resources department if you have one.

My boss has favourites and I am definitely not one of them. As a result, I'm not given essential information and I miss out on good opportunities. How can I change things?

Lack of communication often contributes to workplace misunderstandings. Try approaching your boss with information about what you're doing and talk about your methods and goals. If your boss persists in denying you the information you need, you may have a case of bullying against him or her.

I have a boss who is really moody and bad-tempered, making work almost intolerable. Is there anything I can do to change this?

Observe whether there is a pattern in this behaviour and try to work out how you could influence the situation for the better. Once you've made your observations, you could try giving constructive feedback, letting your boss know how his or her mood swings affect you. Use assertive language and ask if there is anything you can do to alleviate the cause of the problem. If the behaviour persists, you may wish to consult your human resources

department to see if there are any formal procedures in place to deal with such a situation.

MAKING IT HAPPEN

Consider the impact on your own health and happiness

Rather than deal with the problem directly, many people are tempted to live with the difficulties of having a troublesome boss. Instead of addressing the problem, they brush it under the carpet by looking for ways of minimising the impact he or she has on their working lives. However, employing avoidance tactics or finding ways to offset the emotional damage can be time-consuming and stressful. Focusing on your own well-being may encourage you to tackle the issue rationally and try to reach an accommodation that will prevent you from jeopardising your health or feeling that you have to leave your job.

Understand your boss

When you come to look more closely at your relationship with your boss, the first thing to do is to realise how much of it is due to the structure of the organisation – for example, your boss necessarily has to give you tasks, some of which you may not enjoy – and how much is due to truly unreasonable behaviour.

Looking at the wider issues in the organisation may provide the key to the problem. 'Difficult boss syndrome' is rarely caused simply by a personality clash: more often than not, there are broader organisational factors that can go some way to explaining seemingly unreasonable behaviour.

However uncomfortable it may feel, try putting yourself in your boss's shoes. Recognise the objectives that define his or her role and think through the pressures he or she is under. Make a mental list of your boss's strengths, preferred working style, idiosyncrasies, values, and beliefs. Observe his or her behaviour and reactions, and watch where he or she chooses to focus attention. This will help you to deepen your understanding. Very often, when we feel disliked or when we dislike someone, we avoid building this understanding and instead look for ways of avoiding the issues.

Compare the way you both perceive your role

As part of the process of understanding your boss, compare the perceptions you both have of your role and the criteria used to judge your success. You may feel that you're performing well, but if you're putting your energy into tasks that your boss doesn't feel are relevant, you will be seen as performing poorly.

Take the initiative to explore your boss's expectations and agree on your objectives. This will clarify your role and give you a better idea of how to progress in the organisation.

Understand yourself

Having scrutinised your boss and developed a greater understanding of him or her, try doing the same exercise on yourself. Sometimes a lack of self-knowledge leads to us being surprised by our reactions and the feedback we get. Ask for input from your colleagues while you're doing this. Ask them what they observe when you interact with your boss, how you come across to them, and how you could manage your communication differently. Although their perceptions may not represent the absolute truth about you, it nonetheless reflects the image you create.

Think through some of the past encounters you've had with your boss and reflect upon them objectively, perhaps with a friend or colleague who knows you well. Maybe this situation happens over and over again, which suggests that you harbour a value or belief that is being repeatedly compromised. If you can understand what this is, you can learn to manage these situations more effectively. You may need to consider changing some of your behaviour. This often prompts a reciprocal behavioural change in your boss. If you don't change anything about the way you interact with your boss, the relationship will remain unaltered, so this is definitely worth a try.

For example, perhaps you value attention to detail, but your boss is a big-picture person. Every time you ask for more detailed information, you'll be drawing attention to one of your boss's vulnerabilities, and he or she is likely to become unco-operative or irritated by your request. Once you've observed your respective patterns, you can begin to work around them or accommodate them.

Remember that the relationship is mutual

In order to be effective, managers need a co-operative and productive team. But in order to be part of such a team, each member needs their manager to provide the resources and support they need to do their job properly. An unsupportive boss can be just as nightmarish as a vindictive one.

When managers neglect to give their employees the information and feedback they need, employees are forced to second-guess their boss's requirements. This inevitably leads to misunderstandings on both sides. The knock-on effects of this are an atmosphere of distrust and ill-will, and mutual recriminations – not to mention the negative impact on the organisation's productivity levels. Ask for the information and resources you require, or find other ways to get these, as this will put you in control of the situation and protect you from the need to improvise.

Nightmare situations can arise when employees' needs aren't met. Some people become angry and resentful of the manager's authority; some find ways of challenging decisions in order to assert their own power; and others develop agendas of their own that are neither helpful nor productive.

One-sided relationships are a recipe for revolution! It is rare in business to find relationships where there is absolutely *no* reciprocal power. Remember that if you're no longer willing to spend time managing your difficult boss, you still have the ultimate power: you can just walk away.

COMMON MISTAKES

You take your boss's behaviour personally

It is very tempting to take the behaviour of a difficult boss personally. However, it is very unlikely that *you* are the problem. It may be something you do, it may be the values you hold, or it may be that you remind your boss of someone he or she doesn't get on with. The only person who loses out if you take it personally is you.

You don't remain detached

Many difficult relationships deteriorate to the point where they are fraught with contempt and confrontation. This is never helpful in a work setting and only makes matters uncomfortable for everyone. If you find yourself being drawn into an angry exchange, try to remain emotionally detached and listen actively to what is being said to (or shouted at) you. It may provide you with clues about why the situation has developed and allow you to get straight to the point of concern. Ask for a private review afterwards to explore the incident. You may find that this brings to the surface issues that are relatively easy to deal with and that will prevent further outbursts from occurring.

You never confront the issue

Because facing up to difficult people is not an easy thing to do, many people avoid biting the bullet. However, this will only prolong a miserable situation. Acquiescence enables bullying to thrive and allows the aggressors to hold power. Break the cycle by taking responsibility for your share of the problem and examining what it is you're doing to provoke conflict between you and your boss. Doing nothing is not a viable option.

THE BEST SOURCES OF HELP
Book:
McIntyre, Marie G. *Secrets to Winning at Office Politics: How to Achieve Your Goals and Increase Your Influence at Work*. New York: St. Martin's Griffin, 2005.

Websites:
Bully Online: **www.bullyonline.org**
ImproveNow.com: **www.improvenow.com**
Monster.com: **http://midcareer.monster.com/ articles/careerdevelopment/stresseffects**
Unison: **www.unison.org.uk**

Coping with Discrimination

GETTING STARTED
Discrimination against individuals on the basis of their race, age, gender, cultural background, or physical/mental impairment is unlawful. Everyone has an equal right to employment with fair remuneration in an environment that is free from discrimination. There are few experiences more depressing than being treated unfairly because of who you are. Fortunately, there are established ways in which you can tackle any type of discrimination and bring the nightmare to an end.

FAQS

I believe that I have been discriminated against on the basis of my ethnic background. What should I do?

Firstly, don't wait too long; there are time limits for bringing a case under the Race Relations Act. Racial discrimination is not easy to prove, so you'll need to gather as much evidence as possible and create a good record of the incident(s) along with a list of any witnesses. Seek guidance from trusted friends and professional confidants at the earliest opportunity and explore the legal assistance that you may be eligible for. You can go to your union, the Citizens Advice Bureau, or the Equality and Human Rights Commission.

My boss has always been respectful before, but he recently made a sexual advance while we were at an official function and I felt really threatened. Am I able to take action under the Sex Discrimination Act?

If your boss has made even a single sexual advance on you, you may have grounds for a complaint. You don't have to experience persistent sexual harassment before you ask for help – if it's sufficiently serious, one incident can amount to sex discrimination. However, before you start down this road, think about taking your complaint to the human resources department or to a trusted superior to see if there are any internal policies that can support or protect you and help to resolve the situation.

I have discovered that my colleague receives a much better package of benefits than I do, and was recently awarded a bonus that I knew nothing about. Do I have grounds for a claim?

Yes, equal pay law embraces benefits, bonuses, pensions, holiday, and sick pay as well as salary. If you can prove that your job is comparable with that of your colleague, involving the same level of skills and knowledge, then you are likely to have a case. However, you must be able to demonstrate this before you can proceed to a tribunal with your claim.

MAKING IT HAPPEN

Discrimination is a huge subject, and there are many resources you can turn to if you feel that you've been discriminated against. However, the following will provide a useful starting point. More detailed information can be found using the various links at the end of this actionlist.

It may be that you're being discriminated against in more than one way. Take a look at each of the following steps in turn, checking if they apply to you.

Racial discrimination

If you feel you've been discriminated against because of your ethnic background, don't wait too long; there are time limits for bringing a case under the Race Relations Act. Gather as much evidence as possible and create a good record of the incident(s) along with a list of any witnesses. Racial discrimination isn't easy to prove, and the burden of proof will be on you. Also seek guidance from trusted friends and professional confidants at the earliest opportunity and explore the legal assistance that you may be eligible for. You can go to your union, the Citizens Advice Bureau, or the Equality and Human Rights Commission.

Sex discrimination

The Sex Discrimination Act 1975 makes it unlawful for employers to treat women or men less favourably in employment matters because of their sex or marital status.

If you were dismissed for poor performance while a poorly performing colleague of the opposite gender retained their job, you may have a claim for sex discrimination. This would also be the case if you were dismissed for being persistently late while a colleague of the opposite sex with the same timekeeping habits was not.

If you were selected for redundancy, you may have a claim if you can show that the selection criteria used affected one sex more than the other and that there was no rational justification for this.

Equal pay

The issue of pay within the area of sex discrimination is covered specifically by the Equal Pay Act 1970. The Equal Pay Act doesn't cover you for being treated differently from members of the same sex, only the opposite sex, however, because the majority of part-timers still tend to be women, there is also a clause relating to the rights of part-timers.

There are two ways of looking at equal pay. Sometimes a person is paid less than a colleague of the opposite sex for doing the same job. Other times, one individual is paid less than another of the opposite sex for doing work of equivalent value. Both these situations are discriminatory and may be unlawful. Equal pay rights apply to both sexes.

Equal pay legislation extends beyond just wages and salaries; it also covers bonuses, benefits, overtime, holiday pay, sick pay, performance-related pay, and occupational pensions.

There are several ways in which pay discrimination can take place. Here are some examples:

- A woman is appointed on a lower salary than her male counterparts.
- A woman on maternity leave is denied a bonus received by other staff.
- The jobs that women occupy are given different job titles and grades from those of male colleagues doing virtually the same work.
- Part-time staff have no entitlement to sick pay or holiday pay.
- All staff are placed on individual contracts and not allowed to discuss their pay rates.

Your rights to equal pay are set out in the Equal Pay Act 1970. You can take your claim for equal pay to an employment tribunal at any time while you're in the job, or within six months of leaving employment.

Sexual harassment

The Sex Discrimination Act makes it unlawful for employers to treat a woman less favourably than a man (or a man less favourably than a woman) by subjecting her or him to any emotional or physical harm. The Act also applies to individuals undergoing gender reassignment.

You can only make a claim of sexual harassment if the incident(s) took place during 'the course of employment' – that is at work or at a work-related function.

Sexual harassment is defined as unwelcome physical, verbal, or non-verbal conduct of a sexual nature. Cases are most likely to be brought as civil claims in an employment tribunal. Examples of sexual harassment at work include:

- requests or demands for sexual favours by either gender
- comments about your appearance which are derisory or demeaning
- remarks that are designed to cause offence
- intrusive questions or speculations about your sex life
- any behaviour related to gender that creates an intimidating, hostile, or humiliating working environment

Incidents involving touching or more extreme physical threats are criminal offences and should be reported to the police as well as your employer.

Disability discrimination

If you're disabled, or have had a disability, the Disability Discrimination Act (DDA) makes it unlawful for you to be discriminated against in the areas of:

- employment
- access to goods, facilities, and services
- the management, buying, or renting of land or property

The DDA was passed in 1995 to introduce new measures aimed at ending the discrimination which many disabled people face in these areas. It uses the term 'disability' to describe 'anyone with a physical or mental impairment which has a substantial and long-term adverse effect upon their ability to carry out normal day-to-day activities'. This includes:

- **physical impairment** – the weakening or adverse change of a part of the body caused through illness, by accident, or from birth
- **mental impairment** – learning disabilities and all recognised mental illnesses

Ageism

Under the terms of the Employment Equality Act (Age) Regulations 2006, people over the age of 50 must not be discriminated against in education or employment. The Regulations focus in particular on implementing age equality with regard to recruitment, how workers are treated at work, and any redundancy and retirement issues.

Victimisation

Your employer shouldn't discriminate against you because you've taken a case of discrimination to a tribunal. People who have helped you by giving evidence or providing information are also protected.

COMMON MISTAKES
You rush into legislation

Don't rush to make a claim, or threaten to do so, because you believe that you've been discriminated against at work. The process of taking action is lengthy and evidence needs to be produced to back up your claim. Even when this is available, the procedures are stressful and time consuming. It's always best to see if you can find another way around the problem. Start by broaching the subject with the 'perpetrator' or having a discussion with the human resources department.

You think that office parties don't count

Being 'off duty' or away from the work premises with your colleagues does not protect you from being accused of harassment. Under the Sex Discrimination Act, sex discrimination is outlawed in a wide variety of contexts that are related to your employment. Action can be taken if it can be shown that the (social) event at which the incident occurred was linked to your employment.

THE BEST SOURCES OF HELP
Websites:
Age Positive: **www.agepositive.gov.uk**
Equality and Human Rights Commission:
www.equalityhumanrights.com
Global Action on Ageing: **www.globalaging.org/ elderrights/world/uklabor.htm**

Turning Around a Poor Recruitment Decision

GETTING STARTED

There is no failsafe technique for ensuring that someone coming into your business will perform in the way that you expect.

There is no cast-iron way of guaranteeing that the person who wowed you at interview will be a huge success when they start to work for your business. Even if the successful candidate performed well in a battery of tests and came with glowing references from his or her former employer, but you're still not guarded against a poor recruitment decision. The new recruit may have values that do not resonate with those of your organisation, for example; he or she may not get on with their colleagues; or there may be personal problems that spill over into the workplace.

If you're faced with similar problems after hiring someone, don't panic but do act swiftly to remedy the situation.

FAQS

I believe that I have recruited the best person for a particular role, but other members of the team don't see it in this way. How should I tackle this?

You may have recruited someone with a different set of values or way of working from others in your team. If so, you will need to work on integrating the new person. This may mean bringing the team together for some relationship building, and setting expectations around how each will contribute to the team's role in the business. Don't leave this too long. An early intervention will save a lot of time, as relationships that have gone bad are difficult and time-consuming to turn round.

The business brought someone in at a senior level, who had to invest personally and financially in relocating for the job. Unfortunately, the recruitment decision has proved to be wrong. What should I do?

The circumstances surrounding the recruitment decision shouldn't change the nature of the response. It serves no one if you avoid or fudge the issue. Your company's contract with the new recruit should have a clause that spells out the kind of compensation available if they should leave the business. This should be interpreted liberally to minimise the grief and inconvenience the recruit will undoubtedly face. However, once you've decided it was a bad choice, you should bite the bullet and waste little time in giving the person notice.

My new employee has some worrying habits. He frequently smells of alcohol, and his time-keeping is poor. How should I approach this?

Alcohol abuse is dangerous, particularly if the employee has responsibility for machinery, or his or her role involves driving. Whether in the probationary period or not,

disciplinary action should be taken. You'll need to refer to your employee handbook for guidance on the appropriate action to take. It may be that a rehabilitation programme and joining Alcoholics Anonymous would be sufficient. But if your organisation has no such manual, a professional or trade association could be of assistance, or you could contact a government agency that deals with health and safety issues for advice. If all else fails, you probably have little recourse but to terminate the person's employment.

MAKING IT HAPPEN

Face up to the problem

Realising that you have made an incorrect recruitment decision is extremely uncomfortable. You may be embarrassed that you didn't notice something 'obvious' at the interview, and feel that you've wasted precious time and resources. Furthermore, you may feel frustrated and guilty about what lies ahead – the prolonged process of firing one person while beginning recruitment over again.

Once you've acknowledged the problem, there are several stages you should go through before removing the person from his or her post.

Ensure you've given the employee clear objectives

It's not unusual for someone to come into a new role and find that the job requirements are ambiguous. When you suspect that your recruitment decision has been poor, go back to the job description and make sure that everything is clear, and that the new employee understands the demands being placed upon him or her. If there is any aspect of the role that needs to be described in greater detail, make sure this happens, and keep a close coaching eye on how the person responds.

Ensure a satisfactory induction programme is in place

It's not necessarily easy for a newcomer to feel at home in an unfamiliar organisation. Induction programmes can go some way towards addressing teething troubles, but even if these schemes are in place, new employees may step on some sensitive organisational toes and create a poor first impression. This is difficult, because the newcomer may have valuable experience and fresh ideas, which could add value to 'the way things are done around here'. Managers have a delicate balance to strike between promoting innovative ideas while also being sensitive to the organisation's equilibrium.

Satisfy yourself that it isn't a matter of more training

It isn't unusual for there to be a skills or knowledge gap between someone's former experience and new job requirements. The recruitment decision may appear to have been poor when in fact there is merely a need for some additional training and development. This doesn't have to take the form of expensive external training programmes; it may be a question of giving the new employee the opportunity to shadow someone who is successful in the relevant area, and to have some coaching for a short while.

Check the level of support has been appropriate

People coming into new jobs with lots of background experience are often left to get on with it without a lot of supervision. This doesn't always provide the framework necessary for them to meet objectives expected of them. People need supervision, guidance, and support until they develop an understanding of how to meet the expectations of the role. At that point, the level of supervision can be reduced.

Meet the employee to discuss his or her perceptions

A new employee who is performing poorly might have picked up the manager's disappointment and be anxious about his or her future in the business. An early performance appraisal on a one-to-one basis can help. This gives both an opportunity to bring issues to the table. During this discussion, performance targets and time frames for compliance can be set. If the recruitment decision eventually turns out to have been a mistake, it's essential that this confidential meeting has taken place.

Coach them

Coaching is essential if the early signs in someone's employment are disappointing. Although coaching takes time, it's a good investment if the employee's performance turns around. Good coaching techniques encourage the employee's resourcefulness, and are much more helpful than merely telling him or her what to do.

Consider extending their probation period, and forewarn them of the consequences of failing to comply with expectations

From a practical standpoint, it's much easier to reverse a recruitment decision if the new employee is still within the probationary period. Once full employment has been confirmed, the legal requirements that have to be followed are far more convoluted. However, you must still demonstrate that you've given the new employee every opportunity to perform satisfactorily in his or her role.

Create a contingency plan for rapid succession into that job, should the person fail to improve

Most businesses cannot afford to have key roles vacant or in transition for long periods. You may therefore want to consider contingency plans to cover the job should it be vacated again. This may mean bringing in temporary support staff, seconding someone from another team, or allocating parts of the role to others who are able to meet the performance criteria.

If the poor recruitment decision results in the employee's departure from the role, consider other posts in the organisation for which they're better suited. If no such positions exist, you'll have to give them notice, and allow them time to seek other opportunities during this period. If the person is disruptive, you may prefer to compensate them for an early departure.

There is no value in prolonging a poor decision, for either party. It's always best to tackle the issue in a professional way and ensure the least damage – to the business and to morale.

COMMON MISTAKES

You don't explore the situation properly

Try to avoid rushing to the conclusion that a poor recruitment decision has been made before you've considered the context. Hasty decisions can result in a grievance being filed by the new employee, who may feel unfairly treated. It's important to go through the proper processes to explore all aspects of the situation fully.

Communication is poor

When someone isn't performing according to expectations, it often highlights a management issue rather than their inability to do the job. If your organisation's recruitment process doesn't give the new person every opportunity to show themselves in a good light, you may want to examine the process for possible improvements.

Very often, problems occur as a result of poor communication. It's important that expectations are clearly articulated, that processes and systems are properly explained, and that support is on hand to respond to any questions or concerns.

The new recruit isn't given a chance to improve

Disappointment in the new recruit can lead to premature removal. Although the situation shouldn't be left to fester for too long, it's important that the new recruit/employee is dealt with fairly and without ambiguity. They must understand the position they're in so that they can do their part to remedy the situation. This means giving early feedback, guidance, and advice, and setting regular meetings so that progress can be monitored. If the situation can be improved, it's best for everyone.

THE BEST SOURCES OF HELP

Book:

Becker, Brian, Mark Huselid, and Dave Ulrich. *The HR Scorecard: Linking People, Strategy, and Performance*. Boston, Massachusetts: Harvard Business School Press, 2001.

Websites:

BusinessTown.com: **www.businesstown.com/ hiring/hiring-advice.asp**

HRM Guide.co.uk: **www.hrmguide.co.uk/ hrm/chap10/Top**

Succeeding As a New Manager

GETTING STARTED

Congratulations, you've been appointed as a manager – either for the first time, or for the first time at this level. You're likely to be responsible for managing a team of up to 15 people, either in a company you already work for, or in a new organisation. This is obviously very exciting for you, though you may feel somewhat daunted at the prospect, especially if you were previously a member of the team you will now be managing.

However, provided you follow a few basic rules, there is no reason why such fears shouldn't be easily overcome, and your new role will give you excellent scope to stretch your wings and fulfil your potential. This actionlist is intended to give you these basic rules and help to smooth the path forward into this new phase of your working life.

FAQS

I'm afraid I might not be up to the job. How can I overcome this fear?

It's only natural to have some feelings of this kind; most people do when faced with a new challenge. However it's important to get such worries under control, as a crisis of confidence may affect your chance of success. Try some positive self-talk, reminding yourself of your skills and competence to do the job – after all, the company has recognised them, otherwise you wouldn't have been offered the job! It's also important to look after your health: make sure you get plenty of sleep and exercise, so you feel fit and ready to take on anything.

Is it likely that my new job will affect my home life?

Almost certainly, yes. Moving into any new job can be stressful, and even more so when new or extra levels of responsibility are involved. The trick is to make sure you're prepared for it, and face the fact that your life may be more demanding than ever before. Talk this over with your family and friends at an early stage; it will be a huge help if they are ready to lend their support while you get to grips with your new role, and also to keep 'home' distractions to a minimum to let you focus.

Will I need to change my persona at work?

No, not essentially, but you may need to adjust your attitude and the way you think about your job. A lot of management is about standing back from the detail and seeing the 'big picture' of what is happening, so that you can make strategic decisions about how to act. Rather than getting involved in the nitty-gritty of individual tasks (as you may have done as a team member), try to cultivate an objective overview. If you can learn to see the wood for the trees, this will naturally lead to you behaving in a way that suits the circumstances.

MAKING IT HAPPEN

Research and plan your new job

First things first: if you're moving to a new employer, find out everything possible about the company you'll be working for, the department or section you'll be in, the job itself, and anything else you can think of. Don't pre-judge what you're going to find, and don't be bound by what you've done before, or by how any of your previous employers operated. It's also a good idea to find out a bit about your predecessor: why he or she left, what style they preferred, how people responded to that, what may need to be changed, and so on. (If you're staying in the same company, you may know this already, but it's worth doing some extra research.)

From all this information, try to form at least a tentative plan in advance – it's much harder to do this once you're in the position. What do you want to achieve? How might you need to develop yourself to match the new demands? Reflect as honestly as you can on your strengths and weaknesses: how might you use your qualities and experience to the greatest advantage, and compensate for your limitations?

Engage with your team

Once you start your new job, make this your first priority. What is the purpose of your department, team, or unit? What work is being done, what's the current state of play, what customer expectations need to be met? Get all your team members together as soon as possible to introduce yourself, and then arrange meetings with each of them individually. While keeping these meetings as friendly and informal as you can, allow a generous amount of time and plan some kind of framework for the discussion. Listen carefully to what people have to say, and get information about them as individuals. Most importantly, ask each person the question: what should I do or not do to help you to perform your job effectively?

Plan some 'quick wins'

Now is the time to plan a few targets that you can hit quickly and easily, which will help you to feel more at home and on top of things. Achieving these also eases the pressure you feel to perform and create a positive first impression, and begins the relationship-building process. Quick wins might include things like familiarising yourself with systems or ways of working if you're new to the company (for example, the internal e-mail system); setting up an early discussion with your line manager, arranging introductory meetings with suppliers or customers (external and internal), or even taking your team to the pub one lunchtime.

Clarify what expectations others have of you

You may be lucky enough to have been given a detailed job description, but the chances are there are still large gaps in your understanding about the task and priorities, what is or isn't acceptable in the new environment, and on what criteria you will be judged by your boss, peers, customers, and others. Don't be afraid to ask a lot of questions to clarify these issues, and then be very honest with yourself. Can you meet these standards? If not, what might you need to do? Who could help, and what might the price be?

Beware of 'new broom' syndrome

While you will evidently be keen to get going and to make your mark, it is important that you tread delicately – at least to start with. Don't assume that your new team will welcome your style or your ideas with open arms, even if your predecessor was unpopular. They need to feel they can trust you and that you respect what they've been doing previously, before you can count on their support and co-operation. Above all, don't depart too dramatically and quickly from established practice.

Show your commitment to individual development

From your initial meetings with your team, you will know what their individual aspirations and hopes are for their jobs going forward. Follow up by setting a code of management practice that you tell all team members about, and then follow it rigorously. This code might include commitments to assess training needs, to hold regular team meetings and one-to-one sessions, to set specific goals, and to evaluate performance against these goals.

Support this code by the way you yourself behave towards team members. Make a point of appreciating extra time and effort that people put in, listen properly to what they say, and be generous in your praise of their good qualities or achievements. The point is, by demonstrating to your team that you as their manager are on their side and will do everything in your power to support them, you will gain their trust and acceptance, and the performance of the whole team will be greatly enhanced.

Lead by example

An effective manager needs to be a role model, so it almost goes without saying that you must set an example for how you want your team members to behave. Lead by involving people in establishing group objectives, setting standards, and achieving deadlines, and demonstrate your own strong personal commitment to achieving the team's goals. Set an example too by maintaining high standards in your appearance and general behaviour, and by establishing warm, friendly relationships.

Take stock regularly

At the end of your first week, identify issues that need attention and make a plan for the following week. Get into the habit each week of setting aside time for review and planning. Don't let your mistakes lead to self-doubt: everyone makes them, and good managers learn from them, while bad ones repeat them. The pattern of behaviour you set in your first three months will be extremely hard to change later.

COMMON MISTAKES

You make promises that may be difficult or impossible to keep

It is tempting, during the phase of settling in and relationship-building, to make all kinds of promises to your team, boss, or customers in the interests of creating a good impression. However, you will be judged on whether or not those promises are fulfilled, so make sure you exercise caution in what you undertake to deliver. Under-promising and over-delivering are infinitely preferable to the other way round.

You form alliances based on first impressions

Common myth has it that first impressions usually turn out to be accurate, but this is often not true. Your understanding of people and circumstances may change substantially as you learn more about them, and it's important that you don't cement yourself into new relationships that later turn out to be inappropriate or which might alienate other, potentially more useful, allies.

You maintain too close a friendship with former team mates

Although it's important to create cordial relationships with your team members, it's also important to distance yourself a little from those who report to you, so that you can remain objective and unbiased in your actions. This can be difficult when you have previously been a member of the team yourself, but if you don't, you run the danger of being seen as a manager who has 'favourites' and of allowing your personal feelings to affect your judgment. This will not be good for the morale of the team, and you will lose much of your authority. Explain your position to particular friends, be seen to maintain a professional relationship at work, and keep purely social interaction for outside the office.

You allow yourself to be trapped into accepting the status quo

No matter what anyone says about 'the way things are done round here', the old ways are not always the best. Reserve your right to postpone judgment until you are thoroughly familiar with your team and your job and then, if things need changing, change them, remembering, of course, to be sensitive in the way you do it.

THE BEST SOURCES OF HELP
Websites:
HR Guide: **www.hr-guide.com**
HR Village: **www.hrvillage.com**

Motivating Others During Difficult Times

GETTING STARTED

'Difficult times' can take many forms: currently, the global financial crisis is having a wide range of negative effects, but it could be that problems are coming from within your organisation. If a long-standing member of staff has moved on, for example, people who have worked closely with him or her may themselves feel unsettled and out of sorts.

Whatever the reason, if you're steering the ship through choppy waters, it can be a real struggle to keep morale and productivity high. However, as most managers will find themselves in this position at some point in their career, it is worth knowing the best way of getting yourself and your team through, and out the other side.

FAQS

How can I keep my team motivated, even though it's clear to everyone that the outlook is bleak? I try to stay cheerful and optimistic but it's not working.

Maybe you're overdoing it. If your business really is in dire straits, your team can't fail but be aware of the situation and your enthusiasm could end up being construed as desperation. Be candid: call a meeting and explain the bigger situation, then describe your team's importance and explain why you think you should all continue to work productively.

Wages have been frozen and training budgets are non-existent. How can I motivate my team in spite of having no money?

Remember that, although it is a major contributing factor, money isn't the be-all and end-all of a fulfilling job. Your team colleagues need to feel that they are contributing to something valuable, so make an effort to build a sense of community, and to convey the importance of your work to the organisation as a whole.

As a result of recent redundancies, several people will have to take on extra work, which they're not happy about. How can I mollify them?

First of all you need to tackle the inevitable drop in morale that comes after restructuring. People may be relieved to have survived the 'chop' on this occasion, but they've still have a nasty shock, and will (understandably) feel unsure about their future. Most likely there is a very good reason why they *weren't* let go, so you don't want to lose them. Give them the opportunity to tell you about their feelings and fears, in a team meeting or one-on-one – whichever they'd prefer. Be flexible about reallocation of duties and take on board your staff's comments: find out what they'd like to do. One person may be eager to take on a job that another colleague wouldn't want to touch with a

bargepole, and it's only by talking to your team that you can help them to feel empowered and happier about their situation.

MAKING IT HAPPEN

Face the challenge head-on

Although you may want to shield staff from bad news, or feel uncomfortable about broaching the issue with them, it's always a good idea to act early. Tell your team what the state of play is, what you hope may be the outcome, what the likely outcomes are (if they differ from what you'd like to see happen), and how you plan to tackle the crisis. Make sure they understand that your door is open and that you're happy to take their questions there and then, or in private.

Show that you appreciate good work

Your staff aren't telepathic: if they are doing a great job, thank them. Tell them how much you appreciate the effort they're putting in. Even when times are good, while money is one of the main drivers for employees, it's not the only one and we all like to feel valued. When you run a small business, in particular, it is incredibly easy to get caught up in the time-consuming paperwork and the small details of the day-to-day running of the business, but your staff are one of your greatest assets. Don't neglect them, especially if times are tough.

Offer some type of incentive

While you may not have a lot of spare cash to spend if the business is going through a lean time, you can offer other types of incentives to reward your staff for their loyalty. For example, if you work in the manufacturing industry, why not offer anyone who beats their monthly production target by X per cent an extra day's leave? If it's the case that the business is relatively sound but morale is low, giving people time to reach their own personal goals can be very welcome. One of the world's leading pharmaceutical companies allows its staff one day a week to pursue their own research agenda. Could you incorporate that idea (even if not in that form *per se*) into your business?

Realise that some people won't be able to stay the course

In any workplace, bonds are forged that can make staff seem like a family at times: that is very often the case in small businesses, in particular. Be prepared for some of your staff leaving if times become very tough, and don't take it personally: if they have a family or other responsibilities to manage, it may be financially impossible for them to hang on for better times to come if they find another, more stable working environment. Take it on the chin and move on.

Make sure you are meeting basic needs

If the balance sheet looks relatively healthy but morale is low, you need to focus on building long-term job satisfaction for your team rather than get the business through a sticky patch. This means looking at aspects of work that you may take for granted, or not even notice.

The management guru Abraham Maslow identified what he called a 'hierarchy of needs', which were originally offered as general explanations of human behaviour but which are now viewed as key parts of workplace motivation theories. Translated into an everyday workplace setting, make sure you are thinking about the following:

- Can you improve on the fundamentals currently in place, such as salary, canteen, working conditions?
- Is there a bonus, health care, or pension scheme that will demonstrate organisational support and loyalty towards employees?
- Do you provide the resources people need to do their jobs? Do they have the right equipment, budgets, training, and (if appropriate) coaching?
- Are your staff's roles well defined within the organisational hierarchy? Do people know what they are supposed to do and what their level of authority is?
- Are the two-way channels of communication effective? Do people have a place to go to voice their worries and concerns, either individually or collectively?
- Are there ways in which people can be creative/innovative and make a personal contribution to organisational success?
- Are there ways in which you can recognise people's achievements visibly? Does everyone have an area of expertise that they are known and appreciated for?
- Is there a compelling vision or purpose for your organisation's existence?

If all these factors are in place, you'll have a much better chance of making it through a tough time with your team relatively intact, because their basic needs will have been satisfied and they will be ready to put their energy into combating new challenges. In fact, you may find that banding together to get through a challenge will foster improved levels of commitment, ingenuity, and team spirit. If you can paint a picture of the importance that each person plays in getting over the difficulty, whatever it is, and if you can provide the appropriate level of care, concern and support, your business stands a great chance of emerging from a period of turbulence stronger than it was before.

COMMON MISTAKES

You don't lead by example

Feeling gloomy about the future is one thing, but if you see your team leader moping about and looking hopeless, any faith you have left in the future will rapidly vanish. If you are responsible for managing others, to get through a difficult time you'll need to keep positive and have faith in everyone's ability to work together effectively. Put yourself in your team's shoes, and think about what would motivate you if you were in their circumstances. Be confident, competent, and show concern.

You pretend things aren't that bad

While attempting to keep your spirits up during a rough time is something to aim for, going too far and just pretending that the tough time isn't happening at all won't work. Your staff aren't stupid, and they'll be able to tell that something is awry. Be open about the challenges the business is facing, but show that you are committed to tackling these issues.

You become overly controlling

Being a strong leader isn't synonymous with being authoritative and over-demanding. Although you may think that you are appearing to others as being completely in control, you'll probably find that people are feeling cowed by your approach, rather than inspired. Avoid posturing and focus on good, open communication so that you can keep people up to speed with events and lend them an empathetic ear as and when.

THE BEST SOURCES OF HELP

Power Link Dynamics – Self-help tips for professionals: **www.pldynamics.com/archived-self-help-tips-2.php**
Motivation ABC: **www.motivation-abc.com**
Motivation: **http://telecollege.dcccd.edu/mgmt1374/book_contents/4directing/motivatg/motivate.htm**

Creating an Effective Crisis Management Strategy

GETTING STARTED

When companies experience a major problem that threatens their business, they need to react quickly and effectively to protect their reputations. Providing clear information to customers and the media can build support and help the company to recover quickly. An important part of the process is having a crisis management strategy in place before problems occur.

FAQS

Can crises really be managed?

Yes. Remember that you'll be fighting on two fronts to some extent: clearly you need to be tackling the problem that has cropped up so that it is resolved as quickly as possible; you also need to protect your brand and reputation.

While in some cases it is possible to see a problem coming, in many cases difficult situations tend to 'erupt' without any warning. Having a coherent strategy in place to deal with such events can make the difference between your business weathering the storm and it being dealt a knockout blow. Today's 24-hour cycle means that good *and* bad news travels fast, so you need to be prepared and ready to go the minute a crisis hits.

How should we handle media enquiries in difficult times?

So that your organisation presents its side of the issue professionally and calmly, nominate one person (probably someone from your publicity department) to deal with the media. That person should be thoroughly versed in your management plan and well briefed on the crisis being dealt with. Channelling all enquiries via this person will give the media a welcome point of contact and also make sure that a consistent point of view is offered.

MAKING IT HAPPEN

Nip potential crises in the bud

Halting a crisis before it takes hold is the best way of dealing with it. That is, of course easier said than done. Problems like poor financial performance, strikes, product recalls, and distribution problems usually show up on the corporate radar some time before the storm hits, but crises such as extreme weather or acts of God can be nigh on impossible to predict.

The process of planning how to manage a crisis will help you to identify potential risks and – hopefully – make changes that may actually prevent a crisis. Planning for crisis management has three preliminary objectives:

1. identifying problems that may cause a crisis in the first place

2. assessing the potential negative effects on the company or the brand

3. taking positive actions that reduce the risk

DRAW UP A PLAN IN ADVANCE

The key to successfully protecting, and even enhancing, your company's reputation is to have a plan in place and to train your staff for a crisis situation in advance.

Your plan should outline your approach to crisis management and should describe the nature of the brand and the corporate reputation that you want to protect. Thinking through some potential problem situations is a good way to get the ball rolling. For example, what would you do if you found that your organisation was in breach of environmental legislation? How would you deal with the press fall-out surrounding a profits warning? How would you react if fire or flood meant that you couldn't make the deadline on the biggest contract of the year?

The plan should include:

- **assessment of potential risks**
- **the members of the crisis response team**
- **responsibilities of the crisis response team**
- **step-by-step action plan and checklist**
- **crisis communications plan**
- **list of key media**
- **plans for crisis training**
- **media training**
- **development of background material for media information**
- **holding statements for a variety of risk scenarios**

What you're aiming for here is an action-oriented framework that can be adapted to most crisis situations. Don't try to work out an overly prescriptive document that covers every single problem you can think of: it's unrealistic. Also make sure that you take the advice of key people throughout the business as you build the plan: while the senior management team will have a comprehensive overview of how the business functions, they may need help with details and information on how work progresses on a day-to-day basis. Tap into the knowledge of all relevant staff so that your plan doesn't fall at the first hurdle.

Recruit members of the crisis response team

After the hard work involved in creating your crisis management strategy, it's time to identify the people within the business who would be called into action when an emergency arises. First, appoint a team leader, probably a director or senior manager (preferably with some prior experience of this role) who has the necessary clout to get things done. Remember that the team leader will probably have to concentrate on the problem situation when it arises rather than his or her day job, so alert any relevant managers that they will have to step into the breach until the emergency has passed.

The team leader will then need to bring on board representatives from key operational and policy areas of the business and explain to them what their role would be should a crisis hit. A cross-functional team will help you get the most from all the knowledge inside the business. For example, a PR manager will be able to deal confidently with the media; a finance director will be able to monitor budgets and commercial implications; production managers will be able to advise on operational issues.

If your business is relatively small or you don't have functional managers responsible for each of those areas, you may need to identify people with relevant skills or brief an agency to provide standby support.

Your team should be able to meet the information needs of different groups of stakeholders, such as consumers, regulators, the media, employees and shareholders who would each view a crisis from different perspectives.

Prepare an action plan
The action plan should outline clearly what each member of the response team (see below) should do once the crisis happens. Make sure it identifies:
- the point at which the plan will be activated
- who will be alerted when the plan is activated
- how the team will communicate with their main contacts (gathering and then circulating information is crucial, so make sure that the team is equipped with up-to-date contact details for their contacts)

As mentioned above, make sure there is a spokesperson in place who is ready to deal with all questions. In an ideal scenario, that person should have had media training and also be senior enough to make sure that their statements carry some weight. Although you could outsource this role to a PR agency, the action plan should identify the spokesperson who will deal with media and other enquiries. Ideally the spokesperson will have media training, but they should also have the level of responsibility and seniority to make statements that are credible. Although it may seem easier to give responsibility for this front-line role to a public relations consultancy, it may be more appropriate for the company to handle its own media response as this demonstrates commitment to resolving the crisis.

Identify the 'target audience'
Your crisis communication plan should be similar to any other communication plan – who do you want to reach, how will you reach them and what are the key messages. By looking at a range of crisis scenarios in advance, you can prepare a communications plan that will enable you to keep the most important parties informed on progress in dealing with the crisis. Your communications plan should cover contact with:
- customers
- suppliers
- employees
- business partners
- the media
- shareholders

Prepare communications materials in advance
If a crisis happens, you need to be able to respond immediately. The media does not care about the corporate interests of your organisation – they need to get a story in time for their deadline. So it's important to have basic media information ready for release. Although it would be impossible to predict the detailed content, you can prepare background material that fills in the gaps in the crisis story. You can also prepare a 'skeleton press release' that gives you a framework for quickly producing a full release when you need it.

Be prepared for media interest
Crisis management dictates that when a crisis occurs, you will have two priorities:
1. bringing the crisis under control
2. dealing with the intense media and public scrutiny

To keep your organisation's reputation intact, you must be prepared to communicate effectively and respond immediately. When a crisis happens, it's likely that media interest will break as well, so you must be aware of journalists' needs for information and deadlines. Make sure you have nominated someone to act as a spokesperson so that there is two-way communication between journalists and the company

Respond effectively
Your initial press release should state that you have incomplete knowledge of the crisis details, but should describe your general approach to the crisis and promise to update the media when there is new information. Where possible you should explain why the crisis has happened, but without speculating.

As soon as you are in a position to do so, you should state what you are doing to resolve the situation. If possible, you may also be able to describe what you are doing to prevent any similar event from recurring. If necessary, you should explain what you are doing to compensate any parties affected by the crisis. For example, in the event of a product recall, will you be offering customers special deals on future purchases?

Maintain a good reputation
Your company will survive a crisis better if it has established a good reputation – something which is built up over a period of time. When a crisis occurs, it is too late to start building relationships and credibility. Although a good reputation takes time to build, you can either strengthen or destroy goodwill and reputation by the way you manage the crisis. Make sure you have a sound response plan in place and stick to it.

Plan for post-crisis rebuilding
When planning, you should also look ahead to the situation after a crisis. Your medium- and long-term planning should assess the possible damage that might be incurred through a crisis. You should identify how to prevent similar crisis situations while looking to maximise recovery and

minimise the damage. At the same time, you should consider the type of communications programme that would help to restore confidence in your company and its products.

COMMON MISTAKES
You fail to plan in advance
Industry statistics indicate that a high percentage of companies who do not have a response plan in place fail to recover from a crisis. It is essential that you are prepared in advance.

You try to win goodwill when it's too late
A crisis highlights the importance of good relations with the media, your customers, and your shareholders.

If you have already built a good reputation, you are more likely to get a sympathetic response and fair press coverage.

THE BEST SOURCES OF HELP
Book:
Regester, Michael and Larkin, Judy. *Risk Issues and Crisis Management: A Casebook of Best Practice.* 4th ed. London: Kogan Page, 2008.

Website:
Crisis Management:
www.crisismanagement.com

Using Marketing to Increase Competitiveness

GETTING STARTED
A truly effective marketing programme is one that will help you to deliver a product or service which is both profitable *and* competitive. In order to do this, you need to understand what differentiates your business from your competitors' businesses, to know your strengths, to build on your strengths, and to make the most of them through marketing. You'll need to research your market and your customer, and make changes based on the results. This may involve improving your product offering, providing better customer service, or marketing your services more effectively – or a mix of all three. In order to remain competitive, however, you will also need to keep control of your costs.

FAQS
Does 'profitability' require a long-term view?
Of course! The key term here is *customer lifetime value.* You need to put together a picture of your customer base, and to establish which of those customers have the highest lifetime value. You then need to look at ways of maximising that value. In order to retain the customers and lock in the potential for profits, you should focus on developing the products or services which those customers value most.

MAKING IT HAPPEN
Get to know your competitors
Knowledge is strength. In order to compete successfully, you need to know what the alternatives are for your customers.

For each of your competitors, ask yourself the following questions:
- Is this a direct competitor?
- Is this a major competitor?

- What are their main strengths?
- How do our products compare?
- How do our prices compare?
- How does our customer service compare?
- What are customers' attitudes towards this competitor?
- How do these attitudes compare with attitudes towards *our* company?

Remember that, most likely, your competitors will be going through the same processes as you, and will be updating their approach based on the data *they* collect. New competitors may also appear. You must therefore review this information regularly, ensuring that it is always up to date. You should also make the information available to key staff, so that anyone who needs it has access to this crucial knowledge.

Think about customer lifetime value
To remain competitive, you must avoid wasting resources on unprofitable customers. Although customer retention is crucial, you need to recognise that not all customers are profitable. Your current set-up may mean that transactions with certain customers are less profitable than others. It may be that some are given larger discounts or free added extras, while others cost your business in man-hours. Where such relationships have grown up over a long time, it may be that you take them for granted, and have stopped assessing whether they are actually worth keeping.

Customer retention is not just about keeping customers; it's about maintaining the *value* of your customer base. This may involve losing certain customers – but should also help you to focus on gaining new, more valuable customers.

Know your (product) strengths
Once you have identified your most valuable customers, you need to ensure that you retain them by offering

them the products or services that they want – and that you increase their value by encouraging them to buy more from you. You could get them to upgrade (*up-selling*), or you could get them to buy more (*cross-selling*). However, you will need to offer a large enough range of products or services before you can achieve either of these aims.

Extend or enhance your product range

Developing new products isn't the only option; you can also improve your existing product range. Review your products regularly, using your customer- and market-research findings to ensure that you remain focused on your customers' needs.

You could:

- add features and benefits to existing products or services
- add more expensive or cheaper versions
- increase your range (either by developing new products yourself or by buying products in from third parties)
- introduce niche products
- introduce own-brand products
- introduce products in response to competitors' products

Involve your customers

As well as helping you to develop your product development strategy, getting your customers involved will cement your relationship. Ask for opinions on your current products, and for any ideas they may have for new products or services.

You may want to ask:

- How can we improve the current product?
- What problems need to be overcome?
- What new features could we add?
- Would you make more use of a product that includes these features?
- What do you think of our new product ideas?
- What products are missing from our range?

Think about pricing

Pricing directly impacts both your profitability and your competitiveness. To help you to develop a competitive pricing policy, ask yourself the following questions:

- How do our prices compare with those of similar products elsewhere?
- What benefits do customers get from using our products or services?
- How important is price in our customers' buying decisions? (Think about pricing in relation to factors such as speed of delivery, convenience, customer service, and reliability.)
- What value do our customers place on the benefits our products provide (think about the *whole package*)?
- How do our benefits compare with those of our competitors? How do they add value to their products?
- Could we charge a premium if we're first to market, or the exclusive supplier?
- How valuable is our brand?

When making pricing decisions, remember that how your brand or product is *perceived* is also an important factor. In many cases, higher-priced products are perceived as being of higher value – as premium products. This will attract certain customers – but will deter others. It is up to you to decide which of these groups represents the highest lifetime value for your company.

Build your reputation

There are many ways to build your reputation – and one of the least-effective ways is through advertising (advertising is about *presence* and *brand*). Customers are essentially conservative, so you will need to work hard to build your credibility, especially if your company is small, a recent start-up, or moving into a new area. You need to gain the trust of your customers through a *relationship marketing* programme. You will do this by providing consistently good service; but another way of building your reputation with limited resources is by becoming an industry thought leader. Speaking appearances at industry events, articles in respected journals, well-produced customer newsletters, and a good-quality website will all help to position you as a thought leader, creating a favourable attitude towards your company and its products through a recognition that it understands its business, the market, and the needs of its customers.

Reward customer loyalty

Rewarding customer loyalty will strengthen relationships even further. There are several ways of doing this:

- discounts or incentives for repeat/large/frequent purchases
- incentives for buying particular products
- rewards for recommending you to other potential customers

Programmes that reward regular purchases have several benefits: they help to shut out competitors; they provide regular revenue; and they help you to build an accurate picture of your most-valued customers and their requirements. This in turn will help you to tailor your product range and marketing programmes so they appeal even more to these customers. Having a database with details of individual customers and their buying habits will help you to target specific groups of customers with relevant offers, thus increasing their value – and your competitiveness.

Focus on account management

As we have seen, competitiveness requires a long-term approach. In order to build stronger, lasting relationships with your customers, you will need to encourage a change in attitude among your sales staff: a shift from *sales* to *account management*. Rather than focusing on making the sale *now*, for short-term profit, sales staff should be encouraged to get to know customers, and to manage the relationship, thus increasing repeat orders and minimising the time spent following leads which result in single sales.

There are a number of requirements involved in this shift from short-term sales to long-term relationship management:

- focusing on profitability as well as turnover
- moving to a long-term view
- developing an understanding of each customer's business
- building relationships at different levels in the customer's organisation (i.e. not just with purchasing staff)
- understanding and influencing the customer's decision-making process
- recognising the value of customer service

A further outcome of this shift in attitude is that your sales staff will feel more empowered, which should improve their morale.

Keep costs down

The Internet means that businesses now have many options for reducing costs by moving certain activities online. It is important to remember, however, that anything published on the Web must be produced to the same high standard as traditional printed material. It must also be kept up to date.

While **customer service** is crucial in a business's competitiveness, high costs can detract significantly from profitability. Businesses can now offer customers self-service facilities via the Web. The benefits for the customer include convenience (the service is available 24/7) and choice; while the benefits for businesses include reduced customer support costs and flexibility (key staff are freed up to deal with more complicated issues).

Web-based self-service facilities can be offered for a variety of processes:

- delivery of information
- direct sales
- sales administration
- payments
- customer support
- technical support
- direct marketing
- advertising

E-mail and Web **marketing** are extremely flexible, targetable, and cost-effective. E-mails, for example, can be used to keep in touch with a large customer base, or to build a one-to-one relationship with your most profitable customers.

COMMON MISTAKES
You ignore competitor activity

You must always keep in touch with what your competitors are doing, and be willing to adjust your plans or take action if necessary. You must keep an eye out for threats to any of your accounts. Also, before spending money on a marketing campaign or product launch, make sure that none of your competitors is doing anything that might detract from its impact.

THE BEST SOURCES OF HELP
Book:
Hooley, Graham J., Saunders, John A., Piercy, Nigel. *Marketing Strategy and Competitive Positioning.* Harlow: FT Prentice Hall, 2007.

Website:
1000 Ventures: **www.1000ventures.com**

Planning an Advertising Campaign

GETTING STARTED
Any communications campaign needs to have clear, measurable objectives, whether it is designed to communicate product benefits or to support an event. In order to achieve these objectives, it must also be planned carefully. There are eight main stages to consider, from defining the target market to setting a budget.

FAQS
Do I need an advertising campaign?
Often the term 'advertising campaign' is used when the more holistic phrase 'communications campaign' would be more appropriate. Advertising strictly only refers to paid-for space or time in media such as newspapers or radio. On the other hand, direct mail, sales promotions, exhibitions, or any of a range of communication tools can be used in a campaign to support your marketing.

To decide if you need a communications campaign, you should be fairly sure that the problem you want to address can be solved best by communications. For example, finding new customers or prospective customers is often best accomplished by advertising or direct mail, but converting enquirers into customers may be better dealt with by you or your sales team (if you have one) in person.

Who is responsible for campaign planning – the client or the advertising agency?
Both parties contribute. The client sets the overall marketing objectives and the specific communications campaign objectives. The agency develops an advertising strategy based on those, but may seek to modify the campaign objectives. Timings will be determined by the client's product and marketing plans, together with practical considerations such as publication dates and lead times.

Why is it necessary to plan a campaign in so much detail?
To be effective, advertising and communications must meet specific measurable objectives. The objectives affect choice of media, creative strategy, overall budget, and lead times. Overlooking any of those details could weaken the effectiveness of the campaign.

MAKING IT HAPPEN
Set campaign objectives
It is important to set clear objectives for an advertising campaign and identifying a specific task for a specific campaign is essential. This might be:
- raising awareness of a company, product, or service within a clearly identified target market
- communicating the benefits of a product or service
- generating leads for the salesforce or retail network

To ensure you design a cost-effective campaign that delivers results, advertising objectives should be translated into precise, measurable targets.

Identify key planning activities
There are eight main stages in planning an advertising campaign:

1. Define the target market
Who is your campaign aimed at? An understanding of your audience will influence the media you select and the creative treatment of your advertisement. To define your target market, you should ask questions like these:
- Who buys your type of product?
- Who influences the purchasing decision?
- In business buying, who are the important decision-makers?
- Do you need to communicate with the actual buyers or those who influence the purchasing decision?
- How many potential buyers are there?
- How many users are currently buying your product and what is your share of the market?
- Which prospects do you want to reach with the campaign and where are they located?
- What are the characteristics of these people (for example, age, sex, income, job title), and what are their most important considerations in choosing a brand or a supplier?
- What does research tell you about their attitudes towards your company and your products?
- How do they currently receive information about your products?
- What is the role of advertising in reaching the target audience?

2. Select media
There are four important factors to consider in selecting campaign media:
- how closely the audience profile of the medium matches your target audience
- the comparative costs of reaching the target audience through different media

- whether the frequency of the medium matches the timing of your campaign
- the creative opportunities of the medium for the communication of your message

3. Plan campaign timing
When should your campaign run? You have to consider a number of factors first in relation to the purchasing pattern of your products:
- When are your customers making their buying decisions?
- Do you know when your customers hold product/purchasing review meetings?
- If you are launching a new product, when will the product be available?
- Does your advertising campaign have to tie in with the timing of any other marketing activity, for example, an exhibition, direct marketing campaign, or salesforce call?
- How quickly will you be able to follow up the campaign?

You also have to take into account production and media lead times:
- What is the next available publication or broadcasting date?
- When does the media owner require your advertisement?
- How long will it take to produce the advertisement?

4. Decide campaign frequency
Campaigns raise levels of awareness with each appearance. They also move individual respondents further along the decision-making process and maintain contact during an extended process. Campaigns reinforce the impact of the message by repetition and provide an opportunity to communicate multiple or complex messages about the company or the product range.

Frequency is determined by:
- frequency of publication, that is, how often the publication appears
- frequency of broadcast: radio or television commercials can be broadcast many times during the same day
- your budget, although a number of appearances in the same medium will earn a discount
- the behaviour of consumers or buyers: if a buying decision is made only annually, then timing may be more crucial than frequency

5. Plan creative treatment
To achieve good results, you must develop a comprehensive creative brief. The main elements are:
- campaign objectives
- description of the target audience
- the main concerns of the target audience: why they buy, what they consider, how they view different products and suppliers
- the main benefits of the product or service: why the product is different from competitive offerings, what is new, why the benefits are important
- the core message or proposition – what the prospect is being offered: the opportunity to sample or buy, further information, a sales visit, an incentive, or a discount
- the planned response: should the prospect contact the

company, send off an order, wait for a phone call, or simply absorb the information?
- the media – size and mechanical details
- the supporting activities – telemarketing, advertising, sales follow-up, tie-in promotions

6. Develop a response mechanism

Action is a vital ingredient of any advertising campaign and it is essential that you make it easy for your prospects to respond. First, decide which action they are to take:
- to place an order
- to arrange a sales meeting
- to request further information
- to visit your website
- to visit a retail outlet
- to try the product

Review the cost, convenience, and practicality of response options, including telephone, post, fax, e-mail, and website.

7. Set a budget

A campaign budget will include direct, indirect, and variable costs. Direct costs include the production costs of advertisements, including design, writing and production, and media costs. Indirect costs include the cost of setting up response handling, either by internal resources or an external supplier, and the management costs of planning and controlling the campaign. Variable costs include the cost of handling the campaign response, for example, Freephone costs and telephone resources, or costs of Freepost services; the cost of meeting the response – supplying and distributing the material that is requested; and the cost of servicing the response – sales or telemarketing costs in dealing with the potential volume of new business.

8. Set schedules

To set a campaign schedule, work back from the launch date and work out how long each individual activity will take.

COMMON MISTAKES

Poor targeting

Without a clear picture of your target, market advertising can be wasteful. You should always aim for the best match between the audience and your ideal customers – subject, of course, to your budget.

Failing to integrate advertising plans with other marketing activities

Advertising must be integrated with other related marketing tasks. Poor salesforce performance, for example, could waste the contribution of a successful advertising campaign that provided a large number of sales leads.

Trying to achieve advertising objectives with inadequate resources

If companies try to achieve targets without committing the right budget, it will mean either that advertisements do not appear frequently enough to have impact, or that production quality is sacrificed.

THE BEST SOURCES OF HELP

Book:
Steel, Jon. *Truth, Lies, and Advertising: The Art of Account Planning*. Chichester: Wiley, 1998.

Website:
The Advertising Association: **www.adassoc.org.uk**

Selecting and Working with an Advertising Agency

GETTING STARTED

If your budget will stretch, and you are able to engage an advertising agency to help you spread the word about your product or service, you need to choose an agency that can provide the right selection of services. These can include consultancy, strategy, creative work, media, and integration with other communications activities. Important factors in selecting an agency include its approach, reputation, and financial stability. If you choose your agency carefully, you're much more likely to avoid the problems that cause breakdowns in the agency/client relationship.

FAQS

Do I need an advertising agency?

Many small to medium-sized companies don't. However, the skills offered by agencies are just as specialised as those offered by your accountant. Many agencies will be able to offer services other than advertising, including direct marketing, sales promotion, and public relations.

Indeed they may not call themselves an 'advertising' agency at all. Agencies that offer a wide range of skills are often called 'full-service' agencies. If you know what you want to achieve, but are not sure if advertising is the best course, discuss the issues with a number of different agencies.

I want to work with a specific agency, but they already handle the account of a competitor. Should I work with that agency?

This problem occurs frequently, particularly when agency mergers occur, and the new group finds that its client lists include conflicting accounts. The decision to continue handling conflicting accounts is sometimes taken by the agency, and sometimes by the clients. It can be particularly difficult if the agency is seen as an industry specialist, with considerable expertise in a particular market. Sometimes the problem can be resolved by handling the conflicting accounts through separate agency teams.

How do I know that an agency can maintain its standards in day-to-day business, once they have won the initial pitch?

Sometimes agencies field a special senior team to win new business, and then hand the day-to-day account to a completely different team. Since a good relationship between agency and client is so important, you should insist on meeting the team who will actually work on the business.

Is it essential to appoint an agency to handle advertising campaigns?

A full-service agency may not be essential, particularly if you have the resources to handle part of the task internally. Creative consultancies, media specialists, or integrated agencies can take on specialist tasks.

MAKING IT HAPPEN
Choose the right type of agency

Depending on the type of agency, you can use a comprehensive service or specific services, including:
- initial consultancy
- development of an advertising strategy
- creative proposals, copywriting, design, and production of advertisements
- media planning, negotiation, buying, and administration
- integration of advertising with other communications activities

Whatever you decide, ask to see examples of previous campaigns and for an honest appraisal of their effectiveness.

Work with a full-service advertising agency

Full-service agencies handle all aspects of an advertising programme. You should select a full-service agency if you do not have any internal skills or resources for handling advertising, or if extensive advertising is important to the achievement of your marketing objectives.

Use a media independent

A media independent handles only media planning and buying and is likely to be interested only if you are spending a considerable amount on buying space in newspapers and magazines or airtime on TV or radio. By concentrating on media, the independents can often negotiate better deals with them than full-service agencies. Many smaller advertising agencies use media independents to handle their media buying. If you can handle campaign planning and creative work in other ways but do not have any internal skills or resources for media planning and buying, then you should use a media independent.

A media independent could prove useful if you spend a large amount of your budget on media, and you want to take advantage of specialist buying skills to get better positions or lower rates. You may find that certain media will not deal with you, because you are an advertiser. In that case, a media agency can provide valuable support.

Choose creative independents

Creative independents handle only creative work such as copywriting and design. By specialising in this way, the independents can often achieve more effective advertising than full-service agencies. You would have to handle campaign planning and media in other ways. There are three types of creative independent:
- freelance staff, either combined writer/art director teams, or individuals
- design consultancies offering advertising as part of a communications service
- specialist creative independents – small agencies that either have their own creative teams, or manage freelance teams

You should consider using a creative independent if you can handle campaign planning and media in other ways but do not have any internal skills or resources for creative work. If advertising is a small part of your marketing activity, you could develop effective campaigns by taking advantage of specialist creative services.

Work with an integrated agency

Integrated agencies handle all aspects of an advertising programme and integrate advertising with other media. Agencies offer integrated services in two forms, as:
- a single integrated agency, in which all campaigns are handled by the same team
- an agency group, in which non-advertising campaigns are handled by specialist companies within the group

An integrated agency may be suitable if other tools, such as direct marketing, publications, and sales promotion are as important as advertising, and you want all of the activities integrated and handled professionally. Any extra cost incurred will be well worth it.

Use the media's own expertise

One alternative to using an agency is to ask the newspaper, magazine, or radio station to help. Often they will offer basic design or writing services free of charge. However they are rarely as skilled as specialists and you may find it difficult to make your advertising stand out or to maintain consistency over time.

Evaluate advertising agencies

There are a number of important factors in selecting an agency:

- approach: what is the agency's philosophy, and how does it work in practical terms?
- track record: what campaigns has the agency produced, and how effective have they been?
- reputation: does the agency have an established reputation in your market? Are you able to approach other clients to give their assessment of the agency?
- accountability: how does the agency measure the performance of its campaigns?
- client relationships: what is the current client list, and how many of these clients are enjoying long-term relationships? What is the average length of account tenure?
- disciplines: does the agency offer all disciplines from within its own resources, and can it offer the full range of services?
- staff: does the agency have the staff to handle complex, large-scale programmes? What is the consultancy's recruitment and personal development policy?
- financial stability: what is the agency's recent performance? Does it have the stability and resources to sustain an effective level of service over the long term?

Check agency performance

According to Henley Centre research, clients believe the 10 most important questions regarding agency performance are as follows:

- Does it take the trouble to understand your business?
- Can it use creativity effectively to sell your products?
- Does it have real creative flair?
- Does it get work done on time?
- Does it have a good understanding of your consumers?
- Does it believe in defining advertising objectives beforehand?
- Does it keep costs within budget?
- Does it use research to aid its creative work?
- Is it strong on media buying?
- Is it thorough and hard-working?

Obtain information about advertising agencies

There are a number of useful sources of information about agencies:

- The Institute of Practitioners in Advertising and the Marketing Communication Consultants Association publish information about agencies.
- Individual agencies provide videos of their agency credentials or will send, or present in person, their portfolio of work. Larger agencies have their details available through the Advertising Agency Register and most agencies have websites or, at the least, brochures available.
- *Campaign*, *Marketing*, and *Marketing Week* magazines publish regular news about agencies and their clients and your own trade publications may mention agencies which specialise in your market.

- Talk to friends and colleagues, even if in different businesses, to find out which agencies are reliable.

COMMON MISTAKES

Choosing the wrong size of agency

A large agency may have the resources and scale to support national or international campaigns, but if your account is small, you may get poor service from a junior team. It may be more appropriate to work with a smaller agency, where you will get personal service from the senior people.

Choosing the wrong type of agency

Agencies, like any other business, develop specialities. Their expertise may not coincide with your needs. The most important division is between a consumer and a business-to-business agency but, beyond that, agencies develop expertise in certain industries or markets. Look carefully at the agency's client list to find the right match.

Relying on a creative pitch

Agency selection is frequently made on the basis of a pitch – a presentation that shows how an agency would tackle a specific project. Although the presentation gives an insight into the agency's working methods, it is an artificial guide to potential performance.

Not sharing information with the agency

Clients often expect a lot from a new agency, but can be disappointed when the agency does not know something 'obvious' about the client's business. The agency can only know what you know *if you tell them*. If you are concerned about confidentiality, discuss this and get a signed agreement from the agency management.

Not discussing the budget in enough detail

Agencies work for a fee and, like you, will want to make a profit. You will only get good service when they feel your business is worth their while. From the outset discuss how much you plan to spend and what you want to achieve – competent agencies will tell you from the outset what is possible.

THE BEST SOURCES OF HELP

Book:

Cummins, Julian, and Roddy Mullin. *Sales Promotion: How to Create, Implement and Integrate Campaigns That Really Work*. 4th ed. London: Kogan Page, 2008.

Websites:

Institute of Practitioners in Advertising:
www.ipa.co.uk

Public Relations Consultants' Association:
www.prca.org.uk

Preparing an Advertising Brief

GETTING STARTED
To get the most from working with an advertising agency, you need to make a start by putting together a comprehensive creative brief. This must cover all aspects of the project: background, objectives, research, competitors, product information, and the target audience. It's worth spending time on making the briefing information as complete as you can, as otherwise you run the risk of wasting time and money on a campaign that has little impact.

FAQS

Why is a detailed brief important?
It will start the campaign on exactly the right foot. An imprecise and insufficiently detailed brief may mean that the work is aimed at the wrong audience. Provide the agency or consultancy with as much information as possible, so that they can produce a campaign that achieves results.

Who should be involved in setting a creative brief?
The people who evaluate a creative brief should also be involved in setting or approving the brief. It can be difficult to deal with objections and criticism from someone who does not understand the brief. On the client side, the briefing team is likely to include the marketing executive, sales executive, and any relevant marketing specialists such as promotions or direct mail executives. The person who has the final say must be involved in defining the brief. The team should also include specialists to provide detailed information on the product and prospective customers. The agency team should be involved in preparing the brief, although this does not always happen in practice.

Should an agency brief always have measurable objectives?
The more specific the brief, the easier it is to assess the results of the creative work. It is not always possible to set a measurable objective, but this should be the goal. Agencies may argue that results depend on factors outside their control, but it should be possible to isolate the communications objectives and identify a way of measuring them. A direct response campaign, for example, can be measured by the number of responses, while a corporate campaign could be assessed through attitude surveys conducted before and after the campaign.

MAKING IT HAPPEN

Plan the campaign approach
How will you present your message? Most publications and commercial broadcast media carry high volumes of advertising. Your advertisement must achieve immediate impact to succeed. There are three essential checks that can be applied to creative work in any media:
- it must have immediate impact
- it must meet the needs of the reader or viewer
- it must stimulate a response

Provide background information
Your briefing of the agency or consultancy should begin with the background to the project:
- What is the overall aim of the project?
- What threats and opportunities does the business face?
- Why is the project being produced?
- How does the project fit into the overall marketing programme?
- Why is it necessary to advertise, and what is the advertising intended to achieve?

The background material should include any research that you have carried out or used. You should ensure that the project works in the context of other marketing activities carried out by you and your competitors.

Produce a comprehensive brief
Information of this kind enables writers and designers to approach the creative process in a disciplined, logical way. Great creative ideas may occur in a vacuum, but they are more likely to be a response to a clearly defined problem.

The creative brief is important whether you are using external suppliers or carrying out the creative work internally.

Set out objectives
The brief should set out a number of objectives, including the overall corporate objective and the marketing objective. For example, you may want to make potential customers in a new region aware of your product in order that sales staff can work more effectively.

The campaign objectives should be detailed and specific. Examples could include:
- generate 3,000 prospects and convert 3 per cent of them
- ensure that key decision-makers understand the product's business benefits
- raise awareness among 20 per cent of the target audience

Provide access to any research information
The creative team should be aware of any relevant research information, including:
- customer surveys, interviews, or analysis
- industry surveys
- competitor analysis
- product reviews
- press comment on the product or company
- feedback from focus groups
- results of previous campaigns

Include information on competitors
The brief should include detailed information on:
- which competitors provide a similar product or service
- how the competitive offering compares
- the product's key benefits against the competition
- how competitors are perceived by customers

This information can help creative teams to identify some of the key benefits that will differentiate the product from competitors' offerings. It will also show how other companies have tackled the problem of describing the product.

Provide comprehensive product information
The product or service should be described in detail:
- what it is
- what it is used for
- how it operates
- the main benefits for the customer
- the advantages over competitor products

If the team can use or experience for itself your product or service in the same way as a customer, then this will greatly enhance its understanding.

Describe the target audience
Describing the target audience helps the creative team to focus on the key decision-makers:
- What types of company buy the product?
- Which business sectors are they in?
- How big are these companies?
- Who are the main decision-makers?
- What is their role in the decision-making process?
- What are their business concerns?
- What is their perception of your company and its products?

Establish target perceptions
The creative team should be aware of any key messages that are important to the target audience. The task of the creative team is not to invent these messages; it is to communicate them as effectively as possible. The brief should therefore set out the perceptions that the target audience have now and those they should hold once the campaign is finished.

Get approval of the brief
The brief should be circulated to all members of the group involved in briefing and approving the project. No creative work should begin until the brief has been signed off by everyone involved. Once the brief has been approved, members should not be able to change it without good reason.

Be clear about payment terms
Some agencies will present their ideas without expecting payment, but most would rather not. If you cannot pay for initial ideas, make this clear before expecting anything of value from the team. If, however, you *can* pay, agree the amount and establish who will own the ideas once the initial presentation is finished.

Describe the review process
Let the creative team know how their work will be reviewed and evaluated. This can take place at a number of levels:
- review by the agency and client teams
- evaluation in focus groups
- pilot campaigns in test markets

COMMON MISTAKES
Making the brief too specific
It is possible to make a brief too specific, thereby ruling out creative approaches that may achieve outstanding results. For example, setting out the creative approach in the brief before the creative team has had an opportunity to consider it will produce very limited results. The creative team needs information to focus their attention on the problem, not suggestions on how the problem should be solved.

Not integrating creative work
Although the brief should allow the agency creative team complete freedom, it is equally important that creative work across different media should be integrated. If advertising is the dominant medium, and a team is working on direct marketing, they should relate their approach to the advertising theme. Repetition of the same creative theme across different media reinforces the key messages and can improve overall awareness.

Concentrating too hard on creativity, and not enough on results
Creative work should be accountable. The agency may have a brilliant, award-winning creative idea, but if it fails to produce the intended results it may be a waste of money. The creative team should therefore be aware of the specific objectives of the campaign; it is not enough just to get attention.

THE BEST SOURCES OF HELP
Book:
Ogilvy, David. *Ogilvy on Advertising*. London: Prion Books, 1995.

Website:
Institute of Practitioners in Advertising: **www.ipa.co.uk**

Setting Advertising Objectives

GETTING STARTED

Spending a fortune on advertising is expensive for any business, and the owners of small companies should think long and hard before ploughing their hard-earned cash into it. If you do decide to go ahead, setting clear objectives for your campaign is essential. Have them in place well before the campaign begins, so that each campaign has a specific task. In addition, make sure that the desired results can be measured; that way, you'll be able to work out whether you've had a good return on your investment.

FAQS

Should advertising be judged on sales results?

Advertising should certainly be measured, but there may not be a direct correlation between advertising and sales. Advertising may generate a large number of leads, but the sales force may not be able to convert those leads to sales.

Should advertising agencies be judged solely on the results they deliver?

There has been a trend towards judging agencies on measurable results. This has been driven partly by the increasing importance of direct marketing agencies who claim to be driven by results, and partly by the desire of marketing executives to increase accountability. Some agencies have gone so far as to base their fees on results, rather than traditional agency payment. The problem is that results are dependent on so many other aspects of marketing. An agency could claim that it has no control over the performance of the sales force or the quality of the product. It is essential therefore that you agree on a definition of success.

Is it possible to set a number of different objectives for the same advertising campaign, particularly when budgets are limited?

It *is* possible, but it may not be a good idea. An effective campaign has a single focus with a specific measurable result. By mixing objectives, you may achieve only part of the outcome you want.

MAKING IT HAPPEN

Set the right objective

Having clear objectives for your campaign is the only way you'll be able to tell whether you've succeeded! You may have multiple objectives, but it's wise to identify a specific task for a specific campaign. This might be:

- raising awareness of a company, product, or service within a clearly identified target market
- communicating the benefits of a product or service
- generating leads for the sales force or retail network
- encouraging prospects to buy directly through a direct response campaign
- persuading prospects to switch brands
- supporting a special marketing event such as a sale or an exhibition
- ensuring that customers know where to obtain the product
- building confidence in an organisation

Whatever your general objectives, you should be clear how much is dependent on the communications and how much dependent on other aspects of your marketing effort, such as the sales force (if you have one).

Make the objectives measurable

To ensure you design a cost-effective campaign that delivers results, advertising objectives should be translated into precise, measurable targets, as in the following examples.

Consumer product

- target market: 500,000 ABC1 prospects in the South of England
- marketing objective: achieve high level of product understanding
- advertising objective: persuade 15 per cent of targeted prospects to request a free sample

Business product

- target market: 5,000 specialist machinery designers in (specified) industrial processes
- marketing objective: increase market share to 20 per cent (that is, recruit 1,000 new clients)
- advertising objective: persuade 40 per cent of prospects to request product fact file

Raise awareness

This objective is usually the starting point for advertisers and is especially important if your company is entering new markets where you do not have an established reputation, or you are trying to influence important decision-makers who may not be aware of your company. Awareness advertising can also be used if you are launching new products which appeal to specific sectors of your market, or if research shows that customers and prospects are not aware of the full extent of your products and services.

This type of objective would be important for a company launching a new range of products. For example, to raise awareness of its new range, one company planned to advertise in a group of special interest consumer magazines aimed at its target audience. The advertisements included the telephone number of an information line that generated a large number of enquiries. Editorial articles in the same group of publications backed up the advertising by providing more detailed information for consumers. You should, however, be wary of specifying awareness targets. Awareness on its own will not sell products and, if this is your aim, you will have to integrate your campaign carefully with other elements of your marketing to meet your targets. Likewise, awareness amongst the general public is very different from awareness in a very small, specialised market, so you should be clear about who you are trying to reach.

Communicate benefits

Product advertising should lead with benefits. This type of advertising is important when research shows low awareness of product benefits. It should also be used if your products have recently been improved, or if you need to counter competitors who have introduced products with similar or better benefits.

For example, if research shows that your company's products are perceived as old-fashioned or poor value for the money, you need to take action to communicate the real benefits of your products.

Generate sales leads

Advertising's role is to provide leads that can be followed up by a field sales force or telemarketing team. Lead generation is important if marketing success depends on the performance of the sales force. Sometimes, customers or prospects have a complex decision-making structure and you cannot identify some of the decision-makers. Advertising that generates enquiries can identify the right people and open the door for the sales team. It can also be used to identify prospects when you are entering new market sectors where you do not have an established customer base. The final use for this type of campaign is to generate leads for agents, distributors, or retailers who handle your local marketing.

Sell through direct response

Direct response advertising is the most measurable form of advertising. The advertising budget provides a direct return in terms of incremental sales. This objective can be important if customers can only buy direct from you. In an increasing number of markets, customers prefer the convenience of buying direct, and you have to decide whether to bypass your existing distribution channels. If you are targeting niche markets which are not covered by retail outlets, direct response can be used to complement your distribution channels, if appropriate.

In the personal computer market, for example, manufacturers found that businesses and individuals were willing to buy personal computers 'off the page' or via the Internet. The products were regarded as commodities and the resulting price competition put pressure on margins. The result was a considerable growth in the level of direct sales with manufacturers using large format advertisements or inserts in computer and business publications. Direct selling meant that the manufacturers could reduce prices by avoiding the cost of selling through retail outlets.

Encourage brand-switching

Brand-switching advertising plays an important role in winning new customers as the first stage in a customer relationship programme. It helps you to increase market share or maintain share against competitive actions, and is also important if you are introducing new products that offer greater benefits than competitive products.

Support a marketing event

This objective can be important in a number of situations, for example, taking part in an exhibition where an important new product will be launched, or holding a sale, or promoting a seminar or other customer event at which you wish to ensure customer participation. Advertising helps to build traffic for your event and ensures that the event attracts the right prospects. A company that sponsors senior executive seminars as a way of building its credibility could run advertisements in the business press to promote a seminar.

Build customer confidence

Capability advertising or corporate advertising is sometimes dismissed because it is difficult to measure, but is important when a company has been undergoing significant change, or is entering new markets where it is not established. It also provides support when a company is trying to win key account business, or if competitors are threatening important business.

COMMON MISTAKES

Setting objectives that cannot be measured

Advertising objectives should be measurable for two important reasons. First, to ensure that advertising represents an adequate return on investment. Second, to measure the effectiveness of the campaign itself, so that future advertising can be improved or modified to deliver better results.

Setting objectives that are too general

A general objective, such as raising awareness, is important, but often is seen as the only objective. Advertising objectives should be closely linked to marketing objectives so that advertising is used to carry out specific tasks within an overall marketing framework. You should be sure that what you want to achieve is possible with communications and acknowledge the importance of other elements of your marketing, crucially, the product itself or your pricing strategy.

THE BEST SOURCES OF HELP

Book:

Cummins, Julian, and Roddy Mullin. *Sales Promotion: How to Create, Implement and Integrate Campaigns That Really Work*. 4th ed. London: Kogan Page, 2008.

Website:

Institute of Practitioners in Advertising: **www.ipa.co.uk**

Getting Better Results from Your Agency

GETTING STARTED
Agencies emphasise a number of factors when trying to win new business. It is important to review agency performance regularly to see that initial promises are being kept and that the original selection criteria are still valid.

FAQS

Should I place all marketing tasks with a single agency or deal with specialists?
Full-service agencies claim to integrate all aspects of a client's marketing operations so that clients get a better overall return on marketing spend. Specialists, on the other hand, claim to offer a more effective service in critical areas such as creativity, media buying, or below-the-line promotion. If you choose specialists, you have to ensure that they work to consistent standards and do not overlap. If you choose an integrated agency, you may need to compromise on the quality of some of the more specialist areas of activity.

Is agency commission better than a service fee?
Traditionally, agencies were remunerated by the commission received from the media in which they placed advertisements. Any creative, planning, or buying services would be covered by that commission, which meant that these services were effectively free to the advertiser. However, the higher service content of most agency work meant that commission did not adequately cover agency costs. Agencies therefore charged fees to clients and passed some of the media commission to the client. In the absence of fees, agencies might have been forced to reduce service levels.

MAKING IT HAPPEN

Use the right criteria to select an agency
The most popular reasons for a client's choice of agency include:
- seeing advertising they like
- recommendation by a colleague
- information from the marketing/advertising press
- the agency winning an award
- using the services of a selection agency
- using a selection consultant

Agencies emphasise a number of factors when they are trying to win new business. It is essential to see that they are delivering on their initial claims and promises, which commonly include:
- a good understanding of the business
- quality thinking
- involvement of senior staff who will continue to work on the account
- evidence of sound business and account management skills
- a powerful creative idea

Concentrate on the key criteria
In reviewing your agency, you should concentrate on key criteria such as those identified in industry surveys:
- creativity
- value for money
- media buying
- quality of account management
- attentiveness and adaptability
- marketing strategy
- coverage of major world markets

Avoid problems in agency–client relationships
Reports in the trade press highlight a number of factors that create conditions for a breakdown.
- The agency is not devoting enough time or resources to the account.
- The agency is losing enthusiasm for the account.
- The agency may be faced with working on a conflicting account.
- There may be a personality clash.
- The client believes that advertising does not have the planned effect on the marketplace.
- The agency feels that poor results are caused by problems on the client side.
- The client does not like the advertisements for subjective reasons.
- The agency fails to understand the client's business.
- A failure of communication means the agency cannot respond to the client's real needs.
- Frequent changes in the agency team or client team make continuity difficult.
- Poor agency administration lets down good creative work.
- Relationships can become stale.

Schedule regular review meetings
Review agency performance regularly. Many agencies and clients conduct reviews at three-, six-, or 12-month intervals, or after each major campaign, to assess both campaign and agency performance.

Take action to improve performance
If your agency shows poor performance in one or more areas, take remedial action. Suggest a change in remuneration that rewards performance or move part of your account into another type of agency offering specialist services.

Consider paying agencies by results
With the increasing emphasis on accountability, a small but growing number of agencies are including an element of payment by results in their remuneration packages. Variations include:
- part fee and part results-based, for example, based on an increase in sales or awareness

- part fee and part commission, with the fee based on achievement of agreed measurable objectives

Although this orientation towards results is attractive to clients, it can be difficult to relate the contribution of the agency to a measurable result, and this trend seems unlikely to replace traditional forms of remuneration.

Switch to creative independents

If your agency is weak on creative work, you could consider working directly with an independent creative consultancy. Creative independents only handle creative work, such as copywriting and design. By specialising, the independents can often achieve more effective advertising than full-service agencies. There are three types of creative independent:

- freelance staff, either combined writer/art director teams or individuals
- design consultancies offering advertising as part of a communications service
- specialist creative independents – small agencies with their own creative teams or who manage freelance teams

Work with a virtual agency

As clients demand greater flexibility and an increasingly wide range of services, they are attracted by the concept of a virtual agency. In some cases, the agency may simply consist of a planning and management team with all creative, media, and specialist services bought in from independent suppliers. Other agencies maintain a central office with specialists based in satellite operations linked by telecommunications and videoconferencing.

Appoint a brand consultancy

The role of the advertising agency in creating and maintaining brand awareness is being challenged by a new type of marketing services organisation known as a brand consultancy. The brand consultancy brings together skills from a number of different disciplines, including market research, marketing consultancy, management consultancy, and advertising.

The brand consultancy claims a number of advantages over the traditional advertising agency approach:

- a longer-term perspective on the development of brands, because they are not limited by an annual advertising budget
- recognition and integration of the different elements that contribute to brand success
- closer working relationships with the whole client brand team

Choose a media independent

A media independent, as the name suggests, only handles media planning and buying. By concentrating on media, the independents can often negotiate better deals than full-service agencies. In fact, many smaller advertising agencies use media independents to handle their media buying. You would have to handle campaign planning and creative work in other ways.

Appoint an integrated agency

Agencies offer integrated services in a number of forms:

- a single integrated agency where all campaigns are handled by the same team
- an agency group where non-advertising campaigns are handled by specialist companies within the group

COMMON MISTAKES

Failing to review agency performance

Many companies appoint an advertising agency for a fixed period but do not build performance reviews into the agreement. Regular performance reviews provide opportunities to identify and resolve problems before they become too serious.

No performance criteria

If you include performance reviews in your agency agreement, make sure you set out the criteria by which the agency will be assessed. The more precise and measurable the criteria, the easier it will be to carry out an objective assessment. It is too easy to say, 'I don't like their creative work.' If the creative work delivers results and meets targets, it must be judged successful, regardless of personal taste.

Expecting one agency to do everything

Many agencies claim to be good at all types of marketing. They call themselves full-service agencies. However, they may not be able to meet your requirements in all areas, so you should consider appointing specialists to handle specific tasks such as media buying, sales promotion, or product development.

THE BEST SOURCES OF HELP
Website:
Institute of Practitioners in Advertising:
www.ipa.co.uk

Integrating Advertising with Other Campaigns

GETTING STARTED
Advertising is one of a series of interrelated marketing tools that support each other, and in an integrated campaign, advertising becomes a much more flexible medium and can be used wherever it is most effective.

FAQS

Why do some agencies avoid integrated campaigns?
It may be because they do not have the skills to handle the other marketing activities that fall outside the traditional advertising agency role. In some cases, they do not understand how the activities work together.

Is an advertising agency the best choice to handle an integrated campaign?
There are integrated agencies that offer all marketing services from within their own organisation. Others may be part of a larger group who can offer the other, non-advertising services. These types of agency are suitable for handling integrated campaigns. If advertising is not a major part of the integrated campaign, it may be more appropriate to talk to a marketing services company or group that offers all the relevant services.

Why is integration so important? Isn't it better to focus on getting the best results from individual marketing activities?
Results indicate that integration can save money and make better use of a budget. The savings come through multiple use of the same planning and creative work and more efficient use of the available funds. The other major bonus is that integrated activities support each other, improving the efficiency of individual campaign elements against overall objectives.

MAKING IT HAPPEN

Integrate campaigns
Advertising is not a separate activity but one of a series of interrelated marketing tools that support each other. Although campaigns take many different forms, there are core elements that are crucial to the successful development of an integrated marketing strategy. The most important of these are:
- advertising
- direct marketing
- telemarketing
- press information
- relationship marketing
- sales support
- publications

In the integrated approach, the elements support each other. For example, an advertising campaign with reply coupon is integrated with a direct mail programme, which is followed up by telemarketing. Without the support of the other marketing elements, the advertising and direct mail programmes would achieve results; but together they reinforce each other to achieve real impact.

Advertising
With an adequate budget and effective media planning, it would be possible to use advertising alone to launch and market a new product. In this situation, advertising would have a number of objectives, which are:
- raising customer awareness of the new product
- explaining the comparative benefits of the product
- generating initial requests for information

The success of the launch would be directly related to the size of the budget and how efficiently it is used. By integrating advertising with other marketing activities, however, the company can use advertising for specific tasks within the overall programme and make more effective use of its budget. In an integrated programme, advertising is just one of the marketing tools available, and it can be used in whatever capacity is most effective. This could be one of several ways such as:
- a national direct response medium, to generate leads for a corporate direct marketing or telemarketing campaign
- a regional direct response medium, to generate leads for follow-up by local intermediaries
- part of a selective regional sales promotion campaign that offers prospects incentives for providing database information

These options make advertising a much more flexible medium.

Direct marketing
Direct marketing is one of the most flexible tools in an integrated marketing programme. It can be used to reinforce the effectiveness of other marketing tools, or used alone in a variety of different ways. Direct mail advertising, for example, can be a viable alternative to press or broadcast media as a way of reaching specific sectors of the market. In an integrated campaign, it can also be used to follow up prospects who request further information. In addition, it can be employed to maintain effective contact and build long-term relationships with customers.

In an integrated campaign, however, direct marketing must be used to strengthen overall effectiveness. As a first stage, it can be integrated with the consumer advertising campaigns:
- as a follow-up to the direct response advertising campaign. The advertisements provide information on warm prospects, which can be used to form a database for future direct marketing programmes.
- to make differentiated offers to prospects who respond to the advertising campaign
- to supplement the advertising campaign's coverage of different target markets

- to reach sectors that cannot be reached efficiently by other media, or to provide increased reach or frequency
- to reinforce the impact of the advertising campaign by selective follow-up

Telemarketing
Telemarketing can be used to supplement the advertising and direct marketing campaigns through inbound and outbound programmes. It can be used to handle a number of different tasks:

- direct sales to prospects over the telephone
- maintaining contact with current customers
- using the relationship to launch new products
- generating leads from unqualified mailing lists
- following up direct marketing programmes
- winning back lapsed customers by introducing them to new products that may be of greater interest
- following up leads generated through advertising or direct marketing, or via intermediaries
- carrying out market research, using surveys to establish consumer response to products or sales incentives
- maintaining contact with customers as part of a relationship marketing programme

Telemarketing can also provide a point of response for queries generated through advertising or direct marketing campaigns, or to obtain information from respondents as a basis for future database marketing.

Press information
Press activities can be used in the context of a wider public relations campaign. Sponsorship of sporting or entertainment events, for example, can increase awareness and build a high profile for a company, leaving advertising and direct marketing to focus on direct response and brand-building strategies.

Sales support
In an integrated campaign, leads can be generated for the salesforce by advertising and direct marketing. Salesforce productivity can also be improved by using telemarketing to handle routine customer communications. It is essential to back up sales teams with information both on the products and on the marketplace to improve their overall effectiveness. The programme includes:

- direct salesforce and distributor support
- standard and customised presentations for different market sectors
- product/sales guides to improve product knowledge
- information on the advertising and direct marketing support available in each territory
- competitor profiles

Relationship marketing
Relationship marketing builds on the leads generated by advertising and direct marketing. It also enhances the direct contact of the sales force by increasing customer loyalty. These are its key roles in an integrated programme:

- maintaining an existing customer base
- increasing account control
- issuing a regular, planned flow of information
- increasing customer loyalty

Publications
Product publications do not normally form part of an integrated programme. However, they form an important part of the communications programme. Publications are used to:

- reinforce overall branding
- provide benefits-led information
- communicate positioning messages, as well as product information
- act as sales presentation guides

COMMON MISTAKES
Running integrated campaigns through separate agencies
One of the key benefits of integrated marketing is that the client deals with a single agency for all marketing activities. Dealing with multiple agencies can lead to such problems as different creative solutions or duplicated costs. It is essential that one agency plans and produces the entire integrated campaign.

Defining integrated marketing too narrowly
Advertising, sales promotion, and direct marketing are viewed as the mainstream elements in an integrated campaign. However, sales support, telemarketing, public relations, exhibitions, and many other activities may have a key part to play.

Failing to use data to plan and control campaigns
One of the key elements in an integrated campaign is the database. Information from all campaign activities should be used to identify communications needs, target individual communications, measure campaign effectiveness, and track customer responses. Without this underlying control, campaign funds may well be wasted.

THE BEST SOURCES OF HELP
Book:
Smith, Paul, and Jonathan Taylor. *Marketing Communications: An Integrated Approach*. London: Kogan Page, 2004.

Website:
Chartered Institute of Marketing: **www.cim.co.uk**

Measuring Advertising Performance

GETTING STARTED

Advertising is expensive, so it is important to ensure that it provides value for money in terms of effective results. Objectives should be clearly defined; results should then be measured and evaluated in order to establish that these objectives have been achieved.

FAQS

Why is it so important to measure advertising effectiveness?

Advertising budgets represent a major investment for most companies. Measuring advertising allows you to measure the effectiveness of your advertising and your agency. The feedback obtained is invaluable in determining future strategies.

The media publish research on the effectiveness of advertising. Can I use this for my own research purposes?

This type of research is unlikely to be completely objective, since it is designed to promote the medium. However, it can act as a useful guideline for carrying out a preliminary evaluation of the media. You must measure the results of your own advertising campaign.

Some agencies offer a payment-by-results service. Is this the only way to reward agency and advertising effectiveness?

This type of agency typically runs a high proportion of direct response advertising, where results can be measured accurately. There are other important parameters, but they do not lend themselves to the same simple measurement.

MAKING IT HAPPEN

Set measurable objectives

It is important to set clear, measurable objectives for an advertising campaign. There is no single advertising objective, so it is essential to identify a specific task for the campaign:

- to raise awareness of a company, product, or service in a clearly identified target market
- to communicate the benefits of a product or service
- to generate leads for the salesforce or retail network
- to encourage prospects to buy directly through a direct response campaign
- to persuade prospects to switch brands
- to support a special marketing event such as a sale or an exhibition
- to ensure customers know where to obtain the product
- to build confidence in an organisation

Advertising objectives should be measurable for two important reasons: first, to ensure that advertising represents an adequate return on investment and, second, to measure the effectiveness of the campaign itself.

The objectives should be detailed and specific. Examples could include:

- to convert 3 per cent of prospects
- to ensure that key decision-makers understand the product's business benefits
- to raise awareness among 20 per cent of the target audience

An effective campaign should have a single focus with a specific measurable result. By mixing objectives, you may achieve only some of the results you want.

Use research to measure advertising effectiveness

Research should be used to assess how well your advertising has achieved its objectives. This will enable you to fine-tune your advertising plans. You should carry out research before and after a campaign to evaluate:

- changes in customer awareness of the product
- advertising recall
- attitudes to the product
- the responses to different creative approaches

Test creative treatment

There are three vital checks that can be applied to creative work in any medium: it must have immediate impact; it must meet the reader's or viewer's needs; and it must stimulate a response.

Creative work can be tested in a number of ways, of which the most common are a panel of prospects and customers, test marketing, and measuring the response from pilot campaigns. Important variables to test are:

- size of advertisement
- layout
- creative approach
- position in the publication
- timing
- product offer
- price or discount offer
- response mechanism

Measure brand-switching

Brand loyalty is a key marketing objective, helping companies to retain customers and increase their lifetime value. Brand-switching advertising plays an important role in winning new customers as the first stage in a customer relationship programme. It is an important objective that helps you to increase market share or maintain share against competitive actions. It is also important if you are introducing a new product that offers greater benefits than competitors' products. Researching brand-switching is therefore an important long-term measure of advertising effectiveness. Published independent surveys that show market share for different suppliers can be a useful starting point.

Actionlists

Monitor target perceptions

To find out what your customers consider important about your products and your company, carry out a survey or run a focus group. The survey should ask respondents how they rank the different brand values. It should also ask respondents how they believe your company and a number of competitors compare across a number of the brand values. The results should give you an indication of overall ranking as well as an insight into customer perceptions of individual companies. Advertising aims to change those perceptions so that customers hold a positive view of your company.

Customer perceptions change over a period of time, particularly if you are running targeted communications programmes, so you should carry out continuous research to monitor changes in customer attitude. This type of research is known as tracking research, and it helps you to measure the effectiveness of your advertising.

Monitor the right factors

The corporate reputation is the way a company is perceived by customers, suppliers, and other important groups. You should use your tracking research to monitor customer perceptions of factors such as:
- financial performance
- the quality of the management team
- clarity of direction
- market performance
- growth record and potential
- relationships with suppliers and employees
- manufacturing capability

Measure response levels

Direct response advertising is easier to measure than advertising that is designed to change perceptions over a period of time. Your advertisement will include a call to action, such as:
- send for more information
- reply within seven days and receive a free gift
- send for a free report
- take out an annual subscription now and get the first two issues free
- ring for a free consultation
- book now at a special price
- order now and get a big discount
- visit our website and find out more

The most popular mechanisms for press advertisements include website address, e-mail address, Freepost address, and Freephone number. Monitor the response levels from different sources to see which is the most effective.

Check the cost of your response

You can measure the cost of your direct response campaign by dividing the cost of the advertising or marketing programme by the number of responses. You can use the same type of measure to assess factors such as timing, offer, and creative treatment.

Measure Internet advertising

The advantage of the Internet is that, at little or no cost, you can test your campaign on part of your target audience. You can also experiment with different banner ad sizes. The Internet is ideal for testing messages against your target, gauging the appeal of promotional offers and the type of message that attracts customers who buy. Some advertisers measure effectiveness on click-through rates (CTRs). The average CTR for banner advertising on the Internet is currently 0.2 per cent to 0.4 per cent. Commentators believe that banners that get high click-throughs may not be the best at getting conversions, where the user actually signs up for a subscription or makes a purchase. The real success of your campaign should be based on action, so it is more realistic to use conversions as your measure.

Consider paying agencies by results

With the increasing emphasis on accountability, a small but growing number of agencies are including an element of payment by results in their remuneration packages. Variations include:
- part fee and part results-based: for example, based on an increase in sales or awareness
- part fee and part commission, with the fee based on the achievement of agreed measurable objectives

Although this orientation towards results is attractive to clients, it can be difficult to relate the contribution of the agency directly to a measurable result, and this trend seems unlikely to replace traditional forms of remuneration.

COMMON MISTAKES

No objective performance criteria

It is important to set objective criteria for measuring advertising performance. The more precise and measurable the criteria, the easier it will be to carry out an objective assessment.

Failure to measure advertising

Companies in consumer and business markets are prepared to spend millions on advertising campaigns but are reluctant to invest in research to measure the effectiveness of them. This has led to a lack of accountability and to problems in reaching a proper evaluation of advertising and agencies.

Using the wrong measures

The measures you use are determined by your objectives. Corporate campaigns need to measure changes in perception. If you are working on a direct response campaign, measure response rates or direct sales.

THE BEST SOURCES OF HELP

Websites:
Advertising Association: **www.adassoc.org.uk**
Institute of Practitioners in Advertising:
  www.ipa.co.uk

Building One-to-one Relationships

Actionlists

GETTING STARTED
Building one-to-one relationships involves collecting and using information about actual and prospective customers as a basis for a customised selling approach. This provides an efficient and targeted means of maximising sales.

FAQS

Do I have to tell customers that I am collecting personal information?
You are bound by data protection legislation to advise customers about data collection and use. However, it is good commercial practice to publish a clear privacy policy explaining your procedures. You should also tell customers how you intend to use the data. Experience indicates that customers are happy to part with information if they see some tangible benefit. Concerns about security and privacy issues remain major barriers to the development of e-commerce.

Does one-to-one marketing guarantee customer loyalty?
It cannot guarantee loyalty, but it can make an important contribution. Customers will only remain if they continue to recognise the value of your products and the quality of your customer service. That means continually enhancing the customer experience.

Is one-to-one marketing always the best way to deal with customers?
For one-to-one marketing to work effectively, you need the right level of information on customers. You may not always be able to get that level of information on individual customers. However, if you have sufficient information on groups of customers with common needs, you can use techniques such as direct mail to communicate with a degree of precision. As your information on individual customers grows, you can move towards one-to-one communication.

MAKING IT HAPPEN

Refine your target market
The more information you have about your target audience, the more precise you can make your campaign. In an ideal world, direct marketing techniques would allow you to communicate one to one with every prospect, but in practical terms you are more likely to be communicating with groups who share the same characteristics. This enables you to develop a unique relationship that competitors will find very difficult to match. It can also reduce your marketing and customer management costs by reducing wastage to a minimum.

Establish clear objectives
One-to-one marketing is designed to:
- improve the quality of customer service
- strengthen customer relationships
- maximise the profitability of each customer relationship
- increase retention rates for customers
- maximise the return on your investment in marketing and customer service

Set up a database
At the heart of effective one-to-one marketing is a data networking solution that collects, stores, manages, and distributes all relevant customer information via a single, integrated customer database. The database is updated from all customer channels and is accessible by all customer-facing staff.

Keep capturing customer data
The more you know about your customers, the better your chances of increasing lifetime value. Data capture must therefore be an integral part of all your sales, marketing, and customer service campaigns. You can build detailed profiles through campaign responses and customer research, and use the latest database and communications technology to manage, analyse, and distribute information. Take every opportunity to find out more about your customers so that you can build a real competitive edge, based on one-to-one personal relationships.

Invest in personalisation
The rapid development of data storage and data analysis tools means that it is now possible to know far more about your customers – with information well beyond details of income, spending patterns, service preferences, and frequency of use. The information available represents a quantum leap in the ability to profile customers.

Investing in personalisation can increase value and loyalty even further.

At the heart of a personalised service is the customer's individual profile. A basic profile covers:
- name and address
- contact details
- purchase history
- personal interests
- product or service preferences

Let customers add their own personal details
If you offer personal pages on your website, you can allow customers to add further choices to the profile, using a special checklist. However, it is important to use customer information in appropriate ways. Attempts to increase customer interactions and provide more personalised information have made many consumers concerned about privacy issues. It is essential to let customers control the frequency and scope of interaction. Businesses must

understand the difference between using and abusing the information they gather.

Information should be used to meet individual customer needs; customers are aware of the value of their information and are willing to provide it only when they see real benefits. That means giving customers control over their data and the way they interact with your company. To build trust, you must allow customers to choose how they want to interact and to use the information that they provide.

Develop a one-to-one relationship

The contact between buyer and seller on the Internet is moving towards the ultimate one-to-one experience. Database technology supports a level of personalisation that can deliver highly tailored products and services to specific individuals. Each time a customer logs on to a website, for example, the database can pull together purchase history and personal preferences as a basis for a highly personalised response. By giving customers a single point of entry, you can increase customer loyalty and learn more about their purchasing patterns. This provides an excellent basis for adding value and for the development of new products.

Maintain regular, targeted communication

Once you have customer information, it is important to act on it. Maintain regular contact by sending customers information or special offers tailored to their individual needs.

Use e-mail to maintain contact

With e-mail you can deliver individual messages cost-effectively. E-mail also commands immediate attention. Most people check their e-mail routinely and generally read or quickly scan most messages. This makes e-mail a powerful marketing tool with a high potential return for a modest investment. Your e-mail goes straight into the customer's inbox, so you don't have to spend money attracting people to your site. When a customer opts to take regular e-mail from you, you have an opportunity to build a strong relationship. This makes online marketing more predictable and gives you the chance to develop a one-to-one relationship.

Allow customers to customise products

Interactive facilities on a website allow customers to design their own customised products. Cars and computers are good examples. The customer chooses a basic model, and then selects features and options from a database. The system provides a price for the customised product, then gives the customer the choice of ordering now or storing the specification on a personal web page for later modification. The high level of interaction gives customers greater choice and provides you with detailed insight into their needs.

Customise information services

You can use data on customer preferences as a basis for offering personalised information services. Customers specify the type of information they need, and you alert them by e-mail whenever relevant information is available.

Offer different service levels

One-to-one service allows you to offer different levels of service to each category of customer. These could include:
- privileged rewards for top customers
- incentives for regular customers to spend more
- special offers to lapsed customers

COMMON MISTAKES

Ignoring privacy issues

One-to-one marketing is based on the acquisition and use of high levels of personal information. You should publish a privacy policy on your site and you should also ensure that you comply with relevant data protection legislation. When you collect data, tell visitors what you do with the information, and follow best practice on privacy issues.

Failing to develop customer relationships

The primary reason for collecting data is to find out more about customer needs so that you can build long-term relationships and increase customer loyalty. It is essential to act on the information you collect, analyse it, and develop strategies for building a personalised one-to-one service.

Targeting the wrong people

Marketing programmes work most effectively when they are aimed at a specific audience. The more you segment your target audience, the more precisely you can communicate. Different groups within your target market may have different purchasing needs or spending levels. By segmenting your audience and customising your marketing material, you can address individual needs.

THE BEST SOURCES OF HELP
Book:
Peppers, Don, and Martha Rogers. *Return on Customer: Creating and Maximizing Value from Your Scarcest Resource*. London: Cyan Books, 2005.

Website:
Peppers & Rogers: **www.1to1.com**

Strengthening Customer Relationships via an Ethical Sales Approach

GETTING STARTED
A strong and effective sales approach not only results in good income for a company, but also a trusting relationship between supplier and customer. Your sales representatives (reps) are on the front line every day, and for them to succeed, their customers have to want to work with them. If reps base their relationships with others on honesty and commitment to the success of the customer's business, it's a win–win situation for everyone.

FAQS
Do sales reps need to conform to a formal code of ethics?
None exists currently, but organisations often create their own set of standards that their sales teams need to adhere to. It is generally accepted that good practice is founded on accurate and honest descriptions of the products and services in question, but in a sense it's only when a customer or prospect trusts a sales representative enough to make a purchase that you can tell if they really 'buy' their conduct. That sense of the reps being people the customers can do business with is something that can't be won by a formal code of conduct.

MAKING IT HAPPEN
Increase trust levels
While sales of most types are always welcome, the ideal sale is one that leads to an ongoing, profitable relationship with a customer. To that end, it's essential that the sales team build strong, trusting relationships with people who come to view them as a credible supplier. To create this type of relationship, the sales reps will need to show:
- a strong commitment to their company's ethos and products
- inside-out knowledge of products and services
- a desire to understand their customers' needs

The relationship won't be built overnight, but devoting time to it will reap rewards in the long run.

Have all relevant information to hand
Customers will have their trust in a rep enhanced if he or she is comfortable with the details relating to their product or service, and that those details are accurate. Incorrect information can make customers nervous, and you'd have to work hard to repair your relationship. Of course there will be times when the customer has a question that you can't answer: if you can't telephone or e-mail for an immediate answer to the question there and then, it's best for you to say you don't know, but do offer to find out. Give the customer a date when you'll get back to them and stick to it.

Advise honestly
When reps are asked for advice by a customer about a potential purchase, it does put them in what may feel like an invidious position: knocking a competitor may put the customer on the defensive, while singing the praises of their own product without flinching leaves them open to accusations of bias. Again, openness is the best policy here. While getting a sale is their goal, if they're honest enough to say that their product may not be the right one for the customer in a particular set of circumstances, their integrity is enhanced in the eyes of that customer. Giving incorrect or prejudiced information will trip you up in the end.

Think about what the customer wants
Understanding what your customers are looking for is one of the most important ways you can give them outstanding services. Tailoring your sales pitch based on what you know of the business, including its market, size, and bestselling lines can help you work out what your clients want, but by far and the best way is simply to ask them – and listen carefully. You'll find that this will go beyond basic product information: obviously each business will have very specific needs, but they may include regular updates on the progress of an order, training, or support.

Tackle problems honestly
As in any part of life, sorting out difficulties is a big issue for sales reps. Whether the issue be down to late deliveries, quality slips, or cost increases, they need to be tackled effectively for the customer to keep faith with their supplier. It's never a good policy to keep quiet about a problem or change in the hope that the customer won't notice or be that bothered by it; it may well be that they aren't too worried by a small change in specifications (for example), but that's their decision to make, and they should be made fully aware of any potential changes as soon as possible so that alternative arrangements can be made in the event of a serious crisis. Yes, a sale may be lost, but it's a trade-off worth making in some cases if it means that your company doesn't lose the customer for good.

Take responsibility
If a problem crops up and it's your fault, own up to it. If a customer were to find out that even a white lie has been told, your relationship could be fatally holed. Take responsibility, tell the customer how you'll rectify the situation, and move on.

Stick to commitments
Keep on top of the details as well as the big picture. Make sure phone calls are returned, samples sent out as

requested, and that meetings are attended on time. These small points are crucial parts of the larger relationship and show that you value your customer's time and business.

Address objections honestly

While some sales may run smoothly, you are bound to come up against customer objections at one time or another, and the way you handle these questions says a lot about your approach to sales ethics. For example, let's say your photocopier doesn't have the widget a customer is looking for. A rep could counter this by emphasising the widgets the copier does include, and the features thereof. This constitutes an honest approach. Dismissing the feature out of hand is completely the opposite. Sometimes you just have to take it on the chin.

Create an ethical selling culture

Business has never been more competitive, and customers are bombarded with information about new products every day. If they're harassed or short of time, they may fall prey to a particularly aggressive sales person who promises them a quick solution. It may not be the best one, however, and they can be left feeling cheated and frustrated. If you're a manager, you need to understand the pressure your sales team is under and to make sure they understand that you want long, lasting business partnerships with your customers rather than short-term gains. You need to set the context for them. For example, explain that you want to:
- build customer relationships, rather than focus on individual transactions
- simplify product information so the buyer can understand it
- train your sales team so that they can get results without obfuscation

COMMON MISTAKES
You go for sales at all costs

If bonuses are riding on targets being reached, some reps are tempted to encourage customers to buy more than they would normally. This type of unethical behaviour can have far-reaching consequences, however: not only will it be a distorting 'spike' in the sales figures, but customers may not want to do further business with a company they feel has put them under undue pressure.

You avoid ethical conundrums

Sales representatives should always do what is best for the customer, because people like to do business with representatives they can trust, and who give them the very best advice, service, and products. However, when it comes to the difficult decisions about losing a sale by being honest or making excuses for late delivery or other issues, sales representatives may avoid the ethical issues unless it is impossible to avoid doing so.

You knock the competition unfairly

Comparing your product or service to similar ones available is a key part of any sales pitch, but it shouldn't mean that you need to denigrate other companies' offerings unfairly. It is, of course, completely legitimate to explain that your product has added features, a better price, and so on, but don't dismiss the competition as shoddy without being able to back up your claims. Focus on the benefits your product offers and keep your pitch professional.

THE BEST SOURCES OF HELP
Website:
Institute of Sales and Marketing Management:
www.ismm.co.uk

Developing an Effective Marketing Campaign with Partners

GETTING STARTED

In principle, joining forces with partners to make a bigger marketing splash (and to get the best use possible from budgets) can seem like an excellent notion. It can, however, be difficult to create a campaign that delivers mutual benefits.

FAQS
Can co-operative marketing ever be effective?

Yes, but it may be a complex process. For example, it can be difficult to reconcile the objectives and agendas of two organisations, particularly if their relationship dynamics

undermine the effectiveness of the communications. If, however, a strong joint message and branding is decided upon early and the marketing campaign executed well, both parties should reap rewards.

MAKING IT HAPPEN
Get involved

It's often the case in some industries that components suppliers aren't included in their partners' marketing efforts: it may seem to the outside world that only the 'headline' brand is involved in the manufacture of their star products. It doesn't have to be like that, however: look at the amazing profile achieved by Intel via their 'Intel Inside' campaign: their signature tune in particular is instantly recognisable. Could your business try that approach? It's worth approaching your high-profile partner to discuss this with them: some may object, while others may be glad to make your role more public.

Build on strong individual brands

If you're teaming up with a high-profile partner, it can be tempting to hide behind their stronger position in the market. Tempting, but maybe not that wise. Ultimately, you should be aiming to developing your own so that you can stand out from the competition and remind your partner of your business's worth.

Create a single proposition

While it's better for both parties to have strong brand propositions, all communications coming from the partners needs to have one, coherent voice. Each party will, of course, have its own agenda, but consensus needs to be reached if you don't want to run the risk of a muddled message that turns off potential customers.

Sometimes, if negotiations become protracted, partners may settle for a compromise message that actually doesn't suit anyone. If you end up using various corporate logos, straplines, and images indiscriminately, the proposition will become confused.

Design a compelling joint approach

By joining forces to create an outstanding product proposition, partners have the opportunity to achieve outstanding results that they would never be able to reach on their own. There is, of course, a flipside, and that is that before they can get to this potentially very lucrative phase, they have to put aside any differences or clashes. To get things started, each party should appoint a liaison team to deal with preliminary discussions and plans. Remember that if the project is very high profile, it will be difficult for those people to do the liaison work as well as their day job, so you may need to reassign some of their other work until the project is complete.

Consider engaging an external agency

Using an experienced external marketing agency to help arbitrate in any clashes between teams, monitor the budget, and keep the project on schedule may be a massive help. Not only can the agency see issues more objectively than partners may be able to, they can make sure that the customer isn't forgotten and that the marketing message is coming through loud and clear. It's very easy for the campaign to get bogged down in politicking, but if customers don't take any notice, no one will reap the rewards they're hoping for.

Do make sure, however, that the agency you engage has had plenty of experience in dealing with multi-partner projects: managing them well requires special skills and a consultative approach.

Develop benefits

Effective partnership marketing can make budgets work harder and increase sales when partners work together to provide solutions that meet customers' needs. This probably means co-operative product and service development and co-operative marketing, since these kinds of partnerships can deliver an impressive return on investment. Make sure you have a solid understanding of the emotional, commercial and functional drivers of your combined prospect. Just because you've recognised a gap in the market doesn't mean you automatically appeal to the market in the gap. But whatever the arrangement, the parties involved must work hard to assess and address the dynamics of the relationship.

Promote the relationship inside the business too

Key to the success of a joint campaign is the willingness of the staff on each side to make it happen. It's essential that time and effort goes into promoting the benefits of the arrangement to everyone who will be working on it, and that all concerns are addressed in full. Any doubts will eventually be communicated to the public, even if inadvertently. Include all parts of the business: if it's likely that as a result of the campaign you may receive invoicing requests or order amounts that are not the norm, you need to tell the appropriate departments to proceed on this occasion. You want to remove barriers to purchase, not inadvertently put them up!

COMMON MISTAKES

You compete, rather than collaborate

It can be hard to get into a collaborative mindset when marketing is normally focused on just one company's goals, but try not to get into a tit-for-tat situation where you and your partner fight over space or billing. It's important to be pragmatic and to come up with an approach that serves the campaign best and appeals to your customers.

Only one party benefits

Joint marketing efforts should result in joint success. Make sure that from the very outset, both parties explain clearly what success would 'look like' for them. If increased sales or orders are your objectives, think through how those will be managed: which party will be responsible for fulfilment, for example? How will revenue be shared? It may take some time to work out the details, but well worth it to save wrangling and misunderstandings at a later date.

THE BEST SOURCES OF HELP

Book:
Huxham, Chris and Vangen, Siv. *Managing to Collaborate: The Theory and Practice of Collaborative Advantage.* London: Routledge, 2005.

Website:
Partnership Marketing Agency:
www.partnershipmarketing.com

Communicating Customer Service

GETTING STARTED

Your business won't survive without customers, and you need to get across how much you value them. To communicate well externally, you need to have in place a clear, consistent, internal communications strategy too. If you have a team of people working with you, let them know how they each contribute to your business's success, and the way they interact with your customers is a key part of this.

FAQS

Who is responsible for customer service?

Everyone in a business contributes to overall customer satisfaction, even if their jobs do not involve direct customer contact. Broken delivery promises, inaccurate invoices, or poor telephone handling can cancel out the benefits of a good product or service.

Why are award programmes important to the success of customer service?

Customer service staff are in the front line, facing difficult customers and frequent problems. Award programmes can help to maintain motivation and demonstrate that their contribution is important.

Isn't customer service the same as marketing?

Certain aspects of customer service – understanding customer needs, delivering a service, tailoring the offer to meet customer requirements – are the same, but the scope of marketing is much broader.

Is customer service just a set of personal skills?

Personal skills are important, but a company can put in place processes and programmes that improve the customer's experience and make it easier and more convenient for the customer to do business.

MAKING IT HAPPEN

Communicate clearly

When a company changes its focus towards customer service, it is essential that everyone is involved. Change creates an atmosphere of uncertainty, so it is vital that everyone understands the important issues and feels that they can contribute to the success of the change. In an atmosphere of uncertainty, customer service levels can be adversely affected.

Build understanding

Organisational changes can have a significant impact on employees, suppliers, and distributors – so it is vital that they are thoroughly briefed. Change can be a powerful positive factor rather than a cause for concern, and change can demonstrate that a business is committed to improvement and progress.

Encourage commitment

Implementing a customer service policy requires commitment and involvement from all employees. Before implementing a programme, it is sensible to find what the level of commitment is and to include staff in discussion. The most important part of the process is the follow-up. Too many employees believe views will be ignored.

Encourage improvement

As far as possible, training should be offered to all staff to help them understand the importance of customer care. A customer satisfaction guide could be issued, describing the most important elements of customer service and the standards which apply.

Maintain motivation

Motivation and award programmes can help to maintain high levels of interest in the customer service programme and to build a high level of commitment to the programme's success. Award programmes that reward continued improvement in levels of customer satisfaction maintain momentum and give customer service programmes a high profile. They are therefore valuable in building team spirit and a commitment to excellence.

Provide a vision

Clear visions and strong, motivating language focus attention on the importance of customer service programmes. It is also essential that the programme is led from the top. A key figure should be involved personally in every aspect of the programmes – talking to groups of employees, appearing in company intranet broadcasts, and using every public relations opportunity to raise the profile of the programme.

Develop champions

The leader cannot achieve all the objectives alone, so it is essential that other people with influence can take on the role of supporting the message throughout the business. Management commentators often call these people 'champions'. Their task is to build commitment and enthusiasm for change. They may be the very people who could undermine change if left out of the process, though.

COMMON MISTAKES

Treating customer service as a departmental function

Customer service is left to those staff who are directly involved with customers. This is too limited a view, because customer service is relegated to a sales or complaints-handling process.

Managing customer service at departmental level

If customer service is treated as a line management function, staff will not appreciate its critical importance to the success of the business. Customer service must be led from the top, with the direct involvement of a senior manager.

Failure to develop customer service skills

It's a common misconception that customer service quality depends solely on personal skills. Customer service standards can be improved through training and through the introduction of customer service programmes.

Low recognition

Customer service has long suffered from low perceived status. Motivation and reward programmes, together with leadership from the top, can help to redress the balance.

THE BEST SOURCES OF HELP

Books:

Heppell, Michael. *Five Star Service, One Star Budget: How to Create Magic Moments for Your Customers That Get You Noticed, Remembered and Referred.* Harlow: Prentice Hall, 2006.

Reichheld, Frederick F. *The Loyalty Effect: The Hidden Force Behind Growth, Profits, and Lasting Value.* Boston, Massachusetts: Harvard Business School Press, 2001.

Website

Institute of Customer Service: **www.instituteofcustomerservice.com**

Handling Customer Problems

GETTING STARTED

Eventually, even the most professional service companies will inevitably face a problem with a customer that, if left unresolved, may lead to a loss of business. Customers who know that their problems are taken care of are more likely to be fully satisfied with the services that are available. A key factor in resolving customers' problems is the ability to reassure them that help is on the way. Having in place a process to respond quickly and effectively to a problem enables a company to deliver the highest standards of customer care at a time when the customer most needs it.

This process, sometimes called incident management, is particularly suitable for larger companies or if the customer is likely to suffer a great deal of inconvenience because of the incident. However, the principles can be applied to any business, whatever its size.

- In developing a response and support strategy, you should set a wide range of business objectives.
- The incident management approach is to appoint one person, trained in customer service skills, to deal with a customer throughout an incident.
- The role of the personal incident manager is to take responsibility for the provision of appropriate services.
- An incident management programme has two main elements – the infrastructure to deliver the service and the personal skills to provide the right level of customer care.
- Skilled staff are essential to the effective delivery of the service, and training may be necessary.
- Many equipment manufacturers use incident management techniques to support their customers after a disaster.

FAQS

Should incident management form part of all service offerings?

It depends on the type of service that is offered. If the service is critical to the customer's business process – telecommunications or computing, for example – incident management would be important. Disruption to those services could damage the customer's business.

Why is a personal incident manager necessary?

During an incident, effective co-ordination of support services and regular communication with customers are essential. By appointing a single person to take responsibility for co-ordination and communication, you can guarantee continuity and reassure customers by giving them a single point of contact.

Is it possible to plan for future incidents?

It isn't just possible; it is essential. Industry research indicates that a high proportion of companies who did not have a documented plan failed to recover lost business. Planning is just as important as quality support services.

MAKING IT HAPPEN

Deal with customer incidents

Customers who know that their problems are taken care of are more likely to be fully satisfied with the services that are available and will be happier to deal with the same company in the future. Quality experts found that a key factor in delivering time-guaranteed services was the ability to reassure customers that help was on the way. Customers would then be prepared to wait until help or support arrived, even if there was a long gap between reporting the incident and having it resolved. Other research has shown that customers whose complaints are satisfactorily dealt with are likely to be more loyal than those who had no complaint in the first place.

Identify opportunities for incident management
A number of scenarios can be used to identify situations where support like this could be valuable.
- The customer could suffer a great deal of inconvenience and stress as a result of the incident. Reducing the stress and inconvenience would help to demonstrate high levels of care and increase customer satisfaction.
- The incident could threaten the efficiency of the company business, and measures must be taken to limit the damage.
- The customer does not have the skills and resources to resolve the problems on the spot and is dependent on external forms of support.
- The customer has paid for a support package and has agreed to a certain level of response. The company must respond within the agreed levels.
- The speed of response is seen as a competitive differentiation and is positioned as an integral part of the service package.
- Failure to deal with the incident quickly could have a critical effect on the customer's business or personal activities.
- The incident could have legal implications, and the customer needs high levels of advice and guidance.

Set objectives for incident management
In developing a response and support strategy, you should set a wide range of business objectives:
- to provide the highest levels of quality response and customer support throughout an incident
- to minimise inconvenience for the customer
- to ensure that incidents are resolved promptly within agreed time scales
- to ensure that support resources are deployed effectively to maximise customer satisfaction

Introduce incident management
The incident management approach is to appoint one person, trained in customer service skills, to deal with a customer throughout an incident.

Incident management can be applied to any service-led organisation where the customer needs to be kept informed, for example, maintenance and support services for vital equipment or business continuity services where the customer faces difficult and unfamiliar decisions and needs support.

Appoint a personal incident manager
The role of the personal incident manager is to take responsibility for the provision of appropriate services and to reassure the customer that help and support are on the way. In the smaller company, this may be a senior manager, even the managing director, but whoever takes the role must have the authority to take appropriate action. The personal incident manager:

- takes the incoming calls from the customer, establishes the location, and identifies the form of support needed
- provides individual guidance to the customer on action to be taken with an indication of support provided
- deals with the customer's immediate queries
- makes detailed arrangements to put support services into operation
- monitors the progress of support services and keeps the customer up to date if possible

Offer business continuity services
Many equipment manufacturers use incident management techniques to support their customers after an incident such as fire, accident, or system breakdown. If the customer loses essential equipment such as computers or telephones for an extended period, this could seriously threaten the future of their business. Industry research shows that only a minority of companies dependent on the computer have a formal disaster recovery strategy and points out that loss of a system for more than a few days could put them out of business.

Plan and implement business continuity plans
A business continuity programme has a number of stages:
- helping the customer to identify critical activities that should be covered in the event of a disaster
- training staff and managers to prepare for a disaster by simulating the conditions of an emergency
- preparing a contingency plan for business continuity
- providing replacement equipment and services
- providing support and project management resources
- providing full support to restore normal service and maintain business continuity

Throughout a disaster, the customer would have access to an incident manager who would co-ordinate the rescue and recovery activities and provide advice, guidance, and support. The principle is similar to that of the personal incident manager, where customers are given reassurance that incidents will be resolved and that they can be sure of the highest standards of support throughout the incident.

Create the infrastructure for incident management
The programme has two main elements: the infrastructure to deliver the service and the personal skills to provide the right level of customer care. The infrastructure requires a significant investment to ensure that the service can be delivered rapidly and efficiently throughout the country. Depending on the complexity of the project, it might include:
- communications to provide a rapid response to customer queries, and put the service into operation
- a trained support team to deliver the service
- quality-controlled suppliers to support the direct response team
- a control centre to manage the operations and co-ordinate the response

- a network of contacts and suppliers to provide the specialist services that form part of the response

Develop the right skills

Skilled staff are essential to the effective delivery of the service. The skills requirements would include:

- incident management skills, to deal with customers who may be in stressful situations
- project management skills, to co-ordinate and implement a response
- technical skills, to deliver the service
- communications skills, to co-ordinate the elements of the programme

COMMON MISTAKES

Failing to communicate with the customer during an incident

Research shows that customers who receive regular progress updates feel reassured that they are getting the right level of support. Anxiety levels are high during an incident, but regular communication helps customers to deal with the incident and contributes to overall customer satisfaction.

Not having an escalation procedure

A company should have a formal escalation procedure for dealing with customer incidents. If support staff cannot resolve an incident within an agreed time scale, the incident should be reported to a more senior manager, who would then commit more resources. If there is no escalation procedure, the incident can get out of hand and damage customer relationships.

THE BEST SOURCES OF HELP

Books:

Lovelock, Christopher, and Jochen Wirtz. *Services Marketing: People, Technology, Strategy*. 6th ed. Harlow: FT Prentice Hall, 2007.

Wilson, Alan, et al. *Services Marketing*. New York: McGraw-Hill, 2008.

Websites:

Chartered Institute of Marketing: **www.cim.co.uk**
Institute of Customer Service:
 www.www.instituteofcustomerservice.com

Increasing Customer Lifetime Value

GETTING STARTED

'Customer lifetime value' (CLV or LTV) is a way of measuring how much your customers are worth over the time they buy your products and services. Increases in customer retention can increase sales and profits significantly. It is important to retain customers, but not at the cost of other essential marketing activities.

Putting customers into key categories helps to clarify analysis and acts as the basis for marketing activities designed to improve customer lifetime value.

FAQS

What's the difference between customer lifetime value and customer loyalty programmes?

Customer loyalty programmes are designed to retain as many customers as possible, regardless of their real value. The customer lifetime value calculation indicates the contribution individual customers make to profitability.

Why are lapsed customers important?

If they can be 'revived', they tend to behave like new customers and become regular buyers once again, with good potential lifetime value.

Is customer retention more important than acquisition?

Acquisition should never be neglected, because existing business may decline for reasons outside your control. Industry experience indicates, however, that existing customers make a comparatively greater contribution when marketing costs are taken into consideration.

Do we want to retain all our customers?

Not necessarily. Some customers may not be profitable. Using customer lifetime value, you can calculate the cost and contribution of each customer.

MAKING IT HAPPEN

Apply the customer lifetime value concept

Customer lifetime value is a way of measuring how much your customers are worth to you, over the length of time that they remain your customers.

The lifetime for customers will vary from industry to industry, and from brand to brand. The lifetime of customers should come to an end when their contribution ceases to be profitable unless steps are taken to revitalise them.

Benefits from customer lifetime value

Industry experience indicates that a number of benefits apply.

- A 5 per cent increase in customer retention can create a 125 per cent increase in profits.
- A 10 per cent increase in retailer retention can translate to a 20 per cent increase in sales.
- Extending customer life cycles by three years can treble profits per customer.

Identify categories of customer

Before calculating customer lifetime value, it is possible to analyse your customers according to four key attributes. This can help to clarify analysis and act as the basis for marketing activities to improve customer lifetime value:

- frequency – how often they purchase (regular customers are more likely to purchase in the future)
- recency – how much time has elapsed since the last purchase (recent customers are more likely to purchase again)
- amount – how much they spend (higher-spending customers are likely to be more committed)
- category – what sort of product they buy (some products will be more profitable than others and some may be one-off purchases)

Calculate lifetime value

In a consumer business, customer lifetime value is calculated, in practice, by analysing the behaviour of a group of customers who:

- have the same recruitment date
- are recruited from the same source
- bought the same types of product

In a business-to-business environment, a similar approach can be used.

- Isolate particular customers, and examine them individually.
- Analyse the behaviour of different groups, segmenting your customer database by factors such as industry, annual turnover, or staff numbers.

The basic calculation has three stages:

- identify a discrete group of customers for tracking.
- record (or estimate) each revenue and cost for this group of customers, by campaign or season.
- calculate the contribution, by campaign or season.

Refine the calculation

Other factors can be introduced to make the calculation more relevant. In a business-to-business environment, for example, it may be the sales representatives who generate sales. In this case, the calculation should include the representative's 'running costs' and the cost of any centrally produced sales support material.

Evaluate a campaign

The table shows the calculations for a group of customers who were recruited through a direct response advertising campaign that ran in the spring of year 1. The table tracks their expenditure over a five-year period.

Year	Annual customer expenditure	Annual marketing costs	Annual net contribution
0	£12,000	£15,000	£–3,000
1	£10,000	£6,000	£4,000
2	£8,000	£6,000	£2,000
3	£7,000	£6,000	£1,000
4	£6,000	£4,000	£2,000
5	£5,000	£4,000	£1,000
Totals	£48,000	£41,000	£7,000

Divide the total contribution by the number of customers in the group. Say there are one thousand customers: the average lifetime value per customer is £7. But this compares favourably with a short-term analysis which, in the first year, would show a loss of £3 per customer recruited.

Analyse the results

A company may offer different products or brands, which are marketed under different cost centres. If a customer is a customer of more than one cost/profit centre, there is a choice of approaches:

- examine customers of each brand and ignore multi-purchases;
- build a more detailed model that combines and allocates the cumulative costs as well as the cumulative profit in the appropriate proportions.

Use customer lifetime values to improve marketing performance

There are four important applications:

- setting target customer acquisition costs
- allocating acquisition funds
- selecting acquisition offers
- supporting customer retention activities

In the example above, the decision was taken in Year 4 to reduce marketing costs on this group of customers. Equally valid may be an increase in expenditure aimed at reactivating customers – this is a classic retention activity.

Set target customer acquisition costs

If a customer is expected to generate more than one sale, the allowable cost can be greater than the cost allowed for the first sale – the classic loss-leader approach to customer acquisition, illustrated in the table above. However, overspending on customer acquisition can also be ruinous. A reasonable calculation is to recruit only from those sources that yield new customers at less than half the estimated lifetime value. On that basis, the worst sources will have a cost per customer close to a lifetime value, while the average cost per customer should be far lower.

Allocate acquisition funds

Different recruitment sources will provide customers with different lifetime values. After identifying those values, spend more on the best sources.

Select acquisition offers

The lifetime value of a customer may depend on the type and value of their initial purchase. In turn, this can lead to decisions about which products and offers to use when advertising externally, or when considering how to upgrade existing customers.

Support customer retention activities

Once the typical lifetime value of a group of customers is known, companies can decide how hard to work at retaining them. It is not a foregone conclusion that all customers are worth having. Activities should be tailored to the customers who are most valuable.

Increase value with new offers

A financial services company can increase customer lifetime value by cross-selling a range of products and services.

COMMON MISTAKES

Trying to retain the wrong customers

Customer retention costs money in terms of sales and marketing funds, so do bear in mind that not all customers are worth keeping. You should carefully select the customers who are likely to yield the highest returns over a period of time and prioritise the allocation of marketing resources to these.

Offering customers a limited range of products

When you have identified the most valuable customers, you need to have a wide range of products or services to offer them. Cross-selling and up-selling are the best ways to increase customer lifetime value, but this can be difficult with a limited product range. Customers are your company's most valuable asset; think about 'share of customer wallet' rather than just share of market.

Spending too much on acquiring new customers

Customer lifetime value analysis reinforces a traditional marketing rule of thumb, that it costs less to retain existing customers than to acquire new ones. Overemphasis on new business development could be a bad move, since existing customers are easier to sell to.

THE BEST SOURCES OF HELP

Book:
Reichheld, Frederick F. *Loyalty Rules! How Today's Leaders Build Lasting Relationships*. Boston, Massachusetts: Harvard Business School Press, 2003.

Website:
Peppers & Rogers: **www.1to1.com**

Setting Up a Customer Interaction Centre

GETTING STARTED

The best way to retain customers is through proactive relationship management and outstanding customer service. An integrated approach to customer contact is essential and a customer interaction centre integrates people, technology, and customer data. It brings together the staff who deal directly with customers and the support teams into a single, integrated team and gives customers the benefit of a single point of contact. The organisation also benefits, as it is able to create 'virtual teams' that respond rapidly to requests or queries from customers and is also better placed to share best practice between business units.

FAQS

Why isn't a call centre sufficient to handle customer contact?

Call centres were set up to handle telephone calls. They are staffed by people trained in telephone techniques and they are designed to deliver a personal service. Customers who communicate with a company via the Web or e-mail may not receive the same level of personal service because of the way electronic communications are routed through the company.

Isn't it best to concentrate resources on a call centre because most contact is by telephone?

The trends are changing as more and more people recognise the convenience of ordering electronically, 24 hours a day, 7 days a week, when call centres may be closed. Companies who do not offer the full range of facilities may lose business opportunities.

Who should control the customer interaction centre?

The customer interaction centre should be more than an extension of the call centre. It should be an integral part of the sales or marketing department and should be treated as a strategic resource that contributes to long-term customer retention.

Should the interaction centre be limited to telephone and Internet technology?

Customer interaction is getting more and more sophisticated. Multimedia communication is becoming increasingly common in consumer and business markets. The interaction centre should be capable of adapting to new technological developments.

MAKING IT HAPPEN
Retain customer loyalty
Increasingly, companies recognise that the best way to retain customers is through proactive relationship management and outstanding customer service. A key element in that strategy is an integrated approach to customer contact – a customer interaction centre. The interaction centre takes the traditional call centre a stage further, integrating people, technology, and customer data.

Deal with multiple contact
Customers can now contact organisations in many different ways, including the Internet, phone, e-mail, or fax. The integration of the Internet and telephony in multimedia call centres is taking the process even further. On the surface, that level of choice and convenience should lead to better customer service. But, in reality, the opposite is happening. When each channel has its own separate 'information silo' on the customer, there is no integration.

Ensure consistent service standards
If you offer your customers different contact channels and don't integrate your customer information, you could face problems. Here's a situation you might recognise. A customer enters a request via the Web, then calls a customer-service representative in a call centre to get a status report. If the call centre has access only to its own departmental data, it may not even recognise the customer. This could result in an embarrassing phone conversation and possibly a lost customer.

Provide a single point of contact
A customer interaction centre brings together staff who deal directly with customers (customer-facing staff) and support teams in a single, integrated location. Staff, backed by sophisticated information and communication systems, provide customers with a single point of contact and access to the combined skills and resources of the whole company.

Bring together all customer-facing staff
Staff from logistics, credit control, accounting, and administration – as well as customer service and technical support – can work together in a customer interaction centre. By working more closely, the company can create 'virtual teams' that respond rapidly to requests or queries and bring together the right combination of skills for the customer's business. This high level of integration will result in even better alignment between customer service, supply/demand planning and logistics operations. The company can also share best practice more easily between business units.

Speed up communication
The centre should provide a sophisticated technology infrastructure that will make it easier for customers to do business with the company, by supporting a rapid-response and a high-quality service. Integrated telephony systems ensure that when a customer telephones, the call is directed to a named contact with the appropriate skills and knowledge. If the first contact is busy, the customer will be transferred to another team member with the same skills and knowledge. The team member who answers the call will have access to all of the customer's account information on screen, and this information will be updated automatically whenever a customer calls.

Integrate all customer information
At the heart of the infrastructure is an interconnected data networking solution that collects, stores, manages, and distributes all relevant customer information via a single, integrated customer database. The database is updated from all customer channels and is accessible by all customer-facing staff. The aim is to make communications simpler and quicker by giving every member of the customer service team access to the most up-to-date information on a customer's business. The solution can also include business rules and workflow functions to ensure that the right level of resources is applied to different types of customer interaction. A solution like this could, for example, assign priorities to key-account customers or escalate support requests that have not been resolved within agreed service levels.

Make it easy to do business
Your customers will get consistent service, whichever way they contact your organisation. Integrating the centre with electronic commerce systems will simplify the purchasing processes even further. Customers who work with a number of different locations or divisions will now have a single point of contact for all their dealings with the company. This is important because customers are looking for ways of simplifying their own purchasing process. Centralised support is becoming more and more important to customers. By providing a single point of contact for sales and technical and service queries, the company can ensure a rapid, effective response to all customer support requirements.

Develop a more personal service
Many traditional personalisation initiatives have been built on incomplete customer data. A personal web page, for example, would probably have been based only on the customer's Internet interactions, completely ignoring any voice contact through a call centre. With an integrated strategy, an organisation can make full use of all its customer interactions, giving it a significant competitive advantage in the drive for personalisation.

Plan for continued improvement
The centre infrastructure can be scaled up to accommodate growth in demand. It also provides a stable

platform for developing advanced applications that will allow the company to improve customer service even further.

The interaction centre co-ordinates all forms of customer interaction:

- consistently managing customer interactions through multiple communications channels, including phone, fax, e-mail, Web, and video
- defining and applying business rules to customer interactions
- routing customer interactions – according to business rules – to appropriate available resources
- integrating corporate data into customer interactions

This approach brings together all the elements needed to strengthen customer relationships and retain loyalty.

COMMON MISTAKES
Limiting the scope of communications
An interaction centre should cover all forms of communication. It is not a telephone call centre with other technology treated as an add-on. From the outset, the centre should be capable of communicating via traditional and new media. Plans should also be in place to incorporate emerging media.

Concentrating on the wrong standards
If the centre is treated as a technology-led function, customer service may suffer. Companies who want to maintain standards should set quality and performance standards that are focused on customer needs, not technical performance.

Failing to develop a personalised service
A customer interaction centre provides a great deal of valuable customer information that can be used to develop a personalised service. If the information simply stays on file, the company is losing a great opportunity.

Limiting the use of information
The customer interaction centre is only a starting point for information management. The information can be used to support decision-making and business development throughout a company. Linking the information to what Microsoft calls a 'digital nervous system' ensures that people throughout a company are able to act on the very latest information.

THE BEST SOURCES OF HELP
Book:
Dawson, Keith. *The Call Center Handbook: The Complete Guide to Starting, Running and Improving Your Customer Contact Center*. 5th ed. New York: CMP Books, 2004.

Website:
Contact Centre Association: **www.cca.org.uk/cca**

Building a Mailing List

GETTING STARTED
The most important element in a direct marketing programme is the mailing list, and getting hold of a top-quality one is key. There are several routes you can use. If you have the resources, you can use internal sources to compile a valuable mailing list of both customers and prospects. Alternatively, you can rent or purchase existing lists from sources such as list brokers, websites, publishers, or other organisations offering lists of their customers, or you may wish to commission a specially tailored list that matches your requirements exactly. Three of the biggest problems in list management are duplication, incomplete addresses, and out-of-date information.

FAQS
My company has a mailing list of customers and prospects. Can I offer that list to other organisations?
You can market the list to other organisations. However, you should be aware of the implications of data protection legislation. Under the Data Protection Act, customers have a right to know how their data is being used. Always include a clause asking customers if they are willing to allow their data to be passed to other organisations.

Is it better to buy or rent an external mailing list?
It depends how frequently you plan to mail. Rented lists are for a single use only, charged on a cost-per-thousand basis, and the owners have security techniques to counter unauthorised repeat use. A single campaign may be enough, but experience indicates that multiple mailings generally achieve better results. You would need to compare the cost of buying with renting the list for, say, three mailings.

Is a list compiled internally as effective as a list sourced from a direct mail list specialist?
An internal list is only as good as the sources you have available. However, if your target market is existing customers and good prospects, it may be adequate. An external list supplier may not have the same detailed understanding of that market. However, if you are moving into new markets where you have no existing

contacts, it may be more effective to draw on the resources of a company with experience in the market.

MAKING IT HAPPEN
Create an effective list
The most important element in a direct marketing programme is the mailing list. In its simplest form, the list simply includes names, addresses, job titles, and telephone numbers. This can be refined by adding information on buying patterns, lifestyle, and many other factors to provide a comprehensive picture of customers and prospects.

Use internal sources of information
Sometimes your business will already have a mailing list that you could benefit from. Draw on the following sources of information, including:
- customer records
- customer correspondence, including complaints
- website requests for information
- warranty records
- service records
- sales prospect files
- requests for information from the website
- salesforce reports
- records of lapsed customers
- market research surveys
- business information library

Make sure that you are not contravening data protection legislation before you contact these people.

Segment internal lists
Customer records can quickly provide you with names and addresses of individuals, but to get more specific information, you will have to carry out further analysis. Simple segmentation might give you categories such as:
- customers who have bought in the last six months
- lapsed customers
- customers who spend over £X per annum

Identify external sources of information
If you want to compile your own lists, you can use external sources to supplement internal information. External sources include:
- customers' and prospects' websites
- databases and information services available via the Internet
- general or industry-specific trade directories
- membership directories for associations and groups
- local telephone or chamber of commerce directories
- specialist magazines and yearbooks
- business reports and industry surveys in newspapers
- published surveys
- summaries or reports on consumer surveys
- government and industry statistics, including census, industry reports, and trade association statistics

Source external lists
If you do not have the resources to compile your own lists or if you are moving into new markets, you may be able to make use of existing lists. Lists are available from several sources:
- list brokers, who offer different categories of list
- websites
- magazine publishers
- directory publishers
- trade associations or professional institutes
- exhibition and event organisers
- commercial organisations
- retailers

Assess external lists
If you plan to use a ready-made list, you should check the following:
- How closely does the list match your customer profile?
- How much wastage will there be – that is, how much of the list falls outside your customer profile?
- Are there any restrictions on the use of the list?

Commission a list
Standard lists may not give you the degree of match you need, and you may wish to commission a specially tailored list. The success of such a list is directly related to the quality of the brief, and you should provide the supplier with a detailed description of your target audience.

Keep refining your lists
Many standard lists and lists you have compiled yourself may not match your requirements exactly. To improve coverage or to make them more precise, you need to refine them continually. These are some of the actions you can take:
- ensure that new customer and prospect data is added to the list
- include coupons and other reply mechanisms with every form of communication and add the responses to your lists
- encourage the salesforce to provide up-to-date customer and prospect information
- maintain a search programme on the Internet and in publications to identify new prospects for your list

Segment your lists
The strength of direct marketing is that it can provide a high degree of precision, so your lists must be structured carefully. Below is a basic approach to segmenting consumer and business-to-business lists.
   Consumer lists:
- marital status
- income level
- occupation category
- home owner/home value
- car owner/car value
- personal interests
- credit card holder
- shopping patterns
- holiday preferences
- insurance status
- leisure interests

- brand preferences
- recent purchase history
- reading/viewing habits
  Business lists:
- type of business
- size of business
- number of employees
- annual expenditure
- average order size
- purchasing frequency
- head office/local purchasing
- purchasing history
- key contacts
- job title
- budget authority

Check the accuracy of lists
To reduce waste in your mailing campaigns, it is important that you regularly check lists for accuracy. Three of the biggest problems are:
- duplication, where the same individual appears several times, possibly in different guises, for example, Ron Smith, R.T. Smith, Mr Smith. This is not only wasteful, it also irritates the recipient
- incomplete addresses
- out-of-date information

Comply with data protection legislation
The basic premise behind the Data Protection Act is, if you have data, use it properly. The Act works in two ways:
- it places obligations on data users. They must be open about how they use data and follow sound information-handling practice specified in the Act.
- it gives every individual access to information held about them.

Under the Act, all data users must register with the Information Commissioner. Users must:
- obtain and process personal data fairly and lawfully
- hold the data only for the purposes specified in the register entry
- hold only accurate data that is relevant and not excessive for the purpose
- ensure personal data is accurate and kept up to date
- not hold data for longer than necessary

The Information Commissioner has a helpline (01625 545 745) and a useful website at: **www.ico.gov.uk**.

COMMON MISTAKES
Using out-of-date lists
A mailing list is out of date almost as soon as it is compiled. People change jobs, move, or change interests. List maintenance must be a continuous process.

Failing to segment lists
Direct marketing works most effectively when it is aimed at a specific audience. The more you segment your mailing lists, the more precisely you can communicate. Different groups within your target market may have different purchasing needs or spending levels.

THE BEST SOURCES OF HELP
Book:
Tapp, Alan. *Principles of Direct and Database Marketing*. 4th ed. London: FT Prentice Hall, 2008.

Website:
The Direct Marketing Association: **www.dma.org.uk**

Creating Impressive Direct Mail Material

GETTING STARTED
When you are marketing your product or service, you may find you need an effective and precise marketing tool that you can personalise in order to more accurately reflect the needs of customers and prospective customers. If so, direct mail may be what you need. It can be eye-catching and creative, and allows you to include different types of enclosure to provide additional details on the product or service being offered.

Another benefit of direct mail is that it is easy to measure its results precisely, so that you can assess how you've done with a particular campaign or approach. As part of this process, you need to include an easy response mechanism for the customer, such as a reply-paid envelope, or contact details, such as an e-mail address, so that your customers can give you feedback.

FAQS
Don't customers just throw direct mail in the bin?
No, but attitudes vary enormously. Many people may open direct mail, but not all will open and *read it*. Business managers opened 70 per cent of their direct mail but, on average, filed only 20 per cent. Executives are now also starting to employ growing numbers of direct mail 'filterers', who open their mail for them and decide whether it's worth passing on.

Is it possible to create effective direct mail?
Yes, but like any other marketing activity, you'll get the best results from working towards a specific objective. The more information you have, the more focused the work. Direct mail is a very precise medium, so it is possible to create highly customised and attractive mailings that meet the information needs of your chosen prospective customers (prospects).

How far can personalisation go in direct mail?
Of course, mailings to a small number of customers can easily be personalised, and should be. Provided you have the budget, larger mailings can be personalised down to individual level (one-to-one marketing). As an example, you could write individual letters to each of your prospects, or include an incentive tailored to their individual preferences. Practical financial constraints usually prevent this degree of personalisation, so most companies concentrate on limited customisation, addressing specific sector concerns or tailoring special offers to different types of business.

Can the quality of direct mail creative work be measured?
Direct mail is an extremely accountable medium, and the results can be measured precisely, making it possible to judge whether or not a particular creative approach has worked. However, creative work is only one of the factors that influence campaign success, so many companies test different creative approaches to try to identify how they affect results. Remember, though, that the offer's recipient is more important than the presentation of the offer itself, so targeting should be your priority.

MAKING IT HAPPEN
Create good-quality mailing material
Direct mail is the most precise marketing medium, but campaigns will only be effective if they combine precise targeting with good creative work.

In theory anything can be sent by post, but most mailings consist primarily of printed material – letters, leaflets, and brochures. Three-dimensional objects can be mailed and can stimulate interest, but they must be relevant and cost effective. A striking envelope design can also add impact to a mailing. The Post Office has a dedicated team to provide all the information you need to ensure your mailings conform to their regulations and to help to set up Freepost and Business Reply services.

Use direct mail letters effectively
Letters are a universal communications medium and an integral element of any direct mail campaign. They can be used on their own as a personalised form of communication, and can also be used to support and personalise other standard mailing items. Letters can be customised easily and cost-effectively to meet different sector marketing requirements.

Personalise letters
Personalised one-to-one mailings are an ideal form of communication for companies with detailed information on their prospects. The letter should reflect the individual's main interests and concerns, and the offer can be tailored to the individual prospect. Subsequent mailings can build an individual relationship with the prospect.

The key features of this type of letter are:
- it is personalised to the individual reader
- it offers direct and valuable benefits
- it builds future relationships with the customer by promising regular offers

Letters can also be customised by market sector, offering specific benefits to groups of customers.

Use letters to support other mailing material
Direct mail letters can also be used to accompany other material – a product brochure, management guide, or even an invoice, for example. The letter can customise the mailing by including information specific to the individual prospect or market sector, or by making a further offer to the prospect.

Include enclosures
Enclosures can include:
- catalogues
- sales leaflets or brochures
- price lists
- management reports or surveys
- information on special offers
- samples, free gifts, or incentives

There are a number of criteria for selecting enclosures. They should:
- be relevant to the prospect's needs
- not make the mailing impractical or costly because of size or weight
- improve response, size of order, or frequency of order – if they do not, they are an unnecessary cost

Treat envelopes creatively
Postal authorities specify a number of preferred envelope sizes which help them to handle mail more efficiently. Companies that wish to use specific postal response services such as Freepost or Business Reply use the preferred layouts indicated in the authority's design specification. However, using non-standard envelope sizes can add greater impact to a mailing. Envelopes can be designed in a number of ways to achieve greater impact:
- they can include advertising messages
- addresses can be handwritten to add a personal touch
- they can incorporate corporate design elements such as logos or company colours

But be aware of occasions when a clearly, but wrongly identified envelope may depress response, such as if the item looks like a routine statement.

Create three-dimensional enclosures
Three-dimensional enclosures can add impact and novelty value to a mailing. They can be used to send product samples by mail, to send promotional items, or to improve response by creating interest. However, it is important that they are relevant to the prospect's needs, that they do not make the mailing too expensive, and that they do not contravene postal regulations.

Include a response mechanism

If your mailing is designed to stimulate action, it should include an easy-to-use response mechanism, such as a reply-paid card or envelope, or contact details, such as a Freephone telephone number, e-mail address, or website address.

Use professional creative and production services

Quality and impact are essential to the success of a direct mail campaign. Creating an effective direct mail item requires professional skills, and is best handled by suitably experienced people. Although many of the direct mail processes are straightforward, your company may not have the skills or resources to achieve the best possible results. External specialists provide a range of direct mail services, including copywriting and design, printing letters, and producing three-dimensional enclosures.

Specialists include:

- direct mail agencies
- advertising agencies
- marketing communication consultancies
- design consultancies
- creative consultancies
- printers

However, there may be occasions when you decide to create simple direct mail items yourself.

Write persuasive copy

Use a powerful headline to get the attention of the reader. Words such as 'free', 'new', and 'improved' attract attention, while price benefits such as 'sale' and 'reduced' are also useful. Keep your writing style simple, with short sentences and paragraphs; in longer mailing items, use headings and subheadings to make sure that the reader picks up key messages without having to read the complete text. Tell your prospects what they need to know in order to make a decision about your product or service. Your message should deal with your customers' most important concerns and requirements. Describe benefits to the prospect, not features of the product: for example, a power drill that features extremely high operating speeds may be technically interesting, but the benefits to a builder are greater productivity and the opportunity to finish a job quickly. Offer the prospect a clear, powerful proposition. Your copy should encourage the prospect to take action – contact the company for more information, ask for a demonstration, or order immediately to qualify for a promotional offer. Describe your biggest benefit first, then remember that everything that follows should be designed to make the potential customer move on to the next stage.

Create a well-designed layout

Design quality is also important in getting a message to prospects clearly and effectively. To do this:

- keep the layout simple so that the customer can focus on, and understand, the information quickly
- use photographs, diagrams, or illustrations if they help to clarify a point or create impact
- use the most legible type-faces and sizes
- use bold headings or a larger type size for emphasis

COMMON MISTAKES

Using mailing unnecessarily

When customers already know your company and do business with you, it can be off-putting for them to be treated as 'prospects'. Always check that your mailing is an effective means of communicating.

Failing to plan

All mailing activity must be planned with sufficient time and resources. Rushing a mailing can lead to embarrassing and costly mistakes. Not anticipating response can lead to disappointed customers.

Failing to measure

Direct mail campaigns are measured on their results: they should deliver enquiries or sales. If they do not deliver results, even the most creative campaigns should be considered failures. Make sure that you set realistic targets for your campaign. If you do not reach the targets, change the targeting, the offer, the format, or timing until you find one that delivers the results you want.

THE BEST SOURCES OF HELP

Book:
Bird, Drayton. *Commonsense Direct and Digital Marketing.* 5th ed. London: Kogan Page, 2007.

Websites:
The Institute of Direct Marketing:
www.theidm.co.uk
Royal Mail: **www.royalmail.com**

Improving the Response to Direct Mail

GETTING STARTED

Even with the ubiquity of the Internet today, direct mail still has an important role to play: the UK Direct Mail Information Service reports that an estimated £27 billion worth of business is generated by it every year. Someone is clearly making money from it, but are you? This actionlist will help you and your business get a better response rate from a direct mail campaign. Many different factors can affect response rates; it is important to test the variables before committing all your resources to a particular approach, and you should aim for a realistic figure that is within your budget.

- Do try as far as you can to define your target market precisely. The more precisely you target, the better your response rates will be. Make it easy for your prospects to respond, and test your approach before committing resources to the full campaign.
- Performance can be improved by integrating the campaign with other marketing activities.
- If budget allows, you can develop a series of split campaigns. A series of mailings will make sure that you meet your response targets.
- Getting the mailing list right is vital. Check all internal sources of information and be sure that they are up to date. Customer records invariably generate the highest response rates when they are mailed with relevant information.
- If you are moving into new market sectors, internal lists may not provide the information you need. To achieve a high response rate, check how closely the list matches your customer profile.
- You could decide to commission a specially tailored list that matches your requirements exactly.
- Keep refining your lists. To improve response and reduce waste in your mailing campaigns, it is important that your lists are regularly checked for accuracy.
- Personalised one-to-one mailings are an ideal form of communication for companies with detailed information about their prospects.
- Direct mail response levels can increase significantly when telemarketing is used.

FAQS

Why are direct mail responses so low?

The figures quoted are industry averages. They can vary upwards or downwards, depending on the industry and the type of mailing. Remember that a small percentage of a mass mailing can provide you with a reasonable level of new prospects. To put the response rates into perspective, compare the response and the cost of response with an equivalent spend on advertising.

Should direct mailing always be tested?

If it is practical, test direct mail on a small proportion of the market. Although direct mail is a precise medium, testing can refine the process even further. With so many variables in a mailing campaign, you can test different elements individually and plan your full campaign on the basis of the best response rate.

Should direct mail effectiveness be measured by response or by sales?

The ultimate test of any marketing campaign is an increase in profitable sales. However, direct mail, on its own, cannot deliver sales. Sales depend on pricing, the quality of your products, sales representatives, customer service, competitive activity, and many other factors. Direct mail should be given a specific role and measured by how it fulfils that role.

MAKING IT HAPPEN

Set target response levels

- Response levels as low as 1 or 2 per cent are regarded as the industry norm.
- Response rates in the region of 5 per cent are regarded as high.
- Response rates in the region of 10–20 per cent have been reported by companies who have integrated other forms of marketing communications.

Define your target market precisely

Do you want to reach all customers and prospects, or are you targeting specific groups? Direct marketing is a precise medium, so your campaign could be aimed at one key decision-maker or thousands of potential users. The more precisely you target, the better your response rates will be.

Integrate the campaign with other marketing activities

Direct marketing campaigns can run at any time. However, performance can be improved by integrating the campaign with other marketing activities, such as an exhibition, advertising campaigns, or salesforce calls. With integrated campaigns, overall awareness levels among customers and prospects will be much higher. Your direct marketing offer will have a much higher chance of success.

Choose the right campaign frequency

A single mailshot, telephone call, or direct response advertisement may produce results, but a series of quality contacts will have greater impact and make sure you meet your response targets. Multiple direct marketing activities provide a number of benefits:

- they raise levels of awareness with each contact.
- they follow up contacts who have not responded.
- they move individual respondents further along the decision-making process.

Make it easy for prospects to respond

If you want to improve response rates, clearly you have to make it easy for your prospects to respond. Website or e-mail addresses, Freepost, and Freephone facilities provide easy-to-use response mechanisms that can boost response. You should monitor the response levels from different sources to see which is the most effective.

Test your campaign
To guarantee the success of your campaign, you should test your approach before committing resources to the full campaign. There are a number of variables that can be tested:
- the offer
- the creative approach
- the target audience
- the response mechanism
- frequency and timing
- integration with other communications programmes

Use split campaigns
If budget allows, you can develop a series of campaigns that vary by offer, creative approach, response mechanism, frequency, and timing.

Improve your mailing lists
Getting the mailing list right is vital. Basic mailing lists simply include names, addresses, job titles, and phone numbers of customers and prospects. The basic list can be refined by adding information about buying patterns, lifestyle, and many other factors, all of which provide a comprehensive picture of customers and prospects.

Check all internal sources of information
Your customer records are probably your most valuable asset, as existing customers invariably show the highest response rate when they are mailed with relevant information. The most important sources are:
- customer records
- customer correspondence, including complaints
- warranty records
- service records
- sales prospect files
- website registrations
- salesforce reports
- records of lapsed customers

Simple segmentation of your internal lists might give you categories such as:
- customers who have bought in the last six months
- lapsed customers
- customers who spend over £X a year

Add external sources of information
Your internal lists are likely to yield high response rates, but if you're moving into new market sectors, they may not provide the information you need. External lists are available from a number of sources, including list brokers, magazine publishers, directory publishers, trade associations or professional institutes, commercial organisations, and retailers. To achieve a high response rate, check how closely the list matches your customer profile.

Commission a special list
Standard lists may not give you the degree of match you need. The successful preparation of a tailored list is directly related to the quality of the brief, so provide the supplier with a detailed description of your target audience.

Keep refining your lists
- Make sure that the list is kept up to date with new customer and prospect data.
- Include coupons and other reply mechanisms with every communication, and add the responses to your lists.
- Encourage the sales force to provide up-to-date customer and prospect information.
- Maintain an active search programme in appropriate websites, magazines, and newspapers to identify new prospects for your list.

Use personalised letters
Personalised one-to-one mailings are an ideal form of communication for companies with detailed information about their prospects.

Direct mail letters can be personalised in a number of ways, by:
- including the name in the address and greeting only: 'Dear Mr Jones'
- including the name throughout: '. . . and Mr Jones, you'll be glad to know that you've won a special prize. . .'

Use telemarketing
Response levels can increase significantly if direct mail is used in conjunction with telemarketing. It offers a range of benefits because it is:
- selective: contact can be initiated and maintained with all or selected groups of customers and prospects
- precise: the calls can be targeted
- flexible: the offer and the message can be varied
- fast: calls can be made immediately
- responsive: because telemarketing is interactive, it encourages response
- measurable: the effectiveness of a telemarketing campaign can be measured precisely

COMMON MISTAKES
Setting unrealistic response rates
Direct mail is a precise medium, but it's easy to set unrealistic targets for response: figures such as 5 or 6 per cent are seen as extremely high in many industries, for example. If you want a much higher response rate, you may need to use other marketing media or invest more in the campaign.

Failing to integrate direct mail with other activities
Direct mail works most effectively when it is part of an integrated marketing campaign. Advertising can be used to raise the company profile. For example, direct mail would be used to reach specific prospects with a targeted

offer, and telemarketing could be used to back up the mailing with follow-up calls. Response rates from integrated campaigns are generally higher because direct mail is given a specific task in that campaign.

Poor mailing lists

Good response rates depend on the quality of your mailing lists. If your lists contain duplicate addresses, out-of-date information, or incorrect data, response will be poor. Refine your lists continuously to avoid this.

THE BEST SOURCES OF HELP
Book:
Bird, Drayton. *Commonsense Direct and Digital Marketing*. 5th ed. London: Kogan Page, 2007.

Website:
The Institute of Direct Marketing:
www.theidm.co.uk

Planning a Cost-effective Direct Marketing Campaign

GETTING STARTED

For businesses of all sizes, direct marketing works most effectively when it is aimed at a precise audience that cannot be easily reached by any other medium. A campaign should be carefully planned in accordance with the target market and the product or service concerned. Short-term results can be measured accurately and directly by the level of response, so the effectiveness of a campaign can be assessed quickly. There are, however, many different factors that can affect the outcome, such as product price or the quality of the campaign material. As with any direct approach, it is essential to make it as easy as possible for customers to respond.

FAQS

Is direct marketing the same as direct mail?
No. Direct marketing (DM) is any marketing activity that depends on a direct and measurable response. Conventional advertising can be 'direct', as can telephone, fax, e-mail and, of course, the Internet. Direct mail is direct marketing communication sent by post and therefore often has a poor reputation because of the amount of unsolicited mail that people regularly receive.

Can direct marketing be used to sell products?
There are many situations in which you can use direct marketing to build direct sales. You may not have a sales force or a retail network, so customers can only buy direct from you. If you want to sell to niche markets, or if your customers are widely spread or even global, direct marketing may be the only cost-effective way of reaching them. If you decide to sell direct, you must ensure that the products themselves are suitable for selling through direct marketing – that is, that they do not have to be demonstrated, or inspected by the customer.

How does direct marketing build relationships with customers?
The stronger your relationship with your customers, the more opportunities you have to influence the future direction and success of your business. If your company depends on a few key customers for most of its business, you can use direct marketing to improve customer loyalty by building long-term relationships with them. You may also need to use it if your customers want to rationalise the number of suppliers, and you want to remain on the approved list.

Is direct marketing only effective for reaching a small audience?
There are numerous examples of successful large-scale mailings, but the key to direct marketing success is reaching the right people in a cost-effective way. Large-scale mailings based on poorly researched mailing lists may yield results, but there will also be a high level of wastage. The more precise your mailing, the more likely you are to succeed.

MAKING IT HAPPEN
Set campaign objectives
Direct marketing objectives can be initially expressed in general terms:
- encouraging prospects to buy directly in response to a direct marketing campaign
- generating leads for the sales force or retail network
- supporting sales force activity
- improving the effectiveness of other forms of communication
- raising awareness of a company, product, or service among clearly identified customers and prospects
- maintaining effective contact with customers and prospects
- building relationships with customers and prospects

However, these general objectives should be translated into precise, measurable objectives, for example:
- raising awareness of your product range among 35 per cent of technical directors in the mechanical engineering sector
- ensuring that purchasing managers of your 10 top corporate customers are contacted at least once a fortnight
- increasing direct sales of supplies by 15 per cent

Define the target market

Do you want to reach all customers and prospects, or are you targeting specific groups? Direct marketing is a precise medium, so your campaign could be aimed at just a few key decision-makers or thousands of potential users. To plan your direct marketing campaign, you should ask questions such as:

- Who buys your type of product?
- Who influences the purchasing decision?
- How many prospective customers (prospects) do you want to reach with the direct marketing campaign?
- How many prospects can you normally convert to customers, and how long does it take?
- How do they currently get information about your products?
- Is direct marketing the best (or only) way of reaching the target audience?

The more information you have about your target audience, the more precise you can make your campaign. In an ideal world, direct marketing would allow you to communicate one to one with every prospect, but, in practical terms, you are more likely to be communicating with groups that share certain characteristics. For example, you could reasonable expect that 'all fleet managers in the North West of England managing more than 40 vehicles' would have similar needs in respect of their day-to-day job.

Plan campaign timing

A direct marketing campaign can run at any time, so you do not have to consider advertisement publication dates. However, timing may be dictated by other factors – lead times for producing mailing material, seasonal purchasing patterns, product availability, or tender dates. These are some of the factors to consider in planning the timing of your campaign:

- When is your customer likely to be making the buying decision?
- How long is the selling or buying process? How many stages are involved? Who is involved?
- Does your direct marketing campaign have to tie in with the timing of any other marketing activity, such as an exhibition, advertising campaign, or salesforce visit?
- If you are launching a new product, when will the product be available?
- How long will it take to produce the material that is to be mailed?
- When will you be able to follow up the campaign?
- What will you do if you get fewer responses than you need or more than you can handle?

Decide on your contact strategy

A single mailshot, e-mail, telephone call, or direct response advertisement *may* produce results, but a series of appropriate contacts will have greater impact and ensure you meet your objectives. There are several benefits from repeated contacts:

- raising levels of awareness with each contact
- educating potential clients about your product/service
- following up those who have not responded

- moving individual respondents further along the decision-making process
- maintaining contact during extended decision-making processes

There is no hard-and-fast rule about the frequency of individual campaigns; a company trying to get a prospect to make a decision may make contact several times a week, while a company aiming to maintain long-term customer loyalty may only need to contact customers monthly or quarterly.

Develop a response mechanism

Action is a vital ingredient of any direct marketing campaign, and it is essential that you make it easy for your prospects to respond. First, decide if your prospects are to place an order, request a sales visit, or ask for further information. Then decide which of the five basic types of response mechanism is the most appropriate: post, telephone, faxback (rapidly going out of fashion, however), e-mail, or website address.

Keep track of the campaign

You must be prepared to keep records of every aspect of your campaign. You will have to set up the systems to capture data before your campaign (or test campaign) starts. Aim to know at the very least:

- what was sent (the offer, the pack/letter, and so on) and to whom (the lists used and reason for selection)
- the anticipated response (for example, percentage initial response and percentage purchase)
- the actual response
- the costs and the return – in other words, did your campaign make a profit?

Test the campaign

Part of the flexibility of direct marketing is that you can test your approach before committing resources to the full campaign. There are several variables that can be tested:

- the target audience – the most important element
- the offer – what exactly you are offering for sale (including any incentive)
- the creative approach – the look and feel of the communications
- the response mechanism – how easy it is to respond, for example, using a Freephone number or Freepost
- frequency and timing – including the way you follow up enquiries

The test campaign can be carried out in a number of ways:

- on a sample of the target market
- in a defined sales or geographical territory
- in a particular sector of the target market

The most effective test campaign is the one that achieves the highest response levels, and committed DM organisations test continuously to drive down their costs and drive up response rates. Indeed, every campaign should be considered a 'test' to improve on previous campaigns. Each best-performing campaign then becomes the 'control' against which others can be evaluated.

Plan split campaigns

Testing your campaign may reveal that different approaches work more effectively in different market sectors. If budget allows, you can develop a series of campaigns that vary the offer, the creative approach, frequency, timing, or other factors, but ensure you keep track of these variables so that you can use the best-performing campaign format next time.

Set target response levels

In the long term, a campaign may increase awareness, improve customer relations, or cut the cost of sales. However, the simplest and most immediate measure of a direct marketing campaign is the response level it generates. In setting your target response levels, you should aim for a realistic figure that is within budget. Note that:

- response levels as low as 1 or 2 per cent are regarded as the industry norm for large companies sending mail to 'cold' lists
- response rates in the region of 5 per cent are therefore regarded as high
- response rates in the region of 10–20 per cent have been reported by companies who have integrated other forms of marketing communications
- far higher response rates can be experienced by specialist companies communicating vital information to a very committed list of supporters

Many different factors can affect the level of response, including price, quality of the mailing list, the promotional offer, and quality of copy and design. A test is very often the only way to set an initial target response rate for future campaigns.

COMMON MISTAKES

Using DM unnecessarily

While the principles of direct marketing can help any company in its communications and selling, sometimes direct *mail* is used when the existing channels are preferable. Customers who are used to a personal visit and face-to-face negotiations may feel aggrieved if you try to deal with them at a distance.

Failing to set measurable targets

The results of a direct marketing campaign can be measured precisely by the number of responses. This makes it a particularly accountable medium. It is therefore important to set realistic, measurable objectives. If your target is to generate leads from 2 per cent of the target audience, this will determine how many people you mail, the type of offer you make, and the response mechanism you provide. It will also tell you very quickly if your budget balances – how many of those leads need to convert into customers to cover your costs?

Poor audience selection

With direct marketing you can communicate with a single prospect or with 50,000. However, there may be more cost-effective ways of communicating with 50,000 prospects. Direct marketing works most effectively when it is aimed at a precise audience that cannot be easily reached by any other medium, and, crucially, when you want a response. For example, you may find there is a specialist magazine or newsletter that precisely covers your target market.

No integration with other communications

If your marketing budget is split between different communications activities such as advertising, sales promotion, and press and public relations, it is essential that each activity works as effectively as possible. You can use direct marketing in conjunction with other methods of commmunication. If you place advertisements in publications that only reach a general audience, you can reinforce the advertisements with personalised communications to selected prospects. If your advertisements include a response mechanism, keeping to direct marketing principles will ensure effective follow-up. You can also tailor your product and corporate literature to the information needs of different market sectors by including direct marketing material.

THE BEST SOURCES OF HELP

Books:
Bird, Drayton. *Commonsense Direct and Digital Marketing*. 5th ed. London: Kogan Page, 2007.
Tapp, Alan. *Principles of Direct and Database Marketing*. Harlow: Prentice Hall, 2008.

Websites:
Direct Selling Association: **www.dsa.org.uk**
The Institute of Direct Marketing: **www.theidm.co.uk**

Planning a Customer Event

GETTING STARTED

Desk research is no substitute for getting out and meeting customers face to face. Arranging visits or special customer events increases personal contact, and improves customer relationships – although events need to be handled professionally to achieve the right results.

FAQS

Who should organise a customer event?

Few companies have the luxury of a specialist events department, so the task normally falls to the sales, marketing, or public relations department. Events generally form a small part of the overall customer relationship programme, so they may not get the attention or the resources they require. Event organisation is extremely time-consuming, so it may be better to appoint a specialist event company to work with an internal co-ordinator. Invitations and publicity could be handled internally, while the event company takes responsibility for venues, staging, and logistics.

Do events provide a good return on investment?

If events reach the right people and help to strengthen customer relationships, they provide a good return. However, many companies organise events simply to get together with customers. Without a specific objective, the event could be a waste of valuable funds.

How do you decide who should be invited to a customer event?

If resources are limited, you may have to select the most important contacts within a target company. The salesforce can provide advice, but you may still overlook influential people and create resentment. Asking customers to nominate their own delegates shifts some of the responsibility, but they may not choose the people you wish to contact. There is always likely to be a compromise, so make sure you check your records carefully and try to keep up to date with the power structure within a company.

MAKING IT HAPPEN

Get familiar with customers

How well do you know your customers' businesses, their markets, their plans, their competitors, and their strengths and weaknesses? The more you know, the more easily you can identify their real needs and develop a service that wins and keeps business.

Although you can find out a lot about your customers just by looking in your sales records, desk research is no substitute for getting out and meeting customers face to face. The sales team is doing that all the time, but it is unlikely that they will be responsible for delivering customer service. You need to meet the customers yourself by arranging visits or special customer events. These increase personal contact and improve customer relationships.

Manage events professionally

Events such as open evenings, trade shows, and customer receptions are a powerful method of building customer loyalty, but they need to be handled professionally to achieve the right results. By providing the right level of support, you can develop a programme of events that is appropriate for the market. This can include:

- the development of suitable promotional and display material
- choosing the theme for the event
- the generation of mailing lists and selection of people to be invited
- support literature
- personal support by members of the head office team

Arrange an informal customer visit

Many customers will appreciate the interest you are showing in their business if you visit them informally. Alternatively, invite customers to visit your premises. It provides a good chance for customer-facing staff to meet their opposite numbers, and meeting people face to face can help to improve working relationships.

Attend customer exhibitions, seminars, and conferences

You can find out what competitors are up to at the same time. Events like these are a good indicator of what customers believe is important to the success of their business and will give you a good sign of where they see themselves heading.

Make customer care visits

Call on selected customers at intervals to discuss whether they are satisfied with the standard of service they are receiving from you. Ask if they have any specific concerns and ensure that you contact them again with an appropriate response.

Set up regular review meetings

This is a more formal process than the ad hoc customer care visits. Suppliers and customers agree to meet at regular intervals, for example, every year or once a quarter, or monthly, according to the complexity and importance of the business. There is likely to be a set agenda for reviewing performance in specific areas, and there may be agreed standards that are used to measure performance.

Arrange briefing meetings for your customers

Briefings are not for reviewing progress or performance, but for bringing your customers up to date with new developments in your business or industry that might benefit them. For example, you might brief them on a new technical development or on new legislation that is likely to have an impact on them. This type of meeting not only demonstrates your professionalism; it also helps to add value to the customer relationship.

Invite customers to a webcast

If you run webcasts on important subjects, you can invite customers to join the event. Provide time, log-in, and other relevant details to your customers well in advance and explain the format and benefits of the event.

Hold a social event

Many customers enjoy the chance to meet informally and talk shop. A social event could take place after a more formal meeting, or it might be an event in its own right. Although the extravagant side of corporate hospitality has largely disappeared, social events remain an important aspect of business relationships.

Run regional events in retail outlets

When one manufacturer launches a new range of products, the central feature of the launch is a series of customer events run in conjunction with regional retailers around the country. The outlets are given detailed guidelines on the programme and provided with mailing letters inviting customers to the launch event. The outlets put together their own mailing lists using account information, local directories, and database information from head office.

Encourage company staff to attend

At one event, one of the company's senior directors attended to make a brief presentation and talk to customers. A group of company sales and technical staff joined with retailer staff to host the evening and meet customers. The company also provided window displays and free-standing display units to ensure consistent quality. By providing a professional support service, the company was able to ensure a consistent standard and give the retailers the freedom to develop an event that was right for the local market.

Offer events as customer incentives

An incentive scheme for a high street bank offered business customers a structured series of special sporting prizes. Customers were awarded points for using different types of business banking services, and could win a day's free participation and coaching in different sporting activities which had high levels of appeal to the target audience, for example, gliding, water sports, outward bound, and motor racing. The local branches could tailor the awards to their own customer base, but they did not have to provide the resources to manage the events themselves. This was handled by a specialist organisation that could set up the events in different parts of the country.

Sponsored events

Sponsoring an event should be a positive marketing action, not an enforced response to a request for help.

Depending on the type of event and its popularity, sponsorship can:
- build the image of an organisation or product through association with an event that reflects corporate values
- raise awareness of an organisation or product through the exposure associated with an event

There are different levels of sponsorship:
- international, national, regional, or local event
- whole event, with unique or joint sponsorship
- programme or award sponsorship
- hospitality
- participants, as individuals or teams

Make the most of sponsorship
- Issue press releases about the organisation's involvement.
- Advertise on the perimeter or programme.
- Inform employees and customers.
- Use the event for customer hospitality.
- Consider other promotional activities tied in to the event.

COMMON MISTAKES

Poor organisation

At a customer event, the company is on show. The event must be carefully organised and managed to ensure that customers get the right impression of the company. If you are putting on a large or complex event, it may pay to use a professional events organiser. They have the resources and skills to manage all the services and logistics essential to success.

Failing to set objectives for the event

An event must have a specific purpose: for example, to improve relations with key decision-makers or to reward loyal customers. The objectives determine the format of the event and the support services required.

Poor internal communication

The success of an event depends on the participation of staff. Make sure that customer-facing staff are aware of the event, and keep them involved in the planning process. On the day, make sure that everyone is aware of individual responsibilities.

THE BEST SOURCES OF HELP

Books:

Allen, Judi. *Event Planning: The Ultimate Guide to Successful Meetings, Corporate Events, Fundraising Galas, Conferences, Conventions, Incentives and Other Special Events*. 2nd ed. Chichester: Wiley, 2009.

O'Toole, William. *Corporate Event Project Management*. Chichester: Wiley, 2002.

Websites:

Association of British Professional Conference Organisers: **www.abpco.org**

Reed Exhibitions: **www.reedexpo.com**

Getting a Better Return from Customer Events

GETTING STARTED

Customer events are a great way of boosting your profile, but they're complicated and expensive projects. To make sure that you get a strong return on your investment, you'll need to put in the hours before and after the event itself so that you can secure a healthy number of attendees and begin to strengthen your relationship with them. Read on to find out how.

FAQS

In terms of cost, does it make more sense to have in-house staff manage the event, or outsource it?
It all depends on the size and complexity of an event. Outsourcing the work to an events management company may help you keep other costs down in that you can tap into their purchasing power: they probably buy services in bulk, and should be able to pass on some savings to you. If you have the resources in-house, you could appoint someone as the 'point person' for the event and have him or her make the arrangements, but it's unlikely they'd be able to make the arrangements as efficiently. Remember that you'd also have to factor in 'hidden' costs of the co-ordinator's time, labour, and so on.

MAKING IT HAPPEN

Think about your objectives. . . and work out how to measure them
As with any marketing activity, it's essential that you're able to measure how effective an event has been, and this is, of course, tied in to what you're hoping to achieve by holding it. For example, you may want to flag up a new partnership, showcase new products, discuss a new industry initiative, and so on. The metrics you use to gauge success will vary depending on your goals, but some common ones include:
- number of visitors to the event
- number of enquiries at the event
- number of new contacts resulting from the event
- number of new sales leads resulting from the event
- changes in awareness of your company following the event

Consider whether you want to take part or organise
If money is tight, it may be worth your taking part in an industry event rather than hosting one yourself, and inviting customers or prospects to join you there. Although you have less control over this scenario than you would if you were in charge of all the arrangements, you can still achieve corporate goals and achieve a good return on investment. The sections below are useful for both participants and organisers.

Investigate sponsorship opportunities
If hosting an event isn't for you, sponsoring someone else's may be a good option. There are a number of levels at which you can participate, and the benefits will depend on how much money you put in. In general, though, all sponsors should see a boost to their profile and increase levels of public awareness without the hard work involved in pulling the event together. Look at the costs involved carefully to make sure it is worth your while.

Start the ball rolling on registration
Healthy attendance figures offer a better chance of a good financial return. E-mail is a boon here, as you can e-mail many people easily and cost-effectively. It's likely that you'll have to send more than one e-mail invitation to combat inertia, but incentives may also be able to help you encourage prompt registration (see below).

Keep registration simple
Some potential customers may be put off by over-elaborate or time-consuming registration arrangements, so keep it simple. If you issue invitations by e-mail, you could insert a link to a website where visitors can register online. Don't use the website as a surreptitious way of gathering data: people will notice and they will be put off. Ask for the information you need only, such as:
- name
- position
- company
- telephone
- email address
- preferred times/dates (if there is a choice)

Incentivise registration
In some cases, dangling a carrot in the form of incentives for registration could help swell the number of participants. The best ones for your event will, of course, depend on what industry you operate in and what your customer profile is, but some basic incentives can include a discount for 'early bird' registration, a free copy of a valuable industry-specific report, or even promotional offers, such as a theatre trip or meal in a good restaurant.

Promote your organisation in the event brochure
If you are taking part in an event rather than organising your own, flag up your attendance by advertising in the event brochure or guide if the opportunity presents itself. Depending on the space available, you could simply include contact details or (ideally) advertise your range of products and services. If you have a stand or someone from your business is speaking at the event, highlight relevant details.

Publicise!
Take every opportunity to advertise the event in your press releases and any other PR activities. You could issue releases that deal solely with the event, or add footers to

more general releases that encourage readers to attend. Get in touch with trade publications as well, so that you can be sure any adverts or previews are submitted to the magazines at the right time: many will work on a long lead time.

Create a dedicated event website

Posting useful event information online is now essential, but it also saves time and money: no need to stuff endless envelopes with forms and flyers when all the details can go on to a website. If you're hosting an event, make sure the online site features:

- event description
- event dates and times
- travel directions and accommodation
- event programme
- speaker details
- online registration form

If you're taking part in someone else's event, on the other hand, make sure that your logo and contact details are listed on the organiser's website. It's also a good idea to set up a temporary 'micro site' on your own website that visitors can access easily. This will not only highlight your presence at the event, but will also allow you to capture useful contact details of the participants. It will also make their lives a lot easier, and a positive experience at every stage of the proceedings is exactly what you're after.

Increase awareness in-house

To get the best from an event, you need to make sure that everyone working on it in-house understands its objectives, is committed to its success, and is able to communicate their energy and enthusiasm to participants. Well in advance of the event itself, hold some meetings with key staff so that they're clear about their role and what they're working towards; if it's difficult to get everyone together at the same time and in the same place, you could brief them over e-mail or upload useful material on to your company intranet. As the day draws nearer and the guest list is firmed up, pass on visitor information to the sales team so that they can work out how best to target key clients or potential customers. Finally, a quick recap on the morning of the event can refresh everyone's memory and get them focused on their tasks for the next few hours!

Watch literature-related costs

Brochures, programmes, and other event-related literature can be expensive, and it can be difficult to make sure that likely customers (rather than browsers) get it. It's wise to limit the amount of free literature on display and to instead ask visitors to leave contact details with you so that you can post or e-mail it on to them subsequently.

Follow up

Successful events are just one part of the relationship-building process, especially if you're aiming to turn attendees into valued customers. Compiling and circulating a report after the event is one useful way of doing this: it can be sent to key partners who weren't able to attend (include a summary of who was there and what was discussed), and may also encourage participants to attend future events.

Beyond that, make sure all sales leads are followed up and that you keep in touch with visitors via targeted e-mail or telemarketing campaigns. The useful data you captured during the registration process should allow you to do this effectively.

COMMON MISTAKES

You don't promote the event enough

If no one knows about your event, you won't get the visitor numbers you were hoping for! Start the ball rolling in advance so that potential visitors get a sense of it being something you're taking seriously; they're much more likely to get involved that way.

You dismiss the idea of outsourcing out of hand

If your business has a robust programme of events planned, it's likely that you have staff with the strong organisational skills and contacts that you need to create a top-notch corporate event. If that isn't the case, while the idea of doing it yourself may appeal to your bank balance, you could be letting yourself in for a complete nightmare. It is worth talking to a few events management companies to get a quote for their work before you dismiss the idea completely.

You under-invest

Obtaining a healthy return on investment for your event will naturally be one of your objectives, but radical cost-cutting and under-investment may mean you cut off your nose to spite your face. Clearly, managing costs carefully is part of a responsible events management strategy, but you need to have a *realistic* budget that will allow you to present your organisation in the best light, and to really have the 'Wow' factor for potential and existing customers.

THE BEST SOURCES OF HELP

Book:

Allen, Judy. *The Executive's Guide to Corporate Events and Business Entertaining*. Chichester: Wiley, 2007.

Websites:

Council for Hospitality Management Education: **www.chme.org.uk**

Event Management: **www.eventmanagement-uk.co.uk**

Generating More Leads

GETTING STARTED

The constant turnover of customers means that generating new leads is essential to keep a business growing. There are many ways of doing this, depending on the product and customer groups involved, but the primary purpose is to provide data on potential customers which can then be followed up.

FAQS

How important is lead generation?

Lead generation is vital to the development of new business. Customers just stop buying, or they move to competitors; this lost business must be replaced, and new customers added, if sales are to grow. Sales teams must have a constant flow of leads in order to maintain or increase business levels.

What is the best source of new leads?

The best source is the one that produces the highest-quality leads; some publications can produce large numbers of leads, but they could all be poor. A publication, a direct mail programme, or an event that is precisely targeted is likely to produce the most effective source of leads.

Are incentives necessary to a lead generation programme?

They are not essential, but they may help to encourage people to place enquiries. The incentive should not be too generous, since you may attract poor prospects who are more interested in free gifts than in your products.

MAKING IT HAPPEN

Make direct response a priority

To generate leads from your marketing campaigns, include a response mechanism in every communication, and make it easy for prospects to reply. Getting names is a priority, so make sure your communications are designed to deliver.

Generate leads from press advertising

If you want to generate leads, make sure your advertisement includes a call to action, such as:

- send for more information
- reply within seven days and receive a free gift
- send for a free report
- take out an annual subscription now and get the first two issues free
- ring for a free consultation
- book now at a special price
- order now and get a big discount
- visit our website and find out more

Make it easy for prospects to respond

To improve response rates, it is essential to make it easy for prospective customers to respond. The most popular mechanisms for press advertisements are:

- website address
- e-mail address
- Freepost address
- Freephone number

These facilities provide easy-to-use response mechanisms that can boost customer reaction. You should monitor the response levels from different sources to see which is the most effective.

Use enquiry cards

Many publications include a reader response card or helpline number. Readers send back the card to the publication, indicating the products that they are interested in. The usual method is to circle a number which is shown on the advertisement in the publication, for example, 'For more information circle number 15'. The publication then distributes the enquiries to individual advertisers for follow-up.

Run advertorials in the press

An advertorial with a prize is a cost-effective way of generating leads. The advertorial describes a product or service, and customers are offered the opportunity to win a prize in return for supplying basic data or completing a short questionnaire. The questionnaire might take the form of 'give three reasons why product X is the best on the market'. The answers could be multiple choice, based on information in the advertorial, or the customer's own opinion. Free choice questions provide added insight into customer attitudes.

Encourage TV and radio response

More and more television and radio commercials now include a response mechanism, such as a phone number or website address. Some direct the audience to a source of further information, others to a retailer or other outlet. The response mechanism must be clear, because the audience has only a short time to write down the details.

Use direct mail to target prospects

Direct mail can be used at a number of stages in a lead-generation programme. Mailings to lists that have not been qualified should include a response mechanism so that follow-up can begin.

Run offers on packaging

Your product packaging can feature special offers. Buyers send in a coupon or other proof of purchase, together with their name and address. Although the person contacting you is, strictly speaking, already a customer, you need to identify that person to build a relationship. Lead generation is just as important here.

Find out who is visiting retail outlets

Visitors to retail outlets are another potential source of leads. Many retail shoppers who buy from you may remain anonymous, so encourage shoppers to provide names and addresses by running competitions or making other special offers.

Encourage website registration

Website registration provides high levels of information. When customers visit your website, ask them to register their details. The registration form is completed online and submitted by e-mail. In return, you e-mail them regularly with details of products and services that are of interest to them. Incentives such as free reports or free software can encourage higher levels of registration.

Record exhibition visitors

Visitor registration should be an integral part of exhibition planning. Set up a process for capturing data on all stand visitors. Set up a database of exhibition contacts, and use it to plan and monitor a contact programme after the exhibition.

Monitor the business press

Many business publications feature news about recent appointments or interviews with leading executives. This type of information can give you names of potentially valuable contacts. The appointments pages can also alert you to changes in personnel at one of your customer or prospect companies.

Use telemarketing

Telemarketing can be used to generate new leads and qualify existing leads. The telemarketing team can call target companies and ask for the names of decision-makers for follow-up. The team can also call people who have made an initial enquiry, in order to qualify their interest and find out how good the prospects are.

Integrate lead generation with other marketing activities

Lead-generation programmes can be improved by integrating the campaign with other marketing activities such as an exhibition, advertising campaign, or a call by a member of the salesforce. With integrated campaigns, overall awareness levels among customers and prospects will be far higher. Your lead-generation programme will have an even greater chance of success.

Keep refining your contact lists

Many of the contact lists you have developed from internal or external sources may not match your requirements exactly. To improve coverage, or to make them more precise, you must make a continuous effort to refine them. These are some of the actions you can take to improve the coverage of your list:

- ensure that new customer and prospect data are added to the list
- include coupons and other reply mechanisms with every form of communication, and add the responses to your lists
- encourage the salesforce to provide up-to-date customer and prospect information
- maintain an active search programme in appropriate websites, magazines, and newspapers to identify new prospects for your list

COMMON MISTAKES

Overlooking lead generation

Lead generation could be vital to your company's future, especially in these challenging times. Without it, lost customers will not be replaced, and you may miss major opportunities in new or existing market sectors. Only a small proportion of leads become customers, so lead generation must be an ongoing process.

Paying too much for your leads

You can measure the cost of your lead-generation programme by dividing the cost of the advertising or marketing programme by the number of leads. Media for lead generation should be assessed in the same way as media to meet other objectives.

No integration with other relevant marketing programmes

Lead-generation programmes do not work in isolation. Corporate advertising, for example, helps to raise awareness among the target audience, while direct mail and telemarketing can be used to back up lead-generation advertising.

THE BEST SOURCES OF HELP

Books:

Carroll, Brian. *Lead Generation for the Complex Sale: Boost the Quality and Quantity of Leads to Increase Your ROI*. New York: McGraw-Hill, 2006.

Jobber, David, and Geoffrey Lancaster. *Selling and Sales Management*. 8th ed. London: FT Prentice Hall, 2009.

Website:

Institute of Sales and Marketing Management: **www.ismm.co.uk**

Converting Leads into Sales in a Small Business

GETTING STARTED

If you are trying to grow your business, finding leads (that is, potential new customers) is just the beginning. Before they can benefit you in any way, you need to turn those leads into sales. This actionlist offers a systematic approach to doing this and to making sure that the leads are of the right kind in the first place, which will cut down on wasted time and resources.

FAQS

How far can services such as telemarketing take over from the salesforce?

These services can be used to handle many of the sales teams' routine functions: carrying out initial research, qualifying prospective customers, making appointments, and maintaining regular contact. Despite these benefits, they're no substitute for face-to-face selling if that's important to your customer relationships, so make sure they're appropriate for your business.

What is the best way to measure lead conversion?

Measuring sales as a percentage of initial leads is too simplistic an approach: it is more effective to measure at each stage of the process. For example, only 50 per cent of initial leads may turn out to be suitable prospective customers. If the leads have been well qualified, the sales team may be able to convert 20 per cent of the final prospect list. Measuring results at each stage helps you focus the right level of resources and plan future lead-generation programmes.

Should we try to get as many leads as possible?

The quality of the leads is as important as the number. Following up a large number of unsuitable leads is a waste of resources, but getting as many good leads as possible is important to any company that wants to expand its business.

MAKING IT HAPPEN

Qualify your leads

Your lead-generation programme may have given you large numbers of leads, but not all of them will convert to sales. Some may be poor prospects, while others may simply be gathering information rather than planning a purchase. Good prospects have the following characteristics:

- the financial resources to purchase your product
- the authority to make a purchase decision
- a genuine need for your product or service
- the desire to learn more about your product
- plans to make a purchase in the near future

Telemarketing can be used to qualify the leads. Call the contact and ask for more details of their enquiry so that you can send information tailored to their needs. Just sending a brochure, with no accompanying letter and no understanding of the prospective customer's needs, is a waste of money.

Qualifying questions can include:

- Are you the person who makes the purchasing decision? If not, who does?
- Is your company currently buying this product?
- What quantities do you buy, or how much do you spend on the service?
- When are you likely to make your next purchase?
- What information do you need on our product and company?

Choose a one-step or two-step process

In the case of some products and services, the lead-generation and sales-conversion processes can be combined. These are known as one-step programmes, and are equivalent to direct selling operations. They are suitable for:

- inexpensive products
- information services such as newsletter or magazine subscriptions
- office supplies
- software
- low-value financial offers

In a two-step programme, the prospective customer (prospect) requests initial information. You send the information and then continue following up until the prospect is ready to buy. Two-step programmes are suitable for:

- expensive offers
- complex technical products
- professional services
- high-value financial services

Plan the conversion process

Lead conversion can be a long-term continuous process, the duration of which depends on the complexity of the product and of the decision-making process. For example, how many people are involved or how important is the product to the customer (or the customer's business)?

For a complex product, the process could be:

- identifying key decision-makers
- sending information to key decision-makers
- arranging meetings with decision-makers
- providing sample products for evaluation by the customer
- bidding for a contract against competition
- final negotiations
- purchase
- after-sales service and support

You must decide how you will handle each stage of the process, who will be involved in the sales team, and how you will manage communications with the prospect.

Another example could be where the product and the purchasing process are simpler, but the prospect is reluctant to change suppliers. The conversion process could take a long time, so you must plan a programme to

maintain contact and move the prospect away from the existing supplier. Actions could include:
- personalised direct mail with product information
- regular updates on new developments in the company
- targeted special offers to encourage the customer to try the product

Allocate responsibility
Normally, the marketing department generates leads and the sales department follows up. It is important for the two departments to work together to integrate their activities and ensure that the company focuses on the kind of high-quality prospects it really needs. Sales departments frequently complain about the quantity and quality of leads. They want as many leads as possible so that the final number of new sales is high; however, they may also complain if too many of the leads are of poor quality and do not meet the right criteria. Collecting a large number of high-quality leads can be a difficult balancing act. Some sales teams prefer to do their own qualifying, while others prefer to leave that to others so that they can concentrate on face-to-face meetings with prospects.

Back the sales team with telemarketing
Telemarketing can be used to enhance the performance and productivity of the salesforce. The telemarketing team can be responsible for following up sales leads, qualifying prospects, setting up appointments, and maintaining contact with longer-term prospects. This frees the salesforce for increasing the number of face-to-face meetings and for concentrating on the most likely prospects. The integration of telemarketing with the salesforce can play an important part in reducing overall sales costs. The cost of keeping a sales team on the road continues to soar, and it may not always represent the most cost-effective way of reaching the right people.

Maintain a contact diary
A contact diary can help you plan the conversion process and make sure that the sales team does not miss any important contact opportunities. It also ensures that the sales back-up team integrates its follow-up activities with the field salesforce. Computer software is available which allows sales teams to operate a sales diary and record details of meetings and other follow-up activities. The same software can be used by the management team to monitor progress and ensure that no important contacts are overlooked. Contact diaries can include details of the customer, the customer's likes and dislikes, availability for meetings or telephone calls, their buying limits/authorisation, and even personal information that helps to maintain a relationship with them.

Track progress
It is essential to track progress at each stage of the conversion process. If the prospect is important, you may wish to allocate additional resources to win the business. If a

prospect is of only minor importance but is taking time and resources, you may want to refocus the efforts of the salesforce. The progress from initial lead to customer goes through a number of stages:
- raw lead: an initial enquiry from any source
- suspect: an enquiry that has been qualified and has the potential to become a paying customer
- prospect: a lead that has been qualified in more detail
- inactive lead: a prospect who will not buy now but has future potential
- dead lead: a prospect who has little potential to become a customer
- customer

You might also include lapsed customers in this process as a source of qualified leads.

Choose the right contact frequency
A single mailshot, e-mail, telephone call, or direct response advertisement may produce results, but a series of quality contacts will have greater impact and ensure you meet your response targets. Multiple direct marketing activities raise levels of awareness with each contact, follow up contacts who have not responded, and move individual respondents further along the decision-making process.

Use personalised contact
Personalised one-to-one mailings are an ideal form of communication for companies with detailed information on their prospects. The letter reflects the individual prospect's main interests and concerns, and the offer can be tailored to the prospect's needs. Subsequent mailings can build an individual relationship with the prospect.

COMMON MISTAKES
Focusing on the wrong prospects
Sales teams have a natural tendency to deal with friendly prospects and avoid the difficult ones. From a business perspective, however, they may be dealing with the wrong people. The qualifying process should be used to identify the most important prospects in order to improve the targeting of the salesforce.

Poor management
Lead conversion can be a long, complicated process, so it is essential to monitor progress and manage the programme carefully. Lead conversion can use a lot of salesforce and telemarketing resources, and careful planning can make sure that it is carried out effectively.

THE BEST SOURCES OF HELP
Book:
Jobber, David, and Geoffrey Lancaster. *Selling and Sales Management*. 8th ed. London: FT Prentice Hall, 2009.

Website:
Chartered Institute of Marketing: **www.cim.co.uk**

Researching the Size of Your Market

GETTING STARTED

It's important to find out what potential your business has to generate revenues and profits in your chosen market sector, and the only way to do this is to carry out thorough market research. The better the data you have about your market, the better equipped you will be to make informed decisions about your business. Good market research will help you establish the most important objective of all – in other words, your sales targets. Your financial backers, business partners, key staff, and other key stakeholders will also have a keen, if not vested, interest in your sales potential and the market share you believe you can realistically achieve.

Before you can estimate the share of the market you want to attain, you'll need to have researched the *overall* size of the market. Its size could be calculated in terms of its volume (that is to say, the number of buyers), and its value (in terms of annual total spend), or both. This actionlist will help you to do just that.

FAQS

What do I need to know about my customer group?

Assuming you have already accurately profiled the customer group that you consider to be your ideal market audience, you need to know how many potential buyers the group consists of, and how much they currently spend.

What else do I need to know before I set my sales targets?

Once you have found out how many potential buyers you have, and how much they spend at the moment, you need to find out whether your market is growing or declining. You then need to decide what sales levels you are going to aim for.

MAKING IT HAPPEN

Find out the number of potential buyers

Your target audience will be made up of groups of businesses, groups of individuals, or both. Calculating the size of this overall market, that is to say the number of people who could potentially buy from you, will only be possible once you have considered who they are, their unique characteristics, and where they are located. It may be the case in your business situation that your potential customers live close to you as you offer a service that people generally will travel only a short distance to purchase – you could run a sandwich bar or café, for example. For other services, people are prepared to travel a reasonable distance, for example, up to an hour, to buy something. In other instances, distance is not an issue, as consumers will buy by mail order or via the Internet.

You need to ask yourself whether location or proximity to your service is an issue for your target audience. This will help you to scope the potential size of your market when you add this factor into the profile of your customers' buying characteristics. You'll then be able to target the number of buyers you think you can reach with your marketing.

Research how much buyers spend in the market

Establishing how many buyers there are for your service is only part of the equation. You will also need to understand how much these buyers are prepared to spend on a product or service such as yours, in terms of each time they buy, and in terms of how frequently they buy.

Knowing your market size is meaningless unless you can attach a value to the volume of potential buyers you have. That value is also meaningless unless you understand the repeat-purchase rate, in other words how many times they buy or use your service in weeks, months, or over a year. This information is vital when forecasting sales revenues for your business plan or forthcoming budget.

Establish if the market is expanding or declining

Once you know how many buyers you have, how much they spend, and how often they buy, you need to look at the market *potential*. Will your market be the same size in six or 12 months' time, for example? Look at the trends, to see if they suggest that your customers will be spending more, the same, or less. Try to predict whether there will be any more buyers seeking your type of product and service.

There may also be other target audiences with similar buying characteristics and needs that you will be able to access through your marketing. Don't get fixated on the size of your market now; you'll end up missing opportunities to reach a wider audience in a year's time without even realising it. Similarly, watch out for – and act on! – signs that customer numbers are falling or that they're buying less frequently: don't leave it too late.

Think about your target market share

Once you've come up with a target market share to aim for, you can work out the precise marketing effort, methods, channels, and budget you'll need to achieve it. Also remember that you'll need to bear in mind what your competitors are up to: what could you learn from or improve on, based on their approach? If your market is a growing one, it's likely that you'll have more competition as time goes on, so keep on top of trends and try to predict whether your competitors will have new, better value, more innovative services than yours. You will need to keep a very close eye on their marketing activities, for example, special promotions, free gifts, guarantees, after-sales service, and so on. This might give them the edge over your business, and a chance to steal a greater share of the market you have targeted or established for yourself.

Find information about market size and trends

Business and market information is available from a variety of sources. Some is free, but you will probably have to pay for more in-depth statistics, trends, and forecasts. The reference section of your local library will have a business section carrying published market reports on hundreds of sectors. They will also have government statistics, trade magazines, and national and local business directories. If they do not have the publications themselves, they should have a directory of them, together with details of their costs and where you can source them. Contact your local council if you want local population or business information.

The Internet is also a good place to start, but wading through the sheer volume of information available can be time-consuming, especially for the less-experienced Web user. Having said that, using one of the main search engines and carrying out a search using terms containing the name of the market sector you are in, the type of information you need, a product name, geographic area, and suppliers' or competitors' names, should bring up a good range of relevant websites for your business.

For information on market trends in the United Kingdom, try Mintel, KeyNote, or Euromonitor – or the UK Statistics Authority gives information about statistics and trends (website addresses are given below). For details of potential business buyers, there are a number of good directories including Thomson Local, Yellow Pages Online, and the British Chambers of Commerce. If you are just starting up, or are a newly established business, try Enterprise Quest.

COMMON MISTAKES

Not being up to date

Do be 100 per cent sure that your estimates of the size of your market are based on current data and trends. If you make decisions based on out-of-date information, or fail to spot the trends in your sector, you'll either miss the opportunities to obtain a greater share of the overall market, or your competitors will steal your market share.

Taking your eye off the target

Research regularly: it shouldn't be a one-off exercise! If you don't keep tabs on what's happening to the size and structure of your market, you'll lose touch with your existing audiences and potential new customers.

Failing to spot the trends

Do try always to look at the 'bigger picture' in your sector, rather than just one particular aspect of the market, or the statistics relating to it. Look for trends in terms of potential buyers you could reach, the average value of purchase they make, and how often they are buying. Keep an eye out for new entrants in your sector, and the share of the overall market they are taking.

THE BEST SOURCES OF HELP

Websites:

British Chambers of Commerce:
   www.britishchambers.org.uk
Chartered Institute of Marketing:
   www.cim.co.uk
Enterprise Quest: **www.enterquest.net**
Euromonitor: **www.euromonitor.com**
KeyNote: **www.keynote.co.uk**
Mintel: **www.mintel.co.uk**
UK Statistics Authority: **www.statistics.gov.uk**
Yellow Pages: **www.yell.com**

Involving Customers in Product or Service Development

GETTING STARTED

For some people 'new product development' means inventing something new. In reality, though, most new products are modifications of existing ideas. In some cases, 'new product development' can also mean adding an element of service on to a product.

The power of new product development is that your business may be able meet a customer's need more closely than the competition. Involving customers creates the possibility of your product or service being tailor-made for them, thereby encouraging loyalty.

FAQS

Is there a risk in letting customers evaluate new products before launch?

There are two risks. First, the customer may be extremely disappointed with the product if quality is poor. Second, there is a risk that competitors could find out about your plans indirectly. The quality issue is one that you should deal with: if a product is not right, it should not be given to customers in any form – it is not enough simply to promise future improvements. The security risk of a leak to competitors can be minimised through disclosure and confidentiality agreements, although these provide no real guarantee. Having said that, the advantages of involving customers outweigh the risks, so evaluation is worth while.

How practical is it for customers and suppliers to collaborate on product development?

There are different levels of collaboration. Some may involve regular meetings to provide input and review progress. These meetings can be held on site or remotely, using video-conference links. In some cases, customer staff may work alongside the supplier team for all or part of the project. Secondment like this can provide other benefits for the customer by improving the technical knowledge of their staff.

Does pre-announcement put new product launches at risk?

Some companies, particularly in the IT sector, have put themselves under unnecessary pressure by trying to meet a series of pre-announced release dates. The schedule may not allow proper time for development, resulting in failure to meet the date, or the release of a product that is not ready. Don't release a date unless you are sure of it.

MAKING IT HAPPEN

Ask customers before you launch your product

If you are planning a new product or redeveloping an existing one, ask your customers for their views on the existing product and what they would like to see in a new one. By explaining your plans and involving customers in product development, you can strengthen relationships and provide a service that is mutually beneficial. Questions could include:

- How is the product used?
- How can we improve the current product?
- What problems have been encountered?
- What new features would customers welcome?
- Do the plans represent an improvement?
- Would customers make greater use of a product that included the features they have highlighted?

Set up a user group

You can encourage feedback and build a sense of community by setting up a user group which could operate as a 'virtual community' on the Internet or meet at events. The user group can serve as a forum for discussing issues of mutual concern to customers such as quality, performance, standards, and future developments. The group would include representatives from your own company and from a cross-section of your customers. Comments from the user group provide valuable feedback on current performance and help to identify needs that can be met through new product development.

Ask customers to evaluate new products

Customer evaluation, or beta testing, is well established in the software industry. Customers test new products or upgraded versions before they are released to the market. They identify any problems in using the software, thus providing valuable feedback on product performance.

Issue new product announcements

Another valuable practice from the IT industry is to pre-announce new products. For example, a company will set a number of release dates during the coming year when it will release new versions of products. The company outlines the new products and gives customers the opportunity to provide input to the development process. The major benefit for customers is that they can align their own development plans to the release dates. The dates do need to be accurate, though, as mentioned above.

Work in partnership with customers

Product development can be a joint initiative where you work closely with specific customers to develop products that meet their specific needs. This approach is a valuable one where:

- your customers have developed partnership sourcing to take advantage of your technology
- your customers have technology and technical skills that complement your own, and a joint project can produce more-effective results
- you want to strengthen relationships with key customers by working in partnership on joint development projects

The latest networking systems and collaborative software tools make it possible to create 'virtual teams' of key contacts (including suppliers and partners) who can collaborate as appropriate.

Understand your customers' markets

The new products you develop could enable your customers to improve their competitive performance, so it is important to understand their markets. Tell customers about your product plans and ask them for input to your development process. By building a detailed picture of their markets, you can align your own plans with them, and develop products that are tailored to their needs.

- What are their main markets?
- What is their position in the marketplace?
- Who are their main competitors?
- How are their products regarded in the marketplace?
- What are the key success factors in the market?
- What are the long-term product trends?
- What new technical developments will be needed to succeed?
- Could innovation help your customers to succeed?
- Are your customers considering entry into new markets?
- Do you have product development plans that are relevant to the new market?

Understand customer strategies

It is equally important to understand your customers' business strategies: their corporate direction and key objectives, and how they aim to succeed. By aligning your product development objectives with theirs, and showing how your products or services can help them to achieve their strategic business objectives, you can improve the chances of your new products being successful.

There are two possible approaches to customer-focused product development. Where your customers want to become market leaders through innovation, your new product programmes can help them to develop the right level of innovation without investment in their own skills. Where they want to succeed through competitive pricing, you can help them to reduce overall costs by developing cost-effective products.

Assess your products and services

Products that help your customers to meet their strategic business objectives can increase the chances of new product success. The more your customers depend on your new product, the more demanding they will be. If you can, keep up with their demands and try to anticipate and meet them; you'll not only help yourself but also create barriers for your competitors.

Analyse your customers' technical requirements

When you're assessing new product development opportunities, think about how your products can help your customers. They can use your skills in a number of ways, such as:

- improving the performance of their own products and services by using your design and development skills. They may gain privileged access to your technical skills to improve their own competitive performance.
- using your technical expertise to enhance the skills of their own technical staff. This enables them to make a more effective contribution to their own product development process.
- using your technical resources to handle product development on a subcontract basis. This provides your partners with access to specialist resources or to additional research and development capacity to improve the performance of their product development programmes.

- using your technical expertise to develop new products that they could not achieve themselves. This provides your customers with new technology, and allows them to diversify in line with your specialist skills.
- using your design skills to improve through-life costs (the total cost of owning and using a product, including purchase price, maintenance, and any other related costs). By carrying out value engineering studies on your customers' products, you may be able to reduce overall costs and improve reliability by designing components that are easier to assemble and maintain.

COMMON MISTAKES

Not involving your customers sufficiently

Product development should be focused on customer needs. Although most companies carry out research before development, the research may not provide the detailed input that is essential. Product development may also be driven by technology, with no clear market focus. The more your customer depends on your product, the more likely it is to succeed, so involving customers can pay real dividends.

Ignoring user groups

Many companies set up user groups in response to a crisis and then fail to use them. This can be frustrating for customers and wasteful for the companies. User groups provide a valuable perspective on products and services, and their feedback can provide real benefits for the product development process.

THE BEST SOURCES OF HELP

Books:

Charan, Ram. *What the Customer Wants You to Know: How Everybody Needs to Think Differently About Sales.* London: Michael Joseph, 2008.

Ulwick, Anthony W. *What Customers Want: Using Outcome-Driven Innovation to Create Breakthrough Products and Services.* New York: McGraw-Hill, 2005.

Website:

Chartered Institute of Marketing: **www.cim.co.uk**

Profiling Decision-makers

GETTING STARTED

In business purchasing, more than one person influences the choice of supplier. A decision-making team could include a wide range of key personnel, and the influence of team members varies at different stages during the purchasing process. It is important to identify the members of the team and communicate with each at the appropriate stage.

FAQS

How can I identify a purchasing team when my sales representatives only meet the purchasing manager?

You need to find out who within your customer's company is interested in your products. Telephone research, direct mail, or advertising with a response mechanism can help to identify other team members. Be careful about direct approaches: purchasing managers may guard their status and resent approaches to other team members that appear to be undermining their position.

My organisation sells low-value commodity components. Do I need to identify a complete decision-making team?

On the surface, your task should be simple. Just deal with the person who orders the products. However, there may be bigger opportunities. The technical manager may not be happy with the performance of commodity products. The research team or the marketing department may be planning new products, which could change the product specification. You need to monitor changing customer requirements.

My organisation needs to talk to senior directors about the strategic importance of our products. How can we do this when our sales team never gets the opportunity to meet directors?

It is unlikely that directors would have time during the normal working day to meet sales representatives, or regard a sales meeting as high on their list of priorities. You could arrange a seminar or executive briefing session that would appeal to directors. That would ensure you meet the right people and give you the opportunity to find out more about their needs.

MAKING IT HAPPEN

Identify the decision-makers

In business purchasing, more than one person influences the choice of supplier. Individuals make different contributions to the decision-making process and have different information requirements. Many companies have adopted team purchasing structures to deal with high-value purchases and it is important that you communicate effectively with every member of the team.

Depending on the value and complexity of the purchase, a decision-making team could include:

- senior executives
- purchasing professionals
- technical staff
- manufacturing managers
- service providers
- marketing staff
- departmental managers

Assess the importance of the purchase

As a rough guideline, you are likely to be dealing with a powerful purchasing organisation if any of the following conditions apply:

- your product is a vital component, or strategically important to your customers
- your product is technically complex
- your product is of high value

If your product is of relatively low value, purchasing decisions are more likely to revolve around price and delivery, and it is unlikely that a team would be involved.

The influence of team members varies at different stages during the purchasing process:

- purchasing staff and departmental managers may have considerable early influence when a specification is being drawn up
- when proposals are being evaluated, technical staff may be more influential
- senior executives are unlikely to be interested in detail, but they need an overview of the overall business benefits of the product or service

Senior executives

Senior executives need an overview of the business benefits of a product or service, and seek reassurance that your organisation is capable of supplying their long-term needs – any risk could be detrimental to their own business. Many suppliers try to move discussion of their products and services to board level to demonstrate that they are of strategic importance. This can be a useful exercise in developing business, because it can build a level of dependency that is important to account control.

Purchasing professionals

Purchasing professionals are usually the key figures in a purchasing team. While they may not take sole responsibility for decision-making, they are likely to be the team leaders and will remain your main point of contact.

Many companies operate a preferred supplier programme and, to be recognised, you may have to meet a detailed list of criteria. The purchasing department is instrumental in managing the list of approved suppliers. Many of the preferred supplier programmes include rating systems to measure suppliers' performance; these are part of a process of developing effective relationships, so that purchasing professionals can provide an even better service to their internal customers.

Finance executives

Finance executives have ultimate control over purchasing budgets, and they're likely to be involved if purchases are complex or entail major capital expenditure. They seek reassurance that they are getting value for money and that their purchase represents the best return on investment. They may consider alternative methods of financing, and you may be able to improve your competitive position by offering flexible schemes such as leasing or deferred payments.

Technical staff

Technical staff are a vital part of the purchasing team. They are responsible for improving the performance of the company products in order to develop a competitive edge. You therefore need to be closely involved with the technical team at a number of stages. When they are developing new products, you should be involved at the planning stages so you can influence the design. When they are enhancing existing products, you should be developing proposals to improve product performance. If they are moving into new markets, you can support them by handling contract development services, or by training their staff. You can provide them with a range of specialist technical services that enable them to provide a better service to their internal customers.

Manufacturing managers

If you are introducing an innovative product, or you have identified an opportunity to improve your customers' manufacturing operations or reduce costs, you need to influence manufacturing specialists.

Service providers

If you provide professional services rather than products, make sure that you are dealing with a service provider. Service providers are responsible for areas such as maintenance, training, administration, logistics, computers, and other services that enable business processes to operate efficiently. By working with them, you can improve relationships and increase customers' dependency on your organisation.

Marketing staff

Marketing specialists ensure that a product or service adds value and helps the company to develop a stronger competitive position. They will play an important part in decision-making if your customers are seeking to improve their market position or are entering new markets where you have specific expertise.

Departmental managers

Departmental managers are often the users of your products or services. They need to be reassured that they will benefit from dealing with a particular supplier. They play an important role in specifying the product and evaluating the performance of existing suppliers.

Research decision-makers

Although it is simple to list potential decision-makers, it is more complicated to identify who is actually involved in the process. Many decision-makers may not have a direct role in a project team, or may be involved in only part of the purchasing process, so you need to look carefully at your research processes.

Your sales team in regular contact with the customer should be best placed to identify the key decision-makers. There are a number of other techniques for identifying other influencers, such as:

- independent research into how companies buy different types of product or service; the survey may be limited to a specific group of customers, or carried out across a whole industry
- published industry surveys on buying patterns; these provide broad guidelines to the key decision-makers but need to be qualified by specific account research
- direct response advertising, in which responses are analysed to identify decision-making patterns
- joint projects, in which members of the customer team work with members of your team; the relationships and approval procedures that emerge provide useful clues about who are the hidden decision-makers

Research like this should be carried out continuously, because purchasing is a dynamic activity. Members of the decision-making team may change their jobs and, as the process progresses, individual contributions change.

COMMON MISTAKES

Concentrating on the wrong people

Don't focus your sales team on the wrong decision-makers. Companies rarely make it clear who influences the purchasing decisions. Meetings with the purchasing manager could be wasted if someone else draws up the specification.

Communicating at the wrong level

You may think you are just selling your customers a product or a service, but your product may make an important contribution to their business. If it is an innovative component that enables them to develop a new product or enter new markets, your company then becomes a potential strategic partner. Make sure that you communicate this to the right people.

THE BEST SOURCES OF HELP

Book:
Jobber, David, and Geoffrey Lancaster. *Selling and Sales Management.* 8th ed. London: FT Prentice Hall, 2009.

Website:
MRS: **www.marketresearch.org.uk**

Branding a Business Product

GETTING STARTED

Branding is as important in business markets as it is in consumer markets, and buyers feel more confident buying from a reliable company. Indeed, some buyers may be reluctant to buy new products that are not tried and tested.

FAQS

How can I identify brand attributes?

Brand attributes are not always obvious. A good starting point is customer research. What do your customers feel is important when they buy? Compare their requirements against the performance of your own products and your company. Alternatively, look at your competitors and consider your comparative strengths.

What do I do if my brand attributes look poor?

Customers admire a company that is committed to continuous improvement, so start looking for improvements, particularly in the attributes that are most important to customers. Make sure you communicate any improvement.

Is it possible to measure the effect of branding?

In consumer markets, companies use tracking research to monitor changes in customer perceptions of the company. This research can indicate whether customers see your company in a more favourable light. This, in turn, can increase the likelihood of future sales.

My advertising budget is limited. Should I concentrate on product messages or brand-building messages?

Product messages are more likely to generate short-term revenue. That could increase your marketing budget over time. However, it would be wrong to neglect brand-building messages completely. You would be sacrificing long-term business development.

An increasing proportion of sales is coming via the Internet. Does this mean brand values are now less important?

With more and more crowding on the Internet, companies will have to work hard to stand out. Brand values will remain important.

MAKING IT HAPPEN

Why business branding is important

Branding is as important in business markets as in consumer markets. Business buyers, however, look for a different set of brand values. They ask what a product or service can do for their business.

Using the brand values

The following list covers the key attributes. Once you have identified the attributes that are most important to your customers and prospects, you can emphasise them in your communications. If an attribute is important to customers, but is currently weak, you should consider ways of improving performance.

Fitness for purpose

The product should be fit for its purpose. Does it meet the buyer's specification and conform to industry standards? Approval by recognised authorities is important.

Value for money and quality

Value for money may be important to some buyers. That does not mean buyers will always look for the lowest price. Some customers may be happy to pay more for a product with an integral maintenance package. Quality can be an important differentiator. Japanese companies led the way in transforming their brand values with massive improvements in quality. Companies that excel in quality build confidence.

Extendability

If you supply a range of products or services, brand values should be extendable to the entire range. This can help to build incremental business and strengthen customer loyalty.

Company reliability

Buyers feel more confident buying from a reliable company. That means solid financial performance, a strong management team, a good industrial relations record, and a track record in effective products.

Tried and tested products

Some buyers may be reluctant to buy new products that are not tried and tested. They don't like to think that their companies are being treated as proving grounds for product development laboratories.

Investing in product development

Customers want to know that products are being continuously improved. They are not necessarily interested in leading-edge products, but they want to know that they are getting the best products currently available.

Distribution and finance

If distribution is poor, customers can't buy the product. The importance of distribution varies by product, and the recent growth of direct sales via the Internet is reducing its importance. However, certain products, such as components or supplies, continue to depend on effective national distribution. The availability of finance may be important to some customers. Capital goods have long been marketed with a finance package, but finance is also available on many lower-value products. Attractive interest rates or payment terms can differentiate a product.

Service back-up

Service back-up is vital to products that a customer depends on. The loss of a critical process can prove damaging, so a customer wants to know that service response will be rapid.

Training

Training helps customers make effective use of a product. Many companies operate their own training departments or develop distance-learning packages, to ensure that customer staff become familiar with new products.

Customised products

Customised products may represent higher value than standard versions. Customers have individual needs and a standard product may not prove an exact fit. By modifying, you can meet needs more effectively.

Partnership

Working in partnership with a customer can increase the value of the relationship. Partnership may mean working on joint development projects or providing a package of services that support a customer throughout the life cycle of the product. Collaboration on joint projects is now much easier with the growth of videoconferencing and other communications.

Administration and customer service
Efficient administration makes it easier to buy from a company. Lost orders, inaccurate invoices, and poor correspondence do not impress customers. Quality of customer service is a key measure of a company's values. Customer service takes many forms, from the way a customer's initial enquiry is handled to the quality of after-sales service. In a number of companies, customer service is viewed as a strategic activity, with dedicated staff and documented procedures.

Consultancy
Consultancy can move a company from commodity supplier to valued partner. Pre-sales advice is critical with complex or high-value products, and the quality of advice can determine where the order goes.

Technical support
The scope of technical support ranges from advice on the right product for an application, to after-sales user support and problem-solving. In complex products, the quality of technical support can be the most important differentiator.

Environmental issues
Many companies are judged on their environmental performance. Products must conform to appropriate legislation, but companies are also measured by the effects of their processes on the environment. Using materials from non-renewable sources or that contribute to pollution can damage a company's image.

Ordering and product information
Simple ordering procedures make it easier for customers to do business. Many companies have automated their ordering processes to reduce the time a customer has to spend on administration. Quality brochures, detailed product guides, comprehensive information on the Internet, and clear presentations help buyers to make informed decisions.

Delivery
Delivery, like administration, is not seen as a key marketing activity, but it has an impact on brand perceptions.

Customer base
Buyers assess a product by the customers who already use it. A blue-chip customer list demonstrates product quality and approval.

COMMON MISTAKES
Neglecting the 'soft' issues
Many companies communicate their strengths in the 'hard' attributes, such as quality, performance, and price. Customers may take these for granted, particularly in a commodity market. The 'soft' attributes such as customer service or technical support, can prove to be key.

Ignoring branding
Traditionally, branding has been seen as a consumer marketing discipline. Business marketing was seen as different; buyers were assumed to be rational and decisions were believed to depend primarily on price and performance. Research has shown that business purchase decisions are more complex, and companies base their decisions on a variety of factors. Business-to-business companies ignore branding at their peril.

Concentrating on the wrong attributes
It's essential to communicate what customers feel is important. In technology markets, quality of support and commitment to product development may outweigh price and delivery. In commodity markets, support and information can differentiate products with no performance advantage.

THE BEST SOURCES OF HELP
Book:
de Chernatony, Leslie, and Malcolm McDonald. *Creating Powerful Brands*. Oxford: Butterworth-Heinemann, 2003.

Website:
Chartered Institute of Marketing: **www.cim.co.uk**

Raising Awareness of Your Brand

GETTING STARTED
Whatever the size of your business, brand awareness plays an important role when customers make a decision to buy. It's essential that you understand what your brand 'values' are, and they can relate to many areas, from product attributes to less-tangible aspects of a company's reputation such as good customer care or a top-notch website. By identifying the key values of your brand you can establish how your products, your services, and your company are perceived by different types of customer.

FAQS

Can a small company use branding?

Absolutely. You have to understand your own brand, since you will have a brand or corporate image in your market whether you like it or not! Smaller companies increasingly compete with large, well-known, brands – sometimes globally – so the aim of branding is to differentiate your company or product and to convey its unique attributes. Don't be behind the door. Make sure that your name, address, contact details, and logos feature prominently on your website, catalogues, quotes, leader headers, even compliments slips and packing slips.

How important are brand values?

Branding is frequently perceived as a consumer marketing discipline. However, industry experience indicates that business-to-business purchasing is a complex process influenced by intangible perceptions as much as by hard facts on product performance.

MAKING IT HAPPEN

Identify the most important elements of a brand

The key attributes of a business brand may include the following:

- fitness for purpose – is it the best at what it does?
- value for money – if not offered at always the lowest price, does it represent a good deal compared to the competition, even if it isn't better?
- quality – is it simply better built or better managed?
- extendability – does the brand work in many related markets?
- company reliability – does the brand come from a good 'stable'?
- proven products – is the brand associated with established successes?
- investment in product development – is innovation significant?

Find out what is important to your customers

Although these brand values can be applied to business products in general terms, it's vital to understand how individual customers rank the values. This can be determined in several ways, described below.

Talk to customers

This is the simplest way to find out what they value, but take care not to talk exclusively about the physical benefits of a product. There will almost certainly be aspects of service that are as important. You should also ask 'open' questions about the competition for example:

- Who else have you looked at?
- What do you think of them?
- What is their biggest strength or weakness?
- What do other people think of them?

Carry out customer surveys

To find out what your customers consider important, carry out a survey; if your budget runs to it, this should be done through a market research company so that respondents feel the survey is independent. It should ask respondents how they rank the different brand values and how they believe your company and a number of competitors compare across these values.

Run a focus group

Although they're not appropriate for all industries, focus groups can be used to cover the same ground as the customer survey. In addition, they'll enable you to cover the subject in greater depth and to raise issues that you may not anticipate or that would normally be outside the scope of a survey. Focus groups are ideal for identifying branding issues that concern customers, assessing customer reactions to potential changes, or identifying any problems customers are experiencing.

Review industry trends

When you're trying to do a hundred things at once, keeping on top of websites and publications relevant to your industry can seem a luxury, but it is actually essential. Spending a few hours each week finding out about new developments, trends, product ideas and so on can be energising and helpful. Industry associations and publishers also produce regular surveys into buying behaviour in their industry sector, and these can highlight issues that concern the whole market.

Find out about customer purchasing requirements

An increasing number of business customers use formal criteria to evaluate potential suppliers and monitor their performance. These purchasing criteria indicate the factors that your customers believe are important and can help to identify the key messages you should include in your own brand communications.

Communicate through all channels

Advertising and marketing communications are the most important media for raising awareness. However, there are several other direct and indirect channels, including:

- products – the design and brand symbolism can convey significant brand values
- services – the way you deal with customers can demonstrate your commitment to their needs
- packaging – can carry messages regarding your brand
- distribution facilities – can give an impression of your approach and values
- websites – must be consistent with your key brand values
- customer service facilities – must deliver the promise of the brand

Assess your product branding

Do your products communicate your key brand values? The most important values are listed above, but brand values extend to every aspect of your company that your customer may experience.

If customer research shows that you are perceived as poor in any of these areas, or if customers are not aware of your strengths, you must look closely at your product development programme. Also review your customer communications to see how customers build their image of your brand.

Actionlists

Brand your services

Service capability can also help to differentiate a company from its competitors. Many companies have underestimated the importance of service to their customers and as a result haven't adequately communicated their service capabilities. The right services can help customers improve their own business performance and can supplement their own resources, so raising awareness of service capability is an important aspect of brand communication. You can increase awareness through product advertising, product literature, direct marketing, and product public relations, as well as through service communications.

Communicate brand values through packaging

Packaging raises awareness of brand values by the way in which it reflects the corporate identity. The right packaging can visually support your brand through the use of your logo, slogans, promises, and company values.

Don't forget to include your branding distribution facilities

Your distribution facilities can affect awareness of your brand. Again, if your budget allows, vehicles, uniforms, and premises should carry the same logo and key messages as other media of communication.

Distribution is an area that is frequently overlooked in branding programmes, but it can make an important contribution to customer perceptions of your company. For example, the cleanliness of a delivery van shows a level of professionalism.

Build brand values through your website

An effective e-commerce website is one in which the various technical and design components all work together to generate customer interest, build trust, communicate product value, and support convenient profitable transactions. Even if you don't sell directly from your website, the key is that your customers must feel they have gained something from the visit that exceeds the 'cost' (even if only in time) of visiting.

Brand through customer service facilities

Your customer service facilities have a major impact on the way your customers perceive your company. Customer contact takes place both before and after a sale, and these contacts can prove critical in shaping customer attitudes.

When your customer service team handles enquiries, orders, or complaints effectively, it creates awareness of positive brand values.

Monitor levels of brand awareness

Customer perceptions change over a period of time. Continuous research should be carried out to monitor customer attitudes. This type of research is known as tracking research, and it helps to measure the effectiveness of brand communications programmes.

COMMON MISTAKES

Failing to monitor customer perceptions

Regular research is critical. You must know how you are perceived by your customers so that you can plan the way your brand is represented in the future.

Overlooking individual customer preferences

Industry research may give you a broad view of the brand values that are important to customers. However, it's more important to understand how individual customers – particularly your most important customers – rank individual values. This can be achieved only by continuous detailed research into individual customer needs.

Ignoring important communication channels

Brand values are communicated through many different channels, not just advertising and marketing media. Customers' attitudes and perceptions are shaped by packaging, customer service, distribution, and products as well as by other factors. Make sure every aspect of your business reflects the brand values that are important to your customers.

THE BEST SOURCES OF HELP

Book:
Gainess Ross, Lesley. *Corporate Reputation: 12 Steps to Safeguarding and Recovering Reputation.* Chichester: Wiley, 2008.

Websites:
British Brands Group:
   www.britishbrandsgroup.org.uk
Institute of Practitioners in Advertising:
   www.ipa.co.uk

Creating Product Literature

GETTING STARTED
There are many different types of product publication, each of which has a different role in the sales and marketing process.

FAQS
Who should write product literature?

Product and technical specialists should provide the input and content for product literature. However, it is important that this content is edited or rewritten by a professional writer or communications specialist who understands the information needs of the market.

Isn't it easier to produce a single product catalogue rather than a range of publications?

Not necessarily: for example, if the products change frequently, the cost of updating the catalogue could be prohibitive. Where there is a wide range of products and customers in different market sectors, a single publication may not provide the depth of information needed.

Does the Internet make product publications redundant?

The Internet has made it easier to produce, update, and distribute product information. However, the comfort factor means that demand for printed publications remains relatively high.

MAKING IT HAPPEN
Choose the right type of publication

There are many different types of product publication, each with a different role in the sales and marketing process.

Leaflets

Leaflets or flyers are simple forms of communication used in the early stages of customer contact. They summarise the key benefits of a product or service and help to create initial interest. They are economical to produce and can be updated easily.

Catalogues

Catalogues give customers an indication of the scope of a product range. A catalogue provides an overview and should point to other publications that provide more detailed information. It should be clearly laid out so that customers can find the specific information they want quickly and easily.

Product brochures

The contents should cover:

- product description
- how the product is used
- main benefits to the customer
- important achievements
- market position
- related products or services
- company information
- commercial information such as price or availability

Data sheets

Data sheets provide the detailed technical information that customers need in order to evaluate products. They should help customers to understand the benefits of a product and to compare it with competitors' offerings.

Product guides

A product guide provides a highly detailed description of a product and can be issued to the salesforce as well as to customers and prospects. It should include the same information as a product brochure but with a far greater level of detail. It should cover:

- description of the product and its main applications
- analysis of product features
- product operation and necessary skills
- accessories, replacement parts, and support services

Technical updates

Technical updates are used to keep customers up to date with information on the products they have bought. They also communicate a policy of continuous improvement. The information that has changed may be important to customers, so it must be shown clearly. Any important safety information should be highlighted.

Help customers to make informed decisions

Your customers may not evaluate a product in the way you want them to. You must explain benefits carefully, particularly those that are less obvious, such as reduced maintenance costs.

Educate customers

If your product is innovative, you may need to reinforce the product description with customer education in order to explain the product and its potential benefits.

Provide practical guidelines on usage

Your product literature may need to include instructions or guidelines on use to help customers to get the best from the product. You should also include information on sources of technical help or other assistance.

Reassure your customers

Customers may be reluctant to change from an existing product or supplier. Case histories, testimonials from satisfied customers, lists of existing users, or approval by official bodies can help to reassure customers.

Stress price and quality

Customers don't necessarily want the lowest price: they are looking for value for money. Stress the quality of your product and show how it can save your customers money.

Present the complete product range

Customers may be interested in one specific product, but you should refer to your complete range. It may generate cross-selling opportunities, and it also tells customers that they can obtain all their product needs from a single source.

Present benefits, not features

When customers are making an initial assessment of your product, they want to know how it will benefit them. Features become more important when they are comparing your product with competitive offerings.

Recognise your customers' needs

Your copy should demonstrate that you understand your customers' needs. Describe the business and technical issues facing customers, and show how your product helps customers to deal with them.

Brand your products
It is important to build customer confidence in your products and your company. Reinforce the brand values that you have established in your advertising and direct marketing. Product literature should sell as well as inform.

Offer related services
You can add value to your products by offering customers services such as planning, installation, training, and maintenance. These services will help your customers to make more effective use of your products and offer them the benefits of an all-in-one package.

Make effective use of product publications
A brochure may be the most obvious initial suggestion, but the idea should be carefully examined by laying down stringent requirements for in-house users:

- ask them to make out a business case for the brochure
- levy an internal charge on the brochure, which must be covered by an increase in revenue
- ask them to define a specific communications task for the brochure

This process not only eliminates ill-considered requests, it also helps to ensure a precise brief that will improve the value and performance of the communication, whatever form it eventually takes.

Consider alternatives to the brochure
- Customised presentations, where your company has a small number of key customers. A presentation can be customised for each customer and easily updated. The presentation not only provides relevant, highly targeted information, it also increases personal contact with the customer.
- A customer magazine, where you have a larger customer base and your product range or technology changes rapidly. A regular magazine can easily be distributed to the larger target audience.
- A customer handbook, where you work in partnership with a small number of customers. A customer handbook, generally in loose-leaf form, includes information on both

supplier and customer to increase mutual understanding and awareness.
- A customised information pack, where you have a wide product range and a large customer base in many different sectors and where information requirements are therefore highly diversified. An information pack, consisting of a corporate folder or wallet with sector- or customer-specific inserts, provides a flexible communications tool.
- A targeted literature programme, where you have a database that allows you to segment your customer base and track purchasing patterns and campaign response. Use the database to develop a contact strategy that begins with introductory literature and goes on to provide groups or individual customers with product information reflecting their specific needs and purchasing patterns.

COMMON MISTAKES
Producing the wrong type of publication
Different types of publications have specific roles in the sales and marketing process. Giving prospective customers detailed product guides when they are only carrying out a preliminary evaluation represents wasted effort.

Overlooking alternatives to publications
A publication may not always be the most appropriate communications solution. For example, if a prospect has specific product requirements, it may be more appropriate to develop a customised presentation tailored to that prospect.

Producing information that is too technical
Product information is read by a wide group of different decision-makers, including purchasing managers, general managers, technical specialists, and senior executives. The copy must relate to the information needs of each group. Content should reflect all of these interests.

THE BEST SOURCES OF HELP
Website:
Chartered Institute of Marketing: **www.cim.co.uk**

Extending a Product with Service

GETTING STARTED
'Service' is a business concept that's often overlooked or relegated to somewhere in between maintenance and problem-solving. Done properly, though, service can be a key differentiator between your business and the competition. Meeting customer requirements in the most appropriate and efficient way adds enormously to the perceived value of your

product and can sometimes increase the profitability of your relationship. Don't worry if you don't have the skills or resources to deliver extra services yourself: you can either build your own service team through recruitment and training or work in partnership with a specialist organisation which will deliver the service on your behalf.

FAQS

I already offer free installation and maintenance with my products. Does that add value?

Yes. But while some customers may expect this, others may not, or may not value the service. Many companies have recognised the importance of service to certain customers, and have changed their service strategy accordingly. Instead of offering free service to everyone, they have upgraded the services, increased the range of services offered, and therefore, in some cases, started charging customers. Although customers may initially object to being charged for something that seemed to be free, they may see the value of a service that now more closely meets their needs.

I sell in a business-to-business market and my customers have their own internal service people. Why should they want to use my services?

Many companies have internal service departments. They can be expensive to maintain, however, and are sometimes lacking in essential skills. For example, they may not be trained in the latest software. By demonstrating the potential savings and benefits of outsourcing a service, you can persuade them to switch to you.

MAKING IT HAPPEN

Differentiate your product with service

Service is proving to be a key differentiator in many market sectors. In many companies, however, the role of the service department should be more than simply maintenance and problem-solving. For example, a company supplying industrial dishwashers to the restaurant trade has to respond quickly to breakdowns – replacing the machine if necessary rather than simply scheduling a repair visit. So, to take full advantage of the service opportunity, it is important to explain the benefits of effective service to customers, and present your service operations as convenient, cost-effective, and strategically important.

Meet key service attributes

These are some of the key features that customers may be looking for in a service offer:

- one contact point, simplifying contact and service administration
- direct contact with a technical specialist, providing an immediate response to problems or queries wherever the customer is located
- quality support to a standard such as ISO 9000, giving independent reassurance that service standards are high
- support around the clock, meaning that it is available when customers need it, minimises interruption of their business
- service options give a choice of service levels, which can be aligned to customers' needs
- investment in support means long-term commitment to the customer

Provide one contact point for service resources

Whether your customers have a technical query, a service request, or a product enquiry, or need advice, guidance, or information, they should be able to call one number for direct access to all your support resources. Ideally, you'll have specialists on the spot to deal with their requests. If they can't answer the query immediately, make sure that the right person calls the customer back.

Offer direct contact with technical specialists

Your customers may have a technical query, and want to talk to an experienced specialist immediately. When they call the technical help desk, they should be talking to a highly skilled person with extensive technical support and field experience. It may mean locating support staff in accessible locations to be able to make visits quickly and efficiently.

Provide good support

When your customers have a service request, they should be able to contact a central service point where a service co-ordinator ensures that the right specialist help is available. Service co-ordinators should ensure that customers get the fastest and most effective response to their requests. In some cases, service points can deal with requests directly, but if not, they can assign an engineer to visit the customer site within agreed times. All service processes should be assessed with reference to to ISO 9000. If customers have any queries, there should be an 'escalation procedure' to move a customer complaint up to a more senior team member if the person dealing with the complaint initially cannot resolve it. This should ensure a prompt resolution of any problems.

Offer flexible service options

You can provide your customers with a choice of flexible service options to suit their operational needs and to increase their loyalty. If your customers have in-house support, you can support their team with an efficient spares delivery service, or manage their spares for them. You can also offer to enhance the skills of your customer's in-house team with training, advice and guidance, technical support, and access to specialists. You may go as far as offering consultancy on a fee basis, utilising your specialist knowledge to help your customer.

Invest in support

High-quality service for your market may require a significant investment in the service infrastructure: the right premises, efficient service communications, and a sophisticated service management system to enable you to enhance your response and performance even further. It may require you to appoint one person with specific responsibility for customer service or, perhaps, to develop a dedicated support website.

Add value to a product

Improving your customer service may add value and help to differentiate your products and services from the competition. By analysing the products and services in your range (and those of your competitors), you can add relevant value and improve a customer's perception of your business. Some examples are:

- business services that free up customer staff to do more important tasks, or help managers perform their jobs better. Training, for example, can ensure that staff make more effective use of the products the company buys.
- complementary services to make a consumer product more attractive. Film processing could, for example, be offered with a camera.
- convenience services added to a basic service to enhance it. Insurance companies, for example, might add a helpline or list of approved repairers to help their customers to recover more quickly from an accident.

Develop product/service packages
To add value to products and to increase customer loyalty, put together 'bundles' of products and services that reflect customer needs. Examples include:

'Adding-in' services
- specialist package holidays, including flights, hotel, and guides
- a building company includes plans and planning application services

'Leaving-out' services
- 'fastfit' car repair centres, without non-essential services
- specialised conveyancing services without using solicitors

Added value services
- home delivery of fast food or videos
- support and advice through helplines

Changing distribution channels
- direct sales, bypassing retailers, such as organic vegetable 'box schemes'
- electronic delivery, such as delivery of technical drawings and specifications

COMMON MISTAKES
Offering only basic services
Basic services such as installation, maintenance, and upgrades are available from many different service organisations. They do not differentiate you and they do not add value. Higher-value services, requiring skill, knowledge, or experience, are the keys to success.

Failing to invest in a service infrastructure
Customers expect a quality service. That means you have to invest in people and infrastructure. Ideally, your services should conform to recognised industry standards. If you fail to deliver the right standard of service, you could damage customer relationships.

Missing service opportunities
Customers require many different services during the time they own a product. Their requirements could include: advice, consultancy, and design before the sale; installation and training; then maintenance, upgrading, and other after-sales services. Each of these represents an opportunity to earn incremental income and maintain contact with the customer.

THE BEST SOURCES OF HELP
Book:
Lovelock, Christopher, and Jochen Wirtz. *Services Marketing: People, Technology, Strategy*. 6th ed. London: FT Prentice Hall, 2007.

Website:
Chartered Institute of Marketing: **www.cim.co.uk**

Introducing a New Product to Market

GETTING STARTED
New product launches are crucial to the success of a business and need careful planning. Internal communications are vital to the early success of the programme, as is the support of the senior management team.

FAQS
Is it risky to spend money on a high-profile launch? The rate of new-product failure is relatively high.
Actually, failure to launch properly may be a contributory factor to poor performance by new products. Provided the product has been carefully researched and developed, an effective launch should act as a good launch pad. It can't

work miracles, however, and won't rescue a poor product, or one with no defined market.

Why spend money on an internal launch, when it is the customers who will determine success?
Unless you have the commitment of the management team and the people who will be responsible for designing, producing, selling, and distributing the product, it is unlikely to get the support or resources it needs to succeed. Internal communication is key.

If a product is good enough, do I need to run sales incentives during the launch period?
Any product has to fight for attention from the sales team and resellers. An incentive may give the new product a vital push during the critical launch period.

MAKING IT HAPPEN
Plan carefully
New product launches are crucial to the success of a business and reflect a considerable amount of investment. The product launch progresses through a number of important stages:
- internal communications, to ensure high levels of awareness and commitment to the new product
- pre-launch activity, to secure distribution and ensure that retailers have the skills, resources, and knowledge to market the product
- launch events at national, regional, or local level
- post-event activity to help the salesforce and retailers make the most of the event
- launch advertising and other forms of customer communication

Communicate the launch internally
Internal communications are vital to the early success of the programme. The new product development team must sell its concepts to the senior management team who will commit resources to the project. They also need to win the support of a number of departments who will form part of the product launch process – manufacturing, design, research and development, distribution, and marketing. Sales and marketing departments involved in the practical launch of the product should be fully briefed on the product so that they can begin the external communications process. Sales staff should be issued with comprehensive sales and marketing guides so that they can identify the most important prospects. The marketing department will use the specification and objectives of the programme to formulate other marketing programmes and identify the most important sectors for development.

Launch the product to the trade
If a product is sold through a distributor or retail network, pre-launch activity is important. The programme should include a sales and distributor incentive programme to generate high levels of initial interest. Incentives to build high levels of launch stock are essential. If a product is not available in the retail outlets, consumer launch material is wasted. Launch guides will help to give local outlets an indication of all the key activities that should be carried out.

Produce a launch guide
A launch guide ensures that everyone involved in the launch process understands the product, and the launch itself.

Explain the background
The first section of the guide should cover the background to the launch and the market opportunities:
- Why is the new product being launched?
- How does it fit into the company's overall strategy?
- What sort of people will buy the product and how do they differ from traditional customers?

- What new opportunities does this give the local outlet?
- How will competitors respond to this product?

Highlight features and benefits
The second part of the guide should explain the features and benefits of the product. The guide:
- will act as a sales guide for the local outlet staff
- will ensure that they fully understand the product
- should include information about the training and product support available
- will outline the key stages of any training that is to be an integral part of the launch programme
- will identify the people who should be involved in the training programme, together with a training schedule

Describe launch support
The third part of the guide should indicate the level of support available for the launch. This will include the launch event itself. Details should be given of national advertising and promotional programmes, together with any local marketing programmes. Advance notice allows local outlets to order support material, and to plan their own local marketing programme, so that it is fully integrated with the national launch.

Outline launch activities
The final part of the guide should provide a schedule, and a list of key launch activities, so that the management team can meet all the requirements of the launch programme. These launch activities might include:
- stock and ordering details
- a training schedule
- launch events
- dates for national and local advertising
- suggested dates and formats for customer events
- a schedule for launching marketing activities

Announce on the website
Highlight the new product on your website with an announcement on the home page and a link to any product information or launch news stories in the site. You could also add a footer to all e-mail correspondence mentioning the new product and displaying the website address.

Arrange high-profile launch events
Hold a national launch event, attended by all sales staff and all retailers, or hold a series of regional events for local retailers. Alternatively, you can introduce the new product to individual outlets through a series of sales calls, or send mailings to individual outlets.

Maintain momentum through post-launch activity
It is easy to overlook in the emotion of a major launch that the real sales effort has only just begun. Post-launch sales activities can include promotional support for retailers and ongoing incentives for retailers and the

salesforce, as well as direct marketing programmes to help retailers market the new products and local events to reinforce the launch.

Communicate the product to customers

The customer launch can be achieved in a number of different ways, including advertising, direct marketing, trial offers, and exhibitions.

Use other forms of marketing to raise initial awareness and get customers to try the new product.

Use advertising to build interest

Advertising can provide a high-profile launch platform. It can be used in a number of ways:

- to announce the new product in order to raise customer awareness
- to advise customers where to obtain the new product
- to offer customers further information, or a trial of the product, as a way of generating sales leads

Use sales promotion to encourage product trial

Sales promotion activities can also be used to encourage sampling and product trial. Curiosity value and novelty are not sufficient to ensure the success of a new product launch. The promotional campaign must incorporate strong consumer benefits, together with an incentive to buy that might include money off on trial packs.

Target key prospects with direct marketing

Direct marketing to key customer groups will allow the marketing group to target their most important prospects. It can be used to make special offers, or to provide detailed information about the new products and feedback on new product performance. The flexibility of direct marketing means that you can evaluate different launch and marketing approaches.

Communicate at the point of sale

Consumer information at the point of sale is essential for new products sold through retail outlets. It can be used to reach the prospects and customers who may have been missed in the advertising campaign and to reinforce other media. Point-of-sale material provides additional information to customers and prospects and supports sales development through retail outlets.

Use the press

A press information programme will ensure that the new product receives good coverage in the right publications. It can take a number of formats, including tie-in promotions such as reader offers, competitions, and product information in the form of press releases or feature articles.

COMMON MISTAKES
Failing to motivate the salesforce

The salesforce is critical to the success of a product launch. They need to be committed to the product so that they can communicate enthusiastically with customers and resellers. A new product will form only part of their overall sales target, so motivation is essential.

Losing momentum after the launch

A lot of effort and energy goes into a launch, but many companies fail to maintain the sales and distribution momentum. After the initial period, sales may slump to a point where the product fails to recover.

THE BEST SOURCES OF HELP
Book:
Cooper, Robert G. *Winning at New Products: Accelerating the Process from Idea to Launch*. 3rd ed. New York: Perseus, 2001.

Planning a Corporate Public Relations Campaign

GETTING STARTED

Corporate public relations raises awareness of a company and builds confidence. It is important when a company has undergone change or is entering new markets. It can also overcome problems of poor reputation.

The corporate reputation is the way a company is perceived by customers, suppliers, and other important groups. Corporate public relations stresses the positive aspects of an organisation and seeks to correct any misunderstandings.

The first stage in building a positive corporate reputation is to assess current perceptions. An audit identifies key areas for improving communications performance. A corporate press relations programme should communicate:

- professionalism
- technical success
- market success
- corporate stability

It is essential that messages should be communicated consistently in every form of contact with the customer. The programme should include information on:

- new appointments and management changes
- investments and other business developments
- business and financial performance

FAQS

If my company has a poor reputation in the market, can corporate public relations overcome that?

Corporate public relations can help to correct wrong perceptions. However, if the perceptions are based on poor corporate performance, the focus should be on improving performance. Trying to mislead the market can be dangerous.

My company's products have an excellent reputation in the market. Why should I worry about corporate public relations?

Success depends on more than a good product range. Your company may have excellent products but a poor delivery record. If demand is growing, customers will ask if you have the capacity to meet new levels of demand. If your company is not making good profits, customers will ask whether it can invest for the future or even survive in the long term.

Who should deal with press enquiries about corporate matters?

Companies deal with this issue in different ways. Some companies appoint a single spokesperson who handles all enquiries. Others refer enquiries to a senior director. It is essential that telephone operators are aware of the correct press contacts. It can be frustrating for journalists to be passed from person to person. An alternative is to route all press enquiries to a corporate public relations consultancy.

MAKING IT HAPPEN

Plan corporate public relations

Corporate public relations raises awareness of a company and builds the confidence of different groups in the company. It can be important in a number of different business scenarios.

- The company has undergone significant change.
- Research shows that customers are not aware of the company's key strengths.
- The company is entering new markets and there is low awareness among potential customers.
- Research shows that the company has a poor reputation in a number of areas important to its success.
- The company is building key account or partnership relationships and customers need to know that the company can maintain its standard of supply.

Identify the elements of a corporate reputation

The corporate reputation is the way a company is perceived by customers, suppliers, and other important groups. It is based on a number of elements, including:

- financial performance
- the quality of the management team
- clarity of direction
- market performance
- growth record and potential

- relationships with suppliers and employees
- manufacturing capability

Build a positive corporate reputation

Corporate public relations stresses the positive aspects of an organisation and seeks to correct any misunderstandings.

Audit the corporate reputation

The first stage in building a positive corporate reputation is to assess current perceptions of the organisation through research. This is the management summary of a research programme into customer perceptions.

- The company is almost as visible as its competitors but is only rated third in all issues associated with image.
- Contact with the customer at all levels is less than professional. According to the customer, the company does not understand its business and its products, and does not communicate its future strategies.
- There is a legacy of poor reputation which has largely been overcome by increased product reliability, but the image persists in the minds of the customer's senior management team.
- The company is perceived as offering lower quality and lower performance than competitors, and its users are less satisfied than competitors' users.
- The company is seen as losing ground with important decision-makers.
- The company is identified more clearly than competitors with specific product lines, but is not rated most highly as the potential supplier of those products.
- The company's major weakness is perceived as its narrow product line and lack of expertise in certain areas.

An audit like this identifies key areas for improving communications performance. In such circumstances, it is essential that positive messages such as those below should be communicated consistently in every form of contact with the customer.

Communicate professionalism

The company is a professional organisation that understands the customer's business needs and can meet them with a wide range of high-quality products and services. The sample messages below would support this perception:

- The company is investing £X in training over the next year.
- The company is organised into market-focused groups to offer the highest standards of service.
- X number of staff are dedicated to the customer's business.
- The company is committed to total quality.
- The company has developed a broad product range and a full range of support services.
- The new product development programme is providing innovative new products.

Communicate technical success

The company is technically successful in major projects, developing total solutions and delivering value for money, on time, every time. The important messages to support this perception include the following:

- The company has an established reputation for innovation.

- The company's products have been selected for the following demanding applications . . .
- Customers are saving money by using the company's products.
- The company's products conform to international standards.
- The company has a research and development budget in excess of £X, and has a team of X highly skilled people dedicated to technical support.

Communicate market success

The company is winning share from its competitors. The important messages to support this perception include the following:

- The company has been selected to provide products and services to the following customers . . .
- The company has recently won a major order worth £X.
- The company has been selected as a strategic supplier to the following customers . . .
- The company has gained X per cent market share in the last year, while competitors have lost X per cent share in the last year.

Communicate corporate stability

'The company is successful and financially stable, with a sound management team – a good prospective supplier and business partner.' The important messages to support this perception include the following:

- The company's annual results show X per cent growth in orders, revenue, and profits.
- The company is expanding.
- The company is a member of the following international groups . . .
- The company is the leading European supplier.

Introduce a corporate press relations programme

A wide variety of press relations techniques can be used to improve corporate relations. They include:

- regular press releases on new appointments and management changes
- regular press releases on investments and other business developments
- interviews with senior executives in important magazines
- encouraging press visits

COMMON MISTAKES

Ignoring corporate public relations

Many companies fail to recognise the problems caused by a poor corporate reputation. They concentrate on product public relations because corporate matters appear to be intangible. This can make it difficult for a company to rebuild confidence if problems occur.

Waiting until a crisis before investing in corporate public relations

If a company hits a crisis, it may try to limit damage by issuing press information. Journalists usually recognise this type of crisis in public relations and this can make the situation worse. By adopting a policy of continuing public relations, it is possible to build effective relations with the press and gain understanding if there are problems.

Ignoring certain key groups

Successful corporate communication depends on building understanding with all the groups that influence the success of your business. This might include investors, employees, pressure groups, distributors, and suppliers – as well as customers. In planning your campaign, make sure that you cover all the key groups.

THE BEST SOURCES OF HELP

Books:

Alsop, Ron. *The 18 Immutable Laws of Corporate Reputation: Creating, Protecting and Repairing Your Most Valuable Asset*. Rev. ed. London: Kogan Page, 2006.

Gregory, Anne, ed. *Public Relations in Practice*. 2nd ed. London: Kogan Page, 2003.

Websites:

Chartered Institute of Public Relations:
 www.cipr.co.uk
Public Relations Consultants' Organisation:
 www.prca.org.uk

Producing a Corporate Brochure

GETTING STARTED

A corporate brochure is a publication that is designed to provide customers with reassurance. Its aim is to present the company as a solid, well-managed business partner offering an excellent product range and possessing the attributes of financial stability, technological innovation, reliability, and customer focus.

FAQS

How important is the corporate brochure?

Many companies produce a corporate brochure before considering any other publication. It is seen as the face of the company and is particularly popular with the sales-force. Despite its popularity, however, it is not necessarily the most effective form of communication. A corporate brochure has a role to play in communicating company information, but it should not be used as a substitute for targeted communications.

Corporate brochures can be expensive to produce. Should their use be restricted?

The feeling exists that corporate brochures should be high-quality publications because these will reflect a solid company. These expensive brochures are then often given away freely by members of the salesforce. A growing number of companies have introduced internal charging for publications, so that internal customers must now prepare a business case for using publications; the result is that they are used more carefully.

Who should receive corporate brochures?

Corporate brochures can be used as part of an integrated communications programme aimed at customers (actual and prospective), suppliers, business partners, distributors, and investors. They can also be used, selectively, as part of an employee communications programme.

MAKING IT HAPPEN

Present a successful company

A corporate brochure demonstrates corporate success presenting the company as a financially stable, long-term partner. Above all, the corporate brochure should be a statement of confidence: this is a publication that is designed to reassure customers.

A corporate brochure should include the following information about a company:

- a description of its product range
- location, resources, and international activities
- technical and research capability
- manufacturing resources
- success in handling complex projects
- success in terms of innovation or market leadership
- financial performance
- management skills

Present the product range

A company must show that its product range meets current requirements and can be developed in response to changing market conditions. The product range should contain a good balance of market-leading established products and new products with good growth potential.

Communicate innovation

Companies who supply technically advanced products must be seen to be at the leading edge of technology: they must convince their customers that their policy of continuous innovation enables them to offer more advanced products than their competitors.

Demonstrate high-performance products

When customers are trying to improve the performance of their own products, they need to work with companies who can comply with their requirements and meet new technological challenges. High-performance products have to meet stringent quality checks if they are to be accepted. They are often used in safety-critical applications where the margin for error is extremely small.

In presenting company capability, it is important to show how the company conforms to requirements.

Communicate investment in research

Companies should point to their investment in research and development as evidence of their commitment to innovation. A company can enhance its reputation for innovation by becoming involved in industry research and helping to set industry standards. For example, membership of user groups or industry standards associations can help to demonstrate industry leadership and a commitment to progress.

A good research investment record demonstrates that the company is committed to providing increasingly higher standards of service and, in turn, to improving its long-term growth prospects. Investment does not necessarily mean capital expenditure on equipment: investment in people is seen as an increasingly important area for corporate development.

Show that your company is market-focused

Presenting a company as market-focused can have a number of important benefits:

- it shows customers that you are concerned about their business.
- it tells investors that your company has the right priorities.
- it helps build staff commitment to customer service.

Market focus is demonstrated by:

- researching customer requirements
- obtaining customer feedback
- developing a new product programme
- appointing a senior executive responsible for customer service
- focusing the organisation on the customer
- communicating customer benefits
- the right levels of service
- flexibility of production
- staff training in customer care
- participation in user groups

Explain customer focus

A market-focused company must first understand the needs of the market through research and consultation with the customer. New product programmes are essential to any company, but in a market-focused company they are an integral part of the company culture. The whole organisation must reflect the needs of the market, and the principles of market focus must be embodied in a senior executive. A key aspect of market-focused service is that it reflects key customer requirements such as convenience, cost-effectiveness, value for money, and reliability. A product or service does not need to represent an industry as best in every aspect, but it should reflect the key perceptions identified by research.

Demonstrate financial stability

Presenting a company as financially stable can have important benefits:

- reassuring customers that you are a reliable supplier
- helping a company win long-term contracts
- providing a company with access to funds
- telling staff that the company has good long-term prospects

Several factors help to demonstrate financial stability:
- membership of a large group
- serving growing markets
- sound financial controls
- good investment record
- share price performance
- stable customer base
- broadly based product portfolio
- record of profitability
- low cost base

Communicate size and success

Being a member of a major group can help to reassure customers that your company will remain a reliable supplier. Customers need to know that you have the resources to finance work in progress and that you have access to funds for research and for growth investment. The backing of a major group provides the right credentials.

Market success is another indicator of good long-term prospects. For example, a company operating in sectors in overall decline, such as steelmaking or shipbuilding, is unlikely to have the same long-term prospects as a company in the high-technology sector.

Explain company management

A well-managed company should provide a cost-effective service and make reasonable profits to invest in future growth and the development of the service. Key factors to convey include:
- an experienced team
- commitment to excellence
- clear objectives
- an effective recruitment process
- management development programmes

Customers want to know that their suppliers are capable of running their own business effectively and that they understand the business of their customers. A well-managed company should be able to demonstrate a record of sustained growth and profitability and should have a clear sense of direction.

Explain objectives

Good management begins at the top with effective leadership: if the board is committed, the rest of the management team will have clear guidelines to follow. A company should have a clear mission statement which is focused on service to the customer.

When a company has clear objectives, customers are reassured that future developments are in line with their needs. Many companies publish a statement of direction which tells customers how they intend to develop their business in the future; at the same time, it gives managers and staff a clear sense of direction.

COMMON MISTAKES
Unbalanced content

A corporate brochure should present a balanced picture of a company – its skills, products, resources, performance, and track record. Customers and prospects use corporate brochures to assess the suitability of a company as a supplier. The brochure should therefore cover all the factors that customers consider important.

Presentation before content

Many companies concentrate on the presentation of a corporate brochure at the expense of its content on the assumption that customers judge a corporate brochure on its appearance. However, high-quality paper, excellent photography, and good print are no compensation for poor content.

THE BEST SOURCES OF HELP
Books:

Simmons, John. *Twenty-six ways of looking at a blackberry: How to release the creativity of your brand.* London: A&C Black, 2009.

Sullivan, Jenny. *Brochures: Making a Strong Impression – 85 Strategies for Message-driven Design.* Gloucester Massachusetts: Rockport Publishers, 2007.

Producing Press Material

GETTING STARTED

Newspapers, local television, trade press, radio, and Web journalists are constantly looking for stories (or 'copy'). Supply information in the form of press releases, feature articles, or advertorials – in the right format and to the right person – and you can gain great publicity for your organisation.

FAQS
Will the press be interested in us?

Journalists work under great pressure, so a well-written, informative, and current press release is always welcome. They won't, however, be interested in you unless you have a story to tell. Like customers, editors will want to know what makes your company different from others. Local media will be interested in how you fit in with the community; and the trade press will be more interested in new products and ideas.

It is worth developing a relationship with editors in order to understand how you can help them. By concentrating on the kind of news and story they want, you can save yourself time and increase the chances of your story being published.

Should we produce our own press material or use the services of an external agency?

An external agency can take a more objective view of your press material and may have experience in writing for the publications on your distribution list. That means they can tailor material for individual publications and ensure that it is printed. They may, however, lack product knowledge and require considerable training to achieve the right results. If your company produces complex technical products, you may split the task, keeping technical press releases in-house, and using an external agency to produce company or business material. Do check out their rates and fees carefully before you place work with them, though, as their costs may be well outside your budget.

Can we use the same press release for all the publications on our distribution list?

You can issue a single release, but you will increase the chances of getting into print if you tailor information to the needs of individual publications; for example, your local newspaper will have a different take on your news than a trade publication. By talking to journalist, reading previous issues, and studying publishers' readership data, you can identify the type of material that is likely to be printed or broadcast.

What should we do if an editor does not publish the information in a press release?

There's no cast-iron guarantee that your piece will get published, so don't see it as a 'given'. There could be a number of reasons for non-publication that are outside your control, such as lack of space, the release missing the copy date, or another story coinciding with your release. Your story may appear in the next issue if space allows. On the other hand, the editor may have decided simply that your information was wrong for the publication or not newsworthy. A quick call to the editor may help you find out the reason. If your material was unsuitable, you may be able to provide something more relevant for future issues.

MAKING IT HAPPEN

Plan your press release

A press release is a piece of information distributed to Web, print, television, or radio journalists, which is published or broadcast as a piece of news. It can cover a variety of topics, including:

- information on new products or services
- information on developments in a company
- news of recent appointments or promotions

An effective press release should contain news rather than thinly disguised advertising, and it should reflect readers' interests.

The release may be used without modification if it is newsworthy, timely, and if space permits. The press release may be cut to fit available space without any further reference to you. In some cases, a journalist or editor may contact you for further information and rewrite the item in the style of the publication. It is often a good idea to provide additional background information to help journalists in this task. Information such as product specifications, contact details, or alternative photographs are useful. Some companies offer such information specifically for journalists on a section of their website. Sometimes the information may not be used, because it is not newsworthy or not relevant to the readership. Alternatively, although the main press release may not be used, an accompanying photograph may be used with a caption.

Produce your press release

To stand the best chance of getting your press release noticed:

- make sure the text is double spaced
- identify the source of the release clearly
- give a contact name and number for further information
- flag up any limitations on use or timing of publication, such as 'not for publication before. . .'
- put the most important information in the early paragraphs. If an editor is short of space, the press release will be cut as simply and quickly as possible, probably from the bottom upwards.
- include quotes if you can: they're frequently used by editors
- add some photographs or diagrams if appropriate
- check that you match the target publication as much as possible in terms of writing style, even in the length of sentences and paragraphs. The easier you make it for the journalists to use your piece, the more likely it is they'll use it

Distribute your press release

Press releases are most usually sent by e-mail but can also be loaded on to your website so that can be picked up by visiting journalists. Wherever possible, they should be sent to a named individual. Information on editorial contacts, with details of their special interests, is available in the *PR Planner*, which is updated regularly (see below). If you do not want the information published before a certain date for reasons of commercial security, include an embargo – 'not for publication before. . .'

Time your press release

Check the publication dates of magazines or newspapers on your distribution list. This information is available in publications such as BRAD Insight (formerly British Rate and Data; see www.bradinsight.com/brad.aspx), *Willings Press Guide* (www.willingspress.com/default.asp), or the *PR Planner*. An editorial copy date will be indicated. Ensure that your release reaches the editor by that date at the latest.

Actionlists

Plan feature articles

A feature article, which could be 500–2,000 words in length, is published in a magazine and credited to an organisation. The article may be on technical or business developments in an industry, or on other subjects that provide practical or topical information for readers. The article may form part of an industry survey. This type of feature provides an opportunity for organisations to demonstrate their expertise and professionalism.

Feature articles can cover a variety of topics, including surveys of new industry or technical developments, practical 'how to' articles, or reviews of research projects.

If it is reasonably well written, the article may be used without modification; it will be published when space permits, or may be used as part of a special survey. In some cases, a journalist or editor may contact you for further information or rewrite the item in the style of the publication.

Produce feature articles

An effective feature article should reflect readers' interests and contain information that is useful to them. It should also bring them up to date with recent developments.

The following guidelines should help you prepare a feature article.

- Feature articles should be double spaced.
- Length should be discussed with the editor, but is likely to be between 500 and 2,000 words, with 1,000 words as the average.
- A contact name for further information should be provided.
- Photographs or diagrams, with a caption for every item, add value to the article.

Distribute feature articles

Feature articles should only be sent to one publication at a time, although they can be modified for use in other markets. Wherever possible, they should be sent to a named individual. Information on editorial contacts, with details of their special interests, is available in the *PR Planner*, which is updated regularly. In some cases, the initiative may come from the publication and the editor will provide you with details of requirements.

Produce advertorials

An advertorial is a special category of feature article, combining advertising and editorial, which is used to promote products and services. These are the key characteristics of an advertorial, which:

- may include a reader offer, such as a chance to participate in a competition

- should be identified as an 'advertisement feature'
- is produced in the form of an editorial rather than in a conventional advertisement format, even though the space is paid for

The writing guidelines are similar to those for press releases and feature articles but you are paying for the space and you have considerably more control over what is published. Newspapers and journals will often help with the layout.

COMMON MISTAKES

Writing unsuitable material

Spend some time studying the publications that are on your distribution list. Editors know very quickly what is relevant or interesting to their readers. If your material is not suitable, it will not be used. Study the editorial content and check the readership figures, which are usually available from the publication.

Providing news stories that are out of date

'Old news is no news' and that means a story could be wasted. It's easy to get the timing right with a daily or weekly publication, but it can be tricky to decide on the right date to send a news story to a monthly publication. The publication can provide you with the dates when your copy will be required, but you have to make sure that those dates tie in with your own schedules. If you have to release a sensitive news story early to catch a publication date, you can protect your interests by putting an embargo clause on the release, saying 'not for publication before. . . .'

Confusing editorial with advertorial

A press release or feature article should provide factual, newsworthy information. It should not be a blatant advertisement for the company. Editors dislike items that are thinly disguised advertisements.

THE BEST SOURCES OF HELP

Books:

Camp, Lindsay. *Can I Change Your Mind? The Art and Craft of Persuasive Writing*. London: A&C Black, 2007.

Treadwell, Donald, and Jill B. Treadwell. *Public Relations Writing: Principles in Practice*. 2nd ed. London: Sage, 2005.

Website:

Cision (for information on subscriptions to *PR Planner*): **http://uk.cision.com**

Running a Product Public Relations Campaign

GETTING STARTED
Product public relations is the most frequently used public relations activity, which can be used to support a number of different sales and marketing objectives. There are many different opportunities for improving product public relations across a variety of media.

FAQS
Should I hold a press conference every time I launch a new product?
You should only hold a press conference if the product being launched is critical to your company or will be seen as important in the market. Minor product developments or simple range extensions do not warrant a press conference.

Can I handle my own product public relations?
Many manufacturing companies handle product public relations internally. They have a detailed knowledge of products and services that an external consultancy would be unable to match.

Should technical specialists write their own product material?
Technical specialists are in the best position to write feature articles that require detailed product knowledge. However, they may write from a technical perspective, rather than a customer perspective, and this may reduce the value of the article. You can take the specialist's material and edit it as necessary.

MAKING IT HAPPEN
Plan product public relations
Product public relations is the most frequently used public relations activity and can be used to support a number of different sales and marketing objectives:
- as part of a new product launch programme
- to raise awareness of a company's product range
- to correct misunderstandings about a product
- to build understanding of product applications
- to encourage wider use of a product
- as part of a market education programme

Identify opportunities for product public relations
There are many different opportunities for improving product public relations, such as:
- contributing product information to regular product surveys
- issuing press releases on new products and new product developments
- contributing articles on complex product applications
- contributing how-to articles on different aspects of product usage
- contributing articles by technical specialists on new developments in the industry

Support a new product launch
A company marketing a new design software tool that will improve engineering design quality and productivity wants to raise awareness and understanding of the product among a group of decision-makers, including:
- design engineers who would use the product
- managers and senior executives responsible for engineering, who would benefit from improved efficiency and productivity
- marketing directors who would benefit indirectly from better product performance

The programme includes the following elements:
- press releases aimed at publications read by the target audience
- an interview with the company's engineering director, explaining how the product improved internal productivity and performance
- contributions to a number of product surveys on engineering design techniques
- a feature article on developments in engineering design
- a feature article submitted to marketing magazines showing how engineering design influences product and marketing performance

Improve market development
A professional services company marketing project services believes that lack of understanding is a barrier to market growth. The company develops a public relations programme which includes the following elements:
- case histories of companies using a project management service
- feature articles on using project services to improve deployment of staff
- feature articles on the use of project services in outsourcing programmes
- a press release including self-assessment questionnaire, helping prospects to identify the need for project services

Increase use of a product
A materials supplier wants to increase the usage of an advanced material which has not been widely used in general markets. The product was originally developed for use in demanding aerospace applications and is believed to be expensive and too good for conventional applications. The campaign is targeted at designers and application engineers in a wide variety of markets. The campaign includes the following elements:
- a press release on an information pack that describes applications of the product
- a feature article, 'How to design with the material', submitted to horizontal market design and engineering publications
- an editorial competition that enables readers to win a special design software package

• a series of application articles written specifically for vertical market publications

Run a press conference

A press conference provides an opportunity for an organisation to meet journalists and editors in person and give them a detailed briefing on a new product development. However, unless the event is important and the press see a real benefit in attending, press conferences are a waste of time, so planning and preparation are important to ensure success.

• Invite journalists and editors from publications that reach your most important customers and prospects.
• Give the press plenty of notice, and try to plan the timing so that editorial coverage will appear in the next issue of the most important monthly publications.
• Provide press packs that include background information, specific information on the product, photographs, and other relevant material.
• If necessary, ensure that senior executives or other specialists are available for interview or to answer detailed questions.
• If any important press contacts cannot attend, send a press pack and arrange a separate meeting if necessary.

Arrange interviews with key product specialists

An interview with a senior executive or product specialist provides an opportunity for an organisation to meet selected or individual journalists and editors in person and to give them a detailed briefing on a new product development. The advantage to the press is that this process is more selective than a press conference, and it gives them an opportunity for an exclusive interview.

Put information in your online press office

Set up a separate page on your website where journalists can get the latest news about your company's products and download press releases, background information, or feature articles. The press office should have a direct link from the home page, and new stories should be featured on the home page. The press page should also feature e-mail addresses and telephone numbers for key contacts.

Alert journalists by e-mail

Journalists may visit your site regularly if it provides valuable information. You can also alert them to the latest product news by e-mail. Include a link to the press release or feature article on your site, so that it can be easily downloaded.

Issue reprints of published material

If a story about your company's products is covered in the press, television, or radio, include a reprint of the item on your site. Also provide links to the publications that covered the story. Alternatively, e-mail the item to other journalists. This may increase coverage even further. Ask the publisher for permission before you reproduce a complete article.

Run an online press briefing

The problem with conventional press conferences is usually time, but running an online press briefing can overcome that problem. Webcasting allows companies to stream traditional audio and video conferences over the Internet, incorporating multimedia content and adding interactive capability such as slides, polling, and messaging. This enables journalists to attend a virtual press conference without leaving their desks, while the interactive facilities enable them to ask questions – just as they would at a traditional press conference.

Issue material by newsletter

If you issue a large number of product press releases, you can include brief summaries of the latest stories in a regular newsletter distributed by e-mail or post to journalists or customers. The summaries should include a link to the complete release. The frequency of your newsletter depends on the volume of releases you produce each week or month.

COMMON MISTAKES

Concentrating on product news, rather than information for the market

Many companies simply write about their products from an internal point of view, ignoring the implications for the customer. Writing articles about applications or benefits for the market makes the press information more relevant and interesting.

Writing information that is not suitable for a publication

It is vitally important to study the publications that are on your distribution list. Editors know very quickly what is relevant or interesting to their readers and if your material is not suitable, it will not be used. Don't assume that all industry publications will be interested in your product.

Failing to keep journalists up to date

Journalists may not be aware of your company's full product range or of its capabilities. They may receive the latest press releases, but that may give them a limited view of your company. It is important to provide background information as well as the latest product information.

THE BEST SOURCES OF HELP

Books:

Cooper, Robert G. et al. *Portfolio Management For New Products*. 2nd ed. New York: Basic Books, 2002.

Gregory, Anne. *Public Relations in Practice*. 2nd ed. London: Kogan Page, 2003.

Website:

Institute of Public Relations: **www.cipr.co.uk**

Planning Promotions

GETTING STARTED

Consumer promotions account for around 20 per cent of the value of the average shopping basket. Promotions are popular because they meet the demands of powerful retailers, and they help brand managers to meet volume targets. The strength of the retail trade puts increasing emphasis on trade and consumer promotions.

Consumers prefer instant-win promotions to money-back or collector schemes. Instant win has a specific tactical role, but it may not be suitable for more strategic tasks such as brand-switching. Cross-promotion allows complementary products to be promoted in a cost-effective way.

FAQS

Is sales promotion more effective than advertising for building market share?

Sales promotion can deliver short-term gains in market share, but competitor promotions may wipe those out. Longer-term promotions such as collector schemes can encourage customer loyalty for the period of the promotion, but they may also be vulnerable to competitive activity. Advertising, on the other hand, can be used to build longer-term brand awareness and attract new customers. Ideally, the two activities should be integrated, if budgets allow.

I sell my products through retail outlets. Should I run trade promotions rather than consumer promotions?

Trade promotions will help you sell into the retail outlets. If you also give retailers incentives to sell more to consumers, or to improve their standards of service, you may also increase sales to consumers. A consumer promotion may boost sales, but it may not increase sales through your retail outlets.

Who should plan promotions? My advertising agency or a specialist promotions company?

Sales promotion should be integrated with other marketing activities, so it is essential that your advertising agency is aware of the promotion. Your agency may not have the skills or resources to plan and implement the promotion. If you use a specialist company, make sure that the creative theme of the promotion reflects the themes of the advertising and other marketing programmes.

MAKING IT HAPPEN

Take advantage of promotions

In the consumer sector, items under promotion account for around 20 per cent of the value of the average shopping basket. The strength of the retail trade puts increasing emphasis on trade and consumer promotions. In the United States, the strength of the trade means that some retail-dependent brands allocate as much as 75 per cent of budget on promotions. Promotions are popular because they meet the demands of powerful retailers and they help brand managers meet volume targets. They are also easy to justify financially because of immediate measurable results.

Identify promotional benefits

Promotions:
- attract the attention of retail buyers and salesforces, particularly for smaller brands
- generate excitement at the point of sale
- simplify negotiations over margins; promotions may create better volumes than reductions in margins
- increase the effectiveness of trialling. One survey indicated that 30 per cent of consumers had not tried the brand in the last six months. Another reported that 44 per cent of consumers said they would buy a brand they do not normally buy if it is on special offer.

Reflect customer views

An industry report indicates that consumers prefer instant-win promotions to money-back or collector schemes. The survey, which provides useful data for promotion of branded products, could also provide an insight for companies running business-to-business promotions. The report indicates that instant-win has a specific tactical role, but it may not be suitable for more strategic tasks such as brand-switching. Key findings of the report include:
- instant win is most appropriate for products with a high purchase frequency
- only 5 per cent of consumers felt they would switch brands to participate in an instant-win promotion, compared with 41 per cent of consumers who would switch brands for a price-reduction promotion
- the main reasons for liking instant-win promotions were: no waiting; immediate knowledge of success
- the main dislikes were: unlikely to win; likely to be a waste of time

Avoid problems created by a promotional culture

The pressure to run promotions can have an impact on overall marketing performance. A review by a major consumer goods company indicated that a great deal of time was required to design, implement, and oversee promotions. It accounted for 25 per cent of salesforce time and 33 per cent of brand managers' time. Other problems included:
- supply inefficiencies
- cost of changing packs
- cost of promotional material
- cost of running the promotion
- impact on long-term brand building

Set the right promotional objectives

Promotions must be managed carefully to provide long-term benefits. The wrong choice of offer, confusing rules, or poor organisation can undo all the good work. In setting objectives, you should ask:

- Why are we running the programme?
- Do we want to increase overall volume, or sales of specific products?
- Do we want to improve performance in other sales-related areas, such as customer service or participation in training schemes and other business programmes?

Choose an appropriate promotional format
- Promotional offers can be awarded to the biggest spenders or to all consumers.
- Programmes that only reward big spenders or large trade customers can act as a disincentive to others.
- Programmes that reward performance against target give a wider opportunity to win.
- A multi-level programme that offers many lower-value prizes can act as a strong motivator.

Set out the rules clearly
- Set out the scope of the promotion and the offer.
- Explain what is required to win and how to collect prizes.
- Include the closing date for the promotion.
- Specify the availability of the offer, for example, only available in selected retail outlets.
- Set the specific requirements for each participant.

Use cross-promotion
Cross-promotion allows complementary products to be promoted cost-effectively. The project can be handled in-house, the samples are cheap, and the cost of the whole promotion is comparatively low. To be successful, this type of promotion should feature products that are complementary and non-competitive. A database can be used to identify opportunities for cross-promotion – first identify the profile of a product, then look for products with a similar profile.

Maintain momentum throughout the promotion
If you are operating a long-term promotion or a promotion that involves a number of stages, you need to maintain momentum:

- send out teaser incentives or gifts during the promotion to maintain interest
- keep participants informed of their progress
- encourage struggling participants with secondary offers
- publish results and distribute them to all participants

Ensure effective fulfilment
If you are delivering promotional products to homes or businesses, you need to set up an efficient logistics operation. You can either operate your own fleet, tying up capital and personnel, or subcontract the operation to a specialist logistics company.

Appoint a fulfilment agency
If your promotion is likely to generate a large volume of requests, your company may not have the resources to handle fulfilment internally. Fulfilment agencies specialise in high-volume response programmes.

Assess the effectiveness of promotional programmes
- How do you justify spending money on promotions?
- What return on your promotional investment are you looking for?
- What are the related sales objectives?
- How will you quantify them?
- How will you isolate the effect of non-promotional activities?
- Was the promotional impact evenly spread across your business?
- Were there significant account, sector, or regional differences in impact?
- Did the differences relate to techniques, premiums, value, customer appeal, or communications?
- Is it possible to profile people who used previous promotions as a basis for planning?

COMMON MISTAKES
Setting too many short-term promotional objectives
Sales-promotion campaigns are judged on the way they change market share. However, any gains in market share can be lost when the promotion stops or competitive activity increases. It is also possible to create an environment in which consumers and the retail trade expect promotion to be a continuous activity.

Failing to integrate promotion with other activities
Sales promotion works most effectively when it is integrated with other activities. A consumer promotion, backed by a trade or salesforce incentive, ensures that all parties are aware of the promotion. A direct mail campaign in conjunction with a promotional offer can increase the direct mail response rate.

Choosing the wrong type of promotion
If you run a promotional campaign, make sure that it reflects your brand values. A money-off offer, for example, would do little to enhance a premium product. If you can add value with your promotional offer, the campaign is more likely to be successful. You should also choose the right type of campaign. An instant-win campaign can have an immediate impact on market share, while a collector programme encourages longer-term loyalty.

THE BEST SOURCES OF HELP
Book:
Cummins, Julian, and Roddy Mullin. *Sales Promotion: How to Create, Implement and Integrate Campaigns That Really Work.* 4th ed. London: Kogan Page, 2008.

Website:
Institute of Sales Promotion: **www.isp.org.uk**

Running a Price Campaign

GETTING STARTED
Promotional pricing can be used throughout the marketing process, in order to encourage brand loyalty and increase sales among customers. Pricing programmes should be carefully matched to particular marketing tasks.

FAQS
Is pricing more important than brand building?
In the longer term, brand building is likely to be more important. However, price promotions can be used to win market share or quickly establish a new product. They can also be used to rapidly counter competitive activity that could have an impact on market share. Continuing to concentrate on price promotion alone is not a recommended strategy.

Should I always respond to a competitor's price promotion?
If the competitor's promotion is likely to damage your market share, it may be worth responding. However, you should weigh up the impact on profitability. It is easy to get drawn into a damaging price war that has no long-term benefit.

Retailers are demanding price cuts. Should I give in to their demands when I'd rather spend the budget on advertising?
It can be difficult to persuade retailers that advertising, direct marketing, and other brand-building strategies are going to benefit them. They frequently prefer a promotion that offers them an immediate return in terms of increased sales. Again, it is a question of balance, meeting both short- and long-term needs.

MAKING IT HAPPEN
Match the promotion to the marketing programme
Promotional pricing can be used throughout the marketing process for:
- launching new products
- winning competitive business
- protecting market share
- entering new market sectors
- developing niche markets
- protecting volume and profit in mature markets

Choose the right pricing programme
There are five main categories of promotional pricing:
- money off current purchase
- money off next purchase
- cashback
- more product for the same price
- discounts on multiple purchase

Run a money-off promotion
This type of price promotion is one of the most commonly used tactics. It is immediate, easily implemented, and is easily understood by consumers. Results are measurable, and pricing levels can be modified for different market sectors. The programme is also easy to modify in response to demand. Money-off promotions are acceptable to retailers, and easy to promote at the point of sale.

There are disadvantages. The promotion is easily imitated and competitors can respond quickly. It also has a potential long-term impact on manufacturer and retailer profitability. This type of promotion has no effect on long-term branding, minimal impact on customer loyalty, and does not differentiate the product.

Offer money off next purchase
This type of price promotion is designed to encourage repeat purchasing and to contribute to brand and customer loyalty. It is easily understood by consumers and can be measured accurately. The campaign is acceptable to retailers and easy to promote at the point of sale. It helps to build a value-for-money reputation, and contributes to the development of long-term relationships. However, like promotions giving money off the current purchase, it is easily imitated by competitors and has no effect on long-term branding or on product differentiation.

Make a cashback offer
In this type of price promotion, the customer pays the full purchase price, and receives a rebate in the form of cash or a cheque. The customer can also be offered the rebate in a different form – for example, £250 worth of petrol when you buy your next car – although this could be considered a free gift. This type of promotion is designed to encourage purchasers to switch brands, by offering them greater freedom of choice in the way they use the discount.

The promotion has perceived value for both consumers and retailers and encourages brand-switching. It is easily understood by consumers and offers them greater flexibility. The offer can be modified for different market sectors and is easy to modify in response to demand. However, the offer is unrelated to brand values and does not encourage repeat purchase. Again, it is easily imitated and offers no product differentiation.

Offer more product for the same price
This type of price promotion is designed to encourage brand-switching or increase the volume of purchasing by offering the customer greater value for money. However, it can be difficult for customers to recognise the value of the offer when packs of different sizes are compared. Apart from this, it is easily understood and offers customers value for money. Competitors find it difficult to respond quickly to the offer, but it has a number of

disadvantages. You may have to modify the product or the packaging, and that can have a potential long-term impact on both manufacturer and retailer profitability. It can also be confusing to the consumer if competitors offer different pack sizes. Like other price promotions, it has no effect on long-term branding or product differentiation.

Offer discounts on multiple purchase

Although there is overlap between this and extra product promotions, this type of price promotion does not require any physical change to the product or packaging. It is designed to encourage repeat purchase and to increase customer loyalty. The 'Buy One, Get One Free' offer takes the promotion to its logical limit. A number of multiple retailers use this offer as the basis for long-term positioning as a value-for-money supplier. The promotion is easily understood, acceptable to retailers, and builds longer-term loyalty. It can, however, have a potential impact on retailer and manufacturer profitability.

Operate credit deals and finance schemes

Credit deals and finance schemes can increase sales by making it easier for customers to buy. Although the recession of the mid-1990s made consumers more cautious about unlimited credit, finance schemes remain an important method of increasing sales and building customer loyalty. In the business-to-business sector, finance schemes such as leasing are often an integral part of a marketing package.

Finance schemes can take a number of forms:

- store cards – credit cards that can be used only in named stores
- loan schemes – operated on behalf of stores or manufacturers by finance companies
- hire purchase schemes – operated on behalf of stores or manufacturers by finance companies
- business finance or leasing schemes – operated on behalf of companies by finance companies

Finance schemes make it easier for customers to buy and can increase customer loyalty. They can be used to encourage repeat purchasing, while reducing the impact of price competition. An important bonus is that they provide high levels of customer information as a basis for direct marketing. The disadvantage is that they can be complex to administer and they do not support product branding.

COMMON MISTAKES

Relying on price as the only weapon

Price promotions make little contribution to brand building or customer retention. Most promotions are easily imitated by competitors, and this can create a marketplace in which customers regularly switch brands to take advantage of the latest offer.

Running price promotions that are difficult to understand

'Buy One, Get One Free' is a very simple concept. '10 per cent off when you buy more than three in a two-week period' is confusing to customers and retailers. Price promotions must be immediately understandable.

Promotions that are difficult to administer

Retailers prefer promotions that are simple to administer. If they have to return coupons, arrange refunds or rebates, or make complicated adjustments to their own pricing mechanisms, they will be reluctant to run the programme. Consumers, too, prefer simple offers. If the programme involves redeeming coupons, or posting proof of purchase to claim a rebate, it will be less attractive.

Getting caught in a price war

When competitors make similar price offers, this can lead to larger and larger cuts. Although one competitor may gain market share, it may be at the expense of profitability. Since it is difficult to retain loyalty through price promotions, this can be a damaging strategy in the long term.

THE BEST SOURCES OF HELP

Books:
Dolan, Robert J., and Hermann Simon. *Power Pricing: How Managing Price Transforms the Bottom Line.* New York: Free Press, 1997.
Nagle, Thomas, and Reed Holden. *The Strategy and Tactics of Pricing: A Guide to Profitable Decision-Making.* 4th ed. New York: Prentice Hall, 2007.

Website:
Chartered Institute of Marketing: **www.cim.co.uk**

Implementing E-commerce

GETTING STARTED

An effective e-commerce strategy combines many separate elements. E-commerce means selling online with content, and this requires a sophisticated content management system. E-commerce purchase, payment, and support systems are required, perhaps with customer relationship management and localisation. Proper marketing will be needed for success. Underpinning all this will be a requirement for professional website development and management. In implementing e-commerce, keep the following in mind:

- E-commerce is not suitable for every product and service.
- The best e-commerce strategy is a clicks-and-bricks approach, combining offline retail resources with online capabilities.
- E-commerce is complex and expensive to get right: nobody should underestimate the difficulty involved in designing and managing an efficient e-commerce website

FAQS

What products are best suited to e-commerce?

- Digital products such as software and information.
- Products with a high value relative to their cost of fulfilment.
- Products requiring a lot of information, such as books, music, travel products, and banking.
- Products that do not need to be handled or tried on.
- Products that are difficult to find in a consumer's local area.
- Products for which it is more convenient to carry out the transaction online than to go physically to the vendor's location.

How difficult is it to establish an e-commerce website?

It depends on the scope of what you want to do. You must be able to manage stock, fulfilment, payment, and security. You must be able to integrate your e-commerce website efficiently with your offline business. E-commerce software has improved and become more streamlined, but it is still neither cheap nor simple to get everything running smoothly.

If you set up an e-commerce website, will you suddenly be selling to a global marketplace?

No. Selling to a foreign marketplace involves more than setting up an e-commerce website.

MAKING IT HAPPEN

Make sure you have a market

Who is going to buy your products online? The best place to start is your current customer base. Will going online make life easier for them? Are you going to save them time and money by allowing them to purchase online? You probably have a basic website already; are you getting requests for online buying from potential customers? It is never truly possible to judge in advance whether a market exists, but there should be at least some indications of a demand for an online presence.

Use a clicks and bricks strategy if possible

The clicks-and-bricks approach is the most effective and economic. This combines offline resources, such as stores, brands, channels, with an online e-commerce presence. The other option – a pure-play dot-com – is now rare. Consumers are looking for brands that they know and trust. They also like the fact that a business has a physical presence, a place where they can go if something goes wrong. Pure-play dot-coms found that they had to spend a lot of money on marketing just to maintain awareness.

Make sure you integrate the shopping experience

Consumers look to the Web primarily for information; they may use the website initially to find out about the product, then buy by phone or in person. However, repeat purchasers more familiar with the Web are more likely to buy online. They will be able to do this more easily if their personal details and purchase history can be stored for use in subsequent purchases.

Plan how you will deal with content, pricing, stock management, fulfilment, payment, returns, support, and security

These are the basics of any business, but there can be added complications online. You need to address the following.

- **Content** is critical to e-commerce and must be updated frequently.
- **Pricing:** if you are selling direct for the first time, you may have problems with your distributors and retailers, who will not want you to underprice them. If you are selling brands by other manufacturers, there may be problems involved in selling in foreign marketplaces. Are you going to offer prices in a range of currencies? If so, which?
- **Stock management:** are you going to use the same stock base to sell online and through your physical distribution channels? If so, you need an integrated stock management system.
- **Fulfilment:** when fulfilling, precise information on order status is essential. Each order should have a tracking number so that the customer can get information on the status of the order right up to the point of delivery. If you haven't sold by mail order before, you will have to plan for packaging and fulfilment. This can be a major cost, and needs careful management. If, for cost or other reasons, you decide not to fulfil to certain countries, you must make this very clear on the website.
- **Payment:** how will people pay? What credit cards will you accept? How will you manage fraud?
- **Returns:** what is your returns policy? Studies indicate that returns can be a major cost for e-commerce.

- **Support:** how will you support the products you sell online? You must plan for a support section on your website to answer basic questions from customers. Will you also offer telephone and e-mail support?
- **Security:** security will be a central issue in an e-commerce strategy. Fraud and hacking of computer systems are ever-growing problems.

Develop an easy-to-use purchase process

An alarming number of consumers abandon their attempts to buy online. One of the reasons given is a badly designed purchase process. Your purchase process must be robust and very easy to use; a good example is Amazon.com. It is a good idea to tell the consumer upfront how many steps there are in the purchase process, and to keep that information prominently displayed at the top of the Web page. An example of the purchase steps is as follows: 'Shopping cart–Account–Shipping–Payment–Verify–Confirm'.

Consider localisation issues

If you want to sell seriously to foreign marketplaces, you will have to localise the website. Studies indicate that, without localisation, sales will be minimal. More worryingly, returns are very high because of misunderstanding by people who are purchasing in a foreign language. There is also the issue of American versus British English: if you are selling into the American marketplace, the content should be in American English, or Americans will think you are making spelling mistakes.

Consider customer relationship management and personalisation

The Internet offers many opportunities for a better understanding of customers' behaviour and for developing a closer relationship with them. Customer relationship management and personalisation systems allow for the collection and application of comprehensive information to create a more customised environment for the consumer. While the potential of such systems is substantial, they are complex and difficult to implement, and, if not professionally managed, can lead to the abuse of consumer privacy.

Make sure you buy the right software

There is no need to do all the work internally, as there is now a wide range of quality software for e-commerce.

Make sure you have a team in place

An e-commerce website needs day-to-day maintenance. Technical problems must be fixed, new content must be published and old content removed, and the website must be constantly marketed.

If you don't market it, they won't come

Opening up an e-commerce website is rather like setting up shop at the North Pole: nobody knows you are there. It is not enough just to register with search engines; you will need an aggressive marketing campaign to make your target market aware of what you have to offer. The ideal situation is a seamless integration with the marketing strategy of the offline business.

COMMON MISTAKES

Thinking that it's cheap to set up an e-commerce website

It is not. Back-end infrastructure is expensive to set up and maintain. Without an existing business and brand, marketing costs will be very high.

Thinking that an e-commerce website has failed because it didn't deliver direct sales

Not necessarily: many businesses have found that their websites support the purchase process, but that consumers still like to complete the sale offline.

Thinking that e-commerce is just the same as ordinary commerce

It is not, although it has many similarities with mail order. If you have never sold products by mail order before, e-commerce involves a steep learning curve. Packaging and delivery, particularly to many different countries, are difficult to master.

Developing a poor-quality purchase process

A great many websites have poor-quality purchase processes. It is essential to test your purchase process thoroughly to make sure that it is robust and easy to use.

Thinking that all you have to do is put up a product catalogue

E-commerce is selling with content, and you need a content-rich website that is constantly being updated if you want to make sales.

Not dealing professionally with legal and security issues

Many consumers are wary of purchasing online because they feel they have better security in a physical store.

THE BEST SOURCES OF HELP
Website:
Google: **http://directory.google.com/Top/ Business/E-Commerce**

Designing a Website Effectively

GETTING STARTED

For the majority of websites, website design is about information, not graphics. The most successful websites have few graphics. Graphics and other high-bandwidth multimedia slow a website down, but most people view the Web as a library, not a source of entertainment, and they hate being kept waiting. Website design should focus on:

- clean, simple, standardised design that helps people find the content they want without delay
- good page layout that allows people to read the content as easily as possible
- avoiding fancy graphics and multimedia experiences. Most people don't want them.

FAQS

What exactly is website design?

Website design is information design. It's about organising content so that it can be easily found and easily read. Website design is a form of publishing: presenting content in a way that is attractive to visitors.

Why do so many websites seem to be poorly designed?

Because many organisations still don't really understand what their websites are intended to achieve. In addition, if the website is controlled by graphic design or technical staff, the results may be essentially unusable from a consumer's point of view.

Why should an editor be in charge?

The Web is a publishing medium, and a website is a publication. The primary job of an editor is to understand content; the primary purpose of a website is to publish content.

What's the main thing people do on the Web?

They search for information, and they read it. Many websites still do not fully recognise this fact and make the content harder to read than is really necessary. Overly elaborate colour schemes, small fonts, and poor layout are still relatively common. If you think of your website visitors as readers, the function of website design will become far clearer.

MAKING IT HAPPEN

Design for the reader/visitor

Too few websites are designed for the needs of their visitors. Remember that the person who visits your website:

- is there to find some information
- will scan read, moving quickly from one piece of text to another
- is generally in a hurry, and may not wait for elaborate pages to download

- may be sceptical because, on the basis of past experience, they expect a website to be full of useless material

Make sure the content is well written

When writing for the Web:

- keep it factual, with punchy, descriptive headings and summaries.
- keep it short. Documents should be between 500 and 700 words, paragraphs between 40 and 60 words. Sentences should be short. There should be no more than 9 and 12 words per line of text.
- keep it updated. Out-of-date content is no good.

Make sure the content is well organised

Think of your website as a directory. If you have lots of products to sell, you must organise them so that people can browse through them easily. Websites such as Amazon.com and eBay are successful because they organise huge quantities of products properly so that people can find what they want quickly and efficiently.

Metadata, navigation, and search are fundamental to the organisation of content on a website. Metadata delivers essential information on a document or Web page: publication date, author, keywords, title, and summary. Search depends on metadata to be truly effective, and is one of the most common activities people do on a website. Search must be available on every page. Navigation is critical: if people can't easily find their way around a website, they will leave.

Make sure the website is interactive

Comprehensive contact details should be prominently available on the website, covering the appropriate range of e-mail and telephone contacts. Physical addresses, with location maps, should also be provided. Online community options such as chat, discussion boards, and e-mail discussion lists can enhance a visitor's understanding of the organisation and its products. E-mail newsletters can allow the organisation to keep in touch regularly and at low cost.

Ensure that standards are developed and adhered to

Newspaper designers have found that people follow a certain pattern when reading content in a newspaper. This is true of reading content on a website too: people navigate and search in a certain way. It is therefore confusing to have different designs in different sections of a website, or between websites in the same organisation.

Some of the emerging standards and conventions for website design are included in the following list.

- Essential navigation: every web page should have a set of essential navigation that is visible when the first screen loads, containing key areas within the website. This essential navigation (sometimes known as global navigation) should always begin with a link back to the home page of the website. Essential navigation should contain links such as Home, About, Products, Customers, and Contact.

- Slim masthead: the masthead is the top of the page area, and should be slim, like the masthead of a newspaper. This makes the maximum amount of screen space available for the content – the main reason for a website visit. The masthead should contain the logo of the organisation, and may also contain the search box and the set of essential links.
- Three-column layout: in the average website, a three-column layout is the best means of delivering maximum content in the most readable format. Some websites use a four-column layout, particularly on the home page.
- Footer on every page: a footer should go at the bottom of every page; it should contain a copy of the essential links, contact information (address, telephone, fax, e-mail), and links to copyright and privacy policy information.
- Maximum accessibility: minimum accessibility standards for websites are increasingly becoming a legal requirement. In any case, implementing best practice in accessibility design generally leads to a more effective website.
- Effective home-page layout and design: a home page has two central functions. First, it provides visitors with the appropriate navigation and search options to allow them to find content quickly; second, it promotes important content. This is done by using short, punchy headings and summaries.
- Consistent document page layout and design: in general, a three-column approach should be used for Web pages that display documents. Every document should have a heading and a summary. Author and date of publication information should be included where appropriate.
- Large sans serif fonts: it is advisable to use sans serif fonts, such as Verdana and Arial, on the Web, because they are easier to read on a screen than serif fonts. Font sizes should not be lower than 8 point for summaries and headings on home pages. The minimum font size recommended for documents is 10 point. The ideal font colour is black text on a white background.
- No italic, bold, or underline: avoid using italic, which has a poor appearance on screen. Avoid using bold in body text, as people may think it's a link. Never use underline, as people will definitely think it's a link.
- Small graphics: graphics should be small, particularly on the home page. If a larger graphic is necessary, consider using a thumbnail approach, with a small graphic and a larger one linked from it, giving visitors the option to view the larger graphic if they want.
- Compatibility with all browsers: although Internet Explorer now has the largest share of the marketplace, it is still important that the website can be viewed properly in Netscape Navigator. You must therefore test your website using both browsers, as well as with different browser versions.

- Light pages: if your Web pages do not download quickly, people will simply leave. Keep pages under 50K in weight; this means small graphics.
- No frames: frames break up a Web page into separate sections. In the words of Web usability expert, Jakob Nielsen: 'Frames: just say no'.
- No splash pages: a splash page is an introductory or initial page presented to visitors before they can get to the actual home page. It simply forces visitors to go through an extra, redundant stage before they can do what they came to do.
- Lots of hypertext: you should use hypertext liberally, but stick to the standard colours: blue for unclicked, purple for clicked. People are used to these colours. Hypertext is a navigation aid, and changing colours is confusing.
- No tricks: swirling logos, animated e-mail postboxes, automated 'Last updated' information, page counters – these are all signs of an amateur website.

Test, test, and test again

Test out your website with potential visitors, and get as much feedback as possible. This is the best way to find out what's working and what isn't.

COMMON MISTAKES

Thinking that a website is about getting attention

Many marketers are used to creating brochures and advertisements that seek to grab attention. However, when someone visits your website, you've already got their attention. They don't want to see a swirling logo or splash screen before they get to your home page; they want to find out something about your product or service.

Creating brochure ware

Too many people think that website design is just like brochure design. Large graphics simply slow down a website and turn visitors off. Website design must allow you to update your website with new content easily, so it should be designed more like a newspaper than a brochure.

Too many gimmicks

The majority of people come to websites to do things and find out information. Gimmicks may be fun and clever, but too often they get in the way.

THE BEST SOURCES OF HELP
Websites:
Builder.com: **www.builder.com**
Webmonkey: **www.webmonkey.com**

Setting Up a Basic Website

GETTING STARTED

A website is a way of informing customers and other stakeholders of what you have to offer. A basic website involves delivering essential information that is easy to read and well laid out. In website design, simplicity is always best. A website must also be actively promoted to make people aware of its existence. When approaching website design, ask yourself the following important questions:

- Who are the people that I want to communicate with?
- How am I going to structure my information so it is easy to navigate and read?
- How am I going to let people know that my website exists?
- How am I going to keep my website updated and keep people informed of new content?

FAQS

How much information should I include on a website?

Provide the information that your target market needs and is likely to read. Don't fill your website with irrelevant and/or repetitive information. It will clutter your site and make the important information hard to find.

How often should I change website content?

You should change your content whenever you have something new and important to say, and whenever content already on the site is out of date. Ideally you should try to publish fresh content every week.

Can I transfer printed copy to the website?

Printed copy can be used as a starting point for web copy, but the structure and length would probably be unsuitable. People like to read short, punchy copy on the Web, so snappy headings and summaries are important. For a website to be truly effective, you must also use hypertext so that people can click for further information if they need it.

MAKING IT HAPPEN

Know who you want to reach

Before you do anything, decide who you want to reach. Prioritise your information for your most important audiences. Ask yourself:

- Do I want to reach new customers? In new markets?
- What can I say on my website that will turn a potential customer into an actual one?
- Do I want to offer support for existing customers?
- Do I want to provide information to attract new staff?

Keep it simple

Website design is about the design and delivery of information. It is not graphic design. Lack of bandwidth means that fancy graphics and moving images slow a website down and frustrate visitors looking for information. Quality website design has simple layout and rich content that is well organised. The best, most successful websites in the world (eBay, Microsoft, Amazon) don't employ fancy gimmicks; neither should you. Keep it simple. Maximise the content and minimise the presentation.

Structure your information well

When people come to your website, they want to find information quickly. They are task-oriented, impatient, and sceptical. It is therefore essential to make your website as accessible and easy to navigate as possible.

A well-structured website needs quality classification, or links. A good website has a series of links that allow the visitor to navigate to other sections of the site. Without these links, a page becomes a dead end with nowhere to go.

Important website sections and links

You should have at least some of the following sections on your website. Links to these sections should be provided in a set of essential links placed prominently on every page of the website.

Home page

The home page is the first page on your website and the most important, as it is usually the first page visitors see. From a linking point of view, the home page is referred to as 'Home'. It should always be the first link in your set of essential links. The home page itself should be full of punchy, attention-grabbing headings and summaries that quickly inform the visitor of, for example, what you do, what you have to sell, or what special offers you have. The Microsoft home page is a great example of using a home page well (**www.microsoft.com**).

What's new

This section contains information on important news, events, and press releases. Always keep this section updated, and make sure that you date each entry. You should plan to add an entry for this section at least once a week, but remember to remove old items too.

About

This section should contain essential information about your business or organisation. If the section contains a lot of information it should be broken down into manageable subsections. 'About' information includes:

- mission: a short description of the organisation and what it seeks to achieve
- key strengths: key products, market position, manufacturing, skills, distribution
- company background
- management team: pictures and short biographies of key members of the management team

- financial information: annual results
- contact and location details: a link to the Contact section on your website

Products

This is the core part of your website, containing the things you have to sell. It should contain a brief overview of products and services and links to detailed information on specific products or services, containing:
- product/services description
- product applications
- business case and ROI (return on investment): how using your product can make and/or save money
- specifications
- purchase and delivery details
- FAQs
- pricing (be sure to specify currency)
- product reviews
- where you sell to; specify the countries or regions you do or do not sell to

Purchase

This is an essential link if you have an e-commerce facility that allows people to buy direct from your website. Ideally you should also create a small graphic to be displayed prominently, particularly on the home page, informing customers that they can purchase your products online.

Customers

People want to know who your customers are. Include a list of your key customers and a selection of quotes and case studies.

Partners

If you have a number of partners and joint ventures, you should have a section describing them, explaining how they allow you to deliver a better service.

Contact

This section should contain all your essential contact information including:
- e-mail address
- postal address and map of location
- telephone and fax

Search

If your website has more than 50 pages, you need a search engine to enable visitors to find information. If you use search, put the search box on every single page of your website, preferably near the top.

Offer an e-mail newsletter

Every website should offer an e-mail newsletter. If visitors give their e-mail address on their first visit, you can send them a regular weekly or monthly e-mail newsletter to tell them what's new.

Use metadata

Every web page should have a title. Where appropriate, content should have: classification, heading, summary, date of publication, author name, keywords. This is metadata; without it, search engines won't index your website properly, and people won't be able to find quickly what they are looking for.

Make sure you have proper footer information

The bottom of every page should have footer information containing:
- a list of the essential links for the website
- essential contact details: main address, telephone and fax, e-mail
- the copyright notice
- your privacy policy

Remember to promote your website

Promotional strategies include:
- registering with the major search engines (Google and Yahoo), as well as search engines specific to your industry or sector
- making sure that your website and e-mail address is on all your promotional literature

Do it yourself or get a design company?

If you are a competent computer user, you may well be able to do most of the work yourself, using packages such as Microsoft FrontPage or Macromedia's Dreamweaver, but you may require a graphic designer to help you with design issues.

COMMON MISTAKES

Being too clever

Some sites try too hard to entertain without providing hard information. Animation, multimedia, video clips, and other tricks can obscure important data. Many visitors are deterred immediately by a home page that features animation.

Poor classification, navigation, and search

Good classification, navigation, and search are essential for a successful website. Customers expect easy access to the information they want. If they can't find it easily on your site, they will go somewhere else. Structure is critical because it helps people find their way around.

Content that is difficult to read

Many websites try to impress by using lots of colour, but the easiest text to read is black on a white background. Keep paragraphs, line lengths, and documents short.

Building a Website Team

GETTING STARTED

A website is a publication. All good Web publications are fuelled by content, supported by an information architecture and technical infrastructure; the website must also be actively marketed and promoted. On a small website, all these functions will be performed by a part-time resource, but a large website will require dedicated personnel. When building a website team, keep the following in mind:

- a website should be managed by an editor – someone who understands content and knows what readers want
- information architecture skills are vital: the content must be well structured so that it can be quickly found and easily read
- the need for technical support should not be underestimated, particularly in the area of Web security

FAQS

Why should a website be run by an editor?

E-commerce means selling with content, so if the content isn't right, the customer won't buy. Content is not a technical issue but an editorial one. The primary job of the editor is to ensure that the right content is being created, and that it is being edited and published correctly.

What are the core functions of editing and publishing?

Publishing is about getting the right content to the right person at the right time, and the selection process is vital. Editing is therefore a critical quality-control function, rejecting poor content and cutting out unnecessary text. Quality websites get the right content up quickly.

What is information architecture?

Information architecture deals with how content is organised and presented. It refers to the metadata, classification, navigation, search, layout, and design of the website. Maintaining an information architecture for a small website is a relatively simple job but is far more complex for larger websites.

What are the key technical resources required to support a website?

A website that doesn't load quickly and consistently is of little use. Large e-commerce websites require complex technical infrastructure that needs constant monitoring. Technical resources include HTML, programming, and systems administration; security is becoming an increasingly important issue.

MAKING IT HAPPEN

Define the business requirements

It is essential to establish the business requirements for the website and to manage how these requirements are being met. What is the website supposed to achieve? If it is modelled on a traditional publication, it will need to generate revenue through advertising and subscription. However, most websites exist to support the sale of the organisation's products and to promote its brand.

Define the scope of the website

The people and skills required to run the website will depend on its scope. On a small website, one part-time person has to do everything, but a very large website will involve a number of people full-time and many more part-time.

Editorial board

It is advisable to establish an editorial board within the organisation to establish the content objectives and oversee their implementation. All the main departments and sections should be represented, and senior management should be involved.

The role of the managing editor

A single individual, with an editorial background, should be given overall charge of running the website. Specifically the managing editor should:

- manage the content: decide what type of content is to be published, and how often the website is to be updated
- manage the staff: hiring, training, motivation, reward, assessment, and discipline
- champion the visitor: make sure that the website focuses on its key visitors. The editor should encourage and make use of feedback from visitors.
- promote the website to senior management and within the organisation
- report to management on a regular basis
- conduct regular reviews to ensure that the website is achieving its objectives and evolving to meet changing needs

Editor

Among other things, the editor should:

- commission and purchase content: make sure that the right content is commissioned/purchased, and that it is delivered on time and to budget.
- edit the content: make sure that content meets editorial standards, clearly communicates its subject matter, and is well written. The editor should check for libel and other legal issues; make sure the metadata is correct; and review, correct and, where appropriate, delete already published content.
- publish the content: decide what is to be published and what is not. The editor should decide, in conjunction with the managing editor, what content should be highlighted on the home page and other relevant sections of the website.
- manage writers: for many people in the organisation, writing is only a small part of their job, so they will require motivation and training. The editor will also deal with hiring, reward, assessment, and discipline.

Actionlists

- champion the visitor/reader: understand what readers want; note and reply to feedback.

Copy editor

Copy editors check for spelling, grammar, and metadata. They ensure that the content is the right length, and rewrite where appropriate.

Writer

Writers must know their subject matter. They should have an ability and enthusiasm for writing, and should be able to suggest content ideas to the editor.

Contributor

Where the writer is not responsible for adding the metadata to the content, contributors ensure that the content gets to the editor quickly with all the appropriate metadata.

Moderator

Where online community facilities are available (chat, discussion boards, mailing lists), moderators will be required. Moderators mix editorial and chairperson skills, and also champion a particular mailing list or chat forum.

Information architect

The information architect is responsible for the information architecture of the website, which includes the following:

- Metadata: metadata is crucial to the design of websites. How content is classified will directly affect how quickly and effectively it can be found. Defining content templates includes agreeing on vital elements that a particular document should have, such as date of publication, author name, summary, or keywords.
- Navigation: the information architect should decide on the most effective options for navigation of the website. Standards and consistency in navigation design must be maintained. The focus should remain on the main task of navigation – finding an item of content quickly.
- Search: the information architect should design basic and advanced search options where appropriate. Search should be easy to use and deliver accurate results quickly.
- Layout and design: the information architect should ensure that all content is laid out in its most readable format. Simple, elegant design delivers web pages that are fast to download and easy to read. Consistency of design throughout the website is important.
- Usability: the website must work for its visitors. Regular feedback and usability testing are essential.

IT manager/programmer

This skill will usually be supplied by the IT department or outsourced. Skills are needed most when the website design is being implemented, but there is an ongoing need for technical support, so have some sort of programming resource permanently available if possible. A key responsibility of the IT manager is to ensure that the website is secure.

Systems administrator

A large website with a lot of traffic requires constant maintenance and monitoring. Responsibilities include maintaining the network and servers, day-to-day maintenance of all software, backing up the website, testing pages for download speed, and checking for broken links or security breaches.

HTML coder

This skill will vary depending on whether the website is being built in pure HTML (Hypertext Markup Language) or content management software is being used.

Graphic designer

Graphic designers should support the information architect. They should be skilled in creating small, elegant, fast-downloading graphics that support the presentation and readability of navigation, content, and other website elements.

Define the marketing and promotion requirements

The marketing department will usually perform marketing and promotion functions. Resources will be required to deal with specific web-related marketing functions such as ongoing search engine registration, establishing links with third parties, promotion through e-mail newsletters, and development of banner ads.

COMMON MISTAKES

Thinking that a website is a purely technical issue

A website is about communication, and the communications department is where the website should reside, supported by the IT and marketing departments.

Not having an editor in charge

The job of the editor is to ensure that the content makes sense – the single most important role in web design and management. Websites that are run by graphic designers often push this aspect at the expense of readable content.

Treating content as a commodity

Content is the most valuable resource a website has, but it must be handled with discretion. Overlong articles, badly written headings, poor metadata – all these reflect a website that doesn't care about its content or the person who is supposed to read it.

Not rewarding and remunerating writers

Content is written by people. The creation of content should be part of the job function and remunerated accordingly, otherwise results will be poor.

THE BEST SOURCES OF HELP
Book:
McGovern, Gerry. *Killer Web Content*. London: A&C Black, 2006.

Implementing Website Accessibility

GETTING STARTED
Having a good standard of website accessibility means that people with disabilities are able to use your site easily. A minimum level of website accessibility is becoming increasingly demanded by law. However, accessibility design should not be carried out simply because it is legally required. Following best practice in website accessibility can enhance the overall usability of a website for all visitors. When approaching website accessibility issues, keep the following in mind:
- simple, clean design greatly improves accessibility
- consistent design standards are critical from an accessibility point of view

MAKING IT HAPPEN
Focus on simplicity
Good accessibility design is also good website design. Don't try to be too clever or to use too many features. Keep your website design simple, clear, and consistent; the result will be more accessible for everyone.

Understand accessibility standards and their legal implications
Minimum accessibility standards are increasingly becoming legal requirements. Understanding what is required of your website is therefore important, particularly in the case of large organisations that are likely to be the primary targets of any legal action.

Implement proper standards of layout and design
Clear and consistent layout of content is important for accessibility. Black text on a white background improves readability for everyone. Avoid the use of coloured or graphical backgrounds, particularly where substantial quantities of text are presented. It is important that font sizes should be reasonable, and that visitors should be able to change the font size if they wish.

Develop consistent and clear navigation
Implementing consistent and clear navigation allows everyone to move through the website easily and in a logical manner. Navigation design should embrace clarity and simplicity.

Treatment of images
All images should have text associated with them: this is called ALT text. It ensures that a visually impaired person can understand everything that is on a page by means of a screen reader that turns text into audio. Use only client-side image maps.

Avoid screen movement
It is very difficult to read text on a screen that also has moving images. Where animated ads are required, they should animate a couple of times and then stop. Where ticker-tape elements are used, provide a facility that allows the visitor to turn them on or off.

Implement common standards in technologies
Keep all designs and technologies to a common standard where possible. If content has to be delivered that requires some sort of plug-in or other special feature, also provide the content in a standard HTML environment if possible.

Using tables for Web page design
Tables are an increasingly popular method of laying out content on a Web page, but you'll need to make sure that they are properly marked up. Clearly identify row and column headers, for instance. Tables can cause difficulties for those people who use screen readers, so check that your tables make sense when laid out in a linear fashion.

Avoid using frames
The use of frames can create a lot of problems, not simply for people with disabilities but for everyone who uses the Web. Very few of the largest and most popular websites use frames. Frames are not recommended, but if you have to use them, make sure they are properly titled.

Scripts and applets
Where possible, Web pages should be capable of being viewed with a browser that doesn't support applets, scripts, or other programming elements. It may be necessary to create two versions of the Web page in order to achieve this.

Use of multimedia
Studies show that the average consumer is not particularly interested in multimedia features. However, where visual multimedia is required, try to provide an audio or text description of the content presented.

Designing forms
The purpose of a form is to collect information. People with disabilities should be able to use assistive technology to fill out forms, or should be offered an alternative means of providing the information required.

THE BEST SOURCES OF HELP
Websites:
Bobby accessibility test:
   http://webxact.watchfire.com
W3C guidelines on Web Content Accessibility:
   www.w3.org/TR/WCAG10

Managing a Website

GETTING STARTED

A website has to be managed on a day-to-day basis. The amount of maintenance work that needs to be done will depend on the size of the website and the amount of new content that is being published. However, even small websites should be checked briefly each day to ensure that everything is in order. When approaching website management, keep the following in mind.

- Websites are communication vehicles and should be run primarily by people who understand content.
- Security is a growing concern on the Internet; every website should have a comprehensive security policy.
- Outsourcing can work well for website operations, but must be approached with care.
- Visitor feedback should always be encouraged as it will help attune the website more closely to visitors' needs.

FAQS

Why should an editor be in charge of the website?
Editors understand content, and content drives websites. Website success does not depend on technical issues, important as they are. The ability to find the right content quickly is what makes a website work for a visitor. To achieve this, someone is needed who truly understands what the organisation does and can consistently publish content on these activities.

Are websites a security risk?
Yes. Websites can open a door into your computer system. Website management therefore requires stringent security procedures that are actively policed. Hackers are an increasing threat on the Internet, and if your website is not properly secured, the consequences can be very serious.

Why is visitor feedback so important in website management?
A website is not like a physical store where it is easy to see if measures are successful or not. Website logs will give some indication of visitor behaviour, but it is essential to encourage feedback. In this way, you can find out where visitors are having problems and what improvements they would like to see. A website should always be evolving, always seeking to make its processes and structures more customer-friendly.

Isn't outsourcing risky?
It can be: many outsourcing companies have folded. Web hosting is a solid and relatively mature business, with many excellent providers of hosting services, but more care is needed when considering outsourcing other web and Internet functions. Make sure that you are dealing with a stable, well-funded outsource vendor, that you have a comprehensive contract with them, and that they offer quality service and support.

MAKING IT HAPPEN

Hosting your website

Hosting your website means putting it on the Internet so that people can visit it. There are two basic options: internal or external hosting. Internal hosting is often the option when dealing with an intranet, because most of the access to the intranet will be from within the organisation. However, you must ensure that there is sufficient bandwidth so that staff working from home, or from hotel rooms, will be able to download pages quickly.

For most public websites, it makes sense to use a third-party hosting company. Such companies have mastered the complexities of website hosting and can offer excellent, good-value service. When choosing such a hosting company, consider the following:

- Do I need a domain name?
- How many visitors do I expect each month?
- How much space and what access speeds will I need?
- Will I need e-commerce facilities?
- Will I need special programming facilities such as CGI scripts?
- How do I want to deal with e-mail?
- What sort of support is offered?
- What are the price and payment options?

Outsourcing your website operations

Hosting externally is a first step in outsourcing your website operations. Running a large website is a complex technical operation; the key advantage of outsourcing is that it allows you to focus on your core business, while giving you flexibility and removing the need to recruit your own technical staff. When considering outsourcing, keep the following in mind.

- Website operation outsourcing is still a new industry with a high failure rate. Choose a company that is solid and well financed.
- It is important to develop a proper outsourcing strategy. This is a serious activity that can have serious consequences if done wrongly.
- It takes time to choose the right vendor.
- A comprehensive contract must be in place. Assume that if something is not in the contract, it won't be done.
- Proper metrics as well as a plan for day-to-day management of the outsourcing relationship must be in place.
- Your outsourcer must have appropriate security practices.
- Your outsourcer must have a good track record in providing quality service and support.
- Outsourcing is not a technology strategy, so you will still need experienced technical staff to plan your future technology strategy.

Day-to-day maintenance of a website

Websites are not static like a company brochure; they are constantly evolving and therefore require continual maintenance. The level of maintenance will depend on the size of the website: a small website will require less maintenance than a large one. It will also depend on which, if any, of the website's operations have been outsourced. To maintain a website professionally:

- the performance of the website must be constantly monitored. The home page and other major pages should be checked daily, as should website logs, in order to spot any technical problems.
- new content must be published regularly and old content removed. A website with out-of-date content makes a very bad impression.
- all links, forms, and programming elements must be checked regularly
- standards established in the design of the website must be monitored, including navigation, search, layout, and graphic design
- procedures should be in place to ensure regular feedback from visitors. Ideally, usability testing should be carried out regularly.
- website accessibility must be monitored
- website security must be policed

Managing Internet security

Internet security is a major concern, and too many websites have poor security. The Internet is a network, and networks are, by definition, open. When approaching Internet security, keep in mind that if you don't have a defined and actively policed Internet security policy, you don't have Internet security. You should also do the following.

- Be ever-vigilant. There is no such thing as the perfect Internet security system. The security threat is constantly changing, so you must monitor the situation constantly.
- Combine software capabilities and human expertise. The best security software in the world still needs human experience and skills, particularly for larger systems.
- Secure internally as well as externally. Many security threats come from inside the organisation.
- Keep it simple. Less software and fewer options mean less opportunity for a hacker to find a weakness.

Dealing effectively with computer viruses

Computer viruses are a constant and growing threat on the Internet, costing organisations billions of pounds every year. Every day they become more sophisticated and replicate more quickly. It is now possible to get a computer virus by visiting a website or opening an e-mail – previously, you had to open the e-mail attachment. The best approach to computer viruses is that prevention is far, far better than cure. To combat computer viruses:

- install the very latest antivirus software and keep it up to date
- scan your entire computer system regularly with your antivirus software
- get the latest software security patches for your computer; if you don't have them, your antivirus software may well not protect you

- join an e-mail newsletter to get news on new antivirus and software upgrades
- immediately delete e-mails that you are in any way suspicious of
- don't download anything from the Internet except from highly reputable websites
- back up your data regularly
- be vigilant

Managing e-mail professionally

E-mail can be a powerful communications tool, but it must be used properly. Not treating e-mail seriously has two main results. First, so much e-mail is generated that its value as an effective communications tool is diminished. Second, many organisations are very lax in responding to e-mail enquiries from their websites or elsewhere. Not responding to an e-mail quickly is like leaving a phone to ring unanswered – it gives the customer a very poor impression. When managing e-mail, have policies and training in place to ensure that e-mail is used effectively, and implement a policy for responding to e-mails, particularly those received from the website.

COMMON MISTAKES
Out-of-date content

A website that has not been updated with fresh content, and/or that contains content that is no longer relevant, gives a very unprofessional impression of the organisation.

Broken links and other features

Many websites do not have procedures in place to check all the parts of the website to see if they are functioning properly. Broken links are common on the Web. It is also not uncommon to find forms that no longer work properly.

Poor security procedures

Many organisations do not realise how serious a security threat a website can be. Security has, in general, been poor on the Internet; the results of this are seen in the speed with which computer viruses can spread, and the frequency of website break-ins.

Not responding to e-mails

Studies indicate that organisations perform poorly in their responses to people who have contacted them through the website. This gives a very poor impression to actual or potential customers.

THE BEST SOURCES OF HELP
Websites:
Builder.com: **www.builder.com**
Google website Management Links:
   www.directory.google.com/Top/Computers

Maintaining a Website

GETTING STARTED

The amount of website maintenance you will need will depend very much on the size of your website and the amount of new content that is being published on it. Websites are not like brochures or other print material: they change, sometimes because of an action you have taken, and sometimes because of external factors. They must therefore be monitored constantly. Keep the following in mind.

- The performance of the website must be constantly watched.
- New content must be published regularly, and old content removed.
- All links, forms, and programming elements must be checked regularly.
- Standards established in the design of the website must be monitored.
- Procedures should be in place to ensure that regular feedback is obtained from visitors.
- Website security must be policed.

MAKING IT HAPPEN

Test the website from different environments

A website should be checked at least once a day to ensure that everything is working properly. It should also be regularly tested from different computers, browsers, and bandwidth access points, at different times of the day. Web pages may download quickly in the office environment over a fast connection, but how quickly are they downloading at home or in a hotel room? If pages are showing signs of slowing down because of increased traffic, it may be time to seek more bandwidth.

Managing your content

A website that doesn't regularly incorporate new content gives a very poor impression to visitors. Content must be created, edited, and published professionally on the website. Old content, or content that is found to be libellous or otherwise incorrect, must be removed quickly. The publication schedule for the website must be adhered to: if the home page is to be changed on Monday at 10am, then it must be changed every Monday at 10am.

Optimise graphics

New graphics should be checked for size. The objective is to have the graphic looking as good as possible, at the same time keeping it to the minimum possible file size. You must also make sure that the actual graphic size is being kept within agreed standards.

Check Web page download sizes

It's important to establish a range for the total file size of a page, including all graphics. 35Kbytes to 70Kbytes should do it, with the objective of staying well below 70Kbytes, particularly for the home page. Although broadband connections are now more widely available, some customers will still have dial-up connections. Even broadband users appreciate as fast a download as possible.

Keep a website accessible

It is important that your website is accessible to people with disabilities. Minimum accessibility standards are increasingly required by law. Check it regularly to ensure that it is accessible. The Web Accessibility Initiative (WAI) site offers plenty of useful advice if you don't know where to start: **www.w3.org/WAI**.

Check links, forms, and programming elements

Website links, forms, and programming elements break, so it is important to check them regularly. Links may break because the page that you have linked to has changed or been removed. A wide selection of software that will check broken links is available. However, sometimes the page link stays the same but the content that you originally linked to changes, so you must occasionally check key links manually to see if they still go to the intended content.

Forms must be checked on a regular basis (monthly is advised). Put your e-mail address and dummy data into the form, and test that everything works properly. Programming elements can malfunction, so they also have to be checked.

Manage website logs

Website logs are important for tracking visitor behaviour on the website. However, they can also provide very useful technical information. Check whether:

- any page errors occur that might indicate technical problems or broken links
- any spikes in visitor behaviour may be causing bandwidth shortages

Website architecture management

A set of standards should be established with regard to the navigation, search, layout, and design of the website. It is important to monitor these standards to make sure that they are being implemented properly.

Make security a priority

Computer security is an increasingly critical issue for websites. An Internet security policy should be in place, and it should be adhered to strictly.

THE BEST SOURCES OF HELP
Book:
Nielsen, Jakob. *Ensuring Web Usability: Understanding What Users Want*. Indianapolis, Indiana: New Riders, 2006.

Updating Your Website as Your Business Grows

GETTING STARTED
When you start up your business and are pushed for time, you often can't devote as much energy as you'd like to creating the ideal website. Once your business starts to grow, however, having a professional-looking online presence is vital, and adding new content, features, and facilities can make a big difference to your customers and your bottom line.

FAQS
How important is it to use professional services to upgrade a website?
Much depends on what exactly you want to add, but if the changes you want are complex or include adding functionality (such as new ways to pay), getting an experienced designer and programmer on board from the beginning is a good idea. Ask other business owners if they can recommend anyone, rather than plucking the first name you find from an online search. 'Interview' prospective candidates so that you can work out whether you can work well with them, and that they understand exactly what you want and who your target audience is.

MAKING IT HAPPEN
Think about your goals
An important part of the planning process for new features or content is knowing what you are trying to achieve with your website upgrade. Set some specific objectives, including timelines if appropriate, such as:
- boosting the number of visitors by 10 per cent in the first six months
- increasing the amount of business generated by the website by 25 per cent in the first year
- increase the level of business generated through the website
- improving customer service

Refresh the content
Although your focus may be on adding new material and/or features, some existing content could be kept if it's given a spring clean. Remove ancient price lists, photos, or press releases, and think about creating an archive (ordered by year, or by topic) that can house useful items.

Plan upgrades around what your visitors really want
There's no point overhauling your website to find that visitors still can't find what they want or that they preferred it the way it was before. To make your upgrade effective, base it on actual data derived from visitor information. For example, it should be relatively easy to find out what the most popular pages on your website are (you can do this yourself with the right software, or ask your Web hosting service to help), and which are the ones no one has visited since 2001. What can you learn from this? Be ruthless and be ready to drop pages or even whole sections that just aren't working. You'll also need

to be objective: *you* may be fascinated by the five-page section on how your business's widget was developed, but if no one else is, wouldn't it be better to put that space to better use? Finally, take time to visit your competitors' websites. What are they doing that you could emulate? What are they doing that you want to avoid?

Increase self-service
Offering customers self-service as part of your online overhaul can have many benefits: customers can buy more easily at any time of the day, support costs are cut, and fewer staff need to be available to man the phones to offer support. For example, because product features, prices, and availability can be flagged up on your site, customers can glean all the information quickly and easily and they appreciate the convenience that these new services add.

Improve online ordering processes
The best websites reduce barriers to purchase and make things simple for their customers. Streamline the ordering process.
- Make sure that all relevant product information (specifications, prices, delivery times) are included on one single page.
- Place all the details necessary to process the order on the ordering and payment page.
- Allow regular customers to simply add new purchases to an ordering page that has all other contact and payment details in place.

Also make sure that any order forms on your site are well structured, clear, and as brief as possible. Don't fish for information you really don't need at this stage, as you'll put people off. The form should ask for details pertaining to the fulfilment of the order, such as customer name and address, delivery address (if different), and payment option.

The product details, quantity, delivery charges, VAT, or any other amounts chargeable should be very clearly shown on screen before the customer is asked to make their final payment. Many sites use a 'summary' page so that customers can quickly review the order and delivery details before they pay, and this is good practice. If the order is successful, acknowledge it by e-mail, giving a reference number so that customers can track its progress or contact you with queries.

Offer secure payment options
If your site supports online ordering, it's absolutely essential that you have a secure method of processing payments. Contact your bank for help as a first port of call, or you could talk to an independent specialist. If you go down this route, however, ask for details of their security measures and also check that they offer secure payment sites protected by industry-approved protocols. It's also wise to investigate their policy on holding customer credit card details. Ask for full details on the security of their links to other organisations in the payment approval chain, as

they'll have to pass on details to banks, credit reference agencies or other parties, as well as communicating with your company. Each transmission represents a potential security risk. Finally, it would be worth asking potential partners for references before you engage them.

Consider using 'landing pages'
Landing pages are a great way of improving response rates to advertising or marketing efforts. Visitors are directed to them when they click on a link in an online ad or in an e-mail, and they offer information about the product or service being 'pushed' at that time, with the aim of getting the customer to buy. (You've probably seen these as a customer yourself, with companies offering buy one, get one free offer, or a special deal on a new product.) Even if you can't tempt people to buy there and then, you can still use landing pages to request information that you can follow up later. For example, you could ask visitors to:
• subscribe to an e-newsletter
• register for an event
• enter their e-mail address to receive future product updates or offers

Set up a virtual press office
Posting press material on the Internet reduces waste and costs, speeds up distribution, and may also improve relationships with journalists (you're making it easier for them to get hold of information). Get into the habit of uploading your releases on to your site as soon as they're ready. If you tend to issue releases very regularly, it may be worth putting a short summary of the story on the main press page with a hyperlink to the full story to make it easier for people to navigate. As ever, maintenance is important, so regularly archive outdated or older releases to reduce clutter on the Web page. Many organisations today also offer 'news alert' services, which allow journalists to choose the updates and topics they need. You could, for example, offer:
• online press kits
• press releases
• feature articles
• Web casts
• briefings

Establish an online publication library
If your business is a leader in its field in terms of research, making that (non-confidential!) information available online will soon make your site indispensable for consumers and journalists alike. To allow visitors to access the publications easily:
• post a full list of publications on your press information page
• make the documents available as pdfs, which can be downloaded easily
• create a 'library listing' of all the publications available, along with a brief description of each
• place links to publications on pages where you describe relevant products or industry solutions

Create a virtual community
Virtual communities are one way of increasing the 'bond'

between an organisation and its customers, creating one for your business may encourage visitors to return to your site more often. As well as the basics, such as newsletters and blogs, you could also allow members to become part of an online club and enjoy privileged services, using the membership database to offer personalised incentives and promotions.

Discussion groups are a must for virtual communities, so make sure people are able to post messages on your site. You may need to appoint a moderator to make sure that the comments are appropriate and inoffensive. Also offer users the chance to give their objective opinion or feedback on products. The aim here is to encourage other members of the community to suggest answers, provide help or contribute to the discussion of a specific issue, all of which will help to strengthen relationships.

Keep tabs on progress
Website upgrades don't have to be expensive, but they do involve a lot of time and energy as you plan and execute your improvement programme. It's a good idea to evaluate your progress regularly, and ask for feedback from staff, trusted customers, and key partners. You want absolute honesty here, so that you can review or even disregard your changes if they don't get the reception you were looking for.

COMMON MISTAKES
You go over the top
If you've been thinking of overhauling your site for a while, you may feel like adding absolutely every new feature you can think of. Do think carefully about this, though: well-chosen updates can give your business a vibrant, fresh new look, but if the new features make the site slow to download or confusing, you'll turn people off. Keep the content brisk but relevant and introduce new functionality that will really make visitors' lives easier.

You don't do any maintenance
If you plan to add new features and content to your website, it's essential to maintain the existing content at the same time. One of the most important tasks is making sure that all links continue to work as they should. Have these checked regularly and remove any broken links or images and pages that don't load properly. Yes, this is a time-consuming job, but it's a key part of creating and looking after a high-quality site. You want your visitors to come and be delighted by what they see, rather than frustrated and put off by poor maintenance.

THE BEST SOURCES OF HELP
Book:
McGovern, Gerry. *Killer Web Content*. London: A&C Black, 2006.

Website:
Jim Sterne's website: **www.targeting.com**

Creating an Effective Online PR Strategy

GETTING STARTED
The Internet has revolutionised the way we gather information these days, and it's made journalists' lives a lot easier too. It can be hard to attract their attention, so do your business a favour by making it easy for them to find out details about your company and its products and services. Putting well-organised, useful information online is a great way of doing this and these days you don't have to restrict yourself to press releases: audio and visual content can really make you stand out from the crowd.

FAQS
Why is it important to post press information on our website?
Now that the Internet offers global news information 24 hours a day, people don't have time to wait about for the postman to arrive with a sack full of press releases. When they have a story to file, journalists want information NOW. By adapting to their needs and posting useful information online, you'll be helping them to keep up to date with breaking news and get hold of background details if they need them.

MAKING IT HAPPEN
Send out press releases by e-mail
Issue press releases to an e-mail list of journalists to save distribution time. It's best practice to include the release in the body of your message, rather than as an attachment which may block up inboxes. If you decide to send the press release to a smaller, targeted group of journalists (those writing for industry magazines, say), you can also send electronic news alerts to other journalists, giving them links to the full story on your website.

Create a news alert service
New alert facilities allow journalists to choose the updates and topics they need. The service sends the latest news features, audio clips, and so on direct to journalists' inboxes. They can set their own preferences for format and frequency, and access the material at a time that suits them.

Post press releases on your website
As well as distributing press releases by e-mail, it's a good idea to upload copies on to your website, taking care to regularly 'prune' them and remove or archive out-of-date or elderly releases. If you do set up an archive, remember that people will still need a quick and easy way to retrieve the information they want, so have the releases appear in date order and if possible, offer a simple search facility so that journalists can look for key words, phrases, or names.

Some companies issue press releases more frequently than others, so if this is the case for you, put a short summary of the story on the main press page with a hyperlink to the full story so that people can navigate easily.

Consider offering an online photo library
While it may not be appropriate for every company, in some cases you'll get better coverage in the press if your story is accompanied by a powerful or particularly apt image. (If the photograph has been sourced outside your company, make sure you have the rights to use it, however.) If you own a series of good images, you may want to include them in an online photo library. Again, for ease of use, make sure the photos are indexed and that they have a short description. If a certain phrasing needs to be used when the photos are reproduced (such as '© John Smith 2008' or 'reproduced by permission of ACB Holdings Ltd'), make sure this is explained clearly and prominently on the Web page.

Offer journalists contact information
If journalists need more specific information on an issue than your press release can offer, or if they want a quote from your company, they'll need to know the best people to speak to. Make sure your website lists the name of a press contact who can either answer the question themselves or put the journalists in touch with the relevant member of staff. Alternatively, you could provide a complete list of specialist contacts, so that journalists can just get in touch direct. Whichever option you take, include both phone and e-mail information.

It's also a good idea to offer some background information somewhere on the site so that journalists can use it to add context to their stories. For example, you could include a potted history of the company, profiles of key staff members, a brief overview of the product range, a list of your bestsellers, and so on.

Publish a media diary
For larger organisations, an online diary of key events can help journalists plan future news coverage or feature articles. The diary should cover:
- product launch dates
- press conference dates
- announcement of financial results
- dates of events or exhibitions supported by your company
- Web cast dates
- milestones or any significant anniversaries

Organise press conferences over e-mail
Inviting journalists to a press conference by e-mail is an efficient use of resources, but do take care not to bombard people with messages if the event won't be

of interest to them. Target your invitations carefully, or people could start ignoring your messages altogether! Remember to:

- invite journalists and editors from publications that reach your most important customers and prospects. If any important contacts can't make it, send them a press pack to keep them in the loop and set up a separate meeting if appropriate.
- give invitees as much notice as possible and try to plan the timing so that editorial coverage will appear in the next issue of the most important monthly publications.
- confirm dates, times, and location.
- explain the reasons for the conference in advance and ensure that journalists understand the importance of the event.

Consider briefing online

Rather than going to the time and expense of holding a physical press conference, it may be worth briefing selected journalists online. They could watch the briefing live via a Webcast or download it from your website later. Send all invitees the date, time, and Internet address they'll need, remembering to include a password if you feel access should be restricted. Once the briefing is over, post a downloadable version on your website along with a summary of the content and links to any sources of further information or related items.

Feature online interviews with key members of staff

To make online briefings even more effective, you can make them interactive by offering journalists the chance to hold a question and answer session with a product specialist or senior members of staff. The Q & A could take place over a video or phone link, with a moderator asking questions placed by the journalists. Both the event itself and the number of invitees need to be handled carefully to make sure that each journalist is given the opportunity to pose a question.

After the online event, you could post an audio or video download of proceedings on to your site, as well as written transcripts that can be saved and edited without too much fuss. Make sure the transcript includes links to relevant biographical or corporate information.

Create 'cut-and-paste' press packs

As things can become especially hectic around the time of a new product launch or end of year results, producing an online press pack that collates all relevant information will save time and cut down on stress levels for both you and the press. The final make-up of your pack will depend on what you're launching, of course, but you could include any or all of the following:

- general introduction
- press release giving details of the product or event
- audio clips or transcripts of press statements
- photographs

- background information
- company information
- contacts for further information

Supply the material as Word documents or another easily edited format so that it can be dropped into other packages simply by the press.

COMMON MISTAKES

You make the press information too hard to find

Journalists usually work on incredibly tight deadlines, so give them a hand to find information easily by including clear links to it from your home page. As your range of electronic material grows, it would make sense to create an online 'press centre' which the press can visit to access the data quickly. Draw together audio and Web casts, product information, company background information, press releases, interviews and so on. To emphasise brand new material, put the most recent stories as headlines on your home page with links to the full text. To make follow-up easy, make sure a contact e-mail address or website link is included on all press material.

Your content is out of date

Nothing is more off-putting than visiting a website and finding that all the content is covered in (virtual) cobwebs. It will give the impression of a company that's either going nowhere or which doesn't appreciate how information-hungry people are today. Make sure someone is responsible for checking content, removing old material, and posting the most recent, newsworthy stories and images. Archive old material and check that all links are working.

You don't actively manage the press centre

Just because information is appearing online rather than in print doesn't mean that you can afford to let your standards slip. All information should be checked for accuracy, and ask your legal team to check any statements or assertions that may be inflammatory. Leave plenty of time to clear permissions if you are reproducing text or images from another source, so that you aren't caught on the hop at the last minute. Content management aside, it's important to measure your site's performance, so that you can make sure it is doing the job you intended and keeping journalists well fed with good quality information. For example, how many visitors are coming to the press centre? What are the most popular pages or downloads?

THE BEST SOURCES OF HELP
Websites:
Chartered Institute of Public Relations:
  www.cipr.co.uk
International Public Relations Association:
  www.ipra.org

Delivering Good Quality Online Customer Service and Support

GETTING STARTED

Customer service is increasingly seen as a central concern for e-commerce. For many consumers it is a key differentiator between good and bad e-commerce websites. A wide range of online support options is now available to organisations, including e-mail, knowledge base systems, live chat, and phone-back. When designing an online support function, keep in mind:

- that the first step in online customer support is a well-structured website with comprehensive information
- that organisations have a poor record in responding to e-mail queries from their websites; a lack of response damages your reputation
- that online support can cause a significant increase in queries, many of which are flippant or of little value. A strategy must be put in place to deal with these and sift out the important queries.

FAQS

Why offer customer support online?

The best-designed website in the world will never answer every question a consumer has. Research has indicated that up to three-quarters of the people who started an online purchase did not complete it. Websites that have added support facilities have found that the number of people completing transactions increases significantly.

When should you offer support online?

All websites should have at least some level of customer support. Cost is a central issue: the lower the margin on the product, the less support can be afforded.

What savings can online support bring?

There are substantial cost savings to be made by dealing with support queries online. For example, customers may be able to find the information they need on a website; e-mails from customers can be held over for a few hours until there is someone available to deal with them, while telephone calls always have to be dealt with immediately. It is easier to have a set of generic answers (to frequently asked questions) ready for general or vague queries.

However, all support is expensive. Although there are many benefits from it, publishing high-quality material on a support website requires an investment of time and money. It may also be important to ensure that the personal touch remains a part of the relationship between the company and the customer. The key is to target the best-quality, most personalised support at the highest-value customers.

Is online support more suitable for some consumers than others?

It depends on the type of online support. Online support that is text-based, such as live chat and e-mail, is more suitable to computer-literate consumers. Chat and e-mail are thus ideal for technology industry customers, who are frequent users of e-mail. New or infrequent computer users can often barely cope with learning to use the browser; asking them to use chat software might just confuse them. For such people, the option to have someone call them and talk them through the website can be very comforting.

MAKING IT HAPPEN

Ensure you have comprehensive, well-organised website content

A website is often described as a library. Libraries have two key components: a selection of well-organised content and a support centre where people can ask questions. Person-to-person support is expensive, and the website should seek to reduce unnecessary interaction by supplying content that will answer as many questions as possible.

It is widely recognised that quality websites can reduce the number of support calls an organisation receives. While the entire website is there to answer questions, specific support functions include the following:

- Frequently Asked Questions (FAQs): a collection of the most frequently asked questions about a product or service. FAQs should be well written and concise. If there are a lot of them, they should be classified into logical groups, and perhaps provided with a search function.
- Comprehensive help: a Help link should be prominent on every page. This should lead the person to a section containing information on all the support elements on the website. Where people are asked to perform a complex task, such as using an advanced search function, or are performing a purchase process, context-sensitive help should be available: when they click on the Help link, they are brought to the specific page they need.
- Knowledge-based systems: these approaches seek to take the FAQ model much further. The user can type in a question, rather than using keywords. The response may involve asking the person a series of questions in order to narrow down the area of interest. While such systems will not answer every question, they do reduce the number of support calls, and can also ensure that consistent answers are being delivered for specific questions.

E-mail-based support

It is often sufficient to use e-mail as the main channel for support on a website. An e-mail response policy must be established, whereby e-mails are graded where appropriate, and a response-time target is specified for each e-mail.

However, the ease of sending e-mails can often result in frivolous questions. Organisations receiving a high volume of e-mail and working on tight margins often make extensive use of auto-response. The auto-response e-mail, which is generated automatically, may contain an FAQ and links to support material on the website. More sophisticated auto-responders may connect to a knowledge base that will search for keywords in the e-mail and send back a response based on these keywords. It is advisable for these approaches to include a human-based option so that the enquirer can talk to someone if they need to.

Unfortunately, many organisations don't allocate enough resources to e-mail response, and so messages are responded to late or not at all.

Live chat
Also known as instant messaging, live chat allows a customer representative to chat with a website visitor in real time, using text. The benefits of live chat are:
- many people have only one phone line, so if they ring support they will have to disconnect from the Internet: live chat means that they can receive text-based support without having to disconnect
- support is sometimes complex and may take a long time; live chat can avoid the enquirer having to spend hours on the phone, and can solve the problem in a more logical manner
- live chat can be an option for international customers who do not have access to a Freephone number
- an experienced customer representative can handle several chat sessions at the same time

Live chat can have certain drawbacks. Response times can be slow, depending on the connection, and novice computer users may not feel comfortable using it. In addition, the quality of the live chat support is dependent on the typing skills and knowledge of the support staff.

Callback support
With this option the website visitor is informed that if they enter their telephone number and details into a form someone will phone them back. This option is expensive, and is most suitable for high-value items. A related and popular option here is to offer the customer a free or low-cost phone number that they can call.

Co-browsing and page pushing
Software is now available that allows the customer service representative to synchronise their browser with the person requesting support. Using live chat or the telephone, the rep can take the person through a process, changing their web page as they change their own. This is not suitable for the sale of low-value items, but can be a valuable feature if complex processes and information have to be delivered.

The importance of graduating customer service
A fundamental objective of many e-commerce websites is to increase sales while reducing the need for person-to-person interaction, thus increasing profit. If there is too much customer interaction, especially with non-serious or low-value customers, the profit will be eaten away. For certain products, margins are so slim that person-to-person interaction must be kept to a minimum.

As a result, it is important that the customer service component of a website should be graduated. For example, a person seeking support should be guided to the FAQ section first; if they can't find an answer there, they should be offered the option of an e-mail, and finally the option of telephone support.

Outsourcing customer service
Customer service support functions such as live chat and e-mail support can now be outsourced to countries such as India and the Philippines, where well-educated English-speaking labour is available at low cost. While outsourcing support definitely reduces costs, it can have negative implications. The support staff may not have the in-depth knowledge required to answer complex questions.

Integration of support functions
If people are contacting the organisation through a number of support channels, the support function can become dissipated. Planning is required to ensure that a single support knowledge base is used, and that all the technologies work in unison.

Training of staff
Offering a range of support options requires a well-planned training approach and targeting of staff skills. Training will be required to raise skill levels.

COMMON MISTAKES
Not responding to e-mails
Survey after survey indicates that organisations have a poor record in responding to e-mail requests from their websites.

Too many queries
Online support makes it easier for people to communicate with the organisation, and this can substantially increase the number of frivolous queries. Organisations are often not properly prepared to handle the increase in volume, and the important queries can be swamped.

Not being able to answer the question
A key problem with all customer service support is a lack of trained staff. When customers ask questions, they must be answered quickly and comprehensively; otherwise the whole purpose is defeated.

Lack of proper integration
Online support must integrate with the overall support structure. Adding numerous support options increases complexity, and this can lead to integration problems.

Implementing a Customer Relationship Management Strategy

GETTING STARTED

Customer relationship management (CRM) is about using people, processes, and technology to develop long-term, profitable relationships with customers. The Internet is an important medium through which CRM services are delivered. CRM technology tends to be sophisticated and expensive to install and manage. It is generally best suited to organisations with a large customer base. However, CRM is not simply about technology: it requires skilled staff to be able to exploit its features, in order to understand their customers better and deliver just the product or service that such customers require.

FAQS

What makes up a CRM system?

CRM can be a catch-all phrase. However, it generally includes some or all of the following components: customer information systems; personalisation systems; content management systems; call-centre automation; data warehousing; data mining; sales force automation; campaign management systems.

Traditionally, CRM focused internally, delivering information to staff who then used that information to interact better with customers. However, with the emergence of the Web we are seeing what is termed as e-CRM, where there is a strong customer self-service and personalisation focus. Ideally, CRM and e-CRM should integrate seamlessly but, because they often use different technologies, this is not always easy to achieve.

Why is CRM so important to e-commerce?

The Internet is a fickle environment. There is no live interaction between the consumer and the website. Therefore, a website needs to work hard to develop relationships with its customers. It needs to show its customers that it cares about their business. A way of doing this is to understand customer needs. It's about anticipating customer information requirements through personalisation. It's about answering customer questions in a comprehensive and timely manner. It's about delivering exactly what the customer ordered, on time. It's about suggesting to customers new products that they will be genuinely interested in.

What are the key benefits of CRM?

The benefits of CRM include the following:
- better, faster information on customer needs and behaviour
- more cost-effective management of the customer relationship through automating and streamlining of customer processes
- more empowered customers who can quickly find the information they need
- more profitable and loyal customers
- suitability for medium and large organisations

Is CRM right for every business?

No. A small business should be able to know its customers without having to implement lots of technology. CRM is complex and expensive to install. It is best suited to organisations which have a large customer base, and are already customer-centric. They should have a significant salesforce, run a variety of marketing and sales programmes, and have strong internal IT resources and quality infrastructures.

MAKING IT HAPPEN

Develop a long-term vision and strategy

Because of the complexity and expense of CRM, it is not advisable to implement an entire CRM system in one go. Rather, your organisation needs to develop a vision of where it wants to go with CRM over the long term. Then, the CRM implementation should be broken down into manageable sections.

Develop a Return on Investment (ROI) model

Surveys have indicated that a number of organisations are depending on intuition, rather than a clear ROI model, in deciding to implement CRM systems. This is not a good idea. To create an ROI model, establish appropriate metrics and see how they change with the implementation of CRM. Examples of CRM metrics include:
- revenue per sales rep
- cost and length of time it takes to close a lead
- revenue/profitability per customer
- customer satisfaction ratings

Talk to your customers before you implement CRM

In developing a vision and strategy, it's critical to talk to your customers. After all, CRM is about focusing on customer needs, and if you don't understand basic customer needs when designing a CRM solution, then chances are you'll get it wrong.

Talk to staff

It's critical to survey staff internally. CRM covers a broad range of activities, including marketing, sales, support, and IT, so it's vital that key people in all of these areas are engaged. There will always be trade-offs. However, unless you get the varying views and wishes, a rounded set of requirements will not emerge.

CRM can be seen as an IT solution to a sales and marketing problem. Sales and marketing departments can resist such technology-based solutions unless they are brought fully on board and clearly convinced of the benefits of CRM. Of course, there is also the issue of internal rivalries to address. CRM requires a unified approach to the customer, but many departments are daily at loggerheads – for example, support complaining that sales promised too much.

Ensure that staff are properly trained and educated

Well-trained staff make for successful CRM. The key objective of CRM is not so much to train staff in how to use the new software, but rather to have a customer-centric view of the world. If staff are not open to embracing a philosophy of making the customer king, then CRM will become an expensive and wasteful exercise. Staff training is an ongoing process of shifting the way people think about and act towards the customer. Just as customers are becoming more information hungry, so staff also need to become more information hungry about their customers. Customer data is nothing if it is not analysed and turned into information and knowledge. Only highly motivated and trained people can do that.

Create a single view of the customer

A core objective of CRM should be to create a single view of the customer. Historically, organisations have held isolated pockets of information on individual customers. CRM should be about bringing all that information together into a single, well-organised environment. That means departments sharing and collaborating. It also means ensuring that all relevant employees can gain easy access and contribute new information to this single customer profile.

Carefully consider integration issues

Because CRM can cover such a broad range of technologies and activities, integration becomes a key issue. There is likely to be a range of different software in the CRM solution and this will need to integrate properly. Also, the CRM solution will have to integrate with existing systems – trying to implement CRM technologies into a poor IT infrastructure will cause serious problems.

Selecting a CRM supplier

Your organisation should have a detailed understanding of what it wants from CRM before approaching suppliers.Here are some of the key questions that need to be asked:

- Who are the supplier's customers? How happy are they with their implementations? Does the supplier have customers in your industry? (If so, talk to them about their experience.)
- What about support and training, which is just as important as the software itself? What are the means by which it is delivered – in person, by telephone, over the Web)? What support packages are available?
- How long has the supplier been in business? What's their financial situation? Have they been in the news lately? If so why?
- What are the skills and experience of the team that will be involved in implementing the solution?
- What's the pricing? Are payment options available?

The ASP option for CRM

Technology vending is acronym city. An Application Services Provider (ASP) will offer basically to manage the CRM system for you, and will charge an ongoing fee for that service. Because of the complexity and ever-changing nature of CRM, this can be an attractive option. However, because a CRM system embodies the heart of what an organisation does – dealing with customers – the choice of ASP vendor needs to be made very carefully.

COMMON MISTAKES

Forgetting about the C in CRM

Much of the selling of CRM has focused on amazing technology and extraordinary features that do all sorts of fancy things. In all the excitement, the very reason CRM exists – to help organisations develop stronger customer relationships by understanding and meeting customer needs better – is often forgotten.

Not getting the staff approval

The best technology in the world is of little use if the people who are supposed to use it are not properly trained and motivated. If staff do not have a customer focus and a desire to develop long-term relationships with customers, then CRM is dead on arrival.

Inability to adapt CRM solutions quickly

Surveys indicate that a significant number of organisations have had problems in adapting CRM solutions quickly to changing customer needs. Often, because the systems are so complex, managers are dependent on the IT department to make even simple changes.

Lack of senior management's understanding and approval

A CRM implementation is crucial to business functions such as sales, marketing, and support. CRM projects will run into trouble if senior management is not engaged.

Poor integration

Integration problems with CRM software have proved costly and time-consuming for some organisations.

Automation without common sense

CRM can automate many sales and marketing processes, but that doesn't mean it shouldn't be carefully monitored. The story is told of a major car manufacturer whose sales department offered deep discounts to get rid of a backlog of lime-green cars. The cars began to sell briskly. The CRM system noticed the trend and requested the manufacturing plant to make more lime-green cars.

THE BEST SOURCES OF HELP

Websites:
MyCustomer.com: **www.mycustomer.com**
ZDNET CRM Update: **www.techupdate.zdnet.com**

Managing Payments Online

GETTING STARTED

Getting your online payment system right is critical to the success of e-commerce. The system must be easy to use, as consumers dislike having to go through long, cumbersome processes to purchase products. However, it must be as secure as possible, since it is estimated that fraud costs an online business three times as much as an offline one. When considering online payment services, keep the following in mind:

- consumers are wary of giving credit card details and other personal information online. Your first step must be to gain their trust.
- fraud and chargebacks are critical issues that can seriously affect an online business
- there is a wide range of online payment services available, so shop around to make sure you get the best one for you

FAQS

What are the key issues facing online payments?

- Fraud is a critical concern that must be addressed comprehensively.
- There is no cross-border integration of payment systems.
- People develop payment habits and are reluctant to change them.
- Can traditional payment methods adapt to the new environment, or is a brand new payment system required?
- There is still no comprehensive hard data on how people pay online.

What is a payment culture?

Within any particular country, and sometimes within states or regions of a country, there are distinct approaches to payment, depending on:

- the range of payment options available locally
- local payment habits
- local/national payment regulations

MAKING IT HAPPEN

Understand your marketplace

Depending on the country, or the region/state within a country, people pay for things in different ways. Different countries also have different payment processing approaches and legal obligations.

Types of payment option available

It is important to understand the range of payment options available before choosing a particular payment method. The options available include the following:

- credit card payment
- credit transfer
- electronic cheques
- direct debit
- PayPal
- smart cards

- prepaid schemes
- loyalty scheme points-based approaches
- person-to-person payments
- mobile phone schemes

The approach chosen will depend on the target market. For example, where a website targets young people, who often have no credit cards, a prepaid scheme can work well. A particular website may use a variety of payment approaches, depending on its needs, but the ability to process all the major credit cards is almost always essential.

Characteristics of an online payment system

An online payment system should have these key characteristics.

- Efficiency and ease of use: a central advantage of doing business online is that it saves time and cuts costs.
- Robustness and reliability: because payment is such a critical function, it is essential that a payments system is fully reliable. Payment systems cannot afford to be down for any length of time.
- Authentication: much online fraud is caused by the absence of proper authentication.
- Integration: a payment system must be able to integrate properly with relevant internal information systems, so that, for example, a record of the payment can be added to the account details.
- Insurance: facilities such as escrow services must be available to ensure that the seller gets the money and the buyer gets the goods.

Selecting an online payment service

The most suitable type of online payment service will depend on the volume of business you intend doing and the margins you make on each sale. There is a wide choice of payment services, so it is important to shop around to find the best one. However, whatever service you choose must be able to verify the credit card, process the transaction, and deposit the money in your account.

Key factors you must consider are set-up fees, ongoing charges, and software and hardware expenses. Most business banks offer an online payment service, and working with your existing bank can be a good choice. When looking beyond banks, make sure you are dealing with reputable organisations. Those that advertise extremely low charges often have expensive hidden extras. You should take care to choose the payment service which suits the volume of transactions you expect to carry out.

Payment by credit card

There are two distinct methods by which credit card payments are made for Internet purchases: payment directly online, and payment by phoning or faxing credit card details. The first method is by far the most popular (88 per cent), but it is advisable to offer both options to potential consumers.

When implementing an online credit card system, a comprehensive security system using a secure server with encryption technology is essential. It is equally important to have comprehensive security procedures for the storage of the information. A database containing confidential information on thousands of individuals is far more attractive to a criminal than acquiring a single credit card number.

Keep the process simple and fast

Whatever payment system you choose, make sure you keep the process as simple and fast as possible. Studies have indicated that many consumers abandon the online purchase process, often because it is too long and difficult to understand. Streamlining the purchasing process is extremely important where repeat business is concerned. Amazon.com, for example, has implemented a '1-Click' purchase process for repeat customers, avoiding a lot of form filling.

One common way of reducing the number of steps in the payment process is to store customers' personal information from their initial purchase. This usually includes delivery address and credit card details. When the customer makes a repeat purchase, this information does not need to be typed in again.

This type of system must be managed carefully, as it contains sensitive personal information, and raises privacy and other legal issues. More importantly, consumers have become wary of websites that store personal information on them. A clear privacy policy must be developed, and displayed prominently on the website.

Business-to-business (B2B) payment options

While there is a wide range of effective business-to-consumer online payment options, payment for B2B transactions is generally made offline. One reason for this is that the amounts of money involved are usually large. However, one of the key reasons businesses embrace online B2B and join e-marketplaces is to reduce costs and to make transactions more efficient. Not being able to complete the payment online adds cost and inconvenience. A range of systems is available for B2B payment online; they focus on ensuring security and authenticity, and some also offer digital signature facilities.

Running an online auction

If you intend running an online auction for the general public, you encounter quite different payment issues: when consumers are trading with each other, the party selling the goods often does not have the capacity to accept credit cards. To overcome such problems, person-to-person (P2P) payment systems have emerged. Most of the larger auction websites, such as eBay and Yahoo, have such systems and these may also be suited for general payment services. However, P2P systems cause concern for legislators because of their potential for money laundering and other types of fraud, so choosing a system requires great care.

Online escrow services

Online escrow services offer to hold payments while the buyer examines the products purchased. If the buyer is satisfied with the products, they then authorise the payment. An online escrow service incurs extra cost because a fee is charged, but it may be worth while if it is essential to give the buyer as much confidence as possible.

The system operates by giving the escrow service a tracking number for the delivery. You must agree the time period allowed to the buyer for examination of the merchandise; you must also establish who pays the carriage fees if the product is returned.

Fraud and chargebacks are major issues

Some studies estimate that e-tailers are losing as much as 5 per cent of their margin to fraud – a rate three times higher than for businesses operating offline. For e-tailers on small margins this is a very serious issue. There are many different types of fraud, but a particularly common online form is identity theft, where fraudsters acquire confidential information on an individual and use it to purchase products. Because no signature or PIN is collected online, using stolen credit card details to make purchases online is straightforward for fraudsters. Clearly, e-tailers must take great care in this area, otherwise their profits will be eaten away. Fraud detection software is available and should be used.

Chargebacks (where the cardholder claims the transaction was never made or never completed) are also a major concern. Chargebacks are expensive for credit card processors to deal with, and as a result, you are likely to be penalised if there are too many chargebacks against your account. So-called 'friendly fraud', where a customer make a purchase but later claims never to have carried out the transaction is also an increasing problem.

COMMON MISTAKES

Not understanding payment cultures

While credit cards may be very common in the United States, they are not as widely used in Europe. Different countries have different payment habits and payment legislation. Not understanding these is a serious obstacle to online business.

Not securing peace of mind for the consumer

Consumers are very concerned that their credit card numbers will be stolen on the Internet. They are equally concerned that confidential information that they give to a website will not be properly protected. Websites that fail to show clearly the steps taken to protect customer information are likely to lose potential business.

THE BEST SOURCES OF HELP
Website:
Verifone: **www.verifone.com**

Dealing Effectively with Computer Viruses and Spyware

GETTING STARTED

Computer viruses are a growing threat on the Internet and cost companies billions globally every year. If all security updates are not installed on your computers, it is possible to get a computer virus just by visiting a website or opening an e-mail. To combat these threats:

- ensure that you have the very latest antivirus software and that you scan your entire computer regularly
- ensure that you have the very latest software security updates (often called 'patches') for your computer
- immediately delete e-mails that you are in any way suspicious of
- don't download anything from the Internet except from reputable websites
- back up your data regularly

MAKING IT HAPPEN

Understand computer viruses, Trojan horses, and spyware

In its simplest form, a computer virus attaches itself to computer files, and then seeks to replicate itself. Viruses can infect all sorts of files, from program and system files to Word documents and HTML files. The Internet allows viruses to spread with extraordinary speed, usually by sending an e-mail to all the people in the infected computer's address book.

A Trojan horse pretends to serve a useful function, such as a screen saver. However, as soon as it is run, it carries out its true purpose, which can be anything from using the computer as a host to infect other computers, to wiping the entire hard disk of the computer. Never download software over the Internet unless you are sure of its authenticity.

Spyware is software that takes partial control of a computer for the benefit of a third party, without the computer owner's informed consent. For example, your Internet browsing habits might be relayed back to the third party, and this information would be used to target pop-up adverts to you. Spyware is often bundled with otherwise useful applications so that the user does not understand the full implications of installing it.

Prevention is much better than cure

Viruses can be extremely difficult to get rid of. You may think you have cleaned them out with your antivirus software, but they may well have inserted hidden code in your operating system that is almost impossible to detect. It is, therefore, essential to stop viruses from getting into your computer in the first place. You do this by:

- making sure that you have the very latest antivirus software; popular antivirus software types include McAfee and Norton
- joining an e-mail list that will inform you of new virus attacks. As soon as you hear of them, check your vendor for the latest updates.
- scanning your entire computer for viruses at least once a week
- always making sure that you have the very latest security patches for your computer software. Viruses are always at their most potent in the first hours and days after their release, so it is vital to implement software patches as soon as they become available.
- if you use Microsoft Windows 2007 or Windows XP software, checking regularly at www.microsoft.com/security for news and updates
- only downloading software from reputable websites
- deleting e-mails if you are in any way suspicious

If you become infected

Deal with the threat immediately. Never wait; the longer the virus is on your computer the more files it can infect. Some viruses open up your computer system to potential hacking. There is no guaranteed way to know that your system does not contain some malicious code that will be used at a future date, even when the offending virus has been deleted. If a virus has indeed infected your system, and if you want to be absolutely safe, you should consider reformatting your hard disk and reinstalling all your software.

Coping with virus hoaxes

The Internet is full of virus hoaxes that waste time. If you get an e-mail about a new virus, go to the website of your antivirus software provider, and check if the warning is real. How to judge a hoax:

- Does the message come from a reputable source?
- Does it ask you to e-mail it on to anyone you know? If it does, it's probably a hoax.
- Does it have a reputable link for more information?

THE BEST SOURCES OF HELP

Websites:

McAfee antivirus software: **www.mcafee.com**

Microsoft anti-Spyware software: **www.microsoft.com/athome/security/spyware/software/default.mspx**

Norton antivirus software: **www.norton.com**

Trend Micro Housecall, free online virus checker: **http://housecall.trendmicro.com**

Implementing Effective Internet Security

GETTING STARTED

Internet security is a critically important issue. The Internet is, by definition, a network; networks are open, and are thus open to attack. A poor Internet security policy can result in a substantial loss of productivity and a drop in consumer confidence. When developing an Internet security policy, keep the following in mind.

- Be continuously vigilant: the perfect Internet security system will be out of date the next day.
- Combine software and human expertise: security software can only do so much; it must be combined with human expertise and experience.
- Secure internally as well as externally. Many security breaches come from inside the organisation.

FAQS

What are examples of best practice in Internet security?

Consider the following as best practice:

- have a coherent Internet security policy
- if your system has been compromised, seek immediate independent expert help
- for complete safety after an attack, the best course of action is to reformat the hard disk
- strip your computer down to its bare essentials. The more features, options, and software your computer has, the more open it is to attack. This is particularly true for Internet-related software and functions.
- for personal computers, be very careful about always-on connections provided by many broadband suppliers. An always-on connection to the Internet is always open to probing and attack by a hacker.
- do not download software from the Internet unless you are totally confident that it is from a reputable source

Are cookies a security threat?

Cookies collect information on how you browse the Web, and are a relatively low security risk. However, cookies can encourage lazy security practices, since they remember user-names and passwords.

Can you get a virus by opening an e-mail?

Yes. It used to be impossible to be infected by a computer virus transmitted by e-mail unless you opened the e-mail attachment. However, more recent viruses simply require the opening of the e-mail itself. Be very careful about unexpected e-mails from unfamiliar sources. If in doubt, delete without opening.

MAKING IT HAPPEN

Develop an Internet security policy

Keep the following in mind when developing your Internet security policy:

- Many security breaches come from within an organisation. The fewer people with access to the inner workings of the system, therefore, the better. Those who are allowed access must be recorded and given specific access rights. Immediately delete revoked and inactive users, or users who have left the organisation.
- A rigorous procedure should be in place for granting and revoking rights of access.
- Streamline hardware and software: a complex system is more open to attack. In your server software, for example, strip away as many of the optional features as possible.
- Have a password policy. Do not allow simple or obvious passwords, and make sure they are changed regularly.
- Have procedures for data back-up and disaster recovery.
- Have procedures for responding to security breaches.
- Be vigilant. The Internet security threat is constantly changing, and constant vigilance is the best security.
- Have your security policy audited by an external professional organisation, and have them on call should a major breach occur.

The benefits of firewalls

A firewall is software that polices the space between your computer system and the outside world. The design and management of firewalls has become more complex since the advent of the Web because of the vast increase in activity between computers and the Internet. If the firewall is too stringent, it slows everything down and prevents people from carrying out certain legitimate activities; if it is too lax, however, it opens the computer up to attack.

Dealing with viruses

Computer viruses are becoming more sophisticated and widespread. It has been estimated that 15 per cent of all messages sent contained viruses. Quite clearly, then, it's essential to have antivirus software and to keep it up to date. It is equally vital to upgrade your computer with the latest software security patches. For Microsoft software, more information on such patches is available at **www.microsoft.com/security**.

Dealing with hackers

The main objective of a hacker is to gain unauthorised access to another computer. This is done by probing for vulnerabilities on the computer, perhaps the result of flaws in the computer software and/or poor security procedures. The Web is more open than a stand-alone computer, so many hackers now focus on Web-based applications. Many of these applications are still relatively new and have not developed robust security measures. Security breaches can range from the hacker changing the pricing in a shopping cart to the theft of credit card numbers. The only way to deal with hackers is to implement rigorous security procedures and to monitor activity on the network constantly.

Reacting to a security breach

After a security breach there are two basic objectives. First, find out what happened so that you can stop it happening again. Second, find out who did it so that you can prosecute or otherwise deal with them. It is very difficult to prosecute a security breach without hard evidence, and very easy to contaminate or destroy such evidence. In dealing with security breaches, make sure that:

- you get professional advice, particularly if it is the first time your security has been breached
- you protect all log information tracking activity on the system
- the information collected is technically accurate
- information is collected from various sources to develop an overall picture of what happened
- no information is tampered with or modified

In monitoring for security breaches:

- check access and error log files for suspicious activity
- be alert for unusual system commands
- be alert for repeated attempts to enter a password

Denial of service attacks

Denial of service attacks do not seek to break into a computer system, but rather to crash a website by deluging it with phoney traffic. They are difficult to defend against, and have been directed at some of the best-known websites, such as CNN and eBay. Firewalls can be designed to block repeated traffic from a particular source.

Setting up a web server

A web server is potentially an open door into your network: if someone can break into your server, they are closer to breaking into your entire computer system. Before you set up a web server you must ensure that you understand and deal effectively with the various security issues. By definition, web servers interface with the World Wide Web and its potential hazards. They are large, complex software programs that embrace open architecture and that have often been developed at great speed.

From an e-commerce perspective, a secure server is a prerequisite. A secure server uses encryption when transferring or receiving data from the Web. Without a secure server, credit card information, for example, could be easily targeted by a hacker. A secure server will encrypt this information, turning it into special code that will then be decrypted only when it is safely within the server environment.

Equally important is what happens to the confidential information once it has reached the server environment. Once the information has been acted on, it should be stored in encrypted form. In the case of sensitive information, such as credit card details, it should be deleted.

Restricting access to your website

You can restrict access to part or all of your website in a number of ways. The most common is by implementing a user-name and password system. However, you can also restrict access by IP (Internet Protocol) address, so that only people connecting from a certain address or domain can access information. Perhaps the most powerful approach is to use public key cryptography, whereby only the person with the assigned cryptography key can request and read the information.

Security and outsourcing

Outsourcing creates an increased security risk. You must establish that the outsource vendor will adhere to your security policy, and that all work done adheres to proper security procedures. Specific questions that you need to ask your outsourcing vendor include:

- What is its security policy?
- What are its data back-up and disaster-recovery procedures?
- How often are these procedures tested and/or updated?
- How is your data safeguarded from that of other customers?
- How is your data safeguarded from the vendor's own employees?
- How is it insured with regard to security breaches?

COMMON MISTAKES

Dropping your guard

There is no such thing as a perfect security system. Without constant vigilance, computer systems become an open invitation for hackers and viruses. An essential part of such vigilance is having the very latest security patches and antivirus software installed.

Thinking that you won't get a virus

Viruses are becoming increasingly common. If you haven't had one so far, either you are tremendously lucky or you have excellent antivirus procedures. If you fall into the former camp, it's likely that your luck will run out at same point!

Thinking that you are anonymous on the Internet

In general, you are not. When you visit a website, you will provide some or all of the following information:

- IP address
- time of access
- user-name (if a user-name and password are used)
- the URL requested
- the URL you were at just before you visited the website
- the amount of data you downloaded
- the browser and operating system you are using
- your e-mail address

THE BEST SOURCES OF HELP

Website:
CERT Internet Security Center: **www.cert.org**

Outsourcing Your Website and IT Operations

GETTING STARTED

As your business grows, you may need to upgrade your website to a larger and more sophisticated one. Running a large website is a complex operation that requires substantial IT architecture and support. This can take the focus of your business away from its core business of selling, marketing, and supporting your products and services. It will also tie up any technical staff on your team. Outsourcing involves hiring third-party professionals to manage and run your website's operations for an ongoing fee.

When approaching outsourcing, remember to:

- develop a proper strategy: outsourcing needs a serious approach
- ensure that a comprehensive contract is in place, and that there are proper metrics and management structures
- make sure that you choose a robust, well-funded outsourcing vendor with a good track record for service and support

FAQS

What are the key factors that drive outsourcing?

- The need to focus on core business activities rather than on building up a large IT function.
- Lack of sufficiently skilled staff to run complex web operations.
- Flexibility: a quality outsource vendor can respond more quickly to rapid changes in customer demand.

MAKING IT HAPPEN

Develop an outsourcing strategy

If you are considering the outsourcing of Web functions, think about exactly why you want to go down this route.

Do you want to outsource:

- to reduce costs?
- to give greater flexibility?
- because you can't find the right IT skills?
- to guarantee a more reliable service?
- to focus better on your core business?
- to keep your IT department as small as possible?
- to reduce staffing levels?

It's wise to have a clear strategy of your vision and objectives *long* before you start discussions with vendors.

Be prepared

Deciding on an outsourcer is a complex and time-consuming process, so you must think very carefully about what you want to achieve and why. When developing your strategy, it is best not to be too open with outsourcing vendors. They will naturally want to sell you what they have, and may try to shape your thinking in a way that is not appropriate. It is better initially to go to a quality independent consultant who will help you think through all the issues.

When you finally engage with your shortlist of outsourcing vendors, they will have many detailed questions on how your operations are currently run. If you cannot answer these questions you will slow the whole process down, and will encourage the vendor to put forward a less fully and clearly defined contract than if it had had all the required information.

Choose a robust, well-funded outsourcer

Choose a company that has a good reputation, is well funded, and has a good track record. When choosing an outsourcing partner, ask the following questions:

- How stable and well funded is it?
- Has it got a satisfied customer base?
- Has it successfully dealt before with the same needs yours?

Make certain that you receive the right service and support

The more you outsource, the more dependent you become on your outsourcer, so it is vital that your chosen vendor delivers comprehensive service and support.

Remember that choosing an outsourcing vendor takes time

Outsourcing is a major strategic move involving much research and negotiation, so do not impose tight deadlines on yourself.

Have a comprehensive contract drawn up

Once you've chosen the outsourcing partner you want to work with, have a precise contract drawn up that clearly describes exactly what is to be delivered and which also states penalties for non-delivery. Bring in your legal team to advise as soon as possible so that everyone understands the legal implications of everything that is being asked for and promised. However, the IT environment is constantly changing, and the contract needs to cater for this and build in some flexibility so that new developments can be addressed if appropriate.

It would be wise to avoid contracts that tie you up for years, although vendors will argue for them because they will be bearing a high up-front cost. A five to 10-year contract just doesn't make sense in a rapidly changing world; a two-year contract is a more reasonable option.

Determine how this relationship will be managed and measured

You must develop a set of metrics to measure how the outsourcer is meeting the objectives set by the contract. By doing this regularly, and addressing issues as they arise, major disputes can be avoided.

Outsourcing is as much about managing the day-to-day relationship between you and the outsource vendor as it is about managing the technology. While a contract is important, prevention, by management that keeps a regular track of what is expected and what has been delivered, is better than cure.

Have a corporate technology strategy
You are outsourcing your technology, not your technology strategy, and will always need skilled in-house resources to help you plan your direction from a technological point of view. Your outsourcer cannot do this; if they do, their recommendations will reflect their own strategy rather than yours.

Consider the security issues
Outsourcing creates an increased security risk. You must establish that the outsource vendor will adhere to your security policy, and that all work done integrates proper security procedures. Ask yourself:
- What is the outsourcer's security policy?
- What are its data back-up and disaster recovery procedures?
- How is your data safeguarded from its other customers?
- How is your data safeguarded from its own employees?
- How is it insured in relation to security breaches?

COMMON MISTAKES
Forgetting that outsourcing means just that
You can't have the same level of control over the day-to-day running of your IT infrastructure after you outsource it, but some businesses forget that and try to achieve such control. This is counterproductive. You chose your outsourcer because – you hope – they do the job better and more efficiently than you do.

Hiring vendors who promise too much
Outsource vendors have been known to over-promise and under-deliver.

Getting rid entirely of the internal IT web operation
Some internal IT resource is necessary to take a more strategic view of the Web operation in order to plan its future evolution.

Going for the lowest price
Going for the lowest price rarely works out well in the long term. Service and support are critical elements in outsourcing, and the outsourcer that offers the lowest price is also, generally speaking, the one who will offer the least support. Remember too that vendors are prone to over-promising and under-delivering.

Not being able to deliver the right information
To deliver an outsourcing service, the vendor requires very detailed information on your current IT and web set-up. If you can't provide this information, you slow the whole process down, which results in imperfect solutions.

Badly framed contracts
Long-term contracts are too often developed on the basis of short-term financial goals, such as cost cutting. What invariably happens is that the contract is unsuitable and renegotiation is required.

THE BEST SOURCES OF HELP
Websites:
International Association of Outsourcing
   Professionals: **www.firmbuilder.com/home.asp**
Outsourcing Center: **www.outsourcing-center.com**

Hosting or Selecting a Hosting Company

GETTING STARTED
Hosting your website means placing it on the Internet network so that it is available to people who want to visit it. There are two basic choices: internal or external hosting. Hosting a website internally is the general option for intranets, where visitors come only from within your organisation. External hosting is the usual option for public websites.

FAQS
Should I host internally or externally?
External hosting has many advantages; hosting is a complex activity, and there are many things that can go wrong. There are numerous specialist companies who are experts in the field of hosting, and are able to offer excellent service at a reasonable price because of economies of scale.

What are the key issues to consider when choosing a hosting option?
Ask yourself:
- Do I need a domain name?
- How many visitors do I expect each month?
- How much space, and what access speeds, will I require?
- Will I need e-commerce facilities?
- Will I require special programming facilities, such as CGI scripts?
- How do I want to deal with e-mail?
- What sort of support is offered?
- What are the price and payment options?

What is the most popular and cost-effective hosting approach?
Virtual (shared) hosting. For between £15 and £20 a month there are excellent hosting packages that will work well for many small and medium-sized businesses.

If, however, you want to add extra functionality, such as e-commerce, the costs begin to rise.

There are so many hosting companies. How do I choose the right one?

This is not easy. If you have quality technical expertise in-house, you will be able to investigate the various options and choose the one that most closely fits your needs. If not, it is best to go with a big brand.

Key questions to ask are:
- How many customers do they have?
- How long have they been in business?
- How are they funded?
- What is their reputation for support?

MAKING IT HAPPEN
Basic hosting options
- Non-virtual hosting: this is the most basic option, and is provided free by entities such as Geocities. You do not have your own domain name; instead, your address would be: www.hostingcompany.com/yourname. This sort of package is only advisable for very small businesses. One of its most serious drawbacks is the lack of flexibility: you cannot change your hosting company without changing your web address, whereas if you have your own domain name, it is yours for ever (provided you pay your yearly registration fee), and you can move it wherever you want.
- Virtual hosting (sometimes known as shared hosting): you get space on a network vendor's server that is also used by other organisations. This is a popular and very suitable option for many small to medium-sized businesses. The hosting company agrees to deliver minimum access speeds and data transfer rates, and to carry out basic hardware maintenance, but you are responsible for managing the content and software.
- Collocation hosting: this involves placing your own servers with a hosting vendor. You manage everything that happens on your servers: content, software, and the hardware itself. The network provider supplies an agreed access speed to the Internet and an agreed amount of data transfer over a specified period. The network provider will also generally agree to some minimum service, such as ensuring that your server is up and running, and rebooting it should it stop for any reason.
- Managed hosting: this is where the vendor has more responsibility. It can range from the vendor supplying and managing the hardware only, to also supplying and managing the software that runs on it.

Registering a domain name
If you are in business you should really have your own domain name. Most of the popular domain names have already been taken up, particularly those connected with the .com suffix. Keep the following in mind when choosing a domain name:
- the name should be as short and memorable as possible
- it's good to have a .com address, but if your primary markets are outside the United States, a domain name specific to these markets should be considered, for example, .co.uk for Britain or .de for Germany

- to find out where to register your domain name, go to: http://directory.google.com/Top/Computers/Internet/Domain_Names

If you already have a domain name registered and are setting up with a hosting company, a transfer process will be required. This may take a couple of days, and if you already have a website up, or are using e-mail based on your domain, there may be a brief change-over period when your domain is inoperable.

Deciding on network speed
How quickly your web pages download is very important. While the size of your web pages is a major factor here, the network speed offered by your hosting company is another important element. As a rule, the cheaper the hosting package, the slower the speed. If you know that many of your customers are in, for example, the United States, it may make sense to host there so that pages download more quickly. Another key issue is whether the hosting company has back-up and redundancy features, so that if one of its machines or lines to the Internet goes down, it can ensure that service is not interrupted. Network speed depends on more than just the type of the network connection; the overall architecture of the hosting company's systems and how they are connected to the Internet is also critical.

Deciding on disk space
Most web hosting options provide plenty of disk space. However, if you think you may have a substantial amount of content, estimate how many pages you expect to have. Multiply that by 50K average for each page. If you expect to have 400 pages, the disk space you require will therefore be 20 megabytes.

Deciding on the number of website visitors expected
This is difficult to predict. A hosting company measures this by data transfer – the amount of data downloaded from your website. For example, if you expect 1,000 visitors a month, and the average visitor will look at four pages, a total of 4,000 pages will be downloaded. If the average size of a page is 50K, that gives a total data transfer of 200,000K, which would be well within the range of most hosting offers.

Access to e-commerce facilities
While basic web hosting can be very good value, it becomes more expensive if you want to add e-commerce functionality. E-commerce requires special software and programming, so you must ensure that your hosting package supports this. If you want to accept credit card information over the Internet, you will need a merchant account and a secure server over which such credit card information can be transferred.

Special programming features
If you want to do anything with your website that involves special programming, you must make sure that your hosting package supports it. It is essential to check

whether your website is stored on a machine that supports the UNIX or Microsoft operating systems. Basically, before you select a hosting package you must discuss with your programmers or consulting company the potential programming that might be involved.

Extra features that must be considered

There are a number of features, over and above basic hosting, that must be considered when choosing a hosting package. These include the following:

- e-mail management: with your own domain you will want your own e-mail addresses, such as sales@mycompany.com, info@mycompany.com, name@mycompany.com. Depending on your hosting package, you may be allocated a certain number of e-mail addresses. Make sure that this allocation is sufficient.
- e-mail forwarding: you may need e-mail to be forwarded to certain addresses. Check that the hosting package offers this.
- e-mail auto-responders: if you are away from the office you may want to use an auto-response function, whereby if someone sends you an e-mail they receive an automated response informing them that you are away. Check that the hosting company offers this.
- Microsoft FrontPage: if you are using Microsoft FrontPage as the tool to create your website, there are hosting packages available specifically to support this.
- Web statistics: you must be able to access the basic website data easily so that you can use website log analysis software on it.

How the hosting will be paid for

Most hosting packages will require a set-up fee. The payment structure can vary: some companies require payment monthly, others every three or six months, while some will ask for 12 months in advance. It is important to check the cancellation policy for any restrictive conditions.

Make sure of quality support

The quality of support is critical. There will be occasional technical glitches that will affect your website. The more you depend on your website, the more vital it is to get it back up quickly, so if the hosting company doesn't offer quality support you could have serious problems. If you can, find out what sort of reputation the hosting company has in this area. It is always better to pay a little more to ensure quality support.

COMMON MISTAKES

Going for the cheapest option

The cheapest option is rarely the best choice. It is nearly always better to spend a little more to get better infrastructure and support. Remember, the more you depend on your website and e-mail, the less you can afford to have them go down for any length of time.

Not planning ahead

Even if you're not ready to sell off your site today, you may want to do so in six months' time. If that's the case, make sure that the hosting package you choose can provide it or that you can easily migrate to another package with the hosting company. Changing hosting companies is a messy and time-consuming process.

THE BEST SOURCES OF HELP

Websites:
Business2 WebSite Hosting Guide:
 **www.business2.com/b2/webguide/
 0,17811,3713,00.html**
HostReview.com: **www.hostreview.com**

Understanding the Key Principles of Content Management

GETTING STARTED

In a world overloaded with information, content management is about getting the right content to the right person at the right time at the right cost. Content management focuses on the management of digital content. It is a necessary evolution from data management, where the emphasis is on storing content. By using the Web as its primary publication medium, content management allows people to have much greater access to the content they need. When approaching content management, keep in mind:

- that in an information economy full of information workers and consumers, content management is a critical function for a modern organisation
- that content management is about the organisation, classification, and storage of digital content, and the publication, navigation, and search of such content
- those management processes that support the creation, editing, and publication of content

FAQS

Why has content management become so important?

Because there is so much information in the world and so little time. Organisations are producing vast quantities of content every year, and the majority of this content is being produced in digital form. By 2001, it was estimated that there were over 550 billion documents on Internet, intranet, and extranet websites. Without professional content management it becomes almost impossible to find what you are looking for.

Why has the Web become such an important medium for the publication of content?

HTML, the layout language that is used to present content on the Web, has become the standard form in which digital content is now published. The web browser, through which HTML pages are viewed, is a simple yet powerful tool that is used by millions of people around the world every day.

What are the drawbacks of the Web?

As Steve Case, former chairman of AOL Time Warner, has stated, the Web makes every enterprise a publisher. The problem is that this has opened up the floodgates of information overload. Much content that is published on the Web lacks professional publishing standards. The early Web also depended on manual HTML editing and manipulation of HTML files for the management of content. This approach is to content management what hand-knitting is to the fabrics industry – beautiful results can be achieved for small amounts of content, but for large amounts of content it is a slow and expensive process. For large quantities of content, content management software is required that streamlines publishing processes and stores content within a database environment.

MAKING IT HAPPEN

Develop a core business case

Professional content management is an expensive process. Not all content has the same value. You need to establish the business case for publishing content on your intranet or Internet website. A core business case will revolve around statements, such as 'Quality content delivered to our customers will result in more sales and fewer support calls'.

Conduct a situation analysis

Before developing a content management strategy, it is important to understand how content is currently being managed within your organisation and by the wider industry. If there is already a website:
- What content is being published on it?
- Is it up to date and accurate?
- Is it being read?
- What are your competitors doing on their websites?
- Are they being successful?

- Are there any standards emerging for content management within the industry?

Focus on who is going to read the content

Too often, organisations think of content as a low-level commodity that merely needs to be stored. But content is a critical resource, and its value lies in being read. There is no point in having a great technical document on a website if nobody knows it exists and the website is never used. To make content management work, you really need to understand who needs your content. Alternatively, you need to ask potential readers what content they need. And you must always remember that content is consumed by busy people.

Identify the content you need

How much content do you need to manage? What's the 'must-have' versus the 'like-to-have' content?
- How many other languages does it need to be published in?
- What are the media you want to publish it in (Web, e-mail, mobile)?
- What content forms will be required (text, audio, video)?
- Will you need to deal with PowerPoint slides and Word documents? How will these be converted?

Don't get carried away. You may have 50,000 documents, but maybe only 5,000 of them are relevant to the audience you want to reach.

Develop professional create, edit, and publishing functions

There are a number of options available in relation to creating content, including:
- commissioning content, either from internal staff or from freelance authors
- acquiring content from third-party sources such as commercial databases
- using online community-created content, created from, for example, discussion boards, chat forums, or mailing lists

Editing content means preparing it for publication. This will involve ensuring tone and style are appropriate and consistent, checking for correct grammar, checking for such things as libel or copyright infringement, and taking care that the correct metadata is included. Editing also involves correcting content that is already published, and reviewing published content to ensure that it is up to date.

Define the content management team

Content doesn't grow in databases. Content management software can underpin the publishing processes and make them far more efficient and cost-effective, but if you want quality content you need quality people to create, edit, and publish it. Someone with editorial and communication skills should run a content management project. Another core skill a content management team requires is information architecture; other skills will include moderating expertise (if there are online communities) as well as marketing, technical, graphic design, and usability expertise. It's unlikely that you or any single member of your team (if you have one) will have all the necessary skills, so you may need to employ a company that specialises in web publishing.

Design the information architecture

Good design of metadata and classification is crucial to the success of content management. Otherwise, content will end up being piled into a database and it will be almost impossible to find the right content quickly.

Navigation is like a signpost system. It is there to help people to find their way easily and logically around a website. Searching is a basic activity on the Web, and its professional design will be crucial to success. Graphic design and layout should ensure that content is presented in a way that has style but also, most importantly, is easy to read, view, or listen to.

Select the content management software

If the website contains more than a couple of hundred pages and needs to be updated regularly, then it will make sense to acquire content management software. On the basis of the previous sections, a set of specifications can be drawn up covering the various content management processes required to achieve a professional result. These specifications will allow the organisation to judge which content management software can best meet content management needs.

Define how everything is going to be measured

A problem with content is that it is difficult to measure. However, that does not mean that measurables should not be put in place. You need to establish methods for measuring how much content needs to be created each week, the quality of that content, and the time it takes to get content published. Information architecture measures include the quality of the metadata, how easy the site is to navigate, how well the search works, and how quickly pages download.

COMMON MISTAKES

Not having a proper business case

While the Internet boom was in full swing, many content management projects did not have to show a strong business case. The situation is now very different. Without having a clear business case and return-on-investment model it is unlikely that content management projects will receive the required funding to succeed.

Thinking that content management is data management on speed

Content management is not an 'all you can eat' affair. It is not about digitising every document you can find and publishing it on a website. Data management is principally about storing content, but content management should have as its main focus the publication of content. There is a big difference in approach between the two.

Believing that all you have to do is buy some fancy software and your problem is solved

Content management software is vital if large quantities of content are involved, but content follows the classic 'garbage in, garbage out' rule. No amount of great software will turn poor quality content into good.

Allowing out-of-date content to remain on websites

A key problem on the Web today is out-of-date content. Many websites forget to remove old content, which results in a very poor experience for the visitor.

THE BEST SOURCES OF HELP

Book:
McGovern, Gerry. *Killer Web Content*. London: A&C Black, 2006.

Website:
Business 2.0 on CNN Money:
http://money.cnn.com/magazines/business2

Making a Website Easy to Navigate

GETTING STARTED

Web navigation is like a signpost. It should give visitors context and help them to find quickly what they are looking for on a website. Without proper navigation a website becomes just a jumble of content. Navigation is even more critical for large websites: in fact, without proper navigation, the larger the website, the less usable it will become. Navigation design is thus a critical function that must be carefully planned and implemented. Keep the following in mind when approaching navigation design.

- Navigation should provide context for content. It should show all the other content that is related to a particular category or item.
- As a rule, navigation should be simple, unadorned, and of a consistent design.
- People like to navigate through content in different ways, so a variety of navigation options should be provided.

FAQS

What is the key principle when designing navigation?

Functionality, not style. Functionality and plainness of design are what people want. What is important is the place they want to get to, not the navigation itself. Navigation should never be flashy and draw attention to itself. It should work in the background, making it easier for people to get to where they want to go.

What is the connection between navigation and classification?

Classification is how content is organised into manageable groups and subject areas. Navigation is how the classification is presented on a website. For a particular subject area there may be only one classification term, but it may be presented in a variety of different ways.

What is the connection between navigation and search?

There are two ways for people to find content on a website: one is through using search, the other is through using navigation. People often combine navigation and search: they might use search initially to narrow down their options, then use navigation to focus on the content in the subject area they wish to explore.

What would be the print media equivalent of navigation?

A publication's table of contents and index. It is unusual to find a publication without a table of contents. One of the key measures of the professionalism of a larger publication, such as a book or directory, is whether it has a good index. These navigation aids are essential to quality reference publishing.

MAKING IT HAPPEN

Design for the visitor

Navigation is about helping people to find content. Keep the visitor in mind at all times. Keep it simple, avoid being flashy, and test the navigation to see if people find it easy to use.

Give visitors a number of options

Different people have different needs when navigating through content. Some may want to navigate geographically, some may have a particular subject in mind, some may want to get back to the home page as quickly as possible. A set of essential links (known as global navigation), placed near the top of the page, is always helpful. This allows the visitor to get quickly to key sections on the website, regardless of what particular page they are on. There is a variety of other navigation options that need to be employed, depending on the particular focus of the website. For example, if the website is e-commerce-enabled, then it will require a prominent e-commerce navigation system.

Let visitors know where they are on the website

Visitors may enter a website in a variety of ways. It is important for each page to clearly display what part of the overall classification it represents. If it is the home page, for example, this should be made clear. If it is a page dealing with pricing information for Product Z, then a heading at the top of the page should clearly state that. Such clear and unambiguous headings help put visitors at ease.

Let visitors know where they have been

A primary function of hypertext is to indicate to visitors the places that they have already visited on a website. This is why hypertext links change colour from blue to purple, with purple representing a link that has been clicked on. Avoid changing hypertext colours. People are familiar with blue for unclicked and purple for clicked.

Let visitors know where they are going

Navigation should always support visitors in getting around the website, pointing them towards places they want to go and away from places they would like to avoid. There are a number of basic rules here.

- When visitors click on a link, they expect to be taken to a standard HTML page. They do not expect to be asked for a password, or to watch as a video or audio file starts downloading. If a link is to a non-standard page, visitors should be informed in advance. For example, a statement such as 'Password required' could be used if that is the case.
- If an image is a link, for example, a company logo linking to a home page, text should appear with a statement such as 'Company X home page' when visitors place their cursor over that image.
- When visitors are asked to carry out a process, for example the purchase of something, navigation should appear that will indicate to them how many steps there are in the process, and how many steps they have completed.

Provide context for visitors

Studies show that only in a minority of cases do visitors know exactly the type of content they want. Visitors may be interested in buying laptop computers, but they may not know the exact make they require. Navigation assembles all the relevant content for a particular subject area into a well-presented environment. This is where navigation and classification are very much intertwined.

Keep navigation consistent

Avoid creating a website in which the navigation is constantly changing its structure. If the essential links are placed across the top of the page in one section of the website, then keep them across the top of the page in every other section unless you have a very good reason to change them. Lack of navigation consistency is particularly problematic if an organisation has a number of websites, for example in an intranet environment. Departments and sections may feel a need to be distinctive, so they often make great efforts to create a navigation system that is totally different from those used by other sections. The result of this is confusion, and an environment that becomes increasingly chaotic, and difficult and expensive to manage.

Where possible, follow navigation conventions that have emerged on the Web

People who use the Web instinctively see it as a single medium. They like familiarity of navigation design, because what they have learned on one website can be carried over to another. Conventions that have emerged on the Web include:

- essential links (global navigation) that are placed on every page: these begin with a 'Home' link and usually contain links to 'About' and 'Contact'
- the organisation's logo on every page, usually in the top left, and linked back to the home page
- a search box on every page, usually near the top
- a footer on every page containing a copy of the essential links, contact information (address, e-mail, phone), and links to copyright and privacy statements
- the use of standard hypertext colours: blue for unclicked, purple for clicked

Never surprise or mislead visitors

Never take visitors down paths that lead to a dead end. For example, if you don't sell to a particular country, inform people of this with a clear statement early on, not after they have ordered a quantity and filled in their address details. Some US websites ask their visitors from other countries to ring an 800 number, which is impossible to do from outside the United States. Also, not every country has ZIP codes. Give visitors an option.

Back up navigation with quality support

The Web is often compared to a library. If you visit a library, the bookshelves are the navigation system, but librarians are always available to give support if you get lost. If the website is a large one, have a comprehensive help section. Make sure that if visitors e-mail the organisation in search of a specific piece of content, someone gets back to them quickly. A surprising number of websites are extremely poor at responding to visitor queries. Subject-sensitive help is particularly important where you are asking visitors to perform complex tasks. An example would be where a website offers advanced search. If visitors are asked to go

through a process such as filling out a form, try to isolate any mistakes that are made. For example, if they didn't fill in the address, don't send them back to fill in the entire form, but rather isolate the exact mistake that they made.

COMMON MISTAKES
Constantly changing the navigation

It is very frustrating to go back to a website and find that the navigation has been changed. Regular visitors get used to the way a website is laid out. The more regularly they visit, the more they get used to it (and the more likely they are to be valuable customers!). It is therefore important to plan your navigation well and to stick with it unless there is a compelling reason to change.

Designing navigation from a visual point of view

Too many websites treat navigation as some visual branding exercise, rather than as a signpost system for helping visitors to find quickly the content they need. Navigation should be simple and functional. It should be one of the first things to download on a Web page.

Designing an inconsistent navigation

Navigation structures that change depending on the section of the website you are in, purely for the sake of being different, are of absolutely no help to the visitor. If a large organisation with a number of websites does not provide consistent navigation, visitors may give up trying to use them. Inconsistency leads to confusion and a sense of disorganisation, thereby defeating the purpose of creating the websites in the first place.

Making navigation overly complex

New techniques using HTML and Flash make is possible to create sophisticated menus with pull-downs and nested menus. Unless you have a very specific need to use this type of navigation, avoid it if at all possible. Inexperienced users will find it confusing and it is more likely to cause browser compatibility and accessibility headaches later on.

THE BEST SOURCES OF HELP
Book:
McGovern, Gerry. *Killer Web Content*. London: A&C Black, 2006.

Writing Well for the Web

GETTING STARTED

People read differently on the Web, so you need to write differently for the Web. Surprisingly, very few websites take the time to lay out their content in a way that will maximise

its readability. An important point is that it is more difficult to read on a screen than from paper. This means that if you want to be read on the Web, you must write and lay out your content in a simpler, more straightforward manner than you would in print. If you want to ensure that your content has the best chance of being read, focus on:

- shorter sentences, shorter paragraphs, and shorter documents
- plentiful use of short, punchy, and descriptive headings and summaries
- larger font sizes and sans serif fonts, because they are easier to read
- straightforward, factual prose

FAQS

In what way do people read differently on the Web?
They scan, moving quickly across text, always looking in a hurry for the content they need. They are very fact-oriented. People don't read on the Web for pleasure – they read to do business, to be educated, to find out something – so they like to read content that gets to the point quickly.

People like reading short documents, with links to more detailed information as appropriate. If a document is long, and people really have no choice but to read it, a significant number of them will print it out. In general, however, long documents tend to go unread.

Why do so many people regard Web content as poor quality?
People don't trust the content they read on the Web because they come across so many websites with poor publishing standards. The Web gives everyone access to the tools of publishing, but giving someone a word processor does not make them a good writer.

Too many websites lack proper editing standards. They also translate documents that were prepared for print directly to the Web; this may save money in the short term, but if people don't read the content, it is pointless. Some websites deliberately try to mislead people with their content. All this gives a poor impression to people who use the Web.

Is writing for the Web a difficult skill to learn?
It is not easy to learn how to write well, no matter what the medium is. However, writing for the Web is about concentrating on the facts. You don't need flowery prose; instead, you must be able to communicate the really important stuff in as few words as possible. This is not an easy thing to do, but with practice most people can master the basics.

MAKING IT HAPPEN

If you're not read you're dead
The connection between writing and reading is one that is not always considered: a surprising number of organisations create vast quantities of content without asking some obvious questions:

- Is anyone interested in reading this content?
- Is it written in a way that is understandable and easy to read?

- How are we going to let people know that we have just published this content?

Less is more
Writing is rarely about quantity, but it should always be about quality. Less is more, particularly on the Web. It is easier to write 5,000 words of waffle than 500 words that are succinct, but 500 words is what is needed on the Web.

Editing is essential
One of the primary functions of editing is to get a long draft into shape. As George Orwell put it: 'If it is possible to cut a word, always cut it.' We all have pet phrases that we love to put into sentences whenever we can. They may sound good to the writer, but very often add nothing to the meaning of what is being communicated. The Web is about functional writing. Get to the point as quickly as you can. Then stop.

Keep it short
When writing for the Web:

- documents should rarely be longer than 1,000 words: 500 to 700 is a good length to aim for
- paragraphs should be between 40 and 50 words
- try not to let your sentences go over 20 words

Write for the reader, not your ego
When writing, always keep in mind who it is you are writing for. Is it the sales rep, the technician, the support staff, the customer, the investor? Will they understand what you are writing about? Don't write to please yourself – write to please your reader. One mark of a poor writer is the use of big words and convoluted phrases. The good writer is clear and precise.

Focus on the headings
Headings are important on the Web for two central reasons. First, people scan, so the first thing they often do is to look for headings; if the heading doesn't attract their attention, then they probably won't read any further. Second, people use search engines a lot, and the most prominent things in a page of search results are the headings. The heading really has to sell the Web page and convince the person to click for more information.

Writing headings well is an art, but here are a few rules that will help you get the basics right.

- Keep them short. A heading should not be longer than five to eight words.
- Make your point clear. For example, 'Nasdaq crashes to record low' is more informative than 'Apocalypse now for investors!' when talking about a severe stock-market downturn.
- Use strong, direct language. Don't be sensational, but at the same time don't be vague, and don't hedge.
- Don't deceive the reader, for example by using 'Microsoft' in a heading just because you think people will then be more likely to read it. Remember, the job of the heading is to tell the reader succinctly what is in the document.

Use subheadings
In longer documents it is always a good idea to use sub-headings, as they break up the text into the more read-able chunks that readers like. Subheadings should be used every five to seven paragraphs.

Summaries: the who, what, where and when
Next to the heading, the summary is the most important piece of text. It should be descriptive, not wandering or indirect. Tell the reader what the document is about, and who, what, where and when the information relates to.

Getting down to write
'No man but a blockhead ever wrote . . . except for money,' according to Samuel Johnson. Sound advice. Writing is not easy but someone has to do it. The first rule of writing is reading: if you are asked to write a technical paper, read how other people write them. Read how they are written on your own website, on competitors' websites, in indus-try journals. Find a style that works well and copy it; use its techniques and approach to structure. Don't plagiarise, but never feel ashamed of finding quality writing and learning from it.

Learn how to edit
Even if you have an editor, you still want to send them a draft that is well written. Here are a few steps to follow.
- Get a first draft written and don't throw it away.
- Leave it for a while – have a cup of tea – then print it out, or make the font size larger so that the text stands out more.
- Read it as if someone else wrote it. Be severe. Ask questions such as: Is it written in a way that the reader can easily understand it? What is the writer trying to say here? Is this sentence or paragraph necessary? Has the writer covered all the essential facts?
- First drafts are often too long. When preparing the second draft, cut ruthlessly, maybe by as much as half.
- Use your word count carefully. When you are asked to write something, always ask how many words are required. If you are not given a word count then decide on one yourself. Keep it as low as possible.

Explore collaborative writing
Computers and the Internet make collaborative writing far easier, and as a result it is becoming an increasingly popular approach to writing content. Collaborative writ-ing works well if:
- the writers spend time working through the objectives of the writing exercise, and reach agreement on such necessary matters as the style, tone, and length of the piece
- there is a lot of content to be written that can benefit from the input of multiple disciplines

- people can be given defined segments of content to write, and/or the different skills of different people can be used, for example when one person understands the subject well, while another is a good writer
- there are professional processes in place to facilitate collaboration
- the writers know and respect each other

COMMON MISTAKES
Not focusing on the needs of the reader
A surprising number of websites fail to consider who their reader is, simply adding content for its own sake. If you ignore the needs of your reader, then your reader will ignore you.

Putting non-Web formats on to the Web
Translating a 40-page Word document into HTML is a simple task; persuading someone to read it is another job entirely. Have you ever tried reading an Adobe PDF file on a screen? It's a painful experience. How many of your customers have read that PowerPoint presentation you translated into HTML?

Putting every piece of content you can find on the Web
The Web is not a dumping ground for content. You might have 50,000 documents, with only 5,000 suitable for your website. Publishing the other 45,000 simply wastes your readers' time – not something you want to do.

Poor editing
It is almost impossible to create quality content without sending it through a professional editorial process. No matter how good the writer, their content will always benefit by having it checked over by an editor.

Long, rambling documents
If, after reading the heading and summary, the reader hasn't grasped what exactly you are trying to communi-cate, chances are he or she will click the Back button. Online readers are ruthless about their time.

THE BEST SOURCES OF HELP
Book:
McGovern, Gerry. *Killer Web Content*. London: A&C Black, 2006.

Website:
Clickz: **www.clickz.com**

Understanding the Key Principles of Internet Marketing

GETTING STARTED

If your business has an online presence, you need to harness the power of the internet so that your company benefits. Internet marketing is about giving, rather than getting, attention. As an adjunct to traditional marketing, it supports and enhances the overall marketing message by providing comprehensive information that answers consumers' questions about a particular product or service. Internet marketing also exploits the networking capabilities of the Web by leveraging online community activities, linking, affiliate marketing, viral marketing, e-mail marketing, and loyalty programmes. When approaching Internet marketing, keep the following in mind.

- When visitors come to a website they are already aware of the brand. They want information.
- Use Internet technology to understand the needs of your customers, so that you can offer them just the right information and products.
- Remember that the Internet empowers the consumer. A dissatisfied consumer can use the networking capabilities of the Internet to undermine your brand.

FAQS

What sort of products and services is Internet marketing best suited to?

Internet marketing is particularly effective for:

- products and services that require a lot of information to sell. For example, travel and books are ideal for the Internet. Travel is a very information-intensive product. People want times, prices, and information about the destination. When buying books, they are strongly influenced by reviews, opinions of other readers, tables of contents, and sample chapters.
- products and services that people feel strongly about, such as books, music, and films. Fans network with other fans in online communities to discuss their favourites.
- products and services that are bought by the Internet demographic. Although the Internet demographic has broadened, it is still generally the domain of the well educated and better off. Those working in technology and academia are very well represented.

What about online advertising?

As a pure branding tool, online advertising does not have the same impact as television or glossy media, because of bandwidth restrictions. Studies indicate that most consumers avoid interactive ads because they simply take too much time to download.

However, the real power of online advertising is not its mass-marketing impact but, rather, its ability to reach niche markets and target the right consumer with the right product. The contextual advertising services like Google AdWords and Yahoo Search Marketing allow even small-scale advertisers to refine their advertising in this way. Advertising success is also claimed by opt-in e-mail-based marketing, where consumers request information on a particular product or service. In online advertising, the scattershot approach is out and laser-point focus is in.

MAKING IT HAPPEN

Recognise that Internet marketing is part of the overall package

The objective of Internet marketing should be to integrate with the overall marketing strategy, so that it supports and is supported by offline marketing activities. However, that is not to say Internet marketing doesn't have its own unique characteristics. Internet marketing is not about a big idea, some compelling graphics, and a killer catchphrase. Offline marketing brings consumers to the website by using such approaches. Consumers' interest has been aroused. They have questions. Internet marketing answers those questions by providing comprehensive information. Remember, if people have read the brochure offline, they're not coming to the website to read it again.

Understand the consumer better

Effective Internet marketing focuses on getting to know the consumer better. The objective here is to understand consumers' exact needs so that exactly the right products and services can be offered to them at exactly the right time and in exactly the right way. The strength of the Internet is also its weakness, though. While people want information, they also suffer from massive information overload. The Internet marketer who can cut through the overload and bring to time-starved consumers the information they need is much more likely to succeed. Find websites and e-mail databases that attract the exact type of consumer you wish to target. Analyse statistics generated as a result of consumers visiting your website and react appropriately to key trends that these statistics throw up. With more sophisticated websites, you can customise consumers' experiences through personalisation systems, whereby a unique and finely targeted set of information and products is presented to each visitor.

Back it up with e-mail marketing

Since the Web was launched, perceptive marketers have been stressing that every website should have an e-mail marketing strategy. Consider that consumers must actively decide to go to a website, but with e-mail they join a database in which they can be regularly informed of the products, services, and offers that the organisation has available. The key to e-mail marketing success is getting people who want the information to join a database in which they will receive regular e-mail alerts and newsletters. Of course, the information they receive needs to be of a type and quality that they will sign up to get.

Tap into the networking ability of the Internet

The Internet is a community, and it offers a tremendously powerful means for people and organisations to network. Linking is one of the simplest yet most effective Internet marketing devices there is. It underpins affiliate marketing efforts by websites such as Amazon.com. Linking is like embedded word of mouth. If another website links to you, it is essentially recommending you to its own visitors. Viral marketing is a network effect, whereby groups of consumers create a buzz about a product or service by e-mailing friends and/or creating their own websites. Consumers gain a power through Internet networking that they traditionally did not have. There are hundreds if not thousands of websites and activist groups set up by disgruntled consumers with the objective of attacking particular organisations.

Make advertising and promotion highly focused

A website, because it is not a physical store, faces a constant challenge to achieve and maintain awareness among its target market. Traditional offline marketing, such as press advertising or direct mail, plays a key role here, but so, too, do specific online marketing strategies. Registration with a commercial search engine is an obvious one. This is not some simple, one-off task but an ongoing activity, because the rules by which search engines classify sites are constantly changing. Banner ads can be effective if properly targeted. Banner ad design needs to apply the unique characteristics of the medium and not simply apply traditional advertising principles. A specialist agency can advise on suitable creative approaches. Getting other websites to link can be very effective, but this is a slow process, the rewards of which are delivered over time. E-mail signature files can promote a website effectively.

Remember that affiliate marketing and loyalty programmes can deliver

There is no better example of the success of affiliate marketing than that of Amazon.com. Literally hundreds of thousands of websites offer books and other products to their visitors using Amazon's affiliate programme. It's a win–win situation. The website in question offers an extra service that is easy to establish and delivers a certain amount of revenue. The affiliate sponsor opens up a new channel every time another website hooks into it.

However, like all marketing techniques, it's not some magic formula. It needs to be thought through properly and applied professionally.

Loyalty programmes can work on the Internet, though they have been over-hyped. Key elements in the management of loyalty programmes are the use of customer databases and the tracking of customer purchasing behaviour. The Internet facilitates such activities, and can thus be a medium through which loyalty programmes can be run.

Getting the incentive structure right is critical to the success of loyalty programmes.

Use online communities to build loyalty

Using blogs, chat, discussion boards, and e-mail mailing lists to bring people together allows you to have a conversation with customers, hear what they want, and to enhance brand loyalty. It can also be a source of unique and cost-effective content. However, it doesn't work in all situations, and online communities that are not properly managed can quickly lose momentum.

Remember that some old marketing tricks still apply

Discounts, competitions, and free offers work as well online as they do offline. While perhaps too much has been offered free on the Internet in order to build business, these traditional marketing techniques, properly used, can be effective on websites.

COMMON MISTAKES

Not building and leveraging a customer database

Bringing people to a website without strongly encouraging them to join some sort of a database is a serious mistake. Studies indicate that many consumers will visit a website once, rarely if ever to return. It's vital to get them into a database to establish ongoing communication.

Focusing on volume of visitors rather than quality targeting

In the early years of the Web there was a frantic rush to build visitor traffic to a website, without any real focus on issues such as revenue per visitor, and numbers who joined databases. Acquisition costs for visitors were high, and as the large number of visitors did not translate into valuable customers, the business model collapsed for many websites.

Focusing solely on purchase activity on a website

There is a need to understand how a website contributes to the overall purchasing process. For example, a great many people visit car websites before they make a purchase, but very few will actually make the purchase online. The key is to forget about measuring by crude visitor volume numbers and focus on the quality of the targeting, along with the influence that the website and e-mail communications have on purchase behaviour.

THE BEST SOURCES OF HELP

Book:
Scoble, Robert, and Shel Israel. *Naked Conversations: How Blogs are Changing the Way Businesses Talk with Customers.* Chichester: Wiley, 2006.

Websites:
Adventive e-mail mailing lists: **www.adventive.com**
Web marketing information centre:
   www.wilsonweb.com/webmarket

Collecting Consumer Data on the Internet

GETTING STARTED
If your business has a website, you'll find that Internet technologies offer a wealth of ways in which information on consumers can be gathered. Such information can either be collected directly as a result of consumers providing details, or indirectly by analysing consumers' behaviour while on a website. If you decide to gather information on consumers this way, keep the following in mind.
- Privacy is a central concern of people who use the Internet, and they are becoming increasingly wary of websites that seek personal information.
- The benefit to the consumer needs to be made clear. Consumers are much more willing to offer personal information when a clear benefit to them can be articulated.
- It is one thing to gather information on consumers but another to analyse it properly and use it productively.

FAQS
Why has privacy become such a burning issue on the Internet?
The Internet has lacked a common and comprehensive legal infrastructure and this has led to an unfortunate situation in which basic consumer rights have been exploited. Websites have gathered information on visitors in a surreptitious manner. Personal data has been sold on to third parties without making the consumer aware. This behaviour has resulted in a consumer backlash.

What are the key benefits of collecting consumer data?
Getting to know consumers better means that you have a better chance of offering them products and services that are more in tune with their needs. This is a key competitive advantage in an information-driven economy. With more and more products becoming increasingly similar in their physical make-up, competitive advantage is achieved through finding out exactly what the consumer wants and meeting those needs precisely.

Why is it so important to collect information on how a website is performing?
A website is not like a bricks-and-mortar shop in which a manager can walk around and observe what is happening. If there are always long queues at the checkout, and people are leaving the store because of these queues, this will quickly become obvious. People may be dropping out in the middle of a purchase process on a website, but unless proper data is coming through and being analysed, no one will know. The number of people visiting the website may be dropping off. How will this be known without proper data? Websites, like offline stores,

need to monitor their performance continuously and adapt where appropriate. Without proper data and thorough data analysis, this cannot be done.

MAKING IT HAPPEN
Use website logs to analyse consumer behaviour
Website logs (server logs) track activity on a website. For an average website, such log software is simple to install and can be purchased fairly cheaply, though for larger websites it is more complex and expensive. It is strongly advisable to use log software, as it delivers vital information on website performance.

Unless the website is hooked into a personalisation system, website logs are not able to identify who exactly has visited the website. Instead, such logs collect general website activity information. Such information includes:
- total number of visits to the website during a defined period of time.
- visitor frequency: information on the number of people who visited only once during the period (unique visitors), and those who have visited more than once.
- page impressions/views: information on the total numbers of complete web pages visited during the period. This is a key measure for advertisers.
- hits: one of the most abused statistics on the Internet, and a totally unreliable measure of website visitor activity: every web page is made up of a number of components – graphics, text, programming elements. Some pages may have anything from 10 to 20 components. Each of these components is counted as a 'hit'. Therefore, the total number of hits is generally very high and bears little or no relation to the actual visitor activity.
- most frequently visited pages.

Website logs can deliver a mind-numbing array of data. This will seem very exciting when you first install the software, but can become tedious to wade through every day. It's thus important to isolate what are the key measures required to deliver a better picture of how the website is performing.

Use cookie software to track consumers
Cookies are small files that are sent to reside in consumers' browsers in order to track those consumers the next time they visit the website. Cookies are an important component in personalisation. A typical example of the use of cookies can be seen when people have subscribed to a service on a website. Cookies allow the website to remember the user-name and password information, so that they don't have to keep filling it out every time they revisit. This is clearly a benefit for most people. However, cookies have been abused, collecting information on people without their knowing. When using cookies, clearly explain to people why they are being used and how they benefit them.

Be cautious about using Web bugs that track website usage

An alternative technology to cookies is what has become known as web bugs. Web bugs are not detectable by standard browsers, although there is software that can be downloaded to detect them. Web bugs have been controversial because they are often used in a surreptitious manner. Their very design reflects a desire not to let the person know that they are being tracked. Web bugs are adding fuel to the belief that people's privacy rights are being constantly abused on the Internet.

Collect information through the use of website forms

Website forms are used to collect information from a consumer in a structured manner. The following are guidelines to follow when designing a form.

- Keep the forms as short as possible. If you make the form too long, consumers will simply not fill it out, or will skip over large sections of it.
- If forms have to be long, break them up. However, inform the person clearly of how many sections there are in the form.
- Clearly mark mandatory fields. In every form there will be fields, such as e-mail addresses, that must be filled out. The convention is to mark the text associated with these fields in red and/or to place a red asterisk beside the field. At the top of the form, a clear statement needs to be made relating to the mandatory fields.
- Don't demand information a consumer can't give. Offer an alternative, for example: 'If you don't have a ZIP code, please write "None".'
- Ask opinion-type questions first. Where the objective of the form is to collect opinion-type information, start off with these questions. People tend to be more open to giving opinion rather than personal information.
- Isolate errors that are made. Everyone makes mistakes, particularly when they are filling out long forms. Never say, 'There's an error in your form. Go back and fill it out correctly.' Rather say, 'It seems you have not filled out your e-mail address. Please fill it out here'. Alternatively, you could highlight the field that needs to be completed in another colour, which will flag it up quickly for the user.
- Make sure the fields aren't too small. Don't, for example, give people a tiny field when you want their street address, which may be quite long.
- Make sure it's accessible to all. Offer an alternative approach for people with disabilities to complete the information requested; these disabilities can range from issues such as colour blindness to physical impairment. Minimum accessibility standards are increasingly required by law.
- Test regularly. You can't just test your forms once before you launch and then keep your fingers crossed. Forms break. Test them regularly as part of your standard website maintenance.

Follow best practice in consumer data collection

People have become rightly uneasy about the abuse of personal information on the Web. To assuage fears and create a win–win situation, put into practice the following.

- Clearly inform people why the information is being collected and what purposes it will be used for.
- Never use this information in a way that was not originally intended.
- Allow the consumer to find out what information has been collected on them.
- Allow them to delete any or all of this information if they desire.
- Publish a comprehensive privacy statement in a prominent position on the website.

Protect consumer data

Hackers – people who break into computer systems – love to target consumer databases. The reason is that these databases may contain credit card information (it is not advisable to store credit card numbers on a website). More usually, hackers know that publicising the theft of consumer databases will be hugely damaging and embarrassing to the organisation. It is therefore vital that any consumer data collected is properly protected and backed up.

Take care when collecting consumer data on children

The rules for collecting consumer data on children are quite naturally a lot stricter than for adults. While the law is evolving, numerous companies have been fined for collecting too much information on children who visit their websites. It's not enough simply to check your national legislation on this issue. The Web is international and your websites should adhere to international standards when it comes to children's privacy rights.

COMMON MISTAKES

Surreptitiously collecting data

People have become very wary about their privacy on the Internet. Too many websites have collected data on consumers without them knowing. This may produce short-term benefit but has led to an inevitable backlash.

Collecting too much data

Software today can deliver seas of data, and websites with large numbers of visitors can easily get flooded. Not focusing on what is the really important data to collect is a common problem. It's important to remember that analysing data takes time, and that, if tangible benefits are not delivered, then it will be wasted time.

Not protecting consumer data properly

There are numerous high-profile cases in which hackers broke into websites and exposed confidential consumer data. Make sure that your consumer data is properly protected.

THE BEST SOURCES OF HELP
Websites:
Information Commissioner's Office: **www.ico.gov.uk**
Web Accessibility Initiative: **www.w3.org/WAI**

Delivering the Benefits of Affiliate Marketing on the Web

GETTING STARTED

Affiliate marketing is about paying for performance. In short, it is a type of marketing in which one company induces others to place banners and buttons on their websites in return for a commission on purchases made by their customers.

Amazon.com is the pioneer of affiliate marketing. It allows other websites to publish information on their own choices of books. When people click through to Amazon and buy these books, the website in question gets a commission. Affiliate marketing can open up new channels to market for the affiliate sponsor, and be a source of extra revenue for the affiliate website. When investigating affiliate marketing, remember that:

- affiliate marketing is more suited to products than services
- you'll need to work hard with your affiliates if you want it all to work
- a well-designed compensation package will be critical to success

MAKING IT HAPPEN

Work out if your business is suited to affiliate marketing

Keep the following in mind:

- there needs to be a substantial number of websites that are attracting your target market. These websites need to show a willingness to join an affiliate programme. You might be selling medical supplies but that doesn't mean that hospital websites will become affiliates.
- affiliate marketing is better suited to products than to services. It is much harder to track whether another website sent you visitors who, after prolonged negotiation, decide to pay you for your services.
- is the market already saturated with affiliate programmes? It would be difficult to set up an affiliate programme today that offered commission on book sales.

Have a strong value proposition

As with all good ideas, there is a huge number of companies offering affiliate programmes. How is your programme going to attract new members? The level of compensation/commission you will offer will be important. However, on its own it will rarely be enough. You will need to work hard with your members by organising regular competitions, special offers, and other incentives that make for an attractive value proposition both for your affiliate members and the end customer.

Keep in regular touch with your affiliates

Keeping in regular communication with your affiliates is essential in order to build their enthusiasm and trust.

You should plan for an e-mail affiliate newsletter. Your affiliate members are your partners, and unless you treat them as such by working closely with them, they will drift away.

Agree a compensation approach

Critical to the success of your programme will be how the affiliate is compensated. There are various compensation approaches.

- You might pay commission only; for smaller-price items such as books and music, commission is a popular option.
- For more expensive items such as cars, compensation may be based on paying for qualified leads.
- If brand building is also an important objective, then you might also offer compensation every time a visitor clicks through from an affiliate.

When making payments you will need to decide how often you do it. Every month? Every quarter? A problem you may face with partners is that some of them will have achieved very little revenue for a particular period, and it will not be cost-effective to send them a cheque So you need to inform partners that there is a certain threshold before payment is made, and that commission earned in one period, if below the threshold, will be added to the commission for the next period. You will need an affiliate agreement that will cover these and other relevant issues.

Innovate, analyse, test, and adapt

There is a need to innovate constantly so as to find the best approach. Affiliate software delivers substantial data and this needs to be carefully analysed. New initiatives need to be properly tested and you need to be willing to keep adapting and refining your offer until you find something that works for both you and your affiliates.

Decide whether to outsource or buy software

Organisations can have the choice of outsourcing much of the running of the affiliate programme or purchasing software and designing it in-house. It is better to outsource, as it allows you to focus on what you do best – selling and marketing your products and services.

THE BEST SOURCES OF HELP
Websites:
Affiliate Marketing Resource Centre:
  www.affiliatemarketing.co.uk
Associate Programs: **www.associateprograms.com**

Getting the Best from Loyalty Programmes on the Web

GETTING STARTED

Loyalty programmes reward customers who spend more and/or stay longer with an organisation. Like much else about the Web, loyalty programmes were a gigantic trend that crashed pretty severely. However, much of what went wrong does not reflect an inherent fault in the loyalty model itself, but rather in vastly over-hyped expectations for what loyalty programmes can deliver. When considering using loyalty programmes on the Web, keep the following in mind.

- You should implement loyalty programmes on the Web only after you have your e-commerce fundamentals solidly in place.
- Loyalty programmes are long-term projects: it can be disastrous to start a loyalty programme and then stop it within six months.
- Getting the level of incentive right is critical to success – too much and your profits will be hurt; too little and you won't attract members.

MAKING IT HAPPEN

Make sure your e-commerce fundamentals are in place first

At the top of the list for consumers are service, comprehensive information, appropriate returns policies, and quality support. Unless these fundamentals are fully addressed, consumers will see loyalty points only as gimmicks.

Remember that loyalty programmes are long-term projects

A critical issue with regard to loyalty programmes is that, by their very nature, they have to be there for the long term. Loyalty programmes ask two key things of consumers: to collect points that will be redeemed at some future date and to give their loyalty. There is no better way to antagonise a consumer than to start a loyalty programme and then six months later – as the member has collected half the points he or she needs for that coveted flight – to stop the programme. Don't start a loyalty programme unless you're in it for the long haul.

Find out what makes your customer loyal

If you don't know what makes your customers loyal then you cannot develop a programme that will enhance their loyalty. It is also critical to focus on making your most profitable customers more loyal.

Choose the right type of loyalty programme

A selection of loyalty programme approaches are:

- points systems – a very popular approach that gives points to customers based on what they purchase
- premium customer programmes – customers who spend certain amounts of money and are repeat purchasers of a

product or service gain special status. This may involve them receiving special service offers, discounts, exclusive offers, gifts, and so on. The important thing here is to make the customers feel special – make them feel that they are getting things that those who are not part of the programme don't get.

- buyers' clubs – when a certain number of consumers get together to buy a particular product, they will be offered a special volume discount

Get the switching cost right

If you offer too much in your loyalty programme, then your margins will be squeezed, and you will be running to stand still from a profitability point of view. If your incentives are too low, then the switching cost for your customer will remain low, and the very purpose of the loyalty programme will have been negated. It would seem that the problem with a lot of loyalty programmes on the Web was that, fuelled by venture capital, major incentives were offered in the hope of attracting huge numbers of members.

Create a loyalty path for the customer

Customers can take loyalty programmes very seriously. Some customers see it as an important achievement that they have a 'Gold Card', or are seen as a 'Premium Customer'. Key in this sort of loyalty psychology is that there should be a loyalty path for customers. They need to see that the more they spend and the longer they stay with you, the more rewards and better treatment they will get.

Keep the customer informed

Customers need to be able to check up on their status easily – to see, for example, how many points they have currently accumulated. Keep in touch. Send loyalty club members a regular bulletin that creates a continuing buzz about the loyalty programme, announcing competition winners, new competitions, special offers, and so on.

Take privacy seriously

A large amount of personal information about customers and their purchasing patterns may be gathered in regular company records or in a loyalty database. It is critical that customers have confidence that your company will protect their information from improper use. In general, this information should never be shared with third parties. There should be regulations in place to regulate the way in which staff access sensitive or personal information.

THE BEST SOURCES OF HELP

Website:
BizReport.com: **www.bizreport.com/2007/05/ how_to_build_online_customer_loyalty.html**

Applying a Viral Marketing Approach on the Internet

GETTING STARTED

Viral marketing is really another name for 'word of mouth' on the Internet. Viral marketing can work in mysterious ways, but what is clear is that the Internet is a medium that offers significant potential for such a strategy, particularly with the growing popularity of personal websites such as blogs. For example, Yahoo did little or no advertising in its early years – people told others that it was a great resource. News about chat services such as AOL Instant Messenger and Skype and the social networking site Facebook spread like wildfire within universities. Viral marketing works well when:

- the product is new and genuinely different, and is something opinion leaders want to be associated with
- the benefits are real – people are telling their friends; they are putting their reputations on the line
- the product is relevant to a large number of people, and it is relatively easy to communicate the benefits

MAKING IT HAPPEN

Consider incentives

Some viral marketing campaigns use an incentive-based approach. This involves rewarding people if they inform their friends and a percentage of these friends purchase the product or fill out a questionnaire, for example. It's very important to have a 'cap' on the number of people that the first person is asked to inform, though. For example, ask contributors to tell no more than five people about your product or service. If the process is open-ended then people are more likely to send out thousands of spam e-mails to people they don't know in order to increase their rewards. Spam is the bane of the online world, and one thing you definitely don't want to encourage, even inadvertently.

Create useful information that will be quoted and passed on

People see the Internet as an information resource. A powerful way of building a brand is to publish information that you allow people to quote and redistribute. There is no better way to enhance your reputation than for someone to pass your newsletter on to a friend, recommending that they should read it. The objective is that you be seen as an expert on a particular subject that is directly related to a product or service you offer. To encourage this type of process, create an 'e-mail-to-a-friend' function on your website, which allows someone easily to e-mail information on something they have just read.

Recognise that linking is viral marketing

Linking is another form of word of mouth. It's one thing for someone to send an e-mail praising your product or information, but the effect is much better and longer-lasting if the recipient publishes a positive review on their website and links back to you.

Remember that viral marketing works well when there is something free

People love to tell their friends when there is some great new service that is free. The Hotmail free e-mail service and the Geocities free website service grew quickly with little or no marketing spend. The appeal of what is free may be losing some of its lustre as the Internet matures, but it is still a powerful driver of behaviour.

Emulate the Hotmail approach

Hotmail was a pioneer of viral marketing. Its success was not simply based on the fact that it was a free service. It embedded viral marketing into the product itself. Every time someone using Hotmail sent an e-mail, at the bottom of the e-mail was the compelling message: 'Get your private, free e-mail at http://www.hotmail.com'. Thus, the very use of the product became a vehicle for marketing and promotion.

Think about integrating other approaches

Depending on your type of business, you might want to investigate the option of marketing virally via text messages as well as the Internet. Let's say your business provides information about entertainment options in your local area. You could encourage visitors to your website to register their phone numbers with you so that you can keep them up to date with special offers, new information, and so on via text message. This would be particularly popular in an area with a high student population. However, you must be *scrupulous* about the information you send out via text message – don't, for example, send out 'jokey' messages that may be misconstrued in any way by the recipient: in 2004, the games company CE Europe attracted a great deal of negative press when it marketed a 'Resident Evil' computer game by a text message that told users that their phones had been infected by a virus. Remember that you must *not* send unsolicited text messages and you must remove numbers immediately from your list if anyone complains (someone else may have registered their number, for example).

Be wary of inappropriate viral marketing

Done inappropriately, viral marketing can be seen as pyramid selling and/or spam. Every e-mail sent needs to make clear that the business is not involved in spamming or other unethical practices. If you do attract adverse attention from an irate recipient, remain calm and respond to the complainant in a professional manner.

THE BEST SOURCES OF HELP
Website:
Business2.0: **http://money.cnn.com/magazines/ business2**

Generating Content and Building Loyalty Through Online Communities and Blogs

GETTING STARTED

Online communities allow consumers to engage with one another and with your organisation through use of interactive tools such as e-mail, discussion boards, and chat software. (Broader and more social online communities are not the topic of this actionlist.) They are a means by which you can take the pulse of consumers to find out what they are thinking, and to generate unique content. As a stand-alone business, online communities have been found to be weak: they work best when they are supporting the need for the organisation to get ongoing feedback. Online communities:

- allow the consumer an ongoing voice, thus facilitating greater feedback
- require moderation and care if they are not to fizzle out, or turn negative
- offer different options for interaction that reflect the varying ways in which people like to communicate

MAKING IT HAPPEN

Keep it moderated

Online communities rarely work if you simply install some discussion board software on a website and walk away. The discussion will either quickly dry up, or else drift off to topics that have nothing to do with the organisation, and may well be libellous or illegal. Thus, to make a success of an online community, quality moderation is essential. Moderators need to combine editorial and chairperson-type skills. They need to be knowledgeable about the subjects being discussed, be enthusiastic, and encourage debate and quality discussion. They require an understanding of legal (particularly libel and copyright) issues, and should have the ability to deal with negative situations where members become overly virulent. Most of all, they need to care and want to make the community work for everybody involved.

Set up e-mail mailing lists

E-mail mailing lists are an excellent way to discuss complex topics over a longer period of time. Members can be drawn from anywhere in the world and come together to share information and experience on a particular theme or subject area. The success of an e-mail mailing list is down to the quality of the contributions and moderation. Done right, it is a powerful way of transferring knowledge. An e-mail mailing list works as follows:

- A moderator establishes a list with mailing list software (this can be bought or rented; renting is usually the best option).
- The theme and focus of the list is published, and people join, using a website form and/or e-mail address.
- The moderator invites contributions and these are duly published by e-mail.

- Subscribers react to the initial publication with their opinions and feedback; a selection of these reactions then gets published in the next e-mail sent out.
- If successful, a feedback and opinion loop is created, with new topics of discussion being introduced as older topics have received sufficient discussion.

Set up discussion boards

Discussion boards (also known as newsgroups, discussion groups, bulletin boards) are areas on a website that allow people to contribute opinions, ideas, and announcements. They tend to be more general in nature than e-mail mailing lists, and are more suited for casual, one-off interactions. People require less commitment to participate in such boards. They can generally review a discussion topic without subscribing, although they do have to subscribe if they want to contribute something themselves. Moderation is not as essential here, although it is important to watch out for the emergence of 'off-topic' subjects – contributions that are unnecessarily negative and perhaps libellous – and copyright infringement.

A prime example of the success of the discussion board approach is how Amazon.com uses it to allow consumers to publish book reviews. Discussion board software is relatively cheap and easy to install.

Set up a blog

A blog is a regularly updated website, which is usual written and managed by one person. A substantial number of weblogs cover business-related topics and some are actually written by executives on behalf of their employer. One example is the GM Fastlane Blog (**http://fastlane. gmblogs.com**), written by the company's vice chairman and concentrating on the company's range of cars and trucks. The official Google blog (**http://googleblog. blogspot.com**) was ranked the number one corporate blog in 2008 by Technorati. Many blogs of this type receive a large amount of constructive customer feedback about the companies' products and plans. The weblog content provides a focus for the community that builds up around it and the personality behind it provides a bridge to allow comments and feedback to be taken on board by the organisation. Microblogging via services such as Twitter is also gaining in popularity. Although it first came to prominence when used for social networking, many high-profile businesspeople and commercial organisations are now using it to do everything from advertise job vacancies to offer product or service information. Corporate Twitterers include Sir Richard Branson, Cisco Systems, IBM and O_2.

Set up online chat

Online chat is real-time, text-based communication. Online chat can be effective when:

- there is a specific event occurring that is of interest to people
- an expert can be made available to talk about a subject or product

To be productive, online chat needs to be well moderated. It is really only suited to small groups of people (two to 20) at any one time. Online chat software is relatively cheap and easy to install.

Monitor and engage with other online communities

Your online community of customers and users does not exist in a vacuum. You also need to monitor, and if appropriate, interact with users on other websites and mailing lists where your product is discussed. If you do interact with customers in this way, it is very important to be courteous and not to misrepresent yourself in any way. It is also poor practice to use someone else's discussion board to make an open sales approach, and the rules of the discussion board may explicitly forbid this.

THE BEST SOURCES OF HELP

Book:

McGovern, Gerry. *Killer Web Content*. London: A&C Black, 2006.

Websites:

Corporate Blogging: **www.corporateblogging.info**

Twitter: **http://twitter.com**

Promoting Your Website Effectively

GETTING STARTED

Launching a website is like opening up a shop at the North Pole or in the Sahara Desert. Nobody will know that you are there unless you promote yourself! Website promotion is not some one-off event that occurs at launch. It is an ongoing activity that demands a keen understanding of promotional techniques that are unique to the Web. It also requires full integration into offline marketing and promotional activities. When approaching website promotion, consider the following:

- it requires a range of promotional strategies, both online and offline
- it's an ongoing activity
- it should be fully integrated into the overall promotional and marketing strategy

FAQS

Why is website promotion of such importance?

In the property business people talk about 'location, location, location'. Well, a website doesn't really have a location. It's not on a high street where thousands of people walk by every day. Without such physical visibility, a website has a major problem attracting consumers. That is one reason why a clicks-and-mortar strategy (combining physical stores with an Internet presence) is deemed so essential for the success of a website. In a physical store, and in its related marketing and promotional activity, consumers can be exposed to the benefits of the website constantly.

What is banner advertising and does it promote a website well?

Banner advertising is the use of rectangular advertisements or logos across the width of page on an Internet site. Businesses often place advertisements of this type on a third party's site to attract users to visit their own.

The jury is still out on the effectiveness of banner advertising. However, prices for banner advertising have dropped significantly in recent years and there is certainly value to be had. It's really down to the target market you are after and whether that accurately matches the profile of visitors coming to a particular website. Online advertising systems allow for a level of targeting and measurement that is impossible in much offline media. So, if you can get to the right target market at the right price, then the equation makes sense.

Does online advertising and promotion have to cost a lot of money?

No. Online ads have dropped significantly in price and, with proper investigation, very good value can be had. Online promotion requires dedication, but a few hours spent every week can deliver real results in the longer term.

MAKING IT HAPPEN
Get linked

Linking is one of the most powerful means of promoting a website. A link from another website is essentially embedded word of mouth, a recommendation from that site to its visitors also to visit you. The Web is huge, with millions of websites, many of them of poor quality. People who use the Internet have become very sceptical and conservative in their behaviour. Building credibility is thus of key importance to online success. There is no better way to build such credibility than to have many other websites linking to you.

Google, perhaps the Web's most popular search engine, achieved popularity because its search results were seen as more relevant than those of other search engines. The way it achieved better results was by analysing a website and seeing how many external websites had linked to it.

The more links the website had, the higher in the results Google placed it. Thus, if you want your website to feature prominently with Google, the more links you can get the better.

But linking is not simply about getting placed higher in search engine results. Think of each link as another 'road' to your website; another way that the visitor can get to you. Getting links is not easy. It involves finding websites that attract your target market and convincing them to include a link to you. Usually, they will not do this unless you have valuable content that could be of interest to their customers. Another approach is to pay for a link, either through monthly fees or through what is called 'click-through payments' – you pay for every visit that results from a particular link.

Weblogs – or 'blogs' – are an increasingly important source of information. They are sites that express a particular person's point of view. Build relationships with blog owners who are relevant to your area to yield links and reviews of your product.

Register with search engines
Because so many people use commercial search engines, it's extremely important that your website is properly registered. Keep the following in mind.
- There are hundreds of search engines and directories but only a handful that really matter, such as Yahoo and Google.
- Identify specialist search engines and directories for your particular industry. You should register with them.
- All search engines used to be free to register with, but this is no longer the case for an increasing number. You need to consider if the fee is worth it.
- An increasing number of search engines sell special placements in their search results. You can choose a keyword and when that keyword is input by a searcher, a short promotion for your website will appear.
- Search engines need to be monitored regularly, as they can change the rules by which search results are presented. A set of keywords needs to be drawn up and the search engine regularly searched using these keywords. If you find your website is dropping down the results page, you may need to re-register. Also, if you launch a new product or service, you should consider registering that.
- Don't register popular keywords with a website just for the sake of increased visitors. It achieves very little, and some search engines will remove websites that continuously abuse search registration processes.
- Don't go overboard with your campaign to improve your company's search results online (otherwise known as 'search engine optimisation'). While there are known tactics you can use to improve your rank, not all are legitimate. If the search engine company believes that you are maliciously manipulating the rankings, it may penalise you, cut your ranking, or even ban your site altogether.

Use banner and other online advertising
As stated above, banner advertising doesn't work for everyone, but it may work for your business. It's particularly useful where a new website, product, or service is being launched. Banner ads can be paid for either on a cost-per-thousand (CPM) basis or per click-through, where the seller gets paid whenever a visitor clicks on an ad. Online ads should be a call to action, with the key objective being to get the person to click on the ad. There are a variety of online advertising options:
- banner advertisements. These ads can go across the top or bottom of the page or down the side, like wallpaper.
- interstitials. These are ads that appear before the actual web page loads. They certainly get the visitors' attention but can be very frustrating.
- pop-under ads. These ads launch in a separate browser window and have been controversial.

Consider e-mail as a form of advertising
E-mail can be a very effective form of advertising, particularly when the advertiser is reaching a targeted list that has opted in to receive information on particular products or services. The thing to watch out for in e-mail advertising is spam. Spam is mass-distributed e-mail that is unsolicited by the receiver. People are increasingly annoyed at receiving spam, and anti-spam legislation has been enacted or is pending in many countries. It's not simply about whether spam is legal or not – but it is certainly unethical, and no reputable organisation should use such an approach.

Remember e-mail signature files
An e-mail signature is the text at the bottom of an e-mail that contains information about the sender. It is also possible to place a short, two-line ad there (e-mail signatures should not be longer than five lines). E-mail signature promotion was used very effectively when Andersen Consulting changed its name to Accenture. For a period after the name change, every time one of Accenture's 60,000 employees sent an e-mail, there was a short e-mail signature ad notifying the receiver of the change of name.

Integrate with offline marketing and promotion
Every single piece of offline literature should contain the website address and, where appropriate, an e-mail address. This includes: all stationery (letterheads, business cards, compliment slips, receipts, invoices); all product packaging; training and support manuals; all ads that are placed in print, radio, or television. If the organisation has physical stores, then promotional material should be placed prominently within these stores informing visitors of the website. When planning new offline promotional and marketing activities, you should seek ways to get consumers to go to the website. For example, the website could be the place where the consumer enters a competition.

Include competitions and free giveaways
Consumers are as likely to react positively to quality Web-based competitions and special promotions as they do to such tactics in the offline world. Competitions

and special offers give the website a sense of vibrancy. A key objective of such promotions should be to get consumers to join databases, used in the future to inform people of other special offers and relevant information.

COMMON MISTAKES

Seeking quantity of visitors over quality

In the early days of the Web there was a mad rush – fuelled by venture capital – to drive as many visitors as possible to websites. A stream of new brands emerged, each one seeking to out-do the next with ad spend. There is still a tendency to consider quantity over quality when it comes to building visitor numbers to a website. This is a serious and expensive mistake.

Focusing purely on search engines

Search engines are important, but they should still be only a part of an online promotional strategy. Also, abuse of search engines by bombarding them with popular keywords and other visitor-generating techniques merely serves to bulk up visitor figures. It does little or nothing for the bottom line.

Lack of integration with offline marketing

Organisations miss vital and cost-effective ways of promoting their websites by not fully utilising offline resources.

Lack of ongoing commitment

Too many websites have been launched enthusiastically, only to be left to wither in the wilderness of cyberspace. To be successful, promotion must be an ongoing activity.

THE BEST SOURCES OF HELP
Website:
Google: **www.google.com**

Using E-mail Marketing Effectively

GETTING STARTED

E-mail should be an essential part of any Internet marketing strategy. If you have someone's e-mail address, you can send them information directly. But with e-mail it is important that the recipient wants the information you are sending. When considering e-mail, keep the following in mind:

- e-mail is a relatively cheap, but powerful communications tool – you can send thousands of e-mail newsletters in a simple, cost-effective way
- e-mail allows you to keep in regular contact with customers and to build up a rapport with them
- never send unsolicited e-mails (spam). E-mail should only deliver worthwhile information.

FAQS

How often should you contact customers by e-mail?

E-mail is a fast, simple, and cost-effective form of communication, so it is tempting to use it at every opportunity. However, unless the information is valuable, this can become annoying for customers. As a general rule, you should not send e-mail to people more than once a week, unless there is a specific and defined need. People are overloaded and if they see too many e-mails coming from you they will turn off. Whatever the frequency, make sure that you stick to your schedule, as people will be expecting it.

Should newsletters be free or chargeable?

It depends on the focus of your business. If you are publishing information, then it is hard to see how a business model can be developed that is advertising only. However, if you are using the information you send to help sell some other product or service, it is highly unlikely that anyone will be willing to pay for it.

What is spam?

Spam is mass-distributed, unsolicited e-mail. Spam is a major problem on the Internet today in that it is easy to buy a database of millions of e-mail addresses and send out unsolicited e-mails to them. If you want to be seen as a reputable business, you should avoid sending spam. Legislation is pending in a number of countries to make sending spam illegal.

What do the terms 'opt-in' and 'double opt-in' mean?

An opt-in approach is where someone actively decides to give you their e-mail address so that you can send them e-mail. However, the emerging convention is double opt-in. What happens here is that when a person receives a request to subscribe to an e-mail address, they reply to that address for verification that the request did in fact come from there. This ensures that the e-mail address was not maliciously set up by a third party.

Is it better to buy software or can it be rented?

Very often it is better to rent. There are a number of organisations that offer professional e-mail management services. To get a list of such companies, go to **www.directory.google.com/Top/Computers/Internet/ Mailing_Lists/Hosting_Companies**.

MAKING IT HAPPEN

Isolate the information need

The first step in any e-mail strategy is to isolate the information need of your target market. What sort of information would they find useful? Would they like information on new products and special offers? Would they like information on trends within your industry? What sort of information would make them want to give you their e-mail address?

Define your publication scope and schedule

Once you have defined an information need, you must make clear what the scope of your e-mail publication is. What exactly will the person get if they subscribe? Unless you are delivering very time-sensitive information, a weekly publication is usually sufficient.

Make the subscription process prominent on your website

Getting people to subscribe is vital to the success of your e-mail strategy. There should therefore be a prominent subscription box on your website encouraging people to subscribe. Also, include subscription details in every mailing that you send out. Don't ask too many questions in the subscription process.

Many successful e-mail newsletter providers only ask for the e-mail address of the subscriber. That makes it a very easy and quick process for the potential subscriber. You can always ask for more information later on, when you have established a stronger relationship with the subscriber. As a rule, the more valuable the information is to the potential subscriber, the more information you can ask of them.

Make the unsubscription process as easy as possible

It is equally important to ensure that the unsubscription process is easy to use. People can get frustrated and angry if they find it difficult to unsubscribe from a service. Some might think you have started spamming them.

If you're offering a paid-for subscription service, offer a free 'teaser' subscription

If you plan to offer a commercial service where you charge people to subscribe, then it is a good idea to offer a free e-mail that contains brief summaries of what is included in the commercial offering. It may also be an idea to offer a free trial period, so that the subscriber can get an understanding of what you have to offer.

Decide whether you want a plain text or HTML version of your e-mail

There are two basic options for the format you can use when delivering an e-mail to your subscriber base: plain text and HTML. Plain text is just like a normal e-mail. It is the simplest and easiest to produce. HTML is like sending a web page in an e-mail. It will deliver a lot more impact and colour. However, it is more expensive to produce, and a number of older e-mail systems find it hard to read HTML. Thus, if you are going to use an HTML e-mail approach, offer a plain text version as well. Otherwise, a significant number of people may be unable to subscribe to your service.

For plain text e-mail layout keep the line length of text between 65 and 70 characters to avoid breaking lines, which make the layout look very ugly, and keep paragraphs nice and short – five to six lines is optimum. Use capitals for headings. Because plain text e-mails do not allow the use of bold or font sizing, capitalising is the only way to give emphasis. Use a nonproportional font such as Courier, because it remains constant regardless of the e-mail package being used.

Keep the e-mail short and punchy

Think of what you are doing as delivering a publication. You're trying to get people to read something that will make them want to act – to buy your product, for example. Focus on having punchy headings and short summaries. Avoid having articles that are longer than 500–600 words. The entire e-mail should not contain more than 1,500 words, unless you have a dedicated audience that you know is willing to read longer pieces. So keep things short, and always have some sort of call to action.

Have a strong subject line

The subject line is what subscribers see first when they download their e-mail. Because people are so busy they often scan the subject line and, if it's not interesting, delete the e-mail. However, if you are sending out a regular publication you may wish to include the title of the publication and date in the subject line. In the body of the e-mail itself, it's a good idea to have a table of contents near the top that lets the reader know what to expect from the rest of the e-mail.

Using hypertext and e-mail addresses

It's a good idea to use a hypertext to link back to your website, in order to encourage the subscriber to get more information, purchase your product, and so on. However, when writing out a hyperlink (URL) always use the full URL. For example, don't use 'www.mycompany.com'; instead, use 'http://www.mycompany.com'. The reason is that some older e-mail packages will not automatically turn the URL into a link unless you include the full URL. Also, if you have a URL that is more than 65 characters long, put in angle brackets (< , >) on either side of the URL. Otherwise, a number of e-mail packages will break the URL on to two lines and make it unusable. If you are including an e-mail address, put in a 'mailto:' before the e-mail address, as this will turn it into a link to the subscriber's e-mail package. For example: 'mailto:tom@mycompany.com'.

Include the essential things every e-mail mailing should have

Every e-mail you send out should contain the subject line (title) and date, subscription and unsubscription information, copyright and privacy policies (or links to these on the website), e-mail contact details (telephone and address may also be included), links back to the website, and brief information on the publication schedule and scope.

COMMON MISTAKES

Using a 'bait and switch' approach

Be very clear to the potential subscriber about what exactly they are subscribing to. If you specialise in special offers, e-mail and tell them so. Don't pretend that you're going to send valuable updates on a particular industry, and then just send special offers.

Not meeting a real information need

Ask yourself the question: why would anyone want to read this? Too many e-mail mailings are full of useless, repetitive, or out-of-date information.

Not keeping to a publication schedule

You're in the business of publishing and if you say you will deliver an e-mail every Wednesday, then you must deliver an e-mail every Wednesday or risk losing credibility and subscribers.

Not managing the subscription and unsubscription process professionally

Make it difficult for someone to subscribe and they won't subscribe. Make it difficult for people to unsubscribe and they can become very irate.

Spamming people

Never subscribe people against their will or without them knowing. Sending unsolicited e-mail is a 'get rich quick' strategy. It will damage your long-term reputation.

THE BEST SOURCES OF HELP
Book:
MacPherson, Kim. *Permission-Based E-Mail Marketing That Works!*. New York: Dearborn Trade Publishing, 2001.

Website:
Clickz e-mail marketing: **www.clickz.com/ em_mkt/em_mkt**

Exploring Peer-to-peer (P2P) Commerce

GETTING STARTED

Peer-to-peer (P2P) embraces the networking capabilities of the Internet. It allows people to share and publish resources directly, and allows the unused processing capability of computers to be shared and used productively. While the concept of peer-to-peer has in fact been around for many years, it has gained a new lease of life with the advent of the Internet. The peer-to-peer model became particularly well known in connection with the original Napster music-swapping service and later Skype, which provides high-quality voice calls over the Internet.

FAQS

What exactly is peer-to-peer?

Peer-to-peer puts every computer on an equal footing, in that every computer can be both a publisher and consumer of information. The traditional model on the Web is the client–server one. The client is a computer and browser that is able only to receive/consume information. The server, on the other hand, serves/publishes information on a website. Peer-to-peer makes a computer both a server and client.

What are examples of peer-to-peer?

Perhaps the best-known example of peer-to-peer is Skype (**www.skype.com**). Skype allows people to make a voice call directly to any other Skype user in the world.

There is also a plethora of P2P file-sharing programs. File-sharing programs generally work as follows: Person A could search for and download music from Person B's computer, while Person B could search for and download music from Person A's computer. (The problem with these P2P file-sharing programs is that there is generally no means to control the distribution of copyright material.)

What sort of peer-to-peer options are available?

The following are distinct options for the use of peer-to-peer technologies:

- information/content: this is the Napster example. The content on your computer becomes accessible to everyone else in the peer-to-peer environment and vice versa.
- processing sharing: computers with spare processing capacity network together in order to combine their resources. Using a large number of computers, this can create very significant processing capabilities.
- communication: a computer user can communicate in various ways with other people in the peer-to-peer network.

Can client-server and peer-to-peer systems work in harmony?

Yes. One does not exclude the other. The best scenario is to exploit the strengths of the client–server model – order, structure, management – and combine them with the flexibility and enabling capacity of peer-to-peer.

MAKING IT HAPPEN

Making better use of processing power

Studies have indicated that 50 per cent or more of a typical organisation's processing power may be unused. Peer-to-peer is a way of tapping this unused resource for productive purposes. There are indications that commercial organisations see this as one of the most practical uses of peer-to-peer technology. However, bear in mind that such an application of peer-to-peer becomes relevant only if there are major processing needs that an organisation is finding difficult to meet. Where such a situation arises, it can be more efficient and cost-effective to spread processing across the computers in the organisation than to buy powerful new computers.

The main drawback here is that there will be a set-up cost for installing the peer-to-peer technology. Education and training will be needed. When ongoing maintenance is added to this, the costs can begin to mount up, and it may well be that a centralised solution is more cost-effective. Whether peer-to-peer is genuinely cost-effective in such situations depends on the amount of processing that is going to be required. A careful analysis is required to establish when a peer-to-peer approach is worth considering.

Collaboration and communication with peer-to-peer

Driven by the rapid growth in partnerships and the need to be more flexible and adaptive, collaboration is now seen as a key attribute of a progressive organisation. Peer-to-peer can prove useful where people are collaborating and sharing resources and content on an active basis. If there is a need to establish a group that might span several organisations, then peer-to-peer technology can be faster, and easier to implement and run than traditional approaches.

Content publication with peer-to-peer

It is true that most content today resides on individual computers rather than on servers that publish this content to websites. Peer-to-peer allows you to see all the content within the organisation, rather than just what has been published on websites. This may be helpful when you are looking for something very specific, but there are some substantial drawbacks.

Much of the content that exists on an individual's computer is either private, in draft form, out of date, or simply not ready for publication or sharing. There are hundreds of billions of documents published on intranets, extranets, and public websites, which is in itself a vast, unimaginable quantity of content. The quantity of content that is on individual computers around the world would dwarf even this massive amount. Having the capacity to access all this content may sound valuable in theory, but in practice it could make information overload a hundred times worse than it already is.

With regard to content publication, peer-to-peer thinking seems to miss some fundamental rules of publishing.

Publishing is not, and never has been, about following an 'as much as you can read' approach, but is about selecting the best content and publishing it. A quality publishing house will reject 90 per cent of the content presented to it. It will then polish up the final 10 per cent, and publish it in such a way that it is easy to find and easy to read.

File sharing with peer-to-peer

The classic model of file sharing occurs where someone downloads a file from a central server. This approach can put a lot of strain on bandwidth if there is a large number of people who need to download files. Peer-to-peer file sharing seeks to use bandwidth more effectively. Let's say Person A and Person B are close together on the network. A downloads an e-learning course. Later, B wants to download the same course. With peer-to-peer, instead of B's request being acted on by the central server, the system looks to see if there is anyone near B on the network who has downloaded the same course. The system finds that A has. So now, instead of B downloading from the central server, B will download from A's machine. This saves time and network resources.

Security and privacy are major issues

Peer-to-peer thrives in an open network environment. The problem is that hackers and viruses likewise thrive in that very same environment. Within an organisation there may be a whole variety of operating systems and security protocols, and linking them all together in a cohesive and secure manner is not a simple task. Many believe that this is the Achilles' heel of peer-to-peer.

A key aspect of peer-to-peer security is the authentication of users. Knowing that the peer you want to share with is reputable and trustworthy is critical. To improve security, many peer-to-peer interactions now use encryption, which ensures that the communication is secure as it is being passed from computer to computer.

Privacy is a major issue for people whose computers will be used in the peer-to-peer network. Because most computer users are novices from a technical point of view, they become very dependent on their IT department to make sure nothing is going wrong. This situation is not welcomed by the average IT manager.

Equally, for the individual, the idea that someone else can root around within his or her computer can be unnerving. Making sure that their private files are fully protected is only part of the problem. In essence, it means thinking about the computer differently: looking at one part of it as being public domain and another private.

Peer-to-peer and management

Peer-to-peer technology can allow the organisation to investigate its computers and see what resources it has. This could allow an organisation to monitor software continually and to distribute upgrades as they become available. It could also allow it to examine the content being created or downloaded by a particular individual, thus giving it more control.

Setting up a peer-to-peer environment

Certain elements need to be in place for peer-to-peer to function. These include:

- publishing of resources: to make a resource available, it must be published on the computer. This requires that it be identified as a resource that can be shared. Part of this identification involves a proper description that will allow other users to identify it quickly and accurately.
- location of resources: the person who wants a resource must locate it. This can be a major problem in a large peer-to-peer environment where there could be many millions of resources available. Some form of directory classification becomes essential in such an environment.
- utilising the resource: once the resource has been located, there must be a method by which it can be utilised. If the resource is content, such as music, then it can be simply downloaded. However, if it is processing power, it will require a more complex interaction.

COMMON MISTAKES

The security angle is overlooked

Peer-to-peer works best in an open network, but an open network is open to attack. The peer-to-peer structure can allow viruses to spread more easily. If authentication of users is not carried out properly, then hackers or other malicious people can gain access to the network.

You forget the Napster example

Part of the original Napster philosophy was that of bringing unsigned artists to the masses, but the reality was that the majority of people just wanted to hear the major acts. When Napster was stopped from illegally swapping commercial music, its usage dropped dramatically. The theory of peer-to-peer is that people are willing to wade through millions of pieces of content to find that precious gem; in fact, most people just want what is popular.

Lack of standards and support

Standards tend to vary widely in peer-to-peer technologies, thus making it more difficult to share resources. Without proper standards, a peer-to-peer environment can quickly become chaotic. Because P2P applications are not based on open standards and have a complex architecture, they are difficult to support. Unless you are satisfied that the P2P system is willing to give your organisation a support contract, it is unwise to depend on it for business-critical purposes.

THE BEST SOURCES OF HELP

Website:
Open P2P.com: **www.openp2p.com/pub/q/p2p_category**

Legal Issues in E-commerce

GETTING STARTED

In any e-business strategy, it is important to address the key legal issues from the start and comprehensively. At a basic level, these are matters such as copyright and libel; at a more advanced level, such things as unique restrictions pertaining to the sale of your product within particular jurisdictions need to be dealt with. When addressing legal issues on the Web, keep the following in mind.

- Prevention is better than cure. Establishing a sound legal structure early on is much easier than trying to firefight legal problems as they occur.
- Legal systems are getting a grip on the Internet. More and more laws are being passed that deal with doing business online.
- While you can't deal with the unique legal aspects of every jurisdiction, you still need to isolate the key jurisdictions for your online business and make sure you adhere to their relevant laws.

FAQS

Why should you address legal issues from the start?

Because it's important to guard against unpleasant consequences if you get legal things wrong, or just ignore them. Some early e-commerce businesses adopted the latter approach, believing that cyberspace was a kind of *laissez-faire* autonomous zone beyond the reach of terrestrial governments.

Is it not the case that many laws do not apply online?

Nobody believes that fallacy any more. Which is fortunate, because courts and governments around the world have shown no hesitation about claiming jurisdiction over online activity – in some cases, even when the website in question is hosted on another continent. They have applied civil sanctions (such as injunctions and damages) and criminal penalties (fines and even imprisonment) in certain instances.

Is there a pragmatic approach to dealing with legal issues online?

Yes. The practical approach is to get legal advice on three specific types of territory for your website:

- the country (or countries) in which your Web operations are principally based, which will often, but not always, be where the site is hosted
- the countries that are the primary target market of the website
- any other countries which may claim authority over the website, and the breach of whose laws might cause unpleasant consequences. The US is by far the best example of this: its legal regime has a dauntingly long reach.

MAKING IT HAPPEN

The different kinds of website

While there are many different types of website, they can broadly be divided into those with the following attributes:

- shop window websites, which provide information about a company and its products, but without encouraging any significant visitor interaction – rather like an online company brochure
- contributed content websites, which allow visitors to contribute content, such as information about their identity, or postings on message boards
- full e-commerce websites, through which visitors can purchase goods or services, either physical products which are delivered offline, or digitised material which is available for download

Shop window website issues

Even shop window websites have legal issues to address. They comprise various types of digitised content, such as graphics, text, images, music, and coding, that raise issues which apply to all forms of website.

Website owners must assume that all such content is protected: either by copyright – which, in effect, disallows its inclusion in another website without the copyright owner's permission; or, in some cases, by moral rights – which require the author to be attributed, and that the work should not be significantly modified without the owner's permission.

These clearances can take the form of a licence or an assignment of copyright from the relevant rights holder, which might be a third-party website designer, photographer, journalist, or (in the more difficult case of music) two or more rights-holding organisations.

In addition, you must ensure that content on your website satisfies other requirements, including the following.

- Using the registered trademarks of a third party as part of your website's metadata will generally constitute trademark infringement. Even a straightforward reference on a website to a third party's trademark can constitute an infringement.
- Hypertext linking, particularly by means of deep linking or framing, to third-party websites without the consent of those websites should be avoided.
- Misleading price indications, for example where online prices have not been updated, can incur penalties.
- Incorrect product descriptions, where inaccurate statements

are made as to the quantity, size, fitness for purpose, or performance of goods, can also cause repercussions.
- Unfair comparative advertising, such as comparisons between goods or services that are not intended for the same purpose, must be avoided.

As well as guarding against infringement of third parties' rights, it is important for owners to include wording in the terms and conditions of their websites which protects their own copyright and other rights. Usually this is done by means of terms which appear directly on the home page or, more commonly, are linked to/from the home page, as well as at the bottom of all other pages on the website.

Contributed content website issues

Websites that encourage visitors to interact are exposed to several additional forms of legal risk. One of the most basic means of facilitating visitor interaction is a discussion board or chat room. Such environments can pose legal problems, as they are often unchecked and allow visitors to post information without any apparent restriction. You need to recognise that you can find yourself liable, either as a civil matter (where a third party's rights have been infringed) or, more extremely, under the criminal law, unless steps are taken to control material which appears on your website.

Some of the most obvious problems here include:

- defamatory statements
- infringement of copyright material
- obscene, blasphemous, threatening, racially discriminatory, and other legally objectionable material

To avoid liability for such material, you need to establish one or more of the following safeguards:

- proactive moderation of material before it appears on the website
- a documented 'notice and take down' procedure, under which infringing content is removed from the website as soon as it has been notified
- regular reviewing of material which has been posted, and removal of any which appears problematic

These issues all need to be addressed in your website's terms and conditions, so that visitors (and potential third-party complainants) are aware of the steps taken to prevent infringement. Many prudent owners also require visitors to register with the website before they can post messages. This allows the owner to contact the visitor if a problematic posting is made by the visitor, and, in certain circumstances, to provide that visitor's personal and contact information to a wronged third party, or to a law-enforcement authority.

Full e-commerce website issues

Clearly, a wide variety of goods and services are capable of being traded through a website. Further, the seller can be either the website owner or a third party trading through the website, as in an online auction service.

It is impossible to cover here all the issues which the various kinds of products can raise. Many have specific regulations which have been imposed by governments for social, ethical, and fiscal reasons. Examples of these include:

- sale of alcohol
- sale of medicines, particularly prescription-only medicines
- financial services
- betting, gaming, and lotteries
- auctions, particularly in various European countries

Depending on the jurisdiction and type of product being sold, a website may need to adhere to regulations such as:

- provision of clear information to consumers before the conclusion of a contract, including: the identity of the supplier; the main characteristics of what's being sold; payment and delivery arrangements; and the principal terms and conditions of the contract between seller and purchaser
- a minimum period during which a consumer may withdraw from the contract for any reason, and reject whatever has been purchased

Whatever you sell through your e-commerce website, it is important that you form a legally binding contract with the purchaser. For example, you might ensure that such a contract is formed by requiring the visitor to scroll through your terms and conditions and click on an 'I accept' button.

COMMON MISTAKES

Doing nothing because you think it's just too complicated

It is certainly true that a dizzying array of legal issues exist to ponder when trading over the Web. However, that's not an excuse for doing nothing. There is a basic minimum that can and should be addressed. The key is to understand the legal issues that, if not addressed properly and promptly, can have a major impact on your business.

Assuming that the long arm of the law does not reach online

This is a very false assumption. Yes, it is often more difficult to successfully prosecute an organisation that is trading over the Web. However, that does not mean that governments and legal systems are ignoring those who they feel are breaking their laws, just because they happen to be on the Web.

Failing to deal with copyright and libel issues quickly

If a third party accuses you of libel or copyright infringement, it is imperative that you deal with it urgently. In many courts of law, the longer the libel remains published on the website, the greater the penalties.

THE BEST SOURCES OF HELP
Website:
British and Irish Legal Information Institute:
www.bailii.org

Podcasting for Business

GETTING STARTED

Podcasts have taken off massively in recent years, and everything from radio programmes, news updates, and even Prime Minister's questions are now available for listeners to access in this format.

In a business context, podcasts can be used as part of a marketing campaign, giving interested customers the opportunity to receive targeted audio content in an accessible format. They're a great way of increasing customer loyalty and boosting a business's visibility and market 'reach'.

FAQS

Can podcasting reap rewards for all types of company?

Not necessarily, no. Podcasting represents a new way of talking to your customers, but as with any marketing tactic, if you don't have anything useful or compelling to say, the results won't justify the resources you need to produce high-quality content.

Do you need a specialist to help you create a podcast?

You can do it yourself if you have access to good recording equipment and if you're comfortable doing editing work on audio files. If not, it may be worth investing in the skills of a recording engineer or production company to help you create content with a professional edge that will really appeal to your customers.

MAKING IT HAPPEN

Understand what podcasting is. . .and what benefits it offers

Podcasts are audio files stored on the Internet that visitors to your site can download, store on MP3 players or computers, and then listen to at their leisure. Before the advent of podcasting, it was possible to upload audio content on your website, but it's now possible for customers who subscribe to automatically receive new content without having to go to a specific site and download from there. As soon as new content is created, the most recent podcast is immediately delivered to the subscriber via widely available software, so you won't have to worry about sending them an e-mail to download a new MP3.

Not only can podcasting boost your visibility in the marketplace so that you can attract new customers, it can also help you improve your relationship with existing clients by keeping them up to date with new developments. It's an efficient way of contacting subscribers, and also allows you to:

- talk to an international audience
- increase your marketing reach
- talk regularly to customers
- increase loyalty through value-added content, such as conference presentations

For larger organisations, it may also help to establish your company as a 'thought leader', a place that starts trends or discussions that the rest of your industry can't help but follow.

Get in touch with a highly targeted audience

Many marketing campaigns founder because they can't reach the right customers. With podcasts, however, people have to subscribe to them, which means that they already have an interest in your company and what it has to offer. Some of the barriers to purchase are already down, and you have a way of contacting a targeted, potentially high value audience.

Podcasting can also be used to talk to other groups with an interest in your business, and you can employ it to:

- keep your staff up to speed with news – for example, if your sales director has news on a big deal that's just been signed off, you can let people know this way
- talk to your sales team
- distribute content from conferences or seminars to employees who were unavailable on the day itself
- circulate training material

Create a suggestions forum

Employees are a wonderful source of ideas, and whatever the size of your business, you should take time to get them involved in developing products and services. They may be able to pass on customer feedback, or have spotted that improvements can be made in a way you've never even thought of. They will appreciate being asked to contribute to your company's future, so why not create a 'suggestions forum'? Employees can telephone a voicemail number where they can record their hot idea, and the resulting audio files can be edited to create a regular podcast which showcases the best ones. You'll be making great strides towards an innovation culture. You could use the same approach to brainstorm or discuss ideas in more detail: the content can be edited to create a 'to do' list of tasks that need to be done to get the project up and running.

Integrate customer feedback

You can add another dimension to your product or service development programmes by creating podcasts based on customer feedback. You can capture customer comments via audio interviews over the phone or in a studio. You may get more realistic feedback by offering customers digital recorders to use in their own time. You can edit the resulting comments into a programme that can shape your product development programme or customer service initiatives. As well as providing valuable feedback, the involvement can help to strengthen customer relationships and create a collaborative atmosphere.

Inform the sales team

Changes to product information, new guidelines, conference dates, and common customer queries can all be passed on to a team of reps via podcast, rather than relying on photocopied hand-outs. If it's hard to get everyone together at the same time for training or briefing sessions, you can post relevant material this way too.

Get more value from conference presentations

It can be difficult for delegates to attend all the presentations at a busy conference. There may also be people who miss the entire conference, even if they want to attend. Podcasting can help you 'fill in the gaps' and get more value from live presentations. By recording presentations and editing them to a manageable format, you can release them in a number of ways:

- single presentation
- all presentations on a particular theme
- round-up of the day's presentation
- highlights of the entire conference

You can also supplement the traditional post-event feedback forms by recording telephone interviews with delegates and editing their responses into a single podcast that can be distributed to all delegates or used as a promotional tool for future events.

Investigate 'thought leadership' content

If your staff are experts in their field, communicate that expertise to the wider world by creating podcasts that show your team discussing hot topics or offering advice on burning issues. To take this one stage further, you could host discussion groups on similar themes which employees, key partners and customers could attend. If you can, make the activity interactive by soliciting feedback or questions from attendees or other customers, which can all be fed back into the podcast.

Include audio content in press material

Integrating audio clips or longer podcasts can give your press material an added edge. For example, when your end of year results come out, rather than simply issue a press release, you could circulate comments from your top management team. Alternatively, if you have an excellent product review from a high-profile figure in your industry, include that clip. If you run an online press service, this material will be sent automatically to journalists who have subscribed.

Tell the world!

As mentioned above, one of the virtues of podcasting is that all the material is sent to people already interested in the subject; so interested, in fact, that they've taken the time to subscribe to receive this content. At some point, however, you'll want to increase that pool of sub-scribers, so you'll need to promote your podcasts effec-tively. Make sure they're flagged up prominently on your website and in any e-newsletters you send out, that you submit details to online directories (which act as search engines do for websites), and also send a press release to relevant news distribution channels.

Follow best practice

In comparison to other communications methods, pod-casting is still a newcomer, relatively speaking. It is, how-ever, already proving its worth as a valuable way of communicating to both internal *and* external customers as long as you keep the content relevant and your stan-dards high. Keep in mind the best practice guidelines below.

- Focus on your target audience's information needs and interests, not your own.
- Provide unique content to match these.
- Use the appropriate recording equipment and software for high-quality audio (use an audio engineer or specialist company to help, if your budget allows).
- Aim to grow your subscriber base by submitting your podcast to directories and search engines so that you can expand your subscriber base.

COMMON MISTAKES

Your content adds no value

Don't start to create and distribute podcasts before you're absolutely sure you know what your audience wants. Put yourself in their shoes, and think about (for example) the key issues facing your industry, current trends, peren-nial problems, and so on. Remember, you want to send them material they'll actively welcome, not consign to their 'deleted items' with a sigh.

Your product doesn't cut the mustard

Creating a good, focused podcast can strengthen your brand, boost customer satisfaction, and, as a result, improve your customer retention levels. If you get it wrong, however, you'll quickly turn people off: also you run the risk of the poor material being forwarded around their networks, which won't do your public image any favours. Don't cut corners and spend as much time as possible planning and producing podcast content so that it closely matches your customers' interests and needs.

THE BEST SOURCES OF HELP

Books:

Colligan, Paul, Mandossion, Alex and Devlin, Joe. *The Business Podcasting Handbook: Turning Podcasts Into a Force-Multiplier for Your Business.* Larstan Publishing, 2007.

Scott, D. M. *The New Rules of Marketing and PR: How to Use News Releases, Blogs, Podcasting, Viral Marketing and Online Media to Reach Buyers Directly.* Chichester: Wiley, 2007.

Website:

Podcasting News: **www.podcastingnews.com**

Calculating Asset Turnover

WHAT IT MEASURES

The amount of sales generated for every pound's worth of assets over a given period.

WHY IT IS IMPORTANT

Asset turnover measures how well a company is leverag-ing its assets to produce revenue. A well-managed manu-facturer, for example, will make its plant and equipment work hard for the business by minimising idle time for machines.

The higher the number the better – within reason. As a rule of thumb, companies with low profit margins tend to have high asset turnover; those with high profit margins have low asset turnover.

This ratio can also show how capital-intensive a business is. Some businesses, software developers, for example, can generate tremendous sales per pound of assets because their assets are modest. At the other end of the scale, electric utilities, heavy industry manufac-turers, and even cable TV companies need a huge asset base to generate sales.

Finally, asset turnover serves as a tool to keep man-agers conscious of the company's balance sheet along with its profit and loss account.

HOW IT WORKS IN PRACTICE

Asset turnover's basic formula is simply sales divided by assets:

sales revenue / total assets

Most experts recommend using average total assets in

the formula. To determine this figure, add total assets at the beginning of the year to total assets at the end of the year and divide by two.

If, for instance, annual sales totalled £4.5 million, and total assets were £1.84 million at the beginning of the year and £1.78 million at the year end, the average total assets would be £1.81 million, and the asset turnover ratio would be:

4,500,000 / 1,810,000 = 2.49

A variation of the formula is:

sales revenue / fixed assets

If average fixed assets were £900,000, then asset turnover would be:

4,500,000 / 900,000 = 5

TRICKS OF THE TRADE
- This ratio is especially useful for growth companies to gauge whether or not they are growing revenue, for example, turnover, in healthy proportion to assets.
- Asset turnover numbers are useful for comparing competitors within industries. Like most ratios, they vary from industry to industry. As with most numbers, the most meaningful comparisons are made over extended periods of time.
- Too high a ratio may suggest overtrading: too much sales revenue with too little investment. Conversely, too low a ratio may suggest undertrading and an inefficient management of resources.
- A declining ratio may be indicative of a company that overinvested in plant, equipment, or other fixed assets, or is not using existing assets effectively.

THE BEST SOURCES OF HELP
Website:
Biz/ed: **www.bized.co.uk**

Calculating Annual Percentage Rate

WHAT IT MEASURES
The annual percentage rate (APR) measures either the rate of interest that invested money earns in one year, or the cost of credit expressed as a yearly rate.

WHY IT IS IMPORTANT
It enables an investor or borrower to compare like with like. When evaluating investment alternatives, naturally it's important to know which one will pay the greatest return. By the same token, borrowers want to know which loan alternative offers the best terms. Determining the annual percentage rate provides a direct comparison.

HOW IT WORKS IN PRACTICE
To calculate the annual percentage rate (APR), apply this formula:

APR = [1 + i/m]m – 1.0

In the formula, **i** is the interest rate quoted, expressed as a decimal, and **m** is the number of compounding periods per year. For example, if a bank offers a 6 per cent interest rate, paid quarterly, the APR would be calculated this way:

APR = [1 + i/m]m – 1.0

$$= [1 + 0.06/4] \; 4 - 1.0$$

$$= [1 + 0.015] \; 4 - 1.0$$

$$= (1.015) \; 4 - 1.0$$

$$= 1.0614 - 1.0$$

$$= 0.0614$$

$$= 6.14 \text{ per cent APR}$$

TRICKS OF THE TRADE
- As a rule of thumb, the annual percentage rate is slightly higher than the quoted rate.
- When using the formula, be sure to express the rate as a decimal, that is, 6 per cent becomes 0.06.
- When expressed as the cost of credit, remember to include other costs of obtaining the credit in addition to interest, such as loan closing costs and financial fees.
- APR provides an excellent basis for comparing mortgage or other loan rates; lenders are required to disclose it.
- When used in the context of investment APR can also be called the 'annual percentage yield', or APY.

THE BEST SOURCES OF HELP
Website:
Investorguide.com: **www.investorguide.com**

Calculating Bond Yield

WHAT IT MEASURES
The annual return on this certificate (the rate of interest) expressed as a percentage of the current market price of the bond.

WHY IT IS IMPORTANT
Bonds can tie up investors' money for periods of up to 30 years, so knowing their yield is a critical investment consideration. Similarly, bond issuers need to know the price they will pay to incur their debt, so that they can compare it with the cost of other means of raising capital.

HOW IT WORKS IN PRACTICE
Bonds are issued in increments of £1,000. To calculate the yield amount, multiply the face value of the bond by its stated annual rate of interest, expressed as a decimal. For example, buying a new ten-year £1,000 bond that pays 6 percent interest will produce an annual yield amount of £60:

$$1{,}000 \times 0.060 = 60$$

The £60 will be paid as £30 every six months. At the end of ten years, the purchaser will have earned £600, and will also be repaid the original £1,000. Because the bond was purchased when it was first issued, the 6 percent is also called the 'yield to maturity'.

This basic formula is complicated by other factors. First is the 'time-value of money' theory: money paid in the future is worth less than money paid today. A more detailed computation of total bond yield requires the calculation of the present value of the interest earned each year. Second, changing interest rates have a marked impact on bond trading and, ultimately, on yield. Changes in interest rates cannot affect the interest paid by bonds already issued, but they do affect the prices of new bonds.

TRICKS OF THE TRADE
- Yield to call. Bond issuers reserve the right to 'call', or redeem, the bond before the maturity date, at certain times and at a certain price. Issuers often do this if interest rates fall and they can issue new bonds at a lower rate. Bond buyers should obtain the yield-to-call rate, which may, in fact, be a more realistic indicator of the return expected.
- Different types of bond. Some bonds are backed by assets, while others are issued on the strength of the issue's good standing. Investors should know the difference.
- Zero coupon bonds. These pay no interest at all, but are sold at a deep discount, increasing in value until maturity. A buyer might pay £3,000 for a 25-year zero bond with a face value of £10,000. This bond will simply accrue value each year, and at maturity will be worth £10,000, thus earning £7,000. These are high-risk investments, however, especially if they must be sold on the open market amid rising interest rates.
- Interest rates. Bond values fall when interest rates rise, and rise when interest rates fall, because when interest rates rise existing bonds become less valuable and less attractive.

THE BEST SOURCES OF HELP
Website:
The Motley Fool: **www.fool.co.uk**

Calculating Book Value

WHAT IT MEASURES
A company's common stock equity, as it appears on a balance sheet.

WHY IT IS IMPORTANT
Book value represents a company's net worth to its shareholders, based on the difference between assets and liabilities. Typically, book value is substantially different from market value, especially in high-tech and knowledge-based industries whose primary assets are intangible and therefore do not appear on the balance sheet.

When compared with its market value, book value helps to reveal how a company is regarded by the investment community. A market value that is notably higher than book value indicates that investors have a high regard for the company. A market value that is, for example, a multiple of book value suggests that investors' regard may be unreasonably high – as was shown in the painful plunge of dot-com companies in 2000 and 2001.

The reverse is also true, of course; indeed, it may suggest that a company's stock is a bargain.

A companion measure is book value per share. It shows the value of the company's assets that each shareholder theoretically would receive if a company were liquidated.

HOW IT WORKS IN PRACTICE
To calculate book value, subtract a company's liabilities and the value of its debt and preference shares from its

total assets. All of these figures appear on a company's balance sheet. For example:

	£
Total assets	1,300
Current liabilities	–400
Long-term liabilities, preference shares	–250
Book value	**= 650**

Book value per share is calculated by dividing the book value by the number of shares issued. If our example is expressed in millions of pounds and the company has 35 million shares outstanding, the book value per share would be £650 million divided by 35 million:

650 / 35 = £18.57 book value per share

TRICKS OF THE TRADE
- Related terms include:
- **adjusted book value** or **modified book value**, which is book

value after assets and liabilities are adjusted to market value;
- **tangible book value**, which also subtracts intangible assets, patents, trademarks, and the value of research and development.

The rationale is that these items cannot be sold outright.
- Book value can also mean the value of an individual asset as it appears on a balance sheet, in which case it is equal to the cost of the asset minus any accumulated depreciation.
- Though often considered a realistic appraisal, book value can still contain unrealistic figures. For example, a building might be fully depreciated and have no official asset value but could still be sold for millions, or four-year-old computer equipment that is not fully depreciated might have asset value but no market value, given its age and advances in technology.

THE BEST SOURCES OF HELP
Website:
Investopedia.com: **www.Investopedia.com/ dictionary**

Calculating Contribution Margin

WHAT IT MEASURES
The amounts that individual products or services ultimately contribute to net profit.

WHY IT IS IMPORTANT
Contribution margin helps a business to decide how it should direct or redirect its resources.

When managers know the contribution margin – or margins, as is more often the case – they can make better decisions about adding or subtracting product lines, investing in existing products, pricing products or services (particularly in response to competitors' actions), structuring sales commissions and bonuses, where to direct marketing and advertising expenditures, and where to apply individual talents and expertise.

In short, contribution margin is a valuable decision-support tool.

HOW IT WORKS IN PRACTICE
Its calculation is straightforward:

sales price – variable cost = contribution margin

Or, for providers of services:

total revenue – total variable cost = contribution margin

For example, if the sales price of a good is £500 and variable cost is £350, the contribution margin is £150, or 30 percent of sales.

This means that 30 pence of every sales pound remain to contribute to fixed costs and to profit, after the costs directly related to the sales are subtracted.

Contribution margin is especially useful to a company comparing different products or services. For example:

	Product A £	Product B £	Product C £
Sales	260	220	140
Variable costs	178	148	65
Contribution margin	82	72	75
Contribution margin (percent)	31.5	32.7	53.6

Obviously, Product C has the highest contribution percentage, even though Product A generates more total profit. The analysis suggests that the company might do well to aim to achieve a sales mix with a higher proportion of Product C. It further suggests that prices for Products A and B may be too low, or that ly, none of this information appears on a standard income tax return.

Contribution margin can also be tracked over a long period of time, using data from several years of income tax returns. It can also be invaluable in calculating volume discounts for preferred customers, and break-even sales or volume levels.

TRICKS OF THE TRADE
- Contribution margin depends on accurately accounting for all variable costs, including shipping and delivery, or the indirect costs of services. Activity-based cost accounting systems aid this kind of analysis.
- Variable costs include all direct costs (e.g. labour and materials).
- Contribution margin analysis is only one tool to use. It will not show so-called loss leaders, for example. And it doesn't consider marketing factors such as existing penetration levels, opportunities, or mature markets being eroded by emerging markets.

THE BEST SOURCES OF HELP
Website:
Business Owner's Toolkit: **www.toolkit.cch.com**

Calculating Conversion Price

WHAT IT MEASURES
The price per share at which the holder of convertible bonds, or debentures, or preference shares, can convert them into ordinary shares.

Depending on specific terms, the conversion price may be set when the convertible asset is issued.

WHY IT IS IMPORTANT
The conversion price is a key factor in an investment strategy. Knowing it helps investors to determine whether or not it is to their advantage to convert their holdings into shares of stock, sell them on the open market, or retain them until they mature or are called by the issuing company.

At the same time, existing shareholders of the issuing company need to know the point at which the value of their shares could be diluted by the creation of additional shares without the concurrent creation of additional capital.

For companies themselves, a conversion price represents an additional financing option: an opportunity to convert debt into equity, an action that itself has advantages and drawbacks.

HOW IT WORKS IN PRACTICE
If the conversion price is set, it will appear in the indenture, a legal agreement between the issuer of a convertible asset and the holder, that states specific terms. If the conversion price does not appear in the agreement, a conversion ratio is used to calculate the conversion price.

A conversion ratio of 25 : 1, for example, means that 25 shares of stock can be obtained in exchange for each £1,000 convertible asset held. In turn, the conversion price can be determined simply by dividing £1,000 by 25:

$$£1,000 / 25 = £40 \text{ per share}$$

Comparison of a stock's conversion price to its prevailing market price can help to decide the best course of action. If the shares of the company in question are trading at £52 per share, converting makes sense, because it increases the value of £1,000 convertible to £1,300 (£52 × 25 shares). But if the shares are trading at £32 per share, then conversion value is only £800 (£32 × 25) and it is clearly better to defer conversion.

TRICKS OF THE TRADE
- Conversion ratios may change over time, according to the terms of the agreement. This is to ensure that a convertible asset holder is not unduly advantaged and that the value of existing stock is not diluted-which, of course, would anger existing shareholders.
- Shareholders, in turn, need to monitor closely a company that decides to issue a large number of convertible assets, since the value of their shares could ultimately be undermined.
- Convertible bonds closely follow the price of the issuing company's underlying stock. Often, in fact, the respective prices of the bond and the shares to be exchanged are almost equal.

THE BEST SOURCES OF HELP
Website:
Investopedia.com: **www.Investopedia.com**

Calculating Conversion Ratio

WHAT IT MEASURES
The number of ordinary shares an investor will receive upon converting a convertible security – a bond, debenture, or preference share.
   The conversion price may be set when the convertible security is issued, depending on its terms.

WHY IT IS IMPORTANT
Like conversion price, the conversion ratio is an investment strategy tool, which is used to determine what the value of a convertible security would be if it were converted immediately. By knowing a convertible's value, an investor can compare it with the prevailing price of the issuing company's ordinary shares and decide whether it is best to convert or to continue holding the convertible.

By the same token, holders of ordinary shares in the company issuing the convertible can use the conversion ratio to help to monitor the value of their shares. For example, a relatively high ratio could mean that the value of their shares would be diluted if large numbers of convertible holders were to exercise their options in mass.

HOW IT WORKS IN PRACTICE
In the same way as conversion price, the conversion ratio may be established when the convertible is issued. If that is the case, the ratio will appear in the indenture, the binding agreement that details the convertible's terms.

If the conversion ratio is not set, it can be calculated quickly: divide the par value of the convertible security (typically £1,000) by its conversion price.

$$£1,000 \ / \ £40 \text{ per share} \ = \ 25$$

In this example, the conversion ratio is 25 : 1, which means that every bond held with a £1,000 par value can be exchanged for 25 ordinary shares.

Knowing the conversion ratio enables an investor to decide quickly whether his convertibles (or group of them) are more valuable than the ordinary shares they represent. If the stock is currently trading at 30, the conversion value is £750, or £250 less than the par value of the convertible. It would therefore be unwise to convert.

TRICKS OF THE TRADE
- Although it is rare, a convertible's indenture can sometimes contain a provision stating that the conversion ratio will change over the years.
- A conversion ratio that is set when a convertible is issued usually protects against any dilution from scrip issues. However, it does not protect against a company issuing secondary offerings of ordinary shares.
- 'Forced conversion' means that the company can make holders convert into shares at virtually any time. Convertible holders should also pay close attention to the price at which the bonds are callable.
- Conversion ratio also describes the number of ordinary shares of one type to be issued for each outstanding ordinary share of a different type when a merger takes place.

THE BEST SOURCES OF HELP
Website:
Investopedia.com: **www.Investopedia.com**

Calculating Days Sales Outstanding

WHAT IT MEASURES
A company's average collection period, or the average number of days it takes a company to convert its accounts receivable into cash. Commonly referred to as DSO, it is also called the collection ratio.

WHY IT IS IMPORTANT
Knowing how long it takes a company to turn accounts receivable into cash is an important financial indicator. It indicates the efficiency of the company's internal collection, suggests how well a company's customers are accepting its credit terms (net 30 days, for example), and

is a figure that is routinely compared with industry averages.

Ideally, DSOs should be decreasing or constant. A low figure means the company collects its outstanding receivables quickly. Typically, DSO is reviewed quarterly or yearly (91 or 365 days).

DSO also helps to expose companies that try to disguise weak sales. Large increases in DSO suggest that a company is trying to force sales either by accepting poor receivable terms or selling products at discount to book more sales for a particular period. An improving DSO suggests that a company is striving to make its operations more efficient.

Any company with a significant change in its DSO merits examination in greater detail.

HOW IT WORKS IN PRACTICE

Regular DSO requires three figures: total accounts receivable, total credit sales for the period analysed, and the number of days in the period (annual, 365; six months, 182; quarter, 91). The formula is:

accounts receivable / total credit sales for the period × number of days in the period = days sales outstanding

For example: if total receivables are £4,500,000, total credit sales in a quarter are £9,000,000, and number of days is 91, then:

4,500,000 / 9,000,000 × 91 = 45.5

Thus, it takes an average of 45.5 days to collect receivables.

TRICKS OF THE TRADE

• Companies use DSO information with an accounts receivable ageing report. This lists four categories of receivables: 0–30 days, 30–60 days, 60–90 days, and over 90 days. The report also shows the percentage of total accounts receivable that each group represents, allowing for an analysis of delinquencies and potential bad debts – a figure that appears on a profit and loss account.
• A rarely used related calculation, best possible DSO, shows how long it takes a company to collect current receivables. Its formula is:

current receivables / total credit sales for the period × the number of days in the period = best possible DSO

So, current receivables of £3,000,000 and total credit sales of £9,000,000 in a 91-day period would result in a best possible DSO of 30.3 days (3,000,000 / 9,000,000 × 91).

• Only credit sales of merchandise should be used in calculating DSO; cash sales are excluded, as are sales of such items as fixtures, equipment, or land and property.
• Properly evaluating an acceptable DSO requires a standard for comparison. A traditional rule of thumb is that DSO should not exceed a third to a half of selling terms. For instance, if terms are 30 days, acceptable DSO would be 40 to 45 days.
• A single DSO is only a snapshot. A fuller picture would require at least quarterly calculations, and some companies review DSO monthly.
• DSO can vary widely by industry as well as company. For example, clothing wholesalers have to have the goods on retailers' shelves for months before they will be sold and the retailer is able to cover invoices. However, a computer wholesaler with a lengthy DSO suggests trouble, since computers become obsolete quickly.

THE BEST SOURCES OF HELP
Website:
Dun & Bradstreet: **www.dnbcollections.com/kdso.htm**

Calculating Debt-to-Capital Ratio

WHAT IT MEASURES
The percentage of total funding represented by debt.

WHY IT IS IMPORTANT

By comparing a company's long-term liabilities to its total capital, the debt-to-capital ratio provides a review of the extent to which a company relies on external debt finance for its funding and is a measure of the risk to its shareholders.

The debt-to-capital ratio is also a measure of a company's borrowing capacity, and of its ability to pay scheduled financial payments on term debts and capital leases. Bond-rating agencies and analysts use it routinely to assess creditworthiness. The greater the debt, the higher the risk.

However, it can be misleading to assume that the lowest ratio is automatically the best ratio. A company may assume large amounts of debt in order to expand the business. Utilities, for instance, have high capital requirements, so their debt-to-capital ratios will be high as a matter of course. So are those of manufacturing companies, especially those developing a new technology or new product.

At the same time, the higher the level of debt, the more important it is for a company to have positive earnings and steady cash-flow.

HOW IT WORKS IN PRACTICE

Although there are variations on exactly what goes into this ratio, the most common method is to divide total long-term debt by total assets (total long-term debt plus shareholders' funds), or

total liabilities / total assets = debt-to-capital ratio

For example, if the balance sheet of a corporate annual report lists total liabilities of £9,800,000 and total shareholders' equity of £12,800,000, the debt-to-capital ratio is (calculating in thousands):

9,800 / (9,800 + 12,800) = 9,800 / 22,600 = 0.434, or 43.4 percent debt-to-capital ratio

Some formulas distinguish different portions of long-term debt. However, that complicates calculations and many experts regard it as unnecessary. It is also common to express the formula as total debt divided by total funds, which produces the same outcome.

TRICKS OF THE TRADE
- If a company has minority interests in subsidiaries that are consolidated in the balance sheet, they must be added to shareholders' equity.
- Debt calculations should include capital leases.
- One rule of thumb holds that a debt-to-capital ratio of 60 percent or less is acceptable, but another holds that 40 percent is the most desirable.
- A high debt-to-capital ratio means less security for shareholders, because debt holders are paid first in bankruptcies. It still can be tolerable, however, if a company's return on assets exceeds the rate of interest paid to creditors.
- Do not confuse the debt-to-capital ratio with debt-to-capitalisation, which compares debt with total market capitalisation and fluctuates as the company's stock price changes.

THE BEST SOURCES OF HELP
Website:
The Motley Fool: **www.fool.co.uk**

Calculating Debt-to-Equity Ratio

WHAT IT MEASURES
How much money a company owes compared with how much money it has invested in it by principal owners and shareholders.

WHY IT IS IMPORTANT
The debt-to-equity ratio reveals the proportion of debt and equity a company is using to finance its business. It also measures a company's borrowing capacity. The higher the ratio, the greater the proportion of debt – but also the greater the risk.

Some even describe the debt-to-equity ratio as 'a great financial test' of long-term corporate health, because debt establishes a commitment to repay money throughout a period of time, even though there is no assurance that sufficient cash will be generated to meet that commitment.

Creditors and lenders, understandably, rely heavily on the ratio to evaluate borrowers.

HOW IT WORKS IN PRACTICE
The debt-to-equity ratio is calculated by dividing debt by owners' equity, where equity is, typically, the figure stated for the preceding calendar or fiscal year. Debt, however, can be defined either as long-term debt only, or as total liabilities, which includes both long- and short-term debt.

The most common formula for the ratio is:

total liabilities / owners' equity = debt-to-equity ratio

In our example, a company's long-term debt is £8,000,000, its short-term debt is £4,000,000, and owners' equity totals £9,000,000. The debt-to-equity ratio would therefore be (calculating in thousands):

(8,000 + 4,000) / 9,000 = 12,000 / 9,000 = 1.33 debt-to-equity ratio

An alternative debt-to-equity formula considers only long-term liabilities in the equation. Accordingly:

8,000 / 9,000 = 0.889 debt-to-equity ratio

There is also a third method, which is the reciprocal of the debt-to-equity ratio; its formula is:

owners' equity / total funds = debt-to-equity ratio

However, this would be more accurately defined as 'equity-to-debt ratio'.

TRICKS OF THE TRADE
- It is important to understand exactly how debt is defined in the ratio presented.
- Like all ratios, debt-to-equity must be evaluated against those of other companies in a given industry and over a period of time.
- When calculating the ratio, some prefer to use the market value of debt and equity rather than the book value, since book value often understates current value.
- For this ratio, a low number indicates better financial stability than a high one does; if the ratio is high, a company could be at risk, especially if interest rates are rising.
- A ratio greater than one means assets are mainly financed with debt; less than one means equity provides most of the financing. Since a higher ratio generally means that a company has been aggressive in financing its growth with

debt, volatile earnings can result owing to the additional cost of interest.

- Debt-to-equity ratio is somewhat industry-specific, and often depends on the amount of capital investment required.

Calculating Creditor and Debtor Days

WHAT THEY MEASURE

Creditor days is a measure of the number of days on average that a company requires to pay its creditors, while debtor days is a measure of the number of days on average that it takes a company to receive payment for what it sells. It is also called accounts receivable days.

WHY THEY ARE IMPORTANT

Creditor days is an indication of a company's creditworthiness in the eyes of its suppliers and creditors, since it shows how long they are willing to wait for payment. Within reason, the higher the number the better, because all companies want to conserve cash. At the same time, a company that is especially slow to pay its bills (100 or more days, for example) may be a company having trouble generating cash, or one trying to finance its operations with its suppliers' funds. Ultimately, companies whose creditor days soar have trouble obtaining supplies.

Debtor days is an indication of a company's efficiency in collecting monies owed. In this case, obviously, the lower the number the better. An especially high number is a telltale sign of inefficiency or worse. It may indicate bad debts, dubious sales figures, or a company being bullied by large customers out to improve their own cash position at another company's expense. Customers whose credit terms are abused also risk higher borrowing costs and related charges.

Changes in both measures are easy to spot, and easy to understand.

HOW THEY WORK IN PRACTICE

To determine creditor days, divide the cumulative amount of unpaid suppliers' bills (also called trade creditors) by sales, then multiply by 365. So the formula is:

$$(\text{trade creditors} / \text{sales}) \times 365 = \text{creditor days}$$

For example, if suppliers' bills total £800,000 and sales are £9,000,000, the calculation is:

$$(800,000 / 9,000,000) \times 365 = 32.44 \text{ days}$$

The company takes 32.44 days on average to pay its bills.

To determine debtor days, divide the cumulative amount of accounts receivable by sales, then multiply by 365. For example, if accounts receivable total £600,000 and sales are £9,000,000, the calculation is:

$$(600,000 / 9,000,000) \times 365 = 24.33 \text{ days}$$

The company takes 24.33 days on average to collect its debts.

TRICKS OF THE TRADE

- Cash businesses, including most retailers, should have a much lower debtor days figure than non-cash businesses, since they receive payment when they sell the goods. A typical target for non-cash businesses is 40–50 days.
- An abnormally high creditor days figure may not only suggest a cash crisis, but also the management's difficulty in maintaining revolving credit agreements.
- An increasing number of debtor days also suggests overly generous credit terms (to bolster sales) or problems with product quality.

Calculating Payback Period

WHAT IT MEASURES
How long it will take to earn back the money invested in a project.

WHY IT IS IMPORTANT
The straight payback period method is the simplest way of determining the investment potential of a major project. Expressed in time, it tells a management how many months or years it will take to recover the original cash cost of the project – always a vital consideration, and especially so for managements evaluating several projects at once.

This evaluation becomes even more important if it includes an examination of what the present value of future revenues will be.

HOW IT WORKS IN PRACTICE
The straight payback period formula is:

cost of project / annual cash revenues = payback period

Thus, if a project cost £100,000 and was expected to generate £28,000 annually, the payback period would be:

100,000 / 28,000 = 3.57 years

If the revenues generated by the project are expected to vary from year to year, add the revenues expected for each succeeding year until you arrive at the total cost of the project.

For example, say the revenues expected to be generated by the £100,000 project are:

	Revenue	Total
Year 1	£19,000	£19,000
Year 2	£25,000	£44,000
Year 3	£30,000	£74,000
Year 4	£30,000	£104,000
Year 5	£30,000	£134,000

Thus, the project would be fully paid for in Year 4, since it is in that year the total revenue reaches the initial cost of £100,000.

The picture becomes complex when the time-value-of-money principle is introduced into the calculations. Some experts insist this is essential to determine the most accurate payback period. Accordingly, present-value tables or computers (now the norm) must be used, and the annual revenues have to be discounted by the applicable interest rate, 10 percent in this example. Doing so produces significantly different results:

	Revenue	Present value	Total
Year 1	£19,000	£17,271	£17,271
Year 2	£25,000	£20,650	£37,921
Year 3	£30,000	£22,530	£60,451
Year 4	£30,000	£20,490	£80,941
Year 5	£30,000	£18,630	£99,571

This method shows that payback would not occur even after five years.

TRICKS OF THE TRADE
- Clearly, a main defect of the straight payback period method is that it ignores the time-value-of-money principle, which, in turn, can produce unrealistic expectations.
- A second drawback is that it ignores any benefits generated after the payback period, and thus a project that would return £1 million after, say, six years, might be ranked lower than a project with a three-year payback that returns only £100,000 thereafter.
- Another alternative to calculating by payback period is to develop an internal rate of return.
- Under most analyses, projects with shorter payback periods rank higher than those with longer paybacks, even if the latter project higher returns. Longer paybacks can be affected by such factors as market changes, changes in interest rates, and economic shifts. Shorter cash paybacks also enable companies to recoup an investment sooner and put it to work elsewhere.
- Generally, a payback period of three years or less is desirable; if a project's payback period is less than a year, some contend it should be judged essential.

THE BEST SOURCES OF HELP
Website:
Business Owner's Toolkit: **www.toolkit.cch.com**

Calculating Efficiency and Operating Ratios

WHAT IT MEASURES
The portion of operating revenues spent on overhead expenses.

WHY IT IS IMPORTANT
Often identified with banking and financial sectors, the efficiency ratio indicates a management's ability to keep overhead costs low. This measurement is also used by mature industries, such as steel manufacture, chemicals, or car production, that must focus on tight cost controls to boost profitability because growth prospects are generally modest.

In some industries, the efficiency ratio is called the overheads burden: overheads as a percentage of sales.

A different method measures efficiency simply by tracking three other measures: accounts payable to sales, days sales outstanding, and stock turnover, which indicates how fast a company is able to move its merchandise. A general guide is that if the first two of these measures are low and third is high, efficiency is probably high; the reverse is likewise true.

HOW IT WORKS IN PRACTICE
The efficiency ratio is defined as operating overhead expenses divided by turnover. If operating expenses are £100,000, and turnover is £230,000, then:

100,000 / 230,000 = 0.43 efficiency ratio

However, not everyone calculates the ratio in the same way. Some institutions include all non-interest expenses, while others exclude certain charges and intangible asset amortisation.

To find the stock turnover ratio, divide total sales by total stock. If net sales are £300,000 and stock is £140,000, then:

300,000 / 140,000 = 2.14 stock turnover ratio

To find the accounts payable to sales ratio, divide a company's accounts payable by its annual net sales. A high ratio suggests that a company is using its suppliers' funds as a source of cheap financing because it is not operating efficiently enough to generate its own funds. If accounts payable are £42,000 and total sales are £300,000, then:

42,000 / 300,000 = 0.14 × 100 = 14 percent accounts payable to sales ratio

TRICKS OF THE TRADE
- Identifying 'overheads' to calculate the efficiency ratio can itself contribute to overall inefficiency. Some financial experts contend that efficiency can be measured equally well by reviewing earnings per share growth and return on equity.
- Some banks identify amortisation of goodwill expense, and pull it out of their non-interest expense in order to calculate what is called the cash efficiency ratio: non-interest expense minus goodwill amortisation expense divided into revenue.
- In banking, an acceptable efficiency ratio was once in the low 60s. Now the goal is 50, while better-performing banks boast ratios in the mid 40s. Low ratings usually indicate a higher return on equity and earnings.

THE BEST SOURCES OF HELP
Website:
Motley Fool: **www.fool.co.uk**

Calculating Expected Rate of Return

WHAT IT MEASURES
The projected percentage return on an investment, based on the weighted probability of all possible rates of return.

WHY IT IS IMPORTANT
No self-respecting businessperson or organisation should make an investment without first having some understanding of how successful that investment is likely to be.

Expected rate of return provides such an understanding, within certain limits.

HOW IT WORKS IN PRACTICE
The formula for expected rate of return is:

$$Er\Sigma_s P(s)r_s$$

where $E[r]$ is the expected return, $P(s)$ is the probability that the rate r_s occurs, and r_s is the return at s level.

A simple example, as given below, is far easier to grasp, and adequately illustrates the principle which the formula expresses. It will also probably be of more practical use to most of those who need to calculate ERR.

The current price of ABC Ltd stock is £10. At the end of the year, ABC shares are projected to be traded:

- 25 percent higher if economic growth exceeds expectations – a probability of 30 percent
- 12 percent higher if economic growth equals expectations – a probability of 50 percent
- 5 percent lower if economic growth falls short of expectations – a probability of 20 percent

To find the expected rate of return, simply multiply the percentages by their respective probabilities and add the results:

(30 percent × 25 percent) + (50 percent × 12 percent) + (25 percent × –5 percent) = 7.5 + 6 + –1.25 = 12.25 percent ERR

A second example:
- if economic growth remains robust (a 20 percent probability), investments will return 25 percent
- if economic growth ebbs, but still performs adequately (a 40 percent probability), investments will return 15 percent
- if economic growth slows significantly (a 30 percent probability), investments will return 5 percent
- if the economy declines outright (a 10 percent probability), investments will return 0 percent

Therefore:

(20 percent × 25 percent) + (40 percent × 15 percent) + (30 percent × 5 percent) + (10 percent × 0 percent) =

5 percent + 6 percent + 1.5 percent + 0 percent = 12.5 percent ERR

Another method that can be used to project expected return is the Capital Asset Pricing Model (CAPM), which is explained separately.

TRICKS OF THE TRADE
- The probability totals must always equal 100 percent for the calculation to be valid.
- Be sure not to overlook any negative numbers in the calculations, or the results produced will be incorrect and of no use.
- An ERR calculation is only as good as the scenarios considered. Wildly unrealistic scenarios will produce an equally unreliable expected rate of return.

THE BEST SOURCES OF HELP
Website:
Investopedia.com **www.Investopedia.com**

Calculating Future Value

WHAT IT MEASURES
The potential value of a sum of money in the future, given certain parameters.

WHY IT IS IMPORTANT
Future value is a fundamental of investment. Understanding it will help any organisation or individual to determine how a sum will be affected by changes in inflation, interest rates, or currency values. Inflation, for instance, will always reduce a sum's value. Interest rates will always increase it. Exchanging the sum for an identical amount in another currency will increase or decrease it, depending on how the respective currencies perform on the world market.

Armed with this knowledge, an organisation can make more informed decisions about how to generate the maximum value from its funds in a given period of time: would it be best to deposit them in simple interest-bearing accounts, exchange them for funds in another currency, use them to expand operations, or use them to acquire another company?

HOW IT WORKS IN PRACTICE
Start with three figures: the sum in question, the percentage by which it will increase or decrease, and the period of time. In this case: £1,000, 11 percent, and two years.

At an interest rate of 11 percent, our £1,000 will grow to £1,232 in two years:

£1,000 × 1.11 = £1,110 (first year) **× 1.11 = £1,232** (second year, rounded to whole pounds)

Note that the interest earned in the first year generates additional interest in the second year, a practice known as compounding. When large sums are in question, the effect of compounding can be significant.

At an inflation rate of 11 percent, by comparison, our £1,000 will shrink to £812 in two years:

£1,000 / 1.11 = £901 (first year) **/ 1.11 = £812** (second year, rounded to whole pounds)

TRICKS OF THE TRADE
- Express the percentage as 1.11 and multiply and divide by that figure, instead of using 11 percent. Otherwise, errors will occur.

- Calculate each year, quarter, or month separately, as our example illustrates.
- It is important always to use the **annual** rates of interest and inflation.
- A more useful tool is 'present value', which estimates what future value cash flows would be worth if they occurred today.

THE BEST SOURCES OF HELP
Websites:
Investopedia.com: **www.investopedia.com**
The Motley Fool: **www.fool.co.uk**

Calculating Internal Rate of Return

WHAT IT MEASURES
Technically, the interest rate that makes the present value of an investment's projected cash-flows equal to the cost of the project; practically speaking, the rate that indicates whether or not an investment is worth pursuing.

WHY IT IS IMPORTANT
The calculation of internal rate of return (IRR) is used to appraise the prospective viability of investments and capital projects.

Essentially, IRR allows an investor to find the interest rate that is equivalent to the monetary returns expected from the project. Once that rate is determined, it can be compared to the rates that could be earned by investing the money elsewhere, or to the weighted cost of capital. IRR also accounts for the time value of money.

HOW IT WORKS IN PRACTICE
How is IRR applied? Assume, for example, that a project under consideration costs £7,500 and is expected to return £2,000 per year for five years, or £10,000. The IRR calculated for the project would be about 10 percent. If the cost of borrowing money for the project, or the return on investing the funds elsewhere, is less than 10 percent, the project is probably worthwhile. If the alternative use of the money will return 10 percent or more, the project should be rejected, since from a financial perspective it will break even at best.

Typically, managements require an IRR equal to or higher than the cost of capital, depending on relative risk and other factors.

The best way to compute an IRR is by using a spreadsheet (such as Excel) or financial calculator, which do it automatically, although it is crucial to understand how the calculation should be structured. Calculating IRR by hand is tedious and time-consuming, and requires the process to be repeated to run sensitivities.

If using Excel, for example, select the IRR function. This requires the annual cash-flows to be set out in columns and the first part of the IRR formula requires the cell reference range of these cash-flows to be entered. Then a guess of the IRR is required. The default is 10 percent, written 0.1.

If a project has the following expected cash-flows, then guessing IRR at 30 percent returns an accurate IRR of 27 percent, indicating that if the next best way of investing the money gives a return of –20 percent, the project should go ahead.

Now	-2,500
Year 1	1,200
Year 2	1,300
Year 3	1,500

TRICKS OF THE TRADE
- IRR analysis is generally used to evaluate a project's cash-flows rather than income, because, unlike income, cash-flows do not reflect depreciation and therefore are usually more instructive to appraise.
- Most basic spreadsheet functions apply to cash-flows only.
- As well as advocates, IRR has critics who dismiss it as misleading, especially as significant costs will occur late in the project. The rule of thumb 'the higher the IRR the better' does not always apply.
- For the most thorough analysis of a project's investment potential, some experts urge using both IRR and net present value calculations, and comparing their results.

THE BEST SOURCES OF HELP
Website:
**http://hadm.sph.sc.edu/COURSES/ECON/irr/irr.
html** is a thorough and well-written tutorial on IRR.

Calculating Marginal Cost

WHAT IT MEASURES
The additional cost of producing one more unit of product, or providing a service to one more customer.

WHY IT IS IMPORTANT

Sometimes called incremental cost, marginal cost shows how much costs increase from making or serving one more, an essential factor when contemplating a production increase, or seeking to serve more customers.

If the price charged is greater than the marginal cost, then the revenue gain will be greater than the added cost. That, in turn, will increase profit, so the expansion in production or service makes economic sense and should proceed. Of course, the reverse is also true: if the price charged is less than the marginal cost, expansion should not go ahead.

HOW IT WORKS IN PRACTICE

The formula for marginal cost is:

change in cost / change in quantity

If it costs a company £260,000 to produce 3,000 items, and £325,000 to produce 3,800 items, the change in cost would be:

£325,000 – £260,000 = £65,000

The change in quantity would be:

3,800 – 3,000 = 800

When the formula to calculate marginal cost is applied, the result is:

£65,000 / 800 = £81.25

If the price of the item in question were £99.95, expansion should proceed.

TRICKS OF THE TRADE

- A marginal cost that is lower than the price shows that it is not always necessary to cut prices to sell more goods and boost profits.
- Using idle capacity to produce lower-margin items can still be beneficial, because these generate revenues that help cover fixed costs.
- Marginal cost studies can become quite complicated, because the basic formula does not always take into account variables that can affect cost and quantity. There are software programs available, many of which are industry-specific.
- At some point, marginal cost invariably begins to rise; typically, labour becomes less productive as a production run increases, while the time required also increases.
- Marginal cost alone may not justify expansion. It is best to determine also average costs, then chart the respective series of figures to find where marginal cost meets average cost, and thus determine optimum cost.
- Relying on marginal cost is not fail-safe; putting more product on a market can drive down prices and thus cut margins. Moreover, committing idle capacity to long-term production may tie up resources that could be directed to a new and more profitable opportunity.
- An important related principle is contribution: the cash gained (or lost) from selling an additional unit.

Calculating Net Present Value

WHAT IT MEASURES
The projected profitability of an investment, based on anticipated cash flows and discounted at a stated rate of interest.

WHY IT IS IMPORTANT

Net present value (NPV) helps managements or potential investors weigh the wisdom of an investment – in new equipment, a new facility, or other type of asset – by enabling them to quantify the expected benefits. Those evaluating more than one potential investment can compare the respective projected returns to find the most attractive project.

A positive NPV indicates that the project should be profitable, assuming that the estimated cash flows are reasonably accurate. A negative NPV, of course, indicates that the project will probably be unprofitable and therefore should be adjusted, if not abandoned altogether.

Equally significantly, NPV enables a management to consider the time-value of money it will invest. This concept holds that the value of money increases with time because it can always earn interest in a savings account.

Therefore, any other investment of that money must be weighed against how the funds would perform if simply deposited and saved.

When the time-value-of-money concept is incorporated in the calculation of NPV, the value of a project's future net cash receipts in 'today's money' can be determined. This enables proper comparisons between different projects.

HOW IT WORKS IN PRACTICE

Let's say that Global Manufacturing Ltd is considering the acquisition of a new machine. First, its management would consider all the factors: initial purchase and installation costs; additional revenues generated by sales of the new machine's products, plus the taxes on these new revenues. Having accounted for these factors in its calculations, the cash-flows that Global Manufacturing projects will generate from the new machine are:

Year 1:	–100,000 (initial cost of investment)
Year 2:	30,000
Year 3:	40,000
Year 4:	40,000
Year 5:	35,000
Net Total:	145,000

At first glance, it appears that cash-flows total a whopping 45 percent more than the £100,000 initial cost, a strikingly sound investment indeed.

Alas, it's not that simple. Time-value of money shrinks return on the project considerably, since future pounds are worth less than present pounds in hand. NPV accounts for these differences with the help of present-value tables. These user-friendly tables, readily available on the Internet and in references, list the ratios that express the present value of expected cash-flow pounds, based on the applicable interest rate and the number of years in question.

In our example, Global Manufacturing's cost of capital is 9 percent. Using this figure to find the corresponding ratios on the present value table, the £100,000 investment cost, expected annual revenues during the five years in question, the NPV calculation looks like this: NPV is still positive. So, on this basis at least, the investment should proceed.

Year	Cash-flow	Table factor (at 9 percent)	Present value
1	(£100,000) ×	1.000000 =	(£100,000)
2	£ 30,000 ×	0.917431 =	£27,522.93
3	£ 40,000 ×	0.841680 =	£33,667.20
4	£ 40,000 ×	0.772183 =	£30,887.32
5	£ 35,000 ×	0.708425 =	£24,794.88
		NPV =	£16,873.33

TRICKS OF THE TRADE
- Beware of assumptions. Interest rates change, of course, which can affect NPV dramatically. Moreover, fresh revenues (as well as new markets) may not grow as projected. If the cash-flows in years 2–5 of our example fall by £5,000 a year, for instance, NPV shrinks to £5,260.89, which is still positive but less attractive.
- NPV calculations are performed only with cash receipts payments and discounting factors. In turn, NPV is a tool, not *the* tool. It ignores other accounting data, intangibles, sheer faith in a new idea, and other factors that may make an investment worth pursuing despite a negative NPV.
- It is important to determine a company's cost of capital accurately.

THE BEST SOURCES OF HELP
Website:
Business Owner's Toolkit: **www.toolkit.cch.com**

Calculating Rate of Return

WHAT IT MEASURES
The annual return on an investment, expressed as a percentage of the total amount invested. It also measures the yield of a fixed-income security.

WHY IT IS IMPORTANT
Rate of return is a simple and straightforward way to determine how much investors are being paid for the use of their money, so that they can then compare various investments and select the best – based, of course, on individual goals and acceptable levels of risk.

Rate of return has a second and equally vital purpose: as a common denominator that measures a company's financial performance, for example in terms of rate of return on assets, equity, or sales.

HOW IT WORKS IN PRACTICE
There is a basic formula that will serve most needs, at least initially:

[(current value of amount invested – original value of amount invested) / original value of amount invested] × 100 percent = rate of return

If £1,000 in capital is invested in stock, and one year later the investment yields £1,100, the rate of return of the investment is calculated like this:

[(1100 – 1000) / 1000)] × 100 percent = 100 / 1000 × 100 percent = 10 percent rate of return

Now, assume £1,000 is invested again. One year later, the investment grows to £2,000 in value, but after another year the value of the investment falls to £1,200. The rate of return after the first year is:

[(2000 – 1000) / 1000] × 100 percent = 100 percent

The rate of return after the second year is:

[(1200 – 2000) / 2000) × 100 percent = –40 percent

The average annual return for the two years (also known as average annual arithmetic return) can be calculated using this formula:

(rate of return for Year 1 + rate of return for Year 2) / 2 = average annual return

Accordingly:

(100 percent + –40 percent) / 2 = 30 percent

Be careful, however! The average annual rate of return is a percentage, but one that is accurate over only a short period, so this method should be used accordingly.

The geometric or compound rate of return is a better yardstick for measuring investments over the long run, and takes into account the effects of compounding. As one might expect, this formula is more complex and technical, and beyond the scope of this article.

TRICKS OF THE TRADE

- The real rate of return is the annual return realised on an investment, adjusted for changes in the price due to inflation. If 10 percent is earned on an investment but inflation is 2 percent, then the real rate of return is actually 8 percent.
- Do not confuse rate of return with internal rate of return, which is a more complex calculation.
- Some unit trust managers have been known to report the average annual rate of return on the investments they manage. In the second example, that figure is 30 percent, yet the value of the investment is only £200 higher than it was two years ago, or 20 percent. So, read such reports carefully.

THE BEST SOURCES OF HELP
Website:
CNNMoney.com calculator: **http://cgi.money. cnn.com/tools/returnrate/returnrate.jsp**

Calculating Return on Sales

WHAT IT MEASURES
A company's operating profit or loss as a percentage of total sales for a given period, typically a year.

WHY IT IS IMPORTANT
Return on sales (ROS) shows how efficiently management uses the sales pound, thus reflecting its ability to manage costs and overheads and operate efficiently. It also indicates a company's ability to withstand adverse conditions such as falling prices, rising costs, or declining sales. The higher the figure, the better a company is able to endure price wars and falling prices.

Return on sales can be useful in assessing the annual performances of cyclical companies that may have no earnings during particular months, and of companies whose business requires a huge capital investment and thus incurs substantial amounts of depreciation.

HOW IT WORKS IN PRACTICE
The calculation is very basic:

operating profit / total sales × 100 = percentage return on sales

So, if a company earns £30 on sales of £400, its return on sales is:

30 / 400 = 0.075 × 100 = 7.5 percent

TRICKS OF THE TRADE

- While easy to grasp as a concept, return on sales has its limits, since it sheds no light on the overall cost of sales or the four factors that contribute to it: materials, labour, production overheads, and administrative and selling overheads.
- Some calculations use operating profit before subtracting interest and taxes; others use after-tax income. Either figure is acceptable as long as ROS comparisons are consistent. Obviously, using income before interest and taxes will produce a higher ratio.
- The ratio's operating profit figure may also include special allowances and extraordinary non-recurring items, which, in turn, can inflate the percentage and be misleading.

- The ratio varies widely by industry. The supermarket business, for example, is heavily dependent on volume and usually has a low return on sales.
- Return on sales remains of special importance to retail sales organisations, which can compare their respective ratios with those of competitors and industry norms.

THE BEST SOURCES OF HELP
Website:
Investopedia.com: **www.Investopedia.com**

Calculating Return on Assets

WHAT IT MEASURES
A company's profitability, expressed as a percentage of its total assets.

WHY IT IS IMPORTANT
Return on assets measures how effectively a company has used the total assets at its disposal to generate earnings. Because the ROA formula reflects total revenue, total cost, and assets deployed, the ratio itself reflects a management's ability to generate income during the course of a given period, usually a year.

Naturally, the higher the return the better the profit performance. ROA is a convenient way of comparing a company's performance with that of its competitors, although the items on which the comparison is based may not always be identical.

HOW IT WORKS IN PRACTICE
To calculate ROA, divide a company's net income by its total assets, then multiply by 100 to express the figure as a percentage:

net income / total assets × 100 = ROA

If net income is £30, and total assets are £420, the ROA is:

30 / 420 = 0.0714 × 100 = 7.14 percent

A variation of this formula can be used to calculate return on net assets (RONA):

net income / fixed assets + working capital = RONA

And, on occasion, the formula will separate after-tax interest expense from net income:

net income + interest expense / total assets = ROA

It is therefore important to understand what each component of the formula actually represents.

TRICKS OF THE TRADE
- Some experts recommend using the net income value at the end of the given period, and the assets value from beginning of the period or an average value taken over the complete period, rather than an end-of-the-period value; otherwise, the calculation will include assets that have accumulated during the year, which can be misleading.
- While a high ratio indicates a greater return, it must still be balanced against such factors as risk, sustainability, and reinvestment in the business through development costs. Some managements will sacrifice the long-term interests of investors in order to achieve an impressive ROA in the short term.
- A climbing return on assets usually indicates a climbing stock price, because it tells investors that a management is skilled at generating profits from the various resources that a business owns.
- Acceptable ROAs vary by sector. In banking, for example, a ROA of 1 percent or better is a considered to be the standard benchmark of superior performance.
- ROA is an effective way of measuring the efficiency of manufacturers, but can be suspect when measuring service companies, or other companies whose primary assets are people.
- Other variations of the ROA formula do exist.

THE BEST SOURCES OF HELP
Website:
MSN Money: **http://moneycentral.msn.com/ investor/home.asp**

Calculating Return on Investment

WHAT IT MEASURES
In the financial realm, the overall profit or loss on an investment expressed as a percentage of the total amount invested or total funds appearing on a company's balance sheet.

WHY IT IS IMPORTANT
Like return on assets or return on equity, return on investment (ROI) measures a company's profitability and its management's ability to generate profits from the funds investors have placed at its disposal.

One opinion holds that if a company's operations cannot generate net earnings at a rate that exceeds the cost of borrowing funds from financial markets, the future of that company is grim.

HOW IT WORKS IN PRACTICE
The most basic expression of ROI can be found by dividing a company's net profit (also called net earnings) by the total investment (total debt plus total equity), then multiplying by 100 to arrive at a percentage:

net profit / total investment × 100 = ROI

If, say, net profit is £30 and total investment is £250, the ROI is:

30 / 250 = 0.12 × 100 = 12 percent

A more complex variation of ROI is an equation known as the Du Pont formula:

(net profit after taxes / total assets) = (net profit after taxes / sales) × sales / total assets

If, for example, net profit after taxes is £30, total assets are £250, and sales are £500, then:

30 / 250 = 30 / 500 × 500 / 250 = 12 percent = 6 percent × 2 = 12 percent

Champions of this formula, which was developed by the Du Pont Company in the 1920s, say that it helps to reveal how a company has both deployed its assets and controlled its costs, and how it can achieve the same percentage return in different ways.

For shareholders, the variation of the basic ROI formula used by investors is:

net income + (current value – original value) / original value × 100 = ROI

If, for example, somebody invests £5,000 in a company and a year later has earned £100 in dividends, while the value of the shares is £5,200, the return on investment would be:

100 + (5,200 – 5,000) / 5,000 × 100 = (100 + 200) / 5,000 × 100 = 300 / 5,000 = 0.06 × 100 = 6 percent ROI

TRICKS OF THE TRADE
- Securities investors can use yet another ROI formula: net income divided by shares and preference share equity plus long-term debt.
- It is vital to understand exactly what a return on investment measures, for example assets, equity, or sales. Without this understanding, comparisons may be misleading or suspect. A search for 'return on investment' on the Web, for example, harvests everything from staff training to e-commerce to advertising and promotions!
- Be sure to establish whether the net profit figure used is before or after provision for taxes. This is important for making ROI comparisons accurate.

THE BEST SOURCES OF HELP
Websites:
Investopedia.com:
 www.Investopedia.com
The Motley Fool:
 www.fool.co.uk

Calculating Working Capital Productivity

WHAT IT MEASURES
How effectively a company's management is using its working capital.

WHY IT IS IMPORTANT
It is obvious that capital not being put to work properly is being wasted, which is certainly not in investors' best interests.

As an expression of how effectively a company spends

its available funds compared with sales or turnover, the working capital productivity figure helps to establish a clear relationship between its financial performance and process improvement. The relationship is said to have been first observed by the US management consultant George Stalk while working in Japan.

A seldom used reciprocal calculation, the working capital turnover or working capital to sales ratio, expresses the same relationship in a different way.

HOW IT WORKS IN PRACTICE

To calculate working capital productivity, first subtract current liabilities from current assets, which is the formula for working capital, then divide this figure into sales for the period.

sales / (current assets – current liabilities) = working capital productivity

If sales are £3,250, current assets are £900, and current liabilities are £650, then:

3250 / (900 – 650) = 3250 / 250 = 13

In this case, the higher the number the better. Sales growing faster than the resources that are required to generate them is a clear sign of efficiency and, by definition, productivity.

The working capital to sales ratio uses the same figures, but in reverse:

working capital / sales × 100 percent = working capital to sales ratio

Using the same figures in the example above, this ratio would be calculated:

250 / 3250 = 0.077 × 100 percent = 7.7 percent

For this ratio, obviously, the lower the number the better.

TRICKS OF THE TRADE

- By itself, a single ratio means little; a series of them, several quarters' worth, for example, indicates a trend, and means a great deal.
- Some experts recommend doing quarterly calculations and averaging them for a given year to arrive at the most reliable number.
- Either ratio also helps a management compare its performance with that of competitors.
- These ratios should also help to motivate companies to improve processes, such as eliminating steps in the handling of materials and bill collection, and shortening product design times. Such improvements reduce costs and make working capital available for other tasks.

THE BEST SOURCES OF HELP
Website:
The Motley Fool: **www.fool.co.uk**

Calculating Economic Value Added

WHAT IT MEASURES
A company's financial performance, specifically whether it is earning more or less than the total cost of the capital supporting it.

WHY IT IS IMPORTANT
Economic Value Added (EVA) measures true economic profit, or the amount by which the earnings of a project, an operation, or a company exceed (or fall short of) the total amount of capital that was originally invested by the company's owners.

If a company is earning more, it is adding value, and that is good. If it is earning less the company is in fact devouring value, and that is bad, because the company's owners (shareholders, for example) would be better off investing their capital elsewhere.

The concept's champions declare that EVA forces managers to focus on true wealth creation and maximising shareholder investment. By definition, then, increasing EVA will increase a company's market value.

HOW IT WORKS IN PRACTICE
EVA is conceptually simple and easy to explain: from net operating profit, subtract an appropriate charge for the opportunity cost of all capital invested in an enterprise – the amount that could have been invested elsewhere. It is calculated using this formula:

net operating profit less applicable taxes – cost of capital = EVA

If a company is considering building a new plant, and its total weighted cost over ten years is £80 million, while the expected annual incremental return on the new operation is £10 million, or £100 million over ten years, then the plant's EVA would be positive, in this case £20 million:

£100 million – £80 million = £20 million

An alternative but more complex formula for EVA is:

(percent return on invested capital – percent cost of capital) × original capital invested = EVA

TRICKS OF THE TRADE

- EVA is a measure of pound surplus value, not the percentage difference in returns.
- Purists define EVA as 'profit the way shareholders define it'. They further contend that if shareholders expect a 10 percent return on their investment, they 'make money' only when their share of after-tax operating profits exceeds 10 percent of equity capital.

- An objective of EVA is to determine which business units best utilise their assets to generate returns and maximise shareholder value; it can be used to assess a company, a business unit, a single plant, office, or even an assembly line. This same technique is equally helpful in evaluating new business opportunities.

THE BEST SOURCES OF HELP
Website:
Stern Stewart & Co: **www.sternstewart.com**

Calculating Risk-adjusted Rate of Return

WHAT IT MEASURES
How much an investment returned in relation to the risk that was assumed to attain it.

WHY IT IS IMPORTANT
Being able to compare a high-risk, potentially high-return investment with a low-risk, lower-return investment helps to answer a key question that confronts every investor: is it worth the risk?

By itself, the historical average return of an investment, asset, or portfolio can be quite misleading and a faulty indicator of future performance. Risk-adjusted return is a much better barometer.

The calculation also helps to reveal whether the returns of the portfolio reflect smart investment decisions, or the assumptions of excess risk that may or may not have been worth what was gained. This is particularly helpful in appraising the performance of money managers.

HOW IT WORKS IN PRACTICE
There are several ways to calculate risk-adjusted return. Each has its strengths and shortcomings. All require particular data, such as an investment's rate of return, the risk-free return rate for a given period, and a market's performance and its standard deviation.

Which one to use? It often depends on an investor's focus, principally whether the focus is on upside gains or downside losses.

Perhaps the most widely used is the **Sharpe ratio**. This measures the potential impact of return volatility on expected return and the amount of return earned per unit of risk. The higher a fund's Sharpe ratio, the better its historical risk-adjusted performance, and the higher the number the greater the return per unit of risk. The formula is:

(portfolio return – risk-free return) / std deviation of portfolio return = Sharpe ratio

Take, for example, two investments, one returning 54 percent, the other 26 percent. At first glance, the higher figure clearly looks like the better choice, but because of its high volatility it has a Sharpe ratio of 0.279, while the investment with a lower return has a ratio of 0.910. On a risk-adjusted basis the latter would be the wiser choice.

Meanwhile, the **Treynor ratio** also measures the excess of return per unit of risk. Its formula is:

(portfolio return – risk-free return) / portfolio's beta = Treynor ratio

In this formula (and others that follow), beta is a separately calculated figure that describes the tendency of an investment to respond to marketplace swings. The higher beta, the greater the volatility, and vice versa.

A third formula, **Jensen's measure**, is often used to rate a money manager's performance against a market index, and whether or not a investment's risk was worth its reward. The formula is:

(portfolio return – risk-free return) – portfolio beta × (benchmark return – risk-free return) = Jensen's measure

TRICKS OF THE TRADE

- A fourth formula, the **Sortino ratio**, also exists. Its focus is more on downside risk than potential opportunity, and its calculation is more complex.
- There are no benchmarks for these values. In order to be useful the numbers should be compared with the ratios of other investments.
- No single measure is perfect, so experts recommend using them broadly. For instance, if a particular investment class is on a roll and does not experience a great deal of volatility, a return per unit of risk does not necessarily reflect management

Actionlists

genius. When the overall momentum of technology stocks drove returns straight up in 1999, Sharpe ratios climbed with them, and did not reflect any of the sector's volatility that was to erupt in late 2000.

- Most of these measures can be used to rank the risk-adjusted performance of individual stocks, various portfolios over the same time, and unit trusts with similar objectives.

THE BEST SOURCES OF HELP
Websites:
Bizterms.net: **www.bizterms.net/term/**
 Risk-adjusted-return-on-capital-RAROC.html
Investopedia: **www.investopedia.com**

Calculating Exchange Rate Risk

WHAT IT MEASURES
The risk of a gain or loss in the value of a business activity or investment that results from changes in the exchange rates of world currencies.

WHY IT IS IMPORTANT
Each business day seems to bring more international business transactions, generated by an ever-growing number of enterprises from an ever-increasing number of countries. Enterprises in developing nations, especially, are vying for their share of world commerce.

However, the economies of these developing nations can be especially fragile, while economies of mature nations periodically wobble and go into recession. Asia, Latin America, and Eastern Europe have all endured economic turmoil in the past decade, while such regions as the Middle East have been volatile for several decades, principally because of the wide swings in oil prices.

Currency exchange rates can be just as volatile and this clearly poses risks to any enterprise conducting business in foreign markets, and any investor holding either stock in a foreign-based company, or an interest in a unit trust that invests in foreign companies. The effects on a company's earnings, cash-flow, and balance sheet can be significant.

The main exchange rate risk to an operation or investment is that any profits realised will be partially reduced – or wiped out altogether – when they are exchanged for the domestic currency, be it US dollars, pounds sterling, the euro, or Japanese yen.

More often, exchange rate risk will affect a company's price competitiveness in a product or service also offered by a competitor whose costs are incurred in a foreign currency. If the competitor's currency weakens, its relative competitive position improves because its costs decline, enabling the competitor to reduce its price and attract a larger share of a market.

HOW IT WORKS IN PRACTICE
There is a simple way to avoid the risk posed by exchange rates: don't do business abroad! For large companies, as well as an increasing number of small- and medium-sized companies, that would be like sticking one's head in the sand.

A second defence against exchange rate risks is almost as unrealistic: conduct all business in your home currency. Requiring foreign customers to pay up only in, say, pounds sterling, puts the burden of currency fluctuations squarely on the customer's shoulders and completely insulates the selling company from any shrinkage of profits from exchange rate differences. The price for such insulation, however, is likely to be a steady loss of customers.

The practical course of action, then, is to gain a basic understanding of exchange rate risks, if only enough to sort out the reams of opinions on the subject, and to select knowledgeable advisers and use their counsel wisely. This is a sophisticated, complex realm that has been examined for over a century. It is certainly no place for amateurs.

At the same time, however, exchange rates, interest rates, and inflation rates have been linked to one another via a classic set of relationships that can serve as leading indicators of changes in risk. These relationships are:

- The **Purchasing Power Parity** theory (PPP). While it can be expressed differently, the most common expression links the changes in exchange rates to those in relative price indices in two countries:

rate of change of exchange rate = difference in inflation rates

- The **International Fisher Effect** (IFE). This holds that an interest-rate differential will exist only if the exchange rate is expected to change in such a way that the advantage of the higher interest rate is offset by the loss on the foreign exchange transactions. Practically speaking, the IFE implies that while an investor in a low-interest country can convert funds into the currency of a high-interest country and earn a higher rate, the gain (the interest rate differential) will be offset by the expected loss due to foreign exchange rate changes. The relationship is stated as:

the expected rate of change of the exchange rate = the interest-rate differential

- The **Unbiased Forward Rate Theory**. This holds that the

forward exchange rate is the best and unbiased estimate of the expected future spot exchange rate.

the expected exchange rate = the forward exchange rate

Other than these yardsticks, defending against exchange rate risk is largely a matter of observation. In the floating exchange rate environment that has existed for nearly the past 30 years, currency exchange rates respond to a host of factors: political climates, the flow of imports and exports, the flow of capital, inflation rates in various countries, consumer expectations, and confidence levels, to name a few. Frequently, limits are placed on exchange rate fluctuations by government policies – actions that themselves can arouse controversy or debate.

Even so, the exchange rate risks these factors create can be arranged into three primary categories:

- **Economic exposure.** Due to changes in rates, operating costs will rise and make a product uncompetitive in the world market, thus eroding profitability. There's little that can be done about economic risk; it's simply a routine business risk that every enterprise must endure.
- **Translation exposure.** The impact of currency exchange rates will reduce a company's earnings and weaken its balance sheet. In turn, the denominations of assets and liabilities are important, although many experts contend that currency fluctuations have no significant impact on real assets.
- **Transaction exposure.** There will be an unfavourable move in a specific currency between the time when a contract is agreed and the time it is completed, or between the time when a lending or borrowing is initiated and the time the funds are repaid. This is the most common problem that confronts most companies. Requiring payment in advance is rarely practical, and impossible, of course, for borrowing and lending.

To reduce translation exposure, experienced corporate fund managers use a range of techniques known as currency hedging, which amounts to diversifying currency holdings, monitoring exchange rates, and acting accordingly, depending upon specific conditions. Its advocates contend that taking appropriate action can greatly reduce translation risks, if not avoid them altogether. Currency hedging, however, is also technical and sophisticated.

Transaction exposure can be eased by a process known as factoring. Major exporters, in particular, transfer title to their foreign accounts receivable to a third-party factoring house that assumes responsibility for collections, administrative services, and any other services requested. The fee for this service is a percentage of the value of the receivables, anywhere from 5 percent to 10 percent or higher, depending on the currencies involved. Companies often include this percentage in selling prices to recoup the cost.

Commercial and country risks can affect exchange rates, too. Commercial risks include the default or bankruptcy of major foreign customers. While this risk mirrors what can also occur at home, foreign-based firms operate under different laws and relationships with their governments. More worrisome are country risks: political or military interventions and currency restrictions that less stable nations might impose. Insurance is available to address such risks, but it can be costly.

TRICKS OF THE TRADE

- Any number of models have been created to explain and forecast exchange rates. None has proved definitive, largely because the world's economies and financial markets are evolving so rapidly.
- A forward transaction is an agreement to buy one currency and sell another on a date some time beyond two business days. It allows an exchange rate on a given day to be locked in for a future payment or receipt, thereby eliminating exchange rate risk.
- Foreign exchange options are contracts which, for a fee, guarantee a worst-case exchange rate for the future purchase of one currency for another. Unlike a forward transaction, the option does not obligate the buyer to deliver a currency on the settlement date unless the buyer chooses to. These options protect against unfavourable currency movements while allowing retention of the ability to participate in favourable movements.
- A producer facing pricing competition caused by fluctuations in exchange rates can also use currency contracts to try to match competitors' cost structures and reduce costs.
- Companies doing larger volumes of business in a foreign country often establish a local office there to pay expenses and collect revenues in local currencies to reduce the impact of sudden and pronounced exchange rate fluctuations.
- Private-sector subscription services monitor currencies and publish alerts. One US-based service has established numerical ranges that indicate risk, from 100 (no risk) to 200 (extreme risk or an outright currency crisis).
- Exchange rate risks cannot be insured against per se.
- The Department for Business, Enterprise and Regulatory Reform (BERR) may be a source of advice for companies, especially smaller and medium-sized companies, seeking assistance.

THE BEST SOURCES OF HELP
Websites:
BERR:
www.berr.gov.uk
Moneyterms: **http://moneyterms.co.uk/ exchange-rate-risk**

Calculating Price/Earnings Ratio

WHY IT IS IMPORTANT

Since EPS is the annual earnings per share of a company, it follows that dividing the share price by EPS tells us how many years of current EPS are represented by the share price. In the above example then, the P/E of 8.3 tells us that investors at the current price are prepared to pay 8.3 years of historical EPS for the share, or 7.1 years of the forecast next year's EPS. Theoretically the faster a company is expected to grow, the higher the P/E ratio that investors would award it. It is one measure of how cheap or expensive a share appears.

HOW IT WORKS IN PRACTICE

The P/E ratio is predominantly useful in comparisons with other shares rather than in isolation. For example, if the average P/E in the market is 20, there will be many shares with P/Es well above and well below this, for a variety of reasons. Similarly, in a particular sector, the P/Es will frequently vary quite widely from the sector average, even though the constituent companies may all be engaged in broadly similar businesses. The reason is that even two businesses doing the same thing will not always be doing it as profitably as each other. One may be far more efficient, as demonstrated by a history of rising EPS compared with the flat EPS picture of the other over a series of years, and the market might recognise this by awarding the more profitable share a higher P/E.

TRICKS OF THE TRADE

- Take care. The market frequently gets it wrong and many high P/E shares have in the past been the most awful long-term investments, losing investors huge amounts of money when the promise of future rapid growth proved to be a chimera. In contrast many low P/E companies, often in what are perceived as dull industries, have proved over time to be outstanding investments.
- The P/E is an investment tool that is both invaluable, and yet requires extreme caution in its application when comparing and selecting investments. It remains though by far the most commonly utilised ratio in investment analysis.

Calculating the Current Price of a Bond

WHY IT IS IMPORTANT

Current prices of comparable bonds are strong indicators of a bond's buying or selling price. Changes in bond prices are also indicators of economic strength and direction.

HOW IT WORKS IN PRACTICE

The price of a bond depends on several factors:

- interest rates: as rates rise, a bond's price falls, because it pays less interest than current offerings and is thus less attractive. Conversely, a bond becomes more attractive as interest rates fall
- the risk perceived for the issuing entity, reflected in its credit rating from one of the major rating agencies. The price of a bond of a company in bankruptcy, for instance, will be low because the company may never be able to redeem it. The price of a bond from a strong company may include a premium over its face or 'par value' because it is considered a reliable investment: a bond with a face value of £1,000 might sell for £1,050, indicating a £50 premium
- the issuing of new bonds by corporations or other bodies (and the ratings they receive) affects the prices of existing bonds

Daily bond tables vary in format, but list the basic information necessary for comparing prices. Only a small fraction of the outstanding bonds trade on any given day, but these representative prices provide sufficient information to estimate what a fair price would be for the bonds being considered.

When considering bonds, several pieces of information are essential:

- the bond's coupon rate: what it will pay in interest

- how long before the principal amount of the bond matures, or if there is a call date
- its recent price and current yield

Essentially, all the tables provide this basic information. The US Treasury table, for example, would be listed as follows:

Rate	Maturity	Bid	Ask	Yield
7 ¾	Feb. 10	105:12	105:14	5.50
5 ⅜	Feb. 10	99:26	99:27	5.44

In the first row, the security is paying its bondholders 7¾ percent interest and is due to mature in February 2010. Prices in the bid and ask columns are percentages of the bond's face value of $1,000. A bid of 105:12 means that a buyer was willing to pay $1053.75, compared to the seller's lowest asking price, 105:14, or $1054.38, a difference of 63 cents per thousand.

Bond quotes follow certain conventions. Prices are given as percentages of face value, but the digits appearing after the colons are not decimals, being expressed in terms of 1/32. So 12/32nds, for example, would equal $3.75, which is appended to the 105 before the colon.

The bid and ask prices indicate that an investor who bought the bond at par when it was first issued can make a profit of more than 5 percent if it were sold now. The last column gives the yield to maturity, an interest rate summarising the bond's overall investment value.

COMMON MISTAKES
- A bond's yield and its price are not the same. Price is what is paid for a bond; yield expresses the percentage return on the investment. Yield is most useful for comparing fixed income investments for planning purposes, rather than as an exact measure of the return expected from an investment.
- The number of bond issues outstanding at any given time is far greater than stocks, and most bondholders buy with the intent of holding them until maturity, so the amount of trading is limited.
- There are several bond-rating agencies. A bond's rating indicates its level of risk.
- Listing tables also show the volume traded along with the current yield.
- The Internet offers many calculators for quickly determining bond prices and yields.

THE BEST SOURCES OF HELP
Website:
www.investinginbonds.com offers an explanation, with examples, of several different kinds of bonds.

Calculating Asset Utilisation

WHAT IT MEASURES
How efficiently an organisation uses its resources and, in turn, the effectiveness of the organisation's managers.

WHY IT IS IMPORTANT
The success of any enterprise is tied to its ability to manage and leverage its assets. Hefty sales and profits can hide any number of inefficiencies. By examining several relationships between sales and assets, asset utilisation delivers a reasonably detailed picture of how well a company is being managed and led – certainly enough to call attention both to sources of trouble and to role-model operations.

Moreover, since all the figures used in this analysis are taken from a company's balance sheet or profit and loss statement, the ratios that result can be used to compare a company's performance with individual competitors and with industries as a whole.

Many companies use this measure not only to evaluate their aggregate success but also to determine compensation for managers.

HOW IT WORKS IN PRACTICE
Asset utilisation relies on a family of asset utilisation ratios, also called activity ratios. The individual ratios in the family can vary, depending on the practitioner. They include measures that also stand alone, such as accounts receivable turnover and asset turnover. The most commonly used sets of asset utilisation ratios include these and the following measures.

Average collection period is also known as days sales outstanding. It links accounts receivable with daily sales and is expressed in number of days; the lower the number, the better the performance. Its formula is:

accounts receivable / average daily sales = average collection period

For example, if accounts receivable are £280,000 and average daily sales are 7,000, then:

280,000 / 7,000 = 40

Inventory turnover compares the cost of goods sold (COGS) with inventory; for this measure, expressed in 'turns', the higher the number the better. Its formula is:

cost of goods sold / inventory

For example, if COGS is £2 million and inventory at the end of the period is £500,000, then:

2,000,000 / 500,000 = 4

Some asset utilisation repertoires include ratios like debtor days, while others study the relationships listed below.

Depreciation / Assets measures the percentage of assets being depreciated to gauge how quickly product plants are ageing and assets are being consumed.

Depreciation / Sales measures the percentage of sales that is tied up covering the wear and tear of the physical plant.

In either instance, a high percentage could be cause for concern.

Income / Assets measures how well management uses its assets to generate net income. It is the same formula as return on assets.

Income / Plant measures how effectively a company uses its investment in fixed assets to generate net income.

In these two instances, high numbers are desirable.

Plant / Assets expresses the percentage of total assets that is tied up in land, buildings, and equipment.

By themselves, of course, the individual numbers are meaningless. Their value lies in how they compare with the corresponding numbers of competitors and industry averages. A company with an inventory turnover of 4 in an industry whose average is 7, for example, surely has room for improvement, because the comparison indicates it is generating fewer sales per unit of inventory and is therefore less efficient than its rivals.

TRICKS OF THE TRADE

- Asset utilisation is particularly useful to companies considering expansion or capital investment: if production can be increased by improving the efficiency of existing resources, there is no need to spend the sums expansion would cost.
- Like all families of ratios, no single number or comparison is necessarily cause for alarm or rejoicing. Asset utilisation proves most beneficial over an extended period of time.
- Studying all measures at once can take up a lot of time, although computers have trimmed hours into seconds. Management teams in smaller organisations may conduct asset utilisation on a continuing basis, tracking particular measures on a monthly basis to stay abreast of operating trends.

THE BEST SOURCES OF HELP
Website:
Powerinvestor.com: **www.powerinvestor.com**

Calculating Accounts Receivable Turnover

WHAT IT MEASURES
The number of times in each accounting period, typically a year, that a company converts credit sales into cash.

WHY IT IS IMPORTANT
A high turnover figure is desirable, because it indicates that a company collects revenues effectively, and that its customers pay bills promptly. A high figure also suggests that a company's credit and collection policies are sound.

In addition, the measurement is a reasonably good indicator of cash-flow, and of overall operating efficiency.

HOW IT WORKS IN PRACTICE
The formula for accounts receivable turnover is straightforward. Simply divide the average amount of receivables into annual credit sales:

sales / receivables = receivables turnover

If, for example, a company's sales are £4.5 million and its average receivables are £375,000, its receivables turnover is:

4,500,000 / 375,000 = 12

TRICKS OF THE TRADE

- It is important to use the average amount of receivables over the period considered. Otherwise, receivables could be misleading for a company whose products are seasonal or are sold at irregular intervals.
- The measurement is also helpful to a company that is designing or revising credit terms.
- Accounts receivable turnover is among the measures that comprise asset utilisation ratios, also called activity ratios.

THE BEST SOURCES OF HELP
Website:
The Motley Fool: **www.fool.co.uk**

Calculating a Capital Asset Pricing Model

WHAT IT MEASURES
The relationship between the risk and expected return of a security or stock portfolio.

WHY IT IS IMPORTANT
The capital asset pricing model's (CAPM) importance is twofold.

First, it serves as a model for pricing the risk in all securities, and thus helps investors evaluate and measure portfolio risk and the returns they can anticipate for taking such risks.

Secondly, the theory behind the formula also has fuelled – some might say provoked – spirited debate among economists about the nature of investment risk itself. The CAPM model attempts to describe how the market values investments with expected returns.

The CAPM theory classifies risk as being either diversifiable, which can be avoided by sound investing, or systematic, that is, not diversified and unavoidable due to the nature of the market itself. The theory contends that investors are rewarded only for assuming systematic risk, because they can mitigate diversifiable risk by building a portfolio of both risky stocks and sound ones.

One analysis has characterised the CAPM as 'a theory of equilibrium' that links higher expected returns in strong markets with the greater risk of suffering heavy losses in weak markets. Otherwise, no one would invest in high-risk stocks.

HOW IT WORKS IN PRACTICE
CAPM holds that the expected return of a security or a portfolio equals the rate on a risk-free security plus a risk premium. If this expected return does not meet or beat a theoretical required return, the investment should not be undertaken. The formula used to create CAPM is:

risk-free rate + (market return – risk-free rate) × beta value = expected return

The risk-free rate is the quoted rate on an asset that has virtually no risk. The market return is the percentage return expected of the overall market, typically a published index such as Standard & Poor's. The beta value is a figure that measures the volatility of a security or portfolio of securities, compared with the market as a whole. A beta of 1, for example, indicates that a security's price will move with the market. A beta greater than 1 indicates higher volatility, while a beta less than 1 indicates less volatility.

Say, for instance, that the current risk-free rate is 4 percent, and the S&P 500 index is expected to return 11 percent next year. An investment club is interested in determining next year's return for XYZ Software Ltd, a prospective investment. The club has determined that the company's beta value is 1.8. The overall stock market always has a beta of 1, so XYZ Software's beta of 1.8 signals that it is a more risky investment than the overall market represents. This added risk means that the club should expect a higher rate of return than the 11 percent for the S&P 500. The CAPM calculation, then, would be:

4 percent + (11 percent – 4 percent) × 1.8 = 16.6 percent expected return

What the results tell the club is that given the risk, XYZ Software Ltd has a required rate of return of 16.6 percent, or the minimum return that an investment in XYZ should generate. If the investment club doesn't think that XYZ will produce that kind of return, it should probably consider investing in a different company.

TRICKS OF THE TRADE
- As experts warn, CAPM is only a simple calculation built on historical data of market and stock prices. It does not express anything about the company whose stock is being analysed. For example, renowned investor Warren Buffett has pointed out that if a company making Barbie™ Dolls has the same beta as one making pet rocks, CAPM holds that one investment is as good as the other. Clearly, this is a risky tenet.
- While high returns might be received from stocks with high beta shares, there is no guarantee that their respective CAPM return will be realised (a reason why beta is defined as a 'measure of risk' rather than an 'indication of high return').
- The beta parameter itself is historical data and may not reflect future results. The data for beta values is typically gathered over several years and experts recommend that only long-term investors should rely on the CAPM formula.
- Over longer periods of time, high beta shares tend to be the worst performers during market declines.

THE BEST SOURCES OF HELP
Website:
Motley Fool: **www.fool.co.uk**

Calculating Current Ratio

WHAT IT MEASURES
A company's liquidity and its ability to meet its short-term debt obligations.

WHY IT IS IMPORTANT
By comparing a company's current assets with its current liabilities, the current ratio reflects its ability to pay its upcoming bills in the unlikely event of all creditors demanding payment at once. It has long been the measurement of choice among financial institutions and lenders.

HOW IT WORKS IN PRACTICE
The current ratio formula is simply:

current assets / current liabilities = current ratio

Current assets are the ones that a company can turn into cash within 12 months during the ordinary course of business. Current liabilities are bills due to be paid within the coming 12 months.

For example, if a company's current assets are £300,000 and its current liabilities are £200,000, its current ratio would be:

300,000 / 200,000 = 1.5

As a rule of thumb, the 1.5 figure means that a company should be able to get hold of £1.50 for every £1.00 it owes.

TRICKS OF THE TRADE
- The higher the ratio, the more liquid the company. Prospective lenders expect a positive current ratio, often of at least 1.5.

However, too high a ratio is also cause for alarm, because it indicates declining receivables and/or inventory – signs that portend declining liquidity.

- A current ratio of less than 1 suggests pressing liquidity problems, specifically an inability to generate sufficient cash to meet upcoming demands.
- Managements use current ratio as well as lenders; a low ratio, for example, may indicate the need to refinance a portion of short-term debt with long-term debt to improve a company's liquidity.
- Ratios vary by industry, however, and should be used accordingly. Some sectors, such as supermarket chains and restaurants, perform nicely with low ratios that would keep others awake at night.
- One shortcoming of the current ratio is that it does not differentiate assets, some of which may not be easily converted to cash. As a result, lenders also refer to the quick ratio.
- Another shortcoming of the current ratio is that it reflects conditions at a single point in time, such as when the balance sheet is prepared. It is possible to make this figure look good just for this occasion: lenders should not, therefore, appraise these conditions by the ratio alone.
- A constant current ratio and falling quick ratio signal trouble ahead, because this suggests that a company is amassing assets at the expense of receivables and cash.

THE BEST SOURCES OF HELP
Website:
Business Owner's Toolkit: **www.toolkit.cch.com**

Calculating Capitalisation Ratios

WHAT THEY MEASURE
By comparing debt to total capitalisation, these ratios reflect the extent to which a corporation is trading on its equity, and the degree to which it finances operations with debt.

While not the focus here, capitalisation ratio also refers to the percentage of a company's total capitalisation contributed by debt, preferred stock, common stock, and other equity.

WHY THEY ARE IMPORTANT
By itself, any financial ratio is a rather useless piece of information. Collectively, and in context, though, finan-

cial leverage ratios present analysts and investors with an excellent picture of a company's situation, how much financial risk it has taken on, its dependence on debt, and developing trends. Knowing who controls a company's capital tells one who truly controls the enterprise!

HOW THEY WORK IN PRACTICE
A business finances its assets with either equity or debt. Financing with debt involves risk, since debt legally obligates a company to pay off the debt, plus the interest the debt incurs. Equity financing, on the other hand, does not obligate the company to pay anything. It is apt to pay investors dividends – but at the discretion of the board of directors. To be sure, business risk accompanies the

operation of any enterprise. But how that enterprise opts to finance its operations – how it blends debt with equity – may heighten this risk.

Various experts include numerous formulas among capitalisation financial leverage ratios. Three are discussed separately: debt-to-capital ratio, debt-to-equity ratio, and interest cover ratios. What's known as the capitalisation ratio per se can be expressed in two ways:

= long-term debt / long-term debt + owners' equity

and

= total debt / total debt + preferred + common equity

For example, a company whose long-term debt totals 5,000 and whose owners hold equity worth £3,000 would have a capitalisation ratio of:

= 5,000 / 5,000 + 3,000

= 5,000 / 8,000 = 0.625 capitalisation ratio

Both expressions of the capitalisation ratio are also referred to as 'component percentages', since they compare a company's debt with either its total capital (debt plus equity) or its equity capital. They readily indicate how reliant a company is on debt financing.

TRICKS OF THE TRADE

- Capitalisation ratios need to be evaluated over time, and compared with other data and standards. A gross profit margin of 20 percent, for instance, is meaningless – until one knows that the average profit margin for an industry is 10 percent; at that point, 20 percent looks quite attractive. Moreover, if that the historical trend of that margin has been climbing for the last three years, it strongly suggests that a company's management has sound and effective policies and strategies in place.
- Also, all capitalisation ratios should be interpreted in the context of a company's earnings and cash-flow, and those of its competitors.
- Take care in comparing companies in different industries or sectors. The same figures that appear to be low in one industry can be very high in another.
- Some less frequently used capitalisation ratios are based on formulas that use the book value of equity (the stock). When compared with other ratios, they can be misleading, because there usually is little relation between a company's book value and its market value – which is apt to be many times higher, since market value reflects what the investment community thinks the company is worth.

THE BEST SOURCES OF HELP
Website:
Investorwords: **www.investorwords.com**

Calculating Acid-test Ratio

WHAT IT MEASURES
How quickly a company's assets can be turned into cash, which is why assessment of a company's liquidity also is known as the quick ratio, or simply the acid ratio.

WHY IT IS IMPORTANT
Regardless of how this ratio is labelled, it is considered a highly reliable indicator of a company's financial strength and its ability to meet its short-term obligations. Because inventory can sometimes be difficult to liquidate, the acid-test ratio deducts inventory from current assets before they are compared with current liabilities – which is what distinguishes it from the current ratio.

Potential creditors like to use the acid-test ratio because it reveals how a company would fare if it had to pay off its bills under the worst possible conditions. Indeed, the assumption behind the acid-test ratio is that creditors are howling at the door demanding immediate payment, and that an enterprise has no time to sell off its inventory, or any of its stock.

HOW IT WORKS IN PRACTICE
The acid-test ratio's formula can be expressed in two ways, but both essentially reach the same conclusion. The more common expression is:

(current assets – inventory) / current liabilities = acid-test ratio

If, for example, current assets total £7,700, inventory amounts to £1,200, and current liabilities total £4,500, then:

(7,700 – 1,200) / 4,500 = 1.44

A variation of this formula ignores inventories altogether, distinguishes assets as cash, receivables, and short-term investments, then divides the sum of the three by the total current liabilities, or:

cash + accounts receivable + short-term investments / current liabilities = acid-test ratio

If, for example, cash totals £2,000, receivables total

£3,000, short-term investments total £1,000, and liabilities total £4,800, then:

$$(2{,}000 + 3{,}000 + 1{,}000) / 4{,}800 = 1.25$$

There are two other ways to appraise liquidity, although neither is as commonly used: the cash ratio is the sum of cash and marketable securities divided by current liabilities; net quick assets is determined by adding cash, accounts receivable, and marketable securities, then subtracting current liabilities from that sum.

TRICKS OF THE TRADE

- In general, the quick ratio should be 1:1 or better. It means a company has a unit's worth of easily convertible assets for each unit of its current liabilities. A high quick ratio usually reflects a sound, well-managed organisation in no danger of imminent collapse, even in the extreme and unlikely event that its sales ceased immediately. On the other hand, companies with ratios of less than 1 could not pay their current liabilities, and should be looked at with extreme care.
- While a ratio of 1:1 is generally acceptable to most creditors, acceptable quick ratios vary by industry, as do almost all financial ratios. No ratio, in fact, is especially meaningful without knowledge of the business from which it originates. For example, a declining quick ratio with a stable current ratio may indicate that a company has built up too much inventory; but it could also suggest that the company has greatly improved its collection system.
- Some experts regard the acid-test ratio as an extreme version of the working capital ratio because it uses only cash and equivalents, and excludes inventories. An acid-test ratio that is notably lower than the working capital ratio often means that inventories make up a large proportion of current assets. An example would be retail stores.
- Comparing quick ratios over an extended period of time can signal developing trends in a company. While modest declines in the quick ratio do not automatically spell trouble, uncovering the reasons for changes can help to find ways to nip potential problems in the bud.
- Like the current ratio, the quick ratio is a snapshot, and a company can manipulate its figures to make it look robust at a given point in time.
- Investors who suddenly become keenly interested in a company's quick ratio may signal their anticipation of a downturn in the company's business or in the general economy.

THE BEST SOURCES OF HELP
Website:
Business Owner's Toolkit: **www.toolkit.cch.com**

Creating a Balance Sheet

WHAT IT MEASURES
The financial standing, or even the net worth or owners' equity, of a company at a given point in time, typically at the end of a calendar or fiscal year.

WHY IT IS IMPORTANT
The balance sheet shows what is owned (assets), what is owed (liabilities), and what is left (owners' equity). It provides a concise snapshot of a company's financial position.

HOW IT WORKS IN PRACTICE
The format of a company's balance sheet is strictly defined by the 1985 Companies Act. Essentially, assets must be in balance with liabilities and shareholders' equity. In other words, assets must equal liabilities and owners' equity.

Assets include cash in hand and cash anticipated (receivables), inventories of supplies and materials, properties, facilities, equipment, and whatever else the company uses to conduct business. Assets also need to reflect depreciation in the value of equipment such as machinery that has a limited expected useful life.

Liabilities include pending payments to suppliers and creditors, outstanding current and long-term debts, taxes, interest payments, and other unpaid expenses that the company has incurred.

Subtracting the value of aggregate liabilities from the value of aggregate assets reveals the value of owners' equity. Ideally, it should be positive. Owners' equity consists of capital invested by owners over the years and profits (net income) or internally generated capital, which is referred to as 'retained earnings'; these are funds to be used in future operations (see opposite for an example).

TRICKS OF THE TRADE
- The balance sheet does not show a company's market worth, nor important intangibles such as the knowledge and talents of individual people, nor other vital business factors such as customers or market share.
- The balance sheet does not express the true value of some fixed assets. A six-year-old manufacturing plant, for example, is listed at its original cost, even though the price of replacing it could be much higher or substantially lower (because of new technology that might be less expensive or vastly more efficient).
- The balance sheet is not an indicator of past or future

performance or trends that affect performance. It needs to be studied along with two other key reports: the income statement and the cash-flow statement. A published balance sheet needs to include prior period comparatives.

ASSETS £	
Current:	
Cash	8,200
Securities	5,000
Receivables	4,500
Inventory & supplies	6,300
Fixed:	
Land	10,000
Structures	90,000
Equipment (less depreciation)	5,000
Intangibles/other	
TOTAL ASSETS	129,000

LIABILITIES £	
Payables	7,000
Taxes	4,000
Misc.	3,000
Bonds & notes	25,000
TOTAL LIABILITIES	39,000
SHAREHOLDERS' EQUITY (stock, par value × shares outstanding)	80,000
RETAINED EARNINGS	10,000
TOTAL LIABILITIES AND SHAREHOLDERS' EQUITY	129,000

THE BEST SOURCES OF HELP
Website:
Conetic.com: **www.conetic.com**

Creating a Profit and Loss Account

WHAT IT MEASURES
One of three principal financial reports a company issues, the Profit and Loss Account (P&L, or income statement as it is also commonly called), is perhaps the most widely used. It measures a company's sales revenues and expenses over a period, providing a calculation of profits or losses during that time.

WHY IT IS IMPORTANT
Reading a P&L is the easiest way to tell if a business has made a profit or a loss during a given month or year. The most important figure it contains is net profit: what is left over after revenues are used to pay expenses and taxes.

Companies typically issue P&L reports monthly. It is customary for the reports to include year-to-date figures, as well as corresponding year-earlier figures to allow for comparisons and analysis.

HOW IT WORKS IN PRACTICE
A P&L adheres to a simple rule of thumb: 'revenue minus cost equals profit'.

There are two P&L formats, multiple-step and single-step. Both follow a standard set of rules known as Generally Accepted Accounting Principles (GAAP). These rules generally adhere to requirements established by governments to track receipts, expenses, and profits for tax purposes. They also allow the financial reports of two different companies to be compared.

The multiple-step format is much more common, because it includes a larger number of details and is thus more useful. It deducts costs from revenues in a series of

steps, allowing for closer analysis. Revenues appear first, then expenses, each in as much detail as management desires. Sales may be broken down by product line or location, while expenses such as salaries may be broken down into base salaries and commissions.

Expenses are then subtracted from revenues to show profit (or loss). A basic multiple-step P&L is shown below. P&Ls of public companies may also report income on the basis of earnings per share. For example, if the company issuing this statement had 12,000 shares outstanding, earnings per share would be £5.12, that is, £61,440 divided by 12,000 shares.

MULTIPLE-STEP PROFIT & LOSS ACCOUNT (£)	
NET SALES	750,000
Less: cost of goods sold	450,000
Gross profit	300,000
LESS: OPERATING EXPENSES	
Selling expenses	
Salaries & commissions	54,000
Advertising	37,500
Delivery/transportation	12,000
Depreciation/store equipment	7,500
Other selling expenses	5,000
Total selling expenses	116,000

TRICKS OF THE TRADE
- A P&L does not show how a business earned or spent its money.
- One month's P&L can be misleading, especially if a business

General & administrative expenses		
Administrative/office salaries	74,000	
Utilities	2,500	
Depreciation/structure	2,400	
Misc. other expenses	3,100	
Total general & admin expenses		82,000
Total operating expenses		198,000
OPERATING INCOME		102,000
LESS (ADD): NON-OPERATING ITEMS		
Interest expenses	11,000	
Interest income earned	(2,800)	8,200
Income before taxes	93,800	
Income taxes		32,360
Net income		61,440

generates a majority of its receipts in particular months. A retail establishment, for example, usually generates a large percentage of its sales in the final three months of the year, while a consulting service might generate the lion's share of its revenues in as few as two months, and no revenues at all in some other months.

• Invariably, figures for both revenues and expenses reflect the judgements of the companies reporting them. Accounting methods can be quite arbitrary when it comes to such factors as depreciation expenses.

THE BEST SOURCES OF HELP
Website:
Biz/ed: **www.bized.co.uk**

Creating a Cash-flow Statement

WHAT IT MEASURES
Cash inflows and cash outflows over a specific period of time, typically a year.

WHY IT IS IMPORTANT
Cash flow is a key indicator of financial health, and it demonstrates to investors, creditors, and other core constituencies a company's ability to meet obligations, finance opportunities, and generally 'come up with the cash' as needs arise. Cash flow that is wildly inconsistent with, say, net income, often indicates operating or managerial problems.

HOW IT WORKS IN PRACTICE
In its basic form, a cash-flow statement will probably be familiar to anyone who has been a member of a club that collected and spent money. It reports funds on hand at the beginning of a given period, funds received, funds spent, and funds remaining at the end of the period.

That formula still applies to a business today, even if creating a cash-flow document is significantly more complex. Cash flows are divided into three categories: cash from operations; cash-investment activities; and cash-financing activities. Companies with holdings in foreign currencies use a fourth classification: effects of changes in currency rates on cash.

A standard direct cash-flow statement is shown opposite.

CRD Ltd
Statement of Cash-flows
For year ended 31 December 20__

CASH FLOWS FROM OPERATIONS	
£	
Operating Profit	82,000
Adjustments to net earnings	
Depreciation	17,000
Accounts receivable	(20,000)
Accounts payable	12,000
Inventory	(8,000)
Other adjustments to earnings	4,000
Net cash flow from operations	87,000

CASH FLOWS FROM INVESTMENT ACTIVITIES	
Purchases of marketable securities	(58,000)
Receipts from sales of marketable securities	45,000
Loans made to borrowers	(16,000)
Collections on loans	11,000
Purchases of plant and land and property assets	(150,000)
Receipts from sales of plant and land and property assets	47,000
Net cash flow from investment activities:	(-121,000)

CASH FLOWS FROM FINANCING ACTIVITIES	
Proceeds from short-term borrowings	51,000
Payments to settle short-term debts	(61,000)
Proceeds from issuing bonds payable	100,000
Proceeds from issuing capital stock	80,000
Dividends paid	(64,000)
Net cash flow from financing activities	106,000
Net change in cash during period	72,000
Cash and cash equivalents, beginning of year	27,000
Cash and cash equivalents, end of year	99,000

TRICKS OF THE TRADE

- A cash-flow statement does *not* measure net income, nor does it measure working capital.
- A cash-flow statement does not include outstanding accounts receivable, but it does include the preceding year's accounts receivable (assuming these were collected during the year for which the statement is prepared).
- Add to a cash inflow any amounts charged off for depreciation, depletion, and amortisation, since cash was actually spent.
- Cash equivalents are short-term, highly liquid investments, although precise definitions may vary slightly by country.

These should be included when recalculating the movement of cash in the period.
- There are alternative ways to present cash flow from operations. Some texts, for example, omit earnings and adjustments, and list instead cash and interest received, cash and interest paid, and taxes received.

THE BEST SOURCES OF HELP
Website:
International Accounting Standards Consultancy:
www.iasc.co.uk

Reading a Balance Sheet

GETTING STARTED
A balance sheet will tell us something about the financial strength of a business on the day that the balance sheet is drawn up. That situation changes constantly, so you could say it is more like a snapshot than a film. Although the method of producing a balance sheet is standardised, there can be a certain element of subjectivity in interpreting it. Different elements of the balance sheet can tell you different things about the how the business is doing.

This actionlist gives an overview of a balance sheet and looks at a brief selection of the more interesting figures that help with interpretation. It's important to remember that a lot of these figures do not tell you that much in isolation; it is in trend analysis or comparisons between businesses that they talk more lucidly.

FAQS
What is a balance sheet?
A balance sheet is an accountant's view of the book value of the assets and liabilities of a business at a specific date and on that date alone. The term 'balance' means exactly what it says – that those assets and liabilities will be equal. In showing how the balance lies, the balance sheet gives us an idea of the financial health of the business.

What does a balance sheet not do?
A balance sheet is not designed to represent the market value of the business. For example, property in the balance sheet may be worth a lot more than its book value. Plant and machinery is shown at cost less depreciation, but that may well be different from market value. Stock may turn out to be worth less than its balance-sheet value, and so on.

Also there may be hidden assets, such as goodwill or valuable brands, that do not appear on the balance sheet at all. These would all enhance the value of the business in a sale situation, yet are invisible on a normal balance sheet.

MAKING IT HAPPEN
Here is a very simple company balance sheet:

Fixed assets	1,000
Current assets	700
Less current liabilities	400
Net current assets	300
	1,300
Less long-term loans	200
Net assets	1,100
Profit and loss account	500
Share capital	600
Shareholders' funds	1,100

DEFINE THE INDIVIDUAL ELEMENTS
- *Fixed assets* – items that are not traded as part of a company's normal activities but enable it to function, such as property, machinery or vehicles. These are tangible assets (meaning you can kick them). This heading can also include intangible assets (you cannot kick them). A common example is 'goodwill', which can arise upon the acquisition of one business by another.
- *Current assets* – items that form the trading cycle of the business. The most common examples are stock, debtors, and positive bank balances.
- *Current liabilities* – also items that form the trading cycle of the business but represent short-term amounts owed to others. Examples will be trade creditors, taxes, and bank overdrafts –

broadly, any amount due for payment within the next 12 months from the date of the balance sheet.
- *Net current assets* – not a new figure, but simply the difference between current assets and current liabilities, often shown because it may be a useful piece of information.
- *Long-term loans* – debt that is repayable more than one year from the date of the balance sheet.
- *Net assets* – also not a new figure, but the sum of fixed assets plus net current assets less long-term loans. In other words, all of the company assets shown in its books, minus all of its liabilities.
- *Profit and loss account* – the total of all the accumulated profits and losses from all the accounting periods since the business started. It increases or decreases each year by the net profit or loss in that period, calculated after providing for all costs including tax and dividends to shareholders.
- *Share capital* – the number of shares issued, multiplied by their nominal value. The latter is the theoretical figure at which the shares were originally issued and has nothing to do with their market value.
- *Shareholders' funds* – not a new figure, but the sum of the profit and loss account plus the share capital. It represents the total interest of the shareholders in the company.

Learn to interpret them

Note that balance sheets differ between one industry and another as regards the range and type of assets and liabilities that exist. For example, a retailer will have little in the way of trade debtors because it sells for cash, while a manufacturer is likely to have a far larger investment in plant than a service business like an advertising agency. So the interpretation must be seen in the light of the actual trade of the business.

Reading a balance sheet can be quite subjective – accountancy is an art, not a science and, although the method of producing a balance sheet is standardised, there may be some items in it that are subjective rather than factual. The way people interpret some of the figures will also vary, depending on what they wish to achieve and how they see certain things as being good or bad.

Look first at the net assets/shareholders' funds

Positive or negative? Our example, being a healthy business, has net assets of a positive £1,100. Positive is good. If there were 600 shares in issue, it would mean that the net assets per share were £1.83.

If it had negative assets (same thing as net liabilities), this might mean that the business is heading for difficulty unless it is being supported by some party such as a parent company, bank, or other investor. When reading a balance sheet with negative assets, consider where the support will be coming from.

Then examine net current assets

Positive or negative? Again, our example has positive net current assets (NCA) of £300. This means that, theoretically, it should not have any trouble settling short-term liabilities because it has more than enough current

assets to do so. Negative net current assets suggest that there possibly could be a problem in settling short-term liabilities.

You can also look at NCA as a ratio of current assets/current liabilities. Here, a figure over one is equivalent to the NCA having a positive absolute figure. The ratio version is more useful in analysing trends of balance sheets over successive periods or comparing two businesses.

A cut-down version of NCA considers only (debtors + cash)/(creditors) thus excluding stock. The reasoning here is that this looks at the most liquid of the net current asset constituents. Again a figure over one is the most desirable. This is also a ratio that is more meaningful in trends or comparisons.

Understand the significance of trade debtor payments. . .

Within current assets, we have trade debtors. It can be useful to consider how many days' worth of sales are tied up in debtors – given by (debtors × 365) / annual sales. This provides an idea of how long the company is waiting to get paid. Too long, and it might be something requiring investigation. However, this figure can be misleading where sales do not take place evenly throughout the year. A construction company might be an example of such a business: one big debtor incurred near the year end would skew the ratio.

. . .and trade creditor payments

Similar to the above, this looks at (trade creditors × 365)/annual purchases, indicating how long the company is taking in general to pay its suppliers. This is not so easy to calculate, because the purchases for this purpose include not only goods for resale but all the overheads as well.

Recognise what debt means

Important to most businesses, this figure is the total of long and short-term loans. Too much debt might indicate that the company would have trouble, in a downturn, in paying the interest. It's difficult to give an optimum level of debt because there are so many different situations, depending on a huge range of circumstances.

Often, instead of an absolute figure, debt is expressed as a percentage of shareholders' funds and known as 'gearing' or 'leverage'. In a public company, gearing of 100 percent might be considered pretty high, whereas debt of under 30 percent may be seen as on the low side.

COMMON MISTAKES
Believing that balance sheet figures represent market value

Don't assume that a balance sheet represents a valuation of the business. Its primary purpose is that it forms part of the range of accounting reports used for measuring business performance – along with the other common financial reports like profit and loss accounts and cash-flow statements. Management, shareholders, and others such as banks will use the entire range to assess the health of the business.

Forgetting that the balance sheet is valid only for the date at which it is produced

A short while after a balance sheet is produced, things could be quite different. In practice there frequently may not be any radical changes between the date of the balance sheet and the date when it is being read, but it is entirely possible that something could have happened to the business that would not show. For example, a major debtor could have defaulted unexpectedly. So remember that balance sheet figures are valid only as at the date shown, and are not a permanent picture of the business.

Confusion over whether in fact all assets and liabilities are shown in the balance sheet

Some businesses may have hidden assets, as suggested above. This could be the value of certain brands or trademarks, for example, for which money may not have ever been paid. Yet these could be worth a great deal. Conversely, there may be some substantial legal action pending which could cost the company a lot, yet is not shown fully in the balance sheet.

Reading a Profit and Loss Account

GETTING STARTED

A profit and loss account (P&L) is a statement of the income and expenditure of a business over the period stated, drawn up in order to ascertain how much profit the business made. Put simply, the difference between the income from sales and the associated expenditure is the profit or loss for the period. 'Income' and 'expenditure' here mean only those amounts directly attributable to earning the profit and thus would exclude capital expenditure, for example.

Importantly, the figures are adjusted to match the income and expenses to the time period in which they were incurred – not necessarily the same as that in which the cash changed hands.

FAQS

What is a profit and loss account?

A profit and loss account is an accountant's view of the figures that show how much profit or loss a business has made over a period. To arrive at this, it is necessary to allocate the various elements of income and expenditure to the time period concerned, not on the basis of when cash was received or spent, but on when the income was earned or the liability to pay a supplier and employees was incurred. While capital expenditures are excluded, depreciation of property and equipment is included as a non-cash expense.

Thus if you sell goods on credit, you will be paid later but the sale takes place upon the contract to sell them. Equally if you buy goods and services on credit, the purchase takes place when you contract to buy them, not when you when you actually settle the invoice.

What does a profit and loss account not show?

Most importantly, a P&L account is not an explanation of the cash coming into and going out of a business.

MAKING IT HAPPEN

Below is a simple example of a profit and loss account for a particular year.

Sales	1,000
Opening stock	100
Purchases	520
	620
Closing stock	80
Cost of sales	540
Gross profit	460
Wages	120
Other overheads	230
	350
Net profit before tax	110
Tax	22
Net profit after tax	88
Dividends	40
Retained profit	48
Retained profit brought forward	150
Retained profit carried forward	198

Note that the presence of stock and purchases indicates that the business is trading or manufacturing goods of some kind, rather than selling services.

Defining the individual elements

- *Sales* – the invoiced value of the sales in the period.
- *Stock* – the value of the actual physical stock held by the business at the opening and closing of the period. It is always valued at cost, or realisable value if that is lower, never at selling price.
- *Purchases and other direct costs* – the goods or raw materials purchased by the business for resale – not capital items used in the business, only items used as part of the direct cost of its sales. In other words, those costs which vary directly with sales, as distinct from overheads (like rent) which do not.

Where a business holds stock, the purchases figure has to be adjusted for the opening and closing values in order to reach the right income and expenditure amounts for that period only. Goods for resale bought in the period may not have been used purely for that period but may be lying in stock at the end of it, ready for sale in the next. Similarly, goods used for resale in this period will consist partly of items already held in stock at the beginning of it. So take the amounts purchased, add the opening stock, and deduct the closing stock. The resulting adjusted purchase figure is known as 'cost of sales'.

In some businesses there may be other direct costs apart from purchases included in cost of sales. For example, a manufacturer may include some wages if they are of a direct nature (wages of employees directly involved in the manufacturing process, as distinct from office staff, say). Or a building contractor would include plant hire in direct costs, as well as purchases of materials.

- *Gross profit* – the difference between sales and cost of sales. This is an important figure, as it measures how much was actually made directly from whatever the business is selling, before it started to pay for overheads.

The figure is often expressed as a percentage ratio, when it is known as the 'gross profit margin'. In our example the GPM is 460 : 1,000 – or 46 percent. Ratios are really only useful as comparison tools, either with different periods of the same business or with other businesses.

- *Overheads* – the expenses of the business which do not vary directly with sales. They include a wide range of items such as rent, most wages, advertising, phones, interest paid on loans, audit fees, and so on.
- *Net profit before tax* – the result of deducting total overheads from gross profit. This is what the business has made before tax is paid on that profit.
- *Tax (or corporation tax)* – This will not actually have been paid in the year concerned, but is shown because it is due on the profit for that period. Even then the figure shown may not be the actual amount due, for various reasons such as possible overpayments from previous years. Tax can be a very complex matter, being based upon a set of changeable rules.
- *Net profit after tax* – the result after deducting the tax liability – the so-called bottom line. This is the amount that the company can do with as it wishes, possibly paying a dividend out of part of it and retaining the rest. It is the company's reward for actually being in business in the first place.
- *Dividends* – a payment to the shareholders as a reward for their investment in the company. Most publicly listed companies of any size pay dividends to shareholders. Private companies may also do so, but this may be more for tax reasons. The dividend in the example shown is paid out of the net profit after tax, but legally it is not permitted to exceed the total available profit. That total available profit is comprised of both the current year's net profit after tax and the retained profit brought forward from previous years.
- *Retained profit* – the amount kept by the company after paying dividends to shareholders. If there is no dividend, then it is equal to the net profit after tax.
- *Retained profit brought forward* – the total accumulated retained profits for all earlier years of the company's existence.
- *Retained profit carried forward* – the above figure brought forward, plus the current year's retained profit. This new total

will form the profit brought forward in the next accounting period.

How to interpret the figures

A lot of accounting analysis is valid only when comparing the figures, usually with similar figures for earlier periods, projected future figures, or other companies in the same business.

On its own, a P&L account tells you only a limited story, though there are some standalone facts that can be derived from it. What our example does show, even in isolation, is that this business was successful in the period concerned. It made a profit, not a loss, and was able to pay dividends to shareholders out of that profit. Clearly a pretty crucial piece of information.

However, it is in comparisons that such figures start to have real meaning.

The example figures reveal that the gross profit margin was 46 percent, an important statistic in measuring business performance. The net profit margin before tax was 110 : 1,000, or 11 percent. You could take the margin idea further and calculate the net profit after tax ratio to sales as 88 : 1,000, being 8.8 percent. Or you could calculate the ratio of any expense to sales. In our example, the wages to sales ratio is 120 : 1,000 or 12 percent.

If you then looked at similar margin figures for the preceding accounting period, you would learn something about this business. Say the gross margin was 45 percent last year compared with 46 percent this year – there has been some improvement in the profit made before deducting overheads. But then suppose that the net profit margin of 8.8 percent this year was 9.8 percent last year. This would tell you that, despite improvement in profit at the gross level, the overheads have increased disproportionately. You could then check on the ratio of each item of the overheads to sales to see where this arose and find out why. Advertising spending could have shot up, for example, or perhaps the company moved to new premises, incurring a higher rent. Maybe something could be tightened up.

Another commonly-used ratio

Another ratio often used in business analysis is return on capital employed. Here we combine the profit and loss account with the balance sheet by dividing the net profit (either before or after tax as required) by shareholders' funds. This tells you how much the company is making proportionate to money invested in it by the shareholders – a similar idea to how much you might get in interest on a bank deposit account. It's a useful way of comparing different companies in a particular industry, where the more efficient ones are likely to derive a higher return on capital employed.

COMMON MISTAKES
Assuming that the bottom line represents cash profit from trading

It does not! There are a few examples where this is the

case: a simple cash trader might buy something for one price, then sell it for more; his profit then equals the increase in cash. But a business that buys and sells on credit, spends money on items that are held for the longer term, such as property or machinery, has tax to pay at a later date, and so on, will make a profit that is not represented by a mere increase in cash balances held. Indeed, the cash balance could quite easily decrease during a period when a profit was made.

THE BEST SOURCES OF HELP
Website:
The Motley Fool: **www.fool.co.uk**

Reading a Cash-flow Statement

GETTING STARTED
In their annual report, most public companies must publish a cash-flow statement – together with the profit and loss account and a balance sheet. As the name suggests, the purpose of a cash-flow statement is to explain the movement in cash balances or bank overdrafts held by the business from one accounting period to the next.

The balance sheet shows the assets and liabilities at the end of the period, with comparative figures for the start of it. The profit and loss account shows how much profit was generated by the business in the period. The cash-flow statement is the third part of the financial picture of the business over the period.

FAQS
What is a cash-flow statement?
Over an accounting period, the money held by a business at the bank (or its overdrafts) will have changed. The purpose of the cash-flow statement is to show the reasons for this change. If you look at the actionlist on profit and loss (**Reading a Profit and Loss Account (p. 351)**), one of the common mistakes illustrated was the erroneous belief that the profit was equal to the cash generated by a business. It is not, but the cash-flow statement is the link between profit and cash balance movements. It takes you down the path from profit to cash. The figures are derived from those published in the annual accounts, and notes will explain how this derivation is arrived at.

What does a cash-flow statement not show?
In the same way that a profit and loss account does not show the cash made by the business, a cash-flow statement does not show the profit. It is entirely possible for a loss-making business to show an increase in cash, and the other way round too.

MAKING IT HAPPEN
Below is a simple example of a cash-flow statement for a particular year.

Net cash inflow from operating activities	7,020
Returns on investments and finance costs	
Interest paid	820
Less interest received	90
Net cash outflow from finance costs	(730)
Taxation	(1,060)
Capital expenditure	
Sale of fixed assets	760
Less purchase of fixed assets	4,420
Net cash outflow from capital expenditure	(3,660)
Dividends paid	(1,530)
Net cash inflow before financing	40
Financing	
New loans	1,000
Loan repayments	(300)
Finance lease repayments	(100)
Net cash inflow from financing	600
Increase in cash	640

DEFINE THE INDIVIDUAL ELEMENTS
- *Net cash inflow from operating activities* – broadly this is the profit of the business, before depreciation plus the change in debtor and creditor balances. There may also be other items included here. In the statutory annual accounts of companies, there will be an explanation to show how this net cash inflow figure is derived from the profit and loss account and balance sheet. Depreciation is excluded because it does not represent a cash cost.

Debtor and creditor balance changes are included here because they represent an inflow or outflow of cash to the business. Thus, if customers owe you less or more at the end of a period than at the beginning of it, it follows that there must have been cash flowing in or out of the business as a result. A reduction in debtors means that cash has come in to the business, and the reverse for an increase in debtors. The same applies to the creditor balances of suppliers. An increase here means a cash inflow, with a decrease denoting an outflow.

- *Returns on investments and finance costs* – these figures comprise interest received on cash balances, less interest paid on debt. There could be other forms of investment income here, such as dividends on shares owned.

- *Net cash outflow from finance costs* - this is not a new figure but the net result of the above items, identified as returns on investments. In our example the result is an outflow of cash. That is, the interest paid on debt exceeded the interest received on cash. It could in some circumstances be the other way round, where, for example, a business has substantial cash balances earning interest.
- *Taxation*: self explanatory, this is the outflow of cash arising from corporation tax paid by the business. It can on occasion be an inflow, where the company has obtained a repayment of corporation tax for some reason.
- *Capital expenditure* - this is cash expended on fixed assets bought for the business, less cash received from the sale of assets no longer required by the business.
- *Net cash outflow from capital expenditure* - this is not a new figure but the net result of the above items, identified as expenditure on new fixed assets less receipts from the sale of disposals of such items. In our example there is a large outflow, which generally would be the norm. It can happen sometimes, though, that a business realises more from the sale of fixed assets in a particular period than it expends on items acquired.
- *Dividends paid*-self - explanatory; this is the outflow of cash arising from paying dividends to shareholders.
- *Net cash inflow before financing* - this is not a new figure but a subtotal of the items above. In our example, the figure of £40 shown happens to be an inflow but it could just as easily have been an outflow. There is no typical figure here; it is just as common to see net inflows as outflows.

It is important to understand what this figure represents. It is the net cash result of running the business in the period concerned, after paying tax to the government and dividends to the shareholders. However, as its label indicates, it doesn't include any financing.

- *Financing* - this term includes the raising of new loans, the repayment of old ones and other methods of financing such as issuing new shares. In the example the company borrowed £1,000 in new loans, which creates a cash inflow of that sum, and repaid £300 on old debt plus a further £100 on equipment leases (which are another form of finance), making a net inflow on finance of £600.
- *Increase in cash* (the bottom line) - adding the net inflow of £600 from finance to the £40 generated by business operations gives us an overall net cash inflow of £640. This is the bottom line. It means that we have £640 more in the bank at the end of the accounting period than at the beginning of it.

Learn to interpret the figures

As suggested above, the cash-flow statement is the third section of the primary set of accounting documents used to explain and analyse businesses. It is a 'derived schedule', meaning that the figures are pulled from the profit

and loss account and balance sheet statements, linking the two.

Its purpose is to analyse the reasons why the company's cash position changed over an accounting period. For example, a sharp increase in borrowings could have several explanations – such as a high level of capital expenditure, poor trading, an increase in the time taken by debtors to pay, and so on. The cash-flow statement will alert management to the reasons for this, in a way that may not be obvious merely from the profit and loss account and balance sheet.

The generally desirable situation is for the net position before financing to be positive. Even the best-run businesses will sometimes have an outflow in a period (in a year of high capital expenditure for example), but positive is usually good. This becomes more apparent when comparing the figures over a period of time. A repeated outflow of funds over several years is usually an indication of trouble. To cover this, the company must raise new finance and/or sell off assets, which will tend to compound the problem, in the worst cases leading to failure.

Cash is critical to every business, especially in challenging times, so the management must understand where its cash is coming from and going to. The cash-flow statement gives us this information in an abbreviated form. You could argue that the whole purpose of a business is to start with one sum of money and, by applying some sort of process to it, arrive at another and higher sum, continually repeating this cycle.

COMMON MISTAKES
Confusing 'cash' and 'profit'

As mentioned previously, the most common mistake with cash-flow statements is the potential confusion between profit and cash. They are not the same and it's crucial that you quickly learn the difference!

Not understanding the terminology

It is clearly fundamental to an understanding of cash-flow statements that the reader is familiar with terms like 'debtors', 'creditors', 'dividends', and so on. But more than appreciating the meaning of the word 'debtors', it is quite easy to misunderstand the concept that, for example, an increase in debtors is a cash outflow, and equally that an increase in creditors represents an inflow of cash to the business.

THE BEST SOURCES OF HELP
Website:
The Motley Fool: **www.fool.co.uk**

Defining Assets

WHAT THEY MEASURE

Collectively, the value of all the resources a company uses to conduct business and generate profits.

Examples of assets are cash, marketable securities, accounts and notes receivable, inventories of merchandise, buildings and property, machinery and office equipment, natural resources, and intangibles such as patents, legal claims and agreements, and negotiated rights.

WHY THEY ARE IMPORTANT

No business can continue for very long without knowing what assets it has at its disposal, and using them efficiently. Assets are a reflection of organisational strength, and are invariably evaluated by potential investors, banks and creditors, and other stakeholders.

Moreover, the value of assets is also a key figure used to calculate several financial ratios.

HOW THEY WORK IN PRACTICE

Assets are typically broken down into five different categories:

- Current assets. These include cash, cash equivalents, marketable securities, inventories, and prepaid expenses that are expected to be used within one year or a normal operating cycle. All cash items and inventories are reported at historical value. Securities are reported at market value.
- Non-current assets, or long-term investments. These are resources that are expected to be held for more than one year. They are reported at the lower of cost and current market value, which means that their values will vary.
- Fixed assets. These include property, plant and facilities, and equipment used to conduct business. These items are reported at their original value, even though current values might well be much higher.

- Intangible assets. These include legal claims, patents, franchise rights, and accounts receivable. These values can be more difficult to determine. FR10, published by the Accounting Standards Board of the Institute of Chartered Accountants for England and Wales is essential reading for dealing with this issue.
- Deferred charges. These include prepaid costs and other expenditures that will produce future revenue or benefits.

TRICKS OF THE TRADE

- Assets do not necessarily include everything of value, such as the talents of individuals, an organisation's collective expertise, or the value of a customer base.
- Classic definitions of assets also often exclude or undervalue trademarks, even though there is universal agreement that these, for example, the three-point star of Mercedes-Benz or Coca-Cola's red logo, can have enormous value.
- Fixed assets are valued at their original cost, because of the prevailing opinion that they are used for business and are not for sale. Moreover, current market value is essentially a matter of opinion.
- Determining the value of patents can be challenging, because a patent has a finite lifespan, its value declines each year, and its useful life may be even shorter.
- Some experts contend that the principal assets of 'knowledge-based' businesses such as consulting firms or property development companies are, in fact, its people. In turn, their aggregate value should be calculated by subtracting the net value of assets from market value.

THE BEST SOURCES OF HELP

Website:
Investorwords.com: **www.investorwords.com**

Calculating Cost of Goods Sold

WHAT IT MEASURES

For a retailer, cost of goods sold (COGS) is the cost of buying and acquiring the goods that it sells to its customers. For a service firm, COGS is the cost of the employee services it supplies. For a manufacturer, COGS is the cost of buying the raw materials and manufacturing its finished products.

WHY IT IS IMPORTANT

Cost of goods sold may help a company to determine the prices to charge for its products and services, and the volume of business that it needs to maintain in order to operate profitably.

For retailers especially, the cost of the merchandise sold is typically the largest expense, and thus an absolutely critical business factor. However, understanding COGS is an important success factor for any business, because it can reveal opportunities to reduce costs and improve operations.

COGS is also a key figure on an income tax return, and an important consideration in computing income taxes because of its close relationship to inventories, which tax authorities treat as future income.

HOW IT WORKS IN PRACTICE

Essentially, COGS is equal to a company's opening stock of goods and services, plus the cost of goods bought and direct costs incurred during a particular period, minus the closing stock of goods and services.

A critical consideration is the accounting policy that a company adopts to calculate inventory values, especially if raw materials prices change during the year. This may happen often, particularly when inflation is high. The Accounting Standards Board of the Institute of Chartered Accountants in England and Wales publishes Statement of Standards Accounting Practice 9, which deals with stocks and work in progress.

COGS for a manufacturer will include a variety of items, such as raw materials and energy used in production, labour, benefits for production workers, the cost of raw materials in inventory, shipping fees, the cost of storing finished products, depreciation on production machinery used, and factory overhead expenses.

For a retail company such as Marks and Spencer, COGS is generally less complex: the total amount paid to suppliers for the products being sold on its shelves.

COGS is calculated as follows:

Stocks at beginning of period	£20,000
Purchases during period	+ £60,000
Cost of good available for sale	= £80,000
Less inventory at period end	– £15,000
Cost of goods sold (COGS)	= £65,000

Because the counting of inventory is an exhaustive undertaking for retailers, doing it quarterly or monthly would be open to error. Accordingly, tax authorities allow them to estimate cost of goods sold during the year.

Determining these estimates requires details of the gross profit margin (retailers typically use the preceding year's figure). This figure is then used to calculate the cost ratio.

Begin by assuming that net sales are 100 percent, then subtract the gross profit margin, say 40 percent, to produce a cost ratio of 60 percent: 100 percent – 40 percent = 60 percent. A monthly COGS calculation then is shown below.

Inventory at beginning of month	£10,000
Purchases during month	+ £25,000
Cost of goods available for sale	= £35,000
Less net sales during month	– £28,000
Cost ratio 100 percent – 40 percent	= 60 percent
Estimated cost of goods sold	= £16,800 (£28,000 × 60 percent)

There is one sample to review, because calculating COGS for manufacturers requires additional factors:

Inventory at beginning of year	£20,000
Purchases during year	+ £50,000
Cost of direct labour	+ £15,000
Materials and supplies	+ £12,000
Misc. costs	+ £3,000
Total product expenses	= £100,000
Less inventory at year end	– £15,000
Cost of goods sold (COGS)	= £85,000

TRICKS OF THE TRADE

- Anyone who wants to determine COGS must maintain inventories and know their value!
- Because goods returned affect inventory values and, in turn, cost of goods sold, returns of goods must be reflected in COGS calculations.
- Merchandising companies may use different inventory accounting systems, but the choice has no bearing on the actual costs incurred; it only affects allocation of costs.
- COGS should not include indirect costs like administration and marketing costs, or other activities that cannot be directly attributed to producing or acquiring the product.

THE BEST SOURCES OF HELP
Websites:
Biz/ed:
  www.bized.co.uk
Investopedia:
  www.investopedia.com

Calculating Working Capital

WHAT IT MEASURES
The funds that are readily available to operate a business. Working capital comprises the total net current assets of a business, which are its stocks, debtors, and cash – minus its creditors.

WHY IT IS IMPORTANT
Obviously, it is vital for a company to have sufficient working capital to meet all of its requirements. The faster a business expands, the greater will be its working capital needs.

If current assets do not exceed current liabilities, a company may well run into trouble paying creditors who want their money quickly. Indeed, the leading cause of business failure is not lack of profitability, but rather lack of working capital, which helps to explain why some experts advise: 'Use someone else's money every chance you get and don't let anyone else use yours.'

HOW IT WORKS IN PRACTICE
Working capital is also called net current assets or current capital, and is expressed as:

current assets – current liabilities

Current assets are cash and assets that can be converted to cash within one year or a normal operating cycle; current liabilities are monies owed that are due within one year.

If a company's current assets total £300,000 and its current liabilities total £160,000, its working capital is:

£300,000 – £160,000 = £140,000

The working capital cycle describes capital (usually cash) as it moves through a company: it first flows from a company to pay for supplies, materials, finished goods inventory, and wages to workers who produce goods and services. It then flows into a company as goods and services are sold and as new investment equity and loans are received. Each stage of this cycle consumes time. The more time the stages consume, the greater the demands on working capital.

TRICKS OF THE TRADE
- Good management of working capital includes actions like collecting receivables faster and moving inventory more quickly; generating more cash increases working capital.
- While it can be tempting to use cash to pay for fixed assets like computers or vehicles, doing so reduces the amount of cash available for working capital.
- If working capital is tight, consider other ways of financing capital investment, such as loans, fresh equity, or leasing.
- Early warning signs of insufficient working capital may include pressure on existing cash; exceptional cash-generating activities such as offering high discounts for early payment; increasing lines of credit; partial payments to suppliers and creditors; a preoccupation with surviving rather than managing; frequent short-term emergency requests to the bank, for example, to help pay wages, pending receipt of a cheque.
- Several ratios measure how effectively and efficiently working capital is being used. These ratios are explained separately.

THE BEST SOURCES OF HELP
Website:
Investopedia.com: **www.investopedia.com**

Calculating Yield

WHAT IT MEASURES
Shares that pay dividends (note that not all do) will produce an annual cash return to the investor. Simply dividing this cash return by the current share price and expressing that as a percentage is known as the 'yield' – that is, the annual percentage income at the current price. As far as newspapers are concerned, the yield figure published there is usually the historical one.

Analysts will often provide forecasts for dividends in terms of earnings per share (EPS) and thus the forecast yield can then be calculated. Forecasts can, of course, go wrong, and consequently there is some risk in relying upon them.

WHY IT IS IMPORTANT
Yield, after the price/earnings ratio (P/E), is one of the most common methods of comparing the relative value of shares and that is why it is so widely quoted in the press. The majority of investors like to see a cash income from their shares, although to some extent this is a cultural thing. There are more companies in the United States, for example, that pay no dividends than in the United Kingdom.

HOW IT WORKS IN PRACTICE
You can compare yields against the market average or against a sector average, which in turn gives you some idea of the relative value of the share against its peers, much like other ratios. Other things being equal, a higher yield share is preferable to that of an identical company with a lower yield. The higher yield share is cheaper. In practice of course, there may well be good reasons why the market has decided that the higher yielder should be so – possibly it has worse prospects, is less profitable, and so on. This is not always the case; the market is far from being a perfectly rational place.

An additional feature of the yield (unlike many of the other share analysis ratios), is that it enables comparison with cash. When you put cash into an interest-bearing source like a bank account or a government stock, you get a yield – the annual interest payable. This is usually a pretty safe investment. You can compare the yield from this cash investment with the yield on shares, which are far riskier. This produces a valuable basis for share evaluation. If, for example, you can get 4 percent in a bank without capital risk, you can then look at shares and ask yourself how this yield compares – given that, as well as the opportunity for long-term growth of both the share price and the dividends, there is plenty of capital risk.

TRICKS OF THE TRADE

Care is necessary, however, because unlike banks paying interest, companies are under no obligation to pay dividends at all. Frequently, if they go through a bad patch, even the largest, most well-known household name companies will cut dividends or even abandon paying them altogether. So, share yield is greatly less reliable than bank interest or government stock interest yield.

Despite this, yield is an immensely useful feature of share appraisal. It is the only ratio that tells you about the cash return to the investor, and you cannot argue with cash. Earnings per share (EPS), for example, is subject to accountants' opinions but a dividend once paid is an unarguable fact.

THE BEST SOURCES OF HELP
Website:
The Accounting Standards Board UK:
   www.frc.org.uk/asb

Reading an Annual Report

GETTING STARTED

Every company must publish an annual report to its shareholders as a matter of corporate law. The primary purpose of this report is to inform shareholders of the company's performance. As a legal requirement, the report usually contains a profit and loss account, a balance sheet, a cash-flow statement, a directors' report, and an auditors' report. The different elements tell you about different aspects of the company's performance and can be read in particular order to build up a true picture of how it is doing.

   Many companies also provide a lot of other non-statutory information on their affairs, in the interests of general communication. In some cases, this may be little more than gloss, contrived to illustrate the company's wonderful achievements while remaining strangely silent on negative features.

FAQS

Is there any difference between annual reports from private and public companies?
The main difference is usually length. The reports of privately held companies will be far shorter because their mandatory reporting requirements are much reduced. Additionally, they will be less concerned with image and consequently will tend to omit the non-compulsory public relations features that are present in public company reports.

What guarantee is there that an annual report is a true picture of a company's performance and not just propaganda put out by directors?
All annual reports have to include a report from the auditors, independent accountants charged with investigating a company's financial affairs to ensure that the published figures give a true and fair view of performance. Their investigation cannot extend to examining

every single transaction (impossible in a company of any size), so they use statistical sampling and other risk-based testing procedures to assess the quality of the company's systems as a basis for producing the annual report. They are not infallible, but they stand between the shareholders and the directors as a way of trying to ensure probity in the running of the company.

MAKING IT HAPPEN
Understanding the main contents of an annual report
The best way to look at this is to take an example. Standard sections in annual reports can vary from country to country, but the following is the contents list of a medium-sized UK public company – let's call it X plc.
- X world
- Chairman's statement
- Chief executive's review
- Financial review
- X in the community
- Environment, health, and safety
- Board of directors
- Directors' report
- Board report on remuneration
- Directors' responsibilities
- Report of the auditors
- Financial statements
- Five-year record
- Shareholder information

X world – belongs in the PR area. It tells you about the company, its products and markets.

Chairman's statement – comments on the group results for the year and upon future developments. It also provides detail on earnings per share and dividends.

Chief executive's review – goes into more detail about individual divisions, breaking down the operating results from areas around the world. It tells us a bit about discontinued businesses and new ones acquired.

Financial review – expands on the two previous sections in a more quantitative way, looking at things like cash-flow and how it affected group debt; interest charges; the effect of exchange rate fluctuations on profits, assets and liabilities; exceptional items that affect the profits (such as the disposal of a subsidiary company), and so on.

X in the community – tells us about the company's initiatives in third-world employment matters: scholarship programmes at universities in countries where they have a presence, and similar topics.

Environment, health, and safety – describes the company's policies towards these matters and how they are maintained by a system of inspection and monitoring.

Board of directors – lists the directors, with a brief description and possibly a photo of each.

Directors' report – is a compulsory feature of the annual report, discussing important items such as the number of shares controlled by each director and outside major shareholders. It mentions changes on the board, political or charitable contributions made by the company in the year, and a series of other issues.

Board report on remuneration – describes the work of a committee of non-executive directors, who decide the directors' income and that of other senior employees. Their remit includes looking at service contracts, bonus and share option schemes, plus pension plans. It includes an analysis of the pay of each director, with comparable figures for the previous year plus details of share options, and so on.

Directors' responsibilities – is a mandatory statement showing exactly what the directors are obliged to discharge with regard to the annual report, maintaining accurate accounting records, and so on.

Report of the auditors – is simply what it says. Their findings are published using standard language in this report.

Financial statements – are the main purpose of the annual report. In the example of X plc, these consist of:

- Consolidated profit and loss account. The profit and loss account of all the group as one.
- Consolidated and company balance sheets. The former is the group balance sheet and the latter shows the parent company alone.
- Consolidated cash-flow statement. A guide to how the money flowing in and out of the company was utilised.
- Notes to the accounts. These amplify numerous points contained in the figures and are usually critical for anyone wishing to study the accounts in detail.

Five-year record – shows a very abbreviated set of profit and loss and balance sheet figures for the current and previous four years. Some companies provide a ten-year record.

Shareholder information – deals with matters such as the registered office, share registrars, brokers, solicitors, dates for meetings and dividend payments, and other points.

Choosing the right order in which to read the report

One way is simply to read the report from cover to cover, like a book. However, if you are not experienced with these things, that may lead you to giving equal weight to all the contents and, perhaps, overvaluing the glossy PR bits at the expense of the hard facts shown by the figures.

Start with the auditors' report

Remember that this thin grey line of accountants is all that stands between the outside shareholder and the directors. To speed up matters, look at the final paragraph, their opinion. Does that statement give a true and fair view? If so, fine. If not, then it is said to be 'qualified'. Qualifications vary in depth from the disastrous, meaning that the company has got something seriously wrong, to perhaps a difference of opinion between the auditors and the board over some accounting matter. Most auditors' reports are unqualified, but, if there is a qualification present, you will have to judge how much the accounts can be relied upon as a measure of the company's performance.

Next, turn to the five/ten-year review

This is where you build up a mental picture of the company's financial history. Look at earnings per share (EPS) – is it increasing, decreasing, fluctuating wildly? This gives you an idea of how it has been doing over the period. Look at dividends, if any, and consider their pattern. Do they follow EPS or, as is likely, are they showing a smoother picture? Look at company debt, if the information is there, and compare it with shareholders' funds. How is it changing over the years?

Generally, try to build up a view as to whether the company is doing better, worse, or perhaps has no particular pattern over the period. Depending on your reasons for reading the report, a set of prejudices will have begun to develop from this historical picture. If it shows a declining financial situation, this could be a good thing from some points of view – if you wish to acquire the company, for example. If you are an employee though, it would not be very encouraging. So reading reports depends to some extent upon which angle you are coming from.

Now read the chairman's and directors' comments

These will give a deeper feel for the company's business, over and above the raw numerical data. Try to exercise a degree of scepticism in some areas, because it is natural for directors to attempt to play up the good points and play down the less good ones.

Get to the heart of the matter

The kernel of the report comprises the financial statements and the huge number of notes that accompany them. A lot of it is in highly technical accounting terminology, but it gives you the intimate financial detail on the year. Never ignore the notes – they are critical. In fact some investment analysts read the report from the back, because the notes are so important.

Notes have increased dramatically over the years as new legal and accounting standards have been introduced, primarily to enforce standardisation so that accounts are more comparable, but also to avoid 'creative accounting', whereby some companies have tried to conceal (legitimately) financial undesirables.

Relax with the glossy stuff

Having absorbed all that really matters, settle back and read the glossy bits that tell you how wonderful the company is. Just remember to exercise a mild degree of cynicism here – this is the least important, though no doubt the most visually attractive, part of the annual report. The real picture of the company is the numbers, not the photo of the bloke in the hard hat standing on an oil rig!

COMMON MISTAKES

Paying too much attention to pictures and comments and too little to the data

This can give a false view of how well, or badly, the company is doing. Understandably, a large number of people have difficulty in comprehending the figures. But if you want to appreciate annual reports properly, then learning to read accounts is essential.

Some cynics among investment analysts have even expressed the view that there is an adverse relationship between the number of glossy pages in an annual report and the company's actual performance. Maybe that's a little harsh – but there might be something in it.

THE BEST SOURCES OF HELP
Website:
The Accounting Standards Board UK:
  www.frc.org.uk/asb

Calculating Depreciation

GETTING STARTED

Depreciation is a basic expense of doing business, reducing a company's earnings while increasing its cash-flow. It affects three key financial statements: balance sheet; cash-flow; and income (or profit and loss). It is based on two key facts: the purchase price of the items or property in question, and their 'useful life'.

Depreciation values and practices are governed by national tax laws, which must be monitored continuously for any changes that are made. Accounting bodies, too, have developed standard practices and procedures for conducting depreciation.

Depreciating a single asset is not difficult: the challenge lies in depreciating the many assets possessed by even small companies, and is intensified by the impact that depreciation has on income and cash-flow statements, and on income tax returns. It is essential to depreciate with care and to rely on experts, ensuring that they fully understand the current government rules and regulations.

FAQS
What is depreciation?

It is an allocation of the cost of an asset over a period of time for accounting and tax purposes. Depreciation is charged against earnings, on the basis that the use of capital assets is a legitimate cost of doing business. Depreciation is also a non-cash expense that is added into net income to determine cash-flow in a given accounting period.

What is straight-line depreciation?

One of the two principal depreciation methods, it is based on the assumption that an asset loses an equal amount of its value each year of its useful life. Straight-line depreciation deducts an equal amount from a company's earnings throughout the life of the asset.

What is accelerated depreciation?

The other principal method of depreciation is based on the assumption that an asset loses a larger amount of its value in the early years of its useful life. Also known as the 'declining-balance' method, it is used by accountants to reduce a company's tax bills as soon as possible, and is calculated on the basis of the same percentage rate each year of an asset's useful life. Accelerated depreciation also better reflects the economic value of the asset being depreciated, which tends to become increasingly less efficient and more costly to maintain as it grows older.

What can be depreciated?

To qualify for depreciation, assets must:
• be used in the business
• be items that wear out, become obsolete, or lose value over time from natural causes or circumstances
• have a useful life beyond a single tax year

Examples include vehicles, machines and equipment, computers and office furnishings, and buildings, plus major additions or improvements to such assets. Some intangible assets can also be included under certain conditions.

Year	Straight-line Method Annual Depreciation	Year-end Book Value	Declining-balance Method Annual Depreciation	Year-end Book Value
1	£900 × 20 percent = £180	£1,000 – £180 = £820	£1,000 × 40 percent = £400	£1,000 – £400 = £600
2	£900 × 20 percent = £180	£820 – £180 = £640	£600 × 40 percent = £240	£600 – £240 = £360
3	£900 × 20 percent = £180	£640 – £180 = £460	£360 × 40 percent = £144	£360 – £144 = £216
4	£900 × 20 percent = £180	£460 – £180 = £280	£216 × 40 percent = £86.40	£216 – £86.40 = £129.60
5	£900 × 20 percent = £180	£280 – £180 = £100	£129.60 × 40 percent = £51.84	£129.60 – £51.84 = £77.76

What cannot be depreciated?

Land, personal assets, stock, leased or rented property, and a company's employees.

MAKING IT HAPPEN

In order to determine the annual depreciation cost of assets, it is necessary first to know the initial cost of those assets, how many years they will retain some value for the business, and what value, if any, they will have at the end of their useful life.

For example, a company buys a lorry to carry materials and finished goods. The vehicle loses value as soon as it is purchased, and then loses more with each year it is in service, until the cost of repairs exceeds its overall value. Measuring the loss in the value of the lorry is depreciation.

Straight-line depreciation is the most straightforward method, and is still quite common. It assumes that the net cost of an asset should be written off in equal amounts over its life. The formula used is:

(original cost – scrap value) / useful life (years)

For example, if the lorry cost £30,000 and can be expected to serve the business for seven years, its original cost would be divided by its useful life:

(30,000 – 2,000) / 7 = 4,000 per year

The £4,000 becomes a depreciation expense that is reported on the company's year-end income statement under 'operation expenses'.

In theory, an asset should be depreciated over the actual number of years that it will be used, according to its actual drop in value each year. At the end of each year, all the depreciation claimed to date is subtracted from its cost in order to arrive at its 'book value', which would equal its market value. At the end of its useful business life, any un-depreciated portion would represent the salvage value for which it could be sold or scrapped.

For tax purposes, some accountants prefer to use accelerating depreciation to record larger amounts of depreciation in the asset's early years in order to reduce tax bills as soon as possible. In contrast to the straight-line method, the declining-balance method assumes that the asset depreciates more in its earlier years of use. The table above compares the depreciation amounts that would be available, under these two methods, for a £1,000 asset that is expected to be used for five years and then sold for £100 in scrap.

While the straight-line method results in the same deduction each year, the declining-balance method produces larger deductions in the first years and far smaller deductions in the later years. One result of this system is that, if the equipment is expected to be sold for a higher value at some point in the middle of its life, the declining-balance method can produce a greater taxable gain in that year because the book value of the asset will be relatively lower.

The depreciation method to be used for a particular asset is fixed at the time that the asset is first placed in service. Whatever rules or tables are in effect for that year must be followed as long as the asset is owned.

Depreciation laws and regulations change frequently over the years as a result of government policy changes, so a company owning property over a long period may have to use several different depreciation methods.

TRICKS OF THE TRADE

- With rare exceptions, it is not possible to deduct in one year the entire cost of an asset if that asset has a useful life substantially beyond the tax year.
- To qualify for depreciation, an asset must be put into service. Simply purchasing it is not enough. There are rules that govern how much depreciation can be claimed on items put into service after a year has begun.
- It is common knowledge that if a company claims more depreciation than it is entitled to, it is liable for stiff penalties in a tax audit, just as failure to allow for depreciation causes an overestimation of income. What is not commonly known is that if a company does not claim all the depreciation deductions it is entitled to, it will be considered as having claimed them when taxable gains or losses are eventually calculated on the sale or disposal of the asset in question.
- While leased property cannot be depreciated, the cost of making permanent improvements to leased property can be (refurbishing a leased office, for example). There are many rules governing leased assets; they should be depreciated with care.
- Another common mistake is to continue depreciating property beyond the end of its recovery period. Cars are common examples of this.

- Conservative companies depreciate many assets as quickly as possible, despite the fact that this practice reduces reported net income. Knowledgeable investors watch carefully for such practices.

Calculating Amortisation

WHAT IT MEASURES

Amortisation is a method of recovering (deducting or writing off) the capital costs of intangible assets over a fixed period of time. Its calculation is virtually identical to the straight-line method of depreciation.

Amortisation also refers to the establishment of a schedule for repaying the principal and interest on a loan in equal amounts over a period of time. Because computers have made this a simple calculation, business references to amortisation tend to focus more on the term's first definition.

WHY IT IS IMPORTANT

Amortisation enables a company to identify its true costs, and thus its net income, more precisely. In the course of their business, most enterprises acquire intangible assets such as a patent for an invention, or a well-known brand or trademark. Since these assets can contribute to the revenue growth of the business, they can be – and are allowed to be-deducted against those future revenues over a period of years, provided the procedure conforms to accepted accounting practices.

For tax purposes, the distinction is not always made between amortisation and depreciation, yet amortisation remains a viable financial accounting concept in its own right.

HOW IT WORKS IN PRACTICE

Amortisation is computed using the straight-line method of depreciation: divide the initial cost of the intangible asset by the estimated useful life of that asset. For example, if it costs £10,000 to acquire a patent and it has an estimated useful life of 10 years, the amortised amount per year is £1,000.

$$£10,000 / 10 = £1,000 \text{ per year}$$

The amount of amortisation accumulated since the asset was acquired appears on the organisation's balance sheet as a deduction under the amortised asset.

While that formula is straightforward, amortisation can also incorporate a variety of non-cash charges to net earnings and/or asset values, such as depletion, write-offs, prepaid expenses, and deferred charges. Accordingly, there are many rules to regulate how these charges appear on financial statements. The rules are different in each country, and are occasionally changed, so it is necessary to stay abreast of them and rely on expert advice.

For financial reporting purposes, an intangible asset is amortised over a period of years. The amortisable life – 'useful life' – of an intangible asset is the period over which it gives economic benefit. Several factors are considered when determining this useful life; for example, demand and competition, effects of obsolescence, legal or contractual limitations, renewal provisions, and service life expectations.

Intangibles that can be amortised can include:

- **Copyrights,** based on the amount paid either to purchase them or to develop them internally, plus the costs incurred in producing the work (wages or materials, for example). At present, a copyright is granted to a corporation for 75 years, and to an individual for the life of the author plus 70 years. However, the estimated useful life of a copyright is usually far shorter than its legal life, and it is generally amortised over a fairly short period.
- **Cost of a franchise,** including any fees paid to the franchiser, as well legal costs or expenses incurred in the acquisition. A franchise granted for a limited period should be amortised over its life. If the franchise has an indefinite life, it should be amortised over a reasonable period, not to exceed 40 years.
- **Covenants not to compete** an agreement by the seller of a business not to engage in a competing business in a certain area for a specific period of time. The cost of the not-to-compete covenant should be amortised over the period covered by the covenant unless its estimated economic life is expected to be shorter.
- **Easement costs** that grant a right of way may be amortised if there is a limited and specified life.
- **Organisation costs** incurred when forming a corporation or a partnership, including legal fees, accounting services, incorporation fees, and other related services. Organisation costs are usually amortised over 60 months.
- **Patents,** both those developed internally and those purchased. If developed internally, a patent's 'amortisable basis' includes legal fees incurred during the application process. Normally, a patent is amortised over its legal life, or over its remaining life if purchased. However, it should be amortised over its legal life or its economic life, whichever is the shorter.
- **Trademarks, brands, and trade names,** which should be written

off over a period not to exceed 40 years. However, since the value of these assets depends on the changing tastes of consumers, they are frequently amortised over a shorter period.

- Other types of property that may be amortised include certain intangible drilling costs, circulation costs, mine development costs, pollution control facilities, and reforestation expenditures. They can even include intangibles such as the value of a market share or a market's composition: an example is the portion of an acquired business that is attributable to the existence of a given customer base.

TRICKS OF THE TRADE

- Certain intangibles cannot be amortised, but may be depreciated using a straight-line approach if they have a 'determinable' useful life. Because the rules are different in each country and are subject to change, it is essential to rely on specialist advice.
- Computer software may be amortised under certain conditions, depending on its purpose. Software that is amortised is generally given a 60-month life, but it may be amortised over a

shorter period if it can clearly be established that it will be obsolete or no longer used within a shorter time.

- Under certain conditions, customer lists that were purchased may be amortised if it can be demonstrated that the list has a finite useful life, in that customers on the list are likely to be lost over a period of time.
- While leasehold improvements are depreciated for income tax purposes, they are amortised when it comes to financial reporting—either over the remaining term of the lease or their expected useful life, whichever is the shorter.
- Annual payments incurred under a franchise agreement should be expensed when incurred.
- The Internet has many amortisation loan calculators that can automatically determine monthly payment figures and the total cost of a loan.

THE BEST SOURCES OF HELP
Website:
Best Software: **www.bestsoftware.com**

Calculating Activity-based Costing

GETTING STARTED

Activity-based costing (ABC) attempts to create the big picture-crystal – clear, full, and accurate – by painting assorted little pictures.

- ABC identifies the relationship between a business activity and all the resources needed to conduct it by assigning costs to each of those resources, thus presenting the true total expense of the entire activity.
- ABC can account for so-called 'soft' or indirect operating costs, and thus produce a more revealing, and perhaps startlingly different, financial picture than other accounting methodologies such as standard costing might offer.
- Used properly, ABC helps management better to distinguish operations that add value from those that do not, allowing it to make more informed decisions about such matters as pricing, product mix, capital investments, and organisational change.
- In turn, its advocates praise ABC as a more effective tool to identify and control costs, improve productivity, and increase profits.

FAQS

When did ABC start?
ABC came of age in the 1980s amid manufacturers' furious efforts to raise the quality of their products while simultaneously eliminating every unnecessary cost from their operations. The dramatic improvements realised

by manufacturers have led to ABC becoming a widely used tool, especially in the manufacturing industry.

What are the basic steps of ABC?
There are five:
- identify the product or service to be studied
- determine all the resources and processes that are required to create the product or deliver the service, and their respective costs
- determine the 'cost drivers' for each resource: the cost of labour as well as raw materials
- collect cost and other data, such as time taken, for each process and resource
- use the data to calculate the overall cost of the product

What are ABC's principal advantages?
First, ABC can gauge virtually any activity, be it a manufacturing process, a business process, the performance of a service, or an administrative operation. Second, it considers a much wider range of resources and materials than more traditional accounting methodologies, and can thus present a more complete picture.

What are ABC's primary weaknesses?
It can be a very time-consuming exercise because of the volume of data it demands. Also, if not managed properly, ABC can transform every manager into an accountant whose energies become fixed on tracking the costs of the activity, rather than on tracking and perfecting the activity itself.

What kind of business sectors use ABC?

The list ranges from accountants to zoologists. It may be especially helpful to knowledge-based businesses that rely primarily on human services and related resources, whose total costs may be difficult to measure with more traditional accounting yardsticks.

What is critical to ABC's success?

Without gaining and maintaining the enduring commitment of all individuals, even a modestly detailed initiative will probably fail. It's also best to start with pilot projects to demonstrate success.

What preliminary steps are needed?

First, an organisation must understand its activities and the resources that these require. Second, it must understand thoroughly the amount of information required, and the expense of generating that information. It must also determine what level of accuracy will be acceptable.

MAKING IT HAPPEN

Creating an ABC cost-accounting system requires three preliminary steps:

- converting to an accrual basis of accounting
- defining cost centres and cost allocation
- determining process and procedure costs

Businesses have traditionally relied on the cash basis of accounting, which recognises income when received and expenses when paid. ABC's foundation is the accrual-basis income statement. The numbers this statement presents are assigned to the various procedures performed during a given period. Cost centres are a company's identifiable products and services, but also include specific and detailed tasks within these broader activities. Defining cost centres will of course vary by business and method of operation. What is critical to ABC is the inclusion of all activities and all resources. Once these steps have been taken, the results are often more than satisfying.

Banks and financial services firms, for example, have long used ABC-like methods to confirm that investments in automated teller machines would be both cheaper than continuing to rely on tellers and clerks and in their customers' best interests.

Railway companies have used the methodology to determine the cost of processing bills of lading by hand, fax, and the Internet. Studying such costs confirmed the wisdom of using e-commerce, generating annual savings of up to £1 million.

Law firms are better positioned to confirm that the hourly fees they charge – no matter how princely they may at first appear – do, in fact, enable them to provide their services profitably.

Finally, health-care providers use ABC to measure profitability, eliminate unnecessary costs, and plan for change. A medical practice that knows the actual cost of providing a specific service, for example, can make far better decisions about the price of managed health care.

For instance, let's say the Apple-a-Day Medical Clinic includes three doctors, Drs Peel, Core, and Stem. Their clinic has an in-house laboratory and a radiology department. All direct revenues and expenses are allocated to the doctor who performs the service and incurs the expense. Indirect variable overhead costs are allocated to each doctor based on the proportion of total revenues that each generates in a given period. Fixed overhead costs are divided equally among doctors. Because of their respective incomes and expense allocations, each doctor would represent a separate cost centre.

Additional cost centres for this medical practice could be laboratory, radiology, and administration. As cost centres are defined, they could further be classified as, say, 'patient service centres' or 'support centres'. In this example, laboratory, radiology, and each individual doctor's activity would be patient service centres, while administration would be a support centre.

Once cost centres are identified, management teams can begin studying the activities each one engages in and allocating the expenses each one incurs, including the cost of employee services. In this health-care scenario, activities would range from actual treatment by doctors and nurses, X-rays, medical tests and assessments of their results, plus such administrative support services as personnel, book-keeping, rent, utilities, property insurance, office supplies, advertising, telecommunications expenses, and equipment costs related to the administrative function. Rent, utilities, and property insurance are usually allocated on the basis of the square footage that the particular activity covers.

Tracking and allocating the detailed costs of individual activities and procedures can be accomplished by different methods, with various degrees of accuracy. The more detailed the cost analysis, of course, the greater the accuracy of the data. Then again, as the detail increases, so does the time and expense.

The most appropriate method is developed from time studies and direct expense allocation. Management teams who choose this method will need to devote several months to data collection in order to generate sufficient information to establish the personnel components of each activity's total cost. The cost of this exercise itself can be significant, but also worthwhile. Proponents say ABC has resulted in cost savings worth as much as 14 times the cost of the exercise. More importantly, the exercise has provided solid documentation for decisions that 'seemed correct', as a Chrysler Corporation team once reported, 'but could not be supported with hard evidence'.

Time studies establish the average amount of time required to complete each task, plus best- and worst-case performances. Only those resources actually used are factored into the cost computation; unused resources are reported separately. These studies can also advise managements how best to monitor and allocate expenses which might otherwise be expressed as part of general overheads, or go undetected altogether.

Notably, determining how much of an operation's personnel is underused or unused can significantly help management planning, specifically by exposing activities that are overstaffed or understaffed. This can be especially helpful to any knowledge-based business, since payroll is almost always its highest cost. Moreover, in any business, the more efficiently an enterprise deploys its personnel, the more profitable it will be.

COMMON MISTAKES
Getting caught up in the details
Notwithstanding its successes, ABC remains a tool, not an end in itself. Organisations can lose sight of that fact, if they are not careful, and end up allowing it to dominate their working lives.

The enormity and complexity of such a project should never be underestimated. The data requirements alone are daunting. It is all too easy to get caught up in ABC's details and mechanics. In turn, estimating some costs is often recommended, to minimise the level of detail.

At the same time, however, some details are important pre-requisites of objectivity and success. For example, if time studies are not used, some other measure must be used to allocate personnel and related costs, as well as indirect costs such as percentage of revenues or income, or the number of customer calls. These methods require far less time for compiling data and are less costly, but drawbacks abound. For one thing, accuracy suffers, and they are almost always subjective, potentially to the point of compromising the entire initiative. Being far less precise, these alternative methods also do not differentiate between used and unused personnel resources, and will not provide information on unused capacity or trends in procedure costs.

Without the aid of computer software that has been developed to automate the process, ABC can be hopelessly time-consuming. Indeed, unaided by technology, ABC might well be hoist with its own petard and exposed as an outrageous waste of time.

Like any cost-accounting system, activity-based costing is not static. Once established, it needs to be maintained and updated as business conditions and organisations change.

Finally, in delivering its crystal-clear pictures, activity-based costing also has the potential to make individual champions of particular products or services squirm, because it may reveal them to be far more expensive than they might otherwise appear. All the more reason for advocating caution: 'Be careful what you wish for!'

If a management team is to reduce and eliminate costs, it must first identify them and grasp their impact on specific processes or products. Because activity-based costing can paint a single picture that reveals all the individual direct and indirect costs a business incurs in a given operation, it can be a powerful tool for both assessing current operations and guiding prompt and intelligent reactions as circumstances change. In fact, it's also known as activity-based management (ABM).

THE BEST SOURCES OF HELP
Website:
Activity Based Costing Benchmarking Association (ABCBA™): **www.abcbenchmarking.com**

Calculating Price/Sales Ratio

WHAT IT MEASURES
The price/sales ratio (P/S) is another measure, like the price/earnings (P/E) ratio, of the relative value of a share when compared with others.

WHY IT IS IMPORTANT
Like many such price-based ratios, it does not mean too much in isolation but acquires worth when making comparisons. So a figure of 0.33 does not say a lot on its own, until you start to look at how this matches up to the market average or the sector average, for example.

HOW IT WORKS IN PRACTICE
The P/S ratio is obtained by dividing the market capitalisation by the latest published annual sales figure. So a company with a capitalisation of £1 billion and sales of £3 billion would have a P/S ratio of 0.33.

P/S will vary with the type of industry. You would expect, for example, that many retailers and other large-scale distributors of goods would have very high sales in relation to their market capitalisations – in other words, a very low P/S. Equally, manufacturers of high-value items would generally have much lower sales figures and thus higher P/S ratios. Like anything to do with share analysis (this being more of an art than a science), it is not always that clear cut . . . but that would be the general trend. If you rank companies by ascending P/S, you will find usually that supermarket chains figure among the lowest.

A company with a lower P/S is cheaper than one with a higher ratio, particularly if they are in the same sector so that a direct comparison is more appropriate. It means that each share of the lower P/S company is buying you more of its sales than those of the higher P/S company.

Note though, that it is cheaper only on P/S grounds; that does not mean it is necessarily the more attractive share. There will frequently be reasons why it has a lower ratio than another, ostensibly similar company, most commonly because it is less profitable. As far as corporate efficiency goes, this ratio considers only sales, the top line of the profit and loss account. It is a long way from there to the bottom line, the bit that really counts (that is, how much profit the company has made).

TRICKS OF THE TRADE

- A loss-making company would thus still have a P/S ratio, even though it would have no P/E ratio. In consequence, like all

investment analysis tools, P/S has to be used with care – but it can be of use for investors. P/S was cited in an extensive study of the New York Stock Exchange as one leading indicator for selecting very long-term shares that perform well.

THE BEST SOURCES OF HELP
Websites:
Investopedia.com: **www.investopedia.com**
The Motley Tool: **www.fool.co.uk**

Calculating EBITDA

WHAT IT MEASURES
A company's earnings from ongoing operations, before net income is calculated.

WHY IT IS IMPORTANT
EBITDA's champions contend it gives investors a sense of how much money a young or fast-growing company is generating before it pays interest on debt, settles with tax collectors, and accounts for non-cash changes. If EBITDA grows over time, champions argue, investors gain at least a sense of long-term profitability and, in turn, the wisdom of their investment.

Business appraisers and investors also may study EBITDA to help to gauge a company's fair market value, often as a prelude to its acquisition by another company. It also is frequently applied to companies that have been subject to leveraged buyouts – the strategy being that EBITDA will help to cover loan payments needed to finance the transaction.

EBITDA, and EBIT, too, are claimed to be good indicators of cash-flow from business operations, since they report earnings before debt payments, taxes, depreciation, and amortisation charges are considered. However, that claim is challenged by many – often rather vigorously.

HOW IT WORKS IN PRACTICE
EBITDA first appeared as leveraged buyouts soared in popularity during the 1980s. It has since become well established as a financial-analysis measure of telecommunications, cable, and major media companies.

Its formula is quite simple. Revenues less the cost of goods sold, general and administrative expenses, and the deductions of items expressed by the acronym EBITDA:

revenue – expenses (excluding interest, taxes, depreciation, and amortisation) = EBITDA

or:

revenue – expenses (excluding tax and interest) = EBIT

This formula does not measure true cash-flow. A communications company, for example, once reported £698 million in EBIT but just £324 million in cash from operations.

TRICKS OF THE TRADE

- A definition of EBITDA isn't as yet enforced by standards-making bodies, so companies can all but create their own. As a result, EBITDA can easily be manipulated by aggressive accounting policies, which may erode its reliability.
- Ignoring capital expenditures could be unrealistic and horribly misleading, because companies in capital-intensive sectors such as manufacturing and transportation must continually make major capital investments to remain competitive. High-technology is another sector that may be capital-intensive, at least initially.
- Critics warn that using EBITDA as a cash-flow indicator is a huge mistake, because EBITDA ignores too many factors that have an impact on true cash-flow, such as working capital, debt payments, and other fixed expenses. Interest and taxes can and do cost a company cash, they point out, while debt holders have higher claims on a company's liquid assets than investors do.
- Critics further assail EBITDA as the barometer of choice of unprofitable firms because it can present a more optimistic view of a company's future than it has a right to claim. *Forbes* magazine, for instance, once referred to EBIDTA as 'the device of choice to pep up earnings announcements'.
- Even so, EBITDA may be useful in terms of evaluating firms in the same industry with widely different capital structures, tax rates and depreciation policies.

THE BEST SOURCES OF HELP
Websites:
Investopedia: **www.investopedia.com**
The Motley Fool: **www.fool.co.uk**

Calculating Dividend Cover

WHAT IT MEASURES
Dividend cover expresses the number of times a company's dividends to ordinary shareholders could be paid out of its net after-tax profits.

Payout ratio expresses the total dividends paid to shareholders as a percentage of a company's net profit in a given period of time.

WHY IT IS IMPORTANT
Whether defined as dividend cover or payout ratio, it measures the likelihood of dividend payments being sustained, and thus is a useful indication of sustained profitability. However, each ratio must be interpreted independently.

A low dividend cover suggests it might be difficult to pay the same level of dividends in a downturn, and that a company is not reinvesting enough in its future. Negative dividend cover is unusual, and a clear sign of trouble.

The payout ratio, expressed as a percentage or fraction, is an inverse measure: a high ratio indicates a lack of reinvestment in the business, and that current earnings cannot sustain the current dividend payments.

HOW IT WORKS IN PRACTICE
Dividend cover is so named because it shows how many times over the profits could have paid the dividend. To calculate dividend cover, divide earnings per share by the dividend per share:

earnings per share / dividend per share = dividend cover

If a company has earnings per share of £8, and it pays out a dividend of 2.1, dividend cover is:

8 / 2.1 = 3.80

An alternative formula divides a company's net profit by the total amount allocated for dividends. So a company that earns £10 million in net profit and allocates £1 million for dividends has a dividend cover of 10, while a company that earns £25 million and pays out £10 million in dividends has a dividend cover of 2.5:

10,000,000 / 1,000,000 = 10 and 25,000,000 / 10,000,000 = 2.5

The payout ratio is calculated by dividing annual dividends paid on ordinary shares by earnings per share:

annual dividend / earnings per share = payout ratio

Take the company whose earnings per share is £8 and its dividend payout is 2.1. Its payout ratio would be:

2.1 / 8 = 0.263 or 26.3 percent

TRICKS OF THE TRADE
- A dividend cover ratio of 2 or higher is usually adequate, and indicates that the dividend is affordable. By the same token, the payout ratio should not exceed two-thirds of earnings. Like most ratios, however, both vary by industry.
- A dividend cover ratio below 1.5 is risky, and a ratio below 1 indicates a company is paying the current year's dividend with retained earnings from a previous year – a practice that cannot continue indefinitely.
- The higher the dividend cover figure, the less likely it is that the dividend will be reduced or eliminated in the future, should profits fall. Companies that suffer sharp declines or outright losses will often continue paying dividends to indicate that their substandard performance is an anomaly.
- On the other hand, a high dividend cover figure may disappoint an investor looking for income, since the figure suggests directors could have declared a larger dividend.
- A high payout ratio clearly appeals to conservative investors seeking income. However, when coupled with weak or falling earnings it could suggest an imminent dividend cut, or that the company is short-changing reinvestment to maintain its payout.
- A payout ratio above 75 percent is a warning to be heeded. It suggests the company is failing to reinvest sufficient profits in its business, that the company's earnings are faltering, or that it is trying to attract investors who otherwise would not be interested.
- Newer and faster-growing companies often pay no dividends at all in order to reinvest earnings in the company's development.

THE BEST SOURCES OF HELP
Website:
finance-glossary.com: **www.finance-glossary.com**

Calculating Interest Cover

WHAT IT MEASURES
The amount of earnings available to make interest payments after all operating and non-operating income and expenses – except interest and income taxes – have been accounted for.

WHY IT IS IMPORTANT

Interest cover is regarded as a measure of a company's creditworthiness because it shows how much income there is to cover interest payments on outstanding debt. Banks and financial analysts also rely on this ratio as a rule of thumb to gauge the fundamental strength of a business.

HOW IT WORKS IN PRACTICE

Interest cover is expressed as a ratio, and reflects a company's ability to pay the interest obligations on its debt. It compares the funds available to pay interest – earnings before interest and taxes, or EBIT – with the interest expense. The basic formula is:

EBIT / interest expense = interest coverage ratio

If interest expense for a year is £9 million, and the company's EBIT is £45 million, the interest coverage would be:

45 million / 9 million = 5 : 1

The higher the number, the stronger a company is likely to be. Conversely, a low number suggests that a company's fortunes are looking ominous. Variations of this basic formula also exist. For example, there is:

operating cash flow + interest + taxes / interest = cash-flow interest coverage ratio

This ratio indicates the company's ability to use its cash flow to satisfy its fixed financing obligations. Finally, there is the fixed-charge coverage ratio, which compares EBIT with fixed charges:

EBIT + lease expenses / interest + lease expense = fixed charge coverage ratio

'Fixed charges' can be interpreted in many ways, however. It could mean, for example, the funds that a company is obliged to set aside to retire debt, or dividends on preferred stock.

TRICKS OF THE TRADE

- A ratio of less than 1 indicates that a company is having problems generating enough cash flow to pay its interest expenses, and that either a modest decline in operating profits or a sudden rise in borrowing costs could eliminate profitability entirely.
- Ideally, interest coverage should at least exceed 1.5; in some sectors, 2.0 or higher is desirable.
- Interest coverage is widely considered to be more meaningful than looking at total debt, because what really matters is what an enterprise must pay in a given period, not how much debt it has.
- As is often the case, it may be more meaningful to watch interest cover over several periods in order to detect long-term trends.
- Cash flow will sometimes be substituted for EBIT in the ratio, because EBIT includes not only cash but also accrued sales and other unrealised income.
- Interest cover also is called 'times interest earned'.

THE BEST SOURCES OF HELP
Websites:
Investopedia: **www.investopedia.com**
The Motley Fool: **www.fool.co.uk**

Calculating Earnings per Share

WHAT IT MEASURES
The portion of a company's profit allocated to each outstanding share of a company's common stock.

WHY IT IS IMPORTANT

Earnings per share (EPS) is simply a fundamental measure of profitability that shows how much profit was generated on a per-share-of-stock basis. Were the term worded as profit per share, the meaning certainly would be much clearer, if not self-evident.

By itself, EPS doesn't reveal a great deal. Its true value lies in comparing EPS figures across several quarters, or years, to judge the growth of a company's earnings on a per-share basis.

HOW IT WORKS IN PRACTICE

Essentially, the figure is calculated after paying taxes and dividends to preferred shareholders and bondholders.

Barring extraordinary circumstances, EPS data is reported quarterly, half-yearly, and annually.

To calculate EPS, start with net income (earnings) for the period in question, subtract the total value of any preferred stock dividends, then divide the resulting figure by the number of shares outstanding during that period. Or:

net income – dividends on preferred stock / average number of shares outstanding

By itself, this formula is simple enough. Alas, defining the factors used in the formula invariably introduces complexities and – as some allege on occasion – possible subterfuge.

For instance, while companies usually use a weighted average number of shares outstanding over the reporting period, shares outstanding still can be either 'primary' or 'fully diluted'. Primary EPS is calculated using the number of shares that are currently held by investors in the market and able to be traded. Diluted EPS is the result of a complex calculation that determines how many shares would be outstanding if all exercisable warrants and options were converted into common shares at the end of a quarter. Suppose, for example, that a company has granted a large number of share options to employees. If these options are capable of being exercised in the near future, that could alter significantly the number of shares in issue and thus the EPS – even though the E part (the earnings) is the same. Often in such cases, the company might quote the EPS on the existing shares and the fully diluted version. Which one a person considers depends on their view of the company and how they wish to use the EPS figure. In addition, companies can report extraordinary EPS, a figure which excludes the financial impact of unusual occurrences, such as discontinued operations or the sale of a business unit.

Net income or earnings, meanwhile, can be defined in a number of ways, based upon respective nations' generally accepted accounting principles.

For example, 'pro forma earnings', tend to exclude more expenses and income used to calculate 'reported earnings'. Pro forma advocates insist these earnings eliminate all distortions and present 'true' earnings that allow pure apples-to-apples comparisons with preceding periods. However, 'non-recurring expenses' seem to occur with such increasing regularity that one may wonder if a company is deliberately trying to manipulate its earnings figures and present them in the best possible light, rather than in the most accurate light.

'Cash' earnings are earnings from operating cash-flow – notably, not EBITDA. In turn, cash EPS is usually these earnings divided by diluted shares outstanding. This figure is very reliable because operating cash-flow is not subject to as much judgment at net earnings or pro forma earnings.

TRICKS OF THE TRADE

- Given the varieties of earnings and shares reported today, investors need to first determine what the respective figures represent before making investment decisions. There are cases of a company announcing a pro forma EPS that differs significantly from what is reported in its financial statements. Such discrepancies, in turn, can affect how the market values a given stock.
- Investors should check to see if a company has issued more shares during a given period, since that action, too, can affect EPS. A similar problem occurs where there have been a number of shares issued during the accounting period being considered. Which number of issued shares do you use: the opening figure, the closing figure, the mean? In practice the usual method is to use the weighted mean number of shares in issue during the year (weighted, that is, for the amount of time in the year that were in issue).
- 'Trailing' earnings per share is the sum of EPS from the last four quarters, and is the figure used to compute most price-to-earnings ratios.
- Diluted and primary shares outstanding can be the same if a company has no warrants or convertible bonds outstanding, but investors should not assume anything, and need to be sure how 'shares outstanding' is being defined.

THE BEST SOURCES OF HELP
Website:
Investopedia.com: **www.Investopedia.com/ articles/analyst/091901.asp**

Drawing Up a Budget

GETTING STARTED
Every business needs to plan its spending on the basis of what it expects from sales income; without this tool, you can't be sure that your business will survive. Budgeting is simply the name given to the process of working out what you expect your business to earn and spend in a given period. It also gives you the ability to check how the business is doing from week to week, or month to month; without this check, you can easily overspend. This actionlist explains how you can make use of your budget, and how to draw one up.

FAQS

What can I use a budget for?

It's important that you use your budget as a control mechanism. At the end of each month, you should enter the actual figures for sales and expenses next to the figures that were forecast. If there are substantial differences between the budgeted figures and the actual figures, then you need to do something about it. For instance, if your sales are too low, you may need to reconsider your marketing strategies. If sales, on the other hand, are higher than planned, then you may need to reconsider your staffing levels or raw material supplies in order to cope with the rising demand. Also, if your expenditure is too high, you'll need to find ways to bring costs down.

How do I estimate sales and expenditure?

The starting point for drawing up a budget is for you to estimate future sales and expenditure. The sales budget can be split into the number of different products your business plans to sell; the number of units of each product that you plan to sell; the price that you plan to sell each unit for; and the place or area where you plan to sell them.

You'll need to split your expenditure budget into production costs or variable costs (such as materials, power, and subcontractors); overhead costs or fixed costs (such as rent and salaries); and capital costs (equipment).

MAKING IT HAPPEN

Budgeting for sales

If your business is a new one, forecasting sales will be particularly tricky for you, because you don't have actual sales from the past on which you can base your expectations. Instead, you'll have to make sure that your budget is based on good research. It must also be closely tied to a realistic marketing plan that will generate the sales you expect. It's important not just to guess your sales figures. Also, don't start by looking at your planned expenditure and then just deriving a sales forecast to cover the cost.

Make the sales budget as detailed as you can. You need to make it very clear what you plan to sell, and at what price. Set out your expected sales on a monthly or quarterly basis. If your business sells a range of products, make sure that you prepare sales budgets for each of them. If your products are sold in more than one area, then you may find it helpful to have a sales budget for each area.

Budgeting for expenditure

Now that you have prepared the sales budget, you have the basic foundations for working out what your expenditure will be. For your purposes, the expenditure budget can be split into a production budget and an overheads budget. If you know how many products you'll sell, you can work out the direct costs of producing them. These direct costs will then make up the production budget, and will vary with the level of production. The overhead costs will stay more or less constant.

The production budget

The production budget is made up of items like the materials and components that go into the product.

If you have a sales team, you also need to include commission paid to them. (If sales people earn a regular retainer as well, this retainer would normally be regarded as a fixed cost.) Make sure that you include the cost of subcontractors, where people are being paid as independent contractors to perform a certain, defined job.

Discounts are usually shown in the budget as a direct cost.

There are some expenses, such as depreciation, that are usually treated as fixed overheads. However, if you want to be particularly accurate with your production budget, you could include these, especially if you can clearly associate them with specific products.

The overheads budget

Once you have prepared the production budget, you'll need to consider the other costs that the business will incur. These will include the salaries for you and your staff, National Insurance contributions, and pension contributions. You'll also need to include rent and company insurance, and telephone, Internet, and e-mail account costs. Any interest on money that you have borrowed will also need to be included in your overheads.

If your business is in manufacturing, it's likely that the above will represent a relatively small proportion of the total costs. On the other hand, if you have a service sector business, it's likely that overheads will represent a very high proportion of the cost. Include all overhead costs, including interest payments and drawings (how much money you plan to take out of the business). Remember that you are taxed on the total profit (if you are self-employed), so allow for this too. If your business is registered as a company, and you expect to take high dividends, make sure that you budget for this as well.

Your business may aim to allocate the overheads to each product, or may prefer to retain overheads as a single budget. Whichever path you choose, it's important that you ensure that the price for each product makes a reasonable contribution to the overheads.

Budgeting for the full cost of production

You're now in a position to pull together the production budget and the overheads budget into a single production cost budget. If there is more than one product or service, then there will be a production budget for each. There will also be variable overheads for you to add for each product. There is no need for you to split fixed overheads across products at this point, since the object of this exercise is for you to be able to determine the total costs.

Capital expenditure budget

If you expect to buy capital equipment, you'll need to decide how you'll pay for it (whether in cash or through a loan), and make sure that you budget for these payments in the relevant months. This is essential information if an accurate forecast is to be prepared, particularly where the business may have to take out a loan to finance the purchase and will have to meet a repayment schedule that includes interest.

If the business decides to lease equipment, it's important to make sure that you read all the small print. While the selling is carried out by a supplier, the leasing is done by a finance company. Usually the conditions are more favourable for them than for your business. On the other hand, the organisation leasing the equipment to you usually has a responsibility to ensure the equipment keeps working, even if the supplier can no longer support it.

Cash flow

If you operate your business on a cash basis, in other words taking in cash for your sales and paying cash for your purchases, then it's fairly easy to see if you are living within your means because you'll have cash left over at the end of the month if you're making a profit. Very few businesses, however, operate like this. It's far more likely that you'll be selling goods or services in one month, and not receiving payment until the following month, or the month after that. Similarly, you may be buying raw materials one month, but not paying for them for at least another four weeks. A budget will help you keep track of your cash flow in and out of the business, and keep control.

Once the budgets have been prepared, you can use the data that has been accumulated in order to prepare financial forecasts. This will include a cash flow forecast, but you should also include a forecast of the profit and loss statement, and the balance sheet. The cash flow forecast should set out, on a month-by-month basis, all cash inflows and outflows from the business for the following 12 months, will help you to determine your working capital needs. The profit and loss forecast will help you to check that your business remains profitable.

COMMON MISTAKES
Not setting realistic targets
If you set realistic targets, you'll be able to tell whether sales and expenditure have gone to plan, and you'll also be able to foresee problems and opportunities in time to take action.

Not bothering to prepare a cash-flow forecast
It's important to remember that a cash-flow forecast is as important as the budget itself. While the budget can tell you if your business is generally profitable, it might not alert you to cash-flow problems.

THE BEST SOURCES OF HELP
Websites:
Institute of Credit Management: **www.icm.org.uk**
Small Business – Information and Cash Flow:
www.credit-to-cash.com

Coping in a Cash-flow Crisis

GETTING STARTED
Many businesses face a cash-flow crisis at some point in their existence. Good financial management should generally prevent this but there are some circumstances that are difficult to avoid, especially in a company's early days or during challenging financial times. Events such as a major customer refusing – or becoming unable – to pay their debts can often saddle small businesses with serious cash-flow problems.

Running out of cash is probably the biggest cause of small businesses failing. There can be many reasons behind a cash crisis, so it's essential that you understand them and know how to prevent or mitigate short-term problems which might otherwise lead to business failure. No matter how good your balance sheet may look in terms of physical assets and outstanding debtors, your ability to convert these to cash at critical times can make the difference between survival and failure.

FAQS
What are the main causes of cash-flow problems?
Typical causes of cash-flow problems include:
- slow payment by your customers
- a key customer becomes insolvent owing you a large sum of money
- insufficient working capital
- focusing on turnover instead of profit
- poor financial planning
- buying too much stock

How can you spot when you're heading for a crisis?
Sometimes a cash-flow crisis will suddenly jump up and hit you, such as when a major debtor announces out of the blue that they cannot pay what they owe. Clearly, you can't always predict that things like this are going to happen, but you can take some steps to soften the blow. Spotting the problem in advance and doing something about it early is still the best step you can take, though, so try to bear this in mind, especially if you have one or two very large customers that you rely on.

You can spot the warning signs by keeping a close eye on your balance sheet. Is the number of debtors rising when everything else is constant? Are your stock levels, especially of finished goods, rising? If the answer to either of these is yes, then you may need to take remedial action.

You also need to keep a close eye on your profit and loss account, although it may take longer to spot problems. Is your profit falling? Worse, are you losing money? If the answer to either of these is yes, then your available working capital will be reducing, and this spells trouble.

MAKING IT HAPPEN

Make sure that you have procedures in place to safeguard, as far as possible, against cash-flow disasters. Even if these can't be prevented, the procedures you've worked out should enable you to see problems coming and act.

Control your finances effectively

The best form of preparation is an effective and robust system of financial control. Preparing a cash-flow forecast and – crucially! – putting it to good use is the basis for avoiding many cash-flow problems. The forecast allows you to anticipate most cash-flow-related issues that could occur during the normal course of running your business. It allows you to do a 'sensitivity analysis' in which you can test the effect of lower sales or slower payment on your cash flow.

Think about your pricing policy

Make sure that you're costing your products or services accurately and that what you charge for them will let you make a profit. Adopt tight credit-control systems and establish procedures for managing the whole process of giving your customers credit. Start by giving credit only to approved customers; check when their accounts are due for payment and that they pay according to your agreed terms. If you have efficient procedures for raising invoices promptly and sending statements to your customers, you won't be adding to payment delays yourself.

Incentivise prompt payment

Consider encouraging your clients to pay more quickly by offering a discount if they pay either on delivery or within a certain number of days (typically 7–14 days) from the invoice date. Generally the discount is between 2 percent and 5 percent of your sale price, but the exact level will depend on your profit margins and on how important early payment is to you.

Consider factoring

To speed up payments, you could use the services of an invoice discounter or factoring company. These companies enter into an arrangement where they will provide your business with an advance (usually 80 percent) on the value of your invoices as soon as they're raised. Interest is then charged on the balance drawn and there is a service charge. Factoring companies can also take control of collecting payments from your customer

directly, which save you the costs of using your own staff to manage the process. This type of service is particularly suitable for businesses that are growing rapidly because they reduce the likelihood that you'll run out of working capital. However, you may still suffer if a major customer goes down – the factor will usually recover the outstanding debt from you.

Aim to improve terms

As your business grows, you may be able to negotiate better credit terms with your suppliers. Initially, this could be achieved by progressing from paying at the time of purchase, to having a 30-day credit account. If the majority of your customers expect to have 60-day credit accounts, you should aim to agree 60-day payment terms with your suppliers.

An agreed overdraft facility allows you to borrow money as and when required, up to an agreed limit. It's a relatively cheap way to finance working capital if you have large variations in cash flow during the course of a month (or if your business is very seasonal), because you only pay interest on the amount actually borrowed. However, if you're continually relying on your overdraft it can be expensive; more importantly it may also highlight that your business needs a longer-term form of finance. With an overdraft, you're exposed to 'repayment on demand', which means that your lender can ask for full repayment at any time.

If your business needs to invest in new equipment but doesn't have the cash, you may be able to fund this with a term loan, a hire purchase loan, or a leasing deal. This avoids the large cash outflow on the full price of the equipment, and gives you a fixed level of repayment over a set period (usually two to five years). In situations where the asset is being used as security for the finance, it's likely that you will still need to provide a deposit.

It's also sensible to manage your business so that you aren't reliant on just one or two major customers, as you'll be dangerously exposed if one of them has a problem. Spread your customer base as widely as you can, aiming for at least five or six customers.

Build up your working-capital availability by retaining some of the profit in your business. This will provide a reserve when you need to buy equipment or have unexpected expenditure to deal with, but will also provide a cushion against possible cash-flow problems.

Take emergency action if all else fails

If you're hit with a cash-flow crisis you have to act very quickly if the business is to survive. The first thing to do is to make an accurate assessment of the scale of the problem. Prepare an updated cash-flow forecast and decide if you'll be able to trade out of your difficulty. If this seems unlikely, look carefully at how much support you need and whether you can provide this from your own personal resources.

If the answer is no, you'll have to go to the bank and explore the possibility of increasing your overdraft. Even if you think you can trade out of the problem, it may be sensible to inform your bank at an early stage in case you discover later that you do need additional working capital after all.

If the bank is unwilling to help, or can only provide partial support, the next step is to inform your creditors. It's sensible to talk to larger creditors directly, explain your position and ask them for longer to pay. It's especially important to talk to HM Revenue & Customs if you have employees and therefore hand over PAYE monthly. They can be very understanding if they think that you're being straight with them and that a little leniency now will result in full payment later. If necessary, offer them reduced payments now with the outstanding balance in instalments as your business recovers. If they are crucial suppliers, you need to keep them on your side or else you won't be able to continue trading.

You should also consider developing a business disaster plan, which will help the business cope with any unexpected events that could damage cash flow. This enables you to prepare for the aftermath of incidents such as computer viruses, major power cuts, loss of key personnel, natural disasters, and terrorist attacks.

If all these options fail, you may have no alternative but to consider the future of your company. If your business runs into severe financial difficulties and becomes insolvent, you must cease trading. The options then are either to seek the appointment of a receiver or liquidate the business. In commercial law this process can involve terms such as insolvency, receivership, administration, liquidation (winding up), and bankruptcy.

COMMON MISTAKES
Being taken by surprise
Keep a close eye on your balance sheet, your debtors, and your bank balance. Look ahead at your cash-flow requirements for the next few weeks and consider what receipts you expect and what payments you'll have to make. Cash-flow problems are best caught early and the more time you can give yourself to respond the better.

Procrastinating
Cash-flow problems rarely resolve themselves – they require positive action. Talk to your bank and your creditors as soon as you suspect there may be a problem. This way, you assure them you're at least doing your homework, even if there are difficult times ahead. If you don't act you run the risk of affecting relationships with all your key stakeholders including the bank, suppliers, and customers. Your bank will be far more receptive to dealing with your cash-flow problems if you approach them before the problem occurs. It is bound to be a worrying time for you, but burying your head in the sand won't help and you'll feel better for doing something about the problem.

THE BEST SOURCES OF HELP
Website:
Credit to Cash:
www.credit-to-cash.com

Issuing Invoices and Collecting Debts

GETTING STARTED
When your business supplies goods or services to its customers, you need to record these transactions formally with a document called an invoice. This document becomes particularly important when you let your customers defer payment for the transaction, by offering them credit. From the date that the invoice is issued, until it is paid, the value of the invoice is regarded as a debt to the business. This actionlist explains the invoicing procedure and offers advice on how to deal with customers who won't pay up on time.

FAQS
Why do you need to issue invoices?
An invoice is a formal record of trading between two parties. It confirms details of the goods or services supplied, and the prices charged. It is used as the basis for all financial management and accounting processes in a business, and is a key document in business tax records. An invoice that is issued by your business to confirm a sale is then a crucial document for customer, as it acts as proof of purchase.

Are there different types of invoices?
Yes. Three types of invoice documents can be used.
1. Pro-forma invoice – this is issued by a business when it does not have credit facilities set up with its customer, and acts as a request for payment for goods prior to despatch. This ensures that payment is received, and is often used when two businesses have not traded before.
2. Standard invoice – a standard document issued to confirm a trading transaction. It is normally classed as a sales invoice by the business that has sold the goods, and as a purchase invoice by the buyer. When an invoice is issued by a VAT-registered business, it is known as a VAT invoice. This must provide specific information about the rate and amount of VAT charged.

3. Credit note – this is issued to cancel an original invoice or part of an invoice when goods are returned or a pricing error has been made. If the original invoice has been settled prior to the credit note being issued, then the buyer will be entitled to alternative goods up to the value of the credit note.

What details should be included on an invoice?

All invoices need to convey certain key pieces of information as supporting evidence for and VAT purposes, and to avoid queries from customers which may lead to delays in payment. These are

- a unique identifying number
- your business name, address, its legal status, and VAT number (if relevant)
- a date of issue, which becomes the tax point
- your customer's name (or trading name) and address
- a description of the quantity and type of goods or services supplied, along with the price charged, and, where appropriate, the VAT charged
- the payment terms for the invoice

Must an invoice always be issued?

You do not always need to issue an invoice to your customer, but you will need to keep a record of the transaction. For example, many retail businesses issue till receipts to their customers rather than fully-detailed invoices. This is fine for small one-off transactions that are paid for at the time of purchase but most business-to-business transactions require an invoice to be issued, and this is especially important if you and your customer are VAT-registered. The key thing to remember is that the sooner you invoice, the sooner you get paid.

Is there anything that can be done if the customer will not pay the invoice?

First of all, you need to find out as soon as possible why your customer won't pay the invoice. If it is a simple issue, such as a genuine pricing or quantity error, then it should be simple to resolve. However, if the reason given is not acceptable and a compromise cannot be reached, you will need to take action to recover the money owed. This can be done in several ways:

- using the County Courts and the small-claims procedure for debts of less than £5,000
- instructing a solicitor to pursue the debt for you. This may just involve him or her sending a letter on your behalf, or managing the whole process of pursuing your claim through the court process
- engaging the services of a debt collection agency, who will either manage the process for a fixed fee, or work on a commission of the debt that is collected

You need to balance the time that it will take for you to pursue your customer for payment against the costs involved with using the services of a solicitor or debt collection agency.

MAKING IT HAPPEN

If your business only issues a small number of invoices then you can use a computer and word-processing package, or even manually write out the invoices. You will need to produce two copies, one for your customer and one for your own records. This simple approach can work well, but once you start to offer credit or have the complication of being VAT registered, it makes more sense to use an integrated accounts system that manages both invoicing and credit control.

Set up procedures for credit control

If you offer credit to your customers, then issuing a sales invoice is just *part* of the sales process – the transaction is not completed until the invoice has been fully settled. Many businesses are very successful at selling their goods or services and yet still fail because they are unable to collect the money owed to them, so it's vital to set up processes that minimise the risk of your customers failing to pay you.

Make sure that credit is only offered to credit-worthy customers, and that you agree payment terms with them in advance. Check the accuracy of invoices before you send them out, and provide customers with monthly statements showing their account balance. When credit terms are exceeded, send reminder letters and follow up with telephone calls, and be prepared to put a customer's account on hold if there is no good reason for non-payment. Finally, don't be afraid to charge interest under the Late Payment of Commercial Debts (Interest) Act 1998.

Investigate reasons for non-payment

Even when you adopt these procedures there are going to be situations that lead to an invoice not being paid on time. You will then have to decide on the best approach to recover your debt, and a lot will depend on the approach of your customer, their size and importance to your business, and the size of the debt. There are several reasons for non-payment.

Habitual slow payer – Sometimes new customers are won suddenly, and it is only after you've supplied them for a while that you find out why: their previous supplier had closed their account because of continuing problems with late payment. These types of customers will go through long delaying tactics as a matter of course, and can waste a huge amount of your (or your finance department's) time in chasing them. Undertaking credit checks can help to minimise this risk, but often it is only by adopting very tight credit control and setting low credit limits initially that you can limit the problem. If the problems continue you may then have to decide between charging higher prices to reflect your extra costs, or refusing to give your customer credit.

Disputed invoices – Misunderstandings about the terms of a transaction are quite common, and the easiest way to avoid them is to make sure that each stage of the sales process has been documented. If this information is not complete, you may have to face negotiating a compromise with your customer, which should mean that you get paid for at least part of the invoice. If there is no room for compromise and you believe that your case is strong, then you should look at formal recovery of your debt as the best way forward-although the process can be time consuming and expensive. If the dispute does end up in court, you will need to be able to demonstrate that you have explored all avenues to resolve it, so you should document the process carefully.

Financial difficulty – This is probably the most common reason for non-payment of an invoice, and is often masked by your customer behind lots of other reasons. You need to identify whether this is a short-term cash-flow glitch or a major financial problem that is likely to result in your customer becoming insolvent. In situations where a customer faces a short-term difficulty, it may be possible to agree to payments by instalment over a specific period. If you do agree to this approach, make sure you confirm it in writing and then monitor the situation carefully to ensure that your customer maintains these special payments.

If a customer's business faces long-term or extreme cash-flow problems it is likely to be unable to pay your debt. Knowing the legal status of your customer's business is important under these circumstances, because this will determine how you can pursue the recovery of your debt. Often the best that you can hope for is that you can claim title to the goods that you have supplied, which may still have some value to you. For this reason,

you should ensure that a retention-of-title clause is used in all of your terms of sale and all invoices which involve the sale of goods.

COMMON MISTAKES
Delaying sending out invoices
Issue invoices promptly after a sale. Taking too much time will lead to delays in you getting paid because payment terms will be based on the invoice date and not the date on which you supplied the goods or services.

Being overly sympathetic to customers' financial problems
If there's no valid reason for non-payment, don't delay the process of debt collection because you're worried about upsetting your customer. This may just lead to your business being owed more, and possibly not getting paid at all if the customer's business ceases trading.

THE BEST SOURCES OF HELP
Websites:
Court process and forms:
    www.courtservice.gov.uk
Credit Services Association (information about Debt Recovery Agencies): **www.csa-uk.com**
User's guide to the Late Payment Act 1998:
    www.payontime.co.uk

Understanding the Role of Price

GETTING STARTED
The price that you charge for your product or service needs to reflect your costs on the one hand and the strength of the market on the other. Setting a price too high can result in lost sales, while undercharging can eat into your profits and possibly lead to you being unable to deliver on your contracts. This actionlist contains advice on how to go about calculating prices, in a way that will suit both your business and the market. One book on the subject that you might also find useful is *Boosting Sales on a Shoestring* by Bob Gorton (A & C Black, 2007).

FAQS
What is the difference between price and cost?
The *cost* of producing your product or service is the total costs for the business, both direct and fixed, divided by the number of products that you sell. The *price* that you charge depends on what the market will stand, that is, on what the customer will pay. The difference between price and cost is profit-or loss!

How do I work out how much I can charge for my product?
You need to research the market carefully in order to determine the price that you can charge. This is most difficult when you are starting up, since you have little information on which to base your pricing decisions, other than reviewing the prices charged by your competitors and your own market research with potential customers. Once you are in business it becomes easier, since you can adjust your prices and review the effects they have on demand.

Will charging less than my competitors win customers?
Many people have difficulty calculating the cost of their products or services and, as a result, let their competitors effectively set the price, thinking that as long as they undercut that price, then they will succeed. However, cost leadership is a strategy that often fails for small businesses since they lack the economies of scale necessary to make the price really competitive, and end up losing money as a result.

What is gross profit?

The gross profit is the selling price less the direct costs involved in making the product or delivering the service. Direct costs (sometimes known as variable costs, because they vary with the output) include such items as raw materials, bought in components, and sub-contracting. Fixed costs (sometimes known as overheads – items such as rent, utilities, depreciation, and insurance) are then deducted from the gross profit, resulting in the net profit. So you need to sell enough at your chosen price to cover all the direct and fixed costs, and make a profit as well.

What is the breakeven point?

The breakeven point is the point where the income from sales exactly equals all the costs incurred by the business. More sales will result in a profit; fewer sales will result in a loss.

Can I change the price once it is set?

The price can always be changed, but you may encounter customer resistance if hikes are too big.

MAKING IT HAPPEN

Remember the two-step process

There are two steps in setting price: the first step is to determine the costs of delivering a product or service; the second step is to set a price that is high enough to cover the costs, but low enough to be competitive.

Research the market

You need to start with an idea of what you may be able to sell and the price at which you might be able to sell it. This information comes from your market research. It is necessary to have sensible estimate of likely sales volumes, otherwise you will not be able to calculate the direct costs. This is less important if you are selling a service where there are very low, if any, direct costs. But it is very important if you are in manufacturing, particularly if the direct costs (like raw materials) are of a high value. Prepare an income and expenditure forecast using different prices. Estimate what effect a price increase will have on your sales. Consider the prices offered by your competitors. If your prices are much higher, are you offering sufficient extra benefit to entice customers to buy from you?

Calculate the costs

There are a number of different ways of allocating costs to products and services, but the key requirement is to know all the costs – direct and fixed – for an expected level of sales. Don't forget to include depreciation and your deductions if you are self-employed. Once you have the cost, then you have the bare minimum price for a given level of sales.

Provided the costs are less than the price that you set when you did your market research, you will make a

profit – assuming, of course, that you also sell the volumes that you predicted.

Carry out a breakeven analysis

Once you know your costs and estimated selling price, you are in a position to calculate how many products, or hours of your time, you need to sell to break even (that is, to cover all your costs).

One way to calculate the breakeven point is to draw a graph that shows sales volume on the horizontal axis and money on the vertical axis. First show the overhead costs. This will be a horizontal line since these costs are, generally, fixed for all volumes of production.

The direct costs can then be added to the overhead costs to give total costs for a given volume of output. A line representing total costs can be plotted. The sales income can then be plotted to show how much income will be generated for a given volume of sales. Remember that sales income starts at zero for zero sales.

The point where the sales income equals the total cost shows the breakeven point. A higher price will achieve breakeven with fewer sales. A lower price may attract more customers, but will require higher sales to break even. The further above breakeven that a business can operate, the greater its margin of safety.

Set targets

Once you have determined your price and defined the breakeven volume that you need to sell, set an annual target, broken down into monthly targets, designed to generate you a reasonable profit.

It can often be helpful to plot the targets for sales and actual sales on a graph to monitor progress regularly. If the business does not achieve its targets you will need to take remedial action.

Review

Review your sales volumes and income regularly. Ensure that you are making a profit; if you are not, take corrective action, perhaps involving changing the price.

COMMON MISTAKES

Setting the price too low

The greatest danger when setting a price for the first time is to pitch it too low. Raising a price is always more difficult than lowering one, yet there are great temptations to undercut the competition. It is clearly important to compare your prices to your competitors', but it is essential that your price covers all your costs and contributes towards your profit.

Failing to cost accurately

Many businesses run into difficulties, and some fail, because they do not cost their work accurately. They fail to check the actual costs of a job against the estimated costs. While they cannot turn back history and re-price, they can at least amend their prices for future sales. Not doing this is likely to result in failing to achieve targets for profit and profitability.

Under-utilising assets

Many businesses buy expensive equipment and fail to include all the depreciation when they are costing. If you are buying expensive equipment, you need to think carefully about how you will recover the cost.

THE BEST SOURCES OF HELP
Website:
Bizpeponline: **www.bizpeponline.com**

Setting Prices

GETTING STARTED

Setting the price of a product or service is often regarded as a financial issue, but in reality it's also a marketing issue. Clearly the price has to cover all the costs and generate a profit – the business won't survive otherwise – but equally, you won't necessarily want to charge the most that you could get away with because you want customers to think that you offer good value for money, and you want repeat business. This actionlist looks at some of the main issues for you to consider when setting your prices.

FAQS

How do I set the price?

Setting a price is a two-part exercise. First, you need to calculate all of your costs, and then divide this figure by the number of products, or days of service, that you expect to sell. This give the a minimum price at which your business can break even but not make a profit. Second, you need to research the market to determine the maximum price that could be achievable for your product or service. You can then set your actual price somewhere between the two.

If my price is lower than my competitors', will I sell more?

Many businesses believe that this is a strategy guaranteed to win greater market share. This is known as 'cost leadership'. Small businesses, however, are usually too small to achieve the economies of scale necessary to enable them to fix a really competitive price. If you are in this position, you need to 'differentiate' your product or service in order to secure a competitive edge. This could be done on the basis of better quality, better service, or quicker delivery for example. You may find that quicker delivery is an extra benefit for which your customers might be willing to pay.

What happens if I increase my prices?

Fixing a price is a juggling act between strategy, pricing, and cash flow. If your price is too low, the income may not cover all your costs. If the price is too high, even with a well-differentiated product, you may have difficulty attracting enough customers. However, maximising profit does not necessarily mean selling high volumes at low profit. It may be possible to sell low volumes at high profit. The challenge that you face is to find the right balance.

In general, changing the price will cause a change in demand. Small businesses often find that they can put up the price without losing too many customers, thus increasing profitability. But you also need to understand the potential effect that a price change will have on your customers. It's a good idea to warn them that prices are going to rise, and to explain why. A good relationship with your customers can improve their perception of the value you are offering.

How much flexibility do I have?

The amount of flexibility that you have largely depends on the way that your product or service is perceived in the marketplace. A cost leadership strategy gives you almost no flexibility, because you have to respond to the price set by your competitors. A differentiated strategy is based on demonstrating how your product or service is quite different to your competitors; the particular benefits of what you offer give you more flexibility in setting your price.

I know how important pricing is, but should I think about *free* giveaways as well?

It's certainly something to consider. Used carefully, offering existing or prospective customers free access to your product or service can have a real and very positive effect on sales. For example, existing customers will be thrilled that you think so highly of them and this will engender a lot of good will in turn. They'll feel they have more of a bond with you, which will make them less likely to buy from a competitor and much more likely to tell colleagues and friends about your company.

Prospective customers like free giveaways as they can try out new products without risk. The key thing in this situation, though, is to make them want to *stay* with you after the free trial is over. The only way to do this is to be sure that what you're offering is the best option around – if you're not, what are you going to do to change that situation? In both cases, though, you should only do free giveways in such a way that you don't get left hopelessly out of pocket with nothing to show for it. Offer customers something that doesn't cost you very much but which has a high perceived value for them.

MAKING IT HAPPEN
The marketing mix

The marketing mix, often referred to as the four Ps (product, position, price, and promotion), covers the different aspects of marketing. It's the marketing mix that conveys your message to your customers.

Your price needs to reflect the position that you want to adopt in the market place. If you adopt a position of quality, you will want (and will probably need) to charge a premium price. If your product or service is regarded as mass-produced, and therefore of lower quality, then the price should be at the bottom end of the spectrum.

Pricing strategies

There are a number of possible pricing strategies that you could adopt:

- **Cost-based pricing** is when total costs are calculated and a mark-up is added to give the required profit. The mark-up is usually expressed as a percentage of the cost. Different types of businesses will apply varying mark-ups, for example, the mark-up on jewellery is enormous compared to the mark-up on food products.
- **'Skimming'** is where you initially charge a relatively high price to recover investment costs quickly if the product is new. As your competitors follow your lead and launch their own products to compete and enter the market, you lower the price.
- **Negotiating prices individually** with customers, based on the quantities they are prepared to buy. If you wish to sell to a particular market, then you might sell one product or service more cheaply (as a **loss leader**) to gain market entry. You balance this by selling other products or services at a higher price. This can be risky, as the danger is that everything becomes a loss leader.
- **Expected price** involves finding out what the customer expects to pay. If you are selling a high-quality product, do not under-price. Often the customer expects to pay more (for instance, if the product or service has a certain 'snob' value), and you could

diminish the premium value of your product or service if you under-price, making it less attractive to the customer.
- **Differential pricing** is where you charge different segments of your market different prices for the same service; for example, you may decide to offer discounts to certain people, such as pensioners or the unemployed, or charge lower rates for quiet periods.
- **Lifetime pricing** is a technique you can adopt if your product price is higher than your competitors and you want to encourage customers to look at the cost of ownership over the *lifetime* of the product. This might work well if, for example, your product is likely to last longer, thus reducing depreciation. Also, the cost of maintenance may be lower, reducing the annual cost.

COMMON MISTAKES
Relying on cost leadership

Do not simply aim to undercut your competitors; cost leadership is a difficult strategy for small businesses to pursue. Instead, aim to differentiate your product or service.

You aren't selling enough

Ensure that you are selling enough products at your chosen price to cover all of your costs and to generate a profit. Keep a careful eye on your sales and if you are not selling enough at your chosen price, then you need to take remedial action.

Treating price as a simple calculation

It's best to regard price as part of the marketing mix, rather than a straight financial calculation. You need to consider all the parts of the equation carefully. Make sure that you research the market thoroughly, and that you are familiar with your competitors' pricing strategies and your customers' needs.

THE BEST SOURCES OF HELP
Website:
Professional Pricing Society:
   www.pricingsociety.com

Managing Creditors and Debtors

GETTING STARTED

All businesses have trading relationships with both suppliers and customers. At any point in time, those suppliers who are extending credit to your business by letting you pay for goods or services after you have received them, are known as your creditors. Customers who owe you money for goods or services that you have supplied are known as your debtors.

The balance between when you need to pay your creditors and when you receive payment from your debtors has a major effect on the cash flow of your business. Getting the balance right is important in determining what cash will be available to your business in the short term, and for identifying the cash needs (often referred to as 'working capital') of your business as it grows.

FAQS

Why do I need to manage creditors and debtors?

Knowing how much you owe, how much you are owed, and when payments are due to be made or received, allows you to forecast your cash flow over several months and ensures that you will have enough money in the bank for other regular business payments, such as salaries and rent. This can be particularly important for businesses that are seasonal, or that have a high spend with their suppliers several months before their customers pay them.

How does this effect the working capital required by a business?

When the value of your creditors equals the value of your debtors, there is no effect on the working capital needs of your business, assuming payment terms are the same. However if the value of your debtors increases relative to the value of your creditors, then the working capital used by your business rises. This is a typical situation faced by businesses as they grow. If you are able to increase the value of your creditors while maintaining the value of your debtors then you can reduce the working capital needed by your business.

What are standard payment terms?

There are no firm rules for credit terms, but there are accepted practices that are widely adopted. Normally the credit period is either based on the date of the invoice, or on the month of the invoice. The most standard credit term based on the date of invoice is 30 days – that is, the invoice is due for payment 30 days after the date on the invoice. If you are providing several invoices to a customer in any one month, it is normal to use 'net monthly terms'. This means that all invoices for a particular month are grouped and paid together at the end of the following month. Using net monthly terms greatly simplifies the process for both supplier and customer, reducing the payment process to only once a month, irrespective of the number of invoices issued.

What is debtor finance?

For many businesses the amount owed by their debtors is the largest single element of their balance sheet. If your business is trading in a business-to-business environment, there is the potential to use the services of a third-party finance company who will make money available to you, based on the security of your debtor balances. This service is called 'factoring' and can range from the provision of just finance against your debtor list to a full sales ledger and credit-control service. The initial advance payment is usually up to 80 percent of the value of the invoice, with the remaining balance being due either at an agreed maturity date, or when your customer pays the factor. This type of service is especially useful for fast-growing businesses who can suffer from a shortage of working capital.

What is creditor finance?

This is the term used for 'borrowing' money from your creditors to fund your working capital. It is typically used by retail businesses, where you sell your products or services for cash, and yet obtain credit from your suppliers.

Are trade suppliers my only short-term creditors?

Although trade suppliers are usually viewed as being the creditors of your business, you should actually include all of the organisations that you owe money to in the short term. This means that the term 'creditors' is more formally split between trade creditors – which will include your trade suppliers to your business – and other creditors, which will include organisations such as HM Revenue & Customs, if you are an employer and/or VAT registered.

MAKING IT HAPPEN

Managing your creditors and debtors is vitally important to the smooth and effective operation of your business. Doing this effectively will save you money, and may even make the difference between your business surviving or failing.

Manage the relationship with your creditors

Suppliers are vital to the operation of your business and the role that they play is often undervalued. For many suppliers, how you manage the payment of their account is a key to a successful long-term relationship. The main issues for a good working relationship with your suppliers are for you to be:

- professional in your handling of their account, by conforming to the agreed credit terms, and not wasting their time through poor administration
- honest with them if you have cash-flow problems and are unable to meet their normal payment terms
- straightforward in your commercial negotiations – look to negotiate better terms from your suppliers, but base this on the volume of business and how this has grown over a period of time, and the fact that you manage your account well

Use a credit card to obtain credit

In situations where it is difficult to obtain credit from your suppliers, you could consider using a credit card to make payment for goods. This has the effect of giving the supplier immediate payment, but also giving you 30–50 days credit. However, there can be an additional charge added to the invoice of 1–3 percent, and it is *essential* that you pay it off promptly or you will incur further costs.

Manage the relationship with your debtors

If providing credit to your customers is important to your business, then it is vital to set up effective credit-control procedures.

Get your customers to complete an account application form, giving details about their business and its legal structure, and details of references. Supply them with a copy of your standard terms and conditions of sale, and make sure they are aware of (and acknowledge) your payment terms, and what their credit limit is. Keep records of quotations and delivery notes to ensure that disputes can be quickly resolved by you providing the missing information, if needed, and ensure that you have efficient accounts administration systems that allow you to send invoices promptly, and follow up with regular statements and reminders.

Monitor your customers' payments. If you are unhappy with them, speak to the person who places the order as well as the finance department. If they still do not pay, be prepared to halt supplies and to take further action to collect the debt if necessary. You may even decide to withdraw credit facilities if a customer is a persistently poor payer.

It's a good idea to produce a regular debtors list, preferably in balance order, so that you can easily review how much each business owes to you, and how old their debt is. You need to concentrate your efforts on those customers that have the oldest and largest debts to ensure that your time is used most cost effectively.

COMMON MISTAKES
Taking a narrow focus
Do not focus all of your efforts on getting better payment terms from your creditors at the expense of managing your debtors more effectively. If your business regularly struggles to pay its creditors because of slow payment from your debtors, this will be an indication that your business does not have sufficient working capital. You will then need to decide if you can manage your debtors better, and reduce the average credit period given, or whether you will need to get additional finance into the business to increase your available working capital.

THE BEST SOURCES OF HELP
Websites:
Better Payment Practice Campaign:
  www.payontime.co.uk
Asset Based Finance Association (formerly the Factors and Discounters Association): **www.abfa.org.uk**

Management Library

The Age of Discontinuity Peter Drucker

GETTING STARTED

According to Drucker, the manager as knowledge worker was a new breed of thoughtful, intelligent executive. The manager was reincarnated as a responsible individual, paid for applying knowledge, exercising judgment, and taking responsible leadership within the organisation.

The knowledge worker sees him or herself as another professional. While dependent on the organisation for access to income and opportunity, the organisation equally depends on him or her.

Drucker maintains that knowledge, rather than labour, is the new measure of economic society – and the knowledge worker is the true capitalist in the knowledge society. Knowledge is not only power, but also ownership of the means of production.

WHY READ IT?

Peter Drucker predicted the rise of the 'knowledge worker' long before the term came into common usage. His definition is much broader than the IT-led version in current usage. He gives a valuable insight into the changing nature of management roles and responsibilities in the knowledge economy.

CONTRIBUTION

1. The manager as knowledge worker

Drucker coined the term 'knowledge worker'. This was a new breed of executive – a highly trained, intelligent managerial professional who realised his or her own worth and contribution to the organisation. Drucker bade farewell to the concept of the manager as mere supervisor or paper shuffler. The manager was reincarnated as a responsible individual.

Though the knowledge worker is not a labourer, and certainly not proletarian, nor is he or she not a subordinate (in the sense of being told what to do). The knowledge worker is paid, on the contrary, for applying his or her knowledge, exercising judgment, and taking responsible leadership.

2. The nature of the knowledge worker

According to Drucker, the knowledge worker sees him or herself just as another professional, no different from the lawyer, the teacher, the preacher, the doctor, or the government servant of yesterday. He or she has the same education, but more income – and probably greater opportunities as well.

The knowledge worker may well realise that he or she depends on the organisation for access to income and opportunity, and that without the organisation, there would be no job. But there is also the realisation that the organisation depends equally on him or her.

Drucker effectively wrote the obituary for the obedient, grey-suited, loyal, corporate man and woman. The only trouble was, it took this corporate creature another 20 years to die.

3. The impact of knowledge workers

The social ramifications of this new breed of corporate executive were significant. If knowledge, rather than labour, was the new measure of economic society then the fabric of capitalist society had to change. The knowledge worker is both the true capitalist in the knowledge society and dependent on his or her job.

Collectively the knowledge workers – the employed, educated middle class of today's society – own the means of production through pension funds, investment trusts, and so on.

Knowledge was not only power, but it was also ownership.

CONTEXT

The book effectively mapped out the demise of the age of mass, labour-based production and the advent of the knowledge-based, information age. Drucker's realisation that the role of the manager had fundamentally changed was not a sudden one. The foundations of the idea of the knowledge worker can be seen in his description of management by objectives in *The Practice of Management* (1954). Knowledge management, intellectual capital and the like are now the height of corporate fashion. The modern idea of the knowledge worker is a creature of the technological age, the mobile executive, the hot-desker. Drucker provided a characteristically broader perspective, placing the rise of the knowledge worker in the evolution of management into a respectable and influential discipline.

Drucker continued to develop his thinking on the role of knowledge, most notably in his 1992 book, *Managing for the Future*, in which he observed, 'From now on the key is knowledge. The world is becoming not labour intensive, not materials intensive, not energy intensive, but knowledge intensive'.

The Age of Discontinuity was startlingly correct in its predictions. Much of it would fit easily into business books of today.

Prior to Drucker's death, management guru Gary Hamel said, 'Peter Drucker's reputation is as a management theorist. He has also been a management prophet. Writing in 1969, he clearly anticipated the emergence of the knowledge economy. I'd like to set a challenge for would-be management gurus: try to find something to say that Peter Drucker has not said first, and has not said well. This high hurdle should substantially reduce the number of business books clogging the bookshelves of booksellers, and offer managers the hope of gaining some truly fresh insights'.

THE BEST SOURCES OF HELP

Drucker, Peter. *The Age of Discontinuity*. Revised ed. Oxford: Butterworth-Heinemann, 1992.

The Age of Unreason Charles Handy

GETTING STARTED

In the author's view, the age of unreason is a time when the future is shaped by us and for us. At such a time, a number of organisational forms will emerge, as will new working patterns, such as outsourcing, telecommuting, the intellectual capital movement, and the rise of knowledge workers.

The portfolio worker will become more important, contributing to a greater work–life balance.

Handy goes on to state that the social changes resulting from these developments will be reflected in changing patterns of business, with a mix of small enterprises and large conglomerates. There will also be temporary alliances of large and small organisations to deliver a particular project.

WHY READ IT?

Written in 1989, this book includes a number of predictions about the way work would develop. The author provides insights into changing organisational structures and developments such as knowledge working, outsourcing, and strategic alliances – the hallmarks of today's economy.

CONTRIBUTION

1. The concept of an age of unreason

The age of unreason is a time when the future, in so many areas, is to be shaped by us and for us. The only prediction that will hold true is that no predictions will hold true. It will be a time for thinking the unlikely and doing the unreasonable.

2. New organisational forms

The author suggests that a number of organisational forms will emerge in an age of unreason:

• the shamrock organisation
• the federal organisation
• the Triple I organisation

The shamrock organisation is a form of organisation based around a core of essential executives and workers supported by outside contractors and part-time help.

The federal organisation is a form of decentralised set-up, in which the centre's powers are given to it by the outlying groups; the centre therefore co-ordinates, advises, influences, and suggests rather than directs or controls. Federalism is the way to combine the autonomy of individual parts with the economics of co-ordination.

The Triple I organisation is based on Information, Intelligence, and Ideas. This type of organisation resembles a university and seeks to make added value out of knowledge. To achieve this, the Triple I organisation increasingly uses smart machines, with smart people to work with them.

3. New working patterns

Handy anticipated the growth of outsourcing, telecommuting, the intellectual capital movement, and the rise of knowledge workers. He also foresaw how these developments might impact the individual. His concept of the portfolio worker helped redefine the nature of work, as well as questions of work–life balance.

4. Portfolio working

A portfolio describes how the different bits of work in our lives fit together to form a balanced whole. The five main categories of portfolio work are:

• wage work and fee work
• homework, gift work, and study work

Wage (or salary) work represents money paid for time given. Fee work is money paid for results delivered. Employees do wage work; professionals, craftspeople, and freelancers do fee work. Fee work is increasing as jobs move outside the organisation. Some employees now get fees (bonuses) as well as wages. Homework includes tasks that go on in the home, from cooking and cleaning, to children and carpentry. Gift work is work done for free outside the home, for charities and local groups, for neighbours or for the community. Study work done seriously is a form of work, not recreation.

5. A broader portfolio

In the past, for most people, the work portfolio has had only one item in it – their career. This was a risky strategy. Few people would put all their money into one asset, yet that is what most people were doing with their lives. The career had to provide many things at once – interest or satisfaction in the work, interesting people and good company, security, money, and the opportunity for development.

6. Funding the portfolio

Portfolio people think in terms of portfolio money, not salary money. Money comes in fits and starts from different sources, for example a bit of a pension, some part-time work, some fees to charge or things to sell. They lead cash-flow lives not salary lives, planning always to have enough inflows to cover outflows.

Portfolio people think in terms of barter and know that most skills are saleable if you want to sell them.

7. Changing patterns of business

It will be a world of 'fleas and elephants' – large conglomerates and small individual entities, or large political and economic blocs and small countries.

There will also be ad hoc organisations, temporary alliances of large and small organisations to deliver a particular project.

CONTEXT

The book predicts many of the important changes in working patterns which are now commonplace, including outsourcing, telecommuting, and virtual project teams from different organisations.

It also recognises the growing importance of knowledge workers and intellectual capital.

THE BEST SOURCES OF HELP

Handy, Charles. *The Age of Unreason: New Thinking for a New World.* New ed. London: Random House Business Books, 2002.

All the Right Moves Constantinos Markides

GETTING STARTED

Markides describes what makes a strategic position distinctive and how a business can make sure it occupies a unique strategic position within its industry. He demonstrates how established companies can discover and work on new strategic positions in parallel to their old position. On the basis of examples drawn from actual practice, he shows how a company can allow the expiry of an old strategy while simultaneously preparing the ground for a new one.

WHY READ IT?

Bill Gates once remarked that though his company did good work, the problem was that products aged so quickly. It is plain from this that innovative strategies are vital for survival in business; organisations must differentiate themselves clearly from their competitors. They must also develop strategies that enable them to find and occupy a unique position within their own industry, while at the same being constantly on the watch for new strategic positions. In this book, Constantinos Markides guides readers towards discovering the breakthrough strategy that will work best for them.

CONTRIBUTION

1. No strategy without innovation

According to the author, a successful business needs a strategy that enables it to find and occupy a unique position within its own branch of industry. But no position is made to last forever. Ambitious competitors not only copy attractive positions, they create new ones which can threaten established positions. A company that is not permanently striving to discover new positions in its field encourages the competition to do precisely that.

2. Building a unique strategic position

Markides suggests that in order to create a unique strategic position and make the best use of it, a company must first define what business it is in. It must then decide to whom it wishes to appeal and what products or services it intends to offer. The task then is to build up an organisational environment in which these decisions can be implemented. In his view, all this involves looking at:

- Core business: Defining one's own business is the starting point for any strategy. As soon as a definition is arrived at, actions follow from it automatically. However it must continually be questioned and one must always be on the lookout for better alternatives.
- Customers: In deciding who its customers are and what it is selling, the company marks out the terrain that it does not intend to enter: the customers it is not setting out to attract, the investments it is not going to action. Thus the company protects itself against squandering its resources through not having a clear focus or not following a clearly defined path.
- Activities and achieving objectives: The company must try to reach a dynamic understanding with its workforce. It can, for example, encourage internal diversity to develop competences that it then has 'in stock' and promote a type of culture in which changes are welcomed.
- Values and capabilities: The values and capabilities that can give a company a lasting advantage are those that it is difficult for a competitor to achieve.
- Organisation: A company's organisational environment is made up of four elements: culture, structure, incentive systems, and workforce. The company must ensure that it shapes the environment to support their proper functioning.
- Strategy development: The development of a new strategy involves planning and trial and error. The planning is necessary to identify the parameters within which the experiments can take place. The process of strategy formation is made up of two parts: first, the production of ideas; second, assessment, experimentation, learning, and modification.

3. Preparing strategic innovations

As soon as a company occupies a unique position within an industry, it must try to improve it. While improving its current position, it must be vigilant for new and potentially dangerous positions that its competitors may be adopting.

Since it cannot be taken for granted that new positions will harmonise with previously existing ones, it is often a good idea for established companies to set up their own units for that purpose. When a company takes over a new position and intends to concentrate on it entirely at some time in the future, it should separate itself from its old position through a gradual process of transition.

In developing its strategy, a company must be able to envisage itself going through the following cycle:

- First, it identifies a distinctive strategic position within its industry and occupies it.
- Then it does so well in that position that the position becomes more attractive than any other in the industry.
- While carrying the fight to its competitors from its present position, it constantly looks around for new strategic positions in the industry.
- Once it has identified another more promising position, it attempts to maintain the old position and the new one simultaneously.
- As it gradually removes itself from the old position, it completes the transition to the new one and begins the cycle over again.

CONTEXT

The book is based on numerous case studies of companies from different countries over a period of three years. Written from a management perspective, it describes the thought processes that a manager has to go through to find and develop a new and innovative strategy.

THE BEST SOURCES OF HELP

Markides, Constantinos C. *All the Right Moves: A Guide to Crafting Breakthrough Strategy*. Boston: Harvard Business School Press, 1999.

The Art of Japanese Management
Richard Pascale and Anthony Athos

GETTING STARTED

By the late 1990s, growing Japanese superiority threatened the United States' dominant position in world markets. In the authors' view, a major reason in Japan's favour was its managerial ethos. Japanese managers had vision, something thought to be notably lacking in the West. In Japan, visions are dynamic, rather than generic statements of corporate intent. US managers are constrained by their beliefs and assumptions. The seven S framework (strategy, structure, skills, staff, shared values, systems, and style) represents the key categories requiring managers' attention. The Japanese succeeded through attention to the 'soft' Ss – style, shared values, skills, and staff, while the West remained squarely focused on the 'hard' Ss of strategy, structure, and systems.

WHY READ IT?

First published in 1981, this book was one of the first genuine business bestsellers, playing a crucial role in the discovery of Japanese management techniques. In its comparisons of Japanese and US companies, it provides rare insights into the truth behind the mythology of Japanese management and the inadequacy of much Western practice.

CONTRIBUTION

1. Growing Japanese superiority

In 1980, Japan's GNP was third highest in the world and extrapolating trends at the time, it looked likely that it would become the highest by the year 2000.

For the US readership, *The Art of Japanese Management* contains some hard-hitting truths. If anything, the extent of Japanese superiority over the United States in industrial competitiveness had been underestimated.

2. Managerial skills

The visionary managerial style adopted in Japan is a major reason for its success, according to the authors. In contrast, despite having a variety of tools to hand, in the West, vision has been limited: beliefs, assumptions, and perceptions about management frequently constrain US managers. The Western vision of management circumscribes our effectiveness.

In Japan, managers enhance their way of doing business with dynamic visions rather than pallid or generic statements of corporate intent. The working practice of the Matsushita Electric Company (now Panasonic) was a particular focus of interest for the authors.

3. The seven S framework

The book is best known for its central concept: the seven S framework. As a general statement of the issues facing organisations, the framework is unremarkable but it did gain a great deal of attention. The framework is a simple list of the seven important categories that managers should take into account – strategy, structure, skills, staff, shared values, systems, and style.

According to Pascale and Athos, the value of a framework such as the seven Ss is that it imposes an interesting discipline on the researcher.

4. Comparing management styles

The seven Ss presents a framework for comparing Japanese and US management approaches: the Matsushita approach was compared with that of the ITT Corporation. The Japanese succeeded largely because of the attention they gave to the 'soft' Ss – style, shared values, skills, and staff, while the West remained preoccupied with the 'hard' Ss of strategy, structure, and systems. Since the book's publication, however, the general trend of Western managerial thinking has been directed towards the 'soft' Ss, which are particularly helpful when managers and leaders have to deal with ambiguous situations and uncertain times – as many have to.

CONTEXT

The book played a crucial role in the discovery of Japanese management techniques. Its roots lie in Pascale's work with the US National Commission on Productivity. Having initially thought that lessons from Japan were limited for cultural reasons, Pascale and Athos decided it would be more productive to look at Japanese companies in the United States. The research for the book eventually covered 34 companies over six years.

The authors' championing of vision proved highly influential. It was Athos who really started the entire 'visioning' industry in the United States. Soon after *The Art of Japanese*

Management, a flurry of books appeared highlighting so-called visionaries. Today, corporate visions are a fact of life.

Speaking of the book, business author Gary Hamel commented, 'Japan-phobia has subsided a bit, helped by a strong yen, inept Japanese macroeconomic policy, and the substantial efforts of many Western companies to rebuild their competitiveness. While Pascale and Athos undoubtedly overstated the unique capabilities of Japanese management (is Matsushita really that much better managed than Hewlett-Packard?), they successfully challenged the unstated assumption that the United States was the font of all managerial wisdom. Since *The Art of Japanese Management* hit the bookstores, US companies have learned much from Japan. Pascale and Athos deserve credit for setting the learning agenda.'

THE BEST SOURCES OF HELP

Pascale, Richard Tanner, and Anthony Athos. *The Art of Japanese Management*. London: Penguin, 1981.

The Art of War Sun Tzu

GETTING STARTED

Sun Tzu is thought to have lived over 2,400 years ago, at roughly the same time as Confucius. Historians are generally agreed that he was a general who led a number of successful military campaigns in present-day Anhui Province; the state of Wu, under whose sovereign he served, became a dominant power at that time. Since then, it has become standard practice for Chinese military chiefs to familiarise themselves with his writings.

The Art of War (the book's actual title is *Sun Tzu Ping Fa*, literally 'The Military Method of Mr Sun') is a compilation of the legendary general's thinking on the strategies that underlie military success. His anecdotes and thoughts, which fill no more than about 25 pages of text in all, are divided into 13 sections. Not all of them are relevant to modern-day concerns, but some strike a significant chord. Rather like a proponent of judo, Sun Tzu particularly recommends using the momentum of your enemy's own moves to defeat him.

WHY READ IT?

When the post-war achievements of Japanese industry began to make a significant impression in the West, and Western business people began to inquire into the thinking that underlay the success of their Eastern counterparts, Sun Tzu's *The Art of War* was a book that was often mentioned. This may seem surprising as it

was probably written over 2,000 years ago. But military language and imagery have played an important role in the development of management thinking, and if you wish to gain an insight into strategy, leadership, and survival in a hostile, competitive environment, who better to turn to than a general whose name is a byword for sagacity?

CONTRIBUTION

1. Get the strategy right

Sun Tzu, like most good and seasoned generals, is anything but an adventurer and anything but gung-ho. 'Why destroy', he asks, 'when you can win by stealth and cunning? To subdue the enemy's forces without fighting is the summit of skill.'

His advice shows subtlety and restraint: 'A sovereign should not start a war out of anger, nor should a general give battle out of rage. While anger can revert to happiness and rage to delight, a nation that has been destroyed cannot be restored, nor can the dead be brought back to life.'

He continues: 'The best approach is to attack the other side's strategy; next best is to attack his alliances; next best is to attack his soldiers; the worst is to attack cities.'

2. Get information from the right sources

Sun Tzu also gives sound advice on knowing your markets, saying: 'Advance knowledge cannot be gained from ghosts and spirits, but must be obtained from people who know the enemy situation.'

3. Stay focused

His view on strategy leaves no room for sentiment or distraction.

'Deploy forces to defend the strategic points; exercise vigilance in preparation, do not be indolent. Deeply investigate the true situation, secretly await their laxity. Wait until they leave their strongholds, then seize what they love.'

CONTEXT

So what does *The Art of War* have to offer the manager of a small components factory in, for example, Peoria or Nottingham? Sun Tzu's admirers argue that his pithy sayings encapsulate basic and eternal truths. According to Gary Hamel, 'Strategy didn't start with Igor Ansoff; neither did it start with Machiavelli. It probably didn't even start with Sun Tzu. Strategy is as old as human conflict . . !' Anyone, therefore, who has to devise a plan, anyone who has to give a lead, can do with all the help they can get.

Hamel goes on to add '. . . and, if the stakes are high in business, they're rather higher in the military sphere'. One of the attractions of the military analogy and the military role model in business is that they elevate proceedings to a loftier plane. Not only are the issues larger, and the scale more heroic, but it is clear who your enemy is, and when your enemy is clear, the world appears clearer whether you are a military general or a managing director.

Embattled managers in particular may benefit from the stimulus that military authors like Sun Tzu, Clausewitz, or Liddell-Hart, and the writings of modern military leaders like Colin Powell or General Sir Mike Jackson, can give to their civilian imaginations.

Finally, as has often been pointed out, Sun Tzu has long been revered in the East. He is said to be required reading not only for Eastern military tacticians but also for Eastern business people. To know your enemies – or indeed to know your friends, partners, and colleagues – it is useful to have read what they have read.

THE BEST SOURCES OF HELP

Sun Tzu. *The Art of War* (trans. Minford). London: Penguin, 2008.

A Behavioral Theory of the Firm
Richard Cyert and James March

GETTING STARTED

An entire academic discipline, decision science, is devoted to understanding management decision-making. Early thinkers believed that the decision process could be rationalised and systematised, and that decision-making can therefore be distilled into a formula. However, reality is often more confused and messy, and managers make decisions based on a combination of intuition, experience, and analysis.

WHY READ IT?

The book is a powerful introduction to the complex world of decision-making. One of its authors, James March, is one of the foremost decision-making theorists of the 20th century. The book evaluates traditional approaches to decision-making and puts forward real-world alternatives.

CONTRIBUTION

1. The evolution of decision-making theory

Early theories were based on the premise that, under a given set of circumstances, human behaviour is logical and therefore predictable – so the decision process can be rationalised and systematised.

A profusion of models and analytical tools followed, seeking to distil decision-making into a formula. Such models assume that the distilled mass of experience will enable people to make accurate decisions. The danger is in concluding that the solution provided by a software package is the right one.

2. The rational theory of decision-making

The authors suggest that the rational, or synoptic, model of decision-making involves a series of steps:

- identifying and clarifying the problem
- prioritising goals
- generating and evaluating options
- comparing predicted outcomes of each option with the goals
- choosing the option that matches best

These models rely on a number of assumptions about the way in which people will behave when confronted with a set of circumstances. The assumptions allow mathematicians to derive formulae based on probability theory. The decision-making tools include such things as cost/benefit analysis, which aims to help managers evaluate different options.

3. Problems in the rational theory

Reality is often more confused and messy than a neat model can allow for. Underpinning the mathematical

approach are a number of flawed assumptions. The model assumes that decision-making is:
- consistent
- based on accurate information
- free from emotion or prejudice
- rational

4. Real-world decision-making

According to the authors, the reality is that managers make decisions based on a combination of intuition, experience, and analysis. As intuition and experience are impossible to quantify, the temptation is to focus on the analytical – the science rather than the mysterious art.

5. The relevance of decision-making models

This does not mean that decision theory is redundant or that decision-making models should be cast aside.

A number of factors mean that decision-making is becoming ever more demanding. The growth in complexity means that companies no longer encounter simple problems. Managers are having to deal with a flood of information: a 1996 Reuters survey of 1,200 managers worldwide found that 43 percent thought their ability to make decisions was affected as a result of having too much information.

Decision theory and the use of models is reassuring, as they lend legitimacy to decisions that may be based on hunches. However, no models are foolproof; none is universally applicable, or can yet cope with the idiosyncrasies of human behaviour.

6. The challenge for organisational decision-making

Business decision-making theory faces a crucial and immediate problem: individuals have goals; collective groups do not. There is a need, therefore, to create useful organisational goals, while not believing there is such a thing as an organisational mind.

Organisations should be regarded as coalitions that negotiate goals.

Creating goals requires three processes:
- bargaining, which establishes the composition and general terms of the coalition
- internal organisational control, which clarifies and develops the objectives
- the process of adjustment to experience, which alters agreements in accord with changing circumstances

Goals are inconsistent for three reasons:
- decision-making being decentralised
- short-term goals taking most attention
- the resources available to the organisation being insufficient to maintain the coalition

7. A new decision-making model

The authors assert that the five principle goals of the modern organisation are production, inventory, sales, market share, and profit. There are nine steps in the decision process: forecast competitors' behaviour; forecast demand; estimate costs; specify objectives; evaluate plans; re-examine costs; re-examine demand; re-examine objectives; select alternatives. To work successfully, this decision-making model demands that there are standard operating procedures. The procedures can be divided into general ones based on avoiding uncertainty, maintaining the rules, and using simple rules. There are also specifics, such as task performance rules, continuing records and reports, information-handling rules, and plans. These procedures are the link between the individual and organisation. They are the means by which organisations make and implement choices.

CONTEXT

Much of decision science rests on foundations set by early business thinkers, such as computer pioneer, Charles Babbage, and scientific management founder, Frederick W. Taylor, who believed that, under given circumstances, human behaviour was logical and therefore predictable. Based on this premise, models emerged to explain the workings of commerce which, it was thought, could be extended to the way in which decisions were made.

THE BEST SOURCES OF HELP

Cyert, Richard, and James March. *A Behavioral Theory of the Firm*. 2nd ed. Oxford: Blackwell Publishing, 1992.

Built to Last James Collins and Jerry Porras

GETTING STARTED

Values are important in the context of business and corporations, and many companies have long recognised the importance of possessing a set of guiding principles.

In the authors' view, enduring organisations with strong guiding principles have outperformed the general stock market by a factor of 12 since 1925.

Core values are the organisation's essential and enduring tenets, and drive the way the company operates at a level that transcends strategic objectives. Such values don't change, although strategies and practices adapt endlessly to change.

Core ideology defines what the company stands for and its very reason for existing. It complements the envisioned future – what the company aspires to become. Any effective vision must embody the core ideology of the organisation.

WHY READ IT?

According to the authors, companies that enjoy enduring success have core values and a core purpose that remain fixed, while their business strategies and practices endlessly adapt to a changing world. The book shows the importance of developing and sticking to a set of guiding principles, and identifies the qualities essential to building a great and enduring organisation.

CONTRIBUTION

1. The importance of corporate values

Honesty, integrity, wealth, fairness are all values that we may be able to relate to on an individual personal basis. But what about values in the context of business and corporations?

While the term 'corporate values' is a relative newcomer to the business lexicon, the concept of values as an important aspect of corporate life is not. Many companies have long recognised the importance of possessing a set of guiding principles, and the evolution of the concept can be traced through some of the most influential business books over the last 50 years.

Thomas Watson Jr, CEO of IBM, observed that any great organisation that has lasted over the years owes its resiliency to the power of its beliefs and the appeal these beliefs have for its people.

2. The qualities of an enduring organisation

The book sets out to identify the qualities essential to building a great and enduring organisation – the successful habits of truly visionary companies.

The 18 companies chosen as subjects had outperformed the general stock market by a factor of 12 since 1925.

Core values are the organisation's essential and enduring tenets. These are a small set of guiding principles (not to be confused with specific cultural or operating practices), which are never to be compromised for financial gain or short-term expediency.

Values are timeless guiding principles that drive the way the company operates at a level that transcends strategic objectives. For Hewlett-Packard, for example, values include a strong sense of responsibility to the community. For Disney, they include creativity, dreams, and imagination and the promulgation of wholesome American values.

3. Core values don't change

Companies that enjoy enduring success have core values and a core purpose that remain fixed while their business strategies and practices endlessly adapt to a changing world. This constancy is a key factor in the success of companies such as Hewlett-Packard, Johnson & Johnson, Procter & Gamble, and Sony.

4. A model for core values

The authors recommend a conceptual framework to cut through some of the confusion swirling around the issues.

In their model, vision has two components – core ideology and envisioned future. Core ideology, the Yin in their scheme, defines what the company stands for and why it exists. Yin is unchanging and complements Yang, the envisioned future.

The envisioned future is what the company aspires to become, to achieve, to create – something that will require considerable change and progress to attain. Core ideology provides the glue that holds an organisation together through time.

5. An effective vision

Any effective vision must embody the core ideology of the organisation. This has two components – core values (a system of guiding principles and tenets) and core purpose (the organisation's most fundamental reason for existence).

CONTEXT

Built to Last sets out to identify the qualities, or corporate values, essential to building a great and enduring organisation.

The evolution of the concept of corporate values can be traced through some of the most influential business books over the last 50 years, from *A Business and Its Beliefs* to *In Search of Excellence*.

THE BEST SOURCES OF HELP

Collins, James, and Jerry Porras. *Built to Last*. Revised ed. London: Random House, 2005.

A Business and Its Beliefs Thomas Watson Jr

GETTING STARTED

Thomas Watson Jr went to work for IBM in 1946 as a salesman. He was appointed chief executive in 1956 and retired in 1970, after presiding over IBM's rise to pre-eminence at the beginning of the computer age.

IBM's origins lay in the Computing-Tabulating-Recording Company, which Thomas Watson Sr joined in 1914. The company initially made everything from butcher's scales to meat slicers, gradually concentrating on mechanical tabulating machines. It became International Business Machines in 1924.

IBM's development was helped by the 1937 Wages-Hours Act, which required US companies to record hours worked and wages paid. The existing machines couldn't cope; Watson Sr developed a solution, the Mark 1, followed by the Selective Sequence Electronic Calculator in 1947. By then IBM's revenues were $119 million and it was set to make the great leap forward to become the world's largest computer company.

As far as management thinking is concerned, what IBM stood for is more important than what it did. Thomas Watson Jr took on a hugely successful company with a strong corporate culture built around salesmanship and service. Thomas Watson Sr had emphasised people and service obsessively. IBM was a service star in an era of machines that performed badly. This is where the message of this book lies.

WHY READ IT?

A Business and Its Beliefs: The Ideas that Helped Build IBM was written by the son of the founder of IBM's commercial greatness, who himself led the company into the computer age. It describes the origins of one of the world's most successful corporations and shows how its achievements were built on a strong corporate culture and a passionate commitment to customer service.

CONTRIBUTION

1. Core values are critical

Success, in Watson's view, comes through a sound set of beliefs, on which the corporation premises all its policies and actions. Beliefs must always come before policies, practices, and goals. The latter must always be altered if they are seen to violate fundamental beliefs.

Not only should the beliefs be sound, they should be stuck to through thick and thin. The most important single factor in corporate success is faithful adherence to those beliefs. Beliefs never change. Change everything else, but never the basic truths on which the company is based.

However, Watson argued for flexibility in all other areas. If an organisation, he asserted, is to meet the challenges of a changing world, it must be prepared to change everything about itself except its beliefs as it moves through corporate life. The only sacred cow in an organisation should be its basic philosophy of doing business.

2. Develop a corporate culture

The beliefs that mould great organisations frequently grow out of the character, the experience, and the convictions of a single person. In IBM's case that person was Thomas Watson Sr.

The Watsons created a corporate culture that lasted. IBM, Big Blue, became the archetypal modern corporation and its managers the ultimate stereotype, with their regulation sombre suits, plain ties, zeal for selling, and company song.

3. A passion for competing

Behind the corporate culture lay a belief in competing vigorously and providing quality service. Later, competitors complained that IBM's sheer size won it orders. This was only partly true. Its size masked a deeper commitment to managing customer accounts, providing service, building relationships, and to the original values laid out by the Watsons.

4. People matter

The real difference between success and failure in a corporation can very often be traced to the question of how well the organisation brings out the great energies and talents of its people. Giving full consideration to the individual employee was one of the enduring beliefs on which IBM's success was built.

CONTEXT

In this book, the author codified and clarified what IBM stands for. The book is a statement of business philosophy, an extended mission statement for IBM.

Though it was published in the same year as Alfred P. Sloan Jr's *My Years with General Motors* it could not be more different. While Sloan sidelines people, Watson celebrates their potential; while Sloan espouses systems and structures, Watson talks of values.

Business guru Gary Hamel commented, 'Never change your basic beliefs, Watson argued. He may be right. But the dividing line between beliefs and dogmas is a fine one. A deep set of beliefs can be the essential pivot around which the company changes and adapts; or, if endlessly-elaborated, overly-codified, and solemnly worshipped, the manacles that shackle a company to the past.'

THE BEST SOURCES OF HELP

Watson, Thomas Jr. *A Business and Its Beliefs: The Ideas that Helped Build IBM.* Revised ed. New York: McGraw-Hill, 2003.

The Change Masters Rosabeth Moss Kanter

GETTING STARTED

According to the author, 'change masters' are adept at anticipating the need for, and leading, productive change. Companies with a commitment to human resources were significantly ahead in long-term profitability and financial growth.

Kanter goes on to suggest that growth problems in US companies are due to suffocation of the entrepreneurial spirit – innovation is the key to growth. New skills are required to manage effectively in innovation-stimulating environments: power skills, the ability to manage employee participation, and an understanding of how change is managed. Empowerment is critical to corporate success.

WHY READ IT?

This book is regarded as an authoritative work on the factors behind successful corporate change. Kanter's work takes a human relations perspective, and was one of the earliest books to focus on the importance of empowerment.

CONTRIBUTION

1. The nature of change masters

Change masters are those people and organisations adept at the art of anticipating the need for, and leading, productive change. Change resisters are those who remain intent on reining in innovation.

2. The importance of managing people

A research programme asked 65 human resource directors in large organisations to name companies that were progressive and forward-thinking in their systems and practices, in relation to people. Forty-seven companies emerged as leaders in the field. They were then compared to similar companies. The companies with a commitment to human resources were significantly ahead in long-term profitability and financial growth.

The message is that if you manage your people well, you are probably managing your business well.

3. Innovation as the key to growth

Kanter places responsibility for company growth problems on the quiet suffocation of the entrepreneurial spirit in segmentalist companies. She identifies innovation as the key to future growth. The way to develop and sustain innovation is to adopt an integrative approach rather than a segmentalist one.

Three new sets of skills are required to manage effectively in such integrative, innovation-stimulating environments:

- the compelling ability to persuade others to invest information, support, and resources in new initiatives driven by an entrepreneur
- the ability to manage problems associated with increased use of teams and employee participation
- an understanding of how change is designed and constructed in an organisation: how the microchanges introduced by individual innovators relate to macrochanges or strategic re-orientation

4. The importance of empowerment

The extent to which individuals are given the opportunity to use power effectively influences whether a company stagnates or innovates. In an innovative company, people are at centre stage.

CONTEXT

Rosabeth Moss Kanter began her career as a sociologist before her transformation into international business guru. *The Economist* (15 October 1994) commented, 'Kanter-the-guru still studies her subject with a sociologist's eye, treating the corporation not so much as a micro-economy, concerned with turning inputs into outputs, but as a mini-society, bent on shaping individuals to collective ends.'

Kanter's work is a development of the Human Relations School of the late 1950s and 1960s. Through *The Change Masters* (1983) and *When Giants Learn to Dance* (1989), she was partly responsible for the increased interest in empowerment, if not its practice.

The Change Masters has been called 'the thinking man's *In Search of Excellence*'.

Gary Hamel said: 'In a turbulent and inhospitable world, corporate vitality is a fragile thing. Yesterday's industry challengers are today's laggards. Entropy is endemic. Certainly *The Change Masters* is the most carefully researched, and best argued, book on change and transformation to date. While Rosabeth may not have discovered the eternal fountain of corporate vitality, she certainly points us in its general direction.'

THE BEST SOURCES OF HELP

Kanter, Rosabeth Moss. *The Change Masters*. New York: Simon & Schuster, 1983.

Competing for the Future Gary Hamel and C.K. Prahalad

GETTING STARTED

This book argues that traditional strategy is too narrow in its perspective. Far from being a simple annual exercise, strategy is multi-faceted, emotional as well as analytical, and concerned with meaning, purpose, and passion. Few managers spend enough time looking to the future. They should adopt 'strategising' – a new approach for developing complex, robust strategies, focusing on core competencies.

Today the onus is on transforming not just individual organisations, but entire industries. The true challenge is to create revolutions when you are large and dominant.

Downsizing is an easy option – growth comes from creating a difference, and vitality comes from within the organisation, if only executives would listen.

WHY READ IT?

Competing for the Future, named by *Business Week* as the best management book of 1994, is regarded as the definitive book on strategy for contemporary business. It criticises the narrow mechanistic view of strategy and calls for a broader approach that recognises a company's core competencies.

CONTRIBUTION

1. The narrow focus of traditional strategy

The authors assert that strategy has tied itself into a straitjacket of narrow, and narrowing, perspectives:

- A huge proportion of strategists, perhaps 95 per cent, are economists and engineers with a mechanistic view of strategy.
- Strategy is multi-faceted, emotional as well as analytical, concerned with meaning, purpose, and passion.
- Strategy should be regarded as a learning process.
- Today, the onus has shifted to transforming not just individual organisations but entire industries.

2. Strategy is not simple

In the authors' view, executives perceive that the problem with strategy is not creating it, but implementing it. Strategy is not a ritual or a once-a-year exercise. As a result, managers are bogged down in the nitty-gritty of the present – spending less than three per cent of their time looking to the future.

3. Adopt strategising

Instead of talking about strategy or planning, companies should talk of strategising and ask, 'What are the fundamental preconditions for developing complex, variegated, robust strategies?'

4. Focus on core competencies

Core competencies represent the collective learning in the organisation, especially how to co-ordinate diverse production skills and integrate multiple streams of technologies.

Organisations should see themselves as a portfolio of core competencies as opposed to business units. Core competencies are geared to growing opportunity share whereas business units are narrowly focused on market share.

5. Different approaches to strategy

There is a thin dividing line between order and chaos. Neither Stalinist bureaucracy nor Silicon Valley provides an optimal economic system. Silicon Valley is extraordinarily good at creating new ideas, but in other ways is extraordinarily inefficient.

6. Small or large organisations?

Small entrepreneurial offshoots are not the route to organisational regeneration. They are too random, inefficient, and prone to becoming becalmed by corporate indifference. Smaller companies have had a revolutionary impact (IKEA, Body Shop, Swatch, and Virgin), but the true challenge is to create revolutions when you are large and dominant. US companies such as Motorola and Hewlett-Packard are more successful at this than their European counterparts. We are moving to more democratic models of organisation, to which US corporations appear more attuned. In Europe and Japan there is a more elitist sense of knowledge residing at the top – a hierarchy of experience, not of imagination.

7. Rules for success

- A company surrenders today's businesses when it gets smaller faster than it gets better.
- A company surrenders tomorrow's businesses when it gets better without getting different.
- Downsizing is an easy option.
- Growth (the authors prefer to talk of vitality) comes from difference, though there are as many stupid ways to grow as there are to downsize.
- The pressure for growth is usually ignited by a crisis.
- Vitality comes from within, if only executives would listen.
- Companies pay millions of dollars for the opinions of McKinsey's bright 29 year olds, but ignore their own bright 29 year olds.

CONTEXT

The debate on the meaning and application of strategy is long-running. The 1960s gave us the analytical Igor Ansoff; the 1970s, Henry Mintzberg with his cerebral crafting strategy; the 1980s, Michael Porter's rational route to competitiveness.

Nominations for the leading strategic thinkers of the 1990s would certainly include Gary Hamel and C.K. Prahalad. *Competing for the Future* has been called the blueprint for a new generation of strategic thinking. *Business Week* (19 September 1994) said: 'At a time when many companies continue to lay off thousands in massive re-engineering exercises, this is a book that deserves widespread attention. It's a valuable and worthwhile tonic for devotees of today's slash-and-burn school of management.'

The surge of interest in core competencies has tended to enthusiastic oversimplification. They are a very powerful weapon, but can encourage companies to get into businesses simply because they see a link between core competencies rather than ones where they have an in-depth knowledge.

The authors' strategic prognosis falls between two extremes. At one extreme are the arch-rationalists, insisting on a constant stream of data to support any strategy. At the other is the thriving-on-chaos school, with its belief in free-wheeling organisations where strategy is a moveable feast.

THE BEST SOURCES OF HELP

Hamel, Gary, and C.K. Prahalad. *Competing for the Future*. Boston, Massachusetts: Harvard Business School Press, 1996.

The Competitive Advantage of Nations Michael Porter

GETTING STARTED

Michael Porter, author of the modern business classic *Competitive Strategy*, has extensive experience as a consultant to national governments. *The Competitive Advantage of Nations* emerged from his work on US President Ronald Reagan's Commission on Industrial Competitiveness. The research for the book encompassed ten countries: the United Kingdom, Denmark, Italy, Japan, Korea, Singapore, Sweden, Switzerland, the United States, and Germany (then West Germany).

The book can be read on three levels as:
• as a general inquiry into what makes national economies successful
• as a detailed study of eight of the world's main modern economies
• as a series of prescriptions about what governments should do to improve their country's competitiveness

It asks crucial questions. What makes a nation's businesses and industries competitive in global markets and what propels a whole nation's economy to advance? Why is one nation often the home for so many of an industry's world leaders?

At its heart is a radical new perspective of the role of nations. From being military powerhouses they are now economic units whose competitiveness is the key to power.

WHY READ IT?

Many consider *The Competitive Advantage of Nations* to be one of the most ambitious books of our times. Said to do 'for international capitalism what Marx did for the class struggle', it re-examines the nation state, suggesting that its basic role today is an economic one, and that, even in a global economy, it has a key role to play by ensuring the success of the companies operating within its borders who are the actual wealth producers for the population.

CONTRIBUTION

1. Nations, competition, and productivity

According to the author, 'Nations don't compete. Companies compete. Nations can make it hard or easy for them to do so.' When governments deliberately set out to help companies compete, however, their efforts are often counterproductive. The principal economic goal of a nation is to produce a high and rising standard of living for its citizens. The ability to do so depends not on the amorphous notion of competitiveness but on the productivity with which a nation's labour and capital resources are employed.

2. The paradox of globalisation

Companies and industries have become globalised and more international in their scope and aspirations than ever before. This would appear to suggest that the nation has lost its role in the international success of its firms. Companies, at first glance, seem to have transcended countries.

While the globalisation of competition might appear to make the nation less important, instead it seems to make it more so. With fewer impediments to trade to shelter uncompetitive domestic businesses and industries, the home nation takes on growing significance because it is the source of the skills and technology that underpin competitive advantage.

3. The national diamond

To make sense of the dynamics behind national or regional strength in a particular industry, Porter developed the concept of the national diamond made up of four forces.
• Factor conditions – these would once have been restricted to natural resources and plentiful labour; now they embrace data communications, university research, and the availability of scientists, engineers, or experts in a particular field.
• Demand conditions – if there is strong national demand for a product or service, this can give the industry a head start in global competition.
• Related and supporting industries – industries which are strong in a particular country are often surrounded by successful related industries.
• Company strategy, structure, and rivalry – domestic competition fuels growth and competitive strength.

Together, these four determine whether a nation has competitive advantage or not.

4. Clusters

'Nations succeed not in isolated industries, but in *clusters* of industries connected through vertical and horizontal relationships.' Groups of interconnected companies, suppliers, and related industries arising in particular locations contribute substantially to national success. Porter shows how such clusters come into being.

CONTEXT

According to *The Economist* (8 October 1994), this was 'the book that projected Mr Porter into the stratosphere, read by aspiring intellectuals and despairing politicians everywhere.'

Not everyone, however, agrees with Porter on the relationship between the nation and the globalised economy. Kenichi Ohmae believes that the nation state is on its way out, and Gary Hamel commented that Porter's book was backward-looking, and that it does not address the future of competitiveness.

Yet on balance, readers around the world have embraced the challenges outlined in Porter's book, and its status and impact as a classic business text cannot be underestimated.

THE BEST SOURCES OF HELP

Porter, Michael. *The Competitive Advantage of Nations.* Revised ed. New York: Free Press, 1998.

Competitive Strategy Michael Porter

GETTING STARTED

In 1973 Michael Porter became one of the youngest professors ever at the Harvard Business School. He has since acted as a strategy counsellor to many leading US and international companies, and as an adviser to foreign governments.

Competitive Strategy is one of those books that bases its message around significant numbers – in this case three and five, the three generic strategies (every company must adopt one or lose out to its competitors) and the five competitive forces (that determine what a company must do to remain competitive). Over 20 years after its first publication, the current critical consensus seems to be that the competitive forces are truer to reality than the generic strategies.

WHY READ IT?

Competitive Strategy is a modern classic. It claims to provide a solution to a long-running strategic dilemma, and has put strategy at the forefront of management thinking.

CONTRIBUTION

1. Resolving the strategy dilemma

Competitive Strategy presents a rationalist's solution to a long-running strategic dilemma. At one end of the spectrum are the pragmatists, who contend that companies have to respond to their own specific situations. Competitive advantage emerges from immediate, fast-thinking responsiveness. There is no formula for achieving sustainable competitive advantage.

At the other end are those who think that market knowledge is all-important. Any company that masters the intricacies of a particular market can reduce prices and increase market share. Porter proposes a compromise, arguing that there are three strategies for dealing with competitive forces: differentiation, overall cost leadership, and focus.

- Differentiation entails competing on the basis of value added to customers (quality, service, differentiation) so that customers will pay a premium to cover higher costs. It requires creative flair, research capability, and strong marketing.
- Cost-based leadership involves offering products or services at the lowest cost.
- Focus involves combining elements of the previous two strategies and targeting a specific market intensively.

2. Combining the strategies

Companies with a clear strategy outperform those whose strategy is unclear or those that attempt to achieve both differentiation and cost leadership.

Sometimes the company can successfully pursue more than one approach, though this is rarely possible. Effectively implementing any of these generic strategies usually requires total commitment, and organisational arrangements are diluted if there is more than one primary target.

3. The risks of ignoring generic strategies

If a company fails to focus on any of the three generic strategies it is liable to encounter problems. The company stuck in the middle is almost guaranteed low profitability. It either loses the high-volume customers who demand low prices or must bid away its profits to get this business away from low-cost companies. It also loses high-margin businesses, the cream, to the companies who are focused on high-margin targets. In addition, it will also probably suffer from a blurred corporate culture and a conflicting set of organisational arrangements and motivation systems.

4. The five competitive forces

In any industry, whether domestic, international, product- or service-oriented, the rules of competition are embodied in:

- The entry of new competitors. These necessitate some competitive response, which will inevitably use resources and reduce profits.
- The threat of substitutes. If there are viable alternatives to your product or service in the marketplace, the prices you can charge will be limited.
- The bargaining power of buyers. If customers have bargaining power they will use it. This will reduce profit margins.
- The bargaining power of suppliers. Given power over you, suppliers will increase their prices and adversely affect your profitability.
- The rivalry among existing competitors. Competition leads to the need to invest in marketing or R&D, or to price reductions. These will reduce profits.

The collective strength of these five competitive forces determines the ability of companies in an industry to earn, on average, rates of return on investment in excess of the cost of capital.

CONTEXT

When *Competitive Strategy* was published, it offered a rational and straightforward method for companies to extricate themselves from strategic confusion. The reassurance proved short-lived. Less than a decade later, companies were having to compete on all fronts. They had to be differentiated through improved service or speedier development, and be cost leaders, cheaper than their competitors.

Porter's other contribution proved more robust. The five forces are a means whereby a company can understand its particular industry. Initially passively interpreted as statements of the facts of competitive life, they are now usually seen as the rules of the game, which may have to be challenged if an organisation is to achieve any impact.

THE BEST SOURCES OF HELP

Porter, Michael. *Competitive Strategy: Techniques for Analyzing Industries and Competitors*. Revised ed. New York: Free Press, 1998.

Corporate Strategy Igor Ansoff

GETTING STARTED

Corporate Strategy integrated strategic planning concepts invented independently in leading US companies. The book provided a powerful, rational model by which strategic and planning decisions could be made. Ansoff saw strategic planning as a complex sequence, or cascade, of decisions and defined two main concepts essential to understanding its nature, and, therefore, to implementing it successfully. The first of these was 'gap analysis' – the 'gap' being the difference between the current position of an organisation and its strategic objectives. The second was 'synergy' – the concept that 2+2=5.

WHY READ IT?

In *Corporate Strategy*, Ansoff codified and generalised his experiences as a strategist at Lockheed. The book develops a series of concepts and procedures that managers can use to develop a practical method for strategic decision-making within an organisation.

CONTRIBUTION

1. Integrating strategic planning concepts

Corporate Strategy integrated strategic planning concepts which were invented independently in a number of leading US companies, including Lockheed.

Ansoff saw strategic management as a powerful applied

theory, offering a degree of coherence and universality lacking in the more traditional, functionally-dominated management theorising.

2. New theoretical concepts

The book presented several new theoretical concepts such as partial ignorance, business strategy, capability and competence profiles, and synergy. One particular concept, the product-mission matrix, became very popular, because it was simple and – for the first time – codified the differences between strategic expansion and diversification.

3. A rational model for planning decisions

Corporate Strategy provided a rational model by which strategic and planning decisions could be made. The model concentrated on corporate expansion and diversification, rather than on strategic planning as a whole.

The Ansoff Model of Strategic Planning was a complex sequence, or cascade, of decisions. The decisions started with highly aggregated ones and proceeded towards the more specific.

4. The introduction of gap analysis

Central to the cascade of decisions is the concept of gap analysis, which can be summarised as: see where you are, identify where you wish to be, and identify the tasks that will take you there.

The procedure within each step of the cascade is similar:
- a set of objectives is established
- the difference (the gap) between the current position of the organisation and the objectives is estimated
- one or more courses of action (strategy) is proposed
- these are tested for their gap-reducing properties

A course is accepted if it substantially closes the gap; if it does not, new alternatives are put forward and tested.

5. The concept of synergy

Corporate Strategy introduced the word 'synergy' to the management vocabulary. Although the term has become overused, Ansoff's explanation $(2+2=5)$ remains memorably simple.

CONTEXT

Corporate Strategy was published at a time of widespread enthusiasm for strategic planning, and an increasing number of organisations were joining the ranks of its users. Until its publication, strategic planning was a barely-understood, ad hoc concept. It was practised, while the theory lay largely unexplored. Ansoff also examined corporate advantage long before Michael Porter's dissection of the subject in the 1980s.

While *Corporate Strategy* was a remarkable book for its time, its flaws have been widely acknowledged, most honestly by Ansoff himself. It is highly prescriptive and advocates heavy reliance on analysis.

Some companies have encountered what Ansoff called 'paralysis by analysis' – the more information they possess, the more they think they need. This vicious circle dogs many organisations that embrace strategic planning with enthusiasm.

Ansoff regarded strategic planning as an incomplete invention, though he was convinced that strategic planning was an inherently useful management tool. He spent 40 years attempting to prove that this is the case and that, rather than being prescriptive and unwieldy, strategic management can be a dynamic tool able to cope with the unexpected twists of turbulent markets.

Business guru Gary Hamel described Ansoff as 'Truly the godfather of corporate strategy', and went on to say, 'Though Ansoff's approach may now appear overly-structured and deterministic, he created the language and processes that, for the first time, allowed modern industrial companies to explicitly address the deep questions of corporate strategy: how to grow, where to co-ordinate, which strengths to leverage, and so on'.

THE BEST SOURCES OF HELP

Ansoff, Igor. *Corporate Strategy*. New York: McGraw-Hill, 1965.

Corporate-level Strategy Michael Goold, Marcus Alexander, and Andrew Campbell

GETTING STARTED

The authors argue that most large companies are now multibusiness organisations. Research indicates that the benefits of economies of scale and synergy do not, in reality, exist.

Whilst individual businesses within the organisation often have strategies, the corporation as a whole may not. Only a tight fit between the parent organisation and its businesses will add value.

There must be a clear insight about the role of the parent organisation. 'Parents' must concentrate on heartland businesses that they understand.

The parent must only intervene on limited issues, and corporate strategy should be driven by parenting advantage.

WHY READ IT?

Although large conglomerates claim to add value through synergy and economies of scale, the authors suggest

this is not the case. They recommend that multibusiness organisations should aim for a tighter fit between individual company strategies and the overall corporate strategy. The book introduces the concept of heartland businesses and shows how it can help corporations improve their overall performance.

CONTRIBUTION

1. The value of multibusiness organisations

Multibusiness companies, by virtue of their size, should offer economies of scale and synergy between the various businesses, which can be exploited to the overall good. The authors' research suggests that in reality this is not the case.

They calculate that in over half of multibusiness companies, the whole is worth less than the sum of its parts. Instead of adding value, the corporation actually detracts from its value. Its influence, though pervasive, is often counter-productive.

This condemnation is not restricted to conglomerates.

The influence of the corporate parent is also felt in companies with portfolios in a single industry, or in a series of apparently related areas.

2. Lack of overall strategy

A primary cause of this phenomenon is that while individual businesses within the organisation often have strategies, the corporation as a whole may not. The proclaimed strategy is often an amalgam of the individual business strategies given credence by general aspirations.

3. Need for a tight fit

According to the authors, if corporate-level strategy is to add value, there needs to be a tight fit between the parent organisation and its businesses.

Successful corporate parents focus on a narrow range of tasks and create value in those areas, and align the structures, processes, and central functions of the parent accordingly.

4. Success factors for multibusiness organisations

From their analysis of 15 successful multibusiness corporations, the authors identify three corporate essentials:

- The role of the parent must be clear. If the parent does not know how or where it can add value, it is unlikely to do so.
- The parent must have distinctive characteristics. It, too, has a corporate culture and personality.
- It must be recognised that each parent will only be effective with certain sorts of business – described as their 'heartland'.

5. The importance of heartland businesses

'Heartland businesses are well understood by the parent; they do not suffer from inappropriate influence and meddling that can damage less familiar businesses,' say the authors. 'The parent has an innate feel for its heartland that enables it to make difficult judgments and decisions with a high degree of success.'

Heartland businesses are broad ranging and can cover different industries, markets, and technologies. Given this complexity, the ability of the parent to intervene on a limited number of issues is crucial.

6. Core businesses

The concept of heartland businesses is distinct from core businesses.' A core business is often merely a business that the company has decided to commit itself to', they say. Though core businesses may be important and substantial, the parent may not be adding a great deal to them.

7. Building parenting advantage

The authors continue: 'In contrast, the heartland definition focuses on the *fit* between a parent organisation and a business: do the parent's insights and behaviour fit the opportunities and nature of this business? Does the parent have specialist skills in assisting this type of business to perform better?'

Corporate strategy should be driven by 'parenting advantage' to create more value in the portfolio of businesses than would be achieved by any rival. To do so requires a fundamental change in basic perspectives on the role of the parent and of the nature of the multibusiness organisation.

CONTEXT

Most large companies are now multibusiness organisations. The logic behind this fact of business life is generally assumed rather than examined in depth.

The authors' research runs counter to the findings of authors such as Alfred Chandler in *Strategy and Structure* and Peter Drucker in *The Practice of Management*.

Gary Hamel said: 'Chandler and Drucker celebrated large multi-divisional organisations, but as these companies grew, decentralised, and diversified, the corporate centre often became little more than a layer of accounting consolidation. In the worst cases, a conglomerate was worth less than its break-up value. In writing the definitive book on corporate strategy, Goold, Alexander, and Campbell gave hope to corporate bureaucrats everywhere. Maybe it really was possible for the corporate level to add value'.

THE BEST SOURCES OF HELP

Goold, Michael, Marcus Alexander, and Andrew Campbell. *Corporate-level Strategy*. Chichester: Wiley, 1994.

The Dilbert Principle Scott Adams

GETTING STARTED

Writing with a well-sharpened pen and plenty of irony, Adams analyses the stuff of everyday office life. His satirical observations are cartoons featuring Dilbert, who personally suffers the consequences of modern management methods, and the dog, Dogbert. Adams rounds off all 26 chapters with letters from long-suffering employees recounting their own real-life experiences.

WHY READ IT?

A comic book as a source of advice for companies? Well, more a source of anti-advice. Scott Adams offers beleaguered employees a few strategies for self-defence.

CONTRIBUTION

1. The Dilbert Principle

We systematically promote the people with the least ability, says Adams. If nature went about organising things the way modern businesses do, a group of mountain gorillas would have an 'alpha' squirrel as their leader.

2. Humiliation

The frame of mind most conducive to employee productivity can be described, according to Adams, as happy, but with low self-esteem. The annual performance review is a particularly humiliating experience, he says elsewhere. Your boss's strategy is to get you to admit your inadequacies. These are then documented and used to justify you receiving measly salary increases.

3. Business communication

The true object of communication is furthering your own career. An unambiguous communication can get you into trouble, because it's only when you tie yourself down that you can turn out to be wrong.

4. Great lies of management

These include 'The employees are our greatest asset' and 'Your contribution is very important to us'. The following equation, says Adams, applies to management: employee suggestions = more work = bad!

5. Marketing and communications

Good advertising will induce people to buy your product even if it is unsuitable for them. A dollar spent on brainwashing, says Adams, is more cost-effective than a dollar spent on improving your product.

6. The business plan

The business plan lies somewhere in between the boss's hallucinations and the reality of the market. It's made in two stages. First, you collect data. Second, you ignore it.

7. Financial planning

If you change the budget often enough, the employees become frightened of making any moves that might draw attention to themselves. Where fear rules, outgoings are low. Where outgoings are low, there are share options for management, followed by the collapse of the business.

8. Selling

If your firm's products are overpriced and faulty, do not worry, says Adams. This can be compensated for by buyer motivation. Emphasise the 'intangible' economic benefits. Confusion is your friend.

9. Conferences

The secret of success at conferences, according to Adams, is a combination of arrogance and honesty. Your audience has to believe that you are giving serious thought to the problems of other people.

10. Downsizing

The most intelligent people are the ones who are the irst to turn their backs on a shrinking organisation, because they take compensation packages with them. The stupid ones, who stay on, offset that by working longer hours.

11. Re-engineering

Re-engineering was invented as an antidote to quality programmes. In re-engineering all of the natural incompetence stored in the firm is unleashed on a monumental scale.

12. Team-building exercises

Exercises designed to strengthen team spirit, says Adams, can take many forms. Team-building exercises expose the employees to unpleasant situations for so long that they end up either as sworn brothers and sisters or a bunch of car thieves.

13. Managers

A manager is someone who prevails on people to do something for his or her benefit. The most important ability of a manager is to be able to claim the credit for something that happens of its own accord.

CONTEXT

This work is one of the best-selling business books of all time and has attained cult status. Satire and humour are a means here of dispelling employee anxiety in the face of management decisions.

THE BEST SOURCES OF HELP

Adams, Scott. *The Dilbert Principle: A Cubicle's Eye View of Bosses, Meetings, Management Fads, and Other Workplace Afflictions*. London: Boxtree, 2002.

Dynamic Administration Mary Parker Follett

GETTING STARTED

In the author's view, management is a social process and should have a special human dimension. The process is based in human emotions and in the interrelations created by working. The working environment has human problems, with psychological, ethical, and economic dimensions.

She goes on to say that workers should be given greater responsibility, which is the great developer of people – and successful leaders must offer a vision of the future and train followers to become leaders.

Relationships, not just transactions, are important in organisations. Knowing this involves recognising that conflict is a fact of life that we should use to work for us – but integration is the only positive way forward.

WHY READ IT?

The book provides one of the earliest perspectives on business from the point of view of human relationships. It was written at a time when workers were seen simply as part of the mass-production process. The book provides useful background on the development of concepts such as empowerment and visionary leadership.

CONTRIBUTION

1. Management as a social process

'We can never wholly separate the human from the mechanical sides', says Follett. The study of human relations in business and the study of the technology of operating are bound up together. The everyday incidents and problems of management reflect the presence or absence of sound principle.

Management has a special human character. Its nature as a social process is deeply embedded in the emotions of human beings and in the interrelations to which the everyday working of industry necessarily gives rise – both at manager and worker levels and, of course, between the two.

2. Towards empowerment

Mary Parker Follett believed that, 'we should undepartmentalise our thinking in regard to every problem that comes to us'.

She continued, 'I do not think that we have psychological and ethical and economic problems. We have human problems, with psychological, ethical, and economical aspects, and as many others as you like'.

Follett advocated giving greater responsibility to people at a time when the mechanical might of mass production was at its height. 'Responsibility is the great developer of men', she said.

3. Leadership through vision

The most successful leader of all is one who sees another picture not yet actualised – who sees the whole rather than the particular, organises the experiences of the group, offers a vision of the future, and trains followers to become leaders.

Leading should be a two-way, mutually beneficial process. 'We want worked out a relation between leaders and led which will give to each the opportunity to make creative contributions to the situation', Follett wrote.

4. Relationships matter

Relationships, not just transactions, are important in organisations. The reciprocal nature of relationships means that a mutual influence is developed when people work together, however formal authority is defined.

Conflict is a fact of life that we should use to work for us. There are three ways of dealing with confrontation: domination, compromise, or integration. Integration is the only positive way forward. This can be achieved by first uncovering the real conflict and then taking the demands of both sides and breaking them up into their constituent parts.

Outlook is narrowed, activity is restricted, and chances of business success largely diminished when thinking is constrained within the limits of what has been called an either–or situation. 'We should never allow ourselves to be bullied by an either–or', said Follett. There is often the possibility of something better than either of two given alternatives.

CONTEXT

Published eight years after her death, *Dynamic Administration* is a collection of Mary Parker Follett's papers on management gathered from 12 lectures given between 1925 and 1933. Her work stands as a humane counterpoint to that of Frederick Taylor and the proponents of scientific management. Follett was a female, liberal humanist in an era dominated by reactionary males intent on mechanising the world of business.

Bearing in mind she was speaking of the United States in the early 1920s, her thinking can be described as little less than revolutionary, and certainly a generation ahead of its time. During her life, Mary Parker Follett's thinking on management was generally ignored.

To some, Follett remains a utopian idealist, out of touch with reality; to others, she is a torchbearer of good sense whose ideas have sadly not had significant impact on organisations.

THE BEST SOURCES OF HELP

Follett, Mary Parker. *Dynamic Administration*. Revised ed. New York: Buccaneer Books, 1982.

Emotional Intelligence Daniel Goleman

GETTING STARTED

In this international bestseller, Daniel Goleman challenges the traditional view that a high IQ is essential for success. He provides examples of people with high IQs and considerable academic achievement who have failed in business and in life; conversely, he also shows how those who are apparently less intellectually gifted were able to manage and harness their emotional intelligence in order to succeed. Although the book does not specifically relate to behaviour in a business setting, its conclusions highlight patterns that can be used to improve personal performance at work. Emotional intelligence is also one of the 'soft skills' that are increasingly regarded as important in commercial life.

WHY READ IT?

Goleman describes the evolution of the brain and explains how the two main brain functions that influence behaviour – emotion and intelligence – are situated in different parts of the brain. The part of the brain that controls emotions receives external signals before the intelligence functions, and that means that initial reactions to events may be emotional rather than rational. Goleman explains that the brain still retains a primitive 'survival mode' that may trigger reactions and responses that are inappropriate. To succeed, he advises, we need to understand those reactions and learn how to control them.

CONTRIBUTION

1. Overcoming impulses

According to Goleman, emotions have a wisdom of their own that can be harnessed. Although our natural reaction is to respond emotionally, it is important to make use of emotional intelligence to develop more positive responses.

2. A framework of emotional intelligence

Goleman has developed a framework that explains emotional intelligence in terms of five elements:
- self-awareness
- self-regulation
- motivation
- empathy
- social skills

Self-awareness

According to Goleman, this element enables you to develop a better understanding of the way emotions affect your performance. You can also use your values to guide your decision-making. By looking at your strengths and weaknesses and learning from your experiences, you can gain self-confidence and certainty about your capabilities, values, and goals.

Self-regulation

Goleman describes how this element can help you control your temper and reduce stress by acting in a more positive and action-orientated way. This enables you to retain your composure and improves your ability to think clearly under pressure. Through self-regulation, he claims, you can handle your impulses effectively.

Motivation

According to the author, by harnessing this aspect of emotional intelligence, you can enjoy challenge and stimulation, and strive for achievement. You will be committed to the cause and seize the initiative. You will also be guided by your personal preferences in following one set of goals, rather than another.

Empathy

Empathy enables you to understand other points of view, and behave openly and honestly.

Social skills

Goleman describes how social skills such as persuasion, communication, listening, negotiating, and leading can be honed.

3. Emotional intelligence and management

Goleman claims that people with a higher degree of emotional intelligence are more likely to succeed in senior management. He also believes that emotional intelligence can be developed over a period of time, although this has been disputed.

CONTEXT

Daniel Goleman has built on the work in this book to research leadership styles based on different characteristics of emotional intelligence. These range from coercive leaders who are self-motivated and driven to succeed, to democratic leaders who are good at communication and listening, and coaching leaders who listen well and motivate others. The research was reported in the March–April 2000 edition of the *Harvard Business Review*.

Commentators have pointed out a possible contradiction in Goleman's work. He claims that emotional intelligence is inherent, yet suggests that it can be developed.

THE BEST SOURCES OF HELP

Goleman, Daniel. *Emotional Intelligence: Why It Can Matter More Than IQ*. London: Bloomsbury, 1995.

The Fifth Discipline Peter Senge

GETTING STARTED

Peter Senge is director of the Center for Organizational Learning at MIT. *The Fifth Discipline* emerged from extensive research by Senge and his team, but Senge said the 'vision that became *The Fifth Discipline*' came to him one morning during his meditation.

The 'fifth discipline' of the title is systems thinking. Of the five building blocks of a learning organisation, systems thinking connects the other four and enables them to work together for the benefit of business.

WHY READ IT?

This is the book that popularised the concept of the learning organisation. More philosophical in tone than most business-oriented books, it adopts a holistic approach. Learning is both an individual and a group experience, Senge would claim, much deeper than just taking information in. 'It is about changing individuals so that they produce results they care about, accomplish things that are important to them', he wrote.

CONTRIBUTION

1. Learning is vital

In Senge's view, as business becomes more complex and dynamic, work must become more 'learningful'. It is no longer sufficient to have one person learning for the whole organisation. It is no longer possible to figure it out from the top, and have everybody else follow the orders of the grand strategist.

The organisations that will excel in the future will be those that can tap the commitment and capacity to learn of people at all levels within them.

Managers should therefore encourage employees to:
• be open to new ideas
• communicate frankly with each other
• understand thoroughly how their companies operate
• form a collective vision
• work together to achieve their goals

2. The five disciplines

There are five components to a learning organisation:
• systems thinking
• personal mastery
• mental models
• shared vision
• team learning

Systems thinking

Systems thinking is a conceptual framework to make patterns clearer, claims Senge. It requires a shift of mind to see interrelationships rather than linear cause and effect. It can help managers spot repetitive patterns, such as the way certain kinds of problems persist, or the way systems have their own in-built limits to growth.

Personal mastery

This idea is based on the familiar competencies and skills associated with management. But it also includes spiritual growth – opening oneself up to a progressively deeper reality and living life from a creative rather than a reactive viewpoint.

Shared vision

Senge stresses the importance of co-creation and argues that shared vision can only be built on personal vision.

Team learning

The discipline of team learning involves two practices: dialogue and discussion. Dialogue is characterised by its exploratory nature, discussion by the opposite process of narrowing down the field to the best alternative for the decisions that need to be made. The two are mutually complementary, but the benefits of combining them only come from having previously separated them.

3. Creating learning organisations

The author argues that transforming companies into learning organisations has proved problematical, principally because it involves managers surrendering their spheres of power and control to the people who are learning. If people are to learn, they must be allowed to experiment and fail. In a blame-oriented culture, this requires a major change in organisational attitude.

The learning organisation demands trust and involvement, usually notable by their absence. Real commitment is rare in today's organisations. Experience indicates that nearly all of what passes for commitment is compliance. One man reported to Senge that by adopting the learning organisation model, he made what he called 'job-limiting choices'. What he meant was that he could have climbed the corporate ladder faster by rejecting Senge's theories and toeing the company line.

CONTEXT

The Fifth Discipline has proved highly influential. Though the learning organisation has rarely been converted into reality, the idea has fuelled the debate on self-managed development and employability, and has affected the rewards and remuneration strategies of many organisations.

THE BEST SOURCES OF HELP

Senge, Peter. *The Fifth Discipline: The Art and Practice of the Learning Organization*. Revised ed. New York: Doubleday, 2006.

The Functions of the Executive Chester Barnard

GETTING STARTED
The author asserts that an organisation allows people to achieve what they could not achieve as individuals, as they and their actions are interconnected. One essential ingredient for a successful organisation is good, short lines of communication because communication enables everyone to be tied into the organisation's objectives. It is also vital that chief executives nurture goals and values and translate them into action; executives should not just ensure conformance to a code of morals, they should create moral codes for others.

WHY READ IT?
Barnard is regarded as an important management thinker, who, according to Tom Peters and Robert Waterman in *In Search of Excellence*, created 'a complete management theory'. Though his language is dated, much of his thinking – particularly on the importance of communication – is relevant to modern management.

CONTRIBUTION
1. People are interconnected in an organisation
Barnard rejected the concept of an organisation as comprising a rather definite group of people whose behaviour is co-ordinated only because they are linked together by some explicit goal or goals. 'In a community,' he argued 'all acts of individuals and of organisations are directly or indirectly interconnected and interdependent.'

2. The importance of communication
Barnard highlights the need for communication. He argues that everyone needs to know what and where the communications channels are so that every single person can be tied into the organisation's objectives.

Lines of communication should be short and direct. He writes: 'the essential functions are, first, to provide the system of communications; second, to promote the securing of essential efforts; and third, to formulate and define purpose.'

3. The need to nurture goals and values
The chief executive is not a dictatorial figure geared to simple, short-term achievements. Part of his or her responsibility is to nurture the values and goals of the organisation. Values and goals need to be translated into action, rather than meaningless motivational phraseology – 'strictly speaking, purpose is defined more nearly by the aggregate of action taken than by words', he writes.

4. A holistic approach to management
An organisation is simply a means of allowing people to achieve what they could not achieve as individuals. An organisation is a system of consciously co-ordinated activities of forces of two or more persons.

5. A code of management morality
In Barnard's view, the distinguishing mark of the executive responsibility is that it requires not merely conformance to a complex code of morals, but also the creation of moral codes for others.

CONTEXT
Chester Barnard was a rarity: a management theorist who was also a successful practitioner. He won an economics scholarship to Harvard but, before finishing his degree, he joined American Telephone and Telegraph, eventually becoming President of New Jersey Bell in 1927.

The Functions of the Executive collected together his lectures on management. 'It is doubtful if any other book since Taylor's *Scientific Management* has had a deeper influence on the thinking of serious business leaders about the nature of their work', observed Barnard's contemporary, Lyndall Urwick.

Although the language is dated, much of what Barnard argued strikes a chord with contemporary management thinking. His ideas on communication, especially on the importance of short lines of communication, remain relevant. In arguing that there was a morality to management, Barnard played an important part in broadening the managerial role from one simply of measurement, control, and supervision, to one also concerned with more abstract notions and concepts, such as values.

THE BEST SOURCES OF HELP
Barnard, Chester. *The Functions of the Executive*. Revised ed. Boston, Massachusetts: Harvard University Press, 2005.

General and Industrial Management Henri Fayol

GETTING STARTED
Fayol created a system of management in which management was the foundation stone of the organisation.

He believed that to manage is to forecast and plan, to organise, to command, to co-ordinate, and to control. His view of forward planning was one of the first examples of business planning in practice.

WHY READ IT?
Fayol created one of the first systems of management that put management at the centre of the organisation. His system divides a company's activities into six groups, in which managerial activities are distinct from the other five. The book provides a systematic analysis of the process of management, in which he anticipated most of the more recent analyses of modern business practice. His brief résumé of what constitutes management largely held sway throughout the 20th century.

CONTRIBUTION

1. A system of management
Fayol created a system of management encapsulated in *General and Industrial Management*.

'Management plays a very important part in the government of undertakings; of all undertakings, large or small, industrial, commercial, political, religious, or any other', he writes.

2. Division by function
Fayol's system was based on acceptance of, and adherence to, different functions. He said that all activities to which industrial undertakings give rise can be divided into six groups. These are:
- technical activities
- commercial activities
- financial activities
- security activities
- accounting activities
- managerial activities

3. The nature of management
The management function is quite distinct from the other five essential functions. To manage is to forecast and plan, to organise, to command, to co-ordinate, and to control.

Fayol's view of what constitutes management was highly influential throughout the 20th century and has only recently been challenged.

4. Principles of management
From his observations, Fayol also produced general principles of management:

- division of work
- authority and responsibility
- discipline
- unity of command
- unity of direction
- subordination of individual interest to general interest
- remuneration of personnel
- centralisation
- scalar chain (line of authority)
- order
- equity
- stability of tenure of personnel
- initiative
- esprit de corps

5. Forward planning
Fayol talks of ten-yearly forecasts, revised every five years – one of the first instances of business planning in practice.

The maxim 'managing means looking ahead', gives some idea of the importance attached to planning for the future in the business world. It is true that if foresight is not the whole of management, it is at least an essential part of it.

CONTEXT
Fayol created a system that put management at the centre of the organisation in a way never envisaged by contemporaries such as Frederick W. Taylor, author of *Scientific Management*.

Fayol's championing of management was highly important. While Taylor regarded managers as little more than overseers with limited responsibility, Fayol regarded their role as critical to organisational success.

In his faith in carefully defined functions, Fayol was systematising business organisation in ways that worked at the time, but proved too limiting and restraining in the long term.

In *The Principles and Practice of Management*, a 1953 study of early management thinking, E.F.L. Brech notes, 'The importance of Fayol's contribution lay in two features: the first was his systematic analysis of the process of management; the second, his firm advocacy of the principle that management can, and should, be taught. Both were revolutionary lines of thought in 1908, and still little accepted in 1925.'

An extrapolation of Fayol's methods was later exposed by Peter Drucker who observed, 'If used beyond the limits of Fayol's model, functional structure becomes costly in terms of time and effort'.

THE BEST SOURCES OF HELP
Fayol, Henri, revised by Irwin Gray. *General and Industrial Management*. New York: IEEE Press, 1984.

The General Theory of Employment
John Maynard Keynes

GETTING STARTED

Keynes' *General Theory* shows how economic policy can overcome periods of stagnation. He argues in favour of investment being state-directed to ensure full employment. In contrast to the exponents of classical economic theory, he does not believe in the self-healing power of the market. Demand is, for him, the lever of the economy, and in times of crisis it is the state that must operate the lever.

WHY READ IT?

Should the state intervene to combat unemployment? Governments were already asking themselves this question during the 1930s. Keynes was the first to show convincingly why state intervention to boost employment is sensible and necessary. This book, first published in 1936, lays the foundations of Keynesianism, a demand-orientated doctrine that is still hotly debated and highly influential today.

CONTRIBUTION

1. The error in classical economics

According to Keynes, Adam Smith and David Ricardo start out from the assumption that the law of supply and demand regulates the price of goods and of labour. Workers, therefore, are only dismissed when their wages are too high. If they accept lower wages, they are re-employed. The classical economic model always returns to a state of balance: anyone who is unemployed, is so voluntarily.

The world economic crisis of the 1930s could not, however, be explained in this way, Keynes thought. Millions of workers were on the streets, although wages were sinking lower and lower. The 'paradox of poverty in the midst of affluence' needed another explanation. Supply was not decisive in achieving economic success; demand was.

2. Aggregate demand – consumption and investment

Demand across the entire economy – the sum of expenditure on consumer and investment goods – has one essential characteristic, Keynes argues: it is unstable. Expenditure on consumption depends on income: the higher the income the more money is spent. But, above a particular level of income, the tendency to increase consumption declines. Part of the additional income is saved.

Investments are the second element in aggregate demand, because they increase the potential of businesses to produce. Investments, according to Keynes, depend on the 'marginal efficiency of capital'. If this is higher than the standard rate of interest in the market, the investor has an incentive to use credit to implement investment plans. In the opposite case, the costs of credit would be higher than the profit, and the investment would not be made.

3. Imbalance between the markets for goods and capital

The market interest rate for investments, says Keynes, results from the population's inclination towards liquidity, that is, their demand for cash. People save for many reasons; to purchase goods, to protect themselves against hard times, or to speculate. Speculators keep their savings in cash until prices become low and an opportunity arises to enter the stock market.

Harmonisation between the goods and capital markets is the exception; equality of savings and investments a rare and lucky chance. It is not the case, says Keynes, that savings decisions are solely dependent on the rate of interest and that the interest mechanism ensures that all savings are available to be loaned to businesses for the purchase of investment goods. Rather, he argues, businesses expand their production so long as they expect larger sales in the future. More and more investors try to attract the capital of the savers. Interest rates and production costs rise and reduce returns. The suppliers of capital get nervous. Panic grips the markets. The unrealistic expectations of the boom are followed by the hysteria of crisis. Investments fall, employment drops, purchasing power disappears, future prospects become more and more dismal. Businesses do not even invest when interest rates sink to zero. The national economy is caught in the 'liquidity trap'.

4. The state as starter motor of the economy

To free the economy from this disastrous situation and turn it back in the direction of full employment, aggregate demand must rise, says Keynes, until increasing production by businesses offers all workers employment. If the demand for investment goods rises, this leads to more production, more work, and more income. Higher consumption boosts demand for goods and investment, which means that production and income rise further. A chain reaction begins, an 'income multiplier' – an exogenous impulse, perhaps an extra boost to investment, gives rise to a multiple increase in income.

From this, Keynes draws the following conclusion. If entrepreneurs do not invest in sufficient quantities, the state must step forward as an investor to set the economy back in motion. To produce additional investment, the public purse accepts credit and uses it to finance, for example, roads, sewage systems, schools, or hospitals.

CONTEXT

The stock market crash of 1929, the crisis in the world economy, and the Great Depression of the 1930s threw up a number of crucial economic and political questions, which Keynes attempted to answer in this book. It made him the most famous national economist of the 20th century and initiated one of the most influential strands in modern economic thought, Keynesianism. Keynesian ideas provided the framework for the post-war recovery and held sway in many countries during the middle of the last century. Even President Richard Nixon remarked 'We are all Keynesians now'. It was only in the 1970s that the 'monetarist counterrevolution' began, eventually

re-enthroning supply-side economics and the market forces whose fallibility it had been part of Keynes' purpose to demonstrate.

THE BEST SOURCES OF HELP
Keynes, John Maynard. *The General Theory of Employment, Interest, and Money*. BNPublishing.com, 2008.

Getting to Yes Roger Fisher and William Ury

GETTING STARTED
The negotiating principles that the authors claim will lead to successful outcomes are:
- don't bargain over positions
- separate the people from the problem
- focus on interests, not positions
- invent options for mutual gain
- insist on objective criteria

WHY READ IT?
Negotiation is an important skill in many aspects of business and personal life. The authors claim that people can become more effective negotiators by moving from adversarial haggling to constructive joint problem-solving, a solution they call 'principled negotiation'. Both Fisher and Ury have conducted negotiations at extremely high levels in business, politics, diplomacy, law, and international relations. They write with authority and have the experience to offer practical advice and insight into each stage of the negotiating process.

CONTRIBUTION
1. The importance of effective negotiation
Negotiation involves everyone, the authors claim. People use negotiation to handle their differences at work and in personal life. However, they believe that standard negotiating strategies tend to leave one or both parties dissatisfied. They describe two types of negotiators:
- soft negotiators who may make easy compromises to avoid conflict
- hard negotiators who want to win at all costs

The authors propose a third way, using what they call 'principled negotiation'. Its aim is to decide issues on their merits, rather than on the will of the parties involved.

2. Avoid bargaining over positions
Fisher and Ury point out that, traditionally, people take positions and defend them. The matter is only resolved through concessions. This approach can harm relation-

ships, and can be damaging to future negotiations. In this approach, emotions become entangled with logic, so it is important to separate people from problems.

3. Separate people from problems
The authors prompt us to remember that negotiators are people with emotions. Negotiators are therefore just as interested in ongoing relationships as in dealing with the immediate problem. Understanding the emotions of the other side is important, because they can act as a barrier to rational discussion. It is important to understand the other person's perspective and find out what is important to them. Listening actively and acknowledging the other party's perspective is critical.

The authors explain how successful negotiators try to make the other party own the problem so that they fully participate in reaching a satisfactory conclusion. Communication is an important part of this process, helping to build constructive working relationships that can reduce the element of confrontation.

4. Focus on interests, not positions
Fisher and Ury recommend looking for the underlying interest in negotiations. Interests may not conflict, although positions do. They suggest finding out or asking why the other side takes a particular position, and acknowledging those interests as part of the problem.

5. Invent options for mutual gain
The aim of negotiation is a single conclusion, say the authors. Introducing other options may appear to slow down the process, but, they claim, it can make the outcome easier to achieve. Enlarging the pie can help to provide what appears to be mutual gain. They believe that brainstorming can help to determine the options because during brainstorming, no decisions have to be made and creativity is encouraged.

6. Insist on objective criteria
Finally, according to Fisher and Ury, it may be possible to decide on the outcome of negotiations by reference to

an independent or objective authority. The standards adopted should be fair and they must be acceptable to both sides. Comparable criteria from other negotiations may also be acceptable.

CONTEXT

Negotiation is a critical element of business. The book takes a detailed look at the process of negotiation independently of business processes such as sales, customer service, or union negotiations.

The authors build on their own experience of negotiations in politics, diplomacy, and the law. Although not every one of the examples relates directly to business, it is possible to apply the same principles to commercial situations of many types.

THE BEST SOURCES OF HELP

Fisher, Roger, and William Ury. *Getting to Yes*. London: Random House, 2003.

How to Win Friends and Influence People
Dale Carnegie

GETTING STARTED

Carnegie holds that it is essential to handle people effectively, and to make them like you to ensure your own success. His book is littered with illustrative anecdotes from the lives of the famous – Clark Gable, Marconi, Franklin D. Roosevelt, Mary Pickford – and the not so famous.

WHY READ IT?

Dale Carnegie was a highly successful public speaker and author of books on public speaking and confidence development. *How to Win Friends and Influence People* provides practical advice on the universal challenge of face-to-face communication. As the familiarity of the title proves, the book has had a great impact. The first edition had a print run of a mere 5,000, but the book has since sold over 15 million copies.

CONTRIBUTION

1. Handle people effectively
Carnegie presented the fundamental techniques in handling people:
• don't criticise, condemn, or complain
• give honest and sincere appreciation
• arouse in the other person an eager want

2. Make people like you
He added advice on other ways to make people like you:
• become genuinely interested in other people
• smile
• remember that a person's name is to that person the sweetest and most important sound in any language

• be a good listener
• encourage others to talk about themselves
• talk in terms of the other person's interests
• make the other person feel important, and do it sincerely

CONTEXT

How to Win Friends and Influence People is the original self-improvement book, and Carnegie was the first superstar of the self-help genre.

Cashing in on his success, he wrote a plethora of other titles on similar themes, including *Public Speaking and Influencing Men in Business*; *How to Stop Worrying and Start Living*; *How to Enjoy Your Life and Your Job*; and *How to Develop Self-confidence and Influence People by Public Speaking*. His successors included Anthony Robbins and Stephen Covey, who studied US success literature (of which Carnegie's body of work is a prime example) before coming up with *The Seven Habits of Highly Effective People*.

Carnegie had done much the same 50 years before, and his principles have a similar homely ring to those of Covey. Carnegie's books and his company's training programmes continue to strike a chord with managers and aspiring managers, because they deal with the universal challenge of face-to-face communication.

Carnegie was notable in being the first to create a credible long-term business out of his ideas. In creating a flourishing enterprise, Carnegie ensured that his name and ideas should continue to live on and make money after his death.

THE BEST SOURCES OF HELP

Carnegie, Dale. *How to Win Friends and Influence People*. New edition. London: Ebury, 2007.

The HP Way David Packard

GETTING STARTED

According to Packard, the HP secret lay in a simple approach to business. The HP way reflected the culture of the company and the management style they used to run it. It was based on openness and respect for the individual, which was key to the company's success. Management was always available and involved, and conflict had to be tackled through communication and consensus rather than confrontation. Their commitment to people fostered commitment to the company, and HP people at all levels show boundless energy and enthusiasm. The recipe for growth was to make products leaders in their markets. They kept divisions small and didn't do anything too risky. These values worked to save the company when times were hard.

WHY READ IT?

David Packard was half of the partnership that created one of the business and management benchmarks of the 20th century – Hewlett-Packard. In 1937, with a mere $538 and a rented garage in Palo Alto, Bill Hewlett and David Packard created one of the most successful corporations in the world. This book tells the story behind the company.

CONTRIBUTION

1. A simple approach to business

HP's secret lay in the simplicity of their methods. From the very start, Hewlett-Packard was guided by a few fundamental principles:

- it did not believe in long-term borrowing to secure the expansion of the business
- its recipe for growth was simply that its products needed to be leaders in their markets
- it got on with the job

'Our main task is to design, develop, and manufacture the finest [electronic equipment] for the advancement of science and the welfare of humanity. We intend to devote ourselves to that task', said Packard in a 1961 memo to employees.

The duo eschewed fashionable management theory: 'If I hear anybody talking about how big their share of the market is or what they're trying to do to increase their share of the market, I'm going to personally see that a black mark gets put in their personnel folder.'

2. Respect for the individual

The company believed that people could be trusted and should always be treated with respect and dignity.

'We both felt fundamentally that people want to do a good job. They just need guidelines on how to do it.'

HP believed that management should be available and involved – 'Management by wandering about' was the motto.

Rather than the administrative suggestions of management, Packard preferred to talk of leadership. Their legacy, and Packard's proudest achievement, is a management style based on openness and respect for the individual.

3. Keeping it small

Hewlett-Packard was a company built on very simple ideas. While competitors were turning into conglomerates, Hewlett and Packard kept their heads down and continued with their methods. When their divisions grew too big (around 1,500 people) they split them up to ensure that they didn't spiral out of control.

They didn't do anything too risky or too outlandish. For example, Packard was sceptical about pocket calculators though, in the end, the company was an early entrant into the market. They didn't risk the company on a big deal or get into debt.

4. Strong commitment to values

Their values worked to save the company when times were hard. During the 1970s recession, Hewlett-Packard staff hung on and took a 10 percent pay cut and worked 10 percent fewer hours.

As the book documents, if the company hadn't had a long-term commitment to employee stock ownership, perhaps employees wouldn't have been so willing to make sacrifices. Packard claims that commitment to people clearly fostered commitment to the company.

CONTEXT

Hewlett-Packard has pulled off an unusual double – it is admired and successful. When they were assembling their list of excellent companies in the late 1970s, Tom Peters and Robert Waterman included Hewlett-Packard.

When Jerry Porras and James Collins wrote *Built to Last*, their celebration of long-lived companies, there was no doubt that Hewlett-Packard was worthy of inclusion. In the same vein, in 1985, *Fortune* ranked Hewlett-Packard as one of the two most highly-admired companies in the United States. The company is ranked similarly in virtually every other poll on well-managed companies or ones that would be good to work for.

'Wherever you go in the HP empire, you find people talking product quality, feeling proud of their division's achievements in that area. HP people at all levels show boundless energy and enthusiasm', observed Tom Peters and Robert Waterman in *In Search of Excellence*.

According to Louise Kehoe in the *Financial Times*, 'Their legacy, and the achievement that Packard was most proud of, is a management style based on openness and respect for the individual.'

THE BEST SOURCES OF HELP

Packard, David. *The HP Way*. New York: Collins, 1996.

The Human Problems of an Industrial Civilization
Elton Mayo

GETTING STARTED
The Hawthorne Studies offered important insights into the motivation of workers:

- People and their motivation were critical to the success of any business.
- There was a link between morale and output – changes in working conditions led to increased output.
- It is important to restore humanity to the workplace. Workers selected for a test felt that more attention was being paid to them. They felt chosen, and so responded positively. The feeling of belonging to a cohesive group led to an increase in productivity. Informal organisations between groups are a potentially powerful force.

WHY READ IT?
The author was part of the team conducting the Hawthorne Studies at Western Electric's Chicago plant between 1927 and 1932, early studies into motivation in the workplace. The book shows the important link between workforce morale and organisational performance, and paved the way for policies and management theories based on teamwork and effective communication.

CONTRIBUTION
1. The Hawthorne Studies
According to Mayo, the studies offered important insights into the motivation of workers. It was found that changes in working conditions led to increased output, even if the changes didn't obviously improve working conditions.

Whatever the dictates of mass production and scientific management, people and their motivation were critical to the success of any business.

2. The link between morale and output
The researchers were interested in exploring the links between morale and output. The author documents how five women workers were removed to a test room and observed as they worked. The research was initially restricted to physical and technical variables. Sociological factors were not expected to be of any significance. The results proved otherwise.

Removed from their colleagues, the morale of the 'guinea pigs' improved. By virtue of their selection, the women felt that more attention was being paid to them.

3. The importance of group cohesion
Mayo reports that the feeling of belonging to a cohesive group led to an increase in productivity. He comments:

'The desire to stand well with one's fellows, the so-called human instinct of association, easily outweighs the merely individual interest and the logic of reasoning upon which so many spurious principles of management are based'.

Mayo champions the case for teamworking and for improved communications between management and the workforce.

The Hawthorne research revealed informal organisations between groups as a potentially powerful force, which companies could make use of or ignore at their peril.

4. Restoring humanity to the workplace
Mayo's belief that the humanity needed to be restored to the workplace struck a chord at a time when the dehumanising side of mass production was beginning to be more fully appreciated.

'So long as commerce specialises in business methods which take no account of human nature and social motives, so long may we expect strikes and sabotage to be the ordinary accompaniment of industry', Mayo notes.

The research assumed that the behaviour of workers was dictated by the 'logic of sentiment' while that of the bosses was by the 'logic of cost and efficiency'.

CONTEXT
The author is known for his contribution to the famous Hawthorne experiments into the motivation of workers.

The experiments were carried out in 1927–32 at the Chicago division of Western Electric. Although they were celebrated as a major event, their significance lay not so much in their results and discoveries but in the statement they made – that people and their motivation were critical to the success of any business.

The findings influenced the human relations school of thinkers, including Herzberg, McGregor, and Maslow, which emerged in the 1940s and 1950s.

The work of the Hawthorne researchers redressed the balance in management theorising, and the scientific bias of earlier researchers was put into a new perspective.

THE BEST SOURCES OF HELP
Mayo, Elton. *The Human Problems of an Industrial Civilization*. Revised ed. London: Routledge, 2003.

The Human Side of Enterprise Douglas McGregor

GETTING STARTED

Management assumptions about controlling human resources determine an organisation's character. Theory X assumes that workers are inherently lazy, needing to be supervised and motivated. Authority is the central, indispensable means of managerial control. Theory Y assumes that people want and need to work and organisations should develop employees' commitment. McGregor argues that the average human being learns not only to accept but to seek responsibility.

WHY READ IT?

McGregor was a key member of the Human Relations School of Management whose work significantly influenced management styles from the 1960s on. His most famous concept is 'Theories X and Y' which describe two extreme approaches to managing people. The book highlights the potential for a more enlightened approach to human relations management and paved the way for approaches such as empowerment.

CONTRIBUTION

1. The importance of human resources

According to the book, the assumptions management holds about controlling its human resources determine the whole character of the enterprise.

2. Theory X – a traditional management approach

Theory X is built on the assumption that workers are inherently lazy, need to be supervised and motivated, and regard work as a necessary evil.

3. The assumptions behind Theory X

- People inherently dislike work and will avoid it if they can.
- People need to be coerced, controlled, and threatened into making adequate effort toward the organisation's ends.
- People lack ambition, preferring to be directed and to avoid responsibility. Above all they want security.

4. The influence of Theory X

The assumption that authority is the central, indispensable means of managerial control pervades US industry. In the author's view, this is a consequence not of human nature, but of management philosophy, policy, and practice. It is not people who have made organisations, but organisations that have transformed the perspectives, aspirations, and behaviour of people.

5. Theory Y – a humanist approach

Theory Y is based on the principle that people want and need to work. An organisation needs to develop the individual's commitment to its objectives, and then to liberate his or her abilities on behalf of those objectives.

6. The assumptions behind Theory Y

- Work is as natural as play or rest - the typical human being doesn't inherently dislike work.
- External control and threat of punishment are not the only means for bringing about effort.
- Commitment to objectives is a function of the rewards associated with their achievement.
- The most important reward is the satisfaction of ego, which can be the direct product of effort.
- The average human being learns, not only to accept but to seek responsibility.
- The capacity to use imagination, ingenuity, and creativity in the solution of organisational problems is widely distributed in the population.

7. Towards the learning manager

McGregor suggests that four kinds of learning are relevant for managers: intellectual knowledge; manual skills; problem-solving skills; social interaction.

CONTEXT

Despite publishing little in his short life, McGregor's work remains significant. His classic study of work and motivation reflected the concerns of the middle and late 1960s, when the monolithic corporation was at its most dominant and the world at its most questioning. The common complaint against Theories X and Y is that they are mutually exclusive. To counter this McGregor was developing 'Theory Z' when he died in 1964: a theory that synthesised the organisational and personal imperatives. William Ouchi later seized on the concept of Theory Z. In his book of the same name, he analysed Japanese working methods. Here he found fertile ground for many of the ideas McGregor was proposing:

- lifetime employment
- concern for employees including their social life
- informal control
- decisions made by consensus
- slow promotion
- excellent transmittal of information from top to bottom and bottom to top with the help of middle management
- commitment to the company
- high concern for quality

Leading author Gary Hamel commented: '. . .we have been slowly abandoning a view of human beings as nothing more than warm-blooded cogs in the industrial machine. People can be trusted; people want to do the right thing; people are capable of imagination and ingenuity – these were McGregor's fundamental premises, and they underlie the work of modern management thinkers from Drucker to Deming to Peters, and the employment practices of the world's most progressive and successful companies.'

THE BEST SOURCES OF HELP

McGregor, Douglas. *The Human Side of Enterprise.* Revised ed. New York: McGraw-Hill, 2005.

In Search of Excellence
Tom Peters and Robert Waterman

GETTING STARTED

The book emerged from research conducted by Peters and Waterman with the consulting firm, McKinsey. They identified excellent companies, then sought to distil lessons from their behaviour and performance.

The sample was eventually whittled down to 62 (which were not intended to be perfectly representative). The choices were largely unsurprising, including the likes of IBM, Hewlett-Packard, Wal-Mart, and General Electric. The emphasis was exclusively on big companies.

There is a certain irony here, however. Although it celebrated big manufacturing businesses, the book condemned the excesses of dispassionate modern management practice and advocated a return to simpler virtues. The authors later came to feel that their ideas were better embodied in smaller companies.

WHY READ IT?

In Search of Excellence is one of the most popular management book of recent times. Appearing when Japanese competition had brought Western business low, it gave managers new heart and a new direction, reminding them, in Gary Hamel's words, 'that success often comes from doing common things uncommonly well'.

CONTRIBUTION

1. Success builds on first principles

The book attacks the excesses of the rational model and the business strategy paradigm that had come to dominate Western management thinking.

It counsels return to first principles:

- attention to customers
- an abiding concern for people (productivity through people)
- the celebration of trial and error (a bias for action)

'The excellent companies really are close to their customers. That's it. Other companies talk about it; the excellent companies do it.'

2. Achieve productivity through people

The authors quote a General Motors worker laid off after 16 years making Pontiacs: 'I guess I was laid off because I make poor quality cars. But in 16 years, not once was I ever asked for a suggestion as to how to do my job better. Not once.'

Excellent companies encourage and nurture an entrepreneurial spirit among all employees.

3. The management role

The real role of the chief executive is to manage the values of the organisation. Executives nurture and sustain corporate values. Rather than being distant figureheads, they should be there making things happen.

The word 'manager' in lip-service institutions often has come to mean not someone who rolls up his or her sleeves to get the job done right alongside the worker, but someone who hires assistants to do it.

4. Keep things simple

Excellent companies 'stick to the knitting'. They remain fixed on what they know they are good at and are not easily distracted.

One of their key attributes is that they have realised the importance of keeping things simple, despite overwhelming pressures to complicate things.

The authors explain what they call the 'smart–dumb rule' as follows:

'Many of today's managers . . . may be a little bit too smart for their own good. The smart ones . . . shift direction all the time, based upon the latest output from the expected value equation [and] have 200-page strategic plans and 500-page market requirement documents that are but one step in product development exercises. Our dumber friends are different. They just don't understand why every customer can't get personalised service, even in the potato chip business.'

5. Become simultaneously loose and tight

The debate about how to become loose and tight (controlled and empowered; big yet small) has dominated much subsequent business writing. The authors recommend new management vocabulary. Each one turns the tables on conventional wisdom, implying both the absence of clear directions and the simultaneous need for action. They include:

- temporary structures
- ad hoc groups
- fluid organisations
- internal competition
- product champions
- skunk works

CONTEXT

Peter Drucker suggested that the book's simplicity explained its appeal: 'The strength of the Peters book is that it forces you to look at the fundamentals. The book's great weakness – which is a strength from the point of view of its success – is that it makes managing sound so incredibly easy.'

Gary Hamel said, 'The dividing line between simple truths, and simplistic prescription is always a thin one. For the most part, Peters and Waterman avoided the facile and the tautological. Indeed, the focus on operations research, elaborate planning systems, and (supposedly) rigorous financial analysis had, in many companies, robbed management of its soul – and certainly had taken the focus off the customer.'

For such a trailblazing book, it is surprisingly uncontroversial. Peters and Waterman admit that what they have to say is not particularly original. They commented that the ideas they were espousing had been generally left behind, ignored, or overlooked by management theorists.

The criteria for selecting excellence were debatable, as all criteria are, and set the authors up for a good deal of criticism when their excellent companies fell from grace. In 1984 *BusinessWeek* revealed that some had speedily declined into mediocrity and, in some cases, abject failure. But Peters and Waterman had already provided a warning: 'We are asked how we know that the companies we have defined as culturally innovative will stay that way. The answer is we don't.'

In Search of Excellence created the impetus for the deluge of business books and, in the business world, established customer service as a key form of differentiation and advantage.

THE BEST SOURCES OF HELP

Peters, Thomas, and Robert Waterman. *In Search of Excellence*. Revised ed. New York: Collins, 2004.

Innovation in Marketing Theodore Levitt

GETTING STARTED

Historical success encouraged the belief that low-cost production was the key to success, but this inevitably leads to narrow perspectives. According to Ted Levitt's influential book, companies must broaden their view of the nature of their business, and should be marketing-led rather than production-led. The emphasis is on providing customer-creating value satisfactions.

WHY READ IT?

Levitt's views on the importance of marketing are highly regarded. His article 'Marketing Myopia' (reprinted in the book) was one of the most popular *Harvard Business Review* articles ever published. It highlights how narrow perspectives result from companies focusing on production rather than customers.

CONTRIBUTION

1. A focus on customers

Levitt argues that the central preoccupation of corporations should be with satisfying customers rather than simply producing goods. Companies should be marketing-led rather than production-led. Management must think of itself not as producing products but as providing customer-creating value satisfactions. The lead must come from the chief executive and senior management.

2. Problems of production-led companies

Henry Ford's success in mass production fuelled the belief that low-cost production was the key to business success. Ford continued to believe that he knew what customers wanted, long after they had decided otherwise.

Production-led thinking inevitably leads to narrow perspectives.

3. Narrow perspectives

Companies must broaden their view of the nature of their business: otherwise their customers will soon be forgotten. The railways are in trouble today not because the need was filled by others, but because it was not filled by the railways themselves. They let others take customers away from them because they assumed they were in the railway business rather than in the transportation business – they were product-oriented instead of customer-oriented.

The railway business was constrained by a lack of willingness to expand its horizons. Similarly, the film industry failed to respond to the growth of television because it regarded itself as being in the business of making movies rather than providing entertainment.

4. Taking growth for granted

Growth can never be taken for granted, asserts the author. There is no such thing as a growth industry – growth is a matter of being perceptive enough to spot where future growth may lie.

History is filled with companies that fall undetected into decay because:

• they assume that the growth in their particular market will continue for as long as the population grows in size and wealth

• they believe that a product cannot be surpassed

• they tend to put faith in the ability of improved production techniques to deliver lower costs and, therefore, higher profits

5. Problems of mass-production industries

Mass-production industries are impelled by a great drive to produce all they can. The prospect of steeply declining unit costs as output rises is more than most companies can usually resist. The profit possibilities look spectacular, so all effort focuses on production.

Concentration on the product, in Levitt's view, also lends itself to measurement and analysis. The result is that marketing gets neglected.

6. Distinguishing selling and marketing

There is a distinction between the tasks of selling and marketing. Selling concerns itself with the tricks and techniques of getting people to exchange their cash for your product; it is not concerned with the values that the exchange is all about. It does not, as marketing invariably does, view the entire business process as consisting of a tightly integrated effort to discover, create, arouse, and satisfy customer needs.

CONTEXT

Ted Levitt's fame was secured early in his career with 'Marketing Myopia' – a *Harvard Business Review* article which enjoyed unprecedented success and attention, selling over 500,000 reprints.

It has since been reproduced in virtually every collection of key marketing texts. 'Marketing Myopia' is a manifesto rather than a deeply academic article. It embraces ideas that had already been explored by others (Levitt acknowledges his debt to Peter Drucker's book *The Practice of Management*).

In the 1980s when marketing underwent resurgence, companies began to heed Levitt's view that they were too heavily oriented towards production. Levitt's article and his subsequent work pushed marketing to centre stage. In some cases it led to what Levitt called marketing mania, with companies obsessively responsive to every fleeting whim of the customer.

THE BEST SOURCES OF HELP

Levitt, Theodore. *Innovation in Marketing*. New York: McGraw-Hill, 1962.

The Innovator's Dilemma Clayton Christensen

GETTING STARTED

This book examines a range of leading, well-managed companies that have failed to capitalise on innovative technologies. The dilemma is that it is often sound decisions by good managers that lead to failure. The author distinguishes between sustaining technologies, which foster improved performance, and disruptive technologies, which represent a breakthrough, but may initially lead to poorer performance.

Part of the problem, according to Christensen, is that the market may not be ready for the new technology. In other cases, leading customers may not be willing to risk a new product. Companies therefore focus on the safe bets, but may subsequently be overtaken by innovation.

WHY READ IT?

This book faces up to a fundamental problem facing innovative companies – how to deal with breakthrough technologies when customers may not be ready for them. It argues that normal practice – focusing investment and development on the most profitable products, those that are in demand among top customers – may ultimately be damaging. The risk is that companies may reject innovative products that do not meet this criterion. Here Christensen explains how to overcome this problem and manage breakthrough products successfully.

CONTRIBUTION

1. Control by customers

The disk drive industry shows the dilemma in action. New entrants introduced disruptive technologies, such as smaller floppy disks that required new computer architecture. These innovations were, however, initially rejected by customers until they became a proven technology. The author concludes that, to a degree, the larger companies were controlled by their customers.

2. Value networks

Christensen offers a possible explanation for failure in these cases – the concept of the 'value network'. This is a technique companies can use to assess the value of a new technology in relation to their current business and customer base. It asks what rewards the company would obtain from re-allocating resources away from mainstream products.

The author believes that the problem is compounded by the scope of the company's suppliers and subcontractors. Each may have its own value network based on the needs of its own customers. Innovative ideas that come up from subcontractors may be stifled in the same way as internal ideas.

The author explains how the cost and profit structures in a value network can limit the attractiveness of an innovation. If profit margins are low, the emphasis will be on cost cutting across proven technologies. Innovation would be too risky. The other response from established companies is to move upmarket where they can earn more from existing products.

3. Avoiding risk

Christensen points out that new entrants have frequently forced the pace of innovation with disruptive technologies. Established companies only moved in when there was a definite market. Disruptive technologies do not initially represent large, high-margin opportunities for established companies and the decision-making structure can rule out innovative ideas.

The author cites five reasons why successful companies fail to capitalise on disruptive technologies:

- Customers control the pattern of resource allocation.
- Small markets do not solve the growth needs of large companies.
- It can be difficult to identify successful applications in advance.
- Larger organisations rely on their core competencies and values.
- Technology supply may not equal market demand.

4. The importance of spin-offs

Christensen explains how companies who did harness disruptive technologies used a number of management techniques:

- Projects were handled within another 'spin-off organisation' that had customers who needed the new technology.
- Those same project organisations could get excited about small markets and small wins.
- Failure was an acceptable part of the process as companies proceeded by trial and error to the right solution.
- Companies looked for new markets and developed the market where the disruptive technology offered value.

The author gives examples of large corporations that have set up spin-off companies to exploit new technology. Frequently, the corporation pulls the spin-off back into the core business when it proves successful.

CONTEXT

The book claims that overdependence on customer needs can affect a company's success. This argument runs counter to the marketing and customer service books that put customer focus at the top of the corporate agenda.

Books such as *When Giants Learn to Dance* by Rosabeth Moss Kanter (Touchstone, 1990) have pointed out the problems faced by larger corporations who compete in fast-moving technology markets. Christensen's book is unusual in highlighting the problems inherent in what appears to be sound decision-making.

THE BEST SOURCES OF HELP

Christensen, Clayton M. *The Innovator's Dilemma.* Revised ed. New York: HarperBusiness, 2003.

Intellectual Capital Thomas Stewart

GETTING STARTED

Traditional capital had financial or physical characteristics. In the author's view, however, the emphasis now is on an intangible asset, intellectual capital, consisting of human, customer, and structural capital.

The real value comes in being able to capture and deploy intellectual capital, Stewart argues.

WHY READ IT?

The author is widely regarded as the world's leading authority on knowledge management, and his views are valuable to any organisation that wants to improve the return on its 'intellectual capital'. The book is a useful guide to the strategic and practical issues of identifying, capturing, and using knowledge to improve a company's competitive advantage.

CONTRIBUTION

1. The new concept of capital

Traditionally, capital could be viewed in purely financial or physical terms. It showed up in the buildings and equipment owned, and could be found in the corporate balance sheets.

The author suggests that in recent times, the emphasis has switched to an intangible form of asset, intellectual capital.

2. Human capital

Human capital is the knowledge residing in the heads of employees that is relevant to the purpose of the organisation.

Human capital is formed and deployed, when more of the time and talent of employees is devoted to activities that result in innovation. It can grow in two ways: when the organisation uses more of what people know; or when people know more that is useful to the organisation. Unleashing it requires an organisation to minimise mindless tasks, meaningless paperwork, and unproductive infighting.

3. Customer capital

This represents the value of a company's ongoing relationships with the people or organisations to which it sells. Indicators of customer capital include market share, customer retention and defection rates, and profit per customer.

Customer capital is probably the worst managed of all intangible assets. Many businesses don't even know who their customers are.

4. Structural capital

Structural capital is the knowledge retained within the organisation. It belongs to the company as a whole and can be reproduced and shared.

Structural capital includes technologies, inventions, publications, and business processes.

5. Managing intellectual capital

The real value comes in being able to capture and deploy intellectual capital. Knowledge assets exist and are worth cultivating only in the context of strategy. You cannot define and manage intellectual assets unless you know what you want to do with them.

There are ten principles for managing intellectual capital:

- companies don't own human and customer capital. Only by recognising the shared nature of these assets can a company manage and profit from them.
- to create usable human capital, a company needs to foster teamwork, communities of practice, and other social forms of learning
- organisational wealth is created around skills and talents that are proprietary and scarce. Companies must see people with these talents as assets.
- structural assets are the easiest to manage but those that customers care least about
- move from amassing knowledge 'just in case' to having readily available information that customers need
- information and knowledge can, and should, substitute for expensive physical and financial assets
- knowledge work is custom work
- every company should re-analyse its own industry to see what information is most crucial
- focus on the flow of information not the flow of materials
- human, structural, and customer capital work together. It is not enough to invest in them separately.

6. Knowledge working and individual careers

Stewart argues that careers in the 21st century will have a number of characteristics:

- a career is a series of 'gigs', not a series of steps
- project management is the furnace in which successful careers are made
- power flows from expertise, not position
- most roles in an organisation can be performed by either insiders or outsiders
- careers are made in markets not hierarchies
- the fundamental career choice is not between one company and another, but between specialising and generalising

CONTEXT

Thomas Stewart pioneered the field of intellectual capital in a series of articles that earned him an international reputation and *Intellectual Capital* has proved itself as the definitive guide to understanding and managing intangible assets. It explains not only why intellectual capital will be the foundation of corporate success but also offers practical guidance to companies about how to make best use of their intangible assets.

THE BEST SOURCES OF HELP

Stewart, Thomas. *Intellectual Capital: The New Wealth of Organisations*. New York: Doubleday, 1998.

The Knowledge-creating Company
Ikujiro Nonaka and Hirotaka Takeuchi

GETTING STARTED

Nonaka and Takeuchi believe that historical adversity has forced Japanese companies to pursue a policy of continuous innovation. Organisational knowledge, according to them, is the ability of a company to create new knowledge, disseminate it throughout the organisation, and embody it in innovative products, services, and systems. They distinguish between explicit knowledge, such as rules or formulas, and tacit knowledge, which is gained from experience and can rarely be learned. The Japanese, they claim, are very effective at turning tacit knowledge into explicit knowledge that can be shared throughout an organisation.

WHY READ IT?

The book focuses on the development of organisational knowledge in Japanese companies. The authors explain how this knowledge forms the basis of innovations that have enabled Japanese companies to become world lead-

ers in many different market sectors. They show that the ability to acquire and apply knowledge is becoming a key factor for success in the transition from an industrial economy to an information economy.

CONTRIBUTION

1. Characteristics of knowledge creation

According to the authors, there are three key characteristics of knowledge creation:

- metaphor and analogy
- the transition from personal to organisational knowledge
- ambiguity and redundancy

The use of metaphor and analogy helps companies to visualise difficult concepts and explain them to other people within an organisation. The transition from personal to organisational knowledge depends on the successful implementation of teamwork so that individuals can interact with each other. The concept of ambiguity and redundancy means that Japanese companies are happy to take a number of different approaches to innovation, some of which are bound to fail. They use redundancy to encourage creativity and identify what does not work in practical terms.

2. Knowledge management

The authors review theories of knowledge from ancient times onward. They analyse recent management writing to identify attitudes towards the question of knowledge. They cite Peter Drucker's 'knowledge worker' and Peter Senge's 'learning organisation' as important concepts in knowledge creation. They also discuss the concept of core competencies and argue that this can distract companies. Core competencies, they argue, suggest that knowledge is an existing, finite resource within a company. Knowledge creation, on the other hand, emphasises the importance of acquiring and developing knowledge from as many internal and external sources as possible.

3. How knowledge creation works

The authors claim that there are four key processes in knowledge conversion:

- socialisation
- externalisation
- combination
- internalisation

An example of socialisation is the brainstorming camps set up by Honda to solve difficult production problems. Externalisation is the process of using metaphors or analogies to communicate difficult concepts in product development. Combination is the process of sorting, adding, combining, and synthesising new knowledge. Internalisation is like relearning other people's experiences or learning by doing.

4. The environment for knowledge creation

To create a suitable environment for knowledge creation, the authors stress the importance of vision to guide overall direction and autonomy to allow everyone in the organisation to get involved in the process.

They describe a structure called 'middle-up-down management' that underpins knowledge creation. This structure contrasts with the bottom-up or top-down management styles found in Western companies. The Japanese model puts middle managers at the heart of the

process, acting between front-line workers and a visionary senior management team. The authors believe that this type of structure creates dialogue and builds positive relationships between the individual specialists who contribute to a development project.

5. Hypertext organisations

Nonaka and Takeuchi refer to the concept of a 'knowledge crew', consisting of knowledge engineers and knowledge practitioners. Underpinning this is what they call a 'hypertext organisation'. This is an organisation with multiple layers:

- a business system layer
- a project team layer
- a knowledge base layer

The business system layer and project team layer generate different types of knowledge, which are brought together in the knowledge base which can be shared throughout the organisation.

CONTEXT

A number of books have looked at the process of innovation, trying to identify the factors that distinguish a successful innovator. The authors offer both theoretical and practical insight into the way that Japanese companies use knowledge as the basis for innovation. Their findings are in contrast with the widespread Western view that Japanese success is based on access to cheap capital, lifetime employment, culture, or quality.

The authors draw on a wide range of Western management sources to highlight the differences between Japanese and Western practice. Among others, they quote Peter Drucker and Alvin Toffler on the importance of knowledge, and Peter Senge on the concept of the 'learning organisation'.

THE BEST SOURCES OF HELP

Nonaka, Ikujiro, and Hirotaka Takeuchi. *The Knowledge-creating Company: How Japanese Companies Create the Dynamics of Innovation.* Oxford: Oxford University Press, 1995.

Leaders: Strategies For Taking Charge
Warren Bennis and Burt Nanus

GETTING STARTED

Good leaders commit people to action and convert followers into leaders. They are usually ordinary people rather than particularly charismatic, as leadership is all-encompassing and open to all.

Successful leaders also have a vision that other people believe in, and communicate it effectively. Instead of being individual problem solvers, they achieve greatness through working effectively with groups. Devising and maintaining an atmosphere in which others can succeed is the leader's creative act.

WHY READ IT?

Warren Bennis is an academic and regular presidential adviser who brought leadership to a new mass audience. He is regarded as one of the most important contemporary thinkers.

Burt Nanus is the founder and director of the Center of Futures Research at the University of Southern California.

In this book, the authors use an eclectic selection of US leaders to offer the readers key lessons on how to become successful. Their message is that leadership is open to all.

CONTRIBUTION

1. The ordinary leader

In the authors' view, the new leader is one who commits people to action, who converts followers into leaders, and who may convert leaders into agents of change. Leadership is not a rare skill – leaders are made rather than born. They are usually ordinary people, or apparently ordinary, rather than obviously charismatic. Leadership is not solely the preserve of those at the top of an organisation – it is relevant at all levels. Leadership is not about control, direction, and manipulation.

2. Common abilities of leaders

From a survey of 90 US leaders (including Neil Armstrong, the coach of the LA Rams, orchestral conductors, and businesspeople such as Ray Kroc of McDonald's), Bennis and Nanus identified four common abilities:
- management of attention
- management of meaning
- management of trust
- management of self

3. Management of attention

This is a question of vision. Leadership is the capacity to create a compelling vision, translate it into action, and sustain it. Successful leaders have a vision that other people believe in and treat as their own.

4. Management of meaning

A vision is of limited practical use if it is encased in 400 pages of wordy text or mumbled from behind a paper-packed desk. Effective communication relies on use of analogy, metaphor, and vivid illustration as well as emotion, trust, optimism, and hope.

5. Management of trust

Trust is the emotional glue that binds followers and leaders together. Leaders have to be seen to be consistent.

6. Management of self

In the authers' view, leaders do not glibly present charisma or time management as the essence of their success. Instead, the emphasis is on persistence and self-knowledge, commitment and challenge, taking risks and, above all, learning. The learning person looks forward to failure or mistakes, which means that the worst problem in leadership is basically early success. There's no opportunity to learn from adversity and problems.

7. A positive self-regard

In the authors' view, leaders have a positive self-regard, known as emotional wisdom. This is characterised by an ability to accept people as they are. They also have a capacity to approach things in terms of only the present, and an ability to treat everyone, even close contacts, with courteous attention. They need an ability to trust others, and to do without constant approval and recognition.

8. Leaders and group working

Greatness starts with superb people. Great groups don't exist without great leaders, but they give the lie to the persistent notion that successful institutions are the lengthened shadow of a great woman or man. It's not clear that life was ever so simple that individuals, acting alone, solved most significant problems. Instead of the individual problem solver, we have a new model for creative achievement.

9. Changing leadership qualities

According to Bennis and Nanus, the leader is a pragmatic dreamer, a person with an original but attainable vision. He or she knows that this dream can only be realised if others are free to do exceptional work. Typically, the leader is the one who recruits the others, by making the vision so seductive that they see it too, and eagerly sign up.

Inevitably, the leader has to invent a leadership style that suits the group. The standard models, especially command and control, simply don't work. The heads of groups have to act decisively, not arbitrarily. They have to make decisions without limiting the autonomy of other participants.

10. The idealistic leader

Most organisations are dull and working life is mundane, so groups can be an inspiration. Individual leaders can create a human community that will, in the long run, lead to the best organisations. 'A Great Group is more than a collection of first-rate minds. It's a miracle', say the authors. Every person has to make a genuine contribution in their lives and the institution of work is one of the main vehicles to achieving this.

CONTEXT

With the torrent of publications and executive programmes on the subject, it is easy to forget that leadership had been largely overlooked as a topic worthy of serious academic interest until it was revived by Bennis and others in the 1980s. Since then, leadership has become a heavy industry. Concern and interest about leadership development is no longer a US phenomenon: it is truly global. The book stands as a humane counter to much of the military-based hero worship which dogs the subject.

THE BEST SOURCES OF HELP

Bennis, Warren, and Burt Nanus. *Leaders: Strategies for Taking Charge*. 2nd ed. New York: Collins, 2003.

The Long Tail Chris Anderson

GETTING STARTED

The popularity contest between products and services is increasingly becoming more symmetric: while 80% of the American population watched the television sitcom *I Love Lucy* in 1953, no television programme has managed to capture a comparably large audience since. However, while markets are getting smaller, the expanding number of 'niches' creates more opportunity for small distributors and for companies, such as Google and Amazon, who create a market in meeting the needs of specialist audiences. Anderson argues that demand is becoming infinite. Those producing products with small markets can compete more effectively than ever before. Large corporations, on the other hand, benefit from new ways of managing global distribution networks and the promise of a market, somewhere, for the products of their investments in research and development. However, understanding the corollary of this is critical – as markets have fractured into niches, it is increasingly difficult for any single product to achieve universal appeal.

WHY READ IT?

In this book, Chris Anderson's rewriting of the laws of production ushers in a new perspective on innovation. Highlighting the profitability of niche products with small but significant markets over blockbuster ideas, *The Long Tail* argues that low barriers to entry enable firms to capitalise on the 'endless demand curve'. Evolving patterns of production mean that firms can now profitably supply products that have smaller levels of demand. For instance, cult music bands can now be profitable with much smaller audiences than before. The rules of innovation and marketing have changed; the 'long tail' refers to the tail of the graph of business ideas, where a small number of products sell exponentially more than the

overwhelming majority. Understanding that even products with small groups of potential customers in the global marketplace can be successful is critical to entrepreneurs looking to thrive.

CONTRIBUTION

Anderson identifies the three forces flattening the curve of popularity versus number of businesses, creating a flatter playing field – and a longer 'tail'.

1. **Democracy of production.** The flattening of access to the means of production, with improved technology and education, means more entrepreneurs and firms can develop and market their innovations. This is in contrast to times when economies of scale were fundamental to success.

2. **Democracy of marketing.** Secondly, the democratisation of marketing tools means that any firm with a website is a global company. It is no longer expensive to sell things; if a product is really good, customers will latch onto it. The smallest firms can compete with the largest multinationals in reaching specialised audiences, as information networks 'flatten' the asymmetries of marketing budgets. Coca-Cola spends vast sums on its television advertising, but this is no longer fundamental to making sales: viral marketing on the Internet can popularise a product with merit far more cheaply and effectively than more traditional methods.

3. **Connecting.** Connecting niche suppliers to niche markets has radically changed with the growth of the popularity of the Internet and websites that can market products with negligible margin costs. For example, while a book shop can stock only a limited number of books – its finite amount of shelf space means only the most popular products can

be offered – Amazon.com can offer a far greater range at less cost. The Long Tail thrives as a consequence of the falling cost of connecting demand and supply.

CONTEXT
Anderson refers to the theories in James Surowiecki's *The Wisdom of Crowds* as critical to reinforcing the Long Tail. As word of mouth is essential in distributing any product, niche concepts must be able to captivate a crowd, even if it is a small one. In charting how 'the many can be smarter than the few', Surowiecki's theory is important in 'crowdsourcing' business models where a broad coverage is possible because of customers' participation in production. Wikipedia is able to offer such a broad coverage of encyclopaedia entries – far greater than that of the *Encyclopaedia Britannica* – only because its users help generate content. By allowing the crowd to spread products, innovative ideas can reach niche markets without expensive, elite advertising strategies.

THE BEST SOURCES OF HELP
Anderson, Chris. *The Long Tail: How Endless Choice Is Creating Endless Demand*. London: Random House, 2006.

The Machine That Changed the World
James Womack, Daniel Jones, and Daniel Roos

GETTING STARTED
Lean production will supersede the mass production of goods, the authors announce. It can simultaneously double productivity, improve quality, and keep costs low. The book recounts the history of the rise of lean production, describes its essential elements, and presents the prospects for the spread of this revolutionary management initiative.

WHY READ IT?
Lean production was Japan's secret weapon in the trade war, and it went on to conquer the world. In 1984 a team of researchers at the Massachusetts Institute of Technology (MIT) undertook a study of it. Within the framework of an analysis of the situation and problems of car manufacturers worldwide, Womack, Jones, and Roos examined the differences between mass and lean production. This widely read and wisely praised book presents their findings.

CONTRIBUTION
1. The beginnings of lean production
In 1950 Eiji Toyoda, a Japanese engineer whose family had founded the Toyota Motor Company, and Toyota's production manager, Taiichi Ohno, visited the Ford motor works in Detroit, then the biggest and most efficient production plant in the world. The basis of the Ford system was a complete division of labour among a wide variety of specialist operatives. The conveyor belt could never be halted; faults were dealt with in post-production.

Toyoda and Ohno felt that there was waste throughout this system: wasted labour, wasted materials, wasted time. Apart from the assemblers, none of the specialists created any value for the car.

On his return, Ohno grouped his workers in teams, to whom he delegated more tasks and who were to work together on improvements. Each worker had a duty to halt the production line if a problem arose that he or she could not deal with. The whole team would then trace the fault back to its ultimate cause and then think up a solution that would ensure it never happened again. The remedial work required before dispatch was thus reduced to zero, and lean production, the authors say, was born.

2. The elements of lean production
The first element is the organisation of the assembly works. A lean factory, the authors report, has two main organisational characteristics. First, it allots a maximum number of tasks and responsibilities to those workers who create actual value in the product on the line. Secondly, it has a fault detection system installed that quickly traces each fault back to its source.

The second element is product development. Lean production, the authors say, is quicker than mass production. The reason lies in basic differences in construction methods.

- Project leadership works on the *susha* system. The *susha* is the team leader, a position of great power in Japanese businesses. In mass-production companies the system is very different. The position of the development manager is too weak to push projects through. Top management often overrides his or her decisions.
- The *susha* creates a small, close-knit team, whose members are drawn from various specialist departments and who remain in contact with them. For the duration of the development project, however, they remain wholly under the control of the *susha*. In mass-production business, development teams consist of individuals on short-term secondment from specialist departments.

- Communication too is different, say the authors. In Western mass production, it is only at a late stage in the project that there is any co-ordination of different interests. In Japan, team members sign formal undertakings to do exactly what the team as a whole has decided. Any conflicts therefore show up at the very beginning of the crisis.

The third element in lean production is co-ordination of the supply chain. In the lean, *susha*-led product development process, all the necessary suppliers are carefully selected, not on the basis of their bids, but on the basis of earlier relationships and proven performance.

Customer relations form the fourth element. Japanese car manufacturers, the authors point out, have comparatively few sales channels. These are differentiated in terms of their appealing to different types of purchaser. The aim is to establish a direct link between the production system and the customer. Employees in the sales channels are loaned to the development teams, and the dealers have a close relationship with the manufacturer.

The fifth major element in lean production, according to the authors, is the way the lean company is managed. Various framework conditions have to exist:

- There must be money to finance development projects that last several years.
- Career ladders must be available for qualified and motivated employees.
- Decentralised activities must be co-ordinated worldwide.

CONTEXT

The MIT investigation was at the time the most comprehensive study of a single industry ever carried out.

While it showed the undoubted successes of lean production, it also claimed to have uncovered certain deficiencies in the concept. Lean production, it suggests, overemphasises the aspects of savings and mechanisation and neglects categories such as know-how and innovation. Lean management brings a short-term improvement in efficiency, but not a long-term increase in productivity. In addition, the authors argue, it is unsuited to dismantling complexity. Anyone, for example, who wishes to reduce the complexity of serialised production steps through individualised manufacture must understand ever more expansive processes in their entirety. In theory, the highly innovative and flexible business organisation with no hierarchy may count as the company of the future, but in everyday practice the weaknesses of lean production are clearly apparent.

THE BEST SOURCES OF HELP

Womack, James, Daniel Jones, and Daniel Roos. *The Machine That Changed the World: The Story of Lean Production*. London: HarperBusiness, 1991.

Made in Japan Akio Morita

GETTING STARTED

This book charts the re-emergence of Japan as an industrial heavyweight. It helped change the image of 'Made in Japan' from shoddy goods to high quality. Sony invented new markets with a pioneering spirit by bringing out product after product, innovation after innovation. Its most famous success was the Walkman, the development of which was based on instinct, not research. Analysis and education do not necessarily help you to reach the best business decisions; sometimes understanding must come before logic. 'Japanese people tend to be much better adjusted to the notion of work, any kind of work, as honourable', says Morita. Recruitment is 'management's risk and management's responsibility'.

WHY READ IT?

Made in Japan is the story of Sony and reflects the changes that took place in post-war business history. Morita and Sony's story parallels the rebirth of Japan as an industrial power. When Sony was first attempting to make inroads into Western markets, Japanese products were sneered at as being of the lowest quality.

Surmounting that obstacle was a substantial business achievement.

CONTRIBUTION

1. The Japanese renaissance

Morita and Sony's story parallels the rebirth of Japan as a major industrial power. Together, they helped change the image of items 'Made in Japan' from something shoddy to something reputable and desirable. At the time, when Sony first tried to break into the Western electronics market, Japanese products were considered fifth-rate. Morita helped Sony not only to overcome this prejudice, but to reverse it.

2. Inventing new markets

Morita and Sony's gift was to invent new markets with a pioneering spirit. 'Sony is a pioneer and never intends to follow others', says Morita.

'Through progress, Sony wants to serve the whole world. It will always seek the unknown. Sony has a principle of respecting and encouraging one's ability . . . and always tries to bring out the best in a person. This is the vital force of Sony.'

3. The power of innovation

While companies such as Matsushita were inspired followers, Sony set the pace with product after product, innovation after innovation.

Sony brought the world the hand-held video camera, the first home video recorder, and the floppy disk. The blemishes on its record were the Betamax video format, which it failed to license, and colour television systems.

4. Instinct and research

Sony's most famous success was the Walkman, the brainchild of Morita. Morita noticed that young people liked listening to music wherever they went. He put two and two together and made – a Walkman. He did not believe that any amount of market research could have told the company that this would be successful. As he famously said: 'The public does not know what is possible. We do.'

5. Analysis doesn't always pay

Brilliant marketing by instinct was no mere accident.

Morita believes that if you go through life convinced that your way is always best, all the new ideas in the world will pass you by.

Analysis and education do not necessarily help you to reach the best business decisions. You can be totally rational with a machine but if you work with people, sometimes understanding has to come before logic.

6. Japanese culture encourages the work ethic

Morita has emphasised the cultural differences in Japanese attitudes towards work. The Japanese tend to have a much stronger work ethic, and see work as an honourable occupation.

In *Made in Japan*, Morita states his belief that management has ultimate responsibility for its staff. If a recession is looming, profit should be sacrificed rather than employees be laid off.

CONTEXT

The book tells the story of the rise of Sony and it reflects the rise of Japan as a post-war industrial power. It looks at the role of quality and innovation as key factors in the success of Japanese companies. Many Western authors have focused on the role of quality in Japan, particularly the influence of people like Deming and Juran. Richard Pascale and Anthony Athos also look at the phenomenon in *The Art of Japanese Management*.

Morita and Sony took the attitude that global markets were important from the outset. Ken Ohmae writes on that subject from the Japanese perspective in *The Borderless World*.

THE BEST SOURCES OF HELP

Morita, Akio. *Made in Japan*. New York: Dutton, 1986.

Management Teams: Why They Succeed or Fail
R. Meredith Belbin

GETTING STARTED

Corporations have been preoccupied with the qualifications, experience, and achievement of individuals – but it is not the individual but the team that is the instrument of sustained and enduring success in management.

Team performance is influenced by the kinds of people makingup a group, and testing indicates that certain combinations of personality-types perform more successfully than others. Nine archetypal functions make up an ideal team – plant, co-ordinator, shaper, teamworker, completer, implementer, resource investigator, specialist, and monitor evaluator.

Unsuccessful teams can be improved by analysing their composition and making appropriate changes.

WHY READ IT?

Effective teamworking is now seen as key to the success of all types of organisation. Meredith Belbin identified the characteristics of people needed to make a successful team. His recommendations are still used, and the book can therefore help anyone who needs to develop a team.

CONTRIBUTION

1. The preoccupation with individuals

Corporations have been preoccupied with the qualifications, experience, and achievement of individuals, and have applied themselves to their selection, development, training, motivation, and promotion. However commentators believe that the ideal individual for a given job cannot be found, because he or she cannot exist. It is not the individual but the team that is the instrument of sustained and enduring success in management.

2. The contribution of individuals in teams

Belbin was interested in group performance and how it might be influenced by the kinds of people making up a group. He asked members engaged in a business school exercise to undertake a personality and critical-thinking test and, based on the test results, discovered that certain combinations of personality-types performed more successfully than others.

Belbin realised that given adequate knowledge of the personal characteristics and abilities of team members through psychometric testing, he could forecast the likely success or failure of particular teams. Unsuccessful teams can be improved by analysing their team design shortcomings and making appropriate changes.

3. Identifying team characteristics
A questionnaire completed by team members was analysed to show the functional roles the managers thought they performed in a team. From this research, Belbin identified nine archetypal functions which go to make up an ideal team.

4. Successful team composition
- Plant – creative, imaginative, unorthodox; solves difficult problems. Allowable weakness: bad at dealing with ordinary people.
- Co-ordinator – mature, confident, trusting; a good chairman; clarifies goals, promotes decision-making. Not necessarily the cleverest member.
- Shaper – dynamic, outgoing, highly strung; challenges, pressurises, finds ways round obstacles. Prone to bursts of temper.
- Teamworker – social, mild, perceptive, accommodating; listens, builds, averts friction. Indecisive in crunch situations.
- Completer – painstaking, conscientious, anxious; searches out errors; delivers on time. May worry unduly; reluctant to delegate.
- Implementer – disciplined, reliable, conservative, efficient; turns ideas into actions. Somewhat inflexible.
- Resource investigator – extrovert, enthusiastic, communicative; explores opportunities. Loses interest after initial enthusiasm.
- Specialist – single-minded, self-starting, dedicated; brings knowledge or skills in rare supply. Contributes only on narrow front.
- Monitor evaluator – sober, strategic, discerning. Sees all options, makes well-considered judgments. Lacks drive and ability to inspire others.

CONTEXT
The explosion of interest in teamworking during the last decade has prompted greater interest in Belbin's work. The teamworking categories he identified have proved robust and are still used in a variety of organisations. Gary Hamel commented, 'High-performing companies increasingly believe that teams, rather than business units or individuals, are the basic building blocks of a successful organisation. Belbin deserves much credit for helping us understand the basic building blocks of successful teams.'

Antony Jay commented, 'Corporations have been preoccupied with the qualifications, experience, and achievement of individuals . . . it is not the individual but the team that is the instrument of sustained and enduring success in management.'

THE BEST SOURCES OF HELP
Belbin, R. Meredith. *Management Teams: Why They Succeed or Fail*. 2nd ed. Oxford: Butterworth-Heinemann, 2004.

Managing Across Borders
Christopher Bartlett and Sumantra Ghoshal

GETTING STARTED
According to the authors, changing patterns of international management have led to a new global model, in which enabling innovation and disseminating knowledge in globally dispersed organisations is an important challenge.

A number of organisational forms are now prevalent among global companies: multinational companies offer a high degree of local responsiveness; global companies offer scale efficiencies and cost advantages; international companies have the ability to transfer knowledge and expertise to overseas environments that are less advanced; and the transnational company combines local responsiveness with global efficiency and the ability to transfer know-how better, cheaper, and faster.

Integration and the creation of coherent systems for value delivery are the new drivers of organisational structure.

WHY READ IT?
Bartlett and Ghoshal map out the new business reality of globalisation and the kinds of organisations a 'borderless' business world requires. The book is regarded as a classic, and has helped many companies to focus on the type of organisation they need for success in the global economy.

CONTRIBUTION
1. Changing patterns of international management
The traditional international management model was simply to export your own way of doing things elsewhere, and companies believed that global operations were simply a means of achieving economies of scale. Local nuances were overlooked in the quest for global standardisation: global and local were mutually exclusive. In general, organisations either gave local operations autonomy or controlled them rigidly from a distance.

2. A new global model

Global presence with local responsiveness is now key. Companies face the challenge of enabling innovation and disseminating knowledge in globally dispersed organisations. Bartlett and Ghoshal identify a number of organisational forms prevalent among global companies.

3. Multinational companies

The multinational or multidomestic organisation offers a very high degree of local responsiveness. It is a decentralised federation of local businesses, linked together through personal control by expatriates who occupy key positions abroad.

4. Global companies

Global organisations offer scale efficiencies and cost advantages. With global scale facilities, the global organisation seeks to produce standardised products. It is often centralised in its home country, with overseas operations considered as delivery pipelines to tap into global market opportunities. There is tight control of strategic decisions, resources, and information by the global hub.

5. International companies

International companies have the ability to transfer knowledge and expertise to overseas environments that are less advanced. They are co-ordinated federations of local businesses, controlled by sophisticated management systems and corporate employees. The attitude of the parent company tends to be somewhat parochial, fostered by the superior know-how at the centre of the organisation.

6. The transnational companies

Global competition is forcing many businesses to shift to a fourth model, which they call the transnational. This organisation combines local responsiveness with global efficiency and the ability to transfer know-how better, cheaper, and faster. The transnational company is made up of a network of specialised or differentiated units, which focus on managing integrative linkages between local businesses as well as with the centre. The subsidiary becomes a distinctive asset, rather than simply an arm of the parent company. Manufacturing and technology development are located wherever it makes sense, and there is an explicit focus on leveraging local know-how in order to exploit worldwide opportunities.

7. The importance of integration

Integration and the creation of a coherent system for value delivery are the new drivers of organisational structure. Companies cannot be left to their own devices, but have to be brought within the fold – while also keeping in touch with their local business environment.

What binds the companies together is a set of explicit or implicit shared values and beliefs that can be developed and managed effectively. There are three techniques crucial to an organisation's psychology:

1. clear, shared understanding of the company's mission and objectives;
2. the actions and behaviour of senior managers are vital as examples and statements of commitment;
3. corporate personnel policies must be geared up to develop a multi-dimensional and flexible organisation process.

CONTEXT

Managing Across Borders is one of the few business books of recent years that deserves recognition as a classic. When it was published in 1989, understanding of globalisation was in its infancy. With its emphasis on networking across the global organisation and transferring learning and knowledge, the book effectively set the organisational agenda for a decade and created a new organisational model.

The authors effectively signalled the demise of the divisional organisation – which gives divisions independence – first developed by Alfred Sloan of General Motors.

THE BEST SOURCES OF HELP

Bartlett, Christopher, and Sumantra Ghoshal. *Managing Across Borders: The Transnational Solution.* 2nd ed. Boston, Massachusetts: Harvard Business School Press, 2002.

Managing on the Edge Richard Pascale

GETTING STARTED

US managerial history is largely inward-focused and self-congratulatory. Change is a fact of business life, but complacency can cause problems. It is essential to change the management perspective. The incremental approach to change is no longer effective. The new emphasis should be on asking questions. Successful organisations undergo continual renewal by constantly asking questions.

The book argues that four factors drive stagnation and renewal:
- fit
- split
- contend
- transcend

'Contention management' is essential to orchestrate tensions that arise between these four factors. Forces locked in opposition can be used to generate inquiry and adaptation and the manager's job is to maintain a constructive level of debate.

WHY READ IT?

This book challenges traditional management thinking, which Pascale feels is too complacent for an environment driven by change. He sets out a new perspective for 'contention management', which seeks to harness the conflicting energies in an organisation to achieve positive change. The book set the management agenda for a decade after its publication.

CONTRIBUTION

1. The dangers of complacency

Nothing fails like success. Great strengths are inevitably the root of weakness. Of the companies listed in 1985's Fortune 500, 143 had been dropped by 1990. In the author's view, US managerial history is largely inward-focused and self-congratulatory.

2. The need for change

According to Pascale, change is a fact of business life. We are ill-equipped to deal with it and the traditional approach to managing change is no longer applicable. The incremental approach to change is effective when the goal is to obtain more of the same thing. Historically, that has been sufficient. The United States' advantages of plentiful resources, geographical isolation, and absence of serious global competition defined a league in which US companies competed with each other and everyone played by the same rules.

3. Growth of management fads

There have been more than two dozen management fads since the 1950s; a dozen emerged in the five years prior to 1990.

4. Driving stagnation and renewal

Four factors drive stagnation and renewal in organisations:
- fit – pertains to an organisation's internal consistency (unity)
- split-describes a variety of techniques for breaking a bigger organisation into smaller units and providing them with a stronger sense of ownership and identity (plurality)
- contend – refers to a management process that harnesses (rather than suppresses) the contradictions that are inevitable by-products of organisations (duality)
- transcend – alerts people to the higher order of complexity that successfully managing the renewal process entails (vitality).

5. Changing management perspective

Pascale calls for a fundamental shift in perspective. Managerial behaviour is based on the assumption that people should rationally order the behaviour of those they manage. That mindset needs to be challenged. Orderly answers are no longer appropriate, in his view, and the new emphasis should be on asking questions. Strategic planning, at best, is about posing questions, more than attempting to answer them. Successful organisations undergo a continual process of renewal. Central to achieving this is a willingness to ask questions constantly and to harness conflict for the corporate good, through systems that encourage questioning. To facilitate this, Pascale argues that companies must become 'engines of inquiry'.

6. Contention management

Managers are ill-equipped to deal with the contention that arises when fundamental questions are posed, but 'contention management' is essential to orchestrate tensions that arise. Around 50 percent of the time when contention arises, it is smoothed over and avoided.

The forces that we have historically regarded as locked in opposition can be viewed as apparent opposites that generate inquiry and adaptive responses. Pascale holds that each point of view represents a facet of reality, and these realities tend to challenge one another and raise questions. If we redefine the manager's job as maintaining a constructive level of debate, we are, in effect, holding the organisation in the question. This leads to identifying blind spots and working around obstacles. Truth – personally and organisationally – lies in the openness of vigorous debate.

Organisations are, in the last analysis, interactions among people.

CONTEXT

Managing on the Edge presents a formidably researched and argued challenge to complacency and timidity.

Pascale criticises Peters and Waterman's *In Search of Excellence* saying, 'Simply identifying attributes of success is like identifying attributes of people in excellent health during the age of the bubonic plague.'

Managing on the Edge set the tone for much of the management thinking of the decade. Its emphasis on the need for constant change has since been developed by Pascale. He now argues that the issue of managing the way we change is a competence rather than an episodic necessity. The capability to change is a core competence in its own right.

Influential critic Gary Hamel commented, 'In *Managing on the Edge*, Richard Pascale provides a number of useful observations on the sources of corporate vitality. One of the things I've always admired about Richard Pascale is that he focuses not on tools and techniques, but on principles and paradigms. While management bookshelves groan with the weight of simplistic how-to books, Pascale challenges managers to think, and to think deeply. Pascale forces managers to deconstruct the normative models on which they base their beliefs and actions.'

THE BEST SOURCES OF HELP

Pascale, Richard. *Managing on the Edge: How Successful Companies Use Conflict to Stay Ahead.* New York: Simon & Schuster, 1990.

Managing Transitions William Bridges

GETTING STARTED

The author believes that many companies try to impose change, but fail to manage the transition. Transition means recognising that things cannot be the same after an organisational change. People must get used to the new ways of doing things. They do this by going through a 'neutral zone' before emerging into a new beginning.

WHY READ IT?

This book focuses on the human aspects of change management. Change is a situation. What the author calls 'transition' is the psychological process people go through to come to terms with change. The book stresses that change involves people and that managers and leaders must help people deal with the transition. The author shows, through practical examples, how managers should make people feel comfortable and unthreatened during a period of change and offers advice, as well as case studies, on the best way to achieve this.

CONTRIBUTION

1. Letting go

The author explains that transition begins with a process of 'letting go'. However, this is a process that many people in an organisation find difficult. They are comfortable with familiar, proven ways of doing things and they fear the unknown.

The first stage, he suggests, is to identify who is losing what, by analysing what is going to change and identifying the impact on different groups of people. Managers should be aware that people will react in different ways. They should acknowledge the effect of the change on people and, if necessary, make some compensation for their loss. Managers should also acknowledge what was good about the existing processes and emphasise the element of continuity in the most important aspects of the new proposals.

2. The neutral zone

Bridges believes that the 'neutral zone' is the most difficult part of the transition process, because this is where people's uncertainties and anxieties about change are most acute. He advises managers to give people a clear sense of direction, as well as support to help them through this difficult stage. Moving from an existing routine to a new one can prove difficult without the right help.

Bridges argues that managers can reduce the damaging impact of the neutral zone by setting short-term targets that are achievable. He also believes that they should not expect or demand exceptional performance during a period of transition.

Communication is vital, claims Bridges, at this and every stage of transition. It is also important to encourage creativity during the neutral zone, particularly when there is less pressure on people to perform. Creativity can help to overcome the sense of loss people feel about leaving old routines behind.

3. New beginnings

When people move to the new system, uncertainties can remain, according to Bridges. There is always a risk in new ways of doing things. It is therefore essential to set out a clear plan with timings and targets. Managers should ensure that everyone has a clear part to play in the new system.

He recommends clear, regular communications to explain the aims and rationale for the new system. A vision of the future can help to paint a clear picture for people in the organisation. To reinforce the new beginning, Bridges recommends that companies should create a new identity and celebrate success.

The book also includes advice for readers on how to take care of themselves during a period of transition.

CONTEXT

This book is one of a number that deal with the subject of managing the process of change. John Kotter's *Leading*

Change (Harvard Business School Press, 1996), for example, reflects on the themes of leadership, vision, and communication.

Bridges' book looks at the human perspective of change and includes a great deal of practical advice on ways of dealing with the personal issues that people face. It also contains a number of useful studies, case histories, and exercises that could be used in workshops.

As such, the book may be more suitable for people in human resources or line management roles. Senior executives who are concerned with the strategic implications of change might find more value in an author such as Kotter.

THE BEST SOURCES OF HELP
Bridges, William. *Transitions: Making Sense of Life's Changes.* London: Nicholas Brealey, 1996.

FURTHER READING
Bridges, William. *Managing Transitions: Making the Most of Change.* 2nd ed.London: Nicholas Brealey, 2002.
Bridges, William. *Creating You and CO: Be the Boss of Your Own Career.* London: Nicholas Brealey, 1997.

Marketing Management Philip Kotler

GETTING STARTED
Marketing continues to evolve and expand its scope exponentially. The emphasis is shifting from transaction-oriented marketing to relationship marketing – retaining customer loyalty through continually satisfying their needs. Marketing management is the process of planning and executing functions that satisfy customer and organisational objectives.

Customer-delivered value is the difference between total customer value and total customer cost.

Organisations encounter three common hurdles to marketing orientation:
- organised resistance
- slow learning
- fast forgetting

WHY READ IT?
Kotler is one of the leading authorities on marketing. This definitive marketing textbook covers the full scope of contemporary marketing. It is the most widely used marketing book in business schools.

CONTRIBUTION
1. Marketing continues to evolve
The marketing discipline is redeveloping its assumptions, concepts, skills, tools, and systems for making sound decisions.

Marketers must know when to:
- cultivate large markets or niche markets
- launch new brands or extend existing brand names
- push or pull products through distribution
- protect the domestic market or penetrate aggressively into foreign markets
- add more benefits to the offer or reduce the price
- expand or contract budgets for sales force, advertising, and other marketing tools

The scope of marketing is expanding exponentially as is demonstrated by the size and scope of *Marketing Management*. Its contents range over:
- industry and competitor analysis
- designing strategies for the global marketplace
- managing product life cycle strategies
- retailing, wholesaling, and other physical-distribution systems

2. The change to relationship marketing
The emphasis is shifting from transaction-oriented marketing to relationship marketing. Good customers are an asset which, when well managed and served, will return a handsome lifetime income stream.

In the intensely competitive marketplace, the company must retain customer loyalty through continually satisfying their needs in a superior way.

3. Defining the role of marketing
Marketing is the social and managerial process by which individuals and groups obtain what they need and want through creating, offering, and exchanging products of value with others. A market consists of all the potential customers sharing a particular need or want, who might be willing to exchange in order to satisfy that need or want.

Marketing management is the process of planning and executing the conception, pricing, promotion, and distribution of goods, services, and ideas, to create exchanges with target groups that satisfy customer and organisational objectives.

4. Analysing products
A product is anything that can be offered to a market for attention, acquisition, use, or consumption that might satisfy a want or need. A product has five levels:
- the core benefit (marketers must see themselves as benefit providers)

- the generic product
- the expected product (the normal expectations the customer has of the product)
- the augmented product (the additional services or benefits added to the product)
- the potential product (all the augmentations and transformations that this product might undergo in the future)

5. Customer value

Customer-delivered value is the difference between total customer value and total customer cost. Total customer value is the bundle of benefits customers expect from a given product or service. It consists of product value, service value, personnel value, and image value. Total customer cost consists of monetary price, time cost, energy cost, and psychic cost. Combined, the two produce customer-delivered value.

6. Barriers to marketing orientation

In order to become marketing oriented, organisations encounter three hurdles:

- Organised resistance – entrenched functional behaviour tends to oppose increased emphasis on marketing, as it is seen as undermining functional power bases.
- Slow learning – most companies only slowly embrace the marketing concept.
- Fast forgetting – companies that embrace marketing concepts tend, over time, to lose touch with the principles. Various US companies have sought to establish their products in Europe with scant knowledge of different marketplaces.

7. Achieving market leadership

Good companies will meet needs; great companies will create markets. Market leadership is gained by envisioning new products, services, lifestyles, and ways to raise living standards. There is a vast difference between companies offering 'me-too' products and those creating previously unimagined product and service values.

In Kotler's view, marketing at its best is about value creation and raising the world's living standards.

CONTEXT

Marketing Management is the definitive marketing textbook. Tightly argued and all-encompassing, its content has been expanded and brought up to date through various editions. The eighth edition, published in 1994, maps out the emerging challenges to all those involved in marketing.

The very size and scope of *Marketing Management* demonstrates the exponential expansion of marketing. Gary Hamel commented: 'There are few MBA graduates alive who have not ploughed through Kotler's encyclopaedic textbook on marketing, and have not benefited enormously from doing so. I know of no other business author who covers his (or her) territory with such comprehensiveness, clarity, and authority as Phil Kotler. I can think of few other books, even within the vaunted company of this volume, whose insights would be of more practical benefit to the average company than those found in *Marketing Management*.'

THE BEST SOURCES OF HELP

Kotler, Philip, and Kevin Keller. *Marketing Management*. 13th ed. Harlow: Prentice Hall, 2008.

The Mind of the Strategist Kenichi Ohmae

GETTING STARTED

Kenichi Ohmae argues that to a large extent, Japanese success can be attributed to the nature of Japanese strategic thinking. Japanese businesses tend not to have large strategic planning staffs. The customer is at the heart of the Japanese approach to strategy. There are three main players in any business strategy – the corporation itself, the customer, and the competition – collectively called the strategic triangle. Just as events in the real world do not always fit a linear model, the Japanese approach to strategy is irrational and non-linear.

WHY READ IT?

The book illuminates the strategic thinking behind Japanese corporate success. The author shows how and why it differs from the Western approach to strategic thinking and explains that Western companies can adapt to this successful model.

CONTRIBUTION

1. Strategy determines Japanese success

Japanese success can be attributed to the nature of Japanese strategic thinking, according to Ohmae. This is basically creative and intuitive rather than rational, but the necessary creativity can be learned.

Unlike large US corporations, Japanese businesses tend not to have large strategic planning staffs. Instead they often have a single, idiosyncratic, naturally-talented strategist.

From the dynamic interaction of the company, customers, and competition, a comprehensive set of objectives and plans eventually emerges.

2. The customer at the centre
In contrast to the West, the customer is at the heart of the Japanese approach to strategy and the key to corporate values.

3. Strategic triangle
In the construction of any business strategy, three main players must be taken into account: the corporation itself, the customer, and the competition. Collectively they are called the strategic triangle.

The job of the strategist, as Ohmae sees it, is to achieve superior performance. At the same time, the strategist must be sure that his strategy matches the strengths of the corporation with the needs of a clearly defined market. Otherwise, the corporation's long-term viability may be at stake.

4. Strategy is irrational
The central thrust of the book is that strategy as epitomised by the Japanese approach is irrational and non-linear.

In strategic thinking, one first seeks a clear understanding of each element of a situation, and then makes the fullest use of human brain power to restructure the elements in the most advantageous way.

Events in the real world do not always fit a linear model. Hence the most reliable means of dissecting a situation into its constituent parts, and reassembling them in the desired pattern, is not a step-by-step methodology, but the ultimate non-linear thinking tool, the human brain.

True strategic thinking thus not only contrasts sharply with the conventional mechanical systems approach, but also with the purely intuitive approach, which reaches conclusions without any kind of breakdown or analysis.

5. Gaining ground through effective strategy
An effective business strategy is one by which a company can gain significant ground on its competitors at an acceptable cost to itself. There are four main ways of achieving this:
• focusing on the key factors for success (KFS)
• building on relative superiority
• pursuing aggressive initiatives
• utilising strategic degrees of freedom
The principal concern is to avoid doing the same thing, on the same battleground, as the competition.

6. Focusing on key factors for success
Certain functional or operating areas within every business are more critical for success in that particular business environment than others. If you concentrate effort into these areas and your competitors do not, this is a source of competitive advantage. The problem lies in identifying these key factors for success.

Ohmae argues that without exception, successful leaders began by bold deployment of strategies based on KFS.

7. Building on relative superiority
When all competitors are seeking to compete on the KFS, a company can exploit any differences in competitive conditions. For example, it can make use of technology or sales networks not in direct competition with its rivals.

8. Pursuing aggressive initiatives
Frequently, the only way to win against a much larger, entrenched competitor is to upset the competitive environment, by undermining the value of its KFS. That means changing the rules of the game by introducing new KFS.

9. Utilising strategic degrees of freedom
This means that the company should focus upon innovation in areas that are untouched by competitors.

CONTEXT
The author is Japan's only successful management guru. The book was published in the West at the height of interest in Japanese management methods.

Ohmae challenged the simplistic belief that Japanese management was a matter of company songs and lifetime employment. Instead, Japanese success could be attributed to the nature of Japanese strategic thinking.

Bestselling author Gary Hamel commented, 'I loved this book! At a time when most strategy savants were focused either on the process of planning (Ansoff and his followers) or on the determinants of successful, that is, profitable, strategies (Michael Porter), Kenichi Ohmae challenged managers to think in new ways. Strategy doesn't come from a calendar-driven process; it isn't the product of a systematic search for ways of earning above-average profits; strategy comes from viewing the world in new ways. Strategy starts with an ability to think in new and unconventional ways.'

THE BEST SOURCES OF HELP
Ohmae, Kenichi. *The Mind of the Strategist: The Art of Japanese Business*. Revised ed. New York: McGraw-Hill, 1991.

Motivation and Personality Abraham Maslow

GETTING STARTED

There is an ascending scale of needs that provides the basis for motivation. Basic physiological needs come first; once these are met, other needs dominate. At the top of the scale is self-actualisation, where individuals achieve their personal potential. Also high up are social or love needs, and ego or self-esteem needs.

The hierarchy of needs provides a rational framework for motivation, and human nature determines that motivation is intrinsically linked to rewards. First presented over 65 years ago, it is a concept still found useful by managers today.

WHY READ IT?

Maslow introduced the concept of a hierarchy of needs which has formed an integral part of marketing, human resource, motivational, and management literature ever since. The book makes an important contribution to the emergence of human relations as a professional discipline.

CONTRIBUTION

1. The hierarchy of needs

There is an ascending scale of needs, which must be understood if people are to be motivated. First are the fundamental physiological needs of warmth, shelter, and food. It is quite true that man lives by bread alone – when there is no bread.

But what happens when there is plenty of bread?

2. Emerging needs

Once basic physiological needs are met, others emerge to dominate. These can be categorised roughly as the safety needs. If a person's state is sufficiently extreme and chronic, he or she may be characterised as living almost for safety alone.

Next on the hierarchy are social or love needs, and ego or self-esteem needs.

3. Self-actualisation

As each need is satisfied, eventually comes self-actualisation – the individual achieves his or her own potential.

4. From motivation to reward

While the hierarchy of needs provides a rational framework for motivation, its flaw lies in the nature of humanity. People always want more. When asked what salary they would be comfortable with, people routinely – no matter what their income – name a figure that is around twice their current income.

Instead of being driven by punishment and deprivation, motivation became intrinsically linked to reward.

CONTEXT

Abraham Maslow was a member of the Human Relations School of the late 1950s, which also included Douglas McGregor (author of *The Human Side of Enterprise*) and Frederick Herzberg (co-author of *The Motivation to Work*).

Motivation and Personality is best known for its hierarchy of needs – a concept that was first published by Maslow in 1943. He argues that there is an ascending scale of needs, which must be understood if people are to be motivated. While the hierarchy of needs provides a rational framework for motivation, its flaw lies in the nature of humanity.

Maslow's hierarchy of needs contributed to the emergence of human relations as a discipline, and to a sea-change in the perception of motivation.

Gary Hamel commented: 'However subtle and variegated the original theory, time tends to reduce it to its most communicable essence: hence Maslow's hierarchy of needs, Pascale's seven Ss, Michael Porter's five forces, and the Boston Consulting Group's growth/share matrix. Yet there is no framework that has so broadly infiltrated organisational life as Maslow's hierarchy of needs. Perhaps this is because it speaks so directly to the aspirations each of us holds for ourself.'

THE BEST SOURCES OF HELP

Maslow, Abraham. *Motivation and Personality*. 3rd ed. New York: Harper & Row, 1987.

The Motivation to Work Frederick Herzberg, Bernard Mausner, and Barbara Bloch Snyderman

Management Library

GETTING STARTED

Employee motivation can be improved through greater emphasis on human relations.

Research indicates that motivation at work takes two forms – hygiene factors and motivation factors. Hygiene factors include working conditions, benefits, and job security. Motivation factors include achievement, personal development, job satisfaction, and recognition. Improvements in hygiene factors remove the barriers to positive attitudes in the workplace, although hygiene factors alone are not sufficient to provide true motivation to work.

Employers should aim to motivate people through job satisfaction, rather than reward or pressure.

WHY READ IT?

Herzberg's work has had a lasting influence on human resource management. Concepts such as job enrichment, self-development, and job satisfaction have evolved from his insight that motivation comes from within the individual, rather than from a policy imposed by the company.

CONTRIBUTION

1. The importance of employee attitudes

'People are our greatest assets' has become one of the most over-used clichés in business. However, before Herzberg, 'people issues' took a low priority in management literature. Management thinkers rarely sought the opinions of employees, or considered them worthy of study. Herzberg and his colleagues, Mausner and Snyderman, highlighted the importance of employee attitudes through a study of 203 Pittsburgh engineers and accountants. By asking what pleased and displeased people about their jobs, he raised the wider question: 'How do you motivate employees?'

2. Identifying factors that motivate employees

Herzberg made a critical distinction between factors that cause unhappiness at work and factors that contribute to job satisfaction. This distinction was based on his earlier work in public health, where he had concluded that mental health was not the opposite of mental illness. Transferring that concept to the workplace, he suggested that the reverse of the factors that make people happy did not make them unhappy. His research indicated that motivation at work takes two forms – hygiene factors and motivation factors.

3. Hygiene factors

Hygiene factors cover basic needs at work. They include working conditions, supervision levels, company policies, benefits, and job security. If these are poor or deteriorate, they lead to dissatisfaction with work. Conversely, improvements in hygiene factors remove the barriers to positive attitudes in the workplace. However, improvement in hygiene factors alone is not sufficient to provide true job satisfaction.

4. Motivation factors

Herzberg discovered that the factors that lead to dissatisfaction are completely different from those that provide satisfaction. He called the positive factors 'motivation factors'. These meet uniquely human needs and include achievement, personal development, job satisfaction, and recognition. Improving these factors can make people satisfied with work.

5. Challenging the reward process

Herzberg concluded that organisations should aim to motivate people through job satisfaction, rather than reward or pressure.

This led to the concept of job enrichment, which would enable organisations to liberate people from the tyranny of numbers and expand the creative role of an individual within the organisation.

CONTEXT

Herzberg was one of the humanist school of management thinking, which emphasises the human aspects of organisations. The humanist tradition includes Mary Parker Follett, Elton Mayo, Douglas McGregor, Abraham Maslow, Charles Handy, and Tom Peters.

Maslow's hierarchy of needs, formulated in 1943, influenced industrial psychologists like Herzberg by showing that work can be made more satisfying by giving greater emphasis to affection, ego, and self-actualisation needs.

Herzberg's breakthrough was to identify hygiene and motivation factors. His work has also influenced organisations' rewards and remuneration packages.

The trend towards 'cafeteria benefits' reflects Herzberg's belief that people choose the form of motivation that is most important to them. Many organisations believe that money is the sole motivation for workers; Herzberg offers a more subtle approach. There has been much subsequent academic debate on the extent to which pay or other factors are the most important motivators.

THE BEST SOURCES OF HELP

Herzberg, Frederick, Bernard Mausner, and Barbara Bloch Snyderman. *The Motivation to Work*. Revised ed. Chichester: Wiley, 1959.

My Years with General Motors Alfred Sloan

GETTING STARTED

Alfred Sloan, a leading figure at General Motors from 1917, became its chief executive in 1946 and honorary chairman from 1956 until his death in 1966.

When he joined, the automobile market was dominated by Ford, and GM's market share was a mere 12 per cent. GM was then an unwieldy combination of companies with eight models that competed against each other as well as against Ford. Sloan cut the eight models down to five and targeted each at a particular segment of the market. The five ranges were updated regularly and came in more than one colour – unlike Ford's Model T. He also reshaped the organisation so that it was better suited to deliver his aspirations.

He created eight divisions – five car and three component divisions. In today's jargon, these were strategic business units. Each had responsibility for its own commercial operations and its own engineering, production, and sales department. The divisions were supervised by a central staff responsible for overall policy and finance.

Despite GM's recent parlous state (it filed for bankruptcy protection in June 2009), the main interest of *My Years with General Motors* for modern management thinkers lies in how Sloan managed to co-ordinate the semi-autonomous divisions with the centre and balance flexibility with control.

WHY READ IT?

Alfred Sloan is one of the very few figures who undoubtedly changed the world of management. He was also one of the first managers to write an important theoretical book. *My Years with General Motors* is an account of his remarkable career and the creation of a new organisational form that spawned a host of imitators.

CONTRIBUTION

1. Balancing flexibility with control

The policy that Sloan labelled 'federal decentralization' marked the invention of the decentralised, divisionalised organisation.

The multi-divisional form enabled Sloan to utilise the company's size without making it cumbersome. Executives had more time to concentrate on strategic issues and operational decisions were made by people in the front line rather than at a distant headquarters.

By 1925, with its new organisation and commitment to annual changes in its models, GM had overtaken Ford. Sloan's segmentation of the company changed the structure of the car industry and also provided a model for how companies could do the same in other industries.

2. Commitment to employees

The book reveals that Sloan was committed to what at the time would have been regarded as progressive human resource management. In 1947 he established GM's employee-research section to look at employee attitudes, and he invested a large amount of his own time in selecting the right people for the job.

3. Problems in decentralisation

The decentralised structure revolved around a reporting and committee infrastructure that eventually became unwieldy.

As time went by, more and more committees were set up. Stringent targets and narrow measures of success stultified initiative. The organisation proved quite incapable of creating and developing new businesses internally. This inability to manage organic expansion into new areas was caused by many factors:

- Operating responsibilities and measurement systems focused on profit and market share in existing markets.
- Business unit managers were not expected to look for new opportunities
- The boxes in the organisation chart defined their product or geographic scope.
- Small new ventures could not absorb the large central overheads and return the profits needed to justify the financial and human investments.

As Sloan himself put it: 'In practically all our activities we seem to suffer from the inertia resulting from our great size. There are so many people involved and it requires such a tremendous effort to put something new into effect that a new idea is likely to be considered insignificant in comparison with the effort that it takes to put it across.'

CONTEXT

Sloan established GM as a benchmark of corporate might, a symbol of US strength and success. 'What's good for GM is good for America', ran the popular mythology. Peter Drucker and Alfred Chandler celebrated his approach, but the deficiencies of the model were apparent to Sloan himself, and were manifested in the decline of GM.

By the end of the 1960s the delicate balance, which he had brilliantly maintained between centralisation and decentralisation, was lost. Finance emerged as the dominant function, and GM became paralysed by what had once made it great.

Gary Hamel commented: 'Can you be big and nimble? The question is as timely today as it was when Sloan took over General Motors. Despite divisionalisation and decentralisation, Sloan's organisational inventions, GM still fell victim to its size ... [T]he corporate superstructure that emerged to manage GM's independent divisions was more successful in creating bureaucracy than in exploiting cross-divisional synergies. The challenge of achieving divisional autonomy and flexibility on one hand, while reaping the benefits of scale and co-ordination on the other, is one that has eluded not only GM, but many other large companies as well.'

One thing that should not be forgotten is that Sloan believed in managers and management in a way that his great rival Henry Ford did not. Nevertheless, as *The Economist* said: 'Alfred Sloan did for the upper layers of management what Henry Ford did for the shopfloor: he turned it into a reliable, efficient, machine-like process.'

Of the book as a whole, Peter Drucker remarked: 'It is perhaps the most impersonal book of memoirs ever written. And this was clearly intentional. Sloan's book knows only one dimension: that of managing a business so that it can produce effectively, provide jobs, create markets and sales, and generate profits.'

THE BEST SOURCES OF HELP

Sloan, Alfred. *My Years with General Motors*. Revised ed. New York: Doubleday, 1990.

The Nature of Managerial Work Henry Mintzberg

GETTING STARTED

What managers actually do, how they do it, and why, are fundamental questions. Managers believe they deal with big strategic issues – in reality they move from task to task dogged by diversions. Managerial work in general is marked by variety, brevity, and fragmentation.

Managers have three key roles and the prominence of each role varies in different managerial jobs.

WHY READ IT?

Mintzberg is regarded by many as a leading contemporary management thinker, and this book was the first to explore what managers actually do at work. It goes behind the myths and the self-perceptions to describe the day-to-day work of a manager.

CONTRIBUTION

1. What managers do – the myth

There are a number of generally accepted answers. Managers believe:

- that they sit in solitude contemplating the great strategic issues of the day
- that they make time to reach the best possible decisions
- that their meetings are high-powered, concentrating on the meta-narrative rather than the nitty-gritty

The reality largely went unexplored until Henry Mintzberg's book.

2. What managers do – the reality

Mintzberg went in search of the reality. He simply observed what a number of managers actually did. The resulting book blew away the managerial mystique.

Managers did not spend time contemplating the long term. They were slaves to the moment, moving from task to task with every move dogged by another diversion, another call. The median time spent by a manager on any one issue was a mere nine minutes.

3. The characteristics of the manager at work

Mintzberg observed that the typical manager:

- performs a great quantity of work at an unrelenting pace
- undertakes activities marked by variety, brevity, and fragmentation
- has a preference for issues that are current, specific, and non-routine
- prefers verbal rather than written means of communication
- acts within a web of internal and external contacts
- is subject to heavy constraints but can exert some control over the work

4. Managers' key roles

From these observations, Mintzberg identified the manager's work roles as:

- interpersonal
- informational
- decisional

5. Interpersonal roles

- figurehead: representing the organisation/unit to outsiders
- leader: motivating subordinates, unifying effort
- liaiser: maintaining lateral contacts

6. Informational roles

- monitor: overseeing information flows
- disseminator: providing information to subordinates
- spokesman: transmitting information to outsiders

7. Decisional roles

- entrepreneur: initiating and designing change
- disturbance handler: handling non-routine events
- resource allocator: deciding who gets what and who will do what
- negotiator: negotiating

All managerial work encompasses these roles, but the prominence of each role varies in different managerial jobs.

CONTEXT

Henry Mintzberg is perhaps the world's premier management thinker, according to Tom Peters. His reputation has been made not by popularising new techniques, but by rethinking the business fundamentals of strategy and structure, management, and planning.

His work on strategy – in particular his ideas of emergent strategy and grass-roots strategy making – has been highly influential for years.

Bestselling author and management guru Gary Hamel commented: 'Five reasons I like Henry Mintzberg: he is a world class iconoclast. He loves the messy world of real companies. He is a master storyteller. He is conceptual and pragmatic. He doesn't believe in easy answers.'

The Nature of Managerial Work has produced few worthwhile imitators, but Mintzberg's rigour and originality have given his ideas staying power.

THE BEST SOURCES OF HELP

Mintzberg, Henry. *The Nature of Managerial Work.* New York: Harper & Row, 1973.

On Becoming a Leader Warren Bennis

GETTING STARTED

Bennis believes that there is no exact science of leadership. Leaders vary in background, education, and experience. However, he identifies certain characteristics as essential for success. According to Bennis, leaders should know what they want and should be able to communicate what they want to others in order to gain their support. Leaders should also understand their own strengths and weaknesses and use them to achieve their goals. Bennis explains the phenomenon of leadership by defining its distinctive qualities – especially those that set a leader apart from a boss or manager, by highlighting the experiences that were vital to the development of leaders, by identifying the turning points, and by examining the role of failure.

WHY READ IT?

Warren Bennis is widely respected as one of the foremost thinkers on leadership, and this book is regarded as a classic. It explains how people become leaders, how they lead, and how organisations respond to leadership. It is not based on academic theory, but rather offers practical advice based on interviews with a mix of leaders from many different fields.

CONTRIBUTION

1. The importance of leadership

Bennis explains that leaders are important for three reasons:

- they are responsible for the effectiveness of organisations
- they provide a focal point
- they provide a recognisable constant in the midst of rapid change

2. Leading and managing

According to Bennis, the ingredients of leadership are wide-ranging and they include guiding vision, passion, integrity, self-knowledge, trust, and daring. Leaders, he argues, may be highly competent, but can fail to win the hearts and minds of the people they are leading.

Bennis believes that there is a significant difference between a leader and a boss, especially a boss who comes up from a results-driven management role. The drive for short-term results can run counter to the effectiveness of a visionary leader.

There are also many important differences between managers and leaders, he argues. The former have short-term rather than long-term perspectives, focus on systems rather than people, accept the status quo rather than challenging it, and exercise control instead of inspiring trust.

3. Leaders and learning

Leaders, according to Bennis, are their own best teachers. They accept responsibility and gain from their own experience and that of others.

He distinguishes between maintenance learning and shock learning, both of which are familiar to managers, and what he calls innovative learning, which involves listening to others. This type of learning, he explains, means that people are free to express themselves, rather than just explain themselves. True intellect, he believes, is being able to see how things can be different.

4. The value of failure

Bennis suggests that leaders also learn from adversity. Making mistakes should not be punished. Leaders must operate on instinct, a process based on the use of the left- and right-hand sides of the brain. Managers, in contrast, rely on tried and tested processes.

According to Bennis, leaders should try everything, even in the face of failure. Few people venture into uncharted waters because of the risk of failure.

5. Achieving goals

Leaders should be able to shift perspective so that they can see what is most important.

Bennis argues that leadership, unlike any other skill, cannot be broken down into a series of repeatable manoeuvres. The creative process involved in reaching a goal is infinitely complex. As he explains, leaders have to be able to move through chaos and synthesise all the elements needed for success.

6. Gaining support

Bennis argues that leaders must get people on their side to effect change. Empathy is therefore an important characteristic of leadership. This, he explains, is in contrast to theories of leadership by force.

Leadership, he believes, requires persuasion, not giving orders. This requires an understanding of the needs of other people and the ability to communicate a vision.

CONTEXT

Leadership is now one of the most popular topics in management literature and training, and Warren Bennis has made an important contribution. Leadership did not attract serious academic interest until the 1985 publica-

tion of *Leaders: Strategies for Taking Change* written in conjunction with Burt Nanus.

Bennis argues that leadership is not a rare skill. Leaders are made rather than born; leaders are usually ordinary, or apparently ordinary, people rather than obviously charismatic figures. Leadership, moreover, is not solely the preserve of those at the top of the organisation – it is relevant at all levels.

THE BEST SOURCES OF HELP

Bennis, Warren. *On Becoming a Leader*. London: Arrow Books, 1998.

The One Minute Manager
Kenneth Blanchard and Spencer Johnson

Management Library

GETTING STARTED

The 'carrot-and-stick' method of motivating employees does not work, say Blanchard and Spencer. It causes confusion and frustration, for two reasons: firstly it is inconsistent, and, secondly, it is unpredictable. And consistency and predictability are what count in human management. This 'allegory', as the authors describe it, recounts the story of a young beginner who sets out to find a really effective manager to model himself on. He finds what he is looking for in the One Minute Manager, who has three simple secrets: one minute goal-setting, one minute praising, and one minute reprimanding.

WHY READ IT?

Blanchard and Johnson start from the idea that the profession of management is not as complicated as it is sometimes made out to be. Following a few simple rules can guarantee increased productivity, profits, and job satisfaction for the employees. First published in 1982, this book has become a popular management classic. It is short, to the point, and the ideas that it advocates can be put into practice straight away.

CONTRIBUTION

1. The search for the One Minute Manager

Really efficient managers deploy themselves and their employees so that both the business and its staff profit from what they do. Effective management, the authors say, is team-orientated. Managers should by and large keep out of decision-making by employees. They should be equally interested in results and people, because results are only achieved by people. A good manager, they suggest, acts on the principle that only people who feel good about themselves work well.

2. One minute goal-setting

In setting goals the One Minute Manager asks the following questions:

- What goals do I want to achieve?
- What kind of behaviour will best help me achieve these goals?

and goes through the following steps:

- writing each individual goal down on a separate sheet of paper in not more than 30 lines
- reading through the piece of paper setting out the goal again periodically
- scrutinising his or her own working methods several times a day
- deciding, on the basis of self-observation, whether his or her own behaviour is helping to achieve the goal or not

3. One minute praising

Praising is effective, say the authors, if it is done like this.

- Always tell your employees what you think of their work.
- If you can praise someone, do it straight away.
- Tell your people what they have done well. Be concrete and go into detail.
- Let them know how pleased you feel about their good performance.
- Stop for a moment so that the person you are praising can share that feeling.
- Tell your employees to 'keep up the good work', as a way of letting them know that you actively support the professional success.

4. One minute reprimanding

A one minute reprimand works well, Blanchard and Spencer suggest, if this procedure is followed.

- Before the reprimand: tell staff from the outset that you will make absolutely clear to them what you think of their work.

- First part of reprimand: if you have to reprimand someone, do it straight away. Tell the person involved in detail what he or she has done wrong. Stop talking and wait long enough for the silence to become painful, that way the person you are criticising will share some of the feeling behind the reprimand.
- Second part of reprimand: offer your hand or show by some other gesture that, despite the fault, you are still on the person's side. It is important to make it clear to people that you value them as employees and think highly of them – apart from what they have done in this particular instance.
- After the reprimand: do not hark back. Once the reprimand is over, it is over.

5. Why one minute goal-setting works
Many managers, say the authors, act like this. They know what they want from staff, but do not take the trouble to tell them. They assume the employees will know. This is wrong. A manager should never take anything for granted, where goal-setting is concerned. Goals must be fixed in writing, so that employees can always look at them again to check their own performance.

6. Why one minute praising works
Most managers hold back praise until the employees have done something 'exactly right'. Consequently, the authors assert, many people never reach their full potential, because their superiors concentrate on catching them out making mistakes. That is wrong. When employees are introduced to a new task, the vital thing is to 'catch' them doing something 'nearly right', so that they go on to learn how to do it exactly right.

7. Why one minute reprimands work
In many businesses a 'blacklist' system operates. Managers collect up instances of unsatisfactory work they have spotted, and then one day – when giving a performance review or if they happen to be in a bad mood – they let the employee have it all at once. That, say Blanchard and Spencer, is wrong. Proper criticism is basically nothing but prompt feedback. Confront the person involved as soon as you have spotted a fault. Reprimands are fairer and clearer if they apply to someone's current behaviour. Criticism should also be directed only at the employee's behaviour, never at him or her as a person.

CONTEXT
The behavioural perspective in *The One Minute Manager* comes from Blanchard, a behavioural scientist and one of the creators of the situation-determined method of management. The psychological aspects of leadership are dealt with by Johnson, a specialist in social medicine and communications. Reviews praise the book's compact treatment of insights that are often presented at great length.

THE BEST SOURCES OF HELP
Blanchard, Kenneth, and Spencer Johnson. *The One Minute Manager*. London: HarperCollins Business, 2000.

FURTHER READING
Johnson, Spencer. *One Minute For Yourself*. New York: William Morrow, 1998.

The Organization Man William Whyte

GETTING STARTED
William Whyte joined the staff of *Fortune* magazine in 1946 after graduating from Princeton and serving in the US Marines during the Second World War. *The Organization Man* is based on articles he wrote for the magazine. He subsequently left *Fortune* and, in his later years, wrote mainly on the subject of urban sprawl, urban planning, and human behaviour in urban spaces.

In the 1950s, the United States still publicly and privately subscribed to the idea that rugged individualism was the hallmark of the American character and the foundation stone of American success. According to Whyte, this was a delusion. Average citizens in fact subscribed to a collectivist social ethic that was turning them into organisation people – and they needed to realise the fact and do something about it.

WHY READ IT?
From the point of view of the age of uncertainty, the age of downsizing, re-engineering, and 'discontinuous change', the 1950s and 1960s can easily seem like a golden age. The careers enjoyed by corporate executives were built on solid foundations, workers had jobs for life, suburbia was heaven, and everything seemed set to go on and on

and on. William Whyte showed the downside to this corporate utopia. Read his brilliant, witty, and often poignant analysis to get both the post-war past and the present in perspective.

CONTRIBUTION
1. The social ethic
Whyte believed that the condition he was analysing did

not affect the United States alone: he referred to 'a bureaucratization that has affected every country'.

The bureaucratic or collectivist ethic rested on three major principles:
- a belief in the group as the source of creativity
- a belief in 'belongingness' as the ultimate need of every individual
- a belief in the application of science to achieve 'belongingness'

And above all he believed that, 'the fundamental principle of the new model executive is . . . that the goals of the individual and the goals of the organization will work out to be one and the same'.

2. The importance of loyalty

Grey-suited and obedient, corporate man was unstintingly loyal to his employer. He spent his life with a single company and rose slowly, but quietly, up the hierarchy.

Loyalty and solid performance brought job security. This was mutually beneficial.

The executive gained a respectable income and a high degree of security. The company gained loyal, dependable, hard-working executives.

But while loyalty is a positive quality, it can easily become blind. What if the corporate strategy is wrong or the company is engaged in unlawful or immoral acts? The corporation becomes a self-contained and self-perpetuating world supported by a complex array of checks, systems, and hierarchies. The company is right.

In a remark reminiscent of George Orwell's *1984*, Whyte suggested that the organisation man 'must not only accept control, he must accept it as if he liked it'.

3. Low-risk environment

Customers, who exist outside the organisation, are often regarded as peripheral.

In the 1950s, 1960s, and 1970s, it sometimes seems, no executive ever lost his or her job by delivering poor quality or indifferent service. In some organisations, executives only lost their jobs by defrauding their employer or insulting their boss. Jobs for life was the refrain and, to a large extent for executives, the reality.

Clearly, such an environment was hardly conducive to the fostering of dynamic risk-takers. It rewarded the steady foot soldier, the safe pair of hands, the organisation man living with his organisation wife.

CONTEXT

Reviewing the book in the *New York Times*, C. Wright Mills wrote: 'Whyte understands that the work-and-thrift ethic of success has grievously declined, except in the rhetoric of top executives; that the entrepreneurial scramble to success has been largely replaced by the organizational crawl.'

Twenty years after the publication of Whyte's book, things had not changed very much. When she came to examine corporate life for the first time in her 1977 book, *Men and Women of the Corporation*, Rosabeth Moss Kanter found that the central characteristic expected of a manager was dependability.

Fortune founder Henry Luce commented: 'It was *Fortune's* William H. Whyte, Jr who made the "organization man" a household word, and the organization wife too. His was a fine achievement in sociological reporting. In it he related the phenomenon of the business organisation to questions of human personality and values.

Whyte was uneasy about corporate life, which seemed to stifle creativity and individualism. He was uneasy about the subtle pressures in the office and at home that called for smooth performance rather than daring creativity. However, he did not urge the organisation men to leave their secure environment. Rather he urged them to fight against the organisation when necessary, and he was optimistic that the battle could be successful.

THE BEST SOURCES OF HELP

Whyte, William. *The Organization Man*. Revised ed. Philadelphia, Pennsylvania: University of Pennsylvania Press, 2002.

Organizational Culture and Leadership Edgar Schein

GETTING STARTED

Schein is sometimes seen as the inventor of the term 'corporate culture'; he is, at the very least, one of its originators. After a long and distinguished academic career, he is currently the Sloan Fellows' Professor of Management Emeritus at the MIT Sloan School of Management.

In this book, he not only provides a sophisticated definition of culture, but he turns the abstract concept into a tool to assist managers in understanding the dynamics of organisations. In addition, he tackles the vital question of how an existing culture can be changed – one of the toughest challenges for leadership.

WHY READ IT?

Organizational Culture and Leadership clarified the entire area of corporate culture in a way no previous book had. It brought culture into the management debate and paved the way for a plethora of further studies. Even today, its perspectives on culture as a constantly changing force in corporate life remain as disconcerting as they are valuable.

CONTRIBUTION

1. The basis of corporate culture

According to the author culture is a pattern of basic assumptions invented, discovered, or developed by a given group as it learns to cope with its problems of external adaptation and internal integration. These assumptions have worked well enough to be considered valid and, therefore, to be taught to new members as the correct way to perceive, think, and feel in relation to those problems.

They can be categorised into five dimensions.

- Humanity's relationship to nature – while some companies regard themselves as masters of their own destiny, others are submissive, willing to accept the domination of their external environment.
- The nature of reality and truth – organisations and managers adopt a wide variety of methods to reach what becomes accepted as the organisational truth.
- The nature of human nature – organisations differ in their views of human nature. Some follow McGregor's Theory X and work on the principle that people will not do the job if they can avoid it. Others regard people in a more positive light and attempt to enable them to fulfil their potential for the benefit of both sides.
- The nature of human activity – the West has traditionally emphasised tasks and their completion rather than the more philosophical side of work. Achievement is all. Schein suggests an alternative approach – 'being-in-becoming' – emphasising self-fulfilment and development.
- The nature of human relationships – organisations make a variety of assumptions about how people interact with each other. Some facilitate social interaction, while others regard it as an unnecessary distraction.

These five categories are not mutually exclusive, but are in a constant state of development and flux. Culture does not ever stand still for long.

2. Shaping organisational values

Key to the creation and development of corporate culture are the values embraced by the organisation. A single person can shape these values and, as a result, an entire corporate culture. The heroic creators of corporate cultures include such people as Henry Ford and IBM's Thomas Watson Sr.

3. Development of corporate culture

There are three stages in the development of a corporate culture:

- Birth and early growth – the culture may be dominated by the business founder. It is regarded as a source of the company's identity, a bonding agent protecting it against outside forces.
- Organisational mid-life – the original culture is likely to be diluted and undermined as new cultures emerge and there is a loss of the original sense of identity. At this stage, there is an opportunity for the fundamental culture to be realigned and changed.
- Organisational maturity – culture, at this stage, is regarded sentimentally. People are hopelessly addicted to how things used to be done and unwilling to contemplate change. Here the organisation is at its weakest and only through aggressive measures will it survive.

4. Changing corporate culture

Each stage of the culture's growth requires a different method of change.

If culture is to work in support of a company's strategy, there has to be a level of consensus covering five areas: the core mission or primary task; goals; the means to accomplish the goals; the means to measure progress; remedial or repair strategies.

Achieving cultural change is a formidable challenge, one that well-established executives in strong cultures often find beyond them. The exceptional executives who achieve cultural change from within a culture they are closely identified with (such as GE's Jack Welch) are rarities, and are known as cultural hybrids.

CONTEXT

Schein's findings gave rise to a host of other studies of the subject. His basic assumptions are rephrased and reinterpreted elsewhere in a variety of ways. Perhaps Chris Argyris comes closest to him when discussing 'theories-in-use'.

THE BEST SOURCES OF HELP

Schein, Edgar H. *Organizational Culture and Leadership.* 3rd ed. San Francisco, California: Jossey-Bass, 2004.

Organizational Learning Chris Argyris and Donald Schön

GETTING STARTED

Learning is a key business activity. Many organisational models only achieve single-loop learning, which – while this permits a company to carry on its present policies and achieve its current objectives – is limited to detection and correction of organisational error.

Double-loop learning, however, enables organisations to detect and correct errors in ways that involve the modification of underlying norms, policies, and objectives. With double-loop learning, managers can act on information and learn from others. Most organisations do quite well in single-loop learning, but have great difficulties with double-loop learning.

Deutero-learning is the process of inquiring into the learning system by which an organisation detects and corrects its errors. It underpins the concept of the learning organisation.

Increasingly, the art of management is managing knowledge – and effective leadership means creating the conditions that enable people to produce valid knowledge. Success in the marketplace increasingly depends on learning, yet most people don't know how to learn.

WHY READ IT?

This book shows why organisational learning is the ultimate competitive advantage. It also explains two of the central paradoxes of business life – how individual initiative and creativity can work in an organisational environment, where rules will always exist, and how teamworking and individual working can co-exist fruitfully.

CONTRIBUTION

1. The weakness of single-loop learning

The authors investigate two basic organisational models.

Model 1 is based on the premise that we seek to manipulate and form the world in accordance with our individual aspirations and wishes. In Model 1, managers concentrate on establishing individual goals. They keep to themselves and don't voice concerns or disagreements. The onus is on creating a conspiracy of silence in which everyone dutifully keeps their head down. Defence is the prime activity in a Model 1 organisation, though occasionally the best means of defence is attack. Model 1 managers are prepared to inflict change on others, but resist any attempt to change their own thinking and working practices.

Model 1 organisations are characterised by single-loop learning – the detection and correction of organisational error that permits the organisation to carry on its present policies and achieve its current objectives.

2. The importance of double-loop learning

Model 2 organisations emphasise double-loop learning – where organisational error is detected and corrected in ways that involve the modification of underlying norms, policies, and objectives.

In Model 2 organisations, managers act on information. They debate issues and respond to change – as well as being prepared to change themselves. They learn from others. A virtuous circle emerges of learning and understanding.

Most organisations do quite well in single-loop learning, but have great difficulties with double-loop learning.

3. The challenge of deutero-learning

Deutero-learning offers even greater challenges. This is the process of inquiring into the learning system by which an organisation detects and corrects its errors. The examination of learning systems is central to the contemporary concept of the learning organisation.

4. The importance of managing knowledge

Learning is powerfully practical and increasingly, the art of management is managing knowledge. Organisations should not manage people per se, but rather the knowledge that they carry.

Leadership means creating the conditions that enable people to produce valid knowledge, and to do so in ways that encourage personal responsibility. Knowledge must relate to action, rather than knowledge for the purpose of understanding and exploring.

5. The learning imperative

There is a natural temptation for organisations and individuals to limit themselves to single-loop learning rather than its more demanding alternatives. However, the need better to understand learning in all its dimensions is now imperative. Any company that aspires to success in the tougher business environment of the 1990s and beyond must embrace learning – yet most people don't know how to learn. Those members of an organisation who are assumed by many to be the best at learning are, in fact, not very good at it.

CONTEXT

If you wished to trace the roots of the learning organisation, you would invariably find yourself reading *Organizational Learning*.

Argyris's ideas became fashionable following the upsurge of interest in the concept of the learning organisation. *Organizational Learning* first appeared in 1978, but it took the 1990 bestseller from Peter Senge of MIT (Massachusetts Institute of Technology), *The Fifth Discipline*, to propel the learning organisation from an academic concept to mainstream acceptance.

THE BEST SOURCES OF HELP

Argyris, Chris, and Donald Schön. *Organizational Learning*. 2nd ed. New York: Addison-Wesley, 1995.

Out of the Crisis W. Edwards Deming

GETTING STARTED

Deming argues that profit comes from repeat customers – and they respond to good quality.

Statistical quality control produces spectacular results, so senior managers must take charge of quality, and quality training should begin at the top of the organisation.

Quality is a way of living, Deming says: it is not the preserve of the few but the responsibility of all. Deming argued that factory workers already understood the importance of quality but were stymied by managers focused on increasing productivity regardless of quality.

Japanese culture is uniquely receptive to the quality message.

WHY READ IT?

This book is regarded as a classic of literature on quality management. It reflects Deming's experience in introducing quality to Japan, and its aim was to transform the style of American management. Deming is regarded as the leading figure on quality and this book sets out the methods that taught industry the power of quality.

CONTRIBUTION

1. The importance of quality

Profit comes from repeat customers, who boast about your product and service, and who bring friends with them.

Quality is more than statistical control, though this is important. Statistical quality control produces spectacular results by using tools to improve processes in ways that minimise defects and eliminate rejects, rework, and recalls.

Deming's work bridges the gap between science-based application and humanistic philosophy.

2. The quality gospel

The book's quality gospel revolves around a number of basic precepts:

- If consistent quality is to be achieved senior managers must take charge of it.
- Implementation requires a cascade, with training beginning at the top before moving down through the hierarchy.
- The use of statistical methods of quality control is necessary so that, finally, business plans can be expanded to include clear quality goals.
- Quality is a way of living, the meaning of industrial life and, in particular, the meaning of management.

3. Deming's Fourteen Points

- Create constancy of purpose for improvement of product and service.
- Adopt the new philosophy.
- Cease dependence on inspection to achieve quality.
- End the practice of awarding business on the basis of price tag alone. Instead, minimise total cost by working with a single supplier.
- Improve constantly and forever every process for planning, production, and service.
- Institute training on the job.
- Adopt and institute leadership.
- Drive out fear.
- Break down barriers between staff areas.
- Eliminate slogans, exhortations, and targets for the workforce.
- Eliminate numerical quotas for the workforce and numerical goals for management.
- Remove barriers that rob people of pride of workmanship. Eliminate the annual rating or merit system.
- Institute a vigorous programme of education and self-improvement for everyone.
- Put everybody in the company to work to accomplish the transformation.

4. The importance of empowerment

The simplicity of the Fourteen Points disguises the immensity of the challenge, particularly that facing management: quality is not the preserve of the few but the responsibility of all. Deming was anticipating the fashion for empowerment.

People all over the world think that it is the factory worker that causes problems. He or she is not your problem. 'Ever since there has been anything such as industry, the factory worker has known that quality is what will protect his job. He knows that poor quality in the hands of the customer will lose the market and cost him his job. He knows it and lives with that fear every day. Yet he cannot do a good job. He is not allowed to do it because the management wants figures, more products, and never mind the quality.'

5. The problem of management

Management is 90 per cent of the problem, a problem caused in part by the Western enthusiasm for annual performance appraisals. Japanese managers receive feedback every day of their working lives.

The basic cause of sickness in American industry and resulting unemployment is failure of top management to manage. He that sells not can buy not.

The Japanese culture was uniquely receptive to Deming's message for a number of reasons. Its emphasis on group rather than individual achievement enables the Japanese to share ideas and responsibility. It also promotes collective ownership in a way that the West often finds difficult to contemplate, let alone understand.

CONTEXT

W. Edwards Deming has a unique place among management theorists. He had an impact on industrial history that others only dream of.

Deming visited Japan after the second world war on the invitation of General MacArthur, and played a key role in the rebuilding of Japanese industry. During the 1950s, Deming and the other American standard bearer of quality, Joseph Juran, conducted seminars and courses throughout Japan. Deming and Japanese management were eventually discovered by the West in the 1980s.

British author Robert Heller says, 'Deming didn't invent quality but his sermons had a uniquely powerful effect because of this first pulpit and congregation: Japan and Japanese managers. Had his fellow Americans responded with the same intense application, post-war industrial history would have differed enormously.'

Management guru Gary Hamel adds, 'Of all the management gurus . . . there is only one who should be regarded as a hero by every consumer in the world – Dr Deming. He may have taken the gospel of quality to the Japanese first, but thank God his message finally penetrated the smug complacency of American and European companies. No senior executive ever sat through one of Dr Deming's harangues without coming away just a little bit more humble and contrite – a good beginning on the road to total quality.'

THE BEST SOURCES OF HELP

Deming, W. Edwards. *Out of the Crisis*. Revised ed. Bambridge, Massachusetts: MIT Center for Advanced Engineering Study, 2000.

Parkinson's Law C. Northcote Parkinson

GETTING STARTED

Companies grow without thinking of how much they are producing and without making any more money. The time taken to complete a task depends on the person doing the job and his or her unique situation. Work also expands to fill the time available for its completion and officials make work for each other.

WHY READ IT?

Parkinson's Law, like *The Dilbert Principle*, takes a cynical look at business. The book treats the growth of bureaucracy and red tape in a humorous way, but the findings reflect real life situations, particularly in government organisations.

CONTRIBUTION

1. How organisations grow

Parkinson's Law is simply that work expands to fill the time available for its completion. As a result, companies grow without thinking of how much they are actually producing.

Even if growth in numbers doesn't make them more money, companies grow and people become busier and busier.

The author contends that an official wants to multiply subordinates, not rivals, and that officials make work for each other.

2. Work expands to fill the time

The notion of a particular task having an optimum time for completion is wrong. There are no rules – it depends entirely on the person doing the job and his or her unique situation.

An elderly lady of leisure can spend an entire day in writing and dispatching a postcard to her niece at Bognor Regis.

The total effort which would occupy a busy person for three minutes may, in this fashion, leave another person prostrate after a day of doubt, anxiety, and toil.

3. Administration expands

Faced with the decreasing energy of age and a feeling of being overworked, administrators face three options:

• resign
• halve the work with a colleague
• ask for two more subordinates

There is probably no instance in civil service history of choosing any but the third alternative.

The number of admiralty officials in the British Navy increased by 78 per cent between 1914 and 1928 while the number of ships fell by 67 per cent and the number of officers and men by 31 per cent.

The expansion of administrators tends to take on a life of its own.

The conclusion drawn is that officials would have multiplied at the same rate had there been no actual seamen at all.

CONTEXT

Parkinson's Law is an amusing interlude in management literature.

It is a kind of *Catch-22* of the business world, by turns irreverent and humorous, but with a darker underside of acute, critical observation.

The book was written in the late 1950s when the Human Relations School in the United States was beginning to flower and thinkers were actively questioning the bureaucracy that had grown up alongside mass production.

Max Weber's model of a paper-producing bureaucratic machine appeared to have been brought to fruition as the arteries of major organisations became increasingly clogged with layer upon layer of managerial administrators.

Gary Hamel had this to say, 'Yes, I know that bureaucracy is dead. We're not managers any more, we're leaders. We're not slaves to our work, we've been liberated. And all those layers of paper-shuffling administrators between the CEO and the order-takers – they're all gone,

right? Well then, why does a re-reading of *Parkinson's Law*, written in 1958, at the apex of corporate bureaucracy, still ring true? *Parkinson's Law* was to the fifties what *The Dilbert Principle* is to the 1990s.'

THE BEST SOURCES OF HELP

Parkinson, C. Northcote. *Parkinson's Law*. Revised ed. London: Penguin, 2005.

Planning for Quality Joseph M. Juran

GETTING STARTED
Unlike the West, the Japanese have always made quality a priority at the top of the organisation.

The key elements in a quality philosophy are:
- quality planning
- quality management
- quality implementation

Juran contends that quality is nothing new, but it has become increasingly ignored in the West where it is treated as an operational issue. There is more to quality than specification and rigorous testing: it cannot be delegated and has to be the goal of each employee, individually and in teams. Quality can be seen as an invariable sequence of steps. Planning consists of developing processes to meet customers' needs; the human side is just as important.

WHY READ IT?
Juran, like W. Edwards Deming, was one of the key figures in the quality revolution. In this book he stresses that the human aspect of quality management is as important as statistical control. The book underscores the contribution that quality teams and empowerment give to the quality process.

CONTRIBUTION
1. National attitudes to quality matter
Talking to Japanese audiences in the 1950s, Joseph Juran's message was enthusiastically absorbed by groups of senior managers – the Japanese have made quality a priority at the top of the organisation. In the West, Juran's audiences were made up of engineers and quality inspectors. Quality was delegated downwards – an operational rather than a managerial issue.

In the post-war years, US businesses were caught unawares for two reasons:
- They assumed their Asian adversaries were copycats rather than innovators.
- Chief executives were too obsessed with financial indicators to notice or heed any danger signs.

2. The quality trilogy
Juran's quality philosophy is built around a 'quality trilogy' based on 'Company-Wide Quality Management' (CWQM), which aims to create a means of disseminating quality to all. Juran insisted that quality cannot be delegated, and he was an early exponent of what has become known as empowerment.

Quality has to be the goal of each employee, individually and in teams, through self-supervision.

3. The historical context of quality
Manufacturing products to design specifications and then inspecting them for defects to protect the buyer was something the Egyptians had mastered 5,000 years previously when building the pyramids. The ancient Chinese set up a separate department of the central government to establish quality standards and maintain them.

Juran's message is therefore that quality is nothing new. But if it is so elemental and elementary, why had it become ignored in the West?

4. The human side of quality
There is more to quality than specification and rigorous testing for defects; Juran regarded the human side of quality as critical. He developed all-embracing theories of what quality should entail.

5. The quality planning process
Quality planning consists of developing the products and processes required to meet customers' needs. Quality planning includes the following activities:
- identifying the customers and their needs
- developing a product that specifically responds to those needs
- developing a process able to produce that product

Quality planning can be produced through an invariable sequence of steps:
- Identify the customers.
- Determine their needs.
- Translate those needs into our language.
- Develop a product that can respond to those needs.

- Optimise the product features to meet our needs as well as customers' needs.
- Develop a process which is able to produce the product.
- Optimise the process.
- Prove that the process can produce the product under operating conditions.
- Transfer the process to those who will be operating it.

CONTEXT

Juran is critical of Deming (*Out of the Crisis*) as being over-reliant on statistics. His approach is less mechanistic than Deming's and places greater emphasis on human relations. Juran was an early exponent of what has become known as empowerment and believed that quality should be the goal of each employee.

Gary Hamel commented: 'The impact of Juran, and of Deming as well, went far beyond quality. By drawing the attention of Western managers to the successes of Japan, they forced Western managers to challenge some of their most basic beliefs about the capabilities of their employees and the expectations of their customers.'

THE BEST SOURCES HELP

Juran, Joseph M. *Planning for Quality*. New York: Free Press, 1988.

The Practice of Management Peter Drucker

GETTING STARTED

Drucker asserts that management will remain a basic and dominant institution, with managers being at the epicentre of economic activity.

A business's purpose is to create a customer; and the two essential functions of business are marketing and innovation. Organisation is a means to achieving business performance and results.

There are five basics of the managerial role – set objectives; organise; motivate and communicate; measure; and develop people. Management has a moral responsibility, and must be driven by objectives.

WHY READ IT?

Peter Drucker was regarded as the major management and business thinker of the 20th century. *The Practice of Management* is a book of huge range, encyclopaedic in its scope and historical perspectives. It laid the groundwork for many of today's accepted management practices and is an excellent primer in management thinking.

CONTRIBUTION

1. The importance of management

Management will remain a basic and dominant institution perhaps as long as Western civilization itself survives. Drucker places management and managers at the epicentre of economic activity.

Rarely has a new basic institution emerged as fast as has management since 1900, and never before has a new institution proved indispensable so quickly.

2. A marketing attitude is critical

There is only one valid definition of business purpose: to create a customer.

Markets are created by business people. The want they satisfy may have been felt previously by the customer, but it was theoretical. Only when the action of business-people provides a means to satisfy that want is there a customer, a market.

Since the role of business is to create customers, its only two essential functions are marketing and innovation. Marketing is not an isolated function, it is the whole business seen from the customer's point of view.

3. The nature of organisations

Though indispensable, organisation is not an end in itself, but a means to achieving performance and results. The wrong structure will seriously impair performance and may even destroy the business.

The first question in discussing structure must be: what is our business and what should it be? Organisation structure must be designed in such a way that it's possible to achieve business objectives for 5, 10, 15 years hence.

4. The managerial role

There are five basics of the managerial role. These are to:

- set objectives
- organise
- motivate and communicate
- measure
- develop people

The function that distinguishes the manager above all others is educational. The unique contribution he or she must make is to give others vision and ability to perform.

5. The importance of moral responsibility

It is vision and moral responsibility that, in the last analysis, define the manager. This morality is reflected in five areas.

- There must be high performance requirements; no condoning of poor or mediocre performance, and rewards must be based on performance.
- Each management job must be rewarding in itself, rather than just a step on the ladder.
- There must be a rational and just promotion system.
- Management needs clear rules on who has the power to make life-and-death decisions affecting a manager; and there should be some way to appeal to a higher court.
- In its appointments, management must realise that integrity is the one quality that a manager has to bring to the job and cannot be expected to acquire later on.

6. Management by objectives

A manager's job should be based on tasks, the performance of which will help attain the company's objectives. The manager should be directed and controlled by the objectives of performance, rather than by his or her boss.

Drucker argues that the manager must know and understand what the business goals demand of him or her in terms of performance, and his or her superior must judge the manager accordingly.

7. Tasks for future managers

Drucker identified six new tasks for the manager of the future. Given that these were laid down over 40 years ago, their prescience is astounding. Tomorrow's managers must:

1. manage by objectives
2. take more risks for longer
3. be able to make strategic decisions
4. be able to build an integrated team, each member of which is capable of managing his or her own performance in relation to the common objectives

5. be able to communicate information
6. be able to see the business, and the industry, as a whole and to integrate his or her function with it

CONTEXT

The Practice of Management laid the groundwork for many of the developments in management thinking during the 1960s, and is notable for its ideas concerning the tools and techniques of management. The book is also important for the central role it argues management has in modern society.

Drucker coined phrases such as 'privatisation' and 'knowledge worker', and championed concepts such as management by objectives. Many of his innovations have become accepted facts of managerial life. *The Economist* commented, 'In a field packed with egomaniacs and snake-oil merchants, he remains a genuinely original thinker.'

Before Drucker's death in 2005, influential author Gary Hamel said, 'No other writer has contributed as much to the professionalisation of management as Peter Drucker. Drucker's commitment to the discipline of management grew out of his belief that industrial organisations would become . . . the world's most important social organisations – more influential, more encompassing, and often more intrusive than either church or state. Professor Drucker bridges the theoretical and the practical, the analytical and the emotive, the private and the social more perfectly than any other management writer.'

THE BEST SOURCES OF HELP
Drucker, Peter F. *The Practice of Management*. Revised ed. Oxford: Butterworth-Heinemann, 1999.

The Prince Niccolò Machiavelli

GETTING STARTED

Change management, leadership style, motivation, and international management were just as relevant in the 16th century as they are today. Executives continue to see themselves as natural rulers of an organisation, and to the leader, presentation is as important as ability.

Introducing change is extremely difficult. It's essential to keep motivation high – success is not down to luck or genius, but happy shrewdness. Leaders who rise rapidly often fall just as quickly, and people ruling foreign countries should be on the spot to prevent trouble. When necessary, leaders have to practise evil.

WHY READ IT?

Although written almost 500 years ago, Machiavelli's advice to leaders remains relevant to managers today, and covers many popular topics such as motivation, dealing with change, and leadership qualities.

CONTRIBUTION

1. Executives have not changed

Machiavelli covers topics as apparently contemporary as change management, leadership style, motivation, and international management. Like the leaders Machiavelli sought to defend, some executives tend to see themselves as the natural rulers in whose hands organisations can be safely entrusted.

Theories abound on their motivation: is it a defensive reaction against failure, or a need for predictability through complete control? The effect of the power-driven Machiavellian manager is usually plain to see.

2. Presenting the right image
According to Machiavelli, 'It is unnecessary for a prince to have all the good qualities [I have] enumerated, but it is very necessary to appear to have them. It is useful to be a great pretender and dissembler.'

3. Managing change and motivation
Machiavelli writes that 'there is nothing more difficult to take in hand, more perilous to conduct, or more uncertain in its success, than to take the lead in the introduction of a new order of things. A leader ought above all things to keep his men well organised and drilled, to follow incessantly the chase.'

4. Managing internationally
'When states are acquired in a country with a different language, customs, or laws, there are difficulties; good fortune and great energy are needed to hold them. It would be a great help if he who acquired them should go and live there. If one is on the spot, disorders are seen as they spring up, and one can quickly remedy them; but if one is not at hand, they are heard of only when they are great, and then one can no longer remedy them.'

5. The qualities of leadership
In the author's opinion, success is not down to luck or genius, but happy shrewdness. He felt that a Prince 'ought to have no other aim or thought, nor select anything else for his study, than war and its rules and discipline; for this is the sole art that belongs to him who rules'.

'In addition, those who solely by good fortune become princes from being private citizens have little trouble in rising, but much in keeping atop,' says the author. 'They have no difficulties on the way up, because they fly, but they have many when they reach the summit.'

It is all very well being good, the author states, but the leader 'should know how to enter into evil when necessity commands'.

CONTEXT
The Prince is the 16th-century equivalent of Dale Carnegie's *How to Win Friends and Influence People*. Many of its insights are as appropriate to today's managers and organisations as they were half a millennium ago. Antony Jay's 1970 book, *Management and Machiavelli* developed the comparisons.

The book offers something for everyone. It covers topics as apparently contemporary as change management, leadership style, motivation, and international management.

Gary Hamel has said: 'We occasionally need reminding that leadership and strategy are not modern inventions. It's just that in previous centuries they are more often the concerns of princes than industrialists. Yet power is a constant in human affairs, and a central theme of Machiavelli's *The Prince*. It is currently out of fashion to talk about power. We are constantly reminded that in the knowledge economy, capital wears shoes and goes home every night. No place here for the blunt instrument of power politics? But would Sumner Redstone, Bill Gates, or Rupert Murdoch agree? What is interesting is that after nearly 500 years, Machiavelli is still in print. What modern volume on leadership will be gracing bookstores in the year 2500? Does Machiavelli's longevity tell us anything about what are the deep, enduring truths of management?'

THE BEST SOURCES OF HELP
Machiavelli, Niccolò. *The Prince*. Oxford: Oxford University Press, 2005.

The Principles of Scientific Management
Frederick Winslow Taylor

GETTING STARTED
Frederick Winslow Taylor was a US engineer and inventor, whose fame rests chiefly on this book. He shares with Henry Ford the dubious distinction of founding an '-ism'. Taylorism is the practice of the principles of scientific management, which emerged from Taylor's work at the Midvale Steel Works. It involves rigorous measurement of work processes, total objectivity in the assessment of which methods work best, and the consequent mechanisation of work and elimination of the human element. The objective standards arrived at, however, are as binding on managers, who have to enforce them, as on the workers who have to meet them. Like the assembly line, scientific management imposes its discipline on everyone. To most members of the humanistic school of management it is the enemy *par excellence*.

WHY READ IT?

At the time *The Principles of Scientific Management* was published, 'business management as a discrete and identifiable activity had attracted little attention' as Lyndall Urwick, the British champion of scientific management, said. The book put management on the map, and its influence on working methods and managerial attitudes for most of the 20th century, especially in mass-production industries, was enormous. Taylor's principles have been alternately reviled, rejected, and rediscovered. They remain undeniably significant even today.

CONTRIBUTION

1. Measuring work

Taylor's science consisted in the minute examination of individual tasks. Having identified every single movement and action involved in doing something, he could determine the optimum time required to complete a task.

Armed with this information, the manager could determine whether a person was doing the job well.

2. Putting science before opinion

The most obvious consequence of scientific management is a dehumanising reliance on measurement.

The experts, who first analyse and then accurately time the various ways of doing each piece of work, will finally know from exact knowledge, and not from anyone's opinion, which method will accomplish the results with the least effort and in the quickest time.

The exact facts will have in this way been developed and they will constitute a series of laws, which are destined to control the vast multitude of our daily personal acts which, at present, are the subjects of individual opinion.

3. A system with no initiative

The Taylorist system envisages no room for individual initiative or imagination. People are labour, mechanically accomplishing a particular task and doing what they are told.

According to Robert McNamara: 'those who were so important in the early stages of American manufacturing, the foremen and plant managers, were disenfran-chised. Instead of being creators and innovators, as in an earlier era, now they depended on meeting production quotas. They could not stop the line and fix problems as they occurred; they lost any stake in innovation or change.' (quoted in *Promise and Power* by Debora Shapley). Taylor's schemes for objectively determining best practices for every imaginable job could, on the other hand, be said to have freed front-line workers from the capricious discipline of unscientific, turn-of-the-century foremen.

CONTEXT

While Taylor's concepts are now usually regarded in a negative light, the originality of his insights and their importance are in little doubt. He himself announced that he was ushering in a revolution, 'a complete mental revolution on the part of the working man engaged in any particular establishment or industry, a complete mental revolution on the part of these men as to their duties toward their work, toward their fellow men, and toward their employees.'

Peter Drucker observed in *The Practice of Management*: 'Few people had ever looked at human work systematically until Frederick W. Taylor started to do so around 1885. Work was taken for granted and it is an axiom that one never sees what one takes for granted. *Scientific Management* was thus one of the great liberating, pioneering insights.'

Lyndall Urwick added: 'At the time Taylor began his work, business management . . . was usually regarded as incidental to, and flowing from knowledge of . . . a particular branch of manufacturing, the technical know-how of making sausages or steel or shirts. The idea that a man needed any training or formal instruction to become a competent manager had not occurred to anyone.'

THE BEST SOURCES OF HELP

Taylor, Frederick Winslow. *The Principles of Scientific Management*. Revised ed. New York: 1st World Library, 2006.

Purple Cow: Transform Your Business By Being Remarkable Seth Godin

GETTING STARTED

The book's title comes from the story Godin tells about when his family left the city to drive through the countryside and were (initially) excited at the sight of grazing cows. After driving for a few hours, however, looking at cows got boring: the only thing that would have been worth their attention, Godin says, would have been a *purple* cow. This feeling can be translated to a commercial setting. While the inventors of aspirin or the frozen pizza built their fortunes by selling a *new* product, today customers' needs are by and large met and already provided for in an increasingly competitive, saturated market. To succeed, one must market a 'Purple Cow' – an iPod or a Frappucino™. While the original marketing mix included such 'Ps' as Price, Product, Position, Publicity, Promotion, Packaging and Permission, the most important 'P' in the future may prove to be the 'Purple Cow'.

WHY READ IT?

To excel, organisations need to distinguish themselves from the competition: in this book, marketing guru Seth Godin likens the art of being recognised and of leading a market to a cow in a field in the countryside that will only be noticed by a passing driver if it is coloured purple. His book is a manual for creating the remarkable and standing out from the crowd. With customers increasingly satisfied – even spoilt – organisations have to find ways of not just meeting their needs, but *exceeding them* and finding entirely new ways to deliver value.

CONTRIBUTION

1. Death of a salesman

Godin's first contribution is to challenge conventional marketing and public relations wisdom that ascribes success to 'share of voice' in standard media streams, such as newspaper and television advertising. He highlights that even Coca-Cola's fantastically expensive adverts do little to sell more cans of soft drinks and argues that the end of what he calls the 'TV-Industrial Complex', with the saturation of global communication, places more emphasis on being people's first choice, rather than simply a close second.

2. Know your business and be passionate about it

By understanding exactly what your business or product is, you can target your marketing more exactly and prioritise tasks. Godin uses most of *Purple Cow* to explore practical examples of remarkable products and services. What they all had in common – from the maker of the internal combustion engine to a publicist for the plastic surgery industry – was a strategic focus on using their unique selling points to meet a previously unexplored market. A market for luxury iced coffees did not exist when Starbucks

first marketed its Frappucino™, but by doing something different, they created a profitable product. Knowing what makes your business and customers tick will allow you more opportunity for success than ever before.

3. Brainstorm and reinvent

Many marketers and salespeople understand the importance of being passionate about their product, but what about *developing* a product that compels people to make decisions with the same passion? Godin cites salt as an example. For years, it was a commodity manufactured in vast quantities with greater economies of scale but diminishing returns. Manufacturers are increasingly realising the benefits of selling handmade, luxury brands – for instance, those targeted at gourmet restaurants – that add value in new ways and for which they can charge a premium. By developing radical, maverick products, or by re-inventing old products so that they meet new needs in creative ways, marketing is at its most effective.

CONTEXT

The importance of being passionate about your product and of creating remarkable marketing strategies has been discussed by management guru Tom Peters (*The Pursuit of Wow*) and the way ideas travel through populations has been studied by Malcolm Gladwell in *The Tipping Point*. Godin, self-proclaimed 'agent of change', argues that most marketers treat these concepts as fads and fall back on tried and tested but boring channel marketing strategies and advertising, hoping that word of mouth will do the rest. With consumers spoilt for choice in a global marketplace, learning how to create a 'Purple Cow' is essential. In a trouble-beset global economy, the only way to create a truly winning product is to be revolutionary. With increasingly flat, globalised communication, customers reject otherwise decent products, seeking only the most extraordinary and unique.

THE BEST SOURCES OF HELP

Godin, Seth. *Purple Cow: Transform Your Business By Being Remarkable*. London: Penguin, 2005.

Quest for Prosperity Konosuke Matsushita

GETTING STARTED

According to the author, customer service is critical to success – customers want goods that will benefit them. Furthermore, after-sales service is more important than assistance before sales.

Business with a conscience cements loyalty. We are using precious resources that could be better used elsewhere unless we make a good profit. Production efficiency and quality products are key. The mission of a manufacturer should be to overcome poverty, to relieve society as a whole from misery, and to bring it wealth.

WHY READ IT?

This book describes how Konosuke Matsushita built a global business – Panasonic – from nothing. It contains lessons on customer service, business ethics, and marketing that would benefit any business.

CONTRIBUTION

1. Building a winning business

The Matsushita story is one of the most impressive industrial achievements of the 20th century.

The company's first break was an order to make insulator plates. The order was delivered on time and was high quality. Matsushita began to make money. He then developed an innovative bicycle light. Initially, retailers were unimpressed. Then Matsushita had his salesmen leave a light switched on in each shop. This simple product demonstration impressed the retailers, and the business took off.

2. The importance of customer service

The company understood customer service before anyone in the West had even thought about it:

- Don't sell customers goods that they are attracted to. Sell them goods that will benefit them.
- After-sales service is more important than assistance before sales. It is through such service that one acquires permanent customers.

3. Efficiency and quality

Matsushita emphasised the importance of efficient production and good quality products.

Managing stock levels is also esential: should you run out of stock (careless, according to Matsushita), apologise to the customers, ask for their address, and tell them that you will deliver the goods immediately.

4. Risk-taking pays

Matsushita took risks and backed his beliefs at every stage.

The classic example of this is the development of the video cassette. Matsushita developed VHS video and licensed the technology. Sony developed Betamax, which was immeasurably better, but failed to license the technology. Consequently, the world standard is VHS and Betamax is consigned to history.

5. Business with a conscience

Matsushita advocated business with a conscience, reflected in his paternalistic employment practices. During a recession early in its life the company did not make any of its workers redundant. This cemented loyalty.

It is not enough to work conscientiously. No matter what kind of job you are doing, you should think of yourself as being completely in charge of, and responsible for, your own work.

6. The role of the leader

Big things and little things are the leader's job. Middle-level arrangements can be delegated.

Matsushita also explained the role of the leader in more cryptic style: 'The tail trails the head. If the head moves fast, the tail will keep up the same pace. If the head is sluggish, the tail will droop.'

7. The broader aims of business

Matsushita mapped out the broader spiritual aims he believed a business should have. Profit was not enough. The mission of a manufacturer should be to overcome poverty, to relieve society as a whole from misery, and to bring it wealth.

He outlined his basic management objective in the following way: 'Recognising our responsibilities as industrialists, we will devote ourselves to the progress and development of society and the well-being of people through our business activities, thereby enhancing the quality of life throughout the world.'

Failure to make a profit was regarded as a sort of crime against society: 'We take society's capital, we take their people, we take their materials, yet without a good profit, we are using precious resources that could be better used elsewhere.'

According to the author, business is demanding, serious, and crucial: 'Business, we know, is now so complex and difficult, the survival of companies so hazardous in an environment increasingly unpredictable, competitive, and fraught with danger, that their continued existence depends on the day-to-day mobilisation of every ounce of intelligence.'

CONTEXT

Matsushita created a $42-billion revenue business from nothing. He also created Panasonic, one of the world's most successful brands, and amassed a personal fortune of $3 billion.

The book explains the key principles that made his business a global success.

THE BEST SOURCES OF HELP

Matsushita, Konosuke. *Quest for Prosperity.* Kyoto: PHP Institute, 1988.

Reengineering the Corporation James Champy and Michael Hammer

GETTING STARTED

In the authors' view, re-engineering must focus on the fundamental rethinking and radical redesign of key business processes. Dramatic improvements in cost, quality, service, and speed are the objectives, and organisations must make key processes as lean and profitable as possible, discarding peripheral processes and people if necessary.

Re-engineering should go far beyond altering and refining processes: the aim is 'to reverse the Industrial Revolution'. Organisations should start with a blank piece of paper and map out processes to identify how their business should operate. They should then attempt to translate the paper into concrete reality.

Re-engineering puts a premium on the skills and potential of the people at the centre of the organisation, and should also tackle three key areas of management – managerial roles, styles and systems.

WHY READ IT?

Reengineering the Corporation is seen as the key book in the re-engineering revolution. It encourages organisations to take a fresh look at inefficient and outdated processes, and to focus on dramatic improvements in cost, quality, service, and speed. Although the message has been misinterpreted, re-engineering remains a powerful tool for change.

CONTRIBUTION

1. Focus on improving core processes

In the context of a fiercely competitive environment and the ability of IT to transform business processes, the book encourages organisations to take a fresh look at inefficient and outdated processes. Re-engineering, according to the authors, is the fundamental rethinking and radical redesign of business processes.

2. Create a lean organisation

The authors argue that organisations need to identify their key processes and make them as lean and profitable as possible. In some cases, peripheral processes and people need to be discarded.

Unfortunately, many organisations have taken this advice literally and downsized without re-engineering. CSC, the consultancy founded by Champy and Hammer, surveyed more than 600 companies involved in re-engineering projects in 1994. In the United States, an average 336 jobs were lost on each project. In Europe, the figure was 760 jobs per project.

3. Achieve a complete corporate revolution

Simple business process re-engineering is not enough, say the authors. True re-engineering is a recipe for a corporate revolution, and should go far beyond altering and refining processes: the past is history; the future is there to be coerced into the optimum shape.

The authors believe that re-engineering is concerned with rejecting conventional wisdom and received assumptions about the past. However, this can mean ignoring the experiences and lessons of the past. Companies are discouraged from trying to understand why they have been successful and building on that.

4. Transform the future

The authors suggest that organisations should start with a blank piece of paper. They should map out their processes to identify how their business should operate, and then attempt to translate the paper into concrete reality.

In practice, this has proved difficult to achieve. The authors now believe that companies tend not to cast the re-engineering net widely; they find processes that can be re-engineered quickly and stop at that point. They lack a vision for the future and the revolutionary approach to take re-engineering forward.

5. Re-engineer management as well

Part of the problem, they now believe, is that managers fail to impose change on themselves – they concentrate on tearing down processes, but they leave their own jobs and management styles intact. However, the old ways of management could eventually undermine the very structure of their rebuilt enterprise. The re-engineering process should therefore tackle three key areas of management – managerial roles, styles, and systems.

6. Re-engineering should be built on trust, respect, and people

The authors believe that re-engineering actually puts a premium on the people at the centre of the organisation. Once peripheral activities have been cut away, the new environment puts a premium on skills of the people who are left. Experience suggests that this has not happened so far: downsizing creates a difficult environment in which trust is frequently absent.

CONTEXT

Re-engineering is seen by some as an old concept with a new label. Frederick W. Taylor's *Scientific Management* advocated similar change, but at an individual rather than an organisational level. Gary Hamel pointed out that re-engineering followed a line from scientific management, industrial engineering, and business process improvement.

The mechanistic theme has been a key focal point for critics, who have made the point that re-engineering owes more to visions of the corporation as a machine, rather than a human system. Peter Cohan, a former colleague, said the authors ignored the importance of people, describing them as objects who handle processes.

Christopher Lorenz of the *Financial Times* believed that the authors failed to state whether organisations should undertake behavioural and cultural changes in parallel with re-engineering.

It has also been easy to take the book's messages too literally. Re-engineering has been seen as a synonym for redundancy, and the book has been blamed for a wave of downsizing.

THE BEST SOURCES OF HELP
Champy, James, and Michael Hammer. *Reengineering the Corporation*. Revised ed. New York: Collins, 2004.

Relationship Marketing Regis McKenna

GETTING STARTED
Marketing, the author says, is everything. It has moved away from mass marketing to customisation and personalisation. Technology is the enabler in this change, allowing companies to deal with the growing power of the customer and the accelerating pace of change in the marketplace. Products are no longer sufficient. Customers demand solutions. Communication has also moved from monologue to dialogue based on a deeper understanding of customers.

WHY READ IT?
Relationship marketing has become one of the most important determinants of corporate success. Retaining customers and maximising lifetime customer value are critical to long term revenue and profitability. Regis McKenna's book sets out the principles of building successful relationships, using technology to understand and communicate with customers.

CONTRIBUTION
1. Integrating the customer
McKenna believes that technology and the choices it offers are transforming the marketplace. All companies, he claims, are technology companies, using technology to customise and offer unlimited choice. The knowledge and understanding available through technology are changing the nature of marketing. The aim now is to integrate the customer into the company.

2. Dominating markets
A strong brand is the reflection of a successful relationship. Owning the market, not just competing in it, is therefore a key goal. Market dominance, he claims, is vital to attracting customers, business partners and the best employees. The starting point is to define a narrow market and dominate it, before expanding the relationships.

3. Dialogue with customers
McKenna claims that one-way advertising is no longer valid. Companies need to have dialogue with customers using trials, user groups, and other feedback mechanisms. He calls this 'experience-based marketing' founded on a deep understanding of the customer.

4. Merger of products and services
The author points out that, in industries like computing, around 75 per cent of the business consists of services such as consultancy, systems integration, and customer support. These are all essential to customers and form part of a solution that builds relationships.

5. Faster time to market
Companies must reduce time to market as much as possible – delay leads to lost opportunities. The marketplace is changing rapidly so it is important to stay close to customers.

6. Market creation replaces market sharing
Companies must differentiate their products to dominate a market, says the author, which may mean starting with small sectors and acting like entrepreneurs. Market creation also means educating customers and listening to them. However, he points out that quantitative information can distract companies from entering small sectors. Qualitative judgment may be more important.

7. Relationships
Relationships are more important with complex high-risk products. Customers need reassurance, education, support, and services to build and maintain their confidence in a company.

8. Dynamic positioning
The author explains how dynamic positioning differs from traditional positioning.
- Product positioning determines how a product fits into a competitive market.
- Market positioning requires a company to understand the infrastructure, influences, and distribution channels in its market.

- Corporate positioning determines whether a company is perceived as a credible and trusted supplier.

9. Product positioning
Product positioning must be based on an understanding of the market environment, according to McKenna. It must also focus on the intangible factors that are important to customers. Trust, he argues, is the logical outcome where customers have a strong relationship and continue to buy.

10. Product success
McKenna cites ten characteristics of a successful product:
- appeals to a new market
- takes advantage of the best technologies
- depends on the market infrastructure for newly-developed technologies
- timing is right
- adapted to market requirements
- developed by small entrepreneurial teams
- customers involved in development
- adopted by early users
- generates a new language
- used in demonstrations, workshops, and user groups

11. Developing relationships
According to McKenna, successful companies develop relationships with the whole market, not just customers. This is the market infrastructure and it includes analysts, developers, retailers, journalists, suppliers, and other organisations who are mutually dependent. The leaders set the standard for their market and everyone else works

with them. McKenna describes these as structural relationships. Strategic relationships with partners are important. For larger companies, the relationships reduce development costs and speed up time to market. For smaller companies, the relationships provide credibility and access.

12. Selling to the right customers
McKenna places buyers in four categories:
- innovators
- early adopters
- majority
- laggards

CONTEXT
This book was one of the first to highlight the importance of relationships with customers, suppliers, distributors, and other players in the marketplace. The discipline of relationship marketing has now entered mainstream marketing practice and is an essential tool for companies in very field.

Since the book's publication, the practice of relationship marketing has been further refined by the development of personalisation techniques and one-to-one marketing via the Internet. The principles, however, remain the same.

THE BEST SOURCES OF HELP
McKenna, Regis. *Relationship Marketing: Successful Strategies for the Age of the Customer*. Cambridge, Massachusetts: Perseus Books, 1993.

Riding the Waves of Culture Fons Trompenaars and Charles Hampden-Turner

GETTING STARTED
Fons Trompenaars studied at a top American business school where he started thinking about cultural differences. 'I started wondering if any of the American management techniques I was brainwashed with in eight years of the best business education money could buy would apply in the Netherlands, where I came from, or indeed in the rest of the world.'

Charles Hampden-Turner is an international authority on cross-cultural communication who taught for many years in the United States and, like his co-author, worked for Shell.

The book is based on meticulous quantitative research (over 15 years 15,000 people from 50 countries were surveyed) and more than 900 seminars presented in 18 countries. Its main contentions are that basic to understanding other cultures is the awareness of cultural difference; that cultural difference can be systematically analysed; that flexibility, a certain amount of humility, and a sense of humour are needed in dealing with cultures other than our own; and that the reconciliation of difference is the supreme managerial art.

WHY READ IT?
Riding the Waves of Culture is an examination of the cultural imponderables faced by managers in the global vil-

lage. Based on exhaustive research, it systematically 'dimensionalises' cultural differences, identifying seven areas, such as attitude to rules and awareness of time, in which different nations have fundamentally different conceptions. Anyone whose work involves dealing with people from other cultures would benefit from reading it.

CONTRIBUTION

1. Culture

Culture is a series of rules and methods that a society has evolved to deal with the recurring problems it faces. They have become so basic that we no longer think about how we approach or resolve them.

People should be aware, first, that they belong to a culture and have a specific way of doing things, and they should be prepared, second, for a different response from the one they are accustomed to receiving when they do business with someone whose culture differs from theirs.

2. Seven dimensions of culture

In analysing cultural differences, the authors identify seven dimensions in which different or contrasting attitudes are particularly crucial. These are:

- universalism vs particularism
- individualism vs collectivism
- neutral vs emotional
- specific vs diffuse
- achievement vs ascription
- attitude towards time
- attitude towards the environment

3. Universalism and particularism

There are two fundamentally distinct ways of dealing with situations that the book labels 'universalism' and 'particularism'. Universalists (including Americans, Canadians, Australians, and the Swiss) advocate one best way, 'what is good and right can be defined and always applies'. They focus on rules and procedure. Particularists (South Koreans, Chinese, and Malaysians) feel that circumstances dictate how ideas and practices should be applied. They focus on the peculiar nature of any given situation and on particular relationships.

Universalists doing business with particularists should be prepared for meandering or irrelevancies that do not seem to be going anywhere.

Particularists doing business with universalists should be prepared for rational and professional arguments and presentations and little else.

4. Collectivist and individualist

The book also contrasts the collectivist mindset with the individualist one.

The United States again comes at one extreme of the spectrum emphasising the individual before the group. Countries such as Egypt and France are at the other end.

Individualists working with collectivists must tolerate time taken to consult and negotiators who only agree tentatively and may withdraw after consulting with superiors.

5. The role of the international manager

Given the wide range of basic differences in how different cultures perceive the world, it is evident that the international manager is moving in a world riddled with potential pitfalls. There are also profound differences between those who show their feelings (such as the Italians) and those who hide them (such as the Japanese), and those who accord status on the basis of achievement and those who ascribe it on the basis of family and age.

The international manager needs to go beyond awareness of cultural differences. He or she needs to respect these differences and take advantage of diversity through reconciling cross-cultural dilemmas. The international manager reconciles cultural dilemmas. In the end, the only positive route forward is through reconciliation. Those societies that can reconcile better are better at creating wealth.

CONTEXT

Tom Peters called *Riding the Waves of Culture* a masterpiece. 'What's not okay is cultural arrogance. If you come to another's turf with sensitivity and open ears . . . you're halfway home.'

Gary Hamel takes the authors to task for their criticisms of US cultural inflexibility: 'So Americans will never understand foreign cultures? Funny how American companies are out-competing their European competitors in Asia and Latin America . . . Where I agree with Trompenaars is that the future belongs to the cosmopolitans.'

The cultural aspects of managing internationally are likely to gain in importance as the full force of globalisation affects industries and individuals. In this respect the value of the book's contribution is undeniable. It has been argued, however, that its stress on cultural relativism and adaptability might become outmoded if capital markets were to enforce 'global rules of the game' independent of different cultures.

THE BEST SOURCES OF HELP

Trompenaars, Fons, and Charles Hampden-Turner. *Riding the Waves of Culture*. 2nd ed. London: Nicholas Brealey, 1997.

The Rise and Fall of Strategic Planning
Henry Mintzberg

GETTING STARTED

Planning is concerned with analysis; strategy making is concerned with synthesis. Strategic planners tend to make false assumptions that discontinuities can be predicted; the future will resemble the past; and strategy making can be formalised. They tend to be detached from action and the reality of the organisation.

Planners typically gather hard data on their industry, markets, and competitors. Soft data - such as networks of contacts, talking with customers, suppliers, and employees - have been ignored. Strategy formulation has been dominated by logic and analysis. This narrows options. Intuition and creativity need to become part of the process.

WHY READ IT?

Mintzberg shows how over-emphasising analysis and hard facts limits strategic planning. Planning should be something visionary and creative. The book has become an influential classic.

CONTRIBUTION

1. Strategy and planning

Planning codifies, elaborates, and operationalises existing company strategy. In contrast, strategy is either an emergent pattern or a deliberate perspective, and cannot be planned. While planning is concerned with analysis, strategy making is concerned with synthesis.

2. The nature of planners

Planners do have value, but only as strategy finders, analysts, and catalysts. At their most effective, they unearth strategies in unexpected pockets of the organisation, whose potential can then be explored.

3. Problems with planning practices

The three main pitfalls are:
- the assumption that discontinuities can be predicted
- planners are detached from the reality of the organisation
- the assumption that strategy making can be formalised

4. The assumption that discontinuities can be predicted

Forecasting techniques often assume that the future will resemble the past. This gives artificial reassurance, and creates strategies that disintegrate rapidly as they are overtaken by events.

5. Detachment from the reality of the organisation

If the system does the thinking, strategy must be detached from operations, and thinkers from doers. This disassociation of thinking from acting lies at the root of strategic planning's problem.

6. Hard data and soft data

Planners typically gather hard data on their industry, markets, and competitors. Soft data – networks of contacts, talking with customers, suppliers, and employees, using intuition, and using the grapevine – have all but been ignored.

Hard data are often anything but. There is the fallacy of measuring what's measurable. There is a tendency to favour cost-leadership strategies (emphasising operating efficiencies, which are generally measurable) over product-leadership strategies (emphasising innovative design or high quality, which tends to be less measurable).

To gain useful understanding of an organisation's competitive situation, soft data need to be dynamically integrated into the planning process. They may be difficult to analyse, but they are indispensable for synthesis – the key to strategy making.

7. The assumption that strategy making can be formalised

The emphasis on logic and analysis creates a narrow range of options. Alternatives that do not fit into the predetermined structure are ignored.

The right side of the brain needs to become part of the process, with its emphasis on intuition and creativity. Planning defines and preserves categories. Creativity creates categories or rearranges established ones.

Thus strategic planning can neither provide creativity, nor deal with it when it emerges. Mould-breaking strategies grow initially like weeds – they are not cultivated and can take root anywhere.

8. The nature of strategy making

Mintzberg defines strategy making thus:
- It is derived from synthesis.
- It is informal and visionary, rather than programmed and formalised.
- It relies on divergent thinking, intuition, and using the subconscious. This leads to outbursts of right-brain creativity as new discoveries are made.
- It is irregular, unexpected, ad hoc, and instinctive. It upsets stable patterns.
- Managers are adaptive information manipulators – opportunists, rather than aloof conductors.
- It is done in times of instability characterised by discontinuous change.
- It results from an approach that takes in broad perspectives and is, therefore, visionary, and involves a variety of actors capable of experimenting and then integrating the results.

CONTEXT

The book reflects a general dissatisfaction with strategic planning. Research by the US Planning Forum found that only 25 per cent of companies considered that their planning was effective.

The book attracted much attention and debate. It also brought a spirited response from the defenders of strategy. Andrew Campbell, co-author of *Corporate-Level Strategy*, wrote: 'Strategic planning is not futile. Research has shown that some companies – both conglomerates and more focused groups – have strategic planning processes that add real value.' Campbell further argues that the corporate centre must develop a value-creating, corporate-level strategy and build the management processes needed to implement it.

Management guru Gary Hamel commented: 'Henry views strategic planning as a ritual, devoid of creativity and meaning. He is undoubtedly right when he argues that planning doesn't produce strategy. But rather than use the last chapter of the book to create a new charter for planners, Henry might have put his mind to the question of where strategies actually do come from!'

THE BEST SOURCES OF HELP

Mintzberg, Henry. *The Rise and Fall of Strategic Planning*. London: Prentice Hall International, 1994.

Strategy and Structure Alfred Chandler

GETTING STARTED

According to the author, structure should be driven by strategy – and if it isn't, inefficiency results. The structure of many corporations is driven by market forces: recognition that production had to be market-driven led large organisations to change to a looser divisional structure.

Increases in scale also led to business owners having to recruit a new breed of professional manager, as professional management co-ordinates the flow of product to customers more efficiently than market forces can ever do.

A planned economy is important to long-term organisational success.

WHY READ IT?

Chandler's book is regarded by many commentators as a masterpiece. It demonstrates the critical link between a company's strategy and its structure, and played an influential role in the profitable decentralisation of many leading corporations. The book's findings remain relevant to new forms of organisation such as the federated organisation, the multi-company coalition, and the virtual company.

CONTRIBUTION

1. Structure should be driven by strategy

Strategy is the determination of the long-term goals and objectives of an enterprise, and the adoption of courses of action and the allocation of resources necessary for reaching these goals.

A company's structure is dictated by its chosen strategy – and unless structure follows strategy, inefficiency results.

A company should establish a strategy and then seek to create the structure appropriate to achieving it.

2. Structure driven by market forces

Organisational structures in companies such as Du Pont, Sears Roebuck, General Motors, and Standard Oil were driven by the changing demands and pressures of the marketplace.

The market-driven proliferation of product lines in Du Pont and General Motors led to a shift from a functional, monolithic organisational form to a more loosely-coupled divisional structure.

3. The rise of the multi-divisional organisation

The multi-divisional organisation removed the executives responsible for the destiny of the entire enterprise from the more routine operational responsibilities.

It gave them the time, information, and even psychological commitment for long-term planning and appraisal.

4. The professionalisation of management

The managerial revolution was fuelled by a variety of factors: the rapid rise of oil-based energy, the development of the steel, chemical, and engineering industries, and a dramatic rise in the scale of production and the size of companies.

Increases in scale led to business owners having to recruit a new breed of professional manager. The roles of the salaried manager and technician are vital, as the visible hand of management co-ordinates the flow of product to customers more efficiently than Adam Smith's 'invisible hand' of the market.

5. The importance of a planned economy

Organisations and their managements require a planned economy rather than a capitalist free-for-all dominated by the unpredictable whims of market forces.

CONTEXT

The book is based on Chandler's research into major US corporations between 1850 and 1920. Its subtitle is 'Chapters in the history of the American industrial enterprise', but its impact went far beyond that of a brilliantly-researched historical text. Alfred Chandler's *Strategy and Structure* is a theoretical masterpiece which has had profound influence on both practitioners and thinkers.

Chandler was highly influential in the trend among large organisations for decentralisation in the 1960s and 1970s. While in 1950 around 20 per cent of Fortune 500 corporations were decentralised, this had increased to 80 per cent by 1970. In the 1980s, Chandler's thinking was influential in the transformation of AT&T from what was in effect a production-based bureaucracy to a marketing organisation.

Until recent times, Chandler's conclusion that structure follows strategy has largely been accepted as a fact of corporate life. Now, the debate has been rekindled.

Tom Peters said, 'I think he got it exactly wrong. For it is the structure of the organisation that determines, over time, the choices that it makes about the markets it attacks.'

In *Managing on the Edge*, Richard Pascale said, 'The underlying assumption is that organisations act in a rational, sequential manner. Yet most executives will readily agree that it is often the other way around. The way a company is organised, whether functional focused or driven by independent divisions, often plays a major role in shaping its strategy. Indeed, this accounts for the tendency of organisations to do what they best know how to do – regardless of deteriorating success against the competitive realities.'

Gary Hamel, author of *Leading the Revolution*, said, 'Those who dispute Chandler's thesis that structure follows strategy miss the point. Of course strategy and structure are inextricably intertwined. Chandler's point was that new challenges give rise to new structures. The challenges of size and complexity, coupled with advances in communications and techniques of management control, produced divisionalisation and decentralisation. These same forces, several generations on, are now driving us towards new structural solutions – the federated organisation, the multi-company coalition, and the virtual company. Few historians are prescient. Chandler was.'

THE BEST SOURCES OF HELP

Chandler, Alfred. *Strategy and Structure.* Cambridge, Massachusetts: MIT Press, 1962.

The Third Wave Alvin Toffler

GETTING STARTED

Alvin Toffler began his career as a journalist but shot to international fame as a futurologist with the publication of his first book *Future Shock* in 1970. *The Third Wave* appeared ten years later, and *Power Shift* ten years after that.

The 'Third Wave' referred to in the title is the super-industrial society that emerged towards the end of the 20th century and is still taking shape. It succeeded the 'Second Wave', the industrialised society produced by the Industrial Revolution, which itself succeeded the agricultural phase of human development, the 'First Wave'. Each new wave was ushered in by the development of revolutionary new technology. Electronics brought in the third.

Though the various waves followed one another in time, they did not affect the whole of the human race simultaneously – many people are still living under First Wave conditions. Toffler's main concern is with the transition from the Second to the Third Wave in advanced societies, but he also deals with possible areas of friction between people co-existing at different stages of development.

WHY READ IT?

The obvious reason for reading a work of futurology more than 20 years after its publication is to see if the futurologist got it right. In many respects Toffler did. But there is a danger there also. Toffler predicted the electronic office and its effects. Now that most people work in electronic offices and live with their effects, perhaps it seems redundant to read a book simply in order to be able to congratulate the author on his foresight. What is startling about *The Third Wave* is that it was written so recently, and yet the technological leaps made since its publication have been so immense. The intriguing thing now is whether the author's broader analysis encompassed the developments that flowed from the developments he immediately foresaw. For many people Toffler's ideas are still intriguing.

CONTRIBUTION

1. Towards mass customisation

The Third Wave, according to Toffler, is characterised by mass customisation rather than mass production.

The essence of Second Wave manufacture was the long run of millions of identical standardised products. By contrast, the essence of Third Wave manufacture is the short run of partially or completely customised products.

The Second Wave strictly separated consumer and producer. The Third Wave will see the two become almost indistinguishable, as the consumer becomes involved in the actual process of production, expressing choices and preferences.

2. The growth of flexible working

Toffler predicted the demise of the nine to five working day.

Machine synchronisation shackled the human to the machine's capabilities and imprisoned all of social life in a common frame. It did so in capitalist and socialist countries alike. Now, as machine synchronisation grows more precise, humans, instead of being imprisoned, are progressively freed. They are freed into more flexible ways of working, whether it is flexitime or working at home.

3. Changes in working relationships

A partial shift towards the electronic office will be enough to trigger an eruption of social, psychological, and economic consequences. The coming word-quake means more than just new machines. It promises to restructure all the human relationships and roles in the office.

The Third Wave will produce anxiety and conflict as well as reorganisation, restructuring, and, for some, rebirth into new careers and opportunities. The new systems will challenge all the old executive turfs, the hierarchies, the sexual role divisions, the departmental barriers of the past.

4. The impact on the corporation

Instead of clinging to a sharply specialised economic function, the corporation, prodded by criticism, legislation, and its own concerned executives, is becoming a multipurpose institution.

The organisation is being driven to redefinition through five forces:

- Changes in the physical environment. Companies must take greater responsibility for the effect of their operations on the global environment.
- Changes in the line-up of social forces. The actions of companies now have greater impact on those of other organisations such as schools, universities, civil groups, and political lobbies.
- Changes in the role of information. As information becomes central to production, as information managers proliferate in industry, the corporation, by necessity, impacts on the informational environment exactly as it impacts on the physical and social environment.
- Changes in government organisation. The profusion of government bodies means that the business and political worlds interact to a far greater degree than ever before.
- Changes in morality. The ethics and values of organisations are becoming more closely linked to those of society. Behaviour once accepted as normal is suddenly reinterpreted as corrupt, immoral, or scandalous. The corporation is increasingly seen as a producer of moral effects.

The organisation of the future will be concerned with ecological, moral, political, racial, sexual, and social problems, as well as traditional commercial ones.

CONTEXT

Other studies of the future of working life tend to plunge head-first into celebrations of the miracles of technology with little attempt to understand the human implications. Toffler is aware of them.

Many of his ideas have since been developed further by others. Charles Handy, for instance, has done a lot of work on the rise of homeworking.

Gary Hamel, influential author of *Leading the Revolution*, commented: 'The post-industrial society is here! And Alvin Toffler saw it coming in 1980 ... One of the challenges for anyone reading Toffler, or any other seer, is that there is no proprietary data about the future. Your competitors read Toffler, Naisbitt, and Negroponte too! The real challenge is to build proprietary foresight out of public data.'

THE BEST SOURCES OF HELP
Toffler, Alvin. *The Third Wave*. New York: Bantam, 1980.

The Tipping Point Malcolm Gladwell

GETTING STARTED
The spread of some products or ideas while others decline is rarely understood. Gladwell's insight into social dynamics provides concrete laws governing the trends of human behaviour. He likens rapid growth, decline, and coincidence to epidemics. Ideas are 'infectious', fashions represent 'outbreaks', and new ideas and products are 'viruses'. For example, advertising is a way of infecting others. Developing his analogy, Gladwell shows how a factor 'tips', that is, when a critical mass catches the infection and passes it on. This is when a shoe becomes a 'fashion craze', social smoking becomes 'addiction', and crime becomes a 'wave'. *The Tipping Point* is a manual for understanding and directing change: a revolutionary's handbook, in fact.

WHY READ IT?

The Tipping Point explains Gladwell's 'laws of epidemics'. Beyond his entertaining anecdotes and illustrations lies an exploration of the forces driving the spread of products, ideas, and other phenomena. The 'tipping point' is the dramatic moment when everything changes simultaneously because a threshold has been crossed, although the situation might have been building for some time. Epidemics can be either 'good' or 'bad'. The spread of HIV is catastrophic but it thrives on the same mechanism that spreads positive things – like fashions or health warnings. Underpinning this mechanism lie three fundamental forces driving all epidemics.

CONTRIBUTION

1. The law of the few

Epidemics need only a small number of people to transmit their infection to many others. Transmission is not achieved by the majority, or even a large minority; it only takes a very few. This is apparent with the spread of disease: the few people who socialise and travel the most make the difference between a local outbreak and a global pandemic. Word of mouth is a critical form of communication when spreading ideas. Those that speak the most (and speak the best) create epidemics of ideas. Gladwell categorises these decisive people into connectors, mavens, and salespeople.

Connectors bring people together, using their social skills to make connections. This affords them power over the spread of epidemics, as they communicate throughout different 'networks' of people. They are masters of the 'weak tie' (a friendly, superficial connection), and can spread ideas far. Since ordinary people form time-consuming relationships, they make fewer of them and affect fewer people.

Mavens (information specialists) are subtly different. They focus on the needs of others rather than their own, and they have the most to say. Examples of mavens include teachers.

Salespeople concentrate on the relationship, not the message, and are more persuasive because they have better sales skills, mastering nonverbal communication and 'motor mimicry' (the imitation of another's emotions and behaviour to gain trust). The product is not necessarily theirs. An individual might make smoking look 'cool' to an impressionable teenager without owning the cigarette company. Without connectors, mavens, and salespeople, epidemics would not reach a 'tipping point'. Epidemics need surprisingly few such people.

2. The stickiness factor

Whereas the law of the few relates to communication, stickiness is about intrinsic qualities or appeal. With a product or idea, the extent to which it spreads and becomes well known depends as much on its attractiveness as it does on how it is promoted. Its 'stickiness' determines whether it passes by or catches on. The author explains that to reach a tipping point, ideas have to be compelling. If the idea or product is unattractive, it will be rejected irrespective of how it is transmitted. The information age has created a stickiness problem: the 'clutter' of messages we face leads to products and ideas being ignored. For those wishing to create epidemics (such as marketers), it has become increasingly important to pay attention to the message's presentation. If contagiousness is a function of the messenger, stickiness is a property of the message.

3. The power of context

We rarely appreciate how our personal lives are affected by circumstances. Changes in the context of a message can tip an epidemic. An example is the 'broken windows theory'. If people see a single broken window, they may believe there is an absence of control and authority. Consequently, they are more likely to commit other crimes. A broken window or wall covered in graffiti invites crime that is more serious, spawning a crime wave. Yet the origin of the epidemic might not be with the connectors, mavens, or salespeople, nor with the stickiness of the factor (assuming crime is not a necessary human act). It could result from an accident in the environment. Gladwell argues that our circumstances matter as much as character. This means that manipulating the environment can control tipping points.

CONTEXT

Gladwell's experience at the *Washington Post* and the *New Yorker* in business, science, and medicine has left him with some excellent explanations for a diverse range of questions. *The Tipping Point* charts a common course between a range of different phenomena. Successful strategies require improvements in our thinking and a shift from an exclusive focus on cause and effect. Gladwell supports a 'systems-thinking' approach. Behind all successful epidemics rests a belief that change is possible. Tipping points underline the power of intelligent action – always an empowering vision.

THE BEST SOURCES OF HELP

Gladwell, Malcolm. *The Tipping Point*. London: Abacus, 2001.

Toyota Production System Taiichi Ohno

GETTING STARTED

The Toyota Production System was developed to help the company catch up with the United States. US car workers were producing nine times as much as their Japanese counterparts. The Toyota system differed from the Western approach, emphasising a reduction in costs rather than an increase in selling price.

According to the author, the company should be seen as a continuous and uniform whole, including suppliers as well as customers. Asking the question 'why?' five times at each stage helps identify and solve problems before moving on.

WHY READ IT?

Since the 1940s Western carmakers have lurched from one crisis to another, seemingly always one step behind. The company they were often following was the Japanese giant Toyota, and the reasons for this are explained by Taiichi Ohno in *Toyota Production System: Beyond Large-scale Production*. The world's car-makers have suffered dramatically since the global financial crisis kicked in in 2008, but Ohno's findings transcend that industry and still have resonance today.

CONTRIBUTION

1. Catching up with the West

The roots of the Toyota Production System lie in the years immediately after the Second World War. Toyoda Kiichiro, president of Toyoda Motor Company, demanded that the company catch up with the United States and gave it three years in which to do so. Otherwise, he anticipated, the Japanese car industry would cease to exist.

At that time in the car industry, an average US worker produced around nine times as much as a Japanese worker.

2. A different approach to production

The Toyota Production System evolved by Ohno was strikingly different from approaches used in the West. There, selling price was regarded as the combination of actual costs plus profit. Toyota, believing that the consumer actually sets the price, concluded that profit resulted when costs were subtracted from the selling price. Their emphasis therefore was on reducing costs rather than increasing the selling price.

3. The principles of the Toyota system

The system has three simple principles:
- just-in-time production
- wider responsibility for quality
- concept of 'value stream'

Just-in-time production

There is no point in producing cars, or anything else, in the hope that someone, somewhere, will buy them; production has to be closely tied to the market's requirements.

Wider responsibility for quality

Responsibility for quality rests with every individual in an organisation. Any quality defects need to be rectified as soon as they are identified.

Concept of value stream

The company should not be seen as a series of unrelated products and processes, but rather a continuous and uniform whole; a stream including suppliers as well as customers.

4. The five whys

Another central element in Ohno's system was the process of the five whys. This suggested that by asking 'why?' five times about various parts of a problem would help you get the root of it and solve it.

CONTEXT

These concepts were brought to mass Western audiences thanks to work carried out at the Massachusetts Institute of Technology as part of its International Motor Vehicle Programme. The MIT research took five years, covered 14 countries, and looked exclusively at the worldwide car industry.

The researchers concluded that US car-makers remained fixed in the mass-production techniques of the past. In contrast, Japanese management, workers, and suppliers worked to the same goals as each other – resulting in increased production, high quality, happy customers, and lower costs.

This research was the basis for the 1990 bestseller by James Womack, Daniel Jones, and Daniel Roos, *The Machine that Changed the World*. From lean production, Womack and Jones went on to propose the lean enterprise (based on research covering 25 US, Japanese, and German companies) and lean management. As with most management fads, it was wilfully misinterpreted. It became linked to re-engineering and, more worryingly, with downsizing.

The reality is that lean production as introduced by Ohno and Toyota is a highly effective concept. It can provide the economies of scale of mass production, the sensitivity to market and customer needs usually associated with smaller companies, and job enrichment for employees.

The West continues to see lean production as a means of squeezing more production from fewer people. This is a fundamental misunderstanding. Reducing the number of employees is the end rather than the means. Western companies have tended to reduce numbers and then declare themselves as lean organisations.

Womack argues that while lean production requires fewer people, the organisation should then accelerate product development to tap new markets to keep the people in work.

Inevitably, lean production has its downside. The most obvious one is that the car industry is its natural home. It can be more difficult to apply in other industries.

The second obvious problem with lean production is that it fails to embrace innovation and product development. It is one thing to be able to make a product efficiently, but how do you originate exciting and marketable products in the first place?

Womack and Jones suggest that the critical starting point for lean thinking is value, but this is effectively one stage beyond the initial one of generating ideas. Even so, lean production has raised awareness, provided a new benchmark, and brought operational efficiency to a wider audience.

Harvard Business School's Michael Porter argues, 'Organisations did well to employ the most up-to-date equipment, information technology, and management techniques to eliminate waste, defects, and delays. They did well to operate as close as they could to the productivity frontier. But while improving operational effectiveness is necessary to achieving superior profitability, it is not sufficient.'

THE BEST SOURCES OF HELP

Ohno, Taiichi. *Toyota Production System.* Cambridge, Massachusetts: Productivity Press, 1988.

Up the Organization Robert Townsend

GETTING STARTED

Townsend's first concern is for the people who are trapped in rigid organisational structures and unable to realise anything like their full potential. He has no time for the adornments of executive office or indeed anything that separates a management elite off from the experiences of ordinary workers. Turning his attention to more general issues, he suggests that all major organisations are operating on the wrong assumptions.

WHY READ IT?

Like any good satire, *Up the Organization* is not only irreverent and wickedly humorous, it is based on shrewd insight and sound common sense. Its questioning of the ghastly stifling orthodoxies of corporate thinking, corporate behaviour, and corporate society is, many commentators note regretfully, as relevant now as it was when the book was first published over 30 years ago.

CONTRIBUTION

1. The organisational trap

According to Townsend, in the average company, the boys in the mailroom, the president, the vice-presidents, and the girls in the typing pool have three things in common: they are docile, they are bored, and they are dull.

He claims that they are trapped in the pigeonholes of organisation charts and that they have been made slaves to the rules of private and public hierarchies that run mindlessly on and on because nobody can change them.

2. The problems of business schools

Townsend's advice to companies is not to hire Harvard Business School graduates.

He believes that this so-called elite is lacking in some

pretty fundamental requirements for success: humility; respect for people in the firing line; deep understanding of the nature of the business and the kind of people who can enjoy themselves making it prosper; respect from way down the line; a demonstrated record of guts, industry, loyalty, judgment, fairness, and honesty under pressure.

3. The end of executive office perks

All the special perquisites of executive office are anathema to Townsend.

His list of no-nos includes:
- reserved parking spaces
- special-quality stationery for the boss and his elite
- muzak
- bells and buzzers
- company shrinks
- outside directorships and trusteeships for the chief executive
- the company plane

4. The wrong kind of leaders

According to Townsend, those with power, or who think they have power, are dangerous beings.

He claims that there is nothing fundamentally wrong with the United States except that the leaders of all its major organisations are operating on the wrong assumptions.

Townsend believes that the country is in this mess because for the last two hundred years it has been using the Catholic Church and Caesar's legions as the patterns for creating organisations.

He argues that until forty or fifty years ago it made sense. The average churchgoer, soldier, and factory worker was uneducated and dependent on orders from above. And authority carried considerable weight because disobedience brought the death penalty or its equivalent.

CONTEXT

Townsend's genius lies in debunking the modern organisation for its excess, stupidity and absurdity. He collected his material in the course of his successful career as a director of American Express and president of Avis Rent-a-Car, then transformed himself into a witty commentator on the excesses of corporate life.

Up the Organization is subtitled *How to Stop the Corporation from Stifling People and Strangling Profits*. The influential British author Robert Heller called the book the first pop bestseller on business management. It is in the tradition of humorous bestsellers debunking managerial mythology and the high-minded seriousness of the theorists. In the 1950s there was *Parkinson's Law*; at the end of the 1960s came Lawrence Peter and

Townsend; more recently the Dilbert series has followed in their footsteps.

Townsend also belongs in the tradition of people-orientated business writing. His humour should not blind one to the underlying seriousness of his purpose.

Given that over 30 years have passed since its publication, the book still retains its freshness and originality, and its insights into the blind deficiencies of too many organisations remain sadly apt.

THE BEST SOURCES OF HELP

Townsend, Robert. *Up the Organization*. London: Michael Joseph, 1970.

The Wealth of Nations Adam Smith

GETTING STARTED

Adam Smith was a Scottish philosopher. He was professor of logic and professor of moral philosophy at Glasgow University, but left his university posts in order to travel on the continent as tutor to a young nobleman. In France he was greatly influenced by a school of philosophical economists known as the 'physiocrats'. Returning to his native town of Kirkcaldy in Fife, he spent the next ten years preparing *An Inquiry into the Nature and Causes of the Wealth of Nations*, which was published – a significant coincidence perhaps – in the same year as the signing of the American Declaration of Independence, 1776.

His central thesis is that capital can best be used for the creation of both individual and national wealth in conditions of minimal interference by government. The 'invisible hand' of free-market competition ensures, in his view, both the vitality of commercial activity and the ultimate good of all a nation's citizens.

WHY READ IT?

Many books are claimed to be classics or seminal works: *The Wealth of Nations* is indisputably both. It is a broad-ranging exploration of commercial and economic first principles. In it Adam Smith laid the philosophical foundations for modern capitalism and the modern market economy. There are few economists over the last 200 years – and fewer politicians of a free-market persuasion – who have not been influenced by it. Smith has helped shape the economic policies of British prime ministers and chancellors of the exchequer from the days of Lord North (1770–82) to those of Margaret Thatcher – and even Tony Blair.

CONTRIBUTION

1. The invisible hand

According to Smith, conscious and well-meaning attempts to better the lot of a nation and its population are generally doomed to failure. The unintended cumulative effects of self-interested striving are far more effective. As he puts it: 'Every individual is continually exerting to find out the most advantageous employment for whatever he can command ... [and] necessarily labours to render the annual revenue of the society as great as he can. He generally neither intends to promote the public interest nor knows how much he is promoting it. He intends only his own gain, and he is in this, as in many other cases, led by an invisible hand to promote an end which was no part of his intention.'

2. Value and labour

The value of a particular good or service is determined by the costs of production. If something is expensive to produce, then its value is similarly high.

'The real price of everything, what everything really costs to the man who wants to acquire it, is the toil and trouble of acquiring it. What everything is really worth to the man who has acquired it, and who wants to dispose of it or exchange it for something else, is the toil and trouble of which it can save himself, and which it can impose on other people.'

3. The division of labour

Smith's legacy to scientific management was the concept of the division of labour.

'The division of labour occasions in every art a proportionable increase of the productive powers of labour. The separation of different trades and employments from one another seems to have taken place in consequence of this advantage.'

'Men are much more likely to discover easier and readier methods of attaining any object when the whole attention of their minds is directed towards that single object than when it is dissipated among a great variety of things.'

CONTEXT

For a book that is over 200 years old, there is a surprisingly modern-sounding ring to a great deal of what *The Wealth of Nations* has to say. This is mainly owing to the acuteness and lasting value of Smith's analysis – the book was the first comprehensive exploration of the foundations, workings, and machinations of a free market economy – but also to the familiarity of many of its basic concepts. *The Wealth of Nations* continues to have a role as a right-wing manifesto, a gloriously logical exposition of the beauty of market forces. And the appeal is not only to the right wing in politics.

Smith's system of demarcation and functional separation provided the basis for the management theorists of the early twentieth century, such as Frederick Winslow

Taylor, and practitioners such as Henry Ford. They translated the economic rigour of his thinking to practices in the workplace, though in ways and to a scale that Smith could never have imagined.

History has, however, put its own limitations on Smith's theorising.

- Physical labour is no longer so important.
- The 20th century saw the emergence of management as a profession. It is barely acknowledged by Smith.
- Smith wrote without knowledge of the power and scope of modern corporations, let alone the power of brand names and customer loyalty.
- He also wrote in harder times where self-interest was not a choice but a necessity.

THE BEST SOURCES OF HELP

Smith, Adam. *The Wealth of Nations*. London: Penguin Books, 1982.

The Will to Manage Marvin Bower

GETTING STARTED

Marvin Bower's success grew on his principle that building trust with clients is critical to consultancy success. The interests of the client should precede increasing the company's revenues: if you look after the client, the profits look after themselves.

He also believed that using values to help shape and guide an organisation is extremely important. One of those values is that regard for the individual is based not on title, but on competence, stature, and leadership. Instead of experienced consultants, McKinsey recruited graduate students who could learn how to be good problem solvers and consultants. The company also developed 'virtual' project teams, bringing in the best people in the organisation wherever they were based in the world. Clear, simple employment policies and change through empowerment helped to maintain high professional standards.

WHY READ IT?

Marvin Bower is the man who did more than anyone else to create the modern management consulting industry. The book gives a valuable insight into the management practices that made McKinsey and Company such a long-lasting success.

CONTRIBUTION

1. A new way of looking at consultancies

Bower did not change the name of his company, McKinsey, as he shrewdly decided that clients would demand his involvement in projects if his name was up

in lights. His vision was to provide advice on managing to top executives and to do it with the professional standards of a leading law firm. Due to a belief that in all successful professional groups, regard for the individual is based not on title but on competence, stature, and leadership, McKinsey consultants were associates who had engagements, rather than mere jobs, and the firm was a practice rather than a business.

2. Building trust with clients

The entire ethos of McKinsey was to be very respectable, the kind of people CEOs naturally relate to. Bower's gospel was that the interests of the client should precede increasing the company's revenues: unless the client could trust McKinsey, the company could not work with them. If McKinsey looked after the client, the profits would look after themselves. High charges were not a means to greater profits, but a simple and effective means of ensuring that clients took McKinsey seriously.

Other central principles were that consultants should keep quiet about the affairs of clients, should tell the truth, and be prepared to challenge the client's opinion. They should only agree to do work which is both necessary and which they could do well. Using values to help shape and guide an organisation was extremely important.

3. New patterns of recruitment

Instead of hiring experienced executives with in-depth knowledge of a particular industry, Bower recruited graduate students who could learn how to be good problem solvers and consultants. This changed the emphasis of consulting from passing on a narrow range of experience to using a wide range of analytical and problem-solving techniques.

4. Developing virtual project teams

Another element of Bower's approach was the use of teams. He thought of McKinsey as a network of leaders. Teams were assembled for specific projects, and the best people in the organisation were brought to bear on a particular problem, no matter where they were based in the world. McKinsey's culture fostered rigorous debate over the right answer, without that debate resulting in personal criticism.

5. Clear, simple employment policies

The company's policy remains one of the most simple: seniority in McKinsey correlates directly with achievement. If a consultant ceases to progress with the organisation, or is ultimately unable to demonstrate the skills and qualities required of a principal, he or she is asked to leave McKinsey.

6. Change through empowerment

'There have been thousands of changes in methods, but not in command and control. Many companies say they want to change, but they need to empower people below. More cohesion is needed rather than hierarchy,' Bower said in 1995.

CONTEXT

Under Bower's astute direction, McKinsey became the world's premier consulting firm. Recent years have also seen the structure and managerial style of the company receiving plaudits. McKinsey is special because it has developed a self-perpetuating aura that it is unquestionably the best. Marvin Bower was the creator of this organisational magic.

American Express chief, Harvey Golub, says that Bower led McKinsey according to a set of values, and it was the principle of using values to help shape and guide an organisation that was probably the most important thing he took away.

THE BEST SOURCES OF HELP

Bower, Marvin. *The Will to Manage*. New York: McGraw-Hill, 1966.

The Wisdom of Crowds James Surowiecki

GETTING STARTED

Surowiecki uses anecdotes to demonstrate how large crowds make more rational decisions than individuals and smaller groups.

The author's definition of a 'crowd' is very broad, ranging from game-show audiences to large corporations, to herds of cars caught in traffic, and to juries and management teams. He argues that collective intelligence can be applied to a wide variety of problems, but requires three conditions to be 'smart': diversity, independence, and decentralisation.

WHY READ IT?

History tells us that change is always managed by a leader. In *The Wisdom of Crowds*, business journalist James Surowiecki argues that the crowd is often more rational and decisive than the individual. Understanding how people behave *en masse* is critical to analysing any situation and an especially useful tool when it comes to comprehending markets. Studying a wide range of different 'crowds' – including traffic, the scientific community, markets, and political democracies – Surowiecki develops a thesis that can be applied to diverse teams, companies, and problems. Understanding the wisdom of crowds promises to change the way we view our business decisions, structure our political systems, and organise our society. While Adam Smith's 'hidden hand of the market' – the idea that individuals' self interest creates economic efficiency – is widely embraced, looking at how the crowd behaves is vital to understanding how markets function and make decisions.

CONTRIBUTION

1. Diversity of membership

Diversity among the members of the group is important because it helps to generate a wider set of possible solutions and makes it better at problem-solving. It adds perspectives that would otherwise be absent and takes away (or weakens) some of the destructive characteristics of group decision-making. Fostering diversity is actually more important in small groups and in formal organisations than in larger collectives, like markets or electorates, because the sheer size of the latter means usually guarantees a minimum level of diversity. Too often, a few biased individuals exert undue influence, skewing the group's collective decision. Diversity makes it easier for a group to make a decision based exclusively on facts, rather than on emotional biases and allegiances: homogeneous groups are less susceptible to 'groupthink'.

2. Independence of opinion

Independence is a crucial ingredient in effective decisions but is notoriously fragile. By enabling each member of the group to make up his or her own mind, the rationality of a group decision is maintained. The fashion industry provides a good example: a product that sells more but which does not offer good value can still succeed because people want to wear what others are already wearing, so that they'll gain approval. In this case, a lack of independent opinion leads the crowd to buy a product that is worse value than its competitors. Independence keeps the mistakes that people make from becoming correlated and systematic.

3. Decentralisation
Surowiecki argues that crowds must decentralise power and diffuse authority on a reasonably equal basis, to be rational. Decentralisation facilitates independence of opinion, while allowing individuals to co-ordinate their activities and collaborate to solve their problems. However, decentralised systems need mechanisms for going beyond aggregating information to being able to make a co-ordinated judgment. In a democracy, voters base their voting decision on the available information, while the mechanism for pronouncing their judgement is the election itself. However, many crowds lack such a formal decision process, which can create anarchy. While maintaining a decentralised system, a crowd can best tackle a problem where the decision process would otherwise have a bias against individuals.

CONTEXT
As corporations' strategic decisions are increasingly complex, harnessing the wisdom of the crowd is increasingly vital. Too many organisations are hampered by rigid hierarchies which formalise individual leaders' power over their teams, leading to flawed and irrational decision-making. Surowiecki's liberating analysis encourages democracy over despotism. A successful example of a company harnessing the wisdom of crowds is Hewlett-Packard's use of internal 'decision markets', where employees anonymously buy and sell shares to reflect their view of future sales of particular products.

In a commercial context, it is important to differentiate between the wisdom of small and large crowds: small groups are unusual, as individuals have more impact on overall judgements – for example, each individual in a jury has more impact on others than each individual in the crude oil market. However, it seems that few organisations have figured out how to make internal groups work consistently well, preferring to discourage all dissent and in the process continue to make flawed decisions.

THE BEST SOURCES OF HELP
Surowiecki, James. *The Wisdom of Crowds: Why the Many Are Smarter Than the Few*. London: Doubleday, 2004.

The World Is Flat Thomas Friedman

GETTING STARTED
Friedman's position is that the forces which separated individuals and markets are falling and that opportunities are becoming equalised. Due to 'flatteners' (see below), the world is increasingly becoming a level playing field. While Columbus travelled West to show the world was round, the rise of Eastern economies – notably, though not limited to, India and China – has destroyed old Western-based prejudices and empowered individuals and corporations across the world to explore new opportunities.

WHY READ IT?
Geographic barriers are collapsing, creating a freer, faster, 'flatter' global economy. However, to succeed and compete in the new era of globalisation, we must understand what is driving the integration of markets. In this book, Friedman argues that free trade and the emergence of a single, global economy – often viewed as unequal and unfair – have spread opportunity, created new markets, and spawned unimaginable innovations.

CONTRIBUTION
1. The ten flatteners
1. **Falling walls and rising windows.** The fall of the Berlin Wall in 1989 was the symbol of the flattening of the political, commercial, and intellectual barriers between the East and West that had seemed fundamental during the Cold War. Freed markets bred opportunity, igniting a new phase of globalisation.
2. **Netscape.** The invention of the Netscape browser brought the benefits of a modern graphic interface to help increasing numbers of people accessing the Internet. As more people could access and share information, opportunities increased.
3. **Work flow software.** Work flow software has created a global web of production: it has shifted from simply connecting people to the Internet to enabling them to collaborate and innovate. Doing for the service industry what Henry Ford did for manufacturing, business operations as diverse as payroll and sales have become automated and digitised, banishing geographical restraints.
4. **Uploading.** By enabling people to share information for free on the Internet, individuals can access

unprecedented resources and the disparity in opportunities between rich and poor has fallen.

5. **Outsourcing.** By enabling companies to concentrate on their core competencies while getting other essential jobs done cheaply overseas, productivity and innovation have increased, 'flattening' the world.

6. **Offshoring.** With an increasing demand for capital and consumer goods, countries have had to integrate, harmonising both political and economic policy. International Relations theorist Susan Strange termed this 'making the world safe for George Soros'. By reducing international risk, companies are increasingly willing to outsource their operations to third parties in offshore locations. With the People's Republic of China joining the World Trade Organization in 2001, the global economy became an exponentially flatter landscape.

7. **Supply chaining.** With governments in consensus on the merits of free trade, companies can create more efficient, closely integrated supply chains that better serve markets. Friedman cites the example of Dell Computers, whose six factories are serviced by dedicated branches of their suppliers, who share information and can better anticipate market movements.

8. **Insourcing.** By bringing the benefits of a global supply chains and the returns to scale of a large operation to small and medium sized businesses that focus on niche markets and market 'microtrends', even local economies can be part of the global, flat world. Fishermen in India can access reliable weather forecasts on the Internet to improve their catch, while UPS enables small businesses throughout the world to deliver merchandise on bespoke, branded vehicles. By enabling all to employ cutting edge best practice, commercial opportunities are flattened.

9. **In-forming.** On an individual scale, the 'information economy' empowers people to know and do more than was imaginable even a few years ago. The democratisation of information is having a profound effect on society. With the erosion of the 'digital divide', increasing numbers of people can search for information on Wikipedia and search for the solutions to their problems on Google, flattening individuals' access to key resources.

10. **The steroids.** The global economy has flattened so rapidly because of the transformation in communication technology, which has enabled the other nine flatteners to work with far greater force than they may have done otherwise. Friedman argues that these forces, deriving from developments in computing technology, increase the potency of the other flatteners. What is new about the current phase of globalisation is its exponential speed.

2. Playing on a level pitch

With emerging markets offering competitive labour costs and more aggressive companies, there is a fear that the developed world will lose out in the 'flat' world. However, a free, global market will benefit all as innovation spawns new markets and new opportunities. Countries with a relative abundance of knowledge workers will engage in the more value-added sectors, while comparative advantage increases economic efficiency. There is, however, a danger that entire economies may be left behind in a flat world and that, as Naomi Klein argues in *No Logo*, dependency and exploitation may emerge. To avoid this, Friedman argues, education and innovation will become ever more important.

CONTEXT

Friedman feels that globalisation happened in three phases:

1. **1500–1800.** With perceptions of the world shrinking from unimaginably large to just about conceivable, after Columbus discover of the New World, new opportunities and new technologies enabled global trade and integration to accelerate.

2. **1800–2000.** Interrupted only by two world wars, the world shrank from a medium to small size. With the rise of multinational companies, global information networks and supply chains, a consensus emerged enshrining the primacy of democracy and free, regulated markets.

3. **2000-Present.** With the development of global communications networks providing instantaneous information and contact, the 'global village' has become simultaneously competitive and rich with opportunity. A playing field for increasingly powerful corporations, financial institutions, and customers, even the poorest countries have improved their fortunes by harnessing increasingly powerful digital technology. Migration has brought seismic changes in cultural attitudes. New patterns of teleworking, as well as digitisation of even basic tasks, have bolstered productivity, ushered in a 'throw-away society' and eroded geographical limitations.

While the world is now flatter than it has been, Friedman does acknowledge the problem created by persistent, absolute poverty. As the Bill and Melinda Gates Foundation – together with the champions of corporate social responsibility – argue, the world can only become truly flat when a humanitarian push comes from global business. Bill Gates told Friedman of his fear that the world will only be flat for its wealthiest 3 billion residents. Friedman cites Hewlett-Packard as an example of a firm that is not just socially responsible, but which profitably engages in the poorest markets. However, while the push for creating a uniformly flat playing field may come from global business, countries lagging behind must themselves embrace reform. Friedman argues that 'reform wholesale', opening a country to foreign trade and investment via 'top-down' initiatives is not sufficient, but must be followed by 'reform retail' – offering the choice of how to develop infrastructure, regulatory institutions, education, and culture at all points in society.

THE BEST SOURCES OF HELP
Friedman, Thomas. *The World is Flat.* London: Penguin, 2005.

Gurus

Igor Ansoff Father of Corporate Strategy

Igor Ansoff was the originator of the strategic management concept, and was responsible for establishing strategic planning as a management activity in its own right. His landmark book, *Corporate Strategy* (1965), was the first text to concentrate entirely on strategy, and although the ideas outlined are complex, it remains one of the classics of management literature.

1918	Born.
1936	Family emigrates to the United States.
1950	Joins the Rand Corporation.
1957	Publishes article 'Strategies for diversification' that presents the Ansoff Matrix.
1963	Appointed professor of industrial administration at the Carnegie Institute of Technology, Pittsburgh.
1965	*Corporate Strategy* published.
1983	Joins US International University as professor of strategic management.
2000	Retires from academic life.
2002	Dies

LIFE AND CAREER

Igor Ansoff was born in Russia in 1918 and his family emigrated to the United States in 1936. His early academic focus was on mathematics, and he obtained a PhD in applied maths from Brown University, in Rhode Island. He joined the Rand Corporation in 1950, and moved on to the Lockheed Aircraft Corporation, where he eventually became vice-president of plans and programmes, and then vice-president and general manager of the industrial technology division.

In 1963 Ansoff was appointed professor of industrial administration at the Carnegie Institute of Technology in Pittsburgh. He went on to hold a number of positions in universities in both the United States and Europe. He retired from academia in 2000 and was named Distinguished Professor Emeritus at the United States International University.

KEY THINKING

Until the publication of *Corporate Strategy*, companies had little guidance on how to plan for, or make decisions about, the future. Traditional methods of planning were based on an extended budgeting system that used the annual budget, projecting it a few years into the future. By its very nature this system paid little or no attention to strategic issues. However, with the advent of greater competition, higher interest in acquisitions, mergers, and diversification, and greater turbulence in the business environment, strategic issues could no longer be ignored. Ansoff felt that, in developing strategy, it was essential to systematically anticipate future environmen-

tal challenges to an organisation, and draw up appropriate strategic plans for responding to these challenges.

He explored these issues in *Corporate Strategy*, and built up a systematic approach to strategy formulation and strategic decision-making through a framework of theories, techniques, and models.

Strategy decisions

Ansoff identified four standard types of organisational decisions, those related to strategy, to policy, to programmes, and to standard operating procedures. The last three of these, he argued, are designed to resolve recurring problems or issues and, once formulated, do not require an original decision each time. This means that the decision process can easily be delegated. Strategy decisions are different, however, because they always apply to new situations and so need to be made anew every time.

Ansoff developed a new classification of decision-making, partly based on Alfred Chandler's work, *Strategy and Structure* (Cambridge, Massachusetts: MIT Press, 1962). This distinguished decisions as: *strategic* (focused on the areas of products and markets); *administrative* (organisational and resource allocating), or *operating* (budgeting and directly managing). Ansoff's decision classification became known as Strategy-Structure-Systems, or the 3S model. (Sumantra Ghoshal proposed a 3Ps model – purpose, process, and people – to replace it.)

Components of strategy

Ansoff argued that within a company's activities there should be an element of core capability, an idea later adopted and expanded by Hamel and Prahalad. To establish a link between past and future corporate activities (the first time such an approach was undertaken) Ansoff identified four key strategy components as:

- product-market scope – a clear idea of what business or products a company was responsible for (predating the exhortations of Peters and Waterman to 'stick to the knitting')
- growth vector – as explained in the section below on the Ansoff matrix, this offers a way of exploring how growth may be attempted
- competitive advantage – those advantages an organisation possesses that will enable it to compete effectively – a concept later championed by Michael Porter
- synergy – explained by Ansoff as '2+2=5', or how the whole is greater than the mere sum of the parts; it requires an examination of how opportunities fit the core capabilities of the organisation

Ansoff Matrix

Variously known as the 'product – mission matrix' or the '2 x 2 growth vector component matrix', the Ansoff Matrix remains a popular tool for organisations wishing to understand the risk component of various growth strategies –

including product versus market development and diversification. The matrix was first published in a 1957 article called 'Strategies for diversification' and the example below illustrates what such a matrix may look like:

	Present	New
Present	1. Market penetration	2. Market expansion
New	3. Product expansion	4. Diversification

Of the four strategies given in the matrix, *market penetration* requires increasing existing product market share in existing markets; *market expansion* requires the identification of new customers for existing products; *product expansion* requires developing new products for existing customers; and *diversification* requires new products to be produced for new markets.

Ansoff's article focused particularly on diversification as a potentially high-growth but also high-risk strategy that necessitates careful planning and analysis before any decision is taken. In Ansoff's view it requires organisations to 'break with past patterns and traditions' as they enter on 'uncharted paths' where, generally, new skills, techniques, and resources will be required. His matrix offered a method of carefully analysing and evaluating the profit potential of diversification strategies.

Paralysis by analysis

It has sometimes been suggested that the application of the ideas in *Corporate Strategy* can lead to an over-emphasis on analysis. Ansoff himself recognised this possibility, however, and coined the now famous phrase 'paralysis by analysis' to describe the type of procrastination caused by excessive planning.

Turbulence

The issue of turbulence underlies all of Ansoff's work on strategy. One of his key aims in establishing a better framework for strategy formulation was to improve the existing planning processes of the stable, post-war economy of the United States, since he realised these would not be sufficient to cope with the pressures that rapid and discontinuous change would place on them.

By the 1980s change, and the pace of change, had become a key issue for management in most organisations. Ansoff recognised, however, that if some organisations were faced with conditions of great turbulence, others still operated in relatively stable conditions. Consequently, although strategy formulation had to take environmental turbulence into account, one strategy could certainly not be made to fit every industry. These ideas are discussed in *Implanting Strategic Management*, where five levels of environmental turbulence are outlined as:

- repetitive – change is at a slow pace, and is predictable
- expanding – a stable marketplace, growing gradually
- changing – incremental growth, with customer requirements altering fairly quickly

- discontinuous – characterised by some predictable change and some more complex change
- surprising – change that cannot be predicted and that both develops, and develops from, new products or services

IGOR ANSOFF IN PERSPECTIVE

Although Ansoff's work is frequently referred to by strategists, it has not become as generally recognised as that of other theorists. Its complexity its reliance on the disciplines of analysis and planning are perhaps among the reasons why Ansoff is not popularly viewed as belonging to the top echelons of management thinkers.

Other theorists were working on themes similar to those of Ansoff at similar times. In the 1960s Ansoff's notion of competence (which was later developed by Hamel and Prahalad) was not unique and, although Ansoff seems to have been the originator of his 2 x 2 growth vector component matrix, a similar matrix had been published earlier. It is likely that much work done during the 1980s and 1990s by other theorists on strategy formation under conditions of uncertainty or chaos owed something to Ansoff's theory of turbulence, though it is difficult to evaluate the extent of the debt.

A debate between Ansoff and Henry Mintzberg over their differing views of strategy has been reflected in print over many years, particularly in the *Harvard Business Review*. Ansoff has often been criticised by Mintzberg, who dislikes the idea of strategy being built from planning that is supported by analytical techniques. This criticism is based on the belief that Ansoff's reliance on planning suffers from three fallacies: that events can be predicted; that strategic thinking can be separated from operational management; and that hard data, analysis, and techniques can produce novel strategies.

Ansoff was one of the earliest writers on strategy as a management discipline and laid strong foundations for several later writers to build upon, including Michael Porter, Gary Hamel, and C.K. Prahalad. He invented the modern approach to strategy, and his work pulled together various ideas and disparate strands of thought, giving a new coherence and discipline to the concept he described as strategic planning.

THE BEST SOURCES OF HELP

Books:

Ansoff, Igor. *Corporate Strategy*. New York: McGraw-Hill, 1965.

Ansoff, Igor, Roger P. DeClerck and Robert L. Hayes. *From Strategic Planning to Strategic Management*. New York: Wiley/Interscience, 1975.

Ansoff, Igor. *Strategic Management*. London: Macmillan, 1979.

Ansoff, Igor. *Implanting Strategic Management*. Englewood Cliffs, New Jersey: Prentice Hall, 1984.

Ansoff, Igor. *The New Corporate Strategy*. New York: Wiley, 1988. (Revised edition of *Corporate Strategy*)

R. Meredith Belbin Team Builder

R. Meredith Belbin is acknowledged as the father of team-role theory. As a result of research carried out in the 1970s, he identified eight (later extended to nine) useful roles that are necessary for a successful team. His contribution has gained in significance because of the widespread adoption of teamworking in the late 1980s and 1990s.

1926	Born.
1981	Publication of *Management Teams: Why They Succeed or Fail*.
1993	Publication of *The Coming Shape of Organization*.
1997	Publication of *Changing the Way We Work*.
2000	Publication of *Beyond the Team*.
2001	Publication of *Managing without Power*.
2008	Honorary Fellow, Henley Management College.

LIFE AND CAREER

Belbin is an academic who has also spent periods working in industry and who now has his own consultancy company. It was while working at the Industrial Training Research Unit in Cambridge that he was asked by Henley Management College to conduct some research into the operation of management teams. The college's approach to management education was based on group work, and it had been noticed that some teams of individually able executives performed poorly and others well. This impression was reinforced when a business game was introduced to one of the courses. Belbin discovered that it was the contribution of particular personality types, rather than the merits of the individuals themselves, that was important to the success and failure of such teams.

KEY THINKING

There has been a continuing interest in Belbin's work because teamworking is an increasingly important strategy for organisations. There are many reasons for this. Teamworking is variously seen as a means of:
• providing greater worker flexibility and co-operation
• helping to achieve cultural shifts within an organisation
• improving problem-solving and project management
• tapping the talents of everyone in the organisation
There are also different types of team involved in working together: for example, temporary teams, cross-functional teams, top management teams, and self-directed teams. Because of this interest in teams, the issue of team building, including team selection, group dynamics, and team performance, has become particularly vital. Although there are many models of team relationships, such as the Team Management Systems (TMS) developed by Margerison and McCann, Belbin's model is probably the best known.

Team role theory

It is important to remember that Belbin's findings relate to teams of managers rather than other types of team. Belbin's findings were first published in *Management Teams: Why They Succeed or Fail* and later refined in *Team Roles at Work*. In Belbin's own words, a team role 'describes a pattern of behaviour characteristic of the way in which one team member interacts with another where his performance serves to facilitate the progress of the team as a whole'.

The essence of his theory is that, given knowledge of the abilities and characteristics of individual team members, success or failure can be predicted within certain limits (see **www.belbin.com** for a full list). As a result, unsuccessful teams can be improved by analysing their shortcomings and making changes. But it is also important for individuals within the team to understand the roles that others play, when and how to let another team member take over, and how to compensate for shortcomings. Although each of the eight roles has to be filled for a team to work effectively, the eight roles are not needed in equal measure, nor are they needed at the same time. There can be fewer than eight people in a team, since people are capable of taking on back-up roles where there is less need for them to fulfil a primary team role.

The roles themselves are determined largely by the psychological make-up of the individuals who instinctively adopt them. Four principal factors are involved: intelligence; dominance; extroversion/introversion; and stability/anxiety. Each role demands a particular combination of these four, and they can be used to rate any individual. In the list of team role contributions, the ratings for each particular trait are shown.

The self-perception inventory and the *Interplace* system

Belbin devised a self-perception inventory, which has been through several revisions, as a quick and easy way for individual managers to work out what their own team roles should be. It was taken up by organisations and used to determine employees' team types, but it has been questioned whether it is psychometrically acceptable for this purpose. Academics were concerned that it was too subjective and recommended that feedback should come instead from a range of sources. Belbin answered this criticism by reiterating that the inventory was never designed for this purpose and by developing a computerised system called *Interplace* to cater for the wider needs of organisations.

Interplace is a more sophisticated approach to role analysis than the self-perception inventory because it incorporates feedback from other people, not just the individual concerned. The main inputs to the *Interplace* system use data from self-perception exercises, observer assignments, and job requirement evaluations. *Interplace* filters, scores, stores, converts, and interprets the data gathered. It offers advice based on the three inputs with respect to counselling, team role chemistry, career development, and the behaviours needed in certain jobs and team positions. The system works as a diagnostic and development tool for organisations.

Later theories

In the 1990s Belbin extended his work on teams to explore the link between teams and the organisational environment in which they operate. He suggested that an effective model for the new flatter organisation might be a spiral or helix in which individuals and teams move forward on the basis of excellence rather than of function.

He has also very recently devised a system for defining jobs which he calls 'Workset'. Its objective is to define the boundaries and content of a job through an interactive communication process between the manager and the job holder. The system uses colour to denote different aspects of the job. There should be five key outcomes:

- the facilitation of empowerment
- the encouragement of greater job flexibility
- the promotion of teamworking
- the support of cultural change
- a continuous improvement process for jobs and job holders

It is too early to say what impact the Progression Helix theory or Workset system will have. They are undoubtedly a contribution, however, to management in today's delayered organisations and flexible working environments, with their associated need to communicate with and involve staff.

R. MEREDITH BELBIN IN PERSPECTIVE

Although independent recent research has thrown doubt on the existence of eight separate team roles, Belbin's broad findings have not been questioned, nor has the popularity of his theories been disputed. There has been an enduring interest in team role categories on the part of practising managers in a wide variety of organisations. This is because:

- there is an increasing interest in teamworking
- Belbin made his ideas accessible to the lay person
- Belbin is recognised as the first to develop our understanding of the dynamics of teams

THE BEST SOURCES OF HELP

Books:

Key works by Belbin

Belbin, R. Meredith. *Management Teams: Why They Succeed or Fail.* 2nd ed. London: Butterworth-Heinemann, 2004.

Belbin, R. Meredith. *Team Roles at Work.* Oxford: Butterworth-Heinemann, 1993.

Belbin, R. Meredith. *The Coming Shape of Organization.* Oxford: Butterworth-Heinemann, 1996.

Belbin, R. Meredith. *Changing the Way We Work.* Oxford: Butterworth-Heinemann, 1997.

Belbin, R. Meredith. *Beyond the Team.* Oxford: Butterworth-Heinemann, 2000.

Belbin Associates. *The Belbin Guide to Succeeding at Work.* London: A & C Black, 2009.

Journal Articles:

Belbin, Meredith, Barrie Watson, and Cindy West. 'True colours.' *People Management*, 6 March 1997, pp. 36–38, 41.

Furnham, Adrian, Howard Steele, and David Pendleton. 'A psychometric assessment of the Belbin team role self-perception inventory.' *Journal of Occupational and Organizational Psychology*, vol. 66 no 3, 1993, pp. 245–261 (This article includes Belbin's criticism of the research and the response of the authors).

Senior, Barbara. 'An empirically-based assessment of Belbin's team roles.' *Human Resource Management Journal*, vol. 8 no 3, 1998, pp. 54–60.

Website:

www.belbin.com contains a useful list of answers to frequently asked questions about team role theory, as well as an online team analysis and reports service. It also contains helpful information on Belbin's latest work on Work Roles.

Warren Bennis Leadership Guru

Warren Bennis's career has been extremely varied. He has worked as an educator, writer, administrator, and consultant, besides authoring or co-authoring many books on different topics. He has carried out highly respected work in the areas of small group dynamics, change in social systems, T-groups, and sensitivity training, and during the 1960s became a recognised futurologist. Bennis wrote his first article on leadership in 1959, and he has become a widely accepted authority on the subject since 1985, when *Leaders* was published.

1925	Born.
1959	Sets up department for organisational studies at MIT.
1967	Appointed Provost of State University of New York (SUNY).
1971	President of the University of Cincinnati.
1979	Professor of Management at the University of Southern California.
1985	Publication of *Leaders: The Strategies for Taking Charge*.
1989	Publication of *On Becoming a Leader*.
1997	Publication of *Organizing Genius*.

LIFE AND CAREER

Bennis was born in New York in 1925 and educated at Antioch College, Ohio, and the Massachusetts Institute of Technology (MIT). Later, he studied group dynamics, and during the 1950s was involved in the US National Training Laboratories teamworking experiments. His early field of work was organisational development. Bennis was a great admirer of Douglas McGregor and his 'Theory Y' approach to motivation. In fact, Bennis became very close to McGregor and was strongly influenced by him. His career path even followed McGregor's to some extent. First, he was an undergraduate student at Antioch College while McGregor was President there, and later, in 1959, he was recruited by McGregor to set up a new department for organisation studies at MIT. From the late 1960s, Bennis's career moved for a time from academic research and teaching to administration. He became Provost at the State University of New York (SUNY), Buffalo, in 1967, staying there until 1971, when he moved to take on the post of President of the University of Cincinnati.

As an administrative leader from 1967 to 1978, Bennis attempted to put McGregor's motivation theories into practice, and found them unworkable without some adaptation in the form of strengthened structure and direction.

During the 1960s, Bennis became known as a student of the future, and predicted (with co-author Philip Slater in a March 1964 article for the *Harvard Business Review* called 'Democracy is Inevitable') the downfall of communism in the face of inevitable democracy. By the mid-1960s, he was predicting the demise of bureaucratic organisation. His 1968 book, *The Temporary Society*, explored new forms of organisation, advocating an 'adhocracy' of free-moving project teams as a necessity for the future. This idea has since been taken up by other writers, such as Alvin Toffler and Henry Mintzberg.

In an adhocracy, responsibility and leadership are distributed to groups or task forces on the basis of the relevance of members' qualifications or abilities for the specific task or purpose of the group. For Bennis, adhocracy was an important concept as a counter to hierarchy, centralised control, and bureaucratic organisation.

KEY THINKING

In his early book on leadership, *The Unconscious Conspiracy* (1976), Bennis highlights how leaders can positively influence others to bring about change. His most distinctive ideas on the subject, however, partly grew out of the broad, general response to a landmark *Harvard Business Review* article of 1977 by Abraham Zaleznik (then Professor of Social Psychology of Management at Harvard).

The Zaleznik article was entitled 'Managers and leaders-are they different?' Bennis's research and writing were extreme in emphasising a complete, qualitative difference between management and leadership, and he drew up a list of sharp distinctions that ended with the now familiar aphorism: 'Managers do things right, leaders do the right thing.' While Bennis considers that managers can become leaders through learning and development, he is firm about the functional differences between the roles and the approaches involved, and the distinctions he draws echo throughout most of his writings on leadership.

The Leaders study

In 1979, on his return to research and teaching as Professor of Management at the University of Southern California, Bennis sought to unravel the lessons of his practical experience of leadership. He explored the subject through a 1985 serial study that was published as a book co-authored with Burt Nanus, called *Leaders: The Strategies for Taking Charge* (1985). While Bennis has written or cowritten many other books relating to leadership, these largely expand on the ideas developed in *Leaders*.

Leaders aimed to identify common characteristics among 90 successful US leaders who had all, the authors considered, demonstrated 'mastery over present confusion' in their careers. The leaders ranged from an orchestra conductor to Ray Kroc, the founder of McDonald's, and included a baseball player and a tightrope walker, as well as the astronaut Neil Armstrong. It was Bennis's second book on leadership, selling over 300,000 copies, and is still considered an important text on the subject.

In *Leaders*, Bennis and Nanus identify four common factors amongst the subjects, and these form the core of their ideas about leadership.

- Attention through vision – all had an agenda, an intense vision and commitment that drew others in. The leaders also gave much attention to other people.
- Meaning through communication – all had an ability to communicate their vision and bring it to life for others, sometimes using drawings or models as well as metaphor and analogy.
- Trust through positioning – through establishing a position with a set of actions to implement their vision, and staying the course, the leaders established trust.
- The deployment of self through positive self-regard – the creative deployment of self is essential to leadership, involving an honest appreciation of oneself and one's own worth, and instilling confidence in others.

Positive self-regard is related to 'emotional wisdom', and five key skills in emotional wisdom are given as the abilities to:

- accept others as they are
- approach things only in terms of the present
- treat others, even familiar contacts, with courteous attention
- trust others, even where the risk seems high
- do without constant approval and recognition

One common quality that Bennis and Nanus particularly identified in these leaders was their way of responding to failure as a learning experience. Karl Wallenda, the great tightrope aerialist, was taken as a main example. The authors illustrate his manner of putting his energies completely into his task, thinking of failure as a mistake from which he could learn, and viewing this experience (of learning based on failure) as a new beginning, rather than the end, for a project or idea.

'Transformative' leadership

The style of leadership discussed by Bennis and Nanus is termed 'transformative', in that it is said to have an empowering effect on others, enabling them to translate intentions into reality. A transformative leadership style is described as one that motivates through identification with the leader's vision, pulling rather than pushing others on.

Four elements of empowerment are distinguished as:

- significance – a feeling of making a difference
- competence – development and learning 'on the job'
- community – a sense of inter-reliance and involvement in a common cause
- enjoyment – capacity to have fun at work because it is enjoyable and involving

The four major characteristics of transformative leaders identified earlier are linked to strategic approaches through which a leader leads.

- The creation of a compelling vision: a leader must develop and communicate an image, or vision, of a credible and attractive future for the organisation.

- The translation of meaning into social architecture: social architecture is the intangible variable that translates the buzz and confusion of organisational life into meaning. While similar to culture, social architecture is more precise in meaning, in that it can be defined, assessed, and, to some extent, managed. Three styles of social architecture are distinguished as formalistic, collegial, and personalistic.
- The position of the organisation in the outside world: positioning of an organisation is described as the process by which it establishes a viable niche in its environment. It encompasses all that must be done to align the internal and external environments of the organisation.
- The development of organisational learning: good leaders are experts at learning within an organisational context, and their behaviour can help to direct and energise innovative learning within the organisation as a whole.

The end result of transformative leadership is, Bennis and Nanus consider, an empowering environment and accompanying culture, enabling employees to generate a sense of meaning in their work. Higher profits and wages, the authors suggest, inevitably accompany this sort of culture, if it is genuinely established.

At the end of the book, five myths about leadership are identified and contradicted.

- Leadership is a rare skill – it is not.
- Leaders are born – they are not.
- Leaders are charismatic – most are ordinary.
- Leadership can exist only at the 'top' – it is relevant at all levels.
- Leaders control, direct, and manipulate – they do not. Transformative leaders align the energies of others behind an attractive goal.

Later work

A later, prominent book by Bennis, *On Becoming a Leader* (1989), looks at learning to lead, developing leadership qualities, and how leadership can be taught. It uses 29 well-known Americans as case studies to illustrate leadership qualities. Its main message suggests that becoming a leader involves continual learning, development, and the reinvention of the self.

Bennis has since written or co-written many books and articles that expand on and develop his ideas on leadership. His more recent works focus on the important roles of followers and groups, as well as on leadership. In *Organizing Genius* (1997), a collaborative work with Patricia Ward Biederman, Bennis almost returned to his roots in group work. The book looks at the history of seven well-known groups in action, including Walt Disney's animation studios, President Clinton's 1992 election campaign, and Lockheed's 'skunk works'. Common features of these successful groups are highlighted, and the mutually interdependent relationship between great leaders and great groups is stressed.

WARREN BENNIS IN PERSPECTIVE

The importance of Bennis's work in the field of leadership is indisputable, and his informal and easy-mannered style of writing and use of practical illustrations have made his books very approachable. The management writer Stuart Crainer emphasises Bennis's humane approach to leadership. Bennis views leadership as a skill that can be developed by ordinary people and that centres on enabling and empowering others rather than on control and direction. He is sometimes criticised as a romantic in his approach and has himself affirmed (in *The Director* of October 1988), that he is indeed a romantic, if that term accurately describes someone who believes in possibilities, and is optimistic.

THE BEST SOURCES OF HELP
Books:

Bennis, Warren. *The Unconscious Conspiracy: Why Leaders Can't Lead*. New York: AMACOM Press, 1976.

Bennis, Warren, and Burt Nanus. *Leaders: The Strategies for Taking Charge*. New York: Harper & Row, 1985.

Bennis, Warren. *On Becoming a Leader*. Reading, Massachusetts: Addison-Wesley, 1989.

Bennis, Warren. *Why Leaders Can't Lead: The Unconscious Conspiracy Continues*. San Francisco, California: Jossey-Bass, 1989.

Bennis, Warren. *An Invented Life: Reflections on Leadership and Change*. Reading, Massachusetts: Addison-Wesley, 1993.

Bennis, Warren, and Patricia Ward Biederman. *Organizing Genius: The Secrets of Creative Collaboration*. Reading, Massachusetts: Addison-Wesley, 1997.

Bennis, Warren. *Managing People Is Like Herding Cats*. London: Kogan Page, 1998.

Bennis, Warren, and Robert Thomas. *Geeks and Geezers*. Boston, Massachusetts: Harvard Business School Press, 2002.

Bennis, Warren. *The Essential Bennis*. San Francisco, California: Jossey-Bass, 2009.

Kenneth Blanchard The One Minute Manager

The One Minute Manager was first published in the United States in 1982. Lambasted as trite and shallow by academics, it has since sold over 17 million copies worldwide, been translated into over 25 languages, and is frequently found on managers' bookshelves. It launched a new genre of management publishing, providing the model for a host of imitations.

1939	Born.
1982	Publication of *The One Minute Manager*.
1984	Publication of *Putting the One Minute Manager to Work*.

LIFE AND CAREER

Kenneth Blanchard graduated from Cornell University in Government and Philosophy and went on to complete his PhD in Administration and Management. In the early 1980s he was Professor of Leadership and Organizational Behavior at the University of Massachusetts, Amherst. He wrote and researched extensively in the fields of leadership, motivation, and the management of change, and his *Management of Organizational Behaviour: Utilizing Human Resources* (co-authored with Paul Hersey) is now in its 8th edition and has become a classic text. In the Introduction to *The One Minute Manager* (OMM), Blanchard and his co-author Spencer Johnson describe the book as an allegory, a simple compilation of what 'many wise people have taught us and what we have learned ourselves'.

KEY THINKING

One-minute management

The framework story of *The One Minute Manager* imagines a young manager going off in search of that holy grail of the aspiring newcomer-an effective manager on whom to model his own thinking and actions. The novice – a cross between *Le Petit Prince* and *Candide* – is caught between the two extremes of the Scientific and Human Relations schools: some managers get good results (but at a price that few colleagues and subordinates seem willing to support), whilst others (whose people really like them) have results which leave much to be desired. Our hero, however, soon comes across a manager who gets excellent results as a result of-apparently – very little effort on his part – the One Minute Manager. The OMM has three simple secrets that bring about increases in productivity, profits, and satisfaction: one-minute goal-setting, one-minute praising, and one-minute reprimanding.

One-minute goal-setting

Although staff cannot know how well they are doing without clear goals, claims the OMM, many are not clear on priorities, and many are spoken to only when they make a mistake. The OMM requires managers to make it clear what tasks people are to do and what sort of behaviour or performance is expected of t hem, and to get staff to write down their most important goals on a single sheet of paper for continued clarification.

One-minute praising

The second secret – one-minute praising – is the key to improved performance and increased productivity. Instead of catching people out for doing something wrong, the opposite is recommended: 'the key to developing people is to catch them doing something right'. There are three steps in one-minute praising.

- Praise someone as close in time to the good behaviour as possible. If you can't find someone to praise every day, then you should wonder why.
- Be specific. Make it clear what it was that was performed well.
- Share feelings – tell them how you feel about what they did, not what you think about what they did.

One-minute reprimanding

The third secret of the One Minute Manager is the key to changing the attitude of the poor performer. There are four aspects to it.

- Immediacy – when a reprimand is necessary, it is best to deliver it as soon as possible after the instance of poor performance that led to it.
- Be specific – don't tell people about your reactions or give vent to your feelings, tell them what they did wrong; admonish the action, not the person.
- Share feelings – once you have established what was wrong, share your feelings.
- Tell them how good they are – the last step in the reprimand. If you finish on negative feedback, they will reflect on your style of behaviour, not on their own performance.

The development of one-minute management

Putting the One Minute Manager to Work was a follow-up in 1984 by Blanchard and co-author Richard Lorber (an expert in performance improvement) to flesh out some of the basic ideas which had met initial success in *The One Minute Manager*. Subtitled *How to Turn the Three Secrets Into Skills*, the 1984 sequel focuses on the 'ABCs' of management, 'effective reprimanding', and the 'PRICE' system.

The ABCs

- Activators – those things that a manager has to do before anyone else can be expected to achieve anything, such as goal-setting, laying down key areas of accountability, issuing instructions, and setting performance standards.
- Behaviour – or performance – what a person says or does, such as filing, writing, selling, ordering, buying etc.
- Consequence – what a manager does after performance, such as sharing feelings, praising, reprimanding, supporting etc.

Effective reprimanding

A manager has to distinguish between a situation where an employee can't do something – which implies a need for training and signals a return to the activator of goal-setting – and one where an employee won't do something – which implies an attitude problem and a case for a reprimand. Reprimands do not teach skills, they can only change attitudes. Positive consequences on the other hand can influence future performance to the good. Therefore it is important, as *The One Minute Manager* had already suggested, to end a reprimand with praise, making the employee think about his or her own behaviour, not that of the reprimander.

The PRICE system

PRICE takes the three basic secrets of one-minute management and turns them into five distinct steps.

- **Pinpointing** – defining key performance areas in measurable terms-part of one-minute goal-setting.
- **Recording** – gathering data to measure actual performance and keep track of progress.
- **Involving** – sharing the information recorded with whoever is responsible.
- **Coaching** – providing constructive feedback on improving performance.
- **Evaluating** – part of coaching, also part of reprimanding or praising.

Later works

Leadership and the One Minute Manager stresses that there is no single, best method of leadership, but that there are in fact four styles: directing, delegating, coaching, and support. Whichever style is employed depends on the situation to be managed: 'Situational leadership is not something you do to people, but something you do with people.' Blanchard turns conventional leadership thinking on its head, using the analogy of turning the organisational pyramid upside down; instead of staff working for their boss, the boss should work for the staff.

The One Minute Manager Builds High-Performing Teams can be seen as a companion to *Leadership* and concentrates on integrating the simplicity of the one-minute techniques into understanding group dynamics and adjusting leadership style to meet developing circumstances.

The One Minute Manager Meets the Monkey deals with the problems of time management and overload. Paying tribute to Bill Oncken, Blanchard's co-author who created the monkey analogy, Blanchard points the finger at the concept of the manager as the 'hero with all the answers', stressing that bosses are not there to try to tackle every problem themselves, but to get others to come up with solutions. The monkey is the problem being passed from subordinate to superior, making the superior rapidly ineffective; the one-minute manager is not a collector of monkeys; rather a facilitator and coach helping others to solve their own problems.

KENNETH BLANCHARD IN PERSPECTIVE

So where does Blanchard sit in the Hall of Fame of management thinkers?

Much of what Blanchard et al. have to say in the *One Minute Manager* series no longer seems earth-shattering today. Countless publications and endless seminars on leadership, change, delegation, and time management have, unsurprisingly, rendered a glance back to

Blanchard, an entertaining experience, yes, and a comforting one in its confirmation of what one has learned elsewhere, but – like the key message of a contemporaneous publication *In Search of Excellence* (Peters and Waterman, 1982) – one-minute management is no longer the inspiration it was.

When asked why *In Search of Excellence* did so well, critics and commentators argued that its timing was impeccable: it was published at a time when Western business concepts were being rubbished in favour of analyses of the Japanese business boom. If Peters and Waterman were largely about reinvigorating pride in successful US organisations, Blanchard's book was excellently timed for its impact on individual skills and techniques.

It is important to remember that before Blanchard, Peters, and everyone who followed in their wake, management – as far as the hard-nosed manager was concerned – was a stuffy, dry subject reserved for lengthy academic treatises and exposés. Most books – not that there were many of them – focused on building the arguments of the human relations school and tackling the monstrous scientific/bureaucratic establishment so convincingly constructed by Taylor, Ford, and Weber. Books on management were not popular, not widely read, and certainly not best-sellers. It is often claimed that Peters and Waterman changed all that. But Ken Blanchard's contribution was also hugely influential. *The One Minute Manager* may have been panned by the academics, but it did more to make management digestible, readable, and accessible to a wide audience than any of its predecessors. By means of allegory, anecdotes, and allusions, it brought management to a level where many believed they could do it and do it well. Others have followed the story-telling format of OMM, such as *One Page Management* (Khadem) and *Zapp! The Lightning of Empowerment* (Byham) to name but two.

So what is the appeal of *The One Minute Manager*, rejected (like Maslow) by academia, but wholeheartedly adopted (again like Maslow) by practising managers around the world? Blanchard's book was, first and foremost, short and to the point. Moreover, it was written in readable, everyday language, offering practical, everyday solutions to practical, everyday problems. This was no dry, stuffy theory, but a collection of honest sensible techniques to try out straight away. This is where Blanchard scored a first.

Any author who sells over 17 million copies deserves a place in the Management Hall of Fame. For Blanchard, that place has to be broadly in the human relations school alongside the great popularisers of empowerment on the one hand and the self-help school, stretching from Samuel Smiles and Dale Carnegie to present-day figures like Stephen Covey and, latterly, Tom Peters, on the other. Blanchard's message may not be original but few have spread the simple messages more effectively, or to such a wide audience.

THE BEST SOURCES OF HELP

Books:

Blanchard, Kenneth, and Spencer Johnson. *The One Minute Manager*. London: Willow Books, 1983.

Blanchard, Kenneth, and Robert Lorber. *Putting the One Minute Manager to Work*. London: Fontana, 1985.

Blanchard, Kenneth, Patricia Zigarmi, and Drea Zigarmi. *Leadership and the One Minute Manager*. London: Collins, 1986.

Blanchard, Kenneth, William Oncken, and Hal Burrows. *The One Minute Manager Meets the Monkey*. London: Collins, 1990.

Blanchard, Kenneth, Donald Carew, and Eunice Parisi-Carew. *The One Minute Manager Builds High-Performing Teams*. London: Fontana, 1993.

Blanchard, Kenneth, and Margret McBride. *The One Minute Apology*. London: HarperCollins, 2003.

Blanchard, Kenneth. *The Leadership Pill*. London: Simon & Schuster, 2005.

Dale Carnegie How to Win Friends and Influence People

Dale Carnegie's main focus is on dealing with people successfully-making them like you, and making them do what you want without making them dislike you. His best-known work, *How to Win Friends and Influence People* (1936), puts forward the essential principles for doing this; for example, you should never criticise, complain about, or condemn another person; you should give sincere appreciation to others; in order to motivate people, you need to stimulate a specific desire in them.

1888	Born.
1908	Graduates from State Teachers College, Warrensburg, Missouri.
1912	Teaches first public speaking class at YMCA in upper Manhattan.
1912 –1920	Formalises course in public speaking.

1926	Publication of textbook *Public Speaking: A Practical Course for Businessmen*.
1936	Publication of *How to Win Friends and Influence People*.
1939	Introduces sales course.
1955	Dies.

Gurus

LIFE AND CAREER

Dale Carnegie (1888–1955) came from a poor, farming background and had to struggle through college. Looking for a way to distinguish himself, he began to enter speaking contests and, despite a shaky start, was soon winning every contest he entered. On leaving college he worked for some time as a salesman, making his territory the most successful one in the company, before deciding to train and work as an actor. This was another false start, however. He gave up the stage to run his own business, and then eventually decided to write novels and support himself by teaching at night.

Carnegie's first courses on public speaking for business-people at the YMCA schools in New York were run purely on a commission basis, as he was initially refused any pay. The courses did well, however, and their popularity made him a great success. They were so successful, in fact, that he was able to turn them into a series of popular books that extended beyond his initial sphere of public speaking into the realm of human relations in general. The books, which provided simple rules on how to achieve success with people, using examples from his own and others' experiences and stories about historical figures such as Roosevelt and Lincoln, became runaway successes in their turn. Carnegie went on to found the Dale Carnegie Institute of Effective Speaking and Human Relations to spread his ideas yet further. In 1997, over 40 years after his death, *How to Win Friends and Influence People*, the book that made him internationally famous, was still on the bestseller list in Germany.

KEY THINKING

Carnegie believed that criticism was counterproductive and should never be used to try to change or motivate people. In his view, people who are criticised tend to respond by justifying themselves and condemning the critical person in return. Great leaders such as Abraham Lincoln achieved their success partly because they never criticised others. Carnegie recommended instead the practice of self-control, understanding, and forgiveness. Most importantly, he advised that you should always try to see the other person's point of view.

In order to influence people and achieve your aims, Carnegie suggests, it is necessary to understand individual motivation. You need to ask yourself what will motivate a person to want to do a task for you, before you attempt to persuade them to do it. He considers most people to be interested only in their own desires, but suggests that, if they are given what they want, they can help the giver to achieve great success in business.

People may simply want to drive a better car or buy a bigger house. For most people, however, the desire to be important is a main, if not the main motivator. It can inspire them to do great things, such as become important leaders or make their fortune in business. It can also take morbid forms. Sometimes individuals become invalids to gain attention or become insane so that they can live in a dream world where their importance is exaggerated by imagination. In any event the urge to be important should not be ignored. Using very human, anecdotal evidence, Carnegie illustrates how nourishing a person's self-esteem can achieve far better results than criticism eve could.

The rules

How to Win Friends and Influence People has 'in a nutshell' conclusions at the end of each section. In them Carnegie summarises the main messages each section offers in terms of behaviour. Some of these are paraphrased below.

Six ways to make people like you:
1. Show a genuine interest in other people.
2. Be happy and positive.
3. Remember that people love hearing the sound of their own name.
4. Listen to other people and develop good listening skills.
5. Talk about others' interests rather than your own.
6. Give others a sincere sense of their importance.

Twelve ways to win people to your way of thinking:
1. To get the best of a situation, avoid arguments.
2. Always listen to others' opinions and never tell anyone they are wrong.
3. Admit it if you are wrong.
4. Show friendliness.
5. Make statements that the other person can agree with.
6. Let the other person talk more than you.
7. Make the other person feel that an idea is their own.
8. See the other person's point of view.
9. Show empathy with others' ideas and desires.
10. Infuse some drama into your ideas.
11. Appeal to the better nature of others.
12. Finish with a challenge.

Nine ways to change people without arousing resentment:
1. Start with genuine praise and appreciation.
2. Draw attention to people's mistakes gradually.
3. Admit that you have made mistakes and then talk to other people about theirs.
4. Don't give direct orders but ask questions.
5. Never humiliate anyone, and let people keep their pride intact.
6. Use plenty of genuine praise and encouragement when there is the slightest improvement.
7. Give people a reputation to maintain.
8. Encourage people. Show them that their task is easy to accomplish.
9. Suggest what you want them to do and make them happy about it.

BECOMING A GOOD PUBLIC SPEAKER

Some of the advice given by Dale Carnegie at the start of his career, in his writing and training on public speaking, is summarised below.

Preparation

From the beginning, Carnegie suggested, you should generate an enthusiasm within yourself for public speaking, whether you have a financial or a social goal in view. Prepare as much as possible for the speech and have it ready well in advance. Begin planning as soon as you can and look for a topic that you know a lot about. Always try to use your own ideas, but bring the topic of your speech into conversation, so that you can explore any interesting stories on the subject that others may be able to tell you. Think about your talk at every possible opportunity and research it thoroughly, using libraries and other sources and collecting more material than you will need.

Do not memorise the talk word for word, as you will then be more likely to forget it. It may also lose much of its effectiveness if it seems too studied. While you should have plenty of material prepared, you should not try to say too much in the talk itself. Your material needs to be structured simply, so that you can talk as if you were in ordinary conversation.

Most people are nervous about talking in public. If you try to act bravely and pretend that you feel more confident than you really do, you will often actually gain in confidence. Practice will help you to feel more certain of yourself, and it is a good idea to rehearse your speech as much as possible, maybe in front of the mirror, or with family and friends as an audience.

Delivery

Dress the part for your speech. Smile, and make sure you are clearly visible to your audience. Show respect and affection for the audience, and let the first sentence capture their attention. Examples of techniques to help you to achieve this are:

- start with a striking incident or example
- state an arresting fact
- ask for a show of hands
- use an exhibit
- do or say something to generate suspense
- promise to tell the audience how they can get something they want

You should not, however, open a talk with either an apology or a funny story. Humorous stories can fall flat, and this is particularly likely to be the case when you are nervous.

Use statistics or the testimony of experts to support your main ideas, but know your audience and do not use technical terms if you are addressing a lay audience. Be eager to share your talk with your listeners, putting passion into your way of speaking and using your emotions without fear. Represent things visually when possible, turning a fact into a picture to help your audience to understand what you are talking about and using specific instances and concrete examples.

Stress important words and avoid hackneyed expressions or clichés. Once your talk is launched, you may feel freer to be humorous when appropriate, but take care to target any fun at yourself rather than others.

Your talk should have some marked form of closure. Summarise what you have said, then use a finalising climax or close of some sort that is appropriate within the context, for example:

- make an appeal for action
- pay the audience a sincere compliment
- raise a final laugh
- use a fitting verse of poetry or a quotation

Carnegie's concluding advice

- Remember that many famous speakers were originally terrified of speaking in public and that a certain amount of stage fright is useful.
- Predetermine your mind to success and seize every opportunity to practise.
- Remember that as you increase your experience your fear will diminish, so seek opportunities to speak in public, and believe in yourself.

DALE CARNEGIE IN PERSPECTIVE

Carnegie claimed that his theories do really work and that he had seen them transform the lives of many people. Some management writers have, however, dismissed Carnegie's ideas as being simple wisdom dressed up in a commercial coating.

Certainly, Carnegie's ideas are based on common sense and are hardly revolutionary. All his self-help books are based on down-to-earth and simply illustrated basic principles. Despite this simplicity, Carnegie has expressed many general truths which people acknowledge and, whatever his critics may say, the books he wrote are still popular.

In fact, Carnegie created a highly successful business out of his ideas, and his books have sold millions. Even today, much money is still being made from his work, which suggests that people still find him very relevant. Certainly, it is possible to see Carnegie's influence in some of today's ideas about management, particularly in discussions on the treatment of customers, and in approaches to interpersonal skills development.

THE BEST SOURCES OF HELP
Books:

Carnegie, Dale. *How to Win Friends and Influence People*. London: Hutchinson Books, 1994.
Carnegie, Dale. *How to Enjoy Your Life and Your Job*. London: Vermilion, 1990.
Carnegie, Dale. *How to Stop Worrying and Start Living*. London: Vermilion, 1990.

Alfred Chandler Business History As a Management Tool

The US academic Alfred Chandler Jr was the first historian in the modern era to both forge his own subject area and dominate it for almost half a century. When he stumbled on the genre after the Second World War, business history was just a virgin cousin of the emerging and wider-based topic called economic history, a largely theoretical discipline that deals with macrofiscal issues as they affect national and international economies.

1918	Born.
1952	Completes PhD at Harvard.
1962	Publication of *Strategy and Structure.*
1970	Appointed Isidor Strauss Professor of Business History, Harvard Business School.
1977	Publication of *The Visible Hand: The Managerial Revolution in American Business.*
2007	Dies.

LIFE AND CAREER

Chandler was born in 1918 and acquired his first interest in history from Wilbur Fiske Gordy's *Elementary History of the United States*, which his father gave him at the age of seven. He was educated at Phillips Exeter Academy, Harvard College, the University of North Carolina, where he received his MA, and Harvard University, where he completed his PhD in history in 1952. His wartime experience was with a unit responsible for analysing photographs of gunnery exercises by the Atlantic Fleet and bombing raids in the Pacific.

He acquired an interest in sociology and saw the value of explicit concepts, generalisations, and theories in analysing human behaviour, but it was when he came to choose his dissertation topic that his interest in business history was initially sparked. His great-aunt died suddenly, and Chandler and his family moved into her house, in which were stored the personal papers of his grandfather, Henry Varnum Poor. Poor, whose name survives as one half of the business information company Standard and Poor's Corporation, had been one of the people most knowledgeable about US railways, having edited the *American Railway Journal* for nearly 20 years. Using Poor's personal papers, together with the extensive back files of his newspapers and related publications in the Baker Library at Harvard, he produced a classic series of articles, his dissertation, and a book entitled *Henry Varnum Poor: Business Editor, Analyst, and Reformer*. This treatise, a seminal work on US railway companies during their formative years, enabled him to develop – through his genius at widespread comparative analysis – what became his characteristic way of extracting clear historical patterns that tended towards inductively derived theory.

Chandler's career as a working business historian began at the Massachusetts Institute of Technology, where he had the opportunity of working on the individual histories of Du Pont, General Motors, Standard Oil (now Exxon), and Sears, Roebuck & Co-a course of study that culminated in *Strategy and Structure*. At Johns Hopkins University he wrote the biography of Pierre du Pont; and in 1970 he was appointed the Isidor Strauss Professor of Business History at Harvard Business School, the world's only endowed chair in the field at the time. Until his death in May 2007 he led a growing field of teachers and studies; about 200 US academics continue to work on the subject.

KEY THINKING

Until Chandler turned to business history as his principal interest, mainstream economic history predominated as the subject matter of business education. There was, admittedly, a detour, the result of imported Western European attitudes, when both popular journalism and academia started to take an interest in the corrupt practices of businesspeople. The perception emerged that they were 'robber barons', a viewpoint that only started to change when Joseph Schumpeter's *The Theory of Economic Development*, which depicted the businessman as a force for positive advancement, was translated from German into English in 1934. Several notable academics started to re-evaluate the same robber barons as constructive, daring, and far-seeing 'industrial statesmen', who deserved credit for making the United States a predominant economic power able to defend itself and its allies from the totalitarian assaults on freedom of the 20th century. Nevertheless, it was Chandler who made business history a linchpin of the curriculum.

His work was pioneering in several other respects. It was conducted in front of a largely unreceptive audience: the majority of management educators long resisted the concept of using the real example of corporate and business history as a teaching tool. Attached to the more empirical methodologies dominated by macroeconomics and quantitative analysis, they believed that business historians painted with too broad a brush on too wide a canvas and lacked a solid or explicitly stated methodology. They also accused the genre of being largely irrelevant given the perceived pace of change. Chandler's work did much to change these attitudes, although it is instructive to note that business and management teachers – unlike educators in disciplines such as the military, politics, music, architecture, sociology, and so on – still widely resist both the concept and the development of history-based experiential learning in their own discipline. Chandler also spent his life challenging economic thinking, in particular the static equilibrium theory. Although he used the results of quantitative research, he did not employ mathematical notation, remaining sceptical of highly theorised arithmetical manipulations that, he said, while elegantly logical, distort intelligible generalisations about the past.

In shifting the focus of business history, Chandler's work, which in fact specifically addressed the process of evolution and change, uses a systematic and analytical approach that has evolved from an intellectual outlook, which he labelled 'managerial enterprise'. As he explained it, this concept moves in two directions – forward from the past to the present and backward from the present to the past. Using the former perspective, for example, he examined why early 19th-century industry did not employ any managers, a phenomenon which changed decisively and for ever in the second half of the 19th century. Using the latter perspective, he questioned the 1950s moves by industry towards decentralisation of their functionally specialised and multi-departmentalised organisations. His answers – in a landmark book entitled *Strategy and Structure*, published in 1962 – took business history into a new dimension by establishing a fresh framework and rationale for the subject. He introduced the feature of making comparisons within and between industries and over time, and enabled business history to acquire relevance in a wide range of related fields.

In *The Visible Hand*, another milestone book, Chandler used the concept of managerial enterprise to illustrate how Germany became the most powerful industrial nation in Europe before the Second World War, the United States became the most productive country in the world for 40 years until the 1960s, and Japan became its most successful competitor thereafter. For this book he won the Pulitzer Prize. These and other works – including, with Richard Tedlow, *The Coming of Managerial Capitalism* – are routinely used in at least 30 higher educational institutions in the United States and many more abroad.

Business history's role at the operational level, Chandler explains, is not about teaching specific management techniques. It has a more strategic function. Any meaningful analysis of an organisation today, he says, must be based on an accurate understanding of its past. 'Such data has to come from business history based on company records or from historically based case studies. Certainly a restructuring of enterprises to meet changing conditions requires an understanding of both why and how the existing organisation evolved and how and why competitive conditions changed. Managers facing such problems can get insights by observing the working out of such processes in other enterprises.' Companies such as McKinsey & Co and AT & T have applied *Strategy and Structure* to this end. The former, for example, has used it to teach its clients about the timing of strategic change and how to adjust their organisational structures, while the latter put it to use in one of its reorganisations.

At the wider education level, Chandler believed that business history can provide insights into the processes of businesses such as the development of competitive strategy, the restructuring of organisational forms, and the effectiveness of investment and monitoring techniques. His view was that the value of teaching business histories in universities is to make MBA students and those in more advanced management courses aware of recent as well as long-term changes in functional activities such as production, marketing, research and development, finance, labour relations, and the like; also in monitoring and coordinating the activities of the current operations of an enterprise as well as in locating resources for future production and distribution. 'Not only can the students learn something about the nature of the functions, but also the complexities of carrying out change', he said.

ALFRED CHANDLER IN PERSPECTIVE

For students and practitioners alike, Chandler's name may be remembered principally as the pioneer who placed strategy before structure in his seminal work published in 1962. Not only did he champion the systematic study of modern bureaucratic administration in an original way, he also turned what is often dismissed as an artless medium into a valid and powerful educational tool. Using the conglomerate history of individual companies to arrive at a historical theory of big business instead of the mainstream-economic-discipline of the day, he revolutionised the fledgling discipline by refocusing attention away from individual entrepreneurs and seeking patterns in the rise of large-scale modern business. Almost uniquely, his work – which has given rise to the term 'Chandlerianism' – has had a profound effect on historians and business thinking all over the world, particularly in Japan and Germany.

History will no doubt bestow on him with the distinction of giving modern management educators a less theoretical way of teaching the business of business. In essence, he has skilfully recycled the tried and tested past to provide both practising and aspiring managers with an inheritance that has practical corporate application in today's highly competitive world. In truth, history is the only way individuals and companies can learn from experience. And learning from experience is the only way to increase productivity and competitiveness.

THE BEST SOURCES OF HELP
Selected books:

Chandler, Alfred. *Strategy and Structure*. Cambridge, Massachusetts: MIT Press, 1962.

Chandler, Alfred. *The Visible Hand: The Managerial Revolution in American Business*. Cambridge, Massachusetts: Harvard University Press, 1977.

Chandler, Alfred. *The Dynamic Firm*. Oxford: Oxford University Press, 1998.

Chandler, Alfred. *Inventing the Electronic Century*. Cambridge, Massachusetts: Harvard University Press, 2005.

Chandler, Alfred. *Shaping the Industrial Century*. Cambridge, Massachusetts: Harvard University Press, 2005.

REFERENCES: Both quotations are extracts from private correspondence with Chandler.

Stephen Covey The Seven Habits of Highly Effective People

In *The Seven Habits of Highly Effective People*, Stephen Covey offers a holistic approach to life and work that has struck a significant chord with the perplexed manager working in turbulent times. The recurring themes in his various works are the transforming power of principles rooted in unchanging natural laws that govern human and organisational effectiveness; the necessity of adapting every aspect of one's life to accord with these principles; effective leadership; and empowerment.

1932	Born.
1985	Founds Covey Leadership Center.
1989	Publication of *The Seven Habits of Highly Effective People*.
1997	Covey Leadership Center merges with Franklin Quest.

LIFE AND CAREER

Stephen Covey is founder and chairman of the Covey Leadership Center – now part of Franklin Covey – and the Institute for Principle – Centered Leadership in Utah. Born in 1932, he received an MBA from Harvard Business School and a doctorate from Brigham Young University, where he was subsequently Professor of Organizational Behavior and Business Management.

At the Covey Leadership Center, through his writing-chiefly *The Seven Habits of Highly Effective People* (which has sold over five million copies) – and through consultancy (he was invited to Camp David by President Clinton), his message has reached millions of individuals in business, government, and education.

KEY THINKING

The Seven Habits of Highly Effective People

The Seven Habits is addressed to readers not only in their capacity as managers, but also as members of a family, and as social, spiritual, sporting, and thinking individuals. It offers a 'life-transforming prescription', which calls for a rethink of many fundamental assumptions and attitudes (paradigms), and builds on the fundamental concept of interdependence. Covey traces a personal development outline from:

- dependence in childhood (many people never grow out of a dependency culture), through. . .
- independence in adolescence - self-assurance, a developing personality, and a positive mental attitude, to. . .
- interdependence - recognition that the optimum outcome results from each individual giving of his or her best, aiming for a common goal, and sharing the same mission and vision, but having the freedom to use his or her best judgment as to how to go about achieving that common goal.

Habit 1

Be proactive.

Covey distinguishes between proactive people – those who focus their efforts on things which they can do something about – and reactive people, who blame, accuse, behave like victims, pick on other people's weaknesses, and complain about external factors over which they have no control (for example, the weather).

Proactive people are responsible for their own lives. Covey breaks down the word *responsibility* into 'response' and 'ability'. Proactive people recognise their responsibility to make things happen. Those who allow their feelings to control their actions have abdicated responsibility and empowered their feelings. When proactive people make a mistake, they not only recognise it as such and acknowledge it, they also correct it if possible and, most importantly, learn from it.

Habit 2

Begin with the end in mind.

Leadership is about effectiveness – the vision of what is to be accomplished. It calls for direction (in every sense of the word), purpose, and sensitivity. Management, on the other hand, is about efficiency – how best to accomplish the vision. It depends on control, guidance, and rules.

To identify the end, and to formulate one's route or strategy to achieving that end, Covey maintains the need for a 'principle-centred' basis to all aspects of life. Most people adopt something as the basis (or pivotal point) of their life – spouse, family, money, church, pleasure, friends (and, in a perverse way, enemies), sport, etc. Of course all of these have some influence over the life of every individual. However, only by clearly establishing one's own principles, in the form of a personal mission, does one have a solid foundation.

Habit 3

Put first things first.

Covey's first major work, *First Things First*, sets out his views on time management. It argues that the important thing is not managing time, but managing oneself, focusing on results rather than on methods when prioritising within each compartment of work and life.

He breaks down life's activities into four quadrants:

Quadrant 1: Urgent and important – for example, crises, deadlines, unexpected opportunities.

Quadrant 2: Not urgent, but important – for example, planning, recreation, relationship-building, doing, learning.

Quadrant 3: Urgent, but not important – for example, interruptions, meetings.

Quadrant 4: Not urgent and not important – for example, trivia, time wasters, gossip.

Essentially all activity of effective people should focus on the second quadrant, apart from the genuinely unpredictable quadrant 1 events. However, effective planning and doing in Quadrant 2 should minimise the number of occasions on which crises occur.

The outcomes of a Quadrant 2 focus include: vision, perspective, balance, discipline, and control. On the other hand, the results of placing one's main focus on the other quadrants are:

Quadrant 1: stress, burn-out, inability to manage time (and thus loss of control of one's own life).

Quadrant 3: short-termism, loss of control, shallowness, feelings of being a victim of circumstances.

Quadrant 4: irresponsibility, dependency, unsuitability for employment.

Habit 3 is therefore about managing oneself effectively, by prioritising according to the principles adopted in Habit 2. This approach transcends the office diary or day-planner, embracing all roles in life – as manager, mentor, administrator, strategist, and also as parent, spouse, member of social groups, and as an individual with needs and aspirations.

Habits 1–3 are grouped under the banner 'Private Victory'. They are about the development of the personal attributes that provide the foundations for independence. Habits 4–6 are described by Covey as the 'Public Victory', as they are the basic paradigms of interdependence.

Habit 4
Think win/win.

Interdependence occurs when there is co-operation, not competition, in the workplace (or the home). Covey holds that competition belongs in the marketplace.

Covey points out that, from childhood, many people are conditioned to a win/lose mentality by school examinations, by parental approval being rationed to 'success', by external comparisons and league tables. This results in a 'scarcity mentality', a belief that there is only a finite cake to be shared: evident in people who have difficulty in sharing recognition or credit, power or profit. It restricts their ability to celebrate other people's success, and even brings about a perverse satisfaction at others' misfortune.

By contrast Covey advocates an 'abundance mentality' that:
- recognises unlimited possibilities for positive growth and development
- celebrates success, recognising that one person's success is not achieved at the expense, or to the exclusion, of others
- understands and seeks a win/win solution

Covey argues that, to be true to your ideals, it is sometimes necessary to walk away, if the other party is interested only in a win/lose outcome. Covey describes this as 'win/win or no deal'.

Habit 5
Seek first to understand, then to be understood.

'I just can't understand my son . . . he won't listen to me.' The absurdity of this statement is highlighted by Covey in emphasising the importance of listening in order to understand. Clearly, the parent needs to stop and listen to the son if he or she truly wants to understand him.

However, most people want to make their point first, or are so busy looking for their opportunity to butt into the conversation that they fail to hear and understand the other party. Covey defines the different levels of listening as:
- hearing but ignoring
- pretending to listen ('Yes', 'Oh', 'I see. . .')
- selective listening (choosing to hear only what we want to hear)
- attentive listening, without evaluation (e.g. taking notes at a lecture)
- empathetic listening (with intent to understand the other party)

True empathetic listening requires a great deal of personal security, as one is vulnerable to being influenced, to having one's opinions changed. 'The more deeply you understand other people,' Covey says, 'the more you appreciate them, the more reverent you feel about them.'

Likewise, when you feel that someone is genuinely seeking to understand your point of view, you recognise and share their openness and willingness to negotiate and to reach a win/win situation.

Habit 6
Synergise.

The essence of synergy is where two parties, each with a different agenda, value each other's differences. Everything in nature is synergistic, with every creature and plant being interdependent with others.

We also have personal effectiveness where there is synergy at an individual level – where both sides of the brain are working in tandem on a problem or situation, the intuitive, creative, visual right side and the analytical, logical, verbal left side combining to achieve the optimum outcome.

Synergy is lacking in insecure people: they either clone others, or else try to stereotype them. Of such insecurity is born prejudice – racism, bigotry, nationalism, and any other form of prejudging others.

Habit 7
Sharpen the saw.

The seventh and final habit relates to renewal. Just as a motor car or any other sophisticated tool needs regular care and maintenance, so too do the human body and mind.

Covey uses the metaphor of a woodcutter who is labouring painfully to saw down a tree. The saw is obviously in need of sharpening, but when asked why he doesn't stop and sharpen the saw, the woodcutter replies, 'I can't stop – I'm too busy sawing down this tree.'

The warning is quite clear. Everyone can become so engrossed in the task in hand that the basic tools are neglected:

- the physical self – which requires exercise, a sensible and balanced diet, and management of stress
- the social/emotional self – which connects with others through service, empathy, and synergy, and which is the source of intrinsic security
- the spiritual self – which through meditation, reflection, prayer, and study helps to clarify and refine our own values and strengths, and our commitment to them
- the mental self – building on to our formal education through reading, visualising, planning, writing, and maintaining a coherent programme of continuing personal development

STEPHEN COVEY IN PERSPECTIVE

Commentators have both attacked and applauded Covey's approach for mixing the self-help message, which can be traced back to Samuel Smiles, with the positive self-drive of winning friends and influencing people (Dale Carnegie), current management theories, and religious fervour.

In times of change and confusion, however, when failure, redundancy, and unemployment dominate individual thinking and lead to stress, Covey's message offers the individual something to hang on to. *First Things First*, co-authored with Roger and Rebecca Merrill, has achieved twice the sales of *The Seven Habits* over the same period.

He is undoubtedly a philosopher for our times, highlighting the significance of changing industrial and human relations in this post-confrontational era, and recognising the potential of the untapped resources within each individual.

THE BEST SOURCES OF HELP
Books:
Covey, Stephen. *The Seven Habits of Highly Effective People*. London: Simon & Schuster, 1989.
Covey, Stephen. *Principle-centered Leadership*. London: Simon & Schuster, 1992.
Covey, Stephen, A. Roger Merrill and Rebecca R. Merrill. *First Things First*. London: Simon & Schuster, 1996.
Covey, Stephen. *The Eighth Habit: From Effectiveness to Greatness*. London: Simon & Schuster, 2006.
Covey, Stephen. *The Leader in Me: How Schools and Parents Around the World Are Inspiring Greatness, One Child at a Time* London: Simon & Schuster, 2008.

Philip Crosby Zero Defects

Philip Crosby wrote the best-seller *Quality Is Free* at a time when the quality movement was a rising, innovative force in business and manufacturing. In the 1980s, his consultancy was advising 40 percent of the Fortune 500 companies on quality management.

His popularity as a consultant can be partly attributed to his ability to talk about quality management ideas in terms that were easy to understand, and this ability was undoubtedly the result of over 40 years' hands-on management experience.

1926	Born.
1952	After war service, begins his career working on an assembly line.
1961	Establishes 'zero concepts' while working for Martin-Marietta.
1965	Joins ITT.
1979	*Quality is Free* published. Leaves ITT to found Philip Crosby Associates II, Inc.
1984	*Quality without Tears* published.
1988	*The Eternally Successful Organization* published.
1991	Launches Career IV Inc.
2001	Dies.

LIFE AND CAREER

Crosby was born in West Virginia in 1926. A graduate of Western Reserve University, he saw service in the Korean War, and started his working life on the assembly line in 1952, becoming quality manager for Martin-Marietta where he developed the 'zero defects' concept. After working his way up, Crosby was corporate vice-president and director of quality at ITT for 14 years.

As a result of the interest shown in *Quality Is Free* (1979), he left ITT to set up Philip Crosby Associates II, Inc and started to teach organisations quality principles and practice as laid down in his book. In 1985, his company was floated for $30 million. In 1991 he retired from Philip Crosby Associates to launch Career IV Inc, a consultancy advising on the development of senior executives. He died in August 2001.

KEY THINKING

Quality, Crosby emphasised, is neither intangible nor immeasurable. It is a strategic imperative, something that can be quantified and put to work to improve the bottom line. 'Acceptable' quality or defect levels produced by means of traditional quality control measures, for Crosby, represent evidence of failure rather than an assurance of success. The goal is to meet requirements on time, first time, and every time. The emphasis, therefore, should be on prevention, not inspection and cure.

Crosby's approach to quality was unambiguous. In his view, good, bad, high, and low quality are meaningless concepts in the abstract; the meaning of quality is 'conformance to requirements'. What that means is that a product should conform to the requirements that the company has itself established based on its customers' needs. He also believed that the prime responsibility for poor quality lies with management, not with the workers. Management sets the tone for the quality initiative from the top.

Nonconforming products are ones that management has failed to specify or control. The cost of non-conformance equals the cost of not doing it right first time, and not rooting out any defects in processes.

'Zero defects' does not mean that people never make mistakes, but that companies should not begin with 'allowances' or substandard targets with mistakes as an in-built expectation. Instead, work should be seen as a series of activities or processes, defined by clear requirements and carried out to produce identified outcomes. Systems that allow things to go wrong – and that result in those things having to be done again – can cost organisations between 20 percent and 35 percent of their revenues, in Crosby's estimation.

His seminal approach to quality was set out in *Quality Is Free*, and is often summarised as the 'Fourteen Steps'.

The Fourteen Steps

1. Management commitment: the need for quality improvement must be recognised and accepted by management, who then draw up a quality improvement programme with an emphasis on the need for defect prevention. Quality improvement equates to profit improvement. A quality policy is needed which states that '. . . each individual is expected to perform exactly like the requirement or cause the requirement to be officially changed to what we and the customer really need.'

2. The quality improvement team: representatives from each department or function should be brought together to form a quality improvement team. Its members should be people who have sufficient authority to commit the area they represent to action.

3. Quality measurement: the status of quality should be determined throughout the company. This means establishing and recording quality measures for each area of activity in order to show where improvement is possible and where corrective action is necessary. Crosby advocated delegation of this task to the people who actually do the job, thus setting the stage for defect prevention on the job, where it really counts.

4. The cost of quality evaluation: the cost of quality is not an absolute performance measurement, but an indication of where the action necessary to correct a defect will result in greater profitability.

5. Quality awareness: this involves making employees aware of the cost to the company of defects, through training and information, and the provision of visible evidence of the results of a concern for quality improvement. Crosby stressed that this sharing process is a key, or even *the* key, step in the progress of an organisation towards quality.

6. Corrective action: discussion of problems will result in the finding of solutions and will also bring to light other elements that are in need of improvement. People need to see that problems are regularly being resolved. Corrective action should then become a habit.

7. Establishing an ad hoc committee for the zero defects programme: zero defects is not a motivation programme: its purpose is to communicate and instil the notion that everyone should do things right first time.

8. Supervisor training: all managers should undergo formal training on the Fourteen Steps before they are implemented. Managers should understand each of the Fourteen Steps well enough to be able to explain them to their people.

9. Zero defects day: it is important that the commitment to zero defects as the performance standard of the company makes an impact, and that everyone gets the same message in the same way. Zero defects day, when supervisors explain the programme to their people, should make a lasting impression as a 'new attitude' day.

10. Goal setting: all supervisors ask their people to establish specific, measurable goals that they can strive for. Usually, these comprise 30-, 60-, and 90-day goals.

11. Error-cause removal: employees are asked to describe, on a simple, one-page form, any problems that prevent them from carrying out error-free work. Problems should be acknowledged and begin to be addressed within 24 hours by the function or unit to which the memorandum is directed. This constitutes a key step in building trust, as it will make people begin to grow more confident that their problems will be attended to and dealt with.

12. Recognition: it is important to recognise those who meet their goals or perform outstanding acts with a prize or award, although this should not be in financial form. The act of recognition itself is what is important.

13. Quality councils: the quality professionals and team leaders should meet regularly to discuss improvements and upgrades to the quality programme.

14. Doing it over again: during the course of a typical programme lasting from 12 to 18 months, turnover and change will dissipate much of the educational process. It is important to set up a new team of representatives and begin the programme again from the beginning, starting with zero defects day. This 'starting over again' helps quality to become ingrained in the organisation.

PUTTING QUALITY TO THE TEST

Crosby often used stories to convey his message and also used audit techniques and questionnaires to clarify organisational and individual understanding.

Below we reproduce a quick 'true or false' questionnaire that features in *Quality Is Free* (the answers are given at the end of this piece).

1. Quality is a measure of goodness of the product that can be defined as fair, good, excellent.
2. The economics of quality require that management establish acceptable quality levels as performance standards.
3. The cost of quality is the expense of doing things wrong.
4. Inspection and test should report to manufacturing so manufacturing can have the proper tools to do the job.
5. Quality is the responsibility of the quality department.
6. Worker attitudes are the primary cause of defects.
7. I have trend charts that show me the rejection level at every key operation.
8. I have a list of the ten biggest quality problems.
9. Zero defects is a worker motivation programme.
10. The biggest problem today is that customers don't understand.

LATER WORK

In his 1984 book, *Quality Without Tears*, Crosby developed the idea of a 'quality vaccination serum', which would be made up of the following ingredients:

- integrity for the chief executive officer, all managers, and all employees
- systems for measuring conformance, and educating all employees and suppliers so that quality, corrective action, and defect prevention become routine
- communications that enable problems to be identified, progress to be conveyed, and achievement to be recognised
- operations organised in such a way that procedures, products, and systems are proven before they are implemented and are then continually examined
- policies that are clear, unambiguous, and establish the primacy of quality throughout the organisation

The Eternally Successful Organization (1988) presented a broader approach to improvements. In it Crosby identi-fied five characteristics essential for an organisation to be successful:

- people routinely do things right the first time
- change is anticipated and used to advantage
- growth is consistent and profitable
- new products and services appear when needed
- everyone is happy to work there

PHILIP CROSBY IN PERSPECTIVE

Throughout his work, Crosby's thinking was consistently characterised by four absolutes:

- the definition of quality is conformance to requirements
- the system of quality is prevention
- the performance standard is zero defects
- the measurement of quality is the price of non-conformance

The major contribution made by Crosby to management thinking is indicated by the fact that his phrases 'zero defects', 'getting it right first time', and 'conformance to requirements' have now entered not only the vocabulary of quality itself, but also the general vocabulary of management.

When Crosby's name is not mentioned in the very same sentence as the best-known quality thinker of them all, Deming, then it is almost certain to be mentioned in the next. Crosby's practical and easy-to-read books on quality became-and remain-bibles for many, demystifying a great deal of the jargon formerly associated with quality management. His timing was perfect for the quality movement, and his writing has marketed quality to a wide audience.

ANSWERS TO QUESTIONNAIRE

1. F; 2. F; 3. T; 4. F; 5. F; 6. F; 7. T; 8. F; 9. F; 10. F

THE BEST SOURCES OF HELP

Books:

Crosby, Philip. *Quality Is Free: The Art of Making Quality Certain*. New York: McGraw-Hill, 1979.

Crosby, Philip. *Quality Without Tears: The Art of Hassle-Free Management*. New York: McGraw-Hill, 1984.

Crosby, Philip. *The Eternally Successful Organization: The Art of Corporate Wellness*. New York: McGraw-Hill, 1988.

Gurus

W. Edwards Deming Total Quality Management

W. Edwards Deming is widely acknowledged as the leading management thinker in the field of quality. He is credited with being the most influential catalyst of Japan's post-war economic transformation, although it wasn't until much later that the value of his ideas and practices began to be recognised by the US manufacturing and service industries.

1900	Born.
1928	Completes PhD at Yale.
1950	Begins teaching quality management in Japan.
1986	Publication of *Out of the Crisis*.
1987	Receives US National Medal of Technology.
1993	Founds W. Edwards Deming Institute.
1993	Dies.

LIFE AND CAREER

Deming obtained a PhD in mathematical physics from Yale University in 1928 and concentrated on lecturing and writing on mathematics, physics, and statistics for the next ten years. It was only in the late 1930s that he became familiar with the work of Walter Shewhart, who was experimenting with the application of statistical techniques to manufacturing processes. Deming became interested in applying Shewhart's techniques to non-manufacturing processes, particularly clerical, administrative, and management activities. After joining the US Census Bureau in 1939, he applied statistical process control to their techniques, which contributed to a six-fold improvement in productivity. Around this time he also started to run courses for engineers and designers on his – and Shewhart's – evolving methods of statistical process control.

Deming's expertise as a statistician was instrumental in his posting to Japan after the Second World War as an adviser to the Japanese Census. At this time the United States was the leading economic power, with products much envied by the rest of the world; it saw no need for Deming's new ideas. The Japanese, on the other hand, recognised that their own goods were shoddy by international standards. Moreover, after the war, they could not afford the wastage of raw materials that post-production inspection processes brought about and so were looking for techniques to help them address these problems. While in Japan, Deming became involved with the Union of Japanese Scientists and Engineers (JUSE) and his career of lecturing to the Japanese on statistical methods and company-wide quality, a combination of techniques now known as Total Quality Management (TQM), had begun.

It was only in the late 1970s that the United States became aware of his achievements in Japan. The 1980s saw a spate of publications explaining his work and influence. In his US seminars during 1980, Deming talked of the need for the total transformation of Western-style management. In 1986 he published *Out of the Crisis*, which documented the thinking and practice that had led to the transformation of Japanese manufacturing industry. His ideas gained acceptance in the United Kingdom following the foundation of the British Deming Association in 1987. Deming died in 1993.

KEY THINKING

Deming's work and writing constitute not so much a technique as a philosophy of management, one that focuses on quality and continuous improvement, but that has also, justifiably, had a much wider influence.

Below we consider Deming's interest in variation and his approach to systematic problem-solving, which led on to his development of the 14 points that have gained widespread recognition and are central to the quality movement.

Variation and problem-solving

The key to Deming's ideas on quality lies in his recognition of the importance of variation. In *Out of the Crisis* he states that 'the central problem in management and in leadership . . . is failure to understand the information in variation.'

Deming was preoccupied with why things do not behave as predicted. All systems (be they the equipment, the process, or the people) have variation, but, he argued, it is essential for managers to be able to distinguish between special and common causes of variation. He developed a theory of variation: that special causes of variation are usually attributable to easily recognisable factors such as a change of procedure, change of shift or operator, and so on, but that common causes will remain when special causes have been eliminated and are normally inherent in the design, process, or system. These common causes often are recognised by workers, but only managers have the authority to change them to avoid repeated occurrence of the problem. Deming estimated that management was responsible for more than 85 percent of the causes of variation. This formed his central message to the Japanese.

Deming's 14 points for management

Deming created 14 points that provided a framework for developing knowledge in the workplace and guiding long-term business plans and aims. The points constitute not so much an action plan as a philosophical code for management. They have been extensively interpreted, both by commentators on quality control and by experts on other management disciplines.

- Create constancy of purpose towards the improvement of products and services, with the aim of becoming competitive, staying in business, and providing jobs.

- Adopt the new philosophy. Western management must awaken to the challenge, learn its responsibilities, and take on leadership for change.
- Cease dependence on mass inspection. Build quality into the product from the start.
- End the practice of awarding business on the basis of price tag alone. Instead, minimise total cost. Move towards a single supplier for any item, based on a long-term relationship of loyalty and trust.
- Improve constantly and forever the system of production and service to improve quality and reduce waste.
- Institute training and retraining.
- Institute leadership. The aim of supervision should be to lead and help people to do a better job.
- Drive out fear so that everyone may work effectively for the company.
- Break down barriers between departments. People in research, design, sales, and production must work as a team, to foresee and solve problems of production.
- Eliminate slogans, exhortations, and targets for the workforce, as they do not necessarily achieve their aims.
- Eliminate numerical quotas in order to take account of quality and methods, rather than just numbers.
- Remove barriers to pride in workmanship.
- Institute a vigorous programme of education and retraining for both the management and the workforce.
- Take appropriate action to accomplish the transformation. Management and workforce must work together.

These principles are relevant to management in general, not simply to quality and process control. They contributed to Deming's status as a founder of the Quality Management movement, and attracted an audience much wider than the quality lobby.

W. EDWARDS DEMING IN PERSPECTIVE

Naturally enough, no one as universally acclaimed as Deming escapes without criticism. Some have criticised his approach as being good for improvement but uninspiring for creativity and innovation. Others say his approach is not effective in generating new products or penetrating new markets.

Others – particularly Juran, another quality guru – accuse him of over-reliance on statistical methods. Deming's US lectures in the 1980s, however, point time and time again to a mistaken preoccupation with the wrong type of statistics. He argued against figures that focused purely on productivity and control and argued for more evidence of quality, a message that Tom Peters adopted in the 1980s and 1990s.

Deming also stirred up wide interest with his rejection of management by objectives and performance appraisals. Similarly, his attitude toward integrating the workforce led TQM to be perceived as a caring philosophy. Paradoxically, however, his focus on cost-reduction has been pointed to as a cause of downsizing.

Although in the 1980s the United States paid tribute to Deming-not only for what he did in Japan, but also for his thinking and approach to quality management – few US companies use his methods today. One reason for this is perhaps that, by the 1980s, Deming was selling a system that worked, thereby implying that he had discovered the only way to achieve quality; thus he was no longer alert to changes in the problems. In Japan, in the beginning, he had listened to Japanese needs and requirements, showed them respect, and developed his thinking with them. In the United States of the 1980s, he appeared to try to dispense his philosophy rather than readapt it to a different culture.

In 1951, in early recognition of their debt to Deming, the JUSE awarded the Deming prize to Japanese organisations that excelled in company-wide quality. It was not until the 1980s that the United States recognised Deming's achievements in Japan and elevated him to guru status. In 1987 the British Deming Association was founded to disseminate his ideas in the United Kingdom. From the 1990s it seemed as if Deming's legacy was likely to have both a lasting and significant impact on management theory. Why is this?

The first reason must lie in the nature of his achievement. Deming has been universally acclaimed as one of the founding fathers of Total Quality Management, if not the founding father. The revolution in Japanese manufacturing management that led to the economic miracle of the 1970s and 1980s has been attributed largely to him.

Second, if the 14 points make less of an impact today than they did just after the Second World War in Japan, it is probably because many aspects of those points were adopted, assimilated, and integrated into management practice in the 1990s and have been continuously debated and taught in business schools around the world.

The third reason is more complex and lies in the scope of his legacy. Deming's 14 points add up to a code of management philosophy that spans the two major schools of managerial thought that have predominated since the early 20th century: scientific (hard) management on the one hand, and human relations (soft) management on the other. Deming succeeds – despite criticisms of his over-use of statistical techniques – in marrying them together. Over half of his 14 points focus on people as opposed to systems. Many management thinkers veer towards one school or the other. Deming, like Drucker, melds them together.

The originality and freshness of Deming is that he took his philosophy not from the world of management, but from the world of mathematics, and wedded it with a human relations approach that did not come from management theory, but from observation and from seeing what people needed from their working environment in order to contribute their best.

THE BEST SOURCES OF HELP

Book:

Deming, W. Edwards. *Out of the Crisis: Quality, Productivity, and Competitive Position.* Cambridge: Cambridge University Press, 1986.

Peter Drucker The Father of Post-war Management

Peter Drucker was known throughout the world as *the* management guru. He did not claim to have invented management – but conceded that he discovered it as a way of life central to the well-being of society and the economy.

With more than 33 books published over seven decades Drucker was, by common consent, the founding father of modern management studies.

1909	Born.
1927	Commences study at University of Hamburg.
1931	Doctorate in Public and International Law, University of Frankfurt, Germany.
1933	Moves to London to work as an investment banker.
1937	Leaves for United States to become investment adviser and correspondent for *Financial News*.
1939	Publication of *The End of Economic Man*.
1940	Private consultant to business and on government policy; teacher at Sarah Lawrence College; Professor at Bennington College, Vermont.
1943	Spends 18 months interviewing senior management at General Motors, which results in the bestselling *The Concept of the Corporation* (1946).
1950	Professor of Management at New York University Graduate School of Business.
1969	Publication of *The Age of Discontinuity*.
1971	Marie Rankin Clarke Professor of Management, Graduate School, Claremont.
1974	Publication of Management: *Tasks, Responsibilities, Practices*.
1975	Columnist for *Wall Street Journal*.
1990	Founding of The Peter F. Drucker Foundation for Non-Profit Management.
1999	Publication of *Management Challenges for the 21st Century*.
2005	Dies.

LIFE AND CAREER

Peter Ferdinand Drucker was born in Vienna in 1909 into a high-achieving, intellectual family and was surrounded in his early years by members of the pre-war Viennese cultural elite. He commenced his studies at the University of Hamburg, but transferred to the University of Frankfurt, where he obtained a Doctorate in Public and International Law in 1931.

While still a student in Frankfurt he worked on the city's *General Anzeiger* newspaper and rose to the posts of foreign and financial editor. Recognised as a talented writer, he was offered a job in the Ministry of Information.

Observing the Nazis' rise to power with abhorrence, he wrote a philosophical essay condemning Nazism; this was probably instrumental in hastening his departure to England in 1933. It was in 1937 that he left for the United States to become an investment adviser to British industry and correspondent for several British newspapers, including the *Financial Times*, then called the *Financial News*.

His first book, *The End of Economic Man*, appeared in 1939. In 1940 he set up as a private consultant to business and government policy-makers, specialising in the German economy and external politics. From 1940 to 1942 he was a teacher at Sarah Lawrence College, and this was followed by the post of Professor of Philosophy, Politics, History, and Religion at Bennington College, Vermont.

It was in the early stages of this appointment that he was invited by the vice-president of General Motors (GM) to investigate what constitutes a modern organisation, and to examine what the managers running it actually do. Although Drucker was relatively inexperienced in business at the time, his analysis led to the publication, in 1946, of *The Concept of the Corporation* – published as *Big Business* in the United Kingdom – which had a mixed reception but nonetheless confirmed Drucker's future as a management writer.

The period 1950–1972 was a time of prolific writing, teaching, and consulting while he was Professor of Management at New York University Graduate School of Business. In 1971 he was appointed the Marie Rankin Clarke Professor of Social Science and Management at the Graduate School in Claremont, a school that was subsequently named after him. In 1994 he was appointed Godkin Lecturer at Harvard University.

Drucker held decorations from the governments of Austria and Japan as well as 22 honorary doctorates from universities in Belgium, Japan, Spain, Switzerland, the United Kingdom, and the United States. He was also a Fellow of the American Association of Science; an Honorary Member of the National Academy of Public Administration; a Fellow of the American Academy of Arts and Sciences; and a Fellow of the American, British, Irish, and International Academies of Management.

KEY THINKING

Drucker's management writings are phenomenal in their coverage and impressive in their clarity. With over 33 books to his credit, we can provide only a snapshot of his thinking here. His earlier works made a significant contribution to establishing what constitutes management practice; his later works tackle the complexities – and the management implications – of the post-industrial 1980s and beyond. It is that range and development that we have tried to represent in our comments on the books covered here.

The End of Economic Man – 1939

The End of Economic Man concentrates on the politics and economics of the 1930s in general and the rise of Nazism in particular; Drucker signalled a warning about the Holocaust and predicted that Hitler would forge an alliance with Stalin. This was his first book in English as sole author; J.B. Priestley said of it: 'At once the most penetrating and the most stimulating book I have read on the world crisis. At last there is a ray of light in the dark chaos.'

This was followed by *The Future of Industrial Man* (1942), which assumed Hitler's defeat and started to look ahead to peacetime, warning of the dangers of an approach to planning founded on the denial of freedom. It attracted the interest of critics, who argued that it mixed economics with social sciences; it was, in fact, the first book to argue that any organisation is both an economic and social organ. As such it laid the foundations for Drucker's interest in management in general and, as it turned out, General Motors in particular.

The Concept of the Corporation – 1946

When General Motors invited Drucker to write about the company, it was expected that the invitation would result in a glowing description of GM's success. What in fact emerged was something different, something that recognised success but also looked to the future.

General Motors provided Drucker with the opportunity to test in practice the theory he had propounded in *The Future of Industrial Man*, i.e. that an organisation was essentially a social system as well as an economic one. *The Concept of the Corporation* questioned whether what had worked in the past – a foolproof system of objective policies and procedures throughout every layer of the organisation – would continue to work in a future of global competition, changing social values, and automation, and with the drive for quality and the growth of the knowledge worker.

The assembly line, he argued, actually created inefficiency because activity took place at the pace of the slowest. Demotivation was rife because no one saw the end result, and initiative was stifled by the minutiae of checks, rules, and controls. The layers of bureaucracy slowed down decision-making, created adversarial labour relations, and did nothing to create a 'self-governing plant community' (the phrase Drucker used for an empowered workforce). Drucker reported the benefits of decentralised operations – an issue that critics were quick to praise and organisations quick to mimic – but suggested that the GM hierarchy of commands and controls would be slow to respond in a rapidly changing future.

The fundamental difference between Drucker and GM was that GM saw the workforce as a cost in the quest for profits, whereas Drucker saw people as a resource who would be better able to satisfy customers if they had more involvement in their jobs and gained some satisfaction from doing them. *The Concept of the Corporation*, consequently, was decades ahead of its time in terms of its espousal of empowerment and self-management.

Although Alfred Sloan – the chief executive and powerhouse behind General Motors' success – had no time for Drucker's book, Drucker was, in the early 1950s, to advise Sloan on setting up a School of Administration at MIT. His criticism of Sloan was implicit rather than explicit, saying he had vision rather than perspective, and implying that leadership had been sacrificed to the rulebook. Sloan was measured in his reply – after all, at the time, General Motors was the largest and arguably one of the most successful companies in the world. His response came in 1963 with the publication of *My Years with General Motors*, which sets out the scientific credo of GM's philosophy, yet talks little of people, transparently because they had little importance relative to the systems they were following.

Another effect of *The Concept of the Corporation* was the establishment of management as a discipline, bringing to the fore the notions of:

- the social and environmental responsibility of the organisation
- the relationship between the individual and the organisation
- the role of top management and the decision-making process
- the need for continual training and retraining of managers with the focus on their own responsibility for self-development
- the nature of labour relations
- the imperatives of community and customer relations

It is telling that Japanese industry listened to these messages and US industry did not.

The Practice of Management – 1954

The Practice of Management was Drucker's second book on management, and it established him as a leader in his field. It set trends in management for decades, and reputations were built by adopting and expanding on the ideas that he set out. It is still regarded by many as the definitive management text.

Drucker states that there is only one valid purpose for the existence of a business: that is, to create a customer. It is not, he argues, the internal structure, controls, organisation, and procedures that keep a business afloat; rather, it is the customer – who pays, and decides what is important – who fills this role. He sets out eight areas in which objectives should be set and performance should be measured:

- market standing
- innovation
- productivity
- physical and financial resources
- profitability
- managers' performance and development
- workers' performance and attitude
- public responsibility

The Practice of Management is probably best remembered for setting out the principles of Management by Objectives and Self Control (Drucker's term, although he didn't coin it) – a management process that has become the accepted basis for management theory and practice.

The book also identified the seven tasks of the manager of tomorrow. He or she must:

Gurus

- manage by objectives
- take risks and allow risk-taking decisions to take place at lower levels in the organisation
- be able to make strategic decisions
- be able to build an integrated team whose members are capable of managing and measuring their own performance and results in relation to overall objectives
- be able to communicate information quickly and clearly, and motivate employees so as to gain commitment and participation
- be able to see the business as a whole and to integrate his or her function within it
- be able to relate the product and industry to the total environment, to find out what is important and what needs to be taken into account. This perspective must embrace developments outside the company's particular market or country, and the manager must begin to see economic, political, and social developments on a worldwide scale

Management: Tasks, Responsibilities, Practices – 1974
Much of the work in *The Practice of Management* is updated, expanded, and revised in *Management: Tasks, Responsibilities, Practices*, which establishes where management has come from, where it is now, and where it needs to go. It draws upon a wide range of international examples and sets out principles for managers and management. Effectively, it is a complete management handbook.

Moving on from his earlier work, Drucker defines the manager's work in terms of five basic operations. He or she:
- sets objectives
- organises
- motivates and communicates
- measures
- develops people, including him/herself

Top management's tasks are to:
- define the business mission
- set standards
- build and maintain the human organisation
- develop and maintain external relationships
- perform social and civic functions
- know how to get on with the task in hand if and when necessary

Management: Tasks, Responsibilities, Practices is regarded by many as Drucker's finest book. It is the only management book to have been selected by a Desert Island Discs castaway.

The Age of Discontinuity – 1969 (reissued 1992)
It is in *The Age of Discontinuity* that Drucker describes the very changes that he had signalled to General Motors 23 years earlier. He writes in the preface: 'This book does not project trends; it examines discontinuities. It does not forecast tomorrow; it looks at today. It does not ask: "What will tomorrow look like?" It asks instead: "What do we have to tackle today to make tomorrow?"'

The book deals with the forces that change society as new technology impacts old industries, changing social values impact consumer behaviour, and markets become international. Drucker advocates privatisation, pointing out the ineffectiveness of government in leading and stimulating change; he examines the role of organisations in society in an age of discontinuity and looks at different ways of managing the knowledge worker.

Managing in Turbulent Times – 1980
The issues raised in *The Age of Discontinuity* were revisited a decade later in *Managing in Turbulent Times*. Change, uncertainty, and turbulence are the underpinning themes as Drucker highlights the new realities of changing population demographics, global markets, and a 'bisexual' workforce.

Drucker issues challenges to junior, middle, and senior management.
- In the knowledge organisation, the 'supervisor' has to become an 'assistant', a 'resource', and a 'teacher'.
- The very term 'middle management' is becoming meaningless as some will have to learn how to work with people over whom they have no direct control, to work transnationally, and to create, maintain, and run systems – none of which are traditionally middle management tasks
- It is top management that faces the challenge of setting directions for the enterprise, of managing the fundamentals. It is top management that will have to restructure itself to meet the challenges of the 'sea-change', the changes in population structure and population dynamics.
- It is top management that will have to concern itself with the turbulences of the environment, the emergence of the world economy, the emergence of the employee society, and the need for the enterprises in its care to take the lead in respect to political process, political concepts, and social policies.

Drucker said it first
Part of Drucker's success and longevity as a management expert was that he had a remarkable knack of spotting trends that were later picked up and made fashionable by others. Invariably, research will trace the origin back to something Drucker wrote ten years – sometimes 20 years – ago. It is interesting that Drucker noted that one of the key aspects of leadership is timing; he, in fact, upbraided himself for being ten years ahead with his forecasts.

The following section is adapted from work by Clutterbuck and Crainer, who summarised the work of James O'Toole, Professor of Management at the University of Southern California. O'Toole said that Drucker was the first to:
- define the role of top managers as the keepers of corporate culture
- advocate mentoring, career planning, and executive development as top management tasks
- say that success hinges on the vision expressed by the CEO
- show that structure follows strategy
- suggest a reduction of management layers between the top and the bottom
- argue that success comes from sticking to the basics

- state that the primary purpose of the organisation is to create a customer
- say that success boils down to sensitivity to the consumer and the marketing of innovative products
- suggest that quality is a measure of productivity
- describe the coming knowledge worker
- state that new approaches to management would be needed in the post-industrial age

It must be said, however, that Drucker also prophesied the continuing growth of the middle manager as he or she evolved into the knowledge worker of post-industrial society. It has not happened quite like that and the massive delayerings of the early 1990s suggest that Drucker may well have got it wrong . . . so far.

'Druckerisms'

On business:

A business is not defined by the company's name, statutes, or articles of incorporation. It is defined by the want the customer satisfies when he buys a product or service. (*Management: Tasks, Responsibilities, Practices*)

On leadership:

There is no substitute for leadership. But management cannot create leaders. It can only create the conditions under which potential leadership qualities become effective; or it can stifle potential leadership. (*The Practice of Management*)

On management:

The function which distinguishes the manager above all others is his educational one. The one contribution he is uniquely expected to make is to give others vision and ability to perform. It is vision and moral responsibility that, in the last analysis, define the manager. (*The Practice of Management*)

On decision-making:

[In] these specifically managerial decisions, the important and difficult job is never to find the right answer, it is hard to find the right question. For there are few things as useless-if not as dangerous-as the right answer to the wrong question. (*The Practice of Management*)

On the knowledge worker:

Increasingly, the knowledge workers of tomorrow will have to know and accept the values, the goals, and the policies of the organisation – to use current buzzwords, they must be willing – nay, eager-to buy into the company's mission. ('Drucker Speaks His Mind', *Management Review*)

[The knowledge worker] . . . may realise that he depends on the organisation for access to income and opportunity, and that without the investment the organisation has made – and a high investment at that – there would be no opportunity for him. But he also realises, and rightly so, that the organisation equally depends on him. (*The Age of Discontinuity*)

PETER DRUCKER IN PERSPECTIVE

Critical of the business school system in general, Drucker always set himself apart from mainstream management education. He said of himself: 'I have always been a loner.

I work best outside. That's where I'm most effective. I would be a very poor manager. Hopeless. And a company job would bore me to death. I enjoy being an outsider.'

An outsider maybe, but commentators pointed consistently to his gentlemanly old-world charm, his humility, and the fact that he never criticised negatively, always politely and constructively.

Drucker's earlier works no longer strike the reader with the same force that they did in the 1950s, 1960s, and 1970s. But this is entirely to his credit. His thinking was absorbed and adopted as the prevailing wisdom behind the philosophy and practice of modern management.

What does strike the modern reader, however, is the sheer force of his writing, his clear mastery of the subject matter, and the clarity of his expression. It is as well to remember that readable books on management were very few and far between when Drucker wrote *The Concept of the Corporation* and *The Practice of Management*. Texts for managers concentrated usually on technical and industrial engineering, and were too complex to have either a wide readership or the impact or influence that Drucker had.

'For many business leaders across the world . . . he remains the doyen of modern management theory, not so much because he can lay claim to being the founder of any particular concept such as business re-engineering, or total quality management, rather because he has demonstrated a rare ability to apply commonsense understanding to the analysis of management challenges and their solutions.' ('Interview with Peter Drucker', the *Financial Times*)

One of Drucker's achievements lay in the fact that he, a devotee of the human relations school, recognised the value of Taylor's scientific, work-study approach, and succeeded in striking a balance between the two approaches. Management by Objectives, when carried out properly, is an effective marriage of both schools, which attaches significance to culture and to the fact that organisations are held together not just by a dictated vision, but by a shared vision of the future.

So, although Drucker awarded the accolade of 'guru's guru' to F.W. Taylor, the world of management will always attribute it to Drucker himself. His ability to see management with a long historical perspective and in a broad social and political context is very rare in management writers. With his capacity for demystifying the apparent complexities of management for millions worldwide, he stood, as he said of himself, quite alone.

THE BEST SOURCES OF HELP

Books:

Drucker, Peter. *The Future of Industrial Man: A Conservative Approach*. London: Heinemann, 1943.

Drucker, Peter. *The Practice of Management*. London: Heinemann, 1955.

Drucker, Peter. *Managing for Results: Economic Tasks and Risk-taking Decisions*. London: Heinemann, 1964.

Drucker, Peter. *The Concept of the Corporation*. New York: New American Library, 1964.

Drucker, Peter. *The Effective Executive*. London: Heinemann, 1967.

Drucker, Peter. *The End of Economic Man*. New York: Harper & Row, 1969.

Drucker, Peter. *Technology, Management, and Society*. London: Heinemann, 1970.

Drucker, Peter. *Management: Tasks, Responsibilities, Practices*. New York: Harper & Row, 1973.

Drucker, Peter. *Managing in Turbulent Times*. London: Heinemann, 1980.

Drucker, Peter. *The Changing World of the Executive*. London: Heinemann, 1982.

Drucker, Peter. *Innovation and Entrepreneurship: Practice and Principles*. London: Heinemann, 1985.

Drucker, Peter. *The Frontiers of Management: Where Tomorrow's Decisions Are Being Made Today*. London: Heinemann, 1986.

Drucker, Peter. *Managing the Non-Profit Organization: Practices and Principles*. Oxford: Butterworth-Heinemann, 1990.

Drucker, Peter. *Managing for the Future: The 1990s and Beyond*. Oxford: Butterworth-Heinemann, 1992.

Drucker, Peter. *Managing in a Time of Great Change*. Oxford: Butterworth-Heinemann, 1995.

Drucker, Peter. *Management Challenges for the 21st Century*. Oxford: Butterworth-Heinemann, 2002.

Henri Fayol Planning, Organisation, Command, Co-ordination, Control

Henri Fayol remained comparatively unknown outside his native France for almost a quarter of a century after his death. However, in the 1950s, *General and Industrial Management* was published, and he posthumously gained widespread recognition for his work on administrative management. Today Fayol is often described as the founding father of the administration school.

1841	Born.
1872	Appointed director of a group of mines.
1918	Retires.
1925	Dies.
1950s	*General and Industrial Management* published; Fayol's reputation as 'the founding father of the administration school' established over 25 years after his death.

LIFE AND CAREER

Fayol spent his entire career in one company, the French mining and metallurgical combine Comentry-Fourchamboult-Decazeville. He began as a mining engineer, was appointed director of a group of mines in 1872, and became managing director in 1888 – a post which he held until his retirement in 1918. He retained the honorary title until his death.

When Fayol began his career, the financial health of the mining combine was poor. By the time he retired, however, there had been a complete turnaround and the company was prospering. Fayol's success is often attributed to his development and championing of the 'functional principle'. This involved:

• preparing yearly and 10-yearly plans, and acting on them

• preparing organisation charts to demonstrate and encourage order

• recruiting and training carefully to ensure each employee was in the right place

• adhering to the principle of the chain of command

• arranging regular meetings with heads of departments and divisions to ensure coordination

KEY THINKING

Administration Industrielle et Générale-Prévoyance, Organisation, Commandement, Contrôle (General and Industrial Management-Planning, Organisation, Command and Control)

In his writing, Fayol attempted to construct a theory of management that could be used as a basis for formal management education and training. First, he divided all organisational activities into six functions:

• technical: engineering, production, manufacture, adaptation

• commercial: buying, selling, exchange

• financial: the search for optimum use of capital

• security: protecting assets and personnel

• accounting: stocktaking, balance sheets, costs, statistics

• managerial: planning, organising, commanding, coordinating, controlling

Although well understood in their own right, none of the first five functions takes account of drawing up a broad plan of where the business is going and how it will operate; organising people; coordinating all of the business efforts and activities, and monitoring to check that what is planned is actually carried out. Fayol's sixth function, therefore, acts as an umbrella to the previous five.

Fayol argued that to manage is to:

1. Plan: a good plan of action should be flexible, continuous, relevant, and accurate. Its function is to unify the organisation by focusing on the nature, priorities, and condition of the business; the longer-term predictions for the industry and economy; the intuitions of key thinkers; and strategic sector analyses from specialist staff.

For effective planning, managers should be skilled in the art of handling people, and possess considerable energy and a measure of moral courage. It is also important that they have some continuity of tenure; be competent in the specialised requirements of the business; have general business experience; and be able to generate creative ideas.

2. Organise: organising is as much about lines of responsibility and authority as it is about communication flow and the use of resources. Fayol lays down the following organisational duties for managers.

- Ensure the plan is judiciously prepared and strictly carried out.
- See that human and material structures are consistent with objectives, resources, and general operating policies.
- Establish a single guiding authority and lines of communication throughout the organisation.
- Harmonise activities and coordinate efforts.
- Formulate clear, distinct and precise decisions.
- Arrange for efficient personnel selection.
- Define duties clearly.
- Encourage a liking for initiative and responsibility.
- Offer fair recompense for services rendered.
- Make use of sanctions in cases of fault and error.
- Maintain discipline.
- Ensure that individual interests are subordinated to the general interest.
- Pay special attention to the authority of command.
- Supervise both material and human order.
- Have everything under control.
- Fight against excess regulation, red tape, and paperwork.

3. Coordinate: coordination involves determining the timing and sequencing of activities so that they mesh properly; allocating the appropriate resources, time, and priority; and adapting means to ends.

4. Command: managers who are in charge should:

- gain a thorough knowledge of their personnel
- eliminate the incompetent (this is not as final as it sounds! Fayol takes pains to point out that any decision to part with employees should be the result of careful thought; that the employees should have had fairly assigned work for which they were trained; that they should have been appraised fairly and objectively and provided with honest feedback; that they should have been given every opportunity for additional training, offered guidance and – where possible – reassigned to alternative work. Fayol also mentions procedures involving written warnings and protection against bias and 'inequities'.)
- be well versed in the agreements between the business and its employees
- set a good example
- conduct periodic audits of the organisation

- bring together senior assistants to ensure unity of direction and focus of efforts
- not become engrossed in detail
- aim at making energy, initiative, loyalty, and unity prevail among employees

5. Control: controlling means checking that:

- everything occurs according to the plan adopted, the principles established, and the instructions issued
- appropriate corrective action is taken
- weaknesses, errors, and deviations have not slipped in
- the plan is kept up to date (it is not cast in stone but adapts to changing developments)

FAYOL'S PRINCIPLES OF MANAGEMENT

Fayol's five-point approach advises managers on their tasks, duties and activities. From his own experience, he established a number of general principles of management, which lend definition to this approach.

- division of work: specialisation allows the individual to build up expertise and therefore be more productive
- authority: the right to issue commands, along with the appropriate responsibility
- discipline: two-sided-employees obey orders only if managers play their part by providing good leadership
- unity of command: one man, one boss – with no other conflicting lines of command
- unity of direction: staff involved in the same activities should have the same objectives
- subordination of individual interest to the general interest: the good of the organisation must come first over any group, just as the interests of any agreed team should come first over the individual
- remuneration: should be fair and equitable, encouraging productivity by rewarding well-directed effort; it should not be subject to abuse
- centralisation: there is no formula to advocate centralisation or decentralisation; much depends on the optimum operating conditions of the business
- scalar chain: Fayol recognised that although hierarchies are essential, they do not always make for the swiftest communication; lateral communication therefore is also fundamental
- order: avoidance of duplication and waste through good organisation
- equity: a 'combination of kindliness and justice' in dealing with employees
- stability of tenure: the more successful the business, the more stable the management
- initiative: encouraging people to use their initiative is a source of strength for the organisation
- esprit de corps: management must foster and develop the morale of employees and encourage each person to use his or her abilities

HENRI FAYOL IN PERSPECTIVE

It is hard to overestimate the influence Fayol has brought to bear on management thinking and management thinkers. Labelled 'the founding father of the administration school', he was the first author to look at the organisation from the 'top down'; to identify management as a process; to break that process down into logical subdivisions; and to lay out a series of principles to make best use of people-thereby establishing a syllabus for management education.

The fact that Fayol's influence has endured is expressed no better than in the influential classic management formula, POSDCORB, a notion directly derived from his writings. It directs that managers should Plan, Organise, Staff, Direct, Coordinate, Report, and Budget.

Looking more closely at the detail of Fayol's five management activities, it is obvious that the conflicts and concerns, responsibilities and duties, styles, and problems that he identified a century ago are still just as relevant today. How do we 'ensure that individual interests are subordinated to (harmonised with) the general interest'? How do we 'encourage a liking for initiative and responsibility'?

And if the 'fight against an excess of regulation, red tape, and paperwork' was problematic enough for Fayol to regard as a management duty in his day, he would surely be disappointed at how little progress has been made.

Fayol's views have been criticised but his principles of management do not differ greatly from the characteristics of formal organisations as set out by Max Weber. Fayol's influence as the first to describe management as a top-down process based on planning and the organisation of people will ensure his prominence amongst students and practising managers alike.

THE BEST SOURCES OF HELP
Book:
Fayol, Henri, revised by Irwin Gray. *General and Industrial Management*. London: Pitman, 1984.

Mary Parker Follett Prophet of Management

Mary Parker Follett was one of the first people to apply psychological insight and social science findings to the study of industrial organisation. She viewed business as a pioneering field within which solutions to human relations problems were being tested.

After the Second World War her ideas were largely neglected, except in Japan. Yet her work foreshadowed a range of current Western approaches emphasising involvement and cross-functional communications.

1868	Born.
1888	Attends Society for Collegiate Instruction of Women, Harvard.
1896	Publication of *The House of Representatives*.
1890	Spends a year at Newnham College, Cambridge.
1918	Begins writing *The New State*.
1933	Gives inaugural series of lectures for Department of Business Administration (now Department of Industrial Relations) at the London School of Economics.
1933	Dies.

LIFE AND CAREER
Born in Massachusetts to a well-off Boston family, Follett was a brilliant scholar who graduated at the age of 12. She was educated at the Thayer Academy, Boston, and Radcliffe College, Massachusetts. At 20 she attended an annexe of Harvard University called the Society for Collegiate Instruction of Women. In 1890, she spent a year at Newnham College, Cambridge and went on to

Paris as a postgraduate student. Pauline Graham describes Follett as a polymath, and records that she read law, economics, government, and philosophy at Harvard, and history and political science at Newnham. While at Cambridge, Follett gave a paper which she later developed into her first book, *The House of Representatives*. This was taken seriously enough to be reviewed by Theodore Roosevelt in the *American Historical Review* of October 1896.

Follett's family life was difficult. Her father, to whom she was close, died when she was in her early teens. Her mother was an invalid with whom Follett did not get on very well. From an early age Follett ran the household and later she also ran the family housing business.

Eventually, Follett broke all family ties and went to share a home with her friend, Isobella Briggs. Over the next 30 years, Isobella provided a stable domestic background, while her social connections were helpful to Follett's work. When Isobella died in 1926, Follett lost her home life as well as her closest friend. Later that year she met Dame Katherine Furse, an Englishwoman who was strongly involved with the Girl Guide movement. Follett later moved to England to share a house in Chelsea with Furse.

Follett the social worker
Follett was expected to become an academic, but instead she went into voluntary social work in Boston, where her energy and practicality (as well as her financial support on occasions) achieved much in terms of community-building initiatives. For over 30 years, she was immersed in this work, and proved to be an innovative, hands-on

manager whose practical achievements included the original use of schools as out-of-hours centres for community education and recreation. This was Follett's own idea, and the resulting community centres became models for other cities throughout the United States.

Follett set up vocational placement centres in Boston schools, and represented the public on the Massachusetts Minimum Wage Board. From 1924 she began to give regular papers relating to industrial organisation, especially at conferences of the Bureau of Personnel Administration in New York. She became, in effect, an early management consultant, as business people began to seek her advice about their organisational and human relations problems.

In 1926 and 1928, Follett gave papers for the Rowntree Lecture Conference and to the National Institute of Industrial Psychology. In 1933, she gave an inaugural series of lectures for the newly founded Department of Business Administration (now the Department of Industrial Relations) at the London School of Economics (LSE). Later in 1933, Follett returned to the United States, where she died on the 18th December of that year, aged 65.

KEY THINKING

The New State was written during 1918, and argues for group-based democracy as a process of government. Through this book, Follett became widely recognised as a political philosopher. It was based on her social work experience rather than on business organisations, but the ideas it contains were later applied in the business context.

The New State presented an often visionary interpretation of what Follett viewed as the progress of social evolution, and the tone is occasionally infused with poetical, religious feeling. The text argues that democracy 'by numbers' should give way to a more valid process of group-based democracy. This form of democracy is described as a dynamic process through which individual conflicts and differences become integrated in the search for overall group agreement. Through it, people will grow and learn as they adapt to one another's views, while seeking a common, long-term good.

The group process works through the relating of individuals' different ideas to each other and to the common interests of the group as a whole. Appropriate action would, Follett held, become self-evident during the consultation process. This would eventually reveal a 'law of the situation', representing an objective that all could see would be the best course for the group as a whole to pursue. Conflict and disagreement were viewed as positive forces, and Follett considered social evolution to progress through the ever-continuous integration of diverse viewpoints and opinions in pursuit of the common good.

The New State envisages the basic group democratic process following right through to the international level, feeding up from neighbourhoods via municipal and state government into the League of Nations. Sometimes, Follett refers to an almost autonomous group spirit, which develops from the community between people.

The Creative Experience was also written during 1918, and again focused on democratic governance, using examples from business to illustrate ideas. *Dynamic Management-The Collected Papers of Mary Parker Follett* and *Freedom and Co-ordination* were both published posthumously and edited by L. Urwick. *Freedom and Co-ordination* collects together six papers given by Follett at the LSE in 1933, and these represent the most developed and concise distillation of her thoughts on business organisation.

Follett's business writings extended her social ideas into the industrial sphere. Industrial managers, she saw, confronted the same difficulties as public administrators as regards control, power, participation, and conflict. Her later writings focused on management from a human perspective, using the new approach of psychology to deal with problems between individuals and within groups. She encouraged business people to look at how groups formed and how employee commitment and motivation could be encouraged. The participation of everyone involved in decisions affecting their activities is seen as fundamental, in that Follett viewed group power and management through co-operation as the obvious route to achievements that would benefit all.

Views on power, leadership, authority, and control

Follett envisaged management responsibility as being diffused throughout a business rather than wholly concentrated at the hierarchical apex. Degrees of authority and responsibility are seen as spread all along the line. For example, a truck driver can act with more authority than the business owner in terms of knowing more about the best order in which to make his or her deliveries. Leadership skills are required of many people rather than just one person, and final authority, while it does exist, should not be overemphasised. The chief executive's role lies in coordinating the scattered authorities and varied responsibilities that make up the organisation into group action and ideas, and also in foreseeing and meeting the next situation.

Follett's concept of leadership as the ability to develop and integrate group ideas, using 'power with' rather than 'power over' people, is very modern. She understood that the crude exercise of authority based on subordination is hurtful to people, and cannot be the basis of effective, motivational management control. Partnership and co-operation, she sought to persuade people, were of far more ultimate benefit to everyone than hierarchical control and competition.

Follett viewed the group process as a form of collective control, with the experience of all who perform a functional part in an activity feeding into decision-making. Control is thus realised through the coordination of all functions rather than imposed from the outside.

Follett's four fundamental principles of organisation

Follett identified four principles of coordination that she considered basic to effective management.

- Coordination consists in the 'reciprocal relating' of all the factors in a situation.
- Coordination should be by direct contact, operating by means of direct communication between all responsible people involved, whatever their hierarchical or departmental positions.
- Coordination should begin in the early stages. It should involve all the people directly concerned, right from the initial stages of designing a project or forming a policy.
- Coordination should be a continuing process, based on the recognition that there is no such thing as unity, but only the continuous process of unifying.

MARY PARKER FOLLETT IN PERSPECTIVE

The context of evolutionary progress

Follett's thinking was ahead of her time, yet was founded on a conviction of social, evolutionary progress, which the course of subsequent history has shown to be flawed. She lived through momentous times, when social and technological change seemed to make a new order inevitable. The destruction caused by the First World War also seemed to dictate the clear need for a determined effort to create a social order that would not break down so disastrously. Simultaneously, the war created pressures in both England and the United States for labour participation in management, and led to a growth in internationalist ideas and to the birth of the League of Nations.

Like other writers of the time, Follett made leaps of the imagination that grew out of the factual changes that were actually taking place. Her view was rational and progressive, and she could not know the degree to which some things would remain constant, undermining the apparently inevitable dynamic of social 'progress'.

From our modern vantage point, looking back on the whole of the 20th century, of which Follett saw only the beginning, we have all too full a knowledge of the Second World War and countless other conflicts, of the discrediting of Russian Communism, and of worsening ethnic divisions and continuing human barbarities. The progressive, internationalist vision seems to be, from our contemporary perspective, a fast-receding dream.

Yet, while Follett's optimistic expectations of radical social change were largely mistaken, she drew from it the imaginative vision to transform at least some of her convictions into ideas about ways of living and working that have contributed much to both social and management practice. In fact, it is almost disheartening to read Follett and realise that she clearly and strongly stated, so many years ago, ideas that are being proffered as 'new' today and that are still rarely practised in any sustained way.

THE BEST SOURCES OF HELP
Books:

Graham, Pauline, ed. *Mary Parker Follett: Prophet of Management-A Celebration of Writings from the 1920s.* Boston, Massachusetts: Harvard Business School Press, 1995

Parker Follett, Mary. *The Speaker of the House of Representatives.* New York: Longmans, Green & Co, 1896.

Parker Follett, Mary. *The New State: Group Organization-the Solution for Popular Government.* New York: Longmans, Green & Co, 1920.

Parker Follett, Mary. *Creative Experience.* New York: Longmans, Green & Co, 1924.

Ghoshal and Bartlett Managing Across Borders

Pioneering research with collaborator Christopher Bartlett into what makes large global organisations tick, and an enquiring mind committed to management as the wealth creator, contributed to the emergence of the late Sumantra Ghoshal as one of the most respected management thinkers of his generation.

A sought-after consultant, teacher, speaker, and prolific writer, his research played an important role in guiding companies towards the era of globalisation.

LIFE AND CAREER: GHOSHAL

Born in India, Sumantra Ghoshal (1946–2004) took a degree in physics before spending 12 years (1969–81) at the Indian Oil Corporation. He demonstrated his appetite for understanding what makes organisations work by

obtaining two doctorates, one from MIT, champion of the rigorous scientific method, the other from more pragmatic Harvard, whose approach is based on case studies, observation, and practice.

After lecturing at MIT and INSEAD, Ghoshal became professor of business policy at INSEAD in 1992, and professor of strategic leadership at the London Business School in 1994. He first came to international prominence with the publication in 1989 of *Managing Across Borders*, co-authored with Christopher Bartlett.

LIFE AND CAREER: BARTLETT

Christopher Bartlett is the Thomas D. Casserly Jr. Professor Emeritus of Business Administration at Harvard

Business School. Before joining the faculty of Harvard, he was a marketing manager with Alcoa in Australia, a management consultant in McKinsey and Company's London office, and general manager at Baxter Laboratories' subsidiary company in France.

His research interests have focused on the strategic and organisational challenges which managers face in running multinational corporations, and these interests have been reflected in his most successful books.

Managing Across Borders was cited by the *Financial Times* as one of the 50 most influential business books of the century. It remains a classic of the genre.

KEY THINKING

Managing across borders

Ghoshal and Bartlett's thinking begins with two fundamental questions:

- What does strategy mean?
- Why do the time-honoured business models – exemplified by Alfred Sloan's General Motors – no longer work?

Their initial research involved asking over 250 managers in nine multinational companies how their companies were facing up to the complexities of international competition and the growing global marketplace. They identified a pervasive organisational inability to cope, survive, and succeed in the face of growing diversity and accelerating change.

They found three types of organisational model in operation:

- the multinational model, exemplified by Philips or Unilever – a decentralised federation of local companies held together by posting key people from the centre
- the global model, exemplified by Ford and Matsushita – benefiting from large-scale economies and new market opportunities
- a more widespread international model – focusing on technology and the transfer of knowledge to less advanced environments

They concluded that a fourth model was necessary – the transnational – which would combine all the elements of the other three and, in addition, exploit local know-how as the key weapon in identifying opportunities, rather than operating overseas sites as outposts of the centre.

Efficiency versus economic progress

To understand why the old models no longer worked, Ghoshal examined Alfred Sloan's General Motors, the pioneer of the three Ss (Strategy, Structure, Systems), emulated by other companies for decades.

The three Ss were designed to make the management of complex organisations systematic and predictable. The top people in the organisation crafted the strategy, then designed the structure that enabled it to unfold and the systems that made it operational. The information systems they relied on dealt with facts and reduced the human element to a minimum. Employees on Ford's assembly lines, for example, were viewed as replaceable parts; ITT, under Harold Geneen, abolished the possibility of surprise by constantly establishing 'unshakeable facts'.

For years, this systematic approach worked. It started to break down only in the 1980s, when converging technologies, fluctuating markets, overnight competition, and technological innovation combined to make its control systems cumbersome, unresponsive, and ultimately a risk to the survival of the organisation itself. An article by Ghoshal, Bartlett, and Peter Moran in the *Sloan Management Review*, Spring 1999 ('A new manifesto for management', pp. 9–20) pointed out that criticisms of these systems for stifling initiative, creativity, and diversity were valid: 'They were designed for an organisation man who has turned out to be an evolutionary dead end.' (p. 11)

In the same article, the authors implicitly attacked Michael Porter's work. Porter had influenced strategic thinking for over a decade by arguing that organisations must beat the competition by gaining a stranglehold on value, that is, by either reducing competitors' value (perhaps through competitive incremental cost or quality improvements) or buying them out. Ghoshal wrote: 'Porter's theory is static in that it focuses strategic thinking on getting the largest possible share of a fixed economic pie.' (p. 12) For Ghoshal, companies exist not to appropriate value, but to create it – and they get themselves into a position to be able to create value by 'changing the smell of the place'.

Fontainebleau and Calcutta: the 'springtime theory'

Ghoshal developed his 'springtime theory' while teaching business policy at INSEAD in the forest of Fontainebleau, south of Paris. During a summer visit to his home city of Calcutta, he found the humidity oppressive and draining, and likened this to the stultifying atmosphere in control- and system-oriented corporate climates. Later, walking in the woods at Fontainebleau, he realised that the fresh, energising forest reminded him of the cultural atmosphere of more open and dynamic organisations. From this, he went on to propound his 'springtime theory', arguing that managers and approaches to management strongly affect cultures and can create or change the organisational context: in his words, 'the smell of the place'. But how?

The three Ps

Ghoshal considered that modern leading companies are built around the 'three Ps': Purpose, Process, and People. In an interview in *Management Skills and Development*, he claimed that, as shapers of purpose, senior managers need 'to create a shared ambition among their staff, instil organisational values, and provide personal meaning for the work their staff do'. Creating that shared ambition is an active management process that challenges poor performance, establishes a common goal, demonstrates managers' commitment and self-discipline, and provides 'meaning for everyone's efforts'. (p. 40)

In the same interview, Ghoshal also stressed the need for organisations to:

- start thinking outside the 'strategic planning' box and examining how they actually learn
- complement vertical information flows with horizontal personal relationships
- build a trust-based culture by spreading a message of genuine openness
- share all the information that has traditionally been a source of power

He said: 'You cannot have faith in people unless you take action to improve and develop them. The success of businesses depends now more than ever on the talent of people working for them.' (p. 39) In short, organisations need to forge a 'new moral contract' with their people.

The new moral contract

In the past, the contract between organisations and employees promised relative security in return for conformity. In the 1980s and 1990s, however, this changed: job security was undermined by downsizing and re-engineering, while managerial approaches such as Total Quality Management and Customer Focus demanded more involvement and initiative from employees. The new contract Ghoshal proposed is based on developing employability, and providing challenging jobs rather than functional boxes. It should be viewed neither as altruism on the company's part nor as something imposed on employees. It is, rather, a new management philosophy that recognises that personal development both improves employees' performance and makes them more employable in their future working lives, and that market performance stems from the initiative, creativity, and skills of all employees, and not just the wisdom of senior management.

Such a contract involves a great leap for both organisations and employees. Employers must create a working environment with opportunities for personal and professional growth, within a management environment in which it is understood that talented, growing people mean talented, growing organisations. Employees must make greater commitment to continuous learning and development, and accept that, in a climate of constant change and uncertainty, the will to develop is the only hedge against a changing job market.

Companies as value creators

Ghoshal felt strongly that organisations must stop focusing on squeezing out every last cost saving, waste reduction, or improvement in quality or efficiency. That may seem like the ultimate goal of TQM and continuous improvement, but organisations with that sole aim are only good at improving existing activities. Their emphasis is wholly on conservation, which, as Ghoshal pointed out, Jack Welch described as a 'ticket to the boneyard' when he was running GE.

The main message of Ghoshal and Bartlett's more recent book, *The Individualized Corporation* (1998), was that the key to competitive advantage in a turbulent economy is a company's ability to innovate its way out of relentless market pressures. As companies shift emphasis from acquiring value to creating it, managers should shift their focus away from obedience, control, and conformity to initiative, relationship building, and continuous challenge of the status quo. Instead of being cogs in a system, they should become facilitators and people developers, drawing creativity from others.

In an interview published in the *Professional Manager*, Ghoshal pointed out that the modern world has brought about an enormous improvement in the quality of our lives and that this improvement – this value – has been created by business. Politicians create the context; they did not, in Ghoshal's view, create value: this came from companies and managers. From this perspective, management is the most important social profession today; the wealth of the nation depends on it: 'The quality of BT's management matters, perhaps matters more than a quarter per cent change in interest rates, because it creates value. If BT, ICI, or Marks and Spencer are poorly managed . . . the UK loses, because these institutions are the engines of the country's progress. The most important source of a nation's progress is the quality of its management.' ('Professor of the Spring Strategy', *Professional Manager*, May 2000, pp. 20–23)

GHOSHAL AND BARTLETT IN PERSPECTIVE

During the time that Ghoshal came to prominence, his focus shifted from international strategy to the importance of putting people, creativity, and innovation at the top of the agenda and an emphasis on high-quality management as an important social and moral value-creating force. His death in 2004 meant that the management world lost an inspirational teacher, thinker, and collaborator. Christopher Bartlett has the last word: 'Borders never meant much to Sumantra.'

THE BEST SOURCES OF HELP
Books:
Bartlett, Christopher, and Sumantra Ghoshal. *Managing Across Borders*. 2nd ed. London: Hutchinson Business, 1989.
Bartlett, Christopher, and Sumantra Ghoshal. *The Individualized Corporation: A Fundamentally New Approach to Management*. London: Heinemann, 1998.
Journal Articles:
Bartlett, Christopher, and Sumantra Ghoshal. 'Changing the role of top management: beyond strategy to purpose.' *Harvard Business Review*, November/December, 1994, pp. 79–88.
Bartlett, Christopher, and Sumantra Ghoshal. 'Changing the role of top management: beyond structure to processes.' *Harvard Business Review*, January/February, 1995, pp. 86–96.
Bartlett, Christopher, and Sumantra Ghoshal. 'Changing the role of top management: beyond systems to people.' *Harvard Business Review*, May/June, 1995, pp. 132–142.

Gurus

Daniel Goleman Emotional Intelligence

Daniel Goleman is usually credited with challenging the traditional view of the IQ (Intelligence Quotient) by drawing together research on how the brain works and developing this to promote and popularise the concept of emotional intelligence. In *Working with Emotional Intelligence* (1998), Goleman defined emotional intelligence (EI) as a capacity for recognising our own and others' feelings, for motivating ourselves, and for managing our emotions, both within ourselves and in our relationships.

1946	Born.
1984	Joins editorial staff of *New York Times*.
1995	Publication of *Emotional Intelligence*.
1997	Founds Consortium for Research on Emotional Intelligence at Rutgers University.
1998	Publication of *Working with Emotional Intelligence*.

LIFE AND CAREER

Goleman, born in 1946, gained his PhD in psychology from Harvard, where he also taught. His best-selling book, *Emotional Intelligence: Why It Matters More Than IQ*, was published in 1995, and in 1998 this was followed by *Working with Emotional Intelligence*. Goleman has frequently written for the *New York Times* on behavioural science, and is also a founding member of the Consortium for Research on Emotional Intelligence, based at Rutgers University.

Goleman's interest in EI arose from a realisation that a high IQ is not necessarily a prerequisite for having a successful life. In *Emotional Intelligence* he identifies many people who, while brilliant academically, were nevertheless failures socially or in corporate life. Conversely, he identifies others who were not well qualified or distinguished in academic terms, but were still highly successful in terms of their lives and business achievements. Goleman went on to relate business acumen to emotional intelligence. In *Working with Emotional Intelligence* he later identified 25 EI competencies, or surface behaviours, and discussed how high emotional intelligence can make all the difference between success and failure.

KEY THINKING

Emotional intelligence and the brain

In *Emotional Intelligence*, Goleman describes how the evolution of the brain has implications for our emotions and behavioural responses. He outlines how, during its evolution over millions of years, the brain has now come to comprise three main areas.

- The brain stem is situated at the base of the brain and at the top of the spinal cord. It controls bodily functions and instinctive survival responses, and is the most primitive part of the brain.

- The hippocampus evolved after the brainstem and is situated just above it. It includes the amygdala region, the importance of which was identified by Joseph LeDoux during the 1980s. Here, the brain stores emotional, survival-linked responses to visual and other inputs. The amygdala seems able to 'hijack' the brain in some circumstances, taking over people's reactions literally before they have had time to think, and provoking an immediate response to a situation. Mammals or human beings who have had their amygdala removed show no signs of emotional feeling at all. The amygdala can catalyse the sort of impulsive actions that may sometimes overpower rational thought and the capacity for considered reactions.

- The neo-cortex is the large, well-developed, top region of the brain which comprises the centre for our thinking, memory, and reasoning functions.

Because of this course of evolution, our emotions and thinking intelligence – the two main functions of the brain regulating our behaviour – are situated in separate areas. Furthermore, our emotional centres receive 'input' before our thinking centres, and can react very quickly and very strongly in some situations. The results of this for human behaviour can be catastrophic in that, unless we are aware of the situation and practised in controlling our initial feelings, we may allow inappropriate emotional responses to pre-empt behaviour based on consideration of more appropriate options. Our emotions have a 'wisdom' of their own that we should learn to use more, particularly in terms of the intuitive sense they offer. Yet, when people confront stimuli that prompt, for example, extreme fear, anger, or frustration, their first impulse to active response comes from the amygdala. Unless intelligent control is exerted, the brain moves into survival mode, stimulating instinctive actions that, while possibly right for the situation, are not rationally considered, and may be very wrong.

Today, we usually have no need to fight or run away from dangers of the sort faced by prehistoric people. While some instinctive reactions may be wise in given circumstances, we need to be aware of how the primitive response in the brain's emotional centre precedes all rational evaluation and response. Emotional intelligence is largely about understanding this and making use of our EI, while also controlling our responses to take account of it.

Goleman's framework of emotional intelligence

Goleman developed a framework to explain emotional intelligence in terms of five elements he described as self-awareness, self-regulation, motivation, empathy, and social skills. Each of these elements has distinctive characteristics, as outlined below.

- *Self-awareness*: examining how your emotions affect your performance; using your values to guide decision-making; looking at your strengths and weaknesses and learning from your experiences (self-assessment); and being self-confident and certain about your capabilities, values, and goals.

- *Self-regulation*: controlling your temper; controlling your stress by being more positive and action-centred; retaining composure and the ability to think clearly under pressure; handling impulses well; and nurturing trustworthiness and self-restraint.
- *Motivation*: enjoying challenge and stimulation; seeking out achievement; commitment; ability to take the initiative; optimism; and being guided by personal preferences in choosing goals.
- *Empathy*: the ability to see other people's points of view; behaving openly and honestly; avoiding the tendency to stereotype others; and being culturally aware.
- *Social skills*: the use of influencing skills such as persuasion; good communication with others, including employees; listening skills; negotiation; cooperation; dispute resolution; ability to inspire and lead others; capacity to initiate and manage change; and ability to deal with others' emotions-particularly group emotions.

Goleman claims that people who demonstrate these characteristics are more likely to be successful in senior management, citing research from various sources that suggests senior managers with a higher emotional intelligence rating perform better than those without. He gives several anecdotal case studies to illustrate ways in which emotional intelligence can make a real impact in the workplace.

The Emotional Competence Inventory

Goleman believes that emotional intelligence can be developed over a period of time and he developed an Emotional Competence Inventory (ECI), in association with the Hay Group, to use when assessing and developing EQ competencies at work. The ECI reduces the original five components of emotional intelligence to four:

1. Self-awareness
- being aware of your emotions and their significance
- having a realistic knowledge of your strengths and weaknesses
- having confidence in yourself and your capacities

2. Self-management
- controlling your emotions
- being honest and trustworthy
- being flexible and dedicated

3. Social competence
- being empathetic, being able to perceive another's thoughts and points of view
- being aware of and sensing a group's dynamics and inter-relationships
- focusing on others' needs, particularly when they are customers

4. Social skills
- helping others to develop themselves
- effective leadership
- skill in influencing others

- excellent interpersonal communication skills
- change-management skills
- ability to resolve arguments and discord
- ability to nourish and build good relationships
- team-player skills

Leadership styles

Goleman, in association with Hay/McBer, has more recently been involved in researching leadership styles, as he reported in a 2000 *Harvard Business Review* article. On the basis of findings with 3,781 executive participants, the research suggests that leaders gain the best results by using a combination of six leadership styles, each of which has a central characteristic feature and uses different components of emotional intelligence.

- *Coercive leaders* – demand instant obedience. Coercive leaders are self-motivated, initiate change, and are driven to succeed.
- *Authoritative leaders* – energise people towards a goal. Authoritative leaders initiate change and are empathetic.
- *Affiliative leaders* – build relationships. Affiliative leaders are empathetic and have good communication skills.
- *Democratic leaders* – actively encourage team involvement in decision-making. Democratic leaders are good at communication, listening, and negotiation.
- *Pacesetting leaders* – set high standards of performance. Pacesetting leaders use their initiative, and are self-motivated and driven to succeed.
- *Coaching leaders* – expand and develop people's skills. Coaching leaders have the ability to listen well, communicate effectively, and motivate others.

The research evidence suggests that the six leadership styles identified are each appropriate for different types of situation, and also that leadership styles have a direct influence on the working atmosphere of an organisation, which, in turn, influences financial results.

DANIEL GOLEMAN IN PERSPECTIVE

The conviction that success depends to a high degree on interpersonal skills is not new, and Goleman has often been criticised for taking others' ideas, to some extent, and repackaging them as a new concept. Goleman himself, however, freely discusses the origins of his ideas, and acknowledges fellow academics when he uses their work.

A critical article by Charles Woodruffe in 2001 reviewed Goleman's version of EI, and suggested that:

- Goleman contradicts himself in claiming that emotional intelligence is inherent and biologically based, yet is a skill that can be learned and developed
- the self-report measures of emotional intelligence used by Goleman have considerable limitations, particularly in terms of accuracy
- the EI behaviours or competencies put forward by Goleman, such as self-confidence and leadership, are not at all new, and are factors that have often been recognised as commonly associated with high achievement levels

Whatever truth there might be in these criticisms, Goleman has certainly promoted management thinking on the subject of EI. He has taken some quite complex ideas relating to human behaviour and biological evolution, and put these into a more simple and comprehensible format that, under the label of 'emotional intelligence', is easy to understand. As a result, many people have found his core proposition, that we can use intelligence to better manage our emotions and draw on our emotional intuition to guide our thinking, to be a helpful approach in both their lives and their work.

THE BEST SOURCES OF HELP
Books:
Goleman, Daniel. *Emotional Intelligence: Why It Can Matter More Than IQ*. London: Bloomsbury, 1995.
Goleman, Daniel. *Working with Emotional Intelligence*. London: Bloomsbury, 1998.
Goleman, Daniel. *Social Intelligence: The New Science of Human Relationships*. London: Arrow Books, 2007.

Gary Hamel The Search for a New Strategic Platform

Professor Gary Hamel is one of the most respected contributors to the modern debate on strategy. His fresh and often hard-hitting approach to organisational innovation has brought wide acknowledgment from academics and practitioners alike. His reputation developed from the early 1990s, when, with C.K. Prahalad, he began to communicate his revolutionary views on strategy, in the process creating the concepts of organisational core competencies, strategic intent, and strategic architecture.

1954	Born.
1980	Gains a PhD in international business from the University of Michigan, where he meets C.K. Prahalad.
1983	Starts teaching at the London Business School.
1990s	Comes to prominence through journal articles containing revolutionary views on strategy.
1994	Co-writes *Competing for the Future* with C.K. Prahalad.
1995	Establishes Strategos, Inc with C.K. Prahalad.
Present	Visiting professor in strategic management at London Business School.

LIFE AND CAREER
Hamel worked as a hospital administrator until 1978, when he began to study for a PhD in international business at the University of Michigan. While there, he met C.K. Prahalad, who later became his mentor, collaborator, and colleague in research, writing, and business. Hamel first came to prominence through journal articles in the early 1990s, and as the co-author of the 1994 book *Competing for the Future*, written (like most of the articles) with Prahalad.

Perenially at the forefront of thinking on strategy, Hamel is visiting professor in strategic and international management at the London Business School, a former distinguished research fellow at Harvard Business School, and co-founder of Strategos, Inc, the strategy services company he set up with Prahalad in 1995.

KEY THINKING
Why a new approach to strategy?
At the beginning of the 1980s, Hamel argues, organisational development was no longer driven by strategic forces but by incrementalism. Companies were concerned with getting bigger and better through downsizing, delayering, re-engineering, and continuous quality improvement, and their goal became to mimic best practice. The result of all these incremental improvements was to squeeze cost efficiencies to the point where there was nothing left to gain.

At the same time, there were various new forces at work that were changing the nature of competition and the base of traditional industries that had enjoyed primacy in the past. These forces included:

- deregulation and privatisation, particularly in the airline, telecommunications and financial services sectors
- blurring, fragmentation and increase in newcomers to the computer and telecommunications industries
- changing customer expectations, in terms of price, quality and service
- continuous technological growth, particularly with the Internet
- shifting boundaries of control and authority, as workforces became more widely distributed, more empowered and less layered
- changes in traditional loyalties as people became simultaneously the most valuable, but also the most expendable, asset
- the lowered value of experience, as change undermined its relevance for the future

STRATEGIC QUESTIONS TO ADDRESS

Hamel argues that a compelling view of the future is necessary if one is not to be tied to the orthodoxies of the past, and he highlights the number of companies that lost money because they stuck too long to the same game instead of trying to get ahead. Although no view of the future can be accurate or perfect, a view of some sort is essential. This can be developed through addressing questions about the possibility of unleashing the corporate imagination, turning technicians into dreamers, turning planners into strategists, and creating an organisation that really lives and makes its decisions in the future.

In a 1996 article Hamel states that, while we can all recognise a great strategy once it is proved to be successful in action, we find it difficult to generate a great strategy in the first place. He argues that strategy generation is not a purely analytical process, but that it is multifaceted and involves risk, gut feelings, intuition, and emotion, as well as analysis. ('Competing in the new economy: managing out of bounds', with C.K. Prahalad, *Strategic Management Journal*, vol. 17, pp. 237–242.)

Strategy as core competence

The concept of corporate competencies was highlighted by Hamel and Prahalad in journal articles and in the book *Competing for the Future*. In the latter they argued that, for too long, organisational focus had been on returns from individual business units, as opposed to the conditions, processes, and competencies that enabled those returns. They define 'core competencies' as the collective learning in the organisation and, especially, the coordination of diverse production skills and integration of multiple streams of technologies.

Hamel and Prahalad ask organisations to look upon themselves as portfolios of core competencies by analysing what it is that they do better than others. Viewing the organisation as systems of activities and building blocks means asking:

• How does activity X significantly improve the end product for the customer?
• Does activity X offer access to a range of applications and markets?
• What would happen to our competitiveness if we lost our strength in activity X?
• How difficult is it for others to imitate activity X and compete with us?

In order to realise the potential that core competencies create, the organisation's people must have the imagination to visualise new markets and the ability to move into them, ahead of the competition. One of the keys to core competencies and effective competition is, therefore, the process through which an organisation releases corporate imagination. And one of the words that recurs increasingly through Hamel's writing is 'revolution'.

Strategy as revolution

In a seminal article, 'Strategy As Revolution' (*Harvard Business Review*, July/August 1996, pp. 69–82), Hamel sets out 10 principles that strategy generators should bear in mind.

• Strategic planning is not strategic: rather, it is a calendar-driven ritual involving plans and sub-plans, instead of something challenging and innovative that might lead to discovery.
• Strategy making should be subversive: great strategies come from challenging the status quo and doing something different. Anita Roddick, founder of the highly innovative Body Shop, is quoted as saying, 'I watch where the cosmetics industry is going and then walk in the opposite direction.'
• The bottleneck is at the top of the bottle: the most powerful defenders of strategic orthodoxy are senior management, and strategy making needs to be freed from the tyranny of their experience.
• Revolutionaries exist in every company: let everyone have a voice, so that new and young as well as tried and tested contributors are part of strategy making.
• Change is not the problem-engagement is: people will support change and welcome the responsibility for engendering it, if this gives them some control over their own future.
• Strategy making must be democratic: the capability for strategic thinking is not limited to senior people, and it is impossible to predict where a good, revolutionary idea may be lurking.
• Anyone can be a strategy activist: people who care about their organisation do not wait for permission to act.
• Perspective is worth 50 IQ points: subversive strategy means gaining a new perspective on the world, and looking at potential markets through new eyes.
• Top-down and bottom-up are not alternatives: if top-down can achieve unity of purpose among the few involved, bottom-up will bring diversity of perspective. Bring the two together.
• You can't see the end from the beginning: surprises do not appeal to everyone, but delving into discontinuities and identifying potential competencies will bring about unpredictable outcomes. These will probably not fit the orthodox strategic mould – but strategy making is about letting go.

So how do we begin to put these principles into a framework for creating strategy as a systemic capability?

Creating strategy

'Strategy innovation is the only way for newcomers to succeed in the face of enormous resource disadvantages, and the only way for incumbents to renew their lease on success.' ('Strategy, innovation and the quest for value', *Sloan Management Review*, Winter 1998, pp. 7–14)

While some strategies result from analysis and others from inspiration and vision, many strategies also evolve and emerge. To achieve strategies that are neither too random nor too ordered or ritualistic, Hamel suggests we look to the roots of strategy creation, which he regards as a relatively simple phenomenon amid the complexity of organisational life. In 'Strategy, innovation and the quest for value' (cited above), Hamel turns his revolutionary principles into action points, and urges organisations to adopt a new stance through:

- new voices – top management relinquishing its hold on strategy and introducing newcomers; young people and people from different groups bring richness and diversity to strategy formulation
- new conversations – the same people discussing the same issues over and over again leads to sterility; new opportunities arise from juxtaposing formerly isolated people
- new passions – people will go for change when they can steer it and benefit from it
- new perspectives – search for new ways of looking at markets, customers, and organisational capabilities; think differently, see differently
- new experiments – small, low-risk experiments can accelerate the organisation's learning and will indicate what may work and what may not

GARY HAMEL IN PERSPECTIVE

While it is not possible to pigeonhole Hamel, we can place him roughly in the progressive (if sometimes ragged) line of strategic thinking stretching back to Chandler and Ansoff and including Porter and Mintzberg, as well as Hamel's collaborator and colleague, Prahalad. Hamel's curiosity and tendency to challenge the status quo make it difficult to predict where his future research interests may take him next. However, it is likely that he will continue to move in tune with, if not ahead of, the rapidly changing business environment. His recent book, for example, *Leading the Revolution*, is about throwing away the old rule book, imagining a future that others have not seen, and then taking the initiative to act on it.

THE BEST SOURCES OF HELP

Books:

Hamel, Gary, and C.K. Prahalad. *Competing for the Future*. Boston, Massachusetts: Harvard Business School Press, 1994.

Hamel, Gary, and Yves Doz. *Alliance Advantage: The Art of Creating Value Through Partnering*. Boston, Massachusetts: Harvard Business School Press, 1998.

Hamel, Gary. *Strategic Flexibility: Managing in a Turbulent Environment*. Chichester: Wiley, 1998.

Hamel, Gary. *Leading the Revolution: How to Thrive in Turbulent Times*. Boston, Massachusetts: Harvard Business School Press, 2000.

Hamel, Gary. *The Future of Management*. Boston, Massachusetts: Harvard Business School Press, 2007.

Journal Articles:

Hamel, Gary, and C.K. Prahalad. 'Strategy as stretch and leverage.' *Harvard Business Review*, March/April 1993, pp. 75–84.

Hamel, Gary, and C.K. Prahalad. 'The core competence of the corporation.' *Harvard Business Review*, May/June 1990, pp. 79–91.

Charles Handy Understanding the Changing Organisation

Charles Handy is well known for his work on organisations. Culminating in the formation of a vision of the future of work and of the implications of change, his observation of work in modern society has identified discontinuous change as the (paradoxically) continuing characteristic of working lives and organisations. He has forecast a future – so far, with a good deal of accuracy – where half of the United Kingdom's workforce will no longer be in permanent full-time jobs.

1932	Born.
1967	Founder of Sloan Programme, London Business School.
1972	Professor, London Business School.
1974	Governor, London Business School.
1976	Publication of *Understanding Organizations*.
1977	Warden, St George's House, Windsor Castle.
1985	Publication of *Gods of Management*.
1989	Publication of *The Age of Unreason*.
1994	Publication of *The Empty Raincoat*.
1997	Publication of *The Hungry Spirit*.

LIFE AND CAREER

Born in Ireland, Charles Handy is a self-employed writer, teacher, and broadcaster. He is a visiting professor at the London Business School and consultant to a wide range of organisations in government, business, and the voluntary and educational sectors.

After he graduated from Oxford, his working life began in the marketing and personnel divisions of Shell International and as an economist with Anglo-American Corporation. He then returned to academia at the Sloan School of Management of the Massachusetts Institute of Technology. In 1967 he was the founder and director of the Sloan Programme at the London Business School, where he also taught managerial psychology and development. Appointments as professor and governor of the School followed in 1972 and 1974 respectively. In 1977 he was appointed Warden of St George's House in Windsor Castle, a private conference and study centre with a strong focus on the discussion of business ethics. As a teacher he later concentrated on the application of behavioural science to management, the management of change, the structure of organisations,

Gurus

and on the theory and practice of individual learning in life.

He is a past chairman of the Royal Society of Arts; in 1994 he was awarded Business Columnist of the Year. He has also been a regular contributor to 'Thought for the Day' broadcast on the *Today* programme on BBC Radio 4.

KEY THINKING

Four of Handy's books in particular consider the structure of organisations in detail, and offer a perspective on the ways in which they work. These are: *Understanding Organizations* (1976), *Gods of Management* (1985), *The Age of Unreason* (1989), and *The Empty Raincoat* (1994).

Understanding Organizations

Handy's *Understanding Organizations*-described by publishers and commentators alike as 'a landmark study' – is equally valuable for the student of management and for the practising manager. Among the subjects with which it deals are motivation, roles and interactions, leadership, power and influence, the workings of groups and the culture of organisations. They are dealt with both as 'concepts' and 'concepts in application'. A 'Guide to Further Study' points the way for further examination of each concept.

Gods of Management

Handy identifies some established structures in organisations and suggests new forms that are emerging. He perceives that, currently, organisations embrace four basic 'cultures'.

- *Club Culture.* This is represented metaphorically by Zeus, the strong leader who has, likes, and uses power, and graphically by a spider's web. All lines of communication lead, formally or informally, to the leader. Such organisations display strength in the speed of their decision-making; their potential weakness lies in the calibre of the 'one-man bands' running them.
- *Role Culture.* This is personified as Apollo, the god of order and rules, represented by a Greek temple. Such organisations are based on the assumptions that people are rational, and that roles can be defined and discharged with clearly defined procedures. They display stability and certainty, and have great strength in situations marked by continuity; they often display weakness in adapting to, or generating, change.
- *Task Culture.* This is likened to Athena, the goddess of wisdom, and is found in organisations where management is concerned with solving a series of problems. The structure is represented by a net, where resources are drawn from all parts of the organisation to meet the needs of current problems. Working parties, sub-committees, task forces, and study groups are formed on an ad hoc basis to deal with problems. This type of culture is seen to advantage when flexibility is required.
- *Existential Culture.* This is represented by Dionysus, the god of wine and song. Organisations characterised by a culture of this type are those that exist to serve the individual and in which individuals are not servants of the organisation. They consist of groups of professionals, for example, doctors or lawyers, with no 'boss'. Coordination may be provided by a committee of

peers. Such structures are becoming more common as more conventional organisations increasingly contract out work to professionals and specialists whose services are used only as and when required.

The changing organisation

The link between this analysis of organisational structures and Handy's later work is, in part, provided by the development of 'contracting out' – one of a number of changes that he observes in the world of employment. Another major change is the basing of the quest for profit on intelligence and professional skills rather than on manual work and machines. Yet another is that the days of working for one employer and/or in one occupation may be over.

The shamrock organisation

An example of Handy's changing perception of organisations is provided by his use (in *The Age of Unreason*) of the shamrock. He uses this symbol to demonstrate three bases on which people are often employed by organisations today. The people linked to an organisation are beginning to fall into three groups, each with different expectations, each managed and rewarded differently.

The first group is a core of qualified professional technicians and managers. They are essential to the continuity of the organisation, and have detailed knowledge of it and of its objectives and practices. They are rewarded with high salaries and associated benefits, in return for which they must be prepared to give commitment, to work hard, and, if necessary, to work long hours. They must be mobile. They work within a task culture, one within which there is a constant effort to reduce their numbers.

The second group consists of contracted specialists who may be used, for example, for advertising, R&D, computing, catering, or mailing services. They operate in an existential culture; and are rewarded with fees rather than with salaries or wages. Their contribution to the organisation is measured in output rather than in hours, in results rather than in time.

The third group-the third leaf of Handy's shamrock-consists of a flexible labour force, discharging part-time, temporary, and seasonal roles. They operate within a role culture; but, Handy observes, while they may be employed on a casual basis, they must not be managed casually but in a way that recognises their worth to the organisation.

The federal organisation and the inverted doughnut

The concept of the federal organisation was first explored in *The Age of Unreason* and expanded in *The Empty Raincoat*. In it, subsidiaries federate to gain benefits of scale. Federal organisations should not be confused with decentralised organisations, in which power lies in the centre and is exerted downwards and outwards. In the federal organisation the role of top management is redefined as that of providing vision and motivating, inspiring, and coordinating; initiative comes from the components of the organisation. Handy observes and describes the principle of 'subsidiarity' – not handing out or delegating power, but ruling and unifying only with the consent and agreement of equal partners.

In *The Empty Raincoat* Handy uses the metaphor of the inverted doughnut to demonstrate how those in the subsidiaries must constantly seek to extend their roles and associated activities. The hole in the conventional doughnut is filled by the core activities of the subsidiary; the substance of the doughnut represents a diminishing vacuum into which the subsidiary can expand its activities given the necessary drive, will and ability.

Portfolio working and downshifting

Following on from his work on organisational change, Handy studied the effects of such change on the individual. He coined the concept 'portfolio working', based on the assumption that full-time working for one employer will soon be a thing of the past. Embedded in this is the notion of downshifting – the idea that it is possible to exchange some part of income for a better quality of life.

Although Handy has gone on record as saying that more and more individuals will opt out of formal organisations and sell their services at a pace and at a price to suit themselves, he has also admitted that comparatively few may find themselves in a position to take real advantage of this. He argues, however, that there is much that the organisation can do to help the individual to get to grips with the new uncertainty. It was in discussion with the Japanese that Handy coined the 'theory of horizontal fast track'. In Japan, the most talented people are moved around from experience to experience as quickly as possible, so that their talents can be tested in different situations, with different managers and in different cultures. This ensures that they discover what they are really good at and provides a lot of experience.

CHARLES HANDY IN PERSPECTIVE

With his imaginative use of analogy and metaphor, Handy moved us from the past into the future. He argues that federalist and shamrock organisations can really be successful only if businesses are prepared to invest in their workforces and build relationships of trust.

While he is as much concerned with individuals as organisations, his messages are sometimes disquieting.

In *The Hungry Spirit*, he assesses the effects of the competitiveness of capitalism on the individual, suggesting that people can become not only stressed but also selfish and insensitive. But his message is not confined to pessimism about the future. On the contrary, the new capitalism consists of intellectual property-know-how, not merely physical and financial resources; the new knowledge markets enable low-cost entry to those with 'a bit of wit and a bit of imagination' and the new products of the knowledge world are not nearly so destructive to the environment as the industrial products of the past.

Handy stands apart from many other management writers due to his breadth of vision, his setting of management in a wide social and economic context, and the sheer readability of his writing. He is also ready to modify his views in the light of experience and further thought (he has admitted that some of his expectations have been proved wrong). He is not merely an observer of change but increasingly a catalyst who forces people to stand back from their daily routine, take stock and view the future through different glasses, acknowledge change, and address its implications.

THE BEST SOURCES OF HELP
Books:
Handy, Charles. *Understanding Organizations.* London: Penguin Books, 1985.
Handy, Charles. *The Age of Unreason.* London: Random House Business Books, 1989.
Handy, Charles. *The Gods of Management.* London: Arrow, 1995.
Handy, Charles. *The Empty Raincoat.* London: Hutchinson, 1994.
Handy, Charles. *Beyond Certainty.* London: Hutchinson, 1995.
Handy, Charles. *The Hungry Spirit: Beyond Capitalism-A Quest for Purpose in the Modern World.* London: Hutchinson, 1997.
Handy, Charles. *The Elephant and the Flea.* London: Hutchinson, 2001.
Handy, Charles. *Myself and Other More Important Matters.* London: Arrow Books, 2007.
Handy, Charles. *The New Philanthropists.* London: Heinemann, 2007.

Frederick Herzberg The Hygiene–Motivation Theory

Herzberg is best known for his 'hygiene-motivation' or 'two factor' theory of what motivates workers. He invented the acronym KITA (Kick In The Ass) and also coined the term 'job enrichment' to describe a process in which positively motivating factors are built into the design of jobs. Herzberg's work focused on the individual in the workplace and the attitude of individuals to their jobs, but it has also been popular with managers as it emphasises the importance of management knowledge and expertise.

1923	Born.
1945	Enters Dachau concentration camp with US liberating forces.
1946	Graduates from City College of New York.
1951–1957	Research director of psychological services in Pittsburgh, Pennsylvania.
1957	Appointed professor of management at Case Western Reserve University, Cleveland, Ohio.
1959	*The Motivation to Work* published.
1966	*Work and the Nature of Man* published.
1968	'One more time: how do you motivate employees?' published in the *Harvard Business Review*.
1972	Joins University of Utah's College of Business.
2000	Dies.

LIFE AND CAREER

Frederick Herzberg (1923–2000) was a US clinical psychologist who became an influential management thinker through his work on the nature of motivation and the most effective ways of motivating people. The 'over-riding interest in mental health' that led him into a career in psychology stemmed from a belief that 'mental health is the core issue of our times', a conviction prompted by his posting while serving in the US forces during the Second World War to Dachau concentration camp very soon after its liberation. On his return to the United States, he worked for the US Public Health Service before beginning an academic career. His 'hygiene-motivation' theory was first set out in *The Motivation to Work*, published in 1959. From 1972 until his retirement he worked at the University of Utah College of Business.

KEY THINKING

The hygiene-motivation theory

The 'hygiene-motivation' or 'two factor' theory that made Herzberg's name grew out of research he undertook with two hundred Pittsburgh engineers and accountants in the late 1950s.

He asked his subjects to recall times when they had felt exceptionally good about their jobs, why they had had these positive feelings, and what effect they had had both on their performance at work and on their lives outside work. In a second question, he asked them to recall times when their experiences at work had resulted in negative feelings.

Herzberg was struck by the fact that the positive things the respondents had to say about their work experiences were not the opposite of the negative ones. From this, he concluded that there were two factors at work.

He postulated that human beings have two sets of needs:
- lower-level needs as an animal to avoid pain and deprivation
- higher-level needs as a human being to grow psychologically

These needs have to be satisfied at work as much as in any other sphere of life. He concluded from the results of his survey that some factors in the workplace meet the first set of needs but not the second, and vice versa. The former group of factors he called 'hygiene factors' and the latter, 'motivators'.

'Hygiene factors' have to do with the context or environment in which a person works. They include:
- company policy and administration
- supervision
- working relationships
- working conditions
- status
- security
- pay

The most important thing about these factors is that they do not in themselves promote job satisfaction; they serve primarily to prevent job dissatisfaction, in the same way that good hygiene does not in itself produce good health, but a lack of it will usually cause disease. Herzberg also spoke of them as 'dissatisfiers' or 'maintenance factors', because their absence or inadequacy causes dissatisfaction at work, while their presence simply keeps workers reasonably happy without motivating them to better themselves or their performance. Some factors are also not to be regarded as true motivators because they need constant reinforcement. Once introduced, they increasingly come to be regarded as rights to be expected, rather than incentives to greater satisfaction and achievement.

'Motivators' (also referred to as 'growth factors') relate to what a person does at work, rather than to the context in which it is done. They include:
- achievement
- recognition
- the work itself
- responsibility
- advancement
- growth

Herzberg explains that the two sets of factors are separate and distinct because they are concerned with two different sets of needs. They are not opposites.

Herzberg's hygiene-motivation theory is derived from the outcomes of several investigations into job satisfaction and job dissatisfaction, studies that replicated his original research in Pittsburgh. The theory proposes that most of the factors that contribute to job satisfaction are motivators, while most of the factors that contribute to job dissatisfaction are hygiene factors.

Most of the evidence on which Herzberg based his theory is relatively clear-cut. This is particularly the case with regard to achievement and promotion prospects as factors that are potential job satisfiers as well as with regard to supervision and job insecurity as factors that contribute principally to dissatisfaction.

The element that continues to cause some debate is salary/pay, which seems as if it might belong in either group. Herzberg himself placed salary with the dissatisfiers, although the evidence was not so clear in this instance. This would seem to be the more appropriate classification. Although pay may have some short-term motivational value, it is difficult to conceive of it as a long-term motivator of the same order as responsibility and achievement. Most experience (and the history of industrial relations) would point to pay as a dissatisfier and therefore a hygiene factor along with supervision, status, and security.

KITA

In his extremely influential 1968 article for the *Harvard Business Review*, 'One more time: how do you motivate employees?', Herzberg basically lumped all the hygiene factors together with the less pleasant aspects of the working experience under the heading KITA (Kick In The Ass). To explain why managers are unable to motivate employees, he demonstrated again that employees are not motivated by being kicked (figuratively speaking), or by being given more money or benefits, or by a comfortable environment, or by reducing the time they spend at work. These things merely produce movement, the avoidance of pain. What genuinely motivates employees are things that are intangible, or intrinsic to the work.

Adam and Abraham

Herzberg used biblical allusions to illustrate his theory, especially in his book *Work and the Nature of Man*, first published in 1966 and intended as a psychological underpinning to his workplace-oriented studies. He depicted humanity's basic needs as two parallel arrows pointing in opposite directions. One arrow represents the 'Animal-Adam' nature of human beings, concerned with the basic need to avoid physical deprivation (the hygiene factors); the other represents their 'Human-Abraham' nature, which is driven by a need to realise their potential for perfection (the motivation factors).

Job enrichment

Job enrichment was a logical extension of Herzberg's hygiene-motivation theory. Still working on the basic premise that a satisfied workforce is a productive workforce, he proposed that motivators of the type he had always advocated should be built into job design. They included:

- self-scheduling
- control of resources
- accountability
- undertaking specialised tasks in order to become expert in them

He saw it as a continuous function of management to ensure that people were given the opportunity to become more and more responsibly and creatively involved in their jobs.

FREDERICK HERZBERG IN PERSPECTIVE

Herzberg's work – in common with that of Elton Mayo (known for the Hawthorne Experiments), Abraham Maslow (developer of the hierarchy of needs), and Douglas McGregor (creator of Theory X and Theory Y) – can be seen as a reaction to F.W. Taylor's scientific management theories. These focused on techniques which could be used to maximise the productivity of manual workers and on the division of mental and physical work between management and workers. In contrast, Herzberg and his contemporaries believed that workers wanted the opportunity to feel part of a team and to grow and develop.

Although Herzberg's theory is not highly regarded by psychologists today, managers have found in it useful guidelines for action. Its basic tenets are easy to understand and can be applied to all types of organisation. Furthermore, it appears to support the position and influence of management.

More specifically, it has had a considerable impact on reward systems, first, in a move away from payment-by-results systems, and today in the growing proportion of cafeteria benefits schemes, which allow individual employees to choose the fringe benefits which best suit them.

Job enrichment was more theorised about than put into practice. Many schemes that were tried resulted only in cosmetic changes or led to demands for increased worker control and were therefore terminated. Nowadays the concept is more one of people enrichment, although this still owes a great deal to Herzberg's original work. His greatest contribution has been the knowledge that motivation comes mainly from within the individual; it cannot be imposed from the outside by an organisation in accordance with some formula. Many of today's trends – career management, self-managed learning, and empowerment – have their basis in Herzberg's insights.

THE BEST SOURCES OF HELP
Books:
Herzberg, Frederick, Bernard Mausner, and Barbara Bloch Snyderman. *The Motivation to Work*. 2nd ed. New York: Wiley, 1959.
Herzberg, Frederick. *Work and the Nature of Man*. London: Staples Press, 1968.

Herzberg, Frederick. *The Managerial Choice: To Be Efficient and To Be Human*. Homewood, Illinois: Dow Jones-Irwin, 1976.

Journal Articles:

Cameron, Donald. 'Herzberg – Still a key to understanding motivation.' *Training Officer*, July/August 1996, pp. 184–186.

Herzberg, Frederick. 'One more time: how do you motivate employees?' *Harvard Business Review*, January/February 1968, pp. 53–62.

(This article was republished, in *Harvard Business Review*, September/October 1987, pp. 109–120, with a retrospective commentary by the author. By the time of this republication, the article had sold over one million reprints, making it the most requested article in the *Review's* history)

Rosabeth Moss Kanter Pioneer of Empowerment and Change Management

Rosabeth Moss Kanter's writings encompass a wide range of topics. She views herself, however, as a thought leader and developer of ideas, and is best known for her work on change management and innovation although her current area of research is turnaround management.

Much of Kanter's success is due to a combination of rigorous research, practical experience, and an ability to write in a clear and concrete way, using many illustrative examples.

1943	Born.
1977	Publication of *Men and Women of the Corporation*.
1983	Publication of *The Change Masters: Corporate Entrepreneurs at Work*.
1986–present	Moves from Yale to Harvard Business School. Currently Ernest L. Arbuckle professor of business administration.
1989	Publication of *When Giants Learn to Dance: Master the Challenge of Strategy, Management, and Careers in the 1990s*.
1989–1992	Editor, *Harvard Business Review*.
2001	Receives US Academy of Management's Distinguished Career Award.

LIFE AND CAREER

Kanter was born in 1943, in Cleveland, Ohio, and attended the top women's academy, Bryn Mawr. She took her PhD at the University of Michigan and was associate professor of sociology at Brandeis University from 1966 to 1977. Between 1973 and 1974 she was on the Organization Behavior Program at Harvard, and she was a fellow and visiting scholar of Harvard Law School between 1975 and 1976.

From 1977 to 1986 Kanter was professor of sociology and professor of organisational management at Yale, and from 1979 to 1986, she was a visiting professor at the Sloan School of Management, Massachusetts Institute of Technology (MIT). In 1986, she returned to Harvard as the 'class of 1960' professor of entrepreneurship and innovation, and she still holds the post of professor of business administration at Harvard Business School.

Between 1989 and 1992 Kanter was editor of the *Harvard Business Review*, and she acted as a key economic adviser to Michael Dukakis during his 1988 presidential campaign. She has travelled widely as a public speaker, lecturer, and international consultant. In 1977, she and her future husband, Barry Stein, set up a management consultancy called Goodmeasure, which has some large and well-known multinational companies as clients.

KEY THINKING

Kanter has authored or co-authored several books and well over 150 major articles. Her doctoral thesis was on communes, and her first books, written during the early 1970s, were sociological. The three books for which she is best known are *Men and Women of the Corporation*, *The Change Masters* and *When Giants Learn to Dance*. There is a logical progression within them, in that the first studies the stifling effects of bureaucratic organisation on individuals, while the subsequent titles go on to explore ways in which 'post-entrepreneurial' organisations release, and make use of, individuals' talents and abilities. Later books include *The Challenge of Organizational Change* (with Barry Stein and Todd Jick), *World Class: Thriving Locally in the Global Economy*, *The Frontiers of Management*, and *Evolve*.

Men and Women of the Corporation

Men and Women of the Corporation won the C. Wright Mills Award in 1977 as the year's best book on social

Gurus

issues. It is a detailed analysis of the nature and effects of the distribution of power and powerlessness within the headquarters of one large, bureaucratic, multinational corporation (called Industrial Supply Corporation, or Indsco, in the book). The effects of powerlessness on behaviour are explored and the detrimental effects of disempowerment, both for the organisation and individual employees, are made clear. Women were the most obvious group affected by lack of power, though Kanter emphasises that other groups outside the white, male norm, such as ethnic minority members, were also affected.

Three main structural variables explained the behaviours observed within Indsco:

- the structure of opportunity
- the structure of power
- the proportional distribution of people of different kinds

Before this book was published, it was generally assumed that behavioural differences underlay women's general lack of career progress. However Kanter's findings made structural issues central and the implications for change management were significant. If all employees were to become more empowered, organisations rather than people would need to change. Accordingly, the book ends with practical policy suggestions to create appropriate structural changes.

While working on this book, Kanter identified the need for organisational change to improve working life, create more equal opportunities, and make more use of employees' talents within organisations.

The Change Masters

The Change Masters puts forward various approaches to achieving these ends. Kanter compares four traditional corporations like Indsco with six competitive and successful organisations, described as 'change masters'. All findings were weighed against the experiences of many other companies and much other material. From the six innovative organisations, Kanter derives a model for encouraging innovation.

Innovative companies were found to have an 'integrative' approach to management, while companies unlikely to innovate were described as 'segmentalist' in that they were compartmentalised by units or departments. The difference begins with a company's approach to problem-solving, and extends through its structure and culture. Entrepreneurial organisations:

- operate at the edge of their competence, focusing on exploring the unknown rather than on controlling the known
- measure themselves by future-focused visions (how far they have to go) rather than by past standards (how far they have come)

Three clusters of structures and processes are identified as factors that encourage power circulation and access to power: open communication systems, network-forming arrangements, and decentralisation of resources. Their implementation is also discussed by Kanter.

Individuals can also be change masters. 'New entrepreneurs' are people who improve existing businesses rather than start new ones. They can be found in any functional area and are described as, literally, the right people, in the right place, at the right time:

- the right people – those with vision and ideas extending beyond the organisation's normal practice
- the right place – an integrative environment fostering proactive vision, coalitions, and teams
- the right time – a moment in the historical flow when change becomes most possible

The ultimate change masters are corporate leaders, who translate their vision into a new organisational reality.

The Change Masters advocates 'participation management' as the means to greater empowerment. Some major 'building blocks' for productive change are identified, and practical measures to remove 'road blocks' to innovation are discussed.

When Giants Learn to Dance

When Giants Learn to Dance completes Kanter's trilogy on the need for change which, she considered, US corporations had to confront in order to compete more effectively. The global economy is likened to a 'corporate Olympics' of competing businesses, with results determining which nations, as well as organisations, are winners.

The games differ, but successful teams share some characteristics such as strength, skill, discipline, good organisation, and focus on individual excellence. To win, US companies would have to become progressively more entrepreneurial and less bureaucratic. Kanter suggested a model for the 1990s the 'post-entrepreneurial' corporation, in which three shaping forces would play the key roles:

- the context set at the top
- top management values
- project ideas and approaches coming up through the organisation

An 'athletic' organisation of this kind would be lean and flexible, and would seek to create synergies through the use of team and partnership approaches. The organisation would be built on empowerment, and employees would be highly valued within team-based or partnership relationships.

Kanter picks out seven skills, or sensibilities, that characterise individual 'business athletes'. These are:

- the ability to operate and get results without depending on hierarchical authority, position, or status
- the ability to compete in a way that enhances co-operation, rather than destroy competitors
- the high ethical standards needed to support the trust that is crucial for co-operative approaches when competing in the corporate Olympics
- a dose of humility, basic self-confidence being tempered by the understanding that new things will always need to be learnt
- process focus, that is, respect for the process of implementation as well as for the substance of what is implemented

- a multifaceted and ambidextrous approach that makes possible cross-functional or cross-departmental work, the forming of alliances where appropriate, and the cutting of ties where necessary
- a temperament that derives satisfaction from results, and a willingness to be rewarded according to achievements

World Class: Thriving Locally in the Global Economy

World Class: Thriving Locally in the Global Economy focuses on world class companies with employees described as 'cosmopolitan' in type. These people are rich in the 'three Cs' – concepts, competence, and connections – and carry a more universal culture to all the places in which their company operates.

This knowledge-rich breed is set against 'locals', who are set in their ways, and the two groups are viewed as the main classes in modern society. The book is optimistic, in that Kanter believes stakeholders can influence world-class companies to spread best practice around the world.

Globalisation, it is argued, offers an opportunity to develop businesses and give new life to the regions. From her studies of regenerative areas, Kanter suggests that business and local government leaders can work together to draw in the right sort of companies to create prosperity.

Later works

The Challenge of Organizational Change, co-authored with Barry Stein and Todd Jick, draws a distinction between evolutionary and revolutionary change, here described as the 'long march' and 'bold stroke' approaches.

Rosabeth Moss Kanter on the Frontiers of Management collects Kanter's essays and research articles for the *Harvard Business Review* together into one volume.

ROSABETH MOSS KANTER IN PERSPECTIVE

Overall, Kanter's books present some fairly complex ideas in a way that many people seem to find approachable. They are well-argued and supported with a wealth of practical research evidence. Some of her central ideas, once viewed by some as unrealistic, have now become absorbed into general management wisdom. These include empowerment, participative management, and employee involvement. In *The Frontiers of Management*, she is presented as a ground-breaking explorer who has initiated a revolution in terms of new ways of working. Some managers have yet to cross those frontiers, or do so in aspiration rather than actuality.

THE BEST SOURCES OF HELP

Books:

Moss Kanter, Rosabeth. *Men and Women of the Corporation.* New York: Basic Books Inc, 1977.

Moss Kanter, Rosabeth. *The Change Masters: Corporate Entrepreneurs at Work.* London: George Allen & Unwin, 1983.

Moss Kanter, Rosabeth. *When Giants Learn to Dance: Master the Challenge of Strategy, Management, and Careers in the 1990s.* London: Simon & Schuster, 1989.

Moss Kanter, Rosabeth, Barry Stein, and Todd Jick. *The Challenge of Organizational Change: How Companies Experience It and Leaders Guide It.* New York: Free Press, 1992.

Moss Kanter, Rosabeth. *World Class: Thriving Locally in the Global Economy.* New York: Simon & Schuster, 1995.

Moss Kanter, Rosabeth. *Rosabeth Moss Kanter on the Frontiers of Change.* Boston, Massachusetts: Harvard Business School Press, 1997.

Moss Kanter, Rosabeth. *Confidence.* London: Random House Business Books, 2004.

Moss Kanter, Rosabeth. *SuperCorp: How Vanguard Companies Create Innovation, Profits, Growth, and Social Good.* New York: Crown Business, 2009.

Kaplan and Norton The Balanced Scorecard

The name of Robert Kaplan is almost invariably linked with that of his co-author, David Norton, and with the assessment tool they introduced to the business world in the early 1990s – the 'balanced scorecard'. Kaplan and Norton argued that adherence to quarterly financial returns and the bottom line alone could not provide the organisation with an overall strategic view. The balanced scorecard enables the organisation to describe its strategy adequately. It shows how non-financial factors – intangible assets – are tied in with the financial ones.

LIFE AND CAREER

Robert Kaplan is the Baker Foundation Professor at Harvard Business School in Boston. He was previously based at Carnegie Mellon University in Pittsburgh, where he was Dean of the Graduate School of Industrial Administration. Kaplan's research work has focused on performance measurement systems, in particular activity-based costing and the balanced scorecard.

David Norton is a founder, chairman, and chief executive of the Balanced Scorecard Collaborative, based in Lincoln, Massachusetts. He also founded and was President of Renaissance Solutions, a balanced scorecard consulting firm.

They are jointly recognised as the popularisers of the balanced scorecard concept. Their approach to it was first introduced in a 1992 *Harvard Business Review* article ('The balanced scorecard: Measures that drive performance'), which began with a variation of the saying 'What gets measured gets done'; Kaplan and Norton took as their starting point 'What you measure is what you get'.

As the story goes, David Norton coined the term 'Balanced Scorecard' after a conversation with John Thompson, who was then president of IBM Canada. John Thompson, returning from a round of golf, announced he needed a scorecard just like the one he used during his game to measure the performance of his company. The balanced scorecard grew out of that conversation.

KEY THINKING

In creating the balanced scorecard, Kaplan and Norton argued that strategies often fail because they are not converted successfully into actions that employees can understand and apply in their everyday work. The problem comes with the search for realistic measures that are meaningful to those doing the work, relate visibly to strategic direction, and provide a balanced picture of what is happening throughout the organisation, not just of one facet of it. It is this aspect that the balanced scorecard addresses.

It concentrates on measures in four key strategic areas- finance, customers, internal business processes, and learning and innovation – and requires the implementing organisation to identify goals and measures for each of them. Research and experimentation have come up with the following, which seem to be regularly applied in many organisations.

Financial perspective
• Goals: survival, success/growth, prosperity
• Measures: return on capital, cash flow, revenue growth, liquidity, cost reduction, project profitability, performance reliability

Customer perspective
• Goals: customer acquisition, retention, profitability, and satisfaction
• Measures: market share, transaction cost ratios, customer loyalty satisfaction surveys/index, supplier relationships, key accounts

Internal business process perspective
• Goals: core competencies, critical technologies, business processes, key skills
• Measures: efficiency measures of working practices and production processes, cycle times, unit costs, defect rates, time to market

Learning and innovation perspective
• Goals: continuous improvement, new product development
• Measures: productivity of intrapreneurship, new ideas and suggestions from employees, employee satisfaction, skill levels, staff attitude, retention, profitability, and rate of improvement

The scorecard provides a description of the organisation's strategy. It will indicate where problems lie because it shows the interrelationships between goals and the activities that are linked to their achievement. It creates an understanding of what is going on elsewhere in the organisation and shows all employees how they are contributing. As Kaplan has said: 'The business scorecard seeks to empower all levels of the workforce by educating them about their company's strategy and the small steps they can take to achieve their goals.' Providing that accurate and timely information is fed into the system, the scorecard also helps to focus attention where change and learning are needed through the cause and effect relationships it can reveal. Examples of the types of insight achieved were detailed in the article 'Linking the Balanced Scorecard to Strategy'.

• If we increase employee training about products, then they will become more knowledgeable about the full range of products they can sell.
• If employees are more knowledgeable about products, then their sales effectiveness will improve.
• If their sales effectiveness improves, then the average margins of products they sell will increase.

Implementing the balanced scorecard
In 'Putting the balanced scorecard to work' Kaplan and Norton identify eight steps towards building a scorecard:
1. Preparation. Select/define the strategy/business unit to which to apply the scorecard. Think in terms of the appropriateness of the four main perspectives defined above.
2. First interviews. Distribute information about the scorecard to senior managers along with the organisation's vision, mission, and strategy. A facilitator will interview each manager on the organisation's strategic objectives and ask for initial thoughts on scorecard measures.
3. First executive workshop. Match measures to strategy. The management team is brought together to develop the scorecard. After agreeing the vision statement, the team debates each of the four key strategic areas, addressing the following questions: If my vision succeeds, how will I differ? What are the critical success factors? What are the critical measurements? These questions help to focus attention on the impact of turning the vision into reality and what has to be done to make it happen. It is important to represent the views of customers and shareholders, and to gain a number of measures for each critical success factor.
4. Second interviews. The facilitator reviews and consolidates the findings of the workshop and interviews each of the managers individually about the emerging scorecard.
5. Second workshop. Hold a team debate on the proposed scorecard; the participants should discuss

the proposed measures, link ongoing change programmes to the measures, and set targets or rates of improvement for each of the measures. Start outlining the communication and implementation processes.

6. Third workshop. Final consensus on vision, goals, measures, and targets. The team devises an implementation programme to communicate the scorecard to employees, integrate it into management philosophy, and develop an information system to support it.

7. Implementation. The implementation team links the measures to information support systems and databases and communicates the what, why, where and who of the scorecard throughout the organisation. The end product should be a management information system that links strategy to shop-floor activity.

8. Periodic review. Balanced scorecard measures can be prepared for review by senior management at appropriate intervals.

KAPLAN AND NORTON IN PERSPECTIVE

Kaplan and Norton published their first article on the balanced scorecard in early 1992. Since then, elaborating, explaining, and applying the basic concept seems to have become a small industry. The jury is, nevertheless, still out on whether it will be an innovation of lasting importance or merely a passing fad. But an increasing number of organisations are trying it out. David Norton has claimed that 60 per cent of large US companies are now using some sort of scorecard that combines financial with non-financial measures.

The balanced scorecard should not be regarded as a panacea. In 'The design and implementation of the balanced business scorecard: an analysis of three companies in practice', Stephen Letza states that the balanced scorecard should highlight performance as a dynamic, continuous, and integrated process; act as an integrating tool; function as the pivotal tool determining the organisation's current and future direction; and deliver information that forms the backbone of its strategy. He also highlights some of the major drawbacks that may be encountered when using the balanced scorecard and points out the need to:

- avoid being swamped by the minutiae of too many detailed measures and make sure that measures do genuinely relate to the strategic goals of the organisation
- make sure all the organisation's activities are included in the assessment – this ensures that everyone is contributing to the organisation's strategic goals

- watch out for conflict as information becomes accessible to those who were not formerly in a position to see it or act on it, and try to harness conflict constructively

The balanced scorecard can be seen as the latest in a long line of attempts at management control, descending from Taylor through to work measurement systems, quality assurance systems, and performance indicators. Commentators claim that the balanced scorecard could become the management tool of the early 21st century, given that it is flexible and adaptable to each organisation's use, and that it is practical, straightforward, and devoid of obscure theory. Most importantly, it responds to many organisations' requirements to expand strategically on traditional financial measures, and points to areas for change.

THE BEST SOURCES OF HELP

Books:

Kaplan, Robert, and David Norton. *The Balanced Scorecard: Translating Strategy into Action*. Boston, Massachusetts: Harvard Business School Press, 1996.

Kaplan, Robert, and David Norton. *The Strategy-Focused Organization*. Boston, Massachusetts: Harvard Business School Press, 2000.

Kaplan, Robert, and David Norton. *Strategy Maps: Converting Intangible Assets into Tangible Outcomes*. Boston, Massachusetts: Harvard Business School Press, 2004.

Kaplan, Robert, and David Norton. *Execution Premium: Linking Strategy to Operations for Competitive Advantage*. Boston, Massachusetts: Harvard Business School Press, 2008.

Journal Articles:

Kaplan, Robert, and David Norton. 'The balanced scorecard: measures that drive performance.' *Harvard Business Review*, January/February 1992, pp. 71–79.

Kaplan, Robert, and David Norton. 'Putting the balanced scorecard to work.' *Harvard Business Review*, September/October 1993, pp.134–147.

Kaplan, Robert, and David Norton. 'Using the balanced scorecard as a strategic management system.' *Harvard Business Review*, January/February 1996, pp. 75–85.

Kaplan, Robert, and David Norton. 'Linking the balanced scorecard to strategy.' *California Management Review*, Fall 1996, pp. 53–79.

Kaplan, Robert, and David Norton. 'Strategic learning and the balanced scorecard.' *Strategy and Leadership*, September/October 1996, pp. 18–24.

Gurus

Theodore Levitt Marketing

Theodore Levitt made a key contribution to management theory in the marketing field, stimulating debate on the importance of a pervasive marketing mindset within an organisation. Having encouraged an awareness of the marketing concept, Levitt further analysed the benefits and shortfalls of marketing in a series of articles and books over four decades. His talent for expounding his views clearly and for illustrating his arguments with company examples and metaphors makes his work highly accessible.

1925	Born.
1935	Leaves Germany for the United States.
1959	Lecturer in business administration at Harvard Business School.
1960	'Marketing myopia' appears in *Harvard Business Review*.
1965	Edward W. Carter Professor of Business Administration, Harvard Business School.
1990	Resigns post as editor of *Harvard Business Review*.
2006	Dies.

LIFE AND CAREER

Born in Volmerz in Germany, Levitt moved with his parents to the United States in 1935, where he later studied economics. In the late 1950s he worked as a consultant in Chicago, before being approached by the Harvard Business School. In his very first year there he began to teach marketing, although at the time he had reportedly never read a book on the subject.

Levitt's first article was published in 1956. His tenure at Harvard as an academic lasted for more than 30 years. This period included a spell as a somewhat controversial editor of the *Harvard Business Review*, a post from which he resigned in 1990 following an argument over an article on women in management.

KEY THINKING

Levitt emphasises the need for a company to achieve a balanced orientation by including marketing in its strategy. He focuses on the need for a marketing outlook to pervade an organisation and provide a necessary counterbalance to a preoccupation with production. His landmark article expounding this theory, 'Marketing myopia', appeared in the *Harvard Business Review* in 1960 and is one of the most requested reprints from that journal, having sold over 500,000 copies. Subsequently, Levitt reiterated and expanded his theory in several articles and books. These partly focus on the methodology of implementing the marketing mode, including the proposition of a 'marketing matrix' for assessing the degree of marketing orientation existing in a company. They also explore the theory behind the marketing concept and delineate some of its limitations and problems. Other works concentrate on topics such as 'the industrialization of service' (examining the potential benefits of applying the production line and quality control methods of industry to service provision), the nature of the product, advertising, and globalisation.

'Marketing myopia' explored

Levitt himself described his article 'Marketing myopia' as a manifesto. It challenged the conventional thinking of the time by putting forward a persuasive case for the importance of the marketing approach and the short-sightedness of failing to incorporate it into business strategy.

In an era in which post-war shortages contributed to a concentration on production, most companies had developed a product orientation, which, Levitt believed, was too narrow a philosophy to allow continued business success. A drive to increase the efficiency and volume of production took place at the expense of monitoring whether the company was actually producing what the customer wanted. The article stressed that 'customer wants and desires should be a central consideration of any business. The organisation must learn to think of itself not as producing goods or services but as buying customers, as doing the things that will make people want to do business with it'.

In order to achieve this, 'the entire corporation must be viewed as a customer-creating and customer-satisfying organism. Management must think of itself not as providing products but as providing customer-creating value satisfactions. It must push this idea (and everything it means and requires) into every nook and cranny of the organisation'.

Levitt highlighted the need for companies to define what business they are in, as this concentrates attention on customer needs. He used the now famous example of the railways, which, rather than thinking of themselves as being in the business of running trains, should instead have defined themselves as providing transportation. Self-definition along those lines would have helped the railway companies to be aware of changing customer demand; if they had had that awareness, they might not have suffered so greatly from the rise of road and air transport. Focusing on the satisfaction of customer needs, Levitt argues, is a better path to continued business success than concentration on the actual product on offer.

Also presented in 'Marketing myopia', as a warning against complacency, is Levitt's belief that 'in truth there is no such thing as a growth industry'. There are growth opportunities, which can be created or capitalised on, but those companies which believe they are 'riding some automatic growth escalator invariably descend into stagnation'. The belief that a company is in a growth industry and is therefore secure must never be allowed to overshadow or replace awareness of the need to practise marketing and assert a customer orientation. This is the only route through which a company can hope to achieve sustained expansion.

Of a more practical nature is the 'marketing matrix', a device presented by Levitt in *Marketing for Business Growth* to aid the measurement of a company's marketing orientation. A horizontal scale of 1–9 records the degree of customer orientation, and a vertical scale of 1–9 records the degree of company orientation. A score of 9 on both scales is the ideal. Using this method, organisations can assess their incorporation of marketing thinking and determine where steps are needed to improve their strategy and to become more marketing-oriented.

Ways of doing this include the 'industrialisation of service', which involves the measuring and standardising of customer service to a predetermined quality level – in other words, applying industrial-style quality controls to the service process. For example, a production line can be set up for service delivery, and service encounters can be standardised and monitored to ensure that they are of a similar quality. This has been accomplished with great success by the McDonald's fast food chain ('The industrialisation of service'). To recognise this concept is, writes Levitt, to introduce a potentially emancipating new cognitive mode and operating style into modern enterprise' (*The Marketing Imagination*). Another factor that is important in enhancing a marketing orientation is relationship marketing (see 'After the sale is over'). This revolves around the need not only to acquire customers, but also to keep them and form mutually beneficial long-term relationships with them.

In a 1983 article, 'The globalization of markets', Levitt once more produced a forward-looking 'manifesto' with a view of the changing nature of the marketplace and the trend, fuelled by technological advances, towards globalisation. His thesis is that, in order to survive and prosper, companies must offer standardised products around the world, products that incorporate the best in design, reliability, and price. The efficiency of such an approach will outweigh, in his opinion, the benefits of taking into account varying cultural preferences and tailoring products to different national markets. The reason for this is the overlying trend towards world homogenisation. 'Two vectors shape the world-technology and globalisation. The first helps determine human preferences; the second, economic realities. Regardless of how much preferences evolve and diverge, they also gradually converge and form markets where economies of scale lead to reduction of costs and prices.'

Levitt's 1991 book, *Thinking about Management*, contains a distillation of his thinking on effective management, presented in nuggets in the three categories of thinking, changing, and operating. Many of his theories are reiterated here, and the work forms a useful guide to his collected thought.

THEODORE LEVITT IN PERSPECTIVE

A major influence on Levitt's work was the writing of Peter Drucker, who was among the first to see marketing as all-pervasive: 'Marketing is not a function, it is the whole business seen from the customer's point of view' (*The Practice of Management*).

However, although influenced by academic thought, Levitt seems to have drawn his greatest inspiration from the real world, examining the companies around him and distilling the examples of good and bad practice that illustrate much of his writing.

Levitt's influence contributed to the rise of the marketing concept in the 1960s and its increasing incorporation into management thinking, initially in the United States but later also in Europe. His subsequent works may not have achieved the fame of 'Marketing myopia', but they are nevertheless an important part of the evolving pattern of marketing writing that has gathered impetus through recent decades. By pointing out the myopic vision of many managers, Levitt set in motion a vigorous new way of thinking that was taken up by other management writers and practitioners and culminated in the rebirth of marketing in the 1980s. Other marketing gurus such as Philip Kotler acknowledge the influence of Levitt's work, and he is regularly quoted.

In retrospect, Levitt has been proven to have had remarkable foresight in his anticipation of the importance of marketing to organisations, his initial work predating the marketing boom by two decades. He also successfully predicted the value of relationship marketing, a topic which only became an identifiable discipline in the early 1990s, and the concept of the global village, which is now commonplace.

THE BEST SOURCES OF HELP

Books:

Levitt, Theodore. *Innovation in Marketing: New Perspectives for Profit and Growth*. New York: McGraw-Hill, 1962.

Levitt, Theodore. *Marketing for Business Growth*. New York: McGraw-Hill, 1974. (First published in 1969 as *The Marketing Mode: Pathways to Corporate Growth*)

Levitt, Theodore. *The Marketing Imagination*. New York: Free Press, 1983.

Levitt, Theodore. *Thinking about Management*. New York: Free Press, 1991.

Levitt, Theodore. *Ted Levitt on Marketing*. Cambridge, Massachusetts: Harvard Business School Press, 2006.

Journal Articles:

Levitt, Theodore. 'Marketing myopia.' *Harvard Business Review*, July/August 1960, pp. 45–56.

Levitt, Theodore. 'The industrialization of service.' *Harvard Business Review*, September/October 1976, pp. 63–74.

Kurt Lewin Change Management and Group Dynamics

Kurt Lewin's output included studies of leadership styles and their effects and work on group decision-making, and he was responsible for the development of force field theory, the 'unfreeze-change-refreeze' model of change management, the 'action research' approach to research, and the group dynamics approach to training (especially in the form of T Groups). He was behind the founding of the Center for Group Dynamics in the United States.

1890	Born.
1910	Begins formal training in psychology in Berlin.
1914	Graduates as PhD from the University of Berlin.
1914–1916	Active service with the German army; is wounded and awarded the Iron Cross.
1916–1932	Teaches at the University of Berlin.
1932	Leaves Germany to escape persecution by the Nazis.
1935	Appointed professor of child psychology at the University of Iowa.
1944	Co-founds the Research Center for Group Dynamics at MIT. Mother killed in Nazi extermination camp.
1947	Dies.

LIFE AND CAREER

German-born, Lewin was professor of philosophy and psychology at Berlin University until he fled to the United States in 1932 to escape from the Nazis. There, he taught at Cornell University, and then at Iowa, becoming professor of child psychology at the latter's Child Research Station. In 1944 he went on to found, with Douglas McGregor and others, a research centre for group dynamics at the Massachusetts Institute of Technology.

KEY THINKING

Leadership styles and their effects

With his colleagues L. Lippitt and R. White, Lewin studied the effects of three different leadership styles on the outcomes of boys' activity groups in Iowa (1939). Those three styles were classified as 'democratic', 'autocratic', and 'laissez-faire'. It was found that in the group with an autocratic leader, there was more dissatisfaction and behaviours became either more aggressive or apathetic. In the group with a democratic leader, there was more co-operation and enjoyment, while those in the laissez-faire group showed no particular dissatisfaction, although they were not particularly productive, either.

Significantly, when the respective leaders were asked to change their styles, the effects produced by each leadership style remained similar. Lewin was aiming to show that the democratic style achieved better results. The possibility of social and cultural factors influencing the results undermined his findings to some extent; nevertheless, the studies suggested the benefits of a democratic style in a US context. They also showed that it is possible for leaders and managers to change their approach, to improve their leadership through training, and to adopt management styles appropriate to their situation and context.

Group decision-making

After the Second World War, Lewin carried out research for the US government, exploring ways of influencing people to change their dietary habits and eat less popular cuts of meat. He found that, if group members were encouraged to become involved, discuss the issues themselves, and make their own decisions as a group, they were far more likely to change their habits than if they simply attended lectures where they were given information, recipes, and advice.

Force field analysis

Lewin put forward the theory that people's activity is affected by forces in their surrounding environment, or 'field'. Its three main principles are that:
- behaviour is a function of the existing field
- analysis starts from the complete situation and distinguishes its component parts
- a concrete person in a concrete situation can be mathematically represented

A particular feature of Lewin's method of analysing behaviour within a given field (for example, within a situation or an organisation) is its identification of the forces at work there as either 'driving forces', which will tend to promote change, or 'restraining forces', which will tend to hinder it. Such things as ambitions, goals, needs, or fears, that drive a person towards or away from something, constitute driving forces. Restraining forces are different in nature, Lewin asserts, in that they act to oppose driving forces rather than constituting independent forces in themselves.

Force field analysis is used extensively for purposes of organisational and human resources development, because it can help to indicate when the driving and restraining forces affecting people are not in balance, thus creating a situation in which change can occur.

The interplay of the two types of force can produce either stability or instability. Where activities and situations go on from day to day in a regular, stable routine – that is, in what Lewin calls 'quasi-stationary processes' – the forces are more or less balanced out and equalised; they fluctuate around a state of equilibrium. Achieving change, therefore, involves altering the forces that maintain this equilibrium. To bring about an increase in productivity, for example, the forces currently keeping production at its existing quasi-stationary levels would have to be changed. This can be done by taking one of two alternative routes:

- strengthening the driving forces, for example, paying more money for more productivity
- restraining inhibiting factors, for example, simplifying production processes

Strengthening the drives would seem the obvious route to take, but analysis would show that this could lead to the development of countervailing forces, concern among employees about tiredness, or worry about new targets becoming a standard expectation. Reducing restraining forces, for example, through investment in machinery or training to make the process easier, might be a less obvious, but more rewarding approach, bringing about change with less resistance or demoralisation.

Lewin identified two questions to ask when seeking to make changes within the framework of force field analysis:

- Why does a process continue at its current level under the present circumstances?
- What conditions would change these circumstances?

For Lewin, 'circumstances' is a concept with a very broad meaning; it covers anything from the social context and wider environment to subgroups and communication barriers between groups. The position of each of these factors determines a group's structure and 'ecological setting' while the structure and setting together determine a range of possible changes that are dependent on, and can to some degree be controlled by, the pacing and interaction of forces across the entire field.

Model of change: unfreeze – change – refreeze

Lewin believed that, to achieve change effectively, it was necessary to look at all the options for moving from the existing state to a desired future one, then to evaluate the possibilities of each option and decide on the best one, rather than simply identifying a desired goal and taking the straightest and easiest route to it. His change management model is linked to force field analysis and encourages managers to beware of two kinds of force of resistance, the first deriving from 'social habit' or 'custom', and the second from the creation of an 'inner resistance'. These two different kinds of force are rooted in the interplay between a group as a whole and the individuals within it, and only driving forces that are strong enough to break the habits, challenge the interests, or 'unfreeze' the customs of the group will overcome them.

As most members will want to stay within the behavioural norms of the group, individual resistance to change will increase as a person is induced to move further away from current group values. In Lewin's view, this type of resistance can be lowered either by reducing the value the group attaches to something, or by fundamentally changing what the group values. He considered that a complex, stepped process of unfreezing, changing, and refreezing beliefs, attitudes, and values was required to achieve change, with the initial phase of unfreezing

normally involving group discussions in which individuals experience others' views and begin to adapt their own.

Since Lewin's death, 'unfreeze-change-refreeze' has sometimes been applied more rigidly than he intended, for example, by discarding an old structure, establishing a new one, and then 'fixing' the latter into place. Such an inflexible course of action fits badly with more modern attitudes to change as a continuous and flowing process of evolution. Lewin's change model is now often criticised for its linearity, especially from the perspective of more recent research on non-linear, 'chaotic' systems and complexity theory. The model was, however, process-oriented originally. Lewin himself viewed change as a continuing process, recognising that extremely complex forces are at work in group and organisational dynamics.

T-Groups

What is now known as the 'T-Group' (or Training Group) approach was pioneered by Lewin when, in 1946, he was called in to try to develop better relations between Jewish and black communities in Connecticut. Bringing such groups of people together was, Lewin found, a powerful way of exposing areas of conflict, so that established behaviour patterns could 'unfreeze' before potentially changing and 'refreezing'. He called these learning groups T-Groups. This training approach became particularly popular during the 1970s. Some interpreters of the method, however, have used it in a more confrontational way than Lewin may have intended.

Action research

Lewin's 'action research' approach is linked to T-groups. Introduced during the 1940s, it was seen as an important innovation in research methods and was especially used in industry and education. Action research involves experimenting by making changes and simultaneously studying the results, in a cyclic process of planning, action, and fact-gathering. Lewin's approach emphasised the power relationship between the researcher and those researched, and he sought to involve the latter, encouraging their participation in studying the effects of their own actions, identifying their own biases, and working to transform relationships within their communities.

'Action research' centred on the involvement of participants from the community under research and on the pursuit of separate but simultaneous processes of action and evaluation. Different variations of this approach have evolved since Lewin's day, and its validity as a scientific research method for psychology is often questioned. Its strengths, however, in offering groups or communities an involving, self-evaluative, collaborative, and decision-making role are widely accepted.

KURT LEWIN IN PERSPECTIVE

Lewin is widely recognised as a seminal figure in social psychology, although his early death obscured his central role in the development of the managerial human relations movement. In the United States and the United Kingdom (especially through the work of the Tavistock Institute), much subsequent management thinking and research has been influenced by Lewin's approaches and ideas. These, following in the tradition of Mayo's 1920s and 1930s Hawthorne studies, underlie the whole current field of organisational development and change management.

THE BEST SOURCES OF HELP

Books:

Lewin, Kurt. *Resolving Social Conflicts: Selected Papers on Group Dynamics.* New York: Harper and Brothers, 1948.

Lewin, Kurt. *Field Theory in Social Science,* edited by Dorwin Cartwright. London: Tavistock Publications Ltd, 1952, reprinted 1963.

Niccolò Machiavelli The Patron Saint of Power

Throughout most of the five centuries since his death Niccolò Machiavelli has not been a popular figure. There have always been a few people who appreciated his genius, but most have also closely associated him with intrigue and dark deeds. Fortunately, in the last 100 years or so, a more reasoned view of his work has developed, and the enormous value of Machiavelli's philosophy and its remarkable relevance to modern society has emerged.

1469	Born.
1489	Secretary of Second Chancery, Florence.
1512	Falls from grace as Medici family returns to power.
1513	Publication of *The Prince*.
1527	Dies.

LIFE AND CAREER

Niccolò Machiavelli was born in 1469, the son of a Florentine lawyer. He first came to public notice when in 1498, aged 29, he was appointed Secretary of the Second Chancery – part of the complex bureaucracy that ran Florence as a city state. His appointment came after the execution of Savonarola, the friar-politician who, after leading a revolt that expelled the Medicis and established a democratic republic, dominated Florentine life until he fell foul of the papacy and was burned for heresy.

Machiavelli held the post of Secretary for 14 years, during which time his influence was significant. He took part in 30 foreign missions, meeting most of Europe's key politicians and rulers. This opportunity to learn about government, politics, and economics must have been unique. Unfortunately, it was not to last. In 1512 the Medicis returned to power, and Machiavelli lost his post immediately. He was then suspected, quite wrongly, of plotting against the Medicis, for which he was arrested, imprisoned, and tortured. Although eventually found innocent, he was expelled from Florence and forced to spend the rest of his life in exile on an isolated farm. His many attempts to re-enter political life failed and he died

in 1527, still struggling to regain his lost influence. It was more than 300 years later that Italy became unified, as Machiavelli had wanted it to be.

While Machiavelli may not have enjoyed his time in exile, the world has gained immeasurably from it. The enforced idleness allowed him to write prodigiously about his experiences and ideas.

His written works include a history of Florence, several plays, and two books that established him as a great authority on power politics: *The Prince* and *The Discourses*. Professor Max Lerner, in his introduction to the 1950 Random House edition of *The Prince* describes the book as 'a grammar of power'. There can be no more fitting description of this seminal work.

KEY THINKING

Machiavelli presents no instant management theories or clever techniques for solving day-to-day problems. He deals mainly with broad strategies, and to get value from his writing one needs to interpret it and make comparisons. Perhaps the best approach is first to read Jay's introduction on the art of making such comparisons and then to read Machiavelli with a personal checklist of interests and questions.

Some pertinent insights

The following examples show how certain passages in Machiavelli's writing bridge the seemingly huge gap between sixteenth-century politics and twentieth-century business.

Leadership

Machiavelli provides several examples of good leaders and leaves his readers in no doubt about the importance of skilful leadership to the success of any enterprise. He dismisses luck and genius as the key to successful leadership and goes for 'shrewdness'. The dangers and risks a leader faces are dramatically illustrated (happily for us these are less terrifying today than in Renaissance Italy), and comparisons made between the relative ease of getting to a position of leadership and the difficult task of staying there.

Centralisation versus decentralisation

Anyone who thinks that the problem of choosing between centralised or decentralised control is a modern dilemma will be quickly persuaded otherwise by reading *The Prince*. Machiavelli's examples are drawn entirely from government and from military history, but the comparisons with today's business world are easy to make. Perhaps his best advice comes when he is talking about the government of colonies and outposts.

Poor communications in Renaissance times usually made decentralisation the only option in such cases, and Machiavelli's recommendations centre on what today we would call 'selection and training'. A colonial governor must be carefully selected for his experience and loyalty, trained thoroughly in the state's way of doing things and made so familiar with 'best practice' that however isolated from 'head office' guidance he may be, the job will still get done in a highly predictable way. Shades of William Whyte's *Organization Man?*

Takeovers

The equivalent of a takeover in Machiavelli's world was the conquest of another country or the establishment of a colony. In such matters his advice is very clear. One either totally subjugates the original inhabitants, so that rebellion is unlikely and the cost of garrisoning the place reduced to a minimum, or, and Machiavelli makes clear this is his preference, the conqueror puts in a small team of 'key managers'.

This team will displace only a small number of the original inhabitants, who being scattered cannot rebel, and the remainder will quickly toe the new management line since they have everything to gain from co-operation and a clear indication of what happens to those who do not co-operate. Parallels with business takeovers are frighteningly stark.

Change

Machiavelli has little to offer in the way of ideas for coping with change, but shows very clearly that the problems of introducing change were just as awesome and hazardous in the sixteenth century as they are today. In *The Prince* he says: 'It must be considered that there is nothing more difficult to carry out, nor more doubtful of success, nor more dangerous to handle, than to initiate a new order of things.'

Federations and bureaucracies

Machiavelli compared the 'management' of sixteenth-century France and Turkey. He saw France as a 'federal organisation'; a collection of independent baronies in which the retainers regarded their baron, and not the king, as the 'key manager'. Such organisations are difficult to control, impossible to change, and the ruler is easily overthrown. Turkey, on the other hand, was in Machiavelli's time a classic bureaucracy with a highly trained civil service. Civil servants were frequently moved around, hence they developed no local loyalties, and had a strict, hierarchical relationship with 'top management'. The ruler in such a state, being appointed by the 'system', was secure, respected, and powerful. The points of comparison with today's large organisations need little emphasising.

NICCOLÒ MACHIAVELLI IN PERSPECTIVE

The impact of Machiavelli's writing on politics has been accepted for some time, but the relevance of his ideas to business had to wait until the second half of the nineteenth century, when companies began to operate as large, complex organisations – the equivalent in Machiavelli's terms of a move from a tribal society to a corporate state. An English parson, writing in 1820, compares Machiavelli unfavourably with the devil, yet by the 1860s Victor Hugo was able to say, 'Machiavelli is not an evil genius, nor a cowardly writer, he is nothing but the fact . . . not merely the Italian fact, he is the European fact.'

Machiavelli's image is not helped by what many see as an amoral attitude towards power. It is easy to take offence when he unashamedly says, 'A prudent ruler ought not to keep faith when by so doing it would be against his interest, and when the reasons which made him bind himself no longer exist.'

Such statements are easier to accept if we remember they were made in times very different from our own. They were also the words of a man who was a true observer; he reported what he saw and measured results dispassionately in terms of practical success or failure. He had moral views, as can be seen in his other writing, but on political issues he is a cold realist. He had, as Professor Lerner so aptly observed, 'the clear-eyed capacity to distinguish between man as he ought to be and man as he actually is – between the ideal form of institutions and the pragmatic conditions under which they operate'.

By being so linked with intrigue, cruelty, and opportunism, Machiavelli remains rooted in his own age. However, if we set him aside from the harsh realities of sixteenth-century Europe and look at how he observes human nature and organisations, we see a man who was centuries ahead of his time.

THE BEST SOURCES OF HELP
Books:

Jay, Antony. *Management and Machiavelli*. London: Hodder & Stoughton, 1967.

Machiavelli, Niccolò. *The Prince and The Discourses* (introduced by Max Lerner). New York: Random House, 1950.

A number of editions of *The Prince* and *The Discourses* are currently in print.

Whyte, William. *The Organization Man*. Philadelphia, Pennsylvania: University of Pennsylvania Press, 2002.

Gurus

Abraham Maslow The Hierarchy of Needs

Maslow, known principally for his theory of the 'hierarchy of needs', was one of the first people to be associated with the humanistic-as opposed to task-based-approach to management. As people have increasingly come to be appreciated as a key resource in successful companies, Maslow's model has remained a valuable management concept.

1908	Born.
1934	Receives PhD from the University of Wisconsin.
1935	Returns to New York to work at Columbia University.
1937–1951	On the faculty of Brooklyn College.
1943	'Hierarchy of needs' first presented in an article in the *US Psychological Review*.
1951	Becomes head of the psychology department at Brandeis University.
1954	*Motivation and Personality* published.
1970	Dies.

LIFE AND CAREER

Abraham Maslow (1908–1970) was a US psychologist and behavioural scientist. He spent part of his career in industry as well as working as an academic. He liked to say that, whereas most early psychologists studied people with psychological problems, he devoted his attention to successful people. The 'hierarchy of needs' theory, on which his fame chiefly rests, was first presented in 1943 in the *US Psychological Review*, and later developed in his book *Motivation and Personality*, first published in 1954. His concepts were originally offered as general explanations of human behaviour, but quickly came to be regarded as a significant contribution to workplace motivation theory. They are still used by managers today to understand, predict, and influence employee motivation.

KEY THINKING

Maslow grouped human needs into classes and arranged these classes in the form of a hierarchy, ascending from the lowest to the highest. When one set of needs is satisfied, it ceases to be a motivator; motivation is then generated by the unsatisfied needs further up the hierarchy. The classes of needs identified by Maslow are: survival or physiological needs, safety or security needs, social needs, ego-status needs, and self-actualisation needs, and they appear in that order in the hierarchy. Today the hierarchy is usually represented as a pyramid, although Maslow himself did not present it in that way.

The five levels within the hierarchy can be broken down as follows.

• Survival or physiological needs. These are the most primitive of all needs, comprising all the basic animal requirements such as food, water, shelter, warmth, and sleep.

• Security or safety needs. In earlier times, these needs expressed themselves in the form of a desire to be free of physical danger. In the modern context, they have been refined and are now felt in mainly social and financial terms; purely physical requirements have been replaced by the need for things such as job security or a living wage.

• Social needs. Most humans need to belong and to be accepted by others. They are essentially social beings and therefore seek membership of social groups, such as work groups.

• Ego-status needs. Most humans also need to be held in esteem by both themselves and others. This kind of need is satisfied by power, prestige, and self-confidence.

• Self-actualisation needs. The most sophisticated type of need is the desire to maximise one's skills and talents. This embraces self-realisation, self-expression, and self-fulfilment.

There are certain conditions, Maslow wrote, that are immediate prerequisites for satisfying needs, such as the freedom to speak, the freedom to express oneself in other ways, the freedom to defend oneself, justice, fairness, and honesty. Any danger threatening these is perceived almost as if it were a danger to the satisfaction of the needs themselves.

The hierarchy is usually referred to as if it were a fixed order, but Maslow explained that it is not necessarily rigid or universally applicable in its usual form. While most people do experience their basic needs in the order indicated, there are a number of exceptions. Creative people, for example, are often driven by a desire for self-actualisation and give it precedence over the satisfaction of 'lower' needs in a way that the average person perhaps would not. The hierarchy is often presented in simplified terms, giving the false impression that one need must be fully satisfied before the next need emerges. In fact, as Maslow pointed out, man is a continually wanting animal, whose basic needs are for the most part partially satisfied and partially unsatisfied at the same time. Needs continually overlap; for example, social needs are felt by almost everyone, including those people whose basic physiological needs are not being met. As soon as a need is satisfied, however, it will drop out of the equation and cease to be a motivator.

Maslow's intention all along was to define an aspect of the human condition, but his insights are obviously applicable within a business context. If, for example, a manager is able to recognise which level of the hierarchy a worker has reached, then he or she can motivate the employee in the most appropriate way. Peter Drucker, in his book *Management: Tasks, Responsibilities, Practices* (London: Heinemann, 1973), pointed out that although it becomes less satisfying to obtain economic rewards as one moves up the hierarchy, the need for such rewards does not necessarily become less important. This is because, as their impact as a positive incentive decreases, their ability to create dissatisfaction and act as a disincentive increases. Economic rewards come to be seen as entitlements and, if they are not looked after, can act as deterrents.

ABRAHAM MASLOW IN PERSPECTIVE

Maslow is often mentioned in connection with his contemporaries, Douglas McGregor and Frederick Herzberg, who were also developing motivation theories at about the same time. Maslow admired McGregor, the author of Theory X and Theory Y, although he had strong reservations about the validity of Theory Y. Herzberg suggested that hygiene factors – those that may be causes of job dissatisfaction (for example, working conditions, salary, job security, or company policy) but are not in themselves incentives to improve performance – should be separated from motivators–those that lead to positive job satisfaction (such as achievement, recognition, responsibility, or advancement). Herzberg's hygiene factors can be compared with Maslow's levels one, two, and three, and the motivators to levels four and five.

Maslow's influence continues through the work of later psychologists and writers, such as Chris Argyris and Blake and Mouton. Argyris looked at how individual initiatives and creativity can coexist with organisational rules. Blake and Mouton were the authors of the *Managerial Grid*, which created the concept of the manager who balanced a concern for people with a concern for the task.

Practising managers have also, on the whole, found Maslow's concept a valuable and sensible one, which helps to clarify their thoughts. It is often used as a basis for questionnaires and checklists to discover an individual's level of motivation, or cited in support of the idea of empowerment. Twyla Dell, in *How to Motivate People* (London: Kogan Page, 1988), listed the ten qualities that people most

want from their jobs and included two questionnaires to help readers judge how many of the ten qualities they were receiving and giving in their work. She then matched the ten qualities to Maslow's hierarchy.

Maslow's theory only makes complete sense when applied, as he originally intended, to life in general rather than to the workplace in particular. This is because some of the needs of the individual, particularly the higher needs, may be satisfied outside the workplace. This holistic view is nonetheless important within the workplace, as employers increasingly come to realise that individuals have a life outside their job that may impinge on their performance at work. Although Maslow's theory is now over 60 years old, it is still referred to by managers and it offers them useful insights. Along with Herzberg and McGregor, he is recognised as one of the founding fathers of motivation theory.

THE BEST SOURCES OF HELP
Books:

Frick, Willard B. *Humanistic Psychology: Interviews with Maslow, Murphy, and Rogers.* Columbus, Ohio: Charles E. Merrill, 1971.

Hoffman, Edward. *The Right to be Human: a Biography of Abraham Maslow.* Wellingborough: Crucible, 1989.

Lowry, Richard J. *A. H. Maslow: An Intellectual Portrait.* Monterey, California: Brookes Cole, 1973.

Maslow, Abraham. *Motivation and Personality.* 2nd ed. New York: Harper and Row, 1970.

Maslow, Abraham. *The Farther Reaches of Human Nature.* New York: Viking Press, 1971.

Elton Mayo The Hawthorne Experiments

George Elton Mayo (1880–1949) has secured fame as the leader in a series of experiments that became one of the great turning points in management thinking. At the Hawthorne plant of Western Electric, he discovered that job satisfaction increased through employee participation in decisions, rather than through short-term incentives.

1880	Born.
1911	Appointed lecturer in logic, ethics, and psychology (later Professor of Philosophy) at University of Queensland.
1923	Moves to United States and takes a post at Pennsylvania University; conducts experiments on productivity in a spinning mill, related to working conditions.
1924–1932	Experiments are carried out at the Hawthorne plant.

1928	Moves to Harvard as associate professor of industrial research; becomes involved with Hawthorne experiments.
1929–1930	Deduces that a more listening, caring style of supervision raises morale and boosts productivity.
1930–1945	Develops TWI programme.
1947	Retires from Harvard.
1947–1949	Adviser to British government on problems within industry.
1949	Dies.

LIFE AND CAREER

An Australian by birth, Mayo read psychology at Adelaide University and, in 1911, was appointed lecturer in logic, ethics, and psychology (and later Professor of Philosophy) at the University of Queensland.

Anxious to move to the United States for professional reasons, he took a post at Pennsylvania University in 1923. Here, he became involved in one of the investigations that acted as a dry run for Hawthorne. In one department at a spinning mill in Philadelphia, labour turnover was 250 percent, compared with an average of 6 percent in other parts of the company. A series of experimental changes in working conditions was introduced in the department, most notably rest pauses. These changes led to successive increases in productivity and the raising of morale. After one year, labour turnover was down to the average level for the company. It was assumed that this improvement was due to the introduction of rest pauses-a conclusion that was to undergo substantial modification as a result of Hawthorne.

The Hawthorne experiments began in 1924 and Mayo's involvement in them in 1928, after he had moved to the Harvard University School of Business Administration as associate professor of industrial research. Later awarded a chair, he remained at Harvard until his retirement in 1947. During the Second World War, Mayo contributed to the development of supervisor training with his Training Within Industry (TWI) programme, which was widely adopted in the United States. The last two years of his life were spent in the United Kingdom, as an adviser to the British government on problems within industry.

KEY THINKING

Mayo wrote about democracy and freedom, and the social problems of industrialised civilisation. It is as the author of *Human Problems of an Industrial Civilisation*, which reports on the Hawthorne experiments, that he is known for his contribution to management thinking, even though he disclaimed responsibility for the design and direction of the project.

Hawthorne

The Hawthorne plant of Western Electric was located in Chicago. It had some 29,000 employees and manufactured telephones and telephone equipment, principally for AT&T. The company had a reputation for advanced personnel policies and had welcomed a study by the National Research Council into the relationship between workplace lighting and the efficiency of individual workers.

The experiments

The study began in 1924 by isolating two groups of workers in order to test the impact of various incentives on their productivity. Improvements to levels of lighting produced increases in productivity, but so too did reversion to standard lighting and even below-standard lighting in both groups. The initial assumption therefore was that increased output stemmed from variation alone.

Other incentives, including payment incentives and rest pauses, were manipulated at regular intervals and, although output levels varied, the trend was inexorably upwards. Whatever experimentation was applied, output went up. Although it had been fairly conclusively determined that lighting had little to do with output levels, the assistant works manager (George Pennock) agreed that something peculiar was going on, and that experimentation should continue.

Early deductions – supervision and employee attitudes

In the winter of 1927, Pennock invited Clair Turner, professor of biology and public health at Massachusetts Institute of Technology (MIT), to contribute. Turner quickly resolved that rest pauses in themselves were not the cause for increased output, although longer rest pauses gave rise to more social interaction, which in turn affected mental attitudes. Turner attributed the rise in output to the small group; the type of supervision; earnings; the novelty of the experiment; and the increased attention to the workers generated by the experiment itself.

Pennock had been among the first to note that supervisory style was important. The supervisor involved in the illumination experiment had been relaxed and friendly; he got to know the operators well and was not too worried about company policies and procedures. Discipline was secured through enlightened leadership, and an esprit de corps grew up within the group. This was in stark contrast to standard practice before the experiment.

When Pennock invited Turner to participate, he also invited Mayo – although it is not known whether this was as a result of Mayo's achievements at the Philadelphian spinning mill, or because of a desire to involve Harvard. Visits in 1929 and 1930 indicated to Mayo 'a remarkable change of attitude in the group'. Mayo's view was that the test room workers had turned into a social unit, enjoyed all the attention they were getting, and had developed a sense of participation in the project.

In order to understand this further, Mayo instituted a series of interviews. These provided the workers with an opportunity to express their views. It emerged that they would feel better for discussing a situation, even if it did not change. Further exploration revealed that some complaints had little or no basis in fact, but were actually indicators of personal situations causing distress.

By focusing on a more open, listening and caring interview approach, Mayo had struck a chord which linked the style of supervision and the level of morale to levels of productivity.

Further research-social groups

A third stage in the research took place in the bank wiring room, with a similar application of incentives to productivity. Here it emerged that output was restricted:

- the group had a standard for output that was respected by individuals in the group
- the group was indifferent to the employer's financial incentive scheme
- the group developed a code of behaviour of its own, based on solidarity in opposition to the management
- output was determined by informal social groups rather than by management.

Mayo had read the work of F.W. Taylor, who had already established that social groups were capable of exercising very strong control over the work behaviour of individual members (Taylor had called it 'systematic soldiering'). The interesting development that Mayo noted, however, was that whereas in the first set of experiments productivity went up as the project progressed, in the other-the bank wiring room-productivity was restricted.

In *The Human Problems of an Industrial Civilization*, Mayo wrote: 'Human collaboration in work . . . has always depended for its perpetuation upon the evolution of a non-logical social code which regulates the relations between persons and their attitudes to one another. Insistence upon a merely economic logic of production . . . interferes with the development of such a code and consequently gives rise in the group to a sense of human defeat. This . . . results in the formation of a social code at a lower level and in opposition to the economic logic. One of its symptoms is "restriction".'

The question which needed to be asked, therefore, was, 'What was different between the two groups?' The answer was found to lie with the attitude of the observer – where the observer encouraged participation and took the workers into his confidence, productivity went up; where the observer merely watched and adopted the trappings of traditional supervisory practice, output was restricted.

Interpreting Hawthorne

For industry to benefit from the experiments at Hawthorne, Mayo first concluded that supervisors needed training in understanding the personal problems of workers, and also in listening and interviewing techniques. He held that the new supervisor should be less aloof, more people-oriented, more concerned, and skilled in handling personal and social situations.

It was only later, after a period of reflection, that Mayo was able to conclude that:

- job satisfaction increased as workers were given more freedom to determine the conditions of their working environment and to set their own standards of output
- intensified interaction and co-operation created a high level of group cohesion
- job satisfaction and output depended more on co-operation and a feeling of worth than on physical working conditions

In Mayo's view, workers had been unable to find satisfactory outlets for expressing personal problems and dissatisfactions in their work life. The problem was that managers thought the answers to industrial problems resided in technical efficiency, when actually the answer was a human and social one.

Mayo's contribution lies in recognising that the formality of strict rules and procedures spawns informal approaches and groups with their base in human emotions, problems, and interactions. The manager, therefore, should strive for an equilibrium between the technical organisation and the human one, and hence should develop skills in handling human relations and situations. These include diagnostic skills in understanding human behaviour and interpersonal skills in counselling, motivating, leading, and communicating.

ELTON MAYO IN PERSPECTIVE

Mayo has been acclaimed by his followers as the founder of the human relations school of management, and criticised by sociologists for not going far enough in his interpretations.

Reading Mayo's conclusions causes no surprise today; his attitudes are increasingly commonplace among social scientists, trade unionists, and managers alike. But that is perhaps a measure of his achievement, because most commentators agree that he was the first to demonstrate, infer, and provide evidence for the benefits of a shift in management thinking away from the widespread dominance of Taylor's scientific management.

F.J. Roethlisberger said of Mayo that the data were not his; the results were not his; but the interpretations of both were indeed his. Without those interpretations, the results of Hawthorne might still be collecting dust in the archives.

The experiment also gave rise to the term 'Hawthorne effect': a situation which arises because people are 'singled out' for special treatment, or a 'special situation' is created, in which workers can feel free to air their problems.

Mayo's ideas on the emergence of 'informal' organisations were read by Argyris and others as they developed theories about how organisations learned and developed. The discrediting of the 'rabble hypothesis' theory led directly to the work of McGregor.

The conclusions drawn by Mayo from the Hawthorne studies established the beginnings of recognition that management style is a major contributor to industrial productivity; that interpersonal skills are as important as monetary incentives or target-setting, and that a more humanistic approach is an important means of satisfying the organisation's economic and social needs.

THE BEST SOURCES OF HELP
Books:

Mayo, Elton. *The Human Problems of an Industrial Civilization*. Revised ed. London: Routledge, 2003.
Mayo, Elton. *The Social Problems of an Industrial Civilization*. London: Routledge and Kegan Paul, 1949

Gurus

Douglas McGregor Theory X and Theory Y

Developer of Theory X and Theory Y, which describe two views of people at work and two opposing management styles, Douglas McGregor's relatively short career has been a key influence for many of today's management commentators. *The Human Side of Enterprise* marked a watershed in management thinking, and laid the foundations for the modern, people-centred view of management.

1906	Born.
1932	Graduates from Wayne University.
1935	Receives PhD in Experimental Psychology from Harvard University.
1948–1954	President, Antioch College.
1954	Professor of Management, Massachusetts Institute of Technology.
1960	Publication of *The Human Side of Enterprise*.
1964	Dies.
1993	Listed as one of the most popular management writers alongside Henri Fayol.

LIFE AND CAREER

Douglas McGregor (1906–1964) followed a mostly academic career, lecturing at Harvard University, Massachusetts Institute of Technology (MIT) and Antioch College, where he became the first Sloan Fellows professor at MIT. Although he wrote only a few publications before his early death, they have had a great impact.

In 1993 McGregor was listed as one of the most popular management writers alongside Henri Fayol (in *Management Gurus – What Makes Them and How to Become One*). Major US writers such as Rosabeth Moss Kanter, Warren Bennis, and Tom Peters, whose writings have much influence on current learning and practice, agree that much of modern management thinking goes back to McGregor, especially the implications of his writing for theories on leadership.

KEY THINKING

McGregor believed that managers' basic beliefs have a dominant influence on the way that organisations are run, and central to this are managers' assumptions about the behaviour of people. McGregor argues that these assumptions fall into two broad categories – Theory X and Theory Y. His findings were detailed in *The Human Side of Enterprise*, first published in 1960.

Theory X and Theory Y describe two views of people at work and may be used to describe two opposing management styles.

Theory X: the traditional view of direction and control

Theory X is based on the assumptions that:

- the average human being has an inherent dislike of work and will avoid it if at all possible
- because of this human dislike of work, most people must be coerced, controlled, directed, and threatened with punishment to get them to make an adequate effort towards the achievement of organisational objectives
- the average human being prefers to be directed; wishes to avoid responsibility; has relatively little ambition; wants security above all else.

A Theory X management style therefore requires close, firm supervision with clearly specified tasks and the threat of punishment or the promise of greater pay as motivating factors. Managers working under these assumptions will employ autocratic controls that can lead to mistrust and resentment from those they manage. McGregor acknowledges that this approach constitutes a damning statement about the 'mediocrity of the masses'. He acknowledges, too, that the 'carrot and stick' approach can have a place but will not work when the needs of people are predominantly social and egoistic.

Theory Y: the integration of individual and organisational goals

Theory Y is based on the assumptions that:

- the expenditure of physical and mental effort in work is as natural as play or rest. The average human being does not inherently dislike work. Depending upon controllable conditions, work may be a source of satisfaction, or a source of punishment
- external control and the threat of punishment are not the only means for bringing about effort towards achieving organisational objectives. People will exercise self-direction and self-control in the service of objectives to which they are committed
- commitment to objectives is a result of the rewards associated with their achievement. The most significant of such rewards, such as the satisfaction of ego and self-actualisation needs, can be direct products of effort directed towards organisational objectives
- under proper conditions, the average human being learns not only to accept but to seek responsibility. Avoidance of responsibility, lack of ambition, and emphasis on security are generally consequences of experience, not inherent human characteristics
- the capacity to exercise a relatively high degree of imagination, ingenuity, and creativity in the solution of organisational problems is widely, not narrowly, distributed in the population
- under the conditions of modern industrial life, the intellectual potential of the average human being is used only partially.

Theory Y assumptions can lead to more co-operative relationships between managers and workers. A Theory

Y management style seeks to establish a working environment in which the personal needs and objectives of individuals can relate to, and harmonise with, the objectives of the organisation.

In *The Human Side of Enterprise*, McGregor recognises that Theory Y is not a panacea for all ills. But by highlighting such ideas, he hopes instead to achieve an abandonment by management of the limiting assumptions of Theory X and a consideration of the techniques involved in Theory Y.

Theory into practice

Abraham Maslow viewed McGregor as a mentor, and was a strong supporter of theories X and Y. So he decided to put Theory Y (that people want to work, achieve, and take responsibility) into practice in a Californian electronics factory. However, he found that an organisation driven solely by Theory Y could not succeed, as some sense of direction and structure was required. Instead, he advocated an improved version of Theory Y that involved an element of structured security and direction taken from Theory X.

Maslow's negative experience with implementing Theory Y must be balanced against that of McGregor himself at a Procter & Gamble plant in Georgia, where he introduced Theory Y through the concept of self-directed teams. This plant was found to be a third more profitable than any other Procter & Gamble plant; it was kept a trade secret until the mid-1990s.

Before he died, McGregor began to develop a further theory that addressed the criticisms made of theories X and Y – that they were mutually incompatible. Ideas he proposed as part of this theory included lifetime employment; concern for employees (both inside and outside the working environment); decision by consensus; and commitment to quality. He tentatively called it Theory Z. Before it could be widely published, McGregor died and the ideas faded.

Theory Z

The work on Theory Z that McGregor began was not completely forgotten. During the 1970s, William Ouchi began to expound its principles by comparing and contrasting Japanese (Type J) and US (Type A) organisations.

Type A organisations, he proposed, tend to offer short-term employment, specialised careers (with rapid promotion), and individual decision-making and responsibility. Type J companies, on the other hand, mirror the ethos of Japanese society-collectivism and stability rather than individuality. Those US companies that share Type J characteristics, and indeed have more in common with Type J organisations, were described as Type Z (examples included Hewlett-Packard and Procter & Gamble).

Leadership

Before McGregor, the thrust of writing about leadership focused on the qualities and characteristics of 'great people', in the hope that, if those qualities were identified, they could be emulated.

McGregor argued that there were other variables involved in leadership, including the attitudes and needs of the followers, the nature and structure of the organisation itself, and the social, economic, and political environment. For McGregor, leadership was not a property of the individual but a complex relationship among these variables. He was one of the first to argue that leadership was more about the relationship between the leader and the situation he or she faced, than merely the characteristics of the leader alone.

DOUGLAS MCGREGOR IN PERSPECTIVE

The Human Side of Enterprise marked a watershed in management thinking that had previously been dominated by the scientific approach of Taylor, and formed the foundations for the current, people-centred view of management.

Theory Y has been criticised for being too idealistic, but if we examine each of the six tenets of Theory Y in turn, we can trace much modern thinking back to McGregor:

1. Work, as a source of satisfaction, means accepting that people need to know not just what or how, but why; the adoption of meaningful objectives is one of the keys to self-motivation.

2–4. Ownership, commitment, and responsibility are three of the cornerstones of empowerment.

5–6. The encouragement for people to be fully exercised in the solution of organisational problems is central to action learning, total quality management, strategic thinking, and knowledge exploitation.

As mentioned above, Moss Kanter (writing on empowerment), Bennis (on leadership), and Peters (on excellence as well as chaos) all acknowledge their debt to McGregor.

Contemporary and subsequent commentaries on McGregor's theories have tended to see them as black and white. Harold Geneen, former president and CEO of ITT, commented that although Theories X and Y propose a neat summary of business management, no company is run in strict accordance with either one or the other. Peter Drucker said that Theory X sees people as immature, whereas Theory Y sees them striving towards adulthood.

The two contrasting theories are best seen perhaps as two polarising forces with which managers have to grapple. Blake and Mouton expressed this in terms of the managerial grid, where managers constantly have to balance the drives and forces between task (getting things done) and people (how best to get them done for the benefit of the organisation and the individuals doing them).

Although Theory Y has been held up as an unachievable goal-with the individual and the organisation having convergent aspirations-the successful cases in which this aim is being attempted are growing. It is precisely such a goal that organisations are hoping to achieve through continuous improvement, continuous professional development, and participation schemes, operating in climates of empowerment.

It is not going too far to say that *The Human Side of Enterprise* recognises that although we cannot actually motivate people, we do have a responsibility to acknowledge the elements involved in motivation. What we can do is to attempt to create the right climate, environment, or working conditions for motivation to be enabled.

THE BEST SOURCES OF HELP

Books:

Huczynski, Andreas. *Management Gurus-What Makes Them and How to Become One*. London: Routledge, 1992.

McGregor, Douglas. *The Human Side of Enterprise*. Revised ed. New York: McGraw-Hill, 2006.

McGregor, Douglas. *Leadership and Motivation*. Boston, Massachusetts: MIT Press, 1966.

McGregor, Douglas. *The Professional Manager*. New York: McGraw-Hill, 1967.

Ouchi, William G. *Theory Z: How American Business Can Meet the Japanese Challenge*. Reading, Massachusetts: Addison Wesley, 1981.

Henry Mintzberg A Great Generalist

Often regarded as an iconoclast and a rebel, Henry Mintzberg (1939-) has certainly challenged many traditional ideas. But he does not attack people with whom he disagrees; he simply sets about proving them wrong, with devastating clarity. In his writing – the product of a career devoted to understanding how people actually manage – he resists every temptation to pontificate about how anyone ought to manage.

1939	Born.
1961	Receives a B Eng from McGill University.
1961–1963	Operational Research with Canadian National Railways.
1968	Receives a PhD and becomes professor at McGill University; also subsequently becomes director of the Center for Strategic Studies.
1973	Publication of *The Nature of Managerial Work*.
1975	Wins the McKinsey Prize for best article.
1988–1991	President of the Strategic Management Society.
1991–	Holds other positions in management institutions, including that of visiting professor at INSEAD in France.
1995	*Academy of Management* receives the George R. Terry best book of the year award.
1995–2000	Director of International Masters Program in Practicing Management.
1996	Appointed Cleghorn Professor of Management Studies at McGill University.

LIFE AND CAREER

Henry Mintzberg was born in Canada and has spent virtually all his working life there. He studied at McGill University and, after further study at MIT, returned to Canada to take up an appointment with Canadian National Railways in 1961. In 1963 he moved into the academic world and by 1968 was back at McGill University as a professor, a post he holds to the present day. He is also director of the Center for Strategic Studies in Organization at McGill and has held several important positions in other management institutions, including that of visiting professor at INSEAD, the international business school at Fontainebleau in France. He has been a consultant to many organisations throughout the world and from 1988 to 1991 he was president of the Strategic Management Society.

Mintzberg's major impact on the management world began with his book *The Nature of Managerial Work*, published in 1973, and a seminal article in the *Harvard Business Review*, 'The manager's job: folklore and fact', written two years later. Based on detailed research and thoughtful observation, these two works established Mintzberg's reputation by showing that what managers did, when successfully carrying out their responsibilities, was substantially different from much business theory.

KEY THINKING

Unlike many gurus, Mintzberg's contribution to management thinking is not based on one or two clever theories within some narrow discipline. His approach is broad, involving the study of virtually everything managers do and how they do it. His general appeal is further enhanced by a fundamental belief that management is about applying human skills to systems, not applying systems to people, a belief that is demonstrated throughout his writing.

How managers work

In 'The manager's job: folklore and fact', Mintzberg sets out the stark reality of what managers do. 'If there is a simple theme that runs through this article, it is that the pressures of his job drive the manager to be superficial in his actions-to overload himself with work, encourage interruption, respond quickly to every stimulus, seek the tangible and avoid the abstract, make decisions in small increments, and do everything abruptly,' he writes.

Mintzberg uses the article to stress the importance of the manager's role and the need to understand it thoroughly before attempting to train and develop those engaged in carrying it out.

'No job is more vital to our society than that of the manager. It is the manager who determines whether our social institutions serve us well or whether they squander our talents and resources. It is time to strip away the folklore about managerial work, and time to study it realistically so that we can begin the difficult task of making significant improvements in its performance.' In *The Nature of Managerial Work*, Mintzberg proposes six characteristics of management work and ten basic management roles.

- The manager's job is a mixture of regular, programmed jobs and unprogrammed tasks.
- A manager is both a generalist and a specialist.
- Managers rely on information from all sources but show a preference for that which is transmitted orally.
- Managerial work is made up of activities that are characterised by brevity, variety and fragmentation.
- Management work is more an art than a science and is reliant on intuitive processes and a 'feel' for what is right.
- Management work is becoming more complex.

Mintzberg places the ten roles that he believes make up the content of the manager's job into three categories.

Interpersonal

- Figurehead - performing symbolic duties as a representative of the organisation
- Leader - establishing the atmosphere and motivating the subordinates
- Liaiser - developing and maintaining webs of contacts outside the organisation

Information

- Monitor - collecting all types of information that are relevant and useful to the organisation
- Disseminator - transmitting information from outside the organisation to those inside
- Spokesperson - transmitting information from inside the organisation to outsiders

Decision-making

- Entrepreneur - initiating change and adapting to the environment
- Disturbance Handler - dealing with unexpected events

- Resource Allocator - deciding on the use of the organisation's resources
- Negotiator - negotiating with individuals and dealing with other organisations

The Structuring of Organizations

In his 1979 book, *The Structuring of Organizations*, Mintzberg identified five types of 'ideal' organisation structures. These were: simple structure; machine bureaucracy; professional bureaucracy; divisional; and adhocracy. The classification was re-examined and expanded ten years later in *Mintzberg on Management* and the following, more detailed, view of organisation types drawn up:

- the Entrepreneurial Organisation – small staff, loose division of labour, little management hierarchy, informal, with power focused on the chief executive
- the Machine Organisation – highly specialised, routine operating tasks, formal communication, large operating units, tasks grouped under functions, elaborate administrative systems, central decision making, and a sharp distinction between line and staff
- the Diversified Organisation – a set of semi-autonomous units under a central administrative structure. The units are usually called divisions and the central administration referred to as the headquarters
- the Professional Organisation – commonly found in hospitals, universities, public agencies, and firms doing routine work, this structure relies on the skills and knowledge of professional staff in order to function. All such organisations produce standardised products or services
- the Innovative Organisation – this is what Mintzberg sees as the modern organisation: one that is flexible, rejecting any form of bureaucracy and avoiding emphasis on planning and control systems. Innovation is achieved by hiring experts; giving them power; training and developing them; and employing them in multi-disciplinary teams that work in an atmosphere unbounded by conventional specialisms
- the Missionary Organisation – it is the mission that counts above all else in such organisations, and the mission is clear, focused, distinctive, and inspiring. Employees readily identify with the mission, share common values and are motivated by their own zeal and enthusiasm.

Strategy and planning

The relationship between strategy and planning is a constant theme in Mintzberg's writing and his views on the subject are perhaps his most important contribution to current management thinking.

In his 1994 book, *The Rise and Fall of Strategic Planning*, Mintzberg produces a masterly criticism of conventional theory. His main concern is with what he sees as basic failings in our approach to planning.

- processes – the elaborate processes used create bureaucracy and suppress innovation and originality
- data – 'hard' data (the raw material of all strategists) provides information, but 'soft' data provides wisdom. 'Hard information can be no better and is often at times far worse than soft information.'

- detachment – it is no use producing strategies in 'ivory towers'. Effective strategists are not people who distance themselves from the detail of a business '... but quite the opposite: they are the ones who immerse themselves in it, while being able to abstract the strategic messages from it.'
- strategy – it is not 'the consequence of planning but the opposite: its starting point'. Mintzberg has coined the phrase 'crafting strategies' to illustrate his concept of the delicate, painstaking process of developing strategy-a process of emergence that is far removed from the classical picture of strategists grouped around a table predicting the future. He argues that while an organisation needs a strategy, strategic plans are generally useless as one cannot predict two to three years ahead.

HENRY MINTZBERG IN PERSPECTIVE

Henry Mintzberg remains one of the few truly generalist management writers of today. Different readers see him as an expert in different areas. For some people, he is an authority on time management, and he has written some of the most thoughtful and practical advice on this subject; for others he is the champion of hard-pressed managers, surrounded by management theorists telling them how to do their jobs; and for yet another group, he is a leading authority on strategic planning.

For most people, however, Mintzberg is the man who dared to challenge orthodox beliefs and who has changed our ideas about many key business activities.

THE BEST SOURCES OF HELP

Books:

Mintzberg, Henry. *The Nature of Managerial Work.* New York: Harper & Row, 1973.

Mintzberg, Henry. *The Structuring of Organizations: a Synthesis of the Research.* Englewood Cliffs, New Jersey: Prentice Hall, 1979.

Mintzberg, Henry. *Structure in Fives: Designing Effective Organizations.* Englewood Cliffs, New Jersey: Prentice Hall, 1983.

Mintzberg, Henry. *Power In and Around Organizations.* Englewood Cliffs, New Jersey: Prentice Hall, 1983.

Mintzberg, Henry. *Mintzberg on Management: Inside our Strange World of Organizations.* New York: Free Press, 1989.

Mintzberg, Henry. *The Rise and Fall of Strategic Planning.* Hemel Hempstead: Prentice Hall International, 1994.

Mintzberg, Henry, and J. B. Quinn. *The Strategy Process: Concepts, Contexts, Cases.* 3rd ed. London: Prentice Hall International, 1996.

Mintzberg, Henry, Bruce Ahlstrand, and Joseph Lempel. *Strategy Safari.* London: Financial Times Prentice Hall, 1998.

Mintzberg, Henry. *Managers, Not MBAs.* London: Financial Times Prentice Hall, 2004.

Mintzberg, Henry, Bruce Ahlstrand, and Joseph Lempel. *Strategy Bites Back.* London: Financial Times Prentice Hall, 2004.

Mintzberg, Henry. *Tracking Strategies: Towards a General Theory.* Oxford: Oxford University Press, 2007.

Journal Articles:

Mintzberg, Henry. 'The manager's job: folklore and fact.' *Harvard Business Review*, March/April, pp. 163–176. (Originally published in 1975, the article includes a retrospective commentary by the author.)

Mintzberg, Henry. 'The fall and rise of strategic planning.' *Harvard Business Review*, January/February 1994, pp. 107–114.

Mintzberg, Henry. 'Rounding out the manager's job.' *Sloan Management Review*, Autumn 1994, pp. 11–26.

Mintzberg, Henry. 'Musings on management.' *Harvard Business Review*, July/August 1996, pp. 61–67.

Kenichi Ohmae The Art of Japanese Business

Ohmae's fresh approach to business strategy challenged business leaders to think in innovative, simple, and unconventional terms. His work in the late 1970s and 1980s heralded the arrival of Japanese management techniques in the West. Ohmae was the messenger for the Japanese way of doing business, urging managers to think 'out of the box', and challenge accepted norms with clear, simple ideas in order to gain, and sustain, competitive advantage.

1943	Born.
1972	Joins McKinsey & Co.
1975	Publication of *The Mind of the Strategist*.
1987	Publication of *Beyond National Boundaries*.
1990	Publication of *The Borderless World*.
1995	Stands as candidate for governorship of Tokyo.
1995	Publication of *The End of the Nation State*.
1997	Joins UCLA's School of Public and Social Research.

LIFE AND CAREER

Kenichi Ohmae was born in 1943 on the island of Kyushu, and graduated from Waseda University and the Tokyo Institute of Technology before obtaining a PhD in nuclear engineering from the Massachusetts Institute of Technology. In 1972 he joined the consultancy firm McKinsey & Co, becoming managing director of their Tokyo office. As well as being a nuclear physicist, he is an accomplished clarinettist and a politician. In 1995, he stood for election as governor of Tokyo and also acted as an adviser to Japan's then prime minister, Nakasone.

Ohmae lives in Yokohama and advises some of Japan's most successful international companies in a wide spectrum of industries. His special interest and area of expertise is in formulating creative strategies and developing organisational concepts to implement them.

Ohmae's seminal book, *The Mind of the Strategist*, was published in Japan in 1975. It was, however, only when interest in Japanese management methods increased during the early 1980s that the book was published in the United States. This 1982 US edition was given the subtitle *The Art of Japanese Business*. In *The Mind of the Strategist* Ohmae argues that the success of Japanese companies can be attributed to the nature of Japanese strategic thinking. This, contrary to the Western stereotype of Japanese management, was largely creative, intuitive, and vision-driven. Ohmae went on to explain what this creativity involved and how it could be learnt.

The view presented by Ohmae overturned traditional Western perceptions of Japanese managers, and the idea that their success was founded on brilliantly rational, far-sighted thinking. Ohmae heralded a revolution based on creativity and innovation, and showed how, in the hands of a single, talented strategist, creativity could transform a major corporation.

In 1990, Ohmae's book *The Borderless World* challenged Japanese companies and corporations around the world to take account of globalisation in their strategic planning. He urged businesses to focus less on the competitive aspects of strategy (promoted so effectively by Porter and others), and instead to give greater focus to 'country' and 'currency', two key elements that in an interdependent world economy can make or break a business strategy. This approach reflected Ohmae's increasing focus on global business and the relationship between business and the nation state. The latter was also the subject of two other books, *Beyond National Boundaries* (1987) and *The End of the Nation State* (1995).

Just as *The Mind of the Strategist* had encouraged innovation in strategy in the 1980s, so *The Borderless World* highlighted the importance of the global interdependence that dominated trade in the 1990s.

KEY THINKING

The role of the strategist

Ohmae has explored a number of features of successful business strategies (usually Japanese), and compared them with their typical counterparts in the West. He identified several key differences including:

- vision and dynamic leadership. Japanese businesses tend to have a single, driving force in the form of an effective strategist, a leader, or a visionary who possesses what Ohmae has described as an idiosyncratic mode of thinking. Through this, company, customers, and competition (described as the strategic triangle) merge into a dynamic interaction from which a comprehensive set of objectives and plans for action eventually emerges. This approach was in marked contrast to the large, strategic planning bureaucracies that were typical of many large Western corporations of the time (the early 1980s).
- customer focus. The customer is at the heart of Japanese strategy and is virtually enshrined as central to corporate values. The focus of the business needs to be on delivering what the customer wants, or there will be no business.
- methodology. Ohmae perceived that to develop effective strategies, managers must first gain a detailed understanding of the characteristics of each element in a situation, and then develop a holistic plan tying each part of the business, each separate resource, into a competitive and efficient operation. This is not a systems approach based on linear thinking, but instead relies on detailed analysis ('the starting point') and knowledge, combined with innovation, intuition, and creativity.

The strategic triangle

Ohmae claimed that, in constructing any business strategy, the three main players to be taken into account are the corporation itself, the customer, and the competition. Each of these three Cs is a living entity with its own interests and objectives, while collectively they form the strategic triangle. The three Cs influence strategy and planning in a number of important ways.

1. *Strategic business units (SBUs)*. The need for strategic business units that understand all three elements and to which strategic decisions can be delegated is held to be essential, in order to take adequate account of the strategic triangle. This is particularly the case for a large company made up of a number of different businesses selling to different customer groups (probably with different competitors). The definition of a business unit is always likely to be in dispute, so Ohmae suggests asking three key questions as a test:

- Are customer wants well-defined and understood by the industry, and is the market segmented so that differences in those wants are treated differently?
- Is the business unit (an aspect of the corporation) equipped to respond easily to customer wants and needs?
- Do competitors have different sets of conditions that give them a relative advantage over the business unit?

If the business unit seems unable to compete effectively, then it should be redefined to better meet customer needs and competitive threats.

2. *Freedom of operation*. For Ohmae, the SBU must have full freedom of operation across the strategic triangle in order to develop and implement an effective strategy. In devising a strategy the SBU must be able to:

- address the total market for its customers
- encompass all the critical functions of the corporation (i.e. procurement, design, manufacturing, sales, marketing, distribution, and service) in order to respond with maximum freedom to the total needs of the customer
- understand all key aspects of the competitor so that the corporation can seize an advantage when opportunities arise, and exploit any unexpected sources of strength

3. *Matching the corporation with the market*. In the context of the strategic triangle, Ohmae sees the role of the strategist as matching the strengths of the corporation to the needs of a clearly defined market. Such matching, however, is relative to the capabilities of the competition. For this reason, Ohmae defines a successful strategy as one that ensures a better or stronger matching of corporate strengths to customer needs than that provided by competitors.

Four routes to strategic advantage

In *The Mind of the Strategist* Ohmae identifies four ways in which a corporation can gain advantage over its competitors.

- A business strategy based on Key Factors for Success (KFS). The business is required to identify what it does to give it an advantage over its competitors, or where the potential for advantage is greatest, and then concentrate resources there.
- Relative superiority. If a business is still unable to gain an advantage over its competitors and the KFS struggle is being waged equally, then any difference between the two competing businesses can be exploited. This might, for example, mean linking products together through the sales network to provide customers with better offers.
- Aggressive initiatives. When a competitor is established in a stagnant, low-growth industry, then Ohmae advocates an unconventional strategy aimed at upsetting the competitor's KFS. This can be achieved by challenging the accepted ways of doing business in the industry-upsetting the status quo.
- Strategic degrees of freedom. Success in the competitive struggle can be achieved by a business strategy based on the use of innovations. This may involve the vigorous opening up of new markets or the development of new products in areas untouched by the competition.

In each case, Ohmae believes that the main concern is to avoid taking the same approach in the same market as the competition.

KENICHI OHMAE IN PERSPECTIVE

Gary Hamel, among others, has recognised Ohmae's immense influence and contribution, emphasising the impact of his challenge to managers to think in new and unconventional ways. It is a testament to the strength and appeal of Ohmae's work that, although the growth of the Japanese economy faltered during the 1990s, his ideas are still regarded as fundamental contributions to strategic management.

It might be argued that Ohmae's emphasis on strategic creativity helped to lay the foundations for the radical, transforming management approaches of the 1980s and 1990s. Certainly, if one accepts the need for an intuitive, innovative strategist, then it seems likely that there will be widespread changes in the ways that organisations are managed. So it was with the arrival of lean production, business process re-engineering, and strategies for innovation and empowerment. Ohmae's view of the strategist, in fact, is now the widely accepted norm, and the need for a questioning approach that is not constrained by tradition, fear, or habitual patterns of behaviour has filtered down from the strategists themselves to all layers of organisations.

THE BEST SOURCES OF HELP

Books:

Ohmae, Kenichi. *The Mind of the Strategist*. New York: McGraw-Hill, 1982.

Ohmae, Kenichi. *Japan Business: Obstacles and Opportunities*. New York: Wiley, 1983.

Ohmae, Kenichi. *Triad Power: The Coming Shape of Global Competition*. New York: Free Press, 1985.

Ohmae, Kenichi. *The Borderless World: Power and Strategy in the Interlinked Economy*. London: William Collins, 1990.

Ohmae, Kenichi. *The End of the Nation State: The Rise of Regional Economics*. London: Harper Collins, 1995.

Ohmae, Kenichi. *The Next Global Stage: The Challenges and Opportunities in Our Borderless World*. Indianapolis, Indiana: Prentice Hall PTR, 2005.

Robert Owen Pioneer of Personnel Management

Robert Owen is perhaps best known for his model textile factory and village at New Lanark in Scotland. Conditions in early factories were harsh and hazardous. Long working hours were the norm, with children as young as five working under the same conditions as adults. Factory owners placed more importance on the care of their expensive machines than on the well-being of their expendable employees. Owen's strength was that he saw his employees as every bit as important to the success of his enterprise as his machines.

1771	Born.
1781–1790	Works in various drapery businesses in Stamford, London, and Manchester.
1790	Becomes joint owner of textile factory in Manchester.
1799	Purchases mill in New Lanark from his father-in-law, David Dale, and sets about creating a 'model' mill and village.
1808	Keeps the mill open, in spite of the US trade embargo on British goods; mass unemployment elsewhere.
1813	Tries to persuade other manufacturers to follow his example in employment practices.
1815	Attempts to introduce a bill to legislate on working conditions in factories.
1819	Legislation finally introduced, although limited to banning employment of children under nine.
1825	Leaves for the United States; founds New Harmony in Indiana.
1828	Returns to England after project fails due to internal disagreements and bad planning, leaving the settlement in his sons' hands.
1834	Founds the Grand National Consolidated Trades Union.
1858	Dies.

LIFE AND CAREER

By the age of 19, Owen was joint owner of a textile factory in Manchester. Being new to the responsibilities of management, he learnt about the workings of the factory by observing his employees as they carried out their work. He wrote: 'I looked very wisely at the men in their different departments, although I really knew nothing. By intensely observing everything, I maintained order and regularity throughout the establishment, which proceeded under such circumstances much better than I had anticipated.'

In 1799, Owen (with a group of partners) purchased the New Lanark mill from his father-in-law, David Dale. Even though Dale was recognised as a progressive employer,

conditions in and around the factory were still very poor. Children from five or six years old were employed through contracts with the local poorhouse, and working for 15 hours per day was common. Owen immediately withdrew from accepting any further children from the poorhouse, and raised the minimum age of employment to ten. He also banned the beating of children.

KEY THINKING

Although a paternalistic employer, Owen was a businessperson above all else. He made no changes to employment conditions that could not be justified on economic grounds-all social improvements at New Lanark were funded through the profits of the factory. To achieve this, he required improved productivity from his workforce through changes to the working practices and methods of the factory.

For a workforce that was already working very hard, this was not popular. Owen (uniquely for the time) realised he had to gain the trust of his employees in order to get them to co-operate with the changes to the working environment he wished to achieve. He did this (in the language of today) by persuading 'champions'. He wrote: 'I . . . sought out the individuals who had most influence among [the workforce] from their natural powers or position, and to these I took pains to explain what were my intentions for the changes I wished to effect.'

Owen further won the trust of his employees when, in 1808, the United States passed a trade embargo on British goods. Most mills closed and mass unemployment occurred. Unlike other mill owners of the time, Owen kept his employees on full pay just to maintain the factory machinery in a clean, working condition.

This approach of fair management proved to be successful and, as returns from the business grew, Owen began to alter the working environment. Employment of children gradually ceased (as no further children were indentured from the poorhouse) and those still in employment were sent to a purpose-built school in New Lanark. The housing available to his workers was gradually improved, the environment was freed from gin shops, and crime decreased. The first adult night school anywhere in the world also operated in New Lanark. Finally, Owen set up a shop at New Lanark, and the principles behind this laid the basis for the later retail cooperative movement.

Owen the innovator

Owen's innovations, however, did not merely extend to improving working conditions for his employees. The Industrial Revolution (which began in the mid-to-late 1700s) led to a belief in the supremacy of machines. Owen opposed this growing view by seeking to humanise work.

'Many of you have long experiences in your manufacturing operations of the advantage of substantial, well-contrived and well-executed machinery. If, then, due care as to the state of your inanimate machines can produce such beneficial results, what may not be expected if you devote equal attention to your vital machines, which are far more wonderfully constructed,' he wrote.

As already indicated, Owen was one of the first to 'manage' rather than order his workforce, and the first to attempt to gain agreement for his ideas rather than impose them on others (a worker could not be sacked for disagreeing with Owen). Additionally, he required his managers to behave with some autonomy (possibly the first example of empowerment at work); managers (or superintendents) were selected carefully and trained to be able to act in Owen's absence.

Owen developed an aid to motivation and discipline-the silent monitor system – which could be described as a distant ancestor of the appraisal schemes in practice today. Each machine within the factory had a block of wood mounted on it with a different colour – black, blue, yellow, or white-painted on each face. Each day, the superintendents rated the work of their subordinates and awarded each a colour that was then turned to face the aisle so that everyone was able to see all ratings. The intention of this scheme was that high achievers were rewarded and slackers were motivated to improve.

Owen the reformer

The factory at New Lanark was spectacularly profitable, with returns of over 50 percent on investment, and Owen held this to be proof of the validity and importance of his theories. Strengthened by his profitability, he tried to persuade other manufacturers to follow his example in employment practices. This was first attempted through those of influence who visited New Lanark (estimates put the number of visitors at 20,000 between 1815 and 1825) and then, in 1815, via his attempt to introduce a bill to legislate on basic working conditions in factories.

The aims of the bill were to ban the employment of those aged under ten; to ban night shifts for all children; to provide 30 minutes' education a day for those under 18; and to limit the working day to ten and a half hours. This would have been enforced by a system of government factory inspectors. The bill failed to be introduced in its intended form, as its opponents argued that it would be bad for business and that in any case most employers were voluntarily doing what the bill would require. By the time it was finally introduced in 1819, the legislation was limited to banning the employment of those under nine.

In 1825, disillusioned with his failure to introduce far-reaching employment legislation but still enthusiastic about his ideals, Owen left for the United States, where he founded New Harmony in Indiana. This, along with other projects, failed because of internal disagreements and bad planning. He returned to England, where in 1834 he founded (and briefly chaired) the Grand National Consolidated Trades Union and continued to push for social reform and the growth of the co-operative movement. Robert Owen died, aged 87, in 1858.

ROBERT OWEN IN PERSPECTIVE

Owen occupies a curious position in the history of management thinking. Dismissed by his contemporaries and now little recognised apart from the linking of his name with that of New Lanark, his vision and foresight place him as the pioneer of management practices that are taken for granted today.

Although many influential people visited the sites of New Lanark and New Harmony, the ideas Owen propounded failed to win him immediate followers. There is much debate about the reasons behind this. The New Lanark factory was obviously very profitable (although, as Frank Podmore argued, almost any personnel policy could have been profitable then because profits in the cotton spinning industry at the time were so large), but still none of his factory-owning contemporaries adopted his ideas. Possibly the radical nature of his views contributed to this – if he had instead advocated a step-by-step approach towards improving working conditions and relations with employees instead of an 'all-or-nothing' approach, he might have been more successful.

Although it is not too surprising that resistance to his ideas came from factory owners (who may indeed have felt they had much to lose from following them), antipathy was also expressed from across the political spectrum. Some of the most long-lasting criticism was expressed by Marx and Engels in their Communist manifesto. The label of 'Utopian' that they applied to Owen is one by which he is still well known. The manifesto expressed the view that his ideas could not work in practice; his success at New Lanark was, they argued, due to luck rather than judgment.

Against these negative views must be set the experiences of those followers Owen did inspire. Although Owen's own partnership with Quakers and Nonconformists at the end of his time at New Lanark failed (because of their wish to impose religious instruction on all), it was this sector of society that produced the people who were most influenced by his ideas. They included Titus Salt, George Palmer, and Joseph Rowntree.

THE BEST SOURCES OF HELP
Book:
Owen, Robert. *A New View of Society.* New ed. London: Penguin, 2007.

Tom Peters The Guru As Performer

Tom Peters has probably done more than anyone else to shift the debate on management from the confines of boardrooms, academia, and consultancies to a broader, worldwide audience, where it has become the staple diet of the media and managers alike. Peter Drucker wrote more and his ideas have withstood a longer test of time, but it is Peters - as consultant, writer, seminar lecturer, blogger, and stage performer - whose energy, style, influence, and ideas have shaped new management thinking.

1942	Born.
1966–1970	Naval service.
1973	Leaves Stanford with PhD in organisational behaviour; works for White House.
1974–1981	Joins consultancy firm, McKinsey, becoming a partner in 1977.
Late 1970s	Various collaborative research projects; development of the McKinsey 7-S Model.
1982	Publication of *In Search of Excellence*.
1982–present	Writing, lecturing, touring, and changing his mind; formulates ideas for a management agenda for the future

LIFE AND CAREER

Born in Baltimore in 1942, Peters repaid a navy scholarship to Cornell with a degree in civil engineering and four years' service in the navy, spending a term of duty in Vietnam in 1966 before being assigned to the Pentagon in 1968. He left Stanford in 1973 with a PhD in organisational behaviour and worked for the White House for a short while as senior adviser on combatting drug abuse. In 1974 he joined the top consultancy firm, McKinsey.

Exposed to consulting assignments in America's blue-chip companies, Peters's curiosity and imagination led him in the late 1970s into various aspects of collaborative research, which brought about the development of the McKinsey 7-S Model. This model focuses on shared values, staff, systems, strategy, structure, skills, and style. It was in fact the first expression of the shift-characterising all of Peters's work-away from the traditional numbers-centred, rational, analytical, and bureaucratic notion of management of McKinsey and many others towards a more innovative, intuitive, and people-centred approach.

In 1982, Peters co-published with Bob Waterman *In Search of Excellence*, which brought him worldwide fame, and set him off on a new career expounding his theories of excellence. Since then, his life has been a whirlwind of writing, lecturing, touring, and changing his mind.

Peters describes himself as gadfly, curmudgeon, champion of bold failures, prince of disorder, maestro of zest, corporate cheerleader, and irritator. *Fortune Magazine*

calls him the Ur-guru (the original guru) and *The Economist* the Über-guru.

KEY THINKING

In Search of Excellence resulted from the application of the 7-S model in an attempt to discover models of excellence in corporate America. Peters and Waterman identified eight lessons from their research.

- a bias for action - excellent companies get on with doing the job, unconstrained by the bureaucratic trappings
- be close to the customer - this has since become a key business 'must'
- autonomy and entrepreneurship - the entrepreneur has freedom to think, act and invest effort in the organisation
- productivity through people - it was previously believed that large organisations held the key to productivity because only they could handle the economies of scale required for profitability
- be driven by hands - on values-the shared values of the 7-S model that matter to employees, as well as making the business tick with managers who are not afraid to get their hands dirty
- stick to the knitting - companies should stay with their core competencies, not diversifying for the sake of it
- simple form, lean staff - successful companies are not preoccupied with their size or procedures but with keeping things simple
- simultaneous loose - tight properties-examples of excellence derived from the faster-moving, more flexible features of smaller organisations, not the more cumbersome aspects of large ones

When Peters declared in 1987, at the beginning of *Thriving on Chaos*, that there are no excellent companies, it was not only in recognition of the fact that many of the companies he had cited earlier had foundered. It was also because the rules had changed again: there was no single consistent route to excellence. Times change, so companies need to change their approach in order to continue to be successful. Peters has argued consistently that the eight lessons from *In Search of Excellence* remain valid-the companies he cited that later foundered merely failed to follow the lessons through.

A Passion for Excellence was published in 1985, intended as a sequel to *In Search of Excellence*, but this time with the focus on leadership. According to Peters (and his co-author Nancy Austin) the successful leader becomes passionate about getting the most out of people, takes to heart the full people-centred implications of the 7 Ss, and lays the basis for the culture of empowerment. It is also in this book that Peters starts to return time and again to the centrality of the customer.

In *Thriving on Chaos*, Peters was one of the first to describe the emerging world of uncertainty and accelerating change. He was lucky with his timing: it was published in the same month (October 1987) that the stock-market crashes in Wall Street, London, and Tokyo brought chaos to the world's money markets. The book was in fact a rejection of the secure world of the past, and a description of the uncertain world of the future. Some of the book's themes were already there in *In Search of Excellence*: customer responsiveness and flexibility through empowerment, for example. But already in 1987, the world was a fast-changing place where increased competition meant speed to market, and that meant fast-paced innovation. Most of all, Peters understood that organisations would need flexible systems to deal with a topsy-turvy world.

Thriving on Chaos encouraged managers to cast off their old thinking and be prepared for a world of change and uncertainty. But Peters had not yet drawn a map of how to get there. *Liberation Management* was his attempt to draw such a map. He advocated flexible, flowing structures that are anti-hierarchical and based on building up relationships with customers. As he had done in *Thriving on Chaos*, Peters quoted examples of companies that represent the lean, flatter, and responsive organisation required now that the old rule-book had been torn up. Again, he focused on the need to innovate, on closeness to customers, and on empowerment. In *Liberation Management* who asserted that knowledge is becoming the key asset, the working capital of the organisation.

Peters the writer

Drucker may have written more, but Peters was beginning to catch up with him until he started to prefer blogging (see **www.tompeters.com**) to print publishing. *Thriving on Chaos* is over 500 pages long; *Liberation Management* is over 800. In addition, Peters wrote a column for 10 years as a channel for his thoughts, ideas, observations, and continuing flow of examples of companies.

His style of writing, as well as the content of his work, has changed over the years. One of the attractive features of *In Search of Excellence* was its accessible style. Peters's later works take this style to an extreme and reduce the language of management to monosyllabic expressions designed to shock, excite, provoke, and stir the reader out of conventional thinking. Hence his 1994 title – *The Pursuit of Wow!*

The guru as performer

This is an area that Tom Peters has made his own. Many gurus are academics or writers, but few would claim to have the impact of Peters on stage. He has been universally described as a brilliant performer, with great stage presence and unbeatable delivery technique. Sometimes delivering two seminars a day in different cities, Peters is acknowledged for his genuine interest, concern, even passion for getting people to reflect on the way they manage.

The Tom Peters seminar: *The Circle of Innovation*

The message that comes over in *The Circle of Innovation* is one that has taken between 15 and 20 years to develop.

The book attempts to push the management of organisations to anticipate the topsy-turvy markets that are emerging with global markets, the Internet, and the ever greater closeness of customer and producer.

- Beyond change – be prepared to try things out, but do not expect to get things right first time. Peters acknowledges the role of stability and regularity but attaches far greater importance to agility.
- Beyond downsizing – aim to be big and small at the same time, so that you get the benefits of a large organisation (economies of scale, networking, and knowledge-sharing) along with those of the small (speed, independence, and responding to opportunities).
- Beyond empowerment – make every job entrepreneurial.
- Beyond loyalty – everybody learns to think about the future, the customer, and the bottom-line.
- Beyond re-engineering – the conversion of units or departments into full professional service firms with responsibility and accountability.
- Beyond disorganisation – as the organisation spots and responds to opportunities, it becomes a network of partners, distributors, suppliers, and customers with boundaries that are transparent to outsiders.
- Beyond the learning organisation – stimulating curiosity and creativity everywhere in the organisation.
- Beyond TQM – towards sustainable product/service differentiation to escape the sameness of today's markets through design.
- Beyond management – from management to revolutionary leadership.

TOM PETERS IN PERSPECTIVE

Peters did not actually discover the concept of customers with *In Search of Excellence*, but he and Waterman bucked the dominance of strategy to remind management that customers come first. If he seems all for discontinuity and disorganisation, it is principally to remind people not to get stuck in the rut of procedures and routine.

Peters has been criticised for not being thorough or academic enough in support of his assertions, for relying too much on his charisma as a performer, and for 'dumbing down' management to a level of mundaneness and banality. But one of the widely agreed achievements of Tom Peters is that, for a period of 15 years or more, his antennae have sensed where the world of business is heading before it arrives. It is also widely acknowledged that his approach, style, and energy have popularised management ideas to a wider audience than ever before.

Managers from all levels and from all types of organisation say that Peters's influence has been positive rather than negative, and he is spoken of in the same league as Porter, Ohmae, Hamel, Handy, and even Drucker. If he has changed his mind, it is because today's world has altered so radically from that of the 1970s. If he has been inconsistent, he has nonetheless stayed ahead of the management times and foreseen – or helped to set – the management agenda for the fast-changing world of the future.

THE BEST SOURCES OF HELP
Books:

Crainer, Stuart. *Corporate Man to Corporate Skunk: The Tom Peters Phenomenon, A Biography*. Oxford: Capstone Publishing, 2001.

Peters, Tom, and Bob Waterman. *In Search of Excellence: Lessons from America's Best-run Companies*. New York: Harper & Row, 1982.

Peters, Tom, and Nancy Austin. *A Passion for Excellence: The Leadership Difference*. New York: Harper Collins, 1985.

Peters, Tom. *Thriving on Chaos: Handbook for a Management Revolution*. New York: A. Knopf, 1987.

Peters, Tom. *Liberation Management*. New York: A. Knopf, 1992.

Peters, Tom. *The Tom Peters Seminar: Crazy Times for Crazy Organisations*. New York: Vintage Books, 1994.

Peters, Tom. *The Pursuit of Wow! Every Person's Guide to Topsy-Turvy Times*. New York: Vintage Books, 1994.

Peters, Tom. *The Circle of Innovation: You Can't Shrink Your Way to Greatness*. London: Hodder & Stoughton, 1997.

Peters, Tom. *Re-imagine!* London: Dorling Kindersley, 2003.

Michael Porter What Is Strategy?

In an age when management gurus are both lauded by the faithful and hounded by the critics, Michael Porter seems to be one of the few who is well-regarded both academically and in the business world. Porter has been at the leading edge of strategic thinking since his first major publication, *Competitive Strategy* in 1980.

1947	Born.
1969	Completes a degree in aeronautical engineering at Princeton University.
1971	Receives an MBA from Harvard Business School.
1973	Receives a PhD from Harvard University. Joins the Harvard Business School faculty.
1980	Publishes *Competitive Strategy*, which sets him at leading edge of strategic thinking.
1994	Founds The Initiative for a Competitive Inner City, and becomes Chairman and CEO.

LIFE AND CAREER

Born in 1947, Porter completed a degree in aeronautical engineering at Princeton in 1969 and joined the Harvard Business School faculty at the age of 26 after completing a doctorate in economics. He has acted as a consultant to businesses and governments and, like many academics, he has set up a consulting company, Monitor.

KEY THINKING

His thinking on strategy has been supported by precision research into industries and companies. Over a period of almost 20 years, his thinking remains consistent as well as developmental – it has not stood still since *Competitive Strategy* became a corporate bible for many in the early 1980s. Before that time, most strategic thinking focused on either the organisation of a company's internal resources and their adaptation to meet particular circumstances in the marketplace, or improving competitiveness by lowering prices to increase market share. These approaches, derived from the work of Igor Ansoff, were bundled into systems or processes that provided strategy with its place in the organisation.

In *Competitive Strategy*, however, Porter managed to reconcile these approaches and provide management with a fresh way of looking at strategy – not just from the point of view of markets or of organisational capabilities, but from the point of view of industry itself.

Internal capability for competitiveness-the value chain

Porter describes two different types of business activity-primary and secondary. Primary activities are concerned with transforming inputs (raw materials) into outputs (products), and with delivery and after-sales support. These are usually the main 'line management' activities and include:

- inbound logistics – materials handling, warehousing
- operations – turning raw materials into finished products
- outbound logistics – order processing and distribution
- marketing and sales – communication and pricing
- service – installation and after-sales service

Secondary activities support the primary and include:

- procurement – purchasing and supply
- technology development – know-how, procedures and skills
- human resource management – recruitment, promotion, appraisal, reward and development
- company infrastructure – general and quality management, finance, planning

To survive competition and supply what customers want to buy, the company has to ensure that all these value-chain activities link together, even if some of the activities take place outside the organisation. A weakness in any one of the activities will impact on the chain as a whole and affect competitiveness.

Gurus

The five forces

Porter argued that in order to examine its competitive capability in the marketplace, an organisation must choose between three generic strategies:

- cost leadership – becoming the lowest-cost producer in the market
- differentiation – offering something different, extra, or special
- focus – achieving dominance in a niche market

The skill is to choose the right one at the right time. These generic strategies are driven by five competitive forces that the organisation has to take into account:

- the power of customers to affect pricing and reduce margins
- the power of suppliers to influence the organisation's pricing
- the threat of similar products to limit market freedom and reduce prices and thus profits
- the level of existing competition that impacts on investment in marketing and research and thus erodes profits
- the threat of new market entrants to intensify competition and further impact on pricing and profitability

In recent years, Porter has revisited his earlier work. Such is the acceleration of market change that companies now have to compete not on a choice of strategic fronts, but on all fronts at once. Porter has also said that it is a misconception of his approach for a company to try to position itself in relation to the five competitive forces. Positioning is not enough. What companies have to do is ask how the five forces can help to rewrite industry rules in the organisation's favour.

Diversification

Instead of going it alone, an organisation can spread risk and attain growth by diversification and acquisition. While the blue-chip consulting companies such as Boston Consulting Group (market growth/market share matrix) and McKinsey (7-S framework) have developed analytical models for discovering which companies will rise and fall, Porter prefers three critical tests for success.

- The attractiveness test. Industries chosen for diversification must be structurally attractive. An attractive industry will yield a high return on investment, but entry barriers will be high; customers and suppliers will have only moderate bargaining power, and there will be only a few substitute products. An unattractive industry will be swamped by a range of alternative products, high rivalry, and high fixed costs.
- The cost-of-entry test. If the cost of entry is so high that it prejudices the potential return on investment, profitability is eroded before the game has started.
- The better-off test. How will the acquisition provide advantage to either the acquirer or the acquired? Porter argues that one must offer significant advantage to the other.

Porter devised seven steps to tackle these questions.

- As competition takes place at the business unit level, identify the interrelationships among the existing business units.
- Identify the core business that is to be the foundation of the strategy. Core businesses are those in attractive industries and in which competitive advantage can be sustained.
- Create horizontal organisational mechanisms to facilitate interrelationships among core businesses.
- Pursue diversification opportunities that allow shared activities and pass all three critical tests.
- Pursue diversification through a transfer of skills, if opportunities for sharing activities are limited or exhausted.
- Pursue a strategy of restructuring if this fits the skills of management, or if no good opportunities exist for forging corporate partnerships.
- Pay dividends so that shareholders can become portfolio managers.

National competitiveness

Why do some companies achieve consistent improvement in innovation, seeking an ever more sophisticated source of competitive advantage? For Porter, the answer lies in four attributes that affect industries. These attributes are:

- **factor conditions** – the nation's skills and infrastructure capable of enabling a competitive position
- **demand conditions** – the nature of home-market demand
- **related and supporting industries** – presence or absence of supplier/feeder industries
- **company strategy, structure and rivalry** – the national conditions under which companies are created, grow, organise, and manage.

These are the chief determinants that create the environment in which businesses flourish and compete, he suggests. The points on the diamond constitute a self-reinforcing system, in which the effect of one point often depends on the state of the others, and any weakness at one point will impact adversely on an industry's capability to compete.

The new strategic wave

Sometime between 1980 and 1990 a new wave of more subversive strategic thinking – like Gary Hamel's *Strategy as Revolution*, and Mintzberg's 'The fall and rise of strategic planning' (*Harvard Business Review*) – emerged to replace the old rule-book. Porter's main contribution to date, *Competitive Strategy*, argues that strategic planning lost its way because managers failed to distinguish between strategic and operational effectiveness and confused the two.

The old strategic model was based on productivity, increasing market share, and lowering costs. Hence, total quality management, benchmarking, outsourcing, and re-engineering were all at the forefront of change in the 1980s as the key drivers of operational improvements. But continuing incremental improvements to the way things are done tend to bring different players up to the same level, rather than differentiating them. To achieve differentiation therefore means that:

- strategy rests on unique activities, based on customers' needs, customers' accessibility, or the variety of a company's products or services
- the company's activities must fit and link together. In terms of the value chain, one link is prone to imitation but with a chain, imitation is very difficult
- it is important to make trade-offs. Excelling at some things means making a conscious choice not to do others – it's a

question of being a 'master of one trade' to stand out from the crowd, as opposed to being a 'jack of all trades' and lost in the mass. Trade-offs deliberately limit what a company offers. The essence of strategy lies in what *not* to do.

MICHAEL PORTER IN PERSPECTIVE

It is a mark of Porter's achievement that much of his work on *Competitive Strategy*, researched in the 1970s, still has high value and relevance and still shapes mainstream thinking on competition and strategy.

While his work is academically rigorous, his ability to abstract his thinking into digestible chunks for the business world has given him wide appeal to both the academic and business communities. It is now standard practice for organisations to think and talk about 'value chains', and the five forces have entered the curriculum of every management programme.

THE BEST SOURCES OF HELP
Books:

Porter, Michael. *Competitive Strategy: Techniques for Analyzing Industries and Competitors.* New York: Free Press, 1980.

Porter, Michael. *Competitive Advantage: Creating and Sustaining Superior Performance.* Revised ed. New York: Free Press, 1985.

Porter, Michael. *The Competitive Advantage of Nations.* Rev ed. New York: Free Press, 1998.

C.K. Prahalad A New View of Strategy

Gurus

C.K. Prahalad is regarded as one of the most influential thinkers on strategy in the United States. His work stems from a deep concern with the ability of large organisations to maintain competitive vitality when faced with international competition and changing business environments. Many of his ideas on competitive analysis argue against the supremacy of traditional strategic thinking and focus upon the concepts of 'strategic intent', 'core competence', and 'strategy as stretch and leverage'.

1941	Born.
1960–1964	Works as an industrial engineer.
1966	Completes an MBA at the Indian Institute of Management.
1975	Completes a DBA at Harvard Business School.
1975	Visiting Research Fellow, Harvard Business School.
1975–1977	Professor and Chairman, Management Education Programme, Indian Institute of Management.
1981	Visiting Professor, INSEAD, Fontainebleau, France.
1986–	Professor, University of Michigan Business School.
1994	Co-writes *Competing for the Future* with Gary Hamel.
1994	Receives award from Indo-American Society for promoting goodwill, understanding, and friendship between India and the United States.
1995	American Society for Competitiveness recognises his contribution to competitiveness in business.

LIFE AND CAREER

Prahalad came to management thinking from the field of physics – entering the world of the fuzziest of sciences from one of the most precise. He worked as an industrial engineer before completing an MBA at the Indian Institute of Management in 1966 and a DBA at Harvard Business School in 1975. Since then he has been a visiting research fellow at Harvard, a professor at the Indian Institute of Management, and a visiting professor at the European Institute of Business Administration (INSEAD). He is Harvey C. Fruehauf Professor of Corporate Strategy and International Business at the Graduate School of Business Administration, University of Michigan. Over the years he has been a consultant for many large, multinational companies, including Eastman Kodak, AT&T, Honeywell, Philips, Motorola, and Ahlstrom.

Prahalad's contributions to strategic thinking have been widely acknowledged. *Business Week* wrote '. . . a brilliant teacher at the University of Michigan, Prahalad may well be the most influential thinker on corporate strategy today.' In September 1993 the *Wall Street Journal*'s Special Report on Management Education named him as one of the top ten teachers in the world. In 1994 he received the annual award presented by the Indo-American Society for his outstanding contribution towards the promotion of Indo-American goodwill, understanding, and friendship, and in 1995 the American Society for Competitiveness recognised his outstanding academic contribution to competitiveness in business.

KEY THINKING
Competing for the Future

Prahalad sees his book *Competing for the Future* as presenting a new view of competitiveness, strategy, and organisations. It takes the ideas of strategic intent, core competence and strategy as stretch and leverage, and builds on them to create a new strategy model.

Strategic intent

Strategic intent is described as a way of creating an obsession with winning at all levels and across all functions of the organisation. It is a shared competitive agenda for global leadership. Strategic intent uses stretch targets to create competitive advantage. For example, landing a man on the moon by the end of the 1960s provided the stretch target that gave the United States global leadership in space. It is the role of senior management to develop the organisation in a way that closes the gap between ambition and ability. This involves active management processes, which include focusing the organisation's attention on the urgency of winning; motivating people with challenges that require personal effort and commitment; using these challenges to create mid-term competitive advantage, and applying intent consistently to guide resource allocation. Strategic intent provides the focus for 'barrier-breaking' initiatives.

Core competencies

Core competencies are often confused with core capabilities and core technologies. A core competency is an ability that transcends products and markets, and it results when an organisation learns to harmonise multiple technologies, learning, and relationships across levels and functions. Core competencies feed into core products, which themselves can become business units. A core competency provides access to a wide variety of markets, makes a significant contribution to the customer's perceived benefit, and is difficult for competitors to imitate. Examples include Sony's competence in miniaturisation, Philips's optical-media expertise, and Black & Decker's knowledge of small electrical engines. Viewing the organisation as a portfolio of competencies is seen to lead to strategic advantage.

Strategic architecture

A strategic architecture is a framework for leveraging corporate resources towards the strategic intent. It draws upon a variety of information to present a view of the evolution of an industry. A strategic architecture identifies the core competencies to build, and their constituent technologies. It provides a framework within which innovation can be planned and managed.

Corporate imagination

In order to realise the potential that core competencies create, organisations must have the imagination to visualise new markets and the ability to move into them ahead of the competition. The key to competitive advantage is the process through which organisations release corporate imagination, identify and explore new competitive space, and consolidate control over emerging markets. Prahalad suggests that four elements combine to quicken an organisation's imagination:

- escaping the focus on served markets
- searching for innovative product concepts
- overturning assumptions about price and performance relationships
- leading, rather than following, customers

Escaping served markets

Traditionally, organisational concern for existing markets blurs the view of new markets. Such a defensive policy is fine up to a point, but it should not be at the expense of new and potentially lucrative markets.

Innovative product concepts

Dramatic innovations in product concepts reshape markets and industry boundaries, creating new competitive space. Such innovations take one of three forms:

- the addition of a new function to a successful product
- the development of a new form for delivering a proven functionality
- the delivery of a proven functionality through an entirely new product concept

Product innovations flow from organisations that view a market in terms of needs and functionalities. This logical process of dissecting a product or service into its functional components is rare in most organisations.

Price/performance trade-off

Most organisations view products and services as price/performance trade-offs. Radical innovation can be achieved where an organisation pursues those products labelled 'unattainable dreams'. New competitive space can be created by understanding how emerging technologies might allow customers' unmet needs to be satisfied, or their existing needs to be better satisfied.

Leading customers

Leading customers requires a deep insight into the lifestyles, needs, and aspirations of today's and tomorrow's customers. Traditional modes of market research fail to provide such insights: it is through creative human science studies that such an understanding can be gained. Leading customers to where they want to go, before they know it themselves, provides a huge competitive advantage. This approach involves all functions of the organisation. It creates marketeers with technological imagination and technologists with marketing imagination, overcoming the debate about whether an organisation should be market- or technology-led.

Expeditionary marketing

On the premise that being first to market provides a competitive advantage, expeditionary marketing is identified as a tool used by organisations that create competitive space. Expeditionary marketing helps organisations gain an understanding of the particular features, price, and performance of new products that will successfully pen-etrate the market. Such learning can be gained only when a product-imperfect as it might be-is launched. Expeditionary marketing increases the number of successful products an organisation achieves by increasing the number of market opportunities, niches, and product variations explored.

C.K. PRAHALAD IN PERSPECTIVE

The strength of Prahalad's writing lies in the fact that much of it has resulted from debate and development with his joint authors. His belief that there was more to strategy than the existing theories portrayed caught the attention of academics and practising managers alike. Couple this with a strong belief in the need for business school research to have a strong managerial significance, and you begin to realise why Prahalad is held in such high regard.

Consultancy work in corporate America and beyond continually raised the question of how smaller rivals, new to a market, could prevail against much larger, richer organisations. 'Existing theories of strategy and organisation, while providing a solid base for discovery, do not fully answer these questions,' Prahalad argues. These theories help us to understand the structure of an industry, identify the attributes of a transformational leader, and provide a scorecard for monitoring relative competitive advantage. But they do not provide insight into what it takes to redesign an industry, help us understand the role of the leadership team in visualising the future, or explain the process of competence-building. *Competing for the Future* is a work which aims to fill the gap between theory and reality.

Prahalad's ideas developed at a time when corporate strategy was in crisis and in need of a new face. Organisations were more concerned with improving operational efficiency than focusing on the future, and downsizing for short-term gain meant that many businesses were failing to focus on the potential of tomorrow. It was the recognition that such an approach could not continue that has made large organisations receptive to Prahalad's thinking.

THE BEST SOURCES OF HELP

Books:

Prahalad, C.K., and Gary Hamel. *Competing for the Future*. Boston, Massachusetts: Harvard Business School Press, 1994.

Prahalad, C.K. *The Fortune at the Bottom of the Pyramid: Eradicating Poverty Through Profits*. London: Financial Times Prentice Hall, 2004.

Prahalad, C.K., with Venkat Ramaswamy. *The Future of Competition: Co-creating Unique Value with Customers*. Boston, Massachusetts: Harvard Business School Press, 2004.

Prahalad, C.K., and Kenneth Lieberthal. *The End of Corporate Imperialism*. Boston, Massachusetts: Harvard Business School Press, 2008.

Journal Articles:

Prahalad, C.K., and Yves Doz. 'An approach to strategic control in MNCs.' *Sloan Management Review*, vol. 22 no. 4, 1981, pp. 5–13.

Prahalad, C.K., and Gary Hamel. 'Do you really have a global strategy?' *McKinsey Quarterly*, Summer 1986, pp. 34–59.

Prahalad, C.K., Gary Hamel, and Yves Doz. 'Collaborate with your competitors and win.' *Harvard Business Review*, January/February 1989, pp. 133–139.

Prahalad, C.K., and Gary Hamel. 'Strategic intent.' *McKinsey Quarterly*, Spring 1990, pp. 36–61.

Prahalad, C.K., and Gary Hamel. 'Core competence of the corporation.' *Harvard Business Review*, May/June 1990, pp. 79–91.

Prahalad, C.K., and Gary Hamel. 'Corporate imagination and expeditionary marketing.' *Harvard Business Review*, July/August 1991, pp. 81–92.

Prahalad, C.K., and Gary Hamel. 'A strategy for growth: The role of core competencies in the corporation.' *EFMD Forum*, no. 3–4 1993, pp. 3–9.

Prahalad, C.K., and Gary Hamel. 'Competing for the future.' *Harvard Business Review*, vol. 72 no. 4, July/August 1994, pp. 122–128.

Prahalad, C.K., and Gary Hamel. 'Competing in the new economy: managing out of bounds.' *Strategic Management Journal*, Mar 1996, pp. 237–242.

Edgar Schein Careers, Culture, and Organisational Learning

Edgar Schein pioneered the concept of corporate culture with his landmark book *Organizational Culture and Leadership* (1985), which sparked off much research into the subject. He also coined the now much-used phrases 'psychological contract' and 'career anchor'.

1928	Born.
1949	Masters Degree in Psychology, Stanford.
1972–1982	Chairman of the Organization Studies Group of Sloan School of Management, Massachusetts Institute of Technology.
1978–1990	Sloan Fellows Professor of Management, Massachusetts Institute of Technology.
1985	Publication of *Organizational Culture and Leadership*.

LIFE AND CAREER

Currently the Sloan Fellows Professor of Management Emeritus and part-time senior lecturer at the MIT Sloan School of Management, Edgar Schein has had a long and distinguished academic career. He received his PhD in social psychology from Harvard University, collaborated with Douglas McGregor at MIT, and worked for many years with the National Training Laboratory. In addition, he has made a strong contribution to the 'helping' professions, mainly in the areas of organisation development, career development, and organisational culture.

Schein has researched and written extensively about the factors that influence individual and organisational performance. The main themes underlying his work are the identification of culture(s) in the organisation, the relationship between organisational culture and individual behaviour, and the importance of organisational culture for organisational learning. Douglas McGregor invited him to MIT on the basis of his work on the repatriation of POWs following the end of the Korean War. This work strongly influenced Schein's whole career, and re-emerged forcefully in 1999 in an article for the *Learning Organization* on brainwashing and organisational persuasion techniques ('Empowerment, coercive persuasion, and organizational learning: Do they connect?', vol. 6, no. 4, pp. 163–172).

KEY THINKING

Corporate culture

Early in his career Schein found traditional approaches to understanding work behaviour and motivation firstly too simplistic to explain the range of experiences of individuals in organisations and secondly too restrictive, since human and organisational needs vary widely from person to person, place to place, and time to time. In *Organizational Culture and Leadership*, he became the first management theorist to define corporate culture and suggest ways in which culture is the dominant force within an organisation.

In his view, culture is a mix of many different factors, such as:

- observed behavioural regularities when people interact
- norms that evolve in working groups
- dominant values pushed by the organisation
- the philosophy guiding the attitudes of senior management to staff and customers
- organisational rules, procedures, and processes
- the feeling or climate that is conveyed without a word being spoken

In *Organizational Culture and Leadership*, Schein defines culture as a pattern of basic assumptions, and discusses how these fall into five, often oppositional, categories, which are:

- humanity's relationship to nature-some organisations seem to want to dominate the external environment, while others accept its domination
- the nature of reality and truth-the ways and means by which organisations arrive at the 'truth'
- the nature of human nature-some people seem to avoid work if they possibly can, while others embrace it as a way of fulfilling their potential, to both their own and the organisation's benefit
- the nature of human activity-a focus on the completion of tasks on the one hand, and on self-fulfilment and personal development on the other
- the nature of human relationships-some organisations seem to facilitate social interaction, others to regard it as an unnecessary distraction

Organisational socialisation

Schein's thoughts on organisational socialisation were triggered when, after arriving at MIT, he asked McGregor for guidance in the form of previous outlines and notes for a course he was preparing. McGregor politely refused, saying there was no need to rely on history and that Schein should make up his own mind. This lesson in acclimatising to MIT led Schein to argue that companies should be conversant with their socialisation practices and recognise the conflicts they can create for new recruits.

In 'Organizational Socialization and the Profession of Management' (*Sloan Management Review*, Fall 1988, pp. 53–65) Schein discusses how, when a new recruit enters the organisation, a process of socialisation-adaptation or 'fit'-takes place. He argues that this process has more to do with recruits' past experience and values than their qualifications or formal training.

Usually, Schein suggested, organisations create a series of events that work to undo the new recruit's old values to some extent, so that he or she is more open to learning new values. This process of 'undoing' or 'unfreezing' can be unpleasant, and its success may therefore depend upon either a recruit's strong motivation to endure it, or the organisation's perseverance in making recruits endure it. There are three basic responses to this socialisation process:

- rebellion – outright rejection of the organisation's norms and values
- creative individualism – selective adoption of key values and norms
- conformity – acceptance of the organisation's norms and values

Noting similarities between brainwashing experienced by servicemen captured during the Korean War and the socialisation of executives in programmes at MIT, Schein argues that many forms of organisational development involve restructuring and change, and have serious implications for the way people work and their relationship with management.

Schein likens such processes to a form of coercive persuasion, or brainwashing, giving people little choice but to abandon, for example, older norms and values that fit badly with the new learning. If we are in tune with the goals and values of the change this will not be a problem, but if we dislike the values, we are likely to disapprove of the brainwashing. Schein concludes that, because the very concept of organisation involves some restriction of individual freedom to achieve a joint purpose, the concept of a continually learning, innovative organisation is something of a paradox, since creativity and learning are related to individual freedom and growth.

Organisational learning

Organisational learning, Schein considers, needs to be fast in order to cope with growing market pressures, yet seems to be obstructed by a fear of, or anxiety about, facing change, particularly on the part of senior executives. This feeling is associated with reluctance to learn what is new, because it appears too difficult or disruptive. Schein argues that only a new anxiety greater than the existing one can overcome this, and his 'anxiety 2' is the fear, shame, or guilt associated with not learning anything new.

Schein emphasises the need for people to feel psychologically safe, if change is to happen. Achieving organisational learning and transformation therefore depends upon creating a feeling of safety and overcoming the negative effects of past incentives and past punishments- especially the latter. To learn, people need to feel motivated and free to try out new things.

Psychological contract and career anchors

In *Organizational Psychology* Schein highlights a 'psychological contract' (attributing the original concept to Chris Argyris), which he defines as an unwritten set of expectations operating between employees and employing managers and others in an organisation. He stresses how essential it is that both parties' expectations of a contract should match, if a long-term relationship that will benefit both parties is to develop.

Closely linked to the notion of the psychological contract is the concept of the 'career anchor', a guiding force that influences individuals' career choices and is based on their self-perceptions. Schein proposes that, from their varying aspirations and motivations, individuals- perhaps unconsciously – develop one underlying career anchor, which they are unwilling to surrender. On the basis of 44 cases, he distinguishes career anchor groups such as technical/functional competence, managerial competence, creativity, security or stability, and autonomy.

The three cultures of management

Rather than a single culture, Schein identifies three cultures (or communities of interest) within an organisation: the operator culture, which evolves locally within organisations and within operational units; the engineering culture of technicians in search of 'people-free' solutions; and the executive culture, which is focused on financial survival.

The three often conflict rather than work in harmony. For example, while the executive culture must have systems and reporting relationships for evidence that operations are on track, the engineering culture attempts to design systems that cut across lines of control and the people manning these.

In his article 'Three cultures of management: The key to organizational learning' (*Sloan Management Review*, Fall 1996, pp. 9–20) Schein suggests that, in many cases, either operators assume executives and engineers do not understand their work needs and covertly do things in their own way; or executives or engineers assume a need for tighter control over operators and force them to follow policies and procedure manuals. In either case, there is no commonly understood plan, and efficiency and effectiveness suffer.

Schein stresses the need to take the concept of culture more seriously and accept how deeply embedded are the assumptions of executives, engineers, and employees. He proposes that helping executives and engineers learn how to evolve their cultures may be central to organisational learning.

EDGAR SCHEIN IN PERSPECTIVE

Schein's work now spans more than five decades and his great contribution has been in linking culture with individual development and growth, putting the accent on organisations as complex systems and on individuals as whole beings.

Schein was aware that the concept of corporate culture was no cure-all for ailing organisations. The fact, however, that culture is now generally recognised as a central factor in organisational change and development is largely attributable to his work.

THE BEST SOURCES OF HELP

Books:

Schein, Edgar. *Career Dynamics: Matching Individual and Organizational Needs*. Reading, Massachusetts: Addison-Wesley, 1978.

Schein, Edgar. *Organizational Psychology*. 3rd ed. Englewood Cliffs, New Jersey: Prentice Hall, 1980.

Schein, Edgar. *Organizational Culture and Leadership*. 3rd ed. San Francisco, California: Jossey-Bass, 2004.

Schein, Edgar. *The Corporate Culture Survival Guide*. San Francisco, California: Jossey-Bass, 1999.

Schein, Edgar. *How to Offer, Give and Receive Help*. San Francisco, California: Berrett-Koehler, 2009.

Journal Article:

Schein, Edgar. 'How can organizations learn faster? The challenge of entering the green room.' *Sloan Management Review*, Winter 1993, pp. 85–92.

Peter Senge The Learning Organisation

Populariser of the theory of the learning organisation, first suggested by Chris Argyris and Donald Schön, Peter Senge studied how organisations develop adaptive capabilities in a world of increasing complexity and change. His work culminated in the publication of *The Fifth Discipline: The Art and Practice of the Learning Organization*.

1947	Born.
1975–1990	Research at the Sloan School of Management into ways of learning.
1990	Publication of *The Fifth Discipline*.
1999	Named by the *Journal of Business Strategy* as one of the 24 people with the greatest influence on business strategy over the previous century.
Present	Founding chair of the Society of Organizational Learning at the Sloan School of Management, MIT.

LIFE AND CAREER

Peter Senge is senior lecturer at the Sloan School of Management, Massachusetts Institute of Technology (MIT). He graduated in engineering from Stanford before earning a PhD in social systems modelling at MIT. For many years, Senge studied how businesses and organisations develop adaptive capabilities in a world of increasing complexity and change, but the success of his book *The Fifth Discipline* popularised the concept of the 'learning organisation'.

Published in 1990, *The Fifth Discipline* brought the attention of the world to bear on this rather unassuming man, who suddenly found himself the modern equivalent of a medieval crusader seeking dramatically to change corporate America, and indeed the rest of the world, against all the odds. Senge's message was simple- the learning organisation believes that competitive

advantage derives from continued learning, both individual and collective. Furthermore, the new challenges of the information age demand that not only businesses, but also educational institutions and governments, transform themselves radically. Senge describes himself as an 'idealistic pragmatist' and spends much time building learning organisations with the top leaders of companies, education, and government.

Although Senge's ideas are utopian, his Center for Organizational Learning has attracted an impressive list of corporate sponsors who have dug deep into their pockets to fund pilot programmes.

KEY THINKING

The Fifth Discipline

In *The Fifth Discipline*, Senge suggests that there are five basic ingredients for a learning organisation.

Systems thinking: Senge's whole approach to organisations is a 'systems' approach that views the organisation as a living entity, with its own behaviour and learning patterns. He introduces the idea of 'systems archetypes' to help managers spot repetitive patterns that lead to recurrent problems or limits to growth.

Personal mastery: every modern manager recognises the importance of developing skills and competencies in individuals, but Senge takes this notion further by stressing the importance of spiritual growth in the learning organisation. True spiritual growth exposes us to a deeper reality; it teaches us to see the current reality more clearly and, by highlighting the difference between vision and the current reality, generates a creative tension, out of which successful learning arises. In Senge's own words, a learning organisation is 'a group of people who are continually enhancing their capability to create their future' by 'changing individuals so that they produce results they care about, accomplish things that are important to them'.

Mental models: the systems approach is continued with Senge's emphasis on mental models. This discipline requires managers to construct mental models for the driving forces behind the organisation's values and principles. Senge alerts his readers to the impact of acquired patterns of thinking at the organisational level and the need to develop non-defensive mechanisms for examining the nature of these patterns.

Shared vision: according to Senge, true creativity and innovation are based on group creativity, and the shared vision the group depends on can only be built on the personal vision of its members. Shared vision occurs when the vision is no longer seen by the team members as separate from the self.

Team learning: effective team learning involves alternating processes for dialogue and discussion. Dialogue is exploratory and widens possibilities, whereas discussion narrows down the options to find the best alternatives for future decisions. Although these two processes are complementary, they need to be separated. Unfortunately, most teams lack the ability to distinguish between these two modes and to move consciously between them.

Senge's basic premise can be stated very simply: people should put aside their old ways of thinking (mental models); learn to be open with others (personal mastery); understand how the company really works (systems thinking); form a plan everyone can agree on (shared vision); and then work together to achieve that vision (team learning).

Practical tools-*The Fifth Discipline Fieldbook*

Recognising that the ideas contained in *The Fifth Discipline* needed to be made more accessible to practising managers, Senge and his colleagues produced a more practical guide – *The Fifth Discipline Fieldbook*. Throughout the book, the authors stress that anyone who wants to be part of a learning organisation must be willing to go through a personal change. To help this process, Senge and his co-authors provide a set of elaborate personal awareness exercises. The *Fieldbook* was designed as a resource for dipping into and it contains many good ideas and case studies. Even if you find Senge's thinking too general, the *Fieldbook* is well worth scrutinising for references and new ideas. Here are just a few:

System archetypes and causal loops: the *Fieldbook* devotes a lot of time to mapping processes in organisations, analysing feedback loops and identifying typical organisational problems (the system archetypes). This process-mapping tool can help employees to work out how complex systems interact, and to develop their 'mental models' of the organisation. The 'beer game' described in *The Fifth Discipline* is a simulation based on these models.

Left- and right-hand columns: by writing down in meetings what you really think (left-hand column) and what you actually said (right-hand column), you can analyse and identify those personal prejudices that get in the way of really productive work.

The ladder of inference: this exercise provides a step model for analysing our values, beliefs, and actions. Climbing down the ladder helps us to discover why we behave the way we do, and helps us to avoid jumping to dangerous conclusions. The steps on the ladder are:

- I take ACTIONS based on my beliefs
- I adopt BELIEFS about the world
- I draw CONCLUSIONS
- I make ASSUMPTIONS based on the meanings added to my mental models
- I add MEANINGS (cultural and personal)
- I select DATA from what I observe
- I OBSERVE data and experiences

The container: this is a dialogue tool that has proved very effective (if not explosive!) in some organisations. People at a meeting are encouraged to imagine a container that holds everyone's hostile thoughts and feelings. As everyone speaks out, putting their fears, prejudices, and anger on the table, the hostility between different factions is neutralised, because it is exposed in a safe place for all to discuss. In the early days of such experiments, a good facilitator is probably essential.

Learning labs and flight simulators: the *Fieldbook* provides useful references for all those who wish to design effective simulations for training sessions.

PETER SENGE IN PERSPECTIVE

Although Senge's *The Fifth Discipline* was a bestseller, its basic concepts had emerged from extensive research carried out at the influential Sloan School of Management at MIT over 15 years. The success of the 'learning organisation' concept is a reflection of the times. None of the book's concepts is new, but Senge was able to put them all together and to create a simple but very powerful idea.

Senge is a product of his age, probably greatly influenced by the culture of the 1960s in the United States. His systems approach towards organisations shows the same maturity displayed in the systems analysis tools developed by thinkers such as Peter Checkland at Lancaster University. Here the organisation is viewed as a 'superorganism' with its own behaviour patterns, but also profoundly influenced by the nature of its constituent members. The sad fact is that Senge was one of the first management gurus to make the accepted beliefs of a whole generation of social scientists, biologists, and environmentalists credible to the corporate world.

In his own words, Senge says: 'We live under a massive illusion of separation from one another, from nature, from the universe, from everything. We're depleting the earth and we're fragmenting our spirit. The symptoms are pollution, anger, and fear. Everything in our culture is about the management of impressions and appearances, from physical fitness to the way we dress. And yet on another level we know it's all bullshit.' Even having just passed the millennium, there is little evidence that the change in attitude needed to achieve Senge's ideals – of long-term corporate sustainability and freedom for all to achieve personal mastery – is in sight: there are very few organisations that have been able to implement his ideas successfully.

The main criticism that can be levelled at Senge's work is the inherent difficulty of applying his models. Senge was trained as an engineer and then became involved in social research. Both require a systems approach, but this cannot be developed easily. In fact systems thinking is about as easy as learning brain surgery in a three-day course. Nor can most companies afford the luxury of their top executives learning to 'crash land' for too long.

Breaking old corporate habits is very hard, and therefore transforming an enterprise into a learning organisation is highly problematic and not for the faint-hearted. The reason for this is simple-in order to move forward to a new, co-operative learning model, managers have to give up their traditional areas of power and control. They have to hand over power to the learners and allow them to make mistakes. In a blame-oriented culture, this change in attitude remains a major obstacle.

Despite the elusiveness of its ideals, *The Fifth Discipline* has proved highly influential. Its concepts have stimulated the debate and acceptance of issues such as self-managed development, empowerment, and creativity. Its practical impact can be seen in modern human resource management strategies, teamwork principles, and in quality models.

It is more important perhaps to recognise that in life all the most profound truths are deceptively simple, yet almost impossible to apply in practice. The difficulty experienced in applying Senge's ideas does not invalidate them – if anything, it confirms their importance for companies in 21st century.

THE BEST SOURCES OF HELP
Books:
Checkland, Peter. *Systems Thinking, Systems Practice!*. New ed. Chichester: Wiley, 1999.

Gibson, Rowan, ed. *Rethinking the Future*. London: Nicholas Brealey, 1997.

Kleiner, Art. *The Age of Heretics: Heroes, Outlaws, and the Forerunners of Corporate Change*. 2nd ed. San Francisco: Jossey-Bass, 2008.

Senge, Peter. *The Fifth Discipline: The Art and Practice of the Learning Organization*. London: Century Business, 1990.

Senge, Peter, et al. *The Fifth Discipline Fieldbook: Strategies and Tools for Building a Learning Organization*. London: Nicholas Brealey, 1994.

Senge, Peter, et al. *Presence: Exploring Profound Change in People Organizations and Society*. London: Nicholas Brealey, 2005.

Senge, Peter. *The Necessary Revolution: How Individuals and Organisations Are Working Together to Create a Sustainable World*. London: Nicholas Brealey, 2008.

Journal Articles:
Senge, Peter. 'The future of workplace learning and performance.' *Training and Development USA* vol. 48 no. 5, 1994, pp. S36-S47.

Senge, Peter. 'Mr Learning Organization.' *Fortune International* 17 Oct 1994, pp. 75–81.

Senge, Peter. 'Looking ahead: implications of the present.' *Harvard Business Review* September/October 1997, pp. 18–32.

Gurus

Adam Smith Founder of Political Economics

Adam Smith published his best-known book, fully entitled *An Inquiry into the Nature and Causes of the Wealth of Nations* but commonly known as *The Wealth of Nations*, in 1776. This is often described as one of the most important texts of our time, and its two main philosophical points stressed the supreme value of individual liberty, and the pursuit of self-interest as ultimately beneficial for society as a whole.

1723	Born.
1748	Appointed lecturer in literature at Edinburgh University.
1751	Appointed professor of literature at Glasgow University.

1763	Publication of *The Theory of Moral Sentiments*.
1776	Publication of *The Wealth of Nations*.
1778	Accepts post of commissioner of customs in Scotland.
1787	Elected lord rector at Glasgow University.
1790	Dies.

LIFE AND CAREER

Smith was brought up in Kirkcaldy by his widowed mother. At 14, he won a scholarship to study mathematics and moral philosophy at Glasgow University; and then, at 17, to Balliol College, Oxford. In 1748, he was appointed to a lectureship in literature at Edinburgh, and in 1751, became professor of literature at Glasgow University. One year later, he was appointed professor of moral philosophy and, despite a nervous disorder, faltering speech, and a tendency to forgetfulness, became a teacher of high repute. His lectures focused on theology, ethics, and jurisprudence.

In 1763, following the publication of his first book, *The Theory of Moral Sentiments*, Smith was asked to act as tutor and companion to the young Duke of Buccleuch during his 'grand tour' of Europe. Through this he met several great philosophers and thinkers, including Voltaire and Rousseau, and his own ideas took firmer shape. On his return from Europe he retired to Kirkcaldy to concentrate on writing *The Wealth of Nations*.

In 1778, Smith accepted the post of commissioner of customs in Scotland, and was elected lord rector at Glasgow University in 1787. Although Smith had plans to add a third volume (on jurisprudence) to follow the other two, his writings remained limited to reissuing editions of *The Wealth of Nations*.

Smith never married and, despite his impressive mind, became known as somewhat eccentric, largely due to his tendency to forget everyday things, such as changing from his nightclothes into day wear. After the death of Smith's mother, he was looked after by a maiden aunt until his death in 1790.

HISTORICAL BACKGROUND

To understand Smith's thinking fully, it is helpful to know a little about his background. He knew many of the most influential contemporary thinkers, and spent much time debating in the gentlemen's clubs of London. He was a friend of both John Locke and David Hume and was, for a time, a disciple of Quesnay, the leading French physiocrat. *The Wealth of Nations* undoubtedly drew ideas from many such sources.

In the later 17th and 18th centuries, there was increasing interest in the theory of 'natural' law. The natural sciences had become established since the publication of Newton's *Philosophiae Naturalis Principia Mathematica* (1687) and there was a strong drive to uncover the natural laws that were thought to guide people's actions.

At the same time, burdensome government regulations were increasingly criticised, and the theory of natural order was being drawn into ideas about society and government. For example, John Locke's *Treatise on Civil Government* (1691) proposed that men are born free and equal, and are governed by 'natural laws', arguing that, while executive power is necessary, this should be only by consent.

Such revolutionary ideas were taken up by many great thinkers, including Hume, Hutchison, the French physiocrats, and Smith himself. It was, however, impossible to prove the existence of a benevolent 'natural order', ordained by God for men's happiness. While proponents of the concept considered it to be self-evident, it was always, in fact, an intangible hypothesis wide open to challenge.

The idea that human society should be based on a natural order encouraged ideas about individualism to develop further. The concept of an economic system founded on individual self-interest rather than government control is central to *The Wealth of Nations* and to later social, political, and economic change.

THE WEALTH OF NATIONS

Natural law and 'laissez faire'

The Wealth of Nations followed the French physiocrats in arguing that all human powers are subject to immutable, natural moral and physical laws. These laws, divine in origin, were thought to offer a basis for government that could leave things to work naturally, with results that would satisfy both individual and state interests.

Smith never actually used the term 'laissez faire', but his book popularised associated arguments for government non-intervention in social, economic, and commercial matters. 'Laissez faire' was first used by the French, and essentially meant that the government should let things alone, specifically in terms of trade, production of goods, and quantities or quality of products. This philosophy dominated much 18th and 19th century government, and assumed that:

- natural laws, if left to work freely, would create the best possible society
- enlightened individual selfishness was ultimately in the public interest
- men are born equal

The Wealth of Nations took ten years to write, and the ideas within it challenged Smith's contemporary, mercantilist government and its protectionist laws. The author realised that his book would outrage those with vested interests in business or government, because of its arguments for government-enforced competition and against price-fixing.

Although often castigated as such, Smith was neither inhumane nor a proponent of 'the law of the jungle' as an approach to social organisation. He recognised the worst tendencies of some businessmen who 'love to reap where they never sowed', and was extremely aware of how greed could lead to excesses of monopoly and corruption. Smith did, in fact, support some forms of intervention, especially in public areas such as defence. He did not, however, have our benefit of hindsight, or know how the Industrial Revolution would change society, creating some extremely wealthy businessmen, and a mass of extremely poor industrial workers, who would suffer greatly because of their lack of protection from regulatory laws.

The law of labour

Natural law was considered by Smith to encompass a 'law of labour'. According to this, the external environment could provide people with the products necessary for subsistence, in return for their labour, and all people should therefore have the right to carry out activities to preserve their existence. Government's only role should be to promote the existence of natural law and to enable its free working.

The natural laws were assumed to work in the same exacting way as mathematical laws. Left to themselves, they should establish an order that would benefit both individuals and society. Individualism, for Smith and the other economists and philosophers of his time, meant relief from the constraints of mercantilism, the right to economic freedom, and the right of a people to legislate for themselves and be taxed by the government they chose.

The division of labour

Smith gives many examples of the advantages of the division of labour, with each worker focusing upon a single stage of manufacture rather than, as in traditional crafts, being involved in every stage. His ideas were based on life before 1760, and he did not foresee how the introduction of machinery would make the division of labour even more logical and sometimes a harsh necessity.

The free market

Smith's main thesis throughout *The Wealth of Nations* was the inefficiency of government interference, which he demonstrates with reference to the markets for both national and international trade. He envisions a free market as a customer-driven, democratic mechanism through which, by exercising their free choices about purchase or sale prices, people would act to regulate resources fairly. Although it was Dudley North who first related supply to demand and extolled the benefits of free trade, Smith recognised that buyers as well as sellers profit from trade, and saw international commerce as a source of wealth for both importers and exporters.

Smith had a very positive vision of how a free market would eventually realise a state of 'universal opulence' for everyone. He argued that each nation should concentrate on those industrial areas where it enjoyed a 'comparative advantage'. These ideas were taken up by subsequent economists such as Ricardo and Malthus, and can be traced within the thinking of some contemporary strategists, particularly in Michael Porter's work on competitive advantage.

Morality

Smith is often criticised for a lack of moral focus in *The Wealth of Nations* but he did assume that its readers would already know of the moral base given in *The Theory of Moral Sentiments*. The earlier book sought to explore moral judgements within the context of Smith's assumption that people are essentially driven by self-interest, and proposed that we all have 'social propensities' for sympathy, justice, and benevolence.

ADAM SMITH IN PERSPECTIVE

The Wealth of Nations had a profound influence on English history, leading to the end of the mercantilist era and catalysing a social and economic order based on individualism and the 'natural laws' supposedly underlying competition and free market forces.

Smith's ideas have often been castigated for the support they gave to later businesspeople who grew very rich while rejecting any regulations to protect industrial workers. He wrote his masterpiece, however, before the Industrial Revolution began to take effect, and it was intended as a polemic against restrictive government policies and monopolistic abuses, rather than as a panegyric for unregulated business. Also, just as Smith's first book, *The Theory of Moral Sentiments*, supplies a moral aspect to complement *The Wealth of Nations*, it is probable that his intended, but unwritten, third volume on jurisprudence could have contributed ideas for legal safeguards to protect the public from abuses resulting from greed and collusion, since he considered these typically to arise out of people's business activities and contacts.

For his time, Smith was actually a social radical, promoting liberty and equality and denouncing various pillars of the existing establishment. From our modern perspective, it is clear there was no factual base for his ideas about natural law and harmony, and that perfect competition could not erase social problems, particularly when factors from a future that Smith could not have imagined (including giant corporations, economic cycles and depressions, mass unemployment, and mechanical warfare) became more pertinent. Despite this, however, *The Wealth of Nations* remains a 'milestone' book offering a composite analysis that shaped our social and economic world.

THE BEST SOURCES OF HELP
Books:
Haakonssen, Knud, ed. *The Theory of Moral Sentiments*. Cambridge: Cambridge University Press, 2002.
Smith, Kathryn, ed. *Wealth of Nations*. Reissue. Oxford: Oxford University Press, 2008.

Sun Tzu Strategy and *The Art of War*

The quality management techniques used by Japanese companies enabled them to put cheaper and better products into American and British shops than their domestic rivals. This led to an understanding that Japanese business people have a different perspective on the marketplace from their Western counterparts. Further studies showed that Asian business leaders appeared to attach great significance to classical Chinese military strategy and to believe that the principles underpinning it are embedded in various aspects of daily life.

c. 400 BC	Sun Tzu lived and wrote.
1780	First European translation of *The Art of War* published.
1910	English translation published.

LIFE AND CAREER

Although the precise dates of his birth and death are not known, Sun Tzu is thought to have lived over 2,400 years ago, at roughly the same time as Confucius. Brought up in a family of army officers, he became familiar with, and eventually expert in, military affairs. Historians are generally agreed that he was a general who led a number of successful military campaigns in the region currently known as the Anhui Province. It is recorded that the state of Wu, under whose sovereign he served, became a dominant power at that time. Since then, it has become standard practice for Chinese military chiefs to familiarise themselves with Sun Tzu's writings.

KEY THINKING

The Art of War

Sun Tzu's *The Art of War* (the book's actual title is *Sun Tzu Ping Fa*, literally 'The Military Method of Mr Sun') is a compilation of his thinking on the strategies that underlie success in war. It has been translated into many languages, and there are several English versions. This account is based on the translation by Thomas Cleary, published by Shambhala Pocket Classics and available online. Two further editions, published by Tuttle and Wordsworth Editions respectively, were also consulted.

Sun Tzu's anecdotes and thoughts, which fill no more than about 25 pages of text in all, are divided into 13 sections:

1. strategic assessments
2. doing battle
3. offensive strategy
4. formation
5. force
6. emptiness and fullness
7. armed struggle
8. adaptations
9. manoeuvring armies
10. terrain
11. nine grounds
12. attack by fire
13. use of spies

Some of these have less current relevance than others, but they are all worth at least a glance. Hidden among advice such as not to dally in salt marshes when retreating or attacking (11), there is the odd gem that is striking in its modernity. For example: 'when a leader enters deeply into enemy territory with the troops, he brings out their potential.' (11) The advice given in section 10 on how to proceed in narrow or steep terrain (occupy the high and sunny side to await your opponent) can be quickly passed over, but a little further on in the same section Sun Tzu's castigation of poor leadership is much more pertinent: 'When generals are weak and lack authority, instructions are not clear, officers and soldiers lack consistency, and they form battle lines every which way; this is riot.'

On strategy

Many commentaries focus on the first section, strategic assessments, at the expense of the others. It is certainly there that, helped by a little lateral thinking, Sun Tzu seems best to relate to the spirit of modern business. He refers initially to five key factors that determine the result of war:

- politics – that which causes people to be in harmony with their ruler
- weather – the seasons
- terrain – distances, difficulty or ease of travel, opportunities or safety
- leadership – a matter of intelligence, trustworthiness, humanity, courage, and strictness
- discipline – organisation, chain of command, logistics

There are also seven issues to be appraised (the postscript following each question has been added to indicate the line most interpretations take).

- Whose moral influence is the stronger? (Whose followers are more willing to subscribe to common goals?)
- Which leader is the more able? (Who has the ability to combine benevolence and compassion with boldness and strict discipline?)
- Which army has greater advantage of nature and terrain? (Whom do politics, economic cycles, investment, and social and cultural factors favour? Who understands the bigger picture?)
- Whose laws and rules are more effective? (Do people understand what is expected as a result of clear instructions and procedures?)
- Whose troops are stronger? (How can things be arranged so that small can compete effectively with large?)
- Whose soldiers are better trained? (Who uses delegation and training for organisational effectiveness?)
- Whose system of rewards and punishments is clearer? (Who is therefore able to generate higher performance and a better competitive position?)

The theme of strategy is picked up again and again, apparently at random. One interpretation stretches section 6 to make it relate to market presence and strategies of deception employed to fool competitor intelligence. Sun Tzu argues that 'there is no constant good or bad, right or wrong: therefore victory in war is not repetitious, but adapts its form endlessly . . . so a military force has no constant formation, water has no constant shape: the ability to gain victory by changing and adapting according to the opponent is called genius.' (6)

On information and intelligence

'. . .to fail to know the conditions of opponents because of reluctance to give rewards for intelligence is extremely inhuman, uncharacteristic of a true military leader . . . so what enables an intelligent government and a wise military leadership to overcome others and achieve extraordinary accomplishments is foreknowledge . . . [which] must be obtained from people who know the conditions of the enemy.' (13)

On tactics

'Making the armies able to take on opponents without being defeated is a matter of unorthodox and orthodox methods.' (5)

'The difficulty of armed struggle is to make long distances near and make problems into advantages.' (7)

On competition and competitor intelligence

'So if you do not know the plans of your competitors, you cannot make informed alliances.' (7)

'So the rule of military operations is not to count on opponents not coming, but to rely on having ways of dealing with them; not to count on opponents not attacking, but to rely on having what cannot be attacked.' (8)

On leadership and people management

'If they rule armies without knowing the arts of complete adaptivity, even if they know what there is to gain, they cannot get people to work for them.' (8)

'If soldiers are punished before a personal attachment to the leadership is formed, they will not submit, and if they do not submit, they are hard to employ.' (9)

'Look upon your soldiers as you do infants, and they willingly go into deep valleys with you; look upon your soldiers as beloved children, and they willingly die with you.' (10)

'If you are so nice to them that you cannot employ them, so kind to them that you cannot command them, so casual with them that you cannot establish order, they are like spoiled children, useless.' (10)

On communication

'When directives are consistently issued to edify the populace, the populace accepts . . . when directives are consistently issued, there is mutual satisfaction between the leadership and the group.' (9)

SUN TZU IN PERSPECTIVE

Historians tell us that the *Sun Tzu Ping Fa* is the oldest existing military treatise in the world, predating Clausewitz by 2,200 years. But so what? Stuart Crainer asks how *The Art of War* can have any relevance to running a crisp factory in Ipswich. It is a fair question. How can the thoughts of a Chinese general who lived two and a half millennia ago possibly inform, enlighten, or inspire a modern manager, or have any bearing on his or her day-to-day concerns? And even if there are interesting links, do they do any more than show us that ancient Chinese strategists did not differ fundamentally from modern business-people?

Sun Tzu's supporters, however, insist that his concepts are ageless. Although it is easy to stretch interpretation too far and find meaning anywhere if you look hard enough, such things as strategic intelligence, planning, attention to detail, cunning, deception, and theories of leadership in which the leader earns authority with the led, have universal value and are appropriate to any human arena and any period.

If part of Sun Tzu's modern appeal derives from the constant search for any nuggets of intelligence that may give an organisation an edge over the competition, another part lies in the fact that the *Ping Fa* offers an opportunity to gain insights into the Oriental mindset that do not come from someone with a modern axe to grind or reputation to make. In addition, the insights are couched in direct, no-nonsense, hard-hitting language that makes them seem more, not less, pregnant with meaning.

As globalisation brings East closer to West, business relationships will hinge on understanding cultures and attitudes that may appear strange at first. And if the managers of Crainer's crisp factory in Ipswich set strategic goals, sell their goods abroad, or interrelate with their workforce, *The Art of War* may still have something to say to them. It finds its way into many MBA programmes.

THE BEST SOURCES OF HELP

Books:

Kaufman, Stephen F. *The Art of War: The Definitive Interpretation of Sun Tzu's Classic Book of Strategy for the Martial Artist*. Rutland, Vermont: Charles E Tuttle, 1996.

Sun Tzu. *The Art of War*. Trans. Thomas Cleary. Boston, Massachusetts: Shambhala Pocket Classics, 1991.

Journal Articles:

Crainer, Stuart. 'Braingain.' *Management Today*, April 1998, pp. 68–70.

Min Chen. 'Sun Tzu's strategic thinking and contemporary business.' *Business Horizons*, March/April 1994, pp. 42–48.

Frederick Winslow Taylor Father of Scientific Management

Peter Drucker was often called 'the guru's guru'. Drucker himself would have suggested that the accolade should be given to Frederick Winslow Taylor (1856–1917). 'On Taylor's "scientific management" rests, above all, the tremendous surge of affluence in the last 75 years which has lifted the working masses in the developed countries well above any level recorded, even for the well-to-do,' Drucker wrote in *Management: Tasks, Responsibilities, Practices*.

1856	Born.
1874	Becomes an apprentice pattern-maker and machinist at Enterprise Hydraulic Works.
1878	Takes unskilled job at the Midvale Steel Works.
1881	Gains master's degree in mechanical engineering.
1890	Becomes general manager of Manufacturing Investment Company (MIC).
1898	Becomes joint discoverer of the Taylor-White process, a method of tempering steel.
1911	Publication of *The Principles of Scientific Management*.
1915	Dies.

LIFE AND CAREER

Although Taylor passed the entrance examination for Harvard College, failing eyesight meant that he could not take up his place. Instead he took the unusual step for someone of his background of becoming an apprentice pattern-maker and machinist at the Enterprise Hydraulic Works.

Following his apprenticeship, Taylor took up an unskilled job at the Midvale Steel Works. After several different jobs and a master's degree in mechanical engineering, he was appointed chief engineer there. In 1890 he became general manager of Manufacturing Investment Company (MIC), eventually becoming an independent consulting engineer to management.

In 1881, Taylor won the doubles championships of the United States Lawn Tennis Association and a year later, the doubles in the Young American C.C. Lawn Tennis Tournament. Later in his career he developed a passion for golf and, in keeping with his love of experiment, attempted to make a putting green that was reliant on water below the surface rather than on natural rainfall. By the time of his death, Taylor's experiments had led to him filing at least 50 patents and had made him an extremely wealthy man.

KEY THINKING
Scientific management

Taylor's seminal work – *The Principles of Scientific Management*-was published six years before his death. In it, he put forward his ideas of 'scientific management' (sometimes referred to today as 'Taylorism'), which differed from traditional 'initiative and incentive' methods of management. These ideas were an accumulation from his life's work, and included several examples from his places of employment. The four overriding principles of scientific management are as follows.

- Each part of a job is analysed 'scientifically', and the most efficient method for undertaking it is devised-the 'one best way' of working. This consists of examining the implements needed to carry out the work, and measuring the maximum amount a 'first-class' worker can do in a day. Workers are then expected to do this much work every day.
- The most suitable person to undertake the job is chosen, again 'scientifically'. The individual is taught to do the job in the exact way devised. Everyone, according to Taylor, has the ability to be 'first-class' at some job. It is management's role to find out which job suits each employee and train them until they are first-class.
- Managers must co-operate with workers to ensure the job is done in the scientific way.
- There is a clear 'division' of work and responsibility between management and workers. Managers concern themselves with the planning and supervision of the work, and workers carry it out.

Taylor summed up the differences between his principles of management and the traditional method as follows: 'Under the management of "initiative and incentive", practically the whole problem is "up to the workman"; while under the scientific management, fully one-half of the problem is "up to the management" ... The principal object of management should be to secure the maximum prosperity for the employer, coupled with the maximum prosperity for each employee.' Taylor could justify his methods because he felt that his long-term goal would lead to 'diminution of poverty, and the alleviation of suffering'.

His main reason for developing scientific management was that he wished to do away with 'soldiering' or 'natural laziness', as he believed that all workers spent little time putting in full effort. To do this, Taylor aimed to analyse every job in a scientific way so that no one could be in any doubt about how much work could and should be done in a day. He felt that 'every single act of every workman can be reduced to a science'. Much inconclusive argument has ensued as to whether he was the pioneer of time and motion study. Certainly, time study played as important a part in Taylor's scientific job and task analysis as the examination of a worker's movements and the implements he used.

Inherent in Taylor's management style was the setting up of planning departments, staffed by clerks who ensured that 'every labourer's work was planned out well in advance, and the workmen were moved from place to place ... very much as chessmen are moved on a chessboard, a telephone and messenger system having been installed for this purpose.' He concluded that, in this way, 'a large amount of the time lost through having too many men in one place and too few in another, and through waiting between jobs, was entirely eliminated.' Such a policy did, however, require the setting up of a more 'elaborate organisation and system', which sowed the seeds for Max Weber's bureaucratic organisation structure. Taylor's approach constituted one of the first formal divisions between those who do the work (workers) and those who supervise and plan it (managers).

Management and workers

For workers on the shopfloor, scientific management brought a dramatic loss in skill level and autonomy. As well as being subject to increased supervision, workers were no longer able to use their own tools, which they might have spent many years modifying to suit their own style. In many cases, however, Taylor's ideas were extremely effective. In the case of shovellers at the Bethlehem Steel Works, workers earned higher wages and the company saved between $75,000 and $80,000 per year through greater efficiency.

Although Taylor believed that disputes between managers and workers would be eliminated because what 'constitutes a fair day's work will be a question for scientific investigation, instead of a subject to be bargained and haggled over', there were numerous occasions when his ideas came into conflict with labour organisations. His opinion of such unions was invariably derogatory, as he was convinced that their objective was to limit the output of their members. Because of this, Taylor focused on the individual, believing that where a group of workers was formed, peer pressure would be used to ensure each man did not work to his full capacity. In the Bethlehem Steel Works, he decreed that no more than four men could work together in a gang without a special permit.

Even the way he wrote about unskilled workers was condescending. 'Now one of the very first requirements for a man who is fit to handle pig iron as a regular occupation is that he shall be so stupid and phlegmatic that he more nearly resembles in his mental make-up the ox than any other type' is a typical example.

Although Taylor's manner often appeared inhumane, he also wrote: 'If the workman fails to do his task, some competent teacher should be sent to show him exactly how his work can best be done, to guide, help, and to encourage him and, at the same time, to study his possibilities as a workman. So that, under the plan which individualizes each workman, instead of brutally discharging the man or lowering his wages to make good at once, he is given the time and the help required to make him proficient at his present job, or he is shifted to another class of work for which he is either mentally or physically better suited.'

Contemporary reaction to scientific management

It is easy to see why Taylor's work was regarded as inhumane. However good his motives of bringing about the greater good for the worker on the shopfloor, alleviating poverty, and eliminating waste, his methods were extremely hard and sometimes had the opposite effect.

It took him three years to implement some of his methods in the Midvale Steel Works. The workers resorted to breaking their machines in an attempt to prove to management that Taylor was overworking them. In response, he fined anyone whose machine broke, until eventually 'they got sick of being fined, their opposition broke down, and they promised to do a fair day's work'.

FREDERICK WINSLOW TAYLOR IN PERSPECTIVE

Many of Taylor's ideas are relevant to the modern day. Three in particular, taken from *The Principles of Scientific Management*, stand out:

- Rewards: 'A reward, if it is to be most effective in stimulating men to do their best work, must come soon after the work has been done . . . The average workman must be able to measure what he has accomplished and clearly see his reward at the end of each day if he is to do his best.' In Taylor's view, it was pointless to involve the shopfloor workers in end-of-year profit-sharing schemes.
- Quality standards: The use of written documentation for each part of a worker's job, inherent in scientific management, is strikingly prescient of the procedural documentation used in the ISO 9000 series of quality standards. 'In the case of a machine-shop which is managed under the modern system, detailed written instructions as to the best way of doing each piece of work are prepared in advance, by men in the planning department. These instructions represent the combined work of several men in the planning room, each of whom has his own speciality, or function . . . The directions of all of these men, however, are written on a single instruction card, or sheet.' The main difference is that today's best practice means involving staff in drawing up their own procedures.
- Suggestion schemes: Taylor proposed a form of incentive for employees to make suggestions if they felt an improvement could be made, either to the method or the implement used to undertake a task. If, after analysis, the suggestion was implemented, the person suggesting it 'should be given the full credit for the improvement, and should be paid a cash premium as a reward for his ingenuity. In this way the true initiative of the workmen is better attained under scientific management than under the old individual plan.'

At the time of his death in 1917, Taylor's work was the subject of much debate, both for and against it. His approach is now frowned upon as 'Victorian', but it should not be forgotten that he was a man of his times and sought solutions to the problems of his times. The main criticism of Taylor is that his approach was too mechanistic – treating people like machines or as unthinking creatures to be trained like dogs, rather than as human beings.

However, he was one of the first true pioneers of management through his scientific examination of the way work is done, and his thinking led directly to the achievements of other management gurus such as Max Weber and Henry Ford.

THE BEST SOURCES OF HELP
Books:
Kakar, Sudhir. *Frederick Taylor: A Study in Personality and Innovation.* Cambridge, Massachusetts: MIT Press, 1970.
Nelson, Daniel. *Frederick W. Taylor and the Rise of Scientific Management.* Madison, Wisconsin: University of Wisconsin Press, 1980.

Taylor, Frederick Winslow. *Shop Management* in *Scientific Management* (comprising *Shop Management, The Principles of Scientific Management, Testimony before the Special House Committee*). New York: Harper, 1947.
Taylor, Frederick Winslow. *The Principles of Scientific Management.* New York: W.W. Norton, 1967.

Alvin Toffler The Futurologist's Futurologist

One of the world's leading authorities on change, Alvin Toffler is anything but the classical soothsayer. He carefully avoids words such as 'trend' and 'prediction' in his writing, and insists that nobody can tell for certain what will happen in the future. His special gift is an understanding of the effects of change. It comes from a broad and deep knowledge of science, technology, and the arts, and a capacity to deduce what might result when complex technological and social changes impact on entrenched attitudes and vested interests.

1928	Born.
1965	Coins the term 'future shock' in an article in *Horizon*.
1969–1970	Works as consultant for AT&T.
1970	Publication of *Future Shock*.
1977	Co-founds Institute for Alternative Futures with Clement Bezold and James Dator.
1980	Publication of *The Third Wave*.
1986	Helps set up Issyk-Kul Forum, the first non-Communist, non-governmental organisation in the former USSR.
1990	Publication of *Powershift*.
1993	Publication of *War and Anti-War*.
1996	Founds Toffler Associates, an executive advisory firm.

LIFE AND CAREER

Alvin Toffler was born in 1928. Though he has travelled widely, he gained all his education and working experience in the United States. He has been a visiting fellow at the Russell Sage Foundation, a visiting professor at Cornell University, a faculty member of the New School for Social Research, and a highly successful business consultant. He has several honorary degrees, and his books have won many awards.

Much of Toffler's work has been created in collaboration with his wife Heidi – as he is always the first to point out. Theirs is a long-standing partnership: both studied English at New York University and then entered the

heady Bohemian world of post-war Greenwich Village, where their interests were mainly in writing poetry and planning novels.

Not a scientist by first choice, Toffler understood from a very young age the importance of science and technology in the modern world and took a course in the history of technology.

The Tofflers spent several years in journalism, writing for publications ranging from *Fortune* and *Playboy* to the leading political, scientific, and economic journals of the day. In 1960 an invitation from IBM to write a paper on the long-term social and organisational implications of the computer gave them a lengthy exposure to high technology. From this seminal experience grew the all-consuming interest in change, for which they are now world-famous. *Future Shock*, the first book in Toffler's great trilogy on change, was begun shortly after completing the IBM paper.

KEY THINKING

Though he has published many books and countless articles and papers, Toffler's philosophy, and most of his key ideas, are encapsulated in three books: *Future Shock* (1970), *The Third Wave* (1980), and *Powershift* (1990). Each is a self-standing work in its own right, but they combine to form a trilogy that develops Toffler's ideas about change in a seamless dialogue.

Toffler gives his own brief summation of what the trilogy is all about in the preface to *Powershift*: '. . . the central subject is change – what happens to people when their entire society abruptly transforms itself into something new and unexpected. *Future Shock* looks at the process of change – how change affects people and organisations. *The Third Wave* focuses on the directions of change-where today's changes are taking us. *Powershift* deals with the control of changes still to come-who will shape them and how.'

Besides giving a painstaking analysis of change and the many challenges and problems it brings, the trilogy is full of hope. The books argue, convincingly, that the rapid change all around us is not so chaotic or random as it first appears; there are patterns and recognisable forces behind it. Understanding these patterns and forces will allow us to cope 'strategically' with change, and to avoid haphazard responses to individual events as they are encountered.

The Trilogy: *Future Shock*

Toffler has described the effect of too much change occurring too quickly so well, that the expression 'future shock' has entered the world's vocabulary and is now widely used to define the disorientation, confusion, and breakdown of decision-making capacity that afflicts individuals, groups, and whole societies when they are overwhelmed by change.

In his preface to *Powershift*, Toffler contends that 'the acceleration of history carries consequences of its own, independent of the actual direction of change. The simple speed-up of events and reaction times produces its own effects, whether the changes are perceived as good or bad'.

Future Shock was written over 30 years ago, and of Toffler's foresight. What we find is quite remarkable; he anticipated the break-up of the nuclear family, the genetic revolution, the 'throwaway' society, the resurgence of emphasis on education, and the increased importance of knowledge in society.

The Third Wave

This book explores perhaps Toffler's most elegant theory, adding a 'third wave' to the other two great and generally recognised surges in human development.

The first came with the introduction of agriculture, and humankind's revolutionary shift from hunter-gatherer to settled farmer. This released it from the constant struggle for subsistence, providing the stability and security needed to develop the arts and technology that are the basis of civilisation as we know it today.

The second was the industrial revolution, the remarkable leap forward in manufacturing methods and the organisation of labour that created the industrialised world. The exploitation of raw materials, mass production, and an ever more ingenious application of technology brought prosperity and comfort to those countries that could embrace the necessary changes.

Toffler's third wave is the post-industrial, information-based revolution that began, he suggests, in the 1950s, with a number of major technological and social changes.

In *The Third Wave*, Toffler predicted with an uncanny foresight both the profound effects of information technology and biotechnology on the economy, and the changes we can now see taking place in manufacturing methods, marketing, and working patterns. He showed particular prescience in foreseeing the development of niche marketing and the increased power of the consumer. He even invented a new word – 'prosumer' – to designate the fusion of producer and consumer.

In his introduction to the book, Toffler talks of the seemingly chaotic changes of the 1960s that produced 'a culture of warring specialisms, drowned in fragmented data and fine-toothed analysis', and a climate in which synthesis 'is not merely useful – it is crucial'. It was to address this need for synthesis that Toffler conceived *The Third Wave*. It is, he claims, 'a book of large-scale synthesis [that] describes the old civilisation in which many of us grew up, and presents a careful, comprehensive picture of the new civilisation bursting into being in our midst'.

He goes on to say: '. . . the world that is fast emerging from the clash of new values and technologies, new geophysical relationships, new life-styles and modes of communication, demands wholly new ideas and analogies, classifications and concepts. We cannot cram the embryonic world of tomorrow into yesterday's conventional cubby holes'.

Powershift

In this, the final book of the trilogy, Toffler carries forward his earlier analysis with an exploration of how individuals, organisations, and nations will be affected by inevitable changes in the way power is perceived and applied. He talks of a 'new power system replacing that of the industrial past'.

The word 'powershift' in the title means something very different from the usual two-word term 'power shift'. Toffler says that, while a power shift is a transfer of power, a 'powershift' is 'a deep-level change in the very nature of power'. A powershift does not merely transfer power, but also transforms it.

In *Powershift* we are reminded of the three basic sources of power: violence, wealth, and knowledge. All businesses work in what Toffler describes as a 'power-field', where these three 'tools of power' constantly operate. The rising importance of knowledge, so eloquently argued throughout the trilogy, has brought about a profound change in the balance between them.

Powershift gives no hint of an early solution to the problems associated with change. Toffler talks about the struggles to come as individuals, businesses, and national economies move away from their traditional sources of power towards a new dependence on knowledge. In his view, the problems will not be over when these power conflicts are resolved. He sees even greater challenges ahead as divisions develop between 'fast' and 'slow' economies.

Another idea, explored throughout the trilogy but most strongly in *Powershift*, is what Toffler calls 'de-massification'. By this he means a reversal of the trend towards 'mass' solutions prevalent in the late 20th century. He sees mass marketing giving way to niche and micro-marketing; mass production being replaced by increasingly customised production; and large corporations being broken down into small, autonomous units. Even politics and the concept of nationhood, Toffler believes, will be affected by the pressure to 'de-massify', created by the increasing awareness of better-informed individuals and made effective by the unstoppable development of information technology.

ALVIN TOFFLER IN PERSPECTIVE

Influential as Toffler's trilogy continues to be, it must be remembered that the last of the three books was published in 1990; it would be misleading to imply that Toffler's work started or finished at that point. *The Adaptive Corporation*, for example, published in 1985, was built around the report resulting from Toffler's 1969–70 consultancy work for AT&T. Ignored by senior management at the time, this report became influential later, at the time of the Bell divestiture. The book deals with questions of organisational change and adaptation through focusing on the case of AT&T.

Other books and articles have appeared since the trilogy and, from the time of the publication of *Powershift*, Heidi Toffler has allowed her role to be more formally acknowledged; the Tofflers' more recent publications have been under explicit joint authorship.

Their contribution to world politics is something many management commentators neglect. Respected by many world leaders, they have played a significant part in improving East–West relations. Mikhail Gorbachev is an admirer whom they have met several times and greatly influenced.

The Tofflers also visited China and were having a positive effect on Chinese politics until the disastrous reversals following the Tiananmen Square episode. Their books are now banned in China though, of course, banning books often merely serves to increase their influence.

Of the Tofflers' recent major publications, *War and Anti-War* is usually regarded as the most important. It focuses on warfare, suggesting that changes in the way we do business are matched by a parallel revolution in how we make war-and that, like so many in commerce and manufacturing, these military changes derive directly from advances in information technology. Their ideas have already been proved correct in the 1990–91 Gulf War and elsewhere, but Alvin Toffler's most chillingly accurate prediction came in an interview he gave for the *New Scientist* magazine of March 1994, where he spoke of the inadequacy of conventional military force in controlling terrorist action. To illustrate his point, he quoted a former US intelligence officer as saying that, if he had 20 people and a million dollars, he could shut down America. Seven years later the events of 11 September 2001 provided appalling evidence of this statement's credibility.

THE BEST SOURCES OF HELP

Books:

Toffler, Alvin. *Future Shock*. London: Bodley Head, 1970.

Toffler, Alvin. *The Third Wave*. London: Collins, 1980.

Toffler, Alvin. *Powershift*. New York: Bantam Books, 1990.

Toffler, Alvin, and Heidi Toffler. *War and Anti-War*. New York: Little, Brown, 1993.

Toffler, Alvin and Heidi Toffler. *Revolutionary Wealth*. New York: Knopf, 2006.

Gurus

Dictionary

AAA *abbr* FIN American Accounting Association

AAIA *abbr* FIN Associate of the Association of International Accountants

AARF *abbr* FIN Australian Accounting Research Foundation

AAS *abbr* FIN Australian Accounting Standard

AASB *abbr* FIN Australian Accounting Standards Board

AAT *abbr* FIN Association of Accounting Technicians

abandonment option FIN the option of terminating an investment before the time that it is scheduled to end

abandonment value FIN the value that an investment has if it is terminated at a particular time before it is scheduled to end

ABB *abbr* FIN activity-based budgeting

abbreviated accounts FIN a shortened version of a company's annual accounts that a company classified as small or medium-sized under the Companies Act (1989) can file with the Registrar of Companies, instead of having to supply a full version

ABC *abbr* FIN activity-based costing

ABI *abbr* FIN Association of British Insurers

ability-to-pay principle FIN a theory which holds that taxes should be paid only by those who can best afford them

ABM *abbr* FIN activity-based management

ABN *abbr* FIN Australian Business Number: a numeric code that identifies an Australian business for the purpose of dealing with the Australian Tax Office and other government departments. ABNs are part of the tax system that came into operation in Australia in 1998.

abnormal shrinkage FIN the unexpectedly high level of shrinkage that has contributed to an abnormal loss

abnormal spoilage FIN the unexpectedly high level of spoilage that has contributed to an abnormal loss

abnormal waste FIN the unexpectedly high level of waste that has contributed to an abnormal loss

above par FIN used to describe a security that trades above its nominal value

above-the-line FIN **1.** used to describe entries in a company's profit and loss accounts that appear above the line separating those entries that show the origin of the funds that have contributed to the profit or loss from those that relate to its distribution. Exceptional and extraordinary items appear above the line. See also *below-the-line* (sense 1) **2.** in macroeconomics, used to describe a country's revenue transactions. See also *below-the-line* (sense 2)

abridged accounts FIN financial statements produced by a company that fall outside the requirements stipulated in the Companies Act. Abridged accounts are often made public through the media.

ABS *abbr* FIN Australian Bureau of Statistics

absorb FIN to assign an overhead to a particular cost centre in a company's production accounts so that its identity becomes lost. See also *absorption costing*

absorbed account FIN an account that has lost its separate identity by being combined with related accounts in the preparation of a financial statement

absorbed business FIN, GEN a company that has been merged into another company

absorbed costs FIN the indirect costs associated with manufacturing, for example, insurance or property taxes

absorbed overhead FIN an overhead attached to products or services by means of absorption rates

absorption costing FIN an accounting practice in which fixed and variable costs of production are absorbed by different cost centres. Providing all the products or services can be sold at a price that covers the allocated costs, this method ensures that both fixed and variable costs are recovered in full. However, should sales be lost because the resultant price is too high, the organisation may lose revenue that would have contributed to its overheads. See also *marginal costing*

abusive tax shelter FIN a tax shelter that somebody claims illegally to avoid or minimise tax

ACA *abbr* FIN **1.** Australian Communications Authority **2.** Associate of the Institute of Chartered Accountants in England and Wales

Academy of Accounting Historians FIN a US body founded in 1973 that promotes 'research, publication, teaching and personal interchanges in all phases of Accounting History and its interrelation with business and economic history'

ACAS *abbr* FIN Advisory, Conciliation and Arbitration Service

ACAUS *abbr* FIN Association of Chartered Accountants in the United States

ACCA *abbr* FIN **1.** Association of Chartered Certified Accountants **2.** associate of the Association of Chartered Certified Accountants

ACCC *abbr* FIN Australian Competition and Consumer Commission: an independent statutory body responsible for monitoring trade practices in Australia. It was set up in November 1995 as a result of the merger of the Trade Practices Commission and the Prices Surveillance Authority.

accelerated cost recovery system FIN a system used in the United States for computing the depreciation of some assets acquired before 1986 in a way that reduces taxes. *Abbr* **ACRS**

accelerated depreciation ECON, FIN a system used for computing the depreciation of some assets in a way that assumes that they depreciate faster in the early years of their acquisition. Also known as *declining balance method*

acceleration clause FIN a section of a contract which details how a loan may be required to be repaid early if the borrower defaults on other clauses of the contract

acceptance FIN the signature on a bill of exchange, indicating that the drawee (the person to whom it is addressed) will pay the face amount of the bill on the due date

acceptance bonus FIN, HR a bonus paid to a new employee on acceptance of a job. An acceptance bonus can be a feature of a golden hello and is designed both to attract and to retain staff.

acceptance credit FIN a line of credit granted by a bank to an importer against which an exporter can draw a bill of exchange. After acceptance by the bank, the bill can either be sold in the market or held until maturity.

acceptance house ECON, FIN an institution that accepts financial instruments and agrees to honour them should the borrower default

accepting bank FIN the bank that accepts a bill of exchange drawn under a documentary credit

acceptor FIN the person to whom a signed bill of exchange is addressed

access FIN the right to sell goods or services into a particular market without contravening related legislation

access bond *S Africa* FIN a type of mortgage that permits borrowers to take out loans against extra capital paid into the account, home-loan interest rates being lower than interest rates on other forms of credit

ACCI *abbr* FIN Australian Chamber of Commerce and Industry

account FIN 1. a business arrangement involving the exchange of money or credit in which payment is deferred, or a record maintained by a financial institution itemising its dealings with a particular customer 2. a structured record of transactions in monetary terms, kept as part of an accounting system. This may take the form of a simple list or that of entries on a credit and debit basis, maintained either manually or as a computer record.

accountancy bodies FIN professional institutions and associations for accountants

accountancy profession FIN collectively, the professional bodies of accountants that establish and regulate training entry standards and professional examinations, as well as ethical and technical rules and guidelines. These bodies are organised on national and international levels.

accountant FIN a professional person who maintains and checks the business records of a person or organisation and prepares forms and reports for financial purposes

accountant's letter FIN a written statement by an independent accountant that precedes a financial report, describing the scope of the report and giving an opinion on its validity

account day FIN the day on which an executed order is settled by the delivery of securities, payment to the seller, and payment by the buyer.

This is the final day of the accounting period.

account debtor FIN a person or organisation responsible for paying for a product or service

accounting FIN a generic term for all the activities carried out by accountants, for example, book-keeping and financial accounting. Accounting involves the classification and recording of monetary transactions; the presentation and interpretation of the results of those transactions in order to assess performance over a period and the financial position at a given date; and the monetary projection of future activities arising from alternative planned courses of action. Accounting in larger businesses is typically carried out by financial accountants, who focus on formal, corporate issues such as taxation, and management accountants, who provide management reports and guidance.

Accounting and Finance Association of Australia and New Zealand FIN an organisation for accounting and finance academics, researchers, and professionals. The Association has a variety of aims, including the promotion of information on accounting to the public, and the provision of programmes in continual professional development to both members and non-members. The Association's name was changed in 2002 to incorporate the Accounting Association of Australia and New Zealand (AAANZ) and the Australian Association of University Teachers in Accounting (AAUTA). *Abbr* AFAANZ

accounting bases FIN the methods used for applying fundamental accounting concepts to financial transactions and items; preparing financial accounts; determining the accounting periods in which revenue and costs should be recognised in the profit and loss account; and determining the amounts at which material items should be stated in the balance sheet

accounting cost FIN the cost of maintaining and checking the business records of a person or organisation and the preparation of forms and reports for financial purposes

accounting cycle FIN the regular process of formally updating a firm's financial position by recording, analysing, and reporting its transactions during the accounting period

accounting equation FIN a formula in which a firm's assets must be equal to the sum of its liabilities and the owners' equity. Also known as *balance sheet equation*

accounting exposure ECON, FIN the risk that foreign currency held by a company may lose value because of exchange rate changes when it conducts overseas business

accounting insolvency ECON, FIN the condition that a company is in when its liabilities to its creditors exceed its assets

accounting manual FIN a collection of accounting instructions governing the responsibilities of persons, and the procedures, forms, and records relating to the preparation and use of accounting data. There can be separate manuals for the constituent parts of the accounting system, for example, budget manuals or cost accounting manuals.

accounting period FIN a length of time for which businesses may prepare internal accounts so as to monitor progress on a weekly, monthly, or quarterly basis. Accounts are generally prepared for external purposes on an annual basis.

accounting policies FIN the specific accounting bases selected and consistently followed by an entity as being, in the opinion of the management, appropriate to its circumstances and best suited to present fairly its results and financial position. For example, from the various possible methods of depreciation, the accounting policy may be to use straight-line depreciation.

accounting principles FIN the rules that apply to accounting practices and provide guidelines for dealing appropriately with complex transactions

Accounting Principles Board *US* FIN the professional body which issued opinions that formed much of US Generally Accepted Accounting Principles up to 1973, when the Financial Accounting Standards Board (FASB) took over that role. *Abbr* **APB**

accounting procedure FIN an accounting method developed by an individual or organisation to deal with routine accounting tasks

accounting rate of return FIN the ratio of profit before interest and taxation to the percentage of capital employed at the end of a period. Variations include using profit after interest and taxation, equity capital employed, and average capital for the period.

accounting ratio FIN an expression of accounting results as a ratio or percentage, for example, the ratio of current assets to current liabilities

accounting reference date FIN the last day of a company's accounting reference period

accounting standard FIN an authoritative statement of how particular types of transaction and other events should be reflected in financial statements. Compliance with accounting standards will normally be necessary for financial statements to give a true and fair view.

Accounting Standards Board FIN a UK standard-setting organisation established on 1 August 1990 to develop, issue, and withdraw accounting standards. Its aims are 'to establish and improve standards of financial accounting and reporting, for the benefit of users, preparers, and auditors of financial information'. *Abbr* **ASB**

accounting system FIN the means, including staff and equipment, by which an organisation produces its accounting information

accounting year FIN the 12-month accounting period

account reconciliation FIN **1.** a procedure for ensuring the reliability of accounting records by comparing balances of transactions **2.** a procedure for comparing the register of a chequebook with an associated bank statement

accounts payable FIN the amount that a company owes for goods or services obtained on credit. *Abbr* **AP**

accounts receivable FIN the money that is owed to a company by those who have bought its goods or services and have not yet paid for them. *Abbr* **AR**

accounts receivable ageing FIN a periodic report that classifies outstanding receivable balances according to customer and month of the original billing date

accounts receivable factoring US FIN the buying of accounts receivable at a discount with the aim of making a profit from collecting them

accounts receivable financing ECON, FIN a form of borrowing in which a company uses money that it is owed as collateral for a loan it needs for business operations

accounts receivable turnover ECON, FIN a ratio that shows how long the customers of a business wait before paying what they owe. This can cause cash-flow problems for small businesses. The formula for accounts receivable turnover is straightforward. Simply divide the average amount of receivables into annual credit sales:

Sales / Receivables = Receivables turnover

If, for example, a company's sales are £4.5 million and its average receivables are £375,000, its receivables turnover is:

$$4,500,000 / 375,000 = 12$$

A high turnover figure is desirable, because it indicates that a company collects revenues effectively, and that its customers pay bills promptly. A high figure also suggests that a firm's credit and collection policies are sound. In addition, the measurement is a reasonably good indicator of cash flow, and of overall operating efficiency.

accredited investor FIN an investor whose wealth or income is above a particular amount. It is illegal for an accredited investor to be a member of a private limited partnership.

accreted value FIN the value of a bond if interest rates do not change

accretion FIN the growth of a company through additions or purchases of plant or value-adding services

accrual FIN a charge that has not been paid by the end of an accounting period but must be included in the accounting results for the period. If no invoice has been received for the charge, an estimate must be included in the accounting results.

accrual basis FIN see *accrual method*

accrual bond FIN see *zero coupon bond*

accrual concept FIN the idea that income and expense items must be included in financial statements as they are earned or incurred. See also *cash accounting*

accrual method FIN an accounting method that includes income and expense items as they are earned or incurred irrespective of when money is received or paid out. Also known as *accrual basis*

accrual of discount FIN the annual gain in value of a bond owing to its having been bought originally for less than its nominal value

accrue FIN **1.** to include an income or expense item in transaction records at the time it is earned or incurred **2.** to increase and be due for payment at a later date, for example, interest

accrued expense FIN an expense that has been incurred within a given accounting period but not yet paid

accrued income FIN income that has been earned but not yet received

accrued interest FIN the amount of interest earned by a bond or similar investment since the previous interest payment

accruing FIN added as a periodic gain, for example, as interest on an amount of money

accumulated depreciation FIN the cumulative annual depreciation of an asset that has been claimed as an expense since the asset was acquired. Also known as *aggregate depreciation*

accumulated dividend FIN the amount of money in dividends earned by a stock or similar investment since the previous dividend payment

accumulated earnings tax or **accumulated profits tax** FIN the tax that a company must pay because it chose not to pay dividends that would subject its owners to higher taxes

accumulating shares FIN ordinary shares issued by a company equivalent to and in place of the net dividend payable to ordinary shareholders

achievement test HR a type of psychometric test which measures what a person already knows and can do at the time of testing. The two most common types of achievement tests measure verbal reasoning and mathematical ability. There are many test preparation books available. As well as explaining how the questions are structured, they offer test strategies and sample tests. As with other psychometric tests, it has been proven that people perform better at these tests when they are well rested, in good physical shape, and slightly hungry.

acid-test ratio FIN an accounting ratio used to measure an organisation's liquidity. The most common expression of the ratio is:

(Current assets – Inventory) /
Current liabilities = Acid-test ratio

acquirer or **acquiring bank** FIN **1.** a financial institution, commonly a bank, that processes a merchant's credit card authorisations and payments, forwarding the data to a credit card association, which in turn communicates with the issuer. Also known as **clearing house 2.** an organisation or individual that buys a business or asset

acquisition FIN, GEN see **merger**

acquisition accounting FIN the standard accounting procedures that must be followed when one company merges with another

ACRS abbr FIN accelerated cost recovery system

ACT abbr FIN Advance Corporation Tax

active asset FIN an asset that is used in the daily operations of a business

active fund management FIN the managing of a unit trust by making judgments about market movements instead of relying on automatic adjustments such as indexation. See also **passive investment management**

active portfolio strategy FIN the managing of an investment portfolio by making judgments about market movements instead of relying on automatic adjustments

activist fiscal policy FIN the policy of a government or national bank that tries to affect the value of its country's money by such measures as

changing interest rates for loans to banks and buying or selling foreign currencies

activity-based budgeting FIN the allocation of resources to individual activities. Activity-based budgeting involves determining which activities incur costs within an organisation, establishing the relationships between them, and then deciding how much of the total budget should be allocated to each activity. Abbr **ABB**

activity-based costing FIN a method of calculating the cost of a business by focusing on the actual cost of activities, thereby producing an estimate of the cost of individual products or services. An ABC cost-accounting system requires three preliminary steps: converting to an accrual method of accounting; defining cost centres and cost allocation; and determining process and procedure costs. Businesses have traditionally relied on the cash basis of accounting, which recognises income when received and expenses when paid. ABC's foundation is the accrual-basis income statement. The numbers this statement presents are assigned to the various procedures performed during a given period. Cost centres are a company's identifiable products and services, but also include specific and detailed tasks within these broader activities. Defining cost centres will, of course, vary by business and method of operation. What is critical to ABC is the inclusion of all activities and all resources. Once cost centres are identified, management teams can begin studying the activities each one engages in and allocating the expenses each one incurs, including the cost of employee services. The most appropriate method is developed from time studies and direct expense allocation. Management teams who choose this method will need to devote several months to data collection in order to generate sufficient information to establish the personnel components of each activity's total cost. Time studies establish the average amount of time required to complete each task, plus best- and worst-case performances. Only those resources actually used are factored

into the cost computation; unused resources are reported separately. These studies can also advise management teams how best to monitor and allocate expenses that might otherwise be expressed as part of general overheads, or go undetected altogether. Abbr **ABC**

activity-based management FIN a system of management that uses activity-based cost information for a variety of purposes, including cost reduction, cost modelling, and customer profitability analysis. Abbr **ABM**

activity cost pool FIN a grouping of all cost elements associated with an activity

activity driver FIN see **cost driver**

activity driver analysis FIN the identification and evaluation of the activity drivers used to trace the cost of activities to cost objects. It may also involve selecting activity drivers with potential to contribute to the cost management function, with particular reference to cost reduction.

activity indicator ECON a calculation used to measure labour productivity or manufacturing output in an economy

actual cash value FIN the amount of money, less depreciation, that it would cost to replace something damaged beyond repair with a comparable item

actuals FIN earnings and expenses that have occurred rather than being only projected, or commodities that can be bought and used, as contrasted with commodities traded on a futures contract

actual to date FIN the cumulative value realised by something between an earlier date and the present

actual turnover FIN the number of times during a particular period that somebody spends the average amount of money that he or she has available to spend during that period

actuarial age FIN the statistically derived life expectancy for any given person's age, used, for example, to calculate the periodic payments from an annuity

actuarial analysis FIN a life expectancy or risk calculation carried out by an actuary

actuarial science FIN, STATS the branch of statistics used in calculating risk and life expectancy for the administration of pension funds and life assurance policies

actuary FIN, STATS a statistician who calculates probable life spans so that the insurance premiums to be charged for various risks can be accurately determined

ACU *abbr* FIN Asian Currency Unit

adaptive learning GEN a style of organisational learning that focuses on prior successes and the use of these as the basis for developing future strategies and successes. Organisations use adaptive learning to make incremental improvements to existing products, services, and processes in response to the changing business environment. Generative learning is a contrasting approach to organisational learning.

ADDACS *abbr* FIN Automated Direct Debit Amendments and Cancellation Service

addition FIN an arithmetical operation consisting of adding together two or more numbers to make a sum

ADF *abbr* FIN Approved Deposit Fund

adjusted book value FIN the value of a company in terms of the current market values of its assets and liabilities. Also known as *modified book value*

adjusted futures price FIN the current value of a futures contract to buy a commodity at a fixed future date

adjusted gross income FIN the amount of annual income that a person or company has after various adjustments for income or corporation tax purposes. *Abbr* **AGI**

adjusted present value where the capital structure of a company is complex, or expected to vary over time, discounted cash flows may be separated into (i) those which relate to operational items, and (ii) those associated with financing. This treatment enables assessment to be made of the separate features of each area. *Abbr* **APV**

ADR *abbr* FIN American depository receipt: a document that indicates a US investor's ownership of stock in a foreign corporation

ad valorem FIN a tax or commission, for example, Value Added Tax, that is cal-culated on the value of the products or services provided, rather than on their number or size

ad valorem duty or **ad valorem tax** FIN a duty based on the value of a product or service

ad valorem tax FIN see *ad valorem duty*

Advance Corporation Tax FIN formerly, in the United Kingdom, a tax paid by a company equal to a percentage of its dividends or other distributions of profit to its shareholders. It was abolished in 1999. *Abbr* **ACT**

advance payment FIN an amount paid before it is earned or incurred, for example, a prepayment by an importer to an exporter before goods are shipped, or a cash advance for travel expenses

advance payment guarantee or **advance payment bond** FIN a guarantee that enables a buyer to recover an advance payment made under a contract or order if the supplier fails to fulfil its contractual obligations

adverse balance FIN the deficit on an account, especially a nation's balance of payments account

adverse opinion FIN a statement in the auditor's report of a company's annual accounts indicating a fundamental disagreement with the company to such an extent that the auditor considers the accounts misleading

advice of fate FIN immediate notification from a drawer's bank as to whether a cheque is to be honoured or not. This special presentation of a cheque bypasses the normal clearing system and so saves time.

advisory management FIN an advisory service offered by some stockbrokers in which clients are able to discuss a variety of investment options with their broker and receive appropriate advice. No resulting action may be taken, however, without a client's express approval.

AFAANZ *abbr* FIN Accounting and Finance Association of Australia and New Zealand

affiliate FIN, GEN a company that is controlled by another or is a member of a group, or either of two companies that owns a minority of the voting shares of the other

affluent society ECON a community in which material wealth is widely distributed

AFTA *abbr* FIN ASEAN Free Trade Area

after-acquired collateral FIN collateral for a loan that a borrower obtains after making the contract for the loan

after-tax FIN relating to earnings or income from which tax has already been deducted

AG *abbr* FIN Aktiengesellschaft: the German, Austrian, or Swiss equivalent of PLC

against actuals FIN relating to a trade between owners of futures contracts that allows both to reduce their positions to cash instead of commodities

aged debt FIN a debt that is overdue by one or more given periods, usually increments of 30 days

aged debtor FIN a person or organisation responsible for an overdue debt

agent bank *ANZ* FIN a bank that acts on behalf of a foreign bank, or a bank that participates in another bank's credit card programme, acting as a depository for merchants

age pension *ANZ* FIN a sum of money paid regularly by the government to people who have reached the age of retirement

aggregate demand ECON the sum of all expenditures in an economy that makes up its GDP, for example, consumers' expenditure on goods and services, investment in capital stocks, and government spending

aggregate depreciation FIN see *accumulated depreciation*

aggregate income FIN the total of all incomes in an economy without adjustments for inflation, taxation, or types of double counting

aggregate output ECON the total value of all the goods and services produced in an economy. Also known as *aggregate supply*

aggregate supply ECON see *aggregate output*

aggressive FIN relating to an investment strategy marked by willingness to accept high risk while trying to realise higher-than-average gains. Such a strategy involves investing in rapidly growing companies that promise capital appreciation but produce little or no income from dividends and de-emphasises income-producing instruments such as bonds.

aggressive accounting FIN inaccurate or unlawful accounting practices used by an organisation in order to make its financial position seem healthier than it is in reality

aggressive growth fund FIN a unit trust that takes considerable risks in the hope of making large profits

AGI *abbr* FIN adjusted gross income

AGM *abbr* FIN, GEN annual general meeting, a yearly meeting at which a company's management reports the year's results and shareholders have the opportunity to vote on company business, for example, the appointment of directors and auditors. Other business, for example, voting on dividend payments and board- and shareholder-sponsored resolutions, may also be transacted. US term *annual meeting*

agricultural produce FIN see *biological assets*

AICPA *abbr* FIN American Institute of Certified Public Accountants

AIFA *abbr* FIN Association of Independent Financial Advisers

AIM *abbr* FIN Alternative Investment Market: the London market trading in shares of emerging or small companies not eligible for listing on the London Stock Exchange. It replaced the Unlisted Securities Market (USM) in 1995.

air bill FIN a US term for the documentation accompanying a package sent using an express mail service

air waybill FIN a UK term for a receipt issued by an airline for goods to be freighted

AITC *abbr* FIN Association of Investment Trust Companies

Aktb *abbr* FIN Aktiebolaget, the Swedish equivalent of PLC

alien corporation FIN a company which is based in one country, but registered in another

all equity rate FIN the interest rate that a lender charges because of the apparent risks of a project that are independent of the normal market risks of financing it

alligator spread *US* FIN a spread which remains unprofitable even with good market conditions, usually as the result of high commissions paid to brokers or agents *(slang)*

All Industrials Index FIN a subindex of the Australian All Ordinaries Index which includes all the companies from that index that are not involved in resources or mining

All Mining Index FIN a subindex of the Australian All Ordinaries Index which includes all the companies from that index that are involved in the mining industry

allocate FIN to assign a whole item of cost, or of revenue, to a single cost unit, centre, account, or time period

All Ordinaries Accumulation Index FIN a measure of the change in share prices on the Australian Stock Exchange, based on the All Ordinaries Index, but assuming that all dividends are reinvested

All Ordinaries Index FIN the major index of Australian share prices, comprising more than 300 of the most active Australian companies listed on the Australian Stock Exchange. *Abbr All Ords*

All Ords *abbr* FIN All Ordinaries Index

all-or-none underwriting *ANZ* FIN the option of cancelling a public offering of shares if the underwriting is not fully subscribed

All Resources Index FIN a subindex of the Australian All Ordinaries Index which includes all the companies from that index that are involved in the resources industry

alpha rating FIN the return a security or a portfolio would be expected to earn if the market's rate of return were zero. Alpha expresses the difference between the return expected from a stock or unit trust, given its beta rating, and the return actually produced. A stock or trust that returns more than its beta would predict has a positive alpha, while one that returns less than the amount predicted by beta has a negative alpha. A large positive alpha indicates a strong performance, while a large negative alpha indicates a dismal performance. To begin with, the market itself is assigned a beta of 1.0. If a stock or trust has a beta of 1.2, this means its price is likely to rise or fall by 12% when the overall market rises or falls by 10%; a beta of 7.0 means the stock or trust price is likely to move up or down at 70% of the level of the market change. In practice, an alpha of 0.4 means the stock or trust in question outperformed the market-based return estimate by 0.4%. An alpha of –0.6 means the return was 0.6% less than would have been predicted from the change in the market alone. Both alpha and beta should be readily available upon request from investment firms, because the figures appear in standard performance reports. It is always best to ask for them, because calculating a stock's alpha rating requires first knowing a stock's beta rating, and beta calculations can involve mathematical complexities. See also *beta rating*

alpha value FIN a sum paid to an employee when he or she leaves a company that can be transferred to a concessionally taxed investment account such as an Approved Deposit Fund

alternate director FIN a person who is allowed to act for an absent named director of a company at a board meeting

alternative investment FIN an investment other than in bonds or shares of a large company or one listed on a stock exchange

Alternative Investment Market FIN see *AIM*

alternative mortgage instrument FIN any form of mortgage other than a fixed-term amortising loan

AM *abbr* FIN see *asset management*

amalgamation FIN, GEN the process of two or more organisations joining together for mutual benefit, either through a merger or consolidation

ambit claim *ANZ* FIN, GEN a claim made to an arbitration authority for higher pay or improved conditions that is deliberately exaggerated because the claimants know that they will subsequently have to compromise

American Accounting Association FIN a voluntary organisation for those with an interest in accounting research and best practice. Its mission is 'to foster worldwide excellence in the creation, dissemination and application of accounting knowledge and skills'. The AAA was founded in 1916. *Abbr AAA*

American depository receipt FIN see *ADR*

American Institute of Certified Public Accountants FIN founded in New York in 1887, AICPA is the national association for certified public accountants in the United States. *Abbr AICPA*

American option FIN an option contract that can be exercised at any time up to and including the expiry date. Most exchange-traded options are of this style. See also *European option*. Also known as *American-style option*

American Stock Exchange FIN see *AMEX*

American-style option FIN see *American option*

AMEX *abbr* FIN American Stock Exchange: a New York stock exchange listing smaller and less-mature companies than those listed on the larger New York Stock Exchange (NYSE)

amortisation FIN **1.** a method of recovering (deducting or writing off) the capital costs of intangible assets over a fixed period of time. For tax purposes, the distinction is not always made between amortisation and depreciation, yet amortisation remains a viable financial accounting concept in its own right. It is computed using the straight-line method of depreciation: divide the initial cost of the intangible asset by the estimated useful life of that asset. **2.** the payment of the principal and interest on a loan in equal amounts over a period of time

amortise FIN to reduce the value of an asset gradually by systematically writing off its cost over a period of time, or to repay a debt in a series of regular instalments or transfers

amortised value FIN the value at a particular time of a financial instrument that is being amortised

AMPS *abbr* FIN auction market preferred stock

analytical review FIN the examination of ratios, trends, and changes in balances from one period to the next, to obtain a broad understanding of the financial position and results of operations and to identify any items requiring further investigation

angel investor FIN an individual or group of individuals willing to invest in an unproven but well-researched idea. Angel investors are typically the first port of call for start-ups looking for financial backing because they are more inclined to provide early funding than venture capital firms are. After investing in a company, angel investors typically take an advisory role but expect a share in profits.

announcement FIN a statement that a company makes to provide information on its trading prospects, which will be of interest to its existing and potential investors

annual charge FIN a management fee paid yearly to a stockbroker or collective fund manager by a client to cover a range of administrative costs and commission

annual depreciation provision FIN the allocation of the cost of an asset to a single year of the asset's expected lifetime

annual general meeting FIN, GEN see *AGM*

annual meeting *US* GEN = AGM

annual percentage rate or **annualised percentage rate** FIN see *APR*

annual percentage yield FIN the effective or true annual rate of return on an investment, taking into account the effect of compounding. For example, an annual percentage rate of 6% compounded monthly translates into an annual percentage yield of 6.17%. *Abbr APY*

annual report FIN a document prepared each year to give a true and fair view of a company's state of affairs. Annual reports are issued to shareholders and filed at Companies House in accordance with the provisions of company legislation. Contents include a profit and loss account and balance sheet, a cash-flow statement, directors' report, auditor's report, and, where a company has subsidiaries, the company's group accounts. The financial statements are the main purpose of the annual report, and usually include notes to the accounts. These amplify numerous points contained in the figures and are critical for anyone wishing to study the accounts in detail.

annuity FIN a contract in which a person pays a lump-sum premium to an insurance company and in return receives periodic payments, usually yearly, often beginning on retirement. There are several types of annuity. They vary both in the ways they accumulate funds and in the ways they dispense earnings. A fixed annuity guarantees fixed payments to the individual receiving it for the term of the contract, usually until death; a variable annuity offers no guarantee but has potential for a greater return, usually based on the performance of a stock or unit trust; a deferred annuity delays payments until the individual chooses to receive them; a hybrid annuity, also called a combination annuity, combines features of both the fixed and variable annuity.

annuity in arrears FIN an annuity whose first payment is due at least one payment period after the start date of the annuity's contract

anticipation note FIN a bond that a borrower intends to pay off with money from taxes due or money to be borrowed in a later and larger transaction

anticipatory hedging FIN hedging carried out before the transaction occurs to which the hedge applies

anti-dumping ECON intended to prevent the sale of goods on a foreign market at a price below their marginal cost

anti-trust FIN, GEN relating to US legislative initiatives aimed at protecting trade and commerce from monopolistic business practices that restrict or eliminate competition. Anti-trust laws also attempt to curb trusts and cartels and to keep them from employing monopolistic practices to make unfair profits.

ANZCERTA *abbr* FIN Australia and New Zealand Closer Economic Relations Trade Agreement

AP *abbr* FIN accounts payable

APB *abbr* FIN **1.** Auditing Practices Board **2.** US Accounting Principles Board

APEC FIN Asia-Pacific Economic Co-operation, a forum designed to promote trade and economic co-operation among countries bordering the Pacific Ocean. It was established in 1989. Members include Australia, Indonesia, Thailand, the Philippines, Singapore, Brunei, and Japan.

applied economics ECON the practical application of theoretical economic principles, especially in formulating national and international economic policies

appreciation FIN **1.** the value that certain assets, particularly land and buildings, accrue over time. Directors of companies are obliged to reflect this in their accounts. **2.** the increase in value of one currency relative to another

appreciative inquiry GEN an approach to organisational change that focuses and builds on the strengths and potential of an organisation. The concept of appreciative inquiry was developed by David L. Cooperrider and Suresh Srivastva in the course of research into organisational behaviour at Case Western Reserve University, Cleveland Ohio, in the 1980s. They maintain that a change of perspective, such as focusing on and asking questions about the positive characteristics of an organisation rather than focusing on negative aspects such as problems, needs, and deficits, can inspire an image of what the future could be, mobilise positive creative energy and initiate a process of discovery and change within an organisation. Appreciative inquiry has its roots in action research and focuses on organisations as social systems.

appropriation FIN a sum of money that has been allocated for a particular purpose

approved accounts FIN accounts that have been formally accepted by a company's board of directors

Approved Deposit Fund ANZ FIN a concessionally taxed fund managed by a financial institution into which Eligible Termination Payments can be transferred from a superannuation fund. *Abbr* **ADF**

APR *abbr* FIN annual or annualised percentage rate of interest: the interest rate that would exist if it were calculated as simple rather than compound interest. Different investments typically offer different compounding periods, usually quarterly or monthly. The APR allows them to be compared over a common period of time: one year. This enables an investor or borrower to compare like with like, providing an excellent basis for comparing mortgage or other loan rates. In the United Kingdom, lenders are required to disclose it. See also *effective annual rate*. Also known as *annual percentage rate, nominal annual rate*

APRA *abbr* FIN Australian Prudential Regulation Authority

APV *abbr* FIN adjusted present value

APY *abbr* FIN annual percentage yield

AR *abbr* FIN accounts receivable

arbitrage FIN the buying and selling of foreign currencies, products, or financial securities between two or more markets in order to make an immediate profit by exploiting the differences in market prices quoted

arbitrage pricing theory FIN a model of financial instrument and portfolio behaviour that provides a benchmark of return and risk for capital budgeting and securities analysis. It can be used to create portfolios that track a market index, estimate the risk of an asset allocation strategy, or estimate the response of a portfolio to economic developments.

arbitrageur FIN a firm or individual who purchases shares or financial securities to make a windfall profit

arithmetic mean FIN a simple average calculated by dividing the sum of two or more items by the number of items

arm's-length price FIN a price at which an unrelated seller and buyer agree to deal on an asset or a product

articles of association FIN an official document governing the running of a company, that is placed with the Registrar of Companies. The articles of association constitute a contract between the company and its members, set out the voting rights of shareholders and the conduct of shareholders' and directors' meetings, and detail the powers of management of the company. A memorandum of association is a related document. US term *bylaws*

articles of incorporation FIN in the United States, a legal document that creates a corporation and sets forth its purpose and structure according to the laws of the state in which it is established

articles of partnership FIN see *partnership agreement*

ASB *abbr* FIN Accounting Standards Board

ASC *abbr* FIN Accounting Standards Committee

ASEAN Free Trade Area FIN a conceptual regional free trade agreement supported by Singapore to foster trade within the region. *Abbr* **AFTA**

A share FIN **1.** a share in a company issued to raise additional capital without diluting control of the company **2.** in the United States, a class of mutual fund share that is front-end loaded (has a sales charge associated with it). = non-voting share

Asian Currency Unit FIN a bookkeeping unit used for recording transactions made by approved financial institutions operating in the Asian Dollar market. *Abbr* **ACU**

ASIC *abbr* FIN Australian Securities and Investments Commission

ask FIN **1.** the bid price at which a dealer in stocks and shares, commodities, or financial securities is prepared to buy **2.** *US* the price that a security is offered for sale, or the net asset value of a mutual fund plus any sales charges. Also known as *asked price, offering price*

asked price FIN see *ask* (sense 2)

asking price FIN the price that a seller puts on something before any negotiation

assessed loss FIN the excess of tax-deductible expenses over taxable income as confirmed by the South African Revenue Service. It may be carried forward and deducted in determining the taxpayer's taxable income in subsequent years of assessment.

assessed value FIN a value for something that is calculated by a person such as an investment advisor

asset FIN, GEN any tangible or intangible item to which a value can be assigned. Assets can be physical, such as machinery and consumer durables, or financial, such as cash and accounts receivable. Assets are typically broken down into five different categories. Current assets include cash, cash equivalents, marketable securities, inventories, and prepaid expenses that are expected to be used within one year or a normal operating cycle.

All cash items and inventories are reported at historical value. Securities are reported at market value. Non-current assets, or long-term investments, are resources that are expected to be held for more than one year. They are reported at the lower of cost and current market value, which means that their values will vary. Fixed assets include property, plant and facilities, and equipment used to conduct business. These items are reported at their original value, even though current values might well be much higher. Intangible assets include legal claims, patents, franchise rights, and accounts receivable. These values can be more difficult to determine. FR10, published by the Accounting Standards Board of the Institute of Chartered Accountants for England and Wales, is essential reading for dealing with this issue. Deferred charges include prepaid costs and other expenditures that will produce future revenue or benefits.

asset allocation *ANZ* FIN an investment strategy that distributes investments in a portfolio so as to achieve the highest investment return while minimising risk. Such a strategy usually apportions investments among cash equivalents, shares in domestic and foreign companies, fixed-income investments, and property.

asset-backed security ECON, FIN a security for which the collateral is neither land nor a land-based financial instrument

asset-based lending FIN the lending of money with the expectation that the proceeds from an asset or assets will allow the borrower to repay the loan

asset conversion loan FIN a loan that the borrower will repay with money raised by selling an asset

asset coverage FIN the ratio measuring a company's solvency and consisting of its net assets divided by its debt

asset demand ECON the amount of assets held as money, which will be low when interest rates are high and high when interest rates are low

asset financing FIN the borrowing of money by a company using its assets as collateral

asset for asset swap FIN an exchange of one bankrupt debtor's debt for that of another

asset management FIN an investment service offered by some financial institutions that combines banking and brokerage services. *Abbr* **AM**

asset play FIN the purchase of a company's stock in the belief that it has assets that are not properly documented and therefore unknown to others

asset pricing model FIN a pricing model used to determine the profit that an asset will yield

asset protection trust FIN a trust, often set up in a foreign country, used to make the trust's principal inaccessible to creditors

asset restructuring FIN the purchase or sale of assets worth more than 50% of a listed company's total or net assets

asset side FIN the side of a balance sheet that shows the economic resources a firm owns, for example, cash in hand or in bank deposits, products, or buildings and fixtures

assets requirements FIN the assets needed for a business to continue trading

asset-stripping FIN the purchase of a company whose market value is below its asset value, usually so that the buyer can sell the assets for immediate gain. The buyer usually has little or no concern for the purchased company's employees or other stakeholders, so the practice is generally frowned upon.

asset substitution FIN the purchase of assets that involve more risk than those a lender expected the borrower to buy

asset swap FIN an exchange of assets between companies so that they may divest parts no longer required and enter another product area

asset turnover FIN the ratio of a firm's sales revenue to its total assets, used as a measure of the firm's business efficiency

asset valuation FIN the aggregated value of the assets of a firm, usually the capital assets, as entered on its balance sheet

assign FIN to transfer ownership of an asset to another person or organisation

assigned risk FIN a poor insurance risk that a company is required by law to insure against

Associate of the Association of International Accountants FIN *abbr* **AAIA**

Association of British Insurers FIN an association that represents over 400 UK insurance companies to the government, the regulators, and other agencies, as well as providing a wide range of services to its members. *Abbr* **ABI**

Association of Chartered Accountants in the United States FIN a non-profit professional and educational organisation that represents over 6,500 chartered accountants based in the United States. The Association was founded in 1985. *Abbr* **ACAUS**

Association of Chartered Certified Accountants FIN an international accounting organisation with over 325,000 members in more than 170 countries. It was formed in 1904 as the London Association of Accountants. *Abbr* **ACCA**

Association of Independent Financial Advisers FIN a trade association that represents the interests of independent financial advisers. *Abbr* **AIFA**

Association of Unit Trusts and Investment Funds FIN *abbr* **AUTIF**

assumable mortgage FIN a mortgage that the buyer of a property can take over from the seller

assumed bond FIN a bond for which a company other than the issuer takes over responsibility

assured shorthold tenancy FIN a tenancy for a fixed period of at least six months during which the tenant cannot be evicted other than by court order. Any new tenancy without a written agreement is an assured shorthold tenancy.

assured tenancy FIN a tenancy for an indefinite period in which the tenant cannot be evicted other than by court order

ASX *abbr* FIN Australian Stock Exchange

ASX 100 FIN a measure of the change in share prices on the Australian Stock Exchange based on changes in the stocks of the top 100 companies. Similar indexes include the ASX 20, ASX 50, ASX 200, and ASX 300.

asymmetric taxation FIN a difference in tax status between parties to a transaction, typically making the transaction attractive to both parties because of taxes that one or both can avoid

at best FIN an instruction to a stockbroker to buy or sell securities immediately at the best possible current price in the market, regardless of adverse price movements. It is also applicable to the commodity or currency markets. See also *at limit*

at call FIN used to describe a short-term loan that is repayable immediately upon demand

at limit FIN an instruction to a stockbroker to buy or sell a security within certain limits, usually not to sell below or to buy above a set price. A time limit is stipulated by the investor, and, if there has been no transaction within that period, the instruction lapses. It is also applicable to the commodity or currency markets. See also *at best*

ATM FIN automated teller machine: an electronic machine from which bank customers can withdraw paper money using an encoded plastic card

ATO *abbr* FIN Australian Taxation Office

attachment FIN a process that enables a judgment creditor to secure dues from a debtor. A debtor's earnings and/or funds held at his or her bankers may be attached.

attendance bonus *US* HR a financial or non-financial incentive offered to employees by an employer to arrive for work on time

at-the-money FIN used to describe an option with a strike price roughly equivalent to the price of the underlying shares

auction market preferred stock FIN stock in a company owned in the United Kingdom that pays dividends which track a money-market index. *Abbr* **AMPS**

AUD *abbr* FIN Australian dollar

audit FIN a systematic examination of the activities and status of an entity, based primarily on investigation and analysis of its systems, controls, and records

audit committee FIN a committee of a company's board of directors, from which the company's executives are excluded, that monitors the company's finances

audited accounts FIN a set of accounts that have been thoroughly scrutinised, checked, and approved by a team of auditors

Auditor-General *ANZ* FIN an officer of a state or territory government who is responsible for ensuring that government expenditure is made in accordance with legislation

auditor's report FIN a certification by an auditor that a firm's financial records give a true and fair view of its profit and loss for the period

audit trail FIN the records of all the sequential stages of a transaction. An audit trail may trace the process of a purchase, a sale, a customer complaint, or the supply of goods. Tracing what happened at each stage through the records can be a useful method of problem-solving. In financial markets, audit trails may be used to ensure fairness and accuracy on the part of the dealers.

Aussie Mac FIN an informal name for a mortgage-backed certificate issued in Australia by the National Mortgage Market Corporation. The corporation has been issuing such certificates since 1985.

austerity budget FIN a budget imposed on a country by its government with the aim of reducing the national deficit by way of cutting consumer spending

Austrade FIN Australian Trade Commission, a federal government body responsible for promoting Australian products abroad and attracting business to Australia. It currently has 108 offices in 63 countries.

Australia and New Zealand Closer Economic Relations Trade Agreement FIN an accord between Australia and New Zealand designed to facilitate the exchange of goods between the two countries. It was signed on 1 January 1983. *Abbr* **ANZCERTA**

Australian Accounting Standards Board FIN the body that is responsible for setting and monitoring accounting standards in Australia. It was established under Corporations Law in 1988, replacing the Accounting Standards Review Board. *Abbr* **AASB**

Australian Chamber of Commerce and Industry FIN a national council of business organisations in Australia. It represents around 350,000 businesses and its members include state chambers of commerce as well as major national employer and industry associations. *Abbr* **ACCI**

Australian Communications Authority FIN the government body responsible for regulating practices in the communications industries. It was set up in 1997 as a result of the merger of the Australian Telecommunications Authority and the Spectrum Management Agency. *Abbr* **ACA**

Australian Industrial Relations Commission HR an administrative tribunal responsible for settling industrial disputes by conciliation and for setting and modifying industrial awards. It was established in 1988 to replace the Arbitration Commission and other specialist tribunals. *Abbr* **AIRC**

Australian Prudential Regulation Authority FIN a federal government body responsible for ensuring that financial institutions are able to meet their commitments

Australian Securities and Investments Commission FIN an Australian federal government body responsible for regulating Australian businesses and the provision of financial products and services to consumers. It was established in 1989, replacing the Australian Securities Commission. *Abbr* **ASIC**

Australian Stock Exchange FIN the principal market for trading shares and other securities in Australia. It was formed in 1987 as a result of the amalgamation of six state stock exchanges and has offices in most state capitals. *Abbr* **ASX**

Australian Taxation Office FIN a statutory body responsible for the administration of the Australian federal government's taxation system. It is based in Canberra and is also responsible for the country's superannuation system. *Abbr* **ATO**

authorisation FIN the process of assessing a financial transaction, confirming that it does not raise the account's debt above its limit, and allowing the transaction to proceed. This would be undertaken, for example, by a credit card issuer. A positive authorisation results in an authorisation code being generated and the relevant funds being set aside. The available credit limit is reduced by the amount authorised.

authorised capital FIN the money made by a company from the sale of authorised ordinary and preference shares. It is measured by multiplying the number of authorised shares by their par value.

authorised share FIN a share that a company is authorised to issue

authorised share capital FIN the type, class, number, and amount of the shares which a company may issue, as empowered by its memorandum of association. Also known as *nominal share capital, registered share capital*

authorised signatory FIN the most senior issuer of authorisation certificates in an organisation, recognised by a signatory authority and designated in a signatory certificate

AUTIF *abbr* FIN Association of Unit Trusts and Investment Funds

Automated Direct Debit Amendments and Cancellation Service FIN in the United Kingdom, a BACS service that allows paying banks to inform direct debit payees of a change of instruction, for example, an amendment to the customer's account details or a request to cancel the instructions. *Abbr* **ADDACS**

Automated Order Entry System FIN in the United States, a system that allows small orders to bypass the floor brokers and go straight to the specialists on the exchange floor

automated screen trading FIN an electronic trading system for the sale and purchase of securities. Customers' orders are entered via a keyboard; a computer system matches and executes the deals; and prices and deals are shown on monitors, thus dispensing with the need for face-to-face contact on a trading floor.

automated teller machine FIN see *ATM*

automatic debit *US* FIN = standing order

automatic rollover FIN on the London money market, the automatic reinvestment of a maturing fixed-term deposit for a further identical fixed

term, an arrangement that can be cancelled at any time

Auto Pact FIN the informal name for the Agreement Concerning Automotive Products between Canada and the United States, by which duties were reduced on imported cars for US car makers assembling vehicles in Canada. Subsequent provisions of the North American Free Trade Agreement reduced its effect.

availability float FIN money that is available to a company because cheques that it has written have not yet been charged against its accounts

AVCs *abbr* FIN additional voluntary contributions

average accounting return FIN the percentage return realised on an asset, as measured by its book value, after taxes and depreciation

average collection period FIN the mean time required for a firm to liquidate its accounts receivable, measured from the date each receivable is posted until the last payment is received. Its formula is:

Accounts receivable / Average daily sales = Average collection period

For example, if accounts receivable are £280,000, and average daily sales are 7,000, then:

$$280,000 / 7,000 = 40$$

average cost of capital FIN the average of what a company is paying for the money it borrows or raises by selling stock

average nominal maturity FIN the average length of time until a unit trust's financial instruments mature

average option FIN an option whose value depends on the average price of a commodity during a particular period of time

award wage *ANZ* HR a rate of pay set by an industrial court or tribunal for a particular occupation

'aw shucks' FIN see *Sarbanes-Oxley*

BAA *abbr* FIN British Accounting Association

back duty FIN tax relating to a past period that has not been paid because of the taxpayer's failure to disclose relevant information through negligence or fraud. If back duty is found

to be payable, the relevant authorities may instigate an investigation and penalties or interest may be charged on the amount.

back-end loading FIN the practice of charging a redemption fee or deferred sales charge if the holder of an investment decides to sell it. This is used as a discouragement to selling. See also *front-end loading*

backlog depreciation FIN the additional depreciation required when an asset is revalued to make up for the fact that previous depreciation had been calculated on a now out-of-date valuation

back office FIN, GEN the administrative staff of a company who do not have face-to-face contact with the company's customers

back pay HR pay that is owed to an employee for work carried out before the current payment period and is either overdue or results from a backdated pay increase

back-to-back loan FIN an arrangement in which two companies in different countries borrow offsetting amounts in each other's currency and each repays it at a specified future date in its domestic currency. Such a loan, often between a company and its foreign subsidiary, eliminates the risk of loss from exchange rate fluctuations.

back-up FIN a period in which bond yields rise and prices fall, or a sudden reversal in a stock market trend

back-up withholding FIN a withholding tax that a payer sends to the Internal Revenue Service in the United States so that somebody receiving income cannot avoid all taxes on that income

BACS FIN an electronic bulk clearing system generally used by banks and building societies for low-value and/or repetitive items such as standing orders, direct debits, and automated credits such as salary payments. It was formerly known as the Bankers Automated Clearing Service.

BADC *abbr* FIN Business Accounting Deliberation Council of Japan

bad debt FIN a debt which is or is considered to be uncollectable and is, therefore, written off either as a charge to the profit and loss account or against an existing doubtful debt provision

bad debt reserve FIN an amount of money that a company sets aside to cover bad debts

bad debts recovered FIN money formerly classified as bad debts and therefore written off that has since been recovered either wholly or in part

badwill FIN negative goodwill *(slang)*

bailment FIN the delivery of goods from the owner to another person on the condition that they will eventually be returned

balance FIN 1. the state of an account, indicating whether money is owed or owing, i.e. a debit or a credit balance 2. in double-entry book-keeping, the amount required to make the debit and credit figures in the books equal each other 3. the difference between the totals of the debit and credit entries in an account

balance billing FIN the practice of requesting payment from a receiver of a service such as medical treatment for the part of the cost not covered by the person's insurance

balanced budget ECON a budget in which planned expenditure on goods and services and debt income can be met by current income from taxation and other central government receipts

balanced fund FIN a unit trust that invests in a variety of types of companies and financial instruments to reduce the risk of loss through poor performance of any one type

balanced investment strategy FIN the practice of investing in a variety of types of companies and financial instruments to reduce the risk of loss through poor performance of any one type

balanced scorecard FIN, GEN a system that measures and manages an organisation's progress towards strategic objectives. Introduced by Robert Kaplan and David Norton in 1992, the balanced scorecard incorporates not only financial indicators but also three other perspectives: customer, internal business, and learning/innovation. The scorecard shows how these measures are interlinked and affect each other, enabling an organisation's past, present, and potential performance to be tracked and managed.

balanced scorecard approach FIN an approach to the provision of information to management in order to assist strategic policy formulation and implementation to build the long-term value of the business. It emphasises the need to provide the user with a set of information that addresses all relevant areas of performance in an objective and unbiased fashion. The information provided may include financial and non-financial elements and cover areas such as profitability, customer satisfaction, internal efficiency, and innovation. The term originates from the best-selling business book *The Balanced Scorecard*, written by Robert Kaplan and David Norton and published by Harvard Business School Press in 1996. Their approach applies the concept of shareholder value analysis, and is based on the premise that the traditional measures used by managers to see how well their organisations are performing, such as business ratios, productivity, unit costs, growth, and profitability, are only a part of the picture. Traditional measures are seen as providing a narrowly focused snapshot of how an organisation performed in the past, and give little indication of likely future performance. In contrast, the balanced scorecard offers a measurement and management system that links strategic objectives to comprehensive performance indicators.

balance off FIN to add up and enter the totals for both sides of an account at the end of an accounting period in order to determine the balance

balance of payments ECON a list of a country's credit and debit transactions with international financial institutions and foreign countries over a specific period. *Abbr* **BOP**

balance of payments on capital account FIN a system of recording a country's investment transactions with the rest of the world during a given period, usually one year. Among the included transactions are the purchase of physical and financial assets, intergovernmental transfers, and the provision of economic aid to developing nations.

balance of payments on current account FIN a system of recording a country's imports and exports of goods and services during a period, usually one year

balance of trade ECON, FIN the difference between a country's exports and imports of goods and services. *Abbr* **BOT**

balance sheet FIN a financial report stating the total assets, liabilities, and owners' equity of an organisation at a given date, usually the last day of the accounting period. The format of a company's balance sheet is strictly defined by the 1985 Companies Act. The debit side of the balance sheet states assets, while the credit side states liabilities and equity, and the two sides must be equal, or balance. Assets include cash in hand and cash anticipated (receivables), inventories of supplies and materials, properties, facilities, equipment, and whatever else the company uses to conduct business. Assets also need to reflect depreciation in the value of equipment such as machinery that has a limited expected useful life. Liabilities include pending payments to suppliers and creditors, outstanding current and long-term debts, taxes, interest payments, and other unpaid expenses that the company has incurred. Subtracting the value of aggregate liabilities from the value of aggregate assets reveals the value of owners' equity. Ideally, it should be positive. Owners' equity consists of capital invested by owners over the years and profits (net income) or internally generated capital, which is referred to as 'retained earnings'; these are funds to be used in future operations. *Abbr* **B/S**

balance sheet audit FIN a limited audit of the items on a company's balance sheet in order to confirm that it complies with the relevant standards and requirements. Such an audit involves checking the value, ownership, and existence of assets and liabilities and ensuring that they are correctly recorded.

balance sheet equation FIN see *accounting equation*

balance sheet total FIN in the United Kingdom, the total of assets shown at the bottom of a balance sheet and used to classify a company according to size

balancing figure FIN a number added to a series of numbers to make the total the same as another total. For example, if a debit total is higher than the credit total in the accounts, the balancing figure is the amount of extra credit required to make the two totals equal.

balloon loan FIN a loan repaid in regular instalments with a single larger final payment

balloon payment FIN the final larger payment on a balloon loan

ballpark FIN, GEN an informal term for a rough, estimated figure. The term was derived from the approximate assessment of the number of spectators at a sporting event that might be made on the basis of a glance around.

BALO FIN Bulletin des Annonces Légales Obligatoires: a French government publication that includes financial statements of public companies

BAN *abbr* FIN bond anticipation note

bang for the buck *US* FIN, GEN a return on investment *(slang)*

bank FIN a commercial institution that keeps money in accounts for individuals or organisations, makes loans, exchanges currencies, provides credit to businesses, and offers other financial services

bank bill FIN **1.** a bill of exchange issued or accepted by a bank **2.** *US* a banknote

bank card FIN a plastic card issued by a bank and accepted by merchants in payment for transactions. The most common types are credit cards and debit cards. Bank cards are governed by an internationally recognised set of rules for the authorisation of their use and the clearing and settlement of transactions.

bank certificate FIN a document, often requested during an audit, that is signed by a bank official and confirms the balances due to or from a company on a specific date

bank confirmation FIN verification of a company's balances requested by an auditor from a bank

bank credit FIN the maximum credit available to an individual from a particular bank

bank discount FIN the charge made by a bank to a company or customer who pays a note before it is due

bank discount basis FIN the expression of yield that is used for US treasury bills, based on a 360-day year

bank draft FIN see *banker's draft*

bank-eligible issue FIN US Treasury obligations that commercial banks may buy

banker FIN somebody who owns or is a senior executive of a bank

banker's acceptance FIN see *banker's credit*

banker's cheque FIN see *banker's draft*

banker's credit FIN a financial instrument, typically issued by an exporter or importer for a short term, that a bank guarantees. Also known as *banker's acceptance*

banker's draft FIN a bill of exchange payable on demand and drawn by one bank on another. Regarded as being equivalent to cash, the draft cannot be returned unpaid. Also known as *bank draft, banker's cheque*. *Abbr* **B/D**

banker's order FIN an instruction by a customer to a bank to pay a specific amount at regular intervals, usually monthly or annually, until the order is cancelled

banker's reference FIN a written report issued by a bank regarding a particular customer's creditworthiness

bank fee FIN a charge included in most lease transactions that is either paid in advance or is included in the gross capitalised cost. The fee usually covers administrative costs such as the costs of obtaining a credit report, verifying insurance coverage, and checking the lease documentation.

Bank for International Settlements FIN see *BIS*

bank giro FIN see *giro (sense 1)*

bank guarantee FIN a commitment made by a bank to a foreign buyer that the bank will pay an exporter for goods shipped if the buyer defaults

bank holding company FIN a company that owns one or more banks as part of its assets

Banking Code FIN a voluntary code of best practice for the banking and financial services industry, which is

developed and revised by the British Bankers' Association

banking insurance fund FIN in the United States, a fund maintained by the Federal Deposit Insurance Corporation to provide deposit insurance for banks other than savings and savings and loan banks

Banking Ombudsman FIN an official of the Australian or New Zealand government responsible for dealing with complaints relating to banking practices

banking passport FIN a document used to provide somebody with a false identity for banking transactions in another country

banking syndicate FIN a group of investment banks that jointly underwrite and distribute a new security offering

banking system FIN a network of commercial, savings, and specialised banks that provide financial services, including accepting deposits and providing loans and credit, money transmission and investment facilities

bank investment contract FIN a contract that specifies what a bank will pay its investors

Bank of England FIN the central bank of the United Kingdom, established in 1694. Originally a private bank, it became public in 1946 and increased its independence from government in 1997, when it was granted sole responsibility for setting base interest rates.

bank reconciliation FIN a detailed statement reconciling, at a given date, the cash balance in an entity's cash book with that reported in a bank statement

bank reserve ratio FIN a standard established by a central bank governing the relationship between the amount of money that other banks must keep on hand and the amount that they can lend. By raising and lowering the ratio, the central bank can decrease or increase the money supply.

bank reserves FIN the money that a bank has available to meet the demands of its depositors

bankroll FIN the money used as finance for a project

bankrupt FIN a person who has been declared by a court of law as unable to meet his or her financial obligations

bankruptcy FIN the condition of being unable to pay debts, with liabilities greater than assets. There are two types of bankruptcy: involuntary bankruptcy, where one or more creditors bring a petition against the debtor; and voluntary bankruptcy, where the debtor files a petition claiming inability to meet his or her debts.

bank term loan FIN a loan from a bank that has a term of at least one year

bar outside the bar FIN one million pounds sterling *(slang)*

bargain FIN a transaction on a stock market *(slang)*

bargaining chip GEN something that can be used as a concession or inducement in negotiation

bargain tax date FIN the date of a transaction on a stock market

barometer stock FIN a widely held security such as a blue chip that is regarded as an indicator of the state of the market

barren money FIN money that is unproductive because it is not invested

barrier option FIN an option that includes automatic trading in other options when a commodity reaches a specified price

barrier to entry FIN any impediment to the free entry of new competitors into a market

barrier to exit FIN any impediment to the exit of existing competitors from a market

barter ECON, FIN the direct exchange of goods or services between two parties without the use of money as a medium

base currency FIN the currency used for measuring the return on an investment

base date ECON the reference date from which an index number such as the retail price index is calculated

base interest rate FIN in the United States, the minimum interest rate that investors will expect for investing in a non-Treasury security. Also known as *benchmark interest rate*

base pay *US* HR = basic pay

base rate FIN the interest rate at which the Bank of England lends to other banks and which they in turn charge their customers

base rate tracker mortgage FIN a mortgage whose interest rate varies periodically, usually annually, so as to remain a specified percentage above a particular standard rate

base year ECON the year from which an index is calculated

basic pay HR, FIN a guaranteed sum of money given to an employee in payment for work, disregarding any fringe benefits, allowances, or extra rewards from an incentive scheme. US term *base pay*

basic rate FIN the percentage of income that the majority of workers in the United Kingdom pay to HM Revenue & Customs

basic wage HR the minimum rate of pay set by an industrial court or tribunal for a particular occupation

basic wage rate FIN the wages paid for a specific number of hours' work per week, excluding overtime payments and any other incentives

basis point FIN one hundredth of 1%, used in relation to changes in bond interest rates. Thus a change from 7.5% to 7.4% is 10 basis points.

basis risk FIN the risk that price variations in the cash or futures market will diminish revenue when a futures contract is liquidated, or the risk that changes in interest rates will affect re-pricing interest-bearing liabilities

basket of currencies FIN a group of selected currencies used in establishing a standard of value for another unit of currency

bath *&phraseintro;* **take a bath** FIN to suffer a serious financial loss

BBA *abbr* FIN British Bankers' Association

BC *abbr* FIN budgetary control

BCC *abbr* FIN British Chambers of Commerce

BCCS *abbr* FIN Board of Currency Commissioners

B/D *abbr* FIN banker's draft

bear FIN somebody who anticipates unfavourable business conditions, especially somebody who sells stocks or commodities expecting their prices to fall, often with the intention of buying them back cheaply later. See also *bull*

bearer bond FIN a negotiable bond or security whose ownership is not registered by the issuer, but is presumed to lie with whoever has physical possession of the bond

bearer instrument FIN a financial instrument such as a cheque or bill of exchange that entitles the person who presents it to receive payment

bearer security FIN a share or bond that is owned by the person who possesses it. For example, a Eurobond can change hands without registration and so protect the owner's anonymity.

bearish FIN relating to unfavourable business conditions or selling activity in anticipation of falling prices. See also *bullish*

bear market FIN a market in which prices are falling and in which a dealer is more likely to sell securities than to buy them. See also *bull market*

bear raid FIN see *raid*

bear spread FIN a combination of purchases and sales of options for the same commodity or stock with the intention of making a profit when the price falls. See also *bull spread*

bear tack FIN a downward movement in the value of a stock, a part of the market, or the market as a whole

bed and breakfast deal FIN a transaction in which somebody sells shares at the end of one trading day and repurchases them at the beginning of the next. This is usually done to formally establish the profit or loss accrued to these shares for tax or reporting purposes.

before-tax profit margin FIN the amount by which net income before tax exceeds expenditure

beginning inventory *US* FIN = opening stock

behavioural accounting FIN an approach to the study of accounting that emphasises the psychological and social aspects of the profession in addition to the more technical areas

bells and whistles FIN special features attached to a derivatives instrument or securities issue that are intended to attract investors or reduce issue costs *(slang)*

bellwether FIN a security whose price is viewed by investors as an indicator of future developments or trends

below-the-line FIN **1.** used to describe entries in a company's profit and loss account that show how the profit is distributed, or where the funds to finance the loss originate. See also *above-the-line (sense 1)* **2.** in macroeconomics, used to describe a country's capital transactions. See also *above-the-line (sense 2)*

benchmark accounting policy FIN one of a choice of two possible policies within an International Accounting Standard. The other policy is marked as an 'allowed alternative', although there is no indication of preference.

benchmark index FIN an influential index for a particular market or activity

benchmarking the establishment, through data gathering, of targets and comparators, through whose use relative levels of performance (and particularly areas of underperformance) can be identified. By the adoption of identified best practices it is hoped that performance will improve. There are various types of benchmarking. Internal benchmarking is a method of comparing one operating unit or function with another within the same industry. Functional benchmarking compares internal functions with those of the best external practitioners of those functions, regardless of the industry they are in (also known as operational benchmarking or generic benchmarking). Competitive benchmarking gathers information about direct competitors, through techniques such as reverse engineering. Strategic benchmarking is a type of competitive benchmarking aimed at strategic action and organisational change.

benchmark interest rate FIN the lowest interest rate that US investors will accept on securities other than Treasury bills

beneficial interest FIN an arrangement whereby someone is allowed to occupy or receive rent from a house without owning it

beneficial owner FIN somebody who receives all the benefits of a stock, such as dividends, rights, and proceeds of any sale, but is not the registered owner of the stock

beneficiary bank FIN a bank that handles a gift such as a bequest

benefit FIN something that improves the profitability or efficiency of an organisation or reduces its risk, or any non-monetary reward given to employees, for example, paid holidays or employer contributions to pensions

Benford's Law FIN a law proposed in 1938 by Dr Frank Benford, a physicist at the General Electric Company, which shows that in sets of random numbers it is more likely that the set will begin with the number 1 than with any other number

bequest FIN a gift that has been left to somebody in a will

Berhad FIN a Malay term for 'private'. Companies can use 'Sendirian Berhad' or 'Sdn Bhd' in their name instead of 'plc'. *Abbr* **Bhd**

Berne Union FIN see *International Union of Credit and Investment Insurers*

beta FIN a numerical measure of the change in value of something such as a stock

beta coefficient FIN an indication of the level of risk attached to a share. A high beta coefficient indicates that a share is likely to be more sensitive to market movements.

beta rating FIN a means of measuring the volatility (or risk) of a stock or fund in comparison with the market as a whole. The beta of a stock or fund can be of any value, positive or negative, but usually is between +0.25 and +1.75. Stocks of many utilities have a beta of less than 1. Conversely, most high-tech NASDAQ-based stocks have a beta greater than 1; they offer a higher rate of return but are also risky. Both alpha and beta ratings should be readily available upon request from investment firms, because the figures appear in standard performance reports. It is always best to ask for them, because beta calculations can involve mathematical complexities. See also *alpha rating*

BFH FIN Bundesfinanzhof: in Germany, the supreme court for issues concerning taxation

Bhd *abbr* FIN *Berhad*

bid FIN **1.** an offer to buy all or the majority of the capital shares of a company in an attempted takeover **2.** the highest price a prospective buyer for a good or service is prepared to pay

bid-ask quote FIN a statement of the prices that are being offered and asked for a security or option contract

bid bond FIN a guarantee by a financial institution of the fulfilment of an international tender offer

bid costs FIN costs incurred during the takeover of a company as a result of professional advice to the purchasing company from, for example, lawyers, accountants, and bankers

bidding war FIN a competition between prospective buyers for the same stock or security

bid form FIN in the United States, a form containing details of an offer to underwrite municipal bonds

bid-offer spread FIN the difference between the highest price that a buyer is prepared to offer and the lowest price that a seller is prepared to accept

bid price FIN the price a stock exchange dealer will pay for a security or option contract

bid-to-cover ratio FIN a number that shows how many more people wanted to buy US Treasury bills than actually did buy them

bid up 1. FIN to bid for something merely to increase its price **2.** to make successive increases to the bid price for a security so that unopened orders do not remain unexecuted

Big Bang FIN radical changes to practices on the London Stock Exchange implemented in October 1986. Fixed commission charges were abolished, leading to an alteration in the structure of the market, and the right of member firms to act as market makers as well as agents was also abolished. *(slang)*

big bath FIN the practice of making a particular year's poor income statement look even worse by increasing expenses and selling assets. Subsequent years will then appear much better in comparison. *(slang)*

Big Board FIN the New York Stock Exchange *(slang)*. See also *Little Board*

Dictionary

Big Four *ANZ* FIN Australia's four largest banks: the Commonwealth Bank of Australia, Westpac Banking Corporation, National Australia Bank, and *ANZ* Bank

Big GAAP FIN the Generally Accepted Accounting Principles that apply to large companies *(slang)*

Big Three FIN before the merger of Chrysler and Mercedes in 1998, a phrase used to refer to the three largest car manufacturers in the United States: Chrysler, Ford, and General Motors

bilateral facility FIN a loan by one bank to one borrower

bilateral monopoly ECON a market in which there is a single seller and a single buyer

bilateral trade ECON trade between two countries which gives each other specific privileges such as favourable import quotas that are denied to other trading partners

bill broker FIN somebody who buys and sells promissory notes and bills of exchange

bill discount FIN the interest rate that the Bank of England charges banks for short-term loans. This establishes a *de facto* floor for the interest rate that banks charge their customers, usually a fraction above the discount rate.

bill discounting rate FIN the amount by which the price of a US Treasury bill is reduced to reflect expected changes in interest rates

billing cycle FIN the period of time, often one month, between successive requests for payment

bill of entry FIN a statement of the nature and value of goods to be imported or exported, prepared by the shipper and presented to a customs house

bill of exchange FIN **1.** an unconditional order in writing from one person (the drawer) to another (the drawee and signatory), requiring the drawee to pay on demand a sum to a specified person (the payee) or bearer. It is now usually used in overseas trade and the drawee may be a bank as opposed to an importer. The supplier or drawer usually submits the bill with the related shipping documents. It is then accepted by the drawee either as the agreed or implied method of payment. On receipt, the drawee either makes the required payment, or, if payment is to be made at a future date, indicates acceptance by signing it. **2.** a negotiable instrument, drawn by one party on another, for example, by a supplier of goods on a customer, who, by accepting (signing) the bill, acknowledges the debt, which may be payable immediately (a sight draft) or at some future date (a time draft). The holder of the bill can thereafter use an accepted time draft to pay a bill to a third party, or can discount it to raise cash.

bill of goods FIN a consignment of goods, or a statement of their nature and value

bill of lading FIN a document prepared by a consignor by which a carrier acknowledges the receipt of goods and which serves as a document of title to the goods consigned

bill of sale FIN a document confirming the transfer of goods or services from a seller to a buyer

binder *US* FIN a document that an insurance company issues to a customer to serve as a temporary insurance certificate until the issue of the policy itself. Also known as *cover note*

biological assets FIN farm animals and plants classified as assets. International Accounting Standards require that they are recorded on balance sheets at market value. Once they have been slaughtered or harvested, the assets become agricultural produce.

BiRiLiG FIN Bilanzrichtlliniengesetz: the 1985 German accounting directives law

BIS *abbr* FIN Bank for International Settlements: a bank that promotes co-operation between international central banks, provides facilities for international financial operations, and acts as agent or trustee in international financial settlements

BlackBerry® E-COM an electronic device that allows users to pick up their e-mail messages when they are away from their computer. Although very useful for employees who are often out of the office or those taking advantage of flexible working practices, some employees have found it hard to switch off from work during their leisure time and constantly check their BlackBerries for messages. This addictive aspect of the devices has led to their being referred to as 'Crackberries' by some commentators.

black economy ECON economic activity that is not declared for tax purposes and is usually carried out in exchange for cash

black market FIN, GEN an illegal market, usually for goods that are in short supply. Black market trading breaks government regulations or legislation and is particularly prevalent during times of shortage, such as rationing, or in industries that are very highly regulated, such as pharmaceuticals or armaments. Also known as *shadow market*

black market economy FIN **1.** a system of illegal trading in officially controlled goods **2.** an illicit secondary currency market that has rates markedly different from those in the official market

Black Monday FIN either of two Mondays, 28 October 1929 or 19 October 1987, that were marked by the largest stock market declines of the 20th century. Although both market crashes originated in the United States, they were immediately followed by similar market crashes around the world.

black money ECON money circulating in the black economy in payment for goods and services

Black Tuesday FIN 29 October 1929, when values of stocks fell precipitously

blanket bond FIN an insurance policy that covers a financial institution for losses caused by the actions of its employees

blended learning GEN the combination of traditional and online learning methods to maximise the effectiveness of training programmes. In blended learning the training programme is broken down into modules and the most appropriate delivery methods are selected for each and tailored to individual needs. The objective is to take advantage of the best features of each method while avoiding the drawbacks. A variety of media may be used, ranging from traditional workshops, classroom-based teaching, books and other support materials, computer-based training, CD-ROM, and e-learning.

blended rate FIN an interest rate charged by a lender that is between an old rate and a new one

blind entry FIN 1. a book-keeping entry that records a debit or credit but fails to show other essential information 2. *ANZ* a document issued by a supplier that stipulates the amount charged for goods or services as well as the amount of Goods and Services Tax (GST) payable

blind pool FIN a limited partnership in which the investment opportunities the general partner plans to pursue are not specified

blind trust FIN a trust that manages somebody's business interests, with contents that are unknown to the beneficiary. People assuming public office use such trusts to avoid conflicts of interest.

blocked account FIN a bank account from which funds cannot be withdrawn for any of a number of reasons, for example, bankruptcy proceedings, liquidation of a company, or government order when freezing foreign assets

blocked currency FIN a currency that people cannot easily trade for other currencies because of foreign exchange control

blocked funds FIN money that cannot be transferred from one place to another, usually because of exchange controls imposed by the government of the country in which the funds are held

block grant FIN money that the government gives to local authorities to fund local services

blockholder FIN an individual or institutional investor who holds a large number of shares of stock or a large monetary value of bonds in a given company

block investment *ANZ* FIN the purchase or holding of a large number of shares of stock or a large monetary value of bonds in a given company

block trade FIN the sale of a large round number of stocks or large amount of bonds

blog GEN a personal online journal that can be accessed by visitors to the host website. Blogs have developed massively in a very short space of time: according to Technorati.com, there are over 130 million blogs in existence in 81 language. Used initially to record the thoughts and views of private individuals, blogs are beginning to be used by corporate organisations as a means of communicating with staff and customers. Originally, blogs were mainly text-based, but now often feature photographs as well as other image, audio, and video files. Also called *weblog*

blowout *US* FIN the rapid sale of the whole of a new stock issue

Blue Book FIN national statistics of personal incomes and spending patterns in the United Kingdom, published annually

blue chip FIN a description of an equity or company which is of the highest quality and in which an investment would be considered as low risk with regard to both dividend payments and capital values

blue-chip stocks FIN ordinary shares in a company that is considered to be well established, highly successful, and reliable, and is traded on a stock market

Blue List *US* FIN a daily list of municipal bonds and their ratings, published by Standard & Poor

blue-sky law FIN a *US* state law that regulates investments to prevent investors from being defrauded

blue-sky securities FIN stocks and bonds that have no value, being worth the same as a piece of 'blue sky'

BO *abbr* FIN **branch office**

board dismissal FIN, GEN the dismissal and removal from power of an entire board or board of directors

Board of Currency Commissioners FIN the sole currency issuing authority in Singapore, established in 1967. *Abbr* **BCCS**

Board of Customs and Excise FIN see *Her Majesty's Revenue & Customs*

board of directors FIN, GEN the people selected to sit on an authoritative standing committee or governing body, taking responsibility for the management of an organisation. Members of the board of directors are officially chosen by shareholders, but in practice they are usually selected on the basis of the current board's recommendations. The board usually includes major shareholders as well as directors of the company. Also known as *board*

Board of Inland Revenue FIN see *Her Majesty's Revenue & Customs*

board of trustees FIN, GEN a committee or governing body that takes responsibility for managing – and holds in trust – funds, assets, or property belonging to others, for example, charitable or pension funds or assets

board seat FIN, GEN a position of membership of a board, especially a board of directors

board secretary FIN, GEN see *company secretary*

body corporate FIN an association, such as a company or institution, that is legally authorised to act as if it were one person

body of creditors FIN the creditors of a company or individual treated as a single creditor in dealing with the debtor

body of shareholders FIN the shareholders of a company treated as a single shareholder in dealing with the company

bogey *US* FIN a benchmark, often the Standard and Poor's 500 Index, against which unit trust managers or portfolio managers measure their performance *(slang)*

boilerplate *US* FIN, GEN a standard version of a contract that can be used interchangeably from contract to contract *(slang)*

bona fide FIN used to describe a sale or purchase that has been carried out in good faith, without collusion or fraud

bona vacantia FIN the goods of a person who has died intestate and has no traceable living relatives. In the United Kingdom, these goods become the property of the state.

bond FIN 1. a promise to repay with interest on specified dates money that an investor lends a company or government **2.** a certificate issued by a company or government that promises repayment of borrowed money at a set rate of interest on a particular date **3.** *ANZ* a sum of money paid as a deposit, especially on rented premises **4.** *S Africa* a mortgage bond

bond anticipation note FIN a loan that a government agency receives to provide capital that will be repaid from the proceeds of bonds that the agency will issue later. *Abbr* **BAN**

bond covenant FIN part of a bond contract whereby the lender promises not to do certain things, for example, borrow beyond a particular limit

bonded warehouse FIN a warehouse that holds goods awaiting duty or tax to be paid on them

bond equivalent yield FIN the interest rate that an investor would have to receive on a bond to profit as much as from investment in another type of security. Also known as *equivalent bond yield*

bond fund FIN a unit trust that invests in bonds

bondholder FIN an individual or institution owning bonds issued by a government or company. Bondholders are entitled to payments of the interest as due and the return of the principal when the bond matures.

bond indenture FIN a document that specifies the terms of a bond

bond indexing FIN the practice of investing in bonds in such a way as to match the yield of a designated index

bond quote FIN a statement of the current market price of a bond

bond swap FIN an exchange of some bonds for others, usually to gain a tax advantage or to diversify a portfolio

bond value FIN the value of an asset or liability as recorded in the accounts of an individual or organisation

bond-washing FIN the practice of selling a bond before its dividend is due and buying it back later in order to avoid paying tax

bond yield FIN the annual return on a bond (the rate of interest) expressed as a percentage of the current market price of the bond. Bonds can tie up investors' money for periods of up to 30 years, so knowing their yield is a critical investment consideration.

bonus HR a financial incentive given to employees in addition to their basic pay in the form of a one-off payment or as part of a bonus scheme

bonus dividend FIN a one-off extra dividend in addition to the usual twice-yearly payment

bonus issue FIN the capitalisation of the reserves of a company by the issue of additional shares to existing stakeholders, in proportion to their holdings. Such shares are normally fully paid up with no cash called for from the shareholders.

bonus shares FIN **1.** see *scrip issue* **2.** in the United Kingdom, extra shares paid by the government as a reward to founding shareholders who did not sell their initial holding within a certain number of years

book-building FIN the research done among potential institutional investors to determine the optimum offering price for a new issue of stock

book cost FIN the price paid for a stock, including any commissions

book entry FIN an accounting entry indicated in a record somewhere but not represented by any document

book inventory FIN the number of items in stock according to accounting records. This number can be validated only by a physical count of the items.

book-keeper FIN a person who is responsible for maintaining the financial records of a business

book-keeping FIN the activity or profession of recording the money received and spent by an individual, business, or organisation

book-keeping barter FIN the direct exchange of goods between two parties without the use of money as a medium, but using monetary measures to record the transaction

book of original entry FIN see *book of prime entry*

book of prime entry FIN a chronological record of a business's transactions arranged according to type, for example, cash or sales. The books are then used to generate entries in a double-entry book-keeping system. Also called book of original entry

books of account FIN collectively, the ledgers and journals used in the preparation of financial statements

book-to-bill ratio FIN the ratio of the value of orders that a company has received to the amount for which it has billed its customers

book transfer FIN a transfer of ownership of a security without physical transfer of any document that represents the instrument

book value FIN the value of a company's stock according to the company itself, which may differ considerably from the market value. Also known as *carrying amount, carrying value*

book value per share FIN the value of one share of a stock according to the company itself, which may differ considerably from the market value

boom ECON, FIN a period of time during which business activity increases significantly, with the result that demand for products grows, as do prices, salaries, and employment

BOP *abbr* ECON *balance of payments*

border tax adjustment FIN the application of a domestic tax on imported goods while exempting exported goods from the tax in an effort to make the exported goods' price competitive both nationally and internationally

borrowing costs FIN expenses, for example, interest payments, incurred from taking out a loan or any other form of borrowing. In the United States, such costs are included in the total cost of the asset whereas in the United Kingdom, and in International Accounting Standards, this is optional.

Boston Box FIN, GEN a model used for analysing a company's potential by plotting market share against growth rate. The Boston Box was conceived by the Boston Consulting Group in the 1970s to help in the process of assessing in which businesses a company should invest and of which it should divest itself. A business with a high market share and high growth rate is a star, and one with a low market share and low growth rate is a dog. A high market share with low growth rate is characteristic of a cash cow, which could yield significant but short-term gain, and a low market share coupled with high growth rate produces a question mark company, which offers a doubtful return on investment. To be useful, this model requires accurate assessment of a business's strengths and weaknesses, which may be difficult to obtain.

Boston matrix MKT a management technique developed by the Boston Consulting Group for assessing the long-term viability or profitability of products and market sectors. Categories include cash cows, dogs, stars, problem children, and question mark companies. See also *Boston Box*

BOT *abbr* ECON *balance of trade*

bottleneck FIN an activity within an organisation which has a lower capacity than preceding or subsequent activities, thereby limiting throughput. Bottlenecks are often the cause of a build-up of work in progress and of idle time.

bottom line 1. FIN the net profit or loss that a company makes at the end of a given period of time, used in the calculation of the earnings-per-share business ratio **2.** GEN work that produces net gain for an organisation

bottom-of-the-harbour scheme ANZ FIN a tax avoidance strategy that involves stripping a company of assets and then selling it a number of times so that it is hard to trace

bottom out FIN to reach the lowest level in the downward trend of the market price of securities or commodities before the price begins an upward trend again

bottom-up FIN relating to an approach to investing that seeks to identify individual companies that are fundamentally sound and whose shares will perform well regardless of general economic or industry-group trends

bottom-up budgeting FIN see *participative budgeting*

bought-in goods FIN, OPS components and sub-assemblies that are purchased from an outside supplier instead of being made within the organisation

bounce FIN to refuse payment of a cheque because the account for which it is written holds insufficient money *(slang)* Also known as *dishonour*

boundaryless organisation GEN a model that views organisations as having permeable boundaries. An organisation has external boundaries

that separate it from its suppliers and customers, and internal boundaries that provide demarcation to departments. This rigidity is removed in boundaryless organisations, where the aim is to develop greater flexibility and responsiveness to change and to facilitate the free exchange of information and ideas. The boundaryless organisation behaves more like an organism encouraging better integration between departments and closer partnerships with suppliers and customers. The concept was developed at General Electric and described in the book *The Boundaryless Organization: Breaking the Chains of Organizational Structure* by Ron Ashkenas and others, which was published in 1995.

bourse FIN a European stock exchange, especially the one in Paris

boutique investment house FIN see *niche player*

box spread FIN an arbitrage strategy that eliminates risk by buying and selling the same thing

bracket creep *US* FIN the way in which a gradual increase in income moves somebody into a higher tax bracket

Brady bond FIN a bond issued by an emerging nation that has US Treasury bonds as collateral. It is named after Nicholas Brady, banking reformer and former Secretary of the Treasury.

brainsketching GEN a technique for idea generation and problem solving in groups that uses sketching as the primary means of recording ideas. Individuals start to sketch their ideas on a sheet. After a few minutes these are exchanged and they continue on a sheet already started by someone else. These sheets are then placed on a flip chart and used as the inspiration for the generation of new ideas. Brainstorming is a related technique.

branch accounts FIN the books of account or financial statements for the component parts of a business, especially those that are located in a different region or country from the main enterprise

branch office FIN a bank or other financial institution that is part of a larger group and is located in a different geographical area from the parent organisation. *Abbr* **BO**

branch tax FIN a South African tax imposed on non-resident companies that register a branch rather than a separate company

brand architecture MKT the naming and structuring of brands within the product portfolio of an organisation. Brand architectures may be monolithic (the corporate name is used on all products and services), endorsed (sub-brands are linked to the corporate brand by means of either a verbal or visual endorsement), or freestanding (each product or service is individually branded for its target market). Brand architecture is influenced by the overall brand management and brand positioning strategy of the organisation.

breadth-of-market theory FIN the theory that the health of a market is measured by the relative volume of items traded that are going up or down in price

breakeven analysis FIN, GEN a method for determining the point at which fixed and variable production costs are equalled by sales revenue and where neither a profit nor a loss is made. Usually illustrated graphically through the use of a breakeven chart, breakeven analysis can be used to aid decision-making, set product prices, and determine the effects of changes in production or sales volume on costs and profits.

breakeven chart FIN a chart which indicates approximate profit or loss at different levels of sales volume within a limited range

breakeven point FIN the point or level of financial activity at which expenditure equals income, or the value of an investment equals its cost, so that the result is neither a profit nor a loss. *Abbr* **BEP**

breakout FIN a rise in a security's price above its previous highest price, or a drop below its former lowest price, taken by technical analysts to signal a continuing move in that direction

break-up value FIN the combined market value of a firm's assets if each were sold separately, as contrasted with selling the firm as an ongoing business. Analysts look for companies with a large break-up value relative to their market value to identify potential takeover targets.

Bretton Woods ECON an agreement signed at a conference at Bretton Woods in the United States in July 1944 that set up the IMF and the IBRD

bridge financing FIN borrowing that the borrower expects to repay with the proceeds of later, larger loans. See also *takeout financing*

bridge loan *US* FIN = *bridging loan*

bridging FIN the obtaining of a short-term loan to provide a continuing source of financing in anticipation of receiving an intermediate- or long-term loan. Bridging is routinely employed to finance the purchase or construction of a new building or property until an old one is sold.

bridging loan FIN a temporary loan providing funds until further money is received, for example, for buying one property while trying to sell another. US term bridge loan

bring forward FIN to carry a sum from one column or page to the next

British Accounting Association FIN an organisation whose aim is to promote accounting education and research in the United Kingdom. The BAA has more than 800 members, a large proportion of which work in higher education institutions. Founded in 1947, the BAA also organises conferences and publishes *The British Accounting Review*. *Abbr* **BAA**

British Bankers' Association FIN a not-for-profit trading association for the financial services and banking industry. The Association was established in 1919 and has 295 members as well as numerous associate members. It aims to address a variety of industry issues, including the development and revision of the voluntary Banking Code, which aims to set standards of best practice. *Abbr* **BBA**

British Chambers of Commerce FIN a national network of accredited chambers of commerce. The BCC represents over more than 135,000 businesses in the United Kingdom. *Abbr* **BCC**

brokerage FIN **1.** a company whose business is buying and selling stocks and bonds for its clients. Also known

as *brokerage firm, brokerage house* **2.** the business of being a broker **3.** a fee paid to somebody who acts as a financial agent for somebody else

brokerage firm or **brokerage house** FIN see *brokerage (sense 1)*

brokered market FIN a market in which brokers bring buyers and sellers together

broker loan rate FIN the interest rate that banks charge brokers on money that they lend for purchases on margin

B/S *abbr* FIN *balance sheet*

B share *ANZ* FIN a share in a unit trust that has no front-end sales charge but carries a redemption fee, or back-end load, payable only if the share is redeemed. This load, called a CDSC, or contingent deferred sales charge, declines every year until it disappears, usually after six years.

BTI *abbr* FIN *Business Times Industrial index*

bubble economy ECON an unstable boom based on speculation in shares, often followed by a financial crash. This happened, for example, in the 1630s in the Netherlands and in the 1720s in England.

bucket shop *US* FIN a firm of brokers or dealers that sells shares of questionable value

bucket trading FIN an illegal practice in which a stockbroker accepts a customer's order but does not execute the transaction until it is financially advantageous to the broker but at the customer's expense

budget FIN a quantitative statement, for a defined period of time, which may include planned revenues, expenses, assets, liabilities, and cash flows. A budget provides a focus for an organisation, as it aids the co-ordination of activities, allocation of resources, and direction of activity, and facilitates control. Planning is achieved by means of a fixed master budget, whereas control is generally exercised through the comparison of actual costs with a flexible budget.

Budget FIN the UK Government's annual spending plan, which is announced to the House of Commons by the Chancellor of the Exchequer. The Government is legally obliged to present economic forecasts twice a year, and since the 1997 gen-

eral election the main Budget has been presented in the Spring while a Pre-Budget Report is given in the Autumn. This outlines government spending plans prior to the main Budget, and also reports on progress since the last Budget.

budget account FIN a bank account set up to control a person's regular expenditure, for example, the payment of insurance premiums, mortgage, utilities, or telephone bills. The annual expenditure for each item is paid into the account in equal monthly instalments, bills being paid from the budget account as they become due.

budgetary FIN relating to a detailed plan of financial operations, with estimates of both revenue and expenditure for a specific future period

budgetary control FIN the establishment of budgets relating the responsibilities of executives to the requirements of a policy, and the continuous comparison of actual with budgeted results, either to secure by individual action the objectives of that policy or to provide a basis for its revision. *Abbr* **BC**

budget committee FIN the group within an organisation responsible for drawing up budgets that meet departmental requirements, ensuring they comply with policy, and then submitting them to the board of directors

budget deficit FIN the extent by which expenditure exceeds revenue. Also known as *deficit*

budget director FIN the person in an organisation who is responsible for running the budget system

budgeted capacity FIN an organisation's available output level for a budget period according to the budget. It may be expressed in different ways, for example, in machine hours or standard hours.

budgeted revenue FIN the income that an organisation expects to receive in a budget period according to the budget

budget management FIN the comparison of actual financial results with the estimated expenditures and revenues for the given time period of a budget and the taking of corrective action as necessary

budget surplus FIN the extent by which revenue exceeds expenditure. Also known as *surplus*

buffer inventory FIN, OPS the products or supplies of an organisation maintained on hand or in transit to stabilise variations in supply, demand, production, or lead time

buffer stock FIN a stock of materials, or of work in progress, maintained in order to protect user departments from the effect of possible interruptions to supply

building society FIN a financial institution that offers interest-bearing savings accounts, the deposits being reinvested by the society in long-term loans, primarily mortgage loans for the purchase of property

bull FIN somebody who anticipates favourable business conditions, especially somebody who buys particular stocks or commodities in anticipation that their prices will rise, often with the expectation of selling them at a large profit at a later time. See also *bear*

bullet loan FIN a loan that involves specified payments of interest until maturity, when the principal is repaid

bullish FIN conducive to or characterised by buying stocks or commodities in anticipation of rising prices. See also *bearish*

bull market FIN a market in which prices are rising and in which a dealer is more likely to be a buyer than a seller. See also *bear market*

bull spread FIN a combination of purchases and sales of options for the same commodity or stock, intended to produce a profit when the price rises. See also *bear spread*

bundle FIN a package of financial products or services offered to a customer

buoyant market FIN a market which sees plenty of trading activity and on which prices are rising, rather than falling

Business Accounting Deliberation Council FIN in Japan, a committee controlled by the Ministry of Finance that is responsible for drawing up regulations regarding the consolidated financial statements of listed companies

Business Activity Statement FIN a standard document used in Australia to report the amount of GST and other taxes paid and collected by a business. *Abbr* **BAS**

business cluster FIN, GEN a group of small firms from similar industries that team up and act as one body. Creating a business cluster enables firms to enjoy economies of scale usually only available to bigger competitors. Marketing costs can be shared and goods can be bought more cheaply. There are also networking advantages, in which small firms can share experiences and discuss business strategies.

business combinations *US* FIN acquisitions or mergers involving two or more enterprises

Business Council of Australia FIN, GEN a national association of chief executives, designed as a forum for the discussion of matters pertaining to business leadership in Australia. *Abbr* **BCA**

business cycle ECON a regular pattern of fluctuation in national income, moving from upturn to downturn in about five years

business interruption insurance FIN a policy indemnifying an organisation for loss of profits and continuing fixed expenses when some insurable disaster, for example, a fire, causes the organisation to stop or reduce its activities. Also known as *consequential loss policy*

business name FIN in the United Kingdom, the legal term for the name under which an organisation operates

business plan FIN, GEN a document describing the current activities of a business, setting out its aims and objectives and how they are to be achieved over a set period of time. A business plan may cover the activities of an organisation or a group of companies, or it may deal with a single department within the organisation. In the former case, it is sometimes referred to as a corporate plan. The sections of a business plan usually include a market analysis describing the target market, customers, and competitors, an operations plan describing how products and services will be developed and produced, and a financial section providing profit, budget, and cash-flow forecasts, annual accounts, and financial requirements. Businesses may use a business plan internally as a framework for implementing strategy and improving performance or externally to attract investment or raise capital for development plans. A business plan may form part of the overall planning process, or corporate planning, within an organisation and be used for the implementation of corporate strategy.

business property relief FIN in the United Kingdom, a reduction in the amount liable to inheritance tax on certain types of business property

business rate FIN in the United Kingdom, a tax on businesses calculated on the value of the property occupied. Although the rate of tax is set by central government, the tax is collected by the local authority.

business risk FIN the uncertainty associated with the unique circumstances of a particular company, for example, the introduction of a superior technology, as it might affect the price of that company's securities

business segment FIN a distinguishable part of a business or enterprise that is subject to a different set of risks and returns from any other part. Listed companies are required to declare in their annual reports certain information, for example, sales, profits, and assets, for each segment of an enterprise.

business strategy FIN a long-term approach to implementing a firm's business plans to achieve its business objectives

Business Times Industrial index FIN an index of 40 Singapore and Malaysian shares. *Abbr* **BTI**

business transfer relief FIN the tax advantage gained when selling a business for shares of stock in the company that buys it

business unit FIN a part of an organisation that operates as a distinct function, department, division, or stand-alone business. Business units are usually treated as a separate profit centre within the overall, owning business.

bust up FIN to split up a company or a division of a company into smaller units

bust-up proxy proposal FIN an overture to a company's shareholders for a leveraged buy-out in which the acquirer will sell some of the company's assets in order to repay the debt used to finance the takeover

butterfly spread FIN a complex option strategy based on simultaneously purchasing and selling calls at different exercise prices and maturity dates, the profit being the premium collected when the options are sold. Such a strategy is most profitable when the price of the underlying security is relatively stable.

buy and hold FIN an investment strategy based on retaining securities for a long time

buy and write FIN an investment strategy involving buying stock and selling options to eliminate the possibility of loss if the value of the stock goes down

buyback 1. FIN an arrangement whereby a company buys its own shares on the stock market. Also known as share buyback 2. ECON, FIN the repurchase of bonds or shares, as agreed by contract

buy-down FIN the payment of principal amounts that reduce the monthly payments due on a mortgage

buyer FIN 1. somebody who is in the process of buying something or who intends to buy something 2. somebody whose job is to choose and buy goods, merchandise, services, or media time or space for a company, factory, shop, or advertiser

buyer's market FIN a situation in which supply exceeds demand, prices are relatively low, and buyers therefore have an advantage

buy in FIN to buy stock in a company so as to have a controlling interest. This is often done by or for executives from outside the company.

buying economies of scale FIN a reduction in the cost of purchasing raw materials and components or of borrowing money due to the increased size of the purchase

buying manager FIN, OPS see *purchasing manager*

buy on close FIN a purchase at the end of the trading day

buy on opening FIN a purchase at the beginning of the trading day

buy out FIN, GEN 1. to purchase the entire stock of, or controlling financial interest in, a company 2. to pay somebody to relinquish his or her interest in a property or other enterprise

buy-out 1. FIN, GEN the purchase and takeover of an ongoing business. It is more formally known as an acquisition (see *merger*). If a business is purchased by managers or staff, it is known as a management buy-out. 2. FIN, GEN the purchase of somebody else's entire stock ownership in a firm. It is more formally known as an acquisition (see *merger*). 3. FIN, HR an option to transfer benefits of an occupational pension scheme on leaving a company

buy stop order FIN an order to buy stock when its price reaches a specified level

buzz marketing MKT see *word of mouth marketing*

BV *abbr* FIN besloten venootschap: the Dutch term for a limited liability company

by-bidder FIN somebody who bids at an auction solely to raise the price for the seller

bylaws *US* FIN rules governing the internal running of a corporation, such as the number of meetings, the appointment of officers, and so on. Also known as *articles of association*

bypass trust FIN a trust that leaves money in a will in trust to people other than the prime beneficiary in order to gain tax advantage

CA *abbr* FIN chartered accountant *or* certified accountant

c/a *abbr* FIN current account

C/A *abbr* FIN capital account

cage *US* FIN the part of a broking firm where the paperwork involved in the buying and selling of shares is processed (*slang*)

call FIN 1. an option to buy stock. Also known as *call option* 2. a request made to the holders of partly paid-up share capital for the payment of a predetermined sum due on the share capital, under the terms of the original subscription agreement. Failure on the part of the shareholder to pay a call may result in the forfeiture of the relevant holding of partly paid shares. Also known as *call up*

callable FIN a financial instrument with a call provision in its indenture

callable bond FIN a bond that may be bought back by the issuer prior to its maturity. Also known as *redeemable bond*

called-up share capital FIN the amount which a company has required shareholders to pay on shares issued

call money FIN money that brokers use for their own purchases or to help their customers to buy on margin

call option FIN see *call* (sense 1)

call payment FIN an amount that a company demands in partial payment for stock such as a rights issue that is not paid for at one time

call provision FIN a clause in an indenture that lets the issuer of a bond redeem it before the date of its maturity

call up FIN see *call* (sense 2)

Canadian Institute of Chartered Accountants FIN in Canada, the principal professional accountancy body that is responsible for setting accounting standards. *Abbr* **CICA**

cancellation price FIN the lowest value possible in any one day of a unit trust

cap FIN an upper limit such as on a rate of interest for a loan

CAPA *abbr* FIN Confederation of Asian and Pacific Accountants: an umbrella organisation for a number of Asia-Pacific accountancy bodies

capacity usage variance FIN the difference in gain or loss in a given period compared to budgeted expectations, caused because the hours worked were longer or shorter than planned

capacity utilisation 1. OPS a measure of the plant and equipment of a company or an industry that is actually being used to produce goods or services. Capacity utilisation is usually measured over a specific period of time, for example, the average for a month, or at a given point in time. It can be expressed as a ratio, where utilisation = actual output divided by design capacity. This measure is used in both capacity planning and capacity requirements planning processes. 2. ECON the output of an economy, firm, or plant divided by its output when working at full capacity

Caparo case FIN in England, a court decision taken by the House of Lords in 1990 that auditors owe a duty of care to present (not prospective) shareholders as a body but not as individuals

CAPEX *abbr* FIN capital expenditure

capital FIN money that can be invested by an individual or organisation in order to make a profit

capital account FIN the sum of a company's capital at a particular time. *Abbr* **C/A**

capital allowances FIN in the United Kingdom and Ireland, an allowance against income or corporation tax available to businesses or sole traders who have purchased plant and machinery for business use. The rates are set annually and vary according to the type of fixed asset purchased, for example, whether it is machinery or buildings. This system effectively removes subjectivity from the calculation of depreciation for tax purposes.

capital appreciation FIN the increase in a company's or individual's wealth

capital appreciation fund FIN a unit trust that aims to increase the value of its holdings without regard to the provision of income to its owners

capital asset FIN property that a company owns and uses but that the company does not buy or sell as part of its regular trade

capital asset pricing model FIN a theory which predicts that the expected risk premium for an individual stock will be proportional to its beta, such that expected risk premium on a stock = beta × expected risk premium in the market. Risk premium is defined as the expected incremental return for making a risky investment rather than a safe one. *Abbr* **CAPM**

capital budget FIN a subsection of a company's master budget that deals with expected capital expenditure within a defined period. Also known as *capital expenditure budget, capital investment budget*

capital budgeting FIN the process concerned with decision-making with respect to the following issues: the choice of specific investment projects; the total amount of capital expenditure to commit; and the method of financing the investment portfolio

capital consumption FIN in a given period, the total depreciation of a national economy's fixed assets, based on replacement costs

capital controls ECON regulations placed by a government on the amount of capital residents may hold

capital cost allowance FIN a tax advantage in Canada for the depreciation in value of capital assets

capital costs FIN expenses on the purchase of fixed assets

capital deepening ECON the process whereby increasingly capital-intensive production results when a country's capital stock increases but the numbers employed fall or remain constant

capital expenditure FIN the cost of acquiring, producing, or enhancing fixed assets. *Abbr* **CAPEX**. Also known as *capital investment*

capital expenditure budget FIN see *capital budget*

capital expenditure proposal FIN a formal request for authority to undertake capital expenditure. This is usually supported by the case for expenditure in accordance with capital investment appraisal criteria. Levels of authority must be clearly defined and the reporting structure of actual expenditure must be to the equivalent authority level.

capital flight FIN the transfer of large sums of money between countries to seek higher rates of return or to escape a political or economic disturbance

capital formation ECON the process of adding to the stock of a country's real capital by investment in fixed assets

capital funding planning FIN the process of selecting suitable funds to finance long-term assets and working capital

capital gain FIN the financial gain made upon the disposal of an asset. The gain is the difference between the cost of its acquisition and the net proceeds upon its sale.

capital gains distribution FIN a sum of money that, for example, a unit trust pays to its owners in proportion to the owners' share of the organisation's capital gains for the year

capital gains reserve FIN a tax advantage in Canada for money not yet received in payment for something that has been sold

capital gearing FIN the amount of fixed-cost debt that a company has for each of its ordinary shares

capital goods ECON stocks of physical or financial assets that are capable of generating income

capital growth FIN an increase in the value of assets in a fund, or of the value of shares

capital inflow ECON the amount of capital that flows into an economy from services rendered abroad

capital instruments FIN the means that an organisation uses to raise finance, for example, the issue of shares or debentures

capital-intensive FIN using a greater proportion of capital, as opposed to labour

capital investment FIN see *capital expenditure*

capital investment budget FIN see *capital budget*

capitalisation FIN 1. the amount of money invested in a company, or the worth of the bonds and stocks of a company 2. the conversion of a company's reserves into capital through a scrip issue

capitalisation issue FIN a proportional issue of free shares to existing shareholders. US term **stock split**

capitalisation rate FIN the rate at which a company's reserves are converted into capital by way of a capitalisation issue

capitalisation ratio FIN the proportion of a company's value represented by debt, stock, assets, and other items. By comparing debt to total capitalisation, these ratios provide a glimpse of a company's long-term stability and ability to withstand losses and business downturns.

capitalise FIN 1. to provide capital for a business 2. to include money spent on the purchase of an asset as an element in a balance sheet

capitalism ECON an economic and social system in which individuals can maximise profits because they own the means of production

Dictionary

capitalist FIN an investor of capital in a business

capital levy FIN a tax on fixed assets or property

capital loss FIN a loss made through selling a capital asset for less than its market price

capital maintenance concept FIN a concept used to determine the definition of profit, that provides the basis for different systems of inflation accounting

capital market FIN a financial market dealing with securities that have a life of more than one year

capital project management FIN, GEN control of a project that involves expenditure of an organisation's monetary resources for the purpose of creating capacity for production. Capital project management often involves the organisation of major construction or engineering work. Capital projects are usually large scale, complex, need to be completed quickly, and involve capital investment. Different techniques have evolved for capital project management from those used for normal project management, including methods for managing the complexity of such projects and for analysing return on investment afterwards.

capital property FIN under Canadian tax law, assets that can depreciate in value or be sold for a capital gain or loss

capital ratio FIN a company's income expressed as a fraction of its tangible assets

capital rationing FIN 1. the restriction of new investment by a company 2. a restriction on an organisation's ability to invest capital funds, caused by an internal budget ceiling being imposed by management (soft capital rationing), or by external limitations being applied to the company, as when additional borrowed funds cannot be obtained (hard capital rationing)

capital reduction FIN the retirement or redemption of capital funds by a company

capital reserves FIN a former name for undistributable reserves

capital resource planning FIN the process of evaluating and selecting long-term assets to meet strategies

capital stock ECON, FIN the stock authorised by a company's charter, representing no ownership rights

capital structure FIN the relative proportions of equity capital and debt capital in a company's balance sheet

capital sum FIN a lump sum of money that an insurer pays, for example, on the death of the insured person

capital surplus FIN the value of all of the stock in a company that exceeds the par value of the stock

capital tax FIN a tax levied on the capital owned by a company, rather than on its spending

capital transactions FIN transactions affecting non-current items such as fixed assets, long-term debt, or share capital, rather than revenue transactions

capital transfer tax FIN in the United Kingdom, a tax on the transfer of assets that was replaced in 1986 by inheritance tax

capital turnover FIN the value of annual sales as a multiple of the value of the company's stock

capital widening ECON the process whereby capital-intensive production is reduced as a result of an increase in a country's capital stock and the number of people employed

CAPM *abbr* FIN capital asset pricing model

capped rate FIN an interest rate on a loan that may change, but cannot be greater than an amount fixed at the time when the loan is taken out by a borrower

captive finance company FIN an organisation that provides credit and is owned or controlled by a commercial or manufacturing company, for example, a retailer that owns its store card operation or a car manufacturer that owns a company for financing the vehicles it produces

captive insurance company FIN an insurance company that has been established by a parent company to underwrite all its insurance risks and those of its subsidiaries. The benefit is that the premiums paid do not leave the organisation. Many captive insurance companies are established offshore for tax purposes.

cardholder E-COM, FIN an individual or company that has an active credit card account with an issuer with which transactions can be initiated

card-issuing bank E-COM, FIN see *issuer*

card-not-present merchant account E-COM an account that permits e-merchants to process credit card transactions without the purchaser being physically present for the transaction

caring economy ECON an economy based on amicable and helpful relationships between businesses and people

carriage inwards FIN delivery expenses incurred through the purchase of goods

carriage outwards FIN delivery expenses incurred through the sale of goods

carrying amount FIN see *book value*

carrying cost FIN any expense associated with holding stock for a given period, for example, from the time of delivery to the time of dispatch. Carrying costs will include storage and insurance.

carrying value FIN see *book value*

carry-over FIN the stock of a commodity held at the beginning of a new financial year

cartel FIN an alliance of business companies formed to control production, competition, and prices

cash 1. FIN to exchange a cheque for cash 2. ECON, FIN money in the form of banknotes and coins that are legal tender. This includes cash in hand, deposits repayable on demand with any bank or other financial institution, and deposits denominated in foreign currencies.

cash account FIN 1. a brokerage account that permits no buying on margin 2. a record of receipts and payments of cash, cheques, or other forms of money transfer

cash accounting FIN 1. an accounting method in which receipts and expenses are recorded in the accounting books in the period when they actually occur. See also *accrual concept* 2. in the United Kingdom, a system for Value Added Tax that enables the taxpayer to account for tax paid and received during a given period, thus allowing automatic relief for bad debts

cash advance FIN a loan on a credit card account

cash at bank FIN the total amount of money held at the bank by an individual or company

cash available to invest FIN the amount, including cash on account and balances due soon for outstanding transactions, that a client has available for investment with a broker

cashback FIN, MKT a sales promotion technique offering customers a cash refund after they buy a product

cash basis FIN the book-keeping practice of accounting for money only when it is actually received or spent

cash bonus FIN an unscheduled dividend that a company declares because of unexpected income

cashbook FIN a book in which all cash payments and receipts are recorded. In a double-entry book-keeping system, the balance at the end of a given period is included in the trial balance and then transferred to the balance sheet itself.

cash budget FIN a detailed budget of estimated cash inflows and outflows incorporating both revenue and capital items. Also known as *cash-flow projection*

cash contract FIN a contract for actual delivery of a commodity

cash conversion cycle FIN the time between the acquisition of a raw material and the receipt of payment for the finished product. Also known as *cash cycle*

cash cow FIN a product characterised by a high market share but low sales growth, whose function is seen as generating cash for use elsewhere within the organisation

cash crop ECON a crop, for example, tobacco, that can be sold for cash, usually by a developing country

cash cycle FIN see *cash conversion cycle*

cash deficiency agreement FIN a commitment to supply whatever additional cash is needed to complete the financing of a project

cash discount FIN a discount offered to a customer who pays for goods or

services with cash, or who pays an invoice within a particular period

cash dividend FIN a share of a company's current earnings or accumulated profits distributed to shareholders

cash equivalents FIN short-term investments that can be converted into cash immediately and that are subject to only a limited risk. There is usually a limit on their duration, for example, three months.

cash float FIN notes and coins held by a retailer for the purpose of supplying customers with change

cash flow FIN the movement through an organisation of money that is generated by its own operations, as opposed to borrowing. It is the money that a business actually receives from sales (the cash inflow) and the money that it pays out (the cash outflow).

cash-flow coverage ratio FIN the ratio of income to cash obligations

cash flow per common share FIN the amount of cash that a company has for each of its ordinary shares

cash-flow risk FIN the risk that a company's available cash will not be sufficient to meet its financial obligations

cash-flow projection FIN see *cash budget*

cash-flow statement FIN a record of a company's cash inflows and cash outflows over a specific period of time, typically a year. It reports funds on hand at the beginning of the period, funds received, funds spent, and funds remaining at the end of the period. Cash flows are divided into three categories: cash from operations; cash-investment activities; and cash-financing activities. Companies with holdings in foreign currencies use a fourth classification: effects of changes in currency rates on cash.

cash-generating unit FIN the smallest identifiable group of assets that generates cash inflows and outflows that can be measured

cashless pay HR the payment of a weekly or monthly wage through the electronic transfer of funds directly into the bank account of an employee

cashless society ECON a society in which all bills and debits are paid by electronic money media, for example, bank and credit cards, direct debits, and online payments

cash loan company *S Africa* FIN a microlending business that provides short-term loans without collateral, usually at high interest rates

cash offer FIN an offer to buy a company for cash rather than for stock

cash payments journal FIN a chronological record of all the payments that have been made from a company's bank account

cash ratio FIN the ratio of a company's liquid assets such as cash and securities divided by total liabilities. Also known as *liquidity ratio*

cash receipts journal FIN a chronological record of all the receipts that have been paid into a company's bank account

cash sale FIN a sale in which payment is made immediately in cash rather than put on credit

cash settlement FIN 1. an immediate payment on an options contract without waiting for expiry of the normal, usually five-day, settlement period 2. the completion of a transaction by paying for securities

cash surrender value FIN the amount of money that an insurance company will pay to terminate a policy at a particular time if the policy does not continue until its normal expiry date

category killer *US* FIN a major organisation that puts out of business smaller or more specialised companies in a given field by offering goods or services at a lower price, or by using its brand to attract more consumer interest *(slang)*

cats and dogs *US* FIN shares with dubious sale histories *(slang)*

cause and effect diagram FIN a diagram that aids the generation and sorting of the potential causes of variation in an activity or process

CBI *abbr* FIN Confederation of British Industry

CC *abbr S Africa* FIN close corporation

CCA *abbr* FIN current-cost accounting

ccc *abbr* FIN cwmni cyfyngedig cyhoeddus: the Welsh term for a public limited company

Dictionary

CD *abbr* FIN certificate of deposit

CDSC *abbr* FIN contingent deferred sales charge

CEIC *abbr* FIN closed-end investment company

central bank ECON the bank of a country that controls its credit system and its money supply

centralisation FIN, GEN the gathering together, at a corporate headquarters, of specialist functions such as finance, personnel, centralised purchasing, and information technology. Centralisation is usually undertaken in order to effect economies of scale and to standardise operating procedures throughout the organisation. Centralised management can become cumbersome and inefficient, and may produce communications problems. Some organisations have shifted towards decentralisation to try to avoid this.

centralised purchasing FIN, OPS the control by a central department of all the purchasing undertaken within an organisation. In a large organisation centralised purchasing is often located in the headquarters. Centralisation has the advantages of reducing duplication of effort, pooling volume purchases for discounts, enabling more effective inventory control, consolidating transport loads to achieve lower costs, increasing skills development in purchasing personnel, and enhancing relationships with suppliers.

centre FIN a department, area, or function to which costs and/or revenues are charged

certificate of deposit FIN a negotiable instrument which provides evidence of a fixed-term deposit with a bank. Maturity is normally within 90 days, but can be longer. *Abbr* **CD**

certificate of incorporation FIN in the United Kingdom, a written statement by the Registrar of Companies confirming that a new company has fulfilled the necessary legal requirements for incorporation and is now legally constituted

certificate to commence business FIN in the United Kingdom, a written statement issued by the Registrar of Companies confirming that a public limited company has fulfilled the necessary legal requirements regarding its authorised minimum share capital

certified accountant FIN an accountant trained in industry, the public service, or in the offices of practising accountants, who is a member of the Association of Chartered Certified Accountants. Although they are not chartered accountants, they fulfil much the same role and they are qualified to audit company records. *Abbr* **CA**

certified public accountant *US* FIN an accountant trained in industry, the public service, or in the offices of practising accountants, who is a member of the American Institute of Certified Public Accountants. Although they are not chartered accountants, they fulfil much the same role and they are qualified to audit company records. *Abbr* **CPA**

cessation FIN the discontinuation of a business for tax purposes or of its trading on the stock market

CGT *abbr* FIN capital gains tax

CH *abbr* FIN Companies House

chairman's report or **chairman's statement** FIN a statement included in the annual report of most large companies in which the chair of the board of directors gives an often favourable overview of the company's performance and prospects

chamber of commerce FIN an organisation of local businesspeople who work together to promote trade in their area and protect common interests. The British Chambers of Commerce acts as a national association for accredited members.

Chancellor of the Exchequer FIN the United Kingdom's chief finance minister, based at HM Treasury in London. The office of Chancellor dates back to the 13th century. Some of the most famous names in British politics have served in this very senior government position, including Gladstone and Lloyd George.

changeover time FIN the period required to change a workstation from a state of readiness for one operation to a state of readiness for another

channel stuffing FIN the artificial boosting of sales at the end of a financial year by offering distributors and dealers incentives to buy a greater quantity of goods than they actually need *(slang)*

CHAPS *abbr* FIN Clearing House Automated Payment System: a method for the rapid electronic transfer of funds between participating banks on behalf of large commercial customers, where transfers tend to be of significant value

Chapter 11 FIN the US Bankruptcy Reform Act (1978) that entitles enterprises experiencing financial difficulties to apply for protection from creditors and thus have an opportunity to avoid bankruptcy

charge FIN a legal interest in land or property created in favour of a creditor to ensure that the amount owing is paid off

chargeable asset FIN an asset which will produce a capital gain when sold. Assets which are not chargeable include family homes, cars, and some types of investments, such as government stocks.

chargeable gain FIN a profit from the sale of an asset that is subject to capital gains tax

chargeable transfer FIN in the United Kingdom, gifts that are liable to inheritance tax. Under UK legislation, individuals may gift assets to a certain value during their lifetime without incurring any liability to inheritance tax. These are regular transfers out of income that do not affect the donor's standard of living. Additionally, individuals may transfer up to £3,000 a year out of capital. If this exemption is not used in one year, or is only partially used, then the unused allowance may be carried forward to the next year providing the full exemption is then used. Each person may also make small annual gifts of up to £250 per donee. Additionally a parent may give up to £5,000 on the occasion of an offspring's marriage, while a grandparent or more remote ancestor may give up to £2,500, and any other person up to £1,000. Other outright gifts during a lifetime to an individual, and certain types of trust, are known as potentially exempt transfers: there is no inheritance tax to be paid on these at the time of the gift, but a liability arises if the donor dies within seven years, with that liability decreasing the longer the donor survives. If the donor dies within seven years of the gift, then potentially exempt transfers become chargeable transfers for inheritance tax purposes.

charge account FIN a facility with a retailer that enables the customer to buy goods or services on credit rather than pay in cash. The customer may be required to settle the account within a month to avoid incurring interest on the credit. Also known as *credit account*

charge and discharge accounting FIN formerly, a book-keeping system in which a person charges himself or herself with receipts and credits himself or herself with payments. This system was used extensively in medieval times before the advent of double-entry book-keeping.

chargee FIN **1.** a person who holds a charge over a property **2.** a person who has the right to force a debtor to pay

charitable contribution FIN a donation by a company to a charity

charity accounts FIN the accounting records of a charitable institution, that include a statement of financial activities rather than a profit and loss account. In the United Kingdom, the accounts should conform to the requirements stipulated in the Charities Act (1993).

chartered accountant FIN in the United Kingdom, a qualified professional accountant who is a member of an Institute of Chartered Accountants. Chartered accountants are qualified to audit company accounts and some hold management positions in companies. *Abbr* CA

Chartered Association of Certified Accountants FIN the former name of the Association of Chartered Certified Accountants

chartered company or **chartered entity** FIN in the United Kingdom, an organisation formed by the grant of a royal charter. The charter authorises the entity to operate and states the powers specifically granted.

Chartered Institute of Management Accountants FIN see *CIMA*

Chartered Institute of Public Finance and Accountancy FIN see *CIPFA*

Chartered Institute of Taxation FIN in the United Kingdom, an organisation for professionals in the field of taxation, formerly the Institute of Taxation

charting FIN the use of charts to analyse stock market trends and to forecast future rises or falls

chartist FIN an analyst who studies past stock market trends, the movement of share prices, and changes in the accounting ratios of individual companies. The chartist's philosophy is that history repeats itself: using charts and graphs, he or she uses past trends and repetitive patterns to forecast the future. Although the chartist approach is considered narrower than that of a traditional analyst, it nevertheless has a good following.

cheap money FIN low interest rates, used as a government strategy to stimulate an economy either at the initial signs of, or during, a recession

check US FIN = cheque

cheque FIN a bill of exchange drawn on a banker, payable on demand. US term *check*

cheque register FIN a control record of cheques issued or received

Chinese wall FIN, GEN the procedures enforced within a securities firm to prevent the exchange of confidential information between the firm's departments so as to avoid the illegal use of inside information

churn FIN to encourage an investor to change stock frequently because the broker is paid every time there is a change in the investor's portfolio (slang)

churn rate FIN a measure of the frequency and volume of trading of stocks and bonds in a brokerage account

CICA *abbr* FIN Canadian Institute of Chartered Accountants

CIMA *abbr* FIN Chartered Institute of Management Accountants: an organisation that is internationally recognised as offering a financial qualification for business, focusing on strategic business management. Founded in 1919 as the Institute of Cost and Works Accountants, it has offices worldwide, supporting over 170,000 members and students in 165 countries.

CIPFA *abbr* FIN Chartered Institute of Public Finance and Accountancy: in the United Kingdom, one of the leading professional accountancy bodies and the only one that specialises in the public services, for example, local government, public service bodies, and national audit agencies, as well as major accountancy firms. It is responsible for the education and training of professional accountants and for their regulation through the setting and monitoring of professional standards. CIPFA also provides a range of advisory, information, and consultancy services to public service organisations. It is the leading independent commentator on managing accounting for public money.

circuit breaker FIN a rule created by the major US stock exchanges and the Securities and Exchange Commission by which trading is halted during times of extreme price fluctuations (slang)

circular flow of income ECON a model of a country's economy showing the flow of resources when consumers' wages and salaries are used to buy goods and so generate income for manufacturing firms

circularisation of debtors FIN the sending of letters by a company's auditors to debtors in order to verify the existence and extent of the company's assets

City Code on Takeovers and Mergers FIN in the United Kingdom, a code issued on behalf of the Panel on Takeovers and Mergers that is designed principally to ensure fair and equal treatment of all shareholders in relation to takeovers. The Code also provides an orderly framework within which takeovers are conducted. It is not concerned with the financial or commercial advantages or disadvantages of a takeover, nor with those issues, such as competition policy, which are the responsibility of the government. The Code represents the collective opinion of those professionally involved in the field of takeovers on how fairness to shareholders can be achieved in practice.

claim FIN a official request for money, usually in the form of compensation, from an individual or organisation

claims adjuster *US* FIN = loss adjuster

class action FIN a civil law action taken by a group of individuals who have a common grievance against an individual, organisation, or legal entity

classical economics ECON a theory focusing on the functioning of a market economy and providing a rudimentary explanation of consumer and producer behaviour in particular markets. The theory postulates that, over time, the economy would tend to operate at full employment because increases in supply would create corresponding increases in demand.

classical system of corporation tax FIN a system in which companies and their owners are liable for corporation tax as separate entities. A company's taxed income is therefore paid out to shareholders, who are in turn taxed again. This system operates in the United States and the Netherlands. It was replaced in the United Kingdom in 1973 by an imputation system.

classified stock *US* FIN a company's common stock divided into classes such as Class A and Class B

class of assets FIN the grouping of similar assets into categories. This is done because, under International Accounting Standards Committee rules, tangible assets and intangible assets cannot be revalued on an individual basis, only in a class of assets.

clean float ECON a floating exchange rate that is allowed to vary without any intervention from the country's monetary authorities

clean opinion or **clean report** FIN an auditor's report that is not qualified

clean surplus concept FIN the idea that a company's income statement should show the totality of gains and losses, without any of them being taken directly to equity

clearing bank FIN a bank that deals with other banks through a clearing house

clearing house FIN an institution that settles accounts between banks

Clearing House Automated Payment System FIN see *CHAPS*

clearing system FIN the system of settling accounts among banks

clear title FIN see *good title*

clickable corporation E-COM a company that operates on the Internet

clicks-and-bricks or **clicks-and-mortar 1.** GEN a business strategy that involves combining traditional retail outlets with online commerce **2.** E-COM combining a traditional bricks-and-mortar organisation with the click technology of the Internet. Such an organisation has both a virtual and a physical presence. Examples include retailers with physical shops on the high street and also websites where their goods can be bought online.

clientele effect FIN the preference of an investor or group of investors for buying a particular type of security

Clintonomics ECON the policy of former US President Clinton's Council of Economic Advisors to intervene in the economy to correct market failures and redistribute income

CLOB International FIN in Singapore, a mechanism for buying and selling foreign shares, especially Malaysian shares

close company or **closed company** FIN, GEN a company in which five or fewer people control more than half the voting shares, or in which such control is exercised by any number of people who are also directors

close corporation or **closed corporation 1.** *US* FIN, GEN a public corporation in which all of the voting stock is held by a few shareholders, for example, management or family members. Although it is a public company, shares would not normally be available for trading because of a lack of liquidity. **2.** *S Africa* FIN a business registered in terms of the Close Corporations Act of 1984, consisting of not more than 10 members who share its ownership and management. *Abbr* **CC**

closed economy ECON an economic system in which little or no external trade takes place

closed-end credit FIN, GEN a loan, plus any interest and finance charges, that is to be repaid in full by a specified future date. Loans that have property

or motor vehicles as collateral are usually closed-end. See also *open-ended credit*

closed-end fund or **closed-end investment company** FIN a unit trust that has a fixed number of shares. See also *open-ended fund*

closed-end mortgage FIN a mortgage in which no prepayment is allowed. See also *open-ended mortgage.* Also known as *closed mortgage*

closed-loop system FIN a management control system which includes a provision for corrective action, taken on either a feedforward or a feedback basis

closed mortgage FIN see *closed-end mortgage*

closely-held corporation FIN a company whose shares are publicly traded but held by very few people

closely-held shares FIN shares that are publicly traded but held by very few people

Closer Economic Relations agreement FIN see *Australia and New Zealand Closer Economic Relations Trade Agreement*

closing balance FIN **1.** the amount in credit or debit in a bank account at the end of a business day **2.** the difference between credits and debits in a ledger at the end of one accounting period that is carried forward to the next

closing bell *US* FIN the end of a trading session at a stock or commodities exchange

closing entries FIN in a double-entry book-keeping system, entries made at the very end of an accounting period to balance the expense and revenue ledgers

closing price FIN the price of the last transaction for a particular security or commodity at the end of a trading session

closing quote FIN the last bid and offer prices recorded at the close of a trading session

closing rate FIN the exchange rate of two or more currencies at the close of business of a balance sheet date, for example, at the end of the financial year

closing-rate method FIN a technique for translating the figures from a set of financial statements into a different currency using the closing rate. This method is often used for the accounts of a foreign subsidiary of a parent company.

closing sale FIN a sale that reduces the risk that the seller has through holding a greater number of shares or a longer-term contract

closing stock FIN a business's remaining stock at the end of an accounting period. It includes finished products, raw materials, or work in progress and is deducted from the period's costs in the balance sheets.

CN *abbr* FIN credit note

CNCC *abbr* FIN Compagnie Nationale des Commissaires aux Comptes

COB *abbr* FIN Commission des Opérations de Bourse

co-financing FIN the joint provision of money for a project by two or more parties

COGS *abbr* FIN cost of goods sold

cohesion fund FIN, GEN the main financial instrument for reducing economic and social disparities within the European Union by providing financial help for projects in the fields of the environment and transport infrastructure

COLA *abbr* FIN cost-of-living adjustment

collar FIN a contractually imposed lower limit on a financial instrument

collateral FIN property or goods used as security against a loan and forfeited to the lender if the borrower defaults

collateralise FIN to secure a loan by pledging assets. If the borrower defaults on loan repayments, the pledged assets can be taken by the lender.

collateral trust certificate FIN a bond for which shares in another company, usually a subsidiary, are used as collateral

collection ratio FIN the average number of days it takes a firm to convert its accounts receivable into cash. Ideally, this period should be decreasing or constant. A low figure means the company collects its outstanding receivables quickly. Collection ratios are usually reviewed quarterly or yearly. Calculating the collection ratio requires three figures: total accounts receivable, total credit sales

for the period analysed, and the number of days in the period (annual, 365; six months, 182; quarter, 91). Also known as *days' sales outstanding*

collusive tendering FIN the illegal practice among companies making tenders for a job of sharing inside information between themselves, with the aim of fixing the end result

combination annuity FIN see *annuity*

combination bond FIN a government bond for which the collateral is both revenue from the financed project and the government's credit

combined financial statement FIN a written record covering the assets, liabilities, net worth, and operating statement of two or more related or affiliated companies

COMEX *abbr* FIN commodity exchange

comfort letter FIN **1.** in the United States, a statement from an accounting firm provided to a company preparing for a public offering, that confirms that the unaudited financial information in the prospectus follows Generally Accepted Accounting Principles **2.** a letter from the parent company of a subsidiary that is applying for a loan, stating the intention that the subsidiary should remain in business

command economy ECON an economy in which all economic activity is regulated by the government, as in the former Soviet Union or China

commerce FIN the large-scale buying and selling of goods and services, usually applied to trading between different countries

commerce integration FIN the blending of Internet-based commerce capabilities with the legacy systems of a traditional business to create a seamless transparent process

commerce server E-COM a networked computer that contains the programs required to process transactions via the Internet, including dynamic inventory databases, shopping cart software, and online payment systems

commerce service provider E-COM an organisation or company that provides a service to a company to facilitate some aspect of electronic

commerce, for example, by functioning as an Internet payment gateway. *Abbr* **CSP**

commercial 1. FIN relating to the buying and selling of goods and services **2.** MKT an advertising message that is broadcast on television or radio

commercial bank FIN a bank that provides financial services to individuals and businesses, for example savings accounts and loans. See also *merchant bank*

commercial hedger FIN a company that holds options in the commodities it produces

commercialisation FIN the application of business principles to something in order to run it as a business

commercial law FIN, GEN the body of law that deals with the rules and institutions of commercial transactions, including banking, commerce, contracts, copyrights, insolvency, insurance, patents, trademarks, shipping, storage, transportation, and warehousing

commercial loan FIN a short-term renewable loan or line of credit used to finance the seasonal or cyclical working capital needs of a company

commercial paper FIN an unsecured short-term loan note issued by companies and generally maturing within nine months

commercial property FIN buildings and land used for the performance of business activities. Commercial property can include single offices, buildings, factories, and hotels.

commercial report FIN an investigative report made by an organisation such as a credit bureau that specialises in obtaining information regarding a person or organisation applying for something such as credit or employment

commercial substance FIN the economic reality that underlies a transaction or arrangement, regardless of its legal or technical denomination. For example, a company may sell an office block and then immediately lease it back: the commercial substance may be that it has not been sold.

commercial year FIN an artificial year treated as having 12 months of 30 days each, used for calculating such things as monthly sales data and inventory levels

commission FIN, HR a payment made to an intermediary, often calculated as a percentage of the value of goods or services provided. Commission is most often paid to sales staff, brokers, or agents.

Commission des Opérations de Bourse FIN the body, established by the French government in 1968, that is responsible for supervising France's stock exchanges. *Abbr* **COB**

commitment document FIN a contract, change order, purchase order, or letter of intent pertaining to the supply of goods and services that commits an organisation to legal, financial, and other obligations

commitment fee FIN a fee that a lender charges to guarantee a rate of interest on a loan a borrower is soon to make. Also known as *establishment fee*

commitment letter US FIN an official notice from a lender to a borrower that the borrower's application has been approved and confirming the terms and conditions of the loan

commitments basis FIN the method of recording the expenditure of a public sector organisation at the time when it commits itself to it rather than when it actually pays for it

commitments for capital expenditure FIN the amount a company has committed to spend on fixed assets in the future. In the United Kingdom, companies are legally obliged to disclose this amount, and any additional commitments, in their annual report.

Committee on Accounting Procedure FIN in the United States, a committee of the American Institute of Certified Public Accountants that was responsible between 1939 and 1959 for issuing accounting principles, some of which are still part of the Generally Accepted Accounting Principles

commodities exchange FIN a market in which raw materials are bought and sold in large quantities as actuals or futures

commodity ECON an item or service, for example, cotton, wool, or a laptop computer, resulting from a production process

commodity-backed bond FIN a bond tied to the price of an underlying commodity, for example, gold or silver, often used as a hedge against inflation

commodity contract FIN a legal document for the delivery or receipt of a commodity

commodity exchange FIN an exchange where futures are traded, for example, the commodity exchange for metals in the United States. *Abbr* **COMEX**

commodity future FIN a contract to buy or sell a commodity at a predetermined price and on a particular delivery date

commodity paper FIN loans for which commodities are collateral

commodity pool FIN a group of people who join together to trade in options

commodity-product spread FIN co-ordinated trades in both a commodity and a product made from it

common market ECON an economic association, typically between nations, with the goal of removing or reducing trade barriers

common seal FIN see *company seal*

common-size financial statements FIN statements in which all the elements are expressed as percentages of the total. Such statements are often used for making performance comparisons between companies.

common stock FIN a stock that provides voting rights but only pays a dividend after dividends for preferred stock have been paid

common stock ratio FIN a measure of the interest each stockholder has in the company's capital

commorientes FIN the legal term for two or more people who die at the same time. For the purposes of inheritance law, in the event of two people dying at the same time, it is assumed that the older person died first.

Compagnie Nationale des Commissaires aux Comptes FIN in France, an organisation that regulates external audit. *Abbr* **CNCC**

Companies Act FIN an Act of Parliament that regulates the working of companies. Although the first one was passed in 1844, the Acts of 1985 and 1989 consolidated previous legis-

lation and incorporated directives from the European Union.

Companies House FIN in the United Kingdom, the office of the Registrar of Companies. It has three main functions: the incorporation, re-registration, and striking-off of companies; the registration of documents that must be filed under company, insolvency, and related legislation; and the provision of company information to the public. *Abbr* **CH**

companion bond FIN a class of a collateral mortgage obligation that is paid off first when interest rates fall, leading to the underlying mortgages being prepaid. Conversely, the principal on these bonds will be repaid more slowly when interest rates rise and fewer mortgages are prepaid.

company law FIN, GEN the body of legislation that relates to the formation, status, conduct, and corporate governance of companies as legal entities

company limited by guarantee FIN a type of organisation, normally formed for non-profit purposes, in which each member of the company agrees to be liable for a specific sum in the event of liquidation

company report FIN, GEN a document giving details of the activities and performance of a company. Companies are legally required to produce particular reports and submit them to the competent authorities in the country of their registration. These include annual reports and financial reports. Other reports may cover specific aspects of an organisation's activities, for example, environmental or social impact.

company seal FIN the impression of a company's official signature on paper or wax. Certain documents, such as share certificates, have to bear this seal.

company secretary HR, FIN a senior employee in an organisation with director status and administrative and legal authority. The appointment of a company secretary is a legal requirement for all limited companies. A company secretary can also be a board secretary with appropriate qualifications. In the United Kingdom, many company secretaries are members of the Institute of Chartered Secretaries and Administrators.

comparative advantage FIN, GEN an instance of higher, more efficient production in a particular area. A country that produces far more cars than another, for example, is said to have the comparative advantage in car production. David Ricardo originally argued that specialisation in activities in which individuals or groups have a comparative advantage will result in gains in trade.

comparative balance sheet FIN one of two or more financial statements prepared on different dates that lend themselves to a comparative analysis of the financial condition of an organisation

comparative credit analysis FIN an analysis of the risk associated with lending to different companies

compensating balance FIN **1.** the amount of money a bank requires a customer to maintain in a non-interest-bearing account, in exchange for which the bank provides free services **2.** the amount of money a bank requires a customer to maintain in an account in return for holding credit available, thereby increasing the true rate of interest on the loan

compensation package US HR a bundle of rewards including pay, financial incentives, and fringe benefits offered to, or negotiated by, an employee

competition ECON, GEN rivalry between companies to achieve greater market share. Competition between companies for customers will lead to product innovation and improvement, and ultimately, lower prices. The opposite of market competition is either a monopoly or a controlled economy, where production is governed by quotas. A company that is leading the market is said to have achieved competitive advantage.

competitive advantage ECON, FIN, GEN a factor giving an advantage to a nation, company, group, or individual in competitive terms. Used by Michael Porter for the title of his classic text on international corporate strategy, *The Competitive Advantage of Nations* (1990), the concept of

competitive advantage derives from the ideas on comparative advantage of the 19th-century economist David Ricardo.

competitive equilibrium price ECON the price at which the number of buyers willing to buy a good equals the number of sellers prepared to sell it

competitive position FIN the market share, costs, prices, quality, and accumulated experience of an entity or product relative to competition

competitive pricing FIN setting a price by reference to the prices of competitive products

competitor analysis or **competitor profiling** GEN the identification and quantification of the relative strengths and weaknesses of a product or service (compared with those of competitors or potential competitors) which could be of significance in the development of a successful competitive strategy

compliance audit FIN an audit of specific activities in order to determine whether performance conforms with a predetermined contractual, regulatory, or statutory requirement

compliance documentation FIN documents that a share-issuing company publishes in line with regulations on share issues

compliance officer FIN an employee of a financial organisation who ensures that regulations governing its business are observed

component percentage FIN see *capitalisation ratio*

compounding FIN the calculation, payment, or receipt of compound interest

compound interest FIN interest calculated on the sum of the original borrowed amount and the accrued interest. See also *simple interest*

compound rate FIN an interest rate of a loan based on its principal, the amount remaining to be paid, or any interest payments already received

comprehensive auditing FIN see *value for money audit*

compulsory acquisition FIN the purchase, by right, of the last 10% of shares in an issue by a bidder at the offer price

concentration services FIN the placing of money from various accounts into a single account

concepts FIN principles underpinning the preparation of accounting information. See also *fundamental accounting concepts*

concession FIN, GEN **1.** a reduction in price for a particular group of people **2.** the right of a retail outlet to operate within another establishment

concurrent engineering FIN a means of reducing product development time and cost by managing development processes so that they can be implemented simultaneously, rather than sequentially

Confederation of British Industry FIN a corporate membership organisation which aims to promote the interests of UK business. The CBI's headquarters are in London, but it has regional offices throughout the United Kingdom, a European office in Brussels, a Far East office in Beijing, and a US base in Washington DC. *Abbr* **CBI**

confidence indicator FIN a number that gives an indication of how well a market or an economy will fare

conglomerate company FIN, GEN an organisation that owns a diverse range of companies in different industries. Conglomerates are usually holding companies with subsidiaries in wide-ranging business areas, often built up through mergers and takeovers and operating on an international scale.

conglomerate diversification FIN, GEN the diversification of a conglomerate company through the setting-up of subsidiary companies with activities in various areas

consensual relationship agreement HR an agreement signed by employer and employees confirming that a romantic or sexual relationship between employees is voluntary and consensual. A consensual relationship agreement may be used where an employer actively discourages, or requires notification of such relationships, especially between supervisors and junior employees. They have been introduced, primarily in the United States, as an alternative to no-dating policies and to protect the employer against liability in possible claims of sexual harassment should the relationship break down. The agreement may also stipulate that the relationship will not affect or interfere with the work of those involved. Also called *cupid contract*

consequential loss policy FIN see *business interruption insurance*

consignment stock FIN stock held by one party (the 'dealer') but legally owned by another (the 'manufacturer') on terms that give the dealer the right to sell the stock in the normal course of its business, or, at its option, to return it unsold to the legal owner

consistency FIN the idea that a company should apply the same rules and standards to its accounting procedures from year to year. In the United Kingdom, any changes to the rules of recognition, presentation, and measurement must be disclosed in the annual report.

consolidated accounts FIN see *consolidated financial statement*

consolidated balance sheet FIN a listing of the most significant details of a company's finances

consolidated debt FIN the use of a large loan to eliminate smaller ones

consolidated financial statement FIN a listing of the most significant details of the finances of a company and of all its subsidiaries. Also known as *consolidated accounts*

consolidated fund FIN a fund of public money, especially from taxes, used by the government to make interest payments on the national debt and other regular payments

consolidated invoice FIN an invoice that covers all items shipped by one seller to one buyer during a particular period

consolidated loan FIN a large loan, the proceeds of which are used to eliminate smaller ones

consolidated tape FIN a ticker tape that lists all transactions of the New York and other US stock exchanges

consolidated tax return FIN a tax return that covers several companies, typically a parent company and all of its subsidiaries

consolidation FIN 1. the uniting of two or more businesses into one company 2. the combination of several lower-priced shares into one higher-priced one

consolidation accounting FIN the process of adjusting and combining financial information from the individual financial statements of a parent undertaking and its subsidiary undertakings to prepare consolidated financial statements that present financial information for the group as a single economic entity

consortium FIN an association of several entities with a view to carrying out a joint venture

consumer ECON, MKT somebody who uses a product or service. A consumer may not be the purchaser of a product or service and should be distinguished from a customer, who is the person or organisation that purchased the product or service.

consumer price index ECON an index of the prices of goods and services that consumers purchase, used to measure the cost of living or the rate of inflation in an economy. *Abbr* **CPI**

consumer-to-consumer commerce E-COM e-business transactions conducted between two individuals

consumption ECON the quantity of resources that consumers use to satisfy their current needs and wants, measured by the sum of the current expenditure of the government and individual consumers

consumption tax FIN a tax used to encourage people to buy less of a particular good or service by increasing its price. This type of tax is often levied in times of national hardship.

contango FIN a situation where the price of commodities is higher for future delivery than it is for immediate delivery

contestable market ECON a market in which there are no barriers to entry, as when there is perfect competition

contingency plan FIN action to be implemented only upon the occurrence of anticipated future events other than those in the accepted forward plan

contingency tax ECON a one-off tax levied by a government to deal with a particular economic problem, for example, too high a level of imports coming into the country

contingent deferred sales charge FIN *Abbr* **CDSC**. See *B share*

continuous disclosure FIN in Canada, the practice of ensuring that complete, timely, accurate, and balanced information about a public company is made available to shareholders

continuous improvement FIN, GEN, OPS the seeking of small improvements in processes and products, with the objective of increasing quality and reducing waste. Continuous improvement is one of the tools that underpin the philosophies of total quality management and lean production. Through constant study and revision of processes, a better product can result at reduced cost. Kaizen has become a foundation for many continuous improvement strategies, and for many employees it is synonymous with continuous improvement.

continuous inventory or **continuous stocktaking** FIN regular and consistent stocktaking throughout the financial year in order to ensure that the physical reality of the stock situation at any given time tallies with the accounting records such as bin cards. Any discrepancies will highlight errors or losses of stock and the accounts are adjusted to reflect this. Continuous inventory may preclude the need for an annual stocktake.

continuous operation costing or **continuous process costing** FIN the costing method applicable where goods or services result from a sequence of continuous or repetitive operations or processes. Costs are averaged over the units produced during the period, being initially charged to the operation or process.

contract FIN 1. the buying and selling of securities and other financial instruments 2. a mutually agreed, legally binding agreement between two or more parties

contract broker FIN a broker who fills an order placed by somebody else

contract costing FIN a form of specific order costing in which costs are attributed to individual contracts

contracting out HR the withdrawal of employees by an employer from the State Earnings-Related Pension Scheme and their enrolment in an occupational pension scheme that meets specified standards

contract month FIN the month in which an option expires and goods covered by it must be delivered. Also known as *delivery month*

contract note FIN a document with the complete description of a stock transaction

contributed surplus FIN the portion of shareholders' equity that comes from sources other than earnings, for example, from the initial sale of stock above its par value

contribution centre FIN a profit centre in which marginal or direct costs are matched against revenue

contribution margin FIN a way of showing how much individual products or services contribute to net profit

contributions holiday FIN a period during which a company stops making contributions to its pension plan because the plan is sufficiently well funded

control FIN the ability to direct the financial and operating policies of an entity with a view to gaining economic benefits from its activities

control environment FIN the overall attitude, awareness, and actions of directors and management regarding internal controls and their importance to the organisation

controlled disbursement FIN the presentation of cheques only once each day

control procedures FIN the policies and procedures in addition to the control environment which are established to achieve an organisation's specific objectives. They include in particular procedures designed to prevent or to detect and correct errors.

control risk FIN the part of an audit risk that relates to a client's internal control system

conversion FIN 1. a trade of one convertible financial instrument for another, for example, a bond for shares 2. a trade of shares of one unit trust for shares of another in the same family

conversion ratio or **conversion price** FIN 1. an expression of the quantity of one security that can be obtained for another, for example, shares for a convertible bond 2. the number of ordinary shares of one type to be issued for each outstanding ordinary share of a different type when a merger takes place

conversion value FIN the value a security would have if converted into another security

convertible ARM FIN an adjustable-rate mortgage that the borrower can convert into a fixed-rate mortgage under specified terms

convertible bond FIN a bond that the owner can convert into another asset, especially ordinary shares

convertible preference shares FIN shares that give the holder the right to exchange them at a fixed price for another security, usually ordinary shares. Preference shares and other convertible securities offer investors a hedge: fixed-interest income without sacrificing the chance to participate in a company's capital appreciation. When a company does well, investors can convert their holdings into ordinary shares that are more valuable. When a company is less successful, they can still receive interest and principal payments, and also recover their investment and preserve their capital if a more favourable investment appears.

convertibles FIN corporate bonds or preference shares which can be converted into ordinary shares at a set price on set dates

convertible security FIN a convertible bond, warrant, or preference share

convertible term insurance FIN term insurance that the policyholder can convert to fixed life assurance under particular conditions

conveyancing FIN the legal transfer of a property from the seller to the buyer

cooling-off period FIN 1. a period during which someone who is about to enter into an agreement may reflect on all aspects of the arrangement and change his or her mind if necessary 2. in insurance, a period of 10 days during which a person who has signed a life assurance policy may cancel it

co-proprietor FIN a person who owns a property with one other person or more

corporate action FIN a measure that a company takes that has an effect on the number of shares outstanding or the rights that apply to shares

corporate bond FIN a long-term bond with fixed interest issued by a corporation

corporate fraud FIN fraud committed by large organisations, rather than individuals. Auditing practice around the world, but especially in the United States, has come under much scrutiny since the collapse of Enron and WorldCom in 2001 and 2002 respectively. Both companies had overstated their profits, but the auditors, Arthur Andersen, had approved accounts in each case.

corporate governance FIN the system by which companies are directed and controlled. Boards of directors are responsible for the governance of their companies. The shareholders' role in governance is to appoint the directors and the auditors and to satisfy themselves that an appropriate governance structure is in place. The responsibilities of the board include setting the company's strategic aims, providing the leadership to put them into effect, supervising the management of the business, and reporting to the shareholders on their stewardship. The board's actions are subject to laws, regulations, and the wishes of the shareholders in the general meeting.

corporate tribes GEN a group of employees who develop their own languages, traditions, values (core values), and culture. Tribes are broadly classified as generalists (such as sales people) or specialists (such as engineers). The different values and languages of the tribes means that communication between them may be disrupted. It is therefore important for organisations to understand the differences between its tribes and devise ways to enable them to work effectively together.

corporation tax FIN tax chargeable on companies resident in the United Kingdom or trading in the United Kingdom through a branch or agency as well as on certain unincorporated associations. *Abbr* CT

cost FIN the amount of money that is paid to secure a good or service. Cost is the amount paid from the purchaser's standpoint, whereas the price is the amount paid from the vendor's standpoint.

cost account FIN a record of revenue and/or expenditure of a cost centre or cost unit

cost audit FIN the verification of cost records and accounts, and a check on adherence to prescribed cost accounting procedures and their continuing relevance

cost-benefit analysis FIN a comparison between the cost of the resources used, plus any other costs imposed by an activity (for example, pollution, environmental damage) and the value of the financial and non-financial benefits derived

cost centre FIN, GEN a department, function, section, or individual whose cost, overall or in part, is an accepted overhead of a business in return for services provided to other parts of the organisation. A cost centre is usually an indirect cost of an organisation's products or services.

cost-cutting FIN, GEN the reduction of the amount of money spent on the operations of an organisation or on the provision of products and services. Cost-cutting measures such as budget reductions, salary freezes, and staff redundancies may be taken by an organisation at a time of recession or financial difficulty or in situations where inefficiency has been identified. Alternative approaches to cost-cutting include modifying organisational structures and redesigning organisational processes for greater efficiency. Excessive cost-cutting may affect productivity and quality or the organisation's ability to add value.

cost driver FIN, GEN a factor that determines the cost of an activity. Cost drivers are analysed as part of activity-based costing and can be used in continuous improvement programmes. They are usually assessed together as multiple drivers rather than singly. There are two main types of cost driver: the first is a resource driver, which refers to the contribution of the quantity of resources used to the cost of an activity; the second is an activity driver, which refers to the costs incurred by the activities required to complete a particular task or project.

cost-effective FIN, GEN offering the maximum benefit for a given level of expenditure. When limited resources are available to meet specific objectives, the cost-effective solution is the best that can be achieved for that level of expenditure and the one that provides good value for money. The term is also used to refer to a level of expenditure that is perceived to be commercially viable.

cost-effectiveness analysis FIN a method for measuring the benefits and effectiveness of a particular item of expenditure. Cost-effectiveness analysis requires an examination of expenditure to determine whether the money spent could have been used more effectively or whether the resulting benefits could have been attained through less financial outlay.

cost function ECON a mathematical function relating a firm's or an industry's total cost to its output and factor costs

cost of appraisal FIN costs incurred in order to ensure that outputs produced meet required quality standards

cost of conformance FIN the cost of achieving specified quality standards. See also *cost of appraisal, cost of prevention*

cost of external failure FIN the cost arising from inadequate quality discovered after the transfer of ownership from supplier to purchaser

cost of goods sold FIN **1.** for a retailer, the cost of buying and acquiring the goods it sells to its customers **2.** for a service firm, the cost of the employee services it supplies **3.** for a manufacturer, the cost of buying the raw materials and manufacturing its finished products. *Abbr* **COGS**

cost of internal failure FIN the costs arising from inadequate quality which are identified before the transfer of ownership from supplier to purchaser

cost of living FIN the average amount spent by an individual on accommodation, food, and other basic necessities. Salaries are usually increased annually to cover rises in the cost of living.

cost-of-living adjustment *US* FIN a small increase to salaries made to account for rises in the cost of living. *Abbr* **COLA**

cost-of-living allowance FIN a salary supplement paid to some employees to cover rises in the cost of living. The specific amount of the supplement is dictated by the cost of living index.

cost of living index FIN an index which indicates changes in the cost of living by comparing current prices for a variety of goods with the prices paid for them in previous years

cost of non-conformance FIN the cost of failure to deliver the required standard of quality. See also *cost of external failure, cost of internal failure*

cost of prevention FIN the costs incurred prior to or during production in order to prevent substandard or defective products or services from being produced

cost of sales FIN the sum of variable cost of sales plus factory overhead attributable to the sales

cost-plus pricing FIN the determination of price by adding a mark-up, which may incorporate a desired return on investment, to a measure of the cost of the product or service

cottage industry FIN an industry made up of small businesses, often run from the home of the proprietor

council tax FIN a tax paid by individuals or companies to a local authority. Introduced in April 1993 as a replacement for the much-maligned community charge, or 'poll tax', council tax is based on the value of the residential or commercial property occupied

counterparty *US* FIN a person with whom somebody is entering into a contract

counterpurchase ECON see *countertrade*

countertrade ECON a variety of reciprocal trading practices. This umbrella term encompasses the direct exchange of goods for goods (or barter), where no cash changes hands, to more complex variations: counterpurchase, which involves a traditional export transaction plus the commitment of the exporter to buy additional goods or services from that country; and buyback, in which the supplier of plant or equipment is paid from the future proceeds resulting from the use of the plant. Countertrade conditions vary widely from country to country and can be costly and administratively cumbersome.

country risk FIN the risk associated with undertaking transactions with, or holding assets in, a particular country. Sources of risk might be political, economic, or regulatory instability affecting overseas taxation, repatriation of profits, nationalisation, currency stability, etc.

coupon FIN **1.** a piece of paper attached to a government bond certificate that a bondholder presents to request payment **2.** the rate of interest on a bond **3.** an interest payment made to a bondholder **clip coupons** to collect periodic interest on a bond

coupon rate FIN the rate of interest paid on a bond

covenant FIN to agree to pay annually a specified sum of money to a person or an organisation by contract. When payments are made under covenant to a charity, the charity can reclaim the tax paid by the donor.

covered option FIN an option whose owner has the shares for the option

covered warrant FIN a futures contract for shares in a company

cover note FIN a document that an insurance company issues to a customer to serve as a temporary insurance certificate until the issue of the policy itself. US term **binder**

CPA *abbr* FIN **1.** customer profitability analysis **2.** certified public accountant

CPI *abbr* ECON consumer price index

CPIX *ANZ* ECON the consumer price index excluding interest costs, on the basis that these are a direct outcome of monetary policy

crash 1. FIN a precipitous drop in value, especially of the stocks traded in a market **2.** ECON a sudden and catastrophic downturn in an economy. The crash in the United States in 1929 is one of the most famous.

creative accounting FIN the use of accounting methods to hide aspects of a company's financial dealings in order to make the company appear more or less successful than it is in

reality. *(slang)* See also **corporate fraud**

creative destruction GEN, FIN a way of describing the endless cycle of innovation which results in established goods, services, or organisations being replaced by new models. The term was first mentioned by Joseph Schumpeter in *Capitalism, Socialism and Democracy* (1942), but used heavily during the dot-com boom of the late 1990s and early 2000s.

credit FIN **1.** the amount of money left over when an individual or organisation has more assets than liabilities, and those liabilities are subtracted from the total of the assets **2.** the trust that a lender has in a borrower's ability to repay a loan, or a loan itself **3.** a financial arrangement between the vendor and the purchaser of a good or service by which the purchaser may buy what he or she requires, but pay for it at a later date

credit account FIN see **charge account**

credit balance FIN the amount of money that somebody owes on a credit account

credit bureau FIN a company that assesses the creditworthiness of people for businesses or banks in the United States. See also **mercantile agency**

credit capacity FIN the amount of money that a person or organisation can borrow and be expected to repay

credit ceiling FIN see **credit limit**

credit committee FIN a committee that evaluates a potential borrower's creditworthiness

credit co-operative FIN an organisation of people who join together to gain advantage in borrowing

credit creation FIN the collective ability of lenders to make money available to borrowers

credit crunch FIN a situation in which money for borrowing is unavailable. Although the term has been in existence for some time, it has become ubiquitous in recent years as the global economic crisis has taken hold. *(slang)*

credit derivative FIN a financial instrument that transfers a lender's risk to a third party

credit entity FIN a borrower or lender

credit entry FIN an item on the asset side of a financial statement

credit exposure FIN the risk to a lender of a borrower defaulting

credit freeze FIN a period during which lending by banks is restricted by the government

credit granter FIN a person or organisation that lends money

credit history FIN a potential borrower's record of debt repayment. Individuals or organisations with a poor credit history may find it difficult to find lenders who are willing to risk their taking out a loan.

crediting rate FIN the interest rate paid on an insurance policy that is an investment

credit limit FIN the highest amount that a lender will allow somebody to borrow, for example, on a credit card. Also known as **credit ceiling**

credit line FIN see **line of credit**

credit note FIN a document stating that a shop owes somebody an amount of money and entitling the person to goods to the specified value. *Abbr* **CN**

creditor FIN a person or an entity to whom money is owed as a consequence of the receipt of goods or services in advance of payment

creditor days FIN the number of days on average that a company requires to pay its creditors. To determine creditor days, divide the cumulative amount of unpaid suppliers' bills (also called trade creditors) by sales, then multiply by 365. See also **debtor days**

creditor nation ECON a country that has a balance of payments surplus

creditors' committee FIN a group that directs the efforts of creditors to receive partial repayment from a bankrupt person or organisation. Also known as **creditors' steering committee**

creditors' meeting FIN a meeting of those to whom a bankrupt person or organisation owes money

creditors' settlement FIN an agreement on partial repayment to those to whom a bankrupt person or organisation owes money

creditors' steering committee FIN see **creditors' committee**

credit rating agency *US* FIN = credit-reference agency

credit rationing FIN the process of making credit less easily available or subject to high interest rates

credit receipt *US* FIN a document stating that a shop owes somebody an amount of money and entitling the person to goods to the specified value

credit-reference agency FIN a company that assesses the creditworthiness of people on behalf of businesses or banks. US term *credit rating agency*

credit risk FIN the possibility that a loss may occur from the failure of another party to perform according to the terms of a contract

credit sale FIN a sale for which the buyer need not pay immediately

credit scoring FIN a calculation done in the process of credit rating

credit side FIN the part of a financial statement that lists assets. In double-entry book-keeping, the right-hand side of each account is designated as the credit side.

credit squeeze FIN a situation in which credit is not easily available or is subject to high interest rates

credit standing FIN the reputation that somebody has with regard to meeting financial obligations

credit system FIN a set of rules and organisations involved in making loans

credit union FIN a co-operative financial organisation that provides banking services, including loans, to its members at low rates of interest

creditworthy FIN regarded as being reliable in terms of meeting financial obligations

creeping takeover FIN a takeover achieved by the gradual acquisition of small amounts of stock over an extended period of time *(slang)*

creeping tender offer FIN an acquisition of many shares in a company by purchase, especially to avoid US restrictions on tender offers

CREST FIN the paperless system used for settling stock transactions electronically in the United Kingdom

critical success factor 1. FIN an element of organisational activity which is central to its future success. Critical success factors may change over time, and may include items such as product quality, employee attitudes, manufacturing flexibility, and brand awareness. 2. GEN any of the aspects of a business that are identified as vital for successful targets to be reached and maintained. Critical success factors are normally identified in such areas as production processes, employee and organisation skills, functions, techniques, and technologies. The identification and strengthening of such factors may be similar to identifying core competences, and is considered an essential element in achieving and maintaining competitive advantage.

crony capitalism ECON a form of capitalism in which business contracts are awarded to the family and friends of the government in power rather than by open-market tender

cross FIN a transaction in securities in which one broker acts for both parties

cross-border services FIN accountancy services provided by an accountancy firm in one country on behalf of a client based in another country

cross-border trade ECON trade between two countries that have a common frontier

cross-hedging FIN a form of hedging using an option on a different but related commodity, especially a currency

cross listing FIN the practice of offering the same item for sale in more than one place

cross-rate ECON the rate of exchange between two currencies expressed in terms of the rate of exchange between them and a third currency, for example, sterling and the peso in relation to the dollar

cross-sell FIN, MKT to sell customers a range of products or services offered by an organisation at the same time, for example, offering insurance services while selling someone a mortgage

crowding out FIN the effect on markets of credit produced by extraordinarily large borrowing by a national government

crown jewels FIN an organisation's most valuable assets, often the motivation behind takeover bids

CSP *abbr* E-COM customer service provider

cum FIN Latin, meaning 'with'

cum rights FIN an indication that the buyer of the shares is entitled to participate in a forthcoming rights issue

cumulative interest FIN interest which is added annually to capital originally invested

cumulative method FIN a system in which items are added together

cumulative preferred stock FIN preferred stock for which dividends accrue even if they are not paid when due

cupid contract HR see *consensual relationship agreement*

currency FIN the money in circulation in a particular country

currency band FIN exchange rate levels between which a currency is allowed to move without full revaluation or devaluation

currency clause FIN a clause in a contract which avoids problems of payment caused by exchange rate changes by fixing in advance the exchange rate for the various transactions covered by the contract

currency future FIN an option on currency

currency hedging FIN a method of reducing exchange rate risk by diversifying currency holdings and adjusting them according to changes in exchange rates

currency note FIN a bank note

currency risk FIN the possibility of a loss or gain due to future changes in exchange rates

currency swap FIN 1. an agreement to use a certain currency for payments under a contract in exchange for another currency. The organisations bound by the contract may buy one of the currencies at a more favourable rate than the other. 2. the buying or selling of a fixed amount of a foreign currency on the spot market, and the selling or buying of the same amount of the same currency on the forward market

currency unit ECON each of the notes and coins that are the medium of exchange in a country

current account FIN a record of transactions between two parties, for example, between a bank and its customer, or a branch and head office. *Abbr* ***c/a***

current account equilibrium ECON a country's economic circumstances when its expenditure equals its income from trade and invisible earnings

current asset FIN cash or other assets, such as stock, debtors, and long-term investments, held for conversion into cash in the normal course of trading

current assets financing FIN the use of current assets as collateral for a loan

current cash balance FIN the amount, which excludes balances due soon for outstanding transactions, that a client has available for investment with a broker

current cost accounting FIN a method of accounting which notes the cost of replacing assets at current prices, rather than valuing assets at their original cost. *Abbr* **CCA**

current earnings FIN the annual earnings most recently reported by a company

current liabilities FIN liabilities which fall due for payment within one year. They include that part of any long-term loan due for repayment within one year.

current principal factor FIN the portion of the initial amount of a loan that remains to be paid

current ratio FIN a ratio of current assets to current liabilities, used to measure a company's liquidity and its ability to meet its short-term debt obligations. The current ratio formula is a simple one:

Current assets / Current liabilities = Current ratio

Current assets are the ones that a company can turn into cash within 12 months during the ordinary course of business. Current liabilities are bills due to be paid within the coming 12 months. Also known as ***working capital ratio***

current stock value FIN the value of all stock in a portfolio, including stock in transactions that have not yet been settled

current value FIN a ratio indicating the amount by which current assets exceed current liabilities

current yield FIN the interest being paid on a bond divided by its cur-rent market price, expressed as a percentage

cushion FIN money which allows an organisation to pay interest on its borrowings or to survive a loss of some type

cushion bond FIN a bond that pays a high rate of interest but sells at a low premium because of the risk of its being called soon

custodial account US FIN a bank account opened, normally by a parent or guardian, in the name of a minor who is too young to control it

custodian FIN a bank whose principal function is to maintain and grow the assets contained in a trust

customer equity MKT the total asset value of the relationships which an organisation has with its customers. The term was coined by Robert C. Blattberg and John Deighton in their article, 'Manage Marketing by the Customer Equity Test', *Harvard Business Review*, Jul/Aug, vol. 74 no. 4, pp. 136–144. Customer equity is based on customer lifetime value, and an understanding of customer equity can be used to optimise the balance of investment in the acquisition and retention of customers. It is also known as customer capital and forms one component of the intellectual capital of an organisation.

customer knowledge management MKT the acquisition and use of customer-related knowledge to create value for both the organisation and the purchasers of its products and services. Customer knowledge management is a form of knowledge management which focuses on the human aspects of customer knowledge acquired through direct interaction with the customer as well as quantitative transactional data. Some writers restrict the concept to the use of knowledge residing in, or acquired from, customers as opposed to information *about* customers collected by customer relationship management systems. Interactive technologies, conversations with customers and user groups may be used to create knowledge-sharing and partnership between the organisation and its customers.

customer lifetime value MKT the net present value of the profit an organ-isation expects to realise from a customer for the duration of their relationship. Customer lifetime value focuses on customers as assets rather than sources of revenue. The volume of purchases made, customer retention rates, and profit margins are factors taken into account in calculating customer lifetime value. Strategies for increasing customer lifetime value aim to improve customer retention and lengthen the life of the relationship with the customer. Customer lifetime value is a key factor in the customer equity of an organisation.

cyberchondriac E-COM someone who feels physically unwell if he or she spends too much time away from an Internet connection *(slang)*

cybersales E-COM, FIN sales made electronically through computers and information systems

cycle time FIN the total time taken from the start of the production of a product or service to its completion. Cycle time includes processing time, move time, wait time, and inspection time, only the first of which creates value.

cyclical stock FIN a stock whose value rises and falls periodically, for example, according to the seasons of the year or economic cycles

cyclical unemployment ECON unemployment, usually temporary, caused by a lack of aggregate demand, for example, during a downswing in the business cycle

D/A *abbr* FIN deposit account

daily price limit FIN the amount by which the price of an option can rise or fall within one trading day

Daimyo bond FIN a Japanese bearer bond that can be cleared through European clearing houses

D&B *abbr* FIN Dun and Bradstreet

data cholesterol E-COM the clogging up of a computer system with files or traffic to the extent that software programs can no longer run effectively on it *(slang)*

data warehouse 1. GEN a collection of subject-orientated data collected over a period of time and stored on a computer to provide information in support of managerial decision-making.

A data warehouse contains a large volume of information selected from different sources, including operational systems and organisational databases, and brought together in a standard format to facilitate retrieval and analysis. Like Executive Information Systems, data warehouses can be used to support decision-making, but the ways in which they can be searched are not predetermined. Organisations often use data warehouses for marketing purposes, for example, the analysis of customer information, or for market segmentation. Data mining techniques are used to access the information in a data warehouse. **2.** FIN a database in which information is held not for operational purposes, but to assist in analytical tasks such as the identification of new market segments. Data warehouses provide a repository for historical data and collect, integrate, and organise data from unintegrated application systems. The data stored in a data warehouse almost certainly comes from the operational environment, but is always physically separate from it.

dawn raid FIN a sudden, planned purchase of a large number of a company's shares at the beginning of a day's trading. Up to 15% of a company's shares can be bought in this way, and the purchaser must wait for seven days before buying more. A dawn raid may sometimes be the first step towards a takeover.

DAX *abbr* FIN Deutscher Aktienindex: the principal German stock exchange, based in Frankfurt

day order FIN for dollar trading only, an order that is valid only during one trading day

days' sales outstanding FIN see *collection ratio*

day trader FIN somebody who makes trades with very close dates of maturity

day trading FIN the making of trades that have very close dates of maturity

DCF *abbr* FIN discounted cash flow

DCM *abbr* S Africa FIN Development Capital Market

DD *abbr* FIN **1.** direct debit **2.** due diligence

dead cat bounce FIN a short-term increase in the value of a stock fol-lowing a precipitous drop in value (*slang*)

dear money FIN money which has to be borrowed at a high interest rate, thus restricting the borrower's expenditure

debenture FIN the written acknowledgment of a debt by a company, usually given under its seal, and normally containing provisions as to payment of interest and repayment of principal. A debenture may be secured on some or all of the assets of the company or its subsidiaries.

debenture bond FIN **1.** a certificate showing that a debenture has been issued **2.** *US* a long-term unsecured loan

debit FIN an entry in accounts which shows an increase in assets or expenses or a decrease in liabilities, revenue, or capital. It is entered in the left-hand side of an account in double-entry book-keeping.

debit balance FIN the difference between debits and credits in an account where the value of debits is greater

debit card FIN a card issued by a bank or financial institution and accepted by a merchant in payment for a transaction. Unlike the procedure with a credit card, purchases are deducted from the cardholder's account, as with a cheque, when the transaction takes place.

debit column FIN the left-hand side of an account, showing increases in a company's assets or decreases in its liabilities

debit entry FIN an entry on the debit side of an account

debits and credits FIN figures entered in a company's accounts to record increases and decreases in assets, expenses, liabilities, revenues, or capital

debt FIN **1.** an amount of money owed to a person or organisation **2.** money borrowed by a person or organisation to finance personal or business activities

debt collection agency FIN a business that secures the repayment of debts for third parties on a commission or fee basis

debt counselling FIN a service offering advice and support to individuals who are financially stretched

debt/equity ratio FIN the ratio of what a company owes to the value of all of its outstanding shares

debt forgiveness FIN the writing off of all or part of a nation's debt by a lender

debt instrument FIN any document used or issued for raising money, for example, a bill of exchange, bond, or promissory note

debtnocrat FIN a senior bank official who specialises in lending extremely large sums, for example, to developing nations (*slang*)

debtor FIN a person or entity owing money

debtor days FIN the number of days on average that it takes a company to receive payment for what it sells. To calculate debtor days, divide the cumulative amount of accounts receivable by sales, then multiply by 365. See also *creditor days*

debt rescheduling FIN, GEN the renegotiation of debt repayments. Debt rescheduling is necessary when a company can no longer meet its debt payments. It can involve deferring debt payments, deferring payment of interest, or negotiating a new loan. It is usually undertaken as part of turnaround management to avoid business failure. Debt rescheduling is also undertaken in less-developed countries that encounter national debt difficulties. Such arrangements are usually overseen by the International Monetary Fund.

debt/service ratio ECON the ratio of a country's or company's borrowing to its equity or venture capital

declaration date *US* FIN the date when the directors of a company meet to announce the proposed dividend per share that they recommend be paid

declaration of dividend FIN a formal announcement by a company's directors of the proposed dividend per share that they recommend be paid. It is subsequently put to a shareholders' vote at the company's annual general meeting.

declaration of solvency FIN a document, filed with the Registrar of Companies, that lists the assets and liabilities of a company seeking voluntary liquidation to show that the company is capable of repaying its debts within 12 months

declared value FIN the value of goods as entered on a customs declaration

declining balance method ECON, FIN see *accelerated depreciation*

de-diversify FIN to sell off parts of a company or group that are not considered directly relevant to its main area of interest

deductible FIN the part of a commercial insurance claim that has to be met by the policyholder rather than the insurance company. A deductible of £500 means that the company pays all but £500 of the claim for loss or damage. See also *excess*

deduction at source FIN a UK term for the collection of taxes from an organisation or individual paying an income rather than from the recipient, for example, from an employer paying wages, a bank paying interest, or a company paying dividends

deed FIN a legal document, most commonly one that details the transfer or sale of a property

deed of arrangement FIN a legal document which sets out the agreement between an insolvent person and his or her creditors

deed of assignment FIN a legal document detailing the transfer of property from a debtor to a creditor

deed of covenant FIN a legal document in which a person or organisation promises to pay a third party a sum of money on an annual basis. In certain countries this arrangement may have tax advantages. For example, in the United Kingdom, it is often used for making regular payments to a charity.

deed of partnership FIN a legal document formalising the agreement and financial arrangements between the parties that make up a partnership

deed of transfer FIN a legal document which attests to the transfer of share ownership

deed of variation FIN in the United Kingdom, an arrangement that allows the will of a deceased person to be amended, provided certain conditions are met and the amendment is signed by all the original beneficiaries

deep-discount bond FIN a bond offered at a large discount on the face value

of the debt so that a significant proportion of the return to the investor comes by way of a capital gain on redemption, rather than through interest payments

deep-in-the-money call option FIN a call option that has become very profitable and is likely to remain so

deep-in-the-money put option FIN a put option that has become very profitable and is likely to remain so

deep market FIN a commodity, currency, or stock market in which the volume of trade is such that a considerable number of transactions will not influence the market price

defalcation FIN the improper and illegal use of funds by someone who does not own them, but who has been charged with their care

default FIN to fail to comply with the terms of a contract, especially to fail to pay back a debt

default notice FIN a formal document issued by a lender to a borrower who is in default. US term *notice of default*

defended takeover bid FIN a bid for a company takeover in which the directors of the target company oppose the action of the bidder

defensive stock FIN stock that prospers predictably, regardless of external circumstances such as an economic slowdown

deferred coupon FIN a coupon that pays no interest at first, but pays relatively high interest after a specified date

deferred credit or **deferred income** FIN revenue received but not yet reported as income in the profit and loss account, for example, payment for goods to be delivered or services provided at a later date, or government grants received for the purchase of assets. The deferred credit is treated as a credit balance on the balance sheet while waiting to be treated as income. See also *accrual concept*

deferred month FIN a month relatively late in the term of an option

deferred ordinary share FIN 1. a type of share, usually held by founding members of a company, often with a higher dividend that is only paid after other shareholders have received their dividends and, in some cases, only when

a certain level of profit has been achieved 2. a share that pays no dividend for a certain number of years after its issue date but that then ranks with the company's ordinary shares

deficit FIN see *budget deficit*

deficit financing FIN the borrowing of money because expenditure will exceed receipts

deficit spending FIN government spending financed through borrowing rather than taxation

deflation ECON a reduction in the general level of prices sustained over several months, usually accompanied by declining employment and output

deflationary fiscal policy ECON a government policy that raises taxes and reduces public expenditure in order to reduce the level of aggregate demand in the economy

deflationary gap ECON a gap between GDP and the potential output of the economy

deflator ECON the amount by which a country's GDP is reduced to take into account inflation

degearing FIN a reduction in a company's loan capital in relation to the value of its ordinary share plus reserves

degressive tax FIN a tax whose payments depend on an individual's salary. Those on smaller salaries pay a lower percentage of their income than those with larger salaries.

delayed settlement processing E-COM a procedure for storing authorised transaction settlements online until after the merchant has shipped the goods to the purchaser

del credere agent FIN an agent who agrees to sell goods on commission and pay the principal even if the buyer defaults on payment. To cover the risk of default, the commission is marginally higher than that of a general agent.

delinquent US FIN used to refer to an individual who or an organisation which is late in paying an account

delist US FIN to remove a company from the list of companies whose stocks are traded on an exchange

delivery month FIN see *contract month*

demand forecasting FIN, GEN the activity of estimating the quantity of a product or service that consumers will purchase. Demand forecasting involves techniques including both informal methods, such as educated guesses, and quantitative methods, such as the use of historical sales data or current data from test markets. Demand forecasting may be used in making pricing decisions, in assessing future capacity requirements, or in making decisions on whether to enter a new market.

demerge FIN to split up an organisation into a number of separate parts

demonetise FIN to withdraw a coin or note from a country's currency

demurrage FIN compensation paid to a customer when shipment of a good is delayed at a port or by customs

departmental budget FIN see *functional budget*

deposit account FIN an account which pays interest but on which notice usually has to be given to withdraw money. See also *savings account*. *Abbr* **D/A**

depositary FIN a person or organisation which has placed money or documents for safekeeping with a depository

depository FIN a bank or organisation with whom money or documents can be left for safekeeping

deposit protection FIN insurance that depositors have against loss

deposit receipt FIN see *deposit slip*

deposit slip FIN a US term for the slip of paper that accompanies money or cheques being paid into a bank account. Also called deposit receipt

depreciation FIN 1. an allocation of the cost of an asset over a period of time for accounting and tax purposes. Depreciation is charged against earnings, on the basis that the use of capital assets is a legitimate cost of doing business. Depreciation is also a noncash expense that is added into net income to determine cash flow in a given accounting period. **2.** a reduction of a currency's value in relation to the value of other currencies

depression ECON a prolonged slump or downturn in the business cycle, marked by a high level of unemployment

derivative FIN a security, such as an option, the price of which has a strong correlation with an underlying financial instrument

Derivative Trading Facility FIN a computer system and associated network operated by the Australian Stock Exchange to facilitate the purchase and sale of exchange-traded options. *Abbr* **DTF**

designated account FIN an account opened and held in one person's name, but which also features another person's name for extra identification purposes

Deutscher Aktienindex FIN see *DAX*

devaluation ECON a reduction in the official fixed rate at which one currency exchanges for another under a fixed-rate regime, usually to correct a balance of payments deficit

developing country ECON a country, often a producer of primary goods such as cotton or rubber, which cannot generate investment income to stimulate growth and which possesses a national income that is vulnerable to change in commodity prices

Development Capital Market *S Africa* FIN a sector on the JSE Securities Exchange for listing smaller developing companies. Criteria for listing in the Development Capital Market sector are less stringent than for the main board listing. *Abbr* **DCM**

Diagonal Street *S Africa* FIN an informal term for the financial centre of Johannesburg or, by extension, South Africa

digital cash E-COM an anonymous form of digital money that can be linked directly to a bank account or exchanged for physical money. As with physical cash, there is no way to obtain information about the buyer from it, and it can be transferred by the seller to pay for subsequent purchases. Also known as *e-cash*

digital certificate E-COM an electronic document issued by a recognised authority that validates a purchaser. It is used much as a driving licence or passport is used for identification purposes in a traditional business transaction.

digital coins E-COM a form of electronic payment authorised for instant trans-

actions that facilitates the purchase of items priced in small denominations of digital cash. Digital coins are transferred from customer to merchant for a transaction such as the purchase of a newspaper using a smart card for payment.

digital coupon E-COM a voucher or similar form that exists electronically, for example, on a website, and can be used to reduce the price of goods or services

digital economy ECON an economy in which the main productive functions are in electronic commerce, for example, trade on the Internet

digital goods E-COM merchandise that is sold and delivered electronically, for example, over the Internet

digital money E-COM a series of numbers with an intrinsic value in some physical currency. Online digital money requires electronic interaction with a bank to conduct a transaction; offline digital money does not. Anonymous digital money is synonymous with digital cash. Identified digital money carries with it information revealing the identities of those involved in the transaction. Also known as *e-money, electronic money*

digital wallet E-COM software on the hard drive of an online shopper from which the purchaser can pay for the transaction electronically. The wallet can hold in encrypted form such items as credit card information, digital cash or coins, a digital certificate to identify the user, and standardised shipping information. Also known as *electronic wallet*

direct cost FIN, GEN, OPS a variable cost directly attributable to production. Items that are classed as direct costs include materials used, labour deployed, and marketing budget. Amounts spent will vary with output. See also *indirect cost*

direct labour cost percentage rate FIN an overhead absorption rate based on direct labour cost

direct labour hour rate FIN an overhead absorption rate based on direct labour hours

director's dealing FIN the purchase or sale of a company's stock by one of its directors

Dictionary

direct tax FIN a tax on income or capital that is paid directly rather than added to the price of goods or services

dirty float ECON a floating exchange rate that cannot float freely because a country's central bank intervenes on foreign exchange markets to alter its level

dirty price FIN the price of a debt instrument that includes the amount of accrued interest that has not yet been paid

disbursing agent FIN see *paying agent*

discount 1. FIN, GEN a reduction in the price of goods or services in relation to the standard price. A discount is a selling technique that is used, for example, to encourage customers to buy in large quantities or to make payments in cash. It can also be used to improve sales of a slow-moving line. The greater the purchasing power of the buyer, the greater the discounts that can be negotiated. Some companies inflate original list prices to give the impression that discounts offer value for money; conversely too many genuine discounts may harm profitability. **2.** FIN the difference between the share price of an investment trust and its net asset value

discount broker FIN a broker who charges relatively low fees because he or she provides restricted services

discounted bond FIN a bond that is sold for less than its face value because its yield is not as high as that of other bonds

discounted dividend model FIN a method of calculating a stock's value by reducing future dividends to the present value. Also known as *dividend discount model*

discount loan FIN a loan that amounts to less than its face value because payment of interest has been subtracted

discount rate FIN the rate charged by a central bank on any loans it makes to other banks

discount security FIN a security that is sold for less than its face value in lieu of bearing interest

discretionary account FIN a securities account in which the broker has the authority to make decisions about buying and selling without the customer's prior permission

discretionary management FIN an arrangement between a stockbroker and his or her client whereby the stockbroker makes all investment decisions. It is the opposite of an advisory management arrangement.

discretionary order FIN a security transaction in which a broker controls the details, such as the time of execution

discriminating monopoly ECON a company able to charge different prices for its output in different markets because it has power to influence prices for its goods

diseconomies of scale FIN a situation in which increased production increases, rather than decreases, unit costs

disequilibrium price ECON the price of a good set at a level at which demand and supply are not in balance

dishonour FIN to refuse payment of a cheque because the account for which it is written holds insufficient money. Also known as *bounce*

disinflation ECON the elimination or reduction of inflation or inflationary pressures in an economy by fiscal or monetary policies

dispensation FIN an arrangement between an employer and HM Revenue & Customs in which business expenses paid to an employee are not declared for tax

disposable income FIN income that is left for spending after tax and other deductions

dispute benefit HR see *strike pay*

disqualification FIN a court order which forbids a person from being a director of a company. A variety of offences, even those termed as 'administrative', can result in some people being disqualified for up to five years.

distrain FIN to seize assets belonging to a person or organisation in order to pay off a debt

distressed property FIN property purchased with the aid of a loan on which repayments have stopped and the borrower has defaulted

distributions FIN any income arising from a bond fund or an equity

District Bank US FIN one of the 12 banks that make up the Federal Reserve System. Each District Bank is responsible for all banking activity in its area.

diversification FIN, GEN a strategy to increase the variety of business, service, or product types within an organisation. Diversification can be a growth strategy, taking advantage of market opportunities, or it may be aimed at reducing risk by spreading interests over different areas. It can be achieved through acquisition or through internal research and development, and it can involve managing two, a few, or many different areas of interest. Diversification can also be a corporate strategy of investment in acquisitions within a broad portfolio range by a large holding company. One distinct type is horizontal diversification, which involves expansion into a similar product area, for example, a domestic furniture manufacturer producing office furniture. Another is vertical diversification, in which a company moves into a different level of the supply chain, for example, a manufacturing company becoming a retailer. A well-known example of diversification is the move of BIC, the ball-point pen manufacturer, into the production of disposable razors.

diversified investment company FIN a unit trust with a variety of types of investments

divestment FIN the proportional or complete reduction in an ownership stake in an organisation

dividend clawback FIN an agreement that dividends will be reinvested as part of the financing of a project

dividend cover FIN the number of times a company's dividends to ordinary shareholders could be paid out of its net after-tax profits. This measures the likelihood of dividend payments being sustained, and is a useful indication of sustained profitability. If the figure is 3, for example, a firm's profits are three times the level of the dividend paid to shareholders. See also *payout ratio*

dividend discount model FIN see *discounted dividend model*

dividend limitation FIN a provision in a bond limiting the dividends that may be paid

dividend reinvestment plan FIN a plan that provides for the reinvestment of dividends in the shares of the company paying the dividends. *Abbr* **DRIP**

dividend rights FIN rights to receive dividends

dividends-received deduction FIN a tax advantage on dividends that a company receives from a company it owns

dividend yield FIN dividends expressed as a percentage of a share's price

D/N *abbr* FIN debit note

documentary credit FIN an arrangement, used in the finance of international transactions, whereby a bank undertakes to make a payment to a third party on behalf of a customer

dollar cost averaging *US* FIN = pound cost averaging

dollar roll *US* FIN an agreement to sell a stock and buy it back later for a specified price

dollars-and-cents *US* FIN considering money as the determining factor

domicilium citandi et executandi *S Africa* FIN the address where a summons or other official notice should be served if necessary, which must be supplied by somebody applying for credit or entering into a contract

dominant influence FIN influence that can be exercised to achieve the operating and financial policies designed by the holder of the influence, notwithstanding the rights or influence of any other party

dormant account FIN a bank account which is no longer used by the account holder

dormant company FIN a company which has not made any transactions during a specified accounting period

double counting GEN the counting of a cost or benefit element twice when doing analysis. This can happen when calculating the total sales in a market as the sum of all sales made by firms, without deducting the purchases firms make from other firms in the market.

double-entry book-keeping FIN the most commonly used system of book-keeping, based on the principle that every financial transaction involves the simultaneous receiving

and giving of value, and is therefore recorded twice

double indemnity FIN a provision in an insurance policy that guarantees payment of double its face value on the accidental death of the holder

double taxation FIN the taxing of something twice, usually the combination of corporation tax and tax on the dividends that shareholders earn

Dow Jones Averages FIN an index of the prices of selected stocks on the New York Stock Exchange compiled by Dow Jones & Company, Inc

downgrade FIN **1.** to reduce the forecast for a share **2.** to reduce the credit rating for a bond

downsizing FIN organisational restructuring involving outsourcing activities, replacing permanent staff with contract employees, and reducing the number of levels within the organisational hierarchy, with the intention of making the organisation more flexible, efficient, and responsive to its environment

Dow Theory FIN the theory that stock market prices can be forecast on the basis of the movements of selected industrial and transport stocks

draft FIN a written order to pay a particular sum from one account to another, or to a person. See also *sight draft, time draft*

drawee FIN the individual or institution to whom a bill of exchange or cheque is addressed

drawing account FIN an account that permits the tracking of withdrawals

DRIP FIN see *dividend reinvestment plan*

drop lock FIN the automatic conversion of a debt instrument with a floating rate to one with a fixed rate when interest rates fall to an agreed percentage

DSO *abbr* FIN days' sales outstanding. See also *collection ratio*

DTF *abbr* *ANZ* FIN Derivative Trading Facility

dual currency bond FIN a bond that pays interest in a currency other than the one used to buy it

dual economy ECON an economy in which the manufacturing and service sectors are growing at different rates

dual trading FIN the practice of acting as agent for both a broker's firm and its customers

due diligence 1. FIN the examination of a company's accounts prior to a potential takeover by another organisation. This assessment is often undertaken by an independent third party. *Abbr* **DD 2.** GEN the collection, verification, analysis, and assessment of information about the operations and management of a company undertaken by a potential purchaser or investor. Due diligence aims to confirm that the purchaser or investor has an accurate picture of the target company and to identify risks and benefits associated with the prospective deal. Due diligence normally starts after the signing of a letter of intent by both parties and information disclosed during the process is normally protected by the signing of a confidentiality agreement. Due diligence often leads on to negotiations on the detailed terms of the agreement. The process may cover the financial, legal, commercial, technical, cultural, and environmental aspects of the organisation's operations as well as its assets and liabilities, and may be conducted with the assistance of professional advisers.

due-on-sale clause FIN a provision requiring a homeowner to pay off a mortgage upon sale of the property

dumping ECON the selling of a commodity on a foreign market at a price below its marginal cost, either to dispose of a temporary surplus or to achieve a monopoly by eliminating competition

Dun and Bradstreet FIN an international organisation that sources credit information from companies and their creditors which it then makes available to subscribers. *Abbr* **D&B**

duopoly ECON a market in which only two sellers of a good exist. If one decides to alter the price, the other will respond and influence the market's response to the first decision.

Dutch auction FIN an auction in which the lot for sale is offered at an initial price which, if there are no takers, is then reduced until there is a bid

dynamic pricing FIN, GEN pricing that changes in line with patterns of demand

EAA *abbr* FIN European Accounting Association

e-alliance E-COM a partnership forged between organisations in order to achieve business objectives for enterprises conducted over the Web. There has been a surge in such alliances since the Internet took off in the mid-1990s, and studies show that the most successful have been those involving traditional offline businesses and online entities – the clicks-and-mortar strategy – such as that between Amazon.com and Toys 'R' Us. Toys 'R' Us had the physical infrastructure and brand, while Amazon.com had the online infrastructure and experience of making e-commerce work.

E&O *abbr* FIN errors and omissions

early withdrawal FIN the removal of money from a deposit account before the due dates. Early withdrawal often incurs a penalty that the account holder must pay.

earned income FIN money generated by an individual's or an organisation's labour, for example, wages, salaries, fees, royalties, and business profits. See also *unearned income*

earning potential FIN **1.** the amount of money somebody should be able to earn in his or her professional capacity **2.** the amount of dividend that a share potentially can produce

earnings 1. HR a sum of money gained from paid employment, usually quoted before tax, including any extra rewards such as allowances, or incentives. Also known as *pay* **2.** FIN income or profit from a business, quoted gross or net of tax, which may be retained and distributed in part to the shareholders

earnings before interest, tax, depreciation, and amortisation FIN see *EBITDA*

earnings before interest and taxes FIN *Abbr* **EBIT**. See *operating income*

earnings cap FIN the top limit of earnings which can be used in calculating a retirement pension paid from an occupational pension scheme

earnings per share FIN a financial ratio that measures the portion of a company's profit allocated to each outstanding ordinary share. It is the most basic measure of the value of a share, and also is the basis for calculating several other important investment ratios. EPS is calculated by subtracting the total value of any preference shares from net income (earnings) for the period in question, then dividing the resulting figure by the number of shares outstanding during that period. *Abbr* **EPS**

earnings report *US* FIN = published accounts

earnings retained FIN see *retained profits*

earnings surprise FIN a considerable difference in size between a company's actual and anticipated earnings

earnings yield FIN money earned by a company during a year, expressed as a percentage of the price of one of its shares

EASDAQ *abbr* FIN European Association of Securities Dealers Automated Quotations: a stock exchange for technology and growth companies based in Europe and modelled on NASDAQ in the United States

eased FIN used in stock market reports to describe a market that has experienced a slight fall in prices

easy market FIN a market in which fewer people are buying, with the effect that prices are lower than hoped

easy money FIN see *cheap money*

easy money policy FIN a government policy which aims to expand the economy by making money more easily accessible to the public. This is done by strategies such as lowering interest rates and offering easy access to credit.

EBIT *abbr* FIN earnings before interest and taxes. See also *operating income*

EBITDA *abbr* FIN earnings before interest, tax, depreciation, and amortisation: the earnings generated by a business's fundamental operating performance, frequently used in accounting ratios for comparison with other companies. Interest on borrowings, tax payable on those profits, depreciation, and amortisation are excluded on the basis that they can distort the underlying performance.

EBRD *abbr* FIN European Bank for Reconstruction and Development: the bank, which was established in 1991, developed programmes to tackle a range of issues. These included the creation and strengthening of infrastructure; industry privatisation; the reform of the financial sector, including the development of capital markets and the privatisation of commercial banks; the development of productive competitive private sectors of small and medium-sized enterprises in industry, agriculture, and services; the restructuring of industrial sectors to put them on a competitive basis; and encouraging foreign investment and cleaning up the environment. The EBRD had 41 original members: the European Commission, the European Investment Bank, all the then EU countries, and all the countries of Eastern Europe except Albania, which finally became a member in October 1991, followed by all the republics of the former USSR in March 1992.

e-business E-COM a company that conducts business on the Internet

e-cash E-COM see *digital cash*

ECB *abbr* FIN European Central Bank: the financial institution which replaced the European Monetary Institute (EMI) in 1998 and which is responsible for carrying out EU monetary policy and administering the euro

e-commerce E-COM, FIN the exchange of goods, information products, or services via an electronic medium such as the Internet. Originally limited to buying and selling, it has evolved to include such functions as customer service, marketing, and advertising. Also known as *electronic commerce, Web commerce*

econometric model ECON a way of representing the relationship between economic variables as an equation or set of equations with statistically precise parameters linking the variables

econometrics ECON the branch of economics concerned with using mathematical models to describe relationships in an economy, for example, between wage rates and levels of employment

Economic and Monetary Union FIN see *EMU*

economic assumption ECON an assumption built into an economic model, for example, that output will grow at 2.5% in the next tax year

Economic Development Board FIN an organisation established in 1961 that aims to promote investment in Singapore by providing various services and assistance schemes to foreign and local companies. *Abbr* **EDB**

economic goods ECON services or physical objects that can command a price in the market

economic growth ECON an increase in the national income of a country created by the long-term productive potential of its economy

economic indicator ECON a statistic that may be important for a country's long-term economic health, for example, rising prices or falling exports

economic life ECON the conditions of trade and manufacture in a country that contribute to its prosperity or poverty

economic miracle ECON the rapid growth after 1945 in countries such as Germany and Japan, where in 10 years economies shattered by the Second World War were regenerated

economic order quantity FIN the most economic stock replenishment order size, which minimises the sum of stock ordering costs and stock-holding costs. EOQ is used in an 'optimising' stock control system. *Abbr* **EOQ**

economic paradigm ECON a basic unchanging economic principle

Economic Planning and Advisory Council FIN a committee of businesspeople and politicians appointed to advise the Australian government on economic issues

economic pressure ECON a condition in a country's economy in which economic indicators are unfavourable

economics ECON the study of the consumption, distribution, and production of wealth in a society

economic surplus ECON the difference between an economy's output and the costs incurred, for example, wages, raw material costs, and depreciation

economic theory of the firm FIN, GEN the theory that states that the only

duty that a company has to those external to it is financial. The economic theory of the firm holds that shareholders should be the prime beneficiaries of an organisation's activities. The theory is associated with top-down leadership and cost-cutting through rationalisation and downsizing. With immediate share price dominating management activities, economic theory has been criticised as being too short term, as opposed to the longer-term thinking behind stakeholder theory.

economic value added FIN a way of judging financial performance by measuring the amount by which the earnings of a project, an operation, or a company exceed or fall short of the total amount of capital that was originally invested by its owners. EVA is conceptually simple: from net operating profit, subtract an appropriate charge for the opportunity cost of all capital invested in an enterprise – the amount that could have been invested elsewhere. *Abbr* **EVA**

economic welfare ECON the level of prosperity in an economy, as measured by employment and wage levels

economist ECON somebody who studies the consumption, distribution, and production of wealth in a society

economy ECON the distribution of wealth in a society and the means by which that wealth is produced and consumed

economy efficiency principle ECON the principle that if an economy is efficient, no one can be made better off without somebody else being made worse off

ecopreneur FIN, GEN an entrepreneur who is concerned with environmental issues

EDB *abbr* FIN Economic Development Board

e-economy ECON an economy that is characterised by extensive use of the Internet and information technology

effective annual rate FIN the average interest rate paid on a deposit for a period of a year. It is the total interest received over 12 months expressed as a percentage of the principal at the beginning of the period.

effective date FIN the date when an action, such as the issuing of new stock, is effective

effective price FIN the price of a share adjusted to take into account the effects of a rights issue. See also *rights issue*

effective spread FIN the difference between the price of a newly issued share and what the underwriter pays, adjusted for the effect of the announcement of the offering

effective strike price FIN the price of an option at a specified time, adjusted for fluctuation since the initial offering

effective tax rate FIN the average tax rate applicable to a given transaction, whether it is income from work undertaken, the sale of an asset, or a gift, taking into account personal allowances and scales of tax. It is the amount of money generated by the transaction divided by the additional tax payable because of it.

efficiency FIN, GEN the achievement of goals in an economical way. Efficiency involves seeking a good balance between economy in terms of resources such as time, money, space, or materials, and the achievement of an organisation's aims and objectives. A distinction is often made between technical and economic efficiency. Technical efficiency means producing maximum output with minimum input, while economic efficiency means the production and distribution of goods at the lowest possible cost. In management, a further distinction is often made between efficiency and effectiveness, with the latter denoting performance in terms of achieving objectives.

efficiency ratio FIN a way of measuring the proportion of operating revenues spent on overhead expenses. Often identified with banking and financial sectors, the efficiency ratio indicates a management's ability to keep overhead costs low. In banking, an acceptable efficiency ratio was once in the low 60s. Now the goal is 50, while better-performing banks boast ratios in the mid-40s. Low ratings usually indicate a higher return on equity and earnings. This measurement is also used by mature industries, such as steel manufacture, chemicals, or car production, that must focus on tight cost controls to boost profitability because growth prospects are modest. The efficiency ratio is defined as operating overhead expenses divided by turnover.

efficient capital market FIN a market in which share prices reflect all the information available to the market about future economic trends and company profitability

EFT *abbr* FIN electronic funds transfer

EIB *abbr* FIN European Investment Bank: a financial institution whose main task is to further regional development within the EU by financing capital projects, modernising or converting undertakings, and developing new activities

either-way market FIN a currency market with identical prices for buying and selling, especially for the euro

elasticity FIN the measure of the sensitivity of one variable to another. In practical terms, elasticity indicates the degree to which consumers respond to changes in price. It is obviously important for companies to consider such relationships when contemplating changes in price, demand, and supply.

electronic commerce E-COM see *e-commerce*

electronic funds transfer at point of sale FIN the payment for goods or services by a bank customer using a card that is swiped through an electronic reader on the till, thereby transferring the cash from the customer's account to the retailer's or service provider's account

electronic money E-COM see *digital money*

electronic payment system E-COM a means of making payments over an electronic network such as the Internet

electronic retailer E-COM see *e-retailer*

electronic shopping E-COM the process of selecting, ordering, and paying for goods or services over an electronic network such as the Internet. Also known as *online shopping*

electronic trading FIN the buying and selling of investment instruments using computers

electronic wallet E-COM see *digital wallet*

elephant FIN a very large financial institution, such as a bank, which makes trades in high volumes, thereby increasing prices *(slang)*

eligible paper FIN **1.** in the United Kingdom, bills of exchange or securities accepted by the Bank of England as security for loans to discount houses **2.** in the United States, first class paper (such as a bill of exchange or a cheque) acceptable for rediscounting by the Federal Reserve System. See also *lender of last resort*

eligible reserves FIN the sum of the cash held by a US bank plus the money it holds at its local Federal Reserve Bank

eligible termination payment FIN a sum paid to an employee when he or she leaves a company, that can be transferred to a concessionally taxed investment account, such as an Approved Deposit Fund. *Abbr* **ETP**

embargo FIN a government order which stops a type of trade, such as exports to, or imports from, a specified country

embezzlement FIN the illegal practice of using money entrusted to an individual's care by a third party for personal benefit

emerging market FIN a country that is becoming industrialised

EMH *abbr* FIN efficient markets hypothesis

emoluments FIN wages, salaries, fees, or any other monetary benefit derived from employment

e-money E-COM see *digital money*

employee stock fund FIN in the United States, a fund from which money is taken to buy shares of a company's stock for its employees

EMS *abbr* FIN European Monetary System: the first stage of economic and monetary union of the EU, which came into force in March 1979, giving stable, but adjustable, exchange rates

EMU *abbr* FIN Economic and Monetary Union, or European Monetary Union: the timetable for EMU was outlined in the Maastricht Treaty in 1991. The cri-

teria were that national debt must not exceed 60% of GDP; budget deficit should be 3% or less of GDP; inflation should be no more than 1.5% above the average rate of the three best-performing economies of the EU in the previous 12 months; and applicants must have been members of the ERM for two years without having re-aligned or devalued their currency.

encash FIN to exchange a cheque for cash

encumbrance FIN a liability, such as a mortgage or charge, which is attached to a property or piece of land

endorse FIN to sign a bill or cheque on the back to show that its ownership is being passed to another person or company

endowment assurance FIN life cover that pays a specific sum of money on a specified date, or earlier in the event of the policyholder's death. Part of the premium paid is for the life cover element, while the remainder is invested in property and stocks and shares (either a 'with-profits' or 'without-profits' policy) or, in the case of a unit-linked policy, is used to purchase units in a life fund. The sum the policyholder receives at the end of the term depends on the size of the premiums and the performance of the investments. See also *term assurance*

endowment fund FIN a unit trust that supports a non-profit institution

endowment policy FIN an insurance policy that pays a set amount to the policyholder when the policy matures, or to a beneficiary if the policyholder dies before it matures

entail FIN a legal condition which passes ownership of a property to specified persons only

enterprise zone FIN, GEN an area in which the government offers financial incentives, such as tax relief, to encourage new business activities. *Abbr* **EZ**

entertainment expenses HR costs, reimbursable by an employer, that are incurred by an employee in hosting social events for clients or suppliers in order to obtain or maintain their custom or goodwill

entitlement offer FIN an offer that cannot be transferred to anyone else

entrepreneur FIN, GEN somebody who sets up a business or enterprise. An entrepreneur typically demonstrates effective application of a number of enterprising attributes, such as creativity, initiative, risk-taking, problem-solving ability, and autonomy, and will often risk his or her own capital to set up a business.

environmental impact assessment FIN a study, undertaken during the planning phase before an investment is made or an operation started, to consider any potential environmental effects

EOQ *abbr* OPS economic order quantity

equal pay HR the principle and practice of paying men and women in the same organisation at the same rate for like work, or work that is rated as of equal value. Work is assessed either through an organisation's job evaluation scheme or by the judgment of an independent expert appointed by an industrial tribunal. Although many countries have legislation on equal pay, a gap still exists between men's pay and women's pay and is attributed to sexual discrimination in job evaluation and payment systems.

equilibrium price ECON the price at which the supply of and the demand for a good are equal. Suppliers increase prices when demand is high and reduce prices when demand is low.

equilibrium quantity ECON the quantity that regulates supply and demand. Suppliers increase quantity when demand is high and reduce quantity when demand is low.

equilibrium rate of interest ECON the rate at which the expected interest rate in a market equals the actual rate prevailing

equipment trust certificate FIN a bond sold for a 20% down payment and collateralised by the equipment purchased with its proceeds

equity claim FIN a claim on earnings that remain after debts are satisfied

equity contribution agreement FIN an agreement to provide equity under specified circumstances

equity dilution FIN the reduction in the percentage of a company represented by each share for an existing

shareholder who has not increased his or her holding in the issue of new ordinary shares

equity dividend cover FIN an accounting ratio, calculated by dividing the distributable profits during a given period by the actual dividend paid in that period, that indicates the likelihood of the dividend being maintained in future years. See also *capital reserves*

equity floor FIN an agreement for one party to pay another whenever some indicator of a stock market's value falls below a specified limit

equity gearing FIN the ratio between a company's borrowings and its equity

equity multiplier *US* FIN a measure of a company's worth, expressed as a multiple of each dollar of its stock's price

equity sweetener FIN an incentive to encourage people to lend a company money. The sweetener takes the form of a warrant that gives the lender the right to buy shares at a later date and at a specified price.

equivalent annual cash flow FIN the value of an annuity required to provide an investor with the same return as some other form of investment

equivalent bond yield FIN see *bond equivalent yield*

equivalent taxable yield FIN the value of a taxable investment required to provide an investor with the same return as some other form of investment

e-retailer E-COM a business that uses an electronic network such as the Internet to sell its goods or services. Also known as *electronic retailer, e-tailer*

erf *S Africa* FIN a plot of rural or urban land, usually no larger than a smallholding

ERM *abbr* FIN Exchange Rate Mechanism: a system to maintain exchange rate stability used in the past by member states of the European Community

ERR *abbr* FIN expected rate of return

error account FIN an account for the temporary placement of funds involved in a financial transaction known to have been executed in error

errors and omissions FIN mistakes from incorrect record-keeping or accounting. *Abbr* **E&O**

ESC *abbr* FIN European Social Charter: a charter adopted by the European Council of the EU in 1989. The 12 rights it contains are: freedom of movement, employment, and remuneration; social protection; improvement of living and working conditions; freedom of association and collective bargaining; worker information; consultation and participation; vocational training; equal treatment of men and women; health and safety protection in the workplace; pension rights; integration of those with disabilities; and protection of young people.

escalator clause FIN a clause in a contract which allows for regular price increases for a product or service to cover projected cost increases

escrow FIN an agreement between two parties which holds that something, such as a good, document, or amount of money should be held for safekeeping by a third party until certain conditions are fulfilled

escrow account FIN an account where money is held in escrow until certain conditions are met, for example, a contract is signed, or a consignment of goods safely delivered

essential industry FIN an industry regarded as crucial to a country's economy and often supported financially by a government by way of tariff protection and tax breaks

establishment fee FIN see *commitment fee*

estate GEN FIN 1. a substantial area of land that normally includes a large house such as a stately home 2. a deceased person's net assets

estimate FIN 1. an approximate calculation of an uncertain value. An estimate may be a reasonable guess based on knowledge and experience or it may be calculated using more sophisticated techniques designed to forecast projected costs, profits, losses, or value. 2. an approximate price quoted for work to be undertaken by a business

estoppel FIN a rule of evidence whereby someone is prevented from denying or asserting a fact in legal proceedings

e-tailer E-COM see *e-retailer*

e-tailing E-COM the practice of doing business over an electronic network such as the Internet

ethical investment FIN investment only in companies whose policies meet the ethical criteria of the investor. Also known as *socially-conscious investing*

ETP *abbr* FIN eligible termination payment

EU *abbr* FIN European Union: a social, economic, and political organisation of European countries whose aim is integration for all member nations. It has been so called since November 1993 under the Maastricht Treaty, before which it was known as the European Community (EC), and before that as the European Economic Community. Also called single market

EUREX *abbr* FIN Eureka Research Expert System: EUREX was established by Eureka (European Research and Co-ordination Agency) in 1985 on a French initiative for non-military industrial research in advanced technologies in Europe

euro FIN the currency of 12 member nations of the European Union. The euro was introduced in 1999, when the first 11 countries to adopt it joined together in an Economic and Monetary Union and fixed their currencies' exchange rate to the euro. Notes and coins were brought into general circulation in January 2002, although banks and other financial institutions had before that time carried out transactions in euros.

Eurobank FIN a US bank that handles transactions in European currencies

Eurobond FIN a bond specified in the currency of one country and sold to investors from another country. Also known as *global bond*

Euro-commercial paper FIN short-term uncollateralised loans obtained by companies in foreign countries

Eurocredit FIN intermediate-term notes used by banks to lend money to governments and companies

Eurocurrency FIN money deposited in one European country but denominated in the currency of another country

Eurodeposit FIN a short-term deposit of Eurocurrency

Eurodollar FIN a US dollar deposited in a European bank or other bank outside the United States

Euroequity issue FIN a note issued by banks in several European countries

Euroland FIN the area of Europe comprising those countries that have adopted the euro

Euro-note FIN a note in the Eurocurrency market

European Accounting Association FIN an organisation for accounting academics. Founded in 1977 and based in Brussels, the EAA aims to be a forum for European research in the subject. It holds an annual congress and since 1992 has published a journal, *European Accounting Review*. *Abbr* **EAA**

European Association of Securities Dealers Automated Quotations FIN see *EASDAQ*

European Bank for Reconstruction and Development FIN see *EBRD*

European Central Bank FIN see *ECB*

European Economic Community or **European Community** FIN see *EU*

European Investment Bank FIN see *EIB*

European Monetary System FIN see *EMS*

European Monetary Union FIN see *EMU*

European option FIN an option that the buyer can exercise only on the day that it expires. See also *American option*

European Social Charter FIN see *ESC*

European Union FIN see *EU*

Euroyen bond FIN a Eurobond denominated in yen

EVA *abbr* FIN economic value added

evergreen loan FIN a series of loans providing a continuing stream of capital for a project

ex-all FIN having no right in any transaction that is pending with respect to shares, such as a split, or the issue of dividends

excess FIN 1. the part of an insurance claim that has to be met by the policyholder rather than the insurance company. An excess of £50 means that the company pays all but £50 of the claim for loss or damage. See also *deductible* 2. in a financial institu-

tion, the amount by which assets exceed liabilities

excess profits tax FIN a tax levied by a government on a company that makes extraordinarily large profits in times of unusual circumstances, for example, during a war. An excess profits tax was imposed in both the United States and the United Kingdom during the Second World War.

excess reserves FIN reserves held by a financial institution that are higher than those required by the regulatory authorities. As such reserves may indicate that demand for loans is low, banks often sell their excess reserves to other institutions.

exchange FIN 1. the conversion of one type of security for another, for example, the exchange of a bond for shares 2. a market where goods, services, or financial instruments are bought and sold

exchange controls ECON the regulations by which a country's banking system controls its residents' or residents companies' dealings in foreign currencies and gold

exchange equalisation account ECON the Bank of England account that sells and buys sterling for gold and foreign currencies to smooth out fluctuations in the exchange rate of the pound

exchange offer FIN an offer to trade one security for another

exchange rate FIN the rate at which one country's currency can be exchanged for that of another country

Exchange Rate Mechanism FIN see *ERM*

exchange rate parity FIN the relationship between the value of one currency and another

exchange rate risk FIN the risk of suffering loss on converting another currency to the currency of a company's own country

exchange rate spread FIN the difference between the price at which a broker or other intermediary buys and sells foreign currency

Exchequer FIN in the United Kingdom, the government's account at the Bank of England into which all revenues from taxes and other sources are paid

excise duty FIN a tax on goods such as alcohol or tobacco produced and sold within a particular country

exclusive economic zone ECON a zone in a country in which particular economic conditions apply. The Special Economic Zone (SEZ) in China, where trade is conducted free of state control, is an example.

ex dividend FIN used to refer to bonds or shares which, when they are sold, do not provide the buyer with the right to a dividend

execution only FIN used to describe a stock market transaction undertaken by an intermediary who acts on behalf of a client without providing advice. See also *active fund management, discretionary management*

executive pension plan FIN in the United Kingdom, a pension scheme for senior executives of a company. The company's contributions are a tax-deductible expense but are subject to a cap. The plan does not prevent the executive being a member of the company's group pension scheme although the executive's total contributions must not exceed a certain percentage of his or her salary.

executive share option scheme FIN a UK term for an arrangement whereby certain directors and employees are given the opportunity to purchase shares in the company at a fixed price at a future date. In certain jurisdictions, such schemes can be tax efficient if certain local tax authority conditions are met.

executor FIN a person appointed under a will to ensure the deceased's estate is distributed according to the terms of the will

exempt gift FIN a gift that is not subject to US gift tax

exempt investment fund FIN in the United Kingdom, a collective investment, usually a unit trust, for investors who have certain tax privileges, for example, charities or contributors to pension plans

exemption FIN an amount per family member that an individual can subtract when reporting income to be taxed

exempt purchaser FIN an institutional investor who may buy newly issued securities without filing a prospectus with a securities commission

exempt security FIN a security that is not subject to a provision of law such as margin or registration requirements

exempt supply FIN an item or service on which VAT is not levied, for example, the purchase of, or rent on, property and financial services

exercise notice FIN an option-holder's notification to the option's writer of his or her desire to exercise the option

exercise of warrants FIN the use of a warrant to purchase stock

exercise value FIN the amount of profit that can be realised by cashing in an option

Eximbank *abbr* FIN Export-Import Bank: a US bank founded in 1934 that provides loans direct to foreign importers of US goods and services

exit P/E ratio FIN the price/earnings ratio when a company changes hands

exit strategy FIN a plan for disposing of a business and realising the value of the investment made in it. The development of an exit strategy involves establishing the value of the business, identifying and selecting exit options, identifying and removing obstacles, and preparing and implementing a plan. Exit options include the sale of the business, merger, flotation or public listing, management buy-out, franchising, family succession, ceasing to trade, or liquidation.

expected rate of return FIN the projected percentage return on an investment, based on the weighted probability of all possible rates of return. *Abbr* **ERR**. See also *capital asset pricing model*

expenditure switching ECON government action to divert domestic spending from one sector to another, for example, from imports to home-produced goods

expense FIN **1.** a cost incurred in buying goods or services **2.** a charge against a company's profit

expense account HR an amount of money that an employee or group of employees can draw on to reclaim personal expenses incurred in carrying out activities for an organisation

expenses HR personal costs incurred by an employee in carrying out activities for an organisation that are reimbursed by the employer

exploding bonus HR a bonus offered to recent graduates that encourages them to sign for a job as quickly as possible as it reduces in value with every day of delay *(slang)*

exponent FIN the number indicating the power to which a base number is to be raised

Export-Import Bank FIN see *Eximbank*

export-led growth ECON growth in which a country's main source of income is from its export trade

ex-rights FIN for sale without rights, for example, voting or conversion rights. The term can be applied to transactions such as the purchase of new shares.

ex-rights date FIN the date when a stock first trades ex-rights

extendable bond FIN a bond whose maturity can be delayed by either the issuer or the holder

extendable note FIN a note whose maturity can be delayed by either the issuer or the holder

extended fund facility ECON a credit facility of the IMF that allows a country up to eight years to repay money it has borrowed from the fund

Extensible Business Reporting Language FIN *abbr* **XBRL**

external account FIN an account held at a United Kingdom-based bank by a customer who is an overseas resident

external audit FIN a periodic examination of the books of account and records of an entity conducted by an independent third party (an auditor) to ensure that they have been properly maintained, are accurate and comply with established concepts, principles, and accounting standards, and give a true and fair view of the financial state of the entity. See also *internal audit*

external debt ECON the part of a country's debt that is owed to creditors who are not residents of the country

external finance FIN money that a company obtains from investors, for example, by loans or by issuing stock

external funds FIN money that a business obtains from a third party rather than from its own resources

external growth FIN business growth as a result of a merger, a takeover, or through a partnership with another organisation

extraordinary item FIN an item included in a company's accounts that is not likely to occur again, such as an acquisition or a sale of assets. These items are not taken into account when a company's operating profit is calculated.

extraordinary resolution FIN in the United Kingdom, an exceptional issue that is put to the vote at a company's general meeting, for example, a change to the company's articles of association. Also known as *special resolution*

EZ *abbr* FIN enterprise zone

face value FIN the value written on a financial instrument

factoring FIN **1.** the practice of transferring title to foreign accounts receivable to a third-party factoring house that assumes responsibility for collections, administrative services, and any other services requested. Major exporters use factoring as a way of reducing exchange rate risk. The fee for this service is a percentage of the value of the receivables, anywhere from 5% to 10% or higher, depending on the currencies involved. Companies often include this percentage in selling prices to recoup the cost. **2.** the sale of debts to a third party (the factor) at a discount, in return for prompt cash. A factoring service may be with recourse, in which case the supplier takes the risk of the debt not being paid, or without recourse, when the factor takes the risk. See also *invoice discounting*

factor market ECON a market in which factors of production are bought and sold, for example, the capital market or the labour market

fair value FIN the amount for which an asset (or liability) could be exchanged in an arm's length transaction between informed and willing parties, other than in a forced or liquidation sale

fallen angel FIN a stock that was once very desirable but has now dropped in value *(slang)*

falling knife FIN a share whose price has fallen at an alarming rate over a short time period

Fannie Mae US FIN see *FNMA*

far month FIN the latest month for which there is a futures contract for a particular commodity. See also *nearby month*

FASB *abbr* US FIN Financial Accounting Standards Board: a body responsible for establishing the standards of financial reporting and accounting for US companies in the private sector. The Securities and Exchange Commission (SEC) performs a comparable role for public companies.

FASTER FIN Fully Automated Screen Trading and Electronic Registration: a computer-based clearing, settlement, registration, and information system operated by the New Zealand Stock Exchange.

fat cat FIN a derogatory term used to describe a chief executive of a large company or organisation who secures extremely large pay, pension, and termination packages, often causing concern among shareholders

FCA *abbr* FIN Fellow of the Institute of Chartered Accountants in England and Wales

FCCA *abbr* FIN Fellow of the Association of Chartered Certified Accountants

FCM *abbr* FIN futures commission merchant

FCMA *abbr* FIN Fellow of the Chartered Institute of Management Accountants

Fed FIN see *Federal Reserve System*

Federal Funds FIN deposits held in reserve by the US Federal Reserve System

Federal income tax US FIN money deducted from employees' salaries in order to fund Federal services and projects

Federal Reserve bank FIN a bank that is a member of the US Federal Reserve System

Federal Reserve Board US FIN a body of seven governors appointed by Congress on the nomination of the President that supervises the US Federal Reserve System and formulates monetary policy. Appointees to the Board of Governors serve for 14 years. *Abbr* **FRB**

Federal Reserve note FIN a note issued by the US Federal Reserve System to

increase the availability of money temporarily

Federal Reserve System FIN the central banking system of the United States, founded in 1913 by an Act of Congress. The board of governors, made up of seven members, is based in Washington DC and 12 Reserve Banks are located in major cities across the United States. Also known as *Fed*

Fed pass FIN the addition of reserves to the US Federal Reserve System in order to increase credit availability

Fedwire FIN the US Federal Reserve System's electronic system for transferring funds

feedback control FIN the measurement of differences between planned outputs and actual outputs achieved, and the modification of subsequent action and/or plans to achieve future required results

feeding frenzy FIN a period of frantic buyer activity in a market *(slang)*

fee work FIN, GEN work on a project carried out by independent workers or contractors, rather than employees of an organisation

Fellow of the Association of Chartered Certified Accountants FIN *Abbr* **FCCA**

Fellow of the Chartered Institute of Management Accountants FIN *Abbr* **FCMA**

Fellow of the Institute of Chartered Accountants in England and Wales FIN *Abbr* **FCA**

fiat money FIN coins or notes which are not worth much as paper or metal but which are said by the government to have some value

fictitious assets FIN assets, such as prepayments, which do not have a resale value, but which are entered as assets on a company's balance sheet

FID *abbr* ANZ FIN Financial Institutions Duty

fiduciary deposit FIN a bank deposit which is managed for the depositor by the bank

FIFO *abbr* FIN first in first out: a method of stock control in which the stock of a given product first placed in store is used before more recently produced or acquired goods or materials

FIF Tax *abbr ANZ* FIN Foreign Investment Funds Tax

final average monthly salary *US* FIN = pensionable earnings

final closing date FIN the last date for the acceptance of a takeover bid, when the bidder has to announce how many shareholders have accepted his or her offer

final demand FIN a last reminder from a supplier to a customer to pay an outstanding debt. Suppliers often begin legal proceedings if a final demand is ignored.

final discharge FIN the final payment on the amount outstanding on a debt

final dividend FIN the dividend paid at the end of a year's trading. The final dividend must be approved by a company's shareholders.

finance FIN the money needed by an individual or company to pay for something, for example, a project or stocks

finance bill FIN an act passed by a legislature to provide money for public spending

finance company FIN a business that lends money to people or companies against collateral, especially to make purchases by hire purchase

finance house FIN a financial institution

finance lease FIN a lease that is treated as though the leassee had borrowed money and bought the leased assets. US term *capital lease*

financial FIN relating to finance

Financial Accounting Standards Board *US* FIN see *FASB*

financial adviser FIN somebody whose job is to give advice about investments

financial aid FIN monetary assistance given to an individual, organisation, or nation. International financial aid, that is from one country to another, is often used to fund educational, health-related, or other humanitarian activities.

financial analyst FIN see *investment analyst*

financial distress FIN the condition of being in severe difficulties over money, especially being close to bankruptcy

financial economies of scale FIN financial advantages gained by being able to do things on a large scale

financial engineering FIN the conversion of one form of financial instrument into another, such as the swap of a fixed-rate instrument for a floating-rate one

financial institution FIN an organisation such as a bank, building society, pension fund, or insurance company which invests large amounts of money in securities

Financial Institutions Duty *ANZ* FIN a tax on monies paid into financial institutions imposed by all state governments in Australia except for Queensland. Financial institutions usually pass the tax on to customers. *Abbr FID*

financial instrument FIN any contract that gives rise to both a financial asset of one entity and a financial liability or equity instrument of another entity. Financial instruments include both primary financial instruments, such as bonds, debtors, creditors, and shares, and derivative financial instruments, whose value derives from the underlying assets.

financial intermediary FIN an institution which accepts deposits or loans from individuals and lends money to clients. Banks, building societies, and hire purchase companies are all financial intermediaries.

financial planning FIN planning the acquisition of funds to finance planned activities

Financial Planning Association of Australia *ANZ* FIN a national organisation representing companies and individuals working in the Australian financial planning industry. Established in 1992, the Association is responsible for monitoring standards among its members. *Abbr FPA*

Financial Reporting Review Panel FIN a UK review panel established to examine contentious departures from accounting standards by large companies

Financial Reporting Standards Board *ANZ* FIN a body that is responsible for setting and monitoring accounting standards in New Zealand. *Abbr FRSB*

financial risk FIN the possibility of loss in an investment or speculation

Financial Services Authority FIN an independent non-governmental body

formed in 1997 following reforms in the regulation of financial services. Banking and investment services supervision was merged into the remit of the previous regulator, the Securities and Investments Board (SIB), which then changed its name to become the Financial Services Authority. The FSA's four statutory objectives were specified by the Financial Services and Markets Act 2000: maintaining market confidence; increasing public knowledge of the finance system; ensuring appropriate protection for consumers; and reducing financial crime. *Abbr FSA*

financial statements FIN summaries of accounts to provide information for interested parties. The most common financial statements are trading and profit and loss account; profit and loss appropriation account; balance sheet; cash-flow statement; report of the auditors; statement of total recognised gains and losses; and reconciliation of movements in shareholders' funds. See also *annual report*

financial supermarket FIN a company which offers a variety of financial services. For example, a bank may offer loans, mortgages, pensions, and insurance alongside its existing range of normal banking services.

financial year FIN **1.** the 12-month period for which a company produces accounts. A financial year is not necessarily the same as a calendar year. *Abbr FY*. See also *fiscal year* **2.** for corporation tax purposes, the period from 1 April of a given year to 31 March of the following year

financing gap ECON a gap in funding for institutions such as the IMF caused by cancelling the debts of poorer countries such as those in West Africa

finder's fee FIN a fee paid to a person who finds a client for another person or company, for example, someone who introduces a new client to a stockbroking firm

FIRB *abbr ANZ* FIN Foreign Investment Review Board

first in first out FIN see *FIFO*

first-round financing FIN the first infusion of capital into a project

fiscal FIN relating to financial matters, especially in respect of governmental collection, use, and regulation of money through taxation

fiscal balance ECON a taxation policy that keeps a country's employment and taxation levels in balance

fiscal drag FIN the effect that inflation has on taxation in that, as earnings rise, the amount of tax collected increases without a rise in tax rates

fiscal policy ECON the central government's policy on lowering or raising taxation or increasing or decreasing public expenditure in order to stimulate or depress aggregate demand

fiscal year US FIN the 12-month period for which a company produces accounts. A fiscal year is not necessarily the same as a calendar year. *Abbr* **FY**

fixed annuity FIN see *annuity*

fixed asset FIN a long-term asset of a business such as a machine or building that will not usually be traded

fixed assets register FIN a record of individual tangible fixed assets

fixed cost FIN a cost that does not change according to sales volumes, unlike variable costs. Fixed costs are usually overheads, such as rent and utility payments.

fixed exchange rate system FIN a system of currency exchange in which there is no change of rate

fixed-interest loan FIN a loan whose rate of interest does not change

fixed-rate loan FIN a loan with an interest rate that is set at the beginning of the term and remains the same throughout

flat tax FIN a tax levied at one fixed rate whatever an individual's income

flat yield curve FIN a yield curve with the same interest rates for long-term bonds as for short-term bonds

flexed budget FIN a budget which changes in response to changes in sales turnover and output

flexible exchange rate system FIN a system of currency exchange in which rates change from time to time

flexible manufacturing system OPS an integrated, computer-controlled production system which is capable of producing any of a range of parts, and of switching quickly and economically between them. *Abbr* **FMS**

float FIN **1.** to sell shares or bonds, for example, to finance a project **2.** the period between the presentation of a cheque as payment and the actual payment to the payee or the financial advantage provided by this period to the drawer of a cheque **3.** a small cash balance maintained to facilitate low-value cash transactions. Records of these transactions should be maintained as evidence of expenditure, and periodically a float or petty cash balance will be replenished to a predetermined level.

floating debenture FIN a debenture secured on all of a company's assets which runs until the company is wound up

floating debt FIN a short-term borrowing that is repeatedly refinanced

floating rate FIN an interest rate that is not fixed and which changes according to fluctuations in the market

floor FIN a lower limit on an interest rate, price, or the value of an asset

flotation FIN the financing of a company by selling shares in it or a new debt issue, or the offering of shares and bonds for sale on the stock exchange. See also *initial public offering*

flow on FIN, GEN a pay increase awarded to one group of workers as a result of a pay rise awarded to another group working in the same field

FMA *abbr* FIN Fund Managers' Association. See also *Investment Management Association*

FMS *abbr* FIN, OPS flexible manufacturing system

FNMA *abbr* US FIN Federal National Mortgage Association: the largest source of housing finance in the United States, the FNMA trades in mortgages guaranteed by the Federal Housing Finance Board. Created in 1938, the FNMA is a shareholder-owned private company and its stock is traded on the New York Stock Exchange. After weathering the US mortgage crisis for over a year, in September 2008 it was placed under the conservatorship of the Federal Housing Finance Agency. Also known as *Fannie Mae*

Forbes 500 FIN a list of the 500 largest public companies in the United States, ranked according to various criteria by *Forbes* magazine

foreign bill FIN a bill of exchange that is not payable in the country where it is issued

foreign currency ECON the currency or interest-bearing bonds of a foreign country

foreign debt FIN hard-currency debt owed to a foreign country in payment for goods and services

foreign dividend FIN in the United Kingdom, a dividend paid by another country, possibly subject to special rules under UK tax codes

foreign equity market FIN the market in one country for equities of companies in other countries

foreign exchange FIN the currencies of other countries, or dealings in these

foreign exchange option FIN a contract which, for a fee, guarantees a worst-case exchange rate for the future purchase of one currency for another. Unlike a forward transaction, the option does not obligate the buyer to deliver a currency on the settlement date unless the buyer chooses to. These options protect against unfavourable currency movements while preserving the ability to participate in favourable movements.

foreign income dividend FIN a dividend paid from earnings in other countries

Foreign Investment Funds Tax *ANZ* FIN a tax imposed by the Australian government on unrealised gains made by Australian residents from offshore investments. It was introduced in 1992 to prevent overseas earnings being taxed at low rates and never brought to Australia. *Abbr* **FIF Tax**

Foreign Investment Review Board *ANZ* FIN a non-statutory body that regulates and advises the federal government on foreign investment in Australia. It was set up in 1976. *Abbr* **FIRB**

foreign reserve FIN the currency of other countries held by an organisation, especially a country's central bank

foreign tax credit FIN a tax advantage for taxes that are paid to or in another country

forensic accounting FIN the use of accounting records and documents in order to determine the legality or otherwise of past activities

Fortune 500 FIN a list of the 500 largest industrial companies in the United States, compiled annually by *Fortune* magazine

forward contract FIN a private futures contract for delivery of a commodity

forward cover FIN the purchase for cash of the quantity of a commodity needed to fulfil a futures contract

forward interest rate FIN an interest rate specified for a loan to be made at a future date

forward market FIN a market for the buying of foreign currency, shares, or commodities for delivery at a later date at a certain price

forward pricing FIN the establishment of the price of a share in a unit trust based on the next asset valuation

forward rate FIN an estimate of what an interest rate will be at a specified future time

forward transaction FIN an agreement to buy one currency and sell another on a date some time beyond two business days. This allows an exchange rate on a given day to be locked in for a future payment or receipt, thereby eliminating exchange rate risk.

fourth market FIN trading carried out directly without brokers, usually by large institutions

FPA *abbr* FIN Financial Planning Association of Australia

fractional currency FIN the paper money that is in denominations smaller than one unit of a standard national currency

fraud FIN, GEN the use of dishonesty, deception, or false representation in order to gain a material advantage or to injure the interests of others. Types of fraud include false accounting, theft, third party or investment fraud, employee collusion, and computer fraud. See also *corporate fraud*

FRB *abbr* US FIN Federal Reserve Board

free coinage FIN a government's minting of coins from precious metals provided by citizens

free enterprise ECON the trade carried on in a free-market economy, where resources are allocated on the basis of supply and demand

free gold FIN gold held by a government but not pledged as a reserve for the government's currency

free market ECON a market in which supply and demand are unregulated, except by the country's competition policy, and rights in physical and intellectual property are upheld

freeze-out FIN, GEN the exclusion of minority shareholders in a company that has been taken over. A freeze-out provision may exist in a takeover agreement, which permits the acquiring organisation to buy the non-controlling shares held by small shareholders. A fair price is usually set, and the freeze-out may take place at a specified time, perhaps two to five years after the takeover. A freeze-out can still take place, even if provision for it is not made in a corporate charter, by applying pressure to minority shareholders to sell their shares to the acquiring company.

frictional unemployment ECON a situation in which people are temporarily out of the labour market. They could be seeking a new job, incurring search delays as they apply, attending interviews, and relocating.

friction-free market FIN, GEN a market in which there is little differentiation between competing products, so that the customer has exceptional choice

fringe benefits HR rewards given or offered to employees in addition to their wages or salaries and included in their employment contract. Fringe benefits range from share options, company cars, expense accounts, cheap loans, medical insurance, and other types of incentive scheme to discounts on company products, subsidised meals, and membership of social and health clubs. Many of these benefits are liable for tax. A cafeteria benefits scheme permits employees to select from a variety of such benefits, although usually some are deemed to be core and not exchangeable for others. Minor benefits, sometimes appropriated rather than given, are known as perks.

front-end loading FIN the practice of taking the commission and administrative expenses from the early payments made to an investment or insurance plan. See also *back-end loading*

frozen account FIN a bank account whose funds cannot be used or withdrawn because of a court order

FRSB *abbr* ANZ FIN Financial Reporting Standards Board

FSA *abbr* FIN Financial Services Authority

FSB *abbr* FIN Federation of Small Businesses

FTSE 30 *abbr* FIN FTSE 30 Share Index

FTSE 30 Share Index FIN an index showing the share prices of 30 influential companies on the London Stock Exchange. Although in existence since 1935, the 30 Share Index is now one of the less popular indices. *Abbr* **FTSE 30**

FTSE 100 *abbr* FIN FTSE 100 Share Index

FTSE 100 Share Index FIN an index, established in 1984, that is based on the share prices of the 100 most highly capitalised public companies in the United Kingdom. *Abbr* **FTSE 100**

FTSE 250 *abbr* FIN FTSE 250 Index

FTSE 250 Index FIN an index of medium-capitalised companies not included in the FTSE 100 Index. It represents over 17% of UK market capitalisation. *Abbr* **FTSE 250**

FTSE All-Share *abbr* FIN FTSE All-Share Index

FTSE All-Share Index FIN an average of the share prices of all the companies listed on the London Stock Exchange. As this encompasses over 1,000 companies, this index is often used as a reliable barometer of the performance of different companies. This index aggregates the FTSE 100, FTSE 250, and FTSE Small Cap indices. *Abbr* **FTSE All-Share**

FTSE Small Cap *abbr* FTSE Small Cap Index

FTSE Small Cap Index FIN an index which indicates the performance of companies with the smallest market capitalisation, representing roughly 2% of market capitalisation in the United Kingdom. *Abbr* **FTSE Small Cap**

FTSE TMT *abbr* FIN FTSE TMT Index

FTSE TMT Index FIN an index which indicates the performance of companies in three key business areas: technology, media, and telecommunications. *Abbr* **FTSE TMT**

full bank FIN a local or foreign bank permitted to engage in the full range of domestic and international services

full coupon bond FIN a bond whose interest rate is competitive in the current market

fully diluted earnings per (common) share FIN earnings on a share that take into account commitments to issue more shares, for example, as a result of convertibles, share options, or warrants

fully distributed issue FIN an issue of shares sold entirely to investors rather than held by dealers

functional budget FIN a budget of income and/or expenditure applicable to a particular function. A function may refer to a department or a process. Functional budgets frequently include the following: production cost budget (based on a forecast of production and plant utilisation); marketing cost budget; sales budget; personnel budget; purchasing budget; and research and development budget. Also known as *departmental budget*

fundamental accounting concepts FIN broad basic assumptions which underlie the periodic financial accounts of business enterprises. See also *concepts*

funded debt FIN long-term debt or debt that has a maturity date in excess of one year. Funded debt is usually issued in the public markets or in the form of a private placement to qualified institutional investors.

funding risk FIN the risk that an entity will encounter difficulty in realising assets or otherwise raising funds to meet commitments associated with financial instruments. See also *liquidity risk*

fund manager FIN somebody who manages the investments of a unit trust or large financial institution

Fund Managers' Association FIN an association which represents the interests of UK-based institutional fund managers. *Abbr* **FMA**

fund of funds *S Africa* FIN a registered unit trust that invests in a range of underlying unit trusts; subscribers own units in the fund of funds, not in the underlying unit trusts

fungible FIN interchangeable and indistinguishable for business purposes from other items of the same type

future FIN a contract to deliver a commodity at a future date. Also known as *futures contract*

future option FIN a contract in which somebody agrees to buy or sell a commodity, currency, or security at an agreed price for delivery in the future. Also known as *futures option*

futures commission merchant FIN somebody who acts as a broker for futures contracts. *Abbr* **FCM**

futures contract FIN see *future*

futures exchange FIN an exchange on which futures contracts are traded

futures market FIN a market for buying and selling securities, commodities, or currencies that tend to fluctuate in price over a period of time. The market's aim is to reduce the risk of uncertainty about future prices.

futures option FIN see *future option*

future value FIN the value that a sum of money will have in the future, taking into account the effects of inflation, interest rates, or currency values. Future value calculations require three figures: the sum in question, the percentage by which it will increase or decrease, and the period of time. See also *present value*

futuristic planning FIN planning for that period which extends beyond the planning horizon in the form of future expected conditions which may exist in respect of the entity, products/services, and environment, but which cannot usefully be expressed in quantified terms. An example would be working out the actions needed in a future with no motor cars.

FY *abbr* FIN financial or fiscal year

G7 FIN the group of seven major industrial nations established in 1985 to discuss the world economy, consisting of Canada, France, Germany, Italy, Japan, the United Kingdom, and the United States

G8 FIN the group of eight major industrial nations consisting of the G7 plus Russia

G10 *abbr* FIN Group of Ten

GAAP *abbr* FIN Generally Accepted Accounting Principles

GAB *abbr* FIN General Arrangements to Borrow: a fund financed by the Group of Ten that is used when the IMF's own resources are insufficient, for example, when there is a need for large loans to one or more industrialised countries

gap analysis FIN a method of improving a company's financial performance by reducing the gap between current results and long-term objectives

garage FIN 1. a UK term meaning to transfer assets or liabilities from one financial centre to another to take advantage of a tax benefit 2. the annex to the main floor of the New York Stock Exchange

garbatrage *US* FIN stocks that rise because of a takeover but are not connected to the target company (*slang*)

GAS *abbr* FIN Government Accountancy Service

GATT *abbr* FIN General Agreement on Tariffs and Trade: a treaty signed in Geneva in 1947 that aimed to foster multilateral trade and settle trading disputes between adherent countries. Initially signed by 23 nations, it started to reduce trade tariffs and, as it was accepted by more and more countries, tackled other barriers to trade. It was replaced on 1 January 1995 by the World Trade Organization.

gazump FIN in the period between agreeing verbally to sell to one buyer but before the agreement becomes legally binding, to accept a higher offer from another buyer. Gazumping is normally associated with the property market, although it can occur in any market where the prices are rising rapidly.

gazunder FIN in the period between agreeing verbally to buy at one price but before the agreement is legally binding, to offer a lower price. Gazundering is normally associated

Dictionary

with the property market, although it can occur in any market where the prices are falling rapidly.

GDP *abbr* ECON gross domestic product: the total flow of services and goods produced by an economy over a quarter or a year, measured by the aggregate value of services and goods at market prices

GDP per capita ECON GDP divided by the country's population so as to achieve a figure per head of population

GEAR *abbr* S Africa FIN Growth, Employment, and Redistribution: the macroeconomic reform programme of the South African government, intended to foster economic growth, create employment, and redistribute income and opportunities in favour of the poor

geared investment trust FIN an investment trust that borrows money in order to increase its portfolio. When the market is rising, shares in a geared investment trust rise faster than those in an ungeared trust, but they fall faster when the market is falling.

geisha bond FIN see *shogun bond*

General Agreement on Tariffs and Trade FIN see *GATT*

General Arrangements to Borrow FIN see *GAB*

general audit FIN an examination of all books and accounts belonging to a company

General Commissioners FIN a body of unpaid individuals appointed by the Lord Chancellor in England, Wales, and Northern Ireland, and the Secretary of State for Scotland in Scotland, to hear appeals on tax matters

general fund FIN a unit trust with investments in a variety of stocks

general ledger FIN a book that lists all of the financial transactions of a company

general undertaking FIN an agreement signed by all the directors of a company applying for Stock Exchange listing, which promises that they will work within the regulations of the Stock Exchange

generative learning GEN a style of organisational learning that encourages experimentation, risk-taking,

openness, and system-wide thinking. Organisations have successfully used this style of learning to transform themselves in the face of technological, social, and market change. Adaptive learning is a contrasting approach to organisational learning.

gensaki FIN the Japanese term for a bond sale incorporating a repurchase agreement at a later date

gift-leaseback FIN the practice of giving somebody a property and then leasing it back, usually for tax advantage or charitable purposes

gift with reservation FIN a gift with some benefit retained for the donor, for example, the legal transfer of a dwelling when the donor continues in residence

gilt FIN see *gilt-edged security*

gilt-edged security FIN 1. a security issued by the UK government that pays a fixed rate of interest on a regular basis for a specific period of time until the redemption date, when the principal is returned. Their names, for example, Exchequer $10\frac{1}{2}\%$ 2005 (abbreviated to Ex $10\frac{1}{2}\%$ '05) or Treasury $11\frac{3}{4}\%$ 2003–07 (abbreviated to Tr $11\frac{3}{4}\%$ '03–'07) indicate the rate and redemption date. Thought to have originated in the 17th century to help fund the war with France, today they form a large part of the National Debt. Also known as *gilt*. See also *index-linked gilt* 2. a US term used to describe a security issued by a blue-chip company, which is therefore considered very secure

gilt repos FIN the market in agreed sales and repurchase of gilt-edged securities, launched in 1996 by the Bank of England to make gilts more attractive to overseas investors

gilt strip FIN a zero-coupon bond created by unbundling the interest payments from a gilt-edged security so that it produces a single cash payment at maturity

gilt unit trust FIN in the United Kingdom, a unit trust where the underlying investments are gilt-edged securities

Ginnie Mae *US* FIN see *GNMA*

giro FIN 1. a European term for the transfer of money from one bank account to another. Also known as *bank giro* 2. a benefit paid by the state *(slang)*

glamour stock *US* FIN a fashionable security with an investment following

Glass-Steagall Act FIN a US law that enforces the separation of the banking and brokerage industries

global bank FIN a bank that is active in the international markets and that has a presence in several continents

global bond FIN see *Eurobond*

global bond issue FIN an issue of bonds that incorporates a settlement mechanism allowing for the transfer of titles between markets

global co-ordinator FIN the lead manager of a global offering who is responsible for overseeing the entire issue and is usually supported by regional and national co-ordinators

global custody FIN a financial service, usually available to institutional investors only, that includes the safekeeping of securities certificates issued in markets across the world, the collection of dividends, dealing with tax, valuation of investments, foreign exchange, and the settlement of transactions

global hedge FIN see *macrohedge*

global offering FIN the offering of securities in several markets simultaneously, for example, in Europe, the Far East, and North America

GM *abbr* FIN gross margin

GNMA *abbr* FIN Government National Mortgage Association: a US-owned corporation that issues mortgage-backed bonds. Also known as *Ginnie Mae*

gnomes of Zurich FIN a derogatory term for Swiss bankers and currency dealers (who have a reputation for secrecy), often used when unknown currency speculators cause havoc in the currency markets *(slang)*

GNP *abbr* ECON gross national product: GDP plus domestic residents' income from investment abroad less income earned in the domestic market accruing to foreigners abroad

GNP per capita ECON GNP divided by the country's population so as to achieve a figure per head of population

go-go fund FIN a unit trust that trades heavily and predominantly in high-return, high-risk investments

going concern FIN an actively trading company

going plural HR giving up a full-time position in order to take on a variety of part-time roles. The term was coined by Allan Leighton, former chief executive of Asda, in September 2000 when he resigned from a full-time position at Wal-Mart to take over a number of boardroom roles. Going plural has similarities with portfolio working.

going short FIN selling an asset one does not own with the intention of acquiring it at a later date at a lower price for delivery to the purchaser. See also *bear*

gold bond FIN a bond for which gold is collateral, often issued by mining companies

gold card FIN a gold-coloured credit card, generally issued to customers with above-average incomes, that may include additional benefits, for example, an overdraft at an advantageous interest rate, and may have an annual fee

gold certificate FIN a document that shows ownership of gold

golden handcuffs FIN a financial incentive paid to encourage employees to remain in an organisation and dissuade them from leaving for a rival business or to start their own company *(slang)*

golden handshake FIN, HR a sum of money given to a senior executive on his or her involuntary departure from an employing organisation as a form of severance pay. A golden handshake can be offered when an executive is required to leave before the expiration of his or her contract, for example, because of a merger or corporate restructuring. It is intended as compensation for loss of office. It can be a very large sum of money, but often it is not related to the perceived performance of the executive concerned. *(slang)*

golden hello FIN, HR a welcome package for a new employee that may include a bonus and share options. A golden hello is designed as an incentive to attract employees. Some of the contents of the welcome package may be contingent on the performance of the employee.

golden parachute FIN, HR a clause inserted in the contract of employment of a senior employee that details a financial package payable if the employee is dismissed. A golden parachute provides an executive with a measure of financial security and may be payable if the employee leaves the organisation following a takeover or merger, or is dismissed as a result of poor performance. Also known as *golden umbrella*

golden share FIN a controlling shareholding retained by a government in a company that has been privatised after having been in public ownership

golden umbrella HR, FIN see *golden parachute*

gold fix or **gold fixing** FIN the twice-daily setting of the gold price in London, Paris, and Zurich

gold reserve FIN gold coins or bullion held by a central bank to support a paper currency and provide security for borrowing

gold standard FIN a system in which a currency unit is defined in terms of its value in gold

good for the day FIN used to describe instructions to a broker that are valid only for the day given

good for this week/month FIN used to describe instructions to a broker that are valid only for the duration of the week/month given. *Abbr* **GTW / GTM**

Goods and Services Tax FIN **1.** a government-imposed consumption tax, currently of 10%, added to the retail cost of goods and services in Australia **2.** a former Canadian tax on goods and services. It was a value-added tax and was replaced by the harmonised sales tax. *Abbr* **GST**

goods received note FIN a record of goods at the point of receipt

good 'til cancel FIN relating to an order to buy or sell a security that is effective until an investor cancels it, up to a maximum of 60 days. *Abbr* **GTC**

good title FIN the legally unquestionable title to property. Also known as *clear title*

goodwill FIN an intangible asset of a company that includes factors such as reputation, contacts, and expertise, for which a buyer of the company may have to pay a premium

go private FIN to revert from being a public limited company quoted on a stock exchange to a private company without a stock market listing

Government Accountancy Service FIN part of HM Treasury, a service whose remit is to ensure that best accounting practice is observed and conducted across the whole of the Civil Service. *Abbr* **GAS**

Government National Mortgage Association *US* FIN see **GNMA**

government securities/stock FIN securities or stock issued by a government, for example, US Treasury bonds or UK gilt-edged securities

graduated payments mortgage *US* FIN a mortgage with a fixed interest rate but with low payments that gradually increase over the first few years. *Abbr* **GPM**

graduated tax FIN a tax that increases in line with an individual's income

granny bond FIN see *index-linked savings certificate*

grant of probate FIN in the United Kingdom, a document issued by a probate office that pronounces the validity of a will and upholds the appointment of the executor(s)

grantor FIN a person who sells an option

graveyard market FIN **1.** a UK term for a market for shares that are infrequently traded either through lack of interest or because they are of little or no value **2.** a bear market where investors who dispose of their holdings are faced with large losses, as potential investors prefer to stay liquid until the market shows signs of improving

gravy train FIN any type of business activity in which an individual or an organisation makes a large profit without much effort

greater fool theory FIN the investing strategy that assumes it is wise to buy a stock that is not worth its current price. The assumption is that somebody will buy it from you later for an even greater price.

greenmail FIN, GEN the purchase of enough of a company's shares to threaten it with takeover, so that the company is forced to buy back the shares at a higher price to avoid the takeover *(slang)*

green pound ECON the fixed European currency unit (ECU) in which prices

Dictionary

of agricultural goods in the European Union are set

green shoe or **greenshoe option** FIN an option offered by a company raising the capital for the issue of further shares to cover a shortfall in the event of over-allocation. It gets its name from the Green Shoe Manufacturing Company, which was the first to include the feature in a public offering. *(slang)*

green taxes FIN taxes levied to discourage behaviour that will be harmful to the environment

grey wave FIN used to describe a company that is thought likely to have good prospects in the distant future. It gets its name from the fact that investors are likely to have grey hair before they see *their expectations fulfilled*. *(slang)*

gross FIN total, before consideration of taxes

gross domestic product ECON see *GDP*

gross interest FIN the interest earned on a deposit or security before the deduction of tax. See also *net interest*

gross lease FIN a lease that does not require the lessee to pay for things the owner usually pays for. See also *net lease*

gross margin FIN **1.** the differential between the interest rate paid by a borrower and the cost of the funds to the lender. *Abbr GM* **2.** the differential between the manufacturing cost of a unit of output and the price at which it is sold

gross national product ECON see *GNP*

gross profit FIN the difference between an organisation's sales revenue and the cost of goods sold. Unlike net profit, gross profit does not include distribution, administration, or finance costs. Also known as *trading profit*

gross profit margin FIN, GEN see *profit margin*

gross receipts FIN the total revenue received by a business

gross redemption yield FIN see *gross yield to redemption*

gross yield FIN the share of income return derived from securities before the deduction of tax

gross yield to redemption FIN the total return to an investor if a fixed interest security is held to maturity, in other words, the aggregate of gross interest received and the capital gain or loss at redemption, annualised. Also known as *gross redemption yield*. US term *yield to maturity*

group FIN a parent company and all its subsidiaries

group certificate *ANZ* HR a document provided by an employer that records an employee's income, income tax payments, and superannuation contributions during the previous financial year

group investment FIN an investment made by more than one person

group life assurance FIN a life assurance policy that covers a number of people, for example, members of an association or club, or a group of employees at a company

Group of Seven FIN see *G7*

Group of Ten FIN the group of ten countries who contribute to the General Arrangements to Borrow fund: Belgium, Canada, France, Germany, Italy, Japan, the Netherlands, Sweden, the United States, and the United Kingdom. Switzerland joined in 1984. Also known as *Paris Club*. See also *GAB*. *Abbr G10*

Growth, Employment, and Redistribution FIN see *GEAR*

growth and income fund FIN a unit trust that tries to maximise growth of capital while paying significant dividends

growth capital FIN funding that allows a company to accelerate its growth. For new start-up companies, growth capital is the second stage of funding after seed *capital*.

growth company ECON a company whose contribution to the economy is growing because it is increasing its workforce or earning increased foreign exchange for its exported goods

growth equity FIN an equity that is thought to have good investment prospects

growth fund FIN a unit trust that tries to maximise growth of capital without regard to dividends

growth industry FIN an industry that has the potential to expand at a faster rate than other industries

growth rate ECON the rate of an economy's growth as measured by its technical progress, the growth of its labour force, and the increase in its capital stock

growth share or **growth stock** **1.** FIN a share that offers investors the prospect of longer-term earnings, rather than a quick return **2.** GEN a share that has been rising greatly in value, relative to its industry or to the market as a whole

grunt work GEN time and labour-intensive work, often carried out by junior members of staff *(slang)*

GST *abbr* FIN Goods and Services Tax

GTC *abbr* FIN good 'til cancel

guarantee FIN a promise made by a third party, or guarantor, that he or she will be liable if one of the parties to a contract fails to fulfil their contractual obligations. A guarantee may be acceptable to a bank as security for borrowing, provided the guarantor has sufficient financial means to cover his or her potential liability.

guaranteed bond FIN in the United States, a bond on which the principal and interest are guaranteed by a company other than the one that issues them, or a stock in which the dividends are similarly guaranteed. See also *guaranteed stocks*

guaranteed fund FIN a fixed term investment where a third party promises to repay the investors' principal in full should the investment fall below the initial sum invested

guaranteed income bond FIN a bond issued by a UK life assurance company designed to provide an investor with a fixed rate of income for a specified period of time. Changes to the regulations now permit only those policies with an independent third party guarantee to receive this denomination.

guaranteed investment certificate FIN an investment instrument issued by an insurance company that guarantees interest but not the principal originally invested

guaranteed stocks FIN in the United Kingdom, bonds issued by nationalised industries that incorporate an explicit guarantee from the government. See also *guaranteed bond*

guarantor FIN a person or organisation that guarantees repayment of a loan if the borrower defaults or is unable to pay

gun jumping *US* FIN an informal US alternative name for insider trading

haggle FIN to negotiate a price with a buyer or seller by the gradual raising of offers and lowering of asking prices until a mutually agreeable price is reached

hammering the market FIN used to describe a situation where there is intense selling *(slang)*

hand signals FIN the signs used by traders on the trading floors at exchanges for futures and options to overcome the problem of noise

hang-out loan FIN the amount of a loan that is still outstanding after the termination of the loan

Hang Seng index FIN an index of the prices of selected shares on the Hong Kong Stock Exchange

hara-kiri swap FIN an interest rate swap made without a profit margin

hard capital rationing FIN see *capital rationing*

hard commodities FIN metals and other solid raw materials. See also *commodity, soft commodities*

hard currency ECON a currency that is traded in a foreign exchange market and for which demand is persistently high relative to its supply. See also *soft currency*

hard landing ECON the rapid decline of an economy into recession and business stagnation after a sustained period of growth

harmonised sales tax FIN a Canadian tax on goods and services. It is a value-added tax that replaced the Goods and Services Tax. *Abbr* **HST**

harvesting strategy FIN a reduction in or cessation of marketing for a product prior to it being withdrawn from sale, resulting in an increase in profits on the back of previous marketing and advertising campaigns

head and shoulders FIN used to describe a graph plotting a company's share price that resembles the silhouette of a person's head and shoulders. Analysts see this as an early indication of a market fall.

headline rate of inflation ECON a measure of inflation that takes account of home owners' mortgage costs

head tax FIN a tax paid by all inhabitants of a country, regardless of their income

hedge fund FIN a unit trust that takes considerable risks, including heavy investment in unconventional instruments, in the hope of generating great profits

hedging against inflation FIN investing in order to avoid the impact of inflation, thus protecting the purchasing power of capital. Historically, equities have generally outperformed returns from savings accounts in the long term and beaten the Retail Price Index. They are thus considered as one of the best hedges against inflation, although it is important to bear in mind that no stock market investment is without risk.

held order FIN an order that a dealer does not process immediately, often because of its great size

heritage industry GEN an industry centred on the efficient business management of a country's historical monuments, with the aim of encouraging tourism and boosting the local economy

Her Majesty's Revenue & Customs or **HM Revenue & Customs** FIN in the United Kingdom, the government department responsible for theadministration and collection of all forms of tax, including VAT, income tax, and excise duties. HMRC combines the duties of two formerly separate departments, the Inland Revenue and HM Customs and Excise. *Abbr* **HMRC**

hidden tax FIN a tax that is not immediately apparent. For example, while a consumer may be aware of a tax on retail purchases, a tax imposed at the wholesale level, which consequently increases the cost of items to the retailer, will not be apparent.

higher-rate tax FIN in the United Kingdom, the highest of the three bands of income tax. Most countries have bands of income tax with different rates applicable to income within each band.

high-flier or **high-flyer** FIN a heavily traded stock that increases in value quickly over a short period

high-performance work organisation GEN an organisation which has adopted a set of working practices deemed to enhance individual and organisational performance. The concept of the HPWO has evolved from research into the link between human resource management and organisational performance. The characteristics commonly associated with HPWOs and identified in the OECD's definition are: moves towards a flatter and less hierarchical organisation structure; a willingness to adopt new working practices; an emphasis on empowerment and teamwork; and high levels of employee participation and learning. These characteristics are believed to foster motivation, trust, communication, knowledge sharing, and innovation within the organisation. They are also thought to lead to an ability to adapt to the changing business environment and to improvements in performance and quality of working life. *Abbr* **HPWO**. Also called high-performance workplace. See also *high-performance work system*

high-performance workplace GEN see *high-performance work organisation*

high-performance work system GEN a scheme of working practices adopted by a high-performance work organisation

high-premium convertible debenture FIN a convertible bond sold at a high premium that offers a competitive rate of interest and has a long term

high yielder FIN a security that has a higher than average yield and is consequently often a higher risk investment

hire purchase FIN a method of paying for a product or service in which the buyer pays by a series of instalments over a period of time. US term *instalment plan*. *Abbr* **HP**

historical summary FIN in the United Kingdom, an optional synopsis of a company's results over a period of time, often five or 10 years, featured in the annual accounts

historic pricing FIN the establishment of the price of a share in a unit trust on the basis of the most recent values of its holdings

HMCE *abbr* FIN HM Customs and Excise. See also *Her Majesty's Revenue & Customs*

HM Customs and Excise FIN *abbr* **HMCE.** See *Her Majesty's Revenue & Customs*

HMRC *abbr* FIN Her Majesty's Revenue & Customs

HMT *abbr* FIN HM Treasury

HM Treasury FIN the UK government department responsible for managing the country's public revenues. While the incumbent prime minister holds the title of First Lord of the Treasury, the department is run on a day-to-day basis by the Chancellor of the Exchequer.

hockey stick FIN a performance curve typical of businesses in their early stages that descends then rises sharply in a straight line, creating a shape similar to that of a hockey stick

holder FIN the person who is in possession of a bill of exchange or promissory note

holding company GEN, FIN a parent organisation that owns and controls other companies. In the United Kingdom, a holding company has to own over half of the nominal share capital in companies that are then deemed to be its subsidiaries. A holding company may have no other business than the holding of stock in other companies.

home loan FIN a mortgage

home run FIN, GEN **1.** a very great achievement **2.** an investment that produces a high rate of return in a short time

honorarium HR a token sum given in recognition of the recipient's performance of specific, non-onerous duties. An honorarium may take the form of an annual retainer.

horizontal merger GEN, FIN see *merger*

horizontal spread FIN a purchase of two options that are identical except for their dates of maturity

horse-trading FIN hard bargaining that results in one party giving the other a concession

hostile bid FIN a takeover bid that is opposed by the target company. See also *greenmail, knight*

hostile takeover FIN see *takeover*

hot card FIN a credit card that has been stolen

hot issue FIN a new security that is expected to trade at a significant premium to its issue price. See also *hot stock*

hot money FIN **1.** money that has been obtained by dishonest means. See also *money laundering* **2.** money that is moved at short notice from one financial centre to another to secure the best possible return

hot stock FIN a share, usually a new issue, that rises quickly on the stock market. See also *hot issue*

HP *abbr* FIN hire purchase

HPWO *abbr* GEN high-performance work organisation

HR scorecard HR a tool for measuring the contribution of human resource management practices to the financial performance of an organisation. The HR scorecard was developed by academics Bryan Becker, Mark Huselid, and Dave Ulrich and presented in their book *The HR Scorecard: Linking People, Strategy, and Performance* (Harvard Business School Press, 2001). It was intended as a supplementary tool to Kaplan and Norton's balanced scorecard, which does not focus on HR practice. The HR scorecard sees human resource management practices as a strategic asset and provides a road map of six steps designed to help organisations integrate human resource systems with organisational strategy.

HST *abbr* FIN harmonised sales tax

human resource accounting FIN the identification, recording, and reporting of the investment in, and return from the employment of, the personnel of an organisation

hybrid FIN a combination of financial instruments, for example, a bond with warrants attached, or a range of cash and derivative instruments designed to mirror the performance of a financial market

hybrid annuity FIN see *annuity*

hybrid financial instrument FIN a financial instrument such as a convertible bond that has characteristics of multiple types of instruments, often convertible from one to another

hyperinflation ECON a very rapid growth in the rate of inflation so that money loses value and physical goods replace currency as a medium

of exchange. This happened in Latin America in the early 1990s, for example.

hypothecate FIN to use a property as collateral for a loan

IAS *abbr* ANZ FIN instalment activity statement

IASC *abbr* FIN International Accounting Standards Committee

IB *abbr* FIN investment bank

IBOR *abbr* FIN Inter Bank Offered Rate: the rate of interest at which banks lend to each other on the interbank market

IBRC *abbr* FIN Insurance Brokers Registration Council: in the United Kingdom, a statutory body established under the Insurance Brokers Registration Act of 1977 that was deregulated following the establishment of the Financial Services Authority and the General Insurance Services Council. Its complaints and administration functions passed to the Institute of Insurance Brokers.

IBRD *abbr* ECON, FIN International Bank for Reconstruction and Development: a United Nations organisation that provides funds, policy guidance, and technical assistance to facilitate economic development in its poorer member countries

ICAEW *abbr* FIN Institute of Chartered Accountants in England and Wales

ICAI *abbr* FIN Institute of Chartered Accountants in Ireland

Icarus factor GEN the tendency of managers or executives to embark on over-ambitious projects which then fail *(slang)*

ICAS *abbr* FIN Institute of Chartered Accountants of Scotland

ICC *abbr* FIN International Chamber of Commerce: an organisation that represents business interests to governments, aiming to improve trading conditions and foster private enterprise

ICSA *abbr* FIN Institute of Chartered Secretaries and Administrators: an organisation that aims to promote the efficient administration of commerce, industry, and public affairs. Founded in 1891 and granted a royal charter in 1902, it represents the interests of its members to government, publishes journals and other materials, promotes the standing of its members, and provides educational support and qualifying schemes.

IDA *abbr* FIN International Development Association: an agency administered by the IBRD to provide assistance on concessionary terms to the poorest developing countries. Its resources consist of subscriptions and general replenishments from its more industrialised and developed members, special contributions, and transfers from the net earnings of the IBRD.

idea practitioner GEN an individual who specialises in identifying, developing, and implementing business and management ideas. Idea practitioners contribute to the success of an organisation by facilitating innovation, especially with regard to business performance and management. They have the ability to select the most appropriate and timely ideas and to translate the ideas of management theorists into practice in their own organisations. The term was introduced by Thomas Davenport and Laurence Prusak in their book *What's the Big Idea?* (Harvard Business School Press, 2003).

ideation GEN, MKT the thought processes involved in apprehending and expressing a new concept, often in a graphical format. Ideation involves the use of imagination to form new ideas and may be used in an organisational context for problem-solving or in the conceptual phase of new product development.

IEA *abbr* GEN International Energy Authority: an autonomous agency within the OECD whose objectives include improving global energy cooperation, developing alternative energy sources, and promoting relations between oil-producing and oil-consuming countries

IFA *abbr* FIN Institute of Financial Accountants

IFC *abbr* FIN International Finance Corporation: a United Nations organisation promoting private sector investment in developing countries to reduce poverty and improve the quality of people's lives. It finances private sector projects that are profit-oriented and environmentally and

socially sound, and helps to foster development. The IFC has a staff of 2,000 professionals around the world who seek profitable and creative solutions to complex business issues.

IIB *abbr* FIN Institute of Insurance Brokers: in the United Kingdom, the professional body for insurance brokers and the caretaker for the deregulated Insurance Brokers Registration Council's complaints scheme

ILG *abbr* FIN index-linked gilt

illegal parking FIN a stock market practice that involves a broker or company purchasing securities in another company's name though they are guaranteed by the real investor *(slang)*

illiquid FIN **1.** used to describe a person or business that lacks cash or assets such as securities that can readily be converted into cash **2.** used to refer to an asset that cannot be easily converted into cash

IMA *abbr* FIN **1.** *ANZ* investment management agreement **2.** Investment Management Association

IMF *abbr* ECON, FIN International Monetary Fund: the organisation that industrialised nations have established to reduce trade barriers and stabilise currencies, especially those of less-industrialised nations

immediate holding company FIN a company with one or more subsidiaries but which is itself a subsidiary of another company (the holding company)

impact day FIN the day when the terms of a new issue of shares are announced

impaired capital FIN a company's capital that is worth less than the par value of its stock

impairment of capital FIN the extent to which the value of a company is less than the par value of its stock

imperfect competition FIN a situation that exists in a market when there are strong barriers to the entry of new competitors

import duty FIN a tax on goods imported into a country. Although it may simply be a measure for raising revenue, it can also be used to protect domestic manufacturers from overseas competition.

import penetration ECON the situation in which one country's imports dominate the market share of those from other industrialised countries. This is the case, for example, with high-tech imports to the United States from Japan.

imprest account FIN a UK term for a record of the transactions of a type of petty cash system. An employee is given an advance of money, an imprest, for incidental expenses and, when most of it has been spent, he or she presents receipts for the expenses to the accounts department and is then reimbursed with cash to the total value of the receipts.

imputation system FIN a system in which recipients of dividends gain tax advantage for taxes paid by the company that paid the dividends

incentive stock option FIN in the United States, an employee stock option plan that gives each qualifying employee the right to purchase a specific number of the corporation's shares at a set price during a specific time period. Tax is only payable when the shares are sold.

incestuous share dealing FIN share dealing by companies within a group in the shares of the other companies within that group. The legality of such transactions depends on the objective of the deals.

inchoate instrument FIN a negotiable instrument that is incomplete because, for example, the date or amount is missing. The person to whom it is delivered has the prima facie authority to complete it in any way he or she considers fit.

incidence of tax FIN used to indicate where the final burden of a tax lies. For example, although a retailer pays any sales tax to the tax-collecting authority, the tax itself is ultimately paid by the customer.

income FIN **1.** money received by a company or individual **2.** money received from savings or investments, for example, interest on a deposit account or dividends from shares. This is also known as *unearned income*. **3.** money generated by a business

income bond FIN a bond that a company repays only from its profits

income distribution FIN **1.** the UK term for the payment to investors of the income generated by a collective investment, less management charges, tax, and expenses. It is distributed in proportion to the number of units or shares held by each investor. US term *income dividend* **2.** the distribution of income across a particular group, such as a company, region, or country. It shows the various wage levels and gives the percentage of individuals earning at each level.

income dividend *US* FIN = income distribution

income gearing FIN the ratio of the interest a company pays on its borrowing shown as a percentage of its pre-tax profits

income-linked gilt FIN a bond issued by the United Kingdom whose principal and interest track the retail price index

income redistribution ECON a government policy to redirect income to a targeted sector of a country's population, for example, by lowering the rate of tax paid by low-income earners

income shares FIN **1.** ordinary shares sought because of their relatively high yield as opposed to their potential to produce capital growth **2.** certain funds, for example, investment trusts, that issue split level funds where holders of the income element receive all the income (less expenses, charges, and tax), while holders of the capital element receive only the capital gains (less expenses, charges, and tax)

income smoothing FIN a UK term for a form of creative accounting that involves the manipulation of a company's financial statements to show steady annual profits rather than large fluctuations

incomes policy ECON a government policy that seeks to restrain increases in wages or prices by regulating the permitted level of increase

income stream FIN the income received by a company from a particular product or activity

income tax FIN a tax levied directly on the income of a person and paid to the government. *Abbr* **IT**

income tax return FIN a form used for reporting income and computing the tax due on it

income unit FIN a unit in a unit trust that makes regular payments to its unit holders

incorporation FIN the legal process of creating a corporation or company. Incorporated entities have a legal status distinct from that of their owners, and limited liability.

indemnity FIN an agreement by one party to make good the losses suffered by another. See also *indemnity insurance, letter of indemnity*

indemnity insurance FIN an insurance contract in which the insurer agrees to cover the cost of losses suffered by the insured party. Most insurance contracts take this form except personal accident and life assurance policies, where fixed sums are paid as compensation, rather than reimbursement, for a loss that cannot be quantified in monetary terms.

indenture FIN a formal agreement showing the terms of a bond issue

index FIN **1.** a standard that represents the value of stocks in a market, particularly a figure such as the Hang Seng, FTSE 100, or Nikkei average **2.** an amount calculated to represent the relative value of a group of things

indexation FIN the linking of a rate to a standard index of prices, interest rates, share prices, or similar items

index fund FIN a unit trust composed of companies listed in an important stock market index in order to match the market's overall performance. See also *managed fund.* Also known as *index-tracker, tracker fund*

index futures FIN a futures contract trading in one of the major stock market indices, such as the FTSE 100 Share Index. See also *Dow Jones Averages*

index-linked bond FIN a security where the income is linked to an index, such as a financial index. See also *index-linked gilt, index-linked savings certificate*

index-linked gilt FIN an inflation-proof UK government bond, first introduced for institutional investors in 1981 and then made available to the general public in 1982. It is inflation-proof in two ways: the dividend is raised every six months in line with

the Retail Price Index and the original capital is repaid in real terms at redemption, when the indexing of the repayment is undertaken. The nominal value of the stock, however, does not increase with inflation. Like other gilts, ILGs are traded on the market. Price changes are principally dependent on investors' changing perceptions of inflation and real yields. *Abbr* **ILG**

index-linked savings certificate FIN a certificate issued by the UK National Savings & Investments organisation, with a return linked to the rate of inflation. Also known as *granny bond*

index number ECON a weighted average of a number of observations of an economic attribute, such as retail prices expressed as a percentage of a similar weighted average calculated at an earlier period

indicated dividend FIN the forecast total of all dividends in a year if the amount of each dividend remains as it is

indicated yield FIN the yield that an indicated dividend represents

indication price FIN an approximation of the price of a security as opposed to its firm price

indicative price FIN the price shown on a screen-based system for trading securities such as the UK Stock Exchange Automated Quotations system. The price is not firm, as the size of the bargain will determine the final price at which market makers will actually deal.

indirect cost FIN, GEN a fixed or overhead cost that cannot be attributed directly to the production of a particular item and is incurred even when there is no output. Indirect costs may include the cost centre functions of finance and accounting, information technology, administration, and personnel. See also *direct cost*

individual retirement account *US* FIN see *IRA*

Individual Savings Account FIN see *ISA*

industrial production ECON the output of a country's productive industries. Until the 1960s, this commonly related to iron and steel or coal, but since then lighter engineering in motor car or robotics manufacture has taken over.

industrial revenue bond FIN a bond that a private company uses to finance construction

industrial-sector cycle ECON a business cycle that reflects patterns of an old economy rather than the new electronic economy

inflation accounting FIN the adjustment of a company's accounts to reflect the effect of inflation and provide a more realistic view of the company's position

inflationary ECON characterised by excess demand or high costs creating an excessive increase in the country's money supply

inflationary gap ECON a gap that exists when an economy's resources are utilised and aggregate demand is more than the full-employment level of output. Prices will rise to remove the excess demand.

inflationary spiral ECON a situation in which, repeatedly, in inflationary conditions, excess demand causes producers to raise prices and workers to demand wage rises to sustain their living standards

inflation-proof security US FIN a security that is indexed to inflation

inflation rate ECON the rate at which general price levels increase over a period of time

inflation tax ECON an income policy that taxes companies that grant pay rises above a particular level

info rate FIN a money market rate quoted by dealers for information only

informal economy ECON the economy that runs in parallel to the formal economy but outside the reach of the tax system, most transactions being paid for in cash or goods

infotainment GEN television programmes that deal with serious issues or current affairs in an entertaining way

initial offer FIN the first offer that a company makes to buy the shares of another company

initial public offering FIN the first instance of making particular shares available for sale to the public. *Abbr* **IPO**

injunction FIN a court order forbidding an individual or organisation from doing something

inland bill FIN a UK term for a bill of exchange that is payable and drawn in the same country

Inland Revenue FIN see ***Her Majesty's Revenue & Customs***

Inland Revenue Department *ANZ* FIN the New Zealand government body responsible for the administration of the national taxation system. *Abbr* **IRD**

inpatriation GEN, HR the transfer of foreign employees to work in the home country of an international organisation on a temporary or permanent basis. Inpatriation often involves the relocation of employees of a foreign subsidiary company in a developing country to the home base or headquarters of a multinational business in the developed world. The aim may be to fill a skills shortage or to develop a global, multicultural perspective in the organisation. The use of the term has developed by analogy with the term 'expatriate'.

input tax credit *ANZ* FIN an amount paid as Goods and Services Tax on supplies purchased for business purposes, which can be offset against Goods and Services Tax collected

inside information FIN information that is of advantage to investors but is only available to people who have personal contact with a company

inside quote FIN a range of prices for a security, from the highest offer to buy to the lowest offer to sell

insider dealing or **insider trading** FIN profitable, usually illegal, trading in securities carried out using information not available to the public

insolvency FIN, GEN the inability to pay debts when they become due. Insolvency will apply even if total assets exceed total liabilities, if those assets cannot be readily converted into cash to meet debts as they mature. Even then, insolvency may not necessarily mean business failure. Bankruptcy may be avoided through debt rescheduling or turnaround management.

instalment FIN one of two or more payments or repayments for the purchase of an initial public offering

instalment activity statement *ANZ* FIN a standard form used in Australia to report pay-as-you-go instalment

payments on investment income. *Abbr* **IAS**

instalment credit FIN the UK term for a loan that is repaid with fixed regular instalments, and with a rate of interest fixed for the duration of the loan. US term ***instalment loan***

instalment loan *US* FIN = instalment credit

instalment plan or **instalment purchase** FIN see ***hire purchase***

Institute of Chartered Accountants in England and Wales FIN the largest professional accountancy body in Europe, providing qualification by examinations, ensuring high standards of education and training, and supervising professional conduct. *Abbr* **ICAEW**

Institute of Chartered Accountants in Ireland FIN the oldest and largest professional body for accountants in Ireland, the ICAI was founded in 1888. Its many aims include promoting best practice in chartered accountancy and maintaining high standards of professionalism among its members. It publishes a journal, *Accountancy Ireland*, and has offices in Dublin and Belfast. *Abbr* **ICAI**

Institute of Chartered Accountants of Scotland FIN the world's oldest professional body for accountants, based in Edinburgh. *Abbr* **ICAS**

Institute of Chartered Secretaries and Administrators FIN see ***ICSA***

Institute of Directors FIN an individual membership association whose stated aim is to 'serve, support, represent, and set standards for directors'. Founded in 1903 by Royal Charter, the IoD has approximately 55,000 members and is an independent, non-political body. It is based in London, but also has offices in Belfast, Birmingham, Bristol, Edinburgh, Manchester, and Nottingham. *Abbr* **IoD**

Institute of Financial Accountants FIN a professional body, established in 1916, which aims to set technical and ethical standards in UK financial accountancy. *Abbr* **IFA**

Institute of Financial Services FIN the trading name of the Chartered Institute of Bankers

Institute of Insurance Brokers FIN see ***IIB***

institutional investor FIN an institution that makes investments

instrument FIN 1. a generic term for either securities or derivatives. See also *financial instrument, negotiable instrument* 2. an official or legal document 3. a means to an end, for example, a government's expenditure and taxation in its quest for reducing unemployment

insurable risk FIN see *risk*

insurance 1. FIN, GEN an arrangement in which individuals or companies pay another company to guarantee them compensation if they suffer loss resulting from risks such as fire, theft, or accidental damage 2. FIN in financial markets, hedging or any other strategy that reduces risk while permitting participation in potential gains

Insurance and Superannuation Commission ANZ FIN, GEN an Australian federal government body responsible for regulating the superannuation and insurance industries. *Abbr* ISC

insurance broker FIN a person or company that acts as an intermediary between companies providing insurance and individuals or companies who need insurance

Insurance Brokers Registration Council FIN see *IBRC*

Insurance Council of Australia FIN, GEN an independent body representing the interests of businesses involved in the insurance industry. It was set up in 1975 and currently represents around 110 companies. *Abbr* ICA

insurance intermediary FIN an individual or firm that provides advice on insurance or assurance and can arrange policies. See also *IIB, IBRC*

insurance policy FIN, GEN a document that sets out the terms and conditions for providing insurance cover against specified risks

insurance premium tax FIN a tax on household, motor vehicle, travel, and other general insurance

insured FIN covered by a contract of insurance

insured account US FIN an account with a bank or savings institution that belongs to a federal or private insurance organisation

insurer FIN the underwriter of an insurance risk

intangible asset FIN an asset, such as intellectual property or goodwill, that is not physical. Also known as *invisible asset*

intellectual property GEN the ownership of rights to ideas, designs, and inventions, including copyrights, patents, and trademarks. Intellectual property is protected by law in most countries, and the World Intellectual Property Organisation is responsible for harmonising the law across different countries and promoting the protection of intellectual property rights.

Inter Bank Offered Rate FIN see *IBOR*

intercommodity spread FIN a combination of purchase and sale of options for related commodities with the same delivery date

intercompany pricing FIN the setting of prices by companies within a group to sell products or services to each other, rather than to external customers

interest FIN the rate that a lender charges for the use of money that is a loan

interest arbitrage FIN transactions in two or more financial centres in order to make an immediate profit by exploiting differences in interest rates. See also *arbitrage*

interest assumption FIN the expected rate of return on a portfolio

interest cover FIN the amount of earnings available to make interest payments after all operating and non-operating income and expenses – except interest and income taxes – have been accounted for. Interest cover is regarded as a measure of a company's creditworthiness because it shows how much income there is to cover interest payments on outstanding debt.

interest-elastic investment FIN an investment with a rate of return that varies with interest rates

interest-inelastic investment FIN an investment with a rate of return that does not vary with interest rates

interest in possession trust FIN a trust that gives one or more beneficiaries an immediate right to receive any income generated by the trust's assets. It can be used for property,

enabling the beneficiary either to enjoy the rent generated by the property or to reside there, or as a life policy, a common arrangement for Inheritance Tax planning.

interest-only mortgage FIN a long-term loan, usually for the purchase of a property, in which the borrower only pays interest to the lender during the term of the mortgage, with the principal being repaid at the end of the term. It is thus the borrower's responsibility to make provisions to accumulate the required capital during the period of the mortgage, usually by contributing to tax-efficient investment plans such as Individual Savings Accounts or by relying on an anticipated inheritance. See also *mortgage*

interest rate FIN the amount of interest charged for borrowing a sum of money over a specified period of time

interest rate cap FIN an upper limit on a rate of interest, for example, in an adjustable-rate mortgage

interest rate effect ECON the mechanism by which interest rates adjust so that investment is equal to savings in an economy

interest rate exposure FIN the risk of a loss associated with movements in the level of interest rates. See also *bond*

interest rate floor FIN a lower limit on a rate of interest, for example, in an adjustable-rate mortgage

interest rate future FIN see *future*

interest rate guarantee FIN 1. an interest rate cap, collar, or cap and collar 2. a tailored indemnity protecting the purchaser against future changes in interest rates

interest rate option FIN see *option*

interest rate swap FIN an exchange of two debt instruments with different rates of interest, made to tailor cash flows to the participants' different requirements

interest sensitive FIN used to describe assets, generally purchased with credit, that are in demand when interest rates fall but considered less attractive when interest rates rise

interim certificate FIN a document certifying partial ownership of stock that is not totally paid for at one time

interim dividend FIN a dividend whose value is determined on the basis of a

Dictionary

period of time of less than a full fiscal year

interim financial statement FIN a financial statement that covers a period other than a full financial year. Although UK companies are not legally obliged to publish interim financial statements, those listed on the London Stock Exchange are obliged to publish a half-yearly report of their activities and a profit and loss account which may either be sent to shareholders or published in a national newspaper. In the United States, the practice is to issue quarterly financial statements.

interim financing FIN financing by means of bridging loans

interim statement FIN a financial statement relating to a period of time of less than a full fiscal year

intermarket spread FIN a combination of purchase and sale of options for the same commodity with the same delivery date on different markets

intermediary FIN somebody who makes investments for others

internal audit FIN an audit of a company undertaken by its employees. See also *external audit*

internal cost analysis FIN an examination of an organisation's value-creating activities to determine sources of profitability and to identify the relative costs of different processes. Internal cost analysis is a tool for analysing the value chain. Principal steps include identifying those processes that create value for the organisation, calculating the cost of each value-creating process against the overall cost of the product or service, identifying the cost components for each process, establishing the links between the processes, and working out the opportunities for achieving relative cost advantage.

internal growth FIN organic growth created within a business, for example, by inventing new products and so increasing its market share, producing products that are more reliable, offering a more efficient service than its competitors, or being more aggressive in its marketing. See also *external growth*

Internal Revenue Code *US* FIN the complex series of federal tax laws

Internal Revenue Service *US* FIN see *IRS*

International Accounting Standards Board FIN an independent and privately funded accounting standards-setting organisation, based in London. The Board, whose members come from nine countries and a range of backgrounds, is committed to developing a single set of high quality, understandable, and enforceable global standards that require transparent and comparable information in general purpose financial statements. It also works with national accounting standard setters to achieve convergence in accounting standards around the world. *Abbr* **IASB**

International Accounting Standards Committee FIN an organisation based in London that works towards achieving global agreement on accounting standards. *Abbr* **IASC**

International Bank for Reconstruction and Development FIN see *IBRD*

International Centre for Settlement of Investment Disputes FIN one of the five institutions that comprises the World Bank Group. It was established in 1966 to undertake the role previously undertaken in a personal capacity by the President of the World Bank in assisting in mediation or conciliation of investment disputes between governments and private foreign investors. The overriding consideration in its establishment was that a specialist institution could help to promote increased flows of international investment. Although ICSID has close links to the World Bank, it is an autonomous organisation. *Abbr* **ICSID**

International Chamber of Commerce FIN see *ICC*

International Depository Receipt FIN the equivalent of an American depository receipt in the rest of the world, an IDR is a negotiable certificate issued by a bank that indicates ownership of stock. *Abbr* **IDR**

International Development Association FIN see *IDA*

International Energy Authority FIN see *IEA*

International Finance Corporation FIN see *IFC*

international fund FIN a unit trust that invests in securities both inside and outside a country

International Fund for Agricultural Development FIN a specialised United Nations agency with a mandate to combat hunger and rural poverty in developing countries. Established as an international financial institution in 1977 following the 1974 World Food Conference, it has financed projects in over 100 countries and independent territories, to which it has committed US 10.6 billion in grants and loans. *Abbr* **IFAD**

International Monetary Fund FIN see *IMF*

International Organization of Securities Commissions FIN an organisation of securities commissions from around the world, based in Madrid. Its objectives are to promote high standards of regulation, exchange information, and establish standards for and effective surveillance of international securities transactions. *Abbr* **IOSCO**

International Securities Market Association FIN the self-regulatory organisation and trade association for the international securities market. Its primary role is to oversee the fast-changing marketplace through the issuing of rules and recommendations relating to trading and settlement practices. Established in 1969, the organisation has over 600 members from 51 countries. *Abbr* **ISMA**

International Union of Credit and Investment Insurers FIN an organisation that works for international acceptance of sound principles of export credit and foreign investment insurance. Founded in 1934, the London-based Union has 51 members in 42 countries that play a role of central importance in world trade, relating to both exports and foreign direct investments. Also known as Berne Union

Internet commerce E-COM the part of e-commerce that consists of commercial transactions conducted over the Internet

Internet merchant E-COM a businessman or businesswoman who sells a product or service over the Internet

Internet payment system E-COM any mechanism for fund transfer from customer to merchant or business to business via the Internet. There are many payment options available, including credit card payment, credit transfer, electronic cheques, direct debit, smart cards, prepaid schemes, loyalty scheme points-based approaches, person-to-person payments, and mobile phone schemes.

interstate commerce FIN commerce that involves more than one US state and is therefore subject to regulation by Congress. See also *intrastate commerce*

intervention ECON government action to manipulate market forces for political or economic purposes

in the money FIN used to refer to an option with intrinsic value

intrastate commerce FIN commerce that occurs within a single state of the United States. See also *interstate commerce*

intrinsic value FIN the difference between the exercise price of an option and its market value

introducing broker FIN a broker who cannot accept payment from customers

inventory US FIN the total of an organisation's commercial assets

inventory turnover FIN an accounting ratio of the number of times inventory is replaced during a given period. The ratio is calculated by dividing net sales by average inventory over a given period. Values are expressed as times per period, most often a year, and a higher figure indicates a more efficient manufacturing operation. Also known as *stock turns*

inverse floating rate note FIN a note whose interest rate varies inversely with a benchmark interest rate

inverted market FIN a situation in which near-term futures cost more than long-term futures for the same commodity

inverted yield curve FIN a yield curve with lower interest rates for long-term bonds than for short-term bonds. See also *yield curve*

investment analyst FIN an employee of a stock exchange company who researches other companies and identifies investment opportunities for clients. Also known as *financial analyst*

investment bank FIN **1.** a bank that specialises in providing funds to corporate borrowers for start-up or expansion. *Abbr* **IB 2.** US = merchant bank. *Abbr* **IB**

investment bill FIN a bill of exchange that is an investment

investment bond FIN in the United Kingdom, a product where the investment is paid as a single premium into a life assurance policy with an underlying asset-backed fund. The bondholder receives a regular income until the end of the bond's term when the investment – the current value of the fund – is returned to the bondholder.

investment borrowing ECON the borrowing of funds intended to encourage a country's economic growth or to support the development of particular industries or regions by adding to physical or human capital

investment centre FIN a profit centre with additional responsibilities for capital investment, and possibly for financing, whose performance is measured by its return on investment

investment club FIN a group of people who join together to make investments in securities

investment committee US FIN a group of employees of an investment bank who evaluate investment proposals

investment company US FIN a company that pools for investment the money of several investors by means of unit trusts. See also *investment fund*

investment dealer *Canada* FIN a securities broker

investment fund FIN a savings scheme that invests its clients' funds in corporate start-up or expansion projects. See also *investment company*

investment management agreement *ANZ* FIN a contract between an investor and an investment manager required under SIS legislation. *Abbr* **IMA**

Investment Management Association FIN the trade body for the UK investment industry, formed in February 2002 following the merger of the Association of Unit Trusts and Investment Funds (AUTIF) and the Fund Managers' Association. *Abbr* **IMA**

investment manager FIN see *fund manager*

investment portfolio FIN see *portfolio*

investment properties FIN either commercial buildings (for example, shops, factories, or offices) or residential dwellings (for example, houses or apartments) that are purchased by businesses or individuals for renting to third parties

investment revaluation reserve FIN the capital reserve where changes in the value of a business's investment properties are disclosed when they are revalued

investment tax credit US FIN a tax advantage for investment, available until 1986 in the United States

investment trust FIN an association of investors that invests in securities

investomer FIN a customer of a business who is also an investor *(slang)*

investor FIN a person or organisation that invests money in something, especially in shares of publicly owned corporations

invisible asset FIN see *intangible asset*

invisible exports ECON the profits, dividends, interest, and royalties received from selling a country's services abroad

invisible imports ECON the profits, dividends, interest, and royalties paid to foreign service companies based in a particular country

invisibles ECON items such as financial and leisure services, as opposed to physical goods, that are traded by a country

invisible trade ECON trade in items such as financial and other services that are listed in the current account of the balance of payments

invoice date FIN the date on which an invoice is issued. The invoice date may be different from the delivery date.

invoice discounting FIN the selling of invoices at a discount for collection by the buyer

invoice register FIN a list of purchase invoices recording the date of receipt of the invoice, the supplier, the invoice value, and the person to whom the invoice has been passed to ensure that all invoices are processed by the accounting system

invoicing FIN the process of issuing invoices

involuntary liquidation preference FIN a payment that a company must make to holders of its preference shares if it is forced to sell its assets when facing bankruptcy

inward investment FIN investment by a government or company in its own country or region, often to stimulate employment or develop a business infrastructure

IOD *abbr* FIN Institute of Directors

IOSCO *abbr* FIN International Organization of Securities Commissions

IOU FIN a rebus representing 'I owe you' that can be used as legal evidence of a debt, although it is most commonly used by an individual as a reminder that small change has been taken, for example, from a float

IPO *abbr* FIN initial public offering

IRA *abbr* US FIN individual retirement account: a pension plan, designed for individuals without a company pension scheme, that allows annual sums, subject to limits dependent upon employment income, to be set aside from earnings tax-free. Individuals with a company pension may invest in an IRA, but only from their net income. IRAs, including the Education IRA, designed as a way of saving for children's education, may invest in almost any financial security except property.

IRD *abbr* ANZ FIN Inland Revenue Department

IRD number *ANZ* FIN a numeric code assigned to all members of the New Zealand workforce for the purpose of paying income tax

IRR *abbr* FIN internal rate of return

irrevocable letter of credit FIN see *letter of credit*

IRS *abbr* FIN Internal Revenue Service: in the United States, the branch of the federal government charged with collecting the majority of federal taxes

ISA *abbr* FIN Individual Savings Account: a portfolio created according to rules that exempt its proceeds, including dividends and capital gains, from taxes. It was launched in 1999

with the intention that it would be available for at least 10 years. Individuals may invest up to £7,200 each year, £3,000 of which may be invested in a savings account. Either the remaining £4,200, or the entire £7,200, may be invested in the stock market.

ISCID *abbr* International Centre for Settlement of Investment Disputes

ISMA *abbr* FIN International Securities Market Association

issuance costs FIN the underwriting, legal, and administrative fees required to issue a debt. These fees are significant when issuing debt in the public markets, such as bonds. However, other types of debt, such as private placements or bank loans, are cheaper to issue because they require less underwriting, legal, and administrative support.

issue FIN a set of stocks or bonds that a company offers for sale at one time

issue by tender FIN see *sale by tender*

Issue Department FIN the department of the Bank of England that is responsible for issuing currency

issued share capital FIN the type, class, number, and amount of shares held by shareholders

issued shares FIN those shares that comprise a company's authorised capital that has been distributed to investors. They may be either fully paid or partly paid shares.

issue price FIN the price at which securities are first offered for sale

issuer E-COM, FIN a financial institution that issues payment cards such as credit or debit cards, pays out to the merchant's account, and bills the customer or debits the customer's account. The issuer guarantees payment for authorised transactions using the payment card. Also known as *card-issuing bank, issuing bank*

issuer bid FIN an offer made by an issuer for its own securities when it is disappointed by the offers of others

issuing bank E-COM, FIN see *issuer*

issuing house FIN in the United Kingdom, a financial institution that specialises in the flotation of private companies. See also *investment bank, merchant bank*

IT *abbr* FIN *income tax*

item FIN a single piece of information included in a company's accounts

Jensen's measure FIN see *risk-adjusted return on capital*

jikan FIN in Japan, the priority rule relating to transactions on the Tokyo Stock Exchange whereby the earlier of two buy or sell orders received at the same price prevails. See also *kakaku yusen*

job FIN a customer order or task of a relatively short duration

jobber's turn FIN formerly, a term used on the London Stock Exchange for a spread

jobbing backwards FIN a UK term for the analysis of an investment transaction with a view to learning from mistakes rather than apportioning blame

job lot FIN a miscellaneous assortment of items, including securities, that are offered as a single deal

joint account FIN an account, for example, one held at a bank or by a broker, that two or more people own in common and have access to

joint and several liability FIN a legal liability that applies to a group of individuals as a whole and each member individually, so that if one member does not meet his or her liability, the shortfall is the shared responsibility of the others. Most guarantees given by two or more individuals to secure borrowing are joint and several. It is a typical feature of most partnership agreements.

joint float ECON a group of currencies which maintains a fixed internal relationship and moves jointly in relation to another currency

joint life annuity FIN an annuity that continues until both parties have died. They are attractive to married couples as they ensure that the survivor has an income for the rest of his or her life.

joint return FIN a tax return filed jointly by a husband and wife

joint stock bank FIN a term that was formerly used for a commercial bank (one that is a partnership), rather than a High Street bank (one that is a public limited company)

journal FIN a record of original entry, into which transactions are normally transferred from source documents. The journal may be subdivided into: sales journal/day book for credit sales; purchases journal/day book for credit purchases; cash book for cash receipts and payments; and the journal proper for transactions which could not appropriately be recorded in any of the other journals.

JSE *abbr* FIN Johannesburg Stock Exchange: the former unofficial name of the JSE Securities Exchange

judgment creditor FIN in a legal action, the individual or business who has brought the action and to whom the court orders the judgment debtor to pay the money owed. In the event of the judgment debtor not conforming to the court order, the judgment creditor must return to the court to request that the judgment be enforced.

judgment debtor FIN in a legal action, the individual or business ordered to pay the judgment creditor the money owed

jumbo mortgage *US* FIN a mortgage that is too large to qualify for favourable treatment by a US government agency

junior capital FIN capital in the form of shareholders' equity, which is repaid only after secured loans (or senior capital) have been paid if the firm goes into liquidation

junior debt FIN a debt that has no claim on a debtor's assets, or less claim than another debt. See also *senior debt*. Also known as *subordinated debt*

junior mortgage FIN a mortgage whose holder has less claim on a debtor's assets than the holder of another mortgage. See also *senior mortgage*

junk bond FIN a high-yielding bond issued on a low-grade security. The issue of junk bonds has most commonly been linked with takeover activity.

JV *abbr* FIN joint venture

K *abbr* FIN a thousand
kakaku yusen FIN in Japan, the price priority system operated on the Tokyo Stock Exchange whereby a lower price takes precedence over a higher price for a sell order, and vice versa for a buy order. See also *jikan*

kangaroo FIN an Australian share traded on the London Stock Exchange *(slang)*
Kansas City Board of Trade FIN a commodities exchange, established in 1856, that specialises in futures and options contracts for red winter wheat, the Value Line® Index, natural gas, and the ISDEX® Internet Stock Index

Keidanren FIN the Japanese abbreviation for the Japan Federation of Economic Organizations. Established in 1946, it aims to work towards a resolution of the major problems facing the Japanese and international business communities and to contribute to the sound development of their economies. The equivalent of the Confederation of British Industry, its members include over 1,000 of Japan's leading corporations (including over 50 foreign companies) and over 100 industry-wide groups representing such major sectors as manufacturing, trade, distribution, finance, and energy.

Keough Plan FIN a pension subject to tax advantage in the United States for somebody who is self-employed or has an interest in a small company. See also *stakeholder pension*
kerb market FIN a stock market that exists outside the stock exchange. The term originates from markets held in the street.

Keynesian economics ECON the economic teachings and doctrines associated with John Maynard Keynes

kickback FIN a sum of money paid illegally in order to gain concessions or favours *(slang)*

kicker FIN an addition to a standard security that makes it more attractive, for example, options and warrants *(slang)* See also *bells and whistles, sweetener*

killing FIN a considerable profit on a transaction *(slang)*

kite FIN a fraudulent financial transaction, for example, a bad cheque that is dated to take advantage of the time interval required for clearing; **fly a kite** FIN to use a fraudulent financial document such as a bad cheque

kiwibond FIN a Eurobond denominated in New Zealand dollars

knight FIN, GEN a term borrowed from chess strategy to describe a company involved in the politics of a takeover bid. There are three main types of knight. A white knight is a company that is friendly to the board of the company to be acquired. If the white knight gains control, it may retain the existing board of directors. A black knight is a former white knight that has disagreed with the board of the company to be acquired and has set up its own hostile bid. A grey knight is a white knight that does not have the confidence of the company to be acquired.

knock-for-knock FIN used to describe a practice between insurance companies whereby each will pay for the repairs to the vehicle it insures in the event of an accident

knock-out option FIN an option to which a condition relating to the underlying security's or commodity's present price is attached so that it effectively expires when it goes out of the money

Krugerrand FIN a South African coin consisting of one ounce of gold, first minted in 1967, bearing the portrait of 19th-century statesman and South African president Paul Kruger on the obverse

labour-intensive FIN involving large numbers of workers or high labour costs

lagging indicator *US* ECON a measurable economic factor, for example, corporate profits or unemployment, that changes after the economy has already moved to a new trend, which it can confirm but not predict

land bank FIN the land that a builder or developer has that is available for development

land banking *US* FIN the practice of buying land that is not needed immediately, but with the expectation of using it in the future

land tax FIN a form of wealth tax imposed in Australia on the value of residential land. The level and conditions of the tax vary from state to state.

lapse FIN the termination of an option without trade in the underlying security or commodity

lapse rights FIN rights, such as those to a specified premium, owned by the person who allows an offer to lapse

last survivor policy FIN an assurance policy covering the lives of two or more people. The sum assured is not paid out until all the policyholders are deceased. See also *joint life annuity*

launder FIN to pass the profits of illegal activities, such as tax evasion, into the normal banking system via apparently legitimate businesses

laundering FIN the process of making money obtained illegally appear legitimate by passing it through banks or businesses

law of diminishing returns FIN, GEN a rule stating that as one factor of production is increased, while others remain constant, the extra output generated by the additional input will eventually fall. The law of diminishing returns therefore means that extra workers, extra capital, extra machinery, or extra land may not necessarily raise output as much as expected. For example, increasing the supply of raw materials to a production line may allow additional output to be produced by using any spare capacity workers have. Once this capacity is fully used, however, continually increasing the amount of raw material without a corresponding increase in the number of workers will not result in an increase of output.

law of supply and demand ECON see *supply and demand*

LBO *abbr* FIN leveraged buyout

L/C *abbr* FIN letter of credit

LCH *abbr* FIN London Clearing House

LCM *abbr* FIN lower of cost or market

LDC *abbr* ECON less developed country

lead FIN in an insurance policy from Lloyd's, the first named underwriting syndicate

lead bank FIN the main bank in a loan syndicate

leading economic indicator or **leading indicator** ECON an economic variable, such as private-sector wages, that tends to show the direction of future economic activity

lead manager FIN the financial institution with overall responsibility for a new issue including its co-ordination, distribution, and related administration

leads and lags FIN in businesses that deal in foreign currencies, the practice of speeding up the receipt of payments (leads) if a currency is going to weaken, and slowing down the payment of costs (lags) if a currency is thought to be about to strengthen, in order to maximise gains and reduce losses

lead time FIN the time interval between the start of an activity or process and its completion, for example, the time between ordering goods and their receipt, or between starting manufacturing of a product and its completion

lead underwriter *US* FIN = lead manager

LEAPS *abbr* FIN long-term equity anticipation securities: options that expire between one and three years in the future

learning curve FIN the mathematical expression of the phenomenon that when complex and labour-intensive procedures are repeated, unit labour times tend to decrease at a constant rate. The learning curve models mathematically this reduction in unit production time.

learning opportunity GEN a positive way of referring to a mistake that someone has made at work

lease back FIN to sell a property or machinery to a company and then take it back on a lease. This is a popular option among cash-strapped small businesses, as it frees up capital that can then be ploughed back into the company. Also, under many lease agreements, customers are able to upgrade their equipment after an agreed period, which helps them to keep up with their competitors.

ledger FIN 1. a collection of accounts, or book of accounts. Credit sales information is recorded, for example, by debtor, in the sales ledger. 2. a collection of accounts, maintained by transfers from the books of original entry. The ledger may be subdivided as follows: the sales ledger/debtors' ledger contains all the personal accounts of customers; the purchases ledger/creditors' ledger contains all the personal accounts of suppliers; the private ledger contains accounts relating to the proprietor's interest in the business such as capital and drawings; the general ledger/nominal ledger contains all other accounts relating to assets, expenses, revenue, and liabilities.

legacy system E-COM, FIN an existing computer system that provides a strategic function for a specific part of a business. Inventory management systems, for example, are legacy systems.

legal tender FIN banknotes and coins that have to be accepted within a given jurisdiction when offered as payment of a debt. See also *limited legal tender*

lender of last resort FIN a central bank that lends money to banks that cannot borrow elsewhere

less-developed country ECON a country whose economic development is held back by the lack of natural resources to produce goods demanded on world markets. *Abbr* **LDC**

lessee FIN the person who has the use of a leased asset

lessor FIN the person who provides an asset being leased

letter of comfort FIN a letter from a holding company addressed to a bank where one of its subsidiaries wishes to borrow money. The purpose of the letter is to support the subsidiary's application to borrow funds and offer reassurance—although not a guarantee—to the bank that the subsidiary will remain in business for the foreseeable future, often with an undertaking to advise the bank if the subsidiary is likely to be sold. US term *letter of moral intent*

letter of credit FIN a letter issued by a bank that can be presented to another bank to authorise the issue of credit or money. *Abbr* **L/C**. Also known as *irrevocable letter of credit*

letter of indemnity FIN a statement that a share certificate has been lost, destroyed, or stolen and that the shareholder will indemnify the company for any loss that might result from its reappearance after the company has issued a replacement to the shareholder

letter of intent FIN a document in which an individual or organisation indicates an intention to do something, for example, buy a business, grant somebody a loan, or participate in a project. The intention may or may not depend on certain conditions being met and the document is not legally binding. See also *letter of comfort*

letter of licence FIN a letter from a creditor to a debtor who is having problems repaying money owed, giving the debtor a certain period of time to raise the money and an undertaking not to bring legal proceedings to recover the debt during that period

letter of moral intent *US* FIN = letter of comfort

letter of renunciation FIN a form used to transfer an allotment of shares

level term assurance FIN a life assurance policy in which an agreed lump sum is paid if the policyholder dies before a certain date. A joint form of this life cover is popular with couples who have children.

leverage FIN a method of corporate funding in which a higher proportion of funds is raised through borrowing than share issue

leveraged bid FIN a takeover bid financed by borrowed money, rather than by a share issue

leveraged buyout FIN a takeover using borrowed money, with the purchased company's assets as collateral. *Abbr* **LBO**

leveraged required return FIN the rate of return from an investment of borrowed money needed to make the investment worthwhile

liability FIN a debt that has no claim on a debtor's assets, or less claim than another debt

liability insurance FIN insurance against legal liability that the insured might incur, for example, from causing an accident

liability management FIN any exercise carried out by a business with the aim of controlling the effect of liabilities on its profitability. This will typically involve controlling the amount of risk undertaken, and ensuring that there is sufficient liquidity and that the best terms are obtained for any funding needs.

LIBID *abbr* FIN London Inter Bank Bid Rate

LIBOR *abbr* FIN London Inter Bank Offered Rate

licence FIN, GEN a contractual arrangement, or a document representing this, in which one organisation gives another the rights to produce, sell, or use something in return for payment

licensing FIN, MKT the transfer of rights to manufacture or market a particular product to another individual or organisation through a legal arrangement or contract. Licensing usually requires that a fee, commission, or royalty is paid to the licensor.

licensing agreement FIN, MKT an agreement permitting a company to market or produce a product or service owned by another company. A licensing agreement grants a licence in return for a fee or royalty payment. Items licensed for use can include patents, trademarks, techniques, designs, and expertise. This kind of agreement is one way for a company to penetrate overseas markets in that it provides a middle path between direct export and investment overseas.

life annuity FIN an annuity that pays a fixed amount per month until the holder's death

life assurance FIN insurance that pays a specified sum to the insured person's beneficiaries after the person's death. US term *life insurance*. Also known as *life cover*

life assured FIN the person or persons covered by a life assurance policy. The life office pays out on the death of the policyholder.

lifeboat *S Africa* FIN a low-interest emergency loan made by a central bank to rescue a commercial bank in danger of becoming insolvent

life cover FIN see *life assurance*

life-cycle savings motive ECON a reason that a household or individual has for saving or spending during the course of their life, as, for example, spending when starting a family or saving when near retirement

life interest FIN a situation where someone benefits from a property for the entirety of his or her lifetime

life office FIN a company that provides life assurance

life policy FIN a life assurance contract

lifestyle business FIN a typically small business run by individuals who have a keen interest in the product or service offered, for example, handmade greetings cards or jewellery, antique dealing or restoring. Such businesses tend to operate during hours that suit the owners, and generally provide them with a comfortable living.

lifetime transfer FIN see *chargeable transfer*

lifetime value FIN, MKT a measure of the total value to a supplier of a customer's business over the duration of their transactions. In a consumer business, customer lifetime value is calculated by analysing the behaviour of a group of customers who have the same recruitment date. The revenue and cost for this group of customers is recorded, by campaign or season, and the overall contribution for that period can then be worked out. Industry experience has shown that the benefits to a business of increasing lifetime value can be enormous. A 5% increase in customer retention can create a 125% increase in profits; a 10% increase in retailer retention can translate to a 20% increase in sales; and extending customer life cycles by three years can treble profits per customer.

LIFFE *abbr* FIN London International Financial Futures and Options Exchange

LIMEAN *abbr* FIN London Inter Bank Mean Rate

limit FIN an amount above or below which a broker is not to conclude the purchase or sale of a security for the client who specifies it

limit down FIN the most that the price of an option may fall in one day on a particular market

Limited FIN when placed at the end of the company's name, used to indicate that a UK company is a limited company. *Abbr* **Ltd**

limited by guarantee FIN see *public limited company*

limited company FIN a British-registered company in which each shareholder is responsible for the company's debts only to the amount that he or she has invested in the company. Limited companies must be formed by at least two directors.

See also *public limited company*. *Abbr* **Ltd**

limited legal tender FIN in some jurisdictions, low denomination notes and all coins that may only be submitted up to a certain sum as legal tender in any one transaction

limited liability FIN the restriction of an owner's loss in a business to the amount of capital he or she has invested in it

limited market FIN a market in which dealings for a specific security are difficult to transact, for example, because it has only limited appeal to investors or, in the case of shares, because institutions or family members are unlikely to sell them

limit up FIN the most that the price of an option may rise in one day on a particular market

linear programming **1.** GEN a mathematical technique used to identify an optimal solution for the deployment of resources to meet organisational objectives. Linear programming uses graphical and algebraic means to calculate which combination of resources, subject to predicted constraints, is most likely to fulfil a given objective. It was developed during the 1940s for use in military planning. **2.** FIN the use of a series of linear equations to construct a mathematical model. The objective is to obtain an optimal solution to a complex operational problem, which may involve the production of a number of products in an environment in which there are many constraints.

line of credit FIN an agreed finance facility that allows a company or individual to borrow money. Also known as *credit line*

liquid asset ratio FIN the ratio of liquid assets to total assets

liquid assets FIN, ECON cash, and other assets readily convertible into cash

liquidate FIN to close a company by selling its assets, paying off any outstanding debts, distributing any remaining profits to the shareholders, and then ceasing trading

liquidated damages FIN an amount of money somebody pays for breaching a contract

liquidated damages clause FIN, GEN a clause in a contract which sets out

the compensation to be paid in the event of a breach or a default of the terms of the contract. The compensation set out in a liquidated damages clause should be a genuine pre-estimate of the loss suffered as a result of the non-completion of the contract. An example would be an amount payable per day in the event of the non-completion of a building project. If the amount specified is not considered a genuine estimate of the losses incurred, and the clause is perceived to be solely an incentive for the completion of the contract, the clause is deemed a penalty clause and is not legally enforceable. However, liquidated damages clauses are often inaccurately referred to as penalty clauses.

liquidation FIN the winding-up of a company, a process during which assets are sold, liabilities settled as far as possible, and any remaining cash returned to the members. Liquidation may be voluntary or compulsory.

liquidation value FIN the amount of money that a quick sale of all of a company's assets would yield

liquidator FIN the person appointed by a company, its creditors, or its shareholders to sell the assets of an insolvent company. The proceeds of the sale are used to discharge debts to creditors, with any surplus distributed to shareholders.

liquidity FIN a condition in which assets are held in a cash or near cash form

liquidity agreement FIN an agreement to allow conversion of an asset into cash

liquidity preference ECON a choice made by people to hold their wealth in the form of cash rather than bonds or stocks

liquidity ratio FIN see *cash ratio*

liquidity risk FIN the risk that an entity will encounter difficulty in realising assets or otherwise raising funds to meet commitments associated with financial instruments. Also called *funding risk*

liquidity trap FIN a central bank's inability to lower interest rates once investors believe rates can go no lower

liquid market FIN a market in which a large number of trades are being made

list broker FIN, GEN a person or organisation that makes the arrangements for one company to use another company's direct mail list

listed company FIN a company whose shares trade on an exchange

listed security FIN a security listed on an exchange

listing requirements FIN the conditions that have to be met before a security can be traded on a recognised stock exchange. Although exact requirements vary from one exchange to another, the two main ones are that the issuing company's assets should exceed a minimum amount and that the required information about its finances and business should have been published.

Little Board FIN the American Stock Exchange *(slang)* See also *Big Board*

living wage HR a level of pay that provides just enough income for normal day-to-day subsistence

LLC *abbr* GEN limited liability company

LME *abbr* FIN London Metal Exchange

load FIN an initial charge in some investment funds. See also *load fund*

load fund FIN a unit trust that charges a fee for the purchase or sale of shares. See also *no-load fund*

loading *ANZ* HR a payment made to workers over and above the basic wage in recognition of special skills or unfavourable conditions, for example, for overtime or shiftwork

loan FIN a borrowing either by a business or a consumer where the amount borrowed is repaid according to an agreed schedule at an agreed interest rate, typically by regular instalments over a set period of years. However, the principal may be repayable in one instalment. See also *balloon loan, fixed-rate loan, interest-only mortgage, variable interest rate*

loanable funds theory FIN the theory that interest rates are determined solely by supply and demand

loanback FIN the ability of a holder of a pension fund to borrow money from it

loan constant ratio FIN the total of annual payments due on a loan as a fraction of the amount of the principal

Loan Council *ANZ* FIN an Australian federal body, made up of treasurers from the states and the Commonwealth of

Dictionary

Australia that monitors borrowing by state governments

loan loss reserves FIN the money a bank holds to cover losses through defaults on loans that it makes

loan production cycle FIN the period that begins with an application for a loan and ends with the lending of money

loan schedule FIN a list of the payments due on a loan and the balance outstanding after each has been made

loan shark FIN somebody who lends money at excessively, often illegally, high rates of interest

loan stock FIN bonds and debentures

loan to value ratio FIN the ratio of the amount of a loan to the value of the collateral for it

loan value FIN the amount that a lender is willing to lend a borrower

London Chamber of Commerce and Industry FIN in the United Kingdom, the largest chamber of commerce, that aims 'to help London businesses succeed by promoting their interests and expanding their opportunities as members of a worldwide business network'. See also *ICC*

London Clearing House FIN an organisation that acts on behalf of its members as a central counterparty for contracts traded on the London International Financial Futures and Options Exchange, the International Petroleum Exchange, and the London Metal Exchange. When the LCH has registered a trade, it becomes the buyer to every member who sells and the seller to every member who buys, ensuring good financial performance. To protect it against the risks assumed as central counterparty, the LCH establishes margin requirements. See also *margining*. *Abbr* **LCH**

London Commodity Exchange FIN see *London International Financial Futures and Options Exchange*

London Inter Bank Bid Rate FIN on the UK money markets, the rate at which banks will bid to take deposits in Eurocurrency from each other. The deposits are for terms from overnight up to five years. *Abbr* **LIBID**

London Inter Bank Mean Rate FIN the average of the London Inter Bank

Offered Rate and the London Inter Bank Bid Rate, occasionally used as a reference rate. *Abbr* **LIMEAN**

London Inter Bank Offered Rate FIN on the UK money markets, the rate at which banks will offer to make deposits in Eurocurrency from each other, often used as a reference rate. The deposits are for terms from overnight up to five years. *Abbr* **LIBOR**

London International Financial Futures and Options Exchange FIN an exchange for trading financial futures and options. Established in 1982, it offered contracts on interest rates denominated in most of the world's major currencies until 1992, when it merged with the London Traded Options Market, adding equity options to its product range. In 1996 it merged with the London Commodity Exchange, adding a range of soft commodity and agricultural commodity contracts to its financial portfolio. From November 1998, trading gradually migrated from the floor of the exchange to screen-based trading. *Abbr* **LIFFE**

London Metal Exchange FIN one of the world's largest non-ferrous metal exchanges, that deals in aluminium, tin, and nickel. The primary roles of the exchange are hedging, providing official international reference prices, and appropriate storage facilities. Its origins can be traced back to 1571, though in its present form it dates from 1877. *Abbr* **LME**

London Traded Options Market FIN see *London International Financial Futures and Options Exchange*

long FIN having more shares than are promised for sale

long-dated bond FIN a bond issued by the United Kingdom with a maturity at least 15 years in the future

long-dated gilt FIN see *gilt-edged security*

long position FIN a situation in which dealers hold securities, commodities, or contracts, expecting prices to rise

long-term bond FIN a bond that has at least 10 years before its redemption date, or, in some markets, a bond with more than seven years until its redemption date. See also *medium-term bond*

long-term debt FIN loans that are due after at least one year

long-term equity anticipation securities FIN see *LEAPS*

long-term financing FIN forms of funding such as loans or stock issue that do not have to be repaid immediately

long-term lease FIN a lease of at least 10 years

long-term liabilities FIN forms of debt such as loans that do not have to be repaid immediately

lookback option FIN an option whose price the buyer chooses from all of the prices that have existed during the option's life

loss FIN a financial position in which the costs of an activity exceed the income derived from it

loss adjuster FIN, GEN a professional person acting on behalf of an insurance company to assess the value of an insurance claim. Also known as *claims adjuster*

loss assessor FIN in the United Kingdom, a person appointed by an insurance policyholder to assist with his or her claim

loss leader FIN, MKT a product or service that is sold at a loss in order to attract more customers to an organisation

lot FIN **1.** the minimum quantity of a commodity that may be purchased on an exchange, for example, 1,000 ounces of gold on the London Bullion Market **2.** an item or a collection of related items being offered for sale at an auction **3.** *US* a group of shares held or traded together, usually in units of 100 **4.** *US* a piece of land that can be sold

lottery FIN the random method of selecting successful applicants for something, occasionally used when a new share issue is oversubscribed

lower of cost or market FIN a method used by manufacturing and supply firms when accounting for their homogeneous stocks that involves valuing them either at their original cost or the current market price, whichever is lower. *Abbr* **LCM**

low-start mortgage FIN a long-term loan, usually for the purchase of a property, in which the borrower only pays the interest on the loan for the first few years, usually three. After that, the repayments increase to cover the interest and part of the original loan, as in a repayment mortgage. Low-start mortgages are popular with first-time buyers, as the lower initial costs may free up funds for furnishings or home improvements. See also *mortgage*

loyalty bonus FIN in the United Kingdom in the 1980s, a number of extra shares, calculated as a proportion of the shares originally subscribed, given to original subscribers of privatisation issues providing the shares were held continously for a given period of time

lump sum FIN **1.** used to describe a loan that is repayable with one instalment at the end of its term. See also *balloon loan, interest-only mortgage* **2.** an amount of money received in one payment, for example, the sum payable to the beneficiary of a life assurance policy on the death of the policyholder

luxury tax FIN a tax on goods or services that are considered non-essential

machine hour rate FIN an overhead absorption rate based on machine hours

macroeconomics ECON the study of national income and the economic systems of national economies

macroeconomy ECON the broad sectors of a country's economic activity, for example, the financial or industrial sectors, that are aggregated to form its economic system as a whole

macrohedge FIN a hedge that pertains to an entire portfolio. See also *microhedge*. Also known as *global hedge*

magnet employer HR a popular organisation which attracts many job applicants *(slang)*

maintenance bond FIN a bond that provides a guarantee against defects for some time after a contract has been fulfilled

majority shareholder FIN a shareholder with a controlling interest in a company

managed currency fund FIN a unit trust that makes considered investments in currencies

managed economy FIN an economy directed by a government rather than the free market

managed float ECON the position when the exchange rate of a country's currency is influenced by government action in the foreign exchange market

managed fund FIN a unit trust that makes considered investments. See also *index fund*

managed rate FIN a rate of interest charged by a financial institution for borrowing that is not prescribed as a margin over base rate but is set from time to time by the institution

management accountant FIN a person who contributes to management's decision-making processes by, for example, collecting and processing data relating to a business's costs, sales, and the profitability of individual activities

management accounting FIN the application of the principles of accounting and financial management to create, protect, preserve, and increase value so as to deliver that value to the stakeholders of profit and non-profit enterprises, both public and private. Management accounting is an integral part of management, requiring the identification, generation, presentation, interpretation, and use of information relevant to formulating business strategy; planning and controlling activities; decision-making; efficient resource usage; performance improvement and value enhancement; safeguarding tangible and intangible assets; and corporate governance and internal control.

management buy-out FIN, GEN the purchase of an existing business by an individual manager or management group from within that business. *Abbr* **MBO**

management consultancy GEN **1.** the activity of advising on management techniques and practices. Management consultancy usually involves the identification of a problem, or the analysis of a specific area of one organisation, and the reporting of any resulting findings. The consultancy process can sometimes be extended to help put into effect the recommendations made. **2.** a firm of management consultants

managing for value FIN an approach to building the long-term value of a business. The term is most frequently used by businesses that are implementing the balanced scorecard and emphasises the need to make financial and commercial decisions that build the value of the business for its shareholders.

M&A *abbr* FIN mergers and acquisitions

mandatory quote period FIN a period of time during which prices of securities must be displayed in a market

Marché des Options Négotiables de Paris FIN in France, the traded options market. *Abbr* **MONEP**

Marché International de France FIN in France, the international futures and options exchange

margin 1. FIN, GEN the difference between the cost and the selling price of a product or service **2.** *ANZ* HR a payment made to workers over and above the basic wage in recognition of special skills

margin account FIN an account with a broker who lends money for investments

marginal analysis ECON the study of how small changes in an economic variable will affect an economy

marginal cost 1. ECON the amount by which the costs of a firm will be increased if its output is increased by one more unit, or if one more customer is served. If the price charged is greater than the marginal cost, then the revenue gain will be greater than the added cost. That, in turn, will increase profit, so the expansion in production or service makes economic sense and should proceed. The reverse is also true: if the price charged is less than the marginal cost, expansion should not go ahead. **2.** FIN the part of the cost of one unit of product or service which would be avoided if that unit were not produced, or which would increase if one extra unit were produced

marginal costing FIN the accounting system in which variable costs are charged to cost units and fixed costs of the period are written off in full against the aggregate contribution. Its special value is in recognising cost behaviour, and hence assisting in decision-making. Also known as *variable costing*

marginal costs and benefits ECON the losses or gains to an individual or

Dictionary

household arising from a small change in a variable, such as food consumption or income received

marginal lender FIN a lender who will make a loan only at or above a particular rate of interest

marginal private cost ECON the cost to an individual of a small change in the price of a variable, for example, petrol

marginal revenue FIN the revenue generated by additional units of production

marginal tax rate FIN the rate of tax payable on a person's income after business expenses have been deducted

margining FIN the system by which the London Clearing House (LCH) controls the risk associated with a London International Financial Futures and Options Exchange clearing member's position on a daily basis. To achieve this, clearing members deposit cash or collateral with the LCH in the form of initial and variation margins. The initial margin is the deposit required on all open positions (long or short) to cover short-term price movements and is returned to members by the LCH when the position is closed. The variation margin is the members' profits or losses, calculated daily from the marked-to-market-close value of their position (whereby contracts are revalued daily for the calculation of variation margin), and credited to or debited from their accounts.

marked cheque FIN a certified cheque (slang)

marked price FIN the original displayed price of a product in a shop. In a sale, customers may be offered a saving on the marked price.

market 1. ECON, GEN a group of people or organisations unified by a common need **2.** ECON, GEN a gathering of sellers and purchasers to exchange commodities **3.** ECON, FIN the rate at which financial commodities or securities are being sold

market-based pricing FIN setting a price based on the value of the product in the perception of the customer. Also known as *perceived-value pricing*

market bubble FIN a stock market phenomenon in which values in a particular sector become inflated for a short period. If the bubble bursts, share prices in that sector collapse.

market cap *abbr* FIN market capitalisation

market economy ECON an economy in which a free market in goods and services operates

marketeer MKT a small company that competes in the same market as larger companies. Examples of marketeers are restaurants, travel agents, computer software providers, garages, and insurance brokers.

market if touched FIN an order to trade a security if it reaches a specified price. *Abbr* **MIT**

market leader MKT, FIN see *market share*

market logic FIN the prevailing forces or attitudes that determine a company's success or failure on the stock market

market maker FIN **1.** somebody who works in a stock exchange to facilitate trade in one particular company **2.** a broker or bank that maintains a market for a security that does not trade on any exchange

market order FIN an order to trade a security at the best price the broker can obtain

market price ECON in economics, the theoretical price at which supply equals demand

market risk FIN risk that cannot be diversified away, also known as systematic risk. Non-systematic or unsystematic risk applies to a single investment or class of investments, and can be reduced or eliminated by diversification.

market sentiment FIN the mood of those participating in exchange dealings that can range from absolute euphoria to downright gloom and despondency and tends to reflect recent company results, economic indicators, and comments by politicians, analysts, or opinion formers. Optimism increases demand and therefore prices, while pessimism has the opposite effect.

market share FIN one entity's sales of a product or service in a specified market expressed as a proportion of total sales by all entities offering that product or service to the market. It

can be viewed as a planning tool and a performance assessment ratio.

market size FIN the largest number of shares that a market will handle in one trade of a particular security

market valuation FIN **1.** the value of a portfolio at market prices **2.** the opinion of an expert professional as to the current worth of a piece of land or property

market value FIN the price that buyers are willing to pay for a good or service

market value added FIN the difference between a company's market value (derived from the share price), and its economic book value (the amount of capital that shareholders have committed to the firm throughout its existence, including any retained earnings). *Abbr* **MVA**

marking down FIN the reduction by market makers in the price at which they are prepared to deal in a security, for example, because of an adverse report by an analyst, or the announcement or anticipated announcement of a profit warning by a company

massaging FIN the adjustment of financial figures to create the impression of better performance (slang)

master limited partnership FIN a partnership of a type that combines tax advantages and advantages of liquidity

matched bargain FIN the linked sale and repurchase of the same security. See also *bed and breakfast deal*

material facts FIN **1.** information that has to be disclosed in a prospectus. See also *listing requirements* **2.** in an insurance contract, information that the insured has to reveal at the time that the policy is taken out, for example, that a house is located on the edge of a crumbling cliff. Failure to reveal material facts can result in the contract being declared void.

material information FIN = material news

material news FIN price sensitive developments in a company, for example, proposed acquisitions, mergers, profit warnings, and the resignation of directors, that most stock exchanges require a company to announce immediately prior to the exchange. US term *material information*

maturity FIN the stage at which a financial instrument, such as a bond, is due for repayment

maturity date FIN the date when an option expires

maturity yield FIN see *yield*

maximum stock level FIN a stock level, set for control purposes, which actual stockholding should never exceed. It is calculated as follows:

(Reorder level + Economic order quantity) – (Minimum rate of usage × Minimum lead time)

MBIA *abbr* FIN Municipal Bond Insurance Association: a group of insurance companies that insure high-rated municipal bonds

mean reversion FIN the tendency of a variable such as price to return towards its average value after approaching an extreme position

Medicare FIN a US health insurance programme in which the government pays part of the cost of medical care and hospital treatment for people over 65

medium of exchange FIN anything that is used to pay for goods. Nowadays, this usually takes the form of money (banknotes and coins), but in ancient societies, it included anything from cattle to shells.

medium-term bond FIN a bond that has at least five but no more than 10 years before its redemption date. See also *long-term bond*

meltdown FIN an incidence of substantial losses on the stock market. Black Monday (19 October 1987) was described as Meltdown Monday in the press the following day.

member bank FIN a bank that is a member of the US Federal Reserve System

member firm FIN a firm of brokers or market makers that is a member of the London Stock Exchange

member of a company FIN in the United Kingdom, a shareholder whose name is recorded in the register of members

members' voluntary liquidation FIN in the United Kingdom, a special resolution passed by the members of a solvent company for the winding-up of the organisation. Prior to the resolution the directors of the company must make a declaration of solvency. Should the appointed liquidator have grounds for believing that the company is not solvent, the winding-up will be treated as compulsory liquidation. See also *voluntary liquidation*

mercantile ECON relating to trade or commercial activity

mercantile agency FIN a company that evaluates the creditworthiness of potential corporate borrowers. US term *credit bureau*

mercantile paper FIN see *commercial paper*

mercantilism ECON the body of economic thought developed between the 1650s and 1750s, based on the belief that a country's wealth depended on the strength of its foreign trade

merchant account E-COM an account established by an e-merchant at a financial institution or merchant bank to receive the proceeds of credit card transactions

merchant bank FIN a bank that does not accept deposits but only provides services to those who offer securities to investors and also to those investors. US term *investment bank*

merger FIN, GEN the union of two or more organisations under single ownership, through the direct acquisition by one organisation of the net assets or liabilities of the other. A merger can be the result of a friendly takeover, which results in the combining of companies on an equal footing. After a merger, the legal existence of the acquired organisation is terminated. There is no standard definition of a merger, as each union is different, depending on what is expected from the merger, and on the negotiations, strategy, stock and assets, human resources, and shareholders of the players. Four broad types of mergers are recognised. A horizontal merger involves firms from the same industry, while a vertical merger involves firms from the same supply chain. A circular merger involves firms with different products but similar distribution channels. A conglomerate company is produced by the union of firms with few or no similarities in production or marketing but that come together to create a larger economic base and greater profit potential. Also known as *acquisition, one-to-one merger*. See also *consolidation, partnership*

merger accounting FIN a method of accounting which regards the business combination as the acquisition of one company by another. The identifiable assets and liabilities of the company acquired are included in the consolidated balance sheet at their fair value at the date of acquisition, and its results included in the profit and loss account from the date of acquisition. The difference between the fair value of the consideration given and the fair values of the net assets of the entity acquired is accounted for as goodwill.

mergers and acquisitions FIN a blanket term covering the main ways in which organisations change hands. *Abbr* **M&A**

microbusiness GEN a very small business with fewer than 10 employees

microcash E-COM a form of electronic money with no denominations, permitting sub-denomination transactions of a fraction of a penny or cent

microcredit FIN the extension of credit to entrepreneurs and microbusinesses too poor to qualify for conventional bank loans. Also known as *microlending*

microeconomic incentive ECON a tax benefit or subsidy given to a business to achieve a particular objective such as increased sales overseas

microeconomics ECON the branch of economics that studies the contribution of groups of consumers or firms, or of individual consumers, to a country's economy

microeconomy ECON the narrow sectors of a country's economic activity that influence the behaviour of the economy as a whole, for example, consumer choices

microhedge FIN a hedge that relates to a single asset or liability. See also *macrohedge*

microlending FIN see *microcredit*

micromanagement GEN a style of management where a manager becomes over-involved in the details of the work of subordinates, resulting in the manager making every decision in an organisation, no matter how trivial. Micromanagement is a euphemism for meddling, and has the opposite effect to empowerment. Micromanagement can retard the progress of organisational development, as it robs employees of their self-respect.

micromerchant E-COM a provider of goods or services on the Internet in exchange for electronic money

micropayment E-COM, FIN a payment protocol for small amounts of electronic money, ranging from a fraction of a cent or penny to no more than 10 US dollars or euros

middle price FIN a price, halfway between the bid price and the offer price, that is generally quoted in the press and on information screens

MIGA *abbr* FIN Multilateral Investment Guarantee Agency

Miller's rule of seven GEN see *rule of seven*

minimax regret criterion FIN an approach to decision-making under uncertainty in which the opportunity cost (regret) associated with each possible course of action is measured, and the decision-maker selects the activity which minimises the maximum regret, or loss. Regret is measured as the difference between the best and worst possible payoff for each option.

minimum lending rate *US* FIN an interest rate charged by a central bank, which serves as a floor for loans in a country

minimum quote size FIN the smallest number of shares that a market must handle in one trade of a particular security

minimum stock level FIN a stock level, set for control purposes, below which stockholding should not fall without being highlighted. It is calculated as follows:

Re-order level – (Average rate of usage × Average lead time)

minimum subscription FIN the smallest number of shares or securities that may be applied for in a new issue

minimum wage HR an hourly rate of pay, usually set by government, to which all employees are legally entitled

minority ownership FIN ownership of less than 50% of a company's ordinary shares, which is not enough to control the company

MIT *abbr* FIN market if touched

mixed economy ECON an economy in which both public and private enterprises participate in the production and supply of goods and services

MMC *abbr* FIN Monopolies and Mergers Commission

modified accounts FIN see *abbreviated accounts*

modified ACRS FIN a system used in the United States for computing the depreciation of some assets acquired after 1985 in a way that reduces taxes. The ACRS applies to older assets. See also *accelerated cost recovery system*

modified book value FIN see *adjusted book value*

modified cash basis FIN the bookkeeping practice of accounting for short-term assets on a cash basis and for long-term assets on an accrual basis

MONEP *abbr* FIN Marché des Options Négotiables de Paris

monetarism ECON an economic theory that states that inflation is caused by increases in a country's money supply

monetary FIN relating to or involving money, cash, or assets

monetary assets FIN a generic term for accounts receivable, cash, and bank balances – assets that are realisable at the amount stated in the accounts. Other assets, for example, facilities and machinery, inventories, and marketable securities will not necessarily realise the sum stated in a business's balance sheet.

monetary base ECON the stock of a country's coins, notes, and bank deposits with the central bank

monetary base control ECON the restricting of the amount of liquid assets in an economy through government control

monetary policy ECON, FIN government economic policy concerning a country's rate of interest, its exchange rate, and the amount of money in the economy

monetary reserve FIN the foreign currency and precious metals that a country holds, usually in a central bank

monetary system ECON the set of government regulations concerning a country's monetary reserves and its holdings of notes and coins

monetary unit FIN the standard unit of a country's currency

monetise ECON to establish a currency as a country's legal tender

money ECON, FIN a medium of exchange that is accepted throughout a country as payment for services and goods and as a means of settling debts

money at call and short notice FIN 1. in the United Kingdom, advances made by banks to other financial institutions, or corporate and personal customers, that are repayable either upon demand (call) or within 14 days (short notice) 2. in the United Kingdom, balances in an account that are either available upon demand (call) or within 14 days (short notice)

money broker FIN an intermediary who works on the money market

moneyer FIN somebody who is authorised to coin money

money laundering FIN the process of making money obtained illegally appear legitimate by passing it through banks or businesses

moneylender FIN a person who lends money for interest

money market account FIN an account with a financial institution that requires a high minimum deposit and pays a rate of interest related to the wholesale money market rates and so is generally higher than retail rates. Most institutions offer a range of term accounts, with either a fixed rate or variable rate, and notice accounts, with a range of notice periods at variable rates.

money market fund FIN a unit trust that invests in short-term debt securities

money market instruments FIN short-term (usually under 12 months) assets and securities, such as certificates of deposit, and commercial paper and Treasury bills, that are traded on money markets

money national income ECON GDP measured using money value, not adjusted for the effect of inflation

money of account FIN a monetary unit that is used in keeping accounts but is not necessarily an actual currency unit

money order FIN a written order to pay somebody a sum of money, issued by a bank or post office

money purchase pension scheme FIN in the United Kingdom, a pension plan where the fund that is built up is used to purchase an annuity. The retirement income that the beneficiary receives therefore depends on his or her contributions, the performance of the investments those contributions are used to buy, the annuity rates, and the type of annuity purchased at retirement.

money-purchase plan *US* FIN in the United States, a pension plan (a defined benefit plan) in which the participant contributes part and the firm contributes at the same or a different rate

money substitute ECON any goods used as a medium of exchange because of the degree of devaluation of a country's currency

money supply ECON the stock of liquid assets in a country's economy that can be given in exchange for services or goods

Monopolies and Mergers Commission FIN in the United Kingdom, a commission that was replaced by the Competition Commission in April 1999. *Abbr* **MMC**

moratorium FIN a period of delay, for example, additional time agreed by a creditor and a debtor for recovery of a debt

more bang for your buck *US* FIN a better return on your investment *(slang)*

mortgage FIN **1.** a financial lending arrangement whereby an individual borrows money from a bank or another lending institution in order to buy property or land. The original amount borrowed, the principal, is then repaid with interest to the lender over a fixed number of years. **2.** a borrowing arrangement whereby the lender is granted a legal right to an asset, usually a property, should the borrower default on the repayments. Mortgages are usually taken out by individuals who wish to secure a long-term loan to buy a home. See also *interest-only mortgage, low-start mortgage, repayment mortgage*

mortgage-backed security FIN a security for which a mortgage is collateral

mortgage bond *US* FIN a debt secured by land or property

mortgage broker FIN a person or company that acts as an agent between people seeking mortgages and organisations that offer them

mortgage debenture FIN a debenture in which the loan is secured against a company's fixed assets

mortgagee FIN a person or organisation that lends money to a borrower under a mortgage agreement. See also *mortgagor*

mortgage equity analysis FIN a computation of the difference between the value of a property and the amount owed on it in the form of mortgages

mortgage insurance FIN insurance that provides somebody holding a mortgage with protection against default

mortgage lien FIN a claim against a property that is mortgaged

mortgage note FIN a note that documents the existence and terms of a mortgage

mortgage pool FIN a group of mortgages with similar characteristics packaged together for sale

mortgage portfolio FIN a group of mortgages held by a mortgage banker

mortgage rate FIN the interest rate charged on a mortgage by a lender

mortgage tax FIN a tax on mortgages

mortgagor FIN somebody who has taken out a mortgage to borrow money. See also *mortgagee*

most distant futures contract FIN a futures option with the latest delivery date. See also *nearby futures contract*

MRP II *abbr* FIN, OPS manufacturing resource planning: a computer-based manufacturing, inventory planning and control system that broadens the scope of production planning by involving other functional areas that affect production decisions. Manufacturing resource planning evolved from material requirements planning to integrate other functions in the planning process. These functions may include engineering, marketing, purchasing, production scheduling, business planning, and finance.

MSB *abbr* FIN mutual savings bank

multicurrency FIN relating to a loan that gives the borrower a choice of currencies

multifunctional card FIN a plastic card that may be used for two or more purposes, for example, as a cash card, a cheque card, and a debit card

Multilateral Investment Guarantee Agency FIN one of the five institutions that comprise the World Bank Group. MIGA was created in 1988 to promote foreign direct investment into emerging economies with the objective of improving people's lives and to reduce poverty. This is fulfilled by the Agency by offering political risk insurance to investors and lenders and by assisting developing countries to attract and retain private investment. *Abbr* **MIGA**

multinational business or **multinational company** or **multinational corporation** FIN, GEN a company that operates internationally, usually with subsidiaries, offices, or production facilities in more than one country

multinational corporation FIN see *multinational business*

multiple exchange rate FIN a two-tier rate of exchange used in certain countries where the more advantageous rate may be for tourists or for businesses proposing to build a factory

multitasking GEN the practice of performing several different tasks simultaneously *(slang)*

municipal bond or **muni** or **muni-bond** *US* FIN in the United States, a security issued by states, local governments, and municipalities to pay for special projects such as motorways

Municipal Bond Insurance Association FIN see *MBIA*

mutual FIN used to describe an organisation that is run in the interests of its members and that does not have to pay dividends to its shareholders, so surplus profits can be ploughed back into the business. In the United Kingdom, building societies and friendly societies were formed as mutual organisations, although in recent years many have demutualised, either by becoming public limited companies or by being bought by other financial organisations, resulting in members receiving cash or share windfall payments. In the United States, mutual associations, a type of savings and loan association, and state-chartered mutual savings banks are organised in this way.

mutual association *US* FIN see *mutual*

mutual company FIN a company that is owned by its customers who share in the profits

mutual fund *US* FIN = unit trust

mutual insurance FIN an insurance company that is owned by its policyholders who share the profits and cover claims with their pooled premiums

mutual savings bank FIN in the United States, a state-chartered savings bank run in the interests of its members. It is governed by a local board of trustees, not the legal owners. Most of these banks offer accounts and services that are typical of commercial banks. *Abbr* **MSB**

MVA *abbr* FIN market value added

MWCA *abbr* FIN monetary working capital adjustment

naked debenture FIN see *debenture*

naked option FIN an option in which the underlying asset is not owned by the seller, who risks considerable loss if the price of the asset falls

naked position FIN a holding of unhedged securities

naked writer FIN a writer of an option who does not own the underlying shares

name FIN an individual who is a member of Lloyd's of London

NAO *abbr* FIN National Audit Office

narrow market FIN a market where the trading volume is low. A characteristic of such a market is a wide spread of bid and offer prices.

narrow range securities FIN see *trustee investment*

NASD *abbr* FIN National Association of Securities Dealers

NASDAQ or **Nasdaq** *abbr* FIN a computerised quotation system that supports market-making in US-registered equities. It was established by the National Association of Securities Dealers in 1971. NASDAQ International has operated from London since 1992.

NASDAQ Composite Index FIN a specialist US share price index covering shares of high-technology companies

National Association of Investors Corporation *US* FIN a US organisation that fosters investment clubs

National Association of Securities Dealers FIN in the United States, the self-regulatory organisation for securities dealers that develops rules and regulations, conducts regulatory reviews of members' business activities, and designs and operates marketplace services facilities. It is responsible for the regulation of the NASDAQ Stock Market as well as the extensive US over-the-counter securities market. Established in 1938, it operates subject to the Securities Exchange Commission oversight and has a membership that includes virtually every US broker or dealer doing securities business with the public. *Abbr* **NASD**

national bank FIN 1. a bank owned or controlled by the state that acts as a bank for the government and implements its monetary policies 2. *US* a bank that operates under federal charter and is legally required to be a member of the Federal Reserve System

national debt ECON the total borrowing of a country's central government that is unpaid

national demand ECON the total demand of consumers in an economy

National Guarantee Fund *ANZ* FIN a supply of money held by the Australian Stock Exchange which is used to compensate investors for losses incurred when an exchange member fails to meet its obligations

national income ECON the total earnings from a country's production of services and goods in a particular year

national income accounts FIN economic statistics that show the state of a nation's economy over a given period of time, usually a year

National Insurance FIN a compulsory state social insurance scheme to which employees and employers contribute. *Abbr* **NI**

National Insurance contributions FIN payments made by both employers and employees to the government. The contributions, together with other government receipts, are used to finance state pensions and other benefits such as unemployment benefit. *Abbr* **NIC**

National Insurance number FIN a unique number allocated to each UK citizen at the age of 16. It allows HM Revenue & Customs and the Department for Work and Pensions to record contributions and credit to each person's national insurance account.

National Market System FIN in the United States, an inter-exchange network system designed to foster greater competition between domestic stock exchanges. Legislated for in 1975, it was implemented in 1978 with the Intermarket Trading System that electronically links eight markets: American, Boston, Cincinnati, Chicago, New York, Pacific, Philadelphia, and the NASD over-the-counter market. It allows traders at any exchange to seek the best available price on all other exchanges that a particular security is eligible to trade on. *Abbr* **NMS**

National Savings & Investments FIN in the United Kingdom, a government agency accountable to the Treasury that offers a range of savings and investment products directly to the public or through post offices. The funds raised finance the national debt.

National Savings Bank FIN in the United Kingdom, a savings scheme established in 1861 as the Post Office Savings Bank and now operated by National Savings & Investments. *Abbr* **NSB**

National Savings Certificate FIN in the United Kingdom, either a fixed-interest or an index-linked certificate issued for two or five-year terms by National Savings & Investments with returns that are free of income tax. *Abbr* **NSC**

National Society of Accountants *US* FIN a non-profit organisation of some 30,000 professionals who provide accounting, tax preparation, financial and estate planning, and management advisory services to an estimated 19 million individuals and business clients. Most of the NSA's members are individual practitioners or partners in small to mid-size accounting and tax firms. *Abbr* **NSA**

NAV *abbr* FIN net asset value

NBV *abbr* FIN net book value

NCUA *abbr* FIN National Credit Union Administration

NDP *abbr* ECON net domestic product

nearby futures contract FIN a futures option with the earliest delivery date. See also *most distant futures contract*

nearby month FIN the earliest month for which there is a futures contract for a particular commodity. Also known as *spot month*. See also *far month*

near money FIN assets that can quickly be turned into cash, for example, some types of bank deposit, short-dated bonds, and certificates of deposit

negative amortisation FIN an increase in the principal of a loan due to the inadequacy of payments to cover the interest

negative carry FIN interest that is so high that the borrowed money does not return enough profit to cover the cost of borrowing

negative cash flow FIN a cash flow with higher outgoings than income

negative equity FIN a situation in which a fall in prices leads to a property being worth less than was paid for it

negative gearing FIN the practice of borrowing money to invest in property or shares and claiming a tax deduction on the difference between the income and the interest repayments

negative income tax US ECON payments such as tax credits made to households or individuals to make their income up to a guaranteed minimum level

negative pledge clause FIN a provision in a bond that prohibits the issuer from doing something that would give an advantage to holders of other bonds

negative yield curve FIN a representation of interest rates that are higher for short-term bonds than they are for long-term bonds

negotiable certificate of deposit FIN a certificate of deposit with a very high value that can be freely traded

negotiable instrument FIN a document which can be exchanged for cash, for example a bill of exchange, or a cheque

negotiable order of withdrawal FIN a cheque drawn on an account that bears interest

negotiable security FIN a security that can be freely traded

negotiate FIN to transfer financial instruments such as bearer securities, bills of exchange, cheques, and promissory notes, for consideration to another person

negotiated commissions FIN commissions that result from bargaining between brokers and their customers, typically large institutions

negotiated issue FIN see *negotiated offering*

negotiated market FIN a market in which each transaction results from negotiation between a buyer and a seller

negotiated offering FIN a public offering, the price of which is determined by negotiations between the issuer and a syndicate of underwriters. Also known as *negotiated issue*

negotiated sale FIN a public offering, the price of which is determined by negotiations between the issuer and a single underwriter

nest egg FIN assets, usually other than a pension plan or retirement account, that have been set aside by an individual for his or her retirement *(slang)*

net advantage of refunding FIN the amount realised by refunding debt

net advantage to leasing FIN the amount by which leasing something is financially better than borrowing money and purchasing it

net advantage to merging FIN the amount by which the value of a merged enterprise exceeds the value of the pre-existing companies, minus the cost of the merger

net assets FIN the amount by which the value of a company's assets exceeds its liabilities

net asset value FIN a sum of the values of all that a unit trust owns at the end of a trading day. *Abbr* **NAV**

NetBill E-COM a micropayment system developed at Carnegie Mellon University for purchasing digital goods over the Internet. After the goods are delivered in encrypted form to the purchaser's computer, the money is debited from the purchaser's prefunded account and the goods are decrypted for the purchaser's use.

net capital FIN the amount by which net assets exceed the value of assets not easily converted to cash

net cash balance FIN the amount of cash that is on hand

NetCheque™ E-COM a trademark for an electronic payment system developed at the University of Southern California to allow users to write electronic cheques to each other

net current assets FIN the amount by which the value of a company's current assets exceeds its current liabilities

net dividend FIN the value of a dividend after the recipient has paid tax on it

net domestic product ECON the figure produced after factors such as depreciation have been deducted from GDP

net errors and omissions FIN the net amount of the discrepancies that arise in calculations of balances of payments

net fixed assets FIN the value of fixed assets after depreciation

net foreign factor income FIN income from outside a country, constituting the amount by which a country's gross national product exceeds its gross domestic product

net income FIN 1. an organisation's income less the costs incurred to generate it 2. gross income less tax 3. a salary or wage less tax and other statutory deductions, for example, National Insurance contributions

net interest FIN gross interest less tax

net lease FIN a lease that requires the lessee to pay for things that the owner usually pays for. See also *gross lease*

net liquid funds FIN an organisation's cash plus its marketable investments less its short-term borrowings, such as overdrafts and loans

net margin FIN the percentage of revenues that is profit

net operating income FIN the amount by which income exceeds expenses, before considering taxes and interest

net operating margin FIN net operating income as a percentage of revenues

net pay HR see *take-home pay*

net position FIN the difference between an investor's long and short positions in the same security

net present value FIN the value of an investment calculated as the sum of its initial cost and the present value of expected future cash flows. A positive NPV indicates that the project should be profitable, assuming that the estimated cash flows are reasonably accurate. A negative NPV indicates that the project will probably be unprofitable and therefore should be adjusted, if not abandoned altogether. *Abbr* **NPV**

net price FIN the price paid for goods or services after all relevant discounts have been deducted

net proceeds FIN the amount realised from a transaction minus the cost of making it

net profit FIN an organisation's income as shown in a profit and loss account after all relevant expenses have been deducted

net profit margin FIN see *profit margin*

net profit ratio FIN the ratio of an organisation's net profit to its total net sales. Comparing the net profit ratios of companies in the same sector shows which are the most efficient.

net realisable value FIN the value of an asset if sold, allowing for costs

net residual value FIN the anticipated proceeds of an asset at the end of its useful life, less the costs of selling it, for example, transport and commission. It is used when calculating the annual charge for the straight-line method of depreciation. *Abbr* **NRV**

net return FIN the amount realised on an investment, taking taxes and transaction costs into account

net salvage value FIN the amount expected to result from terminating a project, taking tax consequences into consideration

net worth FIN the difference between the assets and liabilities of a person or company

net yield FIN the rate of return on an investment after considering all costs and taxes

new economy ECON a term used in the late 1990s and 2000s to describe the e-commerce sector and the digital economy, in which firms mostly trade online rather than in the bricks and mortar of physical premises in the high street

new issue FIN 1. a new security, for example, a bond, debenture, or share, being offered to the public for the first time. See also *float, initial public offering* 2. a rights issue, or any further issue of an existing security

new issues market FIN the part of the market in which securities are first offered to investors by the issuers. See also *float, initial public offering, primary market*

newly industrialised economy ECON a country whose industrialisation has reached a level beyond that of a developing country. Mexico and Malaysia are examples of newly industrialised economies.

New York Mercantile Exchange FIN the world's largest physical commodity exchange and North America's most important trading exchange for energy and precious metals. It deals in crude oil, petrol, heating oil, natural gas, propane, gold, silver, platinum, palladium, and copper. *Abbr* **NYMEX**

New York Stock Exchange FIN see **NYSE**

New Zealand Stock Exchange FIN the principal market in New Zealand for trading in securities. It was established in 1981, replacing the Stock Exchange Association of New Zealand and a number of regional trading floors. *Abbr* **NZSE**

New Zealand Trade Development Board FIN a government body responsible for promoting New Zealand exports and facilitating foreign investment in New Zealand. Also known as **TRADENZ**

next futures contract FIN an option for the month after the current month

NI *abbr* FIN National Insurance

NIC *abbr* FIN National Insurance contribution

niche player FIN 1. an investment banker specialising in a particular field, for example, management buyouts 2. a broking house that deals in securities of only one industry. Also known as *boutique investment house*

nickel US FIN five basis points (slang)

Nifty Fifty US FIN on Wall Street, the 50 most popular stocks among institutional investors (slang)

Nikkei 225 or **Nikkei Index** FIN the Japanese share price index

nil paid FIN with no money yet paid. This term is used in reference to the purchase of newly issued shares, or to the shares themselves, when the shareholder entitled to buy new shares has not yet made a commitment to do so and may sell the rights instead.

NMS *abbr* US FIN National Market System

no-brainer FIN a transaction so favourable that no intelligence is required when deciding whether to enter into it (slang)

no-dating policy HR a policy introduced by an employer to prohibit or discourage consensual romantic or sexual relationships between employees. No-dating policies are intended to prevent problems arising from employee relationships in the workplace, such as preferential treatment, or claims of sexual harassment in the case of relationship breakdown. The policy defines what constitutes acceptable and unacceptable behaviour and what sanctions will be enforced if the terms of the policy are violated. No-dating policies are not widely used and may raise concerns about employees' rights to privacy. An alternative option is the use of consensual relationship agreements.

noise FIN irrelevant or insignificant data which overload a feedback process. The presence of noise can confuse or divert attention from relevant information; efficiency in a system is enhanced as the ratio of information to noise increases.

no-load fund FIN a unit trust that does not charge a fee for the purchase or sale of shares. See also *load fund*

nominal account FIN a record of revenues and expenditures, liabilities and assets classified by their nature, for example, sales, rent, rates, electricity, wages, or share capital

nominal annual rate FIN see *APR*

nominal capital FIN the total value of all of a company's stock

nominal cash flow FIN cash flow in terms of currency, without adjustment for inflation

nominal exchange rate FIN the exchange rate as specified, without adjustment for transaction costs or differences in purchasing power

nominal interest rate FIN the interest rate as specified, without adjustment for compounding or inflation

nominal ledger FIN a ledger listing revenue, operating expenses, assets, and capital

nominal price FIN the price of an item being sold when consideration does not reflect the value

nominal share capital FIN see *authorised share capital*

nominal value FIN the value of a newly issued share. Also known as *par value*

nominee account FIN an account held not in the name of the real owner of the account, but instead in the name of another person, organisation, or financial institution. Shares can be bought and held in nominee accounts so that the owner's identity is not disclosed.

nominee name FIN a financial institution, or an individual employed by such an institution, that holds a security on behalf of the actual owner. While this may be to hide the owner's identity, for example, in the case of a celebrity, it is also to allow an institution managing any individual's portfolio to carry out transactions without the need for the owner to sign the required paperwork.

non-acceptance FIN on the presentation of a bill of exchange, the refusal by the person on whom it is drawn to accept it

non-business days FIN those days when banks are not open for business, for example, in the West, Saturdays, Sundays, and public holidays

non-cash item FIN an item in an income statement that is not cash, such as depreciation expenses, and gains or losses from investments

non-conforming loan FIN a loan that does not conform to the lender's standards, especially those of a US government agency

non-contributory pension plan *US* FIN = non-contributory pension scheme

non-contributory pension scheme FIN a pension scheme to which the employee makes no contribution

nondeductible FIN not allowed to be deducted, especially as an allowance against income taxes

non-financial asset FIN an asset that is neither money nor a financial instrument, for example, real or personal property

non-interest-bearing bond FIN a bond that is sold at a discount instead of with a promise to pay interest

non-judicial foreclosure FIN a foreclosure on property without recourse to a court

non-linear programming FIN a process in which the equations expressing the interactions of variables are not all linear but may, for example, be in proportion to the square of a variable

non-negotiable instrument FIN a financial instrument that cannot be signed over to anyone else

non-operational balances FIN accounts that banks maintain at the Bank of England without the power of withdrawal

non-optional FIN not subject to approval by shareholders

non-participating preference share FIN the most common type of preference share that pays a fixed dividend regardless of the profitability of the company. See also *participating preference share*

non-performing asset FIN an asset that is not producing income

non-profit organisation GEN, HR an organisation that does not have financial profit as a main strategic objective. Non-profit organisations include charities, professional associations, trade unions, and religious, arts, community, research, and campaigning bodies. These organisations are not situated in either the public or private sectors, but in what has been called the third sector. Many have paid staff and working capital but, according to Peter Drucker, their fundamental purpose is not to provide a product or service, but to change people. They are led by values rather than financial commitments to shareholders.

non-recourse debt FIN a debt for which the borrower has no personal responsibility, typically a debt of a limited partnership

non-recoverable FIN relating to a debt that will never be paid, for example, because of the borrower's bankruptcy

non-recurring charge FIN a charge that is made only once

non-resident FIN used to describe an individual who has left his or her native country to work overseas for a period. Non-residency has tax implications, for example, while a UK national is working overseas only their income and realised capital gains generated within the United Kingdom are subject to UK income tax. During a period of non-residency, many expatriates choose to bank offshore.

Non-Resident Withholding Tax FIN a duty imposed by the New Zealand government on interest and dividends earned by a non-resident from investments. *Abbr* **NRWT**

non-tariff barrier ECON see *NTB*

non-taxable FIN not subject to tax

non-voting share FIN an ordinary share that is paid a dividend from the company's profits, but that does not entitle the shareholder to vote at the Annual General Meeting or any other meeting of shareholders. Such shares are unpopular with institutional investors. Also called A share

normal profit ECON the minimum level of profit that will attract an entrepreneur to begin a business or remain trading

normal yield curve FIN a yield curve with higher interest rates for long-term bonds than for short-term bonds. See also *yield curve*

notes to the accounts FIN an explanation of particular items in a set of accounts

notes to the financial statements FIN an explanation of particular items in a set of financial statements

notice of default *US* FIN = default notice

notional principal amount FIN the value used to represent a loan in calculating interest rate swaps

not negotiable FIN wording on a cheque or bill of exchange to denote that it is deprived of its inherent quality of negotiability. When such a document is transferred from one person to another, the recipient obtains no better title to it than the signatory. See also **negotiable instrument**

novation FIN an agreement to change a contract by substituting a third party for one of the two original parties

NPV *abbr* FIN net present value

NRWT *abbr* FIN Non-Resident Withholding Tax

NSA *abbr* FIN National Society of Accountants

NSB *abbr* FIN National Savings Bank

NSC *abbr* FIN National Savings Certificate

NTB *abbr* ECON non-tariff barrier: a country's economic regulation on something such as safety standards that impedes imports, often from developing countries

numbered account FIN a bank account identified by a number to allow the holder to remain anonymous

nuncupative will FIN a will that is made orally in the presence of a witness, rather than in writing

NYMEX *abbr* FIN New York Mercantile Exchange

NYSE *abbr* FIN New York Stock Exchange: the leading stock exchange in New York, which is self-regulatory but has to comply with the regulations of the US Securities and Exchange Commission

NZSE *abbr* FIN New Zealand Stock Exchange

NZSE10 *abbr* FIN NZSE10 Index

NZSE10 Index FIN a measure of changes in share prices on the New Zealand Stock Exchange, based on the change in value of the stocks of the 10 largest companies. *Abbr* **NZSE10**

NZSE30 Selection Index FIN a measure of changes in share prices on the New Zealand Stock Exchange, based on the change in value of the stocks of the 30 largest companies. *Abbr* **NZSE30**

NZSE40 Index FIN the principal measure of changes in share prices on the New Zealand Stock Exchange, based on the change in value of the stocks of the 40 largest companies. The composition of the index is reviewed every three months.

OBI *abbr* E-COM, FIN open buying on the Internet

OBSF *abbr* FIN off-balance-sheet financing

OCF *abbr* FIN operating cash flow

OCR *abbr* FIN official cash rate

O/D *abbr* FIN overdraft

OECD *abbr* FIN Organisation for Economic Co-operation and Development: a group of 30 member countries, with a shared commitment to democratic government and the market economy, that has active relationships with some 70 other countries via non-governmental organisations. Formed in 1961, its work covers economic and social issues from macroeconomics to trade, education, development, and scientific innovation. Its goals are to promote economic growth and employment in member countries in a climate of stability; to assist the sustainable economic expansion of both member and non-member countries; and to support a balanced and even-handed expansion of world trade.

OEIC *abbr* FIN open-ended investment company

off-balance-sheet financing FIN financing obtained by means other than debt and equity instruments, for example, partnerships, joint ventures, and leases. *Abbr* **OBSF**

offer FIN the price at which a market maker will sell a security, or a unit trust manager in the United Kingdom will sell units. It is also the net asset value of a mutual fund plus any sales charges in the United States. It is the price investors pay when they buy a security. Also known as **ask, offer price, offering price**

offer by prospectus FIN in the United Kingdom, one of the ways available to a lead manager of offering securities to the public. See also **float, initial public offering, new issue, offer for sale**

offer document FIN a description of the loan a lender is offering to provide

offer for sale FIN an invitation by a party other than the company itself to apply for shares in a company based on information contained in a prospectus

offering circular FIN a document which gives information about a company whose shares are being sold to the public for the first time

offering memorandum FIN a description of an offer to sell securities privately

offering price FIN see **ask** (sense 2) and **offer price**

offeror FIN somebody who makes a bid

offer price FIN the price at which somebody offers a share of a stock for sale. Also known as **offering price**

official bank FIN a bank that has a charter from a government

official books of account FIN the official financial records of an institution

official cash rate FIN the current interest rate as set by a central bank. *Abbr* **OCR**

official development assistance FIN money that the Organisation for Economic Co-operation and Development's Development Assistance Committee gives or lends to a developing country

official list FIN in the United Kingdom, the list maintained by the Financial Services Authority of all the securities traded on the London Stock Exchange

official receiver FIN an officer of the court who is appointed to wind up the affairs of an organisation that goes bankrupt. In the United Kingdom, an official receiver is appointed by the Department of Trade and Industry and often acts as a liquidator. The job involves realising any assets that remain to repay debts, for example, by selling property. *Abbr* **OR**

offset FIN a transaction that balances all or part of an earlier transaction in the same security

offset clause FIN a provision in an insurance policy that permits the balancing of credits against debits so that, for example, a party can reduce or omit payments to another party that owes it money and is bankrupt

offshore bank FIN a bank that offers only limited wholesale banking services to non-residents

offshore company FIN a company that is registered in a country other than the one in which it conducts most of its business, usually for tax purposes. For example, many captive insurance companies are registered in the Cayman Islands.

offshore finance subsidiary FIN a company created in another country to handle financial transactions, giving the owning company certain tax and legal advantages in its home country. US term offshore *financial subsidiary*

offshore financial centre FIN a country or other political unit that has banking laws intended to attract business from industrialised nations

offshore financial subsidiary US FIN = offshore finance subsidiary

offshore holding company FIN a company created in another country to own other companies, giving the owning company certain legal advantages in its home country

offshore trading company FIN a company created in another country to handle commercial transactions, giving the owning company certain legal advantages in its home country

offshoring HR the transfer of service operations to foreign countries in order to take advantage of a supply of skilled but relatively cheap labour. Offshoring developed in the early 1990s when IT, data processing, and software programming services were subcontracted to countries such as India. With the development of call centre technologies, an increasing range of transactional services, including financial services and customer inquiry services, have been offshored. Services may be outsourced to a foreign company or a wholly owned foreign subsidiary company may be set up. The main benefit of offshoring is the reduction of costs but concerns about redundancies and job losses in the home countries have been raised.

off-the-shelf company FIN a company for which all the legal formalities, except the appointment of directors, have been completed so that a purchaser can transform it into a new company with relative ease and low cost

OI *abbr* FIN operating income

Old Lady of Threadneedle Street FIN the Bank of England, which is located in Threadneedle Street in the City of London *(slang)*

oligopoly ECON a market in which there are only a few, very large, suppliers

omitted dividend FIN a regularly scheduled dividend that a company does not pay

omnibus account FIN an account of one broker with another that combines the transactions of multiple investors for the convenience of the brokers

on account FIN paid in advance against all or part of money due in the future

on demand FIN 1. used to describe an account from which withdrawals may be made without giving a period of notice 2. used to describe a loan, usually an overdraft, that the lender can request the borrower to repay immediately 3. used to describe a bill of exchange that is paid upon presentation

one-stop shopping FIN the ability of a single financial institution to offer a full range of financial services

one-to-one merger GEN, FIN see *merger*

one-year money FIN money placed on a money market for a fixed period of one year, with either a fixed or variable rate of interest. It can be removed during the fixed term only upon payment of a penalty.

on-target earnings HR the amount earned by a person working on commission who has achieved the targets set. *Abbr* **OTE**

ooda loop GEN a model of the strategic decision-making process, whose elements (observation, orientation, decision, and action) succeed each other in a continuous cycle, each informing and shaping the next. The model was developed by Colonel John Boyd (1927–97) of the United States Air Force, building on the work of military strategists such as Sun Tzu and Karl von Clausewitz. Boyd suggested that it was possible to out-think and outmanoeuvre the enemy by moving through the cycle with variety, rapidity, harmony, and initiative and by thinking inside the enemy's ooda loop. The concept has been applied to organisational decision-making and corporate strategy as a means of gaining competitive advantage in changing environments.

OPEC *abbr* FIN Organization of the Petroleum Exporting Countries: an international organisation of 11 developing countries, each one largely reliant on oil revenues as its main source of income, that tries to ensure there is a balance between supply and demand by adjusting the members' oil output. OPEC's headquarters are in Vienna. The current members, Algeria, Indonesia, Iran, Iraq, Kuwait, Libya, Nigeria, Qatar, Saudi Arabia, the United Arab Emirates, and Venezuela, meet at least twice a year to decide on output levels and discuss recent and anticipated oil-market developments.

open buying on the Internet E-COM, FIN a standard built round a common set of business requirements for electronic communication between buyers and sellers that, when implemented, allows different e-commerce systems to talk to one another. *Abbr* **OBI**. See also *open trading protocol*

open cheque FIN 1. a cheque that is not crossed and so may be cashed by the payee at the branch of the bank where it is drawn 2. *US* a signed cheque where the amount payable has not been indicated

open economy ECON an economy that places no restrictions on the movement of capital, labour, foreign trade, and payments into and out of the country

open-end credit US FIN = open-ended credit

open-ended credit FIN a form of credit that does not have an upper limit on the amount that can be borrowed or a time limit before repayment is due

open-ended fund FIN a unit trust that has a variable number of shares. US term *open-end fund*

open-ended management company FIN a company that sells unit trusts. US term open-end management company

open-ended mortgage FIN a mortgage in which prepayment is allowed. US term *open-end mortgage*

open-end fund US FIN = open-ended fund. See *closed-end fund*

open-end management company US FIN = open-ended management company

open-end mortgage US FIN = open-ended mortgage

opening balance FIN the value of a financial quantity at the beginning of a period of time, such as a day or a year

opening balance sheet FIN an account showing an organisation's opening balances

opening bell FIN the beginning of a day of trading on a market

opening price FIN a price for a security at the beginning of a day of trading on a market

opening purchase FIN a first purchase of a series to be made in options of a particular type for a particular commodity or security

opening stock FIN on a balance sheet, the closing stock at the end of one accounting period that is transferred forward and becomes the opening stock in the one that follows. US term *beginning inventory*

open interest FIN options that have not yet been closed

open loop system FIN a management control system which includes no provision for corrective action to be applied to the sequence of activities

open-market operation FIN a transaction by a central bank in a public market

open-market value FIN the price that an asset or security would realise if it was offered on a market open to all

open trading protocol E-COM, FIN a standard designed to support Internet-based retail transactions, that allows different systems to communicate with each other for a variety of payment-related activities. The open buying on the Internet protocol is a competing standard. *Abbr* **OTP**. See also *open buying on the Internet*

operating cash flow FIN the amount used to represent the money moving through a company as a result of its operations, as distinct from its purely financial transactions. *Abbr* **OCF**

operating income FIN revenue minus the cost of goods sold and normal operating expenses. Also known as *earnings before interest and taxes*. *Abbr* **OI**

operating leverage FIN the ratio of a business's fixed costs to its total costs. As the fixed costs have to be paid regardless of output, the higher the ratio, the higher the risk of losses in an economic downturn.

operating margin FIN see *profit margin*

operating profit FIN the difference between a company's revenues and any related costs and expenses, not including income or expenses from any sources other than its normal methods of providing a good or a service

operating risk FIN the risk of a high operating leverage

opportunity cost ECON, FIN, GEN an amount of money lost as a result of choosing one investment rather than another

optimal portfolio FIN a theoretical set of investments that would be the most profitable for an investor

optimal redemption provision FIN a provision that specifies when an issuer can call a bond

optimise FIN to allocate such things as resources or capital as efficiently as possible

option FIN 1. a contract for the right to buy or sell an asset, typically a commodity, under certain terms. Also known as *option contract* 2. the right of an option holder to buy or sell a specific asset on predetermined terms on, or before, a future date

option account FIN a brokerage account used for trading in options

optionaire FIN a millionaire whose wealth consists of share options *(slang)*

option buyer FIN an investor who buys an option

option class FIN a set of options that are identical with respect to type and underlying asset

option contract FIN see *option*

option elasticity FIN the relative change in the value of an option as a function of a change in the value of the underlying asset

option income fund FIN a unit trust that invests in options

option premium FIN the amount per share that a buyer pays for an option

option price FIN the price of an option

option pricing model FIN a model that is used to determine the fair value of options

options clearing corporation US FIN an organisation responsible for the listing of options and clearing trades in them

option seller FIN see *option writer*

option series FIN a collection of options that are identical in terms of what they represent

options market FIN the trading in options, or a place where options trading occurs

options on physicals FIN options on securities with fixed interest rates

option writer FIN a person or institution that sells an option. Also known as *option seller*

OR *abbr* FIN official receiver

order FIN an occasion when a broker is told to buy or sell something for an investor's own account

order point FIN the quantity of an item that is on hand when more units of the item are to be ordered

orders pending FIN orders that have not yet resulted in transactions

ordinary interest FIN interest calculated on the basis of a year having only 360 days

ordinary shares FIN shares that entitle the holder to a dividend from the company's profits after holders of preference shares have been paid

Organisation for Economic Co-operation and Development FIN see **OECD**

Organization of the Petroleum Exporting Countries FIN see **OPEC**

original face value FIN the amount of the principal of a mortgage on the day it is created

original issue discount FIN the discount offered on the day of sale of a debt instrument

original maturity FIN a date on which a debt instrument is due to mature

origination fee FIN a fee charged by a lender for providing a mortgage, usually expressed as a percentage of the principal

OTC market *abbr* FIN over-the-counter market

other capital FIN capital that is not listed in specific categories

other current assets FIN assets that are not cash and are due to mature within a year

other long-term capital FIN long-term capital that is not listed in specific categories

other prices FIN prices that are not listed in a catalogue

other short-term capital FIN short-term capital that is not listed in specific categories

OTP *abbr* E-COM, FIN open trading protocol

output ECON, FIN anything produced by a company, usually physical products

output gap ECON the difference between the amount of activity that is sustainable in an economy and the amount of activity actually taking place

output method ECON an accounting system that classifies costs according to the outputs for which they are incurred, not the inputs they have bought

output tax *ANZ* FIN the amount of Goods and Services Tax paid to the tax office after the deduction of input tax credits

outsourcing FIN the use of external suppliers as a source of finished products, components, or services

outstanding share FIN a share that a company has issued and somebody has bought

outstanding share capital FIN the value of all of the stock of a company minus the value of retained shares

outwork FIN, GEN work carried out for a company away from its premises, for example, by subcontractors or employees working from home

outworker FIN, GEN a subcontractor or employee carrying out work for a company away from its premises

overall capitalisation rate FIN net operating income other than debt service divided by value

overall market capacity ECON the amount of a service or good that can be absorbed in a market without affecting the price

overall rate of return FIN the yield of a bond held to maturity, expressed as a percentage

overall return FIN the aggregate of all the dividends received over an investment's life together with its capital gain or loss at the date of its realisation, calculated either before or after tax. It is one of the ways an investor can look at the performance of an investment.

overbid FIN **1.** to bid more than necessary **2.** an amount that is bid that is unnecessarily high

overbought market FIN a market where prices have risen beyond levels that can be supported by fundamental analysis. The market for Internet companies in 2001 was overbought and subsequently collapsed when it became clear that their trading performance could not support such price levels.

overcapitalised FIN used to describe a business that has more capital than can profitably be employed. An over-capitalised company could buy back some of its own shares in the market; if it has significant debt capital it could repurchase its bonds in the market; or it could make a large one-off dividend to shareholders.

overdraft FIN the amount by which the money withdrawn from a bank account exceeds the balance in the account. *Abbr* **O/D**

overdraft facility FIN a credit arrangement with a bank, allowing a person or company with an account to use borrowed money up to an agreed limit when nothing is left in the account

overdraft line FIN an amount in excess of the balance in an account that a bank agrees to pay in honouring cheques on the account

overdraft protection FIN the bank service, amounting to a line of credit, that assures that the bank will honour overdrafts, up to a limit and for a fee

overdraw FIN to withdraw more money from a bank account than it contains, thereby exceeding an agreed credit limit

overdrawn FIN in debt to a bank because the amount withdrawn from an account exceeds its balance

overdue FIN an amount still owed after the date due

over-geared FIN used to describe a company with debt capital and preference shares that outweigh its ordinary share capital

overhanging FIN large amounts of commodities or securities that have not been sold and therefore have a negative effect on prices, for example, that part of a new issue left in the hands of the underwriters

overhead absorption rate FIN a means of attributing overhead to a product or service, based for example on direct labour hours, direct labour cost, or machine hours. The choice of overhead absorption base may be made with the objective of obtaining 'accurate' product costs, or of influencing managerial behaviour, for example, overhead applied to labour hours or part numbers appears to make the use of these resources more costly, thus discouraging their use.

overhead costs FIN the indirect recurring costs of running a business that are not linked directly to the goods or service produced and sold. Overhead costs can include payments for the rent of premises, utility bills, and employees' salaries. Also called **overheads**

overhead expenditure variance FIN the difference between the budgeted overhead costs and the actual expenditure

overheads FIN see *overhead costs*

over-insuring FIN insuring an asset for a sum in excess of its market or replacement value. However, it is unlikely that an insurance company will pay out more in a claim for loss than the asset is worth or the cost of replacing it.

over-invested FIN used to describe a business that invests heavily during an economic boom only to find that when it starts to produce an income, the demand for the product or service has fallen

overlap profit FIN profit which occurs in two overlapping accounting periods and on which overlap relief can be claimed

overnight position FIN a trader's position in a security or option at the end of a trading day

overrated FIN used to describe something that is valued more highly than it should be

Overseas Investment Commission FIN an independent body reporting to the New Zealand government that regulates foreign investment in New Zealand. It was set up in 1973 and is funded by the Reserve Bank of New Zealand.

overseas taxation FIN see *double taxation*

oversold FIN used to describe a market or security that is considered to have fallen too rapidly as a result of excessive selling. See also *bear market*

overstocked FIN used to describe a business that has more stock than it needs

over-the-counter market FIN a market in which trading takes place directly between licensed dealers, rather than through an auction system as used in most organised exchanges. *Abbr* **OTC market**

owners' equity FIN a business's total assets less its total liabilities. See also *capital, ordinary shares, common stock*

packaging FIN the practice of combining securities in a single trade

Pac Man defence FIN a strategy to avoid the purchase of a company by making an offer to buy the prospective buyer

paid-up policy FIN **1.** an endowment assurance policy that continues to provide life cover while the cost of the premiums is covered by the underlying fund after the policyholder has decided not to continue paying premiums. If the fund is sufficient to pay the premiums for the remainder of the term, the remaining funds will be paid to the policyholder at maturity. **2.** *US* an insurance policy on which all the premiums have been paid

paid-up share FIN a share for which shareholders have paid the full contractual amount. See also *call, called-up share capital, paid-up share capital, share capital*

paid-up share capital FIN the amount which shareholders are deemed to have paid on the shares issued and called up

painting the tape FIN an illegal practice in which traders break large orders into smaller units in order to give the illusion of heavy buying activity. This encourages investors to buy, and the traders then sell as the price of the stock goes up. *(slang)*

panda FIN one of a series of Chinese gold and silver bullion/collector coins, each featuring a panda, that were first issued in 1982. Struck with a highly polished surface, the smallest gold coin weighs 0.05 ounces, the largest 12 ounces.

P&L FIN see *profit and loss account*

Panel on Takeovers and Mergers FIN see *City Code on Takeovers and Mergers*

panic buying FIN an abnormal level of buying caused by fear or rumours of product shortages or by severe price rises

paper FIN **1.** a certificate of deposits and other securities **2.** a rights issue or an issue of bonds launched by a company to raise additional capital *(slang)* **3.** all debt issued by a company *(slang)*

paper company FIN a company that only exists on paper and has no physical assets

paper millionaire FIN an individual who owns shares that are worth in excess of a million in currency, but which may fall in value. In 2001, many of the founders of dot-com companies were paper millionaires. See also *paper profit*

paper money FIN **1.** banknotes **2.** payments in paper form, for example, cheques

paper profit FIN an increase in the value of an investment that the investor has no immediate intention of realising

PAR *abbr* FIN prime assets ratio

paradox management GEN the holding together in tension of conflicting and contradictory ideas and the balancing of polar opposites in order to achieve a creative synergy which enhances organisational effectiveness. The concept of paradox is based in philosophy. Charles Handy identified nine main paradoxes inherent in modern society in his book, *The Empty Raincoat* (Hutchinson, 1994), and put forward principles for living with paradox. The idea has also been discussed by writers such as Professor Paul Evans of INSEAD, who argues that many contradictions and dilemmas are not problems which can be solved but paradoxes that need to be managed. An organisation which focuses exclusively on a strategy which has brought success in the past runs the risk of subsequent failure.

parallel pricing FIN the practice of varying prices in a similar way and at the same time as competitors, which may be done by agreement with them

parent company FIN a company with one or more subsidiary undertakings

Pareto's Law ECON a theory of income distribution. Developed by Vilfredo Pareto, Pareto's Law states that regardless of political or taxation conditions, income will be distributed in the same way across all countries.

pari passu FIN ranking equally

Paris Club FIN see *Group of Ten*

Paris Inter Bank Offered Rate FIN the French equivalent of the London Inter Bank Offered Rate. *Abbr* **PIBOR**

parity FIN a situation when the price of a commodity, foreign currency, or security is the same in different markets. See also *arbitrage*

parity value FIN see *conversion value*

park FIN to place owned shares with third parties to disguise their ownership, usually illegally

parking FIN **1.** the transfer of shares in a company to a nominee name or the name of an associate, often for non-legitimate or illegal reasons *(slang)* **2.** *US* putting money into safe investments while deciding where to invest the money

Parquet FIN an informal name for the Paris Bourse *(slang)*

participating bond FIN a bond that pays the holder dividends as well as interest

participating insurance FIN a form of insurance in which policy-holders receive a dividend from the insurer's profits

participating preference share FIN a type of preference share that entitles the holder to a fixed dividend and, in addition, to the right to participate in any surplus profits after payment of agreed levels of dividends to ordinary shareholders has been made. See also *non-participating preference share*

participative budgeting FIN a budgeting system in which all budget holders are given the opportunity to participate in setting their own budgets. Also known as *bottom-up budgeting*

partly paid share FIN a share for which shareholders have not paid the full contractual amount. See also *call, share capital*

partnership FIN according to the Partnership Act 1890, the relationship which exists between persons carrying on business in common with a view to profit. The liability of the individual partners is unlimited unless provided for by the partnership agreement. The Limited Partnership Act 1907 allows a partnership to contain one or more partners with limited liability so long as there is at least one partner with unlimited liability. A partnership consists of not more than 20 persons.

partnership accounts FIN the capital and current accounts of each partner in a partnership, or the accounts recording the partnership's business activities

partnership agreement FIN the document that sets up a partnership, detailing the capital contributed by each partner; whether an individual partner's liability is limited; the apportionment of the profit; salaries; and possibly procedures to be followed, for example, in the event of a partner retiring or a new partner joining. In the United Kingdom, when a partnership agreement is silent on any matter, the provisions of the Partnership Act 1890 apply. Also known as *articles of partnership*

par value FIN see *nominal value*

passbook FIN a small booklet issued by banks, building societies, and other financial institutions to record deposits, withdrawals, interest paid, and the balance on savings and deposit accounts. In all but the smaller building societies, it has now largely been replaced by statements.

passing off FIN a form of fraud in which a company tries to sell its own product by deceiving buyers into thinking it is another product

passive investment management FIN the managing of a unit trust or other investment portfolio by relying on automatic adjustments such as indexation instead of making personal judgments. See also *active fund management*

passive portfolio strategy FIN the managing of an investment portfolio by relying on automatic adjustments or tracking an index

pathfinder prospectus FIN a preliminary prospectus used in initial public offerings to gauge the reaction of investors. Also known as *red eye*

pawnbroker FIN a person who lends money against the security of a wide range of chattels, from jewellery to cars. The borrower may recover the goods by repaying the loan and interest by a certain date. Otherwise, the items pawned are sold and any surplus after the deduction of expenses, the loan, and interest is returned to the borrower.

pay HR a sum of money given in return for work done or services provided. Pay, in the form of salary or wages, is generally provided in weekly or monthly fixed amounts, and is usually expressed in terms of the total sum earned per year. It may also be allocated using a piece-rate system, where workers are paid for each unit of work they carry out.

payable to order FIN the legend on a bill of exchange or cheque, used to indicate that it may be transferred

Pay As You Earn HR in the United Kingdom, a system for collecting direct taxes that requires employers to deduct taxes from employees' pay before payment is made. *Abbr* **PAYE**

pay-as-you-go Canada HR a means of financing a pension system whereby benefits of current retirees are financed by current workers

Pay-As-You-Go ANZ FIN a system used in Australia for paying income tax instalments on business and investment income. PAYG is part of the tax system introduced by the Australian government on 1 July 2000. *Abbr* **PAYG**

payback period FIN the length of time it will take to earn back the money invested in a project. The straight payback period method is the simplest way of determining the investment potential of a major project. Expressed in time, it tells a management how many months or years it will take to recover the original cash cost of the project.

PAYE *abbr* HR Pay As You Earn

payee FIN **1.** the person or organisation to whom a cheque is payable. See also *drawee* **2.** the person to whom a payment has to be made

payer FIN the person making a payment

PAYG *abbr* ANZ FIN Pay-As-You-Go

paying agent FIN the institution responsible for making interest payments on a security and repaying capital at redemption. Also known as *disbursing agent*

paying banker FIN the bank on which a bill of exchange or cheque is drawn

paying-in book FIN a book of detachable slips that accompany money or cheques being paid into a bank account

payload FIN the amount of cargo that a vessel can carry

paymaster FIN the person responsible for paying an organisation's employees

payment by results HR a system of pay that directly links an employee's salary to his or her work output. The system is based on the view put forward by Frederick Winslow Taylor that payment by results will increase workers' productivity by appealing to their materialism. The concept is closely related to performance-related pay which rewards employees for behaviour and skills rather than quantifiable productivity measures.

payment gateway E-COM a company or organisation that provides an interface between a merchant's point-of-sale system, acquirer payment systems, and issuer payment systems. *Abbr* **GW**

payment in advance FIN a payment made for goods when they are ordered and before they are delivered. See also *prepayment*

payment in due course FIN the payment of a bill of exchange on a fixed date in the future

payment-in-kind HR an alternative form of pay given to employees in place of monetary reward but considered to be of equivalent value. A payment in kind may take the form of use of a car, purchase of goods at cost price, or other non-financial exchange that benefits the employee. It forms part of the total pay package rather than being an extra benefit.

payment-in-lieu HR payment that is given in place of an entitlement

payment terms FIN the stipulation by a business as to when it should be paid for goods or services supplied, for example, cash with order, payment on delivery, or within a particular number of days of the invoice date

payout ratio FIN an expression of the total dividends paid to shareholders as a percentage of a company's net profit in a given period of time. This measures the likelihood of dividend payments being sustained, and is a useful indication of sustained profitability. The lower the ratio, the more secure the dividend, and the company's future. See also *dividend cover*

PayPal™ E-COM a Web-based service that enables Internet users to send and receive payments electronically. To open a PayPal™ account, users register and provide their credit card or account details. When they decide to make a transaction via PayPal™, their card or account is charged for the transfer.

pay-per-click E-COM see *pay-per-view*

pay-per-play E-COM a website that charges a micropayment to play an interactive game over the Internet

pay-per-view E-COM a website that charges a micropayment to see digital information, for example, an e-book or e-magazine. Also known as *pay-per-click*

payroll HR a record showing for each employee his or her gross pay, deductions, and net pay. The payroll may also include details of the employer's associated employment costs.

payslip HR a document given to employees when they are paid, providing a statement of pay for that period. A payslip includes details of deductions such as income tax, national insurance contributions, pension contributions, and trade union dues.

P/C *abbr* FIN petty cash

PDR *abbr* FIN price/dividend ratio

peg FIN **1.** to fix the exchange rate of one currency against that of another or of a basket of other currencies **2.** to fix wages and salaries during a period of inflation to help prevent an inflationary spiral

penalty FIN an arbitrary pre-arranged sum that becomes payable if one party breaks a term of a contract or an undertaking. The most common penalty is a high rate of interest on an unauthorised overdraft. See also *overdraft*

penalty clause GEN see *liquidated damages clause*

penetration pricing FIN setting prices low, especially for new products, in order to maximise market penetration

penny shares FIN very low-priced stock that is a speculative investment

pension FIN money received regularly after retirement, from a personal pension scheme, occupational pension scheme, or state pension scheme. Also known as *retirement pension*

pensionable earnings FIN in an occupational pension scheme with a defined benefit, the earnings on which the pension is based. Generally, overtime payments, benefits in kind, bonuses, and territorial allowances, for example, payments for working in a large city are not pensionable earnings. US term *final average monthly salary*

PEP *abbr* FIN personal equity plan

P/E ratio *abbr* FIN price/earnings ratio

per capita income ECON the average income of each of a particular group of people, for example, citizens of a country

perceived value pricing FIN see *market based pricing*

per diem HR a rate paid per day, for example, for expenses when an employee is working away from the office

perfect capital market ECON a capital market in which the decisions of buyers and sellers have no effect on market price

perfect competition ECON the condition in which no buyer or seller can influence prices. In practice, perfect markets are characterised by few or no barriers to entry and by many buyers and sellers.

perfect hedge FIN a hedge that exactly balances the risk of another investment

performance bond FIN a guarantee given by a bank to a third party stating that it will pay a sum of money if its customer, the account holder, fails to complete a specified contract

performance criteria FIN the standards used to evaluate a product, service, or employee

performance fund FIN an investment fund designed to produce a high return, reflected in the higher risk involved

performance prism GEN a framework for measuring company performance which takes account of the two-way relationships between an organisation and all its stakeholders. The performance prism was developed by researchers from the Centre for Business Performance at Cranfield School of Management and Accenture. The model takes a similar approach to the balanced scorecard in that non-financial measures of performance are analysed, but it takes account of a wider range of stakeholders including investors, customers, employees, suppliers, regulators, and communities. The factors to be analysed are represented as the five faces of a prism: stakeholder wants and stakeholder contribution at the ends, and strategies, processes, and capabilities as the three internal facets.

period bill FIN a bill of exchange payable on a certain date rather than on demand. Also known as *term bill*

permanent interest-bearing shares FIN shares issued by a building society to raise capital because the law prohibits it from raising capital in more conventional ways. *Abbr* **PIBS**

perpetual bond FIN a bond that has no date of maturity

perpetual debenture FIN a debenture that pays interest in perpetuity, having no date of maturity

perpetual inventory FIN the daily tracking of inventory

personal account FIN a record of amounts receivable from or payable to a person or an entity. A collection of these accounts is known as a sales/debtor ledger, or a purchases/creditors ledger. The terms sales and purchases ledger are preferred. In the United States, the terms receivables ledger and payables ledger are used.

personal allowances FIN the amount of money that an individual can earn without having to pay income tax. The allowances vary according to age, marital status, and whether the person is a single parent.

personal brand GEN the public expression and projection of an individual's identity, personality, values, skills, and abilities. The idea of personal branding has evolved by applying the concept of a product brand or a corporate brand to an individual person. The creation of a personal brand can be used as a tool for personal development as described by Thomas Gad and Anette Rozencreutz in their book, *Managing Brand Me* (Momentum, 2002). It also aims to influence the perceptions of others, emphasising personal strengths and differentiating the individual from others. However, a personal brand should be based on an individual's real identity – who they are and what they stand for, rather than an external image they wish to project.

personal day HR a day when an employee may be absent from work for any reason. In the United States, personal days are usually part of written employment policy and are frequently not distinguished from sick days or annual leave.

personal financial planning FIN short- and long-term financial planning by an individual, either independently or with the assistance of a professional adviser. It will include the use of tax efficient schemes such as Individual Savings Accounts, ensuring adequate provisions are being made for retirement, and examining short- and long-term borrowing requirements such as overdrafts and mortgages.

Personal Identification Number FIN *Abbr* **PIN**

PESTLE MKT an acronym that describes the six influences to which a market is subject, namely, Political, Economic, Social, Technological, Legal, and Environmental

petty cash FIN a small store of cash used for minor business expenses. *Abbr* **P/C**

petty cash account FIN a record of relatively small cash receipts and payments, the balance representing the cash in the control of an individual, usually dealt with under an imprest system

petty cash voucher FIN a document supporting payments under a petty cash system

PFI *abbr* FIN Private Finance Initiative

phantom bid FIN a reported but non-existent attempt to buy a company

phantom income FIN income that is subject to tax even though the recipient never actually gets control of it, for example, income from a limited partnership

phish E-COM to trick someone into providing bank or credit card details by sending a fraudulent e-mail purporting to be from a bank, Internet service provider, or similar, asking for verification of an account number or password

physical asset FIN an asset that has a physical embodiment, as opposed to cash or securities

physical market FIN a market in futures that involves physical delivery of the commodities involved, instead of simple cash transactions

physical price FIN the price of a commodity for immediate delivery

physicals FIN commodities that can be bought and used, as contrasted with commodities traded on a futures contract

physical stocktaking FIN the ascertainment of stocks held (by counting physical objects) for comparison with accounting records. Modern practice is to count different items with different frequencies, classifying items according to the degree of control required. Periodic stocktaking is a process whereby all stock items are counted and valued at a set point in time, usually the end of an accounting period. Continuous stocktaking is the process of counting and valuing selected items at different times, on a rotating basis.

PIBOR *abbr* FIN Paris Inter Bank Offered Rate

PIBS *abbr* FIN permanent interest-bearing shares

picture FIN the price and trading quantity of a particular stock on Wall Street used, for example, in the question to a specialist dealer 'What's the picture on ABC?'. The response would give the bid and offer price and number of shares for which there would be a buyer and seller. *(slang)*

piggyback loan FIN a loan that is raised against the same security as an existing loan

piggyback rights FIN the permission to sell existing shares in conjunction with the sale of like shares in a new offering

PIN *abbr* FIN personal identification number

pink dollar *US* FIN = pink pound

pink pound FIN money spent by the homosexual community. US term *pink dollar*

pit FIN the area of an exchange where trading takes place. It was traditionally an octagonal stepped area with terracing so as to give everyone a good view of the proceedings during open outcry.

pit broker FIN a broker who transacts business in the pit of a futures or options exchange. Also known as *floor broker*

placement FIN see *private placing*

placement fee FIN a fee that a stockbroker receives for a sale of shares

plain vanilla FIN a financial instrument in its simplest form *(slang)*

plastic or **plastic money** FIN a payment system using a plastic card *(slang)* See also *credit card, debit card, multifunctional card*

plc or **PLC** *abbr* FIN public limited company

plenitude ECON a hypothetical condition of an economy in which manufacturing technology has been perfected and scarcity is replaced by an abundance of products

plough back FIN to reinvest a company's earnings in the business instead of paying them out as dividends

plum FIN a successful investment *(slang)*

PN *abbr* FIN promissory note

PO *abbr* FIN purchase order

point *US* FIN a unit used for calculation of a value, such as a hundredth of a percentage point for interest rates

poison pill FIN a measure taken by a company to avoid a hostile takeover, for example, the purchase of a business interest that will make the company unattractive to the potential buyer *(slang)*. Also known as *show stopper*

policyholder FIN a person or business covered by an insurance policy

political economy ECON a country's economic organisation

Dictionary

poop *US* FIN a person who has inside information on a financial deal *(slang)*

pooping and scooping *US* FIN an illegal financial practice in which a person or group of individuals attempts to drive down a share price by spreading false unfavourable information. The advent of the Internet has allowed pooping and scooping to become more widespread. *(slang)*

portable pension FIN a pension plan that moves with an employee when he or she changes employer. See also *stakeholder pension*

portfolio FIN the range of investments, such as stocks and shares, owned by an individual or an organisation

portfolio career HR a career based on a series of varied shorter-term jobs – either concurrently or consecutively – as opposed to one based on a progression up the ranks of a particular profession. The portfolio worker is frequently self-employed, offering his or her services on a freelance or consultancy basis to one or more employers at the same time. However, a portfolio approach can also be taken to full-time employment with a single employer, if the employee chooses to expand his or her experience and responsibilities through taking different roles within the organisation. To critics, the portfolio approach to career development may appear unfocused and directionless. However, it is an excellent opportunity to experience the many different avenues available in modern life. It is important, in general, for the portfolio worker to maintain some overall sense of purpose or strategic direction in the work they undertake, and to view their portfolio career as a unified whole rather than a collection of 'odd jobs'.

portfolio immunisation FIN measures taken by traders to protect their share portfolios *(slang)*

portfolio insurance FIN options that provide hedges against stock in a portfolio

portfolio investment FIN a form of investment that aims for a mixture of income and capital growth

portfolio management FIN the systematic buying and selling shares in order to make the highest-possible profits for a single investor

portfolio manager FIN a person or company that specialises in managing an investment portfolio on behalf of investors

position FIN the number of shares of a security that are owned by an individual or company

position limit FIN the largest amount of a security that any group or individual may own

positive economics ECON the study of economic propositions that can be verified by observing the real economy

possessory action FIN a lawsuit over the right to own a piece of land

post a credit FIN to enter a credit item in a ledger

post Big Bang FIN see *Big Bang*

post-completion audit FIN an objective and independent appraisal of the measure of success of a capital expenditure project in progressing the business as planned. The appraisal should cover the implementation of the project from authorisation to commissioning and its technical and commercial performance after commissioning. The information provided is also used by management as feedback, which helps the implementation and control of future projects.

postdate FIN to put a later date on a document or cheque than the date when it is signed, with the effect that it is not valid until the later date

potential GDP ECON a measure of the real value of the services and goods that can be produced when a country's factors of production are fully employed

potentially exempt transfer FIN see *chargeable transfer*

pot trust FIN a trust, typically created in a will, for a group of beneficiaries

pound cost averaging FIN investing the same amount at regular intervals in a security regardless of its price. US term *dollar cost averaging*

poverty trap FIN a situation whereby low-income families are penalised by a progressive tax system: an increase in income is either counteracted by a

loss of social benefit payments or by an increase in taxation

power of attorney FIN a legal document granting one person the right to act on behalf of another

PPP *abbr* ECON, FIN purchasing power parity

preauthorised electronic debit FIN a scheme in which a payer agrees to let a bank make payments from an account to somebody else's account

prebilling FIN the practice of submitting a bill for a product or service before it has actually been delivered

preceding year FIN the year before the accounting year in question

precious metals FIN gold, silver, platinum, and palladium

predatory pricing FIN the practice of setting prices for products that are designed to win business from competitors or to damage competitors. This may involve dumping, which is selling a product in a foreign market at below cost or below the domestic market price (subject to adjustments for taxation differences, transportation costs, specification differences etc.).

pre-emptive right FIN the right of a stockholder to maintain proportional ownership in a corporation by purchasing newly issued stock

preference share FIN a share which receives its dividend before all other shares and which is repaid first at face value if a company goes into liquidation. Preference shares often have no voting rights. US term *preferred stock*

preferential creditor FIN a creditor who is entitled to payment, especially from a bankrupt, before other creditors

preferential issue FIN an issue of stock available only to designated buyers

preferential payment FIN a payment to a preferential creditor

preferred risk FIN somebody considered by an insurance company to be less likely to collect on a policy than the average person, for example, a non-smoker

pre-financing FIN the practice of arranging funding for a project before the project begins

preliminary prospectus FIN a document issued prior to a share issue that gives details about the company and its financial situation

premarket FIN used to describe transactions between market members carried out prior to the official opening of the market. Also known as *pretrading*

premium FIN **1.** the price a purchaser of an option pays to its writer **2.** the difference between the futures price and the cash price of an underlying asset **3.** the consideration for a contract of insurance or assurance; **at a premium** FIN **1.** of a fixed interest security, at an issue price above its par value **2.** of a new issue, at a trading price above the one offered to investors **3.** at a price that is considered expensive in relation to others

premium income FIN the income earned by a life company or insurance company from premiums

premium pay plan HR an enhanced pay scale for high-performing employees. A premium pay plan can be offered as an incentive to motivate employees, rewarding such achievements as high productivity, long service, or completion of training with an increased pay package.

prepaid interest FIN interest paid in advance of its due date

prepayment FIN the payment of a debt before it is due to be paid

prepayment penalty *US* FIN a charge that may be levied against somebody who makes a payment before its due date. The penalty compensates the lender or seller for potential lost interest.

prepayment privilege FIN the right to make a prepayment, for example, on a loan or mortgage, without penalty

prepayment risk FIN the risk that a debtor will avoid interest charges by making partial or total prepayments, especially when interest rates fall

prescribed payments system *ANZ* FIN a system under which employers are obliged to deduct a certain amount of tax from cash payments made to casual workers. The system was introduced in Australia in 1983.

present value FIN **1.** the amount that a future interest in a financial asset is currently worth, discounted for inflation **2.** the value now of an

amount of money that somebody expects to receive at a future date, calculated by subtracting any interest that will accrue in the interim

preservation of capital FIN an approach to financial management that protects a person's or company's capital by arranging additional forms of finance

pre-syndicate bid FIN a bid made before a group of buyers can offer blocks of shares in an offering to the public

pretax FIN before tax is considered or paid

pretax profit FIN the amount of profit a company makes before taxes are deducted

pretax profit margin FIN the profit made by a company, calculated as a percentage of sales, before taxes are considered

pretrading FIN see *premarket*

price FIN an amount of money that a vendor charges a customer for a good or service

price-book ratio FIN see *price-to-book ratio*

price ceiling FIN the highest price that a buyer is willing to pay

price competition FIN a form of competition based on price rather than factors such as quality or design

price control ECON a government regulation that sets maximum prices for commodities or controls price levels by means of credit controls

price differentiation FIN a pricing strategy in which a company sells the same product at different prices in different markets

price discovery FIN the process by which price is determined by negotiation in a free market

price discrimination ECON the practice of selling the same product to different buyers at different prices

price/dividend ratio FIN the price of a stock divided by the annual dividend paid on a share. *Abbr* **PDR**

price/earnings ratio FIN a company's share price divided by earnings per share (EPS). *Abbr* **P/E** ratio

price effect ECON the impact of price changes on a market or economy

price elasticity of demand ECON the percentage change in demand divided by the percentage change in price of a good

price elasticity of supply ECON the percentage change in supply divided by the percentage change in price of a good

price escalation clause FIN a contract provision that permits the seller to raise prices in response to increased costs

price fixing FIN an often illegal agreement between producers of a good or service in order to maintain prices at a particular level

price floor FIN the lowest price at which a seller is prepared to do business

price index FIN an index, such as the consumer price index, that measures inflation

price indicator ECON a price that is a measurable variable and can be used, for example, as an index of the cost of living

price-insensitive FIN used to describe a good or service for which sales remain constant no matter what its price because it is essential to buyers

price instability ECON a situation in which the prices of goods alter daily or even hourly

price ring FIN a group of traders who make an agreement, often illegally, to maintain prices at a particular level

prices and incomes policy ECON a policy limiting price or wage increases through government regulations

price-sensitive FIN used to describe a good or service for which sales fluctuate depending on its price, often because it is a non-essential item

price-sensitive information FIN as yet unpublished information that will affect a company's share price. For example, the implementation of a new manufacturing process that will substantially cut production costs would have a positive impact, whereas the discovery of harmful side effects from a recently launched drug would have a negative impact.

price stability FIN a situation in which there is little change in the price of goods or services

price support ECON government assistance in keeping market prices from falling below a minimum level

price-to-book ratio FIN the ratio of the value of all of a company's stock to its book value. Also known as *price-book ratio*

price-to-cash-flow ratio FIN the ratio of the value of all of a company's stock to its cash flow for the most recent complete fiscal year

price-to-sales ratio FIN the ratio of the value of all of a company's stock to its sales for the previous 12 months, a way of measuring the relative value of a share when compared with others

price-weighted index FIN an index of production or market value that is adjusted for price changes

primary account number FIN an identifier for a credit card used in secure electronic transactions

primary earnings per (common) share *US* FIN see *earnings per share*

primary liability FIN a responsibility to pay before anyone else, for example, for damages covered by insurance

primary market FIN the part of the market on which securities are first offered to investors by the issuer. The money from this sale goes to the issuer, rather than to traders or investors as it does in the secondary market. See also *secondary market*

primary sector ECON the firms and corporations of the productive sector of a country's economy

prime FIN see *prime rate*

prime assets ratio *ANZ* FIN the proportion of total liabilities which Australian banks are obliged by the Reserve Bank to hold in secure assets such as cash and government securities. *Abbr* **PAR**

prime cost FIN the cost involved in producing a product, excluding overhead costs

prime rate or **prime interest rate** FIN the lowest interest rate that commercial banks offer on loans. Also known as *prime*

principal FIN the original amount of a loan, not including any interest. See also *mortgage*

principal shareholders FIN the shareholders who own the largest percentage of shares in an organisation

prior charge percentage FIN see *priority percentage*

priority percentage FIN the proportion of a business's net profit that is paid in interest to preference shareholders and holders of debt capital. Also known as *prior charge percentage*

prior lien bond FIN a bond whose holder has more claim on a debtor's assets than holders of other types of bonds

private bank FIN 1. a bank that is owned by a single person or a limited number of private shareholders 2. a bank that provides banking facilities to high net worth individuals. See also *private banking* 3. a bank that is not state-owned in a country where most banks are owned by the government

private banking FIN a service offered by certain financial institutions to high net worth individuals. In addition to standard banking services, it will typically include portfolio management and advisory services on taxation, including estate planning.

private cost *US* ECON the cost incurred by individuals when they use scarce resources such as petrol

private debt FIN money owed by individuals and organisations other than governments

private enterprise ECON business or industry that is controlled by companies or individuals rather than the government

private placing FIN the sale of securities directly to institutions for investment rather than resale. US term *private placement*

private sector ECON the section of the economy that is financed and controlled by individuals or private institutions, such as companies, shareholders, or investment groups. See also *public sector*

private sector investment ECON investment by the private enterprise sector of an economy

private treaty FIN the sale of land without an auction

privatisation FIN the transfer of a company from ownership by either a government or a few individuals to the public via the issuance of stock

problem child 1. *US* FIN a subsidiary company that is not performing well or is damaging the parent company in some way 2. MKT a product with a low market share but high growth potential. Problem children often have good long-term prospects, but high levels of investment may be needed to realise the potential, thereby draining funds that may be needed elsewhere.

proceeds FIN the income from a transaction

procurement exchange E-COM a group of companies that act together to buy products or services they need at lower prices

producer price index ECON a statistical measure, the weighted average of the prices of commodities that firms buy from other firms

productivity FIN, GEN, OPS a measurement of the efficiency of production, taking the form of a ratio of the output of goods and services to the input of factors of production. Labour productivity takes account of inputs of employee hours worked; capital productivity takes account of inputs of machines or land; and marginal productivity measures the additional output gained from an additional unit of input. Techniques to improve productivity include greater use of new technology, altered working practices, and improved training of the workforce.

product launch MKT the introduction of a new product to a market. A product launch progresses through a number of important stages: internal communication, which encourages high levels of awareness and commitment to the new product; pre-launch activity, which secures distribution and makes sure that retailers have the resources and knowledge to market the product; launch events at national, regional, or local level; post-event activity, which helps salesforces and retailers make the most of the event; and launch advertising and other forms of customer communication.

product life cycle FIN the period which begins with the initial product specification and ends with the withdrawal from the market of both the product and its support. It is characterised by defined stages, including research, development, introduction, maturity, decline, and abandonment.

profile FIN a description of a company, including its products and finances

profit FIN the difference between the selling price and the purchase price of a security or financial instrument when the selling price is higher

profitability FIN 1. the degree to which an individual, company, or single activity makes a profit 2. the condition of making a profit

profitability index FIN the present value of the money an investment will earn divided by the amount of the investment

profitability threshold FIN the point at which a business begins to make profits

profitable FIN used to refer to a product, service, or organisation which makes money

profit and loss FIN the difference between a company's income and its costs

profit and loss account or **profit and loss statement** FIN the summary record of a company's sales revenues and expenses over a period, providing a calculation of profits or losses during that time. *Abbr* **P&L**

profit before tax FIN the amount that a company or investor has made, without taking taxes into account

profit centre 1. FIN a part of a business accountable for both costs and revenues 2. GEN a person, unit, or department within an organisation that is considered separately when calculating profit. Profit centres are used as part of management control systems. They operate with a degree of autonomy with regard to marketing and pricing, and have responsibility for their own costs, revenues, and profits.

profit distribution FIN the allocation of profits to different recipients such as shareholders and owners, or for different purposes such as research or investment

profiteer FIN an individual or organisation who aims to make excessive profits, often with a detrimental effect on others

profit from ordinary activities FIN profits earned in the normal course of business, as opposed to profits from extraordinary sources such as windfall payments

profit margin FIN sales less cost of sales, expressed either as a value or as a percentage of sales value. The profit margin may be calculated at different stages, hence the terms gross profit margin and net profit margin. The level of profit reported is also influenced by the extent of the application of accounting conventions, and by the method of product costing used, for example, marginal or absorption costing.

profit motive FIN the desire of a business or service provider to make a profit

profit sharing FIN the allocation of a proportion of company profit to employees by an issue of shares or other means

profit-sharing debenture FIN a debenture held by an employee, the payouts from which depend on the employing company's financial success

profit squeeze FIN the inability to maintain an individual or an organisation's profit in a venture, in comparison to previous ventures

profits tax FIN a tax on profits, for example, corporation tax (*slang*)

pro-forma financial statement FIN a projection showing a business's financial statements after the completion of a planned transaction

pro-forma invoice FIN an invoice that does not include all the details of a transaction, often sent before goods are supplied and followed by a final detailed invoice

programme trading FIN the trading of securities electronically, by sending messages from the investor's computer to a market

progressive tax FIN a tax with a rate that increases proportionately with taxable income. See also ***proportional tax, regressive tax***

project creep GEN the gradual slippage of deadlines and targets during a project

project finance FIN money, usually non-recourse finance, raised for a specific self-contained venture, usually a construction or development project

project management FIN the integration of all aspects of a project in order to ensure that the proper

knowledge and resources are available when and where needed, and above all to ensure that the expected outcome is produced in a timely, cost-effective manner. The primary function of a project manager is to manage the trade-offs between performance, timeliness, and cost.

project risk analysis or **project risk assessment** GEN the identification of risks to which a project is exposed, and the assessment of the potential impact of those risks on the project. Project risk analysis forms part of the process of project management and is a specialised type of risk analysis.

promissory note FIN a contract to pay money to a person or organisation for a good or service received. *Abbr* **PN**

property FIN assets, such as land or goods, that an individual or organisation owns

property bond FIN a bond, especially a bail bond, for which a property is collateral

property damage insurance FIN insurance against the risk of damage to property

proportional tax FIN a tax which is strictly proportional in amount to the value of the item being taxed, especially income. See also ***progressive tax, regressive tax***

ProShare FIN a group that acts in the interests of private investors in securities of the London Stock Exchange

prospect theory GEN a branch of decision theory which attempts to explain why individuals make decisions that deviate from rational decision-making by examining how the expected outcomes of alternative choices are perceived. Prospect theory was developed by Daniel Kahneman and Amos Tversky in 1979, in their article 'Prospect Theory: An Analysis of Decision Making under Risk', *Econometrica XX*, pp. 263–291. The theory is based on the premise that people treat risks associated with perceived losses differently from risks associated with perceived gains. Prospect theory has applications in a wide range of fields, including marketing management, where it is relevant to the way in which choices are presented to the consumer.

prospectus FIN a description of a company's operations, financial background, prospects, and the detailed terms and conditions relating to an offer for sale or placing of its shares by notice, circular, advertisement, or any form of invitation which offers securities to the public

protectionism ECON a government economic policy of restricting the level of imports by using measures such as tariffs and NTBs in order to protect a country's domestic industries

protective put buying FIN the purchase of puts for stocks already owned

protective tariff ECON a tariff imposed to restrict imports into a country

protirement HR leaving or retiring from a stressful professional job to focus on a new blend of work and other activities. Protirement is similar to downshifting but is seen as a more positive approach to retirement. It is a lifestyle option increasingly taken by successful people in mid-life or later, sometimes including a new career or educational activities, but most importantly involving a plan for self-enrichment and fulfilment. It may also involve portfolio working. The term was first used in the book *The Adult Years: Mastering the Art of Self Renewal* by F.M. Hudson (Jossey-Bass, 1991).

protocol FIN a set of rules that govern and regulate a process

provision FIN a sum set aside in the accounts of an organisation in anticipation of a future expense, often for doubtful debts. See also *bad debt*

provisional tax FIN tax paid in advance on the following year's income, the amount being based on the actual income from the preceding year

proxy fight FIN the use of proxy votes to settle a contentious issue at a company meeting

proxy statement FIN a notice that a company sends to stockholders, allowing them to vote and giving them all the information they need to vote in an informed way

prudence concept FIN the principle that revenue and profits are not anticipated but are included in the profit and loss account only when realised in the form either of cash or of other assets, the ultimate cash realisation of which can be assessed with reasonable certainty. Provision is made for all known liabilities (expenses and losses) whether the amount of these is known with certainty, or is a best estimate in the light of the information available.

psychometric test HR a series of questions, problems, or practical tasks that provide a measurement of aspects of somebody's personality, knowledge, ability, or experience. There are three main categories of psychometric test: ability or aptitude tests, achievement tests, and personality tests. A test should be both valid – it should measure what it says it measures – and reliable – it should give consistent scores. However, no test can ever be 100% accurate, and should be viewed more as a useful indicator than a definitive verdict on a person's skills or potential. Tests are used in recruitment, to ascertain whether or not a candidate is likely to be a good fit for a job, and in employee development, and their administration and interpretation must be carried out by qualified people. Tests are increasingly taken, scored, and interpreted with the aid of computer-based systems. A test may also be referred to as an instrument, and tests can be grouped into a test battery.

Pty *abbr S Africa* FIN proprietary: used in company names to indicate a private limited liability company

public corporation FIN a state-owned organisation established to provide a particular service, for example, the British Broadcasting Corporation

public debt ECON the money that a government or a set of governments owes

public deposits FIN in the United Kingdom, the government's credit monies held at the Bank of England

public expenditure ECON spending by the government of a country on things such as pension provision and infrastructure enhancement

public finance law FIN legislation relating to the financial activities of government or public sector organisations

public issue FIN a way of making a new issue of shares by offering it for sale to the public. An issue of this type is often advertised in the press. See also *offer for sale, offer by prospectus*

public-liability insurance FIN insurance against the risk of being held financially liable for injury to somebody

public limited company FIN a company in the United Kingdom that is required to have a minimum authorised capital of £50,000 and to offer its shares to the public. A public limited company has the letters 'plc' after its name. In the United Kingdom, only public limited companies can be listed on the London Stock Exchange. US term *publicly held corporation*. Abbr **PLC**

publicly held corporation *US* = public limited company

public monopoly ECON a situation of limited competition in the public sector, usually relating to nationalised industries

public offering FIN a method of raising money used by a company in which it invites the public to apply for shares

public placing FIN placing shares in a public company. See also *private placing*

public sector ECON, FIN the organisations in the section of the economy that is financed and controlled by central government, local authorities, and publicly funded corporations. See also *private sector*

public spending ECON spending by the government of a country on publicly provided goods and services

published accounts FIN a company's financial statements that must by law be published. US term *earnings report*

puff FIN to overstate the virtues of a product, especially a stock *(slang)*

pump priming FIN the injection of further investment in order to revitalise a company in stagnation, or to help a start-up over a critical period. Pump priming has a similar effect to the provision of seed capital.

purchase contract FIN a form of agreement to buy specified products at an agreed price

purchase money mortgage *US* FIN a mortgage whose proceeds the borrower uses to buy the property that is collateral for the loan

purchase order FIN a written order for goods or services specifying quantities, prices, delivery dates, and contract terms

purchase price FIN the price that somebody pays to buy a good or service

purchase requisition GEN an internal instruction to a buying office to purchase goods or services, stating their quantity and description and generating a purchase order

purchasing manager FIN an individual with responsibility for all activities concerned with purchasing. The responsibilities of a purchasing manager can include ordering, commercial negotiations, and delivery chasing. Also known as *buying manager*

purchasing power FIN a measure of the ability of a person, organisation, or sector to buy goods and services

purchasing power parity FIN a theory that the exchange rate between two currencies is in equilibrium when the purchasing power of currency is the same in each country. If a basket of goods costs £100 in the United Kingdom and $150 for an equivalent in the United States, for equilibrium to exist, the exchange rate would be expected to be £1 = $1.50. If this were not the case, arbitrage would be expected to take place until equilibrium was restored. *Abbr* **PPP**

pure competition FIN a situation in which 'there are many sellers in a market and there is free flow of information

pure endowment FIN a gift whose use is fully prescribed by the donor

purpose credit FIN credit used for trade in securities

put or **put option** FIN an option to sell stock within a specified time at a specified price

qualification payment *ANZ* FIN an additional payment sometimes made to employees of New Zealand companies, who have gained an academic qualification relevant to their job

qualified auditor's report FIN see *adverse opinion*

qualified domestic trust *US* FIN a trust for the non-citizen spouse of a US citizen, affording tax advantages at the time of the citizen's death

qualified lead FIN a sales prospect whose potential value has been carefully researched

qualified listed security FIN a security that is eligible for purchase by a regulated entity such as a trust

qualitative analysis FIN the subjective appraisal of a project or investment for which there is no quantifiable data. See also *chartist, quantitative analysis, technical analysis*

qualitative lending guideline FIN a rule for evaluating creditworthiness that is not objective

quality bond FIN a bond issued by an organisation that has an excellent credit rating

quality equity FIN an equity with a good track record of earnings and dividends. See also *blue chip*

quango GEN an acronym derived from quasi-autonomous non-governmental organisation. Established by the government and answerable to a government minister, some, but not all quangos are staffed by civil servants and some have statutory powers in a specified field.

quantitative analysis FIN the appraisal of a project or investment using econometric, mathematical, and statistical techniques. See also *chartist, qualitative analysis, technical analysis*

quantitative research FIN the gathering and analysis of data that can be expressed in numerical form. Quantitative research involves data that is measurable and can include statistical results, financial data, or demographic data.

quantum meruit FIN a Latin phrase meaning 'as much as has been earned'

quarterly report FIN see *interim statement*

quasi-contract FIN a decree by a UK court stipulating that one party has a legal obligation to another, even though there is no legally binding contract between the two parties

quasi-loan FIN an arrangement whereby one party pays the debts of another, on the condition that the sum of the debts will be reimbursed by the indebted party at some later date

quasi-money FIN see *near money*

quasi-public corporation *US* FIN an organisation that is owned partly by private or public shareholders and partly by the government

quasi-rent ECON the short-run excess earnings made by a firm: the difference between production cost (the cost of labour and materials) and selling cost

queuing time OPS the time between the arrival of material at a workstation and the start of work on it

quick asset FIN see *near money*

quick ratio FIN 1. a measure of the amount of cash a potential borrower can acquire in a short time, used in evaluating creditworthiness 2. the ratio of liquid assets to current debts

quid pro quo FIN a Latin phrase meaning 'something for something'

quorum FIN the minimum number of people required in a meeting for it to be able to make decisions that are binding on the organisation. For a company, this is stated in its articles of association, for a partnership, in its partnership agreement.

quota FIN 1. the maximum sum to be contributed by each party in a joint venture or joint business undertaking 2. the maximum number of investments that may be purchased and sold in a given situation or market 3. the maximum amount of a particular commodity, product, or service that can be imported into or exported out of a country

quote FIN a statement of what a person is willing to accept when selling a product or service

quoted company FIN a company whose shares are listed on a stock exchange

quote driven FIN used to describe a share dealing system where prices are initially generated by dealers' and market makers' quotes before market forces come into play and prices are determined by the interaction of supply and demand. The London Stock Exchange's dealing system, as well as those of many over-the-counter markets, have quote driven systems.

quoted securities FIN securities or shares that are listed on a stock exchange

raid FIN the illegal practice of selling shares short to drive the price down. Also known as *bear raid*

raider FIN a person or company that makes hostile takeover bids

rake it in FIN to make a great deal of money *(slang)*

rake-off FIN commission *(slang)*

rally FIN a rise in share prices after a fall

ramp FIN to buy shares with the objective of raising their price. See also *rigged market*

rand FIN the South African unit of currency, equal to 100 cents

Randlord FIN originally a Johannesburg-based mining magnate or tycoon of the late 19th or early 20th centuries, now used informally for any wealthy or powerful Johannesburg businessman

range pricing FIN the pricing of individual products so that their prices fit logically within a range of connected products offered by one supplier, and differentiated by a factor such as weight of pack or number of product attributes offered

ratchet effect ECON the result when households adjust more easily to rising incomes than to falling incomes, as, for example, when their consumption drops by less than their income in a recession

rate cap FIN see *cap*

rate of exchange FIN see *exchange rate*

rate of interest FIN a percentage charged on a loan or paid on an investment for the use of the money

rate of return FIN an accounting ratio of the income from an investment to the amount of the investment, used to measure financial performance. Also known as *return*

ratio analysis FIN the use of ratios to measure financial performance

RBA *abbr* FIN Reserve Bank of Australia

RBNZ *abbr* FIN Reserve Bank of New Zealand

RD *abbr* FIN refer to drawer

RDP *abbr* S Africa FIN Reconstruction and Development Program: a policy framework by means of which the South African government intends to correct the socio-economic imbalances caused by apartheid

RDPR *abbr* FIN refer to drawer please represent

Reaganomics ECON the economic policy of then US President Reagan in the 1980s, who reduced taxes and social security support and increased the national budget deficit to an unprecedented level

real FIN after the effects of inflation are taken into consideration

real asset FIN a non-movable asset such as land or a building

real balance effect ECON the effect on income and employment when prices fall and consumption increases

real capital ECON, FIN assets that can be assigned a monetary value

real exchange rate FIN an exchange rate that has been adjusted for inflation

real GDP ECON GDP adjusted for changes in prices

real growth ECON the growth of a country or a household adjusted for changes in prices

real investment FIN the purchase of assets such as land, property, and plant and machinery as opposed to the acquisition of securities

realise FIN to change an asset into cash by selling it

really simple syndication E-COM a Web feed format that allows users to have updated material from their favourite websites, blogs, or e-mail newsletters sent directly to them as soon as the content is updated. RSS is regarded as a good way of avoiding information overload, as it is up to users to stipulate how much information they want: for example, if users were to subscribe to an RSS feed from a news site, they could download headlines only, or have content classified in a way that suits them best. *Abbr* **RSS**

real purchasing power ECON the purchasing power of a country or a household adjusted for changes in prices

real time credit card processing E-COM the online authorisation of a credit card indicating that the credit

card has been approved or rejected during the transaction

real time transaction E-COM an Internet payment transaction that is approved or rejected immediately when the customer completes the online order form

rebadge MKT to buy a product or service from another company and sell it as part of your own product range

rebate FIN **1.** money returned because a payment exceeded the amount required, for example, a tax rebate **2.** a discount **3.** of a broker, to reduce part of the commission charged to the client as a promotional offer

recapitalise FIN **1.** to increase the capital owned by an individual, company, or industry **2.** to change the organisation of a company's capital, usually in response to a major financial problem, such as bankruptcy

recd *abbr* FIN received

receipt FIN a document acknowledging that something – for example, a payment – has been received

receiver FIN a person appointed to sell the assets of a company that is insolvent. The proceeds of the sale are used to discharge debts to creditors, with any surplus distributed to shareholders.

Receiver of Revenue FIN **1.** S Africa a local office of the South African Revenue Service **2.** an informal term for the South African Revenue Service as a whole

recession ECON a stage of the business cycle in which economic activity is in slow decline. Recession usually follows a boom, and precedes a depression. It is characterised by rising unemployment and falling levels of output and investment.

recessionary gap ECON a shortfall in the amount of aggregate demand in an economy needed to create full employment

reconciliation FIN adjustment of an account, such as an individual's own record of a bank account, to match more authoritative information

recourse agreement FIN an agreement in a hire purchase contract whereby the retailer repossesses the goods being purchased in the event of the hirer failing to make regular payments

recovery ECON the return of a country to economic health after a crash or a depression

recovery fund FIN a fund that invests in recovery stock

recovery stock FIN a share that has fallen in price because of poor business performance, but is now expected to climb as a result of an improvement in the company's prospects

recurring billing transaction E-COM an electronic payment facility based on the automatic charging of a customer's credit card in each payment period

recurring payments E-COM an electronic payment facility that permits a merchant to process multiple authorisations by the same customer either as multiple payments for a fixed amount or recurring billings for varying amounts

red FIN the colour of debit or overdrawn balances in some bank statements; **in the red** FIN in debt, or making a loss

Red Book FIN a copy of the Chancellor of the Exchequer's speech published on the day of the Budget. It can be regarded as the country's financial statement and report.

redeemable bond FIN see *callable bond*

redeemable gilt FIN see *gilt-edged security*

redemption FIN repayment, this term being most frequently used in connection with preference shares and debentures

redemption yield FIN the rate of interest at which the total of the discounted values of any future payments of interest and capital is equal to the current price of a security

red eye US FIN see *pathfinder prospectus (slang)*

redistributive effect FIN the tendency towards equalisation of people's wealth that results from a progressive tax or benefit

red screen market FIN in the United Kingdom, a market where the prices are down and are being shown as red on the dealing screens

red tape GEN excessive bureaucracy

reducing balance depreciation FIN see *depreciation*

redundancy package HR a package of benefits that an employer gives to somebody who is made redundant. US term *severance package*

reference FIN see *banker's reference*

reference rate FIN a benchmark rate, for example, a bank's own base rate or LIBOR. Lending rates are often expressed as a margin over a reference rate.

referred share FIN a share that is ex dividend

refer to drawer FIN to refuse to pay a cheque because the account from which it is drawn has too little money in it. *Abbr* **RD**

refer to drawer please represent FIN in the United Kingdom, written on a cheque by the paying banker to indicate that there are currently insufficient funds to meet the payment, but that the bank believes sufficient funds will be available shortly. See also *refer to drawer*. *Abbr* **RDPR**

refinance FIN to replace one loan with another, especially at a lower rate of interest

refinancing FIN **1.** the process of taking out a loan to pay off other loans **2.** a loan taken out for the purpose of repaying another loan or loans

reflation ECON a method of reducing unemployment by increasing an economy's aggregate demand. See also *recession*

refugee capital FIN people and resources that come into a country because they have been forced to leave their own country for economic or political reasons

regional fund FIN a unit trust that invests in the markets of a geographical region

registered bond FIN a bond, the ownership of which is recorded on the books of the issuer

registered broker FIN a broker registered on a particular exchange

registered capital FIN see *authorised capital*

registered name FIN in the United Kingdom, the name of a company as it is registered at Companies House. It must appear, along with the company's registered number and office, on all its letterheads and orders.

registered number FIN in the United Kingdom, a unique number assigned to a company registered at Companies House. It must appear, along with the company's registered name and office on all its letterheads and orders.

registered security FIN a security where the holder's name is recorded in the books of the issuer. See also *nominee name*

registered share FIN a share, the ownership of which is recorded on the books of the issuer

registered share capital FIN see *authorised share capital*

register of companies FIN in the United Kingdom, the list of companies maintained at Companies House

register of directors and secretaries FIN a record that every registered company in the United Kingdom must maintain of the names and residential addresses of directors and the company secretary together with their nationality, occupation, and details of other directorships held. Public companies must also record the date of birth of their directors. The record must be kept at the company's registered office and be available for inspection by shareholders without charge and by members of the public for a nominal fee.

register of directors' interests FIN a record that every registered company in the United Kingdom must maintain of the shares and other securities that have been issued by the company and are held by its directors. It has to be made available for inspection during the company's annual general meeting.

Registrar of Companies FIN, GEN the person charged with the duty of holding and registering the official start-up and constitutional documents of all registered companies in the United Kingdom

registration statement FIN in the United States, a document that corporations planning to issue securities to the public have to submit to the Securities and Exchange Commission. It features details of the issuer's management, financial status, and activities, and the purpose of the issue. See also *shelf registration*

regressive tax FIN a tax with a rate that decreases proportionally as the value of the item being taxed, especially income, rises. US social security taxes are regressive. See also *progressive tax, proportional tax*

regulated superannuation fund *ANZ* FIN an Australian superannuation fund that is regulated by legislation and therefore qualifies for tax concessions. To attain this status, a fund must either show that its main function is the provision of pensions, or adopt a corporate trustee structure.

regulation FIN the use of laws or rules stipulated by a government or regulatory body, such as the Financial Services Authority, to provide orderly procedures and to protect consumers and investors

regulatory body FIN, GEN an independent organisation, usually set up by government, that regulates the activities of companies in an industry

regulatory pricing risk FIN the risk an insurance company faces that a government will regulate the prices it can charge

reinsurance FIN a method of reducing risk by transferring all or part of an insurance policy to another insurer

reinvestment rate FIN the interest rate at which an investor is able to reinvest income received from another investment

reinvestment risk FIN the risk that it will not be possible to invest the proceeds of an investment at as high a rate as they earned

reinvestment unit trust FIN a unit trust that uses dividends to buy more shares in the company issuing them

rejects FIN, OPS units of output which fail a set quality standard and are subsequently rectified, sold as substandard, or disposed of as scrap

relative income hypothesis ECON the theory that consumers are concerned less with their absolute living standards than with consumption relative to other consumers

relevant interest *ANZ* FIN the legal status held by share investors who can legally dispose of, or influence the disposal of, shares

remuneration HR see *earnings*

renounceable document FIN written proof of ownership for a limited period, for example, a letter of allotment. See also *letter of renunciation*

renting back FIN see *sale and lease-back*

renunciation FIN see *letter of renunciation*

reorder level FIN a level of stock at which a replenishment order should be placed. Traditional 'optimising' systems use a variation on the computation of maximum usage multiplied by maximum lead, which builds in a measure of safety stock and minimises the likelihood of stock running out.

reorganisation bond FIN in the United States, a bond issued to creditors of a business that is undergoing a Chapter 11 form of reorganisation. Interest is normally only paid when the company can make the payments from its earnings.

repayment mortgage FIN a long-term loan, usually for the purchase of a property, in which the borrower makes monthly payments, part of which cover the interest on the loan and part of which cover the repayment of the principal. In the early years, the greater proportion of the payment is used to cover the interest charged but, as the principal is gradually repaid, the interest portion diminishes and the repayment portion increases. See also *mortgage*

replacement cost FIN the cost of replacing an asset or service with its current equivalent

replacement cost accounting FIN a method of valuing company assets based on their replacement cost

replacement ratio ECON the ratio of the total resources received when unemployed to those received when in employment

repo FIN 1. repurchase agreement *(slang)* 2. *US* an open market operation undertaken by the Federal Reserve to purchase securities and agree to sell them back at a stated price on a future date 3. a Bank of England repurchase agreement with market makers in gilt-edged securities. It is used to provide securities for short positions.

report GEN a written or verbal statement analysing a particular issue, incident, or state of affairs, usually with some form of recommendations for future action

repossession FIN the return of goods bought on hire purchase when the purchaser fails to make the required regular payments. See also *recourse agreement*

repudiation FIN a refusal to pay or acknowledge a debt

repurchase FIN of a fund manager, to buy the units in a unit trust when an investor sells

repurchase agreement FIN in the bond and money markets, a spot sale of a security combined with its repurchase at a later date and pre-agreed price. In effect, the buyer is lending money to the seller for the duration of the transaction and using the security as collateral. Dealers finance their positions by using repurchase agreements. Also known as *repo*

required rate of return FIN the minimum return for a proposed project investment to be acceptable

required reserves *US* FIN the minimum reserves that member banks of the Federal Reserve System have to maintain

requisition FIN an official order form used by companies when purchasing a product or service

research FIN the examination of statistics and other information regarding past, present, and future trends or performance that enables analysts to recommend to investors which shares to buy or sell in order to maximise their return and minimise their risk. It may be used either in the top-down approach (where the investor evaluates a market, then an industry, and finally a specific company) or the bottom-up approach (where the investor selects a company and confirms his or her findings by evaluating the company's sector and then its market). Careful research is likely to help investors find the best deals, in particular value shares or growth equities. See also *technical analysis*

reserve bank *US* FIN a bank such as a US Federal Reserve bank that holds the reserves of other banks

Reserve Bank of Australia FIN Australia's central bank, which is responsible for managing the Commonwealth's monetary policy, ensuring financial stability, and printing and distributing currency. *Abbr* **RBA**

Reserve Bank of New Zealand FIN New Zealand's central bank, which is responsible for managing the government's monetary policy, ensuring financial stability, and printing and distributing currency. *Abbr* **RBNZ**

reserve currency FIN foreign currency that a central bank holds for use in international trade

reserve for fluctuations FIN money set aside to allow for changes in the values of currencies

reserve price FIN a price for a particular lot, set by the vendor, below which an auctioneer may not sell

reserve ratio FIN the proportion of a bank's deposits that must be kept in reserve. In the United Kingdom and in certain European countries, there is no compulsory ratio, although banks will have their own internal measures and targets to be able to repay customer deposits as they forecast they will be required. In the United States, specified percentages of deposits – established by the Federal Reserve Board – must be kept by banks in a non-interest-bearing account at one of the 12 Federal Reserve Banks located throughout the country. In Europe, the reserve requirement of an institution is calculated by multiplying the reserve ratio for each category of items in the reserve base, set by the European Central Bank, with the amount of those items in the institution's balance sheets. These figures vary according to the institution.

reserve requirements FIN the requirements an agency levies on a nation's banks to hold reserves

reserves FIN 1. the money that a bank holds to ensure that it can satisfy its depositors' demands for withdrawals 2. profits made by a company in previous accounting periods that have not yet been made available to shareholders 3. a sum of money held by an individual or company to finance unexpected business opportunities. See also *war chest*

residuary legatee FIN the person to whom a testator's estate is left after specific bequests have been made

resolution GEN a proposal put to a meeting, for example, an Annual General Meeting of shareholders, on which those present and eligible can vote. See also *extraordinary resolution*

resource driver FIN a measurement unit which is used to assign resource costs to activity cost pools based on some measures of usage. For example, it may be used to assign office occupancy costs to purchasing or accounting services within a company.

responsibility accounting FIN the keeping of financial records with an emphasis on who is responsible for each item

responsibility centre FIN a department or organisational function whose performance is the direct responsibility of a specific manager

restated balance sheet FIN a balance sheet reframed to serve a particular purpose, such as highlighting depreciation on assets

restricted tender FIN an offer to buy shares only under specified conditions

retail banking FIN services provided by commercial banks to individuals (as opposed to business customers) that include current accounts, deposit and savings accounts, as well as credit cards, mortgages, and investments. In the United Kingdom, although this service was traditionally provided by high street banks, separate organisations, albeit offshoots of established financial institutions, are now providing Internet and telephone banking services.

retail investor FIN an investor who buys and sells shares in retail organisations

retail price index ECON a listing of the average levels of prices charged by retailers for goods or services. The retail price index is calculated on a set range of items, and usually excludes luxury goods. It is updated monthly, and provides a running indicator of changing costs. *Abbr* **RPI**

retained profits FIN the amount of profit remaining after tax and distribution to shareholders that is retained in a business and used as a reserve or as a means of financing expansion or investment. Also known as *earnings retained*

retirement pension FIN see *pension*

retrenchment FIN the reduction of costs in order to improve profitability

retro logistics OPS see *reverse logistics*

return FIN 1. the income derived from an activity 2. see *rate of return* 3. see *tax return*

return logistics OPS see *reverse logistics*

return on assets FIN a measure of profitability calculated by expressing a company's net income as a percentage of total assets. *Abbr* **ROA**

return on equity FIN the ratio of a company's net income as a percentage of shareholders' funds. Return on equity is easy to calculate and is applicable to the majority of industries. It is probably the most widely used measure of how well a company is performing for its shareholders. *Abbr* **ROE**

return on investment FIN a ratio of the profit made in a financial year as a percentage of an investment. *Abbr* **ROI**

return on net assets FIN a ratio of the profit made in a financial year as a percentage of the assets of a company. *Abbr* **RONA**

return on sales FIN a company's operating profit or loss as a percentage of total sales for a given period, typically a year. See also *profit margin*. *Abbr* **ROS**

returns to scale ECON the proportionate increase in a country's or firm's output as a result of increases in all its inputs

revaluation ECON a rise in the value of a country's currency in relation to other currencies

revaluation of assets FIN the revaluation of a company's assets to take account of inflation or changes in value since the assets were acquired. The change in value is credited to the revaluation reserve account.

revaluation of currency FIN an increase in the value of a currency in relation to others. In situations where there is a floating exchange rate, a currency will normally find its own level automatically but this will not happen if there is a fixed exchange rate. Should a government have persistent balance of payment surpluses, it may exceptionally decide to revalue its

Dictionary

currency, making imports cheaper but its exports more expensive.

revaluation reserve FIN money set aside to account for the fact that the value of assets may vary as a result of accounting in different currencies

revenue FIN the income generated by a product or service over a period of time

revenue anticipation note FIN a government-issued debt instrument for which expected income from taxation is collateral

revenue bond FIN a bond that a government issues, to be repaid from the money made from the project financed with it

revenue centre FIN a centre devoted to raising revenue but with no responsibility for costs, for example, a sales centre

revenue ledger FIN a record of all the income received by an organisation

revenue sharing FIN **1.** distribution to states by the US federal government of money that it collects in taxes **2.** the distribution of income within limited partnerships

revenue stamp FIN a stamp that a government issues to certify that somebody has paid a tax

revenue tariff FIN a tax levied on imports or exports to raise revenue for a national government

reversal stop FIN a price at which a trader stops buying and starts selling a security, or vice versa

reverse distribution OPS see *reverse logistics*

reverse leverage FIN **1.** the negative flow of cash **2.** the borrowing of money at a rate of interest higher than the expected rate of return on investing the money borrowed

reverse logistics OPS the flow of goods in the opposite direction to the traditional flow of the supply chain, from producer to consumer, back to a point of recovery or disposal. Reverse logistics is a branch of logistics which involves the collection, transportation and redistribution or disposal of returned, unwanted, damaged, or surplus goods. This may be through reuse, resale, repair, or refurbishment. The term also covers the management of products at the end of their life which contain a haz-

ardous substance needing special treatment for environmental reasons. However, it differs from waste management in that the emphasis is on recapturing value through redistribution, cannibalisation, or recycling, rather than safe disposal. Also called retro logistics, return logistics, reverse distribution

reverse mentoring HR the mentoring of senior personnel by younger people. Reverse mentoring aims to help older, more senior people learn from the knowledge of younger people, usually in the field of information technology, computing, and Internet communications.

reverse mortgage FIN a financial arrangement in which a lender such as a bank takes over a mortgage and then pays an annuity to the home-owner

reverse split FIN the issuing to shareholders of a fraction of one share for every share that they own. See also *split*. Also known as *consolidation*

revolving charge account FIN a charge account with a company for use in buying that company's goods with revolving credit

revolving credit FIN a credit facility which allows the borrower, within an overall credit limit and for a set period, to borrow or repay debt as required

revolving fund FIN a fund the resources of which are replenished from the revenue of the projects that it finances

revolving loan FIN a loan facility whereby the borrower can choose the number and timing of withdrawals against their bank loan and any money repaid may be reborrowed at a future date. Such loans are available both to businesses and personal customers.

rigged market FIN a market where two or more parties are buying and selling securities among themselves to give the impression of active trading with the intention of attracting investors to purchase the shares. This practice is illegal in most jurisdictions.

rights issue FIN the raising of new capital by giving existing shareholders the right to subscribe to new

shares or debentures in proportion to their current holdings. These shares are normally issued at a discount to market price. A shareholder not wishing to take up a rights issue may sell the rights. Also known as *rights offer*

rights offer FIN see *rights issue*

rights offering FIN an offering for sale of a rights issue

ring FIN **1.** a trading pit **2.** a trading session on the London Metal Exchange

ring-fence FIN **1.** to set aside a sum of money for a specific project **2.** to allow one company within a group to go into liquidation without affecting the viability of the group as a whole or any other company within it

ring member FIN a member of the London Metal Exchange

ring trading FIN business conducted in a trading pit

rising bottoms FIN a pattern on a graph of the price of a security or commodity against time that shows an upward price movement following a period of low prices *(slang)*. See also *chartist*

risk FIN a condition in which there exists a quantifiable dispersion in the possible outcomes from any activity

risk-adjusted return on capital FIN return on capital calculated in a way that takes into account the risks associated with income

risk arbitrage FIN arbitrage without certainty of profit

risk-bearing economy of scale FIN conducting business on such a large scale that the risk of loss is reduced because it is spread over so many independent events, as in the issuance of insurance policies

risk capital FIN see *venture capital*

risk-free return FIN the profit made from an investment that involves no risk

risk management FIN the process of understanding and managing the risks that an organisation is inevitably subject to in attempting to achieve its corporate objectives. For management purposes, risks are usually divided into categories such as operational, financial, legal compliance, information, and personnel.

ROA *abbr* FIN return on assets

ROC *abbr* return on capital

rodo kinko FIN in Japan, a financial institution specialising in providing credit for small businesses

ROE *abbr* FIN return on equity

rogue trader FIN a dealer in stocks and shares who uses illegal methods to make profits

ROI *abbr* FIN return on investment

roll up FIN the addition of interest amounts to the principal in loan repayments

ROS *abbr* FIN return on sales

round figures FIN figures that have been adjusted up or down to the nearest 10, 100, 1,000, and so on

routing number *US* FIN = sort code

royalties FIN a proportion of the income from the sale of a product paid to its creator, for example, an inventor, author, or composer

RPI *abbr* ECON retail price index

RPIX FIN an index based on the retail price index that excludes mortgage interest payments and is commonly referred to as the underlying rate of inflation

RPIY FIN an index based on the retail price index that excludes mortgage interest payments and indirect taxation

RSS *abbr* E-COM really simple syndication

rule of 78 FIN a method used to calculate the rebate on a loan with front-loaded interest that has been repaid early. It takes into account the fact that as the loan is repaid, the share of each monthly payment related to interest decreases, while the share related to repayment increases.

rule of seven GEN the generally accepted claim that people can hold approximately seven chunks or units of information in their short-term memory at a time. Sometimes also known as Miller's rule of seven, as G.A. Miller was the first to suggest this memory range in an article entitled 'The magic number seven, plus or minus two: some limits on our capacity for processing information' in the *Psychological Review* (Vol. 63, 1956).

run FIN an incidence of bank customers or owners of holdings in a particular currency simultaneously withdrawing their entire funds because of a lack of confidence in the institution

running account credit FIN an overdraft facility, credit card, or similar system that allows customers to borrow up to a specific limit and reborrow sums previously repaid by either writing a cheque or using their card

running yield FIN see *yield*

SA *abbr* FIN Société Anonyme *or* Sociedad Anónima *or* Sociedade Anónima

SADC *abbr* FIN Southern African Development Community: an organisation that aims to harmonise economic development in Southern Africa. The member countries are Angola, Botswana, Democratic Republic of Congo, Lesotho, Malawi, Mauritius, Mozambique, Namibia, Seychelles, South Africa, Swaziland, Tanzania, Zambia, and Zimbabwe.

safe custody FIN see *safe keeping*

safe hands FIN 1. investors who buy securities and are unlikely to sell in the short to medium term 2. securities held by friendly investors

safe keeping FIN the holding of share certificates, deeds, wills, or a locked deed box on behalf of customers by a financial institution. Securities are often held under the customer's name in a locked cabinet in the vault so that if the customer wishes to sell, the bank can forward the relevant certificate to the broker. A will is also normally held in this way so that it may be handed to the executor on the customer's death. Deed boxes are always described as 'contents unknown to the bank'. Most institutions charge a fee for this service. Also known as *safe custody*

salaried partner FIN a partner, often a junior one, who receives a regular salary, detailed in the partnership agreement

salary HR a form of pay given to employees at regular intervals in exchange for the work they have done. Traditionally, a salary is a form of remuneration given to professional employees on a monthly basis. In modern usage, the word refers to any form of pay that employees receive on a regular basis, and it is often used interchangeably with the term wages. A salary is normally paid straight into an employee's account.

salary ceiling HR the highest level on a pay scale that a particular employee can achieve under his or her contract

salary review HR a reassessment of an individual employee's rate of pay, usually carried out on an annual basis

salary sacrifice scheme HR an agreement between employer and employees by which the employees relinquish a right to future cash in exchange for a non-cash benefit of some sort. This term originated from the practice of contributions to an approved pension scheme being made by employers in return for employees' agreement to forego rights to a future bonus or pay rise.

sale and leaseback FIN the sale of an asset, usually buildings, to a third party that then leases it back to the owner. It is used by a company as a way of raising finance. Also known as *renting back*

sale by instalments FIN see *hire purchase*

sale by tender FIN the sale of an asset to interested parties who have been invited to make an offer. The asset is sold to the party that makes the highest offer.

samurai bond FIN a bond issue denominated in yen and issued in Japan by a foreign institution

sandbag FIN in a hostile takeover situation, to enter into talks with the bidder and attempt to prolong them as long as possible, in the hope that a white knight will appear and rescue the target company *(slang)*

S&L *abbr* FIN savings and loan association

S&P 500 *abbr* FIN Standard & Poor's 500 Index

S&P Index *abbr* FIN Standard & Poor's 500 Index

Santa Claus rally *US* FIN a rise in stock prices in the last week of the year

Sarbanes-Oxley FIN a US corporate governance law which came into effect in 2005. Created in the aftermath of a raft of high-profile financial scandals, including Enron and Worldcom, Sarbanes-Oxley aims to overhaul corporate financial reporting by improving its accuracy and reliability. Accountability standards have

Dictionary

also been considerably tightened, and chief executives are to take full responsibility for the accuracy of all financial results by signing a statement to that effect. This latter aspect effectively dismisses the so-called 'aw shucks' defence strategy adopted by senior executives involved in earlier financial scandals. Under this strategy, the accused maintained that they were simply not aware of the distortion of financial reporting that took place on their watch.

savings FIN money set aside by consumers for a particular purpose, to meet contingencies, or to provide an income during retirement. Savings (money in deposit and savings accounts) differ from investments – for example, on the stock market – in that they are not subject to price fluctuations and are thus considered safer.

savings account FIN an account with a financial institution that pays interest. See also *gross interest, net interest*

savings and loan association FIN a chartered bank that offers savings accounts, pays dividends, and invests in new mortgages. See also *thrift institution*. Abbr *S&L*

savings bank FIN a bank that specialises in managing small investments. See also *thrift institution*

savings bond FIN a US bond that an individual buys from the federal government

savings certificate FIN see *National Savings Certificate*

savings function ECON an expression of the extent to which people save money instead of spending it

savings ratio ECON the proportion of the income of a country or household that is saved in a particular period

SC *abbr* FIN Securities Commission

Scanlon plan HR a type of gain sharing plan that pays a bonus to employees for incremental improvements. The Scanlon plan was developed by Joseph Scanlon in the 1930s. A typical Scanlon plan includes an employee suggestion scheme, a committee system, and a formula-based bonus system. The simplest formula is: base ratio = HR payroll costs

divided by net sales or production value. A Scanlon organisation is characterised by teamwork and employee participation. A bonus is paid when the current ratio is better than that of the base period. A Scanlon plan focuses attention on the variables over which the organisation and its employees have some control.

Schedule C FIN a schedule to the Finance Acts under which tax was charged on income from public sources, such as government stock

scorched earth policy GEN destructive actions taken by an organisation in defence against a hostile takeover. Extreme actions under a scorched earth policy may include voluntary liquidation or selling off critical assets. A scorched earth policy may come into play if the value of the company to be acquired exceeds the value of the company making a hostile bid. *(slang)*

scrip dividend FIN a dividend paid by the issue of additional company shares, rather than by cash

scrip issue FIN a proportional issue of free shares to existing shareholders. US term *stock split*. Also known as *bonus shares, share split*

scripophily FIN the collecting of valueless share or bond certificates

Sdn *abbr* FIN Sendirian

SEAQ *abbr* FIN Stock Exchange Automated Quotations system: the London Stock Exchange's system for UK securities. It is a continuously updated computer database containing quotations that also records prices at which transactions have been struck.

SEAQ International *abbr* FIN Stock Exchange Automated Quotations system International: the London Stock Exchange's system for overseas securities. It is a continuously updated computer database containing quotations that also records prices at which transactions have been struck.

seasonal adjustment FIN an adjustment made to accounts to allow for any short-term seasonal factors, such as Christmas sales, that may distort the figures

seasonal business FIN trade that is affected by seasonal factors, for example, trade in goods such as suntan products or Christmas trees

seasoned equity FIN shares that have traded long enough to have a well-established value

seasoned issue FIN an issue for which there is a pre-existing market. See also *unseasoned issue*

SEATS *abbr* FIN Stock Exchange Automatic Trading System: the electronic screen-trading system operated by the Australian Stock Exchange. It was introduced in 1987.

SEC *abbr* FIN Securities and Exchange Commission

secondary issue FIN an offer of listed shares that have not previously been publicly traded

secondary market FIN a market that trades in existing shares rather than new share issues, for example, a stock exchange. The money earned from these sales goes to the dealer or investor, not to the issuer.

secondary offering FIN an offering of securities of a kind that is already on the market

second mortgage FIN a loan that uses the equity on a mortgaged property as security and is taken out with a different lender from the first mortgage. As the first mortgagee holds the deeds, the second mortgagee has to register its interest with the Land Registry and cannot foreclose without the first mortgagee's permission.

second-tier market FIN a market in stocks and shares where the listing requirements are less onerous than for the main market, as in, for example, London's Alternative Investment Market

Section 21 company *S Africa* FIN a company established as a non-profit organisation

sector index FIN an index of companies in certain parts of a market whose shares are listed on a general or specialist stock exchange

secured FIN 1. used to describe borrowing when the lender has a charge over an asset or assets of the borrower, for example, a mortgage or floating charge 2. used to describe a creditor who has a charge over an asset or assets of the borrower, for example, a mortgage or floating charge. See also *collateral, security*

secured bond FIN a collateralised bond

secure server E-COM a combination of hardware and software that secures e-commerce credit card transactions so that there is no risk of unauthorised people gaining access to credit card details online

securities account FIN an account that shows the value of financial assets held by a person or organisation

securities analyst FIN a professional person who studies the performance of securities and the companies that issue them

Securities and Exchange Commission FIN the US government agency responsible for establishing standards of financial reporting and accounting for public companies. *Abbr* **SEC**

Securities and Futures Authority FIN a self-regulatory organisation responsible for supervising the activities of institutions advising on corporate finance activity, or dealing or facilitating deals in securities or derivatives. *Abbr* **SFA**

Securities Commission FIN a statutory body responsible for monitoring standards in the New Zealand securities markets and for promoting investment in New Zealand. *Abbr* **SC**

securities deposit account FIN a brokerage account into which securities are deposited electronically

Securities Institute of Australia FIN a national professional body that represents people involved in the Australian securities and financial services industry. *Abbr* **SIA**

Securities Investor Protection Corporation FIN in the United States, a corporation created by Congress in 1970 that is a mutual insurance fund established to protect clients of securities firms. In the event of a firm being closed because of bankruptcy or financial difficulties, the SIPC will step in to recover clients' cash and securities held by the firm. The corporation's reserves are available to satisfy cash and securities that cannot be recovered up to a maximum of 500,000, including a maximum of 100,000 on cash claims. *Abbr* **SIPC**

securities lending FIN the loan of securities to those who have sold short

securitisation FIN the process of changing financial assets such as mortgages and loans into securities

security FIN **1.** a tradable financial asset, for example, a bond, stock, a share, or a warrant **2.** the collateral for a loan or other borrowing

security deposit FIN an amount of money paid before a transaction occurs to compensate the seller in the event that the transaction is not concluded and this is the buyer's fault

security investment company FIN a financial institution that specialises in the analysis and trading of securities

seed capital FIN a usually modest amount of money used to convert an idea into a viable business. Seed capital is a form of venture capital. US term *seed money*

selective pricing FIN setting different prices for the same product or service in different markets. This practice can be broken down as follows: category pricing, which involves cosmetically modifying a product such that the variations allow it to sell in a number of price categories, as where a range of brands is based on a common product; customer group pricing, which involves modifying the price of a product or service so that different groups of consumers pay different prices; peak pricing, setting a price which varies according to the level of demand; and service level pricing, setting a price based on the particular level of service chosen from a range.

self-assessment FIN in the United Kingdom, a system that enables taxpayers to assess their own income tax and capital gains tax payments for the fiscal year

self-insurance FIN the practice of saving money to pay for a possible loss rather than taking out an insurance policy against it

self-liquidating FIN providing enough income to pay off the amount borrowed for financing

self-tender FIN in the United States, the repurchase by a corporation of its stock by way of a tender

seller's market FIN a market in which sellers can dictate prices, typically because demand is high or there is a product shortage

selling season FIN a period in which market conditions are favourable to sellers

sell short FIN to sell commodities, currencies, or securities that one does not own in the expectation that prices will fall before delivery to the seller's profit

Sendirian FIN Malay term for 'limited'. Companies can use 'Sendirian Berhad' or 'Sdn Bhd' in their name instead of 'plc'. *Abbr* **Sdn**

senior debt FIN a debt whose holder has more claim on the debtor's assets than the holder of another debt. See also *junior debt*

senior mortgage FIN a mortgage whose holder has more claim on the debtor's assets than the holder of another mortgage with the same mortgagee. See also *junior mortgage*

SERPS *abbr* FIN State Earnings-Related Pension Scheme: in the United Kingdom, a state scheme designed to pay retired employees an additional pension to the standard state pension. Contributions are collected through National Insurance payments, and benefits are related to earnings. Individuals may opt out of SERPS and have their contributions directed to an occupational or personal pension.

service charge FIN a fee for any service provided, or an additional fee for any enhancements to an existing service. For example, banks may charge a fee for obtaining foreign currency for customers. Residents in blocks of flats may pay an annual maintenance fee that is also referred to as a service charge.

service cost centre FIN a cost centre providing services to other cost centres. When the output of an organisation is a service, rather than goods, an alternative name is normally used, for example, support cost centre or utility cost centre.

service/function costing FIN cost accounting for services or functions, for example, canteens, maintenance, or personnel

service level agreement FIN a contract between service provider and customer which specifies in detail the level of service to be provided over the contract period (quality, frequency, flexibility, charges, etc.) as well as the procedures to implement in the case of default

servicing borrowing FIN paying the interest due on a loan

set-aside FIN see *reserves*

set-off FIN an agreement between two parties to balance one debt against another or a loss against a gain

settlement FIN the payment of a debt or charge

settlement date FIN the date on which an outstanding debt or charge is due to be paid

seven-day money FIN funds that have been placed on the money market for a term of seven days

severance package *US* HR = redundancy package

SFA *abbr* FIN Securities and Futures Authority

SFAS *abbr* FIN Statement of Financial Accounting Standards

SFE *abbr* FIN Sydney Futures Exchange

shadow market FIN, GEN see *black market*

shakeout FIN the elimination of weak or cautious investors during a crisis in the financial market *(slang)*

share FIN a fixed identifiable unit of capital which has a fixed nominal or face value, which may be quite different from the market price of the share

share account FIN **1.** an account at a building society where the account holder is a member of the society. Building societies usually offer another type of account, a deposit account, where the account holder is not a member. A share account is generally paid a better rate of interest, but in the event of the society going into liquidation, deposit account holders are given preference. **2.** *US* an account with a credit union that pays dividends rather than interest

share capital FIN the amount of capital that a company raises by issuing shares

share certificate FIN a document that certifies ownership of a share in a company. US term **stock certificate**

share exchange FIN a service provided by certain collective investment schemes whereby they exchange investors' existing individual shareholdings for shares in their funds. This saves the investor the expense of selling holdings, which can be uneconomical when dealing with small shareholdings.

shareholder FIN **1.** a person or organisation that owns shares in a limited company or partnership. A shareholder has a stake in the company and becomes a member of it, with rights to attend the annual general meeting. Since shareholders have invested money in a company, they have a vested interest in its performance and can be a powerful influence on company policy; they should consequently be considered stakeholders as well as shareholders. Some pressure groups have sought to exploit this by becoming shareholders in order to get a particular viewpoint or message across. At the same time, in order to maintain or increase the company's market value, managers must consider their responsibility to shareholders when formulating strategy. It has been argued that on some occasions the desire to make profits to raise returns for shareholders has damaged companies, because it has limited the amount of money spent in other areas (such as the development of facilities, or health and safety). US term **stockholder** **2.** a person who owns shares of a fund or investment trust

shareholders' equity FIN a company's share capital and reserves. US term **stockholder's equity**

shareholders' perks FIN benefits offered to shareholders in addition to dividends, often in the form of discounts on the company's products and services

shareholder value FIN the total return to the shareholders in terms of both dividends and share price growth, calculated as the present value of future free cash flows of the business discounted at the weighted average cost of the capital of the business less the market value of its debt

shareholder value analysis FIN a calculation of the value of a company made by looking at the returns it gives to its shareholders. *Abbr* **SVA**

share incentive scheme HR a type of financial incentive scheme in which employees can acquire shares in the company in which they work and so have an interest in its financial performance. A share incentive scheme is a type of employee share scheme, in which employees may be given shares by their employer, or shares may be offered for purchase at an advantageous price, as a reward for personal or group performance. A share option is a type of share incentive scheme.

share index FIN see *index*

share issue FIN the offering for sale of shares in a business. The capital derived from share issues can be used for investment in the core business or for expansion into new commercial ventures.

shareowner FIN somebody who owns a share of stock

share premium FIN **1.** the amount by which the price at which a company sells a share exceeds its par value **2.** the amount payable for a share above its nominal value. Most shares are issued at a premium to their nominal value. Share premiums are credited to the company's share premium account.

share premium account FIN the special reserve in a company's balance sheet to which share premiums are credited. Expenses associated with the issue of shares may be written off to this account.

share split FIN see *scrip issue*

shark watcher FIN in the United States, a firm specialising in monitoring the stock market for potential takeover activity *(slang)*

shelf registration FIN a registration statement, lodged with the Securities and Exchange Commission two years before a corporation issues securities to the public. The statement, which has to be updated periodically, allows the corporation to act quickly when it considers that the market conditions are right without having to start the registration procedure from scratch.

shell company FIN a company that has ceased to trade but is still registered, especially one sold to enable the buyer to begin trading without having to set up a new company

shibosai FIN the Japanese term for a private placing

shibosai bond FIN a samurai bond sold direct to investors by the issuing company as opposed to a financial institution

shinyo kinku FIN in Japan, a financial institution that provides financing for small businesses

shinyo kumiai FIN in Japan, a credit union that provides financing for small businesses

shogun bond FIN a bond denominated in a currency other than the yen that is sold on the Japanese market by a non-Japanese financial institution. Also known as **geisha bond**. See also **samurai bond**

short FIN 1. a short-dated gilt (slang) 2. an asset in which a dealer has a short position

short covering FIN the purchase of foreign exchange, commodities, or securities by a firm or individual that has been selling short. Such purchases are undertaken when the market has begun to move upwards, or when it is thought to be about to do so.

short-dated gilt FIN see **gilt-edged security**

shorting FIN the act of selling short

short selling FIN see **sell short**

short-term bond FIN a bond on the corporate bond market that has an initial maturity of less than two years

short-term capital FIN funds raised for a period of less than 12 months. See also **working capital**

short-term debt FIN debt with a term of one year or less

short-term economic policy FIN an economic policy with objectives that can be met within a period of months or a few years

show stopper FIN see **poison pill**

shrinkage FIN 1. a reduction in the amount of a company's inventories, often caused by production processes 2. a term used to describe goods that leave a retail outlet but are not logged as sales. Shrinkage can include goods that are stolen by shoplifters, or are damaged or broken.

SIA abbr FIN Securities Institute of Australia

sickness and accident insurance FIN a form of permanent health insurance that may be sold with some form of credit, for example a credit card or personal loan. In the event of the borrower being unable to work because of accident or illness, the policy covers the regular payments to the credit card company or lender.

sight bill FIN a bill of exchange payable on sight

sight deposit FIN a bank deposit against which the depositor can immediately draw

sight draft FIN a bill of exchange that is payable on delivery. See also **time draft**

signature guarantee FIN a stamp or seal, usually from a bank or a broker, that vouches for the authenticity of a signature

signature loan FIN see **unsecured loan**

silent partner US FIN = sleeping partner

simple interest FIN interest charged simply as a constant percentage of the principal and not compounded. See also **compound interest**

simultaneous engineering FIN, OPS see **concurrent engineering**

Singapore dollar FIN Singapore's unit of currency, whose exchange rate is quoted as S$ per US$

Singapore Exchange FIN a merger of the Stock Exchange of Singapore and the Singapore International Monetary Exchange, established in 1999. It provides securities and derivatives trading, securities clearing and depository, and derivatives clearing services. Abbr **SGX**

single currency FIN denominated entirely in one currency

single customs document FIN a standard, universally used form for the passage of goods through customs

single entry FIN a type of bookkeeping where only one entry, reflecting both a credit to one account and a debit to another, is made for each transaction

single market FIN see **EU**

single-payment bond FIN a bond redeemed with a single payment combining principal and interest at maturity

single premium assurance FIN life cover where the premium is paid in one lump sum when the policy is taken out, rather than in monthly instalments

single premium deferred annuity FIN an annuity that is paid for with a single payment at inception and pays returns regularly after a set date. It gives a tax advantage.

single tax FIN a tax that supplies all revenue, especially on land

sinking fund FIN money put aside periodically to settle a liability or replace an asset. The money is invested to produce a required sum at an appropriate time.

SIPC abbr FIN Securities Investor Protection Corporation

six-month money FIN funds invested on the money market for a period of six months

skimming FIN the unethical and usually illegal practice of taking small amounts of money from accounts that belong to other individuals or organisations

Skype E-COM a software program which allows users to call other Skype users for free from their phones, or to phone non-Skype users for a fee. The program was created by two Scandinavian entrepreneurs (Janus Friis and Niklas Zennström) and the first beta version appeared in 2003. In 2005, the company was purchased by eBay. In early 2009, it was estimated that there were over 443 million user accounts around the world.

sleeping partner FIN, GEN a person or organisation that invests money in a company but takes no active part in the management of the business. Although sleeping partners are inactive in the operation of the business, they have legal obligations and benefits of ownership and are therefore fully liable for any debts. US term **silent partner**

slowdown ECON a fall in demand that causes a lowering of economic activity, less severe than a recession or slump

slump ECON a severe downturn phase in the business cycle

slumpflation ECON a collapse in all economic activity accompanied by wage and price inflation. This happened, for example, in the United States and Europe in 1929. (slang)

slush fund FIN a fund used by a company for illegal purposes such as bribing officials to obtain preferential treatment for planned work or expansion

small change FIN a quantity of coins that a person might carry with them

Small Order Execution System FIN on the NASDAQ, an automated execution system for bypassing brokers when processing small order agency executions of NASDAQ securities up to 1,000 shares

smart card E-COM a small plastic card containing a microprocessor that can store and process transactions and maintain a bank balance, thus providing a secure, portable medium for electronic money. Financial details and personal data stored on the card can be updated each time the card is used.

smart market E-COM a market in which all transactions are carried out electronically using network communications

socially conscious investing FIN see *ethical investment*

social marginal cost ECON the additional cost to a society of a change in an economic variable, for example, the price of petrol or bread

social networking E-COM an online method of creating and maintaining personal relationships, whether for private or commercial reasons. Websites such as Facebook, MySpace, and Bebo allow users to share information about themselves and offer users a variety of routes to communicate with each other, including blogs, chat, e-mail, file sharing, and video. Since 2008, Twitter (used by Barack Obama in his US presidential campaign) has also gained in popularity. Social networking sites have become so popular that there has been some concern in workplaces that employees are spending more time visiting the sites than they are on their daily work: since 2004, for example, more than 1,000 public sector workers in the United Kingdom have been dismissed for spending too much time networking online.

Sociedad Anónima FIN the Spanish equivalent of a private limited company. *Abbr* **SA**

Sociedade Anónima FIN the Portuguese equivalent of a private limited company. *Abbr* **SA**

Societàa responsabilitàlimitata FIN an Italian limited liability company that is unlisted. *Abbr* **Srl**

Societàper Azioni FIN an Italian public limited company. *Abbr* **SpA**

Société Anonyme FIN the French equivalent of a private limited company. *Abbr* **SA**

Société à responsabilité limitée FIN a French limited liability company that is unlisted. *Abbr* **SARL**

Société d'investissementà capital variable FIN the French term for collective investment. *Abbr* **SICAV**

Society for Worldwide Interbank Financial Telecommunication FIN see *SWIFT*

socio-economic ECON involving both social and economic factors. Structural unemployment, for example, has socio-economic causes.

soft capital rationing FIN see *capital rationing*

soft commissions FIN brokerage commissions that are rebated to an institutional customer in the form of, or to pay for, research or other services

soft commodities FIN commodities, such as foodstuffs, that are neither metals nor other solid raw materials. Also known as *softs*. See also *future, hard commodities*

soft currency FIN, ECON a currency that is weak, usually because there is an excess of supply and a belief that its value will fall in relation to others. See also *hard currency*

soft landing ECON the situation when a country's economic activity has slowed down but demand has not fallen far enough or rapidly enough to cause a recession

soft loan FIN a loan on exceptionally favourable terms, for example, for a project that a government considers worthy

soft market FIN a market in which prices are falling

softs FIN see *soft commodities*

sole trader GEN a person carrying on business with total legal responsibility for his/her actions, neither in partnership nor as a company

solicit FIN to ask another person or company for money

solvency margin FIN 1. a business's liquid assets that exceed the amount required to meet its liabilities 2. the extent to which an insurance company's assets exceed its liabilities

solvency ratio FIN 1. a ratio of assets to liabilities, used to measure a company's ability to meet its debts 2. in the United Kingdom, the ratio of an insurance company's net assets to its non-life premium income

solvent FIN used to refer to a situation in which the assets of an individual or organisation are worth more than their liabilities

sort code FIN a combination of numbers that identifies a bank branch on official documentation, such as bank statements and cheques

source and application of funds statement FIN see *cash-flow statement*

sources and uses of funds statement FIN see *cash-flow statement*

sovereign loan FIN a loan by a financial institution to an overseas government, usually of a developing country. See also *sovereign risk*

sovereign risk FIN the risk that an overseas government may refuse to repay or may default on a sovereign loan

SpA *abbr* FIN Società per Azioni

spam filter E-COM software available from an Internet service provider which blocks e-mails that contain certain terms or other attributes that identify the message as potential spam

special deposit 1. FIN an amount of money set aside for the rehabilitation of a mortgaged house 2. a large sum of money which a commercial bank has to deposit with the Bank of England

special presentation FIN the sending of a cheque directly to the paying banker rather than through the clearing system. Also known as *special clearing*. See also *advice of fate*

special purpose bond FIN a bond for one particular project, financed by levies on the people who benefit from the project

special resolution FIN see *extraordinary resolution*

specie FIN coins, as opposed to banknotes, that are legal tender

specific charge FIN a fixed charge as opposed to a floating charge

specific order costing FIN the basic cost accounting method applicable where work consists of separately identifiable contracts, jobs, or batches

speculation FIN a purchase made solely to make a profit when the price or value increases

spim E-COM unsolicited e-mail that arrives on a personal computer screen in the form of an instant message

split FIN an issuance to shareholders of more than one share for every share owned. See also *reverse split*

split commission FIN commission that is divided between two or more parties in a transaction

split coupon bond FIN see *zero coupon bond*

spot exchange rate FIN the exchange rate used for immediate currency transactions

spot goods FIN a commodity traded on the spot market

spot interest rate FIN an interest rate that is determined when a loan is made

spot market FIN a market that deals in commodities or foreign exchange for immediate rather than future delivery

spot month FIN see *nearby month*

spot price FIN the price for immediate delivery of a commodity or foreign exchange

spot transaction FIN a transaction in commodities or foreign exchange for immediate delivery

spread FIN **1.** the difference between the buying and selling price of a share on a stock exchange **2.** the range of investments in a portfolio

spreadsheet GEN a computer program that provides a series of ruled columns in which data can be entered and analysed

sprinkling trust FIN a trust with multiple beneficiaries whose distributions occur at the trustees' discretion

squeeze ECON a government policy of restriction, commonly affecting the availability of credit in an economy

Srl *abbr* FIN Società a responsabilità limitata

stabilisation fund ECON a fund created by a government as an emergency savings account for international financial support

stagflation ECON the result when both inflation and unemployment exist at the same time in an economy. There was stagflation in the United Kingdom and the United States in the 1970s, for example.

stakeholder FIN, GEN a person or organisation with a vested interest in the successful operation of a company or organisation. A stakeholder may be an employee, customer, supplier, partner, or even the local community within which an organisation operates.

stakeholder pension FIN, HR a pension, bought from a private company, in which the retirement income depends on the level of contributions made during a person's working life. Stakeholder pensions are designed for people without access to an occupational pension scheme, and are intended to provide a low-cost supplement to the state earnings related pension scheme. A stakeholder pension scheme can either be trust-based, like an occupational pension scheme, or contract-based, similar to a personal pension. Subject to certain exceptions, employers must provide access to a stakeholder pension scheme for employees, although they are not required to establish a stakeholder pension scheme themselves. Membership of a stakeholder pension scheme is voluntary. See also *Keough Plan*

stakeholder theory FIN, GEN the theory that an organisation can enhance the interests of its shareholders without damaging the interests of its wider stakeholders. Stakeholder theory grew in response to the economic theory of the firm, and contrasts with Theory E. One of the difficulties of stakeholder theory is allocating importance to the values of different groups of stakeholders, and a solution to this is proposed by stakeholder value analysis.

stakeholder value analysis FIN, GEN a method of determining the values of the stakeholders in an organisation for the purposes of making strategic and operational decisions. Stakeholder value analysis is one method of justifying an approach based on stakeholder theory rather than the economic theory of the firm. It involves identifying groups of stakeholders and eliciting their views on particular issues in order that these views may be taken into account when making decisions.

stamp duty FIN in the United Kingdom, a duty that is payable on some legal documents and is shown to have been paid by a stamp being fixed to the document

standard FIN a benchmark measurement of resource usage, set in defined conditions. Standards can be set on the following bases: on an ex ante estimate of expected performance; on an ex post estimate of attainable performance; on a prior period level of performance by the same organisation; on the level of performance achieved by comparable organisations; and on the level of performance required to meet organisational objectives. Standards may also be set at attainable levels, which assume efficient levels of operation, but which include allowances for normal loss, waste, and machine downtime, or at ideal levels, which make no allowance for the above losses and are only attainable under the most favourable conditions.

Standard & Poor's 500 Index FIN a US index of 500 general share prices selected by the Standard & Poor agency. *Abbr* **S&P Index**

Standard & Poor's rating FIN a share rating service provided by the US agency Standard & Poor

standard costing FIN a control technique which compares standard costs and revenues with actual results to obtain variances which are used to stimulate improved performance

standard hour FIN the amount of work achievable, at standard efficiency levels, in an hour

standard of living ECON a measure of economic well-being based on the ability of people to buy the goods and services they desire

standby credit ECON credit drawing rights given to a developing country by an international financial institution to fund industrialisation or other growth policies

standby loan ECON a loan given to a developing country by an international financial institution, to fund technology hardware purchase or other growth policies

standing instructions FIN instructions, that may be revoked at any time, for a particular procedure to be carried out in the event of a certain occurrence, for example, for the monies from a fixed-term account that has just matured to be placed on deposit for a further fixed period

standing order FIN an instruction given by an account holder to a bank to make regular payments on given dates to the same payee. US term *automatic debit*

star FIN an investment that is performing extremely well *(slang)*

start-up costs FIN the initial sum required to establish a business or to get a project under way. The costs will include the capital expenditure and related expenses before the business or project generates revenue.

state bank FIN a bank chartered by a state of the United States

state capitalism ECON a way of organising society in which the state controls most of a country's means of production and capital

State Earnings-Related Pension Scheme FIN see *SERPS*

statement FIN a summary of all transactions, such as deposits or withdrawals, that have occurred in an account over a given period of time

statement of account FIN 1. a summary of recent transactions between two parties 2. a list of sums due, usually relating to unpaid invoices, items paid on account but not offset against particular invoices, credit notes, debit notes, and discounts

statement of affairs FIN a statement, usually prepared by a receiver, in a prescribed form, showing the estimated financial position of a debtor or of a company which may be unable to meet its debts. It contains a summary of the debtor's assets and liabilities. The assets are shown at their estimated realisable values. The various classes of creditors, such as preferential, secured, partly secured, and unsecured, are shown separately.

statement of cash flows FIN a statement that documents actual receipts and expenditures of cash

statement-of-cash-flows method FIN a method of accounting that is based on flows of cash rather than balances on accounts

statement of changes in financial position FIN a financial report of a company's incomes and outflows during a period, usually a year or a quarter

Statement of Financial Accounting Standards FIN in the United States, a statement detailing the standards to be adopted for the preparation of financial statements. *Abbr* **SFAS**

statement of source and application of funds FIN see *cash-flow statement*

statistic FIN a piece of information in numerical form

statistical significance FIN the level of importance at which an event influences a set of statistics

statistics FIN information in numerical form and its collection, analysis, and presentation

statute-barred debt FIN a debt that cannot be pursued as the time limit laid down by law has expired

statutory auditor FIN a professional person qualified to carry out an audit required by the Companies Act

STC *abbr S Africa* FIN Secondary Tax on Companies: a secondary tax levied on corporate dividends

sticky floor HR the factors which keep women in low level, non-managerial and support roles and prevent them from seeking or gaining promotion or career development. This term may refer to barriers to the advancement of women such as family commitments, attitudes, stereotyping, and organisational structures but has also been used to focus on circumstances where women are promoted but do not receive commensurate wage rises. It is most likely to be used with reference to women, though it may also apply to other groups of employees. The glass ceiling is a similar concept.

stipend HR a regular remuneration or allowance paid to an individual holding a particular office

stock FIN 1. a form of security that offers fixed interest 2. the capital

made available to an organisation after a share issue

stockalypse FIN a dramatic drop in share price

stockbroker FIN somebody who arranges the sale and purchase of stocks

stock capital FIN an amount of fully paid-up capital, any part of which can be transferred, for example, a block of £1,000 of stock out of a total holding of £15,000

stock certificate *US* FIN = share certificate

stockcount FIN profit gained from ownership of a stock or share

stock exchange FIN a registered market in securities

Stock Exchange Automated Quotations system FIN see *SEAQ*

Stock Exchange Automated Quotations system International FIN see *SEAQ International*

Stock Exchange Automatic Trading System FIN see *SEATS*

stockholder value FIN = shareholder value

stockholder value analysis FIN see *shareholder value analysis*

stock market FIN the trading of stocks, or a place where this occurs

stock option FIN see *option*

stock split *US* FIN = scrip issue

stock symbol FIN a shortened version of a company's name, usually made up of two to four letters, used in screen-based trading systems

stock turns or **stock turnover** FIN see *inventory turnover*

stokvel *S Africa* FIN an informal, widely-used co-operative savings scheme that provides small-scale loans

stop-go ECON the alternate tightening and loosening of fiscal and monetary policies. This characterised the UK economy in the 1960s and 1970s.

stop limit order FIN in the United States, an order to trade only if and when a security reaches a specified price

stop loss *US* FIN an order to trade only if and when a security falls to a specified price

stop order *US* FIN an order to trade only if and when a security rises above or falls below its current price

story stock FIN a stock that is the subject of a press or financial community story that may affect its price

straight-line depreciation FIN a form of depreciation in which the cost of a fixed asset is spread equally over each year of its anticipated lifetime

Straits Times Industrial Index FIN an index of 30 Singapore stocks, the most commonly quoted indicator of stock market activity in Singapore

STRATE *abbr S Africa* FIN Share Transactions Totally Electronic: the electronic share transactions system of the Johannesburg Stock Exchange

strategic capability GEN the competencies, knowledge, and skills that an organisation can apply to achieve success in a competitive environment. The concept is thought to be derived from the core competencies approach to corporate strategy. It is viewed as one of the main pillars of strategic management and focuses on the ability to provide products that customers value or will value in the future. This involves the need to adjust and change in order to 'fit' the changing environment and the need to 'stretch' to exploit organisational resources in ways that are innovative, or that other organisations will find it hard to match.

strategic financial management FIN the identification of the possible strategies capable of maximising an organisation's net present value, the allocation of scarce capital resources among the competing opportunities, and the implementation and monitoring of the chosen strategy so as to achieve stated objectives

strategy FIN a course of action, including the specification of resources required, to achieve a specific objective

strategy mapping GEN the visual representation of an organisation's plans to turn its resources and assets, including intangibles such as knowledge and culture, into tangible outcomes linked to organisational objectives. Strategy maps provide a detailed picture of organisational objectives and the relationships between them. They are used to help organisations manage corporate strategy and realise objectives through improvements in specific areas such as customer retention or faster cycle times. The concept of strategy mapping was developed by Robert Kaplan and David Norton as part of their work on the balanced scorecard.

street name *US* FIN a broker who holds a customer's security in the broking house's name to facilitate transactions

strike pay or **strike benefit** HR a benefit or allowance paid by a trade union to its members during the course of official strike action to help offset loss of earnings. Also known as *dispute benefit*

strike price FIN the price for a security or commodity that underlies an option

stripped bond FIN a bond that can be divided into separate zero-coupon bonds to represent its principal and interest payments

stripped stock FIN stock whose rights to dividends have been separated and sold

strips FIN the parts of a bond that entitle the owner to only interest payments or to only the repayment of principal

structural adjustment ECON the reallocation of resources in response to a change in the output composition of an economy. Also known as *structural change*

structural change ECON see *structural adjustment*

structural fund FIN a unit trust that invests in projects that contribute to the economic development of poorer nations in the European Union

structural inflation FIN inflation that naturally occurs in an economy, without any particular triggering event

structural unemployment ECON unemployment resulting from a change in demand or technology changes so that there is a surplus of labour in a particular location or skills area

stub equity FIN the money raised through the sale of high-risk bonds in large amounts or quantities, as in a leveraged takeover or a leveraged buy-out

subject to collection FIN dependent upon the ability to collect the amount owed

subordinated debt FIN see *junior debt*

subordinated loan FIN a loan that ranks below all other borrowings with regard to both the payment of interest and repayment of the principal. See also *pari passu*

subscribed share capital FIN see *issued share capital*

subscriber FIN 1. a buyer, especially one who buys shares in a new company or new issues 2. a person who signs a company's Memorandum of Association

subscription share FIN a share purchased by a subscriber when a new company is formed

subsidiary account FIN an account for one of the individual people or organisations that jointly hold another account

subsistence allowance HR expenses paid by an employer, usually within pre-set limits, to cover the cost of accommodation, meals, and incidental expenses incurred by employees when away on business

subtreasury FIN a place where some of a nation's money is held

sum FIN 1. an amount of money 2. the total amount of any given item, such as stocks or securities 3. the total arising from the addition of two or more numbers

sum at risk FIN an amount of any given item, such as money, stocks, or securities that an investor may lose

sum insured FIN the maximum amount that an insurance company will pay out in the event of a claim

sum-of-the-year's-digits depreciation FIN accelerated depreciation, conferring tax advantage by assuming more rapid depreciation when an asset is new

sunk cost FIN a cost which has been irreversibly incurred or committed prior to a decision point, and which cannot therefore be considered relevant to subsequent decisions

sunshine law FIN a law that requires public disclosure of a government act

superannuation plan HR a pension plan in Australia

superannuation scheme HR a pension plan in New Zealand

supplier OPS an organisation that delivers materials, components, goods, or services to another organisation

supply and demand ECON the quantity of goods available for sale at a given price, and the level of consumer need for those goods. The balance of supply and demand fluctuates as external economic factors (such as the cost of materials and the level of competition in the marketplace) influence the level of demand from consumers and the desire and ability of producers to supply the goods. Supply and demand is recognised as an economic force, and is often referred to as the law of supply and demand.

supply-side economics ECON the study of how economic agents behave when supply is affected by changes in price

support price ECON the price of a product that is fixed or stabilised by a government so that it cannot fall below a certain level

surety FIN **1.** a guarantor **2.** the collateral given as security when borrowing

surplus FIN see *budget surplus*

surrender value FIN the sum of money offered by an insurance company to somebody who cancels a policy before it has completed its full term

surtax FIN a tax paid in addition to another tax, typically levied on a corporation with very high income

survivalist enterprise *S Africa* FIN a business that has no paid employees, generates income below the poverty line, and is considered the lowest level of microenterprise

sushi bond FIN a bond that is not denominated in yen and is issued in any market by a Japanese financial institution. This type of bond is often bought by Japanese institutional investors. *(slang)*

suspense account FIN an account in which debits or credits are held temporarily until sufficient information is available for them to be posted to the correct accounts

SVA *abbr* FIN shareholder value analysis

swap FIN **1.** an exchange of credits or liabilities. See also *asset swap, bond swap, interest rate swap* **2.** an arrangement whereby two organisations contractually agree to exchange

payments on different terms, for example, in different currencies, or one at a fixed rate and the other at a floating rate

swap book FIN a broker's list of stocks or securities that clients wish to swap

swaption FIN an option to enter into a swap contract *(slang)*

sweep facility FIN the automatic transfer of sums from a current account to a deposit account, or from any low interest account to a higher one. For example, a personal customer may have the balance transferred just before receipt of their monthly salary, or a business may stipulate that when a balance exceeds a certain sum, the excess is to be transferred.

sweetener FIN **1.** a feature added to a security to make it more attractive to investors **2.** a security with a high yield that has been added to a portfolio to improve its overall return. See also *kicker*

SWIFT *abbr* FIN Society for Worldwide Interbank Financial Telecommunication: a non-profit co-operative organisation with the mission of creating a shared worldwide data processing and communications link and a common language for international financial transactions. Established in Brussels in 1973 with the support of 239 banks in 15 countries, it now has over 7,000 live users in 192 countries, exchanging millions of messages valued in trillions of dollars every business day.

swing trading FIN the trading of stock by individuals that takes advantage of sudden price movements that occur especially when large numbers of traders have to cover short sales

switch FIN **1.** to exchange a specific security with another within a portfolio, usually because the investor's objectives have changed **2.** a swap exchange rate. See also *swap*. **3.** to move a commodity from one location to another

Switch FIN a debit card widely used in the United Kingdom

switching FIN the simultaneous sale and purchase of contracts in futures with different expiration dates, as for

example, when a business decides that it would like to take delivery of a commodity earlier or later than originally contracted

switching discount FIN the discount available to holders of collective investments who move from one fund to another offered by the same fund manager. This is usually a lower initial charge compared to the one made to new investors or when existing investors make a further investment.

Sydney Futures Exchange FIN the principal market in Australia for trading financial and commodity futures. It was set up in 1962 as a wool futures market, the Sydney Greasy Wool Futures Exchange, but adopted its current name in 1972 to reflect its widening role. *Abbr* **SFE**

T+ FIN an expression of the number of days allowed for settlement of a transaction

tactical plan FIN a short-term plan for achieving an entity's objectives

tailgating FIN the practice by a broker of buying or selling a security immediately after a client's transaction, in order to take advantage of the impact of the client's deal

take a flyer FIN to speculate *(slang)*

take a hit FIN to make a loss on an investment *(slang)*

take-home pay HR the amount of pay an employee receives after all deductions, such as income tax, national insurance, or pension contributions. Also known as *net pay*

takeout financing FIN loans used to replace bridge financing

takeover FIN the acquisition by a company of a controlling interest in the voting share capital of another company, usually achieved by the purchase of a majority of the voting shares

takeover battle FIN the result of a hostile takeover bid. The bidder may raise the offer price and write to the shareholders extolling the benefits of the takeover. The board may contact other companies in the same line of business, hoping that a white knight may appear. It could also take action to make the company less desirable to the bidder. See also *poison pill*

takeover ratio FIN the book value of a company divided by its market capitalisation. If the resulting figure is greater than one, then the company is a candidate for a takeover. See also *appreciation, asset-stripping*

taker FIN 1. the buyer of an option 2. a borrower

takings FIN a retailer's net receipts

talent management HR the recruitment, selection, identification, retention, management, and development of personnel considered to have the potential for high performance. Talent management is a model of personnel management. It focuses on the skills and abilities of the individual and on his or her potential for promotion to senior management roles. It also assesses how much of a contribution the individual can make to the success of the organisation.

talon FIN a form attached to a bearer bond that the holder of the bond uses to order new coupons when those attached to the bond have been depleted

tangible assets FIN assets that are physical, such as buildings, cash and stock. Leases and securities, although not physical in themselves, are classed as tangible assets because the underlying assets are physical.

tangible book value FIN the book value of a company after intangible assets, patents, trademarks, and the value of research and development have been subtracted

tank FIN to fall precipitously. This term is used especially with reference to stock prices. *(slang)*

tap CD FIN the issue of certificates of deposit, normally in large denominations, when required by a specific investor

tape don't fight the tape FIN don't go against the direction of the market

target cash balance FIN the amount of cash that a company would like to have in hand

target company FIN a company that is the object of a takeover bid

targeted repurchase FIN a company's purchase of its own shares from somebody attempting to buy the company

target savings motive ECON the tendency of people not to save when their families are growing up but to

save when they are in middle age and trying to build up a pension

tariff 1. ECON a government duty imposed on imports or exports to stimulate or dampen economic activity 2. FIN a list of prices at which goods or services are supplied

Tariff Concession Scheme FIN a system operated by the Australian government in which imported goods that have no locally produced equivalent attract reduced duties. *Abbr* **TCS**

tariff office FIN an insurance company whose premiums are determined according to a scale set collectively by several companies

tax FIN a charge levied by a government on individuals and companies to pay for public services. The amount of money required from a person or organisation depends on their income and assets.

taxability FIN the extent to which a good or individual is subject to a tax

taxable FIN subject to a tax

taxable base FIN the amount subject to taxation

taxable income FIN income that is subject to taxes

taxable matters FIN goods or services that can be taxed

tax and price index ECON an index number showing the percentage change in gross income that taxpayers need if they are to maintain their real disposable income

tax auditor FIN a government employee who investigates taxpayers' declarations

tax avoidance FIN the organisation of a taxpayer's affairs so that the minimum tax liability is incurred. Tax avoidance involves making the maximum use of all legal means of minimising liability to taxation.

tax bracket FIN a range of income levels subject to marginal tax at the same rate

tax break FIN an investment that is tax efficient or a legal arrangement that reduces the liability to tax. See also *tax avoidance, tax shelter*

tax consultant FIN a professional who advises on all aspects of taxation from tax avoidance to estate planning

tax-deductible FIN allowed to be subtracted from taxable income before tax is paid

tax-deductible public debt FIN any debt instrument that is exempt from US federal income tax

tax-deferred FIN not to be taxed until a later time

tax dodge FIN an illegal method of paying less tax than an individual or company is obliged to pay

tax domicile FIN a place that a government levying a tax considers to be a person's home

tax-efficient FIN financially advantageous by leading to a reduction of taxes to be paid

tax evasion FIN the illegal practice of paying less money in taxes than is due. See also *tax avoidance*

tax evasion amnesty FIN a governmental measure that affords those who have evaded a tax in some specified way freedom from punishment for their violation of the tax law

tax-exempt FIN not subject to tax

Tax Exempt Special Savings Account FIN a UK savings account in which investors could save up to £9,000 over a period of five years and not pay any tax, provided they made no withdrawals over that time. The advent of the ISA in 1999 meant that no new accounts of this type could be opened. *Abbr* **TESSA**

tax exile FIN a person or business that leaves a country to avoid paying taxes, or the condition of having done this

tax-favoured asset FIN an asset that receives more favourable tax treatment than some other asset

tax file number ANZ FIN an identification number assigned to each taxpayer in Australia. *Abbr* **TFN**

tax-free FIN not subject to tax

tax harmonisation FIN the enactment of taxation laws in different jurisdictions, such as neighbouring countries, provinces, or states of the United States, that are consistent with one another

tax haven FIN a country that has generous tax laws, especially one that encourages non-citizens to base operations in the country to avoid higher taxes in their home countries

tax holiday FIN an exemption from tax granted for a specified period of time. See also *tax subsidy*

taxi industry *S Africa* FIN the privately owned minibus taxi services in

South Africa, which constitute the largest sector of public transport in that country

tax incentive FIN a tax reduction afforded to people for particular purposes, for example, sending their children to college

tax inspector FIN a government employee who investigates taxpayers' declarations

tax invoice ANZ FIN a document issued by a supplier which stipulates the amount charged for goods or services as well as the amount of Goods and Services Tax payable

tax law FIN the body of laws on taxation, or one such law

tax loophole FIN an ambiguity in a tax law that enables some individuals or companies to avoid or reduce taxes

tax loss FIN a loss of money that can serve to reduce tax liabilities

tax loss carry-back FIN the reduction of taxes in a previous year, by subtraction from income for that year of losses suffered in the current year

tax loss carry-forward FIN the reduction of taxes in a future year, by subtraction from income for that year of losses suffered in the current year

tax obligation FIN the amount of tax a person or company owes

tax on capital income FIN a tax on the income from sales of capital assets

tax payable FIN the amount of tax a person or company has to pay

taxpayer FIN an individual or corporation who pays a tax

tax rate FIN the rate at which a tax is payable, usually expressed as a percentage

tax refund FIN an amount that a government gives back to a taxpayer who has paid more taxes than were due

tax relief FIN 1. the reduction in the amount of taxes payable, as for example, on capital goods a company has purchased 2. US money given to a certain group of people by a government in the form of a reduction of taxes

tax return FIN an official form on which a company or individual enters details of income and expenses, used to assess tax liability. Also known as *return*

tax revenue FIN money that a government receives in taxes

tax sale US FIN a sale of an item by a government to recover overdue taxes on a taxable item

tax shelter FIN a financial arrangement designed to reduce tax liability. See also *abusive tax shelter*

tax subsidy FIN a tax reduction that a government gives a business for a particular purpose, usually to create jobs. See also *tax holiday*

tax system FIN a scheme for imposing and collecting taxes

tax treaty FIN an international agreement that deals with taxes, especially taxes by several countries on the same individuals

tax year FIN a period covered by a statement about taxes

T-bill *abbr* FIN Treasury bill

TCS *abbr* FIN Tariff Concession Scheme

TDB *abbr* FIN Trade Development Board

Team Management Wheel™ GEN a visual aid for the efficient co-ordination of teamwork, which can be used to analyse how teams work together, assist in team building, and aid self-development and training. The Team Management Wheel outlines eight main team roles. Team members can determine the main functions of their jobs (what they have to do), by using the 'Types of Work Index', and can determine their own work preferences (what they want to do), using the 'Team Management Index'. They are then assigned one major role and two minor roles on the Team Management Wheel. At the centre of the Wheel are the linking skills common to all team members. The Team Management Wheel was developed by Charles Margerison and Dick McCann in 1984.

teaser e-mail MKT an e-mail message sent to a group of existing or potential customers (who have already given their permission to be contacted) which trails a special offer or piece of news that they will be told about fully at a later date. Teaser e-mails are used to increase the effectiveness of direct marketing campaigns.

teaser rate FIN a temporary concessionary interest rate offered on

mortgages, credit cards, or savings accounts in order to attract new customers

technical analysis FIN the analysis of past movements in the prices of financial instruments, currencies, commodities, etc., with a view to predicting future price movements by applying analytical techniques

technical rally FIN a temporary rise in security or commodity prices while the market is in a general decline. This may be because investors are seeking bargains, or because analysts have noted a support level.

technical reserves FIN the assets that an insurance company maintains to meet future claims

technological risk OPS the risk that a newly designed plant will not operate to specification

Technology and Human Resources for Industry Programme S Africa FIN see *THRIP*

technology stock FIN stock issued by a company that is involved in new technology

telebanking FIN electronic banking carried out by using a telephone line to communicate with a bank

telegraphic transfer FIN a method using telegraphs of transferring funds from a bank to a financial institution overseas. *Abbr* **TT**

telephone banking FIN a system in which customers can access their accounts and a range of banking services up to 24 hours a day by telephone. Apart from convenience, customers usually benefit from higher interest rates on savings accounts and lower interest when borrowing, as providers of telephone banking have lower overheads than traditional high street banks.

teleshopping E-COM the use of telecommunications and computers to shop for and purchase goods and services

teller FIN a bank cashier

tender FIN to bid for securities at auction. The securities are allocated according to the method adopted by the issuer. In the standard auction style, the investor receives the security at the price they tendered. In a Dutch-style auction, the issuer announces a strike price after all the tenders have been examined. This is set at a level where all the issue is sold. Investors who submitted a tender above the strike price just pay the strike price. The Dutch style of auction is increasingly being adopted in the United Kingdom. US Treasury Bills are also sold using the Dutch system. See also *offer for sale, sale by tender*

10-K FIN the filing of a US company's annual accounts with the New York Stock Exchange

tenor FIN the period of time that has to elapse before a bill of exchange becomes payable

10-Q FIN the filing of a US company's quarterly accounts with the New York Stock Exchange

term FIN the period of time that has to elapse from the date of the initial investment before a security or other investment (such as a term deposit or endowment assurance) becomes redeemable or reaches its maturity date

term assurance FIN **1.** a life policy that will pay out upon the death of the life insured, or in the event of the death of the first life insured (with a joint life insurance) **2.** insurance, especially life assurance, that is in effect for a specified period of time

term bill FIN see *period bill*

term deposit FIN a deposit account held for a fixed period. Withdrawals are either not allowed during this period, or they involve a fee payable by the depositor.

terminal date FIN the day on which a futures contract expires

terminal market FIN an exchange on which futures contracts or spot deals for commodities are traded

term loan FIN a loan for a fixed period, usually called a personal loan when it is for non-business purposes. While a personal loan is normally at a fixed rate of interest, a term loan to a business may be at either a fixed or variable rate. Term loans may be either secured or unsecured. An early repayment fee is usually payable when such a loan is repaid before the end of the term. See also *balloon loan, bullet loan*

term share FIN a share account in a building society that is for a fixed period of time. Withdrawals are usually not allowed during this period. However, if they are, then a fee is normally payable by the account holder.

tertiary sector ECON the part of the economy made up of non-profit organisations such as consumer associations and self-help groups

TESSA *abbr* FIN Tax Exempt Special Savings Account

testacy FIN the legal position of a person who has died leaving a valid will

testate FIN used to refer to a person who has died leaving a valid will

testator FIN a man who has made a valid will

testatrix FIN a woman who has made a valid will

TFN *abbr ANZ* FIN tax file number

TFN Withholding Tax *abbr ANZ* FIN Tax File Number Withholding Tax: a levy imposed on financial transactions involving an individual who has not disclosed his or her tax file number

thin market FIN a market where the trading volume is low. A characteristic of such a market is a wide spread of bid and offer prices.

third market FIN a market other than the main stock exchange in which stocks are traded

three steps and a stumble FIN a rule of thumb used on the US stock market that if the Federal Reserve increases interest rates three times consecutively, stock market prices will go down *(slang)*

thrift institution or **thrift** FIN a bank that offers savings accounts. See also *savings and loan association, savings bank*

THRIP *abbr S Africa* FIN Technology and Human Resources for Industry Programme: a collaborative programme involving industry, government, and educational and research institutions that supports research and development in technology, science, and engineering

TIBOR *abbr* FIN Tokyo Inter Bank Offered Rate

tick FIN the least amount by which a value such as the price of a stock or a rate of interest can rise or fall. This could be, for example, a hundredth of a percentage point.

tied loan FIN a loan made by one national government to another on the condition that the funds are used to purchase goods from the lending nation

tiger FIN any of the key markets in the Pacific Basin region, except Japan: Hong Kong, South Korea, Singapore, and Taiwan

tight money ECON a situation where it is expensive to borrow because of restrictive government policy or high demand

TILA *abbr* FIN Truth in Lending Act

time and material pricing FIN a form of cost plus pricing in which price is determined by reference to the cost of the labour and material inputs to the product/service

time bargain FIN a stock market transaction in which the securities are deliverable at a future date beyond the exchange's normal settlement day

time deposit FIN a US savings account or a certificate of deposit, issued by a financial institution. While the savings account is for a fixed term, deposits are accepted with the understanding that withdrawals may be made subject to a period of notice. Banks are authorised to require at least 30 days' notice. While a certificate of deposit is equivalent to a term account, passbook accounts are generally regarded as funds readily available to the account holder.

time draft FIN a bill of exchange drawn on and accepted by a US bank. It is either an after date or after sight bill.

time sheet FIN, HR a record of how a person's time has been spent. It is used to calculate pay, assess the efficient use of time, or charge for work done.

time spread FIN the purchase and sale of options in the same commodity or security with the same price and different maturities

time value FIN the premium at which an option is trading relative to its intrinsic value

tip FIN a piece of useful expert information. Used in the sense of a 'share tip', it is a share recommendation published in the financial press, usually based on research published by a financial institution.

tip-off FIN a warning based on confidential information. See also *insider trading, money laundering*

tipping point GEN the moment in time at which an emerging trend or idea achieves the critical mass which enables it to gain momentum, spread rapidly, and become dominant. The term was introduced by Malcolm Gladwell in his book *The Tipping Point* (Abacus, 2001), which compares the development of trends and fashions to the sudden spread of epidemics and suggests that change is not a gradual process, but takes place in sudden dramatic shifts. In the same way as a small weight will tip the balance of a pair of scales in equilibrium, a small change in organisational strategy may have major effects. The concept has been applied to leadership and change management. A related concept is strategic inflection point.

title FIN a legal term meaning ownership. Deeds to land are sometimes referred to as title deeds. If a person has good title to a property, their proof of ownership is beyond doubt.

toasted FIN used to refer to someone or something that has lost money *(slang)*

toehold *US* FIN a stake in a corporation built up by a potential bidder which is less than 5% of the corporation's stock. It is only when a 5% stake is reached that the holder has to make a declaration to the Securities and Exchange Commission.

Tokyo Inter Bank Offered Rate FIN on the Japanese money markets, the rate at which banks will offer to make deposits in yen with each other, often used as a reference rate. The deposits are for terms from overnight up to five years. *Abbr* **TIBOR**

tombstone FIN a notice in the financial press giving details of a large lending facility to a business. It may relate to a management buyout or to a package that may include an interest rate cap and collars to finance a specific package. More than one bank may be involved. Although it may appear to be an advertisement, technically in most jurisdictions it is regarded as a statement of fact and

therefore falls outside the advertisement regulations. The borrower generally pays for the advertisement, though it is the financial institutions that derive the most benefit.

top slicing FIN **1.** selling part of a shareholding that will realise a sum that is equal to the original cost of the investment. What remains therefore represents potential pure profit. **2.** in the United Kingdom, a complex method used by HM Revenue & Customs for assessing what tax, if any, is paid when certain investment bonds or endowment policies mature or are cashed in early

total absorption costing FIN a method used by a cost accountant to price goods and services, allocating both direct and indirect costs. Although this method is designed so that all of an organisation's costs are covered, it may result in opportunities being missed because of high prices. Consequently sales may be lost that could contribute to overheads. See also *marginal costing*

total-debt-to-total-assets FIN the premium at which an option is trading relative to its intrinsic value

total quality management FIN an integrated and comprehensive system of planning and controlling all business functions so that products or services are produced which meet or exceed customer expectations. TQM is a philosophy of business behaviour, embracing principles such as employee involvement, continuous improvement at all levels, and customer focus, as well as being a collection of related techniques aimed at improving quality, such as full documentation of activities, clear goal-setting, and performance measurement from the customer perspective. *Abbr* **TQM**

total responsibility management GEN systems and procedures to ensure responsible business practices and management. The term was introduced by Waddock, Bodwell, and Graves in their article 'Responsibility: The New Business Imperative', published in the *Academy of Management Executive* in May 2002. It is used to describe the codes of practice and systems that organisations are devel-

oping to manage their social, environmental, and ethical responsibilities in response to pressures from stakeholders, emerging global standards, general social trends, and institutional expectations. Some issues, linked to labour, ecology, and community are included because they are subject to increasing assessment or regulation, while others are raised intermittently as a result of public controversies.

total return FIN the total percentage change in the value of an investment over a specified time period, including capital gains, dividends, and the investment's appreciation or depreciation. The total return formula reflects all the ways in which an investment can earn or lose money, resulting in an increase or decrease in the investment's net asset value (NAV).

touch FIN the difference between the best bid and the best offer price quoted by all market makers for a particular security

touch price FIN the best bid and offer price available

tracker fund FIN see *index fund*

tracking error FIN the deviation by which an index fund fails to replicate the index it is aiming to mirror

tracking stock FIN a stock whose dividends are tied to the performance of a subsidiary of the corporation that owns it

trade balance FIN see *balance of trade*

trade barrier ECON a condition imposed by a government to limit free exchange of goods internationally. NTBs, safety standards, and tariffs are typical trade barriers.

trade bill FIN a bill of exchange between two businesses that trade with each other. See also *acceptance credit*

trade credit FIN credit offered by one business when trading with another. Typically this is for one month from the date of the invoice, but it could be for a shorter or longer period.

trade debt FIN a debt that originates during the normal course of trade

Trade Development Board FIN a government agency that was established in 1983 to promote trade and explore new markets for Singapore products, and offers various schemes of assistance to companies. *Abbr* **TDB**

traded option FIN an option that is traded on an exchange that is different from the one on which the asset underlying the option is traded

trade gap FIN a balance of payments deficit

trade investment FIN the action or process of one business making a loan to another, or buying shares in another. The latter may be the first stages of a friendly takeover.

trade mission FIN a visit by businessmen from one country to another for the purpose of discussing trade between their respective nations

TRADENZ *abbr* FIN New Zealand Trade Development Board

trade point FIN a stock exchange that is less formal than the major exchanges

trade war ECON a competition between two or more countries for a share of international or domestic trade

trade-weighted index ECON an index that measures the value of a country's currency in relation to the currencies of its trading partners

trading account FIN see *profit and loss account*

trading halt FIN a stoppage of trading in a stock on an exchange, usually in response to information about a company, or concern about rapid movement of the share price

trading loss FIN a situation in which the amount of money an organisation takes in sales is less than its expenditure

trading pit FIN see *pit*

trading profit FIN see *gross profit*

tranche CD FIN one of a series of certificates of deposit that are sold by the issuing bank over time. Each of the CDs in a tranche has the same maturity date.

transaction 1. E-COM any item or collection of sequential items of business that are enclosed in encrypted form in an electronic envelope and transmitted between trading partners **2.** FIN a trade of a security

transaction e-commerce E-COM the electronic sale of goods and services, either business-to-business or business-to-customer

transaction history FIN a record of all of an investor's transactions with a broker

transactions motive ECON the motive that consumers have to hold money for their likely purchases in the immediate future

transfer FIN **1.** the movement of money through the domestic or international banking system. See also *BACS, Fedwire, SWIFT* **2.** the change of ownership of an asset

transfer of value FIN see *chargeable transfer*

transferor FIN a person who transfers an asset to another person

transfer-out fee FIN a fee for closing an account with a broker

transfer price FIN the price at which goods or services are transferred between different units of the same company. If those units are located in different countries, the term international transfer pricing is used. The extent to which the transfer price covers costs and contributes to (internal) profit is a matter of policy. A transfer price may, for example, be based upon marginal cost, full cost, market price or negotiation. Where the transferred products cross national boundaries, the transfer prices used may have to be agreed with the governments of the countries concerned.

transfer stamp FIN the mark embossed on to transfer deeds to signify that stamp duty has been paid

transit time FIN the period between the completion of an operation and the availability of the material at the next workstation

transparency FIN the condition in which nothing is hidden. This is an essential condition for a free market in securities. Prices, the volume of trading, and factual information must be available to all.

travel accident insurance FIN a form of insurance cover offered by some credit card companies when the whole or part of a travel arrangement is paid for with the card. In the

event of death resulting from an accident in the course of travel, or the loss of eyesight or a limb, the credit card company will pay the cardholder (or his or her estate) a pre-stipulated sum. See also *travel insurance*

travel insurance FIN a form of insurance cover that provides medical cover while abroad as well as covering the policyholder's possessions and money while travelling. Many travel insurance policies also reimburse the policyholder if a holiday has to be cancelled and pay compensation for delayed journeys. See also *travel accident insurance*

treasurer FIN somebody who is responsible for an organisation's funds

Treasurer *ANZ* FIN the minister responsible for financial and economic matters in a national, state, or territory government

treasuries FIN the generic name for negotiable debt instruments issued by the US government. See also *Treasury bill*

treasury FIN the department of a company or corporation that deals with all financial matters

Treasury FIN in some countries, the government department responsible for the nation's financial policies as well as the management of the economy

Treasury bill FIN a short-term security issued by the government. *Abbr* **T-bill**

Treasury bill rate FIN the rate of interest obtainable by holding a Treasury bill. Although Treasury bills are non-interest bearing, by purchasing them at a discount and holding them to redemption, the discount is effectively the interest earned by holding these instruments. The Treasury bill rate is the discount expressed as a percentage of the issue price. It is annualised to give a rate per annum.

treasury bond *US* FIN a long-term bond issued by the US government that bears interest

treasury management FIN the corporate handling of all financial matters, the generation of external and internal funds for business, the management of currencies and cash flows, and the complex strategies, policies, and procedures of corporate finance

treasury note FIN **1.** a note issued by the US government **2.** a short-term debt instrument issued by the Australian federal government. Treasury notes are issued on a tender basis for periods of 13 and 26 weeks.

treasury stock or **treasury shares** US FIN a company's shares that have been bought back by the company and not cancelled. In the United States, these shares are shown as deductions from equity, in the United Kingdom, they are shown as assets in the balance sheet.

treaty FIN **1.** a written agreement between nations, such as the Treaty of Rome (1957), that was the foundation of the European Union **2.** a contract between an insurer and the reinsurer whereby the latter is to accept risks from the insurer **3.** see *private treaty*

Treynor ratio FIN see *risk-adjusted return on capital*

trickle-down theory ECON the theory that if markets are open and programmes exist to improve basic health and education, growth will extend from successful parts of a developing country's economy to the rest

triple bottom line FIN environmental sustainability and social responsibility used as criteria when judging the overall performance of a company, in addition to purely financial considerations

triple tax exempt US FIN exempt from federal, state, and local income taxes

troubleshooter FIN an independent person, often a consultant, who is called in by a company in difficulties to help formulate a strategy for recovery

troy ounce FIN the traditional unit used when weighing precious metals such as gold or silver. It is equal to approximately 1.097 ounces avoirdupois or 31.22 grams.

true interest cost FIN the effective rate of interest paid by the issuer on a debt security that is sold at a discount

trust 1. FIN a collection of assets held by somebody for another person's benefit **2.** ECON a company that has a monopoly

trust account FIN a bank account that is held in trust for somebody else

trust bank FIN a Japanese bank that acts commercially in the sense of accepting deposits and making loans and also in the capacity of a trustee

trust company FIN a company whose business is administering trusts

trust corporation FIN a US state-chartered institution that may undertake banking activities. A trust corporation is sometimes known as a non-bank bank.

trustee FIN somebody who holds assets in trust

trustee in bankruptcy FIN somebody appointed by a court to manage the finances of a bankrupt person or company

trustee investment FIN an investment that is made by a trustee and is subject to legal restrictions

trusteeship FIN the holding of a trust, or the term of such a holding

trust fund FIN assets held in trust by a trustee for the trust's beneficiaries

trust officer FIN somebody who manages the assets of a trust, especially for a bank that is acting as a trustee

Truth in Lending Act FIN in the United States, a law requiring lenders to disclose the terms of their credit offers accurately so that consumers are not misled and are able to compare the various credit terms available. The Truth in Lending Act requires lenders to disclose the terms and costs of all loan plans, including the following: annual percentage rate; points and fees; the total of the principal amount being financed; payment due date and terms, including any balloon payment where applicable and late payment fees; features of variable-rate loans, including the highest rate the lender would charge, how it is calculated and the resulting monthly payment; total finance charges; whether the loan is assumable; application fee; annual or one-time service fees; prepayment penalties; and, where applicable, confirm the address of the property securing the loan. *Abbr* **TILA**

TT *abbr* FIN telegraphic transfer

turbulence GEN unpredictable and swift changes in an organisation's external or internal environments which affect its performance. The late 20th century was considered a turbulent environment for business because of the rapid growth in technology and globalisation, and the frequency of restructuring and merger activity.

turkey FIN a poorly performing investment or business *(slang)*

turn FIN the difference between a market maker's bid and offer prices

turnaround management FIN, GEN the implementation of a set of actions required to save an organisation from business failure and return it to operational normality and financial solvency. Turnaround management usually requires strong leadership and can include corporate restructuring and redundancies, an investigation of the root causes of failure, and long-term programmes to revitalise the organisation.

turnover 1. GEN The total of value transactions in a specific period, either for the stock market as a whole or for a specific company **2.** FIN the total sales revenue of an organisation for an accounting period. This is shown net of VAT, trade discounts, and any other taxes based on the revenue in a profit and loss account. **3.** HR the rate at which staff leave and are replaced in an organisation

turnover ratio FIN a measure of the number of times in a year that a business's stock or inventory is turned over. It is calculated as the cost of sales divided by the average book value of inventory/stock.

twenty-four hour trading FIN the possibility of trading in currencies or securities at any time of day or night, because there are always trading floors open at different locations in different time zones. A financial institution with offices in the Far East, Europe, and the United States can offer its clients 24-hour trading – either by the clients contacting their offices in each area, or by the customer's local office passing the orders on to another centre.

20-F FIN a document compiled by non-US companies listed on the

New York Stock Exchange for the US SEC that gives detailed corporate information

two-tier tender offer FIN in the United States, a takeover bid in which the acquirer offers to pay more for shares bought in order to gain control than for those acquired at a later date. The ploy is to encourage shareholders to accept the offer. This form of bidding is outlawed in some jurisdictions, including the United Kingdom.

UBR *abbr* FIN uniform business rate

UIF *abbr S Africa* FIN Unemployment Insurance Fund: a system, administered through payroll deductions, that insures employees against loss of earnings through being made unemployed by such causes as retrenchment, illness, or maternity

ultra vires FIN the Latin for 'beyond the powers', used to refer to an activity that normally falls beyond the scope of the instrument from which an organisation's authority is derived, and thus may be challenged by the courts. A company's powers are limited by the objectives in its memorandum of association. Most company's objectives are wide ranging, but, should it act outside of these objectives, any resulting agreement may be unenforceable.

ultra vires activity FIN an act that is not permitted by applicable rules, such as a corporate charter. Such acts may lead to contracts being void.

umbrella fund FIN a collective investment based offshore that invests in other offshore collective investments

unbalanced growth ECON the situation when not all sectors of an economy can grow at the same rate

unbundling FIN the dividing of a company into separate constituent companies, often to sell all or some of them after a takeover

uncalled share capital FIN the amount of the nominal value of a share which is unpaid and has not been called up by the company

uncollected funds FIN money deriving from the deposit of an instrument that a bank has not been able to negotiate

uncollected trade bill FIN an account with an outstanding balance for purchases made from the company that holds it

unconditional bid FIN in a takeover battle, a situation in which a bidder will pay the offered price irrespective of how many shares are acquired

unconsolidated FIN not grouped together, as of shares or holdings

uncontested bid FIN an offering of a contract by a government or other organisation to one bidder only, without competition

UNCTAD *abbr* FIN United Nations Conference on Trade and Development: the focal point within the UN system for the integrated treatment of development and interrelated issues in trade, finance, technology, and investment

underbanked FIN without enough brokers to sell a new issue

underlying asset FIN an asset that is the subject of an option

underlying inflation FIN the rate of inflation that does not take mortgage costs into account

underlying security FIN a security that is the subject of an option

undermargined account FIN an account that does not have enough money to cover its margin requirements, resulting in a margin call

undervalued FIN used to describe an asset that is available for purchase at a price lower than its worth

undervalued currency FIN a currency that costs less to buy with another currency than its worth in goods

underwrite FIN to assume risk, especially for a new issue or an insurance policy

underwriter FIN a person or organisation that buys an issue from a corporation and sells it to investors

underwriters' syndicate FIN a group of organisations that buys an issue from a corporation and sells it to investors

underwriting FIN the buying of an issue from a corporation for the purpose of selling it to investors

underwriting income FIN the money that an insurance company makes because the premiums it collects exceed the claims it pays out

underwriting spread FIN an amount that is the difference between what

an organisation pays for an issue and what it receives when it sells the issue to investors

undistributable reserves FIN in the United Kingdom, reserves that are not legally available for distribution to shareholders as dividends according to the Companies Act (1985)

UNDP *abbr* ECON United Nations Development Programme: the world's largest source of grants for sustainable human development. Its aims include the elimination of poverty, environmental regeneration, job creation, and advancement of women.

unearned income FIN income received from sources other than employment. See also **earned income**.

unearned increment FIN an increase in the value of a property that arises from causes other than the owner's improvements or expenditure

unearned premium FIN the amount repaid by an insurance company when a policy is terminated

uneconomic ECON not profitable for a country, firm, or investor in the short or long term

unemployment ECON the situation in which some members of a country's labour force are willing to work but cannot find employment

unfunded debt FIN short-term debt requiring repayment within a year from issuance

uniform business rate FIN the rate of tax set by the central government that is to be collected from businesses by the local authority. *Abbr* **UBR**

uniform commercial code FIN a set of laws that govern commercial transactions in the United States. The Code has been adopted totally or in part by all 50 states. *Abbr* **UCC**

uniform costing FIN the use by several undertakings of the same costing methods, principles, and techniques

uninsurable FIN considered unsuitable for insurance, especially because of being a poor risk

unissued share capital FIN stock that is authorised but has not been issued. US term **unissued stock**

unissued stock *US* FIN = unissued share capital

unit FIN a collection of securities traded together as one item

unit cost FIN the cost to a company of producing one item that it markets

United Nations Conference on Trade and Development FIN see *UNCTAD*

unit of account ECON a unit of a country's currency that can be used in payment for goods or in a firm's accounting

unit of trade FIN the smallest amount that can be bought or sold of a share of stock, or a contract included in an option

unit trust FIN an investment company that sells shares to investors and invests for their benefit. US term *mutual fund*

unlimited liability FIN full responsibility for the obligations of a general partnership

unlimited risk FIN a risk whose potential loss is unlimited, such as futures trading

unlisted FIN used to refer to a security that is not traded on an exchange

unlisted securities market FIN a market for stocks that are not listed on an exchange. See also *AIM*. *Abbr* **USM**

unquoted FIN having no publicly stated price, usually referring to an unlisted security

unrealised capital gain or **unrealised gain** FIN a profit from the holding of an asset worth more than its purchase price, but not yet sold

unrealised profit/loss FIN a profit or loss that need not be reported as income, for example, deriving from the holding of an asset worth more/less than its purchase price, but not yet sold

unremittable gain FIN a capital gain that cannot be imported into the taxpayer's country, especially because of currency restrictions

unseasoned issue FIN an issue of shares or bonds for which there is no existing market. See also *seasoned issue*

unsecured FIN without collateral

unsecured debt FIN money borrowed without supplying collateral

unsecured loan FIN a loan made with no collateral. Also known as *signature loan*

unstable equilibrium ECON a market situation in which, if there is a movement (of price or quantity) away from the equilibrium, existing forces will push the price even further away

upstairs market FIN the place where traders for major brokerages and institutions do business at an exchange

uptitling HR the change of a job title to make it sound more important, although the job content and level of responsibility remain the same. Uptitling has been seen by some as an attempt by employers to improve job satisfaction without increasing pay.

used credit FIN the portion of a line of credit that is no longer available for use

USM *abbr* FIN unlisted securities market

utopian socialism ECON a form of socialism in which the use and production of all services and goods are held collectively by the group or community, rather than by a central government

value-added reseller FIN a merchant who buys products at retail and packages them with additional items for sale to customers. *Abbr* **VAR**

value-added tax FIN see *VAT*

value chain FIN the sequence of business activities by which, in the perspective of the end user, value is added to products or services produced by an organisation

value driver FIN an activity or organisational focus which enhances the perceived value of a product or service in the perception of the consumer and which therefore creates value for the producer. Advanced technology, reliability, or reputation for customer care can all be value drivers.

value engineering FIN an activity which helps to design products which meet customer needs at the lowest cost while assuring the required standards of quality and reliability

value for customs purposes only FIN what somebody importing something into the United States declares that it is worth

value for money audit FIN an investigation into whether proper arrangements have been made for securing economy, efficiency, and effectiveness in the use of resources. *Abbr* **VFM**. Also known as *comprehensive auditing*

value proposition FIN a proposed scheme for making a profit *(slang)*

value share or **value stock** FIN a share that is considered to be currently underpriced by the market, and therefore an attractive investment prospect

VAR *abbr* FIN value-added reseller

variable annuity FIN see *annuity*

variable costing FIN see *marginal costing*

variable interest rate FIN an interest rate that changes, usually in relation to a standard index, during the period of a loan

variable rate note FIN a note the interest rate of which is tied to an index, such as the prime rate in the United States or the London InterBank Offering Rate (LIBOR) in the United Kingdom. *Abbr* **VRN**

variance FIN the difference between a planned, budgeted, or standard cost and the actual cost incurred. The same comparisons may be made for revenues.

variance analysis FIN the evaluation of performance by means of variances, whose timely reporting should maximise the opportunity for managerial action

VAT *abbr* FIN value added tax: a tax added at each stage in the manufacture of a product. It acts as a replacement for a sales tax in almost every industrialised country outside North America. It is levied on selected goods and services, paid by organisations on items they buy, and then charged to customers.

VAT paid FIN with the VAT already paid

VAT receivable FIN with the VAT for an item not yet collected by a taxing authority

VAT registration FIN the process of listing with a European government as a company eligible for return of VAT in certain cases

VCM *abbr* FIN Venture Capital Market

velocity management OPS the management of processes, people, and systems so that they operate reliably and accurately at high speeds to enable fast responses to orders and inquiries. The development of information and communications technologies has led to faster delivery of value chain information, and velocity management is used to develop the strategies, processes, people, and organisational discipline to fully support and exploit this advantage. Velocity management is a form of process management which has been used in the context of military logistics as well as in business.

velocity of circulation of money ECON the rate at which money circulates in an economy

vendor placing FIN the practice of issuing shares to acquire a business, where an agreement has been made to allow the vendor of the business to place the shares with investors for cash

venture capital FIN, ECON **1.** money used to finance new companies or projects, especially those with high earning potential and high risk. Also known as *risk capital* **2.** the money invested in a new company or business venture

Venture Capital Market FIN a sector on the JSE Securities Exchange for listing smaller developing companies. The criteria for listing in the VCM sector are less stringent than for the DCM (Development Capital Market) sector. See also *Development Capital Market. Abbr* **VCM**

venture funding FIN the round of funding for a new company that follows seed funding, provided by venture capitalists

venturer FIN one of the parties involved in a joint venture

verification FIN in an audit, a substantive test of the existence, ownership, and valuation of a company's assets and liabilities

vertical equity FIN the principle that people with different incomes should pay different rates of tax

vertical form FIN the presentation of a financial statement in which the debits and credits are shown in one column of figures

vertical merger GEN, FIN see *merger*

vested employee benefits FIN employee benefits that are not conditional on future employment

vested rights FIN the value of somebody's rights in a pension in the United States if he or she leaves a job

VFM *abbr* FIN value for money audit

v-form FIN a graphic representation of something that had been falling in value and is now rising

visible trade ECON trade in physical goods and merchandise

voetstoots *S Africa* FIN purchased at the buyer's risk or without warranty

volume of retail sales ECON the amount of trade in goods carried out in the retail sector of an economy in a particular period

volume variances FIN differences in costs or revenues compared with budgeted amounts, caused by differences between the actual and budgeted levels of activity

voluntary arrangement FIN an agreement the terms of which are not legally binding on the parties

voluntary liquidation FIN liquidation of a solvent company that is supported by the shareholders

voluntary registration FIN in the United Kingdom, registration for VAT by a trader whose turnover is below the registration threshold. This is usually done in order to reclaim tax on inputs.

vostro account FIN an account held by a local bank on behalf of a foreign bank

votes on account FIN in the United Kingdom, money granted by Parliament in order to continue spending in a fiscal year before final authorisation of the totals for the year

voting shares FIN shares whose owners have voting rights. US term *voting stock*

voting trust FIN a group of individuals who have collectively received voting rights from shareholders

voucher FIN a document supporting an accounting entry

vouching FIN an auditing process in which documentary evidence is matched with the details recorded in an accounting record in order to check for validity and accuracy

Vredeling Directive FIN a proposal, presented to the European Council

of Ministers in 1980, for obligatory information, consultation, and participation of workers at headquarters level in multinational enterprises

Vulcan nerve pinch GEN the uncomfortable hand position required to reach all the keys for certain computer commands *(slang)*

vulture capitalist FIN a venture capitalist who structures deals on behalf of an entrepreneur in such a way that the investors benefit rather than the entrepreneur *(slang)*

wage earner HR a person in paid employment

wage freeze HR government policy of preventing pay rises in order to combat inflation

wage incentive HR a monetary benefit offered as a reward to those employees who perform well in a specified area

wages HR a form of pay given to employees in exchange for the work they have done. Traditionally, the term wages applied to the weekly pay of manual, or non-professional workers. In modern usage, the term is often used interchangeably with salary.

waiting time FIN the period for which an operator is available for production but is prevented from working by shortage of material or tooling, or by machine breakdown

waiver of premium FIN a provision of an insurance policy that suspends payment of premiums, for example, if the insured suffers a disabling injury

wallet technology E-COM a software package providing digital wallets or purses on the computers of merchants and customers to facilitate payment by digital cash

wallflower FIN an investment that does not attract a lot of interest from potential investors because it has not been profitable enough

wallpaper FIN a disparaging term used to describe a situation where a company issues and sells many new shares in order to finance a series of takeovers

Wall Street FIN **1.** a collective name for the US financial industry **2.** the area of New York City where the financial industry is based and does much of its business

war chest FIN a large amount of money held by a person or a company in reserves that can be used to finance the takeover of other companies (slang)

war loan FIN a government bond that pays a fixed rate of interest and has no redemption date. War loans were originally issued to finance military expenditure.

warrant FIN a contract that gives the right to buy a predetermined number of shares in the future

warrants risk warning notice FIN a statement that a broker gives to clients to alert them to the risks inherent in trading in options

waste FIN discarded material having no value

wasting asset FIN a fixed asset which is consumed or exhausted in the process of earning income, such as a mine or a quarry

watchdog GEN an independent organisation whose remit it is to police a particular industry, ensuring that member companies do not act illegally

watered stock FIN shares in a company that are worth less than the total capital invested

watermark FIN a design inserted into documents to prove their authenticity. For example, banknotes all carry watermarks to prevent forgery.

WDA abbr FIN writing down allowances

WDV abbr FIN written-down value

wealth ECON physical assets such as a house or financial assets such as stocks and shares that can yield an income for their holder

wealth tax FIN a tax on somebody's accumulated wealth, as opposed to their income

wear and tear FIN the deterioration of a tangible fixed asset as a result of normal use. This is recognised for accounting purposes by depreciation.

Web 2.0 E-COM a phrase used to describe what some commentators view as a new generation of Internet services and communities. Web 2.0 does not refer to any technological changes, but rather to a perceived shift in what the Internet can be

used for, with champions of the term arguing that it stands for more collaborative working and information-sharing.

webinar GEN a seminar held on the Internet, linking participants via conference calls and PCs with access to the Internet

WEF abbr FIN World Economic Forum

weighted average cost FIN a method of unit cost determination often applied to stocks. When a new purchase quantity is received, an average unit cost is calculated by dividing the sum of the cost of the opening stock plus the cost of the acquisitions by the total number of units in stock.

weighted average cost of capital FIN The average cost of the company's finance (equity, debentures, bank loans) weighted according to the proportion each element bears to the total pool of capital. Weighting is usually based on market valuations, current yields, and costs after tax. The weighted average cost of capital is often used as the hurdle rate for investment decisions, and as the measure to be minimised in order to find the optimal capital structure for the company.

weighted average cost price FIN a value for the cost of each item of a specific type in an inventory, taking into account what quantities were bought at what prices

weighted average number of ordinary shares FIN the number of ordinary shares at the beginning of a period, adjusted for shares cancelled, bought back, or issued during the period, multiplied by a time-weighting factor. This number is used in the calculation of earnings per share.

Wheat Report FIN a report produced by a committee in 1972 that set out to examine the principles and methods of accounting in the United States. Its publication led to the establishment of the FASB.

whisper number or **whisper estimate** FIN an estimate of a company's earnings that is based on rumours

whisper stock FIN a stock about which there is talk of a likely change in value, usually upwards and often related to a takeover

white coat rule FIN, MKT a US Federal Trade Commission rule prohibiting the use of actors dressed as doctors to promote a product in TV commercials (slang)

white elephant FIN a product or service that has not sold well, despite large amounts of money being pumped into its development

white knight FIN a person or company liked by a company's management, who buys the company when a hostile company is trying to buy it. See also knight

whizz kid FIN a young, exceptionally successful person – especially one who makes a lot of money in large financial transactions, including takeovers

wholesale price FIN a price charged to customers who buy large quantities of an item for resale in smaller quantities to others

wholesale price index FIN a government-calculated index of wholesale prices, indicative of inflation in an economy

wholesale trade MKT trade at wholesale prices

wholly-owned subsidiary FIN a company that is completely owned by another company. A wholly-owned subsidiary is a registered company with board members who all represent one holding company or corporation. Board members may be directly from the holding company or acting as its nominees, or they may be from other wholly owned subsidiaries of the holding company.

widow-and-orphan stock US FIN a stock considered extremely safe as an investment

wiki E-COM computer server software that allows the linking and creation of Web pages. The most famous wiki is Wikipedia, the online encyclopaedia that has been created (and is edited) by a team of users. In a business context, wikis are often used to create 'knowledge banks' by drawing together sources of information with common themes that can be used as a type of intranet. Wikis are meant to be collaborative, but there has been some argument over how reliable they can be when their content can be freely edited and, in the view of some, manipulated.

windfall gains and losses FIN unexpected gains and losses

windfall profit FIN a sudden large profit, subject to extra tax

windfall tax FIN the tax a government levies on a company that makes extraordinarily large profits in times of unusual circumstances, for example, during a war

winding-up FIN the legal process of closing down a company

winding-up petition FIN a formal request to a court for the compulsory liquidation of a company

WIP *abbr* FIN work in progress

witching hour US FIN the time when a type of derivative financial instrument such as a put, a call, or a contract for advance sale becomes due *(slang)*

withdrawal FIN the regular disbursements of dividend or capital gain income from an open-end unit trust

withholding tax FIN **1.** in the United States, the money that an employer pays directly to the government as a payment of the income tax on the employee **2.** the money deducted from a dividend or interest payment that a financial institution pays directly to the government as a payment of the income tax on the recipient

word of mouth marketing MKT a marketing strategy which uses the person-to-person communication of satisfied customers to raise awareness of an organisation's products and services and generate sales. Word of mouth communication spreads through social and business networks and communities, and is regarded as a particularly influential, cost-effective, and speedy means of disseminating information about an organisation's products. Various methods are adopted to promote this process, including customer partnerships and customer referral schemes. Viral marketing and buzz marketing are similar concepts, the latter focusing particularly on the creation of an atmosphere of excitement or 'buzz' about a new product, often within a specific social group.

working capital FIN the funds that are readily available to operate a busi-

ness. Working capital comprises the total net current assets of a business minus its liabilities. Current assets are cash and assets that can be converted to cash within one year or a normal operating cycle; current liabilities are monies owed that are due within one year. If a company's current assets total £300,000 and its current liabilities total £160,000, its working capital is:

£300,000 – £160,000 = £140,000

working capital ratio FIN see *current ratio*

working hours directive HR government regulations that aim to protect employees' health and safety at work by making sure that they do not work for too long, have too little rest, or have disrupted patterns of work. According to the directive, employees must not work more than an average of 48 hours per week, although they may opt out and work longer if they so choose. They must not be forced to work for more than eight hours a night on average. Employees are also legally entitled to one day off each week; 11 hours rest a day; an in-work rest break if they work for more than six hours per day; and four weeks' paid leave annually.

work in process US FIN = work in progress

work in progress FIN any product that is in the process of being made. Such items are included in stocks and usually valued according to their production costs. US term *work in process*. *Abbr* **WIP**

World Bank FIN one of the largest sources of funding for less-developed countries in the world. It is made up of five organisations: the International Bank for Reconstruction and Development, the International Development Association, the International Finance Corporation, the Multilateral Investment Guarantee Agency, and the International Centre for Settlement of Investment Disputes. The World Bank was founded at the 1944 Bretton Woods Conference in the United States and has over 180 member countries. Its head office is based in Washington DC, but

the Bank has field offices in over 100 countries. Its focus has shifted dramatically since the 1980s, when over one-fifth of its lending was made up of investment in the power industry. Its current priorities are education, health, and nutrition in the most economically challenged countries of the world.

world class manufacturing FIN a position of international manufacturing excellence, achieved by developing a culture based on factors such as continuous improvement, problem prevention, zero defect tolerance, customer-driven just-in-time production, and total quality management

World Economic Forum FIN an independent economic organisation whose stated mission is to 'improve the state of the world'. Based in Switzerland, the WEF was formed in the 1970s by Professor Klaus Schwab, who set out to bring together the CEOs of leading European companies in order to discuss strategies that would enable Europe to compete in the global marketplace. Since then, over 1,000 companies around the world have become members of the WEF and its interests have diversified to cover health, corporate citizenship, and peace-building activities. However, it has attracted criticism from some quarters, and anti-globalisation protestors gather regularly at its meetings. *Abbr* **WEF**

world economy ECON the global marketplace that has grown up since the 1970s, in which goods can be produced wherever the production costs are cheapest

wrap fund *S Africa* FIN a registered fund, not itself a unit trust but with similar status to that of a stockbroker's portfolio, which invests in a range of underlying unit trusts, each of which is treated as a discrete holding

write-down FIN **1.** a reduction in the recorded value of an asset to comply with the concept of prudence. The valuation of stock at the lower of cost or net realisable value may require the values of some stock to be written down. **2.** a reduction in the value of an asset as entered in the books of a business

write off FIN a reduction in the recorded value of an asset, usually to zero

writing-down allowance FIN in the United Kingdom, a form of capital allowance giving tax relief to companies acquiring fixed assets which are then depreciated. This allowance forms part of the system of capital allowances. *Abbr* **WDA**

wrongful trading FIN the continuation of trading when a company's directors know that it cannot avoid insolvent liquidation

XBRL *abbr* E-COM, FIN Extensible Business Reporting Language: a computer language for financial reporting. It allows companies to publish, extract, and exchange financial information through the Internet and other electronic means.

Yankee bond FIN a bond issued in the US domestic market by a non-US company

year-end FIN relating to the end of a financial or fiscal (tax) year

year-end closing FIN the financial statements issued at the end of a company's fiscal (tax) year

year to date FIN the period from the start of specified financial year to the current time. A variety of financial information, such as a company's profits, losses, or sales, may be displayed in this way. *Abbr* **YTD**

yield FIN a percentage of the amount invested that is the annual income from an investment. Yield is calculated by dividing the annual cash return by the current share price and expressing that as a percentage. Yields can be compared against the market average or against a sector average, which in turn gives an idea of the relative value of the share against its peers. Other things being equal, a higher yield share is preferable to that of an identical company with a lower yield. An additional feature of the yield (unlike many of the other share analysis ratios) is that it enables comparison with cash. Cash placed in an interest-bearing source

like a bank account or a government stock, produces a yield – the annual interest payable. This is usually a safe investment. The yield from this cash investment can be compared with the yield on shares, which are far riskier. This produces a valuable basis for share evaluation. Share yield is less reliable than bank interest or government stock interest yield, because, unlike banks paying interest, companies are under no obligation at all to pay dividends. Frequently, if they go through a bad patch, even the largest companies will cut dividends or abandon paying them altogether.

yield curve FIN a visual representation of relative interest rates of short- and long-term bonds. It can be normal, flat, or inverted.

yield gap FIN an amount representing the difference between the yield on a very safe investment and the yield on a riskier one

yield management FIN securing maximum profits from available capacity by manipulating pricing to gain business at different times, and from differing market segments. Yield management is used particularly in service industries such as the airline, hotel, and equipment rental industries, where there are heavy fixed overheads and additional revenue has a big impact on bottom line profitability. Increasing computing power has enabled organisations to integrate complex information from different sources (for example, customer travel histories and current information on bookings) and use mathematical models to analyse the possibility of increasing profitability. Hotel businesses, for example, can use price offers to increase 'revenue per available room', or 'RevPAR', on the basis of yield management analysis.

yield to call FIN the yield on a bond at a date when the bond can be called

yield to maturity *US* FIN = gross yield to redemption

YK *abbr* FIN yugen kaisha

YTD *abbr* FIN year to date

yugen kaisha FIN in Japan, a private limited liability corporation. Usually, the number of shareholders must be less than 50. The minimum capital of a limited liability corporation is 3 million yen. The par value of each share must be 50,000 yen or more. *Abbr* **YK**

ZBB *abbr* FIN zero-based budgeting

Z bond FIN a bond whose holder receives no accrued interest until all of the holders of other bonds in the same series have received theirs

zero-balance account FIN a bank account that does not hold funds continuously, but has money automatically transferred into it from another account when claims arise against it

zero-based budgeting FIN a method of budgeting which requires each cost element to be specifically justified, as though the activities to which the budget relates were being undertaken for the first time. Without approval, the budget allowance is zero. *Abbr* **ZBB**

zero coupon bond FIN a bond that pays no interest and is sold at a large discount. Also known as **accrual bond**

zero fund FIN to assign no money to a business project without actually cancelling it *(slang)*

zero growth ECON a fall in output for two successive quarters

zero-rated supplies or **zero-rated goods and services** FIN taxable items or services on which VAT is charged at zero rate, such as food, books, public transport, and children's clothes

zombie *US* FIN a business that continues to trade even though it is officially insolvent *(slang)*

Z score FIN a single figure, produced by a financial model, which combines a number of variables (generally financial statements ratios), whose magnitude is intended to aid the prediction of failure. A Z score model may predict that a company with a score of 1.8 or less is likely to fail within 12 months. Individual companies are scored against this benchmark.

Index

Credits

Best Practice
P18 On Writing As an Essential Business Skill © John Simmons 2006, 2009
P32 How to Get Lucky © Donald N. Sull 2006, 2009
P63 How NLP Can Contribute to Best Management Practice © Joseph O'Connor 2006, 2009
P65 CSR: More Than PR, Pursuing Competitive Advantage in the Long Run © John Surdyk 2006, 2009

Management Library
Ultimate Business Library © Stuart Crainer 2002
Writing the New Economy © John Middleton 2002

Gurus
Business Thinkers © Chartered Management Institute 2002, 2006, 2009

Dictionary
Management terms © Chartered Management Institute 2002, 2006, 2009